The Oxford Handbook of Sexual and Gender Minority Mental Health

Oxford Library of Psychology

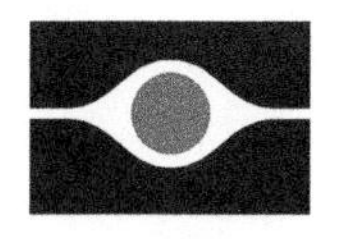

OXFORD LIBRARY OF PSYCHOLOGY

The Oxford Handbook of Sexual and Gender Minority Mental Health

Edited by

Esther D. Rothblum

OXFORD
UNIVERSITY PRESS

2020

OXFORD
UNIVERSITY PRESS

Oxford University Press is a department of the University of Oxford.
It furthers the University's objective of excellence in research, scholarship,
and education by publishing worldwide. Oxford is a registered trade mark of
Oxford University Press in the UK and certain other countries.

Published in the United States of America by Oxford University Press
198 Madison Avenue, New York, NY 10016, United States of America.

Cover art courtesy of Marcia Hill

Library of Congress Cataloging-in-Publication Data
Names: Rothblum, Esther D., editor.
Title: The Oxford handbook of sexual and gender minority mental health /
edited by Esther D. Rothblum.
Description: New York, NY : Oxford University Press, 2020. | Series: Oxford
library of psychology | Includes bibliographical references and index.
Identifiers: LCCN 2020018130 (print) | LCCN 2020018131 (ebook) |
ISBN 9780190067991 (hardback) | ISBN 9780190068011 (epub)
Subjects: LCSH: Sexual minorities—Mental health. | Transgender
people—Mental health.
Classification: LCC RC451.4.G39 O95 2020 (print) | LCC RC451.4.G39 (ebook) |
DDC 616.890086/7—dc23
LC record available at https://lccn.loc.gov/2020018130
LC ebook record available at https://lccn.loc.gov/2020018131

9 8 7 6 5 4 3 2 1

Printed by Sheridan Books, Inc., United States of America

SHORT CONTENTS

CONTRIBUTORS

Edward J. Alessi, PhD, MSW
Associate Professor
School of Social Work
Rutgers, The State University of New Jersey
New Brunswick, NJ

Alishia Alexander, MA
Department of Sociology
University of Illinois at Urbana-Champaign
Urbana, IL

Heather L. Armstrong, PhD
Lecturer
Department of Psychology
University of Southampton
Southampton, United Kingdom

Laura Baams, PhD
Assistant Professor of Pedagogy and Educational Sciences
University of Groningen
Groningen, the Netherlands

Naomi Bird
College of Sustainability
Faculty of Arts & Social Sciences, and School of Planning, Faculty of Architecture & Planning
Dalhousie University
Halifax, Nova Scotia, Canada

Danna Bismar, MS
Graduate Student in Counseling Psychology
University of North Texas
Denton, TX

Wendy B. Bostwick, PhD, MPH
Associate Professor
Health Systems Science Department
College of Nursing
University of Illinois at Chicago
Chicago, IL

Sandra S. Butler, PhD, MSW
Professor
School of Social Work
University of Maine
Orono, ME

Cynthia M. Cabral, PhD
Promoting Resilience, Intersectionality, Diversity, and Equity (PRIDE) Health Research Consortium
Hunter College of the City University of New York
New York, NY

Juan Camarena, PhD
Lecturer, CBB LPCC Program
Executive Director, CCCE Counseling and School Psychology
San Diego State University
San Diego, CA

Alison Cerezo, PhD
Assistant Professor
Department of Counseling, Clinical & School Psychology
University of California, Santa Barbara
Santa Barbara, CA

Gia Chodzen, MA
Graduate Student in Clinical Psychology
Department of Psychology
UCLA BRITE Center for Science, Research and Policy
University of California Los Angeles
Los Angeles, CA

Susan D. Cochran, PhD, MS
Professor
Department of Epidemiology
Fielding School of Public Health
Department of Statistics
University of California Los Angeles
Los Angeles, CA

Phoenix R. Crane, MA
Graduate Student in Experimental Psychology
Texas Tech University
Lubbock, TX

lore m. dickey, PhD
North Country HealthCare
Bullhead City, AZ
Joanne DiPlacido, PhD
Professor of Psychological Science
Central Connecticut State University
New Britain, CT
Cherdsak Duangchan, MSN, RN
Graduate Student
Department of Health and System Sciences
College of Nursing
University of Illinois at Chicago
Chicago, IL
Michele J. Eliason, PhD
Professor of Health Education
Assistant Dean for Faculty Development
College of Health & Social Sciences
San Francisco State University
San Francisco, CA
Carolyn R. Fallahi, PhD
Professor and Chair
Department of Psychological Science
Central Connecticut State University
New Britain, CT
Jessica N. Fish, PhD
Assistant Professor of Family Science
School of Public Health
University of Maryland
College Park, MD
Lourdes Dolores Follins, PhD, LCSW-R
Meliora Consulting LLC
Brooklyn, NY
Anthony M. Foster, MA
Graduate Student in Experimental Psychology
Texas Tech University
Lubbock, TX
David M. Frost, PhD
Associate Professor in Social Psychology
Department of Social Science
University College London
London, United Kingdom
M. Paz Galupo, PhD
Professor of Psychology
Towson University
Towson, MD
Kirsten A. Gonzalez, PhD
Assistant Professor of Psychology
University of Tennessee
Knoxville, TN
Kaitlyn R. Gorman, MA
Graduate Student in Clinical Psychology
University of Massachusetts Boston
Boston, MA
Ann P. Haas, PhD
Professor Emerita of Health Sciences
Lehman College
The City University of New York
New York, NY
Douglas C. Haldeman, PhD
Chair
Doctoral Program in Clinical Psychology
John F. Kennedy University
Pleasant Hill, CA
Kristin A. Hancock, PhD
Professor of Psychology
John F. Kennedy University
Pleasant Hill, CA
Elizabeth A. Harrison, OTD, OTR/L
Graduate Student in Disability Studies
University of Illinois at Chicago
Chicago, IL
Colleen C. Hoff, PhD
Professor of Sexuality Studies
Director of the Center for Research & Education on Gender and Sexuality (CREGS)
San Francisco State University
San Francisco, CA
Cindy Y. Huang, PhD
Assistant Professor of Counseling Psychology
Teachers College
Columbia University
New York, NY
Emily Hunt, MEd, MA
Graduate Student
Counseling Psychology Program
Teachers College
Columbia University
New York, NY
Sarilee Kahn, PhD, MSW
Associate Professor
School of Social Work
McGill University
Montreal, Quebec, Canada

Joshua W. Katz, BA
Graduate Student
Department of Psychology
University of Saskatchewan
Saskatoon, Canada
Laura E. Kuper, PhD
Psychologist
Gender Education and Care
Interdisciplinary Support (GENECIS)
Program at Children's Health
Dallas, TX
Jonathan Mathias Lassiter, PhD
Assistant Professor
Department of Psychology
Muhlenberg College
Allentown, PA
Edward Ou Jin Lee, PhD, MSW
Assistant Professor
School of Social Work
Université de Montréal
Montréal, Quebec, Canada
Abelardo Leon, PhD
Postdoctoral Researcher
School of Social Work
Université de Montréal
Montréal, Quebec, Canada
Chien-Ching Li, PhD
Assistant Professor
Department of Health Systems and
Management
Rush University
Chicago, IL
Tove Lundberg, PhD
Senior Lecturer
Department of Psychology
Lund University
Lund, Sweden
Crystal Madriles, MA
Graduate Student
Department of Counseling and Clinical
Psychology
Teachers College
Columbia University
New York, NY
Meredith R. Maroney, MS
Graduate Student
Counseling Psychology Program
University of Massachusetts Boston
Boston, MA
Jes L. Matsick, PhD
Assistant Professor of Psychology and
Women's, Gender, and Sexuality Studies
The Pennsylvania State University
University Park, PA
Alicia K. Matthews, PhD
Professor
Department of Health and
System Sciences
College of Nursing
University of Illinois at Chicago
Chicago, IL
Vickie M. Mays, PhD, MSPH
Distinguished Professor
Department of Psychology
Director, UCLA BRITE Center for
Science, Research and Policy
University of California Los Angeles
Los Angeles, CA
Mallaigh McGinley, EdM
Graduate Student
Counseling Psychology Program
University of Massachusetts Boston
Boston, MA
Jenifer K. McGuire, PhD
Associate Professor of Family
Social Science
University of Minnesota
St. Paul, MN
Yaser Mirzaei, BA
Graduate Student
Department of Psychology
University of Saskatchewan
Saskatoon, Canada
Todd G. Morrison, PhD
Professor
Department of Psychology
University of Saskatchewan
Saskatoon, Canada
Maggie G. Mortali, MPH
Senior Director
Interactive Screening Program
American Foundation for Suicide
Prevention
New York, NY
Maria Pallotta-Chiarolli, PhD
School of Health and Social Development
Deakin University
Burwood, Victoria, Australia

David W. Pantalone, PhD
Professor of Psychology
University of Massachusetts Boston
Boston, MA

Erin T. Pereida, MA
Graduate Student in Clinical Psychology
University of Massachusetts Boston
Boston, MA

Jayme L. Peta, PhD
Assistant Professor of Psychology
Palo Alto University
Palo Alto, CA

Julie Prud'homme, MSc
Graduate Student in Clinical Psychology
University of Victoria
Victoria, British Columbia, Canada

Amaranta Ramirez, BA
Graduate Student
Department of Counseling, Clinical &
School Psychology
University of California, Santa Barbara
Santa Barbara, CA

Bethany Owens Raymond, BA
Graduate Student in Clinical Psychology
Georgia Southern University
Statesboro, GA

Lauren E. Reid, PhD
Assistant Professor of Psychology
Arcadia University
Glenside, PA

Christina L. Robillard, BSc
Graduate Student in Clinical Psychology
University of Victoria
Victoria, British Columbia, Canada

Margaret Robinson, PhD
Assistant Professor of Sociology and
Social Anthropology
Dalhousie University
Halifax, Nova Scotia, Canada

Katrina Roen, PhD
Professor of Sociology
University of Waikato
Hamilton, New Zealand

Esther D. Rothblum, PhD
Professor
Women's Studies Department
San Diego State University
San Diego, CA

Whit Ryan, MS
Graduate Student
Graduate School of Professional Psychology
University of Denver
Denver, CO

Anna C. Salomaa, MS
Graduate Student in Psychology
The Pennsylvania State University
University Park, PA

Molly Silvestrini, BA
Research Assistant
University of California, San Francisco,
and the Center for Research and
Education on Gender and Sexuality
San Francisco State University
San Francisco, CA

Stacy W. Smallwood, PhD, MPH
Department of Health Policy and
Community Health
Jiann-Ping Hsu College of Public Health
Georgia Southern University
Statesboro, GA

Tyrel J. Starks, PhD
Department of Psychology
Hunter College of the City University
of New York
New York, NY

Vanessa S. Stay, BA
Graduate Student
Counseling Program
Arcadia University
Glenside, PA

Katarina S. Swaringen, MA
Graduate Student in Experimental
Psychology
Texas Tech University
Lubbock, TX

Dawn M. Szymanski, PhD
Professor of Psychology
University of Tennessee
Knoxville, TN

Ali J. Talan, DrPH
Promoting Resilience, Intersectionality,
Diversity, and Equity (PRIDE) Health
Research Consortium
Hunter College of the City University
of New York
New York, NY

Amelia E. Talley, PhD
Associate Professor
Department of Psychological Sciences
Texas Tech University
Lubbock, TX

Samantha L. Tornello, PhD
Assistant Professor of Human Development & Family Studies
The Pennsylvania State University
University Park, PA

Brianna J. Turner, PhD
Assistant Professor of Psychology
University of Victoria
Victoria, British Columbia, Canada

Sarah E. Valentine, PhD
Assistant Professor
Department of Psychiatry
Boston University School of Medicine
Boston, MA

Sean Saifa Wall
Rooted in Research LLC and Intersex Justice Project
Atlanta, GA

Brandon J. Weiss, PhD
Assistant Professor
Department of Psychology
Georgia Southern University
Statesboro, GA

Leo Wilton, PhD, MPH
Department of Human Development
College of Community and Public Affairs
State University of New York at Binghamton
Binghamton, NY

Y. Darin Witkovic, MA
Graduate Student in Clinical Psychology
Palo Alto University
Palo Alto, CA

Somayyeh Zare, MA
Graduate Student
Department of Psychology
University of Saskatchewan
Saskatoon, Canada

CONTENTS

CHAPTER

1 Introduction

Esther D. Rothblum

Abstract

The Oxford Handbook of Sexual and Gender Minority Mental Health provides an overview of the current research on the mental health of sexual and gender minority (SGM) populations. It is aimed at researchers conducting studies on the mental health of SGM populations, clinicians and researchers interested in psychiatric disorders that affect SGM populations, clinicians using evidence-based practice in the treatment of SGM patients/clients, students in mental health programs (clinical psychology, psychiatry, clinical social work, and psychiatric nursing), and policymakers. This chapter defines some terms and provides an overview of current and past SGM research methods.

Keywords: sexual minority, mental health, gender minority, LGBT, research

Terminology: Gender Minorities

The terms *sex* and *gender* are sometimes used interchangeably (and it is unfortunate that in English the word *sex* can also refer to sexual activity, adding to confusion), but usually *sex* refers to biology and *gender* to environment or culture. Thus baldness (more frequent in men) is a sex difference, whereas knitting ability (more frequent in women) is a gender difference. Right away it is impossible to talk about terms without introducing an *intersectional* perspective (Crenshaw, 1990), referring to the fact that there are various forms of social stratification, such as sex, gender, age, race, ethnicity, socioeconomic class, gender identity, sexual orientation, religion, ability, and many others, that are not independent of each other but instead interlock to form each individual's experiences. Thus baldness, which is genetic, is more common among White men (intersection of sex and race), and knitting, which is learned, is more common among older cohorts of women (intersection of gender and age).

The term *intersex* refers to individuals born with variations in sex characteristics, such as sex chromosomes, genitals, or hormones that are outside the appearance or definition of male or female bodies. These variations may be apparent at birth or not until puberty. Cheryl Chase founded the Intersex Society of North American in 1993 (since disbanded) that focused on advocacy to prevent genital surgery of infants with ambiguous genitalia. There are now multiple advocacy groups for intersex individuals such as InterACT for intersex youth, and other organizations around the world.

Gender identity refers to one's own sense of one's gender and can correspond with one's sex assigned at birth or not. *Cisgender* is the term for individuals whose gender identity corresponds to their sex assigned at birth, and, although a fairly new term in the twenty-first century, it is now in wide use, especially on college campuses (Enke, 2012). *Transgender* refers to individuals who do not fully identify with their sex assigned at birth. Some identify with the other gender (to my knowledge, English is the only language using the term "opposite sex," which implies that what one sex does is the complete opposite of the other). The term *trans woman* has replaced earlier terms of transwoman, transgender woman, transsexual woman, or male-to-female individual for a trans individual who considers herself a woman, and *transfeminine* for someone who identifies to some degree with femininity (Stryker, 2017). The term *trans man* replaced earlier terms of transman, transgender man, transsexual man, or female-to-male individual for a trans individual who considers himself a man, and *transmasculine* for someone who identifies to some degree with masculinity (Stryker, 2017). It should also be noted that use of the terms *cisgender* versus *transgender* now reinforces another dichotomy; there are in fact individuals who identify with neither term (Factor & Rothblum, 2017; Stryker, 2017).

But transgender is a broad concept and can include people who are not exclusively masculine or feminine; the term *trans** is used to denote the transgender umbrella. *Gender nonbinary* individuals may experience their gender as changing over time, conceive of gender on a continuum, believe there are more categories than male or female, or "call into question the concept of gender itself" (Bornstein, 1994, p. 122). Other terms used for individuals who view their gender identity outside of the gender binary are *genderqueer*, *agender*, *gender variant*, *gender flexible*, *gender nonconforming*, or *neutrois*. All of these concepts are included in the term *gender minorities* in this *Handbook*.

Whereas some languages do not use gendered pronouns (e.g., Mandarin, Tagalog), others, including English, do, and this has resulted in the use of gender-neutral pronouns (ze, hir, xem in the past; *they* is now commonly used to refer to the single individual; Boylan, 2018). Additionally, words that are gendered—such as Latina and Latino—are now replaced in writing by the gender-neutral term *Latinx* (Stryker, 2017).

Western societies have very binary conceptions of gender, but other cultures have a long history of fluid gender. In North American indigenous cultures in the past, there were people whose gender changed, sometimes in early childhood, who might have special spiritual or healing powers, who often dressed in the clothing of the other gender, who married someone of the other sex, and whose gender might change again over time (Lang, 1999). Lang stated (1999, pp. 95–96):

> Gender variance is as diverse as Native American cultures themselves. About the only common denominator is that in many Native American tribal cultures systems of multiple genders existed, classifying people of either sex according to their occupational preferences and expressions of gender-specific personality traits and mannerisms as either men, women, women-men, or men-women.

Contemporary Native Americans have reclaimed the term *two-spirit* to emphasize the spirituality that was an important aspect of women-men and men-women in the past.

Other cultures outside North America have current terms for genders outside the binary. The Kinnar or Kinner (also known as hijra) in South Asia are officially considered a third gender in India, Bangladesh, Pakistan, and Nepal. Some cultures have an intermediate sex, such as the Bakla in the Philippines, Phuying (also known as Kathoey) in Thailand, Travesti in Brazil, and Onnabe in Japan.

Terminology: Sexual Minorities

Sexual orientation (also referred to as *sexual identity* or *sexuality*) refers to the gender(s) to which one is sexually, romantically, or emotionally attracted. Although a variety of terms are used for same-sex attraction across historical time and across cultures, currently the terms *lesbian woman* for a woman attracted to women, *gay man* for a man attracted to men, *bisexual woman* for a woman attracted to women and men, and *bisexual man* for a man attracted to women and men are in most common use in the research literature. Much of the research on sexual orientation has used a Likert scale (often referred to as the Kinsey Scale) that ranges from exclusively heterosexual to exclusively lesbian/gay, with bisexual in the middle range. Yet researchers then nearly always categorized individuals into lesbian/gay, bisexual, or heterosexual for comparison purposes, sometimes excluding individuals who fell somewhere in between. Research by Vrangalova and Savin-Williams (2012) indicated that respondents who check off "mostly heterosexual" or "mostly lesbian/gay" are an important population to study. For example, Austin, Roberts, Corliss, and Molnar (2008) found that "mostly heterosexual" young women in a primarily Black and Latina sample were more likely to report having been the victims of childhood sexual abuse.

Sexual identity may or may not correspond with *sexual behavior*; for example, some women who identify as lesbian may be currently having sex with men or with both women and men, or may be celibate. Consequently the terms *MSN* (*men who have sex with men*) and *WSW* (*women who have sex with women*) are used by researchers who specifically study sexual behavior.

As these definitions imply, sexual orientation terms are heavily dependent on gender, and, specifically, on binary gender (attraction to women, men, and both women and men). The newer term *pansexual* (also *plurisexual* and *omnisexual*, in contrast to *monosexual*) refers to attraction to people regardless of their sex or gender identity; this can include attraction to people who identify as women, men, or gender nonbinary. *Asexual* refers to people who do not feel sexual attraction to others; some do feel romantic attraction whereas others are *aromantic*.

The term *polyamorous* refers to intimate relationships with more than one partner. In contrast to the term *nonmonogamous*, polyamorous usually includes a consensual aspect to open or multipartner relationships. All of these concepts are included in the term *sexual minorities* in this *Handbook*.

In English, most medical terms are based on Greek and Latin (such as *homosexual*); when minority groups organize they often replace the medical term with something shorter (such as *gay*) or even reclaim a term that was used in pejorative ways (such as *queer*). The commonly used acronym *LGBT* (lesbian, gay, bisexual, and transgender) is now often replaced by *queer* to describe all nonnormative sexual and gender identities. Although *queer* is rarely used in the research literature, it is used in various ways in general discourse: as an umbrella term for all identity labels (American Psychological Association, 2015), as a more radical statement in contrast to the more assimilationist LGBT movements (Miller, Taylor, & Rupp, 2016), and as part of the academic discipline known as queer theory (Sullivan, 2003).

Changes in the Diagnoses of Sexuality and Gender Identity

The first and second editions of the *Diagnostic and Statistical Manual of Mental Disorders* (DSM-I, American Psychiatric Association [APA], 1952; DSM-II; APA, 1968) included "homosexuality" as a "sexual deviation" in the section on personality disorders. Based on early research on homosexuality, advocacy by younger psychiatrists, and protests by gay activists (cf. Drescher, 2015a), the board of trustees of the APA voted (only 58 percent in favor) in December 1973 to remove homosexuality as a diagnosis from the DSM. In the DSM-III (APA, 1980) it was replaced with "ego-dystonic homosexuality" for "homosexual arousal that the individual explicitly states has been unwanted and a persistent source of distress" (p. 282). It was not until 1987 that the DSM-III-R (APA, 1987) eliminated this diagnosis, listing only "sexual disorders not otherwise specified" that included "persistent and marked distress about one's sexual orientation" (p. 295). That was included in the DSM-IV (APA, 1994) and the DSM-IV-Text Revision (APA, 2000) but was finally omitted from the DSM-V (APA, 2013).

Similar changes occurred in the *International Classification of Diseases* (ICD) published by the World Health Organization (cf. Drescher, 2015b; Reed et al., 2016, for reviews). "Homosexuality" was listed in the several editions of the ICD from 1948 to 1975, "lesbianism" was included in editions from 1965 to 1975, and "ego-dystonic sexual orientation" was included in the 1990 edition. It was omitted in 2017.

Regarding gender identity, the DSM-III, DSM-III-R, and ICD-10 included transsexualism, which was changed in the DSM-IV and DSM-IV-TR to gender identity disorder in children, adolescents, or adults. It still exists in the current DSM-V as gender dysphoria (cf. Drescher, 2015b; Reed et al., 2016, for reviews) and in the ICD-11 as gender incongruence of children, adolescents, and adults as a sexual health disorder. Obviously, having these categories in the DSM and ICD continues to generate controversy, and activist groups are hoping to have these removed from diagnostic manuals.

Research on Sexual and Gender Minorities

Few areas of mental health have changed as radically as those affecting sexual and gender minority (SGM) individuals. Fifty years ago publications on (mostly) male and (some) female "homosexuals" consisted of case studies or small samples, and the authors were likely to be clinicians who treated people with severe mental health problems. "Homosexuality" was listed as a mental health disorder in the DSM at the time (APA, 1968), so these studies focused on psychopathology. In 1977, Morin published a review of research on lesbian women and gay men soon after the APA voted to remove "homosexuality" from the DSM in 1973. He noted that studies on lesbians and gay men focused primarily on assessment (e.g., projective techniques), etiology (e.g., parenting styles, negative experiences with the opposite sex, hormones), and adjustment (e.g., comparisons to heterosexuals). Morin pointed out the heterosexist bias in these studies and so did the American Psychological Association's Task Force Report on Heterosexual Bias in Psychotherapy (Garnets, Hancock, Cochran, Goodchilds, & Peplau, 1991).

With the benefit of hindsight, it is easy to point out methodologic problems in these early studies. Lesbian women and gay men often came to therapy as a last resort, to become heterosexual in order to keep or regain their jobs, custody of their children, or the respect of their families. Many other SGM individuals went to therapists but never mentioned their sexual or gender minority identity or attractions, so it was only those least able to "pass" as heterosexual or cisgender, or those who were caught by police in public restrooms or gay bars, who came to the attention of clinicians.

At the same time, fifty years ago, the civil rights movement, the women's liberation movement, and the gay liberation movement were raising awareness about racism, sexism, and heterosexism in societal institutions, including the mental health field. Newsletters and organizations for the LGBT communities began to advertise the services of affirmative therapists, who often had no formal training or degrees in mental health fields but who served as important role models for their SGM clients. As Silverstein (1991) described about this era: "While gays flocked to our services, established professionals, who earned their living by 'curing' gay men and women, saw us as a cabal of reckless incompetents who, when successful, doomed our clients to a life of misery" (p. 5).

This generation of LGBT-affirmative therapists was more informed about the lives of LGBT clients than any researchers of that era, and they began publishing articles about mostly gay and lesbian issues, but from an affirmative rather than a pathological perspective. As I have stated (Rothblum, 2007, p. 443):

> In the early feminist and social issue journals, they described such normative processes in the LGB communities as the coming out process, sex and relationships, adolescence, aging, race and ethnicity, stress and social support, workplace issues, and friendships. They introduced the general mental health professionals reading these articles to concepts such as lesbian "merger," gay bathhouses, bi-phobia, fluid gender identity among Native Americans, and heteronormativity.

This focus by affirmative therapists also had limitations, given that their clients were often middle class, White, highly educated, young, urban, and out about their SGM identity. At the same time the early cohorts of SGM students began to enter programs in counseling, clinical psychology, social work, psychiatry, and psychiatric nursing, often without mentioning their SGM identity during the admissions process. Some of them came out in graduate or medical school and conducted research on SGM topics, often mentored by faculty members with little knowledge of SGM issues.

The 1980s became the era of convenience samples, also of mostly gay and lesbian individuals. The LGBT communities were expanding to include smaller towns and rural areas, campus student groups, religious organizations, feminist and gay bookstores, and periodicals (cf., Rothblum, 1994, for a review). The purpose of *The Gayellow Pages* (http://www.gayellowpages.com/), founded in 1973, was for SGM tourists or new arrivals to find communities and organizations across North America, but it also provided a resource for researchers who could now find local or national groups, including SGM communities of color, to publicize their studies (cf., Rothblum, Factor, & Aaron, 2002). Researchers could also attend events with large numbers of SGM participants, such as gay pride parades, to distribute questionnaires. When Judy Bradford and Caitlin Ryan conducted the National Lesbian Health Care Survey in the mid-1980s (Bradford, Ryan, & Rothblum, 1994), they distributed questionnaires to lesbian and gay organizations, women's centers, feminist bookstores, gay newspapers, prisons, and personal contacts, resulting in 1,917 completed surveys from lesbian and bisexual women.

Interestingly, there was relatively little focus on research about SGM mental health at this time. It was as if the very recent removal of "homosexuality" from the DSM made researchers reluctant to further stigmatize a group that had been pathologized so much in the past.

Studies using convenience samples were viewed as limited even then. First, they recruited participants via LGBT events and organizations, and thus omitted people who were closeted, isolated, or not connected to LGBT communities. Second, these methods of recruitment made it difficult to find comparable heterosexuals. Researchers would compare the LGB sample to published norms, if available, about the "general public," presumed heterosexual. Or they would recruit heterosexual comparison groups via different bookstores, newspapers, or community events.

Third, comparisons of LGB and heterosexual groups usually found demographic differences between these two groups. The LGB group was more highly educated, earned lower incomes relative to their educational level, and was less religious than the heterosexual sample; included more Whites than the general population; and, in the case of gay men, lived in larger cities than did heterosexual men (cf., Badgett, 2001; Morris & Rothblum, 1999). It wasn't possible to know if these demographic differences were the result of the different recruitment methods, or if they represented real differences between these groups. Later on, our research comparing LGBs to heterosexual siblings (Rothblum, Balsam, & Mickey, 2004; Rothblum & Factor, 2001) and transgender (trans women, trans men, and genderqueer individuals) to cisgender siblings (Factor & Rothblum, 2008) showed that many of these difference were in fact real. Lesbian and bisexual women had higher levels of education, LGBs had lower levels of income relative to their educational level, gay men lived in larger cities, LGBs were less likely to have children, and LGBs were less religious and more politically liberal than heterosexuals recruited from siblings (cf. Rothblum, Balsam, Solomon, & Factor, 2005, for a review). Transgender individuals in general had higher levels of education, had lower levels of income relative to their educational level, were less religious, and were less likely to have children than were cisgender siblings (Factor & Rothblum, 2008).

But these studies had a number of strengths. They produced a large amount of data about gay men and lesbian women, though less often about bisexual and transgender individuals. They pointed out trends and topics in the emerging SGM communities, which in turn provided information for more rural, isolated, and closeted individuals as well as for heterosexual and cisgender clinicians and the general public.

As the result of the HIV/AIDS epidemic, by the 1990s population-based surveys were beginning to include one or two items about same-sex behavior, but less commonly items about sexual identity, gender identity, or more details about the lives of SGM respondents. There was concern that any more than a single item or two would offend the general public, who might then refuse to answer the rest of the questionnaire. For example, the 2000 U.S. Census included one item about the gender of partners who were cohabiting (Gates & Ost, 2004), which excluded LGBs who were single or not living with a partner.

This was also a decade when technological advances made surveys more feasible, with such techniques as internet-based surveys, random-digit telephone dialing methods, and portable laptops to complete questionnaires. By 2002, 50 percent of U.S. households had internet access, a percentage that increased to 72 percent by 2013 (Pew Research Center, 2018). Also by 2002 people accessed the internet primarily via personal computers with dial-up modems; by 2013 smartphones and tablets with data plans were in wide use.

Certainly population-based surveys were a large improvement over the snowball sampling methods of prior decades. The samples are more representative of the general population, and the SGM respondents are recruited via the same methods as the heterosexual and cisgender respondents. However, these large-scale surveys are not without challenges. First, the numbers of sexual minority respondents, especially those who are female, are very small. Laumann, Gagnon, Michael, and Michaels (1994) interviewed close to 3,500 individuals using representative sampling and found only 24 women and 49 men in this sample who identified as gay, lesbian, bisexual, or "other." Sandfort and his colleagues (Sandfort, de Graaf, & Bijl, 2003; Sandfort, de Graaf, Bijl, & Schnabel, 2001) conducted a stratified, random-sampling household survey of 7,046 people in the Netherlands who answered one item about sexual behavior in the past year; 82 (2.8 percent) men and 43 (1.4 percent) women reported being sexually active with a member of the same sex in the past year (some of these individuals had been sexually active with opposite-sex partners as well). In the second phase of the National Survey of Midlife Development in the United States (Cochran, Sullivan, & Mays, 2003; Mays & Cochran, 2001), 2,917 respondents answered the single question about sexual orientation; only 41 respondents identified as homosexual and 32 as bisexual. The second part of the National Comorbidity Survey included two items about the number of men and women with whom respondents had had "sexual intercourse" in the past five years (Gilman et al., 2001, p. 934). The sample included 4,785 respondents with exclusively opposite-sex partners, 48 with exclusively same-sex partners (33 men and 15 women), 77 with both same-sex and opposite-sex partners (41 men and 36 women), and 967 who reported no intercourse.

What accounted for these tiny numbers of sexual minorities? How could the National Lesbian Health Care Survey locate close to 2,000 respondents via community organizations and snowball sampling when surveys targeting the general population found just a few dozen? Presumably sexual minorities were reluctant to come out to government agencies (such as the U.S. Census or research funded by the National Institutes of Health), whereas they were eager to participate in research funded by and conducted by members of their own communities.

A second challenge was that, given these small numbers of sexual minorities, researchers often combined lesbian women with bisexual women, and gay men with bisexual men (cf., Cochran et al., 2003; Gilman et al., 2001; Mays & Cochran, 2001). This obscured differences between monosexual and bisexual samples who in fact differ in mental health. Given the earlier focus on lesbian women and gay men, this meant that information specifically about bisexual women and men continued to be sparse.

A third challenge for population-based surveys was the way in which sexual orientation was assessed, especially when researchers could only use one or two items. Some asked about same-sex behavior, others about self-identity, and others (such as the U.S. Census) about cohabiting with a same-sex partner. By the 1990s research was beginning to show that the dimensions of sexual behavior, sexual identity, sexual fantasies, and community participation are not strongly intercorrelated (Laumann et al., 1994; Morris & Rothblum, 1999). Research on lesbian and bisexual women (Morris & Rothblum, 1999) found that Native American, Asian American, and European American women had particularly low interrelationships among the dimensions of self-identity, same-sex relationships, level of outness, years being out, and participation in LGB community events, but even for African American and Latina lesbian and bisexual women these intercorrelations were only moderate. In particular, when population-based surveys asked only about same-sex behavior during a particular timeframe (e.g., the past year), there were often seven or eight times as many respondents who reported no sexual behavior as those who reported same-sex behavior (Gilman et al., 2001; Sandfort et al., 2001, 2003); some of those respondents not currently having sex may have identified as LGB. In particular, lesbian women tended to report having sex less frequently than gay men or heterosexuals (Blumstein & Schwartz, 1983; Peplau, Fingerhut, & Beals, 2004).

Fourth, the way in which gender was assessed in these surveys made it difficult to locate transgender participants. The vast majority of population-based surveys asked only about sex or gender as male or female, which did not include gender nonbinary options. Some surveys included transgender or other as gender options, but this would not identity transgender participants who identified as male or female, for example. The research of Tate, Ledbetter, and Youssef (2013) has demonstrated that including two items, one about current identity and one about sex assigned at birth, provides the most accurate data about the transgender spectrum.

In sum, even today it is impossible to know how many people cannot be reached for SGM research, and/or how many are so closeted that they would not admit to SGM identity or behavior, even on an anonymous survey. That is certainly the case in countries in which it is illegal to be LGBT.

Organization of This Handbook

This *Handbook* consists of three parts. The first section includes chapters on the history of sexual orientation and the history of gender identity. As this overview has shown, SGM mental health and how it has been understood by mental health professionals has changed dramatically in the past half-century.

The second section focuses on SGM mental health via various mental health categories. This includes chapters on depression and mood disorders, anxiety disorders, trauma, body image and eating disorders, alcohol use disorders, drug use, nicotine use, psychotic disorders, sexual disorders, personality disorders, and suicide. Each chapter reviews the current SGM research in that area of mental health. As the chapters will indicate, some categories have a quite substantial research literature whereas others have barely anything. Furthermore, the research continues to focus more on lesbian women and gay men than it does on bisexual individuals. There is often very little focus on gender minorities at all. The samples are often overwhelmingly White, so that People of Color are vastly underrepresented. And very little research has been conducted on the Global South—in Africa, Asia, Latin America, and the Caribbean.

In order to highlight SGM populations that receive less focus in the research literature, the third section includes chapters on specific SGM populations that are underrepresented in the research literature on mental health. This includes chapters specifically on African American SGM, Latinx SGM, Asian American and Pacific Islander SGM, Native American/two-spirit SGM, and biracial and bi-ethnic SGM mental health. There are chapters on the mental health of SGM individuals who identify as bisexual, transgender, gender nonbinary, intersex, asexual, pansexual or queer, and polyamorous. There are also chapters on SGM mental health issues among children and youth, older adults, immigrants and refugees, MSM and WSW, and couples and families. Chapters also focus on HIV/AIDS, the intersection of physical and mental health, individuals with physical or cognitive disabilities, the role of stigma and minority stress, and the role of resilience. A final chapter focuses on challenges in research methods and future directions on SGM mental health. Here too authors are using an intersectional perspective, reviewing the literature (or mentioning its lack) on SGM populations, on People of Color, and on the Global South.

The twenty-first century has seen improvements in sampling, use of longitudinal research, mixed-methods research, statistical methods for research, and funding opportunities for research with SGM populations (cf. Rothblum, Balsam, Riggle, Rostosky, & Wickham, 2019, for a review). Nevertheless, the purpose of this *Handbook* is to point out the gaps in the research as well as the advances, in order to motivate future researchers to expand knowledge about SGM mental health. As this volume goes to press, I am aware that the current sociopolitical context in many nations includes both progress and backlash, with laws and policies including protections for SGM individuals in some countries but denying protections in others. All of these changes will impact SGM individuals, mental health researchers, and especially young people coming of age in this era.

References

American Psychiatric Association. (1952). *The diagnostic and statistical manual of mental disorders* (1st ed.). Washington, DC: American Psychiatric Association.

American Psychiatric Association. (1968). *The diagnostic and statistical manual of mental disorders* (2nd ed.). Washington, DC: American Psychiatric Association.

American Psychiatric Association. (1980). *The diagnostic and statistical manual of mental disorders* (3rd ed.). Washington, DC: American Psychiatric Association.

American Psychiatric Association. (1987). *The diagnostic and statistical manual of mental disorders* (3rd ed., revised). Washington, DC: American Psychiatric Association.

American Psychiatric Association. (1994). *The diagnostic and statistical manual of mental disorders* (4th ed.). Washington, DC: American Psychiatric Association.

American Psychiatric Association. (2000). *The diagnostic and statistical manual of mental disorders* (4th ed., text revision). Washington, DC: American Psychiatric Association.

American Psychiatric Association. (2013). *The diagnostic and statistical manual of mental disorders* (5th ed.). Washington, DC: American Psychiatric Association.

American Psychological Association. (2015). Definitions related to sexual orientation and gender diversity in APA documents. 25 April 2019, Retrieved from https://www.apa.org/pi/lgbt/resources/sexuality-definitions.pdf.

Austin, S. B., Roberts, A. L., Corliss, H. L., & Molnar, B. E. (2008). Sexual violence victimization history and sexual risk indicators in a community-based urban cohort of "mostly heterosexual" and heterosexual young women. *American Journal of Public Health, 98*(6), 1015–20. doi:10.2105/AJPH.2006.099473

Badgett, M. V. L. (2001). *Money, myths, and change: The economic lives of lesbians and gay men.* Chicago, IL: University of Chicago Press.

Blumstein, P., & Schwartz, P. (1983). *American couples: Money, work, sex.* New York: William Morrow.

Bornstein, K. (1994). *Gender outlaw: On men, women, and the rest of us.* New York, NY: Vintage Books.

Boylan, J. F. (9 January 2018). That's what ze said. *New York Times.* Retrieved from https://www.nytimes.com/2018/01/09/opinion/ze-xem-gender-pronouns.html?searchResultPosition=1.

Bradford, J., Ryan, C., & Rothblum, E. D. (1994) National lesbian health care survey: Implications for mental health. *Journal of Consulting and Clinical Psychology, 62,* 228–42. doi:10.1037/0022-006X.62.2.228

Cochran, S. D., Sullivan, J. G., & Mays, V. M. (2003). Prevalence of mental disorders, psychological distress, and mental health services use among lesbian, gay, and bisexual adults in the United States. *Journal of Consulting and Clinical Psychology, 71,* 53–61.

Crenshaw, K. (1990). Mapping the margins: Intersectionality, identity politics, and violence against women of color. *Stanford Law Review, 43,* 1241–99. Retrieved from: http://www.jstor.org/stable/1229039.

Drescher, J. (2015a). Out of DSM: Depathologizing homosexuality. *Behavioral Sciences, 5*(4), 565–75. doi:10.3390/bs5040565

Drescher, J. (2015b). Queer diagnoses revisited: The past and future of homosexuality and gender diagnoses in DSM and ICD. *International Review of Psychiatry, 27*(5), 386–95. doi:10.3109/09540261.2015.1053847

Enke, A. F. (2012). The education of little cis: Cisgender and the discipline of opposing bodies. In A. Enke (Ed.), *Transfeminist perspective: In and beyond transgender and gender studies* (pp. 60–77). Philadelphia, PA: Temple University Press.

Factor, R. J., & Rothblum, E. D. (2008). A study of transgender adults and their non-transgender siblings on demographic characteristics, social support, and experiences of violence. *Journal of LGBT Health Research, 3*(3), 11–30. doi:10.1080/15574090802092879

Factor, R. J., & Rothblum, E. D. (2017). A comparison of trans women, trans men, genderqueer individuals, and cisgender brothers and sisters on the Bem Sex-Role Inventory: Ratings by self and siblings. *Journal of Homosexuality, 64,* 1872–89. doi:10.1080/00918369.2016.1273717

Garnets, L., Hancock, K. A., Cochran, S. D., Goodchilds, J., & Peplau, L. A. (1991). Issues in psychotherapy with lesbians and gay men. *American Psychologist, 46,* 964–72. doi:10.1037/0003-066X.46.9.964

Gates, G. J., & Ost, J. (2004). *The gay and lesbian atlas.* Washington, DC: Urban Institute Press.

Gilman, S. E., Cochran, S. D., Mays, V. M., Hughes, M., Ostrow, D., & Kessler, R. C. (2001). Prevalences of DSM-III-R disorders among individuals reporting same-gender sexual partners in the National Comorbidity Survey. *American Journal of Public Health, 91,* 933–9.

Lang, S. (1999). Lesbians, men-women and two-spirits: Homosexuality and gender in Native American cultures. In E. Blackwood & S. Wieringa (Eds.), *Same-sex relations and female desires: Transgender practices across cultures* (pp. 91–116). New York, NY: Columbia University Press.

Laumann, E. O., Gagnon, J. H., Michael, R. T., & Michaels, S. (1994). *The social organization of sexuality: Sexual practices in the United States.* Chicago, IL: University of Chicago Press.

Mays, V. M., & Cochran, S. D. (2001). Mental health correlates of perceived discrimination among lesbian, gay, and bisexual adults in the United States. *American Journal of Public Health, 91*, 1869–76.

Miller, S. D., Taylor, V., & Rupp, L. J. (2016). Social movements and the construction of queer identity. In R. T. Serpe & J. E. Stets (Series Ed.), *New directions in identity theory and research*. New York, NY: Oxford University Press.

Morin, S. F. (1977). Heterosexual bias in psychological research on lesbianism and male homosexuality. *American Psychologist, 32*(8), 629–37. doi:10.1037/0003-066X.32.8.629

Morris, J. F., & Rothblum, E. D. (1999). Who fills out a "lesbian" questionnaire? The interrelationship of sexual orientation, years "out," disclosure of sexual orientation, sexual experience with women, and participation in the lesbian community. *Psychology of Women Quarterly, 23*, 537–57. doi:10.1111/j.1471-6402.1999.tb00380.x

Peplau, L. A., Fingerhut, A., & Beals, K. P. (2004). Sexuality in the relationships of lesbians and gay men. In J. Harvey, A. Wenzel, & S. Sprecher (Eds.), *Handbook of sexuality in close relationships* (pp. 349–69). Mahway, NJ: Erlbaum.

Pew Research Center (February 28, 2018). Internet/broadband fact sheet. Retrieved from: http://www.pewinternet.org/fact-heet/internet-broadband/.

Reed, G. M., Drescher, J., Krueger, R. B., Atalla, E., Cochran, S. D., First, M. B., . . . Briken, P. (2016). Disorders related to sexuality and gender identity in the ICD-11: Revising the ICD-10 classification based on current scientific evidence, best clinical practices, and human rights considerations. *World Psychiatry, 15*(3), 205–21. doi:10.1002/wps.20354

Rothblum, E. D. (1994). "I only read about myself on bathroom walls": The need for research on the mental health of lesbians and gay men. *Journal of Consulting and Clinical Psychology, 62*, 213–20. doi:10.1037/0022-006X.62.2.213

Rothblum, E. D. (2007). From science fiction to computer-generated technology: Sampling lesbian, gay, and bisexual individuals. Chapter 17 in I. H. Meyer & M.E. Northridge (Eds.), *The health of sexual minorities: Public health perspectives on lesbian, gay, bisexual, and transgender populations* (pp. 442–54). New York, NY: Springer.

Rothblum, E. D., Balsam, K. F., & Mickey, R. M. (2004). Brothers and sisters of lesbians, gay men, and bisexuals as a demographic comparison group: An innovative research methodology to examine social change. *Journal of Applied Behavioral Science, 40*, 283–301. doi:10.1177/0021886304266877

Rothblum, E. D., Balsam, K. F., Riggle, E. D. B., Rostosky, S. S., & Wickham, R. E. (2019). Studying the longest "legal" U.S. same-sex couples: A case of lessons learned. *Journal of GLBT Family Studies* [E-pub before print]. doi:10.1080/1550428X.2019.1626787

Rothblum, E. D., Balsam, K. F., Solomon, S. E., & Factor, R. J. (2005). Siblings and sexual orientation: Products of alternative families or the ones who got away? *Journal of GLBT Family Studies, 1*(2), 71–87. doi:10.1300/J461v01n02_05

Rothblum, E. D., & Factor, R. (2001). Lesbians and their sisters as a control group: Demographic and mental health factors. *Psychological Science, 12*, 63–9. doi:10.1111/1467-9280.00311

Rothblum, E. D., Factor, R., & Aaron, D. (2002). How did you hear about the study? Or, how to reach lesbian and bisexual women of diverse ages, ethnicity, and educational attainment for research projects. *Journal of the Gay and Lesbian Medical Association, 6*, 53–59. doi:10.1023/A:1021993422671

Sandfort, T. G. M., de Graaf, R., & Bijl, R. V. (2003). Same-sex sexuality and quality of life: Findings from the Netherlands Mental Health Survey and Incidence Study. *Archives of Sexual Behavior, 32*, 15–22. doi:10.1023/A:1021885127560

Sandfort, T. G. M., de Graaf, R., Bijl, R. V., & Schnabel, P. (2001). Same-sex sexual behavior and psychiatric disorders: Findings from the Netherlands Mental Health Survey and Incidence Study (NEMESIS). *Archives of General Psychiatry, 58*, 85–91. doi:10.1001/archpsyc.58.1.85

Silverstein, C. (1991). *Gays, lesbians, and their therapists*. New York, NY: W.W. Norton.

Stryker, S. (2017). *Transgender history: The roots of today's revolution*. New York, NY: Seal Press.

Sullivan, N. (2003). *A critical introduction to queer theory*. New York, NY: New York University Press.

Tate, C. C., Ledbetter, J. N., & Youssef, C. P. (2013). A two-question method for assessing gender categories in the social and medical sciences. *Journal of Sex Research, 50*(8), 767–76. doi:10.1080/00224499.2012.690110

Vrangalova, Z., & Savin-Williams, R. C. (2012). Mostly heterosexual and mostly gay/lesbian: Evidence for new sexual orientation identities. *Archives of Sexual Behavior, 41*(1), 85–101. doi:10.1007/s10508-012-9921-y

PART I

History of Sexual and Gender Minority Mental Health

CHAPTER

2 History of Sexual Orientation and Mental Health

Kristin A. Hancock *and* Douglas C. Haldeman

Abstract

Psychology's understanding of lesbian, gay, and bisexual (LGB) people has evolved, become more refined, and impacted the lives of LGB people in profound ways. This chapter traces the history of LGB psychology from the nineteenth century to the present and focuses on major events and the intersections of theory, psychological science, politics, and activism in the history of this field. It explores various facets of cultural and psychological history that include the pathologizing of homosexuality, the rise of psychological science and the political movements in the mid-twentieth century, and the major shifts in policy that ensued. The toll of the AIDS epidemic on the field is discussed as is the impact of psychological research on national and international policy and legislation.

Keywords: sexual orientation, gay/lesbian history, LGBT rights movement, American Psychological Association, American Psychiatric Association, psychological research

How mental health clinicians and researchers understand lesbian, gay, and bisexual (LGB) people has evolved, has become more refined, and has impacted the lives of LGB people in profound ways. In particular, the field of psychology, with its tools and methods, has made significant contributions to the acceptance of LGB people in a heterosexual world. This chapter traces the history of LGB mental health from the nineteenth century to the present and focuses on major events and the intersections of theory, research, politics, and activism in the history of this field. It explores various facets of cultural and psychological history that include the pathologizing of homosexuality, the rise of psychological science and the political movements in the mid-twentieth century, and the major shifts in policy that ensued. The toll of the AIDS epidemic on the field is also discussed, as is the impact of research on national and international policy and legislation.

An Ignominious History

The first mention of same-sex attraction and behavior appeared in the 1886 work *Psychopathia Sexualis* by the Austro-German psychiatrist Richard von Kraft-Ebbing. A notorious cross-dresser himself, Kraft-Ebbing espoused the belief commonly held by ultraconservative religious individuals that the sole legitimate purpose of sexual activity was procreation, and that "homosexuality" was deemed pathological as it served no apparent purpose other than that of sexual pleasure. "With opportunity for the natural satisfaction of the sexual instinct, every expression of it that does not correspond with the purpose of nature—i.e., propagation,—must be regarded as perverse" (Kraft-Ebbing, 1886). He included "masochism, sadism, necrophilia and anilingus" in the same category as homosexuality.

It would not be until the early twentieth century that Kraft-Ebbing's views were challenged publicly by German physician Magnus Hirschfeld. Alarmed at the incidence of depression and suicidality among same-sex–attracted men in his clinical practice, Hirschfeld, along with several others, founded the "Scientific and Humanitarian Committee" in Berlin in 1896. This was the first public organization whose purpose was to end social stigma and repeal laws against homosexuality. The motto of this organization was "Justice through Science." Hirschfeld sought to establish homosexuality as a natural variant of the human experience by scientifically proving that same-sex desire and behavior, by themselves, present no psychological maladjustment other than that which is experienced as a natural response to social opprobrium.

The damage done by Kraft-Ebbing's philosophy and its sociopolitical antecedents, however, was not easily eradicated. The nascent movement among some healthcare professionals to "normalize" homosexuality was eclipsed by the sociopolitical events of the time, most notably the rise of Nazism in the 1930s. Homosexuals were among the first to be sent to concentration camps (Plant, 1986). After a period of relative freedom during the 1920s, at least in large European cities such as Berlin and Paris, homosexuals were driven back into closets. Fear of persecution was common in London as well, where Section 61 of the "Offences against the person" act identified "buggery" as grounds for imprisonment (Crompton, 2009). In North America, New York City police started in 1903 to conduct systematic raids of gay bathhouses and social clubs. As a result, a climate of fear existed among lesbian women and gay men throughout the Western world.

Prohibition of homosexuality was institutionally enshrined in the U.S., Canadian, and other national military organizations. Homosexuality was an exclusion criterion for military service; in World War II, when more soldiers were needed for the war effort, gay men had a choice between concealing their sexual orientation or facing the shame of public identification (Sinclair, 2009). Sigmund Freud stated in his famous 1935 "Letter to an American Mother" that "Homosexuality is assuredly no advantage, but it is nothing to be ashamed of, no vice, no degradation, it cannot be classified as an illness; we consider it to be a variation of the sexual function produced by a certain arrest of sexual development." However, his work was used by psychoanalysts throughout the twentieth century to pathologize same-sex attraction and behavior. Foremost among these are Irving Bieber, Charles Socarides, and Joseph Nicolosi, all of whom used Freud's theory of arrested psychosexual development as the basis for their therapeutic "cures" of homosexuality.

Nicolosi (1991) was the father of the modern-day "conversion therapy" movement as a prolific author and founder of the now-bankrupt National Association for Research and Therapy of Homosexuality (NARTH). Nicolosi contended that same-sex orientation among men could be cured through a corrective relational identification with a male therapist. Numerous other methodologies have been employed through the years to change homosexuals into heterosexuals, including masturbatory reconditioning, visualization and hypnosis, and aversive techniques such as electric shock to the hands and genitals and nausea-inducing drugs—none of which has ever been shown to be effective (American Psychological Association, 2009), and many of which were likely dangerous.

The Midcentury Rise of Psychological Science, Politics, and Activism

After World War II, having discovered that they were not alone, gay men and lesbian women began to locate themselves in and around larger cities in the United States where the odds of finding one another increased substantially. A homosexual subculture developed as gay men and lesbian women met in secrecy socially and at clubs in the larger cities. At this point, homosexuality was regarded more as a mental illness, and some gay men and lesbian women welcomed this perspective because it offered the hope for therapeutic change from an existence that was plagued by harsh legal sanctions and societal ruin (Bayer, 1987). It is important to note that Kinsey's *Sexual Behavior in the Human Male* (1948) was published following World War II and suggested that the number of men who engaged in homosexual behavior had been greatly underestimated.

A number of organizations emerged during this postwar era that provided the foundation for the pursuit of human rights and self-respect for gay men and lesbian women. The most important of these was the Mattachine Society, founded in 1950 by a small group of gay men led by a leftist activist named Harry Hay. The organization went out of its way to oppose "indecent public behavior," pedophilia, violence, and affiliations with political parties (Bayer, 1987). It is important to keep in mind that the early 1950s were fraught with the political paranoia and hysteria created by McCarthyism. Thus, the Mattachine Society sought to educate gay men and lesbian women about the importance of appropriate public behavior. The organization called on psychiatrists and psychologists to educate their clients and the public more thoroughly about homosexuality but did not engage in more aggressive political advocacy as a group. The organization also published *The Mattachine Review*. There were numerous freewheeling debates taken up in this publication—particularly those that represented conflicting perspectives among psychiatrists, psychologists, and other therapists on the etiology of homosexuality, its status as a mental illness, and whether a cure was possible (Bayer, 1987).

Just a few years following the creation of the Mattachine Society, Del Martin and Phyllis Lyon in San Francisco created the Daughters of Bilitis (DOB) in 1955 with four lesbian couples who met in order to socialize privately away from watchful law enforcement. By 1959, DOB had chapters in San Francisco, Los Angeles, Chicago, and Rhode Island. In its mission statement, DOB noted the complete lack of information about female homosexuality and began its own newsletter, *The Ladder*. In every issue of *The Ladder* DOB's four primary goals were printed: educating lesbian women about themselves; educating the public in an effort to break down prejudice and taboos; supporting research conducted by legitimate and responsible psychologists, sociologists, and others regarding homosexuality; and reviewing the penal code as it pertained to homosexuality—suggesting and promoting changes through legislative efforts (Blumenfeld & Raymond, 1988).

Then came a landmark study conducted by Evelyn Hooker (1957), who posited that it was necessary to study nonclinical samples of homosexual males, not simply those who sought or who were referred to treatment, if one were to understand homosexuality. Her groundbreaking investigation of a nonclinical sample of gay men matched with a heterosexual male sample found no significant differences between the two groups on the Rorschach and two other projective tests (Hooker, 1957). This study challenged the notions that homosexuality per se was a mental illness and that projective testing would reveal its existence.

In the two decades that followed, a new generation of psychological research emerged that essentially revealed no significant differences between heterosexual and homosexual individuals on a wide range of variables related to mental health (cf. Hancock & Greenspan, 2010). Scientific evidence that demonstrated the fallacy of the notion of homosexuality as psychopathology began to accumulate.

The 1960s ushered in social unrest, the Vietnam War, and a high level of activism and advocacy among the large proportion of young adults in the United States (the "baby boomers"). Political activism also included antiracism efforts and organizations and political advocacy for women's rights. What followed cannot be fully understood without understanding this tumultuous context.

Earthquakes and Aftershocks

In the 1960s, most of the gay bars in New York City's Greenwich Village were owned by the mafia, and the police were paid to ignore the activities that occurred within these bars. Sometimes the wealthiest patrons were blackmailed by the bar owners in order to keep their sexual activities/orientation secret. Raids still occurred routinely, but police who were paid by the mafia tipped off these bars in advance so that liquor being sold by the mafia could be hidden. In addition, there were state laws about wearing gender-appropriate clothing. Those arrested in the raids had their names printed in the newspapers and often suffered the consequences (e.g., familial disputes, loss of job, divorce).

On June 24, 1969, the Stonewall Inn bar was raided—targeted for operating without a liquor license. Just after midnight on June 28, 1969, the Stonewall Inn was raided again in hopes that the bar would be shut down for good. This time, patrons resisted the raid and those being singled out by the police (mainly those patrons wearing gender-inappropriate attire) called on others to fight back. Within several hours, the crowd had grown so large that the original group of arresting officers had barricaded themselves in the bar. The uprising lasted several days. A year following the Stonewall Inn uprising, a march was organized and proceeded down Christopher Street. As supporters joined in, the crowd eventually numbered into the thousands. Other cities (e.g., San Francisco, Los Angeles, Chicago) in the United States and across the world began to have "pride parades," and gay and lesbian organizations became more activist.

A new generation of gay rights activists began to confront panels (in which there were no gay or lesbian participants) at professional conferences such as the American Psychiatric Association and the American Psychological Association. In 1970, at the American Psychiatric Association convention in San Francisco, Martin Bieber presented on a panel on transsexualism and homosexuality. According to Bayer (1987), Bieber was "unprepared for the kind of rage that greeted him. His efforts to explain his position to his challengers were met with derisive laughter" (p. 102). At the same convention, a paper by Nathaniel McConaghy, a psychiatrist from Australia, described aversive conditioning techniques used with sexual deviation. This presentation was met with "shouts of 'vicious,' 'torture,' and 'where did you take your residency, Auschwitz?' " (Bayer, 1987, p. 103). The American Psychiatric Association convention in 1971 saw more confrontations. One such confrontation occurred when a group of gay activists found an exhibit that was promoting equipment to be used in the aversive conditioning in the treatment of homosexuality (Bayer, 1987).

A panel at the same convention that included gay and lesbian presenters (i.e., Frank Kameny, Del Martin, Larry Littlejohn) revealed a level of anger that caught many members of the American Psychiatric Association by surprise (Bayer, 1987). At the 1972 American Psychiatric Association convention, activists Frank Kameny and Barbara Gittings appeared on a panel entitled "Psychiatry: Friend or Foe to Homosexuals?" with a third panel member, psychiatrist John Fryer. Fryer wore a mask and an oversized tuxedo and spoke about his life as a closeted psychiatrist in a field that classified homosexuality as a mental disorder. A group of gay and lesbian psychologists met at the American Psychological Association convention in 1973 and became the Association of Gay Psychologists (AGP) (Krajeski, 1996).

During this period, other societal "earthquakes" challenged the lives of gay, lesbian, and bisexual people. In 1977, Dade County, Florida, passed an ordinance that banned discrimination based on sexual orientation. Anita Bryant, a singer, former Miss Oklahoma beauty pageant winner, and ambassador for the Florida Citrus Commission, ran a campaign called "Save Our Children" to repeal the ordinance. She believed in the sinfulness of homosexuality and believed that homosexuals recruited children and also molested them. Her campaign helped to mobilize antigay conservative religious groups across the United States, but it also created an enormous backlash among gay, lesbian, and bisexual people. A boycott against orange juice was called for and gay bars across the country stopped serving screwdrivers. Her campaign ignited other efforts to repeal antidiscrimination ordinances in Minnesota, Kansas, and Oregon. In California, the Briggs Initiative sought to fire any public school employee for being gay or making pro-gay statements about homosexuality or homosexual people.

Then, in November 1978, openly gay San Francisco supervisor Harvey Milk was killed along with San Francisco mayor George Moscone by former supervisor Dan White. White was found guilty of voluntary manslaughter by a jury who was convinced that he was depressed and despondent and not responsible for the two murders he committed. The verdict enraged the gay community and a spontaneous protest occurred that night. The march turned violent and when it ended, 61 police officers and 100 protesters were hospitalized (Butler, 1979).

Meanwhile, the American Psychiatric Association became increasingly aware of the "potential and actual discrimination that resulted from psychiatric labeling" (Krajeski, 1996, p. 24). In 1974, with considerable resistance from psychoanalytically oriented psychiatrists, the group voted (with a majority of 58 percent) to drop the diagnosis of homosexuality from the second edition of the *Diagnostic and Statistical Manual of Mental Disorders* (DSM-II) (Bayer, 1987).

A year later, the American Psychological Association adopted similar language to that used by the American Psychiatric Association and added language that urged "all mental health professionals to take the lead in removing the stigma of mental illness that has long been associated with homosexual orientations" (Conger, 1975, p. 633). With the passage of this landmark resolution, the American Psychological Association created a Task Force on the Status of Lesbian and Gay Male Psychologists, the Committee on Gay Concerns was created in 1980, and in 1984 the association approved the formation of a division—the Society for the Psychological Study of Lesbian and Gay Issues (Division 44). Similar efforts in the psychiatric community resulted in the Gay, Lesbian, and Bisexual Caucus of the American Psychiatric Association in 1978. Additionally, within the American Psychiatric Association itself, a Task Force on Gay, Lesbian, and Bisexual Issues created in 1978 became a standing committee in 1981.

Celebrations for the accomplishments in mental health were short-lived, however. When the DSM-III was published in 1980, the diagnosis of "ego-dystonic homosexuality" was introduced, defined as "a desire to acquire or increase heterosexual arousal, so that heterosexual relationships can be initiated or maintained, and a sustained pattern of overt homosexual arousal that the individual explicitly states has been unwanted and a persistent source of distress" (American Psychiatric Association, 1980, p. 281). The lack of empirical evidence for ego-dystonic homosexuality and the irrationality of diagnosing culturally induced internalized stigma were central to the argument to remove it. In the end, this problematic diagnosis was removed from DSM-III-R (American Psychiatric Association, 1987), the revision of DSM-III.

The Treatment of LGB People

In their survey of psychologists as therapists, Pope, Tabachnik, and Keith-Speigel (1987) found that 24 percent of the clinicians admitted that they had treated homosexuality per se as pathological while 42 percent asserted that this practice was ethical.

In 1986, the Task Force on Bias in Psychotherapy with Lesbians and Gay Men conducted a survey of 2,544 psychologists to further examine the treatment of lesbian and gay clients (Garnets, Hancock, Cochran, Goodchilds, & Peplau, 1991). The Bias Study, as it has been called, documented stark examples of biased, inadequate, inappropriate, and even harmful care across various aspects of practice with lesbian and gay clients (i.e., assessment, intervention, identity, relationships, families, and education/expertise). Therapists were described as attributing a lesbian or gay client's presenting problems to their non-heterosexual orientation and focusing upon this orientation when it had nothing to do with the client's presenting problem (Garnets et al., 1991). Therapists expressed beliefs that were insensitive, trivializing, and demeaning. One lesbian client, who presented with issues related to her sexual identity, was told by her therapist "If you have a uterus, don't you think you should use it?" (Garnets et al., 1991, p. 313). The study also documented abrupt referrals upon disclosure of a lesbian or gay sexual orientation, beliefs on the part of therapists that homosexuality per se indicated some form of psychological disturbance, and active efforts to promote or even change a client's lesbian or gay orientation to a heterosexual orientation. These problematic attitudes and behaviors were found to exist by a study conducted over ten years following the adoption of the American Psychological Association's (Conger, 1975) resolution described above. It was clear that additional efforts were needed to facilitate changes in the attitudes, knowledge, and skills of psychologists.

Sexual Orientation Change Efforts

So-called conversion therapies were no longer regarded as consistent with the professional organizations' more affirmative policies regarding homosexuality. Moreover, there was a lack of empirical studies providing any evidence that these approaches change sexual orientation (Haldeman, 1991). Psychologist Gerald Davison (1991) concluded that "change-of-orientation therapy programs are ethically improper and should be eliminated. Their availability only confirms professional and societal biases against homosexuality" (p. 148).

The American Psychological Association (1998) did develop a policy entitled "Resolution on Appropriate Therapeutic Responses to Sexual Orientation" that essentially connected specific ethical standards to working with a client's sexual orientation and requests for change (Hancock & Haldeman, in press). While this policy did not specifically state that psychologists should not use such treatments, largely because of concerns from practitioners that banning any type of therapy was dangerous, it did put the profession on notice that there were serious ethical concerns regarding so-called conversion therapies. Later on, the term *sexual orientation change efforts* (SOCE) would be used instead, since these methods did not constitute a legitimate form of therapy.

A 2009 report entitled "Appropriate Affirmative Responses to Sexual Orientation Distress and Change Efforts" addressed SOCE in a more powerful manner and recommended that such terms as "conversion therapy" or "reparative therapy" no longer be used (American Psychological Association, 2009). This report was also supported by research that found harm to individuals who had experienced SOCE (Shidlo & Schroeder, 2002) that included suicidality, depression, high-risk sexual behaviors when SOCE had failed, and anger toward therapists the individuals had seen for this treatment. Recently, more research has surfaced that reveals sexual identity distress (Dehlin, Gallaher, Bradshaw, Hyde, & Crowell, 2015), dissociation, depression, and anxiety (Jacobsen & Wright, 2014), increased minority stress (Herek & McLemore, 2013), and increased mental health problems—including an increased risk for suicide (Ryan, Toomey, Diaz, & Russell, 2020).

Guidelines for Psychotherapy with Lesbian, Gay, and Bisexual Clients

The *Guidelines for Psychotherapy with Lesbian, Gay, and Bisexual Clients* were adopted in 2000 by the American Psychological Association (Division 44/ Committee on Lesbian, Gay, and Bisexual Concerns Joint Task Force on Guidelines for Psychotherapy with Lesbian, Gay, and Bisexual Clients, 2000) and provided practitioners with LGB-affirmative recommendations for psychotherapy. The guidelines addressed attitudes toward homosexuality and their impact on LGB clients, relationships and family issues, education and training, and issues of diversity. It was the first document of its kind in the mental health professions and served as a model set of guidelines at the state level and internationally.

Klein's 1993 book *The Bisexual Option* challenged the "either/or" categorization of sexual orientation and proposed a new way of measuring sexual orientation (i.e., the Klein Sexual Orientation Grid). In 1998, the American Institute of Bisexuality was formed by Klein in order to educate professionals and the public about bisexuality. With the increasing literature on bisexuality (e.g., Fox, 1995), the authors of the *Guidelines for Psychotherapy with Lesbian, Gay, and Bisexual Clients* (Division 44/Committee on Lesbian, Gay, and Bisexual Concerns Joint Task Force on Guidelines for Psychotherapy with Lesbian, Gay, and Bisexual Clients, 2000) included information relevant to working with bisexual individuals.

The second version of these guidelines was adopted by the American Psychological Association in 2012. The guidelines were updated and expanded, and covered additional areas regarding religion and spirituality, distinguishing sexual orientation issues from those related to gender identity, the issues of differing LGB cohorts, and economic and workplace issues. Each guideline was reviewed and revised in light of the most current literature. The striking feature about the 2012 guidelines is how much the literature on LGB issues evolved in a single decade.

Other Policies in Organized Psychology

The American Psychological Association has adopted a wide range of policies since the original resolution in 1975 (Conger, 1975). At present, there are at least a dozen policies that include, but are not limited to, child custody (Conger, 1977); employment rights for gay teachers (Abeles, 1981); hate crimes (Paige, 2005); use of the diagnoses "homosexuality" and "ego-dystonic homosexuality" (Fox, 1988); SOCE (Anton, 2010; DeLeon, 1998); sexual orientation and marriage (Paige, 2005); sexual orientation, parents, and children (Paige, 2005); sexual orientation and military service (Paige, 2005); opposing discriminatory legislation and initiatives targeting LGB persons (Anton, 2008); marriage equality for same-sex couples (American Psychological Association, 2011); and LGB youths in schools (DeLeon, 1993).

Identity, Diversity, and Descriptive Research

It was initially important to challenge the mental illness model of homosexuality and to demonstrate that LGB individuals are as well adjusted as their heterosexual counterparts. However, the research that followed began to focus more on the lives of LGB people in greater detail and has brought more refinement to the understanding of these populations.

Identity

One of the most important lines of inquiry, theorizing, and research in the post-pathologizing era is identity. Initially, in the 1970s and 1980s, the "coming out" process was examined and described via stage models (e.g., Cass, 1979; Savin-Williams, 1988; Troiden, 1979) that depicted the process by which LGB people come to terms with their same-sex attractions and how these feelings are integrated into a person's identity. Discussions regarding the concepts and issues related to LGB identity development and the challenges to establishing a healthy LGB identity were also a focus (e.g., Brown, 1995; Fox, 1995; Gonsiorek, 1995).

Diversity and Differences

Originally, psychology's understanding of homosexuality was, for the most part, based on male homosexuality, with lesbian women frequently overlooked or ignored in the literature (Hancock, 1986). This androcentric view tended to treat observations and research findings on gay men as though they pertained to anyone attracted to members of the same sex—including lesbian and bisexual individuals (Hancock & Greenspan, 2010). The women's movement in the 1970s helped to raise the cultural consciousness regarding the status of women and was reflected in the creation of the Association for Women in Psychology in 1969 and the creation of the American Psychological Association's Division 35 (Psychology of Women) in 1974.

Important differences between lesbian women and gay men and gender role socialization received more attention in the literature. For instance, gender role socialization was found to have a greater impact than sexual orientation on same-sex relationships (e.g., Kurdek, 1994; Peplau, 1981; Ritter & Terndrup, 2002). Gay male couples were found to be more sexually active than lesbian or heterosexual couples and reported less exclusivity than other couples (e.g., Blumstein & Schwartz, 1983; Kurdek, 1995; Peplau, 1991). Suffice it to say that within-group differences and characteristics emerged as a rapidly growing area of LGB research during this time.

Similarly, just as generalizations about homosexuality were made based on studies of gay men, most conclusions made from early research on LGB people were based on studies of white individuals—particularly white gay men (Chan, 1989, 1992; Greene, 1997). Even after the new attention to gender differences in the literature, findings pertaining to identity development, prejudice, and other important topics were insensitive to the issues experienced by LGB people of color and therefore not necessarily applicable to them (Hancock & Greenspan, 2010). In the 1980s, there was a dramatic increase in writing about and research with racially and ethnically diverse LGB individuals. Authors challenged psychologists to conceptualize identity with more sensitivity and complexity and described how LGB people of color struggled with the difficult and often painful tasks of negotiating multiple stigmatized identities (Chan, 1989, 1992; Martinez & Sullivan, 1998; Mays & Cochran, 1988).

The removal of homosexuality from the diagnostic nomenclature as well as the results of psychological research (e.g., Klein, 1993; Klein, Sepekoff, & Wolf, 1985; Weinberg, Williams, & Pryor, 1994) facilitated the recognition of bisexuality as a viable sexual orientation for some individuals. Following this, the entire notion of sexual orientation in discrete categories was questioned. Firestein (1996) and Rothblum (2000) noted that sexual behavior, identity, and desire are not highly correlated. The literature on bisexuality also began to increase and examine sex differences, attitudes toward bisexuality (e.g., Hertlein, Hartwell, & Munns, 2016), bisexuality in various racial and ethnic populations (e.g., Collins, 2004), and, more recently, sexual fluidity (e.g., Ross, Daneback, & Mansson, 2012).

Intersectionality

More recently, LGB psychology has reflected the more complex understanding of identity introduced by feminists as "intersectionality" (Crenshaw, 1990). As Collins and Bilge (2016) stated:

> Intersectionality is a way of understanding and analyzing the complexity in the world, in people, and in human experiences. The events and conditions of social and political life and the self can seldom be understood as shaped by one factor. They are generally shaped by many factors in diverse and mutually influencing ways. When it comes to social inequality, people's lives and the organization of power in a given society are better understood as being shaped not by a single axis of social division... but by many axes that work together and influence each other.

This framework endeavors to encompass the variables in identity, their interactions with one another, and their impact on a person's behavior and relationships with others. With regard to sexual orientation identity, it is a far cry from linear models without context. It affords the ability to understand and describe the lives of, say, younger Asian American lesbian women or older African American lesbian women.

AIDS

No history of LGB psychology would be complete without mentioning the AIDS epidemic (see also Chapter 33 on HIV/AIDS and mental health in this volume). By the end of 1987, over 50,000 people had been diagnosed with AIDS—95 percent of whom (47,993) had died (Centers for Disease Control and Prevention, 2001). AIDS was viewed as a gay disease, and there was an enormous challenge to even have it recognized as a threat to the larger population. With Ronald Reagan, a Republican conservative, in the White House, AIDS was generally ignored. Meanwhile, exacerbated by the absence of information about AIDS, fear spread rapidly among the gay community.

LGB psychologists, however, were paying attention. The November issue of the *American Psychologist* in 1984 included articles attempting to warn psychologists about the public health hazard and to describe the psychological impact of AIDS on gay men (Batchelor, 1984; Morin, Charles, & Malyon, 1984). In 1990, the American Psychological Association formed an Ad Hoc Committee on Psychology and AIDS dedicated to the development and implementation of the association's response to the epidemic. Psychology was confronted with major challenges during this time: first, the lack of knowledge about the nature of AIDS and how it was transmitted; second, the lack of responsiveness of the federal government and resources to deal with AIDS during the Reagan administration; and third, the attitudes of the general population toward people who were HIV positive or who had full-blown AIDS.

Today, the American Psychological Association's Public Interest directorate provides numerous resources for educators, practitioners, and policymakers through links to blogs and websites, association policies on AIDS, a national database of research, and more. In particular, the association works closely with the Centers for Disease Control and Prevention to track trends in new infection so that prevention programs may be tailored accordingly.

LGB Psychology and the Law: The Research at Work

In this section, we will summarize some of the main issues affecting the lives of LGB people that have been addressed in legislatures and in the courts. Social policies that have the most profound impact on LGB persons, from the regulation of sexual behavior to antidiscrimination statutes to parental custodial rights, have been decided in the judicial and legislative arenas.

The Supreme Court: Bowers v. Hardwick

The first major Supreme Court case to directly affect LGB people was *Bowers v. Hardwick* in 1986. In this case, Michael Hardwick had been involved in consensual homosexual activity with another man in the privacy of his bedroom when an Atlanta police officer, Keith Torick, burst into the room. He had entered Hardwick's home to serve an invalid subpoena for a court appearance regarding an earlier matter unrelated to Hardwick's sexual behavior. Torick arrested both Hardwick and his companion on the spot for violation of Georgia's sodomy statute. The district attorney declined to press charges against Hardwick, but Hardwick sued Georgia attorney general Michael Bowers for a declaratory judgment that Georgia's sodomy law was unconstitutional.

The Supreme Court, in a 5–4 decision, ruled against Hardwick, with Justice Byron White stating, in the majority opinion, that the Constitution did not confer "a fundamental right to engage in homosexual sodomy" (*Bowers v. Hardwick,* 478 U.S., 186, 1986). Chief Justice Warren Burger concurred, stating in his opinion that "To hold that the act of homosexual sodomy is somehow protected as a fundamental right would be to cast aside millennia of moral teaching." (*Bowers v. Hardwick,* 478 U.S. 197, 1986). This ruling was regarded as a serious setback for the gay rights movement, and for LGB psychology in particular, as it relegated "homosexuals" to an inferior status whose right to sexual activity with consensual partners was not constitutionally protected.

Interestingly, however, the ruling ultimately catalyzed greater legal advocacy on behalf of LGB persons. In the years that followed *Bowers*, several states—including Georgia itself—repealed their sodomy laws as unconstitutional. In this seesaw era of progress in—and backlash against—the gay rights movement, a number of jurisdictions enacted both pro- and anti-gay measures on discrimination in housing and employment. For example, in 1989, Colorado governor Roy Romer issued an executive order banning discrimination against people with HIV/AIDS.

Colorado's Amendment 2

The Christian right soon discovered that antigay political initiatives could be a galvanizing force for campaigns to restore "Christian morality" to government and social policies. The most prominent such campaign was Colorado's Amendment 2, which based its platform on the concept of "no special rights" for homosexuals. Gay rights activists argued in vain that antidiscrimination protections were not *special* but were simply an effort to ensure that LGB persons had the same rights as everyone else. The Amendment 2 campaign was successful, and soon other states followed suit in their effort to ensure that LGB people could still be discriminated against in housing and employment.

Lawrence v. Texas

The next major legal decision before the Supreme Court was *Lawrence v. Texas* (2003). In 1998, John G. Lawrence of Houston, Texas, was arrested along with Tyron Garner for engaging in "deviate sex" as sheriff's deputies (who had been tipped off by a jealous lover) invaded Lawrence's apartment. With support from the Lambda Legal organization and amicus briefs from fourteen professional organizations (including American Psychological Association), the Supreme Court in a 6–3 decision struck down the Texas sodomy law as a violation of the due process and equal protection provisions in the Constitution. This was a milestone decision because it not only invalidated the Texas sodomy statute but also automatically invalidated similar laws in thirteen other states, as well as overturning *Bowers v. Hardwick* some thirteen years earlier.

Same-Sex Marriage

Understanding what a valuable enemy LGB persons were for solidifying their base, the religious right turned its attention to enshrining heterosexual marriage and prohibiting same-sex unions or marriages, largely by disseminating scripturally based antigay sentiment. The Republican Party became an eager partner in this effort, and in the U.S. midterm election year of 2006, measures outlawing same-sex marriage passed in twelve states.

At the time, same-sex marriage had only been legalized in one state, Massachusetts, through a 2004 decision of the state supreme court. Therefore, there was little precedent to argue that there was no threat to heterosexual marriage through the legalization of same-sex marriage. At this point, further research was conducted to identify the mental health effects of antigay ballot measures on LGB people. Not surprisingly, Rostosky, Riggle, Horne, and Miller (2009) found that lesbian women and gay men living in states with anti–same-sex marriage initiatives were significantly more likely to be depressed and anxious than their counterparts living in more progressive states. These findings have been replicated by Hatzenbuehler (2010) and others.

American Psychological Association Amicus Briefs

By this time, the American Psychological Association had submitted more amicus briefs in support of LGB issues than all other "social policy" areas put together (Hegarty, 2018). Many of these briefs were submitted on behalf of same-sex parents, using research that Herek (2006) described as "remarkably consistent" in demonstrating that there was no significant difference in mental health or social adjustment between youth raised in same-sex or heterosexual families. Even so, laws regarding same-sex parenting and adoption remained variable throughout the United States. The issue was settled throughout the nation in 2017 when the U.S. Supreme Court struck down an Arkansas law prohibiting adoption by same-sex individuals or couples.

Hate Crimes Legislation and Stigma

Another area in which psychological research has made significant contributions to pro-LGB legislation is that of hate crimes. Herek (1989), in the first major article in the psychological literature on the subject, reported that as many as 92 percent of gay men and 72 percent of lesbian women had experienced some form of antigay harassment. In addition, 24 percent of gay men and 7 percent of lesbian women reported that they had been physically assaulted (Herek, 1989). Herek conducted a large-scale ($n = 2{,}300$) study of hate crime victimization among lesbian women and gay men in the Sacramento, California, area (Herek, 1999), finding that victims of hate crimes appear to be at greater risk for long-term mental health concerns, including depression, stress, and anger, than those who are victims of random crimes.

Meyer's (1995) model of minority stress describes stress processes, including experiences of prejudice, expectations of rejection, hiding, concealing, internalized homophobia, and ameliorative coping processes. Meyer describes this as a normative reaction to experiences of prejudice and discrimination and the expectation thereof, resulting in an elevated stress level, from which the person may develop adaptive or maladaptive coping mechanisms. We mention it here because this theory is widely used in explaining a number of social disparities that are the basis for pro-LGBT legislative initiatives.

"Don't Ask, Don't Tell"

The last bastion of institutionalized discrimination against lesbian women and gay men was the U.S. military. In 1993, President Bill Clinton's attempt to lift the ban on lesbian women and gay men serving in the military was thwarted by an unfriendly Congress, who opposed lifting the ban. What resulted was a compromise that came to be known as "Don't Ask, Don't Tell" (DADT), in which lesbian women and gay men could serve in the armed forces provided that they did not disclose their sexual orientation. This prompted the American Psychological Association to issue a statement at its 2004 meeting: "Empirical evidence fails to show that sexual orientation is germane to any aspect of military effectiveness including unit cohesion, morale, recruitment and retention." That same year, the American Psychological Association Divisions 19 (Military) and 44 (LGBT) issued a joint statement calling for the end of DADT. It would not be until 2010, however, that Congress enacted the "Don't Ask, Don't Tell Repeal Act of 2010," putting an end to the policy.

Obergefell v. Hodges

It is apparent that public opinion about LGBT rights has shifted dramatically in the past twenty years. A recent survey indicates that 63 percent of people in the United States believed that same-sex couples and individuals should have parental and adoptive rights and 73 percent believed that discrimination against LGBT persons in housing and employment should be outlawed (Flores, 2014). The reasons for this rapid shift are not clearly understood, but it is reasonable to speculate that the increased visibility of LGBT people—in the media, as well as in public and private life—has been significant in shaping and reshaping public opinion. In any case, with same-sex marriage legal in 37 states as of 2015, the stage was set for the landmark Supreme Court ruling *Obergefell v. Hodges.*

The Supreme Court was obliged to take up the case of same-sex marriage as there was an amalgam of six separate cases from lower courts with conflicting appeals court rulings. Four of these cases were consolidated in the *Obergefell* decision, with the primary issues centered on the question of whether or not the Fourteenth Amendment's guarantees of due process and equal protection extended to same-sex couples. The court found that the fundamental rights found in the due process clause "extend to certain personal choices central to individual dignity and autonomy, including intimate choices that define personal identity and beliefs" (U.S. Supreme Court, 2015). To date, it is estimated that one in ten self-identified lesbian or gay male individuals are in a same-sex marriage (Pew Research Center, 2019).

Although *Obergefell* might be considered a matter of "settled law" at this point, the current political climate provides ample reason for lesbian women and gay men to be concerned about their hard-won constitutional rights. In a recent antidiscrimination case (*Masterpiece Cake Shop v. Colorado Civil Rights Commission*), the U.S. Supreme Court (2017) found that a baker could deny service to a gay couple based on religious beliefs. The precedent here is chilling and could easily extend beyond bakeries to healthcare facilities, pharmacies, and other services. Furthermore, this ruling could affect women's access to reproductive medicine and other aspects of healthcare—all based on the religious beliefs of service industry workers.

SOCE

As previously mentioned, SOCE have come under scrutiny by the profession as well as by state legislatures, licensing boards, and the courts. In 2012, the first law prohibiting the use of SOCE on minors by licensed mental health professionals was passed in California. As of this writing, seventeen other jurisdictions have passed similar legislation, and state licensing boards are also considering policies to prohibit or limit SOCE. So far, these laws have withstood court challenges from SOCE practitioners.

LGB Psychology Internationally

IPsyNet

In 2005, INET was born (becoming IPsyNet in 2013) to provide a structural mechanism in which international LGBT psychology could develop. Members of IPsyNet include national, multinational, and international psychological associations. The mission of IPsyNet is

> to facilitate and support the contributions of psychological organizations to the global understanding of human sexual and gender diversity, to the health and well-being of people around the world who identify as lesbian, gay, bisexual, transgender, transsexual or intersex (LGBTI), and to the full enjoyment of human rights by people of all sexual orientations, gender expressions, gender identities and sex characteristics. (American Psychological Association, 2018)

International LGB Policies

Legal protections against discrimination in housing and employment for LGBT persons are still a matter of geography and socioeconomic status in the United States, as there is (as yet) no federal antidiscrimination statute. In more progressive and affluent jurisdictions, such protections have been in place for decades, whereas they are still absent in many conservative areas. However, such antidiscrimination laws were nationally instituted decades ago throughout Western Europe, Canada, and several countries in Central and South America.

Long before same-sex marriage became legal in the United States, it was approved in a number of European countries. The frequent predecessor of same-sex marriage, registered domestic partnerships, was first approved in Denmark (1989), with the other Scandinavian countries and the Netherlands soon following suit. In 2001, the Netherlands became the first country in the world to grant full marital rights to same-sex couples. Canada followed suit in 2005.

International laws institutionalizing equality in these areas have generated data indicating that there is no reason for mainstream society to fear such legislation. Antidiscrimination statutes worldwide do not elevate LGBT persons to a "special status," nor do same-sex marriage statutes destroy the heterosexual nuclear family—arguments still heard in opposition to such laws. Legal protections are cited as a central factor in a recent study of "best and worst countries in the world" for LGBT persons (Pew Research Center, 2013). Those countries that have the most comprehensive antidiscrimination protections are, not coincidentally, also ranked as the "best" places for LGBT people, whereas those countries lacking such protections (and even criminalizing same-sex behavior) are ranked as the worst. This is worthy of mention insofar as these data may be used to advance advocacy in the United States.

Refugees

As of this writing, there are still seventy-two countries in the world where same-sex behavior is criminalized (Human Dignity Trust, 2019). In eleven of these countries, most of which are in Africa, the Middle East, and South Asia, same-sex behavior is punishable by death. These circumstances are untenable for LGBT persons living in those countries, so it is not surprising that many of those who are able seek refuge in more tolerant places. At the same time, immigration policies have tightened considerably in recent years, particularly in Western Europe. Most LGBT refugees are fleeing various and complex traumas: violence including rape, often at the hands of the police; being outed by family members; witnessing beatings and murder of loved ones; and more. Often, the voyage itself retraumatizes the refugee prior to arriving in an unfamiliar place with a different culture.

Furthermore, those seeking asylum are often subjected to intrusive and humiliating questioning in order to have a chance to stay in a safe harbor. As a result, a number of international agencies and groups have been created to address what is a humanitarian crisis. The Rainbow Railroad is an organization that helps bring LGBT people from all over the world to safety in the United Kingdom and Canada. Rainbow Street, an organization based in the San Francisco Bay Area, helps LGBT people from the Middle East find safe housing and mental health services. Many European nations have governmental programs designed to help acculturate and advocate for LGBT asylum seekers, such as Gaycamp in Sweden. U.S. mental health professionals have a role to play in this crisis.

Looking Ahead

One of the most important reasons to study history is to learn from past experience—and as we have shown in this chapter, LGB psychology has created a rich history in less than fifty years. If there is one common theme running throughout this necessarily brief review, it is undoubtedly the power of research. Starting with Hooker (1957), research has been the most powerful tool in all of the major policy, legislative, and judicial victories for LGB people, as well as in transforming conceptualization of sexual orientation in theory, practice, and policy. The quality of our research has improved markedly as well. Where once LGB research was primarily in the province of convenience-based samples, more robust data sets are now available through random population-based samples, making it easier to generalize results.

Policies and laws do not change by research alone, however. Visibility has been key in shifting public opinion and public policy. The courage shown by early LGB leaders was central in bringing an end to the "pathology" model of same-sex attraction and behavior; antidiscrimination laws protecting LGB people in housing and employment; healthcare policy; lesbian and gay adoptive and parental rights; protecting vulnerable youth from SOCE; and so much more. None of this would have happened without the courage and energy of LGB leaders and allies—which brings us to the question: Where do we go from here, and how do we get there?

Advocacy is the process by which LGB rights have historically been secured, and we would submit that this will be true going forward as well. As previously mentioned, the database reflecting LGB experiences and attitudes from population-based samples is growing, but more national surveys need to include questions about sexual orientation. The Institutes of Medicine (2011) commissioned a report citing a number of health disparities faced by LGB persons and called for improved data collection with this population. Given the number of LGB people living below the poverty line, particularly in rural areas (where there are less likely to be LGB-competent providers), the Fenway Institute (2014) called on the U.S. Department of Human and Health Services to designate LGB persons a "medically underserved population," which would expand resources available for training and education of healthcare professionals, as well as improving direct service to sexual minority/gender diverse people.

There are several issues for which advocacy will be needed in the legislative arena—most notably that of antidiscrimination protections on the national level in the United States and other nations. Public education campaigns are another vehicle by which research can be used to protect LGB people. Bullying is still seen as a primary cause of queer teen suicidality and depression (Ryan et al., 2020), and both public education and systemic interventions aimed at the institutional level are needed to address this issue. Professional education campaigns are equally important to train and refine the skills of mental health care providers. Whether the care provider is a rural physician seeing an LGB person for the first time, or an expert therapist seeking the latest clinical recommendations for working with LGB people, professional education must keep up with the proliferation of LGB-oriented research. LGB-specific treatment modalities, for example, are being developed (Pachankis, 2018), and the American Psychological Association's practice guidelines are updated every ten years to keep pace with the evolving literature.

Finally, organizational collaboration is essential. The early days of LGB mental health care, and healthcare in general, were marked by organizations and professional associations working independently. Those days have passed, and healthcare policy requires collaboration and integration of effort from the fields of psychology, psychiatry, medicine, nursing, social work, and counseling. Other organizations working to stop bullying, anti-LGBT violence, suicide, and other issues that have a tremendous impact on the collective LGB psyche benefit from collaboration with professional groups.

References

Abeles, N. (1981). Proceedings of the American Psychological Association, Incorporated, for the year 1980: Minutes of the annual meeting of the Council of Representatives. *American Psychologist, 36*, 552–86. doi:10.1037/h0078369

American Psychiatric Association. (1980). *Diagnostic and statistical manual of mental disorders* (3rd ed.). Washington, DC: American Psychiatric Association.

American Psychiatric Association. (1987). *Diagnostic and statistical manual of mental disorders* (3rd ed., revised). Washington, DC: American Psychiatric Association.

American Psychological Association. (2004). Proceedings of the American Psychological Association for the legislative year 2004. Minutes of the meeting of the Council of Representatives, July 28 & 30, Honolulu, HI.

American Psychological Association. (2009). *Report of the Task Force on Appropriate Therapeutic Responses to Sexual Orientation*. Washington, DC: APA Books.

American Psychological Association. (2011). *Resolution on marriage equality for same-sex couples*. Washington, DC: Author.

American Psychological Association. (2012). Guidelines for psychological practice with lesbian, gay, and bisexual clients. *American Psychologist, 67*(1), 10–42. doi:10.1037/a0024659

American Psychological Association. (2018). IPsyU: Mission statement. Retrieved from https://www.apa.org/ipsynet/about.

Anton, B. (2008). Proceedings of the American Psychological Association, Incorporated, for the legislative year 2007: Minutes of the annual meeting of the Council of Representatives. *American Psychologist, 63*, 360–442. doi:10.1037/0003-066X.63.5.360

Anton, B. S. (2010). Proceedings of the American Psychological Association for the legislative year 2009: Minutes of the annual meeting of the Council of Representatives and minutes of the meetings of the Board of Directors. *American Psychologist, 65*, 385–475. doi:10.1037/a0019553

Batchelor, W. (1984). AIDS: A public health and psychological emergency. *American Psychologist, 39*(11), 1279–84. doi:10.1037/0003-066X.39.11.1279

Bayer, R. (1987). *Homosexuality and American psychiatry: The politics of diagnosis*. Princeton, NJ: Princeton University Press.

Blumenfeld, W. J., & Raymond, D. (1988). *Looking at gay and lesbian life*. Boston, MA: Beacon Press.

Blumstein, P., & Schwartz, P. (1983). *American couples: Money, work, sex*. New York, NY: Morrow.

Bowers v. Hardwick, 478 U.S. (1986). Retrieved from https://www.law.cornell.edu/supremecourt/text/478/186.

Brown, L. S. (1995). Lesbian identities: Concepts and issues. In A. R. D'Augelli & C. J. Patterson (Eds.), *Lesbian, gay, and bisexual identities over the lifespan: Psychological perspectives* (pp. 3–23). New York: Oxford University Press.

Butler, K. (1979, May). A bloody protest at city hall: Verdict angers gays. *San Francisco Chronicle*. Retrieved from https://www.sfchronicle.com/news/article/Chronicle-Covers-The-Dan-White-verdict-and-the-7580067.php.

Cass, V. C. (1979). Homosexual identity formation: A theoretical model. *Journal of Homosexuality, 4*, 219–35. doi:10.1300/J082v04n03_01

Centers for Disease Control and Prevention. (2001). HIV and AIDS—United States, 1981–2000. *Morbidity and Mortality Weekly Report*, 50, 430–4. Retrieved from https://www.cdc.gov/mmwr/preview/mmwrhtml/mm5021a2.htm#tab1

Chan, C. (1989). Issues of identity development among Asian-American lesbians and gay men. *Journal of Counseling and Development, 68*, 16–20. doi:10.1002/j.1556-6676.1989.tb02485.x

Chan, C. (1992). Cultural considerations in counseling Asian-American lesbians and gay men. In S. Dworkin & F. Guttierrez (Eds.), *Counseling gay men and lesbians: Journey to the end of the rainbow* (pp. 115–24). Alexandria, VA: American Association of Counseling and Development.

Collins, J. F. (2004). The intersection of race and bisexuality: A critical overview of the literature and past, present, and future directions of the "borderlands." In R. C. Fox (Ed.), *Current research on bisexuality* (pp. 99–116). Binghamton, NY: Harrington Park Press.

Collins, P. H., & Bilge, S. (2016). *Intersectionality*. Malden, MA: Polity Press. Retrieved from https://books.google.com/books?id=wWUnDQAAQBAJ&printsec=frontcover&dq=intersectionality&hl=en&sa=X&ved=0ahUKEwj5uZH6z-LjAhWPsZ4KHdXSAw0Q6AEIKDAA#v=onepage&q=intersectionality&f=false.

Conger, J. J. (1975). Proceedings of the American Psychological Association, Incorporated, for the year 1974: Minutes of the annual meeting of the Council of Representatives. *American Psychologist, 30*, 620–51.

Conger, J. J. (1977). Proceedings of the American Psychological Association, Incorporated, for the year 1976: Minutes of the annual meeting of the Council of Representatives. *American Psychologist, 32*, 408–38. doi:10.1037/h0078511

Crenshaw, K. (1990). Mapping the margins: Intersectionality, identity politics, and violence against women of color. *Stanford Law Review, 43*, 1241–99. http://www.jstor.org/stable/1229039.

Crompton, L. (2009). *Homosexuality and civilization*. Cambridge, MA: Harvard University Press.

Davison, G. C. (1991). Constructionism and morality in therapy for homosexuality. In J. C. Gonsiorek & J. D. Weinrich (Eds.), *Homosexuality: Research implications for public policy* (pp. 137–48). Newbury Park, CA: Sage Publications.

Dehlin, J. P., Galliher, R. V., Bradshaw, W. S., Hyde, D. C., & Crowell, K. A. (2015). Sexual orientation change efforts among current or former LDS church members. *Journal of Counseling Psychology, 62*, 95–105. doi:10.1037/cou0000011

DeLeon, P. H. (1993). Proceedings of the American Psychological Association, Incorporated, for the year 1992: Minutes of the annual meeting of the Council of Representatives. *American Psychologist, 48*, 745–88. doi:10.1037/0003-066X.48.7.745

DeLeon, P. H. (1998). Proceedings of the American Psychological Association, Incorporated, for the legislative year 1997: Minutes of the annual meeting of the Council of Representatives. *American Psychologist, 53*, 882–939. doi:10.1037/0003-066X.53.8.882

Division 44/Committee on Lesbian, Gay, and Bisexual Concerns Joint Task Force on Guidelines for Psychotherapy with Lesbian, Gay, and Bisexual Clients. (2000). Guidelines for psychotherapy with lesbian, gay, and bisexual clients. *American Psychologist, 55*(12), 1440–51. doi:10.1037/0003-066X.55.12.1440

Fenway Institute. (2014). The case for designating LGBT people as a medically underserved population and a health professional shortage area population group. Retrieved from https://fenwayhealth.org/wp-content/uploads.

Firestein, B. (1996). Bisexuality as a paradigm shift: Transforming our disciplines. In *Bisexuality: The psychology and politics of an invisible minority* (pp. 263–91). Thousand Oaks, CA: Sage Publications.

Flores, A. R. (2014). *National trends in public opinion on LGBT rights in the United States.* Los Angeles: Williams Institute. https://williamsinstitute.law.ucla.edu/wp-content/uploads/POP-natl-trends-nov-2014.pdf.

Fox, R. C. (1995). Bisexual identities. In A. R. D'Augelli & C. J. Patterson (Eds.), *Lesbian, gay, and bisexual identities over the lifespan* (pp. 48–86). New York, NY: Oxford University Press.

Fox, R. E. (1988). Proceedings of the American Psychological Association, Incorporated, for the year 1987: Minutes of the annual meeting of the Council of Representatives. *American Psychologist, 43*, 508–31. doi:10.1037/h0091999

Freud, S. (1935). Letter to an American mother. http://www.psychpage.com/gay/library/freudsletter.html.

Garnets, L. D., Hancock, K. A., Cochran, S. D., Goodchilds, J., & Peplau, L. A. (1991). Issues in psychotherapy with lesbians and gay men: A survey of psychologists. *American Psychologist, 46*(9), 964–72. doi:10.1037/0003-066X.46.9.964

Gonsiorek, J. C. (1995). Gay male identities: Concepts and issues. In A. R. D'Augelli & C. J. Patterson (Eds.), *Lesbian, gay, and bisexual identities over the the lifespan: Psychological perspectives* (pp. 24–47). New York: Oxford University Press.

Greene, B. (1997). Ethnic minority lesbians and gay men: Mental health and treatment issues. In B. Greene (Ed.), *Ethnic and cultural diversity among lesbians and gay men* (pp. 216–39). Thousand Oaks, CA: Sage Publications.

Haldeman, D. C. (1991). Sexual orientation conversion therapy for gay men and lesbians: A scientific examination. In J. Gonsiorek & J. D. Weinrich (Eds.), *Homosexuality: Research implications for public policy* (pp. 149–60). Newbury Park, CA: Sage Publications.

Hancock, K. A. (1986, August). *Trends in lesbian psychology: A look at twenty years of empirical and non-empirical research.* Division 44 Presidential Address presented at the meeting of the American Psychological Association, Washington, DC.

Hancock, K. A., & Greenspan, K. (2010). Emergence and development of the psychological study of lesbian, gay, bisexual, and transgender issues. In J. C. Chrisler & D. R. McCreary (Eds.), *Handbook of gender research in psychology* (Vol. 1, pp. 59–78). New York, NY: Springer.

Hancock, K. A., & Haldeman, D. C. (in press). APA's Guidelines for Psychological Practice with Lesbian, Gay, and Bisexual Clients and sexual orientation conversion efforts. In D. C. Haldeman & M. L. Hendricks (Eds.), *Sexual orientation and gender identity change efforts: Evidence, effects, and ethics.* New York, NY: Harrington Park Press.

Hatzenbuehler, M. L. (2010). Social factors as determinants of mental health disparities in LGB populations. *Journal of Social Issues and Policy Review*, 4, 31–62. doi:10.1111/j.1751-2409.2010.01017.x

Hegarty, P. (2018). *A recent history of lesbian and gay psychology: From homophobia to LGBT.* New York, NY: Routledge.

Herek, G. M. (1989). Hate crimes against lesbians and gay men: Issues for research and policy. *American Psychologist*, 44, 216–23. doi:10.1037/0003-066X.446.948

Herek, G. M. (1999). Psychological sequelae of hate crime victimization among lesbian, gay and bisexual adults. *Journal of Consulting and Clinical Psychology*, 67, 945–51. doi:10.1037/0022-006X.67.6.945

Herek, G. M. (2006). Legal recognition of same-sex relationships in the United States: A social science perspective. *American Psychologist, 61*, 607–21. doi:10.1037/0003-066X.61.6.607

Herek, G. M., & McLemore, K. A. (2013). Sexual prejudice. *Annual Review of Psychology, 64*, 309–33. doi:10.1146%2Fannurev-psych-113011-143826

Hertlein, K. M., Hartwell, E. E., & Munns, M. E. (2016). Attitudes toward bisexuality according to sexual orientation and gender. *Journal of Bisexuality, 16*(3), 339–60. doi: 10.1080/15299716.2016.1200510

Hooker, E. (1957). Male homosexuality in the Rorschach. *Journal of Projective Techniques, 21*, 18–31. doi: 10.1080/08853126.1957.10380742

Human Dignity Trust. (2019). Countries where LGBT people are criminalized. Retrieved from https://www.humandignitytrust.org/lgbt-the-law/map-of-criminalisation/?type_filter=death_pen_applies.

Institutes of Medicine. (2011). *The health of lesbian, gay, bisexual and transgender people: Building a foundation for better understanding.* Washington, DC: National Academies Press.

Jacobsen, J., & Wright, R. (2014). Mental health implications in Mormon women's experiences with same-sex attraction: A qualitative study. *The Counseling Psychologist, 42*(5), 664–96. doi:10.1186/1471-244X-8-70

Kinsey, A. C. (1948). *Sexual behavior in the human male.* Philadelphia, PA: Saunders.

Klein, F. (1993). *The bisexual option* (2nd ed.). New York, NY: Harrington Park Press.

Klein, F., Sepekoff, B., & Wolf, T. (1985). Sexual orientation: A multi-variate dynamic process. *Journal of Homosexuality, 11*(1/2), 35–49. doi:10.1300/J082v11n01_04

Kraft-Ebbing, R. V. (1886). *Psychopathia sexualis: A medico-forensic study.* Amsterdam, the Netherlands: Elsevier.

Krajeski, J. (1996). Homosexuality and the mental health professions: A contemporary history. In R. P. Cabaj & T. S. Stein (Eds.), *Textbook of homosexuality and mental health* (pp. 17–31). Washington, DC: American Psychiatric Press.

Kurdek, L. A. (1994). The nature and correlates of relationship quality in gay, lesbian, and heterosexual co-habiting couples: A test of individual difference, interdependence, and discrepancy models. In B. Green & G. M. Herek (Eds.), *Lesbian and gay psychology: Theory, research, and clinical applications* (pp. 133–55). Thousand Oaks, CA: Sage Publications.

Kurdek, L. A. (1995). Lesbian and gay couples. In A. D'Augelli & C. Patterson (Eds.), *Lesbian, gay, and bisexual identities over the lifespan: Psychological perspectives* (pp. 243–61). New York, NY: Oxford University Press.

Martinez, D., & Sullivan, S. (1998). African American gay men and lesbians: Examining the complexity of gay and lesbian identity development. *Journal of Human Behavior in the Social Environment, 1*, 243–64. doi:10.1080/10911359.1998.10530795

Mays, V. M., & Cochran, S. D. (1988). The Black Women's Relationship Project: A national survey of Black lesbians. In M. Shernoff & W. Scott (Eds.), *A sourcebook of lesbian/gay healthcare* (2nd ed., pp. 54–62). Washington, DC: National Lesbian and Gay Health Foundation.

Meyer, I. H. (1995). Minority stress and mental health in gay men. *Journal of Health and Social Behavior, 36*(1), 38–56. doi:10.2307/2137286

Morin, S. F., Charles, K. A., & Maylon, A. K. (1984). The psychological impact of AIDS on gay men. *American Psychologist, 39*(11), 1288–93. doi:10.1037/0003-066X.39.11.1288

Nicolosi, J. (1991). *Therapy of the male homosexual.* Northvale, NJ: Jason Aronson.

Pachankis, J. E. (2018). The scientific pursuit of sexual and gender minority mental health treatments: Toward evidence-based affirmative practice. *American Psychologist, 73*(9), 1207–19. doi:10.1037/amp0000357

Paige, R. U. (2005). Proceedings of the American Psychological Association, Incorporated, for the legislative year 2004: Minutes of the annual meeting of the Council of Representatives. *American Psychologist, 60,* 436–511. doi:10.1037/0003-066X.60.5.436

Peplau, L. A. (1981, May). What homosexuals want. *Psychology Today*, pp. 28–38.

Peplau, L. A. (1991). Lesbian and gay relationships. In J. Gonsiorek & J. Weinrich (Eds.), *Homosexuality: Research implications for public policy* (pp. 177–96). Newbury Park, CA: Sage Publications.

Pew Research Center. (2013). The global divide on homosexuality. Retrieved from https://www.pewresearch.org/global/2013/06/04/the-global-divide-on-homosexuality/. Pew Research Center. (2019). 5 facts about same-sex marriage. Retrieved from https://www.pewresearch.org/fact-tank/2019/06/24/same-sex-marriage.

Plant, R. (1986). *The pink triangle.* London, UK: Macmillan.

Pope, K., Tabachnik, B., & Keith-Spiegel, P. (1987, November). Ethics of practice: The beliefs and behaviors of psychologists as therapists. *American Psychologist, 42*(11), 993–1006. doi:10.1037/0003-066X.42.11.993

Ritter, K. Y., & Terndrup, A. I. (2002). *Handbook of affirmative psychotherapy with lesbians and gay men.* New York, NY: Guilford.

Ross, M. W., Daneback, K., & Mansson, S-A. (2012). Fluid versus fixed: A new perspective on bisexuality as a fluid sexual orientation beyond gender. *Journal of Bisexuality, 12*(4), 449–60. doi:10.1080/15299716.2012.702609

Rostosky, S. S., Riggle, E. D. B., Horne, S. G., & Miller, A. D. (2009). Marriage amendments and psychological distress in lesbian, gay, and bisexual (LGB) adults. *Journal of Counseling Psychology, 56*(1), 56–66. doi:10.1037/a0013609

Rothblum, E. (2000). Sexual orientation and sex in women's lives: Conceptual and methodological issues. *Journal of Social Issues, 56*(2), 193–204. doi:10.1111/0022-4537.00160

Ryan, C., Toomey, R. B., Diaz, R. M., & Russell, S. T. (2020). Parent-initiated sexual orientation change efforts with LGBT adolescents: Implications for young adult mental health and adjustment. *Journal of Homosexuality, 67*(2), 159–73. doi:10.1080/00918369.2018.1538407

Savin-Williams, R. C. (1988). Theoretical perspective accounting for adolescent homosexuality. *Journal of Adolescent Health, 9*(6), 95–104. doi:10.1016/0197-0070(88)90055-1

Shidlo, A., & Schroeder, M. (2002). Changing sexual orientation: A consumer's report. *Professional Psychology: Research and Practice, 33,* 249–59. doi:10.1037/0735-7028.33.3.249

Sinclair, J. D. (2009). Homosexuality and the military: A review. *Journal of Homosexuality, 56,* 701–08. doi:10.1080/00918360903054137

Troiden, R. R. (1979). Becoming homosexual: A model of gay identity acquisition. *Psychiatry, 42,* 362–73. doi:10.1080/00332747.1979.11024039

U.S. Supreme Court. (2015). Retrieved from https://www.supremecourt.gov/opinions/14pdf/14-556_3204.pdf.

U.S. Supreme Court. (2017). *Masterpiece Cake Shop v. Colorado Civil Rights Commission.* Retrieved from https://www.supremecourt.gov/opinions/17pdf/16-111_j4el.pdf.

Weinberg, M., Williams, C., & Pryor, D. (1994). *Dual attraction: Understanding bisexuality.* New York, NY: Oxford University Press.

CHAPTER

3 History of Gender Identity and Mental Health

lore m. dickey

Abstract

In the past fifty years, gender identity has been closely linked to mental health. This is due, in part, to the classification of gender identity disorder and gender dysphoria being listed as mental health disorders in the American Psychiatric Association's *Diagnostic and Statistical Manual of Mental Disorders*. This chapter focuses on the history of the intersection of gender identity and mental health. The author explores first the history addressing the intersection of gender identity and mental health and then evidence-based research exploring this intersection. This includes the ways that mental health has and continues to impact transgender people. The author examines co-occurring mental health concerns such as depression, anxiety, substance abuse, and bipolar disorder as well as the ways that race and ethnicity complicate these disparities. Finally, the author addresses the future directions in the areas of research, clinical practice, and training.

Keywords: history of gender identity, gender identity and mental health, gender identity and diagnosis, transgender history, transgender mental health

In the past fifty years, gender identity has been closely linked to mental health. This is due, in part, to the classification of gender identity disorder and gender dysphoria listed as mental health disorders in the *Diagnostic and Statistical Manual of Mental Disorders* (DSM; American Psychiatric Association, 2000, 2013). In this chapter I first focus on the history of the intersection of gender identity and mental health. Then I explore evidence-based research exploring this intersection, including the ways that mental health research has impacted and continues to impact transgender people. I examine co-occurring mental health concerns such as depression, anxiety, substance abuse, and bipolar disorder. Further, I explore the ways that race and ethnicity complicate these disparities. Finally, I address the future directions in the areas of research.

Historical Figures

In the fields of sexuality and gender identity there are several historical scholars whose work impacted both fields, including Richard von Krafft-Ebing (1840–1902), Magnus Hirschfeld (1868–1935), David O. Cauldwell (1897–1959), Havelock Ellis (1859–1939), and Harry Benjamin (1885–1986). For the purposes of this chapter, my focus on these scholars will address their work regarding transsexualism and transvestism, known today as gender identity and cross dressing, respectively.

By today's standards, the work of these scholars is inconsistent with affirmative approaches to work with trans[1] people. In fact, each of the scholars thought of trans people as having a pathological desire to remove healthy organs (e.g., penis, testes, ovaries, vagina). During the early years of medical treatment of transsexualism there was no mental health diagnosis. Diagnosis of mental health, addressed later in this chapter, arose in the 1970s.

[1] In this chapter I use *trans* in an effort to be as broadly inclusive of people whose gender identity is different than the sex they were assigned at birth.

Activists and scholars today consider the works of von Krafft-Ebing, Hirschfeld, Cauldwell, Ellis, and Benjamin to be problematic in conceptualizing both trans identities and approaches to treatment. However, for their time, these scholars were allies of trans people, and they wanted their patients to feel at ease with their identity even if that identity was inconsistent with societal expectations. Consider the comments of Caudwell: "She would then take male hormones that she thought would, with masculine attire and occupation, solve her problem. I was amazed at such utter simplicity" (Cauldwell, 2006, p. 42). It is possible that the use of cross-sex hormones had never occurred to Cauldwell and even so, this allowed him to understand what has become a common method of treatment. However, Cauldwell goes on to write about the problems associated with surgical interventions. He states that "it would be criminal for any surgeon to mutilate a pair of healthy breasts and . . . to castrate a woman with no disease to the ovaries" (Cauldwell, 2006, p. 42). In what might have been one of the first statements cautioning against reparative therapy, Harry Benjamin stated that "psychotherapy aimed at curing the transsexual person of the desire to change sex is unproductive" (Benjamin, 2006, p. 45).

von Krafft-Ebing was a German psychiatrist who published twelve editions of *Psychopathia Sexualis*. Over time, the edition included over 200 case studies exploring human sexual behavior, primarily sexual deviance; von Krafft-Ebing believed that "any departure from procreative intercourse represent[ed] a form of emotional or physical disease" (2006, p. 21). von Krafft-Ebing regarded homosexuality as a type of gender variance and as such he conflated gender identity and sexual orientation. At the time of his work it was more common to find trans people who were assigned female at birth, which may have been due to the stigma associated with effeminate behaviors in people who were assigned male at birth.

In exploring the case of Sandor (case 131; von Krafft-Ebing, 2006), who was assigned female at birth, some members of Sandor's family were supportive of his male identity and allowed Sandor to attend school dressed as a boy. When Sandor was seen as male he was treated with respect and he interacted with others in a positive manner. Problems arose for Sandor when he was arrested for public deception. Sandor came from a family that was considered to be highly respected and to be eccentric (von Krafft-Ebing, 2006). Sandor was attracted to women, and his problems with the law were about his gender expression and sexuality.

Hirschfeld's contributions to the field of trans studies was his conceptualizations of transvestites. Not unlike von Krafft-Ebing, Hirschfeld believed there was a connection between gender and sexuality. He used the term *sexual intermediaries* to describe trans people and believed they existed on a spectrum from "pure male to pure female" (2006, p. 28). Although this may not be the same as the gender spectrum that is addressed in current discourse it still allowed for a gender to exist outside the restrictive binary. Hirschfeld was also German and his scholarship was considered dangerous by the Nazis, who destroyed his work while he was traveling to give public lectures (Hirschfeld, 2006).

Hirschfeld wrote about the differences between homosexuals and transvestites. Early thoughts about transvestites regarded this behavior as a sexual fetish and for some a type of masochism (Hirschfeld, 2006). Hirschfeld did not accept these explanations, stating that a fetish relates to a sexual attraction to a part of the body rather than the whole body as is the case with people who cross dress. As for masochism, Hirschfeld believed that this was being confused with a "wish for effimination" (2006, p. 32). The terms *transvestite* and *transvestism*, coined by Hirschfeld, are the only terms from that era that are still in use (Stryker, 2008).

Hirschfeld was the first to publish a detailed description of transvestism, consisting of five types: (a) the heterosexual variety, (b) the bisexual variety (being attracted to virile women and effeminate men), (c) the homosexual variety, (d) the narcissistic variety (feminine components of one's nature are consistent with masculine features), and (e) the asexual variety (often impotent and likely to find a role as a woman in everyday life; Crozier, 2000). As can be seen in these descriptions, the patient is described not only by their gender but also by their sexual orientation.

Hirschfeld also described sexual intermediaries as falling into four categories defined by (a) the sexual organs, (b) other physical characteristics, (c) the sex drive, and (d) other emotional characteristics (Hirschfeld, 2006, p. 35). When considering sexual organs, Hirschfeld was referring to people who were 100 percent male or female or those people who had indeterminate genitals (known now as disorders of sex development or intersex). Other physical characteristics referred to men with gynecomastia or women with beards. The third category consisted of transvestites, including men who engaged in sex with women as a woman. The fourth group consisted of men who exhibited womanly emotions. Hirschfeld considered cross dressing to be a rare condition. In coining the term *transvestite*, Hirschfeld admitted that the focus on external behavior (e.g., how a person dresses) was problematic as there are many ways in which person might explore and act on internal cues. Hirschfeld was clear in stating that cross dressing was present for people assigned either male or female at birth. He was not clear about the etiology or the prognosis.

Cauldwell, a U.S. physician, began to popularize the term *transsexual* although Hirschfeld had already used that term. Cauldwell's conceptualization assumed that transsexualism was genetically inherited and influenced by a dysfunctional childhood (Cauldwell, 2006). Cauldwell used terms like "psychopathic transsexual" and "psychologically . . . deficient" (2006, p. 41). Of the scholars in this era, Cauldwell tended to have the least favorable approach to work with trans people. In his mind, trans people were sick and in need of treatment.

Ellis was an English physician said to have reformed the way people thought about sex during the Victorian era (Robinson, 1973). Ellis coined the term *eonism* to identify transvestites in reference to "Chevalier d'Eon" (Crozier, 2000, p. 131). This is similar to the ways in which other sexologists selected names for sexual behaviors (e.g., masochism [Leopold von Sacher-Masoch], sadism [Marquis de Sade]). Although eonism was initially used to describe transvestism it was also used to describe transsexual people, or those who desired to be a member of the opposite sex (Crozier, 2000).

Ellis's work on sex and sexual concerns included developing an understanding of the motives behind deviant sexual behaviors. His intention was not to pathologize the activities a person engaged in but to help raise people's consciousness, with the goal of changing the political landscape in favorable ways.

Benjamin was a German physician who came to the United States prior to World War I. Benjamin first worked with trans people in the 1920s, but it is said that his devotion to the community came after his association with Alfred Kinsey in the late 1940s. Benjamin's conceptualization of transsexuals brought the necessary attention to the health needs of the community that resulted in medical treatment, including hormones and surgery.

Benjamin was the first to develop a list of symptoms that differentiated transsexualism from transvestism. This moved the attention away from assumptions about sexual desire to a focus on the need to change physical features to allow the person to live in a gender role that was different than the sex they were assigned at birth. Benjamin thought of transsexuals as a subset of transvestites and referred to them as *somatopsychic transsexuals*. Early scholars relied heavily on case studies long before the establishment of university-based clinics, and yet the work of university-based clinics was guided by documents such as the Harry Benjamin International Gender Dysphoria Association (HBIGDA) Standards of Care.

From the work of von Krafft-Ebing to the work of Benjamin, much changed in how transsexual people were treated. Still, there was an underlying assumption that the person had a mental illness. The etiology of this mental illness had multiple sources including genetics and childrearing approaches.

Beginning with the work of David Cauldwell (1947), and before him Magnus Hirschfeld (1934, both cited by Bullough, 1975) people are described in the literature who, for the most part, were preoperative transsexuals. Cauldwell's work began with an exploration of men who preferred to dress in female attire, and he is credited, by some, with having first used the terms *transsexual* and *transsexualism* (Ekins & King, 2001). From the outset, cross dressers (known at that time at transvestites) and transsexual people (the only term in use at the time) were pathologized by the medical community. Although trans people were eventually treated medically, this happened through university-based clinics (Devor & Matte, 2004, 2007). The funding for these clinics was predicated on the implementation of research (Devor & Matte, 2004, 2007). At the time, anecdotally, trans people had to agree to participate in research in order to obtain care, and they did not necessarily know the purpose of the research they were participating in.

Benjamin is credited with "being the father of transgender medicine" (Wolf-Gould, 2016). Benjamin (1966) developed a system to categorize transsexual people, consisting of (1) the pseudotransvestite, the fetishistic transvestite, and the true transvestite; (2) nonsurgical transsexuals; and (3) moderate-intensity true transsexuals and high-intensity true transsexuals. Benjamin further described each of these types of people by their dressing habits and social life, sex object and choice of sex life, Kinsey scale, conversion operation, estrogen medication, and psychotherapy. This conceptualization of trans people set up expectations for how a trans person needed to describe their life experience. This also began the expectation that the trans person would engage in psychotherapy. Benjamin

(1966) also described the legal implications of transgender people's lives, making the case that although transsexualism was a crime at the time, the way to "rehabilitate" a person was to provide treatment rather than punishment. Further, Benjamin discussed the challenges that surgeons faced if they decided to perform surgery. At the time the laws had a "mayhem statute" (Benjamin, 1966, p. 172) based on laws that began in England and made amputation of body parts illegal because men were engaging in such behavior with the intention of avoiding military service. Benjamin admitted that he had never heard of a surgeon being prosecuted for genital surgery; however, he and another person he was aware of had received warnings from the courts about not performing trans medical care.

Benjamin's work paved the way for trans people who not only felt alone in their identity but also felt as though there were no options to resolve their gender identity concerns. There are still parts of the world that adhere to the medical model. In addition to being able to describe a gendered history that fits the medical model, trans people are required, in some countries, to be sterilized. Not all trans people want to complete a hysterectomy with oophorectomy (assigned female at birth) or an orchiectomy (assigned male at birth). Yet in countries such as Finland, Latvia, Slovakia, Romania, Serbia, Bulgaria, Montenegro, Bosnia and Herzegovina, Turkey, Georgia, Armenia, and others (Transgender Europe, 2019) sterilization is a requirement for transition. It may seem as though the United States has welcoming policies in this regard. However, most U.S. states require a person to have had genital surgery to change either their driver's license or their birth certificate (Lambda Legal, 2018; National Center for Transgender Equality [NCTE], 2019).

Inherent in the process of eligibility was the determination that a person is in good mental health. Even today, the World Professional Association for Transgender Health's Standards of Care (Coleman et al., 2011) make clear the expectation that co-occurring mental health concerns be "reasonably well-controlled" (p. 187). The challenge in determining whether a mental health concern is "reasonably well-controlled" is that there are a variety of ways in which one might define that. One way is to determine if the client is compliant with treatment recommendations. Another is whether the client is taking medication as prescribed. Finally, is the client asymptomatic? What is mental health? The World Health Organization (WHO, 2019, n.p.) defines health as "a state of complete physical, mental and social well-being and not merely the absence of disease or infirmity." Given this definition, mental health is not simply the absence of a clinical mental health diagnosis. Rather, it implies that a person has well-developed mental health coping skills, is able to be resilient in the face of adversity, and is likely to have positive social experiences (e.g., friendships, employment).

The WPATH Standards of Care (SOC) were first published in 1979 (Berger et al., 1979) and provided a lengthy description about the treatment of transsexual people. In addition to defining transsexualism, the SOC described the types of medical treatment available and the requirements for eligibility for treatment. Currently in the seventh edition (Coleman et al., 2011), the SOC are used by medical providers and insurance companies to dictate medical treatment. In addition, historically trans people were also required to pass a twelve-month "real-life test," which was used to determine a person's resolve to remain in their affirmed gender identity. If a person wavered in their resolve they were required to restart the real-life test clock. This expectation was problematic on several levels. There are legitimate reasons why a person may not be able to meet the real-life test requirements (e.g., costs, preexisting medical concerns). For people intending to make a medical transition, their pretransition self may require the benefit of medical interventions in order to comply with the real-life test expectations. Finally, safety may also be a legitimate concern. Trans people are often exploited, discriminated against, or the victims of violence (James et al., 2016). Although it is no longer a requirement that a trans person complete the real-life test, some providers and insurance companies still adhere to the need for one or more letters of referral by mental health providers prior to initiating care. These referral letters are used to assure the provider or the insurance company that there are no unresolved mental health concerns that could potentially lead to poor results.

Gender Identity in the DSM and International Classification of Diseases

Since the American Psychiatric Association first inclµded *transsexualism* in the third edition of the DSM (American Psychiatric Association, 1980), transgender people have had a diagnosable mental health disorder. Over time, this has become a lightning rod for the community. In order to access care, there had to be a mental health diagnosis. Given the stigma associated with mental health issues, many transgender people have eschewed the use of diagnosis. However, depending on the transition plans a person has there may need to be a diagnosis, which was changed to *gender identity disorder* (American Psychiatric Association, 1994) in the fourth edition of the DSM and to *gender dysphoria* in the fifth edition (American Psychiatric Association, 2013). Corresponding changes in the World Health Organization's International Classification of Diseases (ICD) were *transsexualism* in the tenth edition and *gender incongruence* in the eleventh edition (cf. Reed et al., 2016, for a review).

Gender Identity Today

Gender identity, or how a person defines themselves as a gendered person, is highly individual. People who are not familiar with the process often think that trans people feel as though they "were born in the wrong body." Some trans people may identify with this idea; however, the origin of this arose from the medical model that implied that there was something wrong with a person's body and that in order to correct the situation a person must undergo hormone treatment and surgery, in that order.

Gender is typically considered to fall into two immutable categories: masculine and feminine. Early in the presence of the trans community that expectation was clear. A person was transitioning from either male or female to (and not stopping at any midpoint) female or male, respectively. Over the past two or three decades the concept of nonbinary identities has emerged. Nonbinary identities existed in numerous indigenous cultures. It was not until indigenous communities and cultures were colonized that people began to police the gender of others and, in that time, trans people were told they had only two options. If they chose to live outside of gender binary (e.g., female and male) they were putting their life at risk due to the harsh expectations of colonialism.

Although most nations are no longer subjected to colonial expectations, there are a number of ways that gender continues to be policed. Policing happens when governments consider the implementation of bathroom bills, which carry the expectation that a person only use a restroom that is consistent with the sex that is listed on their birth certificate. There are a number of problems with this expectation, not the least of which is that people rarely carry their birth certificate with them, and no one is posted at restroom access points to check the proper use of the restroom. Moreover, the challenges people face regarding their manner of dress, the activities they engage in, and the kinds of friends they have are problematic expectations about how people perform their gender.

Trans people experience health disparities and differences in other social determinants of health (e.g., housing, public accommodation, employment). The rates at which trans people experience homelessness, unemployment, and discrimination in healthcare are staggering. Cisgender people rarely have to worry about whether their healthcare costs will be covered if they have health insurance. Although not all trans people want to make a medical transition, the costs of such care are rarely covered for those who do.

If a trans person is able to secure coverage and approval for treatment, there may be no providers nearby, or the only providers available are people who have a history of mistreating trans people. Trans people are less likely than their cisgender counterparts to have a primary care provider and are less likely to access care at a doctor's office (dickey, Budge, Katz-Wise, & Garza, 2016). Thus they may primarily rely on urgent care and emergency services; besides the elevated cost of care, using these methods for accessing healthcare does not allow the trans patient to develop a relationship with a provider who knows their health history.

Little research has been conducted on the ways that care, such as hormone treatment, impact a trans person's well-being (Keo-Meier et al., 2015; Meier, Fitzgerald, Pardo, & Babcock, 2011). As a result, physicians and mental health providers cannot rely on research that informs the ways in which hormones might improve a trans person's quality of life. This is a missing aspect of the extant research.

Gender Identity and Mental Health

Rates of mental health concerns tend to be higher among transgender people than in the general population. This includes depression (Clements-Nolle, Marx, & Katz, 2014), anxiety (Bockting, Miner, Swinburne Romine, Hamilton, & Coleman, 2013; Sinnard, Raines, & Budge, 2016), substance abuse (Cochran & Cauce, 2006), self-injury (dickey, Reisner, & Juntunen, 2012), and suicide (Goldblum et al., 2012; Testa et al., 2017). There are numerous reasons for these disparities. First, the mental health concern may or may not be related to a person's gender identity (American Psychological Association, 2015). For example, a nonbinary person may exhibit signs of social anxiety due to the fact that they are consistently misgendered by others. Finally, a client may have symptoms that mimic gender identity concerns but are related to other mental health problems (e.g., delusions or mania; American Psychological Association, 2015).

In recent years, researchers have explored suicidality and nonsuicidal self-injury in the trans community (dickey et al., 2015; Goldblum et al., 2012; Testa et al., 2017). Research on community samples has shown the suicide attempt rates to be as high as 40 percent (James et al., 2016) and nonsuicidal self-injury rates to be as high as 42 percent (dickey et al., 2015). Researchers have called for the need to address these concerns but not necessarily in a way that would interrupt anyone's transition process. Clients with acute suicide and self-injury risks may need to develop coping skills to help them to address emotional dysregulation.

Trauma is a common experience for transgender people. This may be from a parent, guardian, or loved one; as a part of experiencing puberty; or at the hands of a stranger (e.g., sexual assault, attempted murder). Regardless of the source of the trauma, it can have a long-lasting effect (Richmond, Burnes, Singh, & Ferrara, 2017).

Understanding the challenges that a trans person faces will require the provider to engage in trauma-informed counseling (dickey, Singh, & Walinsky, 2017; Richmond et al., 2017). Without retraumatizing their client, providers must explore the ways that trans people have experienced trauma and design treatment plans that are sensitive to the clients' trauma sequelae.

One of the issues with substance abuse is related to how trans people are treated in clinics. The primary concern is related to housing and programming. Ideally, the trans person will be involved in the decision-making process for the choice of housing. However, placing a trans person in a room by themselves limits their involvement in some of the social aspects of treatment.

Although trans people experience mental health disparities, resilience is also seen even in those who are the most marginalized (e.g., trans people of color; Singh, Hays, & Watson, 2011). Resilience can occur on an individual, community, or societal level. Individually, coming out to family, friends, and coworkers is an act of resilience. On a community level, participating in pride marches and memorial events are ways that trans people hold their power in the face of adversity and discrimination. In the broader general public, trans people leverage their relationships with allies to help pass legislation that provides protection in the areas of housing, healthcare, education, public accommodation, and employment. There are few countries that provide broad protections for transgender people, mostly in Europe (Transgender Rights European Union, 2019). The United States continues to maintain that this type of legislation must come from the state or local level. As a result, there is a patchwork of protection in terms of both the geographic location and the type of coverage available.

Intersecting Identities and Mental Health Concerns

There are a number of ways that a person might have an intersecting identity (Crenshaw, 1991). This includes race, disability, socioeconomic status, and other marginalized identities. Trans persons who hold more than one marginalized identity are more likely to experience discrimination, violence, and mistreatment (James et al., 2016). The consequences of holding those identities multiplies the possible adverse consequences such as social determinants of health.

Future Directions

There is an urgent need to understand how mental health concerns impact people who live in the Global South. This must include a deeper understanding of indigenous cultures. It is not safe to assume that treatment approaches that are used in the Western Hemisphere will be appropriate or effective with trans individuals in Africa, Asia, or Latin America.

There is a significant need for additional research about the effectiveness of hormone treatment for people with co-occurring mental health disorders (e.g., depression, anxiety, nonsuicidal self-injury, substance abuse). Understanding the needs of trans people who have HIV/AIDS is also important. In addition to understanding the mental health effects of hormone treatment, researchers also might explore the effects of surgery in a longitudinal study.

The development of evidence-based practices is also critical. At the writing of this chapter, I am aware of only one study that is exploring this topic, and the study is still in the data-collection phase. Critical to this effort is ensuring that the approaches have been studied on trans people with diverse demographic backgrounds.

Finally, there needs to be more focus during training on addressing the needs of trans people. This includes meeting the needs of clients and those of trainees. Infusing this throughout the curriculum is an important first step. Training programs might also consider the development of a course that is designed to address work with trans clients, including a deep understanding of the challenges they face on a day-to-day basis.

Understanding the concerns that a trans person faces will help people to develop some compassion and respect. Without this, trans people will continue to struggle with the challenges that are placed before them, some of which are institutionalized.

References

American Psychiatric Association. (1980). *Diagnostic and statistical manual of mental disorders* (3rd ed.). Arlington, VA: Author.

American Psychiatric Association. (1994). *Diagnostic and statistical manual of mental disorders* (4th ed.). Washington, DC: American Psychiatric Association.

American Psychiatric Association. (2000). *Diagnostic and statistical manual of mental disorders* (4th ed., text revision). Arlington, VA: Author.

American Psychiatric Association. (2013). *Diagnostic and statistical manual of mental disorders* (5th ed.). Washington, DC: Author.

American Psychological Association. (2015). Guidelines for psychological practice with transgender and gender nonconforming people. *American Psychologist, 70,* 832–64. doi:10.1037/a0039906

Benjamin, H. (1966). *The transsexual phenomenon: All the facts about the changing of sex through hormones and surgery.* New York, NY: Warner Books.

Benjamin, H. (2006). Transsexualism and transvestism as psycho-somatic and somato-psychic syndromes. In S. Stryker & S. Whittle (Eds.), *The transgender studies reader* (pp. 45–52). New York, NY: Routledge.

Berger, J. C., Green, R., Laub, D. R., Reynolds, C. L., Walker, P. A., & Wollman, L. (1979). *Standards of care: The hormonal and surgical sex reassignment of gender dysphoric persons.* Galveston, TX: Janus Information Facility.

Bockting, W. O., Miner, M. H., Swinburne Romine, R. E., Hamilton, A., & Coleman, E. (2013). Stigma, mental health, and resilience in an online sample of the US transgender population. *American Journal of Public Health, 103,* 943–51. doi:10.2105/ajph.2013.301241

Bullough, V. (1975). Transsexualism in history. *Archives of Sexual Behavior, 4,* 561–70. doi:10.1007/BF01542134

Cauldwell, D. O. (2006). Psychopathia transexualis. In S. Stryker & S. Whittle (Eds.), *The transgender studies reader* (pp. 40–44). New York, NY: Routledge.

Clements-Nolle, K., Marx, R., & Katz, M. (2014). Attempted suicide among transgender persons. *Journal of Homosexuality, 51,* 53–69. doi:10.1300/J082v51n03_04

Cochran, B. N., & Cauce, A. M. (2006). Characteristics of lesbian, gay, bisexual, and transgender individuals entering substance abuse treatment. *Journal of Substance Abuse Treatment, 30,* 135–46. doi:10.1016/j.jsat.2005.11.009

Coleman, E., Bockting, W., Botzer, M., Cohen-Kettenis, P. DeCuypere, G., Feldman, J., . . . Zucker, K. (2011). Standards of care for the health of transsexual, transgender, and gender-nonconforming people. *International Journal of Transgenderism, 13,* 165–232. doi:10.1080/15532739.2011.700873

Crenshaw, K. (1991). Mapping the margins: Intersectionality, identity politics, and violence against women of color. *Stanford Law Review, 43,* 1241–99. Retrieved from http://www.jstor.org/stable/1229039.

Crozier, I. (2000). Havelock Ellis, Eonism and the patient discourse; or, writing a book about sex. *History of Psychiatry, 11,* 125–54. doi:10.1177/0957154X0001104201

Devor, A., & Matte, N. (2004). One Inc. and Reed Erickson: The uneasy collaboration of gay and trans activism 1964–2003. *GLQ, 10,* 179–209. doi:10.1215/10642684-10-2-179

Devor, A., & Matte, N. (2007). Building a better world for transpeople: Reed Erickson and the Erickson Educational Foundation. *International Journal of Transgenderism, 10,* 47–68. doi:10.1300/J485v10n01_07

dickey, l. m., Budge, S. L., Katz-Wise, S. L., & Garza, M. V. (2016). Health disparities in the transgender community: Exploring differences in insurance coverage. *Psychology of Sexual Orientation and Gender Diversity, 3,* 275–82. doi:10.1037/sgd0000169

dickey, l. m., Reisner, S. L., & Juntunen, C. L. (2015). Non-suicidal self-injury in a large online sample of transgender adults. *Professional Psychology: Research and Practice, 46,* 3–11. doi:10.1037/a0038803

dickey, l. m., Singh, A. A., & Walinsky, D. (2017). Treatment of trauma and nonsuicidal self-injury in transgender adults. *Psychiatric Clinics of North America, 40,* 41–50. doi:10.1016/j.psc.2016.10.007

Ekins, R., & King, D. (2001). Pioneers of transgendering: The popular sexology of David O. Cauldwell. *International Journal of Transgenderism, 5*(2). Retrieved from https://cdn.atria.nl/ezines/web/IJT/97-03/numbers/symposion/cauldwell_01.htm.

Goldblum, P., Testa, R. J., Pflum, S., Hendricks, M. L., Bradford, J., & Bongar, B. (2012). In-school gender-based victimization and suicide attempts in transgender individuals. *Professional Psychology: Research and Practice, 43,* 468–475. doi:10.1037/a0029605

Hirschfield, M. (2006). Selections from: The transvestites: The erotic drive to cross-dress. In S. Stryker & S. Whittle (Eds.), *The transgender studies reader* (pp. 28–39). New York, NY: Routledge. James, S. E., Herman, J. L., Rankin, S., Keisling, M., Mottet, L., & Anafi, M. (2016). *The report of the 2015 U.S. Transgender Survey.* Washington, DC: National Center for Transgender Equality. Retrieved from https://transequality.org/sites/default/files/docs/usts/USTS-Full-Report-Dec17.pdf.

Keo-Meier, C. L., Herman, L. I., Reisner, S. L., Pardo, S. T., Sharp, C., & Babcock, J. C. (2015). Testosterone treatment and MMPI-2 improvement in transgender men: A prospective controlled study. *Journal of Consulting and Clinical Psychology, 83,* 143–56. doi:10.1037/a0037599

Lambda Legal. (2018). *Changing birth certificate sex designation: State-by-state guidelines.* Retrieved from https://www.lambdalegal.org/know-your-rights/article/trans-changing-birth-certificate-sex-designations.

Meier, S. L. C., Fitzgerald, K. M., Pardo, S. T., & Babcock, J. (2011). The effects of hormonal gender affirmation in female-to-male transsexuals. *Journal of Gay & Lesbian Mental Health, 15,* 281–99. doi:10.1080/19359705.2011.581195

National Center for Transgender Equality. (2019). *ID documents center.* Retrieved from: https://transequality.org/documents.

Reed, G. M., Drescher, J., Krueger, R. B., Atalla, E., Cochran, S. D., First, M. B., . . . Briken, P. (2016). Disorders related to

sexuality and gender identity in the ICD-11: Revising the ICD-10 classification based on current scientific evidence, best clinical practices, and human rights considerations. *World Psychiatry, 15*(3), 205–21. doi:10.1002/wps.20354
Richmond, K., Burnes, T. R., Singh, A. A., & Ferrara, M. (2017). Assessment and treatment of trauma with TGNC clients: A feminist approach. In A. A. Singh & L. M. dickey (Eds.), *Affirmative counseling and psychological practice with transgender and gender nonconforming clients* (pp. 191–212). Washington, DC: American Psychological Association.
Robinson, P. A. (1973). Havelock Ellis and modern sexual theory. *Salmagundi, 21*, 27–62. Retrieved from: https://www.jstor.org/stable/40547346.
Singh, A. A., Hays, D. G., & Watson, L. S. (2011). Strength in the face of adversity: Resilience strategies of transgender individuals. *Journal of Counseling & Development, 89*, 20–27. doi:10.1002/j.1556-6678.2011.tb00057.x
Sinnard, M. T., Raines, C. R., & Budge, S. L. (2016). The association between geographic location and anxiety and depression in transgender individuals: An exploratory study of an online sample. *Transgender Health, 1*, 181–86. doi:10.1089/trgh.2016.0020
Stryker, S. (2008). *Transgender history*. Berkeley, CA: Seal Press.
Testa, R. J., Michaels, M. S., Bliss, W., Rogers, M. L., Balsam, K. F., & Joiner, T. (2017). Suicide ideation in transgender people: Gender minority stress and interpersonal theory factors. *Journal of Abnormal Psychology, 126*, 125–36. doi:10.1037/abn0000234c
Transgender Rights European Union. (2019). *Trans rights Europe & Central Asia 2019*. Retrieved from: https://tgeu.org/wp-content/uploads/2019/05/index_TGEU2019.pdf.
Von Krafft-Ebing, R. (2006). Selections from: Psychopathia Sexualis with special reference to contrary sexual instinct. In S. Stryker & S. Whittle (Eds.), *The transgender studies reader* (pp. 21–27). New York, NY: Routledge.
Wolf-Gould, C. (2016). History of transgender medicine in the United States. In A. E. Goldberg (Ed.), *The SAGE encyclopedia of LGBTQ studies* (pp. 507–12). Thousand Oaks, CA: Sage.
World Health Organization. (2019). *WHO constitution*. Retrieved from: https://www.who.int/about/who-we-are/constitution.

PART II

Mental Health Categories

CHAPTER

4

Depression and Mood Disorders among Sexual and Gender Minority Populations

Gia Chodzen, Vickie M. Mays, *and* Susan D. Cochran

Abstract

Sexual and gender minority (SGM) adults have rates of depressive disorders that are higher than those of cisgender or heterosexual adults. These differences are likely due to the ways that SGMs are treated both on an individual and population basis. This chapter begins by discussing evolving conceptualizations of depressive disorders among SGMs with a focus on the dimensionality in symptomatology. Insights are provided into the ways that differences in risk for depressive disorders occur in SGMs by subpopulations with a focus on gender, developmental stages, and geographic context. The authors discuss social risks, examining the ways in which stigma, discrimination, and early life adversity can contribute to depressive disorders in SGMs. This provides a basis for researchers and clinicians to explore and include structural and societal change in addressing mental health disorders in SGMs. The authors also discuss the comorbidity of depressive disorders with several chronic health conditions with particular regard to the health inequities that some subpopulations of SGMs face. Adopting an intersectional approach is useful in studying depressive disorders among SGMs, and the authors suggest pairing this approach with the National Institute of Health's Research Domain Criteria (RDoC) framework. Future directions are suggested to researchers and clinicians to reduce risks of depressive distress in SGM subpopulations.

Keywords: LGBT, mental health, intersectionality, stigma, Global South, RDoC, comorbidity

Over the past two decades, studies of mental health disorders among sexual and gender minority (SGM) populations have found that the rates of mood disorders, particularly depressive disorders, are elevated in comparison to rates seen among similar heterosexual or cisgender individuals (Chaudhry & Reisner, 2019; Cochran, Sullivan, & Mays, 2003). The catalyst for these differences has generally been attributed to the ways in which SGMs are treated on both a group and individual basis (Bostwick, Boyd, Hughes, West, & McCabe, 2014; Mays & Cochran, 2001; Meyer, 2003), resulting in a greater likelihood of developing stress-sensitive disorders. How individuals are treated, what neighborhoods they live in, what their access is to networks of support, and whether there are protective public policies against discrimination can contribute to levels of day-to-day stress. Depending on their stress sensitivity, this chronicity can result in depressive disorders (Hatzenbuehler, Keyes, & Hasin, 2009; Horvath, Iantaffi, Swinburne-Romine, & Bockting, 2014; Jackson, Hackett, Grabovac, Smith, & Steptoe, 2019; Lee, Wimark, Ortiz, & Sewell, 2018; Mays & Cochran, 2001; Nuttbrock et al., 2012). While research has increasingly shown that not all members of the SGM community suffer from mood disorders, those who do are likely to be exposed to chronic stressors, such as stigma and discrimination (Calabrese, Meyer, Overstreet, Haile, & Hansen, 2015; Hatzenbuehler, 2009; Khan, Ilcisin, & Saxton, 2017).

As a function of the brevity of the chapter, we focus on the etiology and prevalence of depressive disorders in primarily lesbian, gay, and bisexual

(LGB) adults, who are the most studied population among SGMs. We will focus on depressive disorders because their development and recurrence are related to a societal context that is often experienced as stressful by SGMs (Colodro-Conde et al., 2018; Hammen, 2015). Unlike depressive disorders, bipolar disorders are believed to be significantly rooted in genetic/biological rather than social and environmental factors (Craddock & Sklar, 2013; Kieseppä, Partonen, Haukka, Kaprio, & Lönnqvist, 2014). While it is not our intention to minimize the often debilitating effects of bipolar disorders among affected LGB adults, the paucity of research on this topic with this population hinders our ability to provide insights into the unique experiences of LGBs with bipolar disorders (Abé et al., 2018; Bostwick, Boyd, Hughes, & McCabe, 2010; Cochran & Mays, 2000; Hellman, Sudderth, & Avery, 2002). We have also chosen not to focus on HIV and depressive disorders as the topic is important enough to warrant stand-alone attention and cannot be covered adequately within the constraints of this chapter. We also note that although suicide risk is elevated among SGMs and that the risk is inherently tied to depressive disorders (Blashill & Calzo, 2019; Blosnich, Nasuti, Mays, & Cochran, 2016), suicide will be covered in Chapter 14 in greater detail. When possible, we will discuss depressive disorders within intersectional subpopulations of SGMs with attention to areas where there are gaps in knowledge.

Evolving Conceptualizations of Depressive Disorders

Recent estimates suggest that 322 million individuals worldwide are affected by depressive disorders (World Health Organization, 2017). Depressive disorders are characterized by the presence of a sad, empty, or irritable mood accompanied by significant impairment in functioning. The two most common depressive disorders are major depressive disorder and persistent depressive disorder (dysthymia) (World Health Organization, 2017). Depressive disorders are considered quite heterogeneous due to the wide range of symptoms that may lead to a depressive disorder diagnosis (Clark, Cuthbert, Lewis-Fernández, Narrow, & Reed, 2017; Goldberg, 2011). Diagnostic conceptualizations of depressive disorders have changed in recent years and will likely continue to evolve in the near future. Currently, depressive disorder diagnoses are given categorically with individuals either meeting diagnostic criteria or not (Clark et al., 2017). In the United States, a formal diagnosis of a depressive disorder can be applied following the protocols outlined in the fifth edition of the American Psychiatric Association's *Diagnostic and Statistical Manual of Mental Disorders* (DSM-5) (American Psychiatric Association, 2013). Internationally, clinicians and researchers may be likely to use the *International Classification of Diseases* (ICD-10 or ICD-11), which similarly uses symptom-based criteria that must exceed a diagnostic threshold (World Health Organization, 2018). Survey research documenting prevalences of depression at the population level typically employ these criteria to arrive at classification of respondents' diagnostic histories.

Despite the current use of categorical classifications of depressive disorders, there is growing scientific evidence among researchers and clinicians that mental health disorders are actually dimensional in nature (Clark et al., 2017; Goldberg, 2000; Kraemer, Noda, & O'Hara, 2004). Depressive disorders, in particular, are experienced on a continuum of severity and with a varied array of symptom presentations (Bjelland et al., 2009; Goldberg, 2011). In addition, mental health disorders may be a function of multiple biological, behavioral, psychosocial, and cultural factors, which all interact with one another as well as an individual's experiences (Clark et al., 2017). Given the complexity of these interactions, the outcome of these etiological variables is likely not a singularly distinct disease, but instead highly variable and complex psychological problems that are currently classified using the DSM/ICD code as a mental health disorder (Clark et al., 2017). Somewhat in line with a dimensional understanding of depressive disorders, some research studies have elected to use continuous scales of depressive psychological distress, such as the Kessler 10 (Kessler et al., 2003).

A step forward in understanding depressive disorders in SGMs would be the use of the National Institute of Mental Health's Research Domain Criteria (RDoC) with its focus on dimensionality (Insel et al., 2010). RDoC is not necessarily intended for clinical use. Rather, RDoC is a research framework in which scholars may draw from several domains and dimensions of mental health in an effort to inform future disease classification efforts (Clark et al., 2017). With regard to depression, researchers have used RDoC to integrate multiple units of analysis to understand several dimensions of behavior, including negative valance systems (Woody & Gibb, 2015).

The RDoC framework's focus on dimensions makes it a particularly promising framework for understanding mental health symptomatology dimensions among SGMs. RDoC provides an approach for conceptualizing how social, environmental, and psychological stressors experienced by SGMs may create a constellation of vulnerabilities for this population (Eaton, 2014). This approach may also yield better understanding of how best to tailor treatments and mental health services for SGMs. For example, research indicates that SGM adults utilize mental health services at elevated rates, but some work suggests that they may not derive similar treatment benefits as heterosexual/cisgender individuals. There may be a number of reasons for this, ranging from differential patterns of symptoms, as predicted by an RDoC approach, to problems of bias in treatment delivery (Cochran et al., 2003; Cochran, Björkenstam, & Mays, 2017; Qureshi et al., 2018).

Prevalence of Depressive Disorders among SGMs

Empirical estimates of the prevalence of depressive disorders among SGMs come from a variety of sources, including federal, state, and local surveillance data; population-based health surveys; cohort studies that contain mental health data; clinical and administrative data; and electronic medical record reviews in specialty clinics. Most broadly, data drawn from national and federal data sets have provided us with prevalence estimates of depressive disorders among large samples of diverse SGMs, especially individuals who identify as LGB. Further, these samples are community-based rather than clinical populations. Thus, many of the respondents are undiagnosed by the healthcare system and may even be unaware that they meet diagnostic criteria for a depressive disorder.

Analyses of federal and state surveillance data consistently indicate that SGMs are more likely to experience depressive disorders than heterosexual and cisgender individuals, with prevalence estimates for SGMs ranging from 3.0 to 26.8 percent (Barnhill, Lee, & Rafferty, 2017; Bostwick et al., 2010; Gonzales & Henning-Smith, 2017; Gonzales, Przedworski, & Henning-Smith, 2016; Streed, McCarthy, & Haas, 2018). Research findings also point to important discrepancies with regard to gender and specific sexual orientation identity in terms of risk of developing a mood disorder. For example, multiple studies have suggested that lesbian and bisexual women experience depressive disorders far more frequently than gay and bisexual men, with estimates between 22.5 and 58.7 percent for women (versus around 13.6 to 42.3 percent for men) (Bostwick et al., 2010; Chaudhry & Reisner, 2019; Frisell, Lichtenstein, Rahman, & Långström, 2010; Gonzales & Henning-Smith, 2017). Further, bisexual women may be at an especially pronounced risk, as their estimated risk for depressive disorders falls within the upper extreme of overall estimates for women: between 35.8 and 58.7 percent (Bostwick et al., 2010; Chaudhry & Reisner, 2019).

Transgender and gender-nonconforming adults are at even greater risk of developing depressive disorders. Overall, they are more likely to experience poor mental health and impairment than cisgender adults, regardless of sex assigned at birth or sexual orientation, particularly within clinical samples (Borgogna, McDermott, Aita, & Kridel, 2019; James et al., 2016; Reisner, White, Mayer, & Mimiaga, 2014; Streed et al., 2018; Witcomb et al., 2018).

Differences also exist within SGM populations in terminology that is reflection of identification versus behavior. For example, in research studies we find evidence that suggests that those who openly identify as LGB experience higher levels of risk for depression than those who are behaviorally classified as LGB (i.e., individuals reporting same-sex attraction or sexual activity but identifying their sexual orientation as heterosexual) (Bostwick et al., 2010; Krueger, Meyer, & Upchurch, 2018). Sometimes this difference reflects factors that predate the individuals' recognition of their SGM status or are a part of a milestone in their sexual orientation identity development (Calzo et al., 2011). Evidence indicates that, among gender minorities, being assigned female at birth is associated with an increased risk for depression. Transgender individuals with female birth assignments were more likely to evidence a current psychiatric diagnosis than those assigned male at birth (Beckwith et al., 2019).

Results from a developmental age perspective of studies with LGB samples have also identified that there are pronounced differences in depressive disorder risk with regard to age in both adolescent/emerging adults and those older than 50. Risk for depression among SGMs is elevated in individuals' younger years. Retrospective studies of SGM individuals find that sexual minority adults may formulate their identity and come out at a young age, and that a faster progression of identity development at a younger age may be associated with a higher risk for developing a depressive disorder (Calzo, Antonucci, Mays, & Cochran, 2011; Rendina,

Carter, Wahl, Millar, & Parsons, 2019). Further, findings from the Healthy Minds Study, an annual survey of adult college students in the United States, demonstrates that risk for depressive disorders is heightened among SGM emerging young adults (Borgogna et al., 2019). LGBs older than 50 may also be at an elevated risk for depressive disorders (Fredriksen-Goldsen, Kim, Barkan, Muraco, & Hoy-Ellis, 2013; Yarns, Abrams, Meeks, & Sewell, 2016). Older LGB adults, particularly gay and bisexual men, are less likely to be partnered or to have raised children compared to heterosexual older adults, thereby leaving them less likely to access key social support networks, and this may contribute to the elevated risk for depressive disorders that we see in some studies (Kim, Fredriksen-Goldsen, Bryan, & Muraco, 2017; Wallace, Cochran, Durazo, & Ford, 2011).

Residential context has also been identified as a shaper of risk for depression among SGMs. For example, SGMs who live in rural areas evidence higher rates of depression than those living in urban areas (Horvath et al., 2014; Whitehead, Shaver, & Stephenson, 2016). One possible explanation for this difference is the dearth of medical services addressing SGM concerns in rural areas, rendering individuals less likely to access necessary culturally specific mental health services (Horvath et al., 2014). However, it is also possible that geographic risk differences may be better accounted for by differences in discrimination exposure and community acceptance. Research demonstrates that those who live in states without policies protecting against hate crimes are at increased risk for negative mental health outcomes (Blosnich, Marsiglio, et al., 2016; Gonzales & Ehrenfeld, 2018; Hatzenbuehler et al., 2009).

Much of the evidence that guides us in our thinking about depressive disorders in SGM populations is derived from research conducted in high-income countries (Wainberg et al., 2017). Yet, some research has suggested that country of residence may be meaningful in terms of risk of depressive disorder, such that those residing in the Global South may exhibit higher rates of depressive disorders than those in high-income countries (Gorjian, Zarenezhad, Mahboubi, Gholamzadeh, & Mahmoudi, 2017; Muller & Hughes, 2016; Safren et al., 2009; Shirdel-Havar, Steensma, Cohen-Kettenis, & Kreukels, 2019; Yang et al., 2015). SGMs living in the Global South are exposed to stressors that can be of dire consequences and result in exacerbating risk for depressive disorders (Polders, Nel, Kruger, and Wells, 2008; Stotzer, 2014). For example, several Global South countries have laws criminalizing consensual same-sex sexual activity (Cochran et al., 2014; United Nations High Commissioner for Human Rights, 2011). Such legislation supports a heterosexist societal climate, leaving SGMs vulnerable to experiencing hate speech, violence, and even death; such a climate is associated with an increased risk of depression (Polders, Nel, Kruger, & Wells, 2008; Stotzer, 2014). SGMs residing in the Global South are also at risk of acts of physical violence, emotional violence, and prejudice (Human Rights Watch, 2011; Muller & Hughes, 2016; Nakkeeran & Nakkeeran, 2018; Peitzmeier et al., 2015; Wells & Polders, 2006). The elevated and consistent incidences of anti-SGM hate crimes, which are the case in many parts of the Global South, are meaningful considerations in a discussion of depressive disorders. Research in SGM and racial/ethnic minority populations finds that victims of hate crimes are at increased risk for experiencing depression (Bell & Perry, 2015; McDevitt, Balboni, Garcia, & Gu, 2001; Stotzer, 2014). Further, the victims are often reluctant to report hate crimes to law enforcement agencies, thereby compounding the distress they already face as well as limiting their opportunities for legal recourse and safety (Human Rights Watch, 2011; Nakkeeran & Nakkeeran, 2018; Rich, 2006; Wells & Polders, 2006). Further investigation into depressive disorders among SGMs in the Global South is warranted, but the current lack of high-quality population-based and longitudinal data on the mental health of SGMs impedes progress in this domain (Cáceres, Konda, Segura, & Lyerla, 2008; Luvuno, Mchunu, Ncama, Ngidi, & Mashamba-Thompson, 2019; Moraes & Casseb, 2017; Reisner, Poteat, Keatley, Cabral, Mothopeng, & Dunham, 2016).

Factors Contributing to the Etiology of Depressive Disorders among SGMs

Increasingly, there is evidence that the development of depressive disorders among SGMs is related to societal factors such as discrimination, stigma, lack of positive affirmation, and impaired social connectedness (Nuttbrock et al., 2012). For example, LGBs experience high rates of discrimination based on their sexual orientation, and these discriminatory experiences have been linked to higher rates of depressive disorders (Bostwick et al., 2014; Khan et al., 2017; Lee, Gamarel, Bryant, Zaller, & Operario, 2016; Mays & Cochran, 2001). Generally, the mechanism causing this elevation is attributed to stress engendered by stigma, prejudice, and discrimination (Meyer, 2003). Studies have indeed shown that SGMs may be exposed to high levels of unpredictable, episodic, and chronic stressors as a function of stigmatization of SGM status (Mays & Cochran, 2001; Williams et al., 2017).

Affirmation of SGM identity may protect against the development of depressive disorders (Ghavami, Fingerhut, Peplau, Grant, & Wittig, 2011; Glynn et al., 2016; Nuttbrock et al., 2012; Sevelius, 2013). Affirmation of SGM identity could be considered to have the opposite effect of stigma on individuals. Affirmation can derive from external sources such as expressions of community inclusion and social acceptance and from internal sources as individuals develop a positive sense of their own SGM identity (Ghavami et al., 2011; Sevelius, 2013; Tajfel & Turner, 1979). Research on minority identity affirmation among gender minorities indicates that gender identity affirmation is a salient protective factor against the development of major depressive disorder (Nuttbrock et al., 2012). Similarly, theorists have suggested that gender identity nonaffirmation, or when one's internal sense of gender identity is not affirmed by others, is related to several psychological morbidities (Nuttbrock et al., 2012; Testa, Habarth, Peta, Balsam, & Bockting, 2015). At least one study has specifically found that greater instances of gender identity nonaffirmation are associated with increased risk for depressive disorders (Nuttbrock et al., 2012). Gender identity nonaffirmation may be more likely to occur for individuals whose gender identity is misinterpreted in social contexts (Beemyn & Rankin, 2011; Bockting & Coleman, 2007; Testa et al., 2015). In its extreme form, gender nonaffirmation can become gender-related psychological and physical abuse, with a profound impact on increasing the risk of depressive disorders among gender minorities (Nuttbrock et al., 2010). Early life experiences of some SGMs are associated with the development of depressive disorders (Balsam, Lehavot, Beadnell, & Circo, 2010; Cook, Valera, Calebs, & Wilson, 2017). The link between childhood maltreatment and depression is well established in non–LGB-specific literature (Norman et al., 2012; Teicher & Samson, 2013), and reports of childhood maltreatment are more common among LGB adults in comparison to heterosexual adults (Corliss, Cochran, & Mays, 2002; Corliss, Cochran, Mays, Greenland, & Seeman, 2009; Hightow-Weidman et al., 2011).

Comorbidity of Depressive Disorders among SGMs

Depressive disorders are often comorbid with many chronic health disorders such as cardiovascular disease, obesity, and chronic pain (Caceres et al., 2017; Compare, Proietti, Germani, & Janeway, 2012; Fishbain, Cutler, Rosomoff, & Rosomoff, 1997; Luppino et al., 2010). Among SGM adults, the connection between cardiovascular disease and depressive disorders is particularly strong for sexual minority women, indicating the fact that this population may particularly benefit from combined psychological and physical health interventions (Caceres et al., 2017). Likewise, SGM women have a greater likelihood to develop cancer, polycystic ovarian syndrome, or obesity (Institute of Medicine, 2011) and thus may be at increased risk for depression. Further, depressive disorders often have harmful effects on the treatment of other diseases, especially with regard to increasing likelihood of medication nonadherence (Goldstein, Gathright, & Garcia, 2017; Gonzalez, Batchelder, Psaros, & Safren, 2011; Grenard et al., 2011). This issue is of particular concern for gay and bisexual men, who are at increased risk for HIV/AIDS, the treatment of which necessitates adherence to highly active antiretroviral therapy (HAART) (Gonzalez, Batchelder, Psaros, & Safren, 2011; Valleroy et al., 2000). One review revealed that even subclinical presentations of depressive symptoms diminished adherence to HAART medication (Gonzalez et al., 2011). Thus, best practices indicate that clinicians treating patients with chronic disorders, including HIV/AIDS, are advised to implement psychological monitoring and intervention targeting depressive symptoms (Gonzalez et al., 2011).

Intersectionality: A Possible Path Forward

The burden of depression among SGM adults is a heterogeneous experience, with rates within this subpopulation varying by individual characteristics, differences in social environments, health status variations, levels of stress and discrimination, and sources of resilience and social capital. One possible path to making sense of this variability is to borrow concepts from the field of intersectionality (Bowleg, 2008, 2012; Carbado, 2012, 2013; Crenshaw, 1991; Mays & Ghavami, 2018). Intersectionality refers to the possible additive and multiplicative effects of disadvantaged social statuses in creating inequities. The theory argues for the essential need to consider how contextually driven power, privilege, and oppression act to create risk clusters at the intersections of identity (Mays & Ghavami, 2018; Mays, Maas, Ricks, & Cochran, 2012). These clusters may then in turn create vulnerabilities for emotional and psychological damages that eventuate in depressive disorders. Concepts from intersectionality pair well with the RDoC approach to conceptualizing mental health disorders. RDoC isolates specific dimensions of symptoms manifested. Whether these dimensions co-vary with risky intersections predicted from intersectionality theory is unknown at this point but could lead to better treatment approaches for different subgroups of SGMs (Mays et al., 2012). For instance, when considering the risk of depressive disorders for racial minority SGMs, additive models derived from the minority stress theory initially failed to predict levels of depression (Kertzner, Meyer, Frost, & Stirratt, 2009). However, recent work taking a more nuanced approach to the question observes that multiple disadvantaged statuses may have cumulative effects (Calabrese et al., 2015; Clark, Mays & Cochran, 2017; Cochran & Mays, 2009; Mays & Ghavami, 2018). An intersectional approach with regard to depressive disorders in SGMs may allow researchers and clinicians to learn how individuals internalize and experience social disadvantage and the ways in which privilege, power, and oppression affect the development of depressive disorders (Mays & Ghavami, 2018). Indeed, intersectionality may provide an avenue for examining depressive disorders among SGMs in terms of the psychological effects of affirming one's minority identity.

Future Directions and Clinical Implications

A multipronged approach is required if we are to succeed in eliminating disparities in stress-related depressive disorders among SGM populations. We offer three primary suggestions for the field.

First, the integration of an RDoC framework with conceptualizations surrounding intersectionality theory may provide new insights into specific vulnerabilities that create a diverse panoply of risks for depression among SGMs. An RDoC approach would also allow researchers to make meaningful connections between constellations of symptoms in subpopulations of SGMs. It would also help to identify the ways in which societal stressors, such as anti-SGM stigma, discrimination, and vulnerability to violence, influence the development of depressive symptoms (Eaton, 2014). This approach may provide great benefits. Indeed, a study by Cochran and Mays (2009) estimated that the burden of mental health morbidity risk in the population could possibly be lessened by 5 to 11 percent if the effects of stigma and discrimination against sexual minorities were addressed.

Second, a growing and important trend in the integrated healthcare setting is the development and use of screening instruments to identify social risk factors (e.g., social determinants of health), such as efforts by the Social Interventions Research and Evaluation Network at the University of California San Francisco (SIREN). The goal is to address the inequities that undermine the well-being of vulnerable populations in the United States (Association of American Medical Colleges, 2016). Over the last two decades, the field of SGM mental health has greatly benefited from the routine inclusion of sexual orientation assessment in national health surveillance surveys. As new ways of measuring the effects of stigma and discrimination in relationship to health outcomes make their way into screening instruments in the integrated care setting, we must ensure that the ways in which sexual orientation and gender identity are associated with negative health outcomes are included in the efforts to develop these screening instruments. It is equally critical that the social stressors likely to affect SGM populations are adequately measured. For example, SIREN is developing clinical social risk factors screening tools for use in the healthcare setting (https://sirenetwork.ucsf.edu/). Henrikson, Sheward, and Cartier (2019) from the Kaiser Foundation Health Plan describe six domains they are using to develop their screening tool: (1) economic stability; (2) education; (3) social and community context; (4) health and clinical care; (5) neighborhood and physical environment; and (6) food security. Frequent input from the SGM community of research scholars is necessary to ensure that these social measures are sensitive to the experiences of diverse SGM populations. Psychologists and others have provided an abundance of scientific evidence for the ways in which social and community contexts are implicated in the development of depressive disorders. Collecting useful data to tie the effects of social and environmental stressors to the mental health of SGM populations is a needed next step (Eaton, 2014; Mays & Cochran, 2019).

With the growing trend in health services delivery to use screening tools and administrative data to improve care, it is important that socially vulnerable and underserved populations, including SGMs, enjoy benefits broadly. While specialty SGM clinics can tailor this work to the needs of the SGM population, most SGM individuals do not have access to this type of specialty care. Hence, all mental health services in the care environment must strive to meet the needs of SGM populations.

Third, clinicians caring for gender minorities are advised to seek education regarding gender-affirming medical interventions, as emerging evidence suggests that access to such interventions may decrease risk of depressive disorders (Colizzi, Costa, & Todarello, 2014; Witcomb et al., 2018). Hormone replacement therapy has been identified as an intervention in decreasing the risk of depression among gender minorities (Beckwith et al., 2019; Witcomb et al., 2018). In some cases, there are no significant differences in terms of depression risk between gender minorities and cisgender individuals after completion of gender-affirming treatment (Dhejne, Van Vlerken, Heylens, & Arcelus, 2016). The timing of beginning hormone replacement therapy may have a significant impact on well-being, such that an earlier age of initiation is associated with better long-term mental health outcomes (Beckwith et al., 2019; Bouman et al., 2016). Other studies have found that gender minority individuals are likely to delay engagement in healthcare due to fear of discrimination, and that this lack of engagement is associated with being over three times more at risk to suffer from major depressive disorder (Seelman, Colón-Diaz, LeCroix, Xavier-Brier, & Kattari, 2017).

Finally, paying attention to the ways in which policies, procedures, and approaches both in the mental health care system and in society more broadly exacerbate daily exposures to inequitable treatment is a form of intervention to reduce depressive disorders. Clinicians and researchers live and participate in social structures to which they can contribute informed activism. However, the first responsibility of do no harm is to ensure that we ourselves are adequately informed by data in order to be prepared to meet the needs of diverse SGM clients. Having evidence-based knowledge facilitates our capacity to provide quality services that can help reduce and address the consequences of depressive disorders in various subpopulations of SGMs.

Acknowledgments

We would like to thank research assistants Jonas Landis and Emily Ng for their efforts in identifying relevant materials for this chapter. Partial support for the work on this chapter comes from MD006932, National Institute of Minority Health and Health Disparities and MH115344, National Institute of Mental Health.

References

Abé, C., Rahman, Q., Långström, N., Rydén, E., Ingvar, M., & Landén, M. (2018). Cortical brain structure and sexual orientation in adult females with bipolar disorder or attention deficit hyperactivity disorder. *Brain and Behavior, 8*(7), e00998. doi:10.1002/brb3.998

American Psychiatric Association. (2013). *Diagnostic and statistical manual of mental disorders* (5th ed.). Washington, DC: Author.

Association of American Medical Colleges. (2016). *Achieving health equity: How academic medicine is addressing the social determinants of health.* Washington, DC: Association of American Medical Colleges.

Balsam, K. F., Lehavot, K., Beadnell, B., & Circo, E. (2010). Childhood abuse and mental health indicators among ethnically diverse lesbian, gay, and bisexual adults. *Journal of Consulting and Clinical Psychology, 78*(4), 459–68. doi:10.1037/a0018661

Barnhill, M. M., Lee, J. G. L., & Rafferty, A. P. (2017). Health inequities among lesbian, gay, and bisexual adults in North Carolina, 2011–14. *International Journal of Environmental Research and Public Health, 14*(8), 835. doi:10.3390/ijerph14080835

Beckwith, N., McDowell, M. J., Reisner, S. L., Zaslow, S., Weiss, R. D., Mayer, K. H., & Keuroghlian, A. S. (2019). Psychiatric epidemiology of transgender and nonbinary adult patients at an urban health center. *LGBT Health, 6*(2), 51–61. doi:10.1089/lgbt.2018.0136

Beemyn, G., & Rankin, S. R. (2011). *The lives of transgender people.* New York, NY: Columbia University Press.

Bell, J. G., & Perry, B. (2015). Outside looking in: The community impacts of anti-lesbian, gay, and bisexual hate crime. *Journal of Homosexuality, 62*(1), 98–120, doi:10.1080/00918369.2014.957133

Bjelland, I., Lie, S. A., Dahl, A. A., Mykletun, A., Stordal, E., & Kraemer, H. C. (2009). A dimensional versus a categorical approach to diagnosis: Anxiety and depression in the HUNT 2 study. *International Journal of Methods in Psychiatry Research, 18*, 128–37. doi:10.1002/mpr.284

Blashill, A. J., & Calzo, J. P. (2019). Sexual minority children: Mood disorders and suicidality disparities. *Journal of Affective Disorders, 246*, 96–8. doi:10.1016/j.jad.2018.12.040

Blosnich, J. R., Marsiglio, M. C., Gao, S., Gordon, A. J., Shipherd, J. C., Kauth, M., . . . Fine, M. J. (2016). Mental health of transgender veterans in US states with and without discrimination and hate crime legal protection. *American Journal of Public Health, 106*(3), 534–40. doi:10.2105/AJPH.2015.302981

Blosnich, J. R., Nasuti, L. J., Mays, V. M., & Cochran, S. D. (2016). Suicidality and sexual orientation: Characteristics of symptom severity, disclosure, and timing across the life course. *American Journal of Orthopsychiatry, 86*(1), 69–78. doi:10.1037/ort0000112

Bockting, W. O., & Coleman, E. (2007). Developmental stages of the transgender coming-out process. In R. Ettner, S. Monstrey, & A. E. Eyler (Eds.), *Principles of transgender medicine and surgery.* Binghamton, NY: Haworth Press.

Borgogna, N. C., McDermott, R. C., Aita, S. L., & Kridel, M. M. (2019). Anxiety and depression across gender and sexual minorities: Implications for transgender, gender nonconforming, pansexual, demisexual, asexual, queer, and questioning individuals. *Psychology of Sexual Orientation and Gender Diversity, 6*(1), 54–63. doi:10.1037/sgd0000306

Bostwick, W. B., Boyd, C. J., Hughes, T. L., & McCabe, S. E. (2010). Dimensions of sexual orientation and the prevalence of mood and anxiety disorders in the United States. *American Journal of Public Health, 100*(3), 468–75. doi:10.2105/AJPH.2008.152942

Bostwick, W. B., Boyd, C. J., Hughes, T. L., West, B. T., & McCabe, S. E. (2014). Discrimination and mental health among lesbian, gay, and bisexual adults in the United States. *American Journal of Orthopsychiatry, 84*(1), 35–45. doi:10.1037/h0098851

Bouman, W. P., Claes, L., Marshall, E., Pinner, G. T., Longworth, J., Maddox, V., . . . Arcelus, J. (2016). Sociodemographic variables, clinical features, and the role of preassessment cross-sex hormones in older trans people. *Journal of Sexual Medicine, 13*(4), 711–19. doi:10.1016/j.jsxm.2016.01.009

Bowleg, L. (2008). When Black + lesbian + woman ≠ Black lesbian woman: The methodological challenges of qualitative and quantitative intersectionality research. *Sex Roles, 59*, 312–25. 10.1007/s11199-008-9400-z

Bowleg, L. (2012). The problem with the phrase "women and minorities": Intersectionality, an important theoretical framework for public health. *American Journal of Public Health, 102*(7), 1267–73. doi:10.2105/AJPH.2012.300750

Caceres, B., Brody, A., Luscombe, R. E., Primiano, J. E., Marusca, P., Sitts, E. M., & Chyun, D. (2017). A systematic review of cardiovascular disease in sexual minorities. *American Journal of Public Health, 107*(4), E13–E21. doi:10.2105/AJPH.2016.303630

Cáceres, C. F., Konda, K., Segura, E. R., & Lyerla, R. (2008). Epidemiology of male same-sex behaviour and associated sexual health indicators in low- and middle-income countries: 2003–2007 estimates. *Sexually Transmitted Infections, 84*(Suppl. 1), I49–I56. doi:10.1136/sti.2008.030569

Calabrese, S. K., Meyer, I. H., Overstreet, N. M., Haile, R., & Hansen, N. B. (2015). Exploring discrimination and mental health disparities faced by black sexual minority women using a minority stress framework. *Psychology of Women Quarterly, 39*(3), 287–304. doi:10.1177/0361684314560730

Calzo, J. P., Antonucci, T. C., Mays, V. M., & Cochran, S. D. (2011). Retrospective recall of sexual orientation identity development among gay, lesbian, and bisexual adults. *Developmental Psychology, 47*(6), 1658–73. doi:10.1037/a0025508

Carbado, A. (2012). *When blood won't tell: An intra-categorical intersectional framework for understanding the construction of race.* Master's thesis, University of California, Los Angeles.

Carbado, D. W. (2013). Colorblind intersectionality. *Signs, 38*(4), 811–45. doi:10.1086/669666

Chaudhry, A. B., & Reisner, S. L. (2019). Disparities by sexual orientation persist for major depressive episode and substance abuse or dependence: Findings from a national probability study of adults in the United States. *LGBT Health, 6*(5), 261–6. doi:10.1089/lgbt.2018.0207

Clark, L. A., Cuthbert, B., Lewis-Fernández, R., Narrow, W. E., & Reed, G. M. (2017). Three approaches to understanding and classifying mental disorder: ICD-11, DSM-5, and the National Institute of Mental Health's Research Domain Criteria (RDoC). *Psychological Science in the Public Interest, 18*(2), 72–145. doi: 10.1177/1529100617727266

Clark, K. A., Mays, V. M. & Cochran, S.D. (2017). Extreme violence and the invisibility of women who murder: The intersectionality of gender, race, ethnicity, sexual orientation, and gender identity equals silence. *Violence and Gender* 117–120. doi: 10.1089/vio.2017.0036

Cochran, S. D., Björkenstam, C., & Mays, V. M. (2017). Sexual orientation differences in functional limitations, disability, and mental health services use: Results from the 2013–2014 National Health Interview Survey. *Journal of Consulting and Clinical Psychology, 85*(12), 1111–21. doi:10.1037/ccp0000243

Cochran, S. D., Drescher, J., Kismödi, E., Giami, A., García-Moreno, C., Atalla, E., . . . Reed, G. M. (2014). Proposed declassification of disease categories related to sexual orientation in the International Statistical Classification of Diseases and Related Health Problems (ICD-11). *Bulletin of the World Health Organization, 92*(9), 672–9. doi:10.2471/BLT.14.135541

Cochran, S. D., & Mays, V. M. (2000). Lifetime prevalence of suicide symptoms and affective disorders among men reporting same-sex sexual partners: Results from NHANES III. *American Journal of Public Health, 90*(4), 573–8. doi:10.2105/ajph.90.4.573

Cochran, S. D. & Mays, V. M. (2009). Burden of psychiatric morbidity among lesbian, gay, and bisexual individuals in the California Quality of Life Survey. *Journal of Abnormal Psychology*, 118 (3), 647–658.

Cochran, S. D., Sullivan, J. G., & Mays, V. M. (2003). Prevalence of mental disorders, psychological distress, and mental health services use among lesbian, gay, and bisexual adults in the united states. *Journal of Consulting and Clinical Psychology, 71*(1), 53–61. doi:10.1037/0022-006X.71.1.53

Colizzi, M., Costa, R., & Todarello, O. (2014). Transsexual patients' psychiatric comorbidity and positive effect of cross-sex hormonal treatment on mental health: Results from a longitudinal study. *Psychoneuroendocrinology, 39*, 65–73. doi:10.1016/j.psyneuen.2013.09.029

Colodro-Conde, L., Couvy-Duchesne, B., Zhu, G., Coventry, W. L., Byrne, E. M., Gordon, S., . . . Martin, N. G. (2018). A direct test of the diathesis-stress model for depression. *Molecular Psychiatry, 23*(7), 1590–96. doi:10.1038/mp.2017.130

Compare, A., Proietti, R., Germani, E., & Janeway, D. (2012). Anxiety and depression: Risk factors for cardiovascular disease. In E. A. Dornelas (Ed.), *Stress proof the heart: Behavioral interventions for cardiac patients* (pp. 139–66). New York, NY: Springer Science + Business Media.

Cook, S. H., Valera, P., Calebs, B. J., & Wilson, P. A. (2017). Adult attachment as a moderator of the association between childhood traumatic experiences and depression symptoms among young Black gay and bisexual men. *Cultural Diversity & Ethnic Minority Psychology, 23*(3), 388–97. doi:10.1037/cdp0000119

Corliss, H. L., Cochran, S. D., & Mays, V. M. (2002). Reports of parental maltreatment during childhood in a United States population-based survey of homosexual, bisexual, and heterosexual adults. *Journal of Child Abuse and Neglect, 26*(11), 1165–78.

Corliss, H. L., Cochran, S. D., Mays, V. M., Greenland, S., & Seeman, T. E. (2009). Age of minority sexual orientation development and risk of childhood maltreatment and suicide attempts in women. *American Journal of Orthopsychiatry, 79*(4), 511–21. doi:10.1037/a0017163

Craddock, N., & Sklar, P. (2013). Genetics of bipolar disorder. *Lancet, 381*(9878), 1654–62. doi:10.1016/S0140-6736.

Crenshaw, K. W. (1991). Mapping the margins: Intersectionality, identity politics, and violence against women of color. *Stanford Law Review, 43*, 1241–99.

Dhejne, C., Van Vlerken, R., Heylens, G., & Arcelus, J. (2016). Mental health and gender dysphoria: A review of the literature. *International Review of Psychiatry, 28*(1), 44–57. doi:10.3109/09540261.2015.1115753

Eaton N. R. (2014). Trans-diagnostic psychopathology factors and sexual minority mental health: Evidence of disparities and associations with minority stressors. *Psychology of Sexual Orientation and Gender Diversity, 1*(3), 244–54. doi:10.1037/sgd0000048

Fishbain, D. A., Cutler, R., Rosomoff, H. L., & Rosomoff, R. S. (1997). Chronic pain-associated depression: Antecedent or consequence of chronic pain? A review. *Clinical Journal of Pain, 13*(2), 116–37. doi:10.1097/00002508-199706000-00006

Fredriksen-Goldsen, K. I., Kim, H. J., Barkan, S. E., Muraco, A., & Hoy-Ellis, C. P. (2013). Health disparities among lesbian, gay, and bisexual older adults: Results from a population-based study. *American Journal of Public Health, 103*(10), 1802–9. doi:10.2105/AJPH.2012.301110

Frisell, T., Lichtenstein, P., Rahman, Q., & Långström, N. (2010). Psychiatric morbidity associated with same-sex sexual behaviour: Influence of minority stress and familial factors. *Psychological Medicine, 40*(2), 315–24. doi:10.1017/S0033291709005996

Ghavami, N., Fingerhut, A., Peplau, L. A., Grant, S. K., & Wittig, M. A. (2011). Testing a model of minority identity achievement, identity affirmation, and psychological well-being among ethnic minority and sexual minority individuals. *Cultural Diversity and Ethnic Minority Psychology, 17*(1), 79–88. doi:10.1037/a0022532

Glynn, T. R., Gamarel, K. E., Kahler, C. W., Iwamoto, M., Operario, D., & Nemoto, T. (2016). The role of gender affirmation in psychological well-being among transgender women. *Psychology of Sexual Orientation and Gender Diversity, 3*(3), 336–44. doi:10.1037/sgd0000171

Goldberg, D. (2000). Plato versus Artistotle: Categorical and dimensional models for common mental disorders. *Comprehensive Psychiatry, 41*(2), 8–13. doi:10.1016/S0010-440X(00)80002-4

Goldberg, D. (2011). The heterogeneity of "major depression." *World Psychiatry, 10*(3), 226–8. doi:10.1002/j.2051-5545.2011.tb00061.x

Goldstein, C. M., Gathright, E. C., & Garcia, S. (2017). Relationship between depression and medication adherence in cardiovascular disease: The perfect challenge for the integrated care team. *Patient Preference and Adherence, 11*, 547–59. doi:10.2147/PPA.S127277

Gonzales, G., & Ehrenfeld, J. M. (2018). The association between state policy environments and self-rated health disparities for sexual minorities in the United States. *International Journal of Environmental Research and Public Health, 15*(6), 1136. doi:10.3390/ijerph15061136

Gonzales, G., & Henning-Smith, C. (2017). Health disparities by sexual orientation: Results and implications from the Behavioral Risk Factor Surveillance System. *Journal of Community Health, 42*(6), 1163–72. doi:10.1007/s10900-017-0366-z

Gonzales, G., Przedworski, J., & Henning-Smith, C. (2016). Comparison of health and health risk factors between lesbian, gay, and bisexual adults and heterosexual adults in the United States. *JAMA Internal Medicine, 176*(9), 1344–51 doi:10.1001/jamainternmed.2016.3432

Gonzalez, J. S., Batchelder, A. W., Psaros, C., & Safren, S. A. (2011). Depression and HIV/AIDS treatment nonadherence: A review and meta-analysis. *Journal of Acquired Immune Deficiency Syndromes, 58*(2), 181. doi:10.1097/QAI.0b013e31822d490a

Gorjian, Z., Zarenezhad, M., Mahboubi, M., Gholamzadeh, S., & Mahmoudi, N. (2017). Depression in patients suffering from gender dysphoria: The hospitalized patients of Legal Medicine Center in southwest of Iran. *World Family Medicine/Middle East Journal of Family Medicine, 15*(7), 62–7.

Grenard, J. L., Munjas, B. A., Adams, J. L., Suttorp, M., Maglione, M., McGlynn, E. A., & Gellad, W. F. (2011). Depression and medication adherence in the treatment of chronic diseases in the United States: A meta-analysis. *Journal of General Internal Medicine, 26*(10), 1175–82. doi:10.1007/s11606-011-1704-y

Hammen, C. L. (2015). Stress and depression: Old questions, new approaches. *Current Opinion in Psychology, 4*, 80–3. doi:10.1016/j.copsyc.2014.12.024

Hatzenbuehler, M. L. (2009). How does sexual minority stigma "get under the skin"? A psychological mediation framework. *Psychological Bulletin, 135*(5), 707–30. doi:10.1037/a0016441

Hatzenbuehler, M. L., Keyes, K. M., & Hasin, D. S. (2009). State-level policies and psychiatric morbidity in lesbian, gay, and bisexual populations. *American Journal of Public Health, 99*(12), 2275–81. doi:10.2105/AJPH.2008.153510

Hellman, R. E., Sudderth, L., & Avery, A. M. (2002). Major mental illness in a sexual minority psychiatric sample. *Journal of the Gay & Lesbian Medical Association, 6*(3–4), 97–106. doi:10.1023/B:JOLA.0000011065.08186.17

Henrikson, N., Sheward, R., & Cartier, Y. (18 July 2019). Examining the validity of clinical social risk screening tools [Webinar]. In *Social Interventions Research & Evaluation Network*. Retrieved from https://sirenetwork.ucsf.edu/sites/sirenetwork.ucsf.edu/files/wysiwyg/Examining-the-validity-of-social-risk-screening-tools-slides.pdf.

Hightow-Weidman, L. B., Phillips, G., Jones, K. C., Outlaw, A. Y., Fields, S. D., & Smith, J. C. (2011). Racial and sexual identity-related maltreatment among minority YMSM: Prevalence, perceptions, and the association with emotional distress. *AIDS Patient Care and STDs, 25*(1), S39–S45. doi:10.1089/apc.2011.9877

Horvath, K. J., Iantaffi, A., Swinburne-Romine, R., & Bockting, W. (2014). A comparison of mental health, substance use, and sexual risk behaviors between rural and non-rural transgender persons. *Journal of Homosexuality, 61*(8), 1117–30. doi:10.1080/00918369.2014.872502

Human Rights Watch. (2011). *"We'll show you you're a woman": Violence and discrimination against black lesbians and transgender men in South Africa.* Retrieved from http://www.hrw.org/reports/2011/12/06/well-show-you-youre-woman.

Insel, T., Cuthbert, B., Garvey, M., Heinssen, R., Pine, D. S., Quinn, K., Sanislow, C., & Wang, P. (2010). Research domain criteria (RDoC): Toward a new classification framework for research on mental disorders. *The American Journal of Psychiatry, 167*(7), 748–751. doi:10.1176/appi.ajp.2010.09091379

Institute of Medicine. (2011). *The health of lesbian, gay, bisexual, and transgender people: Building a foundation for better understanding.* Washington, DC: National Academies Press.

Jackson, S. E., Hackett, R. A., Grabovac, I., Smith, L., & Steptoe, A. (2019). Perceived discrimination, health and wellbeing among middle-aged and older lesbian, gay and bisexual people: A prospective study. *PloS One, 14*(5), e0216497. doi:10.1371/journal.pone.0216497

James, S. E., Herman, J. L., Rankin, S., Keisling, M., Mottet, L., & Anafi, M. (2016). *The report of the 2015 U.S. transgender survey*. Washington, DC: National Center for Transgender Equality.

Kertzner, R. M., Meyer, I. H., Frost, D. M., & Stirratt, M. J. (2009). Social and psychological well-being in lesbians, gay men, and bisexuals: The effects of race, gender, age, and sexual identity. *American Journal of Orthopsychiatry*, *79*(4), 500–10. doi:10.1037/a0016848.

Kessler, R. C., Barker, P. R., Colpe, L. J., Epstein, J. F., Gfroerer, J. C., Hiripi, E., . . . Zaslavsky, A. M. (2003) Screening for serious mental illness in the general population. *Archives of General Psychiatry*, *60*(2), 184–9. doi:10.1001/archpsyc.60.2.184

Khan, M., Ilcisin, M., & Saxton, K. (2017). Multifactorial discrimination as a fundamental cause of mental health inequities. *International Journal for Equity in Health*, *16*(1), 43. doi:10.1186/s12939-017-0532-z

Kieseppä, T., Partonen, T., Haukka, J., Kaprio, J., & Lönnqvist, J. (2014). High concordance of bipolar I disorder in nationwide sample of twins. *American Journal of Psychiatry*, *161*(10), 1814–21. doi: 10.1176/ajp.161.10.1814

Kim, H. J., Fredriksen-Goldsen, K. I., Bryan, A. E., & Muraco, A. (2017). Social network types and mental health among LGBT older adults. *The Gerontologist*, *57*(suppl 1), S84–S94. doi:10.1093/geront/gnw169

Kraemer, H. C., Noda, A., O'Hara, R. (2004). Categorical versus dimensional approaches to diagnosis: Methodological challenges. *Journal of Psychiatric Research*, *38*(1), 17–25. doi:10.1016/S0022-3956(03)00097-9

Krueger, E. A., Meyer, I. H., & Upchurch, D. M. (2018). Sexual orientation group differences in perceived stress and depressive symptoms among young adults in the United States. *LGBT Health*, *5*(4), 242–9. doi:10.1089/lgbt.2017.0228

Lee, J. H., Gamarel, K. E., Bryant, K. J., Zaller, N. D., & Operario, D. (2016). Discrimination, mental health, and substance use disorders among sexual minority populations. *LGBT Health*, *3*(4), 258–65. doi:10.1089/lgbt.2015.0135

Lee, J., Wimark, T., Ortiz, K. S., & Sewell, K. B. (2018). Health-related regional and neighborhood correlates of sexual minority concentration: A systematic review. *PloS One*, *13*(6), e0198751. doi:10.1371/journal.pone.0198751

Luppino, F. S., de Wit, L. M., Bouvy, P. F., Stijnen, T., Cuijpers, P., Penninx, B. W. J. H., & Zitman, F. G. (2010). Overweight, obesity, and depression: A systematic review and meta-analysis of longitudinal studies. *Archives of General Psychiatry*, *67*(3), 220–9. doi:10.1001/archgenpsychiatry.2010.2

Luvuno, Z. P., Mchunu, G., Ncama, B., Ngidi, H., & Mashamba-Thompson, T. (2019). Evidence of interventions for improving healthcare access for lesbian, gay, bisexual and transgender people in South Africa: A scoping review. *African Journal of Primary Health Care & Family Medicine*, *11*(1), e1–e10. doi:10.4102/phcfm.v11i1.1367

Mays, V. M., & Cochran, S. D. (2001). Mental health correlates of perceived discrimination among lesbian, gay, and bisexual adults in the United States. *American Journal of Public Health*, *91*(11), 1869–76. doi:10.2105/ajph.91.11.1869

Mays, V.M. & Cochran, S.D. (2019). Challenges and Opportunities for Modernizing the National Violent Death Reporting System. *American Journal of Public Health*, Am J Public Health. 2019 Feb; 109(2): 192–194. doi:10.2105/AJPH.2018.304891

Mays, V. M., & Ghavami, N. (2018). History, aspirations, and transformations of intersectionality: Focusing on gender. In C. B. Travis, J. W. White, A. Rutherford, W. S. Williams, S. L. Cook, & K. F. Wyche (Eds.), *APA handbook of the psychology of women: History, theory, and battlegrounds* (pp. 541–66). Washington, DC: American Psychological Association. doi:10.1037/0000059-028

Mays, V. M., Maas, R. M., Ricks, J., & Cochran, S. D. (2012). HIV and African American women in the U.S. south: A social determinants approach to population-level HIV prevention and intervention efforts. In A. Baum, T. A. Revenson, & J. Singer (Eds.), *Handbook of health psychology* (2nd ed., pp. 771–801). New York, NY: Psychology Press.

McDevitt, J., Balboni, J., Garcia, L., & Gu, J. (2001). Consequences for victims: A comparison of bias- and non-bias-motivated assaults. *American Behavioral Scientist*, *45*(4), 697–713. doi:10.1177/0002764201045004010

Meyer, I. H. (2003). Prejudice, social stress, and mental health in lesbian, gay, and bisexual populations: Conceptual issues and research evidence. *Psychological Bulletin*, *129*(5), 674–97. doi:10.1037/0033-2909.129.5.674

Moraes, R. P., & Casseb, J. (2017). Depression and adherence to antiretroviral treatment in HIV-positive men in São Paulo, the largest city in South America: Social and psychological implications. *Clinics (Sao Paulo, Brazil)*, *72*(12), 743–9. doi:10.6061/clinics/2017(12)05

Muller, A., & Hughes, T. L. (2016). Making the invisible visible: A systematic review of sexual minority women's health in Southern Africa. *BMC Public Health*, *16*(307), 1–8. doi:10.1186/s12889-016-2980-6

Nakkeeran, N., & Nakkeeran, B. (2018). Disability, mental health, sexual orientation and gender identity: Understanding health inequity through experience and difference. *Health Research Policy and Systems*, *16*(Suppl 1), 1–10. doi:10.1186/s12961-018-0366-1

Norman, R. E., Byambaa, M., De, R., Butchart, A., Scott, J., & Vos, T. (2012). The long-term health consequences of child physical abuse, emotional abuse, and neglect: A systematic review and meta-analysis. *PLoS Medicine*, *9*(11). doi:e1001349.10.1371/journal.pmed.1001349

Nuttbrock, L., Bockting, W., Rosenblum, A., Mason, M., Macri, M., & Becker, J. (2012). Gender identity conflict/affirmation and major depression across the life course of transgender women. *International Journal of Transgenderism*, *13*(3), 91–103. doi:10.1080/15532739.2011.657979

Nuttbrock, L., Hwahng, S., Bockting, W., Rosenblum, A., Mason, M., Macri, M., & Becker, J. (2010). Psychiatric impact of gender-related abuse across the life course of male-to-female transgender persons. *Journal of Sex Research*, *47*(1), 12–23. doi:10.1080/00224490903062258

Peitzmeier, S. M., Yasin, F., Stephenson, R., Wirtz, A. L., Delegchoimbol, A., Dorjgotov, M., & Baral, S. (2015). Sexual violence against men who have sex with men and transgender women in Mongolia: A mixed-methods study of scope and consequences. *PLoS One*, *10*(10), e0139320. doi:10.1371/journal.pone.0139320

Polders, L. A., Nel, J. A., Kruger, P. & Wells, H. L. (2008). Factors affecting vulnerability to depression among gay men and lesbian women in Gauteng, South Africa. *South African Journal of Psychology*, *38*(4), 673–87.

Qureshi, R. I., Zha, P., Kim, S., Hindin, P., Naqvi, Z., Holly, C., Dubbs, W., & Ritch, W. (2018). Health care needs and care utilization among lesbian, gay, bisexual, and transgender populations in New Jersey. *Journal of Homosexuality*, *65*(2), 167-80. doi:10.1080/00918369.2017.1311555

Reisner, S. L., Poteat, T., Keatley, J., Cabral, M., Mothopeng, T., & Dunham, E. (2016). Global health burden and needs of transgender populations: A review. *Lancet, 388*(10042), 412–36. https://doi.org/10.1016/S0140-6736(16)00684-X

Reisner, S. L., White, J. M., Mayer, K. H., & Mimiaga, M. J. (2014). Sexual risk behaviors and psychosocial health concerns of female-to-male transgender men screening for STDs at an urban community health center. *AIDS Care, 26*(7), 857–64. doi:10.1080/09540121.2013.855701

Rendina, H. J., Carter, J. A., Wahl, L., Millar, B. M., & Parsons, J. T. (2019). Trajectories of sexual identity development and psychological well-being for highly sexually active gay and bisexual men: A latent growth curve analysis. *Psychology of Sexual Orientation and Gender Diversity, 6*(1), 64–74. doi:10.1037/sgd0000308

Rich, E. (2006). *Overall research findings on levels of empowerment among LGBT people in the Western cape, South Africa.* Cape Town: Triangle Project and UNISA Centre for Applied Psychology.

Safren, S. A., Thomas, B. E., Mimiaga, M. J., Chandrasekaran, V., Menon, S., Swaminathan, S., & Mayer, K. H. (2009). Depressive symptoms and human immunodeficiency virus risk behavior among men who have sex with men in Chennai, India. *Psychology, Health & Medicine, 14*(6), 705–715. doi:10.1080/13548500903334754

Seelman, K. L., Colón-Diaz, M., J. P., LeCroix, R. H., Xavier-Brier, M., & Kattari, L. (2017). Transgender noninclusive healthcare and delaying care because of fear: Connections to general health and mental health among transgender adults. *Transgender Health, 2*(1), 17–28. doi:10.1089/trgh.2016.0024

Sevelius, J. M. (2013). Gender affirmation: A framework for conceptualizing risk behavior among transgender women of color. *Sex Roles, 68*(11–12), 675–89. doi:10.1007/s11199-012-0216-5

Shirdel-Havar, E., Steensma, T. D., Cohen-Kettenis, P., & Kreukels, B. P. C. (2019). Psychological symptoms and body image in individuals with gender dysphoria: A comparison between Iranian and Dutch clinics. *International Journal of Transgenderism, 20*(1), 108–117. doi:10.1080/15532739.2018.1444529

Stotzer, R. L. (2014). Bias crimes based on sexual orientation and gender identity: Global prevalence, impacts, and causes. In D. Peterson & V. Panfil (Eds.), *Handbook of LGBT communities, 45–64, crime, and justice.* New York, NY: Springer.

Streed, C. G., McCarthy, E. P., & Haas, J. S. (2018). Self-reported physical and mental health of gender nonconforming transgender adults in the United States. *LGBT Health, 5*(7), 443–8. doi:10.1089/lgbt.2017.0275

Tajfel, H., & Turner, J. C. (1979). An integrative theory of intergroup conflict. In W. G. Austin & S. Worschel (Eds.), *The social psychology of intergroup relations,* 33–37. Monterey, CA: Brooks/Cole.

Teicher, M. H., & Samson, J. A. (2013). Childhood maltreatment and psychopathology: A case for ecophenotypic variants as clinically and neurobiologically distinct subtypes. *American Journal of Psychiatry, 170*(10), 1114–33. doi:10.1176/appi.ajp.2013.12070957

Testa, R. J., Habarth, J., Peta, J., Balsam, K., & Bockting, W. (2015). Development of the gender minority stress and resilience measure. *Psychology of Sexual Orientation and Gender Diversity, 2*(1), 65–77. doi:10.1037/sgd0000081

United Nations High Commissioner for Human Rights. (2011). *Discriminatory laws and practices and acts of violence against individuals based on their sexual orientation and gender identity.* New York, NY: United Nations.

Valleroy, L. A., MacKellar, D. A., Karon, J. M., Rosen, D. H., McFarland, W., Shehan, D. A., . . . Janssen, R. S. (2000). HIV prevalence and associated risks in young men who have sex with men. *Journal of the American Medical Association, 284*(2), 198–204. doi:10.1001/jama.284.2.198

Wainberg, M. L., Scorza, P., Shultz, J. M., Helpman, L., Mootz, J. J., Johnson, K. A., . . . Arbuckle, M. R. (2017). Challenges and opportunities in global mental health: A research-to-practice perspective. *Current Psychiatry Reports, 19*(28), 1–10. doi:10.1007/s11920-017-0780-z

Wallace, S. P., Cochran, S. D., Durazo, E. M., & Ford, C. L. (2011). *The health of aging lesbian, gay and bisexual adults in California.* Policy brief. UCLA Center for Health Policy Research, 1–8.

Wells, H., & Polders, L. (2006). Anti-gay hate crimes in South Africa: Prevalence, reporting practices, and experiences of the police. *Agenda: Empowering Women for Gender Equity, 67,* 20–8. https://doi.org/10.1080/10130950.2006.9674694

Whitehead, J., Shaver, J., & Stephenson, R. (2016). Outness, stigma, and primary health care utilization among rural LGBT populations. *PLoS One, 11*(1), e0146139. https://doi.org/10.1371/journal.pone.0146139

Williams, C. C., Curling, D., Steele, L. S., Gibson, M. F., Daley, A., Green, D. C., & Ross, L. E. (2017). Depression and discrimination in the lives of women, transgender and gender liminal people in Ontario, Canada. *Health and Social Care in the Community, 25*(3), 1139–50. doi:10.1111/hsc.12414.

Witcomb, G. L., Bouman, W. P., Claes, L., Brewin, N., Crawford, J. R., & Arcelus, J. (2018). Levels of depression in transgender people and its predictors: Results of a large matched control study with transgender people accessing clinical services. *Journal of Affective Disorders, 235,* 308–15. doi:10.1016/j.jad.2018.02.051

Woody, M. L., & Gibb, B. E. (2015). Integrating NIMH Research Domain Criteria (RDoC) into depression research. *Current Opinion in Psychology, 4,* 6–12. doi:10.1016/j.copsyc.2015.01.004

World Health Organization. (2017). *Depression and other common mental disorders: Global health estimates.* Geneva, Switzerland: World Health Organization.

World Health Organization. (2018). *International statistical classification of diseases and related health problems* (11th revision). https://icd.who.int/browse11/l-m/en

Yang, X., Wang, L., Hao, C., Gu, Y., Song, W., Wang, J., . . . Zhao, Q. (2015). Sex partnership and self-efficacy influence depression in Chinese transgender women: A cross-sectional study. *PLoS One, 10*(9), 1–13. doi:10.1371/journal.pone.0136975

Yarns, B. C., Abrams, J. M., Meeks, T. W., & Sewell, D. D. (2016). The mental health of older LGBT adults. *Current Psychiatry Reports, 18*(60), 1–11. doi:10.1007/s11920-016-0697-y

CHAPTER

5 Anxiety Disorders among Sexual and Gender Minority Populations

Brandon J. Weiss *and* Bethany Owens Raymond

Abstract

Rates of anxiety disorders are significantly elevated among sexual and gender minorities. In this chapter, the minority stress model is discussed as a framework for conceptualizing anxiety among sexual and gender minorities, and the authors review the literature on the relationships between specific minority stressors and symptoms. The authors examine prevalence rates of anxiety disorders among sexual minorities and gender minorities, separately and in comparison to heterosexual and cisgender individuals. Also reviewed is the literature on anxiety disorders among sexual and gender minorities with a racial or ethnic minority status. Current assessment and treatment approaches are identified and reviewed. Finally, limitations to the current literature base are discussed and recommendations are provided for future studies.

Keywords: sexual minorities, gender minorities, anxiety disorders, minority stress, intersectionality

Anxiety disorders are among the most common psychiatric disorders, both in the United States (Kessler et al., 2005) and globally (Kessler et al., 2009). The lifetime prevalence for an anxiety disorder among adults is approximately 31.1 percent in the United States (Kessler et al., 2005), while outside of the United States lifetime prevalence rates range from 4.8 to 25.3 percent (Kessler et al., 2009). However, as discussed in this chapter, these rates are substantially higher for sexual and gender minority (SGM) individuals. This chapter examines the prevalence and clinical features of anxiety disorders among SGM individuals, as well as evidence-based suggestions for assessment and treatment. We focus on social anxiety disorder, generalized anxiety disorder, panic disorder, and specific phobia. We include a focus on racial and ethnic sexual minorities, as well as, when possible, the available literature on SGM individuals residing in the Global South.

Anxiety Disorders among Sexual Minorities

Prevalence

Epidemiological data on anxiety disorders among sexual minorities, particularly data examining diagnostic changes in DSM-5, are sparse. However, studies have reliably shown elevated rates of anxiety disorders among sexual minority individuals compared to their heterosexual counterparts. Using data from the National Epidemiologic Survey on Alcohol and Related Conditions, Bostwick, Boyd, Hughes, and McCabe (2010) found that sexual minority men and women were over twice as likely to experience a lifetime anxiety disorder compared to heterosexual individuals. Among women, lifetime prevalence rates of any anxiety disorder were higher for those who identified as lesbian (40.8 percent) or bisexual (57.8 percent) compared to those who identified as heterosexual (31.3 percent), and rates of panic disorder, social anxiety disorder, specific phobia, and generalized anxiety disorder were higher among sexual minority women than among heterosexual women. Ratings were similar among men, where lifetime prevalence for any anxiety disorder was higher for those who identified as gay (41.2 percent) or bisexual (38.7 percent) compared to those who identified as heterosexual (18.6 percent), along with elevated rates of panic disorder, social anxiety disorder, specific phobia, and generalized anxiety disorder among sexual minority men compared to heterosexual men.

These findings mirror those of other epidemiological studies conducted in the United States. For example, using data from Wave IV of the National Longitudinal Study of Adolescent Health, Strutz, Herring, and Halpern (2015) found higher lifetime prevalence rates of an anxiety disorder among sexual minority men and women compared to heterosexual individuals. Additionally, data from both the MacArthur Foundation National Survey of Midlife Development (Cochran, Sullivan, & Mays, 2003) and the California Quality of Life Survey (Cochran & Mays, 2009) showed a higher twelve-month prevalence rate of generalized anxiety disorder and panic among sexual minority men and women compared to heterosexual individuals. Similarly, elevated rates of anxiety disorders among sexual minority individuals were found in epidemiological studies in the Netherlands (Sandfort, de Graaf, Bijl, & Schnabel, 2001) and Sweden (Bjorkenstam, Bjorkenstam, Andersson, Cochran, & Kosidou, 2017).

While studies on the intersection of race, ethnicity, and sexual orientation on anxiety are sparse, the available data suggest similar or lower rates for racial and ethnic minorities. Using data from the National Latino and Asian American Survey, Cochran, Mays, Alegria, Ortega, and Takeuchi (2007) found higher twelve-month and lifetime prevalence rates of any anxiety disorder among Latino and Asian American sexual minority men compared to their heterosexual counterparts, though lower than among general population-based surveys of sexual minority individuals. Additionally, they found similar rates of twelve-month and lifetime prevalence of any anxiety disorder among both sexual minority and heterosexual Latino and Asian American women. In a community sample of sexual minority individuals in New York City, Meyer, Dietrich, and Schwartz (2008) found equivalent rates of a lifetime anxiety disorder among White and Latino respondents but significantly lower rates of anxiety among Black respondents. In a large sample of sexual minority women, Balsam et al. (2015) found no significant differences in symptoms of generalized anxiety disorder or social anxiety across African American, Latina American, Asian American, and White American participants. Finally, in a sample of sexual minority women experiencing housing instability in San Francisco, California, no significant differences in presence of an anxiety disorder were found between White and non-White (Black/African American, Asian/Pacific Islander, Hispanic/Latina, and multiracial/other) participants (Flentje, Shumway, Wong, & Riley, 2017). While these findings suggest similar rates of anxiety disorders across racial and ethnic sexual minorities, conclusions cannot be drawn without national probability surveys comparing diagnostic rates across the intersections of these groups.

Clinical Features

The frameworks of minority stress (e.g., Meyer, 2003) and sexual stigma (e.g., Herek, 2009) are often used to explain the higher prevalence of anxiety disorders among sexual minority individuals, as well as how such processes maintain anxiety symptoms in this population. Minority stress theory posits that sexual minority individuals experience chronic psychological distress due to perceived prejudice and discrimination, which often becomes internalized and manifested as psychiatric morbidity. This chronic psychological distress might be expressed by processes common to anxiety disorders, such as fear of negative evaluation and worry. For example, some evidence suggests that fear of negative evaluation, the core feature of social anxiety, is higher among gay men compared to heterosexual men (Pachankis & Goldfried, 2006). As such, certain social situations may be particularly salient when individuals perceive stigma related to their sexual orientation. Such stigma can lead to preoccupation and vigilance and, in turn, negative affective states such as anxiety (Pachankis, 2007). This often leads to concealment of one's sexual orientation, which has been found to predict social anxiety symptomatology (Cohen, Blasey, Taylor, Weiss, & Newman, 2016) and poor mental health outcomes (Meidlinger & Hope, 2014). Interestingly, Pachankis, Cochran, and Mays (2015) found that, among sexual minority men, those who had come out more recently had higher odds of generalized anxiety disorder compared to closeted men; however, this relationship was not shared among sexual minority women. Further, increased worry related to perceived discrimination regarding one's sexual orientation is associated with higher depressive symptoms, negative affect, and internalized homophobia and lower positive affect (Weiss & Hope, 2011). It is important, however, for both researchers and clinicians to take into account whether these and other responses to stigma and prejudice are maladaptive (i.e., excessive or unreasonable) or reasonable given the context (e.g., real threat).

Assessment

A number of considerations should be taken into account with regard to assessment and treatment of sexual minority individuals. First, researchers and clinicians should be careful to avoid heterocentric bias in assessment. In order to avoid heterocentrism, Holt, Ralston, and Hope (2019) suggest assessing sexual orientation with all respondents and using such information in case formulations, using assessments that do not include heterocentric language, and distinguishing between adaptive and maladaptive safety behaviors. The use of heterocentric language is particularly relevant with regard to social anxiety, where many widely used measures refer to the opposite sex. Several recent studies have demonstrated psychometrically strong results for alternative items free of heterocentric language in commonly used measures of social anxiety (Lindner, Martell, Bergstrom, Andersson, & Carlbring, 2013; Shulman & Hope, 2016; Weiss, Hope, & Capozzoli, 2013). Failure to use such adaptations risks alienating respondents, perpetuating stigma, and resulting in inaccurate measurement of symptoms. Further considerations for inclusive assessment with SGM can be found in Ortigo and Weiss (2016).

Treatment

The efficacy of cognitive-behavioral therapy for anxiety disorders has been well established (Norton & Price, 2007), but few treatment studies report the sexual orientation of participants. Additionally, there are unique clinical issues among sexual minorities for which treatment adaptations may be helpful (Pachankis & Goldfriend, 2013). Few graduate training programs include formal training for interventions with sexual minority clients (Hope & Chappell, 2015). However, there is an emerging literature demonstrating how evidence-based treatment for anxiety can be adapted for sexual minority clients, when necessary. Case reports by Glassgold (2009) and Walsh and Hope (2010) describe using cognitive restructuring for sexual minority–specific concerns within the context of cognitive-behavioral therapy for social anxiety disorder. Holt, Ralston, and Hope (2019) provide a detailed example of adapting exposure therapy when working with a sexual minority client. Further, in a recent randomized controlled trial, Pachankis, Hatzenbuehler, Rendina, Safren, and Parsons (2015) used a transdiagnostic approach targeting sexual minority–specific stress, demonstrating its utility for reducing anxiety symptoms. Finally, a general overview of adapting evidence-based treatment, including for anxiety disorders, for sexual minority clients can be found in Martell, Safren, and Prince (2003).

Anxiety Disorders among Gender Minorities

Gender minorities, broadly defined, are individuals whose gender identity or gender expression is incongruent with sex assigned at birth. This population is diverse and comprises individuals with multiple different gender identities and expressions (e.g., transgender, male-to-female and female-to-male, cross-dressers, transvestites, drag queens, drag kings, bigender, genderqueer, two-spirit, gender nonbinary, gender nonconforming) (Bockting, Miner, Swinburne Romine, Hamilton, & Coleman, 2017). Epidemiological data regarding prevalence rates of anxiety disorders among this population are currently limited due to small sample sizes and exclusion of control groups (Bouman et al., 2017). An additional barrier is that population-based surveys, medical records, and research studies often do not contain information regarding gender identity (Reisner, Katz-Wise, Gordon, Corliss, & Austin, 2016; Valentine & Shipherd, 2018). The majority of current studies also use measures of anxiety symptoms rather than examining specific types of anxiety disorders (Millet, Longworth, & Arcelus, 2017). Despite these limitations, evidence suggests that gender minorities report higher rates of anxiety compared to non-gender minorities. For instance, a national longitudinal study comparing gender minorities to non-gender minorities found that 38 percent of gender minorities met clinical cutoffs for anxiety symptoms compared to 30 percent of cisgender females and 14 percent of cisgender males (Reisner et al., 2016). An additional study found that transgender respondents reported disproportionally high rates of anxiety symptoms (33.2 percent) compared to community norms (Bockting et al., 2013). One study indicated that transgender people had an almost threefold risk of probable anxiety disorders compared to the general population (Bouman et al., 2017). Another study found that 47 percent of transgender men and 40 percent of transgender women reported significant anxiety symptoms (Budge, Adelson, & Howard, 2013).

Prevalence rates for specific types of anxiety disorders in this population are also limited and vary widely across studies. However, Millet et al. (2017) conducted a systematic review of the literature and found that social anxiety disorder, specific phobias, and panic disorders are most common among the transgender population. Rates of anxiety disorders varied widely across studies, potentially due to differences between the countries in which they were conducted. Among transgender men, reported rates in the literature included specific phobia (25 percent), panic disorder (as high as 13.5 percent), and social anxiety disorder (as high as 11 percent). Among transgender women, the rate of specific phobia was 17 percent and rates of social anxiety disorder were as high as 9.8 percent. Other disorders examined in the literature included agoraphobia (as high as 3.2 percent) and generalized anxiety disorder (as high as 8.8 percent). Although these findings are limited by the sparseness of the literature, the results suggest a higher prevalence of anxiety disorders within the transgender population (Millet et al., 2017).

Minority Stress Model

Anxiety disorders among gender minorities have been largely conceptualized using the minority stress model (Meyer, 2003). According to the minority stress model, individuals with minority statuses experience stigma, discrimination, and oppression. These experiences increase distress and thus contribute to the development of mental health concerns (Meyer, 2003). The model has been adapted to the experiences of gender minorities and delineates several processes through which minority stressors occur (Hendricks & Testa, 2012). First, gender minorities encounter external or distal stressors, which consist of negative events and experiences (Hendricks & Testa, 2012). Research indicates that gender minorities experience high levels of violence, harassment, rejection, discrimination, and social stigma (Badgett, Sears, Lau, & Ho, 2009; Nadal, Whitman, Davis, Erazo, & Davidoff, 2016; Norton & Herek, 2013). Although some of these discrimination experiences likely overlap with those of sexual minorities, gender minorities face unique challenges (Borgogna, McDermott, Aita, & Kridel, 2019). For instance, they might encounter difficulties accessing legal documents due to discrepancies in demographic information within records (e.g., sex, name), refusal of treatment or discrimination when seeking medical care, and difficulties accessing safe public spaces (e.g., restrooms) (Bauer, Scheim, Deutsch, & Massarella, 2014; Borgogna, McDermott, Aita, & Kridel, 2019; Budge, Tebbe, & Howard, 2010; Grant et al., 2010; Scheim, Bauer, & Pyne, 2014). An additional stressor is gender nonaffirmation, which includes the use of incorrect pronouns or names. Nonbinary individuals might face additional stigma regarding the use of gender-neutral pronouns given societal norms of gender (Testa, Habarth, Peta, Balsam, & Bockting, 2015).

In addition to external stressors, gender minorities experience internal, or proximal, stressors related to gender identity. These stressors often arise as a result of external experiences and include expectations of future violence or discrimination (Hendricks & Testa, 2012; Testa et al., 2015; Timmins, Rimes, & Rahman, 2017). In anticipation of negative future events, gender minorities may develop coping strategies such as avoidance of certain environments or hypervigilance to potential threats (Fernie, Wright, Caselli, Nikcevic, & Seda, 2017; Hendricks & Testa, 2012; Timmins, Rimes, & Rahman, 2017). Gender minorities might also internalize negative societal beliefs related to gender nonconformity (e.g., self-stigma, transphobia) (Hendricks & Testa, 2012; Timmins et al., 2017). An additional stressor is concealment, the ability or decision to conceal minority status (Bockting et al., 2013; Testa et al., 2015; Valentine & Shipherd, 2018). Gender is often identified through physical markers, such as body shape, size, and characteristics. As a result, the decision to reveal gender identity status varies depending on physical characteristics, genetics, age, transition status, and medical care. Further, people frequently use gendered pronouns to refer to one another in social contexts, often obligating gender minorities to identify their pronouns. Thus, gender minorities face unique experiences related to disclosing their minority status to others (Testa et al., 2015).

MINORITY STRESS AND ANXIETY DISORDERS

Several studies have examined the relationships between specific gender minority stressors and anxiety. For instance, in one sample of transgender women, higher levels of exposure to trans-related stigma was associated with higher levels of anxiety symptoms (Yang, Manning, van den Berg, & Operario, 2015). Another study demonstrated positive correlations between several minority stressors and social anxiety, including internalized transphobia, active concealment of transgender status, and expectations of rejection (Testa et al., 2015). An additional study found that higher exposure to prejudice events, expectations of rejection, and self-stigma were each correlated with increased symptoms of generalized anxiety (Timmins et al., 2017). In this study the relationship was partially accounted for by rumination, suggesting a potential mechanism for these processes. In a sample of transgender youth, individuals with higher levels of internalized transphobia were more likely to meet criteria for generalized anxiety disorder (Chodzen, Hidalgo, Chen, & Garofalo, 2019). These findings highlight the potential pathways between minority stressors and anxiety symptoms. Both external and internal stressors are associated with anxiety symptoms, which suggests the relevance of the minority stress model in conceptualizing anxiety among gender minorities.

MINORITY STRESSORS FOR SPECIFIC GENDER MINORITIES

The minority stress model posits that all individuals with a gender minority status experience similar stressors and related anxiety, regardless of specific gender identity. However, the diversity within this population results in unique experiences specific to different identity statuses (Borgogna et al., 2019). It has been hypothesized that transgender men and transgender women have differing experiences due to the impact of hormones and societal expectations. For instance, transgender men might receive an increase in social power and privilege after transitioning. Additionally, male hormones might make it easier for transgender men to conceal their minority status (Bockting et al., 2013; Budge et al., 2013). Despite these potential benefits, research demonstrates that among transgender men, lower income and limited education are positively correlated with anxiety, possibly as a result of societal expectations of men (McDowell, White Hughto, & Reisner, 2019). Transgender women might experience a decrease in social power and privilege as a result of transitioning. Also, they might experience increased stigma due to greater societal stigmatization of gender nonconformity among men (Bockting et al., 2013; Yang et al., 2015). Transgender women might also face barriers related to gender, including discrimination, risk of assault, and intimate partner violence (Yang et al., 2015). Gender minorities who identify as nonbinary or gender nonconforming also have unique experiences, such as increased stigmatization for stepping outside of binary gender assumptions (Borgogna et al., 2019).

Prevalence of Anxiety Disorders for Specific Gender Minorities

Considering the unique experiences of specific gender minorities provides a framework for conceptualizing anxiety disorders among these populations. In the literature, gender minorities are often examined as a singular group, which limits the ability to identify potential differences across identity statuses (Borgogna et al., 2019). The current literature regarding the prevalence of anxiety disorders among specific gender minorities is mixed. Some studies indicate that transgender women experience higher rates of anxiety compared to transgender men. For instance, one study found that among transgender participants, the odds of anxiety were 1.36 times as high for transgender women as compared to transgender men (Bockting et al., 2013). Additionally, one study found that transgender women had significantly higher rates of clinician-diagnosed anxiety disorders compared to transgender men (Hoshiai et al., 2010). Some studies found no differences in rates of anxiety between transgender men and transgender women (Colizzi, Costa, & Todarello, 2014; Dhejne, Van Vlerken, Heylens, & Arcelus, 2016). Despite significant variation in results, the majority of large-scale studies indicate that transgender men report higher levels of anxiety than transgender women (Millet et al., 2017). One potential explanation for this finding is that transgender women might be more likely to seek out and use social supports (Pflum, Testa, Balsam, Goldblum, & Bongar, 2015). Additional research is needed to clarify and examine potential differences in prevalence rates between transgender men and transgender women.

An additional limitation of the current literature is that gender minorities are often divided into broad groups, such as trans-female spectrum and trans-male spectrum. As a result, there is a paucity of research examining anxiety among specific gender minorities who do not fit into these categorizations, such as gender nonconforming individuals. Borgogna et al. (2019) compared transgender men, transgender women, gender nonconforming individuals, and cisgender individuals and found that reported anxiety symptoms were high among all gender minority categories. Compared to transgender women and gender nonconforming individuals, transgender men reported the highest levels of anxiety symptoms. Further, gender nonconforming individuals reported higher levels of anxiety than transgender women in this sample (Borgogna et al., 2019). Further research should continue to examine anxiety among specific gender minorities rather than grouping statuses into broad categories.

Risk and Protective Factors

There is some research identifying risk and protective factors associated with anxiety among gender minorities. For instance, a study of transgender and gender nonconforming adults found that social support was negatively correlated with reported anxiety symptoms. Further, trans-community connectedness was negatively associated with anxiety symptoms for trans-female spectrum individuals (Pflum et al., 2015). In terms of risk factors, low self-esteem and interpersonal difficulties have been identified as predictors of increased anxiety symptoms among transgender individuals (Bouman et al., 2017). Future research should continue to identify and further examine risk and protective factors for anxiety disorders. Such knowledge is critical for prevention and intervention within this population.

Intersection of Racial and Ethnic Minority Status and Gender Minority Status

The oppression that gender minorities face can be compounded by stigma associated with intersecting identities (i.e. racial/ethnic minority status) (Díaz, Ayala, Bein, Henne, & Marin, 2001; Yang et al., 2015). Both racism and gender identity–related discrimination are uniquely associated with mental health concerns (Sutter & Perrin, 2016). Additionally, research indicates that transgender People of Color experience more types of discrimination than their White counterparts (Bockting et al., 2013). There is a paucity of research examining the relationship between these intersecting identities and anxiety disorders. However, some studies have found no differences when comparing racial and ethnic minorities to Caucasians. For instance, one study comparing Caucasian gender minorities and gender minorities with an ethnic or racial minority status found no significant differences in reported anxiety symptoms (Pflum et al., 2015). Another study found that the relationship between trans-related stigmatization and anxiety symptoms was not moderated by racial or ethnic identity (Yang et al., 2015). One potential reason for the lack of differences is that community support might counteract experiences of stigma associated with ethnic or racial minority status (Pflum et al., 2015). These processes might also vary across specific ethnic or racial identities. For instance, evidence from a sample of transgender women with a history of sex work suggests that African American and Asian/Pacific Islander gender minority women report higher social support from family, whereas Latina women report needs for increased social support (Nemoto, Bodecker, & Iwamoto, 2011).

Assessment

Culturally competent care of gender minorities requires appropriate, affirmative, and evidence-based assessment tools. However, there is little guidance in the literature regarding assessment practices with this population, and existing measures are often not normed on samples of gender minorities (Keo-Meier & Fitzgerald, 2017; Schulman & Erickson-Schroth, 2017). The gender-affirmative model provides a framework for psychological assessment and intervention within the gender minority population (Hidalgo et al., 2013; Keo-Meier & Fitzgerald, 2017). The major tenets of this model include the affirmation that being transgender is not a disorder and recognition that gender may be fluid and nonbinary. Further, psychopathology is conceptualized as a reaction to hostile environments rather than inherently part of the individual (Hidalgo et al., 2013). Given the evidence that anxiety among gender minorities is influenced by environmental factors, assessment processes should include an evaluation of these experiences (e.g., exposure to minority stressors). This historical information is important for conceptualization and treatment planning (Keo-Meier & Fitzgerald, 2017; Valentine & Shipherd, 2018).

The Gender Minority Stress and Resilience Measure is an assessment tool developed to examine minority stress and resilience among gender minorities (Testa et al., 2015). The assessment measures nine constructs relevant for this population: gender-related discrimination, gender-related rejection, gender-related victimization, nonaffirmation of gender identity, internalized transphobia, negative expectations for future events, nondisclosure, community connectedness, and pride. This measure has demonstrated good psychometric properties, including internal consistency, criterion validity, convergent validity, and discriminant validity (Testa et al., 2015). The use of this measure might provide valuable information for researchers and clinicians working with the gender minority population.

Treatment

Current treatment approaches for anxiety disorders among gender minorities are broadly informed by gender-affirming practices. Such interventions often fit within the framework of the minority stress model through targeting external and internal minority stress processes. For instance, the gender affirmative model posits that psychopathology results from negative environmental experiences (e.g., minority stressors) and is not located within the individual (Hidalgo et al., 2013). Similarly, the gender affirmative lifespan approach (GALA) consists of interventions focused on overcoming internalized oppression, with an emphasis on promoting resiliency, improving gender literacy, promoting positive sexuality, and fostering empowerment through access to gender-affirming medical interventions (Nic Rider et al., 2019). Competent care of gender minorities should be guided by these principles given the literature on the relationship between minority stressors and anxiety.

In addition to overarching frameworks, specific treatments have been developed for this population. Specifically, transgender-affirming cognitive-behavioral therapy is an adaptation of cognitive-behavioral therapy for use with gender minorities (Austin & Craig, 2015). The treatment considers contextual factors relevant for gender minorities, such as stigma and discrimination experiences. Interventions include psychoeducation about minority stress, identification of how internalized transphobic thoughts impact emotions, and cognitive restructuring to challenge internalized transphobic thoughts. Treatment also includes a focus on bolstering social support, resiliency, and empowerment. Further research is necessary to examine the efficacy of this approach in treating anxiety disorders and to identify any further adaptations (Austin & Craig, 2015).

Medical Interventions

Gender-affirming medical interventions (e.g., hormone use, chest surgery, genital surgery, speech therapy, tracheal shave or Adam's apple removal, hair removal) have been demonstrated to reduce symptoms of generalized and social anxiety among gender minorities (Bouman et al., 2017; Butler et al., 2019; Colizzi, Costa, & Todarello, 2014; Gómez-Gil et al., 2012; Tomita, Testa, & Balsam, 2019). Completion of these procedures allows individuals to obtain primary and secondary sex characteristics that align with their gender identity, and thus potentially decrease experiences of minority stress, such as discrimination, rejection, violence, and non-affirmation. Current literature demonstrates that these surgeries are associated with decreased anxiety symptoms, potentially through the reduction of minority stressors (Butler et al., 2019; Testa et al., 2015; Tomita et al., 2019). Given this evidence, increasing access to gender-affirming medical interventions is an important avenue for reducing anxiety symptoms among gender minorities.

Limitations and Directions for Future Research

Given the current state of the literature on anxiety disorders among gender and sexual minorities, there are several important considerations for further research. First, in the anxiety disorder literature more broadly, data on sexual orientation and gender identity should be more regularly collected and reported, even when gender and sexual minorities are not the primary focus of the study. Future studies should also use more rigorous methodology to assess for anxiety disorders, such as diagnostic interviews. The majority of past studies, particularly those focused on gender minorities, have relied on self-report measures of anxiety symptoms, which limit the ability to identify the presence of an anxiety disorder. Self-report measures also create difficulties in determining prevalence rates and distinguishing between specific anxiety disorders. Also, although the literature has conceptualized anxiety disorders using the minority stress model, it is unclear whether or how minority stress processes vary across specific disorders. The use of standardized, diagnostic interviews would thus allow for clarity regarding prevalence rates and potential differences across specific disorders.

Future research should also consider how to separate groups within the sample. For example, gender minorities have been grouped into a singular category and then compared to a singular group of sexual minorities. This limits the ability to draw conclusions regarding specific minority statuses. Also, within the gender minority literature, groups often include female-spectrum and male-spectrum individuals, regardless of how the individual participant self-identifies. Although this method is likely less complex than obtaining groups of specific identity statuses, it excludes certain groups of people, such as gender nonconforming or gender nonbinary individuals. It also might mask potential differences within each broader group.

An additional issue within the gender minority literature is that samples often include individuals at various levels of transitioning. As a result, within the same sample, one participant may have no desire to receive gender-affirming medical interventions, another participant might be awaiting a desired surgery, another participant might have just begun hormone therapy, and another may have received hormone therapy for years. Thus, the diversity among the gender minority population in terms of transition phases requires careful consideration regarding sampling. Although it might be unfeasible to eliminate these differences within a sample, studies should collect and report information regarding transition status.

Further studies should aim to include more diverse samples. First, there is a lack of research examining anxiety disorders among gender and sexual minorities who also have a racial or ethnic minority status. Although some studies have examined anxiety disorders among racial and ethnic groups, sample sizes are often too small to identify potential differences. Also, current research is often limited by grouping all racial and ethnic minorities into a single non-White category. This approach limits the ability to detect unique characteristics among specific racial and ethnic groups. Researchers should focus on recruiting large, diverse samples and examining specific groups of racial and ethnic minorities to expand the literature on these populations. In a similar vein, there is a need for more research examining the relationships between diverse intersecting identities and anxiety disorders. Specifically, factors such as having multiple minority identities (e.g., sexual, gender, racial, ethnic), rurality, and ability status are currently understudied in the literature. Identity statuses do not exist independently but rather interact with the other identities that an individual holds. The intersectionality of identity statuses greatly influences the experiences of the individual and thus may have important impacts on anxiety disorders.

An additional area for research is further identifying risk and protective factors for anxiety disorders among gender and sexual minorities. Given the current use of the minority stress model to conceptualize anxiety disorders in these populations, future studies are needed to identify pathways between specific stressors and anxiety disorders. Examining these pathways would provide valuable information regarding intervention and treatment. Also, current literature regarding the minority stress model suggests that discrimination, prejudice, and stigma are key minority stressors that influence the mental health of gender and sexual minorities (Hendricks & Testa, 2012). Thus, addressing injustices through advocacy and political action is critical for reducing prejudice and discrimination experiences and, in turn, decreasing anxiety among gender and sexual minorities.

Although the literature indicates an increased risk of anxiety among gender and sexual minorities, researchers and clinicians must consider the role of contextual factors. It is well established in the literature that gender and sexual minorities experience stigma, discrimination, and prejudice (Badgett et al., 2009; Nadal et al., 2016; Norton & Herek, 2013), which, in turn, can influence psychological outcomes such as anxiety symptoms (Hendricks & Testa, 2012). Thus, anxiety symptoms might emerge as normative reactions to a hostile and discriminatory environment. For instance, an individual might experience violence and develop hypervigilance in response (Fernie, Shumway, Wong, & Riley, 2017; Hendricks & Testa, 2012; Timmins et al., 2017). Although hypervigilance might be identified as pathological, it might also represent a reasonable response to the realistic possibility of harm. Further, worry and expectations of future negative experiences might be founded in reality. Given the individual's context (e.g., past experiences, political climate, societal stigma), certain responses might serve as adaptive for that environment. Anxiety disorders among gender and sexual minorities therefore require researchers and clinicians to avoid over-pathologizing and to carefully consider past experiences and environmental influences.

In terms of the assessment and treatment literature, guidelines for evidence-based practices should continue to be developed and studied. Certain assessment tools and psychological interventions might require adaptations in order to provide culturally responsive care for gender and sexual minorities. Research on these topics is currently emergent, and further studies are needed to bolster guidelines.

References

Austin, A., & Craig, S. L. (2015). Transgender affirmative cognitive behavioral therapy: Clinical considerations and applications. *Professional Psychology: Research and Practice, 46*, 21–9. doi:10.1037/a0038642

Badgett, M. V. L., Sears, B., Lau, H., & Ho, D. (2009). Bias in the workplace: Consistent evidence of sexual orientation and gender identity discrimination 1998–2008. *Chicago-Kent Law Review, 84*, 559–95. Retrieved from https://scholarship.kentlaw.iit.edu/cklawreview/vol84/iss2/7

Balsam, K. F., Molina, Y., Blayney, J. A., Dillworth, T., Zimmerman, L., & Kaysen, D. (2015). Racial/ethnic differences in identity and mental health outcomes among young sexual minority women. *Cultural Diversity and Ethnic Minority Psychology, 21*, 380–90. doi:1037/a0038680

Bauer, G. R., Scheim, A. I., Deutsch, M. B., & Massarella, C. (2014). Reported emergency department avoidance, use, and experiences of transgender persons in Ontario, Canada: Results from a respondent-driven sampling survey. *Annals of Emergency Medicine, 63*, 713–20. doi:10.1016/j.annemergmed.2013.09.027

Bjorkenstam, C., Bjorkenstam, E., Andersson, G., Cochran, S., & Kosidou, K. (2017). Anxiety and depression among sexual minority women and men in Sweden: Is the risk equally spread within the sexual minority population? *Journal of Sexual Medicine, 14*, 396–403. doi:10.1016/j.jsxm.2017.01.012

Bockting, W. O., Miner, M. H., Swinburne Romine, R. E., Hamilton, A., & Coleman, E. (2013). Stigma, mental health, and resilience in an online sample of the US transgender population. *American Journal of Public Health, 103*, 943–51. doi:10.2105/AJPH.2013.301241

Borgogna, N. C., McDermott, R. C., Aita, S. L., & Kridel, M. M. (2019). Anxiety and depression across gender and sexual minorities: Implications for transgender, gender nonconforming, pansexual, demisexual, asexual, queer, and questioning individuals. *Psychology of Sexual Orientation and Gender Diversity, 6*, 54–63. doi:10.1037/sgd0000306

Bostwick, W. B., Boyd, C. J., Hughes, T. L., & McCabe, S. E. (2010). Dimensions of sexual orientation and the prevalence of mood and anxiety disorders in the United States. *American Journal of Public Health, 100*, 468–75. doi:10.2105/AJPH.2008.152942

Bouman, W. P., Claes, L., Brewin, N., Crawford, J. R., Millet, N., Fernandez-Aranda, F., & Arcelus, J. (2017). Transgender and anxiety: A comparative study between transgender people and the general population. *International Journal of Transgenderism, 18*, 16–26. doi:10.1080/15532739.2016.1258352

Budge, S. L., Adelson, J. L., & Howard, K. A. S. (2013). Anxiety and depression in transgender individuals: The roles of transition status, loss, social support, and coping. *Journal of Consulting and Clinical Psychology, 81*, 545–57. doi:10.1037/a0031774

Budge, S. L., Tebbe, E. N., & Howard, K. A. S. (2010). The work experiences of transgender individuals: Negotiating the transition and career decision-making processes. *Journal of Counseling Psychology, 57*, 377–93. doi:10.1037/a0020472.supp

Butler, R. M., Horenstein, A., Gitlin, M., Testa, R. J., Kaplan, S. C., Swee, M. B., & Heimberg, R. G. (2019). Social anxiety among transgender and gender nonconforming individuals: The role of gender-affirming medical interventions. *Journal of Abnormal Psychology, 128*, 25–31. doi:10.1037/abn0000399

Chodzen, G., Hidalgo, M. A., Chen, D., & Garofalo, R. (2019). Minority stress factors associated with depression and anxiety among transgender and gender-nonconforming youth. *Journal of Adolescent Health, 64*, 467–71. doi:10.1016/j.jadohealth.2018.07.006

Cochran, S. D., & Mays, V. M. (2009). Burden of psychiatric morbidity among lesbian, gay, and bisexual individuals in the California Quality of Life Survey. *Journal of Abnormal Psychology, 118*, 647–58. doi:10.1037/a0016501

Cochran, S. D., Mays, V. M., Alegria, M., Ortega, A. N., & Takeuchi, D. (2007). Mental health and substance use disorders among Latino and Asian American lesbian, gay, and bisexual adults. *Journal of Consulting and Clinical Psychology, 75*, 785–94. doi:10.1037/0022-006X.75.5.785

Cochran, S. D., Sullivan, J. G., & Mayes, V. M. (2003). Prevalence of mental disorders, psychological distress, and mental health services use among lesbian, gay, and bisexual adults in the United States. *Journal of Consulting and Clinical Psychology, 71*, 53–61. doi:10.1037/0022-006X.71.1.53

Cohen, J. M., Blasey, C., Taylor, C. B., Weiss, B. J., & Newman, M. G. (2016). Anxiety and related disorders and concealment in sexual minority young adults. *Behavior Therapy, 41*, 91–101. doi:10.1016/j.beth.2015.09.006

Colizzi, M., Costa, R., & Todarello, O. (2014). Transsexual patients' psychiatric comorbidity and positive effect of cross-sex hormonal treatment on mental health: Results from a longitudinal study. *Psychoneuroendocrinology, 39*, 65–73. doi:10.1016/j.psyneuen.2013.09.029

Dhejne, C., Van Vlerken, R., Heylens, G., & Arcelus, J. (2016). Mental health and gender dysphoria: A review of the literature. *International Review of Psychiatry, 28*, 44–57. doi: 10.3109/09540261.2015.1115753

Díaz, R. M., Ayala, G., Bein, E., Henne, J., & Marin, B. V. (2001). The impact of homophobia, poverty, and racism on the mental health of gay and bisexual Latino men: Findings from 3 US cities. *American Journal of Public Health, 91*(6), 927–32. doi:10.2105/AJPH.91.6.927

Fernie, B. A., Wright, T., Caselli, G., Nikčević, A. V., & Spada, M. M. (2017). Metacognitions as mediators of gender identity-related anxiety. *Clinical Psychology & Psychotherapy, 24*, 264–68. doi:10.1002/cpp.1992

Flentje, A., Shumway, M., Wong, L. H., & Riley, E. D. (2017). Psychiatric risk in unstably housed sexual minority women: Relationship between sexual and racial minority status and human immunodeficiency virus and psychiatric diagnoses. *Women's Health Issues, 27*, 294–301. doi:10.1016/j.whi.2016.12.005

Glassgold, J. M. (2009). The case of Felix: An example of gay-affirmative, cognitive-behavioral therapy. *Pragmatic Case Studies in Psychotherapy, 5*, 1–21. doi:10.14713/pcsp.v5i4.995

Gómez-Gil, E., Zubiaurre-Elorza, L., Esteva, I., Guillamon, A., Godás, T., Almaraz, M. C., & Salamero, M. (2012). Hormone-treated transsexuals report less social distress, anxiety and depression. *Psychoneuroendocrinology, 37*, 662–70. doi:10.1016/j.psyneuen.2011.08.010

Grant, J. M., Mottet, L. A., Tanis, J., Herman, J. L., Harrison, J., & Keisling, M. (2010). *National Transgender Discrimination Survey: Report on health and health care.* Washington, DC: National Center for Transgender Equality and National Gay and Lesbian Task Force. Retrieved from https://transequality.org/issues/us-trans-survey

Hendricks, M. L., & Testa, R. J. (2012). A conceptual framework for clinical work with transgender and gender nonconforming clients: An adaptation of the Minority Stress Model. *Professional Psychology: Research and Practice, 43*, 460–67. doi:10.1037/a0029597

Herek, G. M. (2009). Sexual stigma and sexual prejudice in the United States: A conceptual framework. In D. A. Hope (Ed.), *Contemporary perspectives on lesbian, gay, and bisexual identities: The 54th Nebraska Symposium on Motivation* (pp. 65–111). New York, NY: Springer. doi:10.1007/978-0-387-09556-1_4

Hidalgo, M. A., Ehrensaft, D., Tishelman, A. C., Clark, L. F., Garofalo, R., Rosenthal, S. M., . . . Olson, J. (2013). The gender affirmative model: What we know and what we aim to learn. *Human Development, 56*, 285–90. doi:10.1159/000355235

Holt, N. R., Ralston, A. L., & Hope, D. A. (2019). Anxiety disorders and obsessive-compulsive disorder: Evidence-based considerations for affirmative services for sexual minority clients. In J. E. Pachankis & S. A. Safren (Eds.), *Handbook of evidence-based mental health practice with sexual and gender minorities* (pp. 175–99). New York, NY: Oxford University Press. doi:10.1093/med-psych/9780190669300.001.0001

Hope, D. A., & Chappell, C. L. (2015). Extending training in multicultural competencies to include individuals identifying as lesbian, gay and bisexual: Key choice points for clinical psychology training programs. *Clinical Psychology: Science and Practice, 22*, 105–18. doi:10.1111/cpsp.12099

Hoshiai, M., Matsumoto, Y., Sato, T., Ohnishi, M., Okabe, N., Kishimoto, Y., & Kuroda, S. (2010). Psychiatric comorbidity among patients with gender identity disorder. *Psychiatry and Clinical Neurosciences, 64*, 514–9. doi:10.1111/j.1440–1819.2010.02118.x

Kessler, R. C., Aguilar-Gaxiola, S., Alonso, J., Chatterji, S., Lee, S., Ormel, J., . . . Wang, P. S. (2009). The global burden of mental disorders: An update from the WHO World Mental

Health (WMH) surveys. *Epidemiologia e Psichiatria Sociale, 18*, 23–33. doi:10.1017/S1121189X00001421

Kessler, R. C., Berglund, P., Demler, O., Jin, R., Merikangas, K. R., & Walters, E. E. (2005). Lifetime prevalence and age-of-onset distributions of DSM-IV disorders in the National Comorbidity Survey Replication. *Archives of General Psychiatry, 62*, 593–602. doi:10.1001/archpsyc.62.6.593

Keo-Meier, C. L., & Fitzgerald, K. M. (2017). Affirmative psychological testing and neurocognitive assessment with transgender adults. *Psychiatric Clinics of North America, 40*, 51–64. doi:10.1016/j.psc.2016.10.011

Lindner, P., Martell, C., Bergstrom, J., Andersson, G., & Carlbring, P. (2013). Clinical validation of a non-heteronormative version of the Social Interaction Anxiety Scale (SIAS). *Health and Quality of Life Outcomes, 11*, 209–15. doi:10.1186/1477-7525-11-209

Martell, C. R., Safren, S. A., & Prince, S. E. (2003). *Cognitive-behavioral therapies with lesbian, gay, and bisexual clients.* New York, NY: Guilford Press.

McDowell, M. J., White Hughto, J. M., & Reisner, S. L. (2019). Risk and protective factors for mental health morbidity in a community sample of female-to-male trans-masculine adults. *BMC Psychiatry, 19*, 16. doi:10.1186/s12888-018-2008-0

Meidlinger, P. C., & Hope, D. A. (2014). Differentiating disclosure and concealment in measurement of outness for sexual minorities: The Nebraska Outness Scale. *Psychology of Sexual Orientation and Gender Diversity, 1*, 489–97. doi:10.1037/sgd0000080

Meyer, I. H. (2003). Prejudice, social stress, and mental health in lesbian, gay, and bisexual populations: Conceptual issues and research evidence. *Psychological Bulletin, 129*, 674–97. doi:10.1037/0033-2909.129.5.674

Meyer, I. H., Dietrich, J., & Schwartz, S. (2008). Lifetime prevalence of mental disorders and suicide attempts in diverse lesbian, gay, and bisexual populations. *American Journal of Public Health, 98*, 1004–6. doi:10.2105/AJPH.2006.096826

Millet, N., Longworth, J., & Arcelus, J. (2017). Prevalence of anxiety symptoms and disorders in the transgender population: A systematic review of the literature. *International Journal of Transgenderism, 18*, 27–38. doi:10.1080/15532739.2016.1258353

Nadal, K. L., Whitman, C. N., Davis, L. S., Erazo, T., & Davidoff, K. C. (2016). Microaggressions toward lesbian, gay, bisexual, transgender, queer, and genderqueer people: A review of the literature. *Journal of Sex Research, 53*, 488–508. doi:10.1080/00224499.2016.1142495

Nemoto, T., Bödeker, B., & Iwamoto, M. (2011). Social support, exposure to violence and transphobia, and correlates of depression among male-to-female transgender women with a history of sex work. *American Journal of Public Health, 101*, 1980–8. doi:10.2105/AJPH.2010.197285

Nic Rider, G., Vencill, J. A., Berg, D. R., Becker-Warner, R., Candelario-Pérez, L., & Spencer, K. G. (2019). The gender affirmative lifespan approach (GALA): A framework for competent clinical care with nonbinary clients. *International Journal of Transgenderism, 20*(2-3), 275–88. doi:10.1080/15532739.2018.1485069

Norton, A. T., & Herek, G. M. (2013). Heterosexuals' attitudes toward transgender people: Findings from a national probability sample of US adults. *Sex Roles, 68*, 738–53. doi:10.1007/s11199-011-0110-6

Norton, P. J., & Price, E. C. (2007). A meta-analytic review of adult cognitive-behavioral treatment outcome across the anxiety disorders. *Journal of Nervous and Mental Disease, 195*, 521–31. doi:10.1097/01.nmd.0000253843.70149.9a

Ortigo, K. M., & Weiss, B. J. (2016). Professional training issues in the clinical assessment of sexuality and gender. In V. Brabender & J. Mihura (Eds.), *Handbook of gender and sexuality in psychological assessment* (pp. 605–26). New York, NY: Routledge. doi:10.4324/9781315769387.ch25

Pachankis, J. E. (2007). The psychological implications of concealing a stigma: A cognitive affective-behavioral model. *Psychological Bulletin, 133*, 328–45. doi:10.1037/0033-2909.133.2.328

Pachankis, J. E., Cochran, S. D., & Mays, V. M. (2015). The mental health of sexual minority adults in and out of the closet: A population-based study. *Journal of Consulting and Clinical Psychology, 83*, 890–901. doi:10.1037/ccp0000047

Pachankis, J. E., & Goldfried, M. R. (2006). Social anxiety in young gay men. *Journal of Anxiety Disorders, 20*, 996–1015. doi:10.1016/j.janxdis.2006.01.001

Pachankis, J. E., & Goldfried, M. R. (2013). Clinical issues in working with lesbian, gay, and bisexual clients. *Psychology of Sexual Orientation and Gender Diversity, 1*(S), 45–58. doi:10.1037/2329-0382.1.S.45

Pachankis, J. E., Hatzenbuehler, M. L., Rendina, H. J., Safren, S. A., & Parsons, J. T. (2015). LGB-affirmative cognitive-behavioral therapy for young adult gay and bisexual men: A randomized controlled trial of a transdiagnostic minority stress approach. *Journal of Consulting and Clinical Psychology, 83*, 875–89. doi:10.1037/ccp0000037

Pflum, S. R., Testa, R. J., Balsam, K. F., Goldblum, P. B., & Bongar, B. (2015). Social support, trans community connectedness, and mental health symptoms among transgender and gender nonconforming adults. *Psychology of Sexual Orientation and Gender Diversity, 2*, 281–86. doi:10.1037/sgd0000122

Reisner, S. L., Katz-Wise, S. L., Gordon, A. R., Corliss, H. L., & Austin, S. B. (2016). Social epidemiology of depression and anxiety by gender identity. *Journal of Adolescent Health, 59*, 203–208. doi:10.1016/j.jadohealth.2016.04.006

Sandfort, T. G. M., de Graaf, R., Bijl, R. V., & Schnabel, P. (2001). Same-sex sexual behavior and psychiatric disorders. *Archives of General Psychiatry, 58*, 85–91. doi:10.1001/archpsyc.58.1.85

Scheim, A., Bauer, G. R., & Pyne, J. (2014). Avoidance of public spaces by trans Ontarians: The impact of transphobia on daily life. *Trans PULSE e-Bulletin, 4*. doi:10.13140/RG.2.1.3820.1689

Schulman, J. K., & Erickson-Schroth, L. (2017). Mental health in sexual minority and transgender women. *Psychiatric Clinics of North America, 40*, 309–19. doi:10.1016/j.psc.2017.01.011

Shulman, G. P., & Hope, D. A. (2016). Putting our multicultural training into practice: Assessing social anxiety disorder in sexual minorities. *The Behavior Therapist, 39*, 315–19. Retrieved from http://www.abct.org/docs/PastIssue/39n8.pdf

Strutz, K. L., Herring, A. H., & Halpern, C. T. (2015). Health disparities among young adult sexual minorities in the U.S. *American Journal of Preventative Medicine, 48*, 76–88. doi:10.1016/j.amepre.2014.07.038

Sutter, M., & Perrin, P. B. (2016). Discrimination, mental health, and suicidal ideation among LGBTQ people of color. *Journal of Counseling Psychology, 63*, 98–105. doi:10.1037/cou0000126

Testa, R. J., Habarth, J., Peta, J., Balsam, K., & Bockting, W. (2015). Development of the Gender Minority Stress and Resilience Measure. *Psychology of Sexual Orientation and Gender Diversity, 2*, 65–77. doi:10.1037/sgd0000081

Timmins, L., Rimes, K. A., & Rahman, Q. (2017). Minority stressors and psychological distress in transgender individuals. *Psychology of Sexual Orientation and Gender Diversity, 4,* 328–40. doi:10.1037/sgd0000237

Tomita, K. K., Testa, R. J., & Balsam, K. F. (2019). Gender-affirming medical interventions and mental health in transgender adults. *Psychology of Sexual Orientation and Gender Diversity, 6,* 182–93. doi:10.1037/sgd0000316

Valentine, S. E., & Shipherd, J. C. (2018). A systematic review of social stress and mental health among transgender and gender non-conforming people in the United States. *Clinical Psychology Review, 66,* 24–38. doi:10.1016/j.cpr.2018.03.003

Walsh, K., & Hope, D. A. (2010). LGB affirmative cognitive behavioral treatment for social anxiety: A case study applying evidence-based practice principles. *Cognitive and Behavioral Practice, 17,* 56–65. doi:10.1016/j.cbpra.2009.04.007

Weiss, B. J., & Hope, D. A. (2011). A preliminary investigation of worry content in sexual minorities. *Journal of Anxiety Disorders, 25,* 244–50. doi:10.1016/j.janxdis.2010.09.009

Weiss, B. J., Hope, D. A., & Capozzoli, M. C. (2013). Heterocentric language in commonly used measures of social anxiety: Recommended alternate wording. *Behavior Therapy, 44,* 1–11. doi:10.1016/j.beth.2012.07.006

Yang, M. F., Manning, D., van den Berg, J. J., & Operario, D. (2015). Stigmatization and mental health in a diverse sample of transgender women. *LGBT Health, 2,* 306–12. doi:10.1089/lgbt.2014.0106

CHAPTER

6 Trauma among Sexual and Gender Minority Populations

David W. Pantalone, Kaitlyn R. Gorman, Erin T. Pereida, *and* Sarah E. Valentine

Abstract

This chapter describes the current state of the literature on trauma in sexual minority and transgender and gender-diverse populations. The authors begin by critically defining "trauma" and highlighting some consequences of the way trauma is defined. The authors describe how the subsequent mental health responses are understood and categorized psychiatrically (i.e., posttraumatic stress disorder). The authors describe relevant theoretical contributions to the literature on the cumulative burden of stress on sexual and gender minority individuals. Epidemiologic data are presented showing that trauma—especially in the form of interpersonal victimization—is an unfortunately common experience in the lives of sexual and gender minority individuals, especially those who hold additional devalued and stigmatized identities, such as being a racial or ethnic minority in addition to having a sexual and gender minority identity. Suggestions are presented for future directions for the field of trauma research among sexual and gender minority populations.

Keywords: trauma, posttraumatic stress disorder, PTSD, sexual and gender minorities, mental health, interpersonal victimization

Sexual and gender minority (SGM) individuals endorse high rates of exposure to potentially traumatic events (PTEs), along with myriad other stressful experiences (House, van Horn, Coppeans, & Stepleman, 2011). For many, these experiences can lead to negative health sequalae and the need for clinical intervention (Meyer, Alessi & Martin, 2011; Shipherd, Maguen, Skidmore, & Abramovitz, 2011). Beyond the explicit stressful or traumatic incident, SGM individuals may face a number of barriers to proper assessment and evidence-based intervention. For example, there is currently a debate surrounding what "counts" as a PTE and, by extension, what experiences may warrant intervention with trauma-specific therapy. A narrow definition of PTEs can exclude some extremely stressful events in the lives of many SGM individuals that may contribute to poor mental health in this population.

Understanding Trauma and PTSD

What Is "Trauma"?

Laypeople, and even some professionals, commonly misuse the term "trauma" to refer to *events* as well as *symptoms* of posttraumatic stress disorder (PTSD). However, the term "trauma" correctly refers only to a subset of PTEs (or a series of PTEs), whereas PTSD refers to a cluster of mental health symptoms associated with exposure to such events (Pantalone, Valentine, & Shipherd, 2017). Distinguishing these two concepts is important as the experience of a PTE does not necessarily result in the development of PTSD. Indeed, most individuals have lifetime PTE exposure, and most of them experience a natural recovery, characterized by the dissipation of acute stress symptoms without formal intervention (Keane, Marshall, & Taft, 2006). A diagnosis of PTSD is considered warranted only for those individuals who not recover fully on their own.

The "Trauma" Definition Debate

In the current (fifth) edition of the *Diagnostic and Statistical Manual of Mental Disorders* (DSM-5), a traumatic event—also called a Criterion A event based on its placement in the list of diagnostic criteria for PTSD—is defined as an incident in which a person was exposed to death, the threat of death, threatened or actual serious injury, or sexual violence (American Psychiatric Association, 2013). Similarly, the eleventh edition of the *International Classification of Diseases* (ICD-11; World Health Organization, 2018) defines a traumatic event as exposure to an extremely threatening or horrific event or series of events.

There is an ongoing debate about what types of events are encompassed by Criterion A. Some consider the current DSM-5 and ICD-11 versions too restrictive and, thus, fear that the definition excludes important experiences with the strong potential to lead to mental health symptoms. A narrower definition has benefits, including accuracy in communication and consistency in research, and reduces the potential for excessive heterogeneity in the clinical population and, thus, reduced generalizability of previous research findings. Although many stressful experiences of SGM individuals *do* meet Criterion A (such as bias event, physical assault, or sexual victimization), other stressful experiences *do not*—including microaggressions, bullying, or other forms of overt discrimination. These latter experiences do not rise to the level of threatened death or serious injury that is required in the DSM-5 definition of Criterion A events.

Research on the utility of using a threshold for what is considered a trauma is murky, however. Some data indicate that "non-traumatic" experiences are associated with PTSD symptoms at an equal (Boals & Schuettler, 2009) or greater (Gold, Marx, Soler-Baillo, & Sloan, 2005) severity than threshold-level Criterion A PTEs. For example, a meta-analysis comparing DSM-4-congruent traumas and non-traumas found that Criterion A traumas were associated with a small, significant increase in PTSD symptoms compared to non-traumas, with several individual studies supporting the opposite findings (Larsen & Pacella, 2016). Increased clarity about the most useful definition of traumatic events could improve the ability of practitioners to delineate accurate clinical diagnoses associated with PTE exposures and their sequelae.

The Boundaries of PTEs Are Relevant for Understanding SGM Mental Health

In this chapter, we review the literature on SGM populations regarding exposure and mental health sequelae of both PTEs and other extremely stressful experiences that are common. At first, the debate about defining Criterion A may seem entirely academic. However, this discussion is highly relevant to the lives of SGM individuals, as well as others who hold stigmatized identities for which they face societal discrimination. Day-to-day discrimination would generally not reach the level of a Criterion A trauma, as it frequently does not reach the level of threat to life or bodily harm. The literature documenting the negative impact of discrimination on individuals with marginalized identities has increased substantially over the past decade. For example, perceived racial discrimination is associated with increased risk for numerous psychological disorders (Chou, Asnaani, & Hofmann, 2012). Further, experience with racial or ethnic discrimination may specifically increase the risk of PTSD diagnosis in African American and Latinx individuals (Sibrava et al., 2019).

Similarly, heterosexist discrimination appears to uniquely predict PTSD symptoms in sexual minority individuals (Bandermann & Szymanski, 2014). In a study of 412 transgender and gender-diverse (TGD) individuals, investigators reported that greater incidences of daily discrimination and greater number of attributed reasons for discrimination were independently associated with PTSD symptoms, even after adjusting for prior trauma exposure (Reisner et al., 2016). The impact of numerous traumatic events may have an additive effect, with interpersonal trauma experiences predicting both increased symptoms and risk for additional traumas (Sullivan, Contractor, Gerber, & Neumann, 2017). This pathway may be particularly important for SGM individuals, as many of the stressors reported are interpersonal, such as heterosexist discrimination and family rejection.

Compared to heterosexual cisgender individuals, SGM-identified individuals appear to be at increased risk for PTE exposure using the most stringent definitions (Roberts, Austin, Corliss, Vandermorris, & Koenen, 2010; Shipherd et al., 2011). Additionally, SGM individuals experience high levels of painful stressors that would not meet the strict Criterion A threshold but that nevertheless have important implications for well-being (Kelleher, 2009; Platt & Lenzen, 2013). It is important to be mindful of this distinction when reviewing trauma research, as the interaction between the two categories of stressors is not always considered by clinicians and researchers consuming the academic literature. A casual assessment of the trauma literature may imply that SGM individuals are at greatest risk of singular, horrific events, whereas research increasingly supports the position that the most harmful consequences for SGM individuals are from the "non-traumatic" yet chronic, pervasive, and insidious stressors.

Understanding PTSD as the Central DSM Diagnosis Related to Trauma Exposure

There are a variety of mental health sequelae related to PTE exposure, with none more commonly studied than PTSD, the primary psychological diagnosis used to describe substantial impairment that persists after trauma exposure. In DSM-5, a PTSD diagnosis in adults requires the person to endorse a Criterion A event and then, connected specifically to that event, experienced for one month or more some of the twenty potential symptoms that fall under four headings: intrusions, avoidance, negative alterations in cognitions and mood, and alterations in arousal and reactivity. In addition to trauma exposure, a diagnosis of PTSD requires a client to endorse at least one intrusion symptom, one avoidance symptom, two negative alterations in cognitions and mood symptoms, and two alterations in arousal and reactivity symptoms. Taken together, this cluster of symptoms must result in decrease in functioning. PTSD and related diagnoses are unique in psychiatric nosology, representing pathology as a failure to return to baseline functioning after a stressful event.

The ICD-11 diagnosis of PTSD is characterized by the presence of six symptoms organized under three symptom clusters: re-experiencing of the traumatic event(s), avoidance of traumatic reminders, and a sense of current threat. In the ICD-11 (World Health Organization, 2018), a diagnosis of PTSD requires exposure to an extreme stressor and endorsement of at least one symptom from each cluster. Additionally, symptoms present must be associated with functional impairment for "several weeks." Research examining differences in PTSD prevalence between DSM-5 and ICD-11 have been equivocal; some studies have found higher rates using DSM-5 criteria, some have found higher rates using ICD-11 criteria, and some showed equivalence (Shevlin et al., 2018). Observed differences seen across studies suggests that information is still lacking concerning how to capture consistently the incidence of trauma and its consequences.

In addition to the debate surrounding PTSD diagnostic criteria, the PTSD assessment methods also vary across studies. Currently, the Clinically Administered PTSD Scale (CAPS; Weathers et al., 2018) is widely considered the gold standard for assessing PTSD by major trauma-focused professional organizations (e.g., International Society for Traumatic Stress Studies). However, many studies contributing data on trauma and PTSD rely on self-report measures, which have reduced validity compared to interviewer-administered measures. Some of these measures fail to link PTSD symptoms to the presence of a threshold-level traumatic event, which results in self-report measures capturing general distress but not necessarily PTSD (Shalev, Freedman, Peri, Brandes, & Sahar, 1997).

SGM-Specific Theories on the Cumulative Burden of Stress

Theories such as the sexual minority stress model propose that the cumulative burden of stressors increases PTSD risk for SGM individuals (Meyer, 1995). In Meyer's model, "minority stress" refers to the identity-based stress experienced by members of disadvantaged social groups (in this specific case, SGM individuals), over and above the general life stressors experienced by all members of society. The combination of general and identity-based stressors is hypothesized to lead to heightened risk of negative physical and mental health concerns for SGM individuals. Meyer describes two related categories of minority stress. First, discrimination and victimization refer to overt violent experiences and are considered "distal stressors" in the sexual minority stress model, which directly impact health as well as indirectly impact health through the "proximal stressors." The proximal stressors are considered both to be the consequences of the distal stressors as well as to arise organically via living in a discriminatory society. Proximal stressors include the expectation of rejection, identity concealment, and internalized heterosexism. Per Meyer's model, some experiences of minority stress may reach the level of "traumatic" (i.e., sexual assault) and meet diagnostic criteria for PTSD; however, frequently they will not. The model adds powerfully to the literature suggesting that the cumulative impact of numerous "lower-level" experiences builds to increase vulnerability to poor physical and mental health.

Beyond the accumulation of stigma and discrimination experiences related to their SGM identities and other marginalized statuses that they might hold, SGM individuals are also at increased risk for childhood maltreatment, interpersonal violence, trauma happening to a close friend or relative, and unexpected death of someone close than are heterosexual individuals with no same-sex attractions or partners (Roberts et al., 2010). Experiences of victimization are frequently paired with identity-related stressors, as victimization may be only one part of an individual's experience with discrimination (James et al., 2016). A robust literature has demonstrated that, because of their gender identities, TGD individuals are at high risk for experiencing hostility and other forms of discrimination (Goldblum et al., 2012; James et al., 2016). Similarly, sexual minority individuals report more lifetime and day-to-day discrimination experiences than their heterosexual peers, with approximately 42 percent attributing the discrimination they face to their sexual orientation, in whole or in part (Mays & Cochran, 2001).

Frequent experiences of stigma and discrimination are negatively associated with an individual's access to community and social supports, given experiences of rejection and discrimination. SGM individuals are less likely than heterosexual cisgender individuals to endorse having social support (D'Augelli, Hershberger, & Pilkington, 1998; Factor & Rothblum, 2008). Further, SGM individuals are less likely than heterosexual cisgender individuals to report feeling comfortable interacting with healthcare providers, and report being less likely to see a doctor despite the presence of health concerns (Blosnich, Farmer, Lee, Silenzio & Bowen, 2014; James et al., 2016). Social support and community engagement have been shown to have far-reaching positive implications for SGM individuals and may attenuate the impact of sexual minority stress (Meyer, 2010). For example, TGD individuals who reported that their immediate families were supportive were less likely to report a variety of negative experiences related to economic stability and health, such as experiencing homelessness, attempting suicide, or experiencing serious psychological distress (James et al., 2016). Similarly, perceived support from peers and family mediated the negative association found between sexual minority identity and psychosocial symptoms (Williams, Connolly, Pepler, & Craig, 2005).

Prevalence of PTEs and PTSD in SGM Individuals

PTSD Diagnoses in SGM Individuals

Rates of threshold-level PTSD have been reported to be 12 percent for gay and bisexual men, 11 percent for lesbian and bisexual women, and 18 percent for transgender women specifically—with one study reporting that 39 percent of their TGD sample met criteria for PTSD (Brown & Jones, 2014; Meyer et al., 2011; Shipherd et al., 2011). These figures should generally be considered underestimates, given the narrow definition of Criterion A, although some data are drawn from populations in which a higher prevalence of PTEs is expected, such as veterans. Although data on this topic are limited, there are some published findings on racial/ethnic variability in PTSD showing that sexual minority individuals of color are at higher risk for PTSD compared to their white peers. For example, in a cross-sectional study of 382 sexual minority individuals, 7 percent of white participants, 11 percent of black participants, and 16 percent of Latinx participants met DSM Criterion A (Meyer et al., 2011).

SGM Experiences of PTEs

Based on the minority stress model, it is clear that SGM individuals are at risk for general stressors, as well as additional identity-based stressors, as PTEs. The rate of exposure to PTEs in SGM individuals has been reported at approximately 82 percent (House et al., 2011). For sexual minority men specifically, the rate of PTE exposure appears to be quite high, at 70 percent in one study (House et al., 2011), and even higher for men who identified as gay (85 percent) and bisexual (76 percent) in another study (Roberts et al., 2010). For sexual minority women, the rate of PTE exposure was reported at 79 percent in one study (House et al., 2011); in another study, the rate was even higher for women who identified as lesbian (89 percent) and bisexual (86 percent) (Roberts et al., 2010). For transgender women, the rate of PTE exposure has been reported to be 51 to 74 percent (Wilson, Chen, Arayasirikul, Raymond, & McFarland, 2016). Variability in PTE reports may be driven, in part, by sampling method variability and differences in subpopulations of interest (e.g., TGD women ages 16 to 24 living in the San Francisco Bay area) and may not generalize more broadly.

Some SGM subgroups have received insufficient attention in the empirical literature. Most published research has focused on gay men and other sexual minority populations, and much less has focused on

TGD individuals. More data are needed on these populations. To date, no published studies have reported rates of PTEs specifically for transgender men or for other gender-diverse individuals, such as those who identify outside of the gender binary.

Further, most published data on the PTEs of SGM individuals focus on interpersonal victimization, especially sexual violence. This focus is unsurprising, given that people with stigmatized identities are often identified by perpetrators as especially vulnerable (Gruenewald & Kelly, 2014). However, despite the already high prevalence, these figures are still likely underestimates, given that sexual victimization can go unreported for various reasons, including uncertainty about whether a given experience "counts" as victimization, shame about disclosure or a history of invalidating responses to disclosures, or discomfort with reporting to police or other official supports (e.g., Jackson, Valentine, Woodward, & Pantalone, 2017; Stotzer, 2009). Even in cases of victimization reported to the police, some officers may not have the cultural awareness to classify victims via their chosen identities in official reports (Stotzer, 2012).

Notably, there are also some categories of PTEs included under Criterion A, such as direct or second-hand exposure to death, which appear totally absent from the published literature on SGM individuals. In a study conducted after the 2016 Pulse nightclub shooting in Orlando, Florida, researchers evaluated perceptions of safety in a large sample (N = 1,345) of SGM individuals and found that after the shooting, SGM individuals reported increased safety concern for themselves and their peers (Stults, Kupprat, Krause, Kapadia, & Halkitis, 2017). In another study, authors found that SGM individuals reported a negative impact on their psychological and emotional well-being by learning about the victimization of others from within their communities (Bell & Perry, 2015). Considering the shared cultural awareness of death within SGM communities—especially considering events such as the Pulse shooting, media reports of youth suicide rates, and the widely publicized murders of transgender women in the past year—this category would be especially important for investigators to consider in future research (Khullar, 2018; Stack, 2019; Stults et al., 2017).

The experience of SGM individuals in the Global South is an under-researched area of study. Although prevalence has not been satisfactorily reported, emerging research has explored the experience of SGM refugees from the Middle East, North Africa, and Asia. Although the sample size was limited (N = 37), the majority of participants met criteria for PTSD (65 percent), and many linked their most significant PTE to an SGM identity (Alessi, Kahn, Woolner, & Der Hom, 2018).

Sexual Minority Experiences of Interpersonal Victimization

Rates of childhood maltreatment have been reported at 18 percent for gay men and 12 percent for bisexual men (Roberts et al., 2010). In one large study (N = 720) examining lifetime victimization of sexual minority individuals, Balsam, Rothblum, and Beauchaine (2005) found that 19 percent of gay men and 22 percent of bisexual men reported having experienced childhood psychological abuse, and 14 percent of gay men and 22 percent of bisexual men reported childhood physical abuse. The variability in childhood victimization rates can be attributed to differences in conceptualization and measurement of relevant constructs. For example, in some studies, childhood abuse was clearly labeled as physical abuse, and in other cases it was described more ambiguously as "childhood maltreatment." Among the types of childhood abuse experiences found to be the most common for sexual minority men, childhood sexual abuse has been self-reported by 16 to 59 percent of gay men, and around 44 percent of bisexual men, across samples (Balsam et al., 2005; Rothman, Exner, & Baughman, 2011). Adult sexual abuse has been reported by between 12 and 54 percent of gay men and 12 percent of bisexual men in various observational studies (Balsam et al., 2005; Houston & McKirnan, 2007; Roberts et al., 2010; Rothman et al., 2011). In studies of adult sexual abuse, there is a sizable range because of heterogeneity in conceptualization and measurement. For example, adult sexual abuse is sometimes understood broadly as sexual abuse, and other times more specifically as unwanted sex or sexual activity, coerced intercourse, and attempted rape. Adult physical abuse also appears common, estimated at 19 percent for sexual minority men (Bacchus et al., 2015; Balsam et al., 2005; Houston & McKirnan, 2007). According to the 2010 U.S. National Intimate Partner and Sexual Violence Survey, 40 percent of gay men and 47 percent of bisexual men have experienced sexual violence other than rape, compared to 21 percent of heterosexual men (Black et al., 2011).

Partner abuse was reported by 30 to 45 percent of sexual minority men, across samples (Bacchus et al., 2015; Heintz & Melendez, 2006; Houston &

McKirnan, 2007). In one study of 817 sexual minority men in Chicago, 33 percent of black men, 35 percent of Latino men, and 27 percent of Asian/Pacific Islanders and men from other ethnic groups endorsed lifetime partner abuse (Houston & McKirnan, 2007). Although the rates of partner abuse did not differ significantly across racial or ethnic groups, significant differences were observed between the likelihood of reporting partner abuse for men from low (37 percent) versus high (30 percent) socioeconomic status backgrounds. In another study with a very large sample (N = 51,048; Goldberg & Meyer, 2013), across sexual orientations, Latino men were less likely than white men to report partner abuse (odds ratio [OR] 0.42), and black men were more likely than white men to report partner abuse (OR 1.99).

Childhood psychological and physical abuse was reported by approximately 28 percent of lesbian women and 31 percent of bisexual women (Corliss, Cochran, Mays, Greenland, & Seeman, 2009; Roberts et al., 2010). Childhood sexual abuse has been reported by 23 to 76 percent of lesbian women and 48 to 54 percent of bisexual women across a variety of studies (Balsam et al., 2005; Corliss et al., 2009; Descamps, Rothblum, Bradford, & Ryan, 2000; Roberts et al., 2010; Rothman et al., 2011). In examining the frequency of childhood sexual abuse by race, in one study 45 percent of black lesbian women and 40 percent of Latina lesbian women reported having experienced childhood sexual abuse, rates that were significantly higher than those reported by white lesbian women (27 percent; Descamps et al., 2000). Rates of adult sexual abuse for lesbian women have been reported between 32 and 85 percent (Balsam et al., 2005; Descamps et al., 2000; Roberts et al., 2010; Rothman et al., 2011). The wide range of prevalence estimates can be attributed to differences in recruitment methods and specific populations of interest, as well as the operationalization and measurement of the experiences. In some cases, sexual abuse (or assault) was defined ambiguously; in other cases, it was described explicitly (i.e., coerced intercourse, attempted rape, or completed rape).

According to the National Intimate Partner and Sexual Violence Survey (Black et al., 2011), 44 percent of lesbian and 61 percent of bisexual women experienced rape, physical violence, or stalking by an intimate partner, compared to 35 percent of heterosexual women. When exploring specific types of violence, 46 percent of bisexual women reported being raped, compared to 17 percent of heterosexual women and 13 percent of lesbian women. Similarly, 22 percent of bisexual women have been raped by an intimate partner, compared to 9 percent of heterosexual women (Black et al., 2011). In another study that examined adult sexual abuse prevalence in sexual minority women of color, results indicated racial/ethnic differences in rape prevalence: 45 percent for black lesbian women, 35 percent for Latina lesbian women, and 31 percent for white lesbian women (Descamps et al., 2000). Adult physical abuse has been reported by approximately 44 percent of lesbian women and 48 percent of bisexual women (Balsam et al., 2005). Similarly, partner abuse has been estimated to occur in the lives of 11 to 27 percent of sexual minority women (Descamps et al., 2000; Heintz & Melendez, 2006). For sexual minority women, in addition to less research focused on their victimization experiences, much of the published research dates from the early 2000s and may not reflect current rates of interpersonal victimization.

TGD Experiences of Interpersonal Victimization

Our investigation of the prevalence of interpersonal victimization for TGD individuals may have raised more questions than it answered. During our literature searching, it became apparent quickly that most of the published data focused on TGD populations as if they are a homogeneous group, and that there has been a much greater focus on trans women (sometimes called "male-to-female" trans individuals in older publications) compared to trans men (sometimes called "female-to-male"). One reason for this discrepancy may be that, historically, funding for SGM health was tied to HIV risk, and trans women are at higher risk for HIV acquisition than their trans male peers. In any event, the interpersonal victimization experiences of trans men are no less significant and, thus, deserve to be investigated more thoroughly.

When authors presented data on TGD participants broadly, 55 percent of individuals endorsed childhood abuse experiences (Reisner et al., 2016). In a sample of transgender older adults, 64 percent reported lifetime sexual abuse (Cook-Daniels & Munson, 2010). Adult sexual abuse was reported by 10 to 86 percent of TGD samples, and adult physical abuse was reported by 20 to 86 percent (Mizock & Lewis, 2008; Reisner et al., 2016; Stotzer, 2009). Large ranges in prevalence estimates for adult sexual and physical abuse can be attributed, in part, to variability in data collection methods. Each of the figures came from representative U.S. national samples or literature reviews. In some cases, primary data were collected through self-report surveys; in other cases, the data were gathered from secondary sources, such as surveillance data of the U.S. Department of Justice. The latter might result in underestimates based on social desirability in reporting and reluctance to disclose SGM identities in official settings. Other factors were likely to play a role as well—as with other prevalence estimates noted above—including differences in recruitment methods and specific populations of interest, as well as the operationalization and measurement of the experiences.

In the U.S. Transgender Survey (N = 72,715), 54 percent of TGD individuals endorsed a history of partner abuse (James et al., 2016). In samples focused specifically on TGD women, adult physical abuse was reported by 47 percent (Nuttbrock et al., 2015), and adult sexual abuse was reported by 24 to 85 percent (Budhwani et al., 2018; Kussin-Shoptaw, Fletcher, & Reback, 2017), across samples. Observed differences across TGD subgroups may reflect geographic differences in trans experiences, as the sample in the Budwhani et al. (2018) study recruited trans women in the Dominican Republic and Kussin-Shoptaw et al. (2017) reported data from a sample of urban U.S. TGD women. TGD individuals are also at an increased risk of violence. Current point prevalence estimates for TGD adults are 38 percent for physical assault (Testa et al., 2012) and up to 47 percent for sexual assault (James et al., 2016).

SGM Discrimination Experiences

Discrimination is an unfortunately ubiquitous experience for sexual minority individuals of any gender, with 97 percent reporting having experienced discrimination (House et al., 2011) and 63 percent of surveyed TGD individuals reporting having experienced a serious act of discrimination—events that had a major impact on a person's quality of life, along with the ability to sustain themselves emotionally or financially (James et al., 2016). One fifth of sexual minority men reported psychological abuse in one study (Houston & McKirnan, 2007), and 10 to 13 percent of sexual minority women in another (Roberts et al., 2010). For TGD individuals, 37 to 96 percent of participants reported experiencing discrimination (House et al., 2011; Miller & Grollman, 2015; Mizock & Lewis, 2008; Reisner et al., 2016). In interpreting the reports of discrimination experiences, it is important to consider that, across studies, discrimination was conceptualized and operationalized differently. At times, the researchers reported on discrimination broadly (e.g., House et al., 2011); at other times, discrimination was defined more narrowly, such as workplace or healthcare discrimination.

In this area, also, it appears that racial/ethnic minority SGM individuals fare worse than white-identified SGM individuals. In one study, in comparison to non-Hispanic white TGD participants, multiracial TGD participants were 1.6 times more likely to experience discriminatory events, American Indian TGD participants were 1.8 times more likely, and Latinx TGD individuals were 1.3 times more likely (Miller & Grollman, 2015). One important caveat about the validity of any statistic purporting to represent accurately the frequency of discrimination experiences is that they are often unreported. Some investigators have posed the question about which subgroups of SGM individuals are more versus less likely to report discriminatory experiences. In one study, the results showed that both Black and Asian/Pacific Islander TGD participants were less likely than white TGD participants to report discriminatory events (Miller & Grollman, 2015). At present, there are no published reports that have investigated rates of discrimination or hate crimes within samples of transgender men or individuals with nonbinary or other gender-diverse identities.

SGM Hate Crimes

Based on national survey data, it appears that up to 30 percent of hate crimes reported annually are on sexual orientation (Stotzer, 2012). In one study focused on sexual minority women, 52 percent reported having experienced a hate crime (Descamps et al., 2000). In a more recent study of hate crimes for sexual minority individuals more broadly, findings indicate that at least 33 percent of the sample endorsed hate crime exposure (Burks et al., 2018). Among those hate crimes, 54 percent included physical assault, 30 percent sexual assault, 27 percent robbery, 12 percent burglary, 9 percent vandalism, and 4 percent property damage. In terms of hate crimes experienced by trans women, 47 percent reported having experienced battery/assault, 20 percent reported assault with a weapon, and 12 percent reported robbery/attempted robbery (Stotzer, 2008). In a review that evaluated the frequency of hate crime victimization of trans women, 15 to 33 percent of the samples self-reported having experienced physical violence and 80 to 83 percent experienced verbal abuse. Additionally, trans women reported general harassment at rates between 48 and 69 percent: 23 to 41 percent reported having been robbed or stalked, 20 to 86 percent reported physical assault, and 10 percent reported that they had been assaulted with a weapon (Stotzer, 2009).

SGM Bullying

Although other victimization experiences, such as bullying during childhood or adolescence, may not be considered PTEs by a strict definition of Criterion A, it seems likely that they would contribute to the cumulative burden of stress faced by SGM individuals. Around one third of SM individuals have reported experiencing bullying (Collier, van Beusekom, Boss, & Sandfort, 2013). Based on results from an online national study of TGD youth (ages 13 to 18), rates seem much higher: 75 percent reported verbal harassment, 32 percent reported physical harassment, and 17 percent reported physical assault (Reisner, Greytak, Parsons, & Ybarra, 2015). Additionally, there are some published reports focused on bullying in SGM subgroups. In a cross-sectional study that examined associations between bullying and sexual orientation in a large sample of SM individuals (N = 7,559), bullying was reported by 44 percent of gay men, 40 percent of lesbian women, 36 percent of bisexual men, and 26 percent of bisexual women (Berlan, Corliss, Field, Goodman, & Austin, 2010). In the current era, a significant proportion of bullying happens in virtual/social media contexts. According to data from the Youth Risk Behavior Surveillance study, a nationally representative school-based survey conducted by the U.S. Centers for Disease Control and Prevention, 27 percent of sexual minority individuals endorsed electronic bullying, including 29 percent of lesbian and bisexual young women and 22 percent of gay and bisexual young men (Kann et al., 2018). Verbal bullying was reported by 34 percent, electronic bullying by 17 percent, and relational bullying by 33 percent of SGM youth (Hatzenbuehler, Duncan, & Johnson, 2015).

Future Directions

There is ample evidence of SGM identity–related disparities in discrimination, victimization, and mental health problems, which appear to be driven by the stigmatization of those identities and the societal marginalization faced by the SGM individuals who hold them. There is disagreement in the field about how to conceptualize, measure, and categorize the PTEs that SGM individuals experience, with implications for treatment. Beyond documenting disparities in PTEs and PTSD, researchers should shift the empirical focus to understanding the phenomenology of clinically significant stressors, including discrimination, microaggressions, and other identity-based stressors, and their consequences (social isolation, rejection, shame, concealment), as well as how they contribute to the development and maintenance of specific mental health problems, such as PTSD, depression, substance use, and suicidality. Another useful future direction would be to integrate sexual minority stress models with models of trauma and recovery.

PTSD for SGM Individuals: Theoretical Issues

Recent qualitative work published by a group of SGM-focused researchers at the Veterans Healthcare Administration presented a burgeoning theoretical model that depicts the intersections between a range of clinically significant experiences (Livingston, Berke, Ruben, Matza, & Shipherd, 2019). They argue that an exclusive focus on Criterion A events and PTSD symptoms is insufficient for developing accurate case conceptualizations for SGM clients. Based on their experiences in clinical practice at the Veterans Healthcare Administration, these authors have seen SGM veterans reporting that their distress associated with discrimination, microaggressions, and other minority stressors is dismissed by healthcare providers as unimportant because those experiences fail to reach the Criterion A threshold or they are judged to be less severe than non–identity-based PTEs experienced by cisgender and heterosexual veterans. SGM veterans could understandably experience this dismissal as invalidating of important elements of their victimization history, with the potential to reduce their willingness to engage in mental health services. Livingston et al. (2019) argue that harmful, clinically significant, identity-based experiences can also overlap with traditional PTEs. For example, the experience of a physical assault bias event or hate crime may be both an identity-based discrimination incident and a PTE. More research is needed to further develop this model and to guide assessments, case conceptualization, and intervention development.

Some health disparities researchers have argued for revisiting the definition of Criterion A, either to expand the criteria to include discrimination events ("racial trauma") or to develop a new diagnosis altogether that would capture distress associated with discrete events that do not meet current Criterion

A ("oppression-related distress"; Holmes, Facemire, & DaFonseca, 2016; Watson, DeBlaere, Langrehr, Zelaya, & Flores, 2016). This scientific discussion is controversial yet aptly highlights the limitations in assessing and diagnosing clinical levels of distress that do not fit neatly into the current PTSD criteria. In sum, there is a dire need for the development and testing of strong theoretical models that account for Criterion A and identity-related stressful experiences, and the development or adaptation of assessments that can capture symptoms associated with various types of stressors common in SGM populations.

PTSD for SGM Individuals: Assessment Issues

Standard assessments of mental health disorders often do not adequately incorporate consideration of identity-based stressors, such as discrimination, microaggressions, or other aspects of the minority stress model. In practice, it can be challenging to disentangle the expected distress from these experiences from DSM-defined mental health disorders. During administration of the CAPS-5 (Weathers et al., 2018) in an ongoing research study, we identified that TGD clients often link symptoms—such as strong negative beliefs about themselves and others, hypervigilance, and hyperarousal—to the experience of discrimination or psychological abuse, rather than to a discrete singular physical assault. At present, the DSM does not recognize chronic and persistent discrimination experiences as PTEs. In the context of CAPS assessments, our TGD participants have identified the greatest negative contribution to their mental health as the repeated, pervasive mistreatment they have faced, over and above any singular event (Valentine, 2019). This complicates CAPS administration and the potential validity of the study results related to PTSD prevalence in this and other TGD samples, as CAPS administration guidelines note that symptoms not directly related to the Criterion A index event must be scored as absent. Removal of the contribution of discrimination experiences from the assessment will likely lead to underestimates of legitimate suffering of TGD individuals that may, in turn, lead clinicians to minimize significant distress that does not fall neatly into PTSD criteria. This could result in TGD individuals' significant suffering not being considered in the intervention selection process—meaning that they are un- or under-treated for their trauma symptoms.

Over and above the technical definitions of PTSD excluding what are likely to be the most common and bothersome stressors for SGM individuals, studies of SGM populations have generally not used "gold standard," clinician-administered assessments of PTSD. Often, researchers use self-report measures that do not link reported symptoms directly to Criterion A events. A recent systematic review of the mental health of TGD individuals found that only 3 of 14 studies that purported to measure PTSD symptoms used methods that were sufficient to determine a probable PTSD diagnosis (Valentine & Shipherd, 2018). Without anchoring PTSD symptoms to Criterion A events, self-reported measures can be inflated by general distress (Demirchyan, Goenjian, & Khachadourian, 2014).

Interestingly, Reisner et al. (2016) found that scores on the Primary Care PTSD Screen—the PC-PTSD, a four-item scale designed for use in primary care—were associated with non–Criterion A discrimination, even after controlling for Criterion A exposures (Prins et al., 2016). Although the PC-PTSD fails to identify an index event, and is recommended as a screening measure only and not as a diagnostic measure, these data suggest that there may be commonalities between the types of symptoms that clients report following discrimination (which does not fall under Criterion A) and the sequelae of threshold-level Criterion A PTEs. There are some data to indicate, further, that individuals often link the distress measured by standard PTSD self-report assessments to non–Criterion A events, even if the individuals have also experienced a Criterion A event (Anders, Shallcross, & Frazier, 2012). Studies in this area highlight some of the challenges with accurately assessing PTSD in SGM populations, as well as the need for assessments that can reliably differentiate (or integrate) these forms of distress that are more common yet not officially PTEs.

Epidemiological studies that apply more rigorous methods of assessing for PTSD, with explicit links to Criterion A events, are needed to understand more accurately the prevalence of PTSD in SGM populations. We could identify no published studies focused on the mental health of SGM individuals that used the "gold standard" PTSD measure (CAPS-5). A recent systematic review (Valentine & Shipherd, 2018) identified only one study that applied careful assessment of PTSD, finding that 18 percent of trans individuals who had been assigned male sex at birth evidenced clinical elevations of PTSD, despite 98 percent of the sample reporting exposure to Criterion A events (Shipherd et al., 2011). These data suggest that rates of PTSD among

TGD individuals may be double that of the general population (8 percent prevalence; Kessler et al., 1995); however, more studies are needed across all SGM subgroups for increased certainty about those findings.

PTSD for SGM Individuals: Intervention Development Efforts

Unfortunately, there are currently no interventions that dually address threshold-level PTSD and coping with discrimination. Treatment research on interventions developed for PTSD and discrimination, informed by a solid theoretical framework, is sorely needed. Interventions proposed by researchers to address sexual minority stressors range from simple exercises using cognitive restructuring and affective expression related to sexual minority identities to short-term, skills-based cognitive-behavioral interventions. Although a small number of interventions have shown promise in addressing discrimination and minority stress, they have only been tested in sexual minority men (e.g., Pachankis, Hatzenbuehler, Rendina, Safren, & Parsons, 2015) and, thus, generalizability to other SGM subpopulations is unknown. Sloan, Berke, and Shipherd (2017) propose using a dialectical framework to design interventions for gender minorities, making a compelling argument about how dialectical behavior therapy skills could address the chronic invalidation of living with a stigmatized identity, and the resulting emotion dysregulation that some trans individuals experience. They suggest possible applications of mindfulness and distress tolerance in self-acceptance and affirmation of individuals' gender identities, as well as tolerating chronic discrimination and gender dysphoria. Further, Sloan et al. (2017) describe possible applications of emotion regulation and interpersonal effectiveness to build resilience, coping abilities, effective self-advocacy for validation with others, and recovery from invalidation.

References

Alessi, E. J., Kahn, S., Woolner, L., & Der Horn, R. (2018). Traumatic stress among sexual and gender minority refugees from the Middle East, North Africa, and Asia who fled to the European Union. *Journal of Traumatic Stress, 31*(6), 805–15. doi:10.1002/jts.22346

American Psychiatric Association. (2013). *Diagnostic and statistical manual of mental disorders* (5th ed.). Arlington, VA: Author. doi:10.1176/appi.books.9780890425596.dsm05

Anders, S. L., Shallcross, S. L., & Frazier, P. A. (2012). Beyond Criterion A1: The effects of relational and non-relational traumatic events. *Journal of Trauma & Dissociation, 13*(2), 134–51. doi:10.1080/15299732.2012.642744

Bacchus, L. J., Buller, A. M., Ferrari, G., Peters, T. J., Devries, K., Sethi, G., . . . Feder, G. S. (2015). Occurrence and impact of domestic violence and abuse in gay and bisexual men: A cross-sectional survey. *International Journal of STD and AIDS, 28*(1), 16–27. doi:10.1177/0956462415622886

Balsam, K. F., Rothblum, E. D., & Beauchaine, T. P. (2005). Victimization over the life span: A comparison of lesbian, gay, bisexual, and heterosexual siblings. *Journal of Consulting and Clinical Psychology, 73*(3), 477–87. doi:10.1037/0022-006X.73.3.477

Bandermann, K. M., & Szymanski, D. M. (2014). Exploring coping mediators between heterosexist oppression and posttraumatic stress symptoms among lesbian, gay, and bisexual persons. *Psychology of Sexual Orientation and Gender Diversity, 1*(3), 213–24. doi:10.1037/sgd0000044

Bell, J. G., & Perry, B. (2015). Outside looking in: The community impacts of anti-lesbian, gay, and bisexual hate crime. *Journal of Homosexuality, 62*(1), 98–120. doi:10.1080/00918369.2014.957133

Berlan, E. D., Corliss, H. L., Field, A. E., Goodman, E., & Austin, S. B. (2010). Sexual orientation and bullying among adolescents in the Growing Up Today Study. *Journal of Adolescent Health, 46*(4), 366–71. doi:10.1371/journal.pone.0178059

Black, M. C., Basile, K. C., Breiding, M. J., Smith, S. G., Walters, M. L., Merrick, M. T., . . . Stevens, M. R. (2011). *The National Intimate Partner and Sexual Violence Survey (NISVS): 2010 summary report.* Atlanta, GA: National Center for Injury Prevention and Control, U.S. Centers for Disease Control and Prevention.

Blosnich, J. R., Farmer, G. W., Lee, J. G., Silenzio, V. M., & Bowen, D. J. (2014). Health inequalities among sexual minority adults: Evidence from ten U.S. states, 2010. *American Journal of Preventive Medicine*, 46(4), 337–49. doi:10.1016/j.amepre.2013.11.010

Boals, A., & Schuettler, D. (2009). PTSD symptoms in response to traumatic and non-traumatic events: The role of respondent perception and A2 criterion. *Journal of Anxiety Disorders, 23*(4), 458–62. doi:10.1016/j.janxdis.2008.09.003

Brown, G. R., & Jones, K. T. (2014). Racial health disparities in a cohort of 5,135 transgender veterans. *Journal of Racial and Ethnic Health Disparities, 1*(4), 257–66. doi:10.1007/s40615-014-0032-4

Budhwani, H., Hearld, K. R., Milner, A. N., Charow, R., McGlaughlin, E. M., Rodriguez-Lauzurique, M., . . . Paulino-Ramirez, R. (2018). Transgender women's experiences with stigma, trauma, and attempted suicide in the Dominican Republic. *Suicide and Life-Threatening Behavior, 48*(6), 788–96. doi:10.1111/sltb.12400

Burks, A. C., Cramer, R. J., Henderson, C. E., Stroud, C. H., Crosby, J. W., & Graham, J. (2018). Frequency, nature, and correlates of hate crime victimization experiences in an urban sample of lesbian, gay, and bisexual community members. *Journal of Interpersonal Violence, 33*(3), 402–20. doi:10.1177/0886260515605298

Chou, T., Asnaani, A., & Hofmann, S. G. (2012). Perception of racial discrimination and psychopathology across three U.S. ethnic minority groups. *Cultural Diversity and Ethnic Minority Psychology, 18*(1), 74–81. doi:10.1037/a0025432

Collier, K. L., van Beusekom, G., Boss, H. M. W., & Sandfort, T. G. M. (2013). Sexual orientation and gender identity/expression related peer victimization in adolescence: A systematic review of associated psychoscocial and health outcomes. *Journal of Sex Research, 50*(3–4), 299–317. doi:10.1080/00224499.2012.750639

Cook-Daniels, L., & Munson, M. (2010). Sexual violence, elder abuse, and sexuality of transgender adults, age 50+: Results of three surveys. *Journal of GLBT Family Studies, 6*(2), 142–77. doi:10.1080/15504281003705238

Corliss, H. L., Cochran, S. D., Mays, V. M., Greenland, S., & Seeman, T. E. (2009). Age of minority sexual orientation development and risk of childhood maltreatment and suicide attempts in women. *American Journal of Orthopsychiatry, 79*(4), 511–21. doi:10.1037/a0017163

D'Augelli, A. R., Hershberger, S. L., & Pilkington, N. W. (1998). Lesbian, gay, and bisexual youth and their families: Disclosure of sexual orientation and its consequences. *American Journal of Orthopsychiatry, 68*(3), 361–71. doi:10.1037/h0080345

Demirchyan, A., Goenjian, A. K., & Khachadourian, V. (2014). Factor structure and psychometric properties of the Posttraumatic Stress Disorder (PTSD) Checklist and DSM-5 PTSD symptom set in a long-term post-earthquake cohort in Armenia. *Assessment, 22*(5), 594–606. doi:10.1177%2F1073191114555523

Descamps, M. J., Rothblum, E. D., Bradford, J., & Ryan, C. (2000). Mental health impact of child sexual abuse, rape, intimate partner violence, and hate crimes in the National Lesbian Health Care Survey. *Journal of Gay and Lesbian Social Services, 11*, 27–55. doi:10.1300/J041v11n01_02

Factor, R. J., & Rothblum, E. D. (2008). A study of transgender adults and their non-transgender siblings on demographic characteristics, social support, and experiences of violence. *Journal of LGBT Health Research, 3*(3), 11–30. doi:10.1080/15574090802092879

Gold, S. D., Marx, B. P., Soler-Baillo, J. M., & Sloan, D. M. (2005). Is life stress more traumatic than traumatic stress? *Journal of Anxiety Disorders, 19*(6), 687–98. doi:10.1016/j.janxdis.2004.06.002

Goldberg, N. G., & Meyer, I. H. (2013). Sexual orientation disparities in history of intimate partner violence: Results from the California Health Interview Survey. *Journal of Interpersonal Violence, 28*(5), 1109–18. doi:10.1177/0886260512459384

Goldblum, P., Testa, R. J., Pflum, S., Hendricks, M. L., Bradford, J., & Bongar, B. (2012). The relationship between gender-based victimization and suicide attempts in transgender people. *Professional Psychology: Research and Practice, 43*(5), 468–75. doi:10.1037/a0029605

Gruenewald, J., & Kelley, K. (2014). Exploring anti-LGBT homicide by mode of victim selection. *Criminal Justice and Behavior*, 41(9), 1130–52. doi:10.1177/0093854814541259

Hatzenbuehler, M. L., Duncan, D., & Johnson, R. (2015). Neighborhood-level LGBT hate crimes and bullying among sexual minority youths: A geospatial analysis. *Violence and Victims, 30*(4), 663–75. doi:10.1891/0886–6708.vv-d-13–00166

Heintz, A. J., & Melendez, R. M. (2006). Intimate partner violence and HIV/STD risk among lesbian, gay, bisexual, and transgender individuals. *Journal of Interpersonal Violence, 21*(2), 193–208. doi:10.1177%2F0886260505282104

Holmes, S. C., Facemire, V. C., & DaFonseca, A. M. (2016). Expanding Criterion A for posttraumatic stress disorder: Considering the deleterious impact of oppression. *Traumatology, 22*(4), 314–21. doi:10.1037/trm0000104

House, A. S., van Horn, E., Coppeans, C., & Stepleman, L. M. (2011). Interpersonal trauma and discriminatory events as predictors of suicidal and nonsuicidal self-injury in gay, lesbian, bisexual, and transgender persons. *Traumatology, 17*(2), 75–85. doi:10.1177/1534765610395621

Houston, E., & McKirnan, D. J. (2007). Intimate partner abuse among gay and bisexual men: Risk correlates and health outcomes. *Journal of Urban Health, 84*(5), 681–90. doi:10.1007/s11524-007-9188-0

Jackson, M. A., Valentine, S. E., Woodward, E. N., & Pantalone, D. W. (2017). Sexual minority men's experiences with secondary victimization and disclosure of adult sexual assault: "Victimizing me all over again." *Sexuality Research and Social Policy, 14*(3), 275–88. doi:10.1007/s13178-016-0249-6

James, S. E., Herman, J. L., Rankin, S., Keisling, M., Mottet, L., & Anafi, M. (2016). *The report of the 2015 U.S. Transgender Survey*. Washington, DC: National Center for Transgender Equality.

Kann, L., McManus, T., Harris, W. A., Shanklin, S. L., Flint, K. H., Queen, B.,...Ethier, K. A. (2018). Youth Risk Behavior Surveillance—United States, 2017. *Morbidity and Mortality Weekly Report, 67*(8), 1–114. doi:10.15585/mmwr.ss6708a1

Keane, T. M., Marshall, A. D., & Taft, C. T. (2006). Posttraumatic stress disorder: Etiology, epidemiology, and treatment outcome. *Annual Review of Clinical Psychology, 2*, 161–97. doi:10.1146/annurev.clinpsy.2.022305.095305

Kelleher, C. (2009). Minority stress and health: Implications for lesbian, gay, bisexual, transgender, and questioning (LGBTQ) young people. *Counselling Psychology Quarterly, 22*(4), 373–9. doi:10.1080/09515070903334995

Kessler, R. C., McGonagle, K. A., Zhao, S., Nelson, C. B., Hughes, M., Eshleman, S., . . . Nelson, C. B. (1995). National Comorbidity Survey. *Archives of General Psychiatry, 52*(12), 1048–60.

Khullar, D. (9 October 2018). Stigma against gay people can be deadly. *New York Times*. https://www.nytimes.com/2018/10/09/well/live/gay-lesbian-lgbt-health-stigma-laws.html.

Kussin-Shoptaw, A. L., Fletcher, J. B., & Reback, C. J. (2017). Physical and/or sexual abuse is associated with increased psychological and emotional distress among transgender women. *LGBT Health, 4*(4), 268–74. doi:10.1089/lgbt.2016.0186

Larsen, S. E., & Pacella, M. L. (2016). Comparing the effect of DSM-congruent traumas vs. DSM-incongruent stressors on PTSD symptoms: A meta-analytic review. *Journal of Anxiety Disorders, 38*, 37–46. doi:10.1016/j.janxdis.2016.01.001

Livingston, N. A., Berke, D. S., Ruben, M. A., Matza, A. R., & Shipherd, J. C. (2019). Experiences of trauma, discrimination, microaggressions, and minority stress among trauma-exposed LGBT veterans: Unexpected findings and unresolved service gaps. *Psychological Trauma, 11*(7), 695–703. doi:10.1037/tra0000464

Mays, V. M., & Cochran, S. D. (2001). Mental health correlates of perceived discrimination among lesbian, gay, and bisexual adults in the United States. *American Journal of Public Health, 91*(11), 1869–76. doi:10.2105/AJPH.91.11.1869

Meyer, I. H. (1995). Minority stress and mental health in gay men. *Journal of Health and Social Behavior, 36*, 38–56. doi:10.2307/2137286

Meyer, I. H. (2010). The right comparisons in testing the minority stress hypothesis: Comment on Savin-Williams, Cohen, Joyner, and Rieger (2010). *Archives of Sexual Behavior, 39*(6), 1217–9. doi:10.1007/s10508-010-9670-8

Meyer, I. H., Alessi, E. J, & Martin, J. I. (2011). PTSD and sexual orientation: An examination of Criterion A1 and non-Criterion A1 events. *Psychological Trauma*, 3(4), 149–57. doi:10.1037/a0026642

Miller, L. R., & Grollman, E. A. (2015). The social costs of gender nonconformity for transgender adults: Implications for discrimination and health. *Sociological Forum*, *30*(3), 809–31. doi:10.1111/socf.12193

Mizock, L., & Lewis, T. K. (2008). Trauma in transgender populations: Risk, resilience, and clinical care. *Journal of Emotional Abuse*, *8*(3), 335–54. doi: 10.1080/10926790802262523

Nuttbrock, L., Bockting, W., Rosenblum, A., Hwahng, S., Mason, M., Macri, M., & Becker, J. (2015). Transgender community involvement and the psychological impact of abuse among transgender women. *Psychology of Sexual Orientation and Gender Diversity*, *2*(4), 386. https://psycnet.apa.org/doi/10.1037/sgd0000126

Pachankis, J. E., Hatzenbuehler, M. L., Rendina, H. J., Safren, S. A., & Parsons, J. T. (2015). LGB-affirmative cognitive-behavioral therapy for young adult gay and bisexual men: A randomized controlled trial of a transdiagnostic minority stress approach. *Journal of Consulting and Clinical Psychology*, *83*(5), 875–89. doi:10.1037/ccp0000037

Pantalone, D. W., Valentine, S. E., & Shipherd, J. C. (2017). Working with survivors of trauma in sexual minority and transgender/gender-nonconforming populations. In K. DeBord, T. Perez, A. Fischer, & K. Bieschke (Eds.), *Handbook of sexual orientation and gender diversity in counseling and psychotherapy* (pp. 183–211). Washington, DC: American Psychological Association. doi:10.1037/15959–008

Platt, L. F., & Lenzen, A. L. (2013). Sexual orientation microaggressions and the experience of sexual minorities. *Journal of Homosexuality*, *60*(7), 1011–34. https://psycnet.apa.org/doi/10.1080/00918369.2013.774878

Prins, A., Bovin, M. J., Smolenski, D. J., Mark, B. P., Kimerling, R., Jenkins-Guarnieri, M. A.... Tiet, Q. Q. (2016). The Primary Care PTSD Screen for DSM-5 (PC-PTSD-5): Development and evaluation within a veteran primary care sample. *Journal of General Internal Medicine*, *31*(10), 1206–11. doi:10.1007/s11606-016-3703-5

Reisner, S. L., Greytak, E. A., Parsons, J. T., & Ybarra, M. L. (2015). Gender minority social stress in adolescence: Disparities in adolescent bullying and substance use by gender identity. *Journal of Sex Research*, *52*(3), 243–56. doi:10.1080/00224499.2014.886321

Reisner, S. L., White Hughto, J. M., Gamarel, K. E., Keuroghlian, A. S., Mizock, L., & Pachankis, J. E. (2016). Discriminatory experiences associated with posttraumatic stress disorder symptoms among transgender adults. *Counseling Psychology*, *63*(5), 509–19. doi:10.1037/cou0000143

Roberts, A. L., Austin, S. B., Corliss, H. L., Vandermorris, A. K., & Koenen, K. C. (2010). Pervasive trauma exposure among US sexual orientation minority adults and risk of posttraumatic stress disorder. *American Journal of Public Health*, *100*(12), 2433–41. doi:10.2105/AJPH.2009.168971

Rothman, E. F., Exner, D., & Baughman, A. L. (2011). The prevalence of sexual assault against people who identify as gay, lesbian, or bisexual in the united states: A systematic review. *Trauma, Violence, and Abuse*, *12*(2), 55–66. doi:10.1177/1524838010390707

Shalev, A. Y., Freedman, S., Peri, T., Brandes, D., & Sahar, T. (1997). Predicting PTSD in trauma survivors: Prospective evaluation of self-report and clinician-administered instruments. *British Journal of Psychiatry*, *170*, 558–64. doi:10.1192/bjp.170.6.558

Shevlin, M., Hyland, P., Vallières, F., Bisson, J., Makhashvili, N., Javakhishvili, J.,... & Roberts, B. (2018). A comparison of DSM-5 and ICD-11 PTSD prevalence, comorbidity and disability: An analysis of the Ukrainian Internally Displaced Person's Mental Health Survey. *Acta Psychiatrica Scandinavica*, *137*(2), 138–47. doi:10.1111/acps.12840

Shipherd, J. C., Maguen, S., Skidmore, W. C., & Abramovitz, S. M. (2011). Potentially traumatic events in a transgender sample: Frequency and associated symptoms. *Traumatology*, *17*(2), 56–67. doi:10.1177/1534765610395614

Sibrava, N. J., Bjornsson, A. S., Pérez Benítez, A. C. I., Moitra, E., Weisberg, R. B., & Keller, M. B. (2019). Posttraumatic stress disorder in African American and Latinx adults: Clinical course and the role of racial and ethnic discrimination. *American Psychologist*, *74*(1), 101–16. doi:10.1037/amp0000339

Sloan, C. A., Berke, D. S., & Shipherd, J. C. (2017). Utilizing a dialectical framework to inform conceptualization and treatment of clinical distress in transgender individuals. *Professional Psychology: Research and Practice*, *48*(5), 301–9. doi:10.1037/pro0000146

Stack, L. (3 June 2019). Third transgender woman killed in Dallas: People are afraid. *New York Times*. https://www.nytimes.com/2019/06/03/us/dallas-police-transgender-woman-death.html

Stotzer, R. L. (2008). Gender identity and hate crimes: Violence against transgender people in Los Angeles County. *Sexuality Research & Social Policy*, *5*(1), 43–52. doi:10.1525/srsp.2008.5

Stotzer, R. L. (2009). Violence against transgender people: A review of United States data. *Aggression and Violent Behavior*, *14*(3), 170–9. doi:10.1016/j.avb.2009.01.006

Stotzer, R. L. (2012). *Comparison of hate crime rates across protected and unprotected groups—an update*. Los Angeles, CA: Williams Institute. https://escholarship.org/uc/item/43z1q49r

Stults, C. B., Kupprat, S. A., Krause, K. D., Kapadia, F., & Halkitis, P. N. (2017). Perceptions of safety among LGBTQ people following the 2016 Pulse nightclub shooting. *Psychology of Sexual Orientation and Gender Diversity*, *4*(3), 251–6. doi:10.1037/sgd0000240

Sullivan, E., Contractor, A. A., Gerber, M. M., & Neumann, C. (2017). Examination of polytrauma typologies: A latent class analysis approach. *Psychiatry Research*, *255*, 111–8. doi:10.1016/j.psychres.2017.05.026

Testa, R. J., Sciacca, L. M., Wang, F., Hendricks, M. L., Goldblum, P., Bradford, J., & Bongar, B. (2012). Effects of violence on transgender people. *Professional Psychology: Research and Practice*, *43*(5), 452–9. doi:10.1037/a0029604

Valentine, S. E. (2019). The influence of gender identity-related discrimination on adaptation following exposure to potentially traumatic events among diverse transgender and gender nonconforming (TGNC) persons. Unpublished raw data.

Valentine, S. E., & Shipherd, J. C. (2018). A systematic review of social stress and mental health among transgender and gender non-conforming people in the United States. *Clinical Psychology Review*, *66*, 24–38. doi:10.1016/j.cpr.2018.03.003

Watson, L. B., DeBlaere, C., Langrehr, K. J., Zelaya, D. G., & Flores, M. J. (2016). The influence of multiple oppressions on

women of color's experiences with insidious trauma. *Journal of Counseling Psychology, 63*(6), 656–67. doi:10.1037/cou0000165
Weathers, F. W., Bovin, M. J., Lee, D. J., Sloan, D. M., Schnurr, P. P., Kaloupek, D. G., . . . Marx, B. P. (2018). The Clinician-Administered PTSD Scale for DSM-5 (CAPS-5): Development and initial psychometric evaluation in military veterans. *Psychological Assessment, 30*(3), 383–95. doi:10.1037/pas0000486
Williams, T., Connolly, J., Pepler, D., & Craig, W. (2005). Peer victimization, social support, and psychosocial adjustment of sexual minority adolescents. *Journal of Youth and Adolescence, 34*(5), 471–82. doi:10.1007/s10964-005-7264-x
Wilson, E. C., Chen, Y. H., Arayasirikul, S., Raymond, H. F., & McFarland, W. (2016). The impact of discrimination on the mental health of trans*female youth and the protective effect of parental support. *AIDS and Behavior, 20*(10), 2203–11. doi:10.1007/s10461-016-1409-7
World Health Organization. (2018). *International Statistical Classification of Diseases and Related Health Problems* (11th ed.). https://icd.who.int/browse11/l-m/en

CHAPTER

7 Body Image and Eating Disorders among Sexual and Gender Minority Populations

Todd G. Morrison, Joshua W. Katz, Yaser Mirzaei, *and* Somayyeh Zare

Abstract

This chapter reviews current literature pertaining to body image and pathogenic eating practices among sexual and gender minority populations. The authors begin by detailing three dominant theoretical frameworks that have been used to particularize why some sexual and gender minority persons are at risk of body dissatisfaction and disordered eating—the minority stress model, sociocultural theory, and objectification theory—as well as the pantheoretical model of dehumanization. Then, to highlight dominant trends in the literature, the authors summarize narrative and meta-analytic reviews on body image and eating disorders that target gay men, lesbian women, bisexual persons, and trans persons. The authors conclude by detailing obstacles that prevent researchers from better grasping the corporeal psychology of sexual and gender minority persons. These obstacles include (1) inconsistent and ambiguous operationalizing of constructs such as the "gay community"—constructs that are often invoked to explain why sexual and gender minority persons are at risk; (2) reliance on outdated measures of sexual orientation; (3) the elision of bisexual persons in body image scholarship; (4) the limited attention that is paid to the variability existing *within* sexual and gender minoritized groups; (5) the absence of research focusing on the dynamics of intersectionality as they pertain to the body; and (6) the lack of studies conducted outside of the United States.

Keywords: gay, lesbian, bisexual, transgender, body image, eating disorders, sociocultural, objectification

Body image is a multifactorial construct that may be partitioned into evaluation and investment dimensions (Ryan & Morrison, 2009). Body image evaluation, which denotes individuals' satisfaction or dissatisfaction with their appearance, has been identified as "one of the main contributors towards the onset and maintenance of eating psychopathology" (Jones, Haycraft, Murjan, & Arcelus, 2016, p. 82). Body image investment refers to how engaged individuals are in their appearance—engagement that is evidenced both cognitively and behaviorally (Ryan & Morrison, 2009).

Two groups of people that are susceptible to negative body image evaluation and heightened body image investment are sexual and gender minorities (e.g., Calzo, Blashill, Brown, & Argenal, 2017; Jones et al., 2016). *Sexual minorities* is an umbrella term that refers to individuals who operate outside the boundaries of heterosexuality (e.g., gay, lesbian, bisexual, or pansexual). *Gender minorities* is a similarly broad and complex term; however, at its most basic level, a gender minority person is anyone who is *not* cisgender (e.g., trans, gender-nonconforming, and/or nonbinary).

The purpose of the current chapter is to explore body image (in most cases, body image evaluation) as well as disordered eating among sexual and gender minority (SGM) populations. We begin by reviewing several theoretical frameworks that have dominated the research landscape. The core assumptions of each theory are succinctly outlined and relevant literature is used to delineate how these theories have been applied to SGM groups. We conclude this section by describing the pantheoretical model of dehumanization, which details how sociocultural norms, minority stressors, and objectification jointly function to engender body image dissatisfaction and disordered eating among SGM people. Then, to better understand key findings with respect to SGM people and body image evaluation, body image investment, and disordered eating, we summarize narrative and meta-analytic reviews focusing on four target groups: gay men, lesbian women, bisexual persons, and trans individuals. (When these types of reviews were unavailable, we highlighted relevant standalone studies.) We end this chapter by describing several challenges that confront researchers in this field—challenges that, we believe, must be addressed if SGM persons' attitudes about, and behaviors toward, their bodies are to be fully understood.

Dominant Theoretical Models

In this section we elaborate on those theories that best explain why SGM individuals may be at greater risk of experiencing body dissatisfaction and eating disorder symptoms.

Minority Stress Model

According to Meyer (1995), minority stress is "psychological stress derived from [one's] minority status" (p. 38; see also Brooks, 1981). With regard to the population in question, sexual minority stress refers to the stressors that people experience due to being a member of a sexual minority group (Mason & Lewis, 2016). Such stressors include experiences of discrimination, internalized homonegativity (i.e., shame pertaining to one's sexual orientation), and concealment of one's sexual identity. The minority stress model also can be extended to gender minorities and, in particular, transgender persons (see Hendricks & Testa, 2012). For instance, Brewster, Velez, Breslow, and Geiger (2019) found that minority stressors like anti-transgender discrimination served as an indirect predictor of eating disorders in a sample of 205 American transgender women. Despite such findings, trans people have received limited attention by researchers examining the association between minority stressors and disordered eating (Witcomb et al., 2015). As such, the focus of this subsection is primarily placed on sexual minority individuals.

There are two primary causes of sexual minority stress: (1) distal causes such as discrimination from others and (2) proximal causes like feelings of shame and rejection sensitivity or attempts to hide one's minority status (Mason & Lewis, 2016; Meyer, 2003). Importantly, this stress is repetitive and persists over time (Meyer, 1995); further, minority stress occurs in conjunction with the stress that is experienced daily by all people. Together, these stressors negatively influence physical and mental health, even when taking into consideration the positive impact that minority status can have with regard to strength and resiliency (Mason & Lewis, 2015; Morrison & McCutcheon, 2012). Hatzenbuehler (2009) claims that minority stress results in emotion dysregulation, social and interpersonal problems (e.g., low social support), and cognitive processes that lead to greater risk for psychopathology.

Sexual minority stress has been found to increase susceptibility to eating disorder symptoms and body dissatisfaction. For example, in their study of 116, mainly white, American sexual minority individuals, Wang and Borders (2017) reported that participants were more likely to exhibit eating disorders, as measured by the Eating Attitudes Test (EAT; Garner & Garfinkel, 1979), if they experienced increased levels of minority stressors like discrimination and the need to conceal their sexual orientation. Similarly, Katz-Wise et al. (2015) conducted a longitudinal study and determined that minority stress was correlated with unhealthy eating behaviors in a sample of 1,461 principally white sexual minority youth aged 14 to 28. Using the EAT, Watson, Velez, Brownfield, and Flores (2016) also found the same association in their online sample of 353 American, primarily white, cisgender, bisexual women. In addition, Mason and Lewis (2015) surveyed 164 self-identified lesbian and bisexual women and discerned that minority stress was linked to binge eating behaviors in these groups as well (see also Bayer, Robert-McComb, Clopton, & Reich, 2017).

In terms of body dissatisfaction, Kimmel and Mahalik (2005) found that, for a sample of 357 gay men, minority stressors were linked to negative body image and masculine body ideal distress, which can be defined as stress associated with not meeting the muscular physique that is idealized in Western culture (Kimmel & Mahalik, 2004). In line with these findings, Brewster, Sandil, and DeBlaere (2017) determined that internalized heterosexism (i.e., "the internalization . . . of negative attitudes and assumptions about homosexuality [by sexual minority individuals]"; Szymanski, Kashubeck-West, & Meyer, 2008, p. 510)—a component of sexual minority stress—correlated positively with body shame in a sample of 326 cisgender sexual minority men. Similarly, Badenes-Ribera, Fabris, and Longobardi (2018) found that internalized homonegativity was positively linked to body image dissatisfaction in sexual minority men. The same relationship emerged for sexual minority women with regard to internalized heterosexism (see Watson, Grotewiel, Farrell, Marshik, & Schneider, 2015).

Taking into consideration those who have more than one minority identity, multiple minority stress also has received attention from researchers. Austin, Nelson, Birkett, Calzo, and Everett (2013) describe multiple minority stress as being intersectional in that it focuses on stressors that accompany being minoritized on the dimensions of gender, sexual orientation, and race. According to this model, persons who belong to more than one minority group experience additional stressors and, consequently, are at increased risk for health disadvantages. For instance, a Black lesbian woman may be at greater risk of engaging in pathogenic weight-control practices than a Black heterosexual woman or a white lesbian woman. Following up on prior research findings that sexual minority women were more likely to be classified as overweight (body mass index [BMI] $\geq$ 25) or fat (BMI $\geq$ 30), Yancey, Cochran, Corliss, and Mays (2003) found that lesbian or bisexual African American women were more likely to be classified as fat compared to lesbian or bisexual women of different racial backgrounds. However, these researchers did not measure stressors associated with belonging to minority groups, nor did they measure differences in BMI based on belonging to multiple minority groups (i.e., they only accounted for differences in BMI on the basis of race within the category of sexual minority women and did not survey heterosexual women of any race). Unfortunately, scant attention has been paid to elucidating how multiple minority stressors are associated with eating disorder symptoms or body dissatisfaction.

Sociocultural Theory

In brief, this theory focuses on the messages that media, family, and peers disseminate about physical appearance (Stice, 2002). According to Stice (2002), sociocultural factors leave their imprint on people through one of three processes: social reinforcement, modeling, and social comparison. Social reinforcement occurs when a person internalizes attitudes deemed appropriate by respected others and behaves in ways that those respected others would sanction. Modeling is the process whereby individuals copy the behaviors that they observe other people carrying out. Finally, proponents of social comparison theory (Festinger, 1954) assert that people have an innate drive to evaluate themselves, which leads to comparisons with (preferably similar) others when no objective criteria for evaluation are available (Morrison, Kalin, & Morrison, 2004). Stice (2002) claims that individuals compare themselves to idealized images of beauty and make upward social comparisons (i.e., the target of comparison is judged to be better than the individual on the characteristic of interest; Morrison, Kalin, & Morrison, 2004). All of these processes have the potential to increase a person's susceptibility to develop body dissatisfaction or an eating disorder. Moreover, the three processes described by Stice (2002) appear to map onto the tripartite influence model, which claims that pressure from media, peers, and family members leads individuals to develop body dissatisfaction and eating disorders (Van den Berg, Thompson, Obremski-Brandon, & Coovert, 2002). Specifically, two mediational variables that are included in the model (i.e., internalization of beauty ideals and comparison tendencies) seem to correspond with Stice's notions of social reinforcement and social comparison.

Proponents of sociocultural theory assert that differences between heterosexual and nonheterosexual persons in terms of body dissatisfaction and eating disorder rates stem from norms for sexual minorities, which deal with appearance and physical attributes (Calzo et al., 2017). To illustrate, Wiseman and Moradi (2010) express how sexual objectification by other sexual minority men and pressures to be attractive to potential partners contribute to sexual minority men's heightened susceptibility to develop eating disorders. Heterosexual men do not feel equivalent pressures to be attractive to women (Wiseman & Moradi, 2010). Studies also have shown that exposure to cultural artifacts like sexually explicit media have the potential to increase body dissatisfaction (e.g., Griffiths, Mitchison, Murray, & Mond, 2018).

Sociocultural factors also may increase gender minority persons' susceptibility to eating disorders and body dissatisfaction. In particular, transwomen may be especially vulnerable to internalizing sociocultural norms due to the fact that they are often not deemed to be "real women" and frequently must resort to medical and cosmetic procedures in order to achieve an ideal feminine body (Brewster et al., 2019). In their qualitative study of twenty transgender persons residing in Finland, Ålgars,

Alanko, Santilla, and Sandnabba (2012) discerned that the drive for thinness increased participants' risk of developing an eating disorder. Specifically, this drive, which is motivated in part by sociocultural appearance standards (Izydorczyk & Sitnik-Warchulska, 2018), was linked to attempts to suppress biological gendered characteristics or to enhance those features that are most characteristic of one's desired gender.

SGM individuals do not feel the effects of sociocultural factors to the same extent, though. For example, while gay men have been found, on average, to be more dissatisfied with their bodies than heterosexual men (Peplau et al., 2009), not all gay men are similarly dissatisfied with their appearance. To illustrate: Studies show that gay "bears"—a subset of gay men who are big and typically hairy—are often quite content with their appearance despite deviating from societal beauty norms for gay men (Gough & Flanders, 2009). It is possible that these individuals simply do not internalize sociocultural norms to the same extent as do other groups of gay men. Researchers seem to confirm this notion; they suggest that, despite comparable levels of *awareness* of sociocultural norms pertaining to appearance, individuals differ in the extent to which they *internalize* said norms. For example, studies show that gay men may be more likely than their heterosexual counterparts to be influenced by sociocultural factors (Gigi, Bachner-Melman, & Lev-Ari, 2016), while lesbian women may be less likely to internalize sociocultural beauty norms, such as the thin ideal, when compared to heterosexual women (Huxley, Halliwell, & Clarke 2015; Moore & Keel, 2003). (However, some studies detect no difference between lesbian and straight women [e.g., Koff, Lucas, Migliorini, & Grossmith, 2010; Legenbauer et al., 2009].)

Objectification Theory

Objectification theory serves as a mechanism through which women may experience body dissatisfaction and eating disorders. According to this theory, women are taught by society to view their bodies from an outsider's perspective, which leads to increased levels of body monitoring—a process known as self-objectification (Calogero, 2013)—and other, subsequent, adverse problems (e.g., body dissatisfaction; Fredrickson & Roberts, 1997). According to Fredrickson and Roberts (1997), objectification leads to eating disorders through one of two processes: (1) women may attempt to alleviate the sense of discomfort surrounding their supposed inadequate bodies through submitting to societal standards of attractiveness and altering their bodies accordingly and (2) women may reject what society tells them about their bodies and become the opposite of what mainstream society dictates as being attractive (e.g., fat; Orbach, 1978).

Objectification theory also has been applied to sexual minority persons. In their study of 243 American, primarily white, lesbian women, Watson et al. (2015) found that objectification theory, albeit with some significant alterations, could be used to describe the process whereby sexual minority women experience body dissatisfaction and eating disorders. Watson et al.'s version of objectification theory included heterosexist discrimination and internalized homonegativity, thus blending objectification theory with the minority stress model and sociocultural theory. Brewster et al. (2014) present similar findings with regard to bisexual women (i.e., sexual objectification leads to eating disorders).

Gender minority women, too, have been shown to experience sexual objectification (Garofalo, DeLeon, Osmer, Doll, & Harper, 2006). Interestingly, this is not always perceived as a negative experience (i.e., Nuttbrock et al. [2009] assert that episodes of sexual objectification may serve to affirm transwomen's gender identities by confirming that they are, in fact, women). In this way, objectification is demonstrated to have benefits. Turning to research that focuses on objectification theory and how it relates to eating disorders, one of the few studies to examine this relationship found that objectification served as a direct predictor of eating disorder symptomatology within a sample of transwomen (Brewster et al., 2019). Body surveillance (a component of objectification theory) also emerged as a predictor of body dissatisfaction. Thus, objectification theory may be used to account for disordered eating in gender and sexual minority women alike.

With respect to sexual minority men, Wiseman and Moradi (2010) assessed 231 mostly white, American, gay and bisexual men and determined that objectification theory served as an explanation for body dissatisfaction and eating disorders in this sample. Likewise, Brennan, Craig, and Thompson (2012) assert that objectification accounts for body dissatisfaction in both gay and bisexual men. Unfortunately, little research has explored how objectification impacts transgender men. Velez, Breslow, Brewster, Cox, and Foster (2016) did conduct one notable study that assessed objectification theory within this sample; however, that study is better categorized under the following subsection.

Pantheoretical Model of Dehumanization

The pantheoretical model of dehumanization, as originally outlined by Moradi (2013), serves as the fourth and final theory that will be the focus of this section. Incorporating elements of the prior three theories, it looks at how minority stressors, sociocultural norms, and objectification theory work in concert to increase SGM individuals' susceptibility to negative health outcomes including body dissatisfaction and eating disorder symptoms. While past studies have integrated elements of these theories, the pantheoretical model serves as the first attempt to create one overarching theory that encompasses all aspects of the other frameworks.

In one of the seminal articles evaluating the pantheoretical model, Velez and colleagues (2016) conducted a study of 304, primarily white, transgender men. They incorporated elements of the minority stress model and objectification theory, which included the internalization of sociocultural norms (i.e., sociocultural theory), in order to assess transgender men's compulsive exercising. Their study revealed mixed findings for the theory. Specifically, while internalization of sociocultural norms of attractiveness was directly linked to compulsive exercising, anti-transgender discrimination (a minority stressor) only served as an indirect predictor of body satisfaction and compulsive exercise.

Other studies that have integrated all three of the aforementioned theories have done so without adopting the moniker of the pantheoretical model. For example, in their study of 316 bisexual women, Brewster et al. (2014) assessed all three of these theories. The first major finding was that minority stressors such as anti-bisexual discrimination and internalized binegativity, directed at bisexual women by heterosexual, gay, and lesbian people alike, influenced bisexual women's processing and internalization of sociocultural norms about attractiveness. Another major finding was that sexual objectification experiences and the internalization of sociocultural norms, along with body shame, were each uniquely associated with eating disorders. Thus, it would appear that minority stressors contribute to the internalization of sociocultural norms (see also Brewster et al., 2017), which, alongside experiences of sexual objectification, contribute to the development of eating disorders. In their systematic review of thirty-nine studies on sexual minority women, Mason, Lewis, and Heron (2018) found that sexual objectification, minority stressors, and other similar variables (e.g., adherence to hegemonic gender roles) were linked to the internalization of sociocultural norms, which were then associated with body image concerns and, subsequently, eating disorders. Here, the difference is that objectification contributes to the internalization of sociocultural norms rather than working alongside it to influence body dissatisfaction and eating disorders. Clearly, this is a complex process with many interwoven relationships, and more studies are needed to clarify how exactly these theories work together.

Systematic Reviews of the Literature

In this section, systematic reviews focused on body image and eating disorders across SGM groups are discussed. In general, it appears that sexual minority groups, in comparison to their heterosexual peers, are at elevated risk of developing eating disorders such as anorexia nervosa, bulimia nervosa, and purging (Calzo et al., 2017). For transgender individuals, "body dissatisfaction is core to the distress" they experience, with this distress putting some trans people at risk of eating disorders (Jones et al., 2016, p. 91).

Gay Men

The established view in the area of eating disorders and body image among sexual minority groups is that, in comparison to their heterosexual counterparts, gay men are at heightened risk of developing negative body image. For example, in their meta-analytic review of twenty-seven studies, involving 1,397 heterosexual and 984 gay men, Morrison, Morrison, and Sager (2004) found that gay men evinced lower levels of body satisfaction, though the effect size was small (d = .29). To account for this difference, the authors contended that gay male culture may praise specific body ideals such as the muscular mesomorphic physique, disseminate the message that self-worth is contingent on attaining this ideal appearance, and devalue individuals who deviate from these narrow standards of attractiveness.

In contrast, Kane (2009, 2010) challenged the widely accepted belief that gay men are at higher risk of disordered eating and body image dissatisfaction. He asserts that these conclusions stem from shortcomings in the literature, including researchers' tendencies to pathologize gay men, a reliance on small and unrepresentative samples, and problematic data analysis methods (e.g., treating ordinal data as interval data).

Recent studies have addressed Kane's methodological critiques. For example, Frederick and Essayli (2016) reviewed five national online studies conducted between 2003 and 2012, examining differences between gay and heterosexual men in terms of body image, and the moderating role that BMI plays in the association between sexual orientation and body image. As noted by the authors, these studies sampled large numbers of sexual minority men (*ns* = 111,958 heterosexual and 4,398 gay men) and used homogeneous methods of recruitment (i.e., in contrast to most previous studies in which heterosexual and gay participants were recruited from different sources [e.g., classrooms vs. political activist groups], in the five studies, all participants were recruited from the official website of NBC News). The researchers found that, in comparison to heterosexual men, gay men reported higher levels of body dissatisfaction, greater investment in their appearance and interest in using body modification strategies, more appearance-related pressure, and greater engagement in social comparisons.

In a meta-analytic review of fourteen studies, published up to 2017, Badenes-Ribera et al. (2018) examined the relationship between internalized homonegativity and body image in sexual minority men. The results indicated a positive relationship between internalized homonegativity and different aspects of body image concerns, including muscularity-oriented body dissatisfaction, thinness-oriented body dissatisfaction, body surveillance, and body-related distress. To account for these findings, the authors argue that stereotypical associations between "homosexuality" and femininity, the experience of homonegative discrimination, as well as expectations of stigma may "encourage" gay men to pursue achieving a muscular physique as a coping strategy to appear more masculine and to defend themselves against heterosexism. The authors further contend that, due to these negative experiences, gay men may internalize homonegative attitudes and develop negative feelings about their bodies. However, the authors do issue the caveats that the number of studies sampled is modest and participants were primarily white.

Lesbian Women

The widely accepted view in the realms of body image and eating disorders among sexual minority women is that, compared to their heterosexual peers, lesbian women are less vulnerable to body image and disordered eating. However, available evidence does not uniformly support this position.

In a meta-analytic review of twenty-seven studies (*ns* = 1,391 heterosexual and 1,448 lesbian women), published from 1983 to 2002, Morrison, Morrison, and Sager (2004) investigated differences in body satisfaction between lesbian and heterosexual women. No differences were noted between the two groups. However, when lesbian and heterosexual women of similar weight status, as determined by BMI, were compared, lesbian women were slightly more satisfied with their bodies ($d = -.22$). To explain the negligible difference between these groups, the authors highlighted sociocultural pressures placed on women due to objectification of the female body in Western culture. They argue that while lesbian culture seems to possess more flexible norms about body appearance, this flexibility is unable to overcome the sociocultural messages that bombard women. This explanation remains speculative, however, due to a lack of empirical studies that focus more specifically on the dynamics of gay/lesbian culture.

In their systematic review of forty-five studies (*ns* = 372,256 women), published up to 2017, Meneguzzo et al. (2018) examined eating disorder diagnoses and symptoms in sexual minority women. Only seven studies examined diagnoses of eating disorders using standardized criteria such as the third and fourth editions of the *Diagnostic and Statistical Manual of Mental Disorders* (DSM). The authors found no significant differences between sexual minority and heterosexual women in terms of specific eating disorder diagnoses. Furthermore, in 38 papers that investigated various eating disorder symptoms, the results were inconsistent. For example, no statistically significant differences were found between sexual minority and heterosexual women with regard to symptoms such as dieting, fasting, diet pill use, and disordered eating. However, binging and purging appeared to occur more frequently among sexual minority women. In detail, four papers investigated binge eating: two of them showed no differences and two others showed higher prevalence among sexual minority women. Ten out of 11 papers showed purging was more common among sexual minority women. The results further indicated that the drive for thinness (five papers out of six) and body dissatisfaction (thirteen papers out of 24) were lower in lesbian women. (However, ten out of 24 studies focusing on body dissatisfaction found no differences between the two groups.) Overall, the authors concluded that sexual orientation does not appear to serve as a buffer against susceptibility to eating disorders. An important caveat is that, in some of the studies Meneguzzo et al. (2018) included in their review, lesbian and bisexual women were combined and treated as a homogenous group. More recent studies have identified some differences between these two groups. For example, Maloch, Bieschke, McAleavey, and Locke (2013) examined eating concerns in college women of different sexual orientation identities (*ns* = 1,440 heterosexual women, 830 lesbian women, 1,440 bisexual women, and 550 women questioning their sexual orientation identity). The researchers observed that bisexual women reported higher levels of eating concerns than did lesbian women. Shearer et al. (2015) replicated this finding.

Mason et al. (2018) systematically reviewed 39 studies that examined the correlates of disordered eating and body image concerns in sexual minority women. Their findings revealed that (1) disordered eating and body image issues were strongly interrelated in sexual minority women; (2) the correlates of disordered eating and body image concerns in sexual minority women were similar to those found in heterosexual women; (3) the associations between gender-related factors and disordered eating and body image concerns were unclear, though some studies showed that feminist attitudes, low levels of femininity, high levels of masculinity, and rejection of traditional gender roles were associated with lower levels of disordered eating and fewer body image concerns; and (4) factors related to sexual orientation (e.g., discrimination, internalized homonegativity/binegativity, and stigma consciousness) were related to eating disorders and body image problems.

MacDonald (2011) critically reviewed studies on eating disorders in queer women. The author reported that research in this area is scant, with equivocal findings. MacDonald also highlighted a number of heterosexist assumptions that need to be addressed by researchers. First, despite the heterogeneity of queer women (e.g., their diversity in terms of gender role orientation; namely, masculinity and femininity), they are erroneously deemed to be homogeneous and treated as a uniform group. Second, it is commonly assumed that queer women are protected from hegemonic standards of female beauty because these standards are designed to attract men's sexual attention. Nonetheless, queer women may feel trapped between the dominant standards of mainstream culture and the unique appearance norms that are fostered by the lesbian community. Third, disordered eating is not attributable solely to concerns about appearance; it may be adopted as a coping strategy by queer women in dealing with common stressors such as homonegativity/binegativity, sexism, and racism.

Bisexual Individuals

Unfortunately, there is limited information available about body image and disordered eating among bisexual persons. We could not find any systematic or meta-analytic reviews on eating disorders and body image among bisexual persons; however, some patterns are evident in the available literature.

Davids and Green (2011) compared body dissatisfaction and eating disorders among gay/lesbian (*ns* = 51 women, 96 men), bisexual (*ns* = 139 women, 37 men), and heterosexual (*ns* = 82 women, 34 men) individuals recruited online from forty states in the United States. The researchers found that the level of body dissatisfaction in bisexual men was greater than in heterosexual men, and equivalent to that reported by gay men. However, no statistically significant differences were observed among lesbian, bisexual, and heterosexual women. With regard to eating disorders, bisexual individuals (men and women) showed greater eating disorder symptomatology as compared to heterosexual individuals. For bisexual men, the drive for muscularity was inversely associated with body dissatisfaction, and exercise frequency was significantly related to eating disorders. Moreover, for gay men, BMI, gay community involvement, and maladaptive social comparison predicted body dissatisfaction, and both gay community involvement and body dissatisfaction were statistically significant predictors of eating disorders. For bisexual women, BMI and self-esteem were associated with body dissatisfaction, and gay community involvement and body dissatisfaction were significantly related to eating disorders. Body dissatisfaction also was a significant predictor of eating disorder symptoms in both lesbian and heterosexual women. Similar to bisexual women, higher BMI and lower self-esteem were predictors of body dissatisfaction for heterosexual women.

Transgender People

In general, it seems that two factors are of considerable importance when investigating body image and eating disorders among transgender people: female identity (either assigned at birth or desired) and body parts. A female identity (among both cis and trans persons) has already been shown to be a risk factor for intensified drive for thinness (Castellini, Lelli, Ricca, & Maggi, 2016; Witcomb et al., 2015). Also, while body dissatisfaction appears to be higher in cisgender females than cisgender males, it is higher in transmen than transwomen. The body parts that are reported to cause the most body dissatisfaction are those related to body shape and those associated with "attaining the outward appearance of the gender the person experiences themselves as [being]" (Witcomb et al., 2015, p. 291). Dissatisfaction with body shape (stomach, waist, hips, and buttocks) may, on the surface, suggest a risk for disordered eating because the dissatisfaction is rooted in aspects of the body that could be changed by dietary restriction.

The reviews we surveyed show that trans persons are conspicuously understudied in the literature on body image and disordered eating. To illustrate, we could locate only *one* published systematic review that focused on trans people. Based on their assessment of thirty-nine studies, Jones et al. (2016) concluded that (1) body dissatisfaction is a key factor to the distress trans people experience, which may make them vulnerable to developing eating disorders; (2) gender dysphoria treatment (e.g., hormones and sex reassignment surgery) can elevate body satisfaction among trans people, and this increase is assumed to be the result of sex-specific body parts becoming more in line with gender identity; and (3) trans individuals may develop disordered eating but this does not appear to be clinically significant. To account for these findings, the authors forward several suggestions. First, the gap some trans people feel between their assigned sex at birth and their desired gender seems to be one of the most important factors causing body dissatisfaction. Second, some trans persons might try to align their natal physique with that of their desired gender identity; however, since some of the features of their natal sex cannot be modified (e.g., broad shoulders in transwomen), this may increase their level of body dissatisfaction. Third, transwomen might internalize hegemonic female beauty standards and struggle to appear thinner and more feminine. Finally, despite the high level of body dissatisfaction among trans individuals, the low prevalence of eating disorders among this group may be rooted in dissatisfaction with body parts that cannot be changed through eating behaviors.

Challenges to Current Understanding

Our aforementioned summaries of key theoretical frameworks as well as narrative and meta-analytic reviews of the literature concerning SGM people and body image evaluation, body image investment, and disordered eating indicated some major challenges to understanding. In this section, we discuss each of these challenges separately.

Operationalization/Measurement of Sexual Minority Culture

Many researchers refer to "gay and lesbian culture" to account for differences between gay men versus heterosexual men and lesbian women versus heterosexual women. For example, researchers operate from the assumption that gay male culture exalts adherence to a particular body ideal, and that gay men deviating from this ideal evidence dissatisfaction with their appearance (Morrison, Morrison, & Sager, 2004). In contrast, lesbian culture is presumed to be more lenient with the body standards it promotes, which, in turn, may serve as a buffer against internalizing rigid appearance norms (Mason et al., 2018). These explanations are speculative, and the putative influence of "gay and lesbian culture" on body image and disordered eating is unclear. Although there have been studies documenting gay men's views about the ideal physique as well as the ways in which these views are disseminated (e.g., via cultural products such as media), there is limited insight about the factors that increase versus decrease gay men's acceptance of these messages. Critically, our review of the literature shows that there is no consensus with respect to how terms such as "gay and lesbian culture" and the "LGBT community" should be measured. To illustrate, researchers use different indicators of gay community involvement such as participation in HIV/AIDS and LGBT organizations (Ramirez-Valles, Kuhns, Campbell, & Diaz, 2010); socialization with other gay individuals (Barrett & Pollack, 2005); engagement with gay media such as newspapers, magazines, movies, and television shows (Davids, Watson, Nilsson, & Marszalek, 2015); involvement in social and political movements focusing on sexual minorities (Davids et al., 2015; Ramirez-Valles et al., 2010); and sense of connectedness to the gay community (Frost & Meyer, 2012).

Combining these factors, Foster-Gimbel, Doyle, and Engeln (2018) recently created a new measure entitled the Gay Community Involvement Index (GCII). While the GCII is more comprehensive than older measures, inspection of this scale reveals critical problems. First, many of the items on the GCII are designed for privileged urban gay men who have access to gay organizations, gatherings, clubs, bars, and sports teams (e.g., "I am involved with a sport team/organization for gay men," "I frequent gay bars/clubs"). A gay man who lives in a rural area, for example, would have limited access to many of the activities detailed on the GCII and, consequently, would obtain a low score suggesting minimal involvement with the gay community. Second, the degree to which the activities detailed in the GCII resonate with gay men is unclear. A gay man who does not participate in LGBTQ political activities and has no desire to do so likely differs from a gay man who does not currently participate in said activities yet has a fervent wish to become more involved. One possible solution would be to provide an array of *content valid* items that assess gay community involvement and request that participants select the items that *they* regard as most important (see Bowling, 1995). Respondents then could evaluate their prioritized list in terms of satisfaction with their current level of involvement. Of particular relevance to the domains of body image and disordered eating would be gay men's prioritization of elements of "gay culture" that emphasize appearance (e.g., dating apps). A final limitation of the GCII is that it does not consider "virtual" (i.e., parasocial) involvement with facets of the gay community. Available research suggests this omission may lead to underestimating gay men's involvement with facets of their community. To illustrate, in a national survey examining use of social media, television, radio, and the internet among adults of various sexual orientations, the authors found that LGB respondents reported greater use of online media and significantly greater odds of having several accounts (i.e., three or more) on social media such as Facebook, Twitter, and YouTube (Seidenberg et al., 2017). Large proportions of LGB participants also reported weekly television (>90 percent) and radio (75 percent) use.

Acknowledgment of Intragroup Variability

By focusing on intergroup differences (typically, gay or lesbian versus straight), *intra*group variabilities that, potentially, have different implications for body image and disordered eating have been elided. For example, the umbrella terms *gay* and *lesbian* overshadow discrepancies between subgroups that have their own appearance standards (e.g., "bears" and "daddies" within the gay community). In contrast to mainstream gay culture, the gay "bear" subculture defines large, bulky, hirsute, and bearded men as sexually desirable (Quidley-Rodriguez & Santis, 2017). "Twinks," another subgroup of gay men, are typically young and thin with clean-shaven faces and hairless bodies (Lyons & Hosking, 2014). A few researchers have examined body image in gay and lesbian subgroups. For example, in a qualitative study, McGrady (2016) investigated resistance against weight and sexual orientation stigma in twenty-one bear-identified individuals. The participants described bear culture as a "place of relief" since it had offered them new appearance standards based on which they redefined their bodies from being unattractive and overweight to desirable. With regard to lesbian subcultures, Henrichs-Beck and Szymanski (2017) also examined the influences of various dimensions of gender expression on lesbian women's body dissatisfaction (*ns* = 416 self-identified lesbian women [18 percent butch, 37 percent femme, 21 percent androgynous, and 24 percent none]). These sorts of studies highlight the differences between lesbian and gay subgroups in terms of body image and call for more research to examine *intra*group variability. Moreover, factors that (potentially) have implications for body image and disordered eating including HIV status (Kelly, Langdon, & Serpell, 2009), age (Watson et al. 2016), internalized homonegativity (Wiseman & Moradi, 2010), and physical characteristics such as (non-) sex-related body parts (Becker et al., 2016) have received limited empirical scrutiny.

Measurement of Sexual Orientation

Our review suggests that most studies use Kinsey-type single-item measures of sexual orientation that conceptualize this variable as a single continuum with heterosexual and gay/lesbian sexual orientations located at the two end points and bisexuality situated in the middle. Unfortunately, this type of measure ignores the variety of sexual orientations that fall between these end points, treating them as a homogenous group and often mislabeling them as bisexual (Savin-Williams, 2018). For example, in a qualitative study, Galupo, Mitchell, Grynkiewicz, and Davis (2014) examined 285 sexual minority participants' opinions about two traditional scales (the Kinsey scale and the Klein Sexual Orientation Grid). Respondents, particularly those identifying as plurisexual (i.e., bisexual, pansexual, queer, and fluid) and transgender, claimed that these scales were not representative of their sexual orientation. They criticized traditional conceptualizations of sexuality and sexual orientation that are fixated on dichotomous assumptions of sex/gender and questioned why sexual orientation is presented on a spectrum with attractions to the same or other sex as opposite poles.

To address these sorts of limitations, some researchers have instructed participants to self-identify their sexual orientation. However, this method also can be inaccurate because it disregards aspects of sexual orientation such as attraction and behavior and ignores individuals whose sexual practices might not be congruent with their sexual identity (e.g., men who have sex with men; Mason et al., 2018). Additionally, relying on self-identification may be problematic when participants are young, uncertain about their sexual orientation, and/or afraid of violating dominant heterosexual norms (Kane, 2010; Morrison & McCutcheon, 2012).

Acknowledgment of Bisexuality

The dearth of studies specific to bisexual individuals has resulted in limited and often variable information about body image and eating disorders in this population. Additionally, numerous questions remain unanswered. For example, do bisexual cisgender men and women follow specific beauty norms that make them more or less susceptible to body image dissatisfaction and disordered eating? How does exposure to "gay and lesbian culture" as well as hegemonic heterosexual culture influence their perceptions of their bodies? Do bisexual persons' feelings about their physical appearance vary depending on the sex of their partner? Qualitative research offers some insight on the latter question. Specifically, Chmielewski and Yost (2013) reported that a minority of participants (i.e., two out of six women) reported greater body surveillance with their female partners compared to their male partners. A more recent study conducted by Smith, Telford, and Tree (2019) similarly found that most of their bisexual female participants (i.e., five out of six) believed they would experience greater levels of body dissatisfaction when in a relationship with a female partner (i.e., the similarities between their body and their partner's body would trigger social comparisons on the dimension of appearance). These findings are in contrast to the dominant belief that women in same-sex relationships experience greater levels of body satisfaction.

Recognition of Intersectionality

It is critical to acknowledge that sexual minority individuals simultaneously have other identities related to a host of variables including race, ethnicity, disability, and socioeconomic status. The term *intersectionality*, which is "the mutually constitutive relations among social identities" (Shields, 2008, p. 301), refers to the myriad ways in which these diverse identities intersect. Further, the interrelationships of these identities have the potential to influence body image and eating concerns in multifarious ways. Some researchers have employed an intersectional framework in their studies on sexual minorities' body image. For example, in a qualitative study, Brennan et al. (2013) explored body image among ethnoracialized gay and bisexual men. The participants reported that they were struggling with dual body oppressions. On the one hand, they felt extreme pressure to meet the beauty standards of the predominantly white gay culture. On the other hand, due to racial/ethnic stereotypes, they believed their bodies were either rendered invisible and marginalized or fetishized and objectified. More studies are needed to explore body image and eating disorders in sexual minority individuals of intersectional identities.

Another direction for future research concerns developing measures of intersectionality that are pertinent to the domains of body image and eating disorders. To this aim, researchers should strive to (1) create scales that take multiple (i.e., more than two) identities into consideration (akin to Scheim and Bauer's [2019] Intersectional Discrimination Index) and (2) particularize whether the salience of identities is stable or situationally determined.

Lack of Cross-Cultural Studies

The final challenge facing research on body dissatisfaction and eating disorders as experienced by SGM individuals is the dearth of studies coming from certain countries, primarily located in the Global South (e.g., countries in Africa and South America) but also including nations like China. Indeed, with few exceptions, most of the studies highlighted in this chapter were conducted in the United States. Even those studies that focus on people of Asian or African descent tend to do so within an American context (e.g., Yancey et al., 2003). This is problematic because different countries have different norms, standards, or even laws with regard to what is acceptable in terms of outward expressions of gender and sexuality. Moreover, nations differ in terms of how they treat those who suffer from body dissatisfaction and eating disorders. To this extent, research conducted in the United States might tell us very little about SGM individuals suffering from body dissatisfaction and/or eating disorders in non-Westernized parts of the world. Clearly, more studies are needed from other countries; however, the solution is not as straightforward as one might assume. Take those nations where homosexuality is illegal, for instance. How does one collect data on SGM individuals in a country where belonging to such a group is a punishable offense? Such regions must be taken into consideration, and it is unreasonable to think that data on SGM groups will be available from these countries in the near future.

References

Ålgars, M., Alanko, K., Santilla, P., & Sandnabba, N. K. (2012). Disordered eating and gender identity disorder: A qualitative study. *Eating Disorders, 20*, 300–11. doi:10.1080/10640266.2012.668482

Austin, S. B., Nelson, L. A., Birkett, M. A., Calzo, J. P., & Everett, B. (2013). Eating disorder symptoms and obesity at the intersections of gender, ethnicity, and sexual orientation in US high school students. *Research and Practice, 103*, 16–22. doi:10.2105/AJPH.2012.301150

Badenes-Ribera, L., Fabris, M. A., & Longobardi, C. (2018). The relationship between internalized homonegativity and body image concerns in sexual minority men: A meta-analysis. *Psychology & Sexuality, 9*, 251–68. doi:10.1080/19419899.2018.1476905

Barrett, D. C., & Pollack, L. M. (2005). Whose gay community? Social class, sexual self-expression, and gay community involvement. *Sociological Quarterly, 46*, 437–56. doi:10.1111/j.1533-8525.2005.00021.x

Bayer, V., Robert-McComb, J. J., Clopton, J. R., & Reich, D. A. (2017). Investigating the influence of shame, depression, and distress tolerance on the relationship between internalized homophobia and binge eating in lesbian and bisexual women. *Eating Behaviors, 24*, 39–44. doi:10.1016/j.eatbeh.2016.12.001

Becker, I., Nieder, T. O., Cerwenka, S., Briken, P., Kreukels, B. P., Cohen-Kettenis, P. T., . . . Richter-Appelt, H. (2016). Body image in young gender dysphoric adults: A European multi-center study. *Archives of Sexual Behavior, 45*, 559–74. doi:10.1007/s10508-015-0527-z

Bowling, A. (1995). What things are important in people's lives? A survey of the public's judgements to inform scales of health-related quality of life. *Social Science & Medicine, 41*, 1447–62. doi:10.1016/0277-9536(95)00113-L

Brennan, D. J., Asakura, K., George, C., Newman, P. A., Giwa, S., Hart, T. A., . . . Betancourt, G. (2013). "Never reflected anywhere": Body image among ethnoracialized gay and bisexual men. *Body Image, 10*, 389–98. doi:10.1016/j.bodyim.2013.03.006

Brennan, D. J., Craig, S. L., & Thompson, D. E. A. (2012). Factors associated with a drive for muscularity among gay and bisexual men. *Culture, Health & Sexuality, 14*, 1–15. doi:10.1080/13691058.2011.619578

Brewster, M. E., Sandil, R., & DeBlaere, C. (2017). "Do you even lift, bro?" Objectification, minority stress, and body image concerns for sexual minority men. *Psychology of Men and Masculinity, 18*, 87–98. https://psycnet.apa.org/doi/10.1037/men0000043

Brewster, M. E., Velez, B. L., Breslow, A. S., & Geiger, E. F. (2019). Unpacking body image concerns and disordered eating for transgender women: The roles of sexual objectification and minority stress. *Journal of Counseling Psychology, 66*, 131–42. https://psycnet.apa.org/doi/10.1037/cou0000333

Brewster, M. E., Velez, B. L., Esposito, J., Wong, S., Geiger, E., & Keum, B. T. (2014). Moving beyond the binary with disordered eating research: A test and extension of objectification theory with bisexual women. *Journal of Counseling Psychology, 61*, 50–62. https://psycnet.apa.org/doi/10.1037/a0034748

Brooks, V. R. (1981). *Minority stress and lesbian women*. Lanham, MD: Lexington Books.

Calogero, R. M. (2013). Objects don't object: Evidence that self-objectification disrupts women's social activism. *Psychological Science, 24*, 312–8. doi:10.1177%2F0956797612452574

Calzo, J. P., Blashill, A. J., Brown, T. A., & Argenal, R. L. (2017). Eating disorders and disordered weight and shape control behaviors in sexual minority populations. *Current Psychiatry Reports, 19*, 49–58. doi:10.1007/s11920-017-0801-y

Castellini, G., Lelli, L., Ricca, V., & Maggi, M. (2016). Sexuality in eating disorders patients: Etiological factors, sexual dysfunction and identity issues. A systematic review. *Hormone Molecular Biology and Clinical Investigation, 25*, 71–90. doi:10.1515/hmbci-2015-0055

Chmielewski, J. F., & Yost, M. R. (2013). Psychosocial influences on bisexual women's body image: Negotiating gender and sexuality. *Psychology of Women Quarterly, 37*, 224–41. doi:10.1177%2F0361684311426126

Davids, C. M., & Green, M. A. (2011). A preliminary investigation of body dissatisfaction and eating disorder symptomatology with bisexual individuals. *Sex Roles, 65*, 533–48. doi:10.1007/s11199-011-9963-y

Davids, C. M., Watson, L. B., Nilsson, J. E., & Marszalek, C. M. (2015). Body dissatisfaction among gay men: The roles of sexual objectification, gay community involvement, and psychological sense of community. *Psychology of Sexual Orientation and Gender Diversity, 2*, 376–85. doi:doi/10.1037/sgd0000127

Festinger, L. (1954). A theory of social comparison processes. *Human Relations, 7*, 117–40.

Foster-Gimbel, O., Doyle, D. M., & Engeln, R. (2018). The Gay Community Involvement Index: An exploratory factor analysis and initial validation of a new measure of gay community involvement. *Archives of Sexual Behavior*. doi:10.1007/s10508-018-1271-y

Frederick, D. A., & Essayli, J. H. (2016). Male body image: The roles of sexual orientation and body mass index across five national US studies. *Psychology of Men & Masculinity, 17*, 336–51. https://psycnet.apa.org/doi/10.1037/men0000031

Fredrickson, B. L., & Roberts, T. -A. (1997). Objectification theory: Toward understanding women's lived experiences and mental health risks. *Psychology of Women Quarterly, 21*, 173–206. doi:10.1111/j.1471-6402.1997.tb00108.x

Frost, D. M., & Meyer, I. H. (2012). Measuring community connectedness among diverse sexual minority populations. *Journal of Sex Research, 49*, 36–49. doi:10.1080/00224499.2011.565427

Galupo, M. P., Mitchell, R. C., Grynkiewicz, A. L., & Davis, K. S. (2014). Sexual minority reflections on the Kinsey Scale and the Klein Sexual Orientation Grid: Conceptualization and measurement. *Journal of Bisexuality, 14*, 404–32. doi:10.1080/15299716.2014.929553

Garner, D. M., & Garfinkel, P. E (1979). The Eating Attitudes Test: An index of the symptoms of anorexia nervosa. *Psychological Medicine, 9*, 273–9. doi:10.1017/S0033291700030762

Garofalo, R., Deleon, J., Osmer, E., Doll, M., & Harper, G. W. (2006). Overlooked, misunderstood and at-risk: Exploring the lives and HIV risk of ethnic minority male-to-female transgender youth. *Journal of Adolescent Health, 38*, 230–6. doi:10.1016/j.jadohealth.2005.03.023

Gigi, I., Bachner-Melman, R., & Lev-Ari, L. (2016). The association between sexual orientation, susceptibility to social messages and disordered eating in men. *Appetite, 99*, 25–33. doi:10.1016/j.appet.2015.12.027

Gough, B., & Flanders, G. (2009). Celebrating "obese" bodies: Gay "bears" talk about weight, body image and health. *International Journal of Men's Health, 8*, 235–53. doi:10.3149/jmh.0803.235

Griffiths, S., Mitchison, D., Murray, S. B., & Mond, J. M. (2018). Pornography use in sexual minority males: Associates with body dissatisfaction, eating disorder symptoms, thought about using anabolic steroids and quality of life. *Australian and New Zealand Journal of Psychiatry, 52*, 339–48. doi:10.1177%2F0004867417728807

Hatzenbuehler, M. L. (2009). How does sexual minority stigma get under the skin? A psychological mediation framework. *Psychological Bulletin, 135*, 707–30. https://psycnet.apa.org/doi/10.1037/a0016441

Hendricks, M. L., & Testa, R. J. (2012). A conceptual framework for clinical work with transgender and gender nonconforming clients: An adaptation of the minority stress model. *Professional Psychology: Research and Practice, 43*, 460–7. https://psycnet.apa.org/doi/10.1037/a0029597

Henrichs-Beck, C. L., & Szymanski, D. M. (2017). Gender expression, body–gender identity incongruence, thin ideal internalization, and lesbian body dissatisfaction. *Psychology of Sexual Orientation and Gender Diversity, 4*, 23–33. https://psycnet.apa.org/doi/10.1037/sgd0000214

Huxley, C. J., Halliwell, E., & Clarke, C. (2015). An examination of the tripartite influence model of body image: Does women's sexual identity make a difference? *Psychology of Women Quarterly, 39*, 337–48. doi:10.1177%2F0361684314554917

Izydorczyk, B., & Sitnik-Warchulska, K. (2018). Sociocultural appearance standards and risk factors for eating disorders in adolescents and women of various ages. *Frontiers in Psychology, 9*, 1–11. doi:10.3389/fpsyg.2018.00429

Jones, B. A., Haycraft, E., Murjan, S., & Arcelus, J. (2016). Body dissatisfaction and disordered eating in trans people: A systematic review of the literature. *International Review of Psychiatry, 28*, 81–94. doi:10.3109/09540261.2015.1089217

Kane, G. (2009). Unmasking the gay male body ideal: A critical analysis of the dominant research on gay men's body image issues. *Gay & Lesbian Issues & Psychology Review, 5*(1), 20–33.

Kane, G. D. (2010). Revisiting gay men's body image issues: Exposing the fault lines. *Review of General Psychology, 14*, 311–7. doi:10.1037%2Fa0020982

Katz-Wise, S. L., Calzo, J. P., Scherer, E. A., Sarda, V., Jackson, B., Haines, J. & Austin, S. B. (2015). Sexual minority stressors, internalizing symptoms, and unhealthy eating behaviors in sexual minority youth. *Annals of Behavioral Medicine, 49*, 839–52. doi:10.1007/s12160-015-9718-z

Kelly, J. S., Langdon, D., & Serpell, L. (2009). The phenomenology of body image in men living with HIV. *AIDS Care, 21*, 1560–7. doi:10.1080/09540120902923014

Kimmel, S. B., & Mahalik, J. R. (2004). Measuring masculine body ideal distress: Development of a measure. *International Journal of Men's Health, 3*, 1–10.

Kimmel, S. B., & Mahalik, J. R. (2005). Body image concerns of gay men: The roles of minority stress and conformity to masculine norms. *Journal of Counseling and Clinical Psychology, 73*, 1185–90. https://psycnet.apa.org/doi/10.1037/0022-006X.73.6.1185.

Koff, E., Lucas, M., Migliorini, R., & Grossmith, S. (2010). Women and body dissatisfaction: Does sexual orientation make a difference? *Body Image, 7*, 255–8. doi:10.1016/j.bodyim.2010.03.001.

Legenbauer, T., Vocks, S., Schäfer, C., Schütt-Strömel, S., Hiller, W., Wagner, C., & Vögele, C. (2009). Preference for attractiveness and thinness in a partner: Influence of internalization of the thin ideal and shape/weight dissatisfaction in heterosexual women, heterosexual men, lesbians, and gay men. *Body Image, 6*, 228–34.

Lyons, A., & Hosking, W. (2014). Health disparities among common subcultural identities of young gay men: Physical, mental, and sexual health. *Archives of Sexual Behavior, 43*, 1621–35. doi:10.1007/s10508-014-0315-1

MacDonald, D. E. (2011). Impossible bodies, invisible battles: Feminist perspectives on the psychological research on and treatment of eating disorders in queer women. *Journal of Gay & Lesbian Social Services, 23*, 452–64. doi:10.1080/10538720.2011.611100

Maloch, J. K., Bieschke, K. J., McAleavey, A. A., & Locke, B. D. (2013). Eating concerns in college women across sexual orientation identities. *Journal of College Counseling, 16*, 275–88. doi:10.1002/j.2161-1882.2013.00042.x

Mason, T. B., & Lewis, R. J. (2015). Minority stress and binge eating among lesbian and bisexual women. *Journal of Homosexuality, 62*, 971–92. doi:10.1080/00918369.2015.1008285

Mason, T. B., & Lewis, R. J. (2016). Minority stress, body shame, and binge eating among lesbian women: Social anxiety as a linking mechanism. *Psychology of Women Quarterly, 40*, 428–40. doi:10.1177%2F0361684316635529

Mason, T. B., Lewis, R. J., & Heron, K. E. (2018). Disordered eating and body image concerns among sexual minority women: A systematic review and testable model. *Psychology of Sexual Orientation and Gender Diversity, 5*, 397–422. https://psycnet.apa.org/doi/10.1037/sgd0000293

McGrady, P. B. (2016). "Grow the beard, wear the costume": Resisting weight and sexual orientation stigmas in the bear subculture. *Journal of Homosexuality, 63*, 1698–725. doi:10.1080/00918369.2016.1151695

Meneguzzo, P., Collantoni, E., Gallicchio, D., Busetto, P., Solmi, M., Santonastaso, P., & Favaro, A. (2018). Eating disorders symptoms in sexual minority women: A systematic review. *European Eating Disorders Review, 26*, 275–92. doi:10.1002/erv.2601

Meyer, I. H. (1995). Minority stress and mental health in gay men. *Journal of Health and Social Behavior, 36*, 38–56.

Meyer, I. H. (2003). Prejudice, social stress, and mental health in lesbian, gay, and bisexual populations: Conceptual issues and research evidence. *Psychological Bulletin, 129*, 674–97. https://psycnet.apa.org/doi/10.1037/0033-2909.129.5.674

Moore, F., & Keel, P. K. (2003). Influence of sexual orientation and age on disordered eating attitudes and behaviors in women. *International Journal of Eating Disorders, 34*, 370–4. doi:10.1002/eat.10198

Moradi, B. (2013). *Discrimination, objectification, and dehumanization: Toward a pantheoretical framework.*

Presented at 60th Nebraska Symposium on Motivation, Lincoln, 2013. New York, NY: Springer. doi:10.1007/978-1-4614-6959-9.

Morrison, M. A., Morrison, T. G., & Sager, C. L. (2004). Does body satisfaction differ between gay men and lesbian women and heterosexual men and women? A meta-analytic review. *Body Image, 1,* 127–38. doi:10.1016/j.bodyim.2004.01.002

Morrison, T. G., Kalin, R., & Morrison, M. A. (2004). Body-image evaluation and body-image investment among adolescents: A test of sociocultural and social comparison theories. *Adolescence, 39,* 571–92.

Morrison, T. G., & McCutcheon, J. M. (2012). Body image among gay, lesbian, and bisexual individuals. In T. Cash (Ed.), *Encyclopedia of body image and human appearance* (Vol. 1, pp. 103–7). San Diego, CA: Academic Press.

Nuttbrock, L. A., Bockting, W. O., Hwahng, S, Rosenblum, A., Mason, M., Macri, M., & Becker, J (2009). Gender identity affirmation among male-to-female transgender persons: A life course analysis across types of relationships and cultural/lifestyle factors. *Sexual and Relationship Therapy, 24,* 108–25. doi:10.1080/14681990902926764

Orbach, S. (1978). *Fat is a feminist issue: A self-help guide for compulsive eaters.* New York, NY: Berkley Books.

Peplau, L. A., Frederick, D. A., Yee, C., Maisel, N., Lever, J., & Ghavami, N. (2009). Body image satisfaction in heterosexual, gay, and lesbian adults. *Archives of Sexual Behavior, 38,* 713–25. doi:10.1007/s10508-008-9378-1

Quidley-Rodriguez, N., & De Santis, J. P. (2017). A literature review of health risks in the bear community, a gay subculture. *American Journal of Men's Health, 11,* 1673–9. doi:10.1177%2F1557988315624507

Ramirez-Valles, J., Kuhns, L. M., Campbell, R. T., & Diaz, R. M. (2010). Social integration and health: Community involvement, stigmatized identities, and sexual risk in Latino sexual minorities. *Journal of Health and Social Behavior, 51,* 30–47. doi:10.1177%2F0022146509361176

Ryan, T. A., & Morrison, T. G. (2009). Factors perceived to influence young Irish men's body image investment: A qualitative investigation. *International Journal of Men's Health, 8*(3), 213–34.

Savin-Williams, R. C. (2018). An exploratory study of exclusively heterosexual, primarily heterosexual, and mostly heterosexual young men. *Sexualities, 21,* 16–29. doi:10.1177%2F1363460716678559.

Scheim, A. I., & Bauer, G. R. (2019). The Intersectional Discrimination Index: Development and validation of measures of self-reported enacted and anticipated discrimination for intercategorical analysis. *Social Science & Medicine, 226,* 225–35. doi:10.1016/j.socscimed.2018.12.016

Seidenberg, A., Jo, C., Ribisl, K., Lee, J., Buchting, F., Kim, Y., & Emery, S. (2017). A national study of social media, television, radio, and internet usage of adults by sexual orientation and smoking status: Implications for campaign design. *International Journal of Environmental Research and Public Health, 14,* 450. doi:10.3390/ijerph14040450

Shearer, A., Russon, J., Herres, J., Atte, T., Kodish, T., & Diamond, G. (2015). The relationship between disordered eating and sexuality amongst adolescents and young adults. *Eating Behaviors, 19,* 115–9. doi:10.1016/j.eatbeh.2015.08.001

Shields, S. A. (2008). Gender: An intersectionality perspective. *Sex Roles, 59,* 301–11. doi:10.1007/s11199-008-9501-8

Smith, M. L., Telford, E., & Tree, J. J. (2019). Body image and sexual orientation: The experiences of lesbian and bisexual women. *Journal of Health Psychology, 24*(9), 1178–90. doi:10.1177/1359105317694486

Stice, E. (2002) Sociocultural influences on body image and eating disturbance. In C. G. Fairburn & K. D. Brownell (Eds.), *Eating disorders and obesity: A comprehensive handbook* (pp. 103–7). New York, NY: Guilford Press.

Szymanski, D. M., Kashubeck-West, S., & Meyer, J. (2008). Internalized heterosexism: A historical and theoretical overview. *The Counseling Psychologist, 36,* 510–24. doi:10.1177%2F0011000007309488

Van den Berg, P., Thompson, J. K., Obremski-Brandon, K., & Coovert, M. (2002). The tripartite influence model of body image and eating disturbance: A covariance structure modeling investigation testing the mediational role of appearance comparison. *Journal of Psychosomatic Research, 53,* 1007–20. doi:10.1016/S0022-3999(02)00499

Velez, B. L., Breslow, A. S., Brewster, M. E., Cox, R. Jr., & Foster, A. B. (2016). Building a pantheoretical model of dehumanization with transgender men: Integrating objectification and minority stress theories. (2016). *Journal of Counseling Psychology, 63,* 497–508. https://psycnet.apa.org/doi/10.1037/cou0000136

Wang, S. B., & Borders, A. (2017). Rumination mediates the associations between sexual minority stressors and disordered eating, particularly for men. *Eating and Weight Disorders, 22,* 699–706. doi:10.1007/s40519-016-0350-0

Watson, L. B., Grotewiel, M., Farrell, M., Marshik, J., & Schneider, M. (2015). Experiences of sexual objectification, minority stress, and disordered eating among sexual minority women. *Psychology of Women Quarterly, 39,* 458–70. doi:10.1177%2F0361684315575024

Watson, L. B., Velez, B. L., Brownfield, J., & Flores, M. J. (2016). Minority stress and bisexual women's disordered eating: The role of maladaptive coping. *Counseling Psychologist, 44*(8), 1158–86. doi:10.1177%2F0011000016669233

Wiseman, M. C., & Moradi, B. (2010). Body image and eating disorder symptoms in sexual minority men: A test and extension of objectification theory. *Journal of Counseling Psychology, 57,* 154–66. https://psycnet.apa.org/doi/10.1037/a0018937

Witcomb, G. L., Bouman, W. P., Brewin, N., Richards, C., Fernandez-Aranda, F., & Arcelus, J. (2015). Body image dissatisfaction and eating-related psychopathology in trans individuals: A matched control study. *European Eating Disorders Review, 23,* 287–93. doi:10.1002/erv.2362

Yancey, A. K., Cochran, S. D., Corliss, H. L., & Mays, V. M (2003). Correlates of overweight and obesity among lesbian and bisexual women. *Preventive Medicine, 36,* 676–83. doi:10.1016/S0091-7435(03)00020-3

CHAPTER

8 Alcohol Use Disorders among Sexual and Gender Minority Populations

Phoenix R. Crane, Katarina S. Swaringen, Anthony M. Foster, *and* Amelia E. Talley

Abstract

Sexual and gender minority populations are at a heightened risk of developing alcohol-related problems, such as alcohol use disorder, compared to their heterosexual, cisgender counterparts. The present chapter presents recent prevalence rates of alcohol use disorder and examines how relations among sexual orientation, gender, and alcohol use are influenced by mechanisms relevant to minority stress theory, the intersectionality framework, and other social factors such as racism, sexism, homophobia, sexual victimization, and stigma. This chapter also explores available intervention and treatment initiatives for alcohol misuse in sexual and gender minority populations, suggesting empirically informed approaches to maximize the effectiveness of tailored programs.

Keywords: gay alcohol use disorder, lesbian alcohol use disorder, MSM alcohol use disorder, WSW alcohol use disorder, bisexual alcohol use disorder, transgender alcohol use disorder, LGBT alcohol use disorder

Previous literature has revealed that sexual and gender minority (SGM) populations are at an increased risk of alcohol use disorders (AUD) and other indicators of alcohol misuse (e.g., Green & Feinstein, 2012; McCabe, Hughes, West, Veliz, & Boyd, 2019). This chapter examines the extant literature that focuses specifically on SGM populations, along with other intersecting stigmatized minority identities (Crenshaw, 1989), to highlight the prevalence of AUD and other negative consequences from drinking. Given the disproportionate experiences of prejudice and discrimination reported by various subpopulations of gender and sexual minorities, there has been a recent push in the area to better understand how various sources of minority stress, or stress unique to the experience of SGMs (e.g., Meyer, 2003), contribute to known disparities in alcohol consumption and risk of AUD among SGMs. Ultimately, our goal is to expand research on understudied SGM subpopulations within the alcohol literature and improve alcohol treatment and intervention programs by highlighting unique risk factors.

In our synthesis of this area of SGM research, we attempt to address major limitations in the published literature. Specifically, the extant literature is often limited by combining multiple SGM subgroups (e.g., lesbians and bisexual women) into a single group for the purposes of presenting population-based estimates (Hatzenbuehler, Keyes, & Hasin, 2009), thereby erasing the unique factors that may distinguish these subgroups in terms of typical alcohol consumption, risk of AUD, unique risk factors, and treatment effectiveness. The present chapter overcomes this limitation by presenting findings for each subgroup. In addition, the current work sought to provide suggestions for future research examining risk of AUD and other associated alcohol outcomes among SGM subpopulations as it relates to prevention, intervention, and treatment of alcohol misuse.

Before reviewing the individual studies that have examined rates of AUD among SGM subpopulations, it is important to note how AUD has been defined in the extant literature. AUD was previously classified as either alcohol abuse or alcohol dependence in earlier editions of the *Diagnostic and Statistical Manual of Mental Disorders* (e.g., DSM-IV) (American Psychiatric Association [APA], 1994). The diagnostic criteria for recent (i.e., past year) alcohol abuse in this edition required individuals to meet one or more (out of four) "abuse" criteria (e.g., "continued to drink even though it was causing trouble with your family or friends"), and the diagnostic criteria for past-year alcohol dependence required respondents to meet three or more (out of seven) "dependence" criteria (e.g., "given up or cut back on activities that were important or interesting to you, or gave you pleasure, in order to drink") in the twelve months prior to the assessment. In the fifth edition of the DSM (i.e., DSM-5), the APA (2013) integrated the two separate diagnoses into a single AUD diagnosis. Subclassifications of AUD include mild, moderate, and severe, based on the number of criteria met (i.e., two or three, four or five, or six to eleven criteria, respectively) (U.S. Department of Health and Human Services, 2013). Currently, diagnostic criteria for past-year AUD require that an individual meet at least two of the eleven criteria in the same twelve-month period (e.g., "had times when you ended up drinking more, or longer, than you intended") (DSM-5; APA, 2013). In the current report, we will distinguish between diagnosis rates for AUD versus alcohol abuse and alcohol dependence disorder specifically, whenever relevant, in accordance with the criteria used in the empirical research, at the time of publication. Minor variations in SGM subgroup acronyms (e.g., LGBT, LGB) throughout this chapter are intentional, and, whenever possible, those proffered by authors in their original reports are used.

This chapter will explicitly examine alcohol use outcomes among lesbian, gay, bisexual, transgender (LGBT) subgroups, in turn, including queer/questioning, asexual, pansexual, and gender-nonconforming subgroups. We sought to synthesize the literature on alcohol misuse within four specific subpopulations: (1) gay men/men who have sex with men; (2) lesbians/women who have sex with women; (3) bisexual cisgender men and women; and (4) transgender and gender-nonconforming individuals. Further, we will explore the factors contributing to each subgroup's risk of AUD and related consequences, which have been investigated in the extant literature.

Gay Men/Men Who Have Sex with Men

Findings from an extensive body of work indicate that gay and other homosexually active men (i.e., men who have sex with men [MSM]) report disproportionately higher rates of alcohol use and AUD compared to heterosexual men (e.g., Boyd, Veliz, Stephenson, Hughes, & McCabe 2019; McCabe et al., 2019). Given that studies from other countries have found equivocal evidence to support the conclusion that the quantity-frequency of alcohol use or prevalence of AUD diagnoses among gay men/MSM are generally elevated, compared to heterosexual men (e.g., Bloomfield, Wicki, Wilsnack, Hughes, & Gmel, 2011; Mimiaga et al., 2011), it remains unclear whether AUDs in this population, indeed, constitute a worldwide public health issue.

Young MSM (who may or may not self-ascribe a gay or bisexual identity) are at greater risk for alcohol use and misuse compared to their heterosexual peers in the general population (e.g., Greenwood et al., 2001). Within a large, ethnically diverse sample of young MSM, Wong, Kipke, and Weiss (2008) found a high prevalence of past-month alcohol use (84 percent) within their sample, with 21 percent reporting binge drinking behavior (i.e., five or more alcoholic drinks within a week). Of the subsample of binge drinkers, 40 percent reported *frequent* binge drinking (i.e., binging three or more days a week) (Wong et al., 2008). These findings are largely consistent with extant research examining alcohol use prevalence among adult gay men/MSM. Santos et al. (2018), for example, observed a high prevalence of "hazardous" drinking (i.e., a score of 16 or greater on the Alcohol Use and Disorders Identification Test [AUDIT]; 29.9 percent) and weekly binge drinking (24.9 percent) in a diverse sample of adult gay men/MSM.

In contrast, McCabe et al. (2013) did not find that prevalence rates of lifetime DSM-IV AUD differed across sexual identity subgroups for cisgender adult men (see also Schuler, Rice, Evans-Polce, & Collins, 2018). That is, men who identified as gay (58.7 percent) tended to report a similar prevalence of lifetime DSM-IV AUD diagnosis as men who identified as heterosexual (47.7 percent) or who were "unsure" of their sexual identity (40.9 percent). Past-year DSM-5 AUD prevalence was also found to be equivalent between subgroups. Heterosexual-identified men with no same-sex attraction or behavior (17.1 percent) and heterosexual-identified men with some same-sex attraction or behavior (14.5 percent) both had somewhat lower past-year AUD rates than gay men (26.2 percent) and those who reported being "unsure" about their sexual identity (23.7 percent). Finally, among men who met criteria for past-year AUD, sexual identity subgroups were not different from each other with regard to the probability of endorsing any specific AUD criterion (McCabe et al., 2019).

The outlook for older gay men/MSM appears to be similarly bleak, with available data suggesting that gay men over the age of 50 years old are more likely to engage in excessive drinking behaviors relative to their heterosexual peers (Fredriksen-Goldsen, Kim, Barkan, Muraco, & Hoy-Ellis, 2013). Fredriksen-Goldsen et al. (2012) also found that gay men/MSM tend to report higher rates of risky drinking than older lesbian and bisexual women, suggesting that social determinants of disparities among older adults (e.g., age, sexual orientation), may be potent risk factors for the development of AUDs in gay/MSM subgroups, specifically.

Alcohol Use and AUD Treatment

Despite the relative dearth of research on alcohol use and alcohol-related problems within SGM populations, notable advancements have been made in recent years in the development and implementation of interventions aimed at treating AUD in gay men/MSM (see Wray et al., 2016, for a recent review). There now exist a number of effective interventions for reducing problem drinking in gay men/MSM for those who (a) drink above the recommended weekly levels for men (e.g., Morgenstern et al., 2012), (b) experience alcohol-related problems (e.g., Croff, Clapp, Chambers, Woodruff, & Strathdee, 2012; Velasquez et al., 2009), and (c) are diagnosed with AUD (e.g., Morgenstern et al., 2007; Reback & Fletcher, 2014).

Although research suggests that gay men/MSM report a greater need for alcohol treatment compared to their heterosexual counterparts, Cochran, Keenan, Schober, and Mays (2000) found no differences in treatment utilization for alcohol-related problems between homosexually active and heterosexually active men. Nevertheless, more recent evidence suggests that interventions incorporating aspects of motivational interviewing/enhancement and cognitive-behavioral therapy show promise in reducing problem drinking among gay men/MSM (Wray et al., 2016).

Mechanisms Accounting for Heightened Risk

Recent decades have witnessed an increase in the number of studies examining psychosocial mechanisms that may account for disparities in AUD diagnoses in SGM populations. To date, minority stress is perhaps the most oft-cited risk factor for alcohol misuse among gay men/MSM (e.g., Hatzenbuehler, Nolen-Hoeksema, & Erickson, 2008; Meyer, 1995, 2003). Recent work supports that the frequency with which gay men/MSM experience minority stress due to sexual orientation–based discrimination is related to increased odds of excessive alcohol use and/or AUD (Slater, Godette, Huang, Ruan, & Kerridge, 2017).

Sociocultural contexts and norms that promote and encourage excessive drinking may also play a key role in shaping the drinking behaviors of gay men/MSM. For example, gay-friendly bars/clubs have long been hailed as the proverbial "mecca" for gay men/MSM to congregate and socialize (Adams, McCreanor, & Braun, 2007). Because LGBT-friendly bars/clubs are some of the few places where a gay identity is completely accepted, sexual minority men's reliance on the tolerant drinking norms at such venues may contribute to their heightened risk for AUD (Cochran, Grella, & Mays, 2012). Additional factors such as experiences of abuse, violence, and victimization (e.g., Balsam, Rothblum, & Beauchaine, 2005), internalized heterosexism (e.g., Amadio, 2006), and gay-related rejection sensitivity (e.g., Pachankis, Hatzenbuehler, & Starks, 2014) have also been shown to contribute to alcohol use among gay men/MSM.

Future Directions

Sexual minority men are at substantially greater risk of severe DSM-5 AUD (McCabe et al., 2019). However, the direction and degree of risk for hazardous drinking among gay men/MSM may differ depending on various demographic and geographic factors. For example, whereas young gay/MSM (aged 16 to 20) report more alcohol use when they perceive a relative lack of family support (Newcomb, Heinz, & Mustanski, 2012), older gay men/MSM (aged 50 and older) report more high-risk drinking when encountering day-to-day experiences of discrimination (Bryan, Kim, & Fredriksen-Goldsen, 2017).

Research investigating men's hazardous drinking by sexual orientation and race/ethnicity has found that Black gay men/MSM have lower odds of heavy weekly drinking and binge drinking than both heterosexual White men and their same-race heterosexual peers (Gilbert, Daniel-Ulloa, & Conron, 2015). Among Latino men, research has shown that gay men/MSM have lower odds of lifetime alcohol dependence symptoms compared to White heterosexual men and Latino heterosexual men, suggesting an enhanced protective effect for racial/ethnic minority gay men/MSM living in the United States (Gilbert, Drabble, Daniel-Ulloa, & Trocki, 2017). These findings hold true for both young gay men/MSM (e.g., Wong et al., 2008) as well as older gay men/MSM (e.g., Bryan et al., 2017).

Studies have shown that gay men living in the Global South (i.e., Argentina, Brazil, Costa Rica, Nicaragua, and Uruguay) appear to be at no greater risk of engaging in heavy drinking than heterosexual-identified controls (e.g., Bloomfield et al., 2011). Findings ultimately suggest that general expectations about drinking disparities among gay/MSM subgroups may be misguided without considering the substantial variability in drinking that exists across regions of the world.

In light of these findings, future work in this domain should make a concerted effort to strengthen AUD prevention strategies and improve treatment utilization among gay men/MSM living with profiles of risk that are distinct from general LGB populations. Because gay men/MSM do not appear to be equally affected by alcohol and alcohol-related problems, it may be worthwhile to consider how sociodemographic factors such as age, race/ethnicity, and country of origin uniquely impact the development and risk of AUD in gay/MSM subgroups.

Future research should also be sensitive to the fact that many gay men/MSM may be hesitant to seek LGB-specific treatment options given that the vast majority of gay men/MSM live in countries or regions of the world with anti-gay policies. Unfortunately, extant research suggests that societal norms and policies that discriminate against sexual minorities are those that also increase their risk of AUD (Hatzenbuehler et al., 2009). Because acceptance of same-sex sexuality varies internationally, healthcare providers must implement culturally informed interventions that consider the specific needs of racial/ethnic minorities and populations of gay men/MSM living in regions of the world that are less tolerant of minority sexual identities and behaviors. Thus, more comprehensive measures of sexual orientation dimensions (i.e., attraction, behavior, and identity) should be used for investigating the prevalence of AUD among MSM who may not identify as "gay" for political, religious, and/or safety reasons. Although researchers have made great strides in this area, future work will be necessary to further reduce elevated rates of AUD in gay/MSM populations around the world.

Lesbians/Women Who Have Sex with Women

Lesbian and other women who have sex with women (WSW) also experience disproportionate rates of alcohol use and AUD relative to their heterosexual counterparts. Given previous work showing disparate prevalence of heavy drinking behavior among adolescent (Fish, Schulenberg, & Russell, 2019), young adult (Gruskin, Hart, Gordon, & Ackerson, 2001), and older (Veldhuis, Talley, Hancock, Wilsnack, & Hughes, 2017) sexual minority women, the probability of AUD among lesbians/WSW is quite high. It is also known that sexual minority women, relative to men, tend to show a faster progression from the first use of alcohol to onset of AUD (Agabio, Pisanu, Luigi Gessa, & Franconi, 2017; Hatzenbuehler et al., 2008).

Girls who report same-sex sexual contact (who may or may not self-ascribe a lesbian or bisexual identity) are at greater risk of heavy drinking relative to heterosexual girls (Fish et al., 2019). Using data from the 2015 Youth Risk Behavior Survey study, lesbian-identified girls (11.49 percent) were most likely to have engaged in heavy drinking behaviors, followed by bisexual-identified girls (5.36 percent), girls "not sure" of their sexual identity (5.25 percent), and heterosexual-identified girls (4.38 percent) (Fish et al., 2019). Researchers (e.g., Fish et al., 2019; Hughes, Johnson, Steffen, Wilsnack, & Everett, 2014) posit that these rates are due to school-aged lesbian/WSW girls experiencing more anti-LGB victimization than heterosexual girls. This conjecture was supported by research showing that victimization mediated the relationship between sexual identity and heavy drinking in young lesbians/WSW (e.g., Fish et al., 2019). Newcomb et al. (2012) showed similar findings among young sexual minority women with regard to victimization and increased alcohol use in this same age group.

Extant findings in samples of lesbians/WSW are consistent with predictions derived from minority stress (Meyer, 2003) and intersectionality (Crenshaw, 1989) theories. Specifically, because young lesbian/WSW report multiple, marginalized identities (i.e., being sexual minority and cisgender women), they are believed to be particularly susceptible to alcohol misuse (Hatzenbuehler et al., 2009). That is, lesbians/WSW use alcohol at higher rates because of the compounding effects of being a woman *and* a sexual minority (Anderson & Henderson, 1985). By contrast, Newcomb et al. (2012) did not find that a minority ethnicity or racial identity exacerbated alcohol consumption. Extant findings further indicate young lesbians/WSW, in particular, are at risk for alcohol misuse, compared to their heterosexual counterparts.

In several population-based studies of adult sexual minority women (Diamant, Wold, Spritzer, & Gelberg, 2000; Green & Feinstein, 2012;

Gruskin, et al., 2001), lesbians/WSW report higher levels of alcohol misuse, compared to heterosexual women. For example, women who identified as lesbian/gay (58.6 percent) reported higher rates of lifetime DSM-IV AUD, compared to both heterosexual women (22 percent) and women who were "unsure" of their sexual identity (33 percent) (Hughes et al., 2010). Similarly, women who identified as lesbian/gay (24.5 percent) were more likely to meet criteria for past-year DSM-5 AUD (McCabe et al., 2019), compared to women who identified as heterosexual yet reported same-sex attraction or behavior (18.8 percent) as well as women who identified as heterosexual and reported no same-sex attraction or behavior (8.8 percent). In another national study, lesbians/WSW had greater odds of reporting severe AUD than heterosexual women (Boyd et al., 2019). Finally, results from the National Latino and Asian American Survey showed that 5.2 percent of lesbians/WSW met criteria for lifetime DSM-IV alcohol abuse/dependence compared to 3.2 percent of heterosexual women (Cochran, Mays, Alegria, Ortega, & Takeuchi, 2007).

In addition to examining how ethnicity/race, gender, and sexual orientation characteristics interact to predict AUD and alcohol misuse, researchers have examined the role of aging in SGM women's health and drinking behavior (e.g., Veldhuis et al., 2017). An increase in drinking in older adulthood may worsen alcohol misuse, trigger onset of AUD, or increase risk of mortality (Milic et al., 2018). Despite these admonitions, lesbians/WSW do not seem to drink more as they age. Findings from several studies (e.g., Gruskin et al., 2001; Veldhuis et al., 2017) indicate that younger adult lesbians/WSW drink more heavily than older lesbians/WSW, likely due to a more prominent "bar culture" and accessibility of other substances during young adulthood. More research is needed to understand more clearly how minority stress factors may decline among older lesbians/WSW as well as how to improve alcohol interventions for older sexual minority women.

Alcohol Use and AUD Treatment

Various forms of alcohol treatment-seeking and usage behaviors for lesbians/WSW are relevant. Some research has shown that lesbians and bisexual women have used treatment for alcohol-related issues more compared to heterosexual women (Cochran et al., 2000; Drabble, Midanik, & Trocki, 2005; see also Veldhuis et al., 2017). Unfortunately, however, lesbians/WSW typically report low satisfaction with alcohol treatment and other mainstream health services given that medical providers often have little to no LGBT-cultural sensitivity training or education about LGBT-specific health issues (Bush et al., 2019). Other barriers to treatment, such as socioeconomic strife, childcare, and stigma, affect not only lesbians/WSW but women in general. There have been increasing calls for tailored interventions for lesbians/WSW, and this work is in its early stages. Bush et al. (2019), for example, are currently examining whether an intervention using text messages will decrease alcohol consumption among lesbians/WSW in Australia. Finally, although promising intervention research has attempted to incorporate cognitive-behavioral therapy, contingency management, and motivational interviewing and has shown effectiveness for treating alcohol-related problems among gay men/MSM (see Green & Feinstein, 2012, for a review), it remains to be seen whether efficacy will extend to lesbians/WSW.

Mechanisms Accounting for Heightened Risk

Sexual victimization is a major predictor of hazardous drinking among lesbians/WSW (e.g., Hughes et al., 2010). This is believed to be due to the fact that victimization experiences, which are more often reported by sexual minority women relative to heterosexual women, are major stressors associated with poor mental health outcomes and risk of hazardous drinking (Hughes et al., 2014). Previous work in SGM samples suggests that some lesbians/WSW are inclined to use alcohol and other drugs as a form of self-medication, intended to reduce distress (Welch, Howden-Chapman, & Collings, 1998). Not only are lesbians/WSW more likely to report general risk factors for alcohol misuse, but minority-specific stressors may also be contributing to their risk of AUD. For example, a general risk factor for alcohol misuse, social isolation, has been shown to contribute to increased maladaptive drinking motives in lesbians (Lewis, Winstead, Lau-Barraco, & Mason, 2017). Minority-specific mechanisms being explored by researchers in this area are internalized homophobia (Dorn-Medeiros & Doyle, 2018), or the internalization of the socially prescribed need to be heterosexual, and internalized heterosexism, or the internalization of anti-lesbian/WSW attitudes (Szymanski, 2006). Self-directed stigmatizing thoughts and feelings are expected to lead to negative behavioral health outcomes, such as AUD, so lesbians/WSW are at increased risk of developing alcohol problems as a result of social factors related to their SGM status. Yet, these factors remain understudied, and future research should assess these constructs directly when studying contributors to alcohol misuse and AUD among lesbians/WSW.

Future Directions

Our primary suggestion is the creation of nuanced sexual orientation–based research that distinguishes between subgroups of sexual minority women (e.g., lesbians vs. bisexual women vs. WSW). Additionally, future researchers should be mindful of collecting and analyzing potential moderating factors, related to race/ethnicity, age, nationality, mental health status, and gender. Paying attention to the intersection of various identities (Crenshaw, 1989) is essential to conducting comprehensive research that meets the unique needs of lesbians/WSW. Future research must expand examination of potential protective intersecting identities, such as race/ethnicity (e.g., Newcomb et al., 2012), which may mitigate some risk of alcohol misuse among SGM subgroups, particularly among lesbians/WSW.

Finally, tailored interventions need to be developed and tested for effectiveness in lesbian/WSW subgroups. Promising elements from extant literature that could be incorporated into interventions and treatments include increasing family support (Veldhuis et al., 2017), training educators and caregivers to be more culturally competent (Bush et al., 2019; Ingraham et al., 2016), encouraging safe lesbian/WSW-friendly environments (Drabble & Underhill, 2002), and destigmatizing same-sex sexuality (Lewis et al., 2017; Szymanski, 2006). By adopting these elements and tailoring interventions to lesbians/WSW, alcohol treatment programs may be more effective in retaining clients and helping lesbians/WSW improve their drinking.

Bisexual Cisgender Men and Women

Alcohol research within bisexual communities has sought to examine the prevalence of AUD and better understand risk factors that contribute to their alcohol disparities and consequences relative to their heterosexual and lesbian/gay counterparts (e.g., Schuler et al., 2018). Across various definitions of bisexuality, findings convey the differential risk of lifetime and past-year AUD and alcohol-related harms among those with bisexual identities, behaviors, and attractions, including in longitudinal studies (e.g., McCabe et al., 2013).

Large-scale epidemiological studies from the United States provide useful information on base rates of AUD among adults who identify as bisexual, relative to other sexual identities (McCabe et al., 2013, 2019; Schuler et al., 2018). Findings from these studies suggest increased risk of lifetime and past-year AUD diagnosis, in particular, among bisexual and lesbian-identified women relative to their heterosexual counterparts (e.g., McCabe et al., 2019), and relatively equivalent risk of AUD and alcohol-related harms among men, regardless of sexual identity. Although these studies provide valuable information on overall prevalence, research with targeted samples can inform a more nuanced understanding of alcohol-related harms among bisexual persons.

Bisexual Identity and Alcohol-Related Harms

Equivocal results are often shown in the extant literature with regard to bisexual persons' risk of AUD and other alcohol-related harms, especially when results are collapsed across participant gender. LGBT youth, for example, showed few differences in lifetime AUD diagnosis across persons who identified as gay, as bisexual, or as an "other" sexual minority (Newcomb et al., 2012). In an adult sample, however, Hequembourg and Dearing (2013) showed a trend for bisexual-identified adults to report slightly higher alcohol severity scores, as measured with the AUDIT, compared to gay and lesbian adults. In Italy, bisexual-identified youth showed elevated risk of heavy drinking, compared to their lesbian and gay counterparts (Verrastro et al., 2016), suggesting that, in addition to age and gender, geography may also moderate these associations.

Gender identity appears to play a key role in predicting alcohol consumption and consequences in SGM populations. For example, bisexual college-attending women had greater odds of using alcohol than heterosexual and lesbian college-attending women (e.g., Kerr, Ding, Burke, & Ott-Walter, 2015). Within samples of young sexual minority female drinkers, however, no differences in typical number of drinking days or recent alcohol-related consequences were shown across those with bisexual or lesbian identities (Wilson, Gilmore, Rhew, Hodge, & Kaysen, 2016). Taken together, bisexual identities confer some added risk of alcohol use and related harms compared to those with heterosexual identities, although the effects of gender identity on alcohol outcomes may be more robust, particularly in vulnerable contexts, such as young adulthood.

Discordance among Dimensions of Sexual Orientation

Findings from Talley, Aranda, Hughes, Everett, and Johnson (2015) suggest that discordance among sexual orientation dimensions (identity, attraction, behavior) may contribute to alcohol misuse. Sexual orientation self-concept ambiguity (SSA), or the acknowledgment that dimensions of one's sexual orientation self-concept are incongruent, inconsistent, or in flux, is theorized to be an essential risk factor in predicting alcohol misuse (Talley & Littlefield, 2014). Notably, bisexual individuals are those most likely to report incongruence among facets of their sexual orientation and endorse the highest levels of SSA (Talley & Stevens, 2017). Talley and Stevens found a moderate positive correlation between SSA scores and AUD symptoms in a sample of young adult women.

Alcohol Use and AUD Treatment

McCabe et al. (2013) showed some indication that bisexual individuals (32 percent) may be more likely to access substance use treatment services at some point in their lifetime, compared to "not sure" (20.8 percent) and heterosexual-identified (15.7 percent) persons. Although overall treatment utilization was low (~6 percent), another study showed that bisexual women were more likely than other respondents (i.e., lesbian, gay men, bisexual men) to have sought treatment for alcohol and other drug use (Lea, Reynolds, & de Wit, 2013). Individuals who identify as bisexual or who are behaviorally bisexual are about twice as likely as their peers to access substance treatment services (McCabe et al., 2013). Findings also showed that bisexual persons access substance use treatment in both community venues, such as 12-step meetings (22.5 percent), and medical settings, including alcohol-unit detox wards or clinics (16 percent), suggesting that SGM cultural competency across treatment contexts is key.

Mechanisms Accounting for Heightened Risk

Validation of risk and protective factors for AUDs and treatment outcomes in the bisexual community (e.g., Feinstein, Dyar, & London, 2017) is essential to develop treatment and resilience models. Extant literature has documented that bisexual persons experience bisexual stigma not only from their heterosexual peers but also from their gay and lesbian counterparts (e.g., Bostwick, 2012; see also Herek, 2002). Indeed, higher levels of "outness" (i.e., sexual identity disclosure) and LGBT community involvement have been associated with *greater* risk of AUD for bisexual women, but not lesbian or queer women (Feinstein et al., 2017), with these former associations being partially explained by perceived discrimination. In a national sample of bisexual-identified women (Molina et al., 2015), experience of binegativity, or overt discrimination on the basis of bisexual orientation, was also found to positively predict both binge drinking and alcohol-related consequences. In fact, experienced binegativity accounted for differences in binge drinking and alcohol consequences among bisexual women with a single male and female partner, compared to those with a single female *or* male partner and those with multiple female/male partners.

Bisexual individuals have been found to report high levels of self-directed sexual stigma (i.e., internalized heterosexism, Bostwick, 2012; Hequembourg & Dearing, 2013), even compared to their lesbian/gay peers. Molina et al. (2015) showed that internalized binegativity, or self-directed stigma due to one's bisexual orientation, was positively related to negative alcohol-related consequences. In addition to self-evaluative aspects of one's bisexuality (i.e., self-directed stigma), SSA is argued to independently contribute to risk of alcohol misuse (Talley & Littlefield, 2014) and AUD symptomology (Talley & Stevens, 2017).

Future Directions

In future work within bisexual communities, research might benefit from examinations of intersectionality, beyond gender identity (Crenshaw, 1989). Various research has shown support for differential risk of AUD and related harms based on race/ethnicity in bisexual samples. For example, both gay and bisexual Latino men showed somewhat *lower* odds of lifetime alcohol dependence symptoms (Gilbert et al., 2017) compared to their heterosexual counterparts. However, Black men who identified as heterosexual yet had engaged in some same-sex behavior were found to have three times *greater* log-odds of reporting lifetime AUD symptoms, compared to their heterosexual peers who had only engaged in opposite-sex behavior (Gilbert et al., 2017). These associations may be further influenced by age-related differences in patterns of alcohol use (Pollitt, Mallory, & Fish, 2018). Future work should focus on protective or exacerbating factors impacting risk of AUD and alcohol-related harms in bisexual communities.

Cultural competency training is sorely needed to better serve bisexual individuals who are attempting to access care for problems related to alcohol use (Feinstein et al., 2017). Focus groups with LGBT women in Australia identified "primary areas of consensus" in participants' accounts of services that are needed to improve care, including overcoming heteronormative conventions, providing better training around LBQ issues, and making fewer assumptions (Pennay et al., 2018). Preconceived notions of what a "bisexual" person looks and acts like must be put aside in the treatment of SGM clients struggling with AUD.

Alternative Minority Sexual Identities and AUD Risk

Emergent work within the asexual, pansexual, and other diverse sexual minority communities has been accelerating. A national health survey provided an opportunity for one of the first examinations of queer-identified and pansexual-identified persons with regard to subgroup prevalence for a host of alcohol-related outcomes (Smalley, Warren, & Barefoot, 2016). Queer individuals (21.0 percent) were found to drink alcohol at rates equivalent to gay-identified persons (20.9 percent), whereas pansexual persons (12 percent) were found to drink more on par with lesbian-identified persons (13.5 percent)—both lower than straight-identified individuals (18.4 percent) and bisexual-identified persons (16.4 percent). Gay (10.4 percent) and bisexual (9.9 percent) individuals reported the highest rates of binge drinking, followed by queer (7.8 percent) and pansexual (7.2 percent) persons. Research among smaller subgroups of the LGB+ community are only recently emerging in the available literature. More work is needed to understand the prevalence of AUD and correlates of alcohol misuse in these communities.

Transgender and Gender-Nonconforming Populations

Within the field of LGBT research, transgender and gender nonconforming (TGNC) populations arguably remain some of the most under-researched SGM groups. Specifically, with regard to alcohol use/misuse and AUD, TGNC populations face issues with medical professionals and intervention programs that assume cisgender status or binary gender (Nuttbrock, 2012). As a result, there are difficulties with participant recruitment and the diagnosing of TGNC individuals with AUD (Nuttbrock, 2012; Reisner et al., 2016). Moreover, terminology related to gender and its various identity labels has been in constant flux over the past several decades (Coleman et al., 2011), making it difficult to consistently study these populations over time. For the purposes of this chapter, we use terms that coincide with those advocated for by APA (2015). *TGNC* will be used as an overarching term to include all gender identities that exist outside of the gender binary (i.e., man and woman) or for individuals whose gender does not align or coincide with their natal sex or gender assigned at birth (APA, 2015).

Alcohol Use and AUD Treatment

In recent years, research related to alcohol use in TGNC populations has grown dramatically. With almost 28,000 participants, the 2015 U.S. Transgender Survey (James et al., 2016) provided the most representative examination of TGNC alcohol use within the United States. The majority of participants (57 percent) reported using alcohol fewer than five days during the previous month, 19 percent reported drinking six to ten times during that period, and 23 percent had used alcohol on eleven or more days. For participants engaged in criminalized work (e.g., sex work, drug sales), the use of alcohol rose drastically: Almost half reported binge drinking (i.e., at least five drinks in one sitting) at least once in the past month, and 19 percent reported heavy drinking (i.e., binge drinking five or more times in one month) in the past month. The rest of the sample showed close to half as many reports of binge drinking (27 percent) and heavy drinking (7 percent), which mirrors population rates in the United States (Center for Behavioral Health Statistics and Quality, 2018).

Despite the similar rates of alcohol use within general and TGNC-specific samples, smaller samples of TGNC individuals have yielded wide ranges of reported alcohol-related behaviors. In a systematic review of alcohol research with TGNC samples, Gilbert, Pass, Keuroghlian, Greenfield, and Reisner (2018) found that ranges of behaviors across studies were as follows: binge drinking, 7 to 61 percent; drinking to intoxication, 25 to 58 percent; sexual risk behaviors while intoxicated, 32 to 53 percent; and heightened AUDIT scores, 47 to 48 percent. Differences in prevalence rates across studies are likely related to differences in sampling and measurements of gender identity and alcohol use, none of which have been standardized for TGNC research (Gilbert et al., 2018).

One subset of the TGNC population that remains largely overlooked is TGNC adolescents. In one survey of youth (aged 13 to 18), alcohol use was significantly higher for TGNC youth compared to their cisgender peers (Reisner, Greytak, Parsons, &

Ybarra, 2015). With a sample of over 400 self-identified TGNC adolescents, 49.2 percent reported ever drinking alcohol within the past year, and 21.6 percent reported regularly drinking during the past year. In contrast, cisgender adolescents had less experience with ever drinking alcohol in the past year (38.1 percent among boys; 36.0 percent among girls) and regularly within the past year (17.8 percent among boys; 15.5 percent among girls).

Sexual Risk-Taking Behavior and AUD

A portion of alcohol research with TGNC populations has analyzed the relationship between alcohol use and risky sexual behavior (e.g., condomless sex). When Herrera et al. (2016) recruited transwomen (n = 89) and MSM in Peru who were recently diagnosed with at least one sexually transmitted infection, almost half of transgender participants (47 percent) met qualifications for AUD based on AUDIT scores greater than or equal to 8. At their most recent sexual encounter, 14 percent of participants reported being inebriated and 17 percent reported that their partners were inebriated. The use of alcohol during last sex was correlated with meeting the AUDIT cutoff for AUD, and this relationship increased with AUD severity. Among 205 transwomen in Vietnam, 24 percent reported having at least six drinks per week, and 51 percent met the criteria for a positive AUDIT-3 (Colby et al., 2016).

The relationship between sexual risk-taking behavior and alcohol consumption has been demonstrated similarly in transmen (Reisner, White, Mayer, & Mimiaga, 2014). Medical records were analyzed for twenty-three transmen who had recently undergone testing for a sexually transmitted infection. Of this sample, 65 percent were currently having five or more drinks per week, and this measure of alcohol use was associated with greater levels of sexual risk-taking behaviors during the past three months. Results from samples of transmen and transwomen indicate that risky sexual behavior is positively associated with alcohol use, which may contribute to negative health outcomes for individuals within these populations.

Impact of Discrimination and Distress on Alcohol Use

Based on the tenets of the minority stress model (Meyer, 1995, 2003), TGNC persons who regularly encounter stigma are more likely to report high levels of alcohol use and health impairments. Results from the National Transgender Discrimination Survey supported this model, showing that approximately a quarter (26 percent) of respondents reported using alcohol or other drugs to cope with gender-related discrimination (Grant et al., 2010). Additionally, Reisner et al. (2015) found that TGNC adolescents experience more bullying than their cisgender peers and, subsequently, engaged in more alcohol use. Current research suggests that TGNC individuals may be turning to alcohol to cope with distress resulting from experiences with discrimination (e.g., Nuttbrock et al., 2014).

In further support of the relation between experiences with stigma and alcohol consumption, Livingston, Flentje, Heck, Szalda-Petree, and Cochran (2017) demonstrated, via a fourteen-day diary study, that daily experiences with discrimination likely contributed to subsequent reports of alcohol use. Although the TGNC subsample in this study was small (n = 9), results across various identities showed that participants who had experienced any kind of SGM discrimination were approximately 3.5 times more likely to report substance use, including alcohol use, at the next survey interval. This research provides evidence to support the importance of stigma as a potential risk factor for increased alcohol consumption within TGNC subgroups.

Within samples of TGNC military veterans, the impact of distress and stigma has been associated with increases in alcohol use and AUD diagnosis. Compared to random samples of veterans, TGNC veterans showed a higher rate of AUD (22 percent and 26.2 percent, respectively; Blosnich et al., 2017; Calhoun, Elter, Jones, Kudler, & Straits-Tröster, 2008). Life stressors (e.g., housing instability, financial strain) were correlated with increased odds of being diagnosed with AUD. Additionally, Black TGNC veterans were twice as likely as White TGNC veterans to encounter life stressors and to be diagnosed with AUD, even when controlling for other demographic variables (Blosnich et al., 2017). AUDIT scores within another sample of transgender veterans were positively correlated with experiences of discrimination, shame related to one's gender identity, and suicidal ideation (Lehavot, Simpson, & Shipherd, 2016).

In contrast, Blosnich et al. (2016) found that transgender U.S. veterans were more likely to be formally diagnosed with an AUD when living in areas that provide greater legal protections for SGM persons, related to both equality and nondiscrimination. Because alcohol use was measured with official AUD diagnoses, the researchers posited that

TGNC individuals might feel more comfortable accessing medical care and alcohol treatment in locations that actively promoted awareness and acceptance of LGBT identities. Although further research is needed, focus groups with TGNC participants have shown the importance of comfort and acceptance for this population in help-seeking behavior (Sperber, Landers, & Lawrence, 2005).

Treatment Options

To date, only a few treatment/intervention programs have been targeted to TGNC populations (Glynn & van den Berg, 2017). There is a crucial need for alcohol treatment programs tailored to TGNC individuals who experience social pressures and biological consequences unique to gender minority identities (Nuttbrock, 2012; Sperber et al., 2005). These programs require staff who are educated about, and accepting of, gender minority populations, to ensure that TGNC persons feel secure enough to attend such programs and to disclose pertinent information as it relates to their gender identity (Eliason, 2000).

One of the few intervention programs tailored for TGNC persons demonstrated positive results for both program completion and substance use reduction (Nemoto, Operario, Keatley, Nguyen, & Sugano, 2005). Reducing use and improving coping skills were some of the main treatment goals proffered to transwomen. The program ultimately achieved a completion rate of 30 percent (i.e., 109 of 359 clients completed both the pretest and posttest and attended at least ten out of eighteen sessions). Pretest-to-posttest data showed a marginal reduction in alcohol use for those who completed the course, and reports of past-month alcohol use dropped from 57 percent to 48 percent.

Future Directions

Although alcohol research with TGNC populations has accelerated drastically in recent years, there remains a vast chasm of unexplored questions, particularly with regard to the causes and effects of alcohol use and misuse among TGNC persons. The rapid increase in TGNC alcohol research has been accompanied by methodological concerns related to unstandardized measures (Gilbert et al., 2018). In particular, studies have demonstrated inconsistencies in definitions of TGNC populations and recruitment criteria (Reisner et al., 2016); within recent years, TGNC status has been determined by ICD-9 diagnostic codes (e.g., Blosnich et al., 2016), cross-tabulation of sex assigned at birth and gender identity (Keuroghlian, Reisner, White, & Weiss, 2015), as well as self-identification (James et al., 2016). These differences in methods create issues with accessing participant pools and potential underrepresentation or exclusion of subsets of TGNC (e.g., nonbinary or agender persons). In addition, the interpretation of scores on AUD screening measures requires further research into the cutoff criteria for various populations under the umbrella of TGNC (Gilbert et al., 2018). Because current measures incorporate sex/gender differences in screening cutoffs, research should examine the ways in which gender transitioning (i.e., social or medical) impacts risk of alcohol misuse (e.g., Bradley et al., 2007). Increasing TGNC alcohol research will promote inclusivity and awareness of TGNC individuals, while also benefiting future intervention and treatment programs.

Conclusion

Although this chapter was limited by the scope of available research on SGM populations and alcohol misuse, the collection of work highlighted here paints a comprehensive picture of how SGM subpopulations are uniquely affected by alcohol consumption and disordered use. Moreover, this chapter attempted to dissect social factors and mechanisms that heighten SGM individuals' risk of developing an AUD as well as potential comorbid psychological issues. Although we focused explicitly on four subpopulations of SGMs, discrimination and alcohol use are prevalent among intersecting minority group members as well. It is vital for researchers to consider how individuals with diverse identities are at risk for, or resilient with respect to, AUD and other alcohol-related problems. Researchers must apply their findings to the development and revision of intervention initiatives so that the unique risks and needs of various subpopulations are addressed. By taking such steps, not only can future work help SGM individuals improve their physical and psychological health, but it can also benefit society by resisting systems of discrimination that promote inequality for marginalized populations.

References

Adams, J., McCreanor, T., & Braun, V. (2007). Alcohol and gay men: Consumption, promotion and policy responses. In V. Clarke & E. Peel (Eds.), *Out in psychology: Lesbian, gay, bisexual, trans and queer perspectives* (pp. 369–90). Hoboken, NJ: John Wiley & Sons.

Agabio, R., Pisanu, C., Luigi Gessa, G., & Franconi, F. (2017). Sex differences in alcohol use disorder. *Current Medicinal*

Chemistry, 24, 2661–70. doi:10.2174/092986732366616120 2092908 Amadio, D. M. (2006). Internalized heterosexism, alcohol use, and alcohol-related problems among lesbians and gay men. *Addictive Behaviors, 31*, 1153–62. doi:10.1016/j.addbeh.2005.08.013

American Psychiatric Association. (1994). *Diagnostic and statistical manual of mental disorders* (4th ed.). Washington, D.C: Author. doi:10.1176/appi.books.9780890420249.dsm-iv-tr

American Psychiatric Association. (2013). *Diagnostic and statistical manual of mental disorders* (5th ed.). Arlington, VA: Author. doi:10.1176/appi.books.9780890425596

American Psychological Association. (2015). Guidelines for psychological practice with transgender and gender nonconforming people. *American Psychologist, 70*, 832–64. doi:10.1037/a0039906

Anderson, S. C., & Henderson, D. C. (1985). Working with lesbian alcoholics. *Social Work, 30*(6), 518–25. doi:10.1093/sw/30.6.518

Balsam, K. F., Rothblum, E. D., & Beauchaine, T. P. (2005). Victimization over the life span: A comparison of lesbian, gay, bisexual, and heterosexual siblings. *Journal of Consulting and Clinical Psychology, 73*, 477–87. doi:10.1037/0022-006X.73.3.477

Bloomfield, K., Wicki, M., Wilsnack, S., Hughes, T., & Gmel, G. (2011). International differences in alcohol use according to sexual orientation. *Substance Abuse, 32*, 210–9. doi:10.1080/08897077.2011.598404

Blosnich, J. R., Marsiglio, M. C., Dichter, M. E., Gao, S., Gordon, A. J., Shipherd, J. C., . . . Fine, M. J. (2017). Impact of social determinants of health on medical conditions among transgender veterans. *American Journal of Preventive Medicine, 52*, 491–8. doi:10.1016/j.amepre.2016.12.019

Blosnich, J. R., Marsiglio, M. C., Gao, S., Gordon, A. J., Shipherd, J. C., Kauth, M., . . . Fine, M. J. (2016). Mental health of transgender veterans in US states with and without discrimination and hate crime legal protection. *American Journal of Public Health, 106*, 534–40. doi:10.2105/AJPH.2015.302981

Bostwick, W. (2012). Assessing bisexual stigma and mental health status: A brief report. *Journal of Bisexuality, 12*, 214–22. doi:10.1080/15299716.2012.674860

Boyd, C. J., Veliz, P. T., Stephenson, R., Hughes, T. L., & McCabe, S. E. (2019). Severity of alcohol, tobacco, and drug use disorders among sexual minority individuals and their "not sure" counterparts. *LGBT Health, 6*, 15–22. doi:10.1089/lgbt.2018.0122

Bradley, K. A., DeBenedetti, A. F., Volk, R. J., Williams, E. C., Frank, D., & Kivlahan, D. R. (2007). AUDIT-C as a brief screen for alcohol misuse in primary care. *Alcoholic Clinical and Experimental Research, 31*, 1208–17. doi:10.1111/j.1530-0277.2007.00403.x

Bryan, A. E., Kim, H. J., & Fredriksen-Goldsen, K. I. (2017). Factors associated with high-risk alcohol consumption among LGB older adults: The roles of gender, social support, perceived stress, discrimination, and stigma. *The Gerontologist, 57*, S95–S104. doi:10.1093/geront/gnw100

Bush, R., Brown, R., McNair, R., Orellana, L., Lubman, D. I., & Staiger, P. K. (2019). Effectiveness of a culturally tailored SMS alcohol intervention for same-sex attracted women: Protocol for an RCT. *BMC Women's Health, 19*, 29. doi:10.1186/s12905-019-0729-y

Calhoun, P. S., Elter, J. R., Jones, E. R., Jr., Kudler, H., & Straits-Tröster, K. (2008). Hazardous alcohol use and receipt of risk-reduction counseling among U.S. veterans of the wars in Iraq and Afghanistan. *Journal of Clinical Psychiatry, 69*, 1686–93. doi:10.4088/JCP.v69n1103

Center for Behavioral Health Statistics and Quality. (2018). *2017 National survey on drug use and health: Detailed tables*. Rockville, MD: Substance Abuse and Mental Health Services.

Cochran, S. D., Grella, C. E., & Mays, V. M. (2012). Do substance use norms and perceived drug availability mediate sexual orientation differences in patterns of substance use? Results from the California Quality of Life Survey II. *Journal of Studies on Alcohol and Drugs, 73*, 675–85. doi:10.15288/jsad.2012.73.675

Cochran, S. D., Keenan, C., Schober, C., & Mays, V. M. (2000). Estimates of alcohol use and clinical treatment needs among homosexually active men and women in the US population. *Journal of Consulting and Clinical Psychology, 68*, 1062–71. doi:10.1037/0022-006X.68.6.1062

Cochran, S. D., Mays, V. M., Alegria, M., Ortega, A. N., & Takeuchi, D. (2007). Mental health and substance use disorders among Latino and Asian American lesbian, gay, and bisexual adults. *Journal of Consulting and Clinical Psychology, 75*, 785. doi:10.1037/0022-006X.75.5.785

Colby, D., Nguyen, N. A., Le, B., Toan, T., Thien, D. D., Huyen, H. T., . . . Stall, R. (2016). HIV and syphilis prevalence among transgender women in Ho Chi Minh City, Vietnam. *AIDS & Behavior, 20*, S379–S385. doi:10.1007/s10461-016-1485-8

Coleman, E., Bockting, W., Botzer, M., Cohen-Kettenis, P., DeCuypere, G., Feldman, J., . . . Fraser, L. (2011). Standards of care for the health of transsexual, transgender, and gender-nonconforming people, version 7. *International Journal of Transgenderism, 13*, 165–232. doi:10.1080/15532739.2011.700873

Crenshaw, K. (1989). Demarginalizing the intersection of race and sex: A black feminist critique of antidiscrimination doctrine, feminist theory and antiracist politics. *University of Chicago Legal Forum, 1989*, article 8. https://chicagounbound.uchicago.edu/uclf/vol1989/iss1/8

Croff, J. M., Clapp, J. D., Chambers, C. D., Woodruff, S. I., & Strathdee, S. A. (2012). Brief field-based intervention to reduce alcohol-related problems among men who have sex with men. *Journal of Studies on Alcohol and Drugs, 73*, 285–9. doi:10.15288/jsad.2012.73.285

Diamant, A. L., Wold, C., Spritzer, K., & Gelberg, L. (2000). Health behaviors, health status, and access to and use of health care: A population-based study of lesbian, bisexual, and heterosexual women. *Archives of Family Medicine, 9*,

Dorn-Medeiros, C. M., & Doyle, C. (2018). Alcohol as coping: Internalized homophobia and heterosexism's role in alcohol use among lesbians. *Journal of LGBT Issues in Counseling, 12*, 142–57. doi:10.1080/15538605.2018.1488230

Drabble, L., Midanik, L. T., & Trocki, K. (2005). Reports of alcohol consumption and alcohol-related problems among homosexual, bisexual and heterosexual respondents: Results from the 2000 National Alcohol Survey. *Journal of Studies on Alcohol, 66*, 111–20. doi:10.15288/jsa.2005.66.111

Drabble, L., & Underhill, B. L. (2002). Effective interventions and treatment for lesbians. In S. L. A Straussner & S. Brown (Eds.), *Handbook for addiction treatment for women: Theory and practice* (pp. 399–422). San Francisco, CA: Jossey-Bass.

Eliason, M. J. (2000). Substance abuse counselor's attitudes regarding lesbian, gay, bisexual, and transgendered clients.

Journal of Substance Abuse, 12, 311–28. doi:10.1016/S0899-3289(01)00055-4

Feinstein, B. A., Dyar, C., & London, B. (2017). Are outness and community involvement risk or protective factors for alcohol and drug abuse among sexual minority women? *Archives of Sexual Behavior, 46,* 1411–23. doi:10.1007/s10508-016-0790-7

Fish, J. N., Schulenberg, J. E., & Russell, S. T. (2019). Sexual minority youth report high-intensity binge drinking: The critical role of school victimization. *Journal of Adolescent Health, 64,* 186–93. doi:10.1016/j.jadohealth.2018.07.005

Fredriksen-Goldsen, K. I., Emlet, C. A., Kim, H. J., Muraco, A., Erosheva, E. A.,... & Hoy-Ellis, C. P. (2012). The physical and mental health of lesbian, gay male, and bisexual (LGB) older adults: The role of key health indicators and risk and protective factors. *The Gerontologist, 53,* 664–75. doi:10.1093/geront/gns123

Fredriksen-Goldsen, K. I., Kim, H. J., Barkan, S. E., Muraco, A., & Hoy-Ellis, C. P. (2013). Health disparities among lesbian, gay, and bisexual older adults: Results from a population-based study. *American Journal of Public Health, 103,* 1802–9. doi:10.2105/AJPH.2012.301110

Gilbert, P. A., Daniel-Ulloa, J., & Conron, K. J. (2015). Does comparing alcohol use along a single dimension obscure within-group differences? Investigating men's hazardous drinking by sexual orientation and race/ethnicity. *Drug and Alcohol Dependence, 151,* 101–9. doi:10.1016/j.drugalcdep.2015.03.010

Gilbert, P. A., Drabble, L., Daniel-Ulloa, J., & Trocki, K. F. (2017). Alcohol outcomes by sexual orientation and race/ethnicity: Few findings of higher risk. *Journal of Studies on Alcohol and Drugs, 78,* 406–14. doi:10.15288/jsad.2017.78.406

Gilbert, P. A., Pass, L. E., Keuroghlian, A. S., Greenfield, T. K., & Reisner, S. L. (2018). Alcohol research with transgender populations: A systematic review and recommendations to strengthen future studies. *Drug and Alcohol Dependence, 186,* 138–45.

Glynn, T. R., & van den Berg, J. J. (2017). A systematic review of interventions to reduce problematic substance use among transgender individuals: A call to action. *Transgender Health, 2,* 45–59. doi:10.1089/trgh.2016.0037

Grant, J. M., Mottet, L. A., Tanis, J., Herman, J. L., Harrison, J., & Keisling, M. (2010). *National transgender discrimination survey: Report on health and health care.* Washington, DC: National Center for Transgender Equality and National Gay and Lesbian Task Force.

Green, K. E., & Feinstein, B. A. (2012). Substance use in lesbian, gay, and bisexual populations: An update on empirical research and implications for treatment. *Psychology of Addictive Behaviors, 26,* 265–78. doi:10.1037/a0025424

Greenwood, G. L., White, E. W., Page-Shafer, K., Bein, E., Osmond, D. H., Paul, J., & Stall, R. D. (2001). Correlates of heavy substance use among young gay and bisexual men: The San Francisco Young Men's Health Study. *Drug and Alcohol Dependence, 61,* 105–12. doi:10.1016/S0376-8716(00)00129-0

Gruskin, E. P., Hart, S., Gordon, N., & Ackerson, L. (2001). Patterns of cigarette smoking and alcohol use among lesbians and bisexual women enrolled in a large health maintenance organization. *American Journal of Public Health, 91,* 976. doi:10.2105/ajph.91.6.976

Hatzenbuehler, M. L., Keyes, K. M., & Hasin, D. S. (2009). State-level policies and psychiatric morbidity in lesbian, gay, and bisexual populations. *American Journal of Public Health, 99,* 2275–81. doi:10.2105/AJPH.2008.153510

Hatzenbuehler, M. L., Nolen-Hoeksema, S., & Erickson, S. J. (2008). Minority stress predictors of HIV risk behavior, substance use, and depressive symptoms: Results from a prospective study of bereaved gay men. *Health Psychology, 27,* 455–62. doi:10.1037/0278-6133.27.4.455

Hequembourg, A. L., & Dearing, R. L. (2013). Exploring shame, guilt, and risky substance use among sexual minority men and women. *Journal of Homosexuality, 60,* 615–38. doi:10.1080/00918369.2013.760365

Herek, G. M. (2002). Heterosexuals' attitudes toward bisexual men and women in the United States. *Journal of Sex Research, 39,* 264–74. doi:10.1080/00224490209552150

Herrera, M. C., Konda, K. A., Leon, S. R., Deiss, R., Brown, B., Calvo, G. M.,... Klausner, J. D. (2016). Impact of alcohol use on sexual behavior among men who have sex with men and transgender women in Lima, Peru. *Drug and Alcohol Dependence, 161,* 147–54. doi:10.1016/j.drugalcdep.2016.01.030

Hughes, T. L., Johnson, T. P., Steffen, A. D., Wilsnack, S. C., & Everett, B. (2014). Lifetime victimization, hazardous drinking, and depression among heterosexual and sexual minority women. *LGBT Health, 1,* 192–203. doi:10.1089/lgbt.2014.0014

Hughes, T. L., Szalacha, L. A., Johnson, T. P., Kinnison, K. E., Wilsnack, S. C., & Cho, Y. (2010). Sexual victimization and hazardous drinking among heterosexual and sexual minority women. *Addictive Behaviors, 35,* 1152–6. doi:10.1016/j.addbeh.2010.07.004

Ingraham, N., Eliason, M. J., Garbers, S., Harbatkin, D., Minnis, A. M., McElroy, J. A., & Haynes, S. G. (2016). Effects of mindfulness interventions on health outcomes in older lesbian/bisexual women. *Women's Health Issues, 26,* S53–S62. doi:10.1016/j.whi.2016.04.002

James, S. E., Herman, J. L., Rankin, S., Keisling, M., Mottet, L., & Anafi, M. (2016). *The report of the 2015 U.S. Transgender Survey.* Washington, DC: Center for Transgender Equality.

Kerr, D., Ding, K., Burke, A., & Ott-Walter, K. (2015). An alcohol, tobacco, and other drug use comparison of lesbian, bisexual, and heterosexual undergraduate women. *Substance Use & Misuse, 50,* 340–9. doi:10.3109/10826084.2014.980954

Keuroghlian, A. S., Reisner, S. L., White, J. M., & Weiss, R. D. (2015). Substance use and treatment of substance use disorders in a community sample of transgender adults. *Drug and Alcohol Dependence, 152,* 139–46. doi:10.1016/j.drugalcdep.2015.04.008

Lea, T., Reynolds, R., & de Wit, J. (2013). Alcohol and other drug use, club drug dependence and treatment seeking among lesbian, gay and bisexual young people in Sydney. *Drug and Alcohol Review, 32,* 303–11. doi:10.1111/dar.12004

Lehavot, K., Simpson, T. L., & Shipherd, J. C. (2016). Factors associated with suicidality among a national sample of transgender veterans. *Suicide and Life-Threatening Behavior, 46,* 507–24. doi:10.1111/sltb.12233

Lewis, R. J., Winstead, B. A., Lau-Barraco, C., & Mason, T. B. (2017). Social factors linking stigma-related stress with alcohol use among lesbians. *Journal of Social Issues, 73,* 545–62. doi:10.1111/josi.12231

Livingston, N. A., Flentje, A., Heck, N. C., Szalda-Petree, A., & Cochran, B. N. (2017). Ecological momentary assessment of daily discrimination experiences and nicotine, alcohol, and drug use among sexual and gender minority individuals. *Journal of Consulting and Clinical Psychology, 85,* 1131–43. doi:10.1037/ccp0000252

McCabe, S. E., Hughes, T. L., West, B. T., Veliz, P., & Boyd, C. J. (2019). DSM-5 alcohol use disorder severity as a function of sexual orientation discrimination: A national study. *Alcoholism: Clinical and Experimental Research, 43,* 497–508. doi:10.1111/acer.13960

McCabe, S. E., West, B. T., Hughes, T. L., Boyd, C. J. (2013). Sexual orientation and substance abuse treatment utilization in the United States: Results from a national survey. *Journal of Substance Abuse Treatment, 44,* 4–12. doi:10.1016/j.jsat.2012.01.007

Meyer, I. H. (1995). Minority stress and mental health in gay men. *Journal of Health and Social Behavior, 36,* 38–56. doi:10.2307/2137286

Meyer, I. H. (2003). Prejudice, social stress, and mental health in lesbian, gay, and bisexual populations: Conceptual issues and research evidence. *Psychological Bulletin, 129,* 674–97. doi:10.1037/0033-2909.129.5.674

Milic, J., Glisic, M., Voortman, T., Borba, L. P., Asllanaj, E., Rojas, L. Z., . . . Franco, O. H. (2018). Menopause, ageing, and alcohol use disorders in women. *Maturitas, 111,* 100–9. doi:10.1016/j.maturitas.2018.03.006

Mimiaga, M. J., Thomas, B., Mayer, K. H., Reisner, S. L., Menon, S., Swaminathan, S., . . . Safren, S. A. (2011). Alcohol use and HIV sexual risk among MSM in Chennai, India. *International Journal of STD & AIDS, 22,* 121–5. doi:10.1258/ijsa.2009.009059

Molina, Y., Marquez, J. H., Logan, D. E., Leeson, C. J., Balsam, K. F., & Kaysen, D. L. (2015). Current intimate relationship status, depression, and alcohol use among bisexual women: The mediating roles of bisexual-specific minority stressors. *Sex Roles, 73,* 43–57. doi:10.1007/s11199-015-0483-z

Morgenstern, J., Irwin, T. W., Wainberg, M. L., Parsons, J. T., Muench, F., Bux Jr, D. A., . . . Schulz-Heik, J. (2007). A randomized controlled trial of goal choice interventions for alcohol use disorders among men who have sex with men. *Journal of Consulting and Clinical Psychology, 75,* 72–84. doi:10.1037/0022-006X.75.1.72

Morgenstern, J., Kuerbis, A. N., Chen, A. C., Kahler, C. W., Bux Jr, D. A., & Kranzler, H. R. (2012). A randomized clinical trial of naltrexone and behavioral therapy for problem drinking men who have sex with men. *Journal of Consulting and Clinical Psychology, 80,* 863–75. doi:10.1037/a0028615

Nemoto, T., Operario, D., Keatley, J., Nguyen, H., & Sugano, E. (2005). Promoting health for transgender women: Transgender resources and neighborhood space (TRANS) program in San Francisco. *American Journal of Public Health, 95,* 382–4.

Newcomb, M. E., Heinz, A. J., & Mustanski, B. (2012). Examining risk and protective factors for alcohol use in lesbian, gay, bisexual, and transgender youth: A longitudinal multilevel analysis. *Journal of Studies on Alcohol and Drugs, 73,* 783–93. doi:10.15288/jsad.2012.73.783

Nuttbrock, L. A. (2012). Culturally competent substance abuse treatment with transgender persons. *Journal of Addictive Diseases, 31,* 236–41. doi:10.1080/10550887.2012.694600

Nuttbrock, L., Bockting, W., Rosenblum, A., Hwahng, S., Mason, M., Macri, M., & Becker, J. (2014). Gender abuse, depressive symptoms, and substance use among transgender women: A 3-year prospective study. *American Journal of Public Health, 104,* 2199–206. doi:10.2105/AJPH.2014.302106

Pachankis, J. E., Hatzenbuehler, M. L., & Starks, T. J. (2014). The influence of structural stigma and rejection sensitivity on young sexual minority men's daily tobacco and alcohol use. *Social Science & Medicine, 103,* 67–75. doi:10.1016/j.socscimed.2013.10.005

Pennay, A., McNair, R., Hughes, T. L., Leonard, W., Brown, R., & Lubman, D. I. (2018). Improving alcohol and mental health treatment for lesbian, bisexual and queer women: Identity matters. *Australian and New Zealand Journal of Public Health, 42,* 35–42.

Pollitt, A. M., Mallory, A. B., & Fish, J. N. (2018). Homophobic bullying and sexual minority youth alcohol use: Do sex and race/ethnicity matter? *LGBT Health, 5,* 412–20. doi:10.1089/lgbt.2018.0031

Reback, C. J., & Fletcher, J. B. (2014). HIV prevalence, substance use, and sexual risk behaviors among transgender women recruited through outreach. *AIDS and Behavior, 18,* 1359–67.

Reisner, S. L., Deutsch, M. B., Bhasin, S., Bockting, W., Brown, G. R., Feldman, J., . . . Goodman, M. (2016). Advancing methods for U.S. transgender health research. *Current Opinion in Endocrinology, Diabetes and Obesity, 23*(2), 198–207. doi:10.1097/MED.0000000000000229

Reisner, S. L., Greytak, E. A., Parsons, J. T., & Ybarra, M. L. (2015). Gender minority social stress in adolescence: Disparities in adolescent bullying and substance use by gender identity. *Journal of Sex Research, 52,* 243–56. doi:10.1080/00224499.2014.886321

Reisner, S. L., White, J. M., Mayer, K. H., & Mimiaga, M. J. (2014). Sexual risk behaviors and psychosocial health concerns of female-to-male transgender men screening for STDs at an urban community health center. *AIDS Care, 26,* 857–64. doi:10.1080/09540121.2013855701

Santos, G. M., Rowe, C., Hern, J., Walker, J. E., Ali, A., Ornelaz, M., . . . Raymond, H. F. (2018). Prevalence and correlates of hazardous alcohol consumption and binge drinking among men who have sex with men (MSM) in San Francisco. *PloS One,* 13, 1–23. doi:10.1371/journal.pone.0202170

Schuler, M. S., Rice, C. E., Evans-Polce, R. J., & Collins, R. (2018). Disparities in substance use behaviors and disorders among adult sexual minorities by age, gender, and sexual identity. *Drug & Alcohol Dependence, 189,* 139–46. doi:10.1016/j.drugalcdep.2018.05.008

Slater, M. E., Godette, D., Huang, B., Ruan, W. J., & Kerridge, B. T. (2017). Sexual orientation based discrimination, excessive alcohol use, and substance use disorders among sexual minority adults. *LGBT Health, 4,* 337–44. doi:10.1089/lgbt.2016.0117

Smalley, K. B., Warren, J. C., & Barefoot, K. N. (2016). Differences in health risk behaviors across understudied LGBT subgroups. *Health Psychology, 35,* 103–14.

Sperber, J., Landers, S., & Lawrence, S. (2005). Access to health care for transgendered persons: Results of a needs assessment in Boston. *International Journal of Transgenderism, 8,* 75–91.

Szymanski, D. M. (2006). Does internalized heterosexism moderate the link between heterosexist events and lesbians' psychological distress? *Sex Roles, 54,* 227–34.

Talley, A. E., Aranda, F., Hughes, T. L., Everett, B., & Johnson, T. P. (2015). Longitudinal associations among discordant sexual orientation dimensions and hazardous drinking in a cohort of sexual minority women. *Journal of Health and Sexual Behavior, 56,* 225–45.

Talley, A. E., & Littlefield, A. K. (2014). Pathways between concealable stigmatized identities and substance misuse. *Social and Personality Psychology Compass, 8,* 569–82.

Talley, A. E., & Stevens, J. E. (2017). Sexual orientation self-concept ambiguity: Scale adaptation and validation. *Assessment, 24,* 632–45. doi:10.1177/1073191115617016

U.S. Department of Health and Human Services, National Institutes of Health, National Institute on Alcohol Use and Alcoholism. (2013). *Alcohol use disorder: A comparison between DSM-IV and DSM-5* (NIH Publication No. 13-7999). http://pubs.niaaa.nih.gov/publications/dsmfactsheet/dsmfact.pdf

Velasquez, M. M., von Sternberg, K., Johnson, D. H., Green, C., Carbonari, J. P., & Parsons, J. T. (2009). Reducing sexual risk behaviors and alcohol use among HIV-positive men who have sex with men: A randomized clinical trial. *Journal of Consulting and Clinical Psychology, 77*, 657–67. doi:10.1037/a0015519

Veldhuis, C. B., Talley, A. E., Hancock, D. W., Wilsnack, S. C., & Hughes, T. L. (2017). Alcohol use, age, and self-rated mental and physical health in a community sample of lesbian and bisexual women. *LGBT Health, 4*, 419–26. doi:10.1089/lgbt.2017.0056

Verrastro, V., Fontanesi, L., Petruccelli, I., Santamaria, F., Laghi, F., . . . Baiocco, R. (2016). Binge drinking and internalized sexual stigma among Italian lesbian, gay, and bisexual young adults. *Nordic Studies on Alcohol and Drugs, 33*, 437–46. doi:10.1515/nsad-2016-0035

Welch, S., Howden-Chapman, P., & Collings, S. C. (1998). Survey of drug and alcohol use by lesbian women in New Zealand. *Addictive Behaviors, 23*, 543–8. doi:10.1016/S0306-4603(98)00036-7

Wilson, S. M., Gilmore, A. K., Rhew, I. C., Hodge, K. A., & Kaysen, D. L. (2016). Minority stress is longitudinally associated with alcohol-related problems among sexual minority women. *Addictive Behaviors, 61*, 80–3. doi:10.1016/j.addbeh.2016.05.017

Wong, C. F., Kipke, M. D., & Weiss, G. (2008). Risk factors for alcohol use, frequent use, and binge drinking among young men who have sex with men. *Addictive Behaviors, 33*, 1012–20. doi:10.1016/j.addbeh.2008.03.008

Wray, T. B., Grin, B., Dorfman, L., Glynn, T. R., Kahler, C. W., Marshall, B. D., . . . Operario, D. (2016). Systematic review of interventions to reduce problematic alcohol use in men who have sex with men. *Drug and Alcohol Review, 35*, 148–57. doi:10.1111/dar.12271

CHAPTER

9 Drug Use among Sexual and Gender Minority Populations

Tyrel J. Starks, Cynthia M. Cabral, *and* Ali J. Talan

Abstract

Based on current epidemiological data, sexual and gender minorities present with significantly higher rates of drug use disorders compared with their heterosexual or cisgender counterparts. Using minority stress theory and syndemics theory, the current chapter discusses prevalence rates, psychosocial correlates, and health comorbidities observed in research among men who have sex with men, women who have sex with women, and transgender populations. The authors also highlight how HIV transmission risk has fueled much of the research on drug use disorders with sexual and gender minorities, resulting in a paucity of research on drug use in lesbian and bisexual women and transgender men, as well as other areas for further study.

Keywords: gay drug use, lesbian drug use, bisexual drug use, sexual minority drug use, transgender drug use, LGBT drug use

Drug Use among Sexual and Gender Minority Populations

A significant amount of research on drug use and drug use disorders has included sexual and gender minority populations. While this overall trend is promising, and yields a body of research that we review in this chapter, it also masks subgroup variability in the understanding of drug use. The field has been influenced substantially by an emphasis on links between drug use and human immunodeficiency virus (HIV) infection. As a result, there is considerably more information about the psychosocial correlates and health consequences of drug use available for those SGM populations at highest risk of infection—sexual minority men and transwomen—compared to those with lower HIV infection risk (i.e., sexual minority women and transmen).

The language used in this chapter reflects recent developments in the conceptualization of substance use disorders and also a conventional focus on drug use in much of the research literature. The fifth edition of the *Diagnostic and Statistical Manual of Mental Disorders* (DSM-5) (American Psychiatric Association, 2013) saw substantive changes to categories associated with drug use. Previous editions of the DSM (American Psychiatric Association, 2000) distinguished between "substance abuse disorder" and "substance dependence." DSM-5 introduced a dimensional conceptualization in which substance use disorders are formulated on a continuum from mild to severe. We have generally framed this chapter in terms of substance use disorder, consistent with the current DSM. We use the general term *drug use disorder* to avoid conflation with alcohol-related findings. Any references to abuse and dependence are a reflection of terminology in the original research.

There is, to some extent, a disconnection between the measurement of drug use in research—where the emphasis is often placed on quantifying the amount or frequency of use—and the DSM formulation of substance use disorder. Many research studies, including many treatment outcome studies, gather detailed data on the occurrence, amount, and frequency of drug use for specific substances. While informative, the assessment of use alone does not provide the data necessary to determine whether drug use occurs in the context of a substance use disorder. We therefore restrict discussions to drug use in instances where study methodology does not support inferences about diagnostic status.

Drug Use and Minority Stress

Minority stress theory has had a defining influence on the study of drug use and associated comorbid conditions. The theory proposes that members of marginalized groups experience unique and chronic stressors above and beyond their nonmarginalized peers (Meyer, 2003). These stressors include both distal (e.g., violence, victimization, and discrimination as the result of prejudice) and proximal (e.g., self-stigmatization, concealment of identity, and expectations of rejection) experiences. Hatzenbuehler (2009) suggested that these stressors influence intrapsychological factors, such as emotion regulation and cognition, which subsequently increase risk for the development of psychopathology.

The literature discussed in this chapter consistently illustrates that experiences of minority stress are associated with drug use among SGM in pervasive ways. Social discrimination such as experiences of rejection by family and peers and occurrences of physical, sexual, and child sexual abuse are ubiquitous predictors of drug use across sexual minority groups (e.g., Bostwick, Boyd, Hughes, West, & McCabe, 2014; Grant et al., 2011; McCabe, Bostwick, Hughes, West, & Boyd, 2010). Mental health problems—comorbid sequelae of minority stress—commonly accompany drug use and tend to exacerbate adverse consequences (e.g., Benotsch et al., 2013; Goldbach, Tanner-Smith, Bagwell, & Dunlap, 2014; Lehavot & Simoni, 2011). Our review highlights recent applications of syndemics theory to define common psychological vulnerabilities shared by drug use and other comorbid psychological disorders arising from minority stress (Pachankis, 2014, 2015) and the cumulative impact of drug use and other co-occurring conditions on HIV-related risk specifically (Stall et al., 2003).

Sexual Minority Men: Gay Men, Bisexual Men, and Other Men Who Have Sex with Men

Data consistently indicate that sexual minority men report drug use, drug-related problems, and drug use disorders at higher rates than their heterosexual peers. Data from the 2015–2016 National Survey on Drug Use and Health (NSDUH; Medley et al., 2016) conducted in the United States indicated that 39.1 percent of gay men and 34.6 percent of bisexual men reported the use of any illicit drug in the past year, compared to the male national average of 21.1 percent. Available rates for specific drugs mirrored this overall trend. Rates of marijuana use were 28.2 percent and 28.6 percent among gay and bisexual men respectively, compared to 16.9 percent among men overall. Rates of prescription pain reliever misuse were 9.1 percent and 7.6 percent among gay and bisexual men respectively, compared to 5.2 percent among men overall. Follow-up analyses indicated that the odds of lifetime use of hallucinogens, cocaine, and inhalants were uniformly elevated among gay men relative to age-matched heterosexual men between the ages of 18 and 49. Among bisexual men, there was some indication that disparities increased with age (Schuler, Stein, & Collins, 2019).

Disparities in drug use between sexual minority men and heterosexual men emerge early and are observed across studies in the United States and globally. Recent data from the Youth Risk Behavior Surveillance (YRBS) in the United States indicated that rates of use for all illicit drugs except marijuana were higher among those male respondents who identified as gay or bisexual compared to heterosexual males. Those male youth who were unsure of their sexual identity also reported elevated rates of most illicit drugs relative to heterosexual boys (Kann et al., 2018). These data continue trends observed in earlier meta-analyses, which included studies of samples from outside the United States. Sexual minority youth generally were as much as 190 percent more likely to use substances than their heterosexual counterparts. Moderate to large effect sizes were observed for lifetime use of marijuana (odds ratio = 2.6), cocaine (odds ratio = 3.1), and injection drugs (odds ratio = 7.2) specifically. Disparities were greater for bisexual youth compared to those who identified as lesbian and gay. When outliers were removed, differences between effects observed in U.S. and global samples were not significant (Marshal et al., 2008).

Observed disparities in drug use disorders mirror those observed in drug use generally. Data from the NSDUH indicated that 19.3 percent of gay and 16.4 percent of bisexual men met criteria for a substance use disorder in the past year, compared to the U.S. national average of 10.5 percent for men (Medley et al., 2016). McCabe, Hughes, Bostwick, West, and Boyd (2009) disaggregated risk for DSM-IV alcohol and substance use dependence in the National Epidemiological Survey on Alcohol and Related Conditions (NESARC) data set. Rates of past-year marijuana dependence were comparable across heterosexual-, gay-, and bisexual-identified groups but higher among those who were unsure of their sexual identity. In contrast, gay- and bisexual-identified groups were 4.2 and 6.3 times more likely than heterosexual men to meet criteria for a use disorder for other drugs compared to heterosexual men (McCabe et al., 2009).

Research on drug use among sexual minority men has been propelled in large part by its association with HIV infection risk in this population. Sexual minority men tend to be sexually riskier when they have sex under the influence of drugs (e.g., Rendina, Moody, Ventuneac, Grov, & Parsons, 2015; Vosburgh, Mansergh, Sullivan, & Purcell, 2012). Not only does drug use predict HIV infection risk among sexual minority men, but rates of drug use are elevated among HIV-positive sexual minority men. Research in both the United States and internationally indicates that HIV-positive sexual minority men use drugs at higher rates than HIV-negative sexual minority men. The drugs most commonly used by HIV-positive sexual minority men vary by study, but those often observed include marijuana, methamphetamine, cocaine, gamma-hydroxybutyrate (GHB), ketamine, and Ecstasy (Mimiaga et al., 2013; Parsons, Kutnick, Halkitis, Punzalan, & Carbonari, 2005). These elevated rates may arise because sexual minority men who use drugs are more likely to seroconvert and then subsequently continue to use (Menza, Hughes, Celum, & Golden, 2009; Ostrow et al., 2009; Plankey et al., 2007). They may also arise because the added psychosocial stressor of HIV-related stigma provides an additional motivation for use (Rendina, Millar, & Parsons, 2018).

Studies have consistently indicated that drug use is associated with sexual agreements (Hoff & Beougher, 2010)—or the understandings male couples create to define the rules and boundaries around sex with partners outside their primary relationship. Couples in non-monogamous relationships, where sex with outside partners is permitted, tend to use drugs more frequently than monogamous couples (Brown, Turner, Hern, & Santos, 2017; Gamarel, Woolf-King, Carrico, Neilands, & Johnson, 2015; Mitchell, 2016; Parsons & Starks, 2014; Starks et al., 2019).

Global research on drug use and related disorders among sexual minority men varies considerably, and conclusions are hampered by methodological variability and the failure to disaggregate data by sexual orientation. Several recent reviews support the broad conclusion that rates of illicit drug use are higher among sexual minority men compared to heterosexual men globally (Bourne & Weatherburn, 2017; Sanford et al., 2017). Among sexual minority men in Africa, the most consistent findings were related to high rates of cannabis and injection drug use. Rate estimates for other drugs varied widely across countries and studies (Sanford et al., 2017). In contrast, some evidence from a large online study of sexual minority men living in nine countries in Asia indicated that rates of at least some stimulant drugs (e.g., methamphetamine, 4.0 percent; Ecstasy, 8.1 percent) were comparable to or higher than marijuana use (3.6 percent) (Wei, Guadamuz, Lim, Huang, & Koe, 2012).

Drug Use Motivation

A large body of research has emerged examining the motivational factors—or reasons why—sexual minority men may use drugs. Similar to heterosexual populations, sexual minority men commonly report the use of drugs to feel good or get high and to escape from everyday problems and stressors (Jerome, Halkitis, & Siconofli, 2009; Starks, Golub, Kelly, & Parsons, 2010). Consistent with minority stress theory, research on drug use motivations for sexual minority men also indicates a subset of motivations specifically related to being a sexual minority. Drug use among sexual minority men has been identified as a mechanism to cope with psychological pain associated with being non-heterosexual (Green & Feinstein, 2012; Moody, Starks, Grov, & Parsons, 2018). In contrast to the use of drugs as a maladaptive coping strategy, drug use among sexual minority men may facilitate interpersonal relationships and a greater sense of community belonging (Green & Feinstein, 2012; McKay, McDavitt, George, & Mutchler, 2012). Similar findings have been observed in research on sexual minority men globally (Bourne & Weatherburn, 2017).

There is evidence to suggest that sexual factors represent an additional source of motivation for drug use among sexual minority men. In some instances, they may use drugs to enhance sexual pleasure (Halkitis, Fischgrund, & Parsons, 2005; Jerome et al., 2009; Palamar & Halkitis, 2006). Some sexual minority men use drugs to decrease anxiety or inhibitions around engaging in same-gender sexual behavior (Lelutiu-Weinberger et al., 2013). Some HIV-negative sexual minority men believe that the use of drugs during sex enhances intimacy and results in sexual experiences that are more likely to lead to a relationship (Starks, Millar, Tuck, & Wells, 2015). In other instances, the use of specific drugs—for example stimulants (e.g., methamphetamine, cocaine, or crack) or "club drugs" (e.g., Ecstasy, GBH, and ketamine)—is linked to particular kinds of sexual encounters within subcultures of sexual minority men such that social norms and expectations may provide an additional motivation for use (Bourne et al., 2015; Grov, Hirshfield, Remien, Humberstone, & Chiasson, 2013; Mattison, Ross, Wolfson, & Franklin, 2001).

Drug Use Comorbidities and Health

Drug use does not occur in isolation from an individual's overall functioning. A large body of research has documented the co-occurrence of several mental and physical health problems, including drug use, among the SGM community. Consistent with general principles of minority stress theory, syndemics theory suggests that adverse health conditions in marginalized populations are systematically interconnected (Singer & Clair, 2003; Singer et al., 2006).

Stall et al. (2003) applied syndemics theory to illustrate the cumulative effect of drug use (polydrug use specifically) in conjunction with three other commonly comorbid conditions (depression, childhood sexual abuse, and intimate partner violence) on HIV risk among sexual minority men. The odds of HIV infection increased with the number of syndemic conditions present. Among HIV-negative sexual minority men, syndemic burden was positively associated with HIV sexual risk-taking behavior. The general finding that cumulative syndemic burden is associated with HIV-related risk has been replicated in multiple studies of U.S.-based samples of sexual minority men (e.g., Mimiaga et al., 2019; Mustanski, Garofalo, Herrick, & Donenberg, 2007; Parsons, Grov, & Golub, 2012; Parsons et al., 2017; Starks, Tuck, Millar, & Parsons, 2016).

Sexual Minority Women: Lesbian Women, Bisexual Women, and Other Women Who Have Sex with Women

While some have suggested that sexual minority women may be less likely to manifest drug use disorders and more likely to manifest internalizing problems such as mood and anxiety disorders (Lee, Gamarel, Bryant, Zaller, & Operario, 2016), a substantial body of epidemiological data indicates the presence of significant disparities in drug use among sexual minority women compared to heterosexual women. Data from the 2015–2016 NSDUH indicated that 29.8 percent of lesbian and 47.8 percent of bisexual women reported the use of any illicit drug in the past year, compared to the national average of 15.2 percent for all women. Rates of marijuana use were 24.7 percent and 38.9 percent for lesbian and bisexual women, respectively, compared to 11.0 percent among women overall. Rates of prescription pain reliever misuse were 6.5 percent and 14.7 percent among lesbian and bisexual women, respectively, compared to 3.9 percent among heterosexual women (Medley et al., 2016). Follow-up analyses indicated that the odds of lifetime use of hallucinogens, cocaine, and inhalants were uniformly elevated among both lesbian and bisexual women relative to age-matched heterosexual women from ages 18 to 49; however, trends indicated these disparities were greatest among younger lesbian women and older bisexual women (Schuler et al., 2019).

Epidemiological studies of youth indicate that disparities in drug use emerge early. YRBS data indicated that the prevalence of marijuana use was higher among lesbian and bisexual (54.3 percent) youth compared to heterosexual (34.7 percent) youth and those who were unsure of their sexual identity (29.9 percent). The trend was persistent across illicit drugs (Kann et al., 2018).

Observed disparities in drug use disorders mirror those observed in use generally. Data from the NSDUH indicated that 10.1 percent of lesbian and 17.4 percent of bisexual women met criteria for either alcohol use disorder or a substance use disorder in the past year, compared to 5.6 percent of women nationally (Medley et al., 2016). Data from multiple waves of NESARC indicated that when alcohol and drug use disorders are examined separately, sexual minority women are significantly more likely to meet criteria for a drug use disorder (Kerridge et al., 2017; McCabe et al., 2009).

As evidenced by the prevalence data reviewed previously, there is a consistent trend in which bisexuality is uniquely associated with increased drug use among sexual minority women, particularly in adulthood, a similar trend has been observed among sexual minority men but with far less consistency (Schuler, Rice, Evans-Polce, & Collins, 2018). Studies that have examined multiple components of sexual orientation (identity, attraction, and behavior) have generally found that bisexuality is associated with increased risk for drug use relative to both lesbian and heterosexual forms of monosexuality (Hughes, Wilsnack, & Kristjanson, 2015; Kerr, Ding, Burke, & Ott-Walter, 2015; McCabe et al., 2009;

Paschen-Wolff et al., 2019); however, there is some evidence to indicate that risk is related to attraction and behavior more than identity per se (Kerr et al., 2015; Paschen-Wolff et al., 2019). It is particularly marked among sexual minority women for whom identity, attraction, and behavior are incongruent (Hughes et al., 2015; Kerr et al., 2015; Paschen-Wolff et al., 2019).

Several explanations have been posited for the unique risk faced by bisexual women. Women who express attraction to both men and women without assuming a bisexual identity may experience discrimination and rejection from both lesbian/gay and heterosexual communities (Israel & Mohr, 2004), less social support (Balsam & Mohr, 2007), diminished benefits of "coming out" on reductions in internalized stigma, and more internalized stigma due to stereotypes about the transient nature of non-monosexual identities (Paschen-Wolff et al., 2019). Schuler et al. (2018) review a body of literature that suggests that the lesbian movement's historical connections to feminism potentially frame bisexual women's receptivity to relationships with men as anathema, thereby exacerbating tensions between lesbian and bisexual women in a manner not experienced by gay and bisexual men.

Motivations for Drug Use

Research on gender and coping indicates that women are more likely to use emotion-focused and avoidant coping strategies compared to men (Matud, 2004). Emotion-focused coping has been linked to drug use in studies of women generally (Boyd et al., 2002; Roberts, 2001; Scott, Hides, Allen, & Lubman, 2013) and sexual minority women specifically (Hughes et al., 2015; Rosario, Scrimshaw, & Hunter, 2008). Citing research on the comorbidity of intimate partner violence and drug use, some have hypothesized that drug use may serve as a mechanism by which sexual minority women modulate or avoid emotional pain arising from minority stress (Lewis, Milletich, Kelley, & Woody, 2012). Lesbian identity has been linked to the use of active coping among Black and African American women (Bowleg, Craig, & Burkholder, 2004), suggesting the possibility that sexual identity differences in coping may help to explain increased rates of drug use among bisexual women.

Rosario et al. (2008) observed that sexual minority women who identified as butch were more likely to use drugs than their femme counterparts, and speculated that drug use may constitute one aspect of masculine role adherence for some sexual minority women. Similarly, Lehavot and Simoni (2011) found that butch/masculine sexual minority women were more likely to experience some forms of sexual minority discrimination, leading to associations with increased drug use–related problems.

Drug Use Comorbidities and Health

The study of drug use as a correlate of HIV risk has received considerably less attention among sexual minority women compared to other SGM subgroups. Perhaps owing to this, syndemics theory has been applied less frequently to understand comorbid psychosocial problems among sexual minority women. There is evidence to suggest that the application of syndemics theory has the potential to guide inquiry and direct much-needed attention toward the sexual health of sexual minority women. Coulter, Kinsky, Herrick, Stall, and Bauermeister (2015) found that marijuana, Ecstasy, and hallucinogen use as well as prescription drug misuse loaded onto a latent syndemic factor that also included depression, heavy episodic alcohol consumption, having multiple sexual partners, and a history of sexually transmitted infections. Consistent with the suggestion that co-occurring syndemic conditions arise as a function of minority stress, they also found that the latent syndemic factor was predicted by sexual orientation discrimination.

Several other aspects of the existing literature on drug use comorbidities point to the utility of applying a syndemics framework to examine how minority stress might influence not only the occurrence of individual conditions, but also the co-occurrence of multiple health challenges. One promising pathway implied in existing research may involve emotion-focused coping. As mentioned earlier in the chapter, substantial research has demonstrated that interpersonal victimization in both childhood and adulthood is associated with drug use among sexual minority women (Bimbi, Palmadessa, & Parsons, 2008; Hughes, McCabe, Wilsnack, West, & Boyd, 2010; Otis, Oser, & Staton-Tindall, 2016) and emotion-focused coping has been proposed as a potential mechanism linking these experiences for women (Lewis et al., 2012).

Transgender and Gender-Nonconforming Populations

The National Transgender Discrimination Survey Report on Health and Health Care (NTDS; Grant et al., 2011) gathered data from 6,450 transgender-identified persons living in the United States. Eighteen percent of respondents indicated they misused alcohol or drugs at some point in their lives to cope with discrimination. Follow-up analyses found that nonbinary gender identity (genderqueer, etc.) was uniquely associated with a significant increase in the odds of using alcohol or drugs to cope (Klein & Golub, 2016).

Unfortunately, the NTDS data released do not distinguish between drug and alcohol use. Furthermore, because the NTDS only assesses alcohol and drug misuse specifically as a coping strategy, this may underestimate the proportion of transgender people overall who are using drugs or who experience associated problems. Project VOICE (Keuroghlian, Reisner, White, & Weiss, 2015), a study of 452 transgender adults in Massachusetts, found that 39.6 percent of respondents used marijuana in the past twelve months and 19.0 percent used some illicit drug other than marijuana in the past twelve months. Prescription painkillers (8.6 percent), "downers" (6.4 percent), and hallucinogens (5.8 percent) were the most commonly reported illicit drugs after marijuana. Use of stimulants (3.3 percent) and club drugs (4.2 percent) was relatively less common. Limited research among transgender youth indicates that a substantial proportion of transgender people initiate drug use early in life. YRBS data indicated that at least a quarter of transgender youth used cocaine (27.1 percent), heroine (26.1 percent), methamphetamine (24.9 percent), and prescription opioids (35.9 percent) in their lifetime (Johns et al., 2019). Information about the prevalence of drug use disorders among transgender people is limited by a lack of data that has systematically disaggregated alcohol and drug use. Herbst et al. (2008) estimated that between 11.2 percent and 16.3 percent of transgender people experienced problems with either alcohol or drug use.

Similar to research on sexual minority men, drug use among transgender women and those on the male-to-female spectrum has received particular attention due to associations with HIV risk. The overall mean prevalence estimate for HIV in transwomen is 18.8%, as compared to 2% in transmen (Becasen, Denard, Mullins, Higa, & Sipe, 2019). The use of drugs in conjunction with sex is commonly reported, with estimates ranging from 15.4 percent to 63.6 percent (Reisner et al., 2009; Santos et al., 2014). Drug use before sex has been associated with an increased likelihood of condomless anal sex in studies of transwomen (Brennan et al., 2012; Nemoto, Operario, Keatley, Han, & Soma, 2004; Operario, Nemoto, Iwamoto, & Moore, 2011).

Studies of transwomen at high risk of HIV infection in the United States illustrate the salience of stimulant use, particularly methamphetamine, among those who are HIV positive. While estimates of marijuana use range between roughly a quarter and two thirds, there is little indication that rates differ by HIV status (Reback & Fletcher, 2014; Rose, Santos, McFarland, & Wilson, 2015; Santos et al., 2014). In contrast, there is consistent evidence indicating that HIV-positive transwomen are more likely to use stimulants compared to their HIV-negative counterparts. In their study of 2,136 transwomen, Reback and Fletcher (2014) found that those who were HIV positive were significantly more likely to report use of methamphetamine (odds ratio = 2.01) and crack (odds ratio = 2.19). Similarly, Santos et al. (2014) found HIV-positive transwomen were more likely to report methamphetamine use generally and in conjunction with sex compared to HIV-negative transwomen.

Motivations for Drug Use

As illustrated in data from the NTDS, the use of drugs to cope with gender-related discrimination is commonly reported among gender minority people generally. There is specific evidence that the use of drugs to cope with emotional pain is a mechanism linking life stress to HIV-related risk in transwomen. Young transwomen who experienced gender-related discrimination had significantly increased odds of drug use (odds ratio = 2.28) generally as well as use before or during sex (odds ratio = 2.35) (Rose et al., 2015). Complementary findings suggest that drug use mediates pathways linking life stress with condomless anal sex among young transwomen (Hotton, Garofalo, Kuhns, & Johnson, 2013).

Sexual factors appear to serve as an important source of motivation for drug use among transgender women. Many report using drugs to manage anxiety and mitigate emotional distress during sex (Nemoto et al., 2004; Sausa, Keatley, & Operario, 2007). Some use drugs to facilitate specific kinds of sex (e.g., transactional sex) (Reisner et al., 2009; Sausa et al., 2007).

Drug Use Comorbidities and Health

Similar to sexual minority men, transgender people face multiple social and psychological challenges that occur in addition to drug use. Injection hormone treatments may increase HIV risk in instances where needle-sharing is involved (Herbst et al., 2008; Keuroghlian et al., 2015). Additional evidence illustrates the cumulative deleterious impact of myriad factors on the health of transgender people, these include housing instability, engagement in sex work, economic disadvantage, social isolation, interpersonal violence (physical and sexual abuse in childhood and adulthood), and unmet mental health needs (Herbst et al., 2008; Keuroghlian et al., 2015; Reisner, Hughto, Pardee, & Sevelius, 2016).

As with sexual minority men, a syndemics framework has been applied to study the additive impact of these effects on HIV risk. While this research is limited by an emphasis on U.S.-based samples of transwomen and a dearth of population-based data (Poteat, Scheim, Xavier, Reisner, & Baral, 2016), available evidence indicates the utility of the framework. Brennan et al. (2012) tested the additive effect of five syndemic factors in a sample of young transgender women in Chicago. Syndemic stress was positively associated with HIV-positive serostatus, condomless anal sex, and also associated psychosocial stressors of incarceration and sex work. Similarly, Parsons et al. (2018) found that polydrug use, depression, childhood sexual abuse, and intimate partner violence additively predicted sexual HIV transmission risk behavior and exchange sex in a sample of 212 transwomen recruited in New York City.

Perhaps as a result of a focus on HIV risk, transmen and transmasculine individuals are underrepresented in the study of drug use comorbidities—and their collective impact on health. For example, the Herbst et al. (2008) meta-analyses included twenty-eight studies, but only five included transmale respondents. This is concerning because there is at least some evidence from the United States and globally that transmen who have sex with men are at elevated risk of HIV infection. Reisner et al. (2016) found that—for transmasculine men who reported sex with cisgender men and who lived full time in their identified (male) gender—syndemic stressors (i.e., binge drinking, drug use, anxiety, depression, childhood sexual abuse, and intimate partner violence) were associated with indicators of HIV-related sexual risk taking in a cumulative way in a manner similar to sexual minority men.

Limitations and Future Directions

The existing literature on drug use has been shaped in profound ways by the prioritization of risk factors for HIV infection. This emphasis has accelerated research among those subpopulations of SGM people at highest risk of infection, specifically sexual minority men and transwomen; however, even within these high-risk subgroups, much of the research on substance use and sexual health, particularly HIV prevention and treatment, has centered around the experiences of younger, sexually active, sexual minority men (Heath, Lanoye, & Maisto, 2012). Unfortunately, the identification of factors associated with drug use—and the development of tailored interventions that address those salient factors—for sexual minority women and transgender men has lagged behind.

There is a need for greater attention to aspects of physical health beyond HIV and sexually transmitted infections. While sexual health is an essential component of overall well-being, it is not the only aspect of physical health that is impacted by drug use. For example, a 2017 systematic review found that sexual minority adults (both women and men) who used illicit drugs were at increased risk of cardiovascular disease (Caceres et al., 2017). It is entirely plausible that syndemics theory could be used to conceptualize the impact of drug use and related comorbidities on health problems beyond HIV infection. There may be substantial public health benefits to such investigations.

Conclusions

The existing literature consistently illustrates that SGM populations experience serious health disparities related to drug use in the United States and globally. Across SGM populations, these disparities arise in part as a result of minority stress. Recent applications of syndemics theory point to the potential to use the large body of research on minority stress—and the psychological pathways by which it impacts health outcomes—to understand drug use and related comorbidities, potentially leading to the development of novel interventions for SGM. While promising, the existing literature points to the urgent need to extend research efforts for gender minority populations and sexual minority women. These groups have received substantially less attention to date, which has contributed to the relative lack of tailored intervention options available for them relative to sexual minority men.

References

American Psychiatric Association. (2000). *Diagnostic and statistical manual of mental disorders* (4th ed.). Arlington, VA: American Psychiatric Association.

American Psychiatric Association. (2013). *Diagnostic and statistical manual of mental disorders* (5th ed.). Arlington, VA: American Psychiatric Association.

Becasen, J. S., Denard, C. L., Mullins, M. M., Higa, D. H., & Sipe, T. A. (2019). Estimating the prevalence of HIV and sexual behaviors among the US transgender population: A systematic review and meta-analysis, 2006–2017. *American Journal of Public Health, 109*(1), e1–e8. doi:10.2105/AJPH.2018.304727

Benotsch, E. G., Zimmerman, R., Cathers, L., McNulty, S., Pierce, J., Heck, T., ... Snipes, D. (2013). Non-medical use of prescription drugs, polysubstance use, and mental health in transgender adults. *Drug and Alcohol Dependence, 132*(1–2), 391–4. doi:10.1016/j.drugalcdep.2013.02.027

Bimbi, D., Palmadessa, N., & Parsons, J. T. (2008). Substance use and domestic violence among urban gays, lesbians, and bisexuals. *Journal of LGBT Health Research, 3*(2), 1–7. doi:10.1300/J463v03n02_01

Bostwick, W. B., Boyd, C. J., Hughes, T. L., West, B. T., & McCabe, S. E. (2014). Discrimination and mental health among lesbian, gay, and bisexual adults in the United States. *American Journal of Orthopsychiatry, 84*(1), 35–45. doi:10.1037/h0098851

Bourne, A., Reid, D., Hickson, F., Torres-Rueda, S., Steinberg, P., & Weatherburn, P. (2015). "Chemsex" and harm reduction need among gay men in South London. *International Journal of Drug Policy, 26*(12), 1171–6. doi:10.1016/j.drugpo.2015.07.013

Bourne, A., & Weatherburn, P. (2017). Substance use among men who have sex with men: Patterns, motivations, impacts and intervention development need. *Sexually Transmitted Infections, 93*(5), 342–6. doi:10.1136/sextrans-2016-052674

Bowleg, L., Craig, M. L., & Burkholder, G. (2004). Rising and surviving: A conceptual model of active coping among Black lesbians. *Cultural Diversity and Ethnic Minority Psychology, 10*(3), 229–40. doi:10.1037/1099-9809.10.3.229

Boyd, M. R., Bland, A., Herman, J., Mestler, L., Murr, L., & Potts, L. (2002). Stress and coping in rural women with alcohol and other drug disorders. *Archives of Psychiatric Nursing, 16*(6), 254–62. doi:10.1053/apnu.2002.37280

Brennan, J., Kuhns, L. M., Johnson, A. K., Belzer, M., Wilson, E. C., & Garofalo, R. (2012). Syndemic theory and HIV-related risk among young transgender women: The role of multiple, co-occurring health problems and social marginalization. *American Journal of Public Health, 102*(9), 1751–7. doi:10.2105/AJPH.2011.300433

Brown, R. E., Turner, C., Hern, J., & Santos, G. M. (2017). Partner-level substance use associated with increased sexual risk behaviors among men who have sex with men in San Francisco, CA. *Drug and Alcohol Dependence, 176*, 176–80. doi:10.1016/j.drugalcdep.2017.02.016

Caceres, B. A., Brody, A., Luscombe, R. E., Primiano, J. E., Marusca, P., Sitts, E. M., & Chyun, D. (2017). A systematic review of cardiovascular disease in sexual minorities. *American Journal of Public Health, 107*(4), e13–e21. doi:10.2105/AJPH.2016.303630

Coulter, R. W. S., Kinsky, S. M., Herrick, A. L., Stall, R. D., & Bauermeister, J. A. (2015). Evidence of syndemics and sexuality-related discrimination among young sexual-minority women. *LGBT Health, 2*(3), 250–7. doi:10.1089/lgbt.2014.0063

Gamarel, K. E., Woolf-King, S. E., Carrico, A. W., Neilands, T. B., & Johnson, M. O. (2015). Stimulant use patterns and HIV transmission risk among HIV serodiscordant male couples. *Journal of Acquired Immune Deficiency Syndromes (1999), 68*(2), 147–51. doi:10.1097/QAI.0000000000000418

Goldbach, J. T., Tanner-Smith, E. E., Bagwell, M., & Dunlap, S. (2014). Minority stress and substance use in sexual minority adolescents: A meta-analysis. *Prevention Science, 15*(3), 350–63. doi:10.1007/s11121-013-0393-7

Grant, J. M., Mottet, L. A., Tanis, J. E., Harrison, J., Herman, J. L., & Keisling, M. (2011). *Injustice at every turn: A report of the national transgender discrimination survey*. Washington, DC: National Center for Transgender Equality and National Gay and Lesbian Task Force. https://www.transequality.org/sites/default/files/docs/resources/NTDS_Report.pdf

Green, K. E., & Feinstein, B. A. (2012). Substance use in lesbian, gay, and bisexual populations: An update on empirical research and implications for treatment. *Psychology of Addictive Behaviors, 26*(2), 265–78. doi:10.1037/a0025424

Grov, C., Hirshfield, S., Remien, R. H., Humberstone, M., & Chiasson, M. A. (2013). Exploring the venue's role in risky sexual behavior among gay and bisexual men: An event-level analysis from a national online survey in the US. *Archives of Sexual Behavior, 42*(2), 291–302. doi:10.1007/s10508-011-9854-x

Halkitis, P. N., Fischgrund, B. N., & Parsons, J. T. (2005). Explanations for methamphetamine use among gay and bisexual men in New York City. *Substance Use & Misuse, 40*(9–10), 1331–45. doi:10.1081/JA-200066900

Hatzenbuehler, M. L. (2009). How does sexual minority stigma "get under the skin"? A psychological mediation framework. *Psychological Bulletin, 135*(5), 707–30. doi:10.1037/a0016441

Heath, J., Lanoye, A., & Maisto, S. A. (2012). The role of alcohol and substance use in risky sexual behavior among older men who have sex with men: A review and critique of the current literature. *AIDS and Behavior, 16*(3), 578–89. doi:10.1007/s10461-011-9921-2

Herbst, J. H., Jacobs, E. D., Finlayson, T. J., McKleroy, V. S., Neumann, M. S., & Crepaz, N. (2008). Estimating HIV prevalence and risk behaviors of transgender persons in the United States: A systematic review. *AIDS and Behavior, 12*(1), 1–17. doi:10.1007/s10461-007-9299-3

Hoff, C. C., & Beougher, S. C. (2010). Sexual agreements among gay male couples. *Archives of Sexual Behavior, 39*(3), 774–87. doi:10.1007/s10508-008-9393-2

Hotton, A. L., Garofalo, R., Kuhns, L. M., & Johnson, A. K. (2013). Substance use as a mediator of the relationship between life stress and sexual risk among young transgender women. *AIDS Education and Prevention, 25*(1), 62–71. doi:10.1521/aeap.2013.25.1.62

Hughes, T. L., McCabe, S. E., Wilsnack, S. C., West, B. T., & Boyd, C. J. (2010). Victimization and substance use disorders in a national sample of heterosexual and sexual minority women and men. *Addiction, 105*(12), 2130–40. doi:10.1111/j.1360-0443.2010.03088.x

Hughes, T. L., Wilsnack, S. C., & Kristjanson, A. F. (2015). Substance use and related problems among U.S. women who identify as mostly heterosexual. *BMC Public Health, 15*, 803. doi:10.1186/s12889-015-2143-1

Israel, T., & Mohr, J. J. (2004). Attitudes towards bisexual women and men: Current research, future directions. *Journal of Bisexuality, 4*(1–2), 117–34. doi:10.1300/J159v04n01_09

Jerome, R. C., Halkitis, P. N., & Siconolfi, D. E. (2009). Club drug use, sexual behavior, and HIV seroconversion: A qualitative study of motivations. *Substance Use & Misuse, 44*(3), 431–47. doi:10.1080/10826080802345036

Johns, M. M., Lowry, R., Andrzejewski, J., Barrios, L. C., Demissie, Z., McManus, T., ... Underwood, J. M. (2019). Transgender identity and experiences of violence victimization, substance use, suicide risk, and sexual risk behaviors among high school students—19 states and large urban school districts, 2017. *Morbidity and Mortality Weekly Report, 68*(3), 67–71. doi:10.15585/mmwr.mm6803a3

Kann, L., McManus, T., Harris, W. A., Shanklin, S. L., Flint, K. H., Queen, B., . . . Thornton, J. (2018). Youth risk behavior surveillance—United States, 2017. *MMWR Surveillance Summaries, 67*(8), 1–114. doi:10.15585/mmwr.ss6708a1

Kerr, D., Ding, K., Burke, A., & Ott-Walter, K. (2015). An alcohol, tobacco, and other drug use comparison of lesbian, bisexual, and heterosexual undergraduate women. *Substance Use & Misuse, 50*(3), 340–9. doi:10.3109/10826084.2014.980954

Kerridge, B. T., Pickering, R. P., Saha, T. D., Ruan, W. J., Chou, S. P., Zhang, H., . . . Hasin, D. S. (2017). Prevalence, sociodemographic correlates and DSM-5 substance use disorders and other psychiatric disorders among sexual minorities in the United States. *Drug and Alcohol Dependence, 170*, 82–92. doi:10.1016/j.drugalcdep.2016.10.038

Keuroghlian, A. S., Reisner, S. L., White, J. M., & Weiss, R. D. (2015). Substance use and treatment of substance use disorders in a community sample of transgender adults. *Drug and Alcohol Dependence, 152*, 139–46. doi:10.1016/j.drugalcdep.2015.04.008

Klein, A., & Golub, S. A. (2016). Family rejection as a predictor of suicide attempts and substance use among transgender and gender nonconforming adults. *LGBT Health, 3*(3), 193–9. doi:10.1089/lgbt.2015.0111

Lee, J. H., Gamarel, K. E., Bryant, K. J., Zaller, N. D., & Operario, D. (2016). Discrimination, mental health, and substance use disorders among sexual minority populations. *LGBT Health, 3*(4), 258–65. doi:10.1089/lgbt.2015.0135

Lehavot, K., & Simoni, J. M. (2011). The impact of minority stress on mental health and substance use among sexual minority women. *Journal of Consulting and Clinical Psychology, 79*(2), 159–70. doi:10.1037/a0022839

Lelutiu-Weinberger, C., Pachankis, J. E., Golub, S. A., Ja'Nina, J. W., Bamonte, A., & Parsons, J. T. (2013). Age cohort differences in the effects of gay-related stigma, anxiety and identification with the gay community on sexual risk and substance use. *AIDS and Behavior, 17*(1), 340–9. doi:10.1007/s10461-011-0070-4

Lewis, R. J., Milletich, R. J., Kelley, M. L., & Woody, A. (2012). Minority stress, substance use, and intimate partner violence among sexual minority women. *Aggression and Violent Behavior, 17*(3), 247–56. doi:10.1016/j.avb.2012.02.004

Marshal, M. P., Friedman, M. S., Stall, R., King, K. M., Miles, J., Gold, M. A., . . . Morse, J. Q. (2008). Sexual orientation and adolescent substance use: A meta-analysis and methodological review. *Addiction, 103*(4), 546–56. doi:10.1111/j.1360-0443.2008.02149.x

Mattison, A. M., Ross, M. W., Wolfson, T., & Franklin, D. (2001). Circuit party attendance, club drug use, and unsafe sex in gay men. *Journal of Substance Abuse, 13*(1–2), 119–26.

Matud, M. P. (2004). Gender differences in stress and coping styles. *Personality and Individual Differences, 37*(7), 1401–15. doi:10.1016/S0899-3289(01)00060-8

McCabe, S. E., Bostwick, W. B., Hughes, T. L., West, B. T., & Boyd, C. J. (2010). The relationship between discrimination and substance use disorders among lesbian, gay, and bisexual adults in the United States. *American Journal of Public Health, 100*(10), 1946–52. doi:10.2105/AJPH.2009.163147

McCabe, S. E., Hughes, T. L., Bostwick, W. B., West, B. T., & Boyd, C. J. (2009). Sexual orientation, substance use behaviors and substance dependence in the United States. *Addiction, 104*(8), 1333–45. doi:10.1016/j.jsat.2012.01.007

McKay, T. A., McDavitt, B., George, S., & Mutchler, M. G. (2012). "Their type of drugs": Perceptions of substance use, sex and social boundaries among young African American and Latino gay and bisexual men. *Culture, Health, and Sexuality, 14*(10), 1183–96. doi:10.1080/13691058.2012.720033

Medley, G., Lipari, R. N., Bose, J., Cribb, D. S., Kroutil, L. A., & McHenry, G. (2016). Sexual orientation and estimates of adult substance use and mental health: Results from the 2015 National Survey on Drug Use and Health. NSDUH Data Review. https://www.samhsa.gov/data/sites/default/files/NSDUH-SexualOrientation-2015/NSDUH-SexualOrientation-2015/NSDUH-SexualOrientation-2015.htm

Menza, T. W., Hughes, J. P., Celum, C. L., & Golden, M. R. (2009). Prediction of HIV acquisition among men who have sex with men. *Sexually Transmitted Diseases, 36*(9), 547–55. doi:10.1097/OLQ.0b013e3181a9cc41

Meyer, I. H. (2003). Prejudice, social stress, and mental health in lesbian, gay, and bisexual populations: Conceptual issues and research evidence. *Psychological Bulletin, 129*(5), 674–97. doi:10.1037/0033-2909.129.5.674

Mimiaga, M. J., Hughto, J. M. W., Biello, K. B., Santostefano, C. M., Kuhns, L. M., Reisner, S. L., & Garofalo, R. (2019). Longitudinal analysis of syndemic psychosocial problems predicting HIV risk behavior among a multicity prospective cohort of sexually active young transgender women in the United States. *Journal of Acquired Immune Deficiency Syndromes, 81*(2), 184–92. doi:10.1097/QAI.0000000000002009

Mimiaga, M. J., Reisner, S. L., Grasso, C., Crane, H. M., Safren, S. A., Kitahata, M. M., . . . Mayer, K. H. (2013). Substance use among HIV-infected patients engaged in primary care in the United States: Findings from the Centers for AIDS Research Network of Integrated Clinical Systems cohort. *American Journal of Public Health, 103*(8), 1457–67. doi:10.2105/AJPH.2012.301162

Mitchell, J. W. (2016). Differences in relationship characteristics between HIV-negative male couples who used and did not use substances with sex. *AIDS and Behavior, 20*(3), 667–78. doi:10.1007/s10461-015-1148-1

Moody, R. L., Starks, T. J., Grov, C., & Parsons, J. T. (2018). Internalized homophobia and drug use in a national cohort of gay and bisexual men: Examining depression, sexual anxiety, and gay community attachment as mediating factors. *Archives of Sexual Behavior, 47*(4), 1133–44. doi:10.1007/s10508-017-1009-2

Mustanski, B., Garofalo, R., Herrick, A., & Donenberg, G. (2007). Psychosocial health problems increase risk for HIV among urban young men who have sex with men: Preliminary evidence of a syndemic in need of attention. *Annals of Behavioral Medicine, 34*(1), 37–45. doi:10.1007/bf02879919

Nemoto, T., Operario, D., Keatley, J., Han, L., & Soma, T. (2004). HIV risk behaviors among male-to-female transgender persons of color in San Francisco. *American Journal of Public Health, 94*(7), 1193–9. doi:10.2105/ajph.94.7.1193

Operario, D., Nemoto, T., Iwamoto, M., & Moore, T. E. (2011). Unprotected sexual behavior and HIV risk in the context of primary partnerships for transgender women. *AIDS and Behavior, 15*(3), 674–82. doi:10.1007/s10461-010-9795-8

Ostrow, D. G., Plankey, M. W., Cox, C., Li, X., Shoptaw, S., Jacobson, L. P., & Stall, R. C. (2009). Specific sex-drug combinations contribute to the majority of recent HIV seroconversions among MSM in the MACS. *Journal of Acquired Immune Deficiency Syndromes (1999), 51*(3), 349–55. doi:10.1097/QAI.0b013e3181a24b20

Otis, M. D., Oser, C. B., & Staton-Tindall, M. (2016). Violent victimization and substance dependency: Comparing rural incarcerated heterosexual and sexual minority women. *Journal of Social Work Practice in Addictions, 16*(1–2), 176–201. doi:10.1080/1533256X.2016.1143372

Pachankis, J. E. (2014). Uncovering clinical principles and techniques to address minority stress, mental health, and related health risks among gay and bisexual men. *Clinical Psychology: Science and Practice, 21*(4), 313–30. doi:10.1111/cpsp.12078

Pachankis, J. E. (2015). A transdiagnostic minority stress treatment approach for gay and bisexual men's syndemic health conditions. *Archives of Sexual Behavior, 44*(7), 1843–60. doi:10.1007/s10508-015-0480-x

Palamar, J. J., & Halkitis, P. N. (2006). A qualitative analysis of GHB use among gay men: Reasons for use despite potential adverse outcomes. *International Journal of Drug Policy, 17*(1), 23–8. doi:10.1016/j.drugpo.2005.11.002

Parsons, J. T., Antebi-Gruszka, N., Millar, B. M., Cain, B. M., Cain, D., & Gurung, S. (2018). Syndemic conditions, HIV transmission risk behavior, and transactional sex among transgender women. *AIDS and Behavior, 22,* 2056–67. doi:10.1007/s10461-018-2100-y

Parsons, J. T., Grov, C., & Golub, S. A. (2012). Sexual compulsivity, co-occurring psychological health problems, and HIV risk among gay and bisexual men: Further evidence of a syndemic. *American Journal of Public Health, 102*(1), 156–62. doi:10.2105/AJPH.2011.300284

Parsons, J. T., Kutnick, A. H., Halkitis, P. N., Punzalan, J. C., & Carbonari, J. P. (2005). Sexual risk behaviors and substance use among alcohol abusing HIV-positive men who have sex with men. *Journal of Psychoactive Drugs, 37*(1), 27–36. doi:10.1080/02791072.2005.10399746

Parsons, J. T., Millar, B. M., Moody, R. L., Starks, T. J., Rendina, H. J., & Grov, C. (2017). Syndemic conditions and HIV transmission risk behavior among HIV-negative gay and bisexual men in a U.S. national sample. *Health Psychology, 36*(7), 695–703. doi:10.1037/hea0000509

Parsons, J. T., & Starks, T. J. (2014). Drug use and sexual arrangements among gay couples: Frequency, interdependence and associations with sexual risk. *Archives of Sexual Behavior, 43*(1), 89–98. doi:10.1007/s10508-013-0237-3

Paschen-Wolff, M. M., Kelvin, E., Wells, B. E., Campbell, A. N., Grosskopf, N. A., & Grov, C. (2019). Changing trends in substance use and sexual risk disparities among sexual minority women as a function of sexual identity, behavior and attraction: Findings from the National Survey of Family Growth 2002–2015. *Archives of Sexual Behavior, 48*(4), 1137–58. doi:10.1007/s10508-018-1333-1

Plankey, M. W., Ostrow, D. G., Stall, R., Cox, C., Li, X., Peck, J. A., & Jacobson, L. P. (2007). The relationship between methamphetamine and popper use and risk of HIV seroconversion in the multicenter AIDS cohort study. *Journal of Acquired Immune Deficiency Syndromes (1999), 45*(1), 85–92. doi:10.1097/QAI.0b013e3180417c99

Poteat, T., Scheim, A., Xavier, J., Reisner, S. L., & Baral, S. (2016). Global epidemiology of HIV infection and related syndemics affecting transgender people. *Journal of Acquired Immune Deficiency Syndromes (1999), 72*(Suppl 3), S210–S219. doi:10.1097/QAI.0000000000001087

Reback, C. J., & Fletcher, J. B. (2014). HIV prevalence, substance use, and sexual risk behaviors among trangender women recruited through outreach. *AIDS and Behavior, 18*(7), 1359–67. doi:10.1007/s10461-013-0657-z

Reisner, S. L., Hughto, J. M. W., Pardee, D., & Sevelius, J. (2016). Syndemics and gender affirmation: HIV sexual risk in female-to-male trans masculine adults reporting sexual contact with cisgender males. *International Journal of STD & AIDS, 27*(11), 955–66. doi:10.1177/0956462415602418

Reisner, S. L., Mimiaga, M. J., Bland, S., Mayer, K. H., Perkovich, B., & Safren, S. A. (2009). HIV risk and social networks among male-to-female transgender sex workers in Boston, Massachusetts. *Journal of the Association of Nurses in AIDS Care, 20*(5), 373–86. doi:10.1016/j.jana.2009.06.003

Rendina, H. J., Millar, B. M., & Parsons, J. T. (2018). Situational HIV stigma and stimulant use: A day-level autoregressive cross-lagged path model among HIV-positive gay and bisexual men. *Addictive Behaviors, 83,* 109–15. doi:10.1016/j.addbeh.2018.01.003

Rendina, H. J., Moody, R. L., Ventuneac, A., Grov, C., & Parsons, J. T. (2015). Aggregate and event-level associations of substance use and sexual behavior among gay and bisexual men: Comparing retrospective and prospective data. *Drug and Alcohol Dependence, 154,* 199–207. doi:10.1016/j.drugalcdep.2015.06.04

Roberts, A. C. (2001). Coping behaviors of cocaine dependent women. *Journal of Social Work Practice in the Addictions, 1*(4), 83–99. doi:10.1300/J160v01n04_06

Rosario, M., Scrimshaw, E. W., & Hunter, J. (2008). Butch/femme differences in substance use and abuse among young lesbian and bisexual women: Examination and potential explanations. *Substance Use & Misuse, 43*(8–9), 1002–15. doi:10.1080/10826080801914402

Rose, C., Santos, G. M., McFarland, W., & Wilson, E. C. (2015). Prevalence and correlates of substance use among transfemale youth ages 16–24 years in the San Francisco Bay area. *Drug and Alcohol Dependence, 147,* 160–6. doi:10.1016/j.drugalcdep.2014.11.023

Sanford, T. G. M., Knox, J. R., Alcala, C., El-Bassel, N., Kuo, I., & Smith, L. R. (2017). Substance use and HIV risk among men who have sex with men in Africa: A systematic review. *Journal of Acquired Immune Deficiency Syndromes (1999), 76*(2), e34–e46. doi:10.1097/QAI.0000000000001462

Santos, G. M., Rapues, J., Wilson, E. C., Macias, O., Packer, T., Colfax, G., & Raymond, H. F. (2014). Alcohol and substance use among transgender women in San Francisco: Prevalence and association with human immunodeficiency virus infection. *Drug and Alcohol Review, 33*(3), 287–95. doi:10.1111/dar.12116

Sausa, L. A., Keatley, J., & Operario, D. (2007). Perceived risks and benefits of sex work among transgender women of color in San Francisco. *Archives of Sexual Behavior, 36*(6), 768–77. doi:10.1007/s10508-007-9210-3

Schuler, M. S., Rice, C. E., Evans-Polce, R. J., & Collins, R. L. (2018). Disparities in substance use behaviors and disorders among adult sexual minorities by age, gender, and sexual identity. *Drug and Alcohol Dependence, 189,* 139–46. doi:10.1016/j.drugalcdep.2018.05.008

Schuler, M. S., Stein, B. D., & Collins, R. L. (2019). Differences in substance use disparities across age groups in a national cross-sectional survey of lesbian, gay, and bisexual adults. *LGBT Health*, *6*(2), 68–76. doi:10.1089/lgbt.2018.0125

Scott, R. M., Hides, L., Allen, J. S., & Lubman, D. I. (2013). Coping style and ecstasy use motives as predictors of current mood symptoms in ecstasy users. *Addictive Behaviors*, *38*(10), 2465–72. doi:10.1016/j.addbeh.2013.05.005

Singer, M. C., & Clair, S. (2003). Syndemics and public health: Reconceptualizing disease in bio-social context. *Medical Anthropology Quarterly*, *17*(4), 423–41.

Singer, M. C., Erickson, P. I., Badiane, L., Diaz, R., Ortiz, D., Abraham, T., & Nicolaysen, A. M. (2006). Syndemics, sex and the city: Understanding sexually transmitted diseases in social and cultural context. *Social Science & Medicine*, *63*(8), 2010–21. doi:10.1016/j.socscimed.2006.05.012

Stall, R., Mills, T. C., Williamson, J., Hart, T., Greenwood, G., Paul, J., . . . Catania, J. A. (2003). Association of co-occurring psychosocial health problems and increased vulnerability to HIV/AIDS among urban men who have sex with men. *American Journal of Public Health*, *93*(6), 939–42. doi:10.2105/ajph.93.6.939

Starks, T. J., Golub, S. A., Kelly, D. K., & Parsons, J. T. (2010). The problem of "just for fun": Patterns of use situations among active club drug users. *Addictive Behaviors*, *35*(12), 1067–73. doi:10.1016/j.addbeh.2010.07.007

Starks, T. J., Millar, B. M., Tuck, A. N., & Wells, B. E. (2015). The role of sexual expectancies of substance use as a mediator between adult attachment and drug use among gay and bisexual men. *Drug and Alcohol Dependence*, *153*, 187–93. doi:10.1016/j.drugalcdep.2015.05.028

Starks, T. J., Robles, G., Bosco, S. C., Dellucci, T. V., Grov, C., & Parsons, J. T. (2019). The prevalence and correlates of sexual arrangements in a national cohort of HIV-negative gay and bisexual men in the United States. *Archives of Sexual Behavior*, *48*(1), 369–82. doi:10.1007/s10508-018-1282-8

Starks, T. J., Tuck, A. N., Millar, B. M., & Parsons, J. T. (2016). Linking syndemic stress and behavioral indicators of main partner HIV transmission risk in gay male couples. *AIDS and Behavior*, *20*(2), 439–48. doi:10.1007/s10461-015-1248-y

Vosburgh, H. W., Mansergh, G., Sullivan, P. S., & Purcell, D. W. (2012). A review of the literature on event-level substance use and sexual risk behavior among men who have sex with men. *AIDS and Behavior*, *16*(6), 1394–410. doi:10.1007/s10461-011-0131-8

Wei, C., Guadamuz, T. E., Lim, S. H., Huang, Y., & Koe, S. (2012). Patterns and levels of illicit drug use among men who have sex with men in Asia. *Drug and Alcohol Dependence*, *120*(1–3), 246–9. doi:10.1016/j.drugalcdep.2011.07.016

CHAPTER

10 Nicotine Use among Sexual and Gender Minority Populations

Alicia K. Matthews, Cherdsak Duangchan, *and* Chien-Ching Li

Abstract

The prevalence of tobacco use disorders among sexual and gender minorities remains consistently high despite the overall reduction of tobacco use in the United States and other parts of the world. This chapter begins by describing the criteria for tobacco use disorders in the fifth edition of the American Psychiatric Association's *Diagnostic and Statistical Manual of Mental Disorders*. The authors discuss rates of tobacco use based on sexual orientation and gender identity and summarize the literature describing risk and protective factors for tobacco use among sexual and gender minorities. Strategies are highlighted for reducing the overall public health threat of tobacco use in sexual and gender minority populations.

Keywords: nicotine, LGBT, tobacco use disorder, smoking cessation, e-cigarettes

Introduction

Nicotine is a highly addictive substance found in tobacco products and is the most common source of addiction in the United States (American Society of Addiction Medicine, 2008; Onor et al., 2017). In the United States there are approximately 50 million people who are addicted to the nicotine found in tobacco products such as cigarettes, cigars, chewing tobacco, and snuff (Hu et al., 2016). With the advent of newer nicotine-delivery systems such as electronic cigarettes (also known as e-cigarettes, e-vaporizers, or electronic nicotine-delivery systems), the number of nicotine-addicted non-tobacco users, especially among adolescents, is on the rise (U.S. Department of Health and Human Services, 2016). Estimates put societal costs (healthcare costs and lost productivity) of nicotine addiction in the United States at approximately $193 billion a year (Xu, Bishop, Kennedy, Simpson, & Pechacek, 2015).

Large disparities in tobacco use have been documented among sexual and gender minorities in the United States (Drope et al., 2018; Jamal et al., 2018; Max, Stark, Sung, & Offen, 2016). Consistent with the recommendations of the Institutes of Medicine (Graham et al., 2011), additional research is needed to understand the origins of these disparities and to develop interventions to narrow observed differences in health risk behaviors and outcomes. In this chapter we focus on the differences in tobacco use and tobacco use disorders among adults in the United States based on sexual orientation and gender identity. Information regarding risk factors for elevated use of tobacco will be reviewed. We will also describe the literature related to tobacco prevention and control activities in these populations and make recommendations for reducing the tobacco-related health inequalities observed.

Tobacco Use Disorders

As described in the fifth edition of the *Diagnostic and Statistical Manual of Mental Disorders* (DSM-5; American Psychiatric Association, 2013), tobacco use disorder refers to a problematic pattern of tobacco use leading to impairment or distress. The DSM-5 criteria for tobacco use disorder include a combination of symptoms of dependence (i.e., larger quantities of tobacco over a longer period than intended are consumed), the biological symptoms of tolerance (i.e., the need for increasingly larger doses of nicotine to obtain desired effect), withdrawal (i.e., withdrawal symptoms upon cessation of use), and craving (i.e., a strong urge to use tobacco) occurring within a 12-month period (Herie, Dragonetti, & Selby, 2012). Research findings suggest that sexual minority adults are more likely to meet criteria for DSM-5 tobacco use disorder compared to heterosexual adults (Boyd, Veliz, Stephenson, Hughes, & McCabe, 2019; Slater, Godette, Huang, Ruan, & Kerridge, 2017). For example, using data from the National Epidemiologic Survey on Alcohol and Related Conditions-III, McCabe et al. (2018) found elevated rates of past-12-month tobacco use disorder among sexual minorities (28.0 percent for lesbian, 35.2 percent for bisexual, and 14.2 percent for heterosexual women). A similar pattern was observed among men with past-year tobacco use disorder: 32.0 percent for gay, 43.0 percent for bisexual, and 21.4 percent for heterosexual men. To date, no studies have examined specific criteria for tobacco use disorder for gender minority populations, thus prohibiting exploration of the influence of gender identity on prevalence of tobacco use disorder.

Current Smoking Trends

Nicotine use is the primary risk factor for tobacco use disorder, and cigarettes are the most commonly used nicotine-delivery product. Cigarette use among adults in the United States is at a fifty-year low, with 14.1 percent of adults reporting current smoking (Wang et al., 2018). Despite progress in reducing use of combustible tobacco products such as cigarettes, increases in the use of e-cigarettes have occurred in the past decade (King, Patel, Nguyen & Dube, 2015). A recent study of adults reported that the prevalence of e-cigarettes was 4.5 percent (Mirbolouk et al., 2018). In that same study, 15 percent of current e-cigarette users had never smoked cigarettes, indicating the penetration of e-cigarette usage among individuals with no prior history of tobacco use. Additionally, e-cigarettes are the most commonly used form of tobacco among youth in the United States. From 2017 to 2018, any past-30-day use of e-cigarettes by high school students increased 78 percent, from 11.7 to 20.8 percent (Cullen, Ambrose, Gentzke, Apelberg, Jamal, & King, 2018). Finally, smokeless tobacco, including snuff, chewing tobacco, and snus (a smokeless tobacco product), is used by an estimated 3.8 percent of adults, with use among men considerably higher than women (6.8 percent vs. 1.0 percent) (Wang et al., 2018).

Nicotine and Tobacco Use in Sexual Minority Populations

Although tobacco use rates are declining (Ng et al., 2014), there has been far less progress in reducing observed inequalities in tobacco use (Drope et al., 2018). For example, researchers consistently document that sexual minorities as a whole are at substantially higher risk for tobacco use (Drope et al., 2018; Jamal et al., 2018; Max et al., 2016). Recent data suggest that rates of smoking among LGB individuals are 21.8 percent compared to 14.6 percent among heterosexual individuals (Hoffman, Delahanty, Johnson, & Zhao, 2018). Gender also plays a role in smoking among sexual minorities, with bisexual and lesbian women smoking at higher rates than heterosexual women and gay, bisexual, and heterosexual males (Hoffman et al., 2018). Additionally, data suggest that smoking among LGBT persons starts at an earlier age (Corliss et al., 2012), is characterized by higher-frequency smoking (Watson, Lewis, Fish, & Goodenow, 2018), and persists later into adulthood compared to heterosexual populations (Matthews, McCabe, Lee, & Veliz, 2018). For example, using data from the National Epidemiologic Survey on Alcohol and Related Conditions-III, Matthews, McCabe, et al. (2018) found that overall, 17.5 percent of older LGB and non-LGB adult respondents (aged 55 and older) reported past-year smoking. Rates of past-year cigarette smoking were influenced by both gender and sexual orientation, with older men reporting higher rates compared to women. Among both men and women, smoking was most prevalent among bisexual individuals, mimicking elevated risk among bisexually identified individuals across a range of health risks.

Data on smoking patterns among sexual minorities of color are much more limited than among white sexual minority populations. In one study, researchers reported on differences in smoking behaviors between African American and white sexual and gender minority participants in the "Out, Proud and Healthy" survey (N = 639) (Jordan, Everett, Ge, & McElroy, 2015). In that study, current smoking rates among African Americans and whites were similar (36.3 percent vs. 37.7 percent, respectively). However, African Americans were more likely to be never smokers (58.6 percent vs. 47.3 percent) and less likely to be former smokers (5.2 percent vs. 15.1 percent) compared to whites. Among current smokers, African American sexual and gender minority smokers were more likely to be trying to quit smoking (22.0 percent vs. 12.7 percent) or planning to quit in the next month (24.2 percent vs. 18.9 percent) compared to white sexual and gender minority smokers. Another multisite study reported on the smoking patterns of sexual minority women compared to heterosexual women (Hughes, Johnson, & Matthews, 2008). White sexual minority women smoked at rates similar to heterosexual women; however, African American sexual minority women were more likely to smoke compared to all other women in the study, regardless of race/ethnicity or sexual orientation. One additional study examined readiness to quit among current smokers in a sample of sexual minority men based on race/ethnicity (N = 208) (Matthews, Hotton, et al., 2014). In multivariate analyses, Latino sexual minority men were more likely to be in the precontemplation stage of readiness to quit (not currently thinking about or planning to make a quit attempt) compared to African American or white sexual minority men. In that study, racial/ethnic differences persisted even after controlling for important demographic factors such as education. No studies could be identified that look at smoking patterns among Asian sexual or gender minority populations.

In addition to the United States, large disparities in tobacco use have been documented among sexual minorities in other Western countries, including Canada (Clarke & Coughlin, 2012; Haley et al., 2014), Australia (Roxburgh, Lea, de Wit, & Degenhardt, 2016), and England (Bourne, Davey, Hickson, Reid, & Weatherburn, 2017). However, less research has been conducted in countries representing the Global South where homosexuality remains highly stigmatized or criminalized. One example is the scoping review of sexual minority women's health in Latin America and the Caribbean conducted by Caceres, Jackman, Ferrer, Cato, and Hughes (2019). They were able to identify only eighteen unique studies, with the majority published in Brazil and Mexico. Although the studies were not primarily focused on tobacco use, evidence of tobacco use disparities was reported. Increasing research efforts in tobacco control are especially important given trends showing that the tobacco industry is targeting lower-income and developing countries for tobacco sales (Yach & Bettcher, 2000).

Nicotine and Tobacco Use in Gender Minority Populations

Data on tobacco use among transgender populations is more limited compared to sexual minorities (Fallin, Goodin, Lee, & Bennett, 2015). However, over the past five years, several nationally representative studies have documented rates of tobacco use as more prevalent among transgender compared to cisgender adults. One of the first and largest studies reporting on tobacco use among gender minorities was the National Trans Discrimination Survey (N = 6,400) (Grant et al., 2011). In that study, 30 percent of respondents reported tobacco use compared to national estimates of 20.6 percent for the general population during that same time period (American Lung Association, 2010). More recently, Buchting et al. (2017) reported on data from a nationally representative sample of adults in the United States. In that study, transgender respondents were more likely to report any past-30-day tobacco use (39.7 percent vs. 25.1 percent) and current cigarette smoking (35.5 percent vs. 20.7 percent) compared to cisgender adults. With few exceptions, transgender male respondents had the highest use patterns across all the tobacco products (cigars, cigarettes, e-cigarettes) compared to cisgender males and females and transgender female respondents (Buchting et al., 2017).

Currently, very little is known about racial/ethnic differences in tobacco use among transgender adults. In 2016, the National Center for Transgender Equality released the findings from the 2015 National Transgender Survey (James, Herman, Rankin, Keisling, Mottet, & Anafi, 2016). In that study, overall smoking rates reported for study participants were 22 percent compared to general population estimates of 21 percent. Among current smokers, estimates of daily smoking among survey respondents were lower than the general population (38 percent vs. 59 percent). Racial/ethnic differences in smoking status (i.e., never, former, current) were not reported. However, smoking frequency among daily smokers based on race/ethnicity was described. High-frequency smoking, defined as smoking one or more packs of cigarettes per day, varied substantially by race/ethnicity, with the highest frequency of smoking reported by American Indians (44 percent), whites (40 percent), and Asian Americans (22 percent). The lowest frequency of smoking among daily smokers was among African American (14 percent) and Latinx respondents (18 percent). These findings mirror national estimates showing that African American smokers consume fewer cigarettes per day compared to other racial/ethnic groups (Trinidad et al., 2009).

Due to increased tobacco-control efforts in the United States, the tobacco industry has increased its targeting of cigarette sales to low- and middle-income countries around the world (Lee, Ling, &

Glantz, 2012). Reisner et al. (2016) conducted a systematic review of the global health burden and needs of transgender populations. The authors reported that about 7 percent of the articles identified (N = 14 data points) were focused on tobacco use and none of the articles published were from countries representing the Global South. Due to methodological limitations of the studies reviewed and heterogeneity in the types of and ways that questions were asked, the authors were not able to provide global estimates of health behaviors including tobacco use.

Risk Factors Associated with Tobacco Use among Sexual and Gender Minorities

Many factors influence tobacco use among adults. For example, demographic characteristics are strongly associated with smoking behaviors in the general population. Cisgender males, younger age, and lower education and income levels are consistently found to predict smoking patterns (Drope et al., 2018). Higher prevalence of tobacco use has also been found to co-vary with psychosocial risk factors such as depression and substance use (Weinberger et al., 2017). With few exceptions, research suggests that these same patterns hold for sexual and gender minority populations as well (Drescher et al., 2018; Hughes et al., 2008; Matthews, Steffen, et al., 2017). For example, data from the Chicago Health and Life Experiences of Women study (2010–2012, N = 726) were used to examine predictors of smoking behaviors among sexual minority women (Matthews, Steffen, et al., 2017). In that study, a history of ever smoking was associated with lower educational attainment, having a partner who smokes, heavy drinking, and illicit drug use.

Beyond these general influences, unique risk factors for smoking have also been identified for tobacco use among sexual and gender minorities. These include more permissive social norms related to smoking and the cultural significance of bars as social venues (Blosnich, Lee, & Horn, 2013; Lee, Matthews, McCullen, & Melvin, 2014; Offen, Smith, & Malone, 2008). Further, LGBT communities have been disproportionately targeted by the tobacco industry in terms of direct marketing (Yamey, 2003) and funding of LGBT pride and other community events (Dilley, Spigner, Boysun, Dent, & Pizacani, 2008), resulting in more same-sex couples residing in areas with higher tobacco retailer density (Lee, Pan, Henriksen, Goldstein, & Ribisi, 2016). In addition, data from qualitative studies of sexual and gender minority smokers have identified several culturally specific factors associated with smoking behaviors. In the first study, a racially and ethnically diverse sample of LGB smokers (N = 31) reported that cultural factors including nonjudgmental community norms regarding smoking, the perception of smoking as part of gay culture, and smoking as rebellion against antismoking attitudes were identified as barriers to smoking cessation (Matthews, Cesario, Ruiz, Ross, & King, 2017). In a second study of African American men who have sex with men and who were HIV positive (N = 31), smoking was seen as ubiquitous in the low-income and segregated communities in which the study participants resided. Participants reported perceived associations between smoking and the gay culture, including personal characteristics such as "masculinity," "sexy," and "rebellious." Older study participants reported viewing smoking as very much associated with the "gay life." However, younger study participants felt that smoking was antithetical to the current gay male culture of physical attractiveness (Matthews, Vargas, Kuhns, Shappiva, & King, 2014).

Consistent with the minority stress model (Meyer, 2003), smoking rates among sexual and gender minorities have also been shown to be associated with minority-specific stress. For example, McCabe et al. (2017) reported that sexual minorities who experienced higher levels of past-year sexual orientation discrimination had higher probability of past-year cigarette smoking, any tobacco/nicotine use, and tobacco use disorder relative to sexual minorities who experienced lower levels of discrimination. Exposure to bias-based stressors also extends to LGBT youth, who experience higher rates of familial rejection, homelessness, and bullying compared to their heterosexual peers (Palmer & Greytak, 2017). LGBT youth of color may be at an even higher risk for engagement in health risk behaviors due to the corrosive influences of bullying and race-based discrimination (Rivera et al., 2019). These unique stressors experienced at the interpersonal, community, and institutional levels have direct implications for both short- and long-term health risk behaviors such as smoking.

Tobacco Prevention and Control Initiatives

Tobacco prevention and control efforts consist of multipronged strategies including outreach and awareness campaigns, targeted resources for minority populations, access to smoking cessation interventions, and public policy (Centers for Disease

Control and Prevention, 2014). Despite these disparities, gender and sexual minorities are not systematically included in most tobacco prevention and control efforts (Lee et al., 2014). We will provide a summary of activities in the four primary tobacco prevention and control domains. Evidence of effectiveness is reported when available.

Awareness and Outreach Initiatives

Smoking cessation campaigns have played an important role in raising awareness about the harms associated with smoking and available smoking cessation resources. The Mautner Project, a national lesbian health organization, sponsored a Delicious Lesbian Kisses campaign that urged lesbians to stop smoking. In the early 2000s, similar projects have taken place in other metropolitan areas such as Chicago and San Francisco. More recently, the U.S. Food and Drug Administration has sponsored "This Free Life" for LGBTQ young adults aged eighteen to twenty-four who use tobacco occasionally and the "Real Cost Campaign" (U.S. Food and Drug Administration, 2019a, 2019b), which focused on changing LGBT young adults' social norms around tobacco use. However, Lee et al. (2014) highlighted the absence of peer-reviewed information about the impact of media campaigns directly linked to cessation services. One rare exception is the reported outcomes from an antismoking campaign, *The Break-Up*, for sexual minorities conducted by the Los Angeles County Health Department. *The Break-Up* was a social marketing and outreach campaign aimed at reducing smoking prevalence (Plant et al., 2017). Evaluation of the intervention suggested the campaign was associated with a slight increase (0.07 percent) in calls to the state tobacco quitline from LGB-identified callers (Plant et al., 2017).

The extant literature is mixed as it relates to awareness among LGBT populations about tobacco control campaigns. Data from the National Adult Tobacco Survey (2009–2010) showed that the majority of both LGBT and non-LGBT individuals had seen at least one tobacco cessation ad in the past thirty days (Fallin, Lee, Bennett, & Goodin, 2016). However, the same study indicated that among current smokers, gay and bisexual men reported less awareness of smoking cessation resources such as tobacco quitlines compared to heterosexuals; no differences by sexual orientation were found for females. In an earlier study of awareness of anti-tobacco media campaigns among LGBT community members, a higher proportion of participants reported awareness of anti-tobacco messages in general media outlets compared to LGBT-specific media outlets (Matthews, Balsam, et al., 2014). Additional efforts will be required to increase the inclusion of targeted anti-tobacco messages in mainstream media and increasing the number of LGBT media highlighting anti-tobacco messaging.

LGBT Smoking Cessation Resources

A range of LGBT-specific resources have been developed to support smoking cessation efforts. One example is *MPOWERED: Best and Promising Practices for LGBT Tobacco Prevention and Control* (Buchting et al., 2012). This document, developed by the Network for LGBT Health Equity, was modeled after the World Health Organization (2008)'s framework model outlining key tobacco control strategies. MPOWER is an acronym for Monitor the epidemic; Protect from secondhand smoke; Offer support to quit; Warn of the dangers of tobacco use; Enforce protections; and Raise tobacco taxes. The network added two additional letters: E for Evaluate (and disseminate) and D for Diversify. This resource represents an important roadmap for making progress toward tobacco prevention and control in LGBTQ communities.

Smoking Cessation Interventions

Despite known smoking-related disparities, funded research to promote smoking cessation research among the LGBT population is limited (Coulter, Kenst, Bowen, & Scout, 2014; Lee et al., 2014). A systematic review of smoking cessation interventions for LGBT adults (Lee et al., 2014) and a scoping review (a type of research synthesis aimed at mapping a particular area of research in terms of concepts, gaps, and evidence) of tobacco use cessations for LGBTQ youth and young adults (Baskerville, et al., 2017) reported similar findings regarding the paucity of evidence-based interventions. The limited available research suggests that evidence-based treatments (e.g., individual counseling, pharmacotherapy) recommended in the U.S. Public Health Service's *Clinical Practice Guideline: 2008 Update* (Fiore et al., 2008) are as effective for sexual minorities—if they are used (Covey, Weissman LoDuca, & Duan, 2009; Grady et al., 2014; Lee et al., 2014). For example, results from a large randomized control trial (Matthews et al., 2019), found that evidence-based cognitive-behavioral treatments combined with nicotine replacement had benefits for LGBT smokers on par with those achieved in other populations of smokers. These results suggest that continued efforts should be made to increase awareness of and access to evidence-based smoking cessation treatments among LGBT smokers.

Public Policy

Tobacco control policies, including monitoring of use, taxation, increases in purchasing age, and clean-air statutes, have played important roles in reducing the prevalence of tobacco use nationally (Levy, Tam, Kuo, Fong, & Chaloupka, 2018). Understanding the impact of tobacco control policy interventions is limited by gaps in knowledge and systems as they relate to sexual and gender minorities (P. A. Matthews et al., 2018). For example, monitoring of tobacco use at the local, state, and national levels does not systematically include gender and sexual minorities (Buchting et al., 2012). Comprehensive and valid sexual orientation and gender identity questions are often omitted from the demographic sections of surveys. There is also a lack of systematic clinical data and outcomes data on smoking-related death and disease among LGBT populations (P. A. Matthews et al., 2018). Further, there is a lack of regulation by the U.S. Food and Drug Administration of the menthol-flavored tobacco products that are used by higher percentages of LGBT smokers (Fallin, Goodin, & King, 2015). Despite the absence of comprehensive inclusion of sexual and gender minorities in surveillance efforts, one study found that sexual minorities residing in states with more restrictive tobacco environments (e.g., tobacco tax, tobacco control funding, and policies and tobacco prevalence/norms) were less likely to smoke than sexual minorities residing in more permissive tobacco environments (Hatzenbuehler, Keyes, Hamilton, & Hasin, 2014). Although these results are promising, a more comprehensive and inclusive strategy for determining the impact of tobacco control efforts among high-risk populations such as gender and sexual minorities is required to effectively reduce inequalities.

Limitations and Future Directions

In the past two decades there has been a proliferation of health research related to tobacco use among sexual and gender minorities. Despite these gains, limitations in the research associated with tobacco and tobacco use disorders exist. To date, the majority of data associated with tobacco use were gathered as part of larger health surveys not specifically designed to comprehensively assess smoking behaviors. As such, the preponderance of tobacco use information is descriptive data focused on smoking prevalence rates. Future research is needed to obtain more nuanced information about smoking use patterns in order to develop outreach and intervention approaches aimed at reducing known tobacco use disparities among sexual and gender minorities. Standardized tobacco use measures should be included in future research, including level of nicotine dependency, withdrawal symptoms, craving, readiness to quit smoking, and engagement in evidence-based smoking cessation treatment programs.

Another limitation is the low representation of non-white participants in LGBT tobacco research. National surveys rarely have large enough samples of sexual and gender minorities of color to permit subgroup analyses. Community surveys often include larger samples of racial/ethnic minorities but typically include only African American or Latinx respondents (Lee et al., 2014). Increasing the inclusion of LGBT individuals of color is vitally important given the current research in the general population demonstrating important differences in smoking behaviors based on race/ethnicity (Drope et al., 2018). In addition to race/ethnicity, socioeconomic indicators including education and income levels are persistent drivers of smoking inequalities nationally (Drope et al., 2018). The extant literature suggests that rates of poverty among same-sex couples (Schneebaum & Badgett, 2019) and gender minorities (Crissman, Berger, Graham, & Dalton, 2017) are elevated compared to heterosexual and cisgender individuals. Given the known differences in wealth and income inequality in the United States based on race (Kimmel, Fwu, Abbot, Ratner, & Eggers, 2016), rates of poverty among sexual and gender minorities of color are likely pronounced. As such, future research is needed to determine the influence of sexual orientation, gender identity, race/ethnicity, and economic level on smoking patterns among LGBT populations. To achieve those goals, overcoming barriers to research involvement of sexual and gender minorities of color will be needed. At least part of the problem of recruitment of LGBT individuals of color relates to historical distrust of research and white researchers in communities of color. However, other factors likely include the lack of cultural competency of researchers, failure to use evidence-based and proven approaches to recruit and retain persons of color, and research protocols that include exclusion criteria that disproportionately impact participants of color (i.e., smoking frequency), to name just a few challenges (Matthews, Ross, Lee, & Aranda, 2015).

Tobacco use data on transgender populations are also limited. Although limited evidence exists that gender minorities smoke at higher rates than cisgender individuals (Conron, Scott, Stowell, & Landers, 2012; King, Dube, & Tynan, 2012; McElroy, Everette, & Zanilette, 2011), research relevant to understanding the influence of gender identity on a range of tobacco use dimensions remains spare. When examining potential differences in smoking patterns and behaviors among young adults, transgender identity was associated with a higher frequency of smoking compared to cisgender and nonbinary persons (Vogel, Humfleet, Meacham, Prochaska, & Ramo, 2019). Discrimination has been found to be a contributor to smoking among sexual minority persons (McCabe et al., 2017). At least one study has reported on the effects of structural discrimination (i.e., denied access to housing) and smoking status among a national sample of transgender respondents (Shires & Jaffee, 2015). In addition, existing smoking cessation interventions inclusive of sexual minorities are less likely to report inclusion of gender minority participants (Berger & Mooney-Somers, 2016). As such, further research is needed to examine factors associated with smoking initiation, persistence, and cessation among gender minority populations in order to develop targeted outreach and cessation interventions.

Progress in reducing smoking inequalities among sexual and gender minority populations will require more systematic and rigorous research. Many of the existing frameworks for understanding individual-level predictors of health risk behaviors among adults in general can also be applied to research on LGBT populations (i.e., transtheoretical model of behavioral change) (Prochaska & Velicer, 1997). In addition to individual-level factors, social factors including education, racial segregation, and poverty account for over a third of the total deaths in the United States each year (Galea, Tracy, Hoggatt, Dimaggio, & Karpati, 2011). In response, health disparity researchers are moving beyond the exclusive focus on individual-level predictors of risk to evaluate the influence of social determinants on health inequalities. Similarly, there have been recent calls for the systematic study of the influence of social determinants (economic stability, neighborhood and physical environment, education, community and social context, and the healthcare system) on LGBT health inequalities (Matthews, Breen, & Kittiteerasack, 2018).

Finally, research is needed to better understand the health implications of smoking among LGBT populations in the United States as well as the Global South. A higher prevalence of smoking across the lifespan exposes LGBT populations to elevated risk for lung cancer. However, with the exception of research among HIV-positive individuals (i.e., Reddy et al., 2017), research on lung cancer risk among LGBT individuals is limited (Matthews, McCabe, et al., 2018). A major barrier for evaluating rates of smoking-related diseases in LGBT patients is that cancer registries do not collect information on sexual orientation or gender identity (Burkhalter et al., 2016), thus limiting examination of the influence of smoking on cancer-related incidence and mortality.

Two recent studies reported on the eligibility of LGB older adults for low-dose computed tomography (LDCT) lung cancer screening (a proxy for chronic high-frequency smoking and an indicator of elevated risk for lung cancer) (Wood et al., 2018). In the first study, Matthews, McCabe, et al. (2018), using population-based data sets, examined the overall prevalence of U.S. Centers for Medicare and Medicaid Services (CMS) eligibility for LDCT lung cancer screening among older adults based on sexual orientation (Matthews, McCabe, et al., 2018). Overall, 11.2 percent of older U.S. adults met CMS eligibility criteria for LDCT lung cancer screening. Eligibility for LDCT lung cancer screening was associated with sexual orientation; the highest rates of eligibility were among bisexual women and men (26.9 and 24.5 percent, respectively). In a separate study using data from the Behavioral Risk Factors Survey Study, investigators reported that LGB respondents were more likely to meet CMS guidelines for eligibility for LDCT compared to heterosexuals but less likely to have received a screening test for lung cancer (Veliz et al., 2019). Together, the two studies demonstrate the need for lung cancer screening interventions for LGB smokers.

Conclusions

Research consistently documents that sexual and gender minorities as a whole are at substantially higher risk for tobacco use and tobacco use disorders than their heterosexual and cisgender counterparts. Further efforts are needed to reduce tobacco use and the risk for tobacco use disorders among gender and sexual minorities across the lifespan. Particular emphasis will be needed on inclusion of LGBT persons of color in order to obtain a better understanding of the role of race/ethnicity on tobacco use behaviors among gender and sexual minorities. Additional research is needed that focuses on countries in the Global South to have a better understanding of potential geographic and cultural influences on tobacco and tobacco use disorders among sexual and gender minorities.

Acknowledgments

Dr. Matthews's efforts in the development of this manuscript were supported by funds from the University of Illinois Cancer Center. Efforts on this publication were also supported by the National Institute on Minority Health and Health Disparities of the National Institutes of Health under Award Number U54MD012523. The content is solely the responsibility of the authors and does not necessarily represent the official views of the National Institutes of Health.

References

American Lung Association. (2010). *Smoking out a deadly threat: Tobacco use in the LGBT community*. http://www.lungusa.org/assets/documents/publications/lung-disease-data/lgbt-report.pdf

American Psychiatric Association. (2013). *Diagnostic and statistical manual of mental disorders* (5th ed.). Arlington, VA: American Psychiatric Association. doi:10.1176/appi.books.9780890425596

American Society of Addiction Medicine. (2008). Public policy statement on nicotine addiction and tobacco. https://www.asam.org/advocacy/find-a-policy-statement/view-policy-statement/public-policy-statements/2011/12/15/nicotine-addiction-and-tobacco

Baskerville, N. B., Dash, D., Shuh, A., Wong, K., Abramowicz, A., Yessis, J., & Kennedy, R. D. (2017). Tobacco use cessation interventions for lesbian, gay, bisexual, transgender and queer youth and young adults: A scoping review. *Preventive Medicine Reports, 6*, 53–62. doi:10.1016/j.pmedr.2017.02.004

Berger, I., & Mooney-Somers, J. (2016). Smoking cessation programs for lesbian, gay, bisexual, transgender, and intersex people: A content-based systematic review. *Nicotine and Tobacco Research, 19*(12), 1408–17. doi:10.1093/ntr/ntw216

Blosnich, J., Lee, J. G., & Horn, K. (2013). A systematic review of the aetiology of tobacco disparities for sexual minorities. *Tobacco Control, 22*(2), 66–73. doi:10.1136/tobaccocontrol-2011-050181

Bourne, A., Davey, C., Hickson, F., Reid, D., & Weatherburn, P. (2017). Physical health inequalities among gay and bisexual men in England: A large community-based cross-sectional survey. *Journal of Public Health, 39*(2), 290–6. doi:10.1093/pubmed/fdw029

Boyd, C. J., Veliz, P. T., Stephenson, R., Hughes, T. L., & McCabe, S. E. (2019). Severity of alcohol, tobacco, and drug use disorders among sexual minority individuals and their "Not sure" counterparts. *LGBT Health, 6*(1), 15–22. doi:10.1089/lgbt.2018.0122

Buchting, F. O., Emory, K. T., Kim, Y., Fagan, P., Vera, L. E., & Emery, S. (2017). Transgender use of cigarettes, cigars, and e-cigarettes in a national study. *American Journal of Preventive Medicine, 53*(1), e1–e7. doi:10.1016/j.amepre.2016.11.022

Buchting, F. O., Furmanski, W. L., Lee, G. J., Matthews, A., Matthews-Trigg, D., Scout.,... Torrez, G. (2012). MPOWERED: Best and promising practices for LGBT tobacco prevention and control. https://www.lgbthealthlink.org/Assets/U/documents/mpowered.pdf

Burkhalter, J., Margolies, L., Sigurdsson, H., Walland, J., Radix, A., Rice, D.,... Maingi, S. (2016). The national LGBT cancer action plan: A white paper of the 2014 national summit on cancer in the LGBT communities. *LGBT Health, 3*(1), 19–31. doi:10.1089/lgbt.2015.0118

Caceres, B. A., Jackman, K. B., Ferrer, L., Cato, K. D., & Hughes, T. L. (2019). A scoping review of sexual minority women's health in Latin America and the Caribbean. *International Journal of Nursing Studies, 94*, 85–97. doi:10.1016/j.ijnurstu.2019.01.016

Centers for Disease Control and Prevention. (2014). *Best practices for comprehensive tobacco control Programs—2014*. Atlanta, GA: U.S. Department of Health and Human Services, Centers for Disease Control and Prevention, National Center for Chronic Disease Prevention and Health Promotion, Office on Smoking and Health.

Clarke, M. P., & Coughlin, J. R. (2012). Prevalence of smoking among the lesbian, gay, bisexual, transsexual, transgender and queer (LGBTTQ) subpopulations in Toronto—the Toronto rainbow tobacco survey (TRTS). *Canadian Journal of Public Health, 103*(2), 132–6. doi:10.1007/BF03404218

Conron, K. J., Scott, G., Stowell, G. S., & Landers, S. J. (2012). Transgender health in Massachusetts: Results from a household probability sample of adults. *American Journal of Public Health, 102*(1), 118–22. doi:10.2105/AJPH.2011.300315

Corliss, H. L., Wadler, B. M., Jun, H. J., Rosario, M., Wypij, D., Frazier, A. L., & Austin, S. B. (2012). Sexual-orientation disparities in cigarette smoking in a longitudinal cohort study of adolescents. *Nicotine & Tobacco Research, 15*(1), 213–22. doi:10.1093/ntr/nts114

Coulter, R. W. S., Kenst, K. S., Bowen, D. J., & Scout, S. (2014). Research funded by the national institutes of health on the health of lesbian, gay, bisexual, and transgender populations. *American Journal of Public Health, 104*(2), e105–e112. doi:10.2105/AJPH.2013.301501

Covey, L. S., Weissman, J., LoDuca, C., & Duan, N. (2009). A comparison of abstinence outcomes among gay/bisexual and heterosexual male smokers in an intensive, non-tailored smoking cessation study. *Nicotine and Tobacco Research, 11*(11), 1374–7. doi:10.1093/ntr/ntp137

Crissman, H. P., Berger, M. B., Graham, L. F., & Dalton, V. K. (2017). Transgender demographics: A household probability sample of US adults, 2014. *American Journal of Public Health, 107*(2), 213–5. doi:10.2105/AJPH.2016.303571

Cullen, K. A., Ambrose, B. K., Gentzke, A. S., Apelberg, B. J., Jamal, A., & King, B. A. (2018). Notes from the field: Use of electronic cigarettes and any tobacco product among middle and high school students—United States, 2011–18. *Morbidity and Mortality Weekly Report, 67*(45), 1276–7. doi:10.15585/mmwr.mm6745a5

Dilley, J. A., Spigner, C., Boysun, M. J., Dent, C. W., & Pizacani, B. A. (2008). Does tobacco industry marketing excessively impact lesbian, gay and bisexual communities? *Tobacco Control, 17*(6), 385–90. doi:10.1136/tc.2007.024216

Drescher, C., Lopez, E., Griffin, J., Toomey, T., Eldridge, E., & Stepleman, L. (2018). Mental health correlates of cigarette use in LGBT individuals in the southeastern United States. *Substance Use & Misuse, 53*(6), 891–900. doi:10.1080/10826084.2017.1418087

Drope, J., Liber, A. C., Cahn, Z., Stoklosa, M., Kennedy, R., Douglas, C. E.,... Drope, J. (2018). Who's still smoking? Disparities in adult cigarette smoking prevalence in the

United States: Disparities in adult smoking prevalence in the US. *CA: A Cancer Journal for Clinicians, 68*(2), 106–15. doi:10.3322/caac.21444
Fallin, A., Goodin, A. J., & King, B. A. (2015). Menthol cigarette smoking among lesbian, gay, bisexual, and transgender adults. *American Journal of Preventive Medicine, 48*(1), 93–7. doi:10.1016/j.amepre.2014.07.044
Fallin, A., Goodin, A., Lee, Y. O., & Bennett, K. (2015). Smoking characteristics among lesbian, gay, and bisexual adults. *Preventive Medicine, 74*, 123–30. doi:10.1016/j.ypmed.2014.11.026
Fallin, A., Lee, Y. O., Bennett, K., & Goodin, A. (2016). Smoking cessation awareness and utilization among lesbian, gay, bisexual, and transgender adults: An analysis of the 2009–2010 national adult tobacco survey. *Nicotine and Tobacco Research, 18*(4), 496–500. doi:10.1093/ntr/ntv103
Fiore, M. C., Jaén, C. R., Baker, T. B., Bailey, W. C., Benowitz, N. L., Curry, S. J., . . . Leitzke, C. (2008). *Treating tobacco use and dependence: 2008 update. Clinical practice guideline.* Rockville, MD: U.S. Department of Health and Human Services, Public Health Service.
Galea, S., Tracy, M., Hoggatt, K. J., Dimaggio, C., & Karpati, A. (2011). Estimated deaths attributable to social factors in the United States. *American Journal of Public Health, 101*(8), 1456–65. doi:10.2105/AJPH.2010.300086
Grady, E. S., Humfleet, G. L., Delucchi, K. L., Reus, V. I., Muñoz, R. F., & Hall, S. M. (2014). Smoking cessation outcomes among sexual and gender minority and nonminority smokers in extended smoking treatments. *Nicotine and Tobacco Research, 16*(9), 1207–15. doi:10.1093/ntr/ntu050
Graham, R., Berkowitz, B., Blum, R., Bockting, W., Bradford, J., de Vries, B., & Makadon, H. (2011). *The health of lesbian, gay, bisexual, and transgender people: Building a foundation for better understanding.* Washington, DC: Institute of Medicine, 89–139.
Grant, J. M., Mottet, L. A., Tanis, J., Harrison, J. Herman, J. S., & Keisling, M. (2011). *Injustice at every turn: A report of the National Transgender Discrimination Survey.* Washington, DC: National Center for Transgender Equality and National Gay and Lesbian Task Force.
Haley, L., Wong, J., Moore, D., Chan, K., Michelow, W., Dawar, M., . . . Team, T. (2014). Prevalence and correlates of cigarette smoking among men who have sex with men (MSM) in Vancouver, Canada: A cross-sectional survey. *Journal of Behavioral Health, 3*(1), 1–8. doi:10.5455/jbh.20131217011519
Hatzenbuehler, M. L., Keyes, K. M., Hamilton, A., & Hasin, D. S. (2014). State-level tobacco environments and sexual orientation disparities in tobacco use and dependence in the USA. *Tobacco Control, 23*(e2), e127–e132. doi:10.1136/tobaccocontrol-2013-051279
Herie, M., Dragonetti, R., & Selby, P. (2012). Alcohol and tobacco use problems. In A. Khenti, J. Sapag, S. Mohamound, & A. Ravindran (Eds.), *Collaborative mental health: An advanced manual for primary care professionals* (pp. 195–214). Toronto, ON: Centre for Addiction and Mental Health.
Hoffman, L., Delahanty, J., Johnson, S. E., & Zhao, X. (2018). Sexual and gender minority cigarette smoking disparities: An analysis of 2016 behavioral risk factor surveillance system data. *Preventive Medicine, 113*, 109–15. doi:10.1016/j.ypmed.2018.05.014
Hu, S., Neff, L., Agaku, I., Cox, S., Day, H., Holder-Hayes, E., & King, B. (2016). Tobacco product use among adults—United States, 2013–2014. *Morbidity and Mortality Weekly Report, 65*(27), 685–91. doi:10.15585/mmwr.mm6527a1
Hughes, T. L., Johnson, T. P., & Matthews, A. K. (2008). Sexual orientation and smoking: Results from a multisite women's health study. *Substance Use & Misuse, 43*(8–9), 1218–39. doi:10.1080/10826080801914170
Jamal, A., Phillips, E., Gentzke, A. S., Homa, D. M., Babb, S. D., King, B. A., & Neff, L. J. (2018). Current cigarette smoking among adults—United States, 2016. *Morbidity and Mortality Weekly Report, 67*(2), 53–9. doi:10.15585/mmwr.mm6702a1
James, S. E., Herman, J. L., Rankin, S., Keisling, M., Mottet, L., & Anafi, M. (2016). *Executive summary of the Report of the 2015 U.S. Transgender Survey.* Washington, DC: National Center for Transgender Equality.
Jordan, J. N., Everett, K. D., Ge, B., & McElroy, J. A. (2015). Smoking and intention to quit among a large sample of black sexual and gender minorities. *Journal of Homosexuality, 62*(5), 604–20. doi:10.1080/00918369.2014.987569
Kimmel, P. L., Fwu, C., Abbott, K. C., Ratner, J., & Eggers, P. W. (2016). Racial disparities in poverty account for mortality differences in US Medicare beneficiaries. *SSM—Population Health, 2*, 123–9. doi:10.1016/j.ssmph.2016.02.003
King, B. A., Dube, S. R., & Tynan, M. A. (2012). Current tobacco use among adults in the United States: Findings from the national adult tobacco survey. *American Journal of Public Health, 102*(11), e93–e100. doi:10.2105/AJPH.2012.301002
King, B. A., Patel, R., Nguyen, K. H., & Dube, S. R. (2015). Trends in awareness and use of electronic cigarettes among US adults, 2010–2013. *Nicotine and Tobacco Research, 17*(2), 219–27. doi:10.1093/ntr/ntu191
Lee, J. G., Matthews, A. K., McCullen, C. A., & Melvin, C. L. (2014). Promotion of tobacco use cessation for lesbian, gay, bisexual, and transgender people: A systematic review. *American Journal of Preventive Medicine, 47*(6), 823–31. doi:10.1016/j.amepre.2014.07.051
Lee, J. G. L., Pan, W. K., Henriksen, L., Goldstein, A. O., & Ribisl, K. M. (2016). Is there a relationship between the concentration of same-sex couples and tobacco retailer density? *Nicotine and Tobacco Research, 18*(2), 147–55. doi:10.1093/ntr/ntv046
Lee, S., Ling, P. M., & Glantz, S. A. (2012). The vector of the tobacco epidemic: Tobacco industry practices in low- and middle-income countries. *Cancer Causes & Control, 23*(1), 117–29. doi:10.1007/s10552-012-9914-0.
Levy, D. T., Tam, J., Kuo, C., Fong, G. T., & Chaloupka, F. (2018). The impact of implementing tobacco control policies: The 2017 tobacco control policy scorecard. *Journal of Public Health Management and Practice, 24*(5), 448–57. doi:10.1097/PHH.0000000000000780
Matthews, A. K., Balsam, K., Hotton, A., Kuhns, L., Li, C., & Bowen, D. J. (2014). Awareness of media-based antitobacco messages among a community sample of LGBT individuals. *Health Promotion Practice, 15*(6), 857–66. doi:10.1177/1524839914533343
Matthews, A. K., Breen, E., & Kittiteerasack, P. (2018). Social determinants of LGBT cancer health inequities. *Seminars in Oncology Nursing, 34*(1), 12–20. doi:10.1016/j.soncn.2017.11.001
Matthews, A. K., Cesario, J., Ruiz, R., Ross, N., & King, A. (2017). A qualitative study of the barriers to and facilitators of smoking cessation among lesbian, gay, bisexual, and

transgender smokers who are interested in quitting. *LGBT Health, 4*(1), 24–33. doi:10.1089/lgbt.2016.0059.

Matthews, A. K., Hotton, A., Aranda, F., Kuhns, L., Lee, J. G., & Ross, N. (2014). Predictors of readiness to quit among a diverse sample of sexual minority male smokers. *Journal of Health Disparities Research and Practice, 7*(5), 9.

Matthews, A. K., McCabe, S. E., Lee, J. G. L., & Veliz, P. (2018). Differences in smoking prevalence and eligibility for low-dose computed tomography (LDCT) lung cancer screening among older U.S. adults: Role of sexual orientation. *Cancer Causes & Control, 29*(8), 769–74. doi:10.1007/s10552-018-1044-x

Matthews, A. K., Ross, N., Lee, M., & Aranda, F. (2015). The needs of racial/ethnic LGBT individuals across the cancer care continuum. In U. Boehmer & R. Elk (Eds.), *Cancer and the LGBT community: Unique perspectives from risk to survivorship* (pp. 261–74). Cham, Switzerland: Springer. doi:10.1007/978-3-319-15057-4_16

Matthews, A. K., Steffen, A., Hughes, T., Aranda, F., & Martin, K. (2017). Demographic, healthcare, and contextual factors associated with smoking status among sexual minority women. *LGBT Health, 4*(1), 17–23. doi:10.1089/lgbt.2016.0039

Matthews, A. K., Steffen, A. D., Kuhns, L. M., Ruiz, R. A., Ross, N. A., Burke, L. A., . . . King, A. C. (2019). Evaluation of a randomized clinical trial comparing the effectiveness of a culturally targeted and nontargeted smoking cessation intervention for lesbian, gay, bisexual, and transgender smokers. *Nicotine and Tobacco Research, 21*(11), 1506–16. doi:10.1093/ntr/nty184

Matthews, A. K., Vargas, M., Kuhns, L., Shappiva, N., & King, A. C. (2014). A qualitative examination of barriers and motivators to smoking cessation among HIV positive African American MSM smokers. *Journal of Health Disparities Research and Practice, 7*(2), 4.

Matthews, P. A., Blok, A. C., Lee, J. G. L., Hitsman, B., Sanchez-Johnsen, L., Watson, K., . . . Winn, R. (2018). SBM recommends policy support to reduce smoking disparities for sexual and gender minorities. *Translational Behavioral Medicine, 8*(5), 692–5. doi:10.1093/tbm/ibx017

Max, W. B., Stark, B., Sung, H., & Offen, N. (2016). Sexual identity disparities in smoking and secondhand smoke exposure in California: 2003–2013. *American Journal of Public Health, 106*(6), 1136–42. doi:10.2105/AJPH.2016.303071

McCabe, S. E., Hughes, T. L., Matthews, A. K., Lee, J. G., West, B. T., Boyd, C. J., & Arslanian-Engoren, C. (2017). Sexual orientation discrimination and tobacco use disparities in the United States. *Nicotine and Tobacco Research, 21*(4), 523–31. doi:10.1093/ntr/ntx283

McCabe, S. E., Matthews, A. K., Lee, J. G. L., Veliz, P., Hughes, T. L., & Boyd, C. J. (2018). Tobacco use and sexual orientation in a national cross-sectional study: Age, race/ethnicity, and sexual identity–attraction differences. *American Journal of Preventive Medicine, 54*(6), 736–45. doi:10.1016/j.amepre.2018.03.009

McElroy, J. A., Everett, K. D., & Zaniletti, I. (2011). An examination of smoking behavior and opinions about smoke-free environments in a large sample of sexual and gender minority community members. *Nicotine and Tobacco Research, 13*(6), 440–8. doi:10.1093/ntr/ntr021

Meyer, I. H. (2003). Prejudice, social stress, and mental health in lesbian, gay, and bisexual populations: conceptual issues and research evidence. *Psychological Bulletin, 129*(5), 674. doi:10.1037/0033-2909.129.5.674

Mirbolouk, M., Charkhchi, P., Kianoush, S., Uddin, S. M. I., Orimoloye, O. A., Jaber, R., . . . Blaha, M. J. (2018). Prevalence and distribution of e-cigarette use among U.S. adults: Behavioral risk factor surveillance system, 2016. *Annals of Internal Medicine, 169*(7), 429–38. doi:10.7326/M17-3440

Ng, M., Freeman, M. K., Fleming, T. D., Robinson, M., Dwyer-Lindgren, L., Thomson, B., . . . Gakidou, E. (2014). Smoking prevalence and cigarette consumption in 187 countries, 1980–2012. *Journal of the American Medical Association, 311*(2), 183–92. doi:10.1001/jama.2013.284692

Offen, N., Smith, E. A., & Malone, R. E. (2008). Is tobacco a gay issue? Interviews with leaders of the lesbian, gay, bisexual and transgender community. *Culture, Health & Sexuality, 10*(2), 143–57. doi:10.1080/13691050701656284

Onor, I. O., Stirling, D. L., Williams, S. R., Bediako, D., Borghol, A., Harris, M. B., . . . Sarpong, D. F. (2017). Clinical effects of cigarette smoking: Epidemiologic impact and review of pharmacotherapy options. *International Journal of Environmental Research and Public Health, 14*(10), 1147. doi:10.3390/ijerph14101147

Palmer, N. A., & Greytak, E. A. (2017). LGBTQ student victimization and its relationship to school discipline and justice system involvement. *Criminal Justice Review, 42*(2), 163–87. doi:10.1177/0734016817704698

Plant, A., Montoya, J. A., Tyree, R., Aragon, L., Weber, M., Le Veque, M., . . . Kent, C. (2017). The break up: Evaluation of an anti-smoking educational campaign for lesbians, gays, and bisexuals in Los Angeles county. *Journal of Health Communication, 22*(1), 29–36. doi:10.1080/10810730.2016.1247485

Prochaska, J. O., & Velicer, W. F. (1997). The transtheoretical model of health behavior change. *American Journal of Health Promotion, 12*(1), 38–48. doi:10.4278/0890-1171-12.1.38

Reddy, K. P., Kong, C. Y., Hyle, E. P., Baggett, T. P., Huang, M., Parker, R. A., . . . Walensky, R. P. (2017). Lung cancer mortality associated with smoking and smoking cessation among people living with HIV in the united states. *JAMA Internal Medicine, 177*(11), 1613–21. doi:10.1001/jamainternmed.2017.4349

Reisner, S. L., Poteat, T., Keatley, J., Cabral, M., Mothopeng, T., Dunham, E., . . . Baral, S. D. (2016). Global health burden and needs of transgender populations: a review. *Lancet, 388*(10042), 412–36. doi:10.1016/S0140-6736(16)00684-X

Rivera, E., Poldruhi, M., Ward, C., Jenkins, G., Nichols, E., & Pinter, A. (2019). *The black at the end of the rainbow: Online discrimination among LGBTQ African Americans.* Conference poster, iConference proceedings. doi:10.21900/iconf.2019.103350

Roxburgh, A., Lea, T., de Wit, J., & Degenhardt, L. (2016). Sexual identity and prevalence of alcohol and other drug use among Australians in the general population. *International Journal of Drug Policy, 28*, 76–82. doi:10.1016/j.drugpo.2015.11.005

Schneebaum, A., & Badgett, M. V. L. (2019). Poverty in US lesbian and gay couple households. *Feminist Economics, 25*(1), 1–30. doi:10.1080/13545701.2018.1441533

Shires, D. A., & Jaffee, K. D. (2015). Structural discrimination is associated with smoking status among a national sample of transgender individuals. *Nicotine and Tobacco Research, 18*(6), 1502–8. doi:10.1093/ntr/ntv221

Slater, M. E., Godette, D., Huang, B., Ruan, W. J., & Kerridge, B. T. (2017). Sexual orientation-based discrimination, excessive alcohol use, and substance use disorders among sexual minority adults. *LGBT Health, 4*(5), 337–44. doi:10.1089/lgbt.2016.0117

Trinidad, D. R., Pérez-Stable, E. J., Emery, S. L., White, M. M., Grana, R. A., & Messer, K. S. (2009). Intermittent and light daily smoking across racial/ethnic groups in the United States. *Nicotine & Tobacco Research, 11*(2), 203–10. doi:10.1093/ntr/ntn018

U.S. Department of Health and Human Services. (2016). *E-cigarette use among youth and young adults: A report of the Surgeon General.* Atlanta, GA: U.S. Department of Health and Human Services, Centers for Disease Control and Prevention, National Center for Chronic Disease Prevention and Health Promotion, Office on Smoking and Health.

U.S. Food and Drug Administration. (2019a). This Free Life campaign. https://www.fda.gov/tobacco-products/public-health-education-campaigns/free-life-campaign

U.S. Food and Drug Administration. (2019b). The real cost campaign. https://www.fda.gov/tobacco-products/public-health-education-campaigns/real-cost-campaign

Veliz, P., Matthews, A. K., Arslanian-Engoren, C., Evans-Polce, R. J., Lee, J. G. L., Boyd, C. J.,... McCabe, S. E. (2019). LDCT lung cancer screening eligibility and use of CT scans for lung cancer among sexual minorities. *Cancer Epidemiology, 60*, 51–4. doi:10.1016/j.canep.2019.03.009

Vogel, E. A., Humfleet, G. L., Meacham, M., Prochaska, J. J., & Ramo, D. E. (2019). Sexual and gender minority young adults' smoking characteristics: Assessing differences by sexual orientation and gender identity. *Addictive Behaviors, 95*, 98–102. doi:10.1016/j.addbeh.2019.03.005

Wang, T. W., Wang, T. W., Asman, K., Asman, K., Gentzke, A. S., Gentzke, A. S.,... King, B. A. (2018). Tobacco product use among adults—United States, 2017. *Morbidity and Mortality Weekly Report, 67*(44), 1225–32. doi:10.15585/mmwr.mm6744a2

Watson, R. J., Lewis, N. M., Fish, J. N., & Goodenow, C. (2018). Sexual minority youth continue to smoke cigarettes earlier and more often than heterosexuals: Findings from population-based data. *Drug and Alcohol Dependence, 184*, 64–70. doi:10.1016/j.drugalcdep.2017.11.025

Weinberger, A. H., Kashan, R. S., Shpigel, D. M., Esan, H., Taha, F., Lee, C. J.,... Goodwin, R. D. (2017). Depression and cigarette smoking behavior: A critical review of population-based studies. *American Journal of Drug and Alcohol Abuse, 43*(4), 416–31. doi:10.3109/00952990.2016.1171327

Wood, D. E., Kazerooni, E. A., Baum, S. L., Eapen, G. A., Ettinger, D. S., Hou, L.,... Hughes, M. (2018). Lung cancer screening, version 3.2018. *Journal of the National Comprehensive Cancer Network, 16*(4), 412–41. doi:10.6004/jnccn.2018.0020

World Health Organization. (2008). *WHO report on the global tobacco epidemic, 2008: The MPOWER package.* Geneva, Switzerland: World Health Organization.

Xu, X., Bishop, E. E., Kennedy, S. M., Simpson, S. A., & Pechacek, T. F. (2015). Annual healthcare spending attributable to cigarette smoking: An update. *American Journal of Preventive Medicine, 48*(3), 326–33. doi:10.1016/j.amepre.2014.10.012

Yach, D., & Bettcher, D. (2000). Globalisation of tobacco industry influence and new global responses. *Tobacco Control, 9*(2), 206–16. doi:10.1136/tc.9.2.206

Yamey, G. (2003). Gay tobacco ads come out of the closet. *BMJ, 327*(7409), 296. doi:10.1136/bmj.327.7409.296

CHAPTER

11 Schizophrenia Spectrum and Other Psychotic Disorders among Sexual and Gender Minority Populations

Jayme L. Peta

Abstract

Despite robust evidence that barriers exist for sexual and gender minority (SGM) individuals in accessing mental health care, and evidence that these populations are at higher risk for mental health concerns in general, there is a lack of literature on schizophrenia spectrum and other psychotic disorders in SGM populations or specific adaptations and changes needed to engage and treat SGM individuals with these disorders in a culturally competent manner. This chapter outlines key areas of research regarding SGM populations with schizophrenia spectrum and other psychotic disorders, including important considerations for differential diagnosis and suggestions for cultural competence. Also covered are the unique needs of SGM populations with these disorders and the needs of subpopulations (transgender and gender nonbinary individuals, people of color, and transition-age youth). Directions for future research are discussed.

Keywords: psychosis, schizophrenia, HIV, substance use, LGBT, gay, lesbian, bisexual, transgender, gender nonbinary

Introduction

Schizophrenia, psychosis, and related disorders are among the most challenging disorders for mental health clinicians to diagnose and treat. And despite evidence that sexual and gender minority (SGM) individuals struggle to obtain satisfactory mental health treatment, very little research has addressed the unique needs of the SGM population with serious mental illness (Avery, Hellman, & Sudderth, 2001).

Schizophrenia Spectrum Disorders

The schizophrenia spectrum and other psychotic disorders (SSOPDs) of the *Diagnostic and Statistical Manual* (5th ed., American Psychiatric Association, 2013) comprise disorders that share impairments in the domains of delusions, hallucinations, disorganized speech, abnormal behavior, and negative symptoms. They are heterogenous, with psychosis as the primary symptom. These disorders include schizophrenia, schizoaffective disorder, schizophreniform disorder, brief psychotic disorder, substance-induced psychotic disorders, and psychotic disorder due to another medical condition (American Psychiatric Association, 2013). Schizotypal personality disorder is also included.

Schizophrenia and schizoaffective disorder are often considered to be "serious mental illnesses" due to their chronicity and potential for long-term disability. "Psychosis," while a symptom and a key symptom of the SSOPDs, is not a diagnosis in itself. However, it is often used to describe general symptoms associated with schizophrenia and SSOPDs, although those who have experienced brief psychotic disorder or an episode of psychosis related to substance use, for example, are unlikely to have the same needs or concerns as do those who have been diagnosed with schizophrenia and treated for it for decades. Much of the research on "psychosis" is focused on schizophrenia and schizoaffective disorders, and much of the research on treatment of "serious mental illness" will be applicable when reviewing considerations for those with schizophrenia or schizoaffective disorder. For the purposes of this chapter, the focus will be on schizophrenia or schizoaffective disorder, with some discussion of substance-induced psychosis and psychotic disorder related to a medical condition. Clinicians are urged to use caution in diagnosing clients with psychotic symptoms to avoid over- or misdiagnosing.

Prevalence of SSOPDs among the SGM Population

There are a number of limitations to studies of prevalence of SSOPDs among the SGM population. Commonly, studies of SGM individuals and mental health do not specify serious mental illness, including SSOPDs (Gilman et al., 2001; Kidd, Howison, Pilling, Ross, & McKenzie, 2016). Further, studies on serious mental illness shy away from including questions or information on sexuality in general. Very often, as observed by Barber (2009), those with serious mental illness are regarded as asexual or childlike; thus, the sexuality or gender identity of those with serious mental illness is rarely studied and is commonly seen to be irrelevant to treatment or, worse, viewed as a symptom.

There are general obstacles to studying SGM persons with SSOPDs, including dramatic differences in how to define gender and sexual minority identity or behavior, and differences in what symptoms constitute meeting the threshold for psychosis or an SSOPD. However, there are some studies examining the prevalence of SSOPD among SGM persons. Generally, SGM samples tend to have higher overall rates of mental health symptoms and distress (Carmel & Erickson-Schroth, 2016; Cochran, Sullivan, & Mays, 2003; Gilman et al., 2001). This suggests that higher rates of psychotic disorders are also likely, although schizophrenia and schizoaffective disorders do have a larger genetic contribution to onset, perhaps partly explaining the uneven results in the studies described later in this chapter.

In a 2002 study of prevalence of major mental illness in a small clinical sample, no difference was found between LGBT and control groups in psychotic disorder diagnoses (Hellman, Sudderth, & Avery, 2002). When controlling for sex, men in the LGBT group had lower rates of SSOPDs, while no statistically significant differences were found between LGBT women and the control sample (Hellman et al., 2002). However, this study was completed using a clinical sample rather than a community sample, which may have resulted in confounds related to SGM individuals being less willing to seek treatment or to discuss their gender or sexuality. As Mizock and Fleming (2011) point out, barriers to treatment for gender minorities may result in underreporting of transgender/nonbinary identities among those who also have mental illness.

A study of completed suicides by LGBT-identified individuals in Queensland, Australia, found an underrepresentation of those with psychosis among the sample as compared with the heterosexual control group (Skerett, Kolves, & De Leo, 2015). This again may be due to those with psychosis being less willing to be open about their gender or sexual orientation.

However, a population-based study in the United States found that 9.3 percent of gay men and 2.1 percent of bisexual men were found to have a psychotic disorder while 2.7 percent of heterosexual-identified men were diagnosed with a psychotic disorder. Among women, 3.4 percent of heterosexual women and 9.2 percent of bisexual women had a psychotic disorder. The difference between heterosexual and lesbian women with psychosis was not significant, with 2.9 percent of lesbian women being diagnosed with a psychotic disorder (Bolton & Sareen, 2011). A study in the Netherlands found an increased risk for psychotic symptoms among those with a sexual minority identity (Gevonden et al. 2014). This was a larger study from a community sample and focused on psychotic symptoms rather than specific diagnoses. The authors also found that much of the association was at least partly mediated by childhood trauma, peer bullying, and discrimination. Together, the population-based data sets suggest that there may be higher rates of SSOPD among SGM persons, and that these disparities may be due to experiences of minority stress.

Contributors to SSOPD Disparities among SGM Individuals

Trauma

The possibility that experiences of childhood trauma, peer bullying, and adult trauma, discrimination, or victimization are associated with psychosis for SGM individuals is upheld by a growing number of studies. First, that childhood adverse and childhood stressful experiences are higher in SGM populations has been well established as a driver for adult anxiety, depression, and substance use (Austin et al., 2008; Balsam, Molina, Beadnell, Simoni, & Walters, 2011; Schneeberger, Dietl, Muenzenmaier, Huber, & Lang, 2014). In the general population, childhood trauma is also well established as strongly linked to schizophrenia and similar disorders (Read, van Os, Morrison, & Ross, 2005; Van Os, Linscott, Myin-Germeys, Delespaul, & Krabbendam, 2009), suggesting that childhood adverse experiences are likely a driver of SSOPDs in SGM adults. Thus, while no studies have established a direct association between adverse childhood (or adult) experiences and psychosis in SGM populations, it is highly likely that the increased prevalence of psychotic experiences in population-based studies of SGM individuals is connected to the increased likelihood of a history of childhood trauma and bullying, as well as adult trauma, discrimination, and victimization.

Substance Use

However, there are other possible contributors to the link between SGM identity and SSOPDs. SGM populations are found to have higher rates of substance use disorders (Cochran et al., 2003; Gilman et al., 2001; Herbst et al., 2008; Sandfort et al., 2014). More recently, this connection has been conceptualized as mediated by sexual and gender minority stress—Meyer's (2003) framework for understanding mental health disparities in sexual minorities as directly related to unique experiences of victimization, discrimination, and rejection (Lehavot & Simoni, 2011; McCabe, Bostwick, Hughes, West, & Boyd, 2010; Mereish, O'Cleirigh, & Bradford, 2014; Reisner, Gamarel, Nemoto, & Operario, 2014).

These higher rates of substance use disorders are significant for those treating SGM populations because symptoms of psychosis are often comorbid with substance use, creating difficulty in differential diagnosis and treatment (Buckley, Miller, Lehrer, & Castle, 2008). Additionally, certain substances, such as cannabis and methamphetamines, can cause acute psychotic symptoms and must be ruled out before a diagnosis of schizophrenia or schizoaffective disorder can be made (American Psychiatric Association, 2013). Further, growing evidence shows that long-term use of methamphetamines can lead to chronic psychotic symptoms possibly indistinguishable from schizophrenia (Bramness et al., 2012). Recent cannabis research shows a "kindling effect": cannabis use may hasten the onset of schizophrenia in vulnerable individuals (Di Forti et al., 2015; Gage, Hickman, & Zammit, 2016). Substance use and abuse not only make important contributions to the higher rates of psychosis among SGM populations but are important considerations in diagnosis of acute and chronic psychotic symptoms in SGM persons.

Medical Conditions

It is also important that the clinician observing psychotic symptoms screen for medical conditions that may explain a psychotic presentation. In particular, HIV/AIDS, which continues to heavily impact men who have sex with men and transgender women, is linked to psychosis in important ways (Centers for Disease Control and Prevention, 2018, 2019). First, psychosis secondary to HIV can appear in late-stage HIV (Angelino & Treisman, 2008; Watkins & Treisman, 2012). Some medications frequently used in the treatment of HIV and HIV-related infections can have side effects of psychotic symptoms (Angelino & Treisman, 2008). In addition, the presence of schizophrenia and other preexisting psychotic disorders can cause difficulty in managing HIV, including deficits in managing medication schedules, recognizing and reporting symptoms, and staying current with medical appointments (Watkins & Treisman, 2012). Notably, the interaction between psychosis and HIV is also significant due to studies showing that presence of a psychotic disorder is a risk factor for contracting HIV (Watkins & Treisman, 2012). HIV represents a significant complication to diagnosis and treatment of the client also experiencing psychotic symptoms.

There is some evidence that introduction of gender-affirming hormones or their abrupt discontinuation may result, rarely, in psychotic symptoms (Coleman et al., 2012; Dhillon, Bastiampillai, Krishnan, Opray, & Tibrewal, 2011; Summers & Onate, 2014). Clinicians should be alert to this possibility and ensure that hormone-related psychotic symptoms are ruled out. Many clients using gender-affirming hormones may be using hormones acquired from friends, the black market, or other sources, and may not be using a dose or form of the hormone that is appropriate for them. These clients may need assistance in finding a transgender/nonbinary (TGNB)-knowledgeable physician to help them obtain a prescription, adjust dosages, and rule out the possibility that hormones may be playing a part in inducing psychosis.

Populations of Special Concern

Certain populations under the SGM umbrella require special considerations with regard to SSOPDs. In particular, TGNB individuals face multiple obstacles when seeking care both for mental health and for TGNB-specific healthcare. When working with or assessing SGM persons of color, cultural considerations are crucial, as is addressing the additional barriers to treatment. Early intervention programs working primarily with youth and transition-age youth should pay special attention to the sexual and gender identity development needs of their clients.

TGNB Individuals with SSOPDs

A major consideration for many clinicians treating those who identify as TGNB who have also been diagnosed with SSOPD is how and when to support gender-affirmative medical interventions (GAMIs). A number of areas of concern and potential for diagnostic bias exist. Historically, transgender identities were assumed to be expressions of psychotic symptoms (J. K. Meyer, 1982; Origgi & Vial, 2013). Even as great progress has been made in depathologizing TGNB identities, diagnosing and treating gender identity disorder with cultural competency as a disorder distinct from gender identity, and implementing affirming therapies for TGNB clients, when gender identity concerns overlap with psychotic symptoms, many clinicians become reluctant to support GAMIs or affirm the TGNB identity (Baltieri & De Andrade, 2009; Borras, Huguelet, & Eytan, 2007).

Not only does the historical bias continue to hold sway, but cases of individuals who have experienced sexual delusions that include a strong desire to be another sex and other gender-related delusions have been documented (Borras et al., 2007). Thus, clinicians face the challenge of potentially incorrectly assuming that gender identity is a symptom, and harmfully determining that non-heterosexual sexual orientation or TGNB identity are really symptoms of psychosis. This is further complicated by the finding that many patients do not reveal their TGNB identity until their first psychotic episode due to the disinhibiting effects of psychosis, and due to the fact that the age of disclosing a TGBN identity in early adulthood often overlaps with the average age of the first psychotic break (Meijer, Eeckhout, van Vlerken, & de Vries, 2017; Smith, Goldhammer, & Keuroghlian, 2018). This can contribute to the erroneous conclusion that the TGNB identity is secondary to the psychotic symptoms. For many clinicians, this results in taking a default conservative stance that TGNB identity must be ruled out as a symptom before it can be acknowledged or before GAMIs can be initiated. However, for many clients, symptoms of psychosis will never fully remit, leaving the client in a state of waiting for GAMIs, or simply waiting to be addressed by the chosen name or pronoun. This results in experiences that can be unaffirming, distressing, and even harmful (Mizock & Fleming, 2011). In a series of case studies, Meijer et al. (2017) found that TGNB clients reported the most distress not from waiting for GAMIs, but from not knowing why they were being prevented from obtaining GAMIs.

Studies suggest a few important guidelines when working with TGNB individuals with psychosis. For those who are not requesting GAMIs, an affirmative approach to gender identity is recommended. Mizock and Fleming (2011) suggest that simply affirming gender identity regardless of evidence of whether the gender is related to a psychotic delusion or a TGNB identity will strengthen rapport. Other common suggestions include extended evaluation of symptoms, history of gender identity disorder, and current gender dysphoria to obtain a better understanding of the meaning of the identity to the client, and to track any changes over time (Mizock & Fleming, 2011; Smith et al., 2018).

However, for the clinician evaluating a client with psychosis for GAMIs, a more complex process is needed. An overall affirmative stance toward gender identity is recommended. However, before recommending GAMIs, the clinician needs to ensure that the gender identity is not secondary to psychosis but also to confirm that TGNB individuals with psychosis have realistic expectations of GAMIs and are able to make informed decisions (Borras et al., 2007; Meijer et al., 2017). Tracking delusions separately from gender dysphoria is important in differentiating between psychotic symptoms and a TGNB identity (Meijer et al., 2017; Smith et al., 2018). Any gender beliefs secondary to psychosis should remit along with other symptoms. Meijer et al., (2017) provide a nuanced look at possible complexities and specific recommendations for GAMI treatment in cases with coexisting psychosis, including the important suggestion of staging out GAMI treatment with longer intervals to monitor changes in gender dysphoria, social role, and psychosis. Smith et al. (2018) recommend GAMIs for any client who wants them, is competent to make medical decisions, and meets criteria for gender dysphoria, due to the growing evidence that psychosis tends to improve after GAMI.

SGM People of Color with SSOPDs

It is well documented that Latino and Black Americans are more likely to be misdiagnosed with a psychotic disorder than their White counterparts

(Schwartz & Blankenship, 2014). Further, SGM people of color experience multiple barriers to receiving mental health services (Burns, Ryan, Garofalo, Newcomb, & Mustanski, 2015; Cochran et al., 2003; Kenagy, 2005; Kenagy & Bostwick, 2005; Xavier, Bobbin, Singer, & Budd, 2005). SGM people of color may also experience multiple forms of discrimination both from the larger SGM community and their racial/ethnic communities, as well as minority stress in everyday life, all of which contribute to poorer mental health outcomes (Balsam et al., 2011; I. H. Meyer, 2010). Recent needs assessments have found that TGNB people of color have a higher risk for HIV, have experienced more violence, and are more likely to be struggling with substance abuse (Nemoto, Operario, & Keatley, 2005; Xavier et al., 2005). Further, sexual minority people of color with a serious mental illness report experiencing both racism and heterosexism as well as stigma related to having a serious mental illness when accessing mental health services (Holley, Tavassoli, & Stromwall, 2016). Thus, it is extremely important that clinicians treating SGM people of color who also have been diagnosed with an SSOPD become aware of the complex needs of this population. Because no cultural adaptations have been made for treating SGM clients of color with psychosis, clinicians are urged to obtain consultation and to adapt evidence-based treatments for psychosis to meet the unique needs of this population. Additionally, according to Holley et al., (2016), a respectful, caring attitude and a team approach were commonly named as supportive and helpful to sexual minority people of color diagnosed with serious mental illness.

SGM Youth and Early Intervention Programs

Early intervention for psychosis programs have been successful in engaging transition-age youth in treatment rapidly after a first psychotic episode. Research has supported these interventions as successful in returning youth to family, work, and educational roles, as well as increasing treatment engagement and improving quality of life (Petersen et al., 2005). However, special considerations are needed for SGM transition-age youth in early intervention programs. As noted, those with SSOPDs are often seen as asexual, which may be especially harmful to SGM youth who are in the process of exploring and understanding their gender and/or sexual identity (Barber, 2009). Further, SGM individuals in general face barriers of discrimination when attempting to access mental health services (Israel, Walther, Gortcheva, & Perry, 2011; S. Rosenberg, Rosenberg, Huygen, & Klein, 2005). Together this represents a need for special considerations for SGM transition-age youth experiencing first episodes of psychosis. As discussed by Lamoureux and Joseph (2014), SGM transition-age youth are in need of safe spaces to discuss and explore their sexual and gender identity, including when they are seeking mental health services for psychosis. Affirming, collaborative practices for SGM transition-age youth with psychosis are needed to ensure that these clients can access services, remain in services, and do the important identity development work that is appropriate to their life stage (Craig, Dentato, & Iacovino, 2015).

Treatment and SGM-Adapted Approaches

The American Psychological Association has called for clinicians to provide culturally competent TGNB and sexual minority mental health treatment (American Psychological Association, 2012, 2015; Byne et al., 2012). A number of resources describe the techniques and approaches needed for culturally competent care for SGM individuals (Bieschke, Perez, & DeBord, 2007; Hendricks & Testa, 2012; Logan & Barret, 2006; Pachankis, 2016). However, there are very few resources for those treating SGM individuals with SSOPDs or other serious mental illness, and specific suggestions for treating SGM individuals with SSOPDs remain sparse.

SGM persons with psychosis face a "dual stigma" that represents a significant barrier to services (S. Rosenberg et al., 2005). Rosenberg et al. (2005) note that LGBT people with serious mental illness are often subject to rejection from LGBT communities due to their mental illness, and at the same time experience minority stress (discrimination and rejection on the basis of sexual and gender identity) when attempting to access services for serious mental illness. Given that rejection has been shown to be an important driver of minority stress, as well as connectedness, a crucial resilience factor, this dual stigma represents a significant obstacle to resilience and recovery from SSOPDs (I. H. Meyer, 2003, 2015). Very often, as noted earlier in the chapter, people with serious mental illness are stigmatized as childlike or as having no sexuality (Cook, 2000). This stigma appears to be compounded for LGB people of color seeking mental health services, according to a small study by Holley et al. (2016).

Reviews show that SGM-specific or adapted services available for SGMs with serious mental illness are few, with limited evidence (Kidd et al., 2016).

Evidence-based treatments for psychosis such as cognitive-behavioral therapy and early intervention programs have rarely incorporated SGM-affirmative treatment. Likewise, books and publications about SGM-affirmative treatment have typically not included approaches to SSOPDs. Clinicians should become familiar with both modalities to create integrated treatment (Holttum, 2015).

Not only has treatment for SGM people with serious mental illness been lacking, but SGM populations with serious mental illness have been underserved in a number of other ways. One such concern is that SGM-affirming therapists, as well as peer-led support groups, often have little specialty in serious mental illness, forcing SGM persons with serious mental illness to choose between expertise and acceptance (Lucksted, 2004). Further, LGBT centers and groups are often stigmatizing toward those with serious mental illness (Drescher & Hellman, 2004). Lucksted (2004) also recorded widespread experiences with anti-SGM bias within the public mental health system, including inappropriate assumption of sexual or gender identity as a symptom of psychosis. Notably, many participants reported that attempts to explore gender or sexuality were regarded negatively or even as evidence of pathology. Participants also reported problems with harassment by peers and even, at times, staff. Kidd, Veltman, Gately, Chan, and Cohen (2011) found also that not only are SGM individuals stigmatized on the basis of their identity, but that due to their mental illness they are assumed to be unable to truly know or represent their identity. They are considered to be confused about their sexual orientation or gender identity. Further, they found that stigma appears to negatively impact mental health and creates barriers to recovery and wellness. Thus, clinics and systems working with SGM people with serious mental illness must address issues of discrimination, rejection, and harassment as an important mental health concern.

Adapting Existing Models

While there are few, if any, evidence-based treatments specifically for SGM with SSOPDs, there have been some suggestions regarding how to adapt models to be more welcoming to SGM people with serious mental illness. Lucksted (2004), in a study commissioned by the Center for Mental Health Studies, made some general suggestions such as the need for openness toward and acceptance about SGM clients in treatment as helpful in promoting focus on these clients' abilities to focus on improving symptoms. Additionally, the author notes respondents indicated that integrating SGM identities improved treatment planning and helped to address clients' needs more effectively.

More specific suggestions have been made from those attempting to adapt existing models to be more affirming to SGM individuals. One such suggestion involves normalizing SGM identities. Rosenberg, Rosenberg, Huygen, and Klein (2005) present an affirming model for addressing the needs of LGBT people with serious mental illness in their article on the Rainbow Heights Club, a modified clubhouse approach. They describe using tenets of normalizing LGBT identity through using non-gendered language about partners in paperwork and in addressing others, incorporating partners into treatment, and avoiding eliding sexual or gender identity with symptoms of serious mental illness. They specifically address awareness of the dual stigma of the participants who have often lost status in their families and communities for their gender or sexual identity as well as their illness. The ability to connect with other SGM individuals with serious mental illness also appears to have positive effects on both treatment outcomes and overall satisfaction (J. Rosenberg et al., 2013; Wong, Stanton, & Sands, 2014).

Use of affirming language and other early signs of welcoming SGM clients was an important concern raised by multiple authors with regard to affirmative treatment for SGM people with psychosis (or serious mental illness in general). Many authors indicated that using gender-neutral language such as "Are you dating anyone?" versus "Do you have a boyfriend?" signals to clients that their gender and sexuality may be accepted. Clinicians are advised to review intake paperwork and questions to make sure they are inclusive to same-sex relationships as well as TGNB identities. Ensuring that SGM-specific posters, magazines, or other signs of affirmation of SGM clients are visible in waiting and treatment rooms is also suggested (Kidd et al., 2011, 2016; Lamoureux & Joseph, 2014; J. Rosenberg et al., 2013).

A whole-client approach that includes recognizing and normalizing the sexuality of clients was also named as crucial. Because many clients with serious mental illness are seen as childlike, discussion of sexuality or gender identity is often written off as unnecessary or even harmful, thus stigmatizing those who most need to have a safe place to discuss SGM identities (Barber, 2009; Kidd et al., 2016). This is especially important given that for many clients, sexual and gender identity was disrupted by the onset of serious mental illness in late adolescence (Barber, 2009). Kidd et al. (2016) note the therapeutic importance of contexts where identity is fully acknowledged and accepted as a way to attend to the isolation and impact of stigma. Holley et al. (2016) go farther to emphasize the need to incorporate the ideas and opinions of SGM people of color in their treatment. Others noted the importance of normalizing and welcoming disclosure of gender or sexual orientation identities (J. Rosenberg et al., 2013).

Ensuring the safety of SGM people with serious mental illness in treatment was also central to many studies and reviews. Microaggressions as well as overt homophobia and transphobia from peers and clinic or hospital staff have been reported by clients (Kidd et al., 2016). Most authors strongly recommended training, systemic review, and strategic change in order to address racism, transphobia, and homophobia; protect SGM clients from victimization by peers; and assess the needs of SGM clients (Barber, 2009; Kidd et al., 2016; Lamoureux & Joseph, 2014). Holley et al. (2016) emphasize the need for racial and ethnic cultural competence as well, including representation on staff by people of color, and the need for staff training, but also organization-level changes to address discrimination and microaggressions. The authors also suggest incorporating the views and opinions of SGM people of color into services and attending to intersecting identities of sexuality, gender, race, and ethnicity.

Inpatient Considerations

Inpatient and residential treatment requires special considerations for SGM clients. Lucksted (2004) noted that residential mental health treatment can be the most challenging for SGM clients. The close proximity to others, lack of privacy, and relative isolation from affirming family and friends can present numerous opportunities for the SGM patient to be subject to discrimination, harassment, or even violence (Huygen, 2006; Lucksted, 2004). For all SGM clients, harassment, violence, and lack of affirmation are associated with poorer mental health outcomes (I. H. Meyer, 2003; Testa, Habarth, Peta, Balsam, & Bockting, 2015).

For TGNB patients, the risk for transphobic discrimination, harassment, and being misgendered (e.g., being housed under the wrong gender) is high and creates an even more serious risk for harm (Huygen, 2006; Mizock & Fleming, 2011). TGNB residential and inpatient clients have reported being denied the ability to dress according to their gender identity, nurses and other staff using former names and incorrect pronouns, being forced to attend groups of the incorrect gender, or being refused gender-affirming activities such as putting on makeup or putting on a chest binder (Cochran & Cauce, 2006; Israel et al., 2011; Saw, 2017). Therefore, it is crucial that inpatient facilities employ the SGM-affirming suggestions as indicated earlier in the chapter and ensure that staff are well educated on SGM cultural competence. However, further measures are needed to ensure safety for SGM patients in residential or inpatient settings.

For clinicians making referrals to residential or inpatient care, it is important to advocate for SGM clients, especially TGNB clients. For example, working with the facility to ensure that the client will be housed according to the client's gender identity, finding out the facility's policies on use of gender-affirming name, or confirming that the facility has some cultural competence in working with TGNB clients may be needed (Holman & Goldberg, 2006). Some clinicians may need to educate staff at a facility on the needs of the client. Working collaboratively to determine the client's preferences rather than assuming what clients want and need is crucial (Holman & Goldberg, 2006).

Saw (2017) outlines three important areas of consideration for inpatient facilities to become more affirming for the TGNB patient. This includes ensuring that the client is assigned a private room or, if sharing a room, is assigned a roommate of the client's gender identity. Using the client's preferred name and pronoun and allowing the client access to gender-affirming items such as chest binders or makeup are also crucial to minimizing harm. Saw also emphasizes that clients should be administered their hormone treatment unless otherwise contraindicated. Saw adds specific guidelines for an affirming intake process, including taking time to understand the client's full gender journey. Other suggestions include ensuring that the client's affirming support system be involved in discharge planning, which will often include those outside the family of origin (Huygen, 2006).

Directions for Future Research

Despite the SGM population's higher rates of mental health concerns, and the amount of literature published on SSOPDs, surprisingly little is known about the treatment experiences of SGM persons with serious mental illness (Gilman et al., 2001; Kidd et al., 2011; 2016). Especially as the collaborative, whole-person approach of early intervention programs gains popularity outside of Europe, it will become essential to understand the distinct needs of SGM patients experiencing SSOPDs (Lamoureux & Joseph, 2014). Additionally, even fewer studies address the experiences of SGM people of color with serious mental illness. Qualitative and mixed-methods approaches may be especially useful in gathering additional information about the needs and experiences of SGM people of color seeking treatment for SSOPDs, and the impact of intersecting identities.

Additionally, while minority stress has been well established as a contributor to depression and distress for SGM, little research has investigated the link between minority stress and psychosis or SSOPDs (I. H. Meyer, 2003; Testa et al., 2015). The few studies that have been published focus on sexual minority individuals (Gevonden et al., 2014). Given that trauma and other stressors have been robustly connected to SSOPDs, it stands to reason that further research may uncover connections between SGM stress and psychosis (Austin et al., 2008; Gevonden et al., 2014; Schneeberger et al., 2014).

Lastly, treatments for schizophrenia and psychosis, including cognitive-behavioral therapy for psychosis, and comprehensive early intervention programs such as NAVIGATE have not addressed gender and sexual identities. As of now, there are no evidence-based adapted treatments for psychosis in SGM clients. Development of specific evidence-based treatment adaptations for SGM is crucial for ensuring that SGM persons are able to access treatment and to receive treatment that affirms and does not pathologize their identity.

References

American Psychiatric Association. (2013). *Diagnostic and statistical manual of mental disorders* (5th ed.). Arlington, VA: Author.

American Psychological Association. (2012). Guidelines for psychological practice with lesbian, gay, and bisexual clients. *American Psychologist, 67*(1), 10–42. doi:10.1037/a0024659

American Psychological Association. (2015). Guidelines for psychological practice with transgender and gender nonconforming people. *American Psychologist, 70*(9), 832–64. doi:10.1037/a0039906

Angelino, A. F., & Treisman, G. J. (2008). Issues in co-morbid severe mental illnesses in HIV infected individuals. *International Review of Psychiatry, 20*(1), 95–101. doi:10.1080/09540260701861989

Austin, S. B., Jun, H.-J., Jackson, B., Spiegelman, D., Rich-Edwards, J., Corliss, H. L., & Wright, R. J. (2008). Disparities in child abuse victimization in lesbian, bisexual, and heterosexual women in the Nurses' Health Study II. *Journal of Women's Health, 17*(4), 597–606. doi:10.1089/jwh.2007.0450

Avery, A. M., Hellman, R. E., & Sudderth, L. K. (2001). Satisfaction with mental health services among sexual minorities with major mental illness. *American Journal of Public Health, 91*(6), 990–1. doi:10.2105/ajph.91.6.990

Balsam, K. F., Molina, Y., Beadnell, B., Simoni, J., & Walters, K. (2011). Measuring multiple minority stress: The LGBT People of Color Microaggressions Scale. *Cultural Diversity and Ethnic Minority Psychology, 17*(2), 163–74. doi:10.1037/a0023244

Baltieri, D. A., & De Andrade, A. G. (2009). Schizophrenia modifying the expression of gender identity disorder. *Journal of Sexual Medicine, 6*(4), 1185–8. doi:10.1111/j.1743-6109.2007.00655.x

Barber, M. E. (2009). Lesbian, gay, and bisexual people with severe mental illness. *Journal of Gay & Lesbian Mental Health, 13*(2), 133–42. doi:10.1080/19359700902761305

Bieschke, K. J., Perez, R. M., & DeBord, K. A. (2007). *Handbook of counseling and psychotherapy with lesbian, gay, bisexual, and transgender clients* (2nd ed.). Washington, DC: American Psychological Association.

Bolton, S.-L., & Sareen, J. (2011). Sexual orientation and its relation to mental disorders and suicide attempts: Findings from a nationally representative sample. *Canadian Journal of Psychiatry, 56*(1), 35–43. doi:10.1177/070674371105600107

Borras, L., Huguelet, P., & Eytan, A. (2007). Delusional "pseudotranssexualism" in schizophrenia. *Psychiatry: Interpersonal and Biological Processes, 70*(2), 175–9. doi:10.1521/psyc.2007.70.2.175

Bramness, J. G., Gundersen, Ø. H., Guterstam, J., Rognli, E. B., Konstenius, M., Løberg, E.-M., . . . Franck, J. (2012). Amphetamine-induced psychosis: A separate diagnostic entity or primary psychosis triggered in the vulnerable? *BMC Psychiatry, 12*(221). doi:10.1186/1471-244X-12-221

Buckley, P. F., Miller, B. J., Lehrer, D. S., & Castle, D. J. (2008). Psychiatric comorbidities and schizophrenia. *Schizophrenia Bulletin, 35*(2), 383–402. doi:10.1093/schbul/sbn135

Burns, M. N., Ryan, D. T., Garofalo, R., Newcomb, M. E., & Mustanski, B. (2015). Mental health disorders in young urban sexual minority men. *Journal of Adolescent Health, 56*(1), 52–8. doi:10.1016/j.jadohealth.2014.07.018

Byne, W., Bradley, S., Coleman, E., Eyler, A. E., Green, R., Menvielle, E. J., . . . Tompkins, D. A. (2012). Report of the APA Task Force on treatment of gender identity disorder. *American Journal of Psychiatry, 169*(8, data supplement), 1–35. doi:10.1007/s10508-012-9975-x

Carmel, T. C., & Erickson-Schroth, L. (2016). Mental health and the transgender population. *Psychiatric Annals, 46*(6), 346–9. doi:10.3928/02793695-20161208-09

Centers for Disease Control and Prevention. (2018). HIV and gay and bisexual men.

Centers for Disease Control and Prevention. (2019, April). HIV and gay and transgender people.

Chakraborty, A., McManus, S., Brugha, T. S., Bebbington, P., & King, M. (2011). Mental health of the non-heterosexual population of England. *British Journal of Psychiatry, 198*(2), 143–8. doi:10.1192/bjp.bp.110.082271

Cochran, B. N., & Cauce, A. M. (2006). Characteristics of lesbian, gay, bisexual, and transgender individuals entering substance abuse treatment. *Journal of Substance Abuse Treatment, 30*(2), 135–46. doi:10.1016/j.jsat.2005.11.009

Cochran, S. D., Sullivan, J. G., & Mays, V. M. (2003). Prevalence of mental disorders, psychological distress, and mental health services use among lesbian, gay, and bisexual adults in the United States. *Journal of Consulting and Clinical Psychology, 71*(1), 53–61. doi:10.1037/0022-006x.71.153

Coleman, E., Bockting, W., Botzer, M., Cohen-Kettenis, P., DeCuypere, G., Feldman, J., . . . Zucker, K. (2012). Standards of care for the health of transsexual, transgender, and gender-nonconforming people, version 7. *International Journal of Transgenderism, 13*(4), 165–232. doi:10.1080/15532739.2011.700873

Cook, J. A. (2000). Sexuality and people with psychiatric disabilities. *Sexuality and Disability, 18*(3), 195–206. doi:10.1023/A:1026469832339

Craig, S. L., Dentato, M. P., & Iacovino, G. E. (2015). Patching holes and integrating community: A strengths-based continuum of care for lesbian, gay, bisexual, transgender and questioning youth. *Journal of Gay & Lesbian Social Services, 27*(1), 100–15. doi:10.1080/10538720.2015.988317

Dhillon, R., Bastiampillai, T., Krishnan, S., Opray, N., & Tibrewal, P. (2011). Transgender late onset psychosis: the role of sex hormones. *Australian and New Zealand Journal of Psychiatry, 45*(7), 595. doi:10.3109/00048674.2011.580452

Di Forti, M., Marconi, A., Carra, E., Fraietta, S., Trotta, A., Bonomo, M., . . . Murray, R. M. (2015). Proportion of patients in south London with first-episode psychosis attributable to use of high potency cannabis: A case-control study. *Lancet Psychiatry, 2*(3), 233–8. doi:10.1016/S2215-0366(14)00117-5

Drescher, J., & Hellman, R. (2004). *Handbook of LGBT issues in community mental health.* Binghamton, NY: Haworth Medical Press.

Gage, S. H., Hickman, M., & Zammit, S. (2016). Association between cannabis and psychosis: Epidemiologic evidence. *Biological Psychiatry, 79*(7), 549–56. doi:10.1016/j.biopsych.2015.08.001

Gevonden, M. J., Selten, J. P., Myin-Germeys, I., de Graaf, R., ten Have, M., van Dorsselaer, S., . . . Veling, W. (2014). Sexual minority status and psychotic symptoms: Findings from the Netherlands Mental Health Survey and Incidence Studies (NEMESIS). *Psychological Medicine, 44*(02), 421–33. doi:10.1017/S0033291713000718

Gilman, S. E., Cochran, S. D., Mays, V. M., Hughes, M., Ostrow, D., & Kessler, R. C. (2001). Risk of psychiatric disorders among individuals reporting same-sex sexual partners in the National Comorbidity Survey. *American Journal of Public Health, 91*(6), 933–9. doi:10.2105/AJPH.91.6.933

Hellman, R. E., Sudderth, L., & Avery, A. M. (2002). Major mental illness in a sexual minority psychiatric sample. *Journal of the Gay and Lesbian Medical Association, 6*(3/4), 97–106. doi:10.1023/B:JOLA.0000011065.08186.17

Hendricks, M. L., & Testa, R. J. (2012). A conceptual framework for clinical work with transgender and gender nonconforming clients: An adaptation of the minority stress model. *Professional Psychology: Research and Practice, 43*(5), 460–7. doi:10.1037/a0029597

Herbst, J. H., Jacobs, E. D., Finlayson, T. J., McKleroy, V. S., Neumann, M. S., & Crepaz, N. (2008). Estimating HIV prevalence and risk behaviors of transgender persons in the United States: A systematic review. *AIDS and Behavior, 12*(1), 1–17. doi:10.1007/s10461-007-9299-3

Holley, L. C., Tavassoli, K. Y., & Stromwall, L. K. (2016). Mental illness discrimination in mental health treatment programs: Intersections of race, ethnicity, and sexual orientation. *Community Mental Health Journal, 52*(3), 311–22. doi:10.1007/s10597-016-9990-9

Holman, C. W., & Goldberg, J. M. (2006). Social and medical transgender case advocacy. *International Journal of Transgenderism, 9*(3–4), 197–217. doi:10.1300/J485v09n03_09

Holttum, S. (2015). Coping with cognitive behaviour therapy for psychosis, adapting it for another culture, and community inclusion. *Mental Health and Social Inclusion, 19*(3), 107–13. doi:10.1108/MHSI-05-2015-0018

Huygen, C. (2006). Understanding the needs of lesbian, gay, bisexual, and transgender people living with mental illness. *Medscape General Medicine, 8*(2), 29. https://www.ncbi.nlm.nih.gov/pmc/journals/239/

Israel, T., Walther, W. A., Gortcheva, R., & Perry, J. S. (2011). Policies and practices for LGBT clients: Perspectives of mental health services administrators. *Journal of Gay & Lesbian Mental Health, 15*(2), 152–68. doi:10.1080/19359705.2010.539090

Kenagy, G. P. (2005). Transgender health: Findings from two needs assessment studies in Philadelphia. *Health & Social Work, 30*(1), 19–26. doi:10.1093/hsw/30.1.19

Kenagy, G. P., & Bostwick, W. B. (2005). Health and social service needs of transgender people in Chicago. *International Journal of Transgenderism, 8*(2–3), 57–66. doi:10.1300/J485v08n02_06

Kidd, S. A., Howison, M., Pilling, M., Ross, L. E., & McKenzie, K. (2016). Severe mental illness in LGBT populations: A scoping review. *Psychiatric Services, 67*(7), 779–83. doi:10.1176/appi.ps.201500209

Kidd, S. A., Veltman, A., Gately, C., Chan, K. J., & Cohen, J. N. (2011). Lesbian, gay, and transgender persons with severe mental illness: Negotiating wellness in the context of multiple sources of stigma. *American Journal of Psychiatric Rehabilitation, 14*(1), 13–39. doi:10.1080/15487768.2011.546277

Lamoureux, A., & Joseph, A. J. (2014). Toward transformative practice: Facilitating access and barrier-free services with LGBTTIQQ2SA populations. *Social Work in Mental Health, 12*(3), 212–230. doi:10.1080/15332985.2013.875092

Lehavot, K., & Simoni, J. M. (2011). The impact of minority stress on mental health and substance use among sexual minority women. *Journal of Consulting and Clinical Psychology, 79*(2), 159–170. doi:10.1037/a0022839

Logan, C. R., & Barret, R. (2006). Counseling competencies for sexual minority clients. *Journal of LGBT Issues in Counseling, 1*(1), 3–22. doi:10.1300/J462v01n01_02

Lucksted, A. (2004). Lesbian, gay, bisexual, and transgender people receiving services in the public mental health system: Raising issues. *Journal of Gay & Lesbian Psychotherapy, 8*(3–4), 25–42. doi:10.1080/19359705.2004.9962378

McCabe, S. E., Bostwick, W. B., Hughes, T. L., West, B. T., & Boyd, C. J. (2010). The relationship between discrimination and substance use disorders among lesbian, gay, and bisexual adults in the United States. *American Journal of Public Health, 100*(10), 1946–52. doi:10.2105/AJPH.2009.163147

Meijer, J. H., Eeckhout, G. M., van Vlerken, R. H. T., & de Vries, A. L. C. (2017). Gender dysphoria and co-existing psychosis: Review and four case examples of successful gender affirmative treatment. *LGBT Health, 4*(2), 106–14. doi:10.1089/lgbt.2016.0133

Mereish, E. H., O'Cleirigh, C., & Bradford, J. B. (2014). Interrelationships between LGBT-based victimization, suicide, and substance use problems in a diverse sample of sexual and gender minorities. *Psychology, Health & Medicine, 19*(1), 1–13. doi:10.1080/13548506.2013.780129

Meyer, I. H. (2003). Prejudice, social stress, and mental health in lesbian, gay, and bisexual populations: Conceptual issues and research evidence. *Psychological Bulletin, 129*(5), 674–97. doi:10.1037/0033-2909.129.5.674

Meyer, I. H. (2010). Identity, stress, and resilience in lesbians, gay men, and bisexuals of color. *Counseling Psychologist, 38*(3), 442–54. doi:10.1177/0011000009351601

Meyer, I. H. (2015). Resilience in the study of minority stress and health of sexual and gender minorities. *Psychology of Sexual Orientation and Gender Diversity, 2*(3), 209–13. doi:10.1037/sgd0000132

Meyer, J. K. (1982). The theory of gender identity disorders. *Journal of the American Psychoanalytic Association, 30*(2), 381–418. doi:10.1177/000306518203000204

Mizock, L., & Fleming, M. Z. (2011). Transgender and gender variant populations with mental illness: Implications for clinical care. *Professional Psychology: Research and Practice, 42*(2), 208–13. doi:10.1037/a0022522

Nemoto, T., Operario, D., & Keatley, J. (2005). Health and social services for male-to-female transgender persons of color in San Francisco. *International Journal of Transgenderism, 8*(2–3), 5–19. doi:10.1300/J485v08n02_02

Origgi, G., & Vial, S. M. (2013). Transgender trouble: A transdisciplinary approach to transsexual rights. *Verifiche, 42*(1–3), 119–37. http://www.verificheonline.net/

Pachankis, J. (2016). *Mindfulness and acceptance for gender and sexual minorities: A clinician's guide to fostering compassion, connection, and equality using contextual strategies.* Oakland, CA: New Harbinger Publications.

Petersen, L., Jeppesen, P., Thorup, A., Abel, M.-B., Øhlenschlaeger, J., Christensen, T. Ø., . . . Nordentoft, M. (2005). A randomised multicentre trial of integrated versus standard treatment for patients with a first episode of psychotic illness. *BMJ, 331*(602), 1–7. doi:10.1136/bmj.38565.415000.E01

Read, J., van Os, J., Morrison, A. P., & Ross, C. A. (2005). Childhood trauma, psychosis and schizophrenia: A literature review with theoretical and clinical implications. *Acta Psychiatrica Scandinavica, 112*(5), 330–50. doi:10.1111/j.1600-0447.2005.00634.x

Reisner, S. L., Gamarel, K. E., Nemoto, T., & Operario, D. (2014). Dyadic effects of gender minority stressors in substance use behaviors among transgender women and their non-transgender male partners. *Psychology of Sexual Orientation and Gender Diversity, 1*(1), 63–71. doi:10.1037/0000013

Rosenberg, J., Rosenberg, S. J., Huygen, C., & Klein, E. (2013). Marginal no more: Serious mental illness, sexual orientation, and gender preference. In J. Rosenberg & S. J. Rosenberg (Eds.), *Community mental health: Challenges for the 21st century* (pp. 22–32). New York, NY: Taylor & Francis.

Rosenberg, S., Rosenberg, J., Huygen, C., & Klein, E. (2005). No need to hide: Out of the closet and mentally ill. *Best Practices in Mental Health, 1*(1), 72–85. https://thedavidfollmergroup.com/best-practices-in-mental-health/

Sandfort, T. G., de Graaf, R., ten Have, M., Ransome, Y., & Schnabel, P. (2014). Same-sex sexuality and psychiatric disorders in the second Netherlands Mental Health Survey and Incidence Study (NEMESIS-2). *LGBT Health, 1*(4), 292–301. doi:10.1089/lgbt.2014.0031

Saw, C. (2017). Transgender patient care on the inpatient psychiatric unit. *American Journal of Psychiatry Residents' Journal, 12*(11), 7–8. doi:10.1176/appi.ajp-rj.2017.121103

Schneeberger, A. R., Dietl, M. F., Muenzenmaier, K. H., Huber, C. G., & Lang, U. E. (2014). Stressful childhood experiences and health outcomes in sexual minority populations: A systematic review. *Social Psychiatry and Psychiatric Epidemiology, 49*(9), 1427–45. doi:10.1007/s00127-014-0854-8

Schwartz, R. C., & Blankenship, D. M. (2014). Racial disparities in psychotic disorder diagnosis: A review of empirical literature. *World Journal of Psychiatry, 4*(4), 133–40. doi:10.5498/wjp.v4.i4.133

Skerett, D. M., K. Kolves, & De Leo, D. (2015). Are LGBT populations at higher risk for suicidal behaviors in Australia? Research findings and implications. *Journal of Homosexuality, 62*(7), 883–901. doi:10.1080/00918369.2014.1003009

Smith, W. B., Goldhammer, H., & Keuroghlian, A. S. (2018). Affirming gender identity of patients with serious mental illness. *Psychiatric Services, 70*(1), 65–7. doi:10.1176/appi.ps.201800232

Summers, S. M., & Onate, J. (2014). New-onset psychosis following abrupt discontinuation of hormone replacement therapy in a trans woman. *Journal of Gay & Lesbian Mental Health, 18*(3), 312–9. doi:10.1080/19359705.2014.915463

Testa, R. J., Habarth, J., Peta, J., Balsam, K., & Bockting, W. (2015). Development of the Gender Minority Stress and Resilience Measure. *Psychology of Sexual Orientation and Gender Diversity, 2*(1), 65–77. doi:10.1037/sgd0000081

Van Os, J., Linscott, R. J., Myin-Germeys, I., Delespaul, P., & Krabbendam, L. (2009). A systematic review and meta-analysis of the psychosis continuum: Evidence for a psychosis proneness–persistence–impairment model of psychotic disorder. *Psychological Medicine, 39*(2), 179–95. doi:10.1017/S0033291708003814

Watkins, C. C., & Treisman, G. J. (2012). Neuropsychiatric complications of aging with HIV. *Journal of Neurovirology, 18*(4), 277–90. doi:10.1007/s13365-012-0108-z

Wong, Y.-L. I., Stanton, M. C., & Sands, R. G. (2014). Rethinking social inclusion: Experiences of persons in recovery from mental illness. *American Journal of Orthopsychiatry, 84*(6), 685–95. doi:10.1037/ort0000034

Xavier, J. M., Bobbin, M., Singer, B., & Budd, E. (2005). A needs assessment of transgendered people of color living in Washington, DC. *International Journal of Transgenderism, 8*(2–3), 31–47. doi:10.1300/J485v08n02_04

CHAPTER

12 Sexual Disorders among Sexual and Gender Minority Populations

Heather L. Armstrong

Abstract

Sexual disorders and dysfunction are common among people of all sexual orientations and gender identities. And while definitions and conceptions of sexual health are typically broad, the clinical and research perspectives on sexual function and dysfunction have traditionally relied on the four-phase model of sexual response and disorders are generally classified as "male" or "female." This chapter reviews the diagnostic criteria for specific sexual dysfunctions and presents a summary of existing research among sexual and gender minority populations. Overall, research on sexual dysfunction among sexual and gender minority people is limited, and this is especially true for transgender and gender nonconforming individuals. Understanding these often complex disorders requires that individuals, clinicians, and researchers consider a range of biopsychosocial factors that can affect and be affected by one's sexual health and sexuality.

Keywords: sexual function, sexual dysfunction, sexual health, sexual orientation, gender identity

When people consider sexual health, often the first thing that comes to mind is prevention of sexually transmitted infections. This is especially true when considering the sexual health of gay, bisexual, and other men who have sex with men (gbMSM) where the HIV/AIDS epidemic has been the predominant focus of public health, epidemiology, and sexual behavior research for nearly forty years. However, sexual health is so much more than just the presence or absence of symptoms or infection. The World Health Organization (WHO, 2006) defines sexual health as

> a state of physical, emotional, mental and social well-being in relation to sexuality; it is not merely the absence of disease, dysfunction or infirmity. Sexual health requires a positive and respectful approach to sexuality and sexual relationships, as well as the possibility of having pleasurable and safe sexual experiences, free of coercion, discrimination and violence. For sexual health to be attained and maintained, the sexual rights of all persons must be respected, protected and fulfilled.

This is an important definition because it includes a broad understanding of the many components that affect sexual health, including physical, emotional, mental, relational, and social factors. It is also important to recognize that this definition of sexual health is inclusive of all people; no distinctions or exclusions are made on the basis of sexual orientation or gender identity.

Sexual health has a complex association with mental health. One the one hand, if people are dealing with poor sexual health or if they are struggling with certain aspects of their sexuality, this can have a clinically significant impact on their mental health, as well as on the mental health of their sexual and relationship partners. However, one's mental health, and that of one's partners, can also have a significant effect on one's sexual health. For example, if one is experiencing a time of depression or high anxiety, interest in sexual activity can decrease or cease completely. Thus, the relationship between sexual health and mental health is intertwined. However, as noted in the WHO definition, mental health is not the only cause and effect of sexual health: physical, relational, social, and environmental factors also need to be considered. Because of this, sexual health is best considered using a biopsychosocial approach that recognizes the complex interactions among biological, psychological, and social factors that both affect, and are affected, by sexual health.

Sexual health also occurs within the context of an individual's sexuality. The WHO working definition of sexuality (2006) is as follows:

> A central aspect of being human throughout life encompasses sex, gender identities and roles, sexual orientation, eroticism, pleasure, intimacy and reproduction. Sexuality is experienced and expressed in thoughts, fantasies, desires, beliefs, attitudes, values, behaviours, practices, roles and relationships. While sexuality can include all of these dimensions, not all of them are always experienced or expressed. Sexuality is influenced by the interaction of biological, psychological, social, economic, political, cultural, legal, historical, religious and spiritual factors.

Again, it is important to note the very broad range of factors that can influence, and be influenced by, one's sexuality. Thus, while one's sexuality is a distinct concept from one's sexual health, the two can only be understood and considered in relation to each other. Every individual has a unique sexuality and unique sexual health needs, and these will change, grow, and develop throughout the course of their entire life. This definition of sexuality is also inclusive of all people and specifically recognizes that sex, sexual orientation, and gender identity are important components of sexuality, along with eroticism, pleasure, intimacy, and reproduction. It also notes that while all of these *can* make up a person's sexuality, they are not always experienced or expressed. It is also important to recognize that many of these factors are not fixed and can change or be expressed in different ways throughout a person's life. Consequently, one's sexuality, and relatedly one's sexual health, varies with age, time, and circumstance, just as one's physical and mental health fluctuates over time and space.

Despite the broad consideration of sexual health and sexuality by the WHO, in research and in clinical practice sexual health is often defined as sexual function, or more specifically the lack of sexual dysfunction. Researchers and clinicians, especially in North America, most often rely on the *Diagnostic and Statistical Manual of Mental Disorders* (DSM) in order to define sexual dysfunctions. The DSM, which is published by the American Psychiatric Association (APA), is now in its fifth edition (DSM-5; APA, 2013) and provides criteria that are used extensively by clinicians in order to make diagnoses about sexual dysfunctions and by researchers in order to explore and better understand the complexities of these disorders. Note that the descriptions of each of the disorders rely heavily on how they have been defined in the DSM-5. The remainder of this chapter aims to describe each of the sexual dysfunction categories, as presented in the DSM-5, and then to summarize and review the existing literature as it relates to sexual and gender minority (SGM) individuals.

Delayed Ejaculation

People with penises may experience delayed ejaculation, a marked delay or inability to ejaculate, despite a desire and sufficient sexual stimulation (APA, 2013). Studies among gbMSM suggest a prevalence of difficulties with or an inability to experience orgasm of 5.6 to 36 percent (Hirshfield et al., 2010; Lau, Kim, & Tsui, 2006; 2008; Peixoto & Nobre, 2015a; 2016; Rosser, Metz, Bockting, & Buroker, 1997; Seibel, Rosser, Horvath, & Evans, 2009). In an internet sample of 7,001 sexually active U.S. gbMSM, inability to experience orgasm was less common among African American gbMSM versus white gbMSM; no other racial/ethnic differences were observed (Hirshfield et al., 2010). In this same study, gbMSM living with HIV were significantly more likely to report inability to experience orgasm, as were single gbMSM and older gbMSM (Hirshfield et al., 2010). Among a telephone sample of fifty-five Chinese men in Hong Kong who reported a male sexual partner in the past twelve months, 0 percent of men aged eighteen to thirty-nine and 22.7 percent of men aged forty to fifty-nine reported inability to have an orgasm for a period of at least three consecutive months over the past year (Lau et al., 2006). Further, in another sample of Chinese MSM in Hong Kong, 5.6 percent reported inability to have an orgasm for a period of at least three consecutive months over the past year, and this was associated with not being employed full time; having a bisexual, heterosexual, or other sexual identity as compared with a gay identity; past-year substance use; engaging in commercial sex work including anal sex; reporting discrimination because of sexual orientation; feeling ashamed of one's sexual orientation; and not fully accepting one's sexual orientation (Lau et al., 2008).

Whether or not delayed ejaculation is more prevalent among gbMSM as compared to heterosexual men is unclear. In a sample of 909 Portuguese men (473 heterosexual, 435 gay), no significant differences were found between sexually active gay and heterosexual men: 12.5 percent of gay men reported delayed ejaculation during sex 50 percent of the time or more compared with 11.4 percent of heterosexual men (Peixoto & Nobre, 2015a). Similarly, no significant difference was noted in prevalence of distress: of those who reported delayed ejaculation, 42.6 percent of gay men and 37.0 percent of heterosexual men reported moderate to severe distress (Peixoto & Nobre, 2015a). Finally, after controlling for distress, this study found no difference in prevalence between gay and heterosexual men experiencing distressing delayed ejaculation, with a prevalence of 5.3 percent among gay men and 4.2 percent among heterosexual men (Peixoto & Nobre, 2015a). In contrast, in a survey of 561 non-heterosexual men and 933 heterosexual men in Croatia, delayed ejaculation was reported significantly more often by non-heterosexual men (17.5 percent) compared with heterosexual men (12.0 percent) (Ivanković, Šević, & Štulhofer, 2015). However, delayed ejaculation was considered equally distressing among all men is this sample (42.0 percent non-heterosexual, 38.8 percent heterosexual) (Ivanković et al., 2015).

Delayed ejaculation among transgender or gender variant individuals has not been well studied. Among transgender or gender minority individuals who were born with penises, prevalence of delayed ejaculation could be expected to be similar to that of cisgender men with penises. However, there are additional factors that need to be considered and that may contribute to higher levels of delayed ejaculation. If the individual is taking anti-androgens and/or estrogen, erectile and testicular function, including ejaculation, can be affected. In one study of 232 U.S. trans women after vaginoplasty and clitoroplasty, 85 percent experienced orgasm and 55 percent experienced ejaculation (Lawrence, 2005). Among trans men who have phalloplasty, ability to experience orgasm is typically not affected and orgasm can be had through self-stimulation and penetrative sex (Garcia, Christopher, De Luca, Spilotros, & Ralph, 2014). However, ejaculation via the neophallus does not occur. Finally, body image can affect ability to ejaculate and orgasm, so if the individual holds negative attitudes toward their body in general, or their genitals in particular, this may contribute to the presence of delayed ejaculation. More research is needed.

Finally, substance use and alcohol use during sex is common among some cisgender and transgender gbMSM. Subcultures of chemsex and party and play are prevalent, especially in urban areas. While the specific drugs available and preferred may vary by person and geographic location, typical substances include crystal methamphetamine, mephedrone, gamma-hydroxybutrate (GHB), and gamma-butyrolactone (GBL). Chemsex drugs and alcohol are known to interfere with the ability to ejaculate. However, typically these effects are limited to the timeframe in which substances are consumed and, as such, a diagnosis of delayed ejaculation is not warranted.

Erectile Disorder

People with penises may experience erectile disorder. The primary complaint of erectile disorder is the repeated inability to obtain or maintain an erection during partnered sexual activity (APA, 2013). Difficulties with erection are often associated with low self-esteem, low self-confidence, a decreased sense of masculinity, and depressed mood. Symptoms and associated feelings can lead to fear and avoidance of sexual activities and can cause decreased sexual satisfaction and low sexual desire in the individual and their partner(s). At present, as per the DSM-5, the diagnosis is only given to men (APA, 2013). However, there is no distinction based on sexual orientation, and erectile disorder can be diagnosed in men with partners of any gender/sex.

Studies among gbMSM suggest a prevalence of erectile difficulties between 4.8 and 45 percent (Hart et al., 2012; Hirshfield et al., 2010; Lau et al., 2006, 2008; Peixoto & Nobre, 2015a, 2016; Rosser et al., 1997; Seibel et al., 2009). In an internet sample of 7001 sexually active U.S. gbMSM, no racial/ethnic differences were observed in reported erection problems; however, gbMSM living with HIV and single gbMSM were significantly more likely to report problems (Hirshfield et al., 2010). Among participants enrolled in a longitudinal study of 612 gbMSM living with HIV and 728 gbMSM not living with HIV in the United States, 21 percent of gbMSM living with HIV reported erectile dysfunction compared with 16 percent of HIV-negative gbMSM (Hart et al., 2012). In this study, in addition to age, being black, smoking, taking hypertensive medication, and taking antidepressant medication were associated with increased erectile dysfunction. Among a telephone sample of 55 Chinese men in Hong Kong who reported a male sexual partner in the past twelve months, 3.0 percent of men aged eighteen to thirty-nine and 20.0 percent of men aged forty to fifty-nine reported trouble with erection for a period of at least three consecutive months over the past year (Lau et al., 2006). Further, in another sample of Chinese MSM in Hong Kong, 6.3 percent reported erectile dysfunction for a period of at least three consecutive months over the past year, and this was associated with lower educational attainment, past-year substance use, past-year HIV-related risk behavior, engaging in commercial sex work including anal sex, and reporting discrimination because of sexual orientation (Lau et al., 2008). Additionally, erectile dysfunction has been associated with history of childhood abuse among gbMSM (Seibel et al., 2009). Erectile difficulties are also a common side effect of alcohol and substance use, which may be common among gbMSM, especially among those who engage in chemsex and party and play. Finally, in a survey of 2,640 gbMSM (80 percent of whom were living in North America), moderate to severe erectile dysfunction was more common among gbMSM living with HIV, gbMSM who were not in a steady relationship, and those who reported greater sexual dissatisfaction (Shindel, Vittinghoff, & Breyer, 2012).

It is unclear if there are differences in frequency of erectile dysfunction between heterosexual men and gbMSM. In a sample of 909 Portuguese sexually active gay and heterosexual men (473 heterosexual, 435 gay), 7.3 percent of gay men reported a marked decrease in erectile rigidity, or inability to obtain/maintain an erection until the completion of sexual activity 50 percent of the time or more over the past six months compared with 7.6 percent of heterosexual men, and similar levels of distress were reported (Peixoto & Nobre, 2015a). After controlling for distress, this study found no difference in prevalence of distressing erectile difficulties between gay and heterosexual men: 4.8 percent versus 5.1 percent, respectively (Peixoto & Nobre, 2015a). Similarly, in a survey of 561 non-heterosexual men and 933 heterosexual men in Croatia, difficulties with erection lasting for at least two months during the previous twelve months were reported by 20.1 percent of non-heterosexual men and 25.2 percent of heterosexual men (12.0 percent); similar levels of distress related to the erectile difficulties were also reported (Ivanković et al., 2015). However, in a recent meta-analysis that included results from four quantitative studies on erectile dysfunction among gay (n=18,070) and heterosexual (n = 4,055) men, gay men had 1.5 times higher odds of reporting erectile dysfunction (Barbonetti et al., 2019).

Erection difficulties among transgender and gender nonbinary people with penises may occur if individuals are taking anti-androgens and/or estrogen (Coxon & Seal, 2018). Among trans men, erection of the neophallus is typically controlled via penile implants. As such, erectile dysfunction should not occur if the device is operating correctly. To date, little research has focused on erectile disorder among gender minority individuals.

Female Orgasmic Disorder

Studies examining prevalence of female orgasmic disorder among women who have sex with women (WSW) are limited. Among a sample of 100 U.S. women involved in a lesbian relationship, 28 percent experienced difficulty with orgasm (Meana, Rakipi, Weeks, & Lykins, 2006). In an online survey of 390 lesbian and 1,009 Portuguese heterosexual women, 14.6 percent of lesbian women and 25.8 percent of heterosexual women reported difficulties with orgasm 50 percent of the time or more over the past six months (Peixoto & Nobre, 2015b). After distress was considered, reported prevalence of distressing difficulties with orgasm was 6.7 percent among lesbian women and 11.5 percent among heterosexual women; however, after controlling for relationship length, no difference in prevalence was found (Peixoto & Nobre, 2015b). Among a telephone sample of ninety-five Chinese women in Hong Kong who reported a female sexual partner in the past twelve months, 24.7 percent reported difficulty with orgasm for a period of at least three consecutive months over the past year (Lau et al., 2006). And, in a large sample of Finnish women with same-sex experience (n = 814), the prevalence estimate for distressing difficulty with orgasm was 8.4 percent (Burri et al., 2012). Finally, among studies that have compared WSW and heterosexual women, lesbian and bisexual women report higher levels of orgasm compared to heterosexual women (Beaber & Werner, 2009; Blair, Cappell, & Pukall, 2018; Bressler & Lavender, 1986; Breyer et al., 2010; Garcia, Lloyd, Wallen, & Fisher, 2014).

There is at present no research that has examined female orgasmic disorder among trans women. Among trans women who have experienced vaginoplasty and clitoroplasty, 15 percent report being unable to orgasm following surgery (Lawrence, 2005; Selvaggi et al., 2007); however, level of associated distress was not considered in these studies.

Female Sexual Interest/Arousal Disorder

Female sexual interest/arousal disorder may be diagnosed if a woman reports a persistent lack of sexual interest/arousal, accompanied by personal distress. Prevalence of female sexual interest/arousal disorder among WSW is unknown, partly because of minimal research but also because of the change in the DSM-5 diagnostic category. In previous editions of the DSM, "hypoactive sexual desire disorder" was diagnosed if there was an absence or reduction in the frequency or intensity of interest in sexual activity. In the DSM-5 (APA, 2013), the diagnosis of female sexual interest/arousal disorder recognizes that sexual desire and arousal frequently occur together. In a large sample of Finnish women with same-sex experience (n = 814), the prevalence estimates were 9.9 percent for distressing lack of sexual desire, 6.5 percent for distressing arousal difficulties, and 6.4 percent for distressing lubrication difficulties (Burri et al., 2012). Among a sample of 100 U.S. women involved in a lesbian relationship, 15 percent experienced difficulty becoming aroused and 14 percent reported difficulties maintaining arousal (Meana et al., 2006). In an online survey of 390 lesbian and 1,009 Portuguese heterosexual women, 10.3 percent of lesbian women and 27 percent of heterosexual women reported absent or reduced sexual excitement or pleasure from sexual activity and 21 percent of lesbian women and 24 percent of heterosexual women reported experiencing absent or markedly reduced interest in sexual activity 50 percent or more of the time over the past six months (Peixoto & Nobre, 2015b). After distress was considered, reported prevalence of distressing lack of sexual interest among lesbian women was 6.7 percent and reported prevalence of distressing lack of sexual excitement or pleasure was 8.9 percent; however, after controlling for relationship length, no differences in prevalence were found (Peixoto & Nobre, 2015b). Other studies have found that lesbian and bisexual women score significantly higher on sexual function scales for arousal (Beaber & Werner, 2009) and desire (Breyer et al., 2010; Burri et al., 2012). Finally, among a telephone sample of ninety-five Chinese women in Hong Kong who reported a female sexual partner in the past twelve months, 39.3 percent reported lubrication difficulties and 30.7 percent reported a lack of sexual interest for a period of at least three consecutive months over the past year (Lau et al., 2006).

Only a few studies have explored sexual desire among transgender individuals, primarily before and after hormone therapy and/or sex reassignment surgery, and results are mixed. Overall, rates of hypoactive sexual desire disorder appear similar between trans women and cis women (Klein & Gorzalka, 2009); however, in a sample of fifty Belgian trans women who had had sex reassignment surgery, trans women scored poorly on a sexual function measure of arousal and lubrication compared with previously published scores of cis women (Weyers et al., 2009). Among trans women who choose to use estrogen therapy, decreased sexual desire (libido) and decreased spontaneous erections are expected changes and generally begin within one to three months after the start of treatment (Coxon & Seal, 2018). In a sample of twenty-two Italian trans women, decreases in desire were reported after twelve months on estrogen and before sex reassignment surgery but increased above baseline following surgery (Carriero, Dellino, Campanelli, Licchelli, & Loverro, 2016). Similar results were reported in a large sample of 401 European trans women (Defreyne et al., 2019). However, in a cross-sectional study of 214 trans women in Belgium, 62.4 percent reported a decrease in desire after sex reassignment therapy and 73 percent reported that they never or rarely experienced desire (Wierckx et al., 2014). In this study, a third reported that this lack of desire was distressing, and so a 22 percent prevalence of hypoactive sexual desire disorder was determined. Finally in this study, those who had completed vaginoplasty reported more spontaneous desire compared to those who were planning surgery (Wierckx et al., 2014). (Please see the section on male hypoactive sexual desire disorder later in the chapter for considerations among trans men.)

Finally, female sexual interest/arousal disorder is distinct from an asexual sexual orientation. If a cis gender or trans gender woman self-identifies as asexual and is not distressed by her lack of sexual interest/arousal, a diagnosis of female sexual interest/arousal disorder is not made.

Genito-Pelvic/Penetration Disorder

In DSM-5, female sexual pain disorders have been combined into the broad category of genito-pelvic pain/penetration disorder (GPPPD). This overarching diagnosis includes four commonly comorbid dimensions of female sexual pain: difficulty having intercourse, genito-pelvic pain, fear of pain or penetration, and pelvic floor muscle tension (APA, 2013). GPPPD can be diagnosed if any of the four symptom dimensions are present (APA, 2013).

By definition, only people with vaginas can be diagnosed with GPPPD. If men present with symptoms consistent with GPPPD, they may be diagnosed with other specified or unspecified sexual dysfunction as research on this condition with men is limited at present (APA, 2013).

Sexual pain among WSW has not been well studied. In an online survey of 390 lesbian and 1,009 heterosexual Portuguese women, sexual pain over the past six months was the most common sexual problem reported: 17.4 percent of lesbian women and 18.6 percent of heterosexual women experienced pain 50 percent of the time or more (Peixoto & Nobre, 2015b). After distress was considered, reported prevalence of distressing sexual pain was 9.8 percent among lesbian women and 13.3 percent among heterosexual women; however, after controlling for relationship length, no difference in prevalence of distressing pain was found (Peixoto & Nobre, 2015b). Among a telephone sample of ninety-five Chinese women in Hong Kong who reported a female sexual partner in the past twelve months, 23.6 percent reported sexual pain for a period of at least three consecutive months over the past year (Lau et al., 2006). And, in a large sample of Finnish women with same-sex experience (n = 814), the prevalence estimate for distressing sexual pain was 5.9 percent (Burri et al., 2012). Finally, in an online survey of 839 heterosexual, lesbian, and bisexual women aged eighteen to forty-five years, bisexual women were more likely to report genital pain (38.5 percent), compared with heterosexual (28.2 percent) and lesbian (23.3. percent) women (Blair, Pukall, Smith, & Cappell, 2015). Among the bisexual women in this study, those in mixed-sex relationships were more likely to report pain during sex (45.7 percent) compared with those who were single (28.3 percent) and those who were in same-sex relationships (25.8 percent). Bisexual women in mixed-sex relationships were also more likely to report pain than heterosexual women in mixed-sex relationships; however, there were no statistically significant differences between bisexual women in same-sex relationships and lesbian women in same-sex relationships (Blair et al., 2015). Characteristics of pain were similar for all women, regardless of sexual orientation (Blair et al., 2015). Among same-sex couples, better communication was associated with the perception that pain had less effect on their relationships (Blair et al., 2015).

Research on sexual pain among gender minority individuals is limited. In a sample of fifty Belgian trans women who had had sex reassignment surgery, trans women scored poorly on a measure of sexual pain compared with previously published scores of cis women (Weyers et al., 2009). Much more research is needed.

Male Hypoactive Sexual Desire Disorder

Male hypoactive sexual desire disorder is a sexual dysfunction in which a male experiences markedly reduced or absent desire for sex and deficient/absent sexual thoughts and fantasies. By definition, male hypoactive sexual desire disorder is diagnosed in men.

Studies among gbMSM suggest a prevalence of low (or lack of) sexual desire between 8.3 and 57 percent (Hirshfield et al., 2010; Lau et al., 2006; 2008; Peixoto & Nobre, 2015a; 2016; Rosser et al., 1997; Seibel et al., 2009). In an internet sample of 7,001 sexually active U.S. gbMSM, low sexual desire was the most commonly reported sexual dysfunction (57 percent) and was more common among those under forty-nine years, those who were living with HIV, and those who were single; no differences were observed by race/ethnicity (Hirshfield et al., 2010). Among a telephone sample of fifty-five Chinese men in Hong Kong who reported a male sexual partner in the past twelve months, 20.0 percent of men aged eighteen to fifty-nine reported hypoactive sexual desire for a period of at least three consecutive months over the past year (Lau et al., 2006). Further, in another sample of Chinese MSM in Hong Kong, 8.3 percent reported hypoactive sexual desire for a period of at least three consecutive months over the past year, and this was more likely among those who were not employed full time and those who reported substance use; there were no differences among those who reported discrimination, nonacceptance, or poor social support (Lau et al., 2008). However, among gay men, internalized homophobia, interpersonal problems, lack of adequate sex education, and early life trauma may all be contributing factors (APA, 2013).

Lack of sexual interest appears similar between gbMSM and heterosexual men. In a sample of 909 Portuguese men (473 heterosexual, 435 gay), sexually active gay men reported significantly more lack of sexual desire than heterosexual men (18.9 percent vs. 9.7 percent) (Peixoto & Nobre, 2015a). However, gay men with lack of desire were less likely to report distress (30.5 percent) than heterosexual men (43.5 percent) (Peixoto & Nobre, 2015a).

After controlling for distress, prevalence of distressing lack of sexual desire was comparable, with prevalence rates of 5.7 percent among gay men and 4.2 percent among heterosexual men (Peixoto & Nobre, 2015a). Likewise, in a survey of 561 non-heterosexual men and 933 heterosexual men in Croatia, lack of sexual interest was reported by 26.2 percent and 26.5 percent of non-heterosexual and heterosexual men, respectively, and similar levels of distress were also reported (Ivanković et al., 2015).

Only a few studies have explored sexual desire among transgender individuals, primarily before and after hormone therapy and/or sex reassignment surgery. Among individuals who choose to use estrogen therapy, decreased sexual desire (libido) and decreased spontaneous erections are expected changes and generally begin within one to three months of the start of treatment (Coxon & Seal, 2018). (Please see the section on female sexual interest/arousal disorder earlier in the chapter for more research on sexual desire disorder among trans women.) Among individuals who choose to use testosterone, increased sexual desire can be expected (Carriero et al., 2016; Irwig, 2017). In a large study of 264 European trans men, sexual desire initially increased during the first year but decreased comparable to baseline after thirty-six months (Defreyne et al., 2019). In a cross-sectional study of 138 trans men in Belgium, 71 percent reported an increase in sexual desire after sex reassignment therapy; however, one third reported never or rarely feeling desire while one third reported often or always feeling desire (Wierckx et al., 2014). When distress was considered, 5 percent of trans men met the criteria for hypoactive sexual desire disorder, and this was more common among those who were less satisfied with their phalloplasty (Wierckx et al., 2014).

Finally, male hypoactive sexual desire disorder is distinct from an asexual sexual orientation. If a cis gender or trans gender man self-identifies as asexual and is not distressed by his lack of sexual desire, a diagnosis of male hypoactive sexual desire disorder is not made.

Premature (Early) Ejaculation

Studies among gbMSM suggest a prevalence of premature (early) ejaculation between 10.4 and 34 percent (Hirshfield et al., 2010; Lau et al., 2006; 2008; Peixoto & Nobre, 2015a; 2016; Rosser et al., 1997; Seibel et al., 2009; Shindel et al., 2012). Among a telephone sample of fifty-five Chinese men in Hong Kong who reported a male sexual partner in the past twelve months, 21.8 percent of men aged eighteen to fifty-nine reported premature (early) ejaculation for a period of at least three consecutive months over the past year (Lau et al., 2006). Further, in another sample of Chinese MSM in Hong Kong, 10.4 percent reported premature (early) ejaculation for a period of at least three consecutive months over the past year; this was not associated with age, education, or employment, but it was more commonly reported by those who engaged in anal sex (with and without condom use), who reported commercial sex work including anal sex, who found sex partners online, who reported discrimination because of sexual orientation, who reported greater nonacceptance of their sexual orientation, and who reported poor support among family and friends (Lau et al., 2008). In an internet sample of 7,001 sexually active U.S. gbMSM, premature (early) ejaculation was more common among those under thirty-nine years compared to those fifty and older; no differences were observed by race/ethnicity, income, HIV status, or relationship status (Hirshfield et al., 2010). Finally, in a survey of 2640 gbMSM (80 percent of whom were living in North America), premature (early) ejaculation was more common among gbMSM living with HIV, those with urination difficulties, those with fewer than six lifetime sexual partners, and those who reported greater sexual dissatisfaction (Shindel et al., 2012).

In a sample of 909 Portuguese men (473 heterosexual, 435 gay), sexually active heterosexual men were more likely to report premature (early) ejaculation than gay men: 12.5 percent of gay men reported premature (early) ejaculation over the last six months compared with 14 percent of heterosexual men (Peixoto & Nobre, 2015a). Heterosexual men were also more likely to report that their experience of premature (early) ejaculation was distressing: of those who reported premature (early) ejaculation, 27.8 percent of gay men and 59.1 percent of heterosexual men reported moderate to severe distress (Peixoto & Nobre, 2015a). After controlling for distress, prevalence of distressing premature (early) ejaculation was 3.4 percent among gay men and 8.2 percent among heterosexual men (Peixoto & Nobre, 2015a). Likewise, in a survey of 561 non-heterosexual men and 933 heterosexual men in Croatia, premature (early) ejaculation was reported significantly more often by heterosexual men (18.9 percent) compared with heterosexual men (26.8 percent); however, similar proportions of both groups found their symptoms to be destressing (Ivanković et al., 2015).

Premature (early) ejaculation among transgender or gender-variant individuals has not been studied. Among gender minority individuals who were born with penises, prevalence of premature (early) ejaculation could be expected to be similar to that of cisgender men with penises. However, if the individual is taking anti-androgens and/or estrogen, erectile and testicular function, including ejaculation, can be affected, potentially making premature (early) ejaculation less likely. In a longitudinal study of genital sensitivity after sex reassignment surgery (both phalloplasties and vaginoclitoridoplasties), all trans men and 85 percent of trans women reported orgasm following surgery (Selvaggi et al., 2007). Some trans women also continue to ejaculate following genital surgery (Lawrence, 2005) and as such may experience premature (early) ejaculation, but more research is needed. As previously mentioned, among trans men who have phalloplasty, ability to orgasm is typically not affected and orgasm can be experienced through self-stimulation and penetrative sex (Garcia, Christopher, et al., 2014). However, ejaculation via the neophallus does not occur.

Substance/Medication-Induced Sexual Dysfunction

Prevalence of substance/medication-induced sexual dysfunction is unclear. Approximately 15 to 80 percent of individuals taking certain classes of antidepressants (i.e., monoamine oxidase inhibitors, tricyclic antidepressants, serotonergic antidepressants, and combined serotonergic and adrenergic antidepressants) report sexual side effects, as do approximately 50% of individuals taking antipsychotic medications (APA, 2013).

Prevalence of substance/medication-induced sexual dysfunction among SGM individuals is unknown. Studies indicate higher levels of substance use among SGM individuals (e.g., Day, Fish, Perez-Brumer, Hatzenbuehler, & Russell, 2017; Keuroghlian, Reisner, White, & Weiss, 2015; Lachowsky et al., 2017; Lehavot & Simoni, 2011; Roth et al., 2018; Schmidt et al., 2016), and as such, associated substance/medication-induced sexual dysfunction may be more common. Likewise, mental health conditions like depression and anxiety have been shown to have elevated prevalence among SGM individuals (e.g., Conchran, Sullivan, & Mays, 2003; Crissman, Stroumsa, Kobernik, & Berger, 2019; Lachowsky et al., 2017; Lehavot & Simoni, 2011; Roth et al., 2018; Veale, Watson, Peter, & Saewyc, 2017). Given the association between medication for treatment of these conditions and substance/medication-induced sexual dysfunction, this may also contribute to elevated rates in these populations, but more research is needed to explore these hypotheses.

Discussion

Sexual health is complex and can affect and be affected by a multitude of biopsychosocial factors. At present, our understanding of sexual health is limited by restrictive definitions and classifications that rely heavily on sexual function and response. This is problematic as these existing categories may not accurately reflect sexual response and function for all people, especially for SGM individuals.

Understanding of sexual dysfunction and sexual health also needs to be expanded beyond the current male/female binary. The existing classification scheme of the DSM-5 (APA, 2013) relies heavily on "male" and "female" disorders. For instance, only male individuals can be diagnosed with premature (early) ejaculation (APA, 2013). Recent research has begun to explore premature (early) orgasm in women, and one study using general population data from the British National Survey of Sexual Attitudes and Lifestyles found that 2.3 percent of women aged sixteen to seventy-four reported a problem with having orgasm too soon (Mitchell, 2019). This is consistent with previous data from the Global Study of Sexual Attitudes and Behaviors, which found that 7.7 to 26.3 percent of women, depending on geographic location, reported having orgasm too quickly (Laumann et al., 2005). Despite these preliminary findings, this is not yet recognized as a sexual dysfunction and much more research, which includes WSW, is needed. Likewise, the DSM-5 lacks a sexual pain disorder category for men. Anodyspareunia, frequent and severe pain during receptive anal intercourse (Damon & Rosser, 2005), has been reported by 16 to 30.6 percent of gbMSM (Peixoto & Nobre, 2015a; Rosser et al, 1997), with a lifetime prevalence of up to 61 percent (Rosser et al, 1997), and more than half (58.2 percent) of the gbMSM in one sample reported this as moderately to extremely distressing (Peixoto & Nobre, 2015a). Further, 5.7 to 14 percent of gbMSM report lifetime prevalence of genital pain during insertive sexual acts (Rosser et al, 1997; Siebel et al., 2009), which is likewise not recognized as a sexual disorder in the DSM. Finally, it should be readily apparent that individuals who do not fit neatly into the boxes of "male" and "female," because of either gender (e.g., transgender, gender nonbinary) or sex (e.g., intersex), have been vastly overlooked in the study and classification of sexual dysfunction.

The present understanding and classification of sexual disorders is also largely focused on heterosexual individuals. While sexual minority people are not explicitly excluded from DSM-5 categories (APA, 2013), the vast majority of research on sexual disorders has focused on heterosexual people. As such, we do not fully understand how the sexual health of sexual minority individuals may be differentially affected by biopsychosocial factors. For example, minority stress as the result of sexual minority status and associated stigma, prejudice, discrimination, and victimization has been shown to negatively affect sexual function and sexual health in sexual minority men and women (Cohen & Byers, 2015; Ivanković et al., 2015; Lau et al., 2008). While it should be expected that the sexual health of gender minority individuals will also be affected by minority stress, research in this area is lacking.

Particular consideration should also be paid to the sexual function of SGM individuals living with HIV. While some research has explored differences by HIV status (e.g., Hart et al., 2012; Shindel et al., 2012), a better understanding is still needed. Individuals living with HIV may experience sexual side effects from both HIV-related and non–HIV-related medication (e.g., Colson et al., 2002). Further, HIV stigma can have detrimental effects on the individual, as well as on their sexual and romantic relationships. Research exploring HIV stigma and sexual behavior is mixed (e.g., Varni, Miller, & Solomon, 2012), and research on how stigma might affect sexual function is lacking. The few studies that do consider sexual health and function among SGM individuals tend to group all SGM individuals together. This is problematic as it assumes that the experiences of all SGM individuals are the same. Bisexual and other sexual minority individuals who do not identify as gay or lesbian are likely to have differing experiences of sexual function and dysfunction, as are individuals of varying gender identities.

Finally, the sexual health and function of asexual individuals have been largely overlooked in research on sexual disorders. To be clear, asexuality itself is not a sexual disorder, and some asexual individuals do engage in partnered sexual activities and masturbation frequency has been reported as similar to sexual individuals (Brotto, Knudson, Inskip, Rhodes, & Erskine, 2010). As such, their sexual health needs and function must also be considered, and far more research is needed.

Moving forward, researchers and physical and mental health care providers need to be more cognizant of the unique sexual health needs of SGM individuals, and SGM individuals need to actively participate and be actively included in research, policy, and public health initiatives. From a research perspective, more attention is needed to make sure that measures of sexual function are either validated or created for use with SGM populations. Additionally, research needs to expand to include racial/ethnic minorities and populations from the Global South. Large global studies have shown that there are significant cultural differences in sexual function around the world (e.g., Laumann et al., 2005); as such, the sexual health of individuals who have both a racial/ethnic minority identity and an SGM identity will be differentially affected by various biopsychosocial factors. A more comprehensive understanding of sexual health should also include individuals with polyamorous and other non-monogamous sexual orientations, as these individuals are also likely to have differing sexual health needs and have been largely ignored in the current sexual health landscape.

Regardless of a person's sexual orientation or the genitals that they possess, sexual disorders and dysfunctions are very common. However, sexual health encompasses so much more than sexual function and any associated distress. Individuals, clinicians, and researchers need to expand their concept of sexual health and function to incorporate the vast array of biopsychosocial factors, including satisfaction and pleasure, that influence and are affected by sexual health. This needs to be done with awareness, understanding, and inclusivity of all people whatever their genders, orientations, and relationship status.

References

American Psychiatric Association. (2013). *Diagnostic and statistical manual of mental disorders* (5th ed.). Arlington, VA: Author.

Barbonetti, A., D'Andrea, S., Cavallo, F., Martorella, A., Francavilla, S., & Francavilla, F. (2019). Erectile dysfunction and premature ejaculation in homosexual and heterosexual men: A systematic review and meta-analysis of comparative studies. *Journal of Sexual Medicine, 16*(5), 624–32. doi: 10.1111/j.1743-6109.2011.02599.x

Beaber, T. E., & Werner, P. D. (2009). The relationship between anxiety and sexual functioning in lesbians and heterosexual women. *Journal of Homosexuality, 56*(5), 639–54. doi:10.1080/00918360903005303

Blair, K. L., Cappell, J., & Pukall, C. F. (2018). Not all orgasms were created equal: Differences in frequency and satisfaction of orgasm experiences by sexual activity in same-sex versus mixed-sex relationships. *Journal of Sex Research, 55*(6), 719–33. doi:10.1080/00224499.2017.1303437

Blair, K. L., Pukall, C. F., Smith, K. B., & Cappell, J. (2015). Differential associations of communication and love in heterosexual, lesbian, and bisexual women's perceptions and experiences of chronic vulvar and pelvic pain. *Journal of Sex & Marital Therapy, 41*(5), 498–524. doi:10.1080/0092623X.2014.931315

Bressler, L. C., & Lavender, A. D. (1986). Sexual fulfillment of heterosexual, bisexual, and homosexual women. *Journal of Homosexuality, 12*(3–4), 109–22. doi:10.1300/J082v12n03_10

Breyer, B. N., Smith, J. F., Eisenberg, M. L., Ando, K. A., Rowen, T. S., & Shindel, A. W. (2010). The impact of sexual orientation on sexuality and sexual practices in North American medical students. *Journal of Sexual Medicine, 7*(7), 2391–400. doi:10.1111/j.1743-6109.2010.01794.x

Brotto, L. A., Knudson, G., Inskip, J., Rhodes, K., & Erskine, Y. (2010). Asexuality: A mixed-methods approach. *Archives of Sexual Behavior, 39*(3), 599–618.

Burri, A., Rahman, Q., Santtila, P., Jern, P., Spector, T., & Sandnabba, K. (2012). The relationship between same-sex sexual experience, sexual distress, and female sexual dysfunction. *Journal of Sexual Medicine, 9*(1), 198–206. doi:10.1111/j.1743-6109.2011.02538.x

Carriero, C., Dellino, M., Campanelli, F. D., Licchelli, M., & Loverro, G. (2016). Psychosexual assessment of transgender individuals during the sex reassignment process: Sexual desire, activity, and satisfaction. *Health, 8,* 1975–81. doi:10.4236/health.2016.811111

Cochran, S. D., Sullivan, J. G., & Mays, V. M. (2003). Prevalence of mental disorders, psychological distress, and mental health services use among lesbian, gay, and bisexual adults in the United States. *Journal of Consulting and Clinical Psychology, 71*(1), 53. doi:10.1037/0022-006X.71.1.53

Cohen, J. N., & Byers, E. S. (2015). Minority stress, protective factors, and sexual functioning of women in a same-sex relationship. *Psychology of Sexual Orientation and Gender Diversity, 2*(4), 391–402. doi:10.1037sgd0000108

Colson, A. E., Keller, M. J., Sax, P. E., Pettus, P. T., Platt, R., & Choo, P. W. (2002). Male sexual dysfunction associated with antiretroviral therapy. *Journal of Acquired Immune Deficiency Syndromes (1999), 30*(1), 27–32. doi:10.1097/00042560-200205010-00004

Coxon, J., & Seal, L. (2018). Hormone management of trans women. *Trends in Urology & Men's Health, 9*(6), 10–14. doi:10.1002/tre.663

Crissman, H. P., Stroumsa, D., Kobernik, E. K., & Berger, M. B. (2019). Gender and frequent mental distress: Comparing transgender and non-transgender individuals' self-rated mental health. *Journal of Women's Health, 28*(2), 143–51. doi:10.1089/jwh.2018.7411

Damon, W., & Rosser, B. S. (2005). Anodyspareunia in men who have sex with men. *Journal of Sex & Marital Therapy, 31*(2), 129–41. doi:10.1080/00926230590477989

Day, J. K., Fish, J. N., Perez-Brumer, A., Hatzenbuehler, M. L., & Russell, S. T. (2017). Transgender youth substance use disparities: Results from a population-based sample. *Journal of Adolescent Health, 61*(6), 729–35. doi:10.1016/j.jadohealth.2017.06.024

Defreyne, J., Kreukels, B., T'Sjoen, G., Heijer, M. D., Heylens, G., & Elaut, E. (2019). Sexual desire in transgender persons in relation with gender affirming hormone treatment: Results from the ENIGI, a large multicentre prospective cohort study in transgender people. *Endocrine Abstracts, 63,* OC12.5. doi:10.1530/endolabs.63.OC12.5

Garcia, J. R., Lloyd, E. A., Wallen, K., & Fisher, H. E. (2014). Variation in orgasm occurrence by sexual orientation in a sample of US singles. *Journal of Sexual Medicine, 11*(11), 2645–52. doi:10.1111/jsm.12669

Garcia, M. M., Christopher, N. A., De Luca, F., Spilotros, M., & Ralph, D. J. (2014). Overall satisfaction, sexual function, and the durability of neophallus dimensions following staged female to male genital gender confirming surgery: The Institute of Urology, London U. K. experience. *Translational Andrology and Urology, 3*(2), 156–62. doi:10.3978/j.issn.2223-4683.2014.04.10

Hart, T. A., Moskowitz, D., Cox, C., Li, X., Ostrow, D. G., Stall, R. D., . . . Plankey, M. (2012). The cumulative effects of medication use, drug use, and smoking on erectile dysfunction among men who have sex with men. *Journal of Sexual Medicine, 9,* 1106–13. doi:10.1111/j.1743-6109.2011.02648.x

Hirshfield, S., Chiasson, M. A., Wagmiller, R. L., Remien, R. H., Humberstone, M., Scheinmann, R., & Grov, C. (2010). Sexual dysfunction in an internet sample of U.S. men who have sex with men. *Journal of Sexual Medicine, 7,* 3104–14. doi:10.1111/j.1743-6109.2009.01636.x

Irwig, M. S. (2017). Testosterone therapy for transgender men. *Lancet Diabetes & Endocrinology, 5*(4), 301–11. doi:10.1016/S2213-8587(16)00036-X

Ivanković, I., Šević, S., & Štulhofer, A. (2015). Distressing sexual difficulties in heterosexual and non-heterosexual Croatian men: Assessing the role of minority stress. *Journal of Sex Research, 52*(6), 647–58. doi:10.1080/00224499.2014.909381

Keuroghlian, A. S., Reisner, S. L., White, J. M., & Weiss, R. D. (2015). Substance use and treatment of substance use disorders in a community sample of transgender adults. *Drug and Alcohol Dependence, 152,* 139–46. doi:10.1016/j.drugalcdep.2015.04.008

Klein, C., & Gorzalka, B. B. (2009). Continuing medical education: Sexual functioning in transsexuals following hormone therapy and genital surgery: A review. *Journal of Sexual Medicine, 6*(11), 2922–39. doi:10.1111/j.1743-6109.2009.01370.x

Lachowsky, N. J., Dulai, J. J., Cui, Z., Sereda, P., Rich, A., Patterson, T. L., . . . Moore, D. M. (2017). Lifetime doctor-diagnosed mental health conditions and current substance use among gay and bisexual men living in Vancouver, Canada. *Substance Use & Misuse, 52*(6), 785–97. doi:0.1080/10826084.2016.1264965

Lau, J. T. F., Kim, J. H., & Tsui, H. Y. (2006). Prevalence and factors of sexual problems in Chinese males and females having sex with the same-sex partner in Hong Kong: A population-based study. *International Journal of Impotence Research, 18,* 130–40. doi:10.1038/sj.ijir.3901368

Lau, J. T. F., Kim, J. H., & Tsui, H. Y. (2008). Prevalence and sociocultural predictors of sexual dysfunction among Chinese men who have sex with men in Hong Kong. *Journal of Sexual Medicine, 5,* 2766–79. doi:10.1111/j.1743–6109.2008.00892.x

Laumann, E. O., Nicolosi, A., Glasser, D. B., Paik, A., Cingell, C., Moreira, E., & Wang, T. (2005). Sexual problems among women and men aged 40–80 y: Prevalence and correlated identified in the Global Study of Sexual Attitudes and Behaviors. *International Journal of Impotence Research, 17*, 39–57. doi:10.1038/sj/ijir.3901250

Lawrence, A. A. (2005). Sexuality before and after male-to-female sex reassignment surgery. *Archives of Sexual Behaviour, 34*(2), 147–66. doi:10.1007/s10508-005-1793-y

Lehavot, K., & Simoni, J. M. (2011). The impact of minority stress on mental health and substance use among sexual minority women. *Journal of Consulting and Clinical Psychology, 79*(2), 159–70. doi:10.1037/a0022839

Meana, M., Rakipi, R. S., Weeks, G., & Lykins, A. (2006). Sexual functioning in a non- clinical sample of partnered lesbians. *Journal of Couple & Relationship Therapy, 5*(2), 1–22. doi:10.1300/J398v05n02_01

Mitchell, K. (June, 2019). Early orgasm in women: Is there a problem? Presented at the scientific meeting of the British Association of Sexual Health and HIV, London, UK.

Peixoto, M. M., & Nobre, P. (2015a). Prevalence of sexual problems and associated distress among gay and heterosexual men. *Sexual and Relationship Therapy, 30*(2), 211–25. doi:10.1080/14681994.2014.986084

Peixoto, M. M., & Nobre, P. (2015b). Prevalence of sexual problems and associated distress among lesbian and heterosexual women. *Journal of Sex & Marital Therapy, 41*(4), 427–39. doi:10.1080/0092623X.2014.918066

Peixoto, M. M., & Nobre, P. (2016). Distressing sexual problems and dyadic adjustment in heterosexuals, gay men, and lesbian women. *Journal of Sex & Marital Therapy, 42*(4), 369–81. doi:10.1080/0092623X.2015.1053020

Rosser, B. R. S., Metz, M. E., Bockting, W. O., & Buroker, T. (1997). Sexual difficulties, concerns, and satisfaction in homosexual men: An empirical study with implication for HIV prevention. *Journal of Sex & Marital Therapy, 23*(1), 61–73. doi:10.1080/00926239708404418

Roth, E. A., Cui, Z., Wang, L., Armstrong, H. L., Rich, A. J., Lachowsky, N. J., . . . Olarewaju, G. (2018). Substance use patterns of gay and bisexual men in the Momentum Health study. *American Journal of Men's Health, 12*(5), 1759–73. doi:10.1177/1557988318786872

Schmidt, A. J., Bourne, A., Weatherburn, P., Reid, D., Marcus, U., Hickson, F., & Network, T. E. (2016). Illicit drug use among gay and bisexual men in 44 cities: Findings from the European MSM Internet Survey (EMIS). *International Journal of Drug Policy, 38*, 4–12. doi:10.1016/j.drugpo.2016.09.007

Seibel, S. L., Rosser, S., Horvath, K. J., & Evans, C. D. (2009). Sexual dysfunction, paraphilias and their relationship to childhood abuse in men who have sex with men. *International Journal of Sexual Health, 21*(2), 79–86. doi:10.1080/19317610902773062

Selvaggi, G., Monstrey, S., Ceulemans, P., T'Sjoen, G., De Cuypere, G., & Hoebeke, P. (2007). Genital sensitivity after sex reassignment surgery in transsexual patients. *Annals of Plastic Surgery, 58*(4), 427–33. doi:10.1097/01.sap.0000238428.91834.be

Shindel, A. W., Vittinghoff, E., & Breyer, B. N. (2012). Erectile dysfunction and premature ejaculation in men who have sex with men. *Journal of Sexual Medicine, 9*, 576–84. doi:10.1111/j.1743-6109.2011.02585.x

Varni, S. E., Miller, C. T., & Solomon, S. E. (2012). Sexual behaviour as a function of stigma and coping with stigma among people with HIV/AIDS in rural New England. *AIDS and Behavior, 16*(8), 2330–9. doi:10.1007/s10461-012-0239-5

Veale, J. F., Watson, R. J., Peter, T., & Saewyc, E. M. (2017). Mental health disparities among Canadian transgender youth. *Journal of Adolescent Health, 60*(1), 44–9. doi:10.1016/j.jadohealth.2016.09.014

Weyers, S., Elaut, E., De Sutter, P., Gerris, J., T'Sjoen, G., Heylens, G., . . . Verstraelen, H. (2009). Long-term assessment of the physical, mental, and sexual health among transsexual women. *Journal of Sexual Medicine, 6*(3), 752–60. doi:10.1111/j.1743-6109.2008.01082.x

Wierckx, K., Elaut, E., Van Hoorde, B., Heylens, G., De Cuypere, G., Monstrey, S., . . . T'Sjoen, G. (2014). Sexual desire in trans persons: Associations with sex reassignment treatment. *Journal of Sexual Medicine, 11*(1), 107–18. doi:10.1111/jsm.12365

World Health Organization. (2006). *Defining sexual health: Report of a technical consultation on sexual health, 28–31 January 2002, Geneva.* Geneva, Switzerland: Author.

CHAPTER

13 Personality Disorders among Sexual and Gender Minority Populations

Julie Prud'homme,* Christina L. Robillard,* *and* Brianna J. Turner

Abstracts

Research examining the prevalence, impact, and course of personality disorders in sexual and gender minority populations is sparse; however, the available literature suggests that personality pathology is more prevalent in sexual and gender minorities compared to those who identify as heterosexual and/or cisgender. Although research is limited, several competing hypotheses have attempted to explain this disparity, including environmental, developmental, minority stress, and dual marginalization theories, as well as critical theories that point to possible roles of diagnostic, clinician, and cultural biases. This chapter highlights three critical future directions. First, rigorous longitudinal research needs to be conducted to evaluate competing etiological hypotheses of personality disorders in sexual and gender minorities. Second, future personality research should examine through an intersectional lens how additional aspects of one's identity (e.g., ethnicity, class) interact with sexual orientation and gender to influence the experiences of these groups. Finally, clinicians and researchers must be sensitive to both the need to accurately document personality pathology, and the need to avoid unnecessarily pathologizing the experiences of sexual and gender minorities. Ultimately, addressing these future directions would enhance clinicians' and researchers' understanding of and ability to respond to the mental health needs of sexual and gender minority populations.

Keywords: personality disorders, sexual minorities, gender minorities, gender dysphoria, gender identity disorder, minority stress theory, developmental theories, environmental theories, intersectionality

What Are Personality Disorders?

The current (fifth) edition of the American Psychiatric Association's (APA) *Diagnostic and Statistical Manual of Mental Disorders* (DSM) defines a personality disorder as "an enduring pattern of inner experience and behavior that deviates markedly from the expectations of the individuals' culture, is pervasive and inflexible, has an onset in adolescence or early adulthood, is stable over time, and leads to distress or impairment" (APA, 2013, p. 645). Descriptions of maladaptive personality traits that profoundly impair emotional, cognitive, and social functioning can be traced at least as far back as ancient Chinese and Greek texts (c. 500–300 BCE) that ascribed such impairments to supernatural, biological, or moral imbalances or failings (Crocq, 2013). Maladaptive personality traits were first formally proposed as causal agents of psychiatric illness between the late eighteenth and early twentieth centuries (Crocq, 2013). Since the introduction of personality disorders in the DSM (APA, 1980), their classification and conceptualization have noticeably evolved. Beginning with the third edition of the DSM, for example, personality disorders were classified on a separate axis from other clinical syndromes to emphasize their uniquely persistent course (APA, 1980), but this multi-axial diagnostic model was later removed due to concerns regarding the lack of clear

* These authors contributed equally to this work and are listed alphabetically.

boundaries between the axes (APA, 2013). The fifth edition of the DSM introduced a dimensional, trait-specific model to complement the traditional categorical diagnostic model used in previous editions (APA, 2013). Three core assumptions that have endured throughout this evolution are that (1) personality-related psychopathology is *persistent*, usually beginning in adolescence or early adulthood and affecting the individual for years or decades; (2) *pervasive*, affecting multiple functional domains in a person's life; and (3) *pathological*, meaning that these traits must result in significant distress or impairment. Unlike other clinical syndromes that may emerge in response to specific situational stressors or follow a relapsing–remitting course, personality disorders are expected to be stable and inflexible and to substantially impact a person's functioning.

The DSM-5 includes ten specific personality disorders, grouped into three descriptive clusters: (1) paranoid, schizoid, and schizotypal personality disorders make up the Cluster A disorders, which are characterized by odd or eccentric behaviors; (2) antisocial, borderline, histrionic, and narcissistic personality disorders make up the Cluster B disorders, which are characterized by impulsive or dramatic behavior; and (3) avoidant, dependent, and obsessive-compulsive disorders make up the Cluster C disorders, which are characterized by anxious or fearful behavior (APA, 2013). The alternative dimensional model included in DSM-5 Section III provides trait-specified criteria for six of these disorders (i.e., antisocial, avoidant, borderline, narcissistic, obsessive-compulsive, and schizotypal), based on the presence of impairment in personality functioning and five pathological personality traits (antagonism, disinhibition, detachment, negative affectivity, and psychoticism). Regardless of which diagnostic model is used, criteria also require that the maladaptive patterns of inner experience and behavior that typify personality disorders be inflexible, pervasive, stable, distressing, or impairing and should not be better explained by another psychiatric, physiological, or medical condition.

Personality disorders are estimated to affect roughly 12 percent of adults in the general population (Volkert, Gablonski, & Rabung, 2018). These disorders are significantly overrepresented in clinical and institutional settings, especially mental health services, psychiatric hospitals, and correctional and criminal justice settings, where their estimated prevalence ranges from 25 to 65 percent (Beckwith, Moran, & Reilly, 2014; Fazel & Danesh, 2002; Newton-Howes et al., 2010; Zimmerman, Rothschild, & Chelminski, 2005). Personality disorders are highly comorbid with one another (e.g., approximately three quarters of individuals with borderline personality disorder (BPD) have at least one other personality disorder; Grant et al., 2008) and with other clinical syndromes and concerns, including other psychiatric disorders, alcohol and substance use problems, histories of interpersonal trauma, self-harm and suicidality, aggression, poor physical health, and premature mortality (Fok, Hayes, Chang, Stewart, Callard, & Moran, 2012; Frankenburg & Zanarini, 2004; Grant et al., 2008; Moran et al., 2016; Hiroeh, Appleby, Mortensen, & Dunn, 2001). Individuals with personality disorders have lower educational and occupational achievement, more interpersonal difficulties, and higher mortality compared to people without these disorders (Jackson & Burgess, 2004; Moran et al., 2016; Skodol et al., 2002; Skodal, Johnson, Cohen, Sneed, & Crawford, 2007). While early research and clinical literature frequently emphasized the substantial challenges associated with building and maintaining therapeutic rapport, premature termination of treatment, and poor therapeutic outcomes for people with personality disorders (e.g., Karterud et al., 1992; Lewis & Appleby, 1988; Shea, Pilkonis, Beckham, & Collins, 1990; Woody, McLellan, Luborsky, & O'Brien, 1985), recent longitudinal studies suggest that rates of naturalistic remission of personality disorders are much higher than previously assumed (Zanarini, Frankenburg, Reich, & Fitzmaurice, 2012), and systematic reviews show a variety of treatment approaches that can be considered efficacious and effective for personality disorders (Dixon-Gordon, Turner, & Chapman, 2011). This recent evidence has fueled renewed optimism and redoubled efforts to understand, prevent, and reduce these important disorders.

How Common Are Personality Disorders in Sexual Minority Adults?

Large, high-quality, representative epidemiological surveys are an important source of information regarding the prevalence and sociodemographic distributions of personality disorders in the population. Because these studies seek a representative sampling of the broader population, they can overcome several biases that affect clinical or convenience samples, including help-seeking, referral, and diagnostic biases. Unfortunately, despite several methodologically rigorous epidemiological studies that document the prevalence of personality disorders (e.g., Coid, Yang, Tyrer, Roberts, & Ullrich, 2006;

Dereboy, Güzel, Dereboy, Okyay, & Eskin, 2014; Lenzenweger, Lane, Loranger, & Kessler, 2007; Samuels et al., 2002) or examine mental health concerns among individuals who identify as gay, lesbian, bisexual, queer, or unsure of their sexual orientation (hereafter referred to as sexual minorities) (e.g., Cochran & Mays, 2000; Mathy, 2002; Sandfort, de Graaf, & Bijl, 2003), few such studies have been used to examine the prevalence of personality disorders among sexual minority individuals, seemingly because few studies rigorously evaluate both personality disorders and sexual orientation using appropriate measures.

A notable exception to these limitations is the National Epidemiologic Survey on Alcohol and Related Conditions (NESARC; Grant et al., 2004), a multi-wave, nationally representative survey of the civilian, non-institutionalized adult population in the United States. Analyses of Waves 2 and 3 of the NESARC revealed that, compared to an estimated 23 percent of heterosexual adults, between 35 and 46 percent of sexual minority adults met diagnostic criteria for a personality disorder (Bolton & Sareen, 2011; Kerridge et al., 2017). This elevated risk of personality disorders in sexual minority adults is found even when adjusting for numerous potential sociodemographic confounds, including age, marital status, education, income, race/ethnicity, region, and urbanicity (Bolton & Sareen, 2011; Kerridge et al., 2017). Moreover, risk for personality disorders appears to be unevenly distributed in this population: personality disorders are significantly more prevalent among bisexual women compared to heterosexual women, lesbian women, and gay men (Bolton & Sareen, 2011; Kerridge et al., 2017). In addition, Cluster A and Cluster C personality disorders are overrepresented in adults who identify as gay or who are questioning their sexual orientation, while Cluster B personality disorders are overrepresented in adults who identify as bisexual or questioning, relative to adults who identify as heterosexual. Overall, these findings align with research showing a higher burden of mental health concerns among individuals, especially women, who identify as bisexual (e.g., Bostwick, Boyd, Hughes, & McCabe, 2010; McCabe, Hughes, Bostwick, West, & Boyd, 2009). Although the reasons for this disparity are unclear, one plausible explanation is that the process of *dual marginalization* (Ochs, 1996), whereby bisexual individuals encounter discrimination from both heterosexual and gay/lesbian communities, contributes to the especially high prevalence and risk of personality disorders in this sexual minority group.

An important criticism of the DSM-5 is that the discrete diagnoses it describes often fail to explain the high rates of comorbidity between mental health disorders (e.g., Eaton, South, & Krueger, 2010). As such, investigations that rely on this disorder-by-disorder approach cannot account for potentially important overlap in psychopathology. In response to this criticism, some authors advocate for a transdiagnostic approach to psychopathology, with latent or dimensional factors that account for various diagnoses. One widely used model posits that two latent factors, *internalizing* psychopathology and *externalizing* psychopathology, account for the covariance of many mental health disorders, including some personality disorders (for a review, see Eaton et al., 2010; Krueger & Markon, 2006). Eaton (2014) applied this approach to examine the association between these transdiagnostic factors and sexual minority orientations using Wave 2 of the NESARC. Two central findings emerged. First, Eaton (2014) demonstrated that the transdiagnostic latent structure of psychopathology was invariant across sexual orientations. In other words, the internalizing (indicated by major depressive, dysthymic, generalized anxiety, panic, posttraumatic stress, and BPD, and social and specific phobias) and externalizing (indicated by alcohol, marijuana, nicotine, and other substance dependence diagnoses, and antisocial and borderline personality disorders) factors could be used to capture comorbidity patterns in individuals who identify as gay, lesbian, and bisexual just as effectively as in individuals who identify as heterosexual. Second, Eaton (2014) found that individuals who identify as gay, lesbian, and bisexual had higher average levels of internalizing and externalizing psychopathology compared to their heterosexual counterparts, suggesting that elevations in general psychopathology may account for the higher prevalence of personality disorders in sexual minority adults.

Although analysis of the NESARC data has provided important information regarding the prevalence and risk of personality disorders in sexual minority individuals, there are several limitations that should be noted. First, while the NESARC attempted to draw a representative sample of non-institutionalized adults living in the United States, including those residing in boarding or rooming houses, shelters, non-transient hotels and motels, college housing, and group homes, it did not include individuals who were homeless. Given the disproportionately high rates of homelessness affecting sexual minority individuals (National Alliance to End

Homelessness, 2015) and high rates of psychiatric illness in homeless populations (Scott, 1993), the overall results may underestimate the prevalence of personality disorders in sexual minority adults.

Second, the assessment of sexual orientation in these surveys was based on a single question that required the person to self-identify as heterosexual, gay or lesbian, bisexual, or not sure. As sexual orientation is a multifaceted construct composed of sexual attraction, sexual behavior, and sexual identity (Savin-Williams, 2006), measures that separate these components may provide a more nuanced understanding of an individual's sexual orientation.

Third, the cross-sectional design of the NESARC precludes examining the stability of personality disorders in sexual minority populations over time and makes it difficult to examine underlying mechanisms that might explain *why* sexual minority populations are at greater risk for personality disorders.

These limitations aside, it is evident that a significant disparity in the prevalence and risk of personality disorders exists among sexual minority adults, at least among those living in the United States. This represents an important public health concern deserving future research to clarify the nature of this association.

How Common Are Personality Disorders in Sexual Minorities Presenting to Treatment?

While epidemiological surveys provide valuable information about the prevalence of personality disorders among sexual minority adults in the general population, clinicians, healthcare administrators, and policymakers are often interested in slightly different questions—for example, where are sexual minority populations seeking and receiving mental health treatment and what are their service needs? Unfortunately, similar to the epidemiological literature, rigorous studies that can inform these questions are scarce. Moreover, the majority of clinical studies examine only a subset of personality disorder diagnoses, most frequently BPD, limiting the ability to draw conclusions about the broader burden of personality pathology. Nonetheless, a few important conclusions can be drawn from the extant literature. First, clinical surveys consistently find an overrepresentation of BPD in sexual minority men relative to men who identify as heterosexual, but do not consistently find an association between sexual orientation and BPD in women (Dulit, Fyer, Miller, Sacks, & Frances, 1993; Paris, Zweig-Franke, & Guzder, 1995; Stone, 1990; Zubenko, George, Solof, & Schultz, 1987). For example, Dulit et al. (1993) found that male psychiatric inpatients with BPD were significantly more likely to identify as gay relative to male inpatients without BPD. Among female inpatients, there was no association between sexual orientation and BPD pathology. In a similar vein, although Schulte-Herbrüggen et al. (2009) found that female inpatients with BPD showed a trend toward more often identifying as bisexual compared to healthy controls, the distribution of bisexual and lesbian orientation did not significantly differ between female inpatients with and without BPD. In contrast, Zubenko et al. (1987) found that male inpatients with BPD were ten times more likely to identify as gay, and women inpatients with BPD were six times more likely to identify as lesbian, compared to inpatients with major depression. Likewise, Reich and Zanarini (2008) found that inpatients with BPD were 75 percent more likely to identify as gay, lesbian, or bisexual compared to patients with other personality disorders, and found no significant difference in this overrepresentation of sexual minority identities between men and women with BPD. Overall, these findings suggest that service providers for people with BPD or people who identify as sexual minorities should be aware of the overlap between these populations and tailor their referrals, staff trainings, resources, and interventions accordingly. A major shortcoming of many clinical studies, however, is that sexual orientation was often measured based on inferences or documentation from clinicians regarding sexual behavior or attraction. Consequently, these judgments may not necessarily align with individuals' self-identified sexual orientation and should be interpreted with caution.

Preliminary research also suggests that inpatients with BPD may show less congruence between their self-reported sexual identity and their sexual and romantic behavior, relative to inpatients with other personality disorders. For instance, a ten-year longitudinal study of 362 inpatients with various personality disorders showed that about 9 percent of men and women with BPD endorsed having same-sex intimate relationships without identifying as gay, lesbian, or bisexual (Reich & Zanarini, 2008). Moreover, although people with BPD were no more likely to report a change in sexual identity over the ten-year period than patients with other personality disorders, they were significantly more likely to report a change in the gender of their intimate partners (Reich & Zanarini, 2008). This tentatively suggests that the link between sexual identity and romantic/sexual behavior may not be as tightly linked in patients with BPD relative to those with other personality disorders. Alternatively, people with BPD may be more reluctant to self-identify or report a sexual minority identity. Finally, it is possible that romantic and sexual attraction may be more fluid over time in patients with BPD compared to people with other personality disorders. Ultimately, this is the only longitudinal study that has tracked sexual identity and romantic or sexual behavior in people with personality disorders, limiting the conclusions that can be drawn.

How Common Are Personality Disorders in Sexual Minority Youth?

Prior to the DSM-5, diagnostic criteria prohibited or discouraged diagnosing adolescents under the age of nineteen with personality disorders (APA, 1994). Starting with the DSM-5, however, adolescents may receive personality disorder diagnoses, with the exception of antisocial personality disorder, if their maladaptive personality traits are pervasive and persistent for at least one year and unlikely to be better explained by a particular developmental stage or other psychopathology (APA, 2013). Consistent with this shift, emerging evidence documents an overrepresentation of BPD symptoms in sexual minority youth relative to youth who identify as heterosexual. Marshal et al. (2012) examined 527 heterosexual and sexual minority girls using data from the Pittsburgh Girls Study and found that sexual minority girls reported higher past-year BPD symptoms compared to heterosexual girls. Likewise, a more recent investigation by Reuter, Kalpackci, Choi, and Temple (2016) investigated the link between sexual minority orientation and BPD in an ethnically diverse sample of adolescents. By controlling for other forms of psychopathology, Reuter et al. (2016) were able to test whether the higher prevalence of BPD symptoms in sexual minority youth can be explained by the shared variance between BPD and other forms of psychopathology or whether a unique relationship exists between BPD symptoms and sexual minority orientation. Results revealed that adolescents who self-identified as gay, lesbian, or bisexual scored significantly higher on BPD features compared to heterosexual adolescents, over and above depression and anxiety (Reuter et al., 2016). Thus, it appears that the association between BPD symptoms and sexual orientation in community adolescents cannot be fully explained by higher rates of other forms of psychopathology.

Why Are Personality Disorders More Common in Sexual Minority Populations?

Overall, the extant research substantiates a higher prevalence of personality disorders in sexual minority adults and youth in both clinical and community settings, relative to adults and youth who identify as heterosexual. An important question, therefore, is why this disparity exists. Although several theories have been put forth, many hypotheses are speculative and lack empirical support. One set of theories proposes that the link between sexual orientation and personality pathology can be explained by the social stigma that sexual minority individuals face. Research shows that sexual minority individuals are more likely to experience traumatic stressors or adverse childhood experiences (Andersen & Blosnich, 2013), which have been shown to increase risk for personality pathology (Björkenstam, Ekselius, Burström, Kosidou, & Björkenstam, 2017). For example, Kalichman et al. (2001) found that gay and bisexual men who reported experiencing sexual coercion also endorsed a greater number of BPD symptoms compared to those who did not. Another hypothesis is that, because of the dominant heteronormativity of many cultures, sexual minority youth experience more identity confusion and have more difficulty resolving identity conflicts during identity formation (Silverstein, 1988; see also Cass, 1979; McCarn & Fassinger, 1996; and Troiden, 1989 for detailed models of sexual identity formation in minority populations). Identity disturbance, which is characterized by a markedly and persistently unstable self-image or sense of self, is a major component of personality disorders, most notably BPD (APA, 2013). As such, the confusion experienced by sexual minority youth during identity development may at times resemble the identity disturbances associated with personality pathology. In a similar vein, Reuter et al. (2016) hypothesized that the negative social consequences of "coming out" may trigger intense fear regarding real or imagined abandonment, which is one of nine possible symptoms of BPD (APA, 2013). Thus, according to some theorists, the process of forming and disclosing a sexual minority identity may mimic or even cause symptoms that are consistent with personality pathology as defined in the DSM.

Minority stress theories expand on the idea that sexual minorities experience higher rates of psychopathology due to the stigma and discrimination they encounter in their daily lives by describing specific mediators in this process (Meyer, 1995). According to the minority stress theory, experiences of discrimination, isolation, and negative implicit and explicit messages about sexual minorities generate substantial stress over time and persistently invalidate an individual's experiences, which in turn increases vulnerability to rumination, internalized homophobia, and expectations of rejection in social situations. These processes can then lead to impaired self-functioning, such as chronic feelings of emptiness, identity disturbance, or emotional reactivity (Reuter et al., 2016). Consistent with this theory, Eaton (2014) found that history of discrimination based on sexual orientation was associated with more severe internalizing and externalizing psychopathology, of which borderline and antisocial personality disorder were components. Together, these theories suggest that examining the role of discrimination, prejudice, and harassment as a potential etiological pathway to personality pathology in sexual minorities warrants further examination.

Developmental theories can also provide a framework for understanding the link between personality pathology and sexual orientation. According to Linehan's (1993) cognitive-behavioral model of BPD, a child's biological predisposition toward emotional reactivity interacts with a chronic invalidating environment to elevate risk of BPD. Over time, chronic dismissal of the child's emotional and cognitive experiences is believed to impede their ability to manage their own internal experiences, ultimately contributing to the extreme dysregulation characteristic of BPD. Interestingly, amygdala connectivity, which plays an important role in emotion regulation, has been found to differ between heterosexual and sexual minority individuals (Savic & Lindstrom, 2008). Thus, it has been hypothesized that some sexual minority individuals may possess biological or genetic factors that increase their risk for BPD when combined with invalidating environments early in life (Reuter et al., 2016). That said, prospective studies are needed to determine whether invalidation in early childhood, or its converse, explains the elevated prevalence of BPD pathology in sexual minority adolescents and young adults.

An alternative set of theories questions whether stigma, prejudice, or discrimination has created bias in the research evidence that has been marshaled to suggest a higher prevalence of personality pathology in sexual minorities, rather than reflecting a true difference or a causal mechanism. For instance, research has documented clinical biases in the way personality disorders are commonly diagnosed. Clinicians are more likely to diagnose BPD in women compared to men with identical symptoms (Becker & Lamb, 1994). It has been hypothesized that this gender bias may extend to gay and bisexual men who are perceived as feminine or as breaking heterosexual male norms, which could contribute to an apparently higher prevalence of BPD in the absence of a true difference in symptom severity or presentation. Similarly, Falco (1991) proposed that individuals who are confused or uncertain or have difficulty accepting their sexual orientation, as well as those who experience rejection when they share their sexual orientation, often experience impulsivity, affective instability, anger, and intense or chaotic relationships as they navigate this "coming out" process, all of which correspond with BPD symptoms. In fact, a study by Eubanks-Carter and Goldfried (2006) presented psychologists with a vignette depicting a hypothetical client whose problems could be interpreted as either BPD or a struggle with sexual identity, and found that clinicians were more likely to diagnose BPD in male clients whom they perceived as likely to be gay or bisexual, as well as male clients with partners of an unspecified gender. This finding lends credence to the idea that clinician misdiagnosis may be one of the factors that contributes to the apparently higher prevalence of personality pathology in sexual minority populations. Critical research that seeks to disentangle the multiple roles that stigma, prejudice, and discrimination may play in these relationships is sorely needed.

How Common Are Personality Disorders in Gender Minorities?

Research on the prevalence, impact, and course of personality disorders in gender minority populations is even scarcer than research on sexual minorities. To date, no large-scale epidemiological studies have examined the prevalence of personality disorders in gender minorities. What studies exist have predominately examined personality pathology among clinical samples of patients with formal diagnoses of gender identity disorder (now gender dysphoria) and who have received and/or requested gender reassignment therapy (see Lingiardi, Giovanardi, Fortunato, Nassisi, & Speranza, 2017; see Madeddu, Prunas, & Hartman, 2009). Other gender minority populations, such as individuals who are not seeking gender reassignment therapy and/or identify as nonbinary/genderqueer, bigender, genderfluid, or agender, have been grossly overlooked by personality research. Accordingly, much of the current literature only represents the lived experiences of some gender minorities who, de facto, may be experiencing greater gender dysphoria and psychological distress (including personality pathology) than their peers who are not seeking clinical services (see Lawrence & Zucker, 2012; Lingiardi et al., 2017; Madeddu et al., 2009).

The estimated prevalence of personality disorders in people with gender identity disorder or gender dysphoria ranges from 15 to 65 percent (Cole, O'Boyle, Emory, & Meyer, 1997; Deiana et al., 2016; Haraldsen & Dahl, 2000; Hepp, Kraemer, Schnyder, Miller, & Delsignore, 2005; Heylens et al., 2014; Lingiardi et al., 2017; Madeddu et al., 2009; Miach, Berah, Butcher, & Rouse, 2000). Although few studies formally compare these estimates to a comparable control group without gender dysphoria, these rates far exceed the estimated 10 percent prevalence of personality disorders in nonclinical populations (e.g., Grant et al., 2004; see Lawrence, & Zucker, 2012). In fact, personality pathology appears to be significantly more prevalent in individuals with gender dysphoria than in cisgender, heterosexual populations (Bodlund & Kullgren, 1996; Duišin et al., 2014). Adults with a diagnosis of gender identity disorder also have significantly higher rates of comorbid personality pathology compared to their cisgender, heterosexual counterparts (Bodlund & Kullgren, 1996; Duišin et al., 2014). In terms of specific diagnoses, Cluster B personality disorders are more common in individuals with gender identity disorder compared to Cluster A or Cluster C personality disorders (e.g., Bodlund & Kullgren, 1996; Haraldsen & Dahl, 2000; Hepp et al., 2005; Madeddu et al., 2009; Meybodi, Hajebi, & Jolfaei, 2014; Miach et al., 2000), with estimated prevalences of 8 to 23 percent for Cluster B disorders, 2 to 16 percent for Cluster A disorders, and 6 to 19 percent for Cluster C disorders. It is worth noting, however, that a more recent cross-European study of individuals seeking gender reassignment therapy revealed Cluster C personality disorders to be most common (63 percent of personality disorders reported), followed by Cluster B (45 percent) and Cluster A (41 percent), with borderline (5 percent), avoidant (4 percent), and schizoid (7 percent) personality disorders as most frequently reported (Heylens et al., 2014).

While a handful of studies have compared the prevalence of personality pathology in trans men versus trans women, findings so far are mixed. Most studies have found no significant differences between trans men and trans women (e.g., Cole et al., 1997; Hepp et al., 2005; Madeddu et al., 2009), yet some results do not support this pattern. For instance, in a sample of twelve trans men and thirty-nine trans women who requested gender reassignment therapy, Levine (1980) reported a higher prevalence of personality disorders in trans women (74.4 percent) than trans men (41.67 percent), with a total of forty-three personality disorder diagnoses given to twenty-nine trans women and a total of six diagnoses given to five trans men. A study by Meybodi et al. (2014) also revealed significantly more personality disorders in trans women (89.7 percent) than in trans men (71 percent) requesting gender reassignment therapy, with significantly greater frequency of schizoid, schizotypal, and avoidant personality disorders in trans women than in trans men. Finally, Deiana et al. (2016) found significantly more features of histrionic personality disorder in trans women than in trans men undertaking gender reassignment therapy at a university clinic. Overall, small studies of clinical populations indicate a high burden of personality pathology among gender minorities, especially among trans women. However, given the unrepresentative nature of these small clinical samples, these results may not generalize to nonclinical and other understudied populations of gender minorities. More research on personality disorder prevalence should therefore be conducted to better capture the diversity in lived experience among gender minority populations.

Why Might Personality Disorders Be More Common in Gender Minority Populations?

By far the most common explanation for the high rates of personality pathology observed in treatment-seeking gender minority individuals is that both personality pathology and gender dysphoria arise from the persistent psychosocial distress that many gender minorities experience (e.g., Haraldsen & Dahl, 2000; Singh, McMain, & Zucker, 2011; Smith, Cohen, & Cohen-Kettenis, 2002). In fact, some clinicians posit that personality disorders may emerge as a maladaptive way of coping with gender dysphoria, or with the extremely high rates of prejudice, discrimination, and violence or threats of violence that affect gender minorities (see Bockting, Knudson, & Goldberg, 2006; Haraldsen & Dahl, 2000; Kockott & Fahrner, 1988). Compounding this relationship, studies suggest that personality pathology is an important predictor of difficulties in adapting to life during and after gender reassignment therapy (e.g., Bodlund & Kullgren, 1996; Duišin, Rakić, Barisić, & Nikolić-Balkoski, 2008; Landén, Wålinder, Hambert, & Lundström, 1998). Further research on the etiology of comorbid personality pathology and gender dysphoria, as well as research into personality functioning among gender minority individuals who do not experience gender dysphoria, is needed to inform care for gender minorities.

Given the suggestive findings that gender minorities may experience much higher rates of personality psychopathology relative to cisgender individuals, some researchers have proposed that symptoms of gender dysphoria may be explained by an underlying personality pathology, namely BPD, at least in some individuals (Beatrice, 1985; Lothstein, 1984; see Singh et al., 2011). Unstable identity has been conceptualized as a key feature of BPD (Jørgensen, 2006; 2010), with "identity disturbance" forming a diagnostic criterion for borderline personality disorder since the DSM-III-R (APA, 1987). While the DSM-5 (APA, 2013) includes no specific examples of disturbances in identity, earlier versions of the DSM explicitly listed gender (or sexual) identity as a potential type of identity disturbance (see APA, 1987, 1994). As such, earlier researchers have questioned the validity of gender dysphoria as a separate nosological entity and instead conceptualized it as a part or variant of BPD (e.g., Beatrice, 1985; Lothstein, 1984), even recommending the abandonment of gender reassignment therapy in gender minorities with comorbid gender dysphoria and personality disorders (see Levine, 1980). Despite these suggestions, empirical studies have largely failed to confirm this view. For instance, in a clinical vignette study, ninety clinicians were asked to assess thirty-five possible indicators of identity disturbance, including gender identity conflict, in outpatients with BPD, another personality disorder, or no personality disorder (Wilkinson-Ryan & Westen, 2000). Patients with BPD were evaluated as significantly more "conflicted or unsure about [their] own gender" relative to patients without personality pathology; however, of the thirty-five indicators in total, gender identity conflict received a relatively low ranking (rank 32), suggesting that uncertainty with gender identity may not be a particularly salient aspect of identity disturbance associated with BPD (Wilkinson-Ryan & Westen, 2000). Additionally, a study by Singh et al. (2011) examined the presence of gender identity disturbances in a sample of a hundred clinic-referred cisgender women newly diagnosed with BPD using a well-validated self-report measure of past-year gender dysphoria. The results did not show evidence of marked gender identity disturbances in cisgender women with BPD (Singh et al., 2011). Taken together, these findings support the independence of gender dysphoria and BPD.

What Is Needed to Advance This Field?

Research regarding the prevalence, causes, and consequences of personality pathology among sexual and gender minorities is still in its infancy. So far, however, personality disorders appear to be more prevalent in sexual and gender minorities, relative to individuals who identify as heterosexual and/or cisgender, and this overrepresentation does not seem to be fully accounted for by overall higher rates and severity of psychopathology in sexual and gender minorities. The reasons for the higher burden of personality pathology in sexual and gender minorities, however, remain unclear.

Accordingly, this chapter highlights three future directions for research and clinical practice that are critical for advancing this field. First, it is important to keep in mind that the DSM specifies that personality disorders should be diagnosed "when inner experience or behavior *differ markedly from the expectations of the individual's culture*" (APA, 2013, p. 645, emphasis added) and that "judgements about personality functioning must take into account the individual's ethnic, cultural, and social background" (APA, 2013, p. 648). Making an appropriate diagnosis of personality disorders in sexual or gender minorities will therefore require a nuanced understanding of normal identity, emotional, behavioral, and interpersonal functioning within these cultural groups. Clinicians must be cautious not to impose their own values or norms about what is "normal" versus "pathological" onto clients whose social backgrounds differ from their own and should be mindful of their cultural competencies in working with diverse populations. In the absence of more developed research regarding unique subcultural norms, clinicians may wish to seek consultation, training, supervision, or informants from the client's own cultural group in order to determine whether a particular symptom violates the norms or expectancies of that group. Familiarity with major theories of identity formation in sexual and gender minorities (e.g., Cass, 1979; McCarn & Fassinger, 1996; Troiden, 1989) may help clinicians disentangle pathological from normative personality development and functioning. Clinicians and researchers alike must be sensitive to both the need to accurately document the mental health needs of sexual and gender minorities, and the need to avoid inaccurately or unnecessarily pathologizing or stigmatizing the experiences of an already vulnerable population. Dimensional models of personality pathology, which are increasingly being adopted by researchers and clinicians, may facilitate more nuance regarding specific domains of risk and resilience, and promote early identification of personality pathology and its treatment (Reuter et al., 2016).

A second area in which need for clinical competence is likely to outpace extant research is in applying an intersectional lens to understanding personality functioning in sexual and gender minority populations. In brief, intersectionality examines and acknowledges how multiple aspects of social and political stigma, prejudice, and discrimination may impact an individual's experience, particularly when an individual identifies with multiple minority groups (Crenshaw, 1989). Nearly all of the studies reviewed in this chapter are drawn from WEIRD (i.e., Western, educated, industrialized, rich, democratic; Henrich, Heine, & Norenzayan, 2010) countries, and most examine only one salient aspect of identity at a time (e.g., comparing transgender people to cisgender people, without examining how race or ethnicity might moderate the experiences of these groups). Research that includes a broader range of specific gender and sexual identities (e.g., genderqueer, nonbinary, asexual), ideally with large, diverse samples that are adequately powered to examine moderating effects, is sorely needed.

Finally, there is a critical need for increased research into the etiology of personality pathology in sexual and gender minority populations using rigorous longitudinal designs that can elucidate both risk and protective factors. As noted in this chapter, several competing hypotheses have been put forth to explain the apparent surplus of personality disorders in sexual and gender minority populations. Some of these hypotheses go so far as to question whether this overabundance of personality pathology is genuine, or whether it could be better explained by diagnostic, clinician, or cultural biases, whereas others posit various environmental, developmental, and interpersonal explanations. However, these hypotheses should be met with keen and rigorous testing. Given that personality pathology is thought to emerge during adolescence and early adulthood (APA, 2013), studies focusing on this developmental period could drastically help us better understand when and why personality pathology develops in sexual and gender minorities. Moreover, longitudinal designs might help us untangle how the processes of sexual and gender identity formation impact personality functioning, and vice versa, during a critically sensitive developmental window. This research, in turn, would have significant implications for support and prevention efforts that could be offered to at-risk youth. Together, addressing these three future directions would substantially enhance researchers' and clinicians' understanding of and ability to respond to the needs of sexual and gender minority populations.

References

American Psychiatric Association. (1980). *Diagnostic and statistical manual of mental disorders* (3rd ed.). Washington, DC: American Psychiatric Association.

American Psychiatric Association. (1987). *Diagnostic and statistical manual of mental disorders* (3rd ed., text rev.). Washington, DC: American Psychiatric Association.

American Psychiatric Association. (1994). *Diagnostic and statistical manual of mental disorders* (4th ed.). Washington, DC: American Psychiatric Association.

American Psychiatric Association. (2013). *Diagnostic and statistical manual of mental disorders* (5th ed.). Arlington, VA: American Psychiatric Association.

Andersen, J. P., & Blosnich, J. (2013). Disparities in adverse childhood experiences among sexual minority and heterosexual adults: Results from a multi-state probability-based sample. *PLoS One*, *8*(1), e54691. doi:10.1371/journal.pone.0054691

Beatrice, J. (1985). A psychological comparison of heterosexuals, transvestites, preoperative transsexuals, and postoperative transsexuals. *Journal of Nervous and Mental Disease*, *173*(6), 358–65. doi:10.1097/00005053-198506000-00006

Becker, D., & Lamb, S. (1994). Sex bias in the diagnosis of borderline personality disorder and posttraumatic stress disorder. *Professional Psychology: Research and Practice*, *25*(1), 55. doi:10.1037/0735-7028.25.1.55

Beckwith, H., Moran, P. F., & Reilly, J. (2014). Personality disorder prevalence in psychiatric outpatients: A systematic literature review. *Personality and Mental Health*, *8*(2), 91–101. doi:10.1002/pmh.1252

Björkenstam, E., Ekselius, L., Burström, B., Kosidou, K., & Björkenstam, C. (2017). Association between childhood adversity and a diagnosis of personality disorder in young adulthood: A cohort study of 107,287 individuals in Stockholm County. *European Journal of Epidemiology*, *32*(8), 721–31. doi:10.1007/s10654-017-0264-9

Bockting, W., Knudson, G., & Goldberg, J. M. (2006). Counselling and mental health care of transgender adults and loved ones [PDF file]. (Vancouver Coastal Health, Trenscend Transgender Support & Education Society, and the Canadian Rainbow Health Coalition). http://www.amsa.org/AMSA/Libraries/Com-mitteeDocs/CounselingAndMentalHealthCareOfTransgend-erAdultsAndLovedOnes.sflb.ashx.

Bodlund, O., & Kullgren, G. (1996). Transsexualism—general outcome and prognostic factors: A five-year follow-up study of nineteen transsexuals in the process of changing sex. *Archives of Sexual Behavior*, *25*(3), 303–16. doi:10.1007/BF02438167

Bolton, S. L., & Sareen, J. (2011). Sexual orientation and its relation to mental disorders and suicide attempts: Findings from a nationally representative sample. *Canadian Journal of Psychiatry, 56*(1), 35–43. doi:10.1177/070674371105600107

Bostwick, W. B., Boyd, C. J., Hughes, T. L., & McCabe, S. E. (2010). Dimensions of sexual orientation and the prevalence of mood and anxiety disorders in the United States. *American Journal of Public Health, 100*(3), 468–75. doi:10.2105/AJPH.2008.152942

Cass, V. (1979). Homosexual identity formation: A theoretical model. *Journal of Homosexuality, 4*, 219–35. doi:10.1300/J082v04n03_01

Cochran, S. D., & Mays, V. M. (2000). Relation between psychiatric syndromes and behaviorally defined sexual orientation in a sample of the US population. *American Journal of Epidemiology, 151*(5), 516–23. doi:10.1093/oxfordjournals.aje.a010238

Coid, J., Yang, M., Tyrer, P., Roberts, A., & Ullrich, S. (2006). Prevalence and correlates of personality disorder in Great Britain. *British Journal of Psychiatry, 188*, 423–31. doi:10.1192/bjp.188.5.423

Cole, C. M., O'Boyle, M., Emory, L. E., & Meyer III, W. J. (1997). Comorbidity of gender dysphoria and other major psychiatric diagnoses. *Archives of Sexual Behavior, 26*(1), 13–26. doi:10.1023/A:1024517302481

Crenshaw, K. (1989). Demarginalizing the intersection of race and sex: A black feminist critique of antidiscrimination doctrine, feminist theory, and antiracist politics. *University of Chicago Legal Forum, 1989*(1), 139–67. https://chicagounbound.uchicago.edu/cgi/viewcontent.cgi?article=1052&context=ucl

Crocq, M. (2013). Milestones in the history of personality disorders. *Dialogues in Clinical Neuroscience, 15*(2), 147–53.

Deiana, V., Corda, E., Bandecchi, C., Pintore, S., Pinna, F., Pusceddu, R.,... Carpiniello, B. (2016). Personality traits and personality disorders in gender dysphoria. *European Psychiatry, 33*(Suppl.), S734. doi:10.1016/j.eurpsy.2016.01.2191

Dereboy, C., Güzel, H. S., Dereboy, F., Okyay, P., & Eskin, M. (2014). Personality disorders in a community sample in Turkey: Prevalence, associated risk factors, temperament and character dimensions. *International Journal of Social Psychiatry, 60*(2), 139–47. doi:10.1177/0020764012471596

Dixon-Gordon, K. L., Turner, B. J., & Chapman, A. L. (2011). Psychotherapy for personality disorders. *International Review of Psychiatry, 23*(3), 282–302. doi:10.3109/09540261.2011.586992

Duišin, D., Batinić, B., Barišić, J., Djordjevic, M. L., Vujović, S., & Bizic, M. (2014). Personality disorders in persons with gender identity disorder. *The Scientific World Journal, 2014*, 1–7. doi:10.1155/2014/809058

Duišin, D., Rakić, Z., Barisić, J., & Nikolić-Balkoski, G. (2008). A transsexual patient searching for adjustment. *Serbian Archives of Medicine, 136*(7–8), 406–9. doi:10.2298/SARH0808406D

Dulit, R. A., Fyer, M. R., Miller, F. T., Sacks, M. H., & Frances, A. J. (1993). Gender differences in sexual preference and substance abuse of inpatients with borderline personality disorder. *Journal of Personality Disorders, 7*, 182–5. doi:10.1521/pedi.1993.7.2.182

Eaton, N. R. (2014). Trans-diagnostic psychopathology factors and sexual minority mental health: Evidence of disparities and associations with minority stressors. *Psychology of Sexual Orientation and Gender Diversity, 1*(3), 244–54. doi:10.1037/sgd000004

Eaton, N. R., South, S. C., & Krueger, R. F. (2010). The meaning of comorbidity among common mental disorders. In T. Millon, R. F. Krueger, & E. Simonsen (Eds.), *Contemporary directions in psychopathology: Scientific foundations of the DSM-V and ICD-11* (pp. 223–41). New York, NY: Guilford Press.

Eubanks-Carter, C., & Goldfried, M. R. (2006). The impact of client sexual orientation and gender on clinical judgements and diagnosis of borderline personality disorder. *Journal of Clinical Psychology, 62*(6), 751–70. doi:10.1002/jclp.20265

Falco, K. L. (1991). *Psychotherapy with lesbian clients: Theory into practice*. New York, NY: Brunner/Mazel.

Fazel, S., & Danesh, J. (2002). Serious mental disorder in 23000 prisoners: a systematic review of 62 surveys. *Lancet, 359*(9306), 545–50. doi:10.1016/S0140-6736(02)07740-1

Fok, M. L., Hayes, R. D., Chang, C. K., Stewart, R., Callard, F. J., & Moran, P. (2012). Life expectancy at birth and all-cause mortality among people with personality disorder. *Journal of Psychosomatic Research, 73*(2), 104–7. doi:10.1016/j.jpsychores.2012.05.001

Frankenburg, F. R., & Zanarini, M. C. (2004). The association between borderline personality disorder and chronic medical illnesses, poor health-related lifestyle choices, and costly forms of health care utilization. *Journal of Clinical Psychiatry, 65*(12), 1660–5. doi:10.4088/JCP.v65n1211

Grant, B. F., Chou, S. P., Goldstein, R. B., Huang, B., Stinson, F. S., Saha, T.D.,... Ruan, W. J. (2008). Prevalence, correlates, disability, and comorbidity of DSM-IV borderline personality disorder: Results from the Wave 2 National Epidemiologic Survey on Alcohol and Related Conditions. *Journal of Clinical Psychiatry, 69*(4), 533–45. doi:10.4088/JCP.v69n0701

Grant, B. F., Hasin, D. S., Stinson, F. S., Dawson, D. A., Chou, S. P., Ruan, W. J., & Pickering, R. P. (2004). Prevalence, correlates, and disability of personality disorders in the United States: Results from the National Epidemiologic Survey on Alcohol and Related Conditions. *Journal of Clinical Psychiatry, 65*(7), 948–58. doi:10.4088/JCP.v65n0711

Haraldsen, I. R., & Dahl, A. A. (2000). Symptom profiles of gender dysphoric patients of transsexual type compared to patients with personality disorders and healthy adults. *Acta Psychiatrica Scandinavica, 102*(4), 276–81. doi:10.1034/j.1600-0447.2000.102004276.x

Henrich, J., Heine, S. J., & Norenzayan, A. (2010). The weirdest people in the world? *Behavioral and Brain Sciences, 33*(2/3), 1–75. doi:10.1017/S0140525X0999152X

Hepp, U., Kraemer, B., Schnyder, U., Miller, N., & Delsignore, A. (2005). Psychiatric comorbidity in gender identity disorder. *Journal of Psychosomatic Research, 58*, 259–61. doi:10.1016/j.jpsychores.2004.08.010

Heylens, G., Elaut, E., Kreukels, B. P. C., Paap, M. C. S., Cerwenka, S., Richter-Appelt, H.,... De Cuypere, G. (2014). Psychiatric characteristics in transsexual individuals: A multi-centre study in four European countries. *British Journal of Psychiatry, 204*, 151–6. doi:10.1192/bjp.bp.112.121954

Hiroeh, U., Appleby, L., Mortensen, P. B., & Dunn, G. (2001). Death by homicide, suicide, and other unnatural causes in people with mental illness: A population-based study. *Lancet, 358*(9299), 2110–2. doi:10.1016/S0140-6736(01)07216-6

Jackson, H. J., & Burgess, P. M. (2004). Personality disorders in the community: Results from the Australian National Survey of Mental Health and Well-being Part III. Relationships between specific type of personality disorder, Axis 1 mental disorders and physical conditions with disability and health consultations. *Social Psychiatry and Psychiatric Epidemiology, 37*(6), 251–60. doi:10.1007/s001270200017

Jørgensen, C. R. (2006). Disturbed sense of identity in borderline personality disorder. *Journal of Personality Disorders, 20*(6), 618–44. doi:10.1521/pedi.2006.20.6.618

Jørgensen, C. R. (2010). Invited essay: Identity and borderline personality disorder. *Journal of Personality Disorders, 24*(3), 344–64. doi:10.1521/pedi.2010.24.3.344.

Kalichman, S. C., Benotsch, E., Rompa, D., Gore-Felton, C., Austin, J., Luke, W., . . . Simpson, D. (2001). Unwanted sexual experiences and sexual risks in gay and bisexual men: Associations among revictimization, substance use, and psychiatric symptoms. *Journal of Sex Research, 38*, 1–9. doi:10.1080/00224490109552065

Karterud, S., Vaglum, S., Friis, S., Irion, T., Johns, S., & Vaglum, P. (1992). Day hospital therapeutic community treatment for patients with personality disorders. *Journal of Nervous and Mental Disorders, 180*(4), 238–43. doi:10.1097/00005053-199204000-00005

Kerridge, B. T., Pickering, R. P., Saha, T. D., Ruan, W. J., Chou, S. P., Zhang, H., . . . Hasin, D. S. (2017). Prevalence, sociodemographic correlates and DSM-5 substance use disorders and other psychiatric disorders among sexual minorities in the United States. *Drug and Alcohol Dependence, 170*, 82–92. doi:10.1016/j.drugalcdep.2016.10.038

Kockott, G., & Fahrner, E.-M. (1988). Male-to-female and female-to-male transsexuals: A comparison. *Archives of Sexual Behavior, 17*(6), 539–46. doi:10.1007/BF01542341

Krueger, R. F., & Markon, K. E. (2006). Reinterpreting comorbidity: A model-based approach to understanding and classifying psychopathology. *Annual Review of Clinical Psychology, 2*, 111–33. doi:10.1146/annurev.clinpsy.2.022305.095213

Landén, M., Wålinder, J., Hambert, G., & Lundström, B. (1998). Factors predictive of regret in sex reassignment. *Acta Psychiatrica Scandinavica, 97*(4), 284–9. doi:10.1111/j.1600-0447.1998.tb10001.x

Lawrence, A., & Zucker, K. J. (2012). Gender identity disorders. In M. Hersen & D. C. Beidel (Eds.), *Adult psychopathology and diagnosis* (6th ed., pp. 601–35). Hoboken, NJ: Wiley.

Lenzenweger, M. F., Lane, M. C., Loranger, A. W., & Kessler, R. C. (2007). DSM-IV personality disorders in the National Comorbidity Survey Replication. *Biological Psychiatry, 62*(2), 553–64. doi:10.1016/j.biopsych.2006.09.019

Levine, S. B. (1980). Psychiatric diagnosis of patients requesting sex reassignment surgery. *Journal of Sex & Marital Therapy, 6*(3), 164–73. doi:10.1080/00926238008406081

Lewis, G., & Appleby, L. (1988). Personality disorder: The patients psychiatrists dislike. *British Journal of Psychiatry, 153*, 44–59. doi:10.1192/bjp.153.1.44

Linehan, M. M. (1993). *Diagnosis and treatment of mental disorders. Cognitive-behavioral treatment of borderline personality disorder.* New York, NY: Guilford Press.

Lingiardi, V., Giovanardi, G., Fortunato, A., Nassisi, V., & Speranza, A. M. (2017). Personality and attachment in transsexual adults. *Archives of Sexual Behavior, 46*, 1313–23. doi:10.1007/s10508-017-0946-0

Lothstein, L. M. (1984). Psychological testing with transsexuals: A 30-year review. *Journal of Personality Assessment, 48*(5), 500–7. doi:10.1207/s15327752jpa4805_9

Madeddu, F., Prunas, A., & Hartmann, D. (2009). Prevalence of Axis II disorders in a sample of clients undertaking psychiatric evaluation for sex reassignment surgery. *Psychiatric Quarterly, 80*, 261–7. doi:10.1007/s11126-009-9114-6

Marshal, M. P., Sucato, G., Stepp, S. D., Hipwell, A., Smith, H. A., Friedman, M. S., . . . Markovic, N. (2012). Substance use and mental health disparities among sexual minority girls: Results from the Pittsburgh Girls Study. *Journal of Pediatric and Adolescent Gynecology, 25*, 15–8. doi:10.1016/j.jpag.2011.06.011

Mathy, R. M. (2002). Suicidality and sexual orientation in five continents: Asia, Australia, Europe, North America, and South America. *International Journal of Sexuality and Gender Studies, 7*(2–3), 215–25. doi:10.1023/A:1015853302054

McCabe, S. E., Hughes, T. L., Bostwick, W. B., West, B. T., & Boyd, C. J. (2009). Sexual orientation, substance use behaviors and substance dependence in the United States. *Addiction, 104*(8), 1333–45. doi:10.1111/j.1360-0443.2009.02596.x

McCarn, S. R., & Fassinger, R. E. (1996). Revisioning sexual minority identity formation: A new model of lesbian identity and its implications for counseling and research. *The Counseling Psychologist, 24*(3), 508–34. doi:10.1177/0011000096243011

Meybodi, A. M., Hajebi, A., & Jolfaei, A. G. (2014). The frequency of personality disorders in patients with gender identity disorder. *Medical Journal of the Islamic Republic of Iran, 28*(1), 582–7.

Meyer, I. H. (1995). Minority stress and mental health in gay men. *Journal of Health and Social Behavior, 36*(1), 38–56. doi:10.2307/2137286

Miach, P. P., Berah, E. F., Butcher, J. N., & Rouse, S. (2000). Utility of the MMPI-2 in assessing gender dysphoric patients. *Journal of Personality Assessment*, 75(2), 268–79. doi:10.1207/S15327752JPA7502_7

Moran, P., Romaniuk, H., Coffey, C., Chanen, A., Degenhardt, L., Borschmann, R., & Patton, G. C. (2016). The influence of personality disorder on the future mental health and social adjustment of young adults: A population-based, longitudinal cohort study. *Lancet, 3*(7), 636–45. doi:10.1016/S2215-0366(16)30029-3

National Alliance to End Homelessness. (2015). *How can we prevent the sexual exploitation of LGBT youth.* https://endhomelessness.org/how-can-we-prevent-the-sexual-exploitation-of-lgbt-youth/

Newton-Howes, G., Tyrer, P., Anagnostakis, K., Cooper, S., Bowden-Jones, O., Weaver, T. & COSMIC study team (2010). The prevalence of personality disorder, its comorbidity with mental state disorders, and its clinical significance in community mental health teams. *Social Psychiatry and Psychiatric Epidemiology, 45*(4), 453–60. doi:10.1007/s00127-009-0084-7.

Ochs, R. (1996). Biphobia: It goes more than two ways. In B. A. Firestein (Ed.), *Bisexuality: The psychology and politics of an invisible minority* (pp. 217–39). Thousand Oaks, CA: Sage.

Paris, J., Zweig-Frank, H., & Guzder, J. (1995). Psychological factors associated with homosexuality in males with borderline personality disorder. *Journal of Personality Disorders, 9*, 56–61. doi:10.1521/pedi.1995.9.1.56

Reich, D. B., & Zanarini, M. C. (2008). Sexual orientation and relationship choice in borderline personality disorder over ten years of prospective follow-up. *Journal of Personality Disorders, 22*(6), 564–72. doi:10.1521/pedi.2008.22.6.564.

Reuter, T. R., Sharp, C., Kalpackci, A. H., Choi, H. J., & Temple, J. R. (2016). Sexual orientation and borderline personality disorder features in a community sample of adolescents. *Journal of Personality Disorders, 30*(5). 694–707. doi:10.1521/pedi_2015_29_2

Samuels, J., Eaton, W. W., Bienvenu, O. J., Brown, C. H., Costa, P. T., & Nestadt, G. (2002). Prevalence and correlates of personality disorders in a community sample. *British Journal of Psychiatry, 180,* 536–42. doi:10.1192/bjp.180.6.536

Sandfort, T. G., De Graaf, R., & Bijl, R. V. (2003). Same-sex sexuality and quality of life: Findings from the Netherlands Mental Health Survey and Incidence Study. *Archives of Sexual Behavior, 32*(1), 5–22. doi:10.1023/A:1021885127560

Savic, I., & Lindström, P. (2008). PET and MRI show differences in cerebral asymmetry and functional connectivity between homo- and heterosexual subjects. *Proceedings of the National Academy of Sciences of the United States of America, 105*(27), 9403–8. doi:10.1073/pnas.0801566105

Savin-Williams, R. C. (2006). Who's gay? Does it matter? *Current Directions in Psychological Science, 15*(1), 40–4. doi:10.1111/j.0963-7214.2006.00403.x

Schulte-Herbrüggen, O., Ahlers, C. J., Kronsbein, J. M., Ruter, A., Bahri, S., Vater, A., & Roepke, S. (2009). Impaired sexual function in patients with borderline personality disorder is determined by history of sexual abuse. *Journal of Sexual Medicine, 6,* 3356–63. doi:0.1111/j.1743-6109.2009.01422.x

Scott, J. (1993). Homelessness and mental health. *British Journal of Psychiatry, 162*(3), 314–24. doi:10.1192/bjp.162.3.314

Shea, M. T., Pilkonis, P. A., Beckham, E., & Collins, J. F. (1990). Personality disorders and treatment outcome in the NIMH treatment of depression collaborative research program. *American Journal of Psychiatry, 147*(6), 711–8. doi:10.1176/ajp.147.6.711

Silverstein, C. (1988). The borderline personality disorder and gay people. *Journal of Homosexuality, 15*(1–2), 185–212. doi:10.1300/J082v15n01_13

Singh, D., McMain, S., & Zucker, K. J. (2011). Gender identity and sexual orientation in women with borderline personality disorder. *Journal of Sexual Medicine, 8,* 447–57. doi:10.1111/j.1743-6109.2010.02086.x

Skodol, A. E., Gunderson, J. G., McGlashan, T. H., Dyck, I. R., Stout, R. L., Bender, D. S.,... Oldham, J. M. (2002). Functional impairment in patients with schizotypal, borderline, avoidant, or obsessive-compulsive personality disorder. *American Journal of Psychiatry, 159*(2), 276–83. doi:10.1176/appi.ajp.159.2.276

Skodol, A. W., Johnson, J. G., Cohen, P., Sneed, J. R., & Crawford, T. N. (2007). Personality disorder and impaired functioning from adolescence to adulthood. *British Journal of Psychiatry, 190,* 415–20. doi:10.1192/bjp.bp.105.019364

Smith, Y. L. S., Cohen, L., & Cohen-Kettenis, P. T. (2002). Postoperative psychological functioning of adolescent transsexuals: A Rorschach study. *Archives of Sexual Behavior, 31*(3), 255–61. doi:10.1023/A:1015200919860

Stone, M. H. (1990). *The fate of borderline patients.* New York, NY: Guilford Press.

Troiden, R. R. (1989). The formation of homosexual identities. *Journal of Homosexuality, 17*(1–2), 43–73. doi:10.1300/J082v17n01_02

Volkert, J., Gablonski, T. C., & Rabung, S. (2018). Prevalence of personality disorders in the general adult population in Western countries: Systematic review and meta-analysis. *British Journal of Psychiatry, 213*(6), 709–15. doi:10.1192/bjp.2018.202.

Wilkinson-Ryan, T., & Westen, D. (2000). Identity disturbance in borderline personality disorder: An empirical investigation. *American Journal of Psychiatry, 157,* 528–41. doi:10.1176/appi.ajp.157.4.528

Woody, G. E., McLellan, T., Luborsky, L. L., & O'Brien, C. P. (1985). Sociopathy and psychotherapy outcome. *Archives of General Psychiatry, 42,* 1081–6. doi:10.1001/archpsyc.1985.01790340059009

Zanarini, M. C., Frankenburg, F. R., Reich, D. B., & Fitzmaurice, G. (2012). Attainment and stability of sustained symptomatic remission and recovery among patients with borderline personality disorder and axis II comparison subjects: A 16-year prospective follow-up study. *American Journal of Psychiatry, 169*(5), 476–483. doi:10.1176/appi.ajp.2011.11101550

Zimmerman, M., Rothschild, L., & Chelminski, I. (2005). The prevalence of DSM-IV personality disorders in psychiatric outpatients. *American Journal of Psychiatry, 162*(10), 1911–8. doi:10.1176/appi.ajp.162.10.1911

Zubenko, G. S., George, A. W., Soloff, P. H., & Schulz, S. (1987). Sexual practices among patients with borderline personality disorder. *American Journal of Psychiatry, 144,* 748–52. doi:10.1176/ajp.144.6.748

CHAPTER

14 Suicidal Behavior among Sexual and Gender Minority Populations

Ann P. Haas *and* Maggie G. Mortali

Abstract

This chapter examines the research literature about suicide and suicide attempts in sexual and gender minority (SGM) populations, comparing this information, where possible, with current knowledge of suicidal behavior in general populations. Drawing on studies across several decades, the authors identify the key research strategies used to study the prevalence and patterns of SGM suicide deaths and attempts, and discuss their contributions and limitations. Theoretical models for understanding SGM suicidal behavior and their implications for suicide prevention are also discussed. The chapter describes how understanding of SGM suicidal behavior has been limited, in particular, by the lack of routine, systematic identification of decedents' sexual orientation and gender identity at the time of death and insufficient attention to the impact of sociocultural and structural factors on SGM suicide risk.

Keywords: sexual and gender minorities, LGBT, suicide death, suicide attempt, minority stress

Suicidal behavior is not a separate diagnostic entity but co-occurs with many different mental health disorders. To improve recognition and treatment across the diverse populations in which it is observed, some experts have proposed elevating suicidal behavior to the status of a distinct mental health disorder (Oquendo & Baca-Garcia, 2014). In the fifth edition of the *Diagnostic and Statistical Manual of Mental Disorders* (American Psychiatric Association, 2013), *suicidal behavior disorder* is listed as a condition needing further study as a potential diagnosis.

As currently defined, suicidal behavior encompasses both suicide deaths and non-fatal suicide attempts. We begin this chapter with a brief discussion of suicide deaths and attempts in general populations as a background for interpreting what is known, and not known, about suicidal behavior in sexual and gender minority (SGM) populations.

Suicidal Behavior in General Populations

In the United States, data on suicide deaths are collected primarily by the National Vital Statistics System in conjunction with state vital registration systems. These systems routinely and systematically identify decedents' age, sex, race/ethnicity, and other personal and demographic characteristics, but do not identify sexual orientation and gender identity (SOGI).

In 2017, the latest year for which data are available, the age-adjusted suicide rate in the United States was 14.0; that is, 14 suicides occurred for every 100,000 people in the population (Hedegaard, Curtin, & Warner, 2018). The suicide rate in males (22.4) was about three times higher than the rate in females (6.1). Overall, the suicide rate has increased 33 percent since 1999, putting the United States among the 20 percent of the world's countries with the highest reported suicide rates (World Health Organization, 2019). In sharp contrast to trends in the United States, between 1990 and 2016 the average age-adjusted global suicide rate decreased by almost 33 percent, falling to 11.2 suicides for every 100,000 people (Naghavi, 2019).

Non-fatal suicide attempts are less systematically counted than suicide deaths but are estimated to be twenty-five to fifty times more common (Oquendo

& Baca-Garcia, 2014). In the United States, suicide attempt surveillance relies heavily on government-supported population-based surveys. Based on survey estimates, the prevalence of suicide attempts has remained fairly stable in recent decades, with about 4 to 5 percent of U.S. adults and adolescents reporting at least one lifetime suicide attempt (Kessler, Borges, & Walters, 1999; Nock et al., 2013). An estimated 0.6 percent of adults and 7 to 9 percent of adolescents report making a suicide attempt in the past twelve months (Center for Behavioral Health Statistics and Quality, 2018; Centers for Disease Control and Prevention [CDC], 2018; Kessler, Berglund, Borges, Nock, & Wang, 2005). Among both adults and adolescents, females are two to three times more likely to attempt suicide than males of comparable age.

Suicide Causation and Prevention

The most recent U.S. National Strategy for Suicide Prevention (National Action Alliance for Suicide Prevention, 2012) described suicide as a complex outcome influenced by a mix of risk and protective factors within four domains: the individual, relationships with family and others, community, and the broader society. This conceptualization is widely accepted as a guide to suicide prevention across the world, although countries vary considerably in the relative emphasis placed on each domain. In the United States and other countries in the Global North, suicide research and prevention has long emphasized individual-level factors, in particular mental health disorders, as the primary cause of suicide. Although a 2018 CDC report found that less than half (46 percent) of people who died by suicide had a known mental health condition (Stone et al., 2018), U.S. suicide prevention continues to focus largely on identifying and referring suicidal and at-risk individuals to mental health treatment (Zalsman et al., 2016).

In contrast, the recent dramatic decrease in the global suicide rate has largely occurred in the context of macro-level social, economic, and policy changes. In China, for example, the suicide rate has declined by almost two thirds over the last thirty years as a result of urbanization and the accompanying improvement in the socioeconomic status of rural women, who previously accounted for the majority of the country's suicide deaths (Wang, Chan, & Yip, 2014). In China and other countries in the Global South, policies restricting access to pesticides, a common and highly lethal method of suicide, have also played a significant role in reducing suicide at a population level (Yip et al., 2012).

Suicide Deaths in SGM Populations

No country in the world routinely and systematically identifies sexual orientation and gender identity at the time of death (Haas, Lane, Blosnich, Butcher, & Mortali, 2019). Because we lack universal surveillance data, what is known about the prevalence and patterns of suicide in SGM people has come from studies in a number of countries in the Global North, which have used a variety of research approaches.

Psychological Autopsy Studies

Several studies have used "psychological autopsy" interviews with surviving family and friends to determine whether sexual minority persons are overrepresented among suicide decedents (Renaud, Berlim, Begolli, McGirr, & Turecki, 2010; Rich, Fowler, Young, & Blenkush, 1986; Shaffer, Fisher, Hicks, Parides, & Gould, 1995). This research method was initially designed to investigate psychiatric diagnoses in decedents that may not have been identified prior to suicide (Isometsä, 2001; Kelly & Mann, 1996).

Using a limited number of consecutive suicide cases drawn from single locales in the United States (Rich et al., 1986; Shaffer et al., 1995) or Canada (Renaud et al., 2010), studies have found few informants willing or able to identify the decedent as sexual minority. In the two studies that used living control samples (Renaud et al., 2010; Shaffer et al., 1995), no sexual minority control subjects were identified. All three studies reported that minority sexual orientation was not disproportionately found among suicide decedents, although this conclusion has been challenged on methodological grounds (Plöderl et al., 2013). Nonetheless, these studies by established suicide researchers drew attention to a topic that prior to the mid-1980s had not been systematically studied.

Follow-Up Studies of Sexual Minority Survey Respondents

Using data from the Third National Health and Nutrition Examination Survey, a U.S. population-based survey administered to young and middle-aged adults beginning in the late 1980s, Cochran and Mays (2011) examined subsequent suicide mortality in the eighty-five men who reported any lifetime same-sex sexual partners. These presumably sexual minority men were matched with data from the National Death Index, a centralized database of state-level death records developed for approved health research. None of the men were found to have died by suicide during the eighteen year period from 1988 to 2006.

In a later study, Cochran and Mays (2015) examined suicide mortality in a cohort of almost 18,000 adults who provided information about the sex of their sexual partners in a General Social Survey between 1988 and 2002. Using National Death Index data up through 2008, the study was able to identify suicide mortality in participants during an average of almost twelve years after the survey. No significant difference in suicide mortality was found between men who reported any same-sex sexual partners (N = 424) and men with only opposite-sex sexual partners (N = 7,456). However, women with any same-sex sexual partners (N = 429) were six times more likely to die by suicide than women with only opposite-sex partners (N = 9,577).

A limitation of these studies is that the classification of the sample groups was based on sexual behavior reported some time in the past, which may not have matched participants' sexual behavior or orientation at the time of death. Further, the study design required a considerable time lag for observation of mortality in a sufficient number of participants, which limits the utility of findings for timely intervention.

Scandinavian Universal Register Studies

Denmark's universal registers, which contain a voluminous amount of integrated sociodemographic, economic, and health-related information about individual residents, have long been a valuable resource for suicide researchers. In 1989, when Denmark became the first country to recognize same-sex domestic partnerships, its registers became a potential source of information about sexual minority suicide. In 2003, a Danish register-based study (Qin, Agerbo, & Mortensen, 2003) reported that persons in same-sex registered partnerships were three to four times more likely than heterosexual married persons to die by suicide, although no corroborating data were presented. A subsequent analysis (Mathy, Cochran, Olsen, & Mays, 2011) found that men who entered a same-sex partnership between 1990 and 2001 were eight times more likely to die by suicide than men in heterosexual marriages, and twice as likely as never-married men. Higher prevalence of suicide was not found, however, among same-sex partnered women. A later study using register data up to 2011 (Frisch & Simonsen, 2013) confirmed an eightfold higher prevalence of suicide in same-sex partnered men compared to men in heterosexual marriages, and also found that same-sex partnered women were six times more likely to die by suicide than women in heterosexual marriages.

Sweden also registered same-sex domestic partners for several years before recognizing same-sex marriages in 2009. Reviewing the Swedish register database of almost 6,500 men and women who entered a same-sex partnership or marriage between 1996 and 2009, researchers found same-sex partnered/married individuals had significantly greater risk of suicide in the years 1996 to 2011, compared to different-sex partnered/married individuals (Björkenstam, Andersson, Dalman, Cochran, & Kosidou, 2016). An almost threefold higher risk was found in same-sex partnered/married men, and a twofold risk in same-sex coupled women.

Collectively, these findings from relatively progressive countries provide strong evidence of elevated suicide risk in same-sex partnered individuals, although these studies have not explored underlying reasons. Further, partnership/marital status may be an uncertain marker of sexual orientation at the time of death, particularly among bisexual individuals and persons who entered a partnership or marriage many years ago. In addition, these studies exclude the majority of sexual minority people who are not legally recognized as partnered.

Swedish register data have also been used to examine suicide deaths in the subset of gender minority persons who receive surgery for gender affirmation (termed "sex reassignment" in most of the research literature). Combining medical, legal, and mortality records, one large study (Dhejne et al., 2011) examined suicide mortality in 324 persons who were assigned a new legal sex following surgery in the years 1973 to 2003. Overall, the study tracked these individuals an average of eleven years after surgery. After controlling for two variables found to be significantly higher in persons receiving gender-related surgery (immigrant status and presurgery hospitalization for psychiatric morbidity other than gender identity disorder), the researchers found suicide mortality to be nineteen times higher in the surgery group compared to controls of the same birth sex. Similar results were found when individuals who had gender-related surgery were compared to controls matched on current legal sex. Within the surgery group, no significant difference in prevalence of suicide was found in persons whose current legal sex was female, compared to male.

The design of the Dhejne et al. (2011) study provided more precise findings than were previously reported in clinical follow-up studies of persons who received gender-affirming treatments in the

Netherlands (Asscheman, Giltay, Megens, van Trotsenburg, & Gooren, 2011; Asscheman, Gooren, & Eklund, 1989). However, the Swedish study sample included many participants who were treated decades earlier, limiting the generalizability of the findings to present-day gender minority people in Sweden or other countries where the accessibility and outcomes of gender affirmation treatments have improved, and the associated stigma has decreased. In addition, findings from this study cannot be generalized to gender minority people other than those who have received gender-affirming surgery.

Studies Using Official Postmortem Data

Since 1990, the Queensland Suicide Register in Australia has accumulated cases of recorded suicide deaths among that state's 4.6 million residents. Although Australia does not systematically identify SOGI at the time of death, such information may be noted in narrative reports. Reviewing records of about six thousand suicides from 2000 to 2009, a team of researchers identified thirty-five "likely LGBT" adults, representing 0.6 percent of the suicide cases (Skerrett, Kõlves, & De Leo, 2014). Almost two thirds were gay men. Classifying all other suicide decedents as "non-LGBT," the study created a control group by selecting three non-LGBT decedents, matched on age and gender to each LGBT decedent. In their comparative review of death records, the researchers found evidence of psychosis in about 12 percent of non-LGBT cases, but in none of the LGBT cases. LGBT decedents, however, showed greater evidence of depression compared to non-LGBT controls (71 vs. 52 percent), as well as more relationship problems (31 vs. 10 percent) and recent stressful life events (35 vs. 20 percent).

In the United States, the National Violent Death Reporting System (NVDRS) provides a similar database of records from official investigations of deaths from suicide, homicide, and other types of violence (Fowler, Jack, Lyons, Betz, & Petrosky, 2018). Designed to guide prevention activities, this state-based system collects documents and reports on each violent death and codes them into over seven hundred data elements related to the decedent and the circumstances of the death. Established in 2002, NVDRS began collecting data from six states in 2003 but was not funded in all U.S. states until 2017.

In 2013, transgender status and sexual orientation were added to the codebook used by state abstractors (CDC, 2015). In coding SOGI-related variables, abstractors are instructed to look for specific evidence in the reports submitted by the local coroner, medical examiner, or law enforcement that the decedent self-identified as transgender or received medical treatments for gender transition (for transgender status), or self-identified as heterosexual, gay, lesbian, or bisexual (for sexual orientation). Since SOGI information is not required to be collected by death investigators, it is infrequently included in death reports, and when reported, may not be supported by clear evidence. Nevertheless, two recent studies have attempted to use NVDRS data to illuminate LGBT suicide.

One analysis by CDC personnel (Lyons et al., 2019) examined over 123,000 suicide cases in persons aged fifteen years and older, reported from the eighteen U.S. states where NVDRS was funded during its first eleven years (2003 to 2014). The timeframe covered only a single year in which the system coded SOGI-related items, allowing the researchers to set their own less restrictive indicators of LGBT status (e.g., decedent was perceived to be LGBT by family members or friends; autopsy showed decedent to be transgender). Using keyword searches of death records, the researchers identified 621 LGBT decedents. This represented 0.5 percent of the suicide cases, almost the exact percentage identified as LGBT in the Queensland Suicide Register study (Skerrett et al., 2014).

Among the LGBT decedents, about 54 percent were gay males, 28 percent lesbian females, 10 percent transgender, and 8 percent bisexual individuals. Similar to procedures used in the Queensland study, all decedents who did not meet the criteria for identification as LGBT were included as a "non-LGBT" control group, divided into non-gay male and non-lesbian female subgroups. Due to inadequate numbers of bisexual and transgender decedents, data analyses focused on examining differences in factors contributing to the suicides of gay compared to non-gay males, and lesbian compared to non-lesbian females. Overall, both gay male and lesbian decedents were found to have higher prevalence of depressed mood, other mental health problems, suicide attempt histories, and disclosure of suicide intent to others, compared to their non-gay and non-lesbian counterparts. Noting the finding of a contemporaneous, nationally representative survey that 4.1 percent of U.S. adults identified as LGBT (Gates, 2011), Lyons et al. (2019) acknowledged that their identification of LGBT status in only 0.5 percent of suicide decedents was likely a substantial underestimate. They also acknowledged that some control decedents may have been erroneously classified as non-LGBT due to incomplete information, in particular bisexual decedents. In addition to the issues noted by the researchers, it is possible that anecdotal information found in the death records may have disproportionately identified LGBT persons with clinical histories. In any case, these concerns substantially limit confidence in the study's reported findings.

A second recent study to examine LGBT suicide using NVDRS data looked specifically at deaths of LGBT youth and young adults aged twelve to twenty-nine years (Ream, 2019). This study used NVDRS data collected in eighteen U.S. states during the three-year period after transgender status and sexual orientation were added to the NVDRS codebook (2013 to 2015). The study data set included 10,311 suicide cases of which 2,209 (21.4 percent) had been coded by a state abstractor for transgender status and/or sexual orientation. Among the coded decedents, 215 were identified as LGBT, 2.1 percent of all young suicide decedents. The researcher divided this group into six categories: gay males (43 percent), lesbian females (30 percent), bisexual males (8 percent), bisexual females (6 percent), transgender males (7 percent), and transgender females (6 percent). The other 1,994 young suicide decedents who had been SOGI-coded were divided into two categories: non-LGBT males (80 percent) and non-LGBT females (20 percent). Analyses of differences across the resulting eight categories of decedents identified mental health diagnoses to be especially prevalent among bisexual females (92 percent) and transgender males (67 percent). These two groups also ranked highest in prevalence of prior suicide attempts (42 and 50 percent, respectively). The validity of these percentages is limited, however, by the small number of decedents identified as bisexual female (n = 12) or transgender male (n = 16).

The study also looked at the prevalence of LGBT individuals among decedents of different ages, finding that almost a quarter (24 percent) of the youngest suicide decedents (aged twelve to fourteen) were LGBT. Also noted was that LGBT prevalence steadily decreased as age increased, falling to 8 percent of the oldest decedents (aged twenty-five to twenty-nine years). The study conclusions emphasized the implications of these percentages for estimating the prevalence of LGBT youth among young suicide decedents. These figures, however, were based on the small number of decedents in each age group who were able to be coded for transgender status and/or sexual orientation, and are subject to the biases and limitations inherent in the procedures through which NVDRS currently identifies SOGI in all decedents, including those who were cisgender and heterosexual (Clark, Blosnich, Haas, & Cochran, 2019). Data reported by the Ream (2019) study indicate that the 215 decedents identified as LGBT represented 2.1 percent of the total sample of 10,311 young suicide decedents but 9.7 percent of the 2,209 decedents who were SOGI-coded, suggesting that NVDRS abstractors more frequently found specific evidence in the death reports that identified the decedent as transgender, gay, lesbian, or bisexual, than cisgender and heterosexual. This would not be surprising given the lack of routine, systematic SOGI inquiry in death investigations, but a systematic bias of underidentifying cisgender, heterosexual individuals in the death records has the effect of inflating the percentage of decedents identified as LGBT.

Suicide Attempts in SGM Populations

In the United States and other areas of the Global North, information on suicide attempts in SGM populations has been collected for many decades, initially through relatively small community-based studies and increasingly in population-based studies.

Meta-analyses of Sexual Minority Suicide Attempt Data

A 2008 meta-analysis of fifteen international population-based studies of adolescents and adults that measured sexual orientation and suicide attempts found lifetime suicide attempt prevalence to be four times higher among male respondents who identified as gay or bisexual than among heterosexual males, and twice as high among female respondents who identified as lesbian and bisexual compared to heterosexual women (King et al., 2008). Respondents who identified as LGB were also more than twice as likely as heterosexual respondents to report a suicide attempt in the past twelve months.

More recently, a team of Canadian researchers undertook a broader meta-analysis that sought to balance the likely underreporting of sexual minority identity or same-sex sexual behavior in population-based studies (especially when they are government-administered) with the enriched sexual minority samples of community-based studies (Hottes, Bogaert, Rhodes, Brennan, & Gesink, 2016). Pooling data from thirty cross-sectional studies conducted in nonclinical settings in the United States, Canada, Europe, Australia, and New Zealand that included over 21,000 sexual minority adults, Hottes et al. (2016) found lifetime suicide attempt prevalence estimates of 4 percent for heterosexual respondents in population surveys, 11 percent for LGB respondents in population surveys, and 20 percent for LGB respondents in community surveys. While both population and community surveys showed significantly higher prevalence of lifetime suicide attempts in LGB compared to heterosexual respondents, the researchers attributed the markedly higher attempt prevalence found in LGB community samples to greater disclosure of sexual minority identity and suicidal behavior. They noted, however, that more research is needed to determine potential biases in community samples administered by LGB-affiliated organizations, which may overrepresent individuals with strong LGB community attachment (Hottes et al., 2016).

Population-Based Studies of Sexual Orientation Differences in Suicide Attempts

Studies using data from single population-based surveys have reported clear differences in prevalence of suicide attempts among sexual minority subgroups defined by sex and sexual orientation identification. In a study of data from the 2004–2005 National Epidemiologic Survey of Alcohol and Related Conditions, Bolton and Sareen (2011) found that 2 percent of the target group of adults aged twenty years and older identified as gay or lesbian (0.9 percent), bisexual (0.6 percent), or unsure (0.5 percent). While the heterosexual sample was slightly more female than male (52 vs. 48 percent), gay/lesbian respondents were about 40 percent female, bisexual respondents were 67 percent female, and not-sure respondents were 58 percent female. Among all male respondents, the prevalence of lifetime suicide attempts was highest among bisexual men (10.0 percent), followed by gay men (9.8 percent) and men who were not sure (8.5 percent); heterosexual men had the lowest attempt prevalence (2.1 percent). Female respondents showed the same pattern across sexual orientation groups, with the highest prevalence of lifetime suicide attempts found among bisexual women (24.4 percent), followed by lesbian women (10.9 percent), women who were not sure (9.9 percent), and heterosexual women (4.2 percent). Comparing lifetime prevalence of suicide attempts between male and female respondents in each sexual orientation group, prevalence among heterosexual women was double that among heterosexual men (4.2 and 2.1 percent, respectively). Similarly, attempt prevalence of bisexual women was slightly more than double that of bisexual men (24.4 and 10 percent, respectively). In contrast, attempt prevalence was only marginally higher among lesbian women compared to gay men (10.9 and 9.8 percent, respectively) and among women who were not sure of their sexual orientation compared to men who were not sure (9.9 and 8.5 percent, respectively). The study found all sexual minority groups to have notably higher prevalence of lifetime suicide attempts, compared with heterosexual respondents, although prevalence was highest in bisexual respondents, especially in bisexual women (Bolton & Sareen, 2011).

The Youth Risk Behavior Survey, which began asking a sexual identity question in 2015, provides a picture of sexual orientation differences in twelve-month suicide attempt prevalence among students in grades nine through twelve. An analysis of this survey's findings from that year (Kann et al., 2016) found that 8.6 percent of students reported at least one suicide attempt during the past twelve months. Among students who identified as LGB, the prevalence of past-twelve-month suicide attempt (29.4 percent) was more than four times higher than that of heterosexual students (6.4 percent). Students who identified as not sure had a suicide attempt prevalence of 13.7 percent, significantly higher than among heterosexual students and significantly lower than among LGB students (Kann et al., 2016).

Among female students, the study found that those who identified as lesbian or bisexual had a past-twelve-month suicide attempt prevalence almost four times higher (32.8 percent) than those who identified as heterosexual (8.4 percent) and almost three times higher than those who identified as not sure (11.7 percent). Male students who identified as gay or bisexual had a past-twelve-month suicide attempt prevalence of 19.4 percent, about four times higher than among heterosexual students (4.5 percent) and slightly higher than among students who identified as not sure (16.0 percent). Further, the prevalence of suicide attempts within the past twelve months was found to be significantly higher among lesbian/bisexual females (32.8 percent) than gay/bisexual males (19.4 percent).

Studies of Suicide Attempts Among Sexual Minority Persons in the Global South

In conjunction with a developing emphasis on LGBT psychology in the Philippines (Manalastas & Torre, 2016), efforts have been made to replicate findings from global research on sexual minority suicidal behavior. Using data from a population-based survey of over eight thousand Filipino youth aged fourteen to twenty-four years, an early study found that young sexual minority males were twice as likely to report suicidal ideation than young heterosexual males, although sexual minority males did not show higher prevalence of suicide attempts (Manalastas, 2013). Suicidal ideation in sexual minority males was found to be linked to depression, recent suicide attempt of a friend, and experiences of victimization. A subsequent study (Manalastas, 2016), which repeated these analyses using data from young females who completed the same survey, showed that sexual minority females had a significantly higher prevalence of both suicide ideation and attempts than heterosexual females. These findings are especially concerning in light of the researchers' recent analysis of the World Values Survey data, which found that, among six Southeast Asian countries, Filipinos reported the lowest percentage (28 percent) of respondents who expressed lack of acceptance of lesbians and gay men (Manalastas et al., 2017). In a related study of a convenience sample of 185 young self-identified lesbian women (n = 61) and gay men (n = 124) living in Manila, suicidal behavior was found to increase as a function of both perceived stigma and internalized self-stigma (Reyes et al., 2017).

An online study that explored sexual orientation differences in the mental health of almost a thousand young adult women in Japan and Taiwan (Kuang & Nojima, 2005) found marginally higher lifetime prevalence of suicide attempts among women in both countries who identified as lesbian compared to those who identified as heterosexual (20 vs. 15 percent, respectively, in Japan; 35 vs. 27 percent, respectively, in Taiwan). Only the Taiwanese difference was established to be significant, likely because a larger sample was recruited from that country (n = 545 vs. 415). A 2008 Japanese study of over two thousand youth aged fifteen to twenty-four, who were recruited using street-intercept techniques in the Osaka metropolitan area, found that 6 percent of males and 11 percent of females reported making a prior suicide attempt (Hidaka et al., 2008). Among young males, those who identified as gay or bisexual were five times more likely to report a prior suicide attempt (24.5 percent) than those who identified as heterosexual (4.7 percent). Young females who identified as sexual minority were also more likely to report a prior attempt (20.7 percent) compared to females who identified as heterosexual (11.2 percent), although this difference was not significant.

Similar findings were reported in a study of almost 2,300 youth aged twelve to twenty in three cities in Brazil (Teixeira-Filho & Rondini, 2012). Among the 4.5 percent of youth who were defined as non-heterosexual based on sexual behavior, the prevalence of lifetime suicide attempt was 19.8 percent, almost three times higher than among heterosexual youth (6.8 percent).

Surveys of Suicide Attempts in Gender Minority People

Multiple non-random community surveys of transgender people have found that up to one third of respondents reported making at least one lifetime suicide attempt (Clements-Nolle, Marx, & Katz, 2006; Grossman & D'Augelli, 2007; Kenagy, 2005; Xavier, Honnold, & Bradford, 2007). In the past decade, improved outreach techniques have resulted in recruitment of larger, more representative samples in surveys of transgender people. In 2009, the U.S. National Transgender Discrimination Survey of over six thousand transgender adults found that 41 percent reported making at least one lifetime suicide attempt, almost nine times the 4 to 5 percent lifetime prevalence of suicide attempts in the general population (Haas, Rodgers, & Herman, 2014). Lifetime suicide attempt prevalence was 46 percent among respondents who identified as female-to-male transgender, compared to 42 percent of those who identified as male-to female transgender, and 37 percent of those who identified as gender nonconforming. The 2015 U.S. Transgender Survey, which had over 27,000 transgender adult participants from all U.S. states, similarly reported a 40 percent prevalence of lifetime suicide attempts (James et al., 2016). In addition, this survey found that 7 percent of participants had made a suicide attempt in the past twelve months, almost twelve times higher than the rate of 0.6 percent in the general adult population.

A 2017 meta-analysis of thirty-two U.S. and Canadian studies of transgender suicidality found a somewhat lower prevalence of lifetime suicide attempts (Adams, Hitomi, & Mooney, 2017). Overall, the meta-analysis found that an average of 28.9 percent of transgender participants reported at least one lifetime suicide attempt, including about 32 percent of those who identified as female-to-male transgender, 31 percent of those who identified as male-to-female transgender, and 26 percent of those who identified as gender nonconforming or nonbinary. Based on combined data from the five studies that measured suicide attempts in the past twelve months, an average of 10.7 percent of participants reported making a past-year suicide attempt, almost eighteen times higher than the estimated prevalence among U.S. adults.

An analysis of data from a general population survey of adolescents, which included a specific measure of gender identity, found similarly high prevalence of suicide attempts in gender minority youth (Toomey, Syvertsen, & Shramko, 2018). Among the more than 120,000 youth aged eleven to nineteen who participated in the survey between 2012 and 2015, lifetime suicide attempts were reported by 50.8 percent of those who identified as female-to-male transgender, 41.8 percent of those who identified as not exclusively male or female, 29.9 percent of those who identified as male-to-female transgender, and 27.9 percent of youth who identified as gender-questioning. In comparison, lifetime suicide attempts were reported by 17.6 percent of cisgender female youth and 9.8 percent of cisgender male youth.

Causes of SGM Suicidal Behavior

Studies of SGM populations dating back to the 1970s have found suicidal behavior to be strongly associated with mental health disorders (Haas et al., 2011). In the meta-analysis of international studies by King et al. (2008), higher rates of suicide attempts among sexual minority adolescents and adults were linked to higher rates of depression, anxiety disorders, and substance use disorders than were found among heterosexual people of the same age and gender. In contrast to gender patterns among the general population, rates of depression and panic disorder were especially marked in sexual minority males, while substance dependence was found to be especially prevalent in sexual minority females. Lower association of suicidal behavior to mood and anxiety disorders in lesbian women, compared to gay men, has been reported by U.S. population-based studies (Haas et al., 2011). However, inconsistencies in the way studies have measured sexual orientation and the relatively small numbers of sexual minority participants in population-based studies have limited conclusions about these relationships. Further, studies have not clearly established that higher prevalence of mental health disorders in sexual minority people is causally linked to suicidal behavior.

Over the past two decades, explanations of suicidal behavior in SGM people have been strongly influenced by the minority stress model developed by Meyer (1995, 2003). As conceptualized, this model posited that sexual minority individuals are exposed to excess stressful events and conditions due to their disadvantaged position in heteronormative societies, which generates "minority stress processes" through which rejection becomes expected, sexual orientation is concealed, and stigma is internalized. Unless buffered by protective factors such as positive identity as a sexual minority individual, well-developed coping skills, and peer and community support, these stress processes heighten the likelihood of negative health outcomes, including mental health disorders and suicidal behavior.

By increasing awareness of the pervasive psychological effects of sexual orientation–based marginalization and discrimination, the minority stress model has improved understanding of the elevated prevalence of mental health disorders and suicidal behavior in sexual minority people. In recent years, the model has been shown to be comparably useful for understanding these outcomes in gender minority populations (Testa, Habarth, Peta, Balsam, & Bockting, 2015). In addition, it has stimulated research on stigma and discrimination among sexual minorities across the globe, including parts of the Global South. In Hong Kong, for example, researchers have developed a culturally sensitive Self-Stigma Scale (Mak & Cheung, 2010), and in South Africa, studies have documented the negative impact of family rejection of black men in rural townships who disclose same-sex sexual attraction and behavior (Gyamerah, Collier, Reddy, & Sandfort, 2019).

In the United States, the premises of the minority stress model are reflected in a limited number of targeted suicide prevention initiatives, including the Family Acceptance Project, a family education and intervention program rooted in research showing a strong association between experiencing SOGI-based family rejection during adolescence and suicidal behavior and other negative outcomes in young adulthood (Ryan, Huebner, Diaz, & Sanchez, 2009). The project has produced high-quality videos and instructional booklets, which have been recognized as a best practice in youth suicide prevention (Suicide Prevention Resource Center, 2019). It also provides training and consultation to schools, social service agencies, and faith-based organizations on developing and implementing family-based services for SGM children and adolescents (Family Acceptance Project, 2019). Recent research by Ryan, Toomey, Diaz, and Russell (2018) reporting an association between conversion therapy and suicidal behavior in SGM youth has supported advocacy initiatives to ban therapeutic practices that seek to change a person's sexual orientation or gender identity (The Trevor Project, 2019).

As researchers, advocates, and SGM people themselves have come to increasingly link suicidal behavior to discrimination and other minority stressors, tensions have emerged about whether this emphasis may increase the risk of "suicide contagion" in these populations; that is, the transmission of suicidal behavior from one person to another by way of personal contact or exposure to media coverage. General population studies from the past five decades have provided extensive evidence that when suicide is sensationalized or portrayed as a normative response to a distressing life experience, "copycat" suicides can be triggered in other vulnerable people (e.g., Gould, 1990; Motto, 1970; Niederkrotenthaler et al., 2009; Phillips, 1974, 1979; Stack, 2002). Contagion as a cause of suicide has not been systematically studied in SGM populations. The process has been observed in SGM contexts, however, most notably in 2010 when media accounts that graphically linked the suicides of young SGM people to anti-LGBT bullying were followed by additional suicides among gay and transgender adolescents. This prompted a coalition of suicide prevention and LGBT organizations to develop a guide for talking safely about suicide in LGBT populations (Haas, 2017).

In another vein, the minority stress model has been criticized for its conceptualization of stress as a psychological problem of affected individuals, and its relative inattention to the institutionalized nature of the stressors experienced by SGM individuals (Riggs & Treharne, 2017). Like other psychologically based suicide frameworks, critics note, the model largely leads to helping SGM people become more resilient rather than dismantling the sociocultural, institutional, and political forces from which minority stress emanates. Outside the United States, a growing research literature has developed challenging Western suicide prevention to move from its narrow focus on individual pathology toward a more contextualized, ecological, political, and social justice–oriented perspective on suicide risk in SGM and other marginalized populations (e.g., Cover, 2012; McDermott & Roen, 2016; White, 2016).

Rejecting the notion that suicidal behavior in SGM youth stems solely from internal "medicalized" factors such as mental health disorders, or external social stressors, Australian writer Rod Cover (2012) has argued that contemporary queer culture has become increasingly "homonormative" in an attempt to make itself palatable to the broader society, privileging white gay males, gender conformity, physical fitness, affluence and consumerism, and "assimilationist" relationship patterns like marriage. Caught between these restrictive "homonorms" and the prevailing heteronormativity of the broader culture, queer youth face a choice of "relative misery," which, especially for those who are racially, ethnically, or sexually diverse, gender nonconforming, poor, or homeless, contributes to a sense that their lives are not livable. Cover cites extensive anecdotal evidence for his culture-based theory, but it has not been formally tested.

In Canada, prevention researchers Kral and Idlout (2016) have called for an "indigenous suicidology" that emphasizes an understanding of suicide in high-risk minority communities from the perspectives of their culture, history, and unmet needs. Working with Inuit communities in the Canadian Arctic, these researchers have documented how community-based participatory research can identify root causes of suicide and empower community-driven suicide prevention solutions. Their findings that self-reliant interventions by Inuit communities have been more effective in decreasing lives lost to suicide than outside professional programs may hold promise for reducing suicidal behavior in SGM and other minority populations.

Future Directions for Understanding and Preventing SGM Suicidal Behavior

Despite decades of research, it is still not known how many SGM people die by suicide each year, or which sexual minority and gender minority groups are most at risk. Neither is it known how prevalence of SGM suicide varies by age or any other demographic variables, or whether the patterns of suicide death in SGM people are similar to or different from patterns of suicide attempts.

In the general population, vital statistics, used in conjunction with population estimates derived from census data, provide clear answers to these questions, while supplementary information from NVDRS and targeted research studies help to illuminate underlying causes. Perhaps the clearest lesson from the accumulated literature on SGM suicide is that research is not an adequate substitute for a universal surveillance system in which all decedent characteristics that evidence suggests are related to suicide mortality, including SOGI, are routinely and systematically identified. As long as SOGI is ignored or poorly identified by suicide surveillance systems, understanding of SGM suicide will remain inadequate to guide meaningful actions toward preventing suicide among SGM people.

Since 2014, we have been working to improve SOGI identification through NVDRS by developing a systematic method for death investigators and other relevant personnel to use in their investigations of suicides, homicides, and other violent deaths (Haas et al., 2015, 2019). Working with coroners and medical examiners in several states, we have designed and are pilot testing an accredited program to train death investigators in SOGI data collection (www.lgbtmortality.com). We are also collaborating with LGBT advocates to encourage states to require collection of SOGI data at the time of death. While a standardized method of collecting decedents' SOGI information is essential, changes also need to be made in NVDRS coding procedures to ensure broader identification of SGM decedents using behavioral information in addition to self-identification. In addition, the range of death-related circumstances identified by NVDRS should be expanded to include a wider range of community and societal-level factors that may increase risk for suicide and other violent deaths in SGM people and contribute to understanding individual- and relationship-level factors such as prior suicide attempts and intimate partner problems.

Although much of the Western world continues to view suicide largely through the lens of individual psychopathology, there are promising signs of increasing awareness that, in addition to mental health treatment, cultural, structural, and political interventions are needed to address and prevent the conditions that contribute to elevated suicide risk in SGM people.

References

Adams, N., Hitomi, M., & Moody, C. (2017). Varied reports of adult transgender suicidality: Synthesizing and describing the peer-reviewed and gray literature. *Transgender Health, 2*(1), 60–75. doi:10.1089/trgh.2016.0036

American Psychiatric Association. (2013). *Diagnostic and statistical manual of mental disorders* (5th ed.). Arlington, VA: Author.

Asscheman, H., Giltay, E. J., Megens, J. A. J., van Trotsenburg, M. A. A., & Gooren, L. J. G. (2011). A long-term follow-up study of mortality in transsexuals receiving treatment with cross-sex hormones. *European Journal of Endocrinology, 164*(4), 635–42. doi:10.1530/EJE-10-1038

Asscheman, H., Gooren, L. J. G., & Eklund, P. L. E. (1989). Mortality and morbidity in transsexual patients with cross-gender hormone treatment. *Metabolism, 38*(9), 869–73. doi:10.1016/0026-0495(89)90233-3

Björkenstam, C., Andersson, G., Dalman, C., Cochran, S., & Kosidou, K. (2016). Suicide in married couples in Sweden: Is the risk greater in same-sex couples? *European Journal of Epidemiology, 31*(7), 685–690. doi:10.1007/s10654-016-0154-6

Bolton, S. L., & Sareen, J. (2011). Sexual orientation and its relation to mental disorders and suicide attempts: Findings from a nationally representative sample. *Canadian Journal of Psychiatry, 56*(1), 35–43. doi:10.1177/070674371105600107

Center for Behavioral Health Statistics and Quality. (2018). *Results from the 2017 National Survey on Drug Use and Health: Detailed tables.* Rockville, MD: Author. https://www.samhsa.gov/data/sites/default/files/cbhsq-reports/NSDUHDetailedTabs2017/NSDUHDetailedTabs2017.pdf

Centers for Disease Control and Prevention. (2015). National Violent Death Reporting System (NVDRS) coding manual revised. https://www.cdc.gov/violenceprevention/datasources/nvdrs/coding-manual.html

Centers for Disease Control and Prevention. (2018). 1991–2017 High School Youth Risk Behavior Survey (YRBS) data. https://nccd.cdc.gov/Youthonline/App/Default.aspx

Clark, K. A., Blosnich, J. R., Haas, A. P., & Cochran, S. D. (2019). Estimate of lesbian, gay, bisexual, and transgender youth suicide is inflated. *Journal of Adolescent Health, 64*(6), 810. doi:10.1016/j.jadohealth.2019.03.003

Clements-Nolle, K., Marx, R., & Katz, M. (2006). Attempted suicide among transgender persons: The influence of gender-based discrimination and victimization. *Journal of Homosexuality, 51*(3), 53–69. doi:10.1300/J082v51n03_04

Cochran, S. D., & Mays, V. M. (2011). Sexual orientation and mortality among US men aged 17 to 59 years: Results from the National Health and Nutrition Examination Survey III. *American Journal of Public Health, 101*(6), 1133–8. doi:10.2105/AJPH.2010.300013

Cochran, S. D., & Mays, V. M. (2015). Mortality risks among persons reporting same-sex sexual partners: Evidence from the 2008 General Social Survey-National Death Index data set. *American Journal of Public Health, 105*(2), 358–64. doi:10.2105/AJPH.2014.301974

Cover, R. (2012). *Queer youth suicide, culture and identity: Unliveable lives?* London: SAGE Publications. doi:10.4324/9781315603261

Dhejne, C., Lichtenstein, P., Boman, M., Johansson, A. L., Långström, N., & Landén, M. (2011). Long-term follow-up of transsexual persons undergoing sex reassignment surgery: Cohort study in Sweden. *PLoS One, 6*(2). doi:10.1371/journal.pone.0016885

Family Acceptance Project. (2019). The Family Acceptance Project, San Francisco State University. https://familyproject.sfsu.edu/

Fowler, K. A., Jack, S. P., Lyons, B. H., Betz, C. J., & Petrosky, E. (2018). Surveillance for violent deaths: National Violent Death Reporting System, 18 states, 2014. *MMWR Surveillance Summaries, 67*(2), 1–36. doi:10.15585/mmwr.ss6702a1

Frisch, M., & Simonsen, J. (2013). Marriage, cohabitation and mortality in Denmark: National cohort study of 6.5 million persons followed for up to three decades (1982–2011). *International Journal of Epidemiology, 42*(2), 559–78. doi:10.1093/ije/dyt024

Gates, G. J. (2011). *How many people are lesbian, gay, bisexual, and transgender?* Williams Institute, University of California, Los Angeles School of Law. http://www3.law.ucla.edu/williamsinstitute/pdf/How-many-people-are-LGBT-Final.pdf.

Gould, M. S. (1990). Suicide clusters and media exposure. In S. J. Blumenthal & D. J. Kupfer (Eds.), *Suicide over the life cycle* (pp. 517–32). Washington, DC: American Psychiatric Press.

Grossman, A. H., & D'Augelli, A. R. (2007). Transgender youth and life-threatening behaviors. *Suicide and Life-Threatening Behavior, 37*(5), 527–37. doi:10.1521/suli.2007.37.5.527

Gyamerah, A. O., Collier, K. L., Reddy, V., & Sandfort, T. G. (2019). Sexuality disclosure among Black South African MSM and responses by family. *Journal of Sex Research, 56*(9), 1203–18. doi:10.1080/00224499.2018.1559917

Haas, A. P. (2017). What we know now: Updating best practices for talking about suicide and LGBT populations. https://pflag.org/blog/what-we-know-now-updating-best-practices-talking-about-suicide-lgbt-populations

Haas, A. P., Eliason, M., Mays, V. M., Mathy, R. M., Cochran, S. D., D'Augelli, A. R., . . . Clayton, P. (2011). Suicide and suicide risk in lesbian, gay, bisexual, and transgender populations: Review and recommendations. *Journal of Homosexuality, 58*(1), 10–51. doi:10.1080/00918369.2011.534038

Haas, A. P., Lane, A. D., Blosnich, J. R., Butcher, B. A., & Mortali, M. G. (2019). Collecting sexual orientation and gender identity information at death. *American Journal of Public Health, 109*(2), 255–9. doi:10.2105/AJPH.2018.304829

Haas, A. P., Lane, A., & Working Group for Postmortem Identification of SO/GI. (2015). Collecting sexual orientation and gender identity data in suicide and other violent deaths: A step towards identifying and addressing LGBT mortality disparities. *LGBT Health, 2*(1), 84–7. doi:10.1089/lgbt.2014.0083

Haas, A. P., Rodgers, P. L., & Herman, J. L. (2014). *Suicide attempts among transgender and gender non-conforming adults.* Williams Institute, University of California, Los Angeles. https://williamsinstitute.law.ucla.edu/wp-content/uploads/AFSP-Williams-Suicide-Report-Final.pdf.

Hedegaard, H., Curtin, S. C., & Warner, M. (2018). Suicide mortality in the United States, 1999–2017. *NCHS Data Brief, 330,* 1–8. http://www.salishfysprt.org/uploads/1/1/3/4/11346130/db330-h.pdf.

Hidaka, Y., Operario, D., Takenaka, M., Omori, S., Ichikawa, S., & Shirasaka, T. (2008). Attempted suicide and associated risk factors among youth in urban Japan. *Social Psychiatry and Psychiatric Epidemiology, 43*(9), 752–7. doi:10.1007/s00127-008-0352-y

Hottes, T. S., Bogaert, L., Rhodes, A. E., Brennan, D. J., & Gesink, D. (2016). Lifetime prevalence of suicide attempts among sexual minority adults by study sampling strategies: A systematic review and meta-analysis. *American Journal of Public Health, 106*(5), 1–12. doi:10.2105/AJPH.2016.303088

Isometsä, E. (2001). Psychological autopsy studies—a review. *European Psychiatry, 16*(7), 379–85. doi:10.1016/S0924-9338(01)00591-6

James, S., Herman, J., Rankin, S., Keisling, M., Mottet, L., & Anafi, M. A. (2016). *The report of the 2015 U.S. Transgender Survey.* Washington, DC: National Center for Transgender Equality. https://transequality.org/sites/default/files/docs/usts/USTS-Full-Report-Dec17.pdf

Kann, L., Olsen, E. O. M., McManus, T., Harris, W. A., Shanklin, S. L., Flint, K. H., . . . Thornton, J. (2016). Sexual identity, sex of sexual contacts, and health-related behaviors among students in grades 9–12: United States and selected sites, 2015. *MMWR Surveillance Summaries, 65*(9), 1–202. doi:10.15585/mmwr.ss6509a1

Kelly, T. M., & Mann, J. J. (1996). Validity of DSM-III-R diagnosis by psychological autopsy: A comparison with clinician antemortem diagnosis. *Acta Psychiatrica Scandinavica, 94*(5), 337–43. doi:10.1111/j.1600–0447.1996.tb09869.x

Kenagy, G. P. (2005). Transgender health: Findings from two needs assessment studies in Philadelphia. *Health & Social Work, 30*(1), 19–26. doi:10.1093/hsw/30.1.19

Kessler, R. C., Berglund, P., Borges, G., Nock, M., & Wang, P. S. (2005). Trends in suicide ideation, plans, gestures, and attempts in the United States, 1990–1992 to 2001–2003. *Journal of the American Medical Association, 293*(20), 2487–95. doi:10.1001/jama.293.20.2487

Kessler, R. C., Borges, G., & Walters, E. E. (1999). Prevalence of and risk factors for lifetime suicide attempts in the National Comorbidity Survey. *Archives of General Psychiatry, 56*(7), 617–26. doi:10.1001/archpsyc.56.7.617

King, M., Semlyen, J., Tai, S. S., Killaspy, H., Osborn, D., Popelyuk, D., & Nazareth, I. (2008). A systematic review of mental disorder, suicide, and deliberate self-harm in lesbian, gay and bisexual people. *BMC Psychiatry, 8*(1), 70–86. doi:10.1186/1471-244X-8–70

Kral, M., & Idlout, L. (2016). Indigenous best practices: Community-based suicide prevention in Nunavut, Canada. In J. White, I. Marsh, M. Kral, & J. Morris (Eds.), *Critical suicidology: Transforming suicide research and prevention for the 21st century* (pp. 229–243). Vancouver: UBC Press.

Kuang, M. F., & Nojima, K. (2005). The mental health and sexual orientation of females: A comparative study of Japan and Taiwan. *Kyushu University Psychological Research, 6,* 141–8. doi:10.15017/15690

Lyons, B. H., Walters, M. L., Jack, S. P., Petrosky, E., Blair, J. M., & Ivey-Stephenson, A. Z. (2019). Suicides among lesbian and gay male individuals: Findings from the National Violent Death Reporting System. *American Journal of Preventive Medicine, 56*(4), 512–21. doi:10.1016/j.amepre.2018.11.012

Mak, W. W., & Cheung, R. Y. (2010). Self-stigma among concealable minorities in Hong Kong: Conceptualization and unified measurement. *American Journal of Orthopsychiatry, 80*(2), 267–81. doi:10.1111/j.1939–0025.2010.01030.x

Manalastas, E. J. (2013). Sexual orientation and suicide risk in the Philippines: Evidence from a nationally representative sample of young Filipino men. *Philippine Journal of Psychology, 46*(1), 1–13.

Manalastas, E. J. (2016). Suicide ideation and suicide attempt among young lesbian and bisexual Filipina women: Evidence for disparities in the Philippines. *Asian Women, 32*(3), 101–120. doi:10.14431/aw.2016.09.32.3.101

Manalastas, E. J., Ojanen, T. T., Torre, B. A., Ratanashevorn, R., Hong, B. C. C., Kumaresan, V., & Veeramuthu, V. (2017). Homonegativity in Southeast Asia: Attitudes toward lesbians and gay men in Indonesia, Malaysia, the Philippines, Singapore, Thailand, and Vietnam. *Asia-Pacific Social Science Review, 17*(1), 25–33.

Manalastas, E. J., & Torre, B. A. (2016). LGBT psychology in the Philippines. *Psychology of Sexualities Review, 7*(1), 60–72.

Mathy, R. M., Cochran, S. D., Olsen, J., & Mays, V. M. (2011). The association between relationship markers of sexual orientation and suicide: Denmark, 1990–2001. *Social Psychiatry and Psychiatric Epidemiology, 46*(2), 111–7. doi:10.1007/s00127-009-0177-3

McDermott, E., & Roen, K. (2016). *Queer youth, suicide and self-harm: Troubled subjects, troubling norms.* London: Palgrave MacMillan.

Meyer, I. H. (1995). Minority stress and mental health in gay men. *Journal of Health and Social Behavior, 36*(1), 38–56. doi:10.2307/2137286
Meyer, I. H. (2003). Prejudice, social stress, and mental health in lesbian, gay, and bisexual populations: Conceptual issues and research evidence. *Psychological Bulletin, 129*(5), 674–697. doi:10.1037/0033–2909.129.5.674
Motto, J. A. (1970). Newspaper influence on suicide: A controlled study. *Archives of General Psychiatry, 23*(2), 143–8. doi:10.1001/archpsyc.1970.01750020047006
Naghavi, M. (2019). Global, regional, and national burden of suicide mortality 1990 to 2016: Systematic analysis for the Global Burden of Disease Study, 2016. *British Medical Journal, 364*(8186), 94–104. doi:10.1136/bmj.l94
National Action Alliance for Suicide Prevention. (2012). *2012 national strategy for suicide prevention: Goals and objectives for action: A report of the U.S. Surgeon General and of the National Action Alliance for Suicide Prevention.* Washington, DC: U.S. Department of Health & Human Services. https://www.ncbi.nlm.nih.gov/books/NBK109917/.
Niederkrotenthaler, T., Till, B., Kapusta, N. D., Voracek, M., Dervic, K., & Sonneck, G. (2009). Copycat effects after media reports on suicide: A population-based ecologic study. *Social Science & Medicine, 69*(7), 1085–90. doi:10.1016/j.socscimed.2009.07.041
Nock, M. K., Green, J. G., Hwang, I., McLaughlin, K. A., Sampson, N. A., Zaslavsky, A. M., & Kessler, R. C. (2013). Prevalence, correlates, and treatment of lifetime suicidal behavior among adolescents: Results from the National Comorbidity Survey Replication Adolescent Supplement. *JAMA Psychiatry, 70*(3), 300–10. doi:10.1001/2013.jamapsychiatry.55
Oquendo, M., & Baca-Garcia, E. (2014). Suicidal behavior disorder as a diagnostic entity in the DSM-5 classification system: Advantages outweigh limitations. *World Psychiatry, 13*(2), 128–30. doi:10.1002/wps.20116
Phillips, D. P. (1974). The influence of suggestion on suicide: Substantive and theoretical implications of the Werther effect. *American Sociological Review, 39*(3), 340–54. doi:10.2307/2094294
Phillips, D. P. (1979). Suicide, motor vehicle fatalities, and the mass media: Evidence toward a theory of suggestion. *American Journal of Sociology, 84*(5), 1150–74. doi:10.1086/226904
Plöderl, M., Wagenmakers, E.-J., Tremblay, P., Ramsay, R., Kralovec, K., Fartacek, C., & Fartacek, R. (2013). Suicide risk and sexual orientation: A critical review. *Archives of Sexual Behavior, 42*(5), 715–27. doi:10.1007/s10508-012-0056-y
Qin, P., Agerbo, E., & Mortensen, P. B. (2003). Suicide risk in relation to socioeconomic, demographic, psychiatric, and familial factors: A national register-based study of all suicides in Denmark, 1981–1997. *American Journal of Psychiatry, 160*(4), 765–72. doi:10.1176/appi.ajp.160.4.765
Ream, G. L. (2019). What's unique about lesbian, gay, bisexual, and transgender (LGBT) youth and young adult suicides? Findings from the National Violent Death Reporting System. *Journal of Adolescent Health, 64*(5), 602–7. doi:10.1016/j.jadohealth.2018.10.303
Renaud, J., Berlim, M. T., Begolli, M., McGirr, A., & Turecki, G. (2010). Sexual orientation and gender identity in youth suicide victims: An exploratory study. *Canadian Journal of Psychiatry, 55*(1), 29–34. doi:10.1177/070674371005500105
Reyes, M. E. S., Davis, R. D., David, A. J. A., Del Rosario, C. J. C., Dizon, A. P. S., Fernandez, J. L. M., & Viquiera, M. A. (2017). Stigma burden as a predictor of suicidal behavior among lesbians and gays in the Philippines. *Suicidology Online, 8*(2), 1–10. http://www.suicidology-online.com
Rich, C. L., Fowler, R. C., Young, D., & Blenkush, M. (1986). San Diego suicide study: Comparison of gay to straight males. *Suicide and Life-Threatening Behavior, 16*(4), 448–57. doi:10.1111/j.1943-278X.1986.tb00730.x
Riggs, D. W., & Treharne, G. J. (2017). Decompensation: A novel approach to accounting for stress arising from the effects of ideology and social norms. *Journal of Homosexuality, 64*(5), 592–605. doi:10.1080/00918369.2016.1194116
Ryan, C., Huebner, D., Diaz, R. M., & Sanchez, J. (2009). Family rejection as a predictor of negative health outcomes in white and Latino lesbian, gay, and bisexual young adults. *Pediatrics, 123*(1), 346–52. doi:10.1542/peds.2007–3524
Ryan, C., Toomey, R. B., Diaz, R. M., & Russell, S. T. (2018). Parent-initiated sexual orientation change efforts with LGBT adolescents: Implications for young adult mental health and adjustment. *Journal of Homosexuality, 123*(1), 346–52. doi:10.1080/00918369.2018.1538407
Shaffer, D., Fisher, P., Hicks, R. H., Parides, M., & Gould, M. (1995). Sexual orientation in adolescents who commit suicide. *Suicide and Life-Threatening Behavior, 25*(2), 64–71. doi:10.1111/j.1943-278X.1995.tb00491.x
Skerrett, D. M., Kõlves, K., & De Leo, D. (2014). Suicides among lesbian, gay, bisexual, and transgender populations in Australia: An analysis of the Queensland Suicide Register. *Asia-Pacific Psychiatry, 6*(4), 440–6. doi:10.1111/appy.12128
Stack, S. (2002). Media coverage as a risk factor in suicide. *Injury Prevention, 8*(Suppl. 4), iv30–iv32. doi:10.1136/ip.8.suppl_4.iv30
Stone, D. M., Simon, T. R., Fowler, K. A., Kegler, S. R., Yuan, K., Holland, K. M., . . . Crosby, A. E. (2018). Vital signs: Trends in state suicide rates—United States, 1999–2016 and circumstances contributing to suicide—27 states, 2015. *Morbidity and Mortality Weekly Review, 67*(22), 617–24. doi:10.15585/mmwr.mm6722a1
Suicide Prevention Resource Center. (2019). *Finding programs and practices.* Waltham, MA: Education Development Center. https://www.sprc.org/strategic-planning/finding-programs-practices
Teixeira-Filho, F. S., & Rondini, C.A. (2012). Suicide thoughts and attempts of suicide in adolescents with hetero and homoerotic sexual practices. *Saúde e Sociedade, 21*(3), 651–67. doi:10.1590/S0104-12902012000300011
Testa, R. J., Habarth, J., Peta, J., Balsam, K., & Bockting, W. (2015). Development of the gender minority stress and resilience measure. *Psychology of Sexual Orientation and Gender Diversity, 2*(1), 65–77. doi:10.1037/sgd0000081
The Trevor Project. (2019). Rep. Lieu introduces federal ban on LGBTQ conversion therapy. https://www.thetrevorproject.org/trvr_press/rep-lieu-introduces-federal-ban-on-lgbtq-conversion-therapy/
Toomey, R. B., Syvertsen, A. K., & Shramko, M. (2018). Transgender adolescent suicide behavior. *Pediatrics, 142*(4), e20174218. doi:10.1542/peds.2017–4218
Wang, C. W., Chan, C. L. W., & Yip, P. S. F. (2014). Suicide rates in China from 2002 to 2011: An update. *Social Psychiatry and Psychiatric Epidemiology, 49*(6), 929–41. doi:10.1007/s00127-013-0789-5
White, J. (2016). Reimagining youth suicide prevention. In J. White, I. Marsh, M. Kral, & J. Morris (Eds.), *Critical*

suicidology: Transforming suicide research and prevention for the 21st century (pp. 244–263). Vancouver: UBC Press.
World Health Organization. (2019). Suicide rate estimates, age standardized: Estimates by country. http://apps.who.int/gho/data/view.main.MHSUICIDEASDRv?lang=en.
Xavier, J., Honnold, J. A., & Bradford, J. (2007). *The health, health related needs, and life-course experiences of transgender Virginians*. Richmond, VA: Virginia Department of Health.
Yip, P. S. F., Caine, E. D., Yousuf, S., Chang, S. S., Wu, K. C. C., & Chen, Y. Y. (2012). Means restriction for suicide prevention. *Lancet, 379*(9834), 2393–9. doi:10.1016/S0140-6736(12)60521–2
Zalsman, G., Hawton, K., Wasserman, D., van Heeringen, K., Arensman, E., Sarchiapone, M., & Zohar, J. (2016). Suicide prevention strategies revisited: 10-year systematic review. *Lancet, 3*(7), 646–59. doi:10.1016/S2215-0366(16)30030-X

PART III

Specific Sexual and Gender Minority Populations

III

CHAPTER

15 Black U.S. Sexual and Gender Minority Mental Health

Jonathan Mathias Lassiter, Lourdes Dolores Follins, Stacy W. Smallwood, Leo Wilton, Alishia Alexander, *and* Sean Saifa Wall

Abstract

This chapter provides a comprehensive and nuanced review and critique of the extant scholarship related to Black sexual and gender minority (SGM) mental health in the United States. The authors highlight the determinants of mental health, the prevalence of mental health problems and inequities, and protective and resilience factors related to Black SGM mental health within five different subgroups: transgender people, intersex people, bisexual people, lesbians, and gay/same-gender-loving men. An intersectional approach is used to draw attention to how racial, gender, socioeconomic, and sexual orientation identities at the individual level influence experiences of oppression at the structural level to synergistically impact mental health. The chapter concludes with a discussion of the gaps in the literature related to Black SGM mental health and recommendations for addressing them.

Keywords: African American, Black, sexual minority, transgender, intersex, mental health

Introduction

Black[1] sexual and gender minority (SGM) people's mental health has been understudied and seldom discussed in larger scientific and popular discourses related to health. Several comprehensive reviews of the scientific literature point to the fact that when it comes to Black SGMs, our bodies are usually the focal point (Huang et al., 2010; Munoz-Laboy, 2019). When research is conducted about the mental health of Black SGMs, findings are presented as if Black SGMs are a monolith. Specifically, a significant proportion of research about Black SGMs is conducted with samples of Black people across distinct sexual and gender identities who are then combined to form one larger group (Follins & Lassiter, 2017). Given the federal government's HIV research funding priorities (Wade & Harper, 2017), most research that focuses on Black SGMs' mental health is conducted with Black gay, same-gender-loving men (BG/SGLM)[2], bisexual men and transwomen due to the HIV-related inequities found among these groups (Wade & Harper, 2017). As a result, these methodological and structural decisions have hindered the scientific investigation of the mental health of

[1] Black is used in this chapter to describe people with sub-Saharan African ancestral origins with brown or black complexions. This term denotes a heterogeneous group of people with roots on the African continent regardless of whether they were displaced via any one of the slave trades starting in the fifteenth century or remained on the African continent. This term is used as opposed to "African American" to highlight the heterogeneity of this group, because the term "African American" does not include groups of people who are Black and living in the United States but may not have experienced slavery in the United States. Our intentional use of the term "Black" emphasizes the sociocultural experience of being treated as "Black" and the sociopolitical consequences of such treatment instead of focusing on country of origin.

[2] The terms "gay" and "same-gender-loving" are used to describe men who have same-sex attractions and sexual behaviors. Many Black people choose not to identify as "gay" due to multiple factors, including but not limited to the absence of African diasporic culture and values within the larger sexual minority communities, as well as experiences of racism within the White gay male community (Lassiter, 2014). Therefore, the term "same-gender-loving" was coined in the 1990s by Cleo Manago as an alternative term that embraces both same-sex desire and an affirmation of African American culture (Lassiter, 2014).

BG/SGLM, bisexual men, and transwomen outside of sexually pathological lens. Similarly, and perhaps more egregiously, these decisions have contributed to a dearth of information about Black lesbians, bisexual women, transmen, and intersex people's mental health. These gaps severely impair scientists' and mental health providers' abilities to develop, disseminate, and integrate culturally responsive mental health research into their work with Black SGMs.

Due to their multiple, intersecting marginalized identities, Black SGMs face being ostracized in each community to which they belong, including transphobia and homonegativity within Black communities, and cisgenderism, monosexism, and racism within SGM communities (Earnshaw et al., 2019; Follins & Lassiter, 2017). However, they are also extremely resilient. Because many Black people undergo racial socialization before becoming aware of their sexual identity, Black SGMs may develop more positive feelings about their racial identity (Follins, Walker, & Lewis, 2014). These positive feelings, along with the psychological resources that they gain from their communities of origin to resist oppression, have been shown to positively impact psychological well-being and resiliency for Black SGMs (Bowleg, Huang, Brooks, Black, & Burkholder, 2003; Graham, Braithwaite, Spikes, Stephens, & Edu, 2009). As a result, Black SGMs are often resilient in the midst of multilevel stressors (e.g., intersectional oppression, violence, financial strain). However, this fact is rarely highlighted in empirical investigations about these communities. This lack of attention to resilience could have negative effects for Black SGMs' mental health. In her groundbreaking work, *Black LGBT Health in the United States: The Intersection of Race, Gender, and Sexual Orientation*, Follins (2017) wrote about the importance of integrating a strengths-based perspective into scientific and clinical work with Black SGMs. She explained:

> Understanding how Black LGBT individuals overcome various biopsychosocial and spiritual barriers and lead healthy lives can help community members, researchers, and providers develop interventions and strategies to promote the growth and development of Black LGBT individuals and their communities. (p. x)

The authors of this chapter have worked to heed Follins's genius and interweave findings related to Black SGMs' resiliency and strengths into our literature review. We hope that readers will finish the chapter with an understanding of not only what risks and negative mental health outcomes Black SGMs navigate, but also how they resist and thrive in the midst of intersectional oppression.

This chapter provides a nuanced review and critique of the available scholarship related to Black SGMs' mental health. We highlight the determinants of mental health, the prevalence of mental health problems, mental health protective and resilience factors, and gaps in the literature related to the mental health concerns of five different subgroups within the Black SGM community: transgender people, intersex people, bisexual people, lesbians, and BG/SGLM. This review provides a complex understanding of the heterogeneity of Black SGMs. We use an intersectional approach to draw attention to how racial, gender, socioeconomic, and sexual orientation identities at the individual level influence experiences of oppression at the structural level to synergistically impact mental health (Bowleg, 2013). Intersectionality recognizes that identities are not isolated and additive; rather, they are interrelated and mutually constitutive (Bowleg, 2012, 2013). By using this theoretical framework, readers will be able to better understand the complexity of multilevel factors that contribute to mental health issues in and enhance the psychological well-being of Black SGM people.

Review of the Current Literature

Determinants of Mental Health

Black SGMs share several determinants of mental health at the societal, structural, interpersonal, and individual levels. The most pervasive determinants of Black SGMs' mental health are intersectional discrimination and oppression. Anti-blackness, white supremacy, transphobia, heterosexism, patriarchy, economic disenfranchisement, and state-sanctioned violence under capitalism interlock in pervasive and chronic ways that distinctly affect Black SGMs' lives (Follins & Lassiter, 2017). For example, intersectional discrimination (e.g., based on race, sexual orientation, and gender) has been found to be related to the likelihood of Black bisexual individuals being diagnosed with a mental health disorder (Bostwick, Boyd, Hughes, West, & McCabe, 2014). Bostwick et al. (2014) found that sexual minorities who had experienced dual discrimination (due to gender and race) and triple discrimination (based on race, sexual orientation, and gender) were, respectively, 4.3 and 3.13 times more likely to have been diagnosed with mood and anxiety disorders than those who had experienced no discrimination. These forms of discrimination are harmful to Black SGMs' mental health even when examined by themselves. Black transgender people have reported high rates of insufficient income (e.g., household income of less than $10,000 per year; 38 percent), homelessness (41 percent), and unemployment (26 percent; Grant et al., 2011). These socioeconomic factors are often coupled with poor access to mental health treatment, incarceration, violence, and racial and gender-based stigma and discrimination. These factors coalesce to contribute to higher rates of psychological distress for this group when compared to the general population (Reisner et al., 2016; Wilton, 2017). Additionally, discrimination because of one's body size is also detrimental (Wilson, 2009a). Weight discrimination and oppression have been linked to health providers' negative attitudes toward Black bisexual women as well as depression and poor perceived physical health among this population (Wilson, Okwu, & Mills, 2011). These societal injustices are detrimental, but are not the only factors that contribute to poor mental health among Black SGMs.

Biological trauma and adverse childhood experiences are also associated with poor mental health for Black SGMs. Being identified as intersex at birth is the initial site of trauma for many Black intersex people. Depending on the variation, Black intersex infants and children are subject to invasive medical examinations and surgical procedures designed to "correct" their genitals and bodies (Meyer-Bahlburg, Khuri, Reyes-Portillo, & New, 2017). These traumatic experiences lead to internalized shame and stigma, which can affect mental health (Ginicola, 2017). Other forms of adverse childhood experiences also negatively impact mental health. Sexual, emotional, and physical abuse have all been found to increase the odds (at least twofold) of BG/SGLM having poor mental health as adults (Ports, Lee, Raiford, Spikes, Manago, & Wheeler, 2017). Cook, Valera, Calebs, and Wilson (2017) found that young BG/SGLM who were bullied or physically abused by a non-family member during childhood suffered from anxiety in their adult relationships more than those who were not bullied or physically abused. Furthermore, experiencing adverse childhood experiences may have a more severe impact for Black SGMs. Balsam, Lehavot, Beadnell, and Circo (2010) found that the association between emotional abuse, anxiety, and posttraumatic stress disorder was significantly stronger for Black participants compared to Whites. These studies suggest that early experiences of trauma negatively impact mental health across the lifespan.

These early experiences of trauma may negatively impact one's sense of self, which in turn can be a barrier to psychological well-being. Researchers have examined Black lesbians' sexual identity disclosure and their decision-making processes around this, as well as the effects of victimization (i.e., racism, homonegativity, heterosexism, misogynoir) on their mental health outcomes (Aranda et al., 2015; Balsam et al., 2015; Woody, 2015). Dibble, Eliason, and Crawford (2012) found that 66.7 percent of their sample of Black lesbians were out to their families of origin, 81.3 percent were out to friends, 55.7 percent were out to their healthcare providers, and 36.1 percent were out to clergy or a spiritual advisor. Ramsey, Hill, and Kellam's (2010) Black lesbian needs assessment found that 63.7 percent of their sample were out to varying degrees and that 48 percent reported that they had been rejected or discriminated against because of their sexual identity. In Woody's (2015) study of Black lesbians aged fifty-seven to seventy-two, participants did not come out unless it was deemed necessary in order to "stay safe in a sexist, racist, and ageist world" (p. 53). Research suggests that intersectional stigma is associated with difficulty in developing a healthy, integrated identity for BG/SGLM as well (Graham et al., 2009). Because of racial socialization, BG/SGLM may develop more positive feelings toward their racial identity, while holding negative attitudes about their sexual identity. A lack of identity integration then becomes a source of stress for BG/SGLM that contributes to negative mental and social health outcomes such as mood disorders, anxiety, psychological distress, lower self-esteem, and lower life satisfaction (Graham et al., 2009). Internalization of stigma in the form of internalized homonegativity also has been associated with increased depressive distress among BG/SGLM (Amola & Grimmett, 2015; Boone, Cook, & Wilson, 2016; Smallwood, Spencer, Ingram, Thrasher, & Thompson-Robinson, 2017a). Overall, the extant literature suggests that intersectional oppression and stigma are often internalized by Black SGMs and contribute to hypervigilance related to potential discrimination and a lack of identity integration, all of which contribute to poor mental health.

Prevalence of Mental Health Problems

There is consensus that Black SGMs typically experience more societal discrimination and stressors than their White counterparts. However, this exposure does not necessarily contribute to more diagnosed mental health problems (Feinstein, Turner, Beach, Korpak, & Phillips, 2019; Meyer, Dietrich, & Swartz, 2008; Reisner et al., 2016). For example, despite having higher incidences of childhood and adult adversities (including intimate partner violence [IPV]), Black bisexual women reported fewer depressive and posttraumatic stress symptoms compared to White lesbians (Alexander, Volpe, Abboud, & Campbell, 2016; Bostwick, Hughes, Steffen, Veldhuis, & Wilsnack, 2019). Black transgender women also reported lower prevalence of mental health and substance use disorders (Reisner et al., 2016). It appears that Black bisexuals and transgender women report fewer mental health problems than would be expected given their high levels of experiences with discrimination and adversity.

However, research findings about the prevalence of mental health problems among Black lesbians, BG/SGLM, and transgender people suggest a more complex narrative, especially when comparing their mental health with their Black heterosexual counterparts. Black lesbians have reported higher rates of depression and poorer psychological well-being than their White lesbian or Black heterosexual female counterparts due to their more frequent experiences with multiple types of oppression (Aranda et al., 2015; Calabrese, Meyer, Overstreet, Haile, & Hansen, 2015). Some Black lesbians reported similar or lower levels of depressive symptoms, eating disorders, and anxiety as their White and Latina lesbian or Black heterosexual female peers (Balsam et al., 2015; Cooperman, Simoni, & Lockhart, 2003; Feldman & Meyer, 2007; Kertzner, Meyer, Frost, & Stirrat, 2009). Also, studies have found that Black sexual minority male adolescents experienced higher levels of depression than their heterosexual adolescent male counterparts (Consolacion, Russell, & Sue, 2004). These contradictory findings indicate that there is still much work to be done to determine the true burden of mental health problems in Black SGM communities.

One mental health problem that does seem to be more prevalent among Black SGMs is suicide. A limited number of studies have examined the occurrence of suicide ideation and attempts among Black transgender people. Grant et al. (2011) reported that 49 percent of Black transgender people in their sample reported a history of suicide attempts. In another study, 36.6 percent of the young BG/SGLM and Black transwomen surveyed reported a history of lifetime suicidal thoughts and 16.1 percent reported prior suicide attempts (cisgender men: 91 percent; transwomen: 9 percent; Wilton et al., 2018). Similarly, Meyer et al. (2008) found that BG/SGLM, Black lesbians, and Black bisexuals reported slightly higher odds of having a serious suicide attempt than their white counterparts, but these odds were not significantly different. These findings indicate that suicide often occurs in the absence of diagnosed mental health disorders and is a serious mental health issue that should be studied more carefully among this group.

When examining intragroup differences among Black sexual minorities, researchers have found that bisexual people report more mental health problems than their monosexual counterparts (Friedman et al., 2019). Black bisexual men had more problems with substance use, depressive symptoms, and experiences of IPV or physical assault compared to gay-identified Black men. Black bisexual men were also more likely to report having concealed their sexuality and feeling disconnected from the gay community (Friedman et al., 2019). Black bisexual men have disclosed experiencing low self-esteem and self-worth related to feeling a lack of acceptance and fearing rejection and judgment because of their bisexuality in their communities (Dodge et al., 2012). There are also gender differences in mental health prevalence within the Black sexual minority community. For example, Black bisexual women have reported poorer psychological and social well-being than BG/SGLM, and this was related to higher reports of discrimination (Calabrese et al., 2015). These findings highlight the fact that the intersections of oppression due to gender and sexual orientation affect mental health in ways that cannot be accounted for when only examining differences between BG/SGLM and bisexuals and Black lesbians and bisexuals, or conflating Black bisexual and monosexual people.

Protective and Resilience Factors

Research on protective and resilience factors for Black SGMs is growing (Follins et al., 2014; Garret-Walker & Longmire-Avital, 2018). Protective and resilience factors among this group include universal ones such as social support and religion and spirituality (Lassiter, 2014; 2016; Smallwood, Spencer, Ingram, Thrasher, & Thompson-Robinson, 2017b; Teti et al., 2012). In addition, this group has also reported using culturally specific factors such as racial socialization, an African consciousness, and the integration of intersecting marginalized identities (Follins et al., 2014) to resist and persist in spite of intersectional oppression. These factors may account for the lower prevalence of mental health problems among Black SGM people compared to their White counterparts, despite their higher levels of exposure to negative determinants of mental health.

Black Transgender People's Protective and Resilience Factors

Black transgender people employ several protective and resilience strategies. In a qualitative study of Black transmen, Poteat and Follins (2017) found that coping, resiliency, and social support were helpful resources in navigating structural barriers related to mental health concerns, health care maltreatment, intersectional stigma and discrimination, and violence. Further, Bailey (2019) has highlighted the positive role of House-ballroom communities (i.e., networks or groups of individuals that are connected through 'houses', which serve as familial, cultural, and supportive systems) for BG/SGLM and transgender people of color. He found that House-ballroom communities disseminated health-protective messages to their members, such as emphasizing the importance of gender and sexuality exploration and expression in a safe environment. Follins et al. (2014, p. 200) also noted several other themes of resilience among Black transgender people: "a self-generated definition of oneself; embracing one's self-worth; recognizing and negotiating gender and ethnoracial oppression; pride in one's ethnoracial identity; and purposefully seeking out supportive communities." These cognitive and behavioral strategies highlight the necessity of engaging in deep exploration and integration of one's stigmatized social identities by reframing negatives into positives. These processes allow one to forge a healthy integrated identity that is strengths-based, and that connects one with an affirming community that can provide support during subsequent challenges.

Black Lesbians' Protective and Resilience Factors

Black lesbians' individual protective resources include internal factors such as self-esteem, racial identity, lesbian group identity, religiosity and spirituality, feelings of uniqueness, behavioral and social competencies, happiness, optimism, and humor (Bowleg, Brooks, & Ritz, 2008; Bowleg et al., 2003). These internal factors predict active coping when Black lesbians face oppression in their communities of origin, at work, and at school (Bowleg et al., 2003). Active coping for Black lesbians includes, but is not limited to, constructing protective environments, being out and managing that, assessing their power to change situations, not allowing others to define their reality, choosing not to bear the burden of others' bigotry, covering or concealing their sexual identity, engaging in cognitive reframing, confronting and educating coworkers, and engaging in psychotherapy (Bowleg et al., 2008; Mays, Cochran, & Roeder, 2003). Research on the impact of religiosity and spirituality on Black lesbians' mental health is mixed, however. Drabble, Veldhuis, Riley, Rostosky, and Hughes (2017) found that highly religious Black lesbians reported higher rates of hazardous drinking, while Walker and Longmire-Avital's (2013) study of Black sexual minority emerging adults found that religious faith contributed to resiliency when participants struggled with high internalized homonegativity.

As for Black lesbians' interpersonal protective and resilience resources, research has found that social support, the perception of available SGM resources, interactions with families and Black communities that buffer against multiple minority stress, and supportive relationships with SGM friends, heterosexual allies, partners, and religious communities are all protective factors for those surveyed (Bowleg et al., 2003; Wilson, 2009b). Zimmerman, Darnell, Rew, Lee, and Kaysen (2015) found that the Black emerging adult lesbians in their study reported lower connectedness to an SGM community, but not lower collective self-esteem about being lesbian. It is unclear how connectedness to a *Black* SGM community affects Black lesbian mental health.

BG/SGLM's Protective and Resilience Factors

A growing body of research examines the role of resilience in fostering positive mental health outcomes among BG/SGLM. Wilson et al. (2016) examined patterns of resilience among a sample of 226 young BG/SGLM. Their findings suggested that poor mental health outcomes in the sample "appeared to be most influenced by low levels of self-efficacy and hardiness/adaptive coping skills" (p. 153). More recently, the concept of resilience has been expanded to include the construct of "grit" (i.e., perseverance and passion for long-term goals; Duckworth, Peterson, Matthews, & Kelly, 2007), which is thought to be more forward-focused in nature than resilience, with an emphasis on achieving future goals (Winiker, Tobin, Davey-Rothwell, & Latkin, 2019). Another study of 239 BG/SGLM found that two thirds of the men surveyed reported high levels of grit, which in turn was associated with fewer depressive symptoms and reduced substance use (Winiker et al., 2019). The study also found that BG/SGLM with higher levels of grit also reported having more gay or bisexual male friends, suggesting that being part of social networks with similar experiences may lend itself to more social support, which could mediate mental health outcomes (Winiker et al., 2019). Another emerging area of study examines the ways in which sociopolitical involvement may be a coping strategy for stress related to discrimination among sexual minority people of color. Some studies suggest that through organizing with others of similar identity and engaging in activism, members of SGM groups can resist the oppression they experience based on their identities and develop more positive self-appraisals (DeBlaere et al., 2014; Santos & VanDaalen, 2018).

Black Intersex and Bisexual People's Protective and Resilience Factors

We found no studies that specifically focused on protective and resilience factors in Black intersex and bisexual people's lives. More research is needed in this area.

Gaps in the Literature and Suggestions for Future Directions

The scientific literature is replete with gaps in knowledge about Black SGM mental health and the factors that impact it. These gaps exist within the domains of content, sampling, and methodology. There are narrow conceptualizations related to which mental health problems and their associated factors are studied, which subgroups' mental health is investigated, and how mental health is examined among Black SGMs. Overall, there is a lack of nuance, cultural consideration, and comprehensiveness concerning Black SGM mental health and treatment.

Gaps in Content

Too often Black SGM mental health is only studied in the context of sexual health or risk factors, or is ignored altogether (Wade & Harper, 2017). While some of these subpopulations have a disproportionate HIV burden and risk, there are additional mental health issues faced by Black SGMs that should be given due attention. Furthermore, a continued focus solely on HIV-related factors reinforces the idea that HIV is a "Black disease," particularly among BG/SGLM and transwomen (Villarosa, 2017). This in turn contributes to stigma and discrimination that negatively impact Black SGMs' mental health.

Future research should also move beyond the individual to examine interpersonal and structural factors and their associations with Black SGM mental health. With the loss of physical spaces for Black SGMs to come together as a community and the increased use of digital platforms (e.g., social media, geosocial mobile applications) for constructing social networks, the impact of these structural changes on these communities' overall mental health should be considered. The way in which family structures and relations influence Black SGMs' mental health should be explored in more depth. Black lesbians are more likely to report having ever been a parent than their non-Black lesbian peers (Ramsey et al., 2010). How might these relationships contribute to mental health outcomes (e.g., stress, resilience, anxiety related to parenting while Black) among this group? More information is needed on how parenting in a country where virulent anti-Black racism exists alongside anti-LGBTQ parenting legislation influences Black lesbians' and other Black SGMs' mental health. Overall, research about how familial relationships and dynamics, intimate partners, and community members impact Black SGM mental health is also largely absent in the scientific literature.

Similarly, research on the associations between racial, sexual, and gender identity development and psychological distress is virtually absent from research about Black SGM mental health. For example, most discussions about Black intersex people have focused on nonconsensual surgeries; other aspects of Black intersex people's lived experiences, such as how they embody or shun racialized intersex identities, warrant further exploration. Likewise, other than the work of Bowleg et al. (2003, 2008), the effects of racial identity on Black sexual minority women's mental health have not been explored. However, exploring identity development could present an opportunity to broaden understanding of Black SGM mental health (Graham et al., 2009).

In addition, a focus on the intersecting identities of Black SGMs and intragroup differences is lacking. For example, much of the scientific literature about Black transgender people's mental health has focused on transgender women and has largely neglected transgender men. Additional research is needed to explore how Black SGMs manage stigma that originates from within their communities (e.g., stigma held by Black transmen about Black transwomen. Also, the authors were unable to find any mental health studies that focused on Black SGM with physical and cognitive disabilities or who were immigrants. More research is needed in these areas to expand our knowledge of the strengths and vulnerabilities of these groups. This attention to the heterogeneity of Black SGM communities will help researchers and clinicians develop more tailored and effective mental health interventions.

Despite the plethora of research about the factors that lead to mental health challenges in these communities, with only two exceptions (Haynes & Dale, 2017; Hergenrather, Geishecker, Clark, & Rhodes, 2013), there is no published research about the design, implementation, and efficacy of mental health treatments for Black SGMs. Hergenrather et al. (2013) developed an intervention to improve mental health and employment outcomes for BG/SGLM who were living with HIV/AIDS. Their intervention included seven three-hour-long group sessions that were conducted over seven weeks. Men in this group worked on building goal-setting skills, problem-solving skills, health-promoting behaviors, and employment-seeking behaviors. Haynes and Dale (2017) described the development of an open, integrative psychotherapy group, *Shades of Black*, which aimed to cultivate resilience among BG/SGLM. The group also provided a space where men could work at integrating their social identities, increasing their self-esteem and self-acceptance, and reducing social isolation. This intervention (Haynes & Dale, 2017) represents the only psychotherapeutic intervention outside of the realm of HIV or another physical health intervention that directly addresses mental health for BG/SGLM. No other culturally specific mental health treatments were found for this group or other segments of the Black SGM community. Researchers are encouraged to expand their efforts in this area.

Gaps in Sampling

When studying the mental health of racially and ethnically diverse SGM samples, there is a tendency to condense people of color into one category, thus delimiting the focus on Black SGMs as a heterogeneous group. For example, one of the challenges in sampling in HIV prevention science is the merging of gender and sex; as a result, BG/SGLM and transgender women are often conflated in studies, often due to the recruitment of these two groups in overlapping social and sexual network venues (Poteat, German, & Flynn, 2016). When conducting research with Black transgender and intersex people, researchers should look beyond the places where they typically recruit cisgender SGMs and commit to establishing trust, integrity, and credibility with these organizations and safe spaces that specifically serve Black transgender and intersex groups. Furthermore, there is also a tendency to combine Black lesbians with Black bisexual women and other sexual minority women of color into a "sexual minority women of color" group that obscures the profound and demonstrable differences between these communities (Cooperman et al., 2003). One example of this is Morris and Balsam's (2003) study of lesbian and bisexual women's experience of victimization. The researchers boasted that "the diversity of race and ethnicity of the sample allowed us to examine victimization factors for African American, Latina, Native American, Asian American, and European American women, separately" (p. 70). However, the data were combined for most analyses and there was no examination of the differences between lesbian and bisexual women, or the differences between the ethnoracial groups (except for the types of victimization and highest levels of trauma experienced).

There are similar conflations of bisexual people with monosexual SGMs. Research related to Black bisexual mental health has largely been conducted in conjunction with studies examining health among larger groups of Black SGMs or racially diverse samples of SGMs (Bostwick et al., 2014; Calabrese et al., 2015). Few studies have focused solely on Black bisexual samples or disaggregated their data to examine the unique experiences of Black bisexual people (Alexander et al., 2016). Furthermore, there is an absence of research related to the mental health of Black bisexuals with intersectional identities beyond race, gender, and HIV status. We were unable to find any mental health studies that focused on Black bisexual people with physical and cognitive disabilities, who were intersex, or who were immigrants. More research is needed in this area to expand our knowledge of the strengths and vulnerabilities of these groups.

There is a lack of attention to diversity (e.g., in sexual orientation identity, age, class, language, ability, intersex identities) among Black SGMs when recruiting samples to participate in mental health research. This review found that no research exists about Black intersex people's mental health. Several articles included intersex in their title, but not in the content (Jones, 2018). This leads to a huge gap in the understanding of this community and hinders researchers and clinicians from effectively serving them. Another gap is the dearth of attention given to disaggregation of the various gender identities and presentations when sampling Black SGMs. For example, Black lesbians use myriad identifiers to describe their sexuality (i.e., femme,[3] stud,[4] masculine of center,[5] stemme,[6] butch[7]). The mental health of these different subgroups should not be assumed to be understood in studies that survey general samples of Black lesbians without specifically assessing these labels (Reed & Valenti, 2012).

Similarly, older Black SGMs are rarely represented in the mental health literature. Woody (2015) noted: "For many Black lesbians... becoming older or being perceived as old marks the beginning of another chapter of oppression... However, there is little scholarship... that captures the complexities of being a Black woman who is a lesbian, and who is aging" (p. 50). Seelman, Adams, and Poteat's (2016) study of older Black lesbians revealed how the "overlapping axes" of age, gender, race, and sexual orientation "contribute to the unique, intersectional needs of this population in relation to healthy aging" (p. 530). Finally, decisions to only recruit English-speaking samples is a barrier to learning more about Black SGM people who immigrate from Francophone and Portuguese- and Spanish-speaking African and Caribbean nations (Cooperman et al., 2003) and about the effects of acculturation (Corliss et al., 2014).

Gaps in Methodology

Research about Black SGM mental health tends to be either quantitative or qualitative and cross-sectional. There is a general lack of mixed-methods, population-based, epidemiological studies, ecological momentary assessments, randomized controlled trials, and biomarker research with Black SGMs. Furthermore, there have been no nationwide databases aimed at collecting robust data about Black SGM mental health. For example, incidence and prevalence rates of mental health for Black transgender people have traditionally been gleaned from medical records or national data sets with general populations that do not collect data on Black transgender people specifically (Crissman, Berger, Graham, & Dalton, 2017). Thus, researchers are at risk of misclassifying Black transgender people and underestimating mental health disease burden in this group. Large-scale, well-funded, multisite research projects that focus on Black SGM mental health are needed (Lassiter, 2017). These studies will allow for focused and nuanced research inquiry (e.g., questions about intersectionality and group heterogeneity) and resource- and time-intensive methods (e.g., daily diary studies, longitudinal biomarker collection; hierarchal class analyses) that are often infeasible due to small sample sizes and budget limitations due to biased funding practices (Ginther et al., 2011).

There is a need for exploration of culturally specific and congruent frameworks of Black SGM mental health. Existing conceptualizations and measures of mental health and psychological distress may not be culturally specific enough to fully explain the ways in which and why mental health problems manifest among Black SGMs. More formative research should be conducted in this area. Along these lines, community-based participatory research and Afrocentric psychological frameworks have the potential to discover and harness cultural resources to help Black SGMs thrive. Community-based participatory research centers the voices of community members and engages them as co-researchers and co-producers of knowledge. Such research methodologies emphasize collaborating with Black SGM activists and community insiders and openly discussing the intersections of race and SGM identities in a holistic context to ensure that methodologies and findings are relevant to and disseminated in the communities from which the participants originated. Afrocentric psychology, which grounds itself in the cultural values (e.g., interconnectivity and spirituality) that were found among ancient African societies (e.g., Kemetic, Dogara, Anunian) (Akbar, 2003; Azibo, 1996; McAllister, 2014), may also be a useful paradigm to explore Black SGM mental health. Afrocentric psychology has the potential to remove conceptualizations of Black SGMs' experiences of psychological distress out of a framework based on deviations from a Eurocentric norm. An Afrocentric model allows for focus on (a) transcendence of limitations in one's physical and social environments and (b) growth using the cultural gifts of improvisation (e.g., resilience), orality (e.g., self-definition), and spirituality (Jones, 2003). There is much work

[3] Femme is a term used to describe a woman whose gender identity is female and who presents as more stereotypically female and feminine.

[4] Stud is a term used to describe a person assigned female at birth who presents as stereotypically male and masculine.

[5] Masculine of center is a term that "recognizes the breadth and depth of identity for lesbian/queer/womyn who tilt toward the masculine side of the gender scale and includes a wide range of identities such as butch, stud, aggressive/AG, dom, macha, tomboi, trans-masculine etc." (From https://www.butchvoices.com/faqs/, accessed June 5, 2019.)

[6] Stemme is a term used to describe SGL Black women who purposefully present themselves as a blend of femininity and masculinity.

[7] Butch is a term used to describe a woman whose gender identity is female and who presents as more stereotypically masculine.

to be done to be able to better describe, assess, diagnose, and treat mental health problems among Black SGMs within and beyond a biopsychosocial framework.

Conclusion

Black SGM mental health is understudied. Most research about Black SGMs focuses on BG/SGLM and transgender women. The research about these subgroups is often solely in the context of sexual health. This chapter presents a nuanced and thorough review of what is known and not known about the mental health of Black SGMs. The authors focus on mental health risk and resilience and subgroup analyses, in an effort to highlight the complexity of this group. The authors also provide recommendations for areas of future scientific investigation related to Black SGM mental health. The authors hope that this chapter stimulates more comprehensive and culturally responsive mental health study and treatment for these populations.

References

Akbar, N. (2003). *Akbar papers in African psychology.* Tallahassee, FL: Mind Productions & Associates.

Alexander, K., Volpe, E., Abboud, S., & Campbell, J. (2016). Reproductive coercion, sexual risk behaviors, and mental health symptoms among young low-income behaviorally bisexual women: Implications for nursing practice. *Journal of Clinical Nursing, 25*(23–24), 3533–44. doi:10.1111/jocn.13238

Amola, O., & Grimmett, M. A. (2015). Sexual identity, mental health, HIV risk behaviors, and internalized homophobia among Black men who have sex with men. *Journal of Counseling & Development, 93*(2), 236–46. doi:10.1002/j.1556-6676.2015.00199.x

Aranda, F., Matthews, A. K., Hughes, T. L., Muramatsu, N., Wilsnack, S. C., Johnson, T. P., & Riley, B. B. (2015). Coming out in color: Racial/ethnic differences in the relationship between level of sexual identity disclosure and depression among lesbians. *Cultural Diversity & Ethnic Minority Psychology, 21,* 247–57. doi:10.1037/a0037644

Azibo, D. (1996). *African psychology in historical perspective & related commentary.* Trenton, NJ: Africa World Press.

Bailey, M. M. (2019). Whose body is this? On the cultural possibilities of a radical Black sexual praxis. *American Quarterly, 71,* 161–9. doi:10.1353/aq.2019.0009.

Balsam, K., Lehavot, K., Beadnell, B., & Circo, E. (2010). Childhood abuse and mental health indicators among ethnically diverse lesbian, gay, and bisexual adults. *Journal of Consulting and Clinical Psychology, 78*(4), 459–68. doi:10.1037/a0018661

Balsam, K., Molina, Y., Blayney, J., Dillworth, T., Zimmerman, L., & Kaysen, D. (2015). Racial/ethnic differences in identity and mental health outcomes among young sexual minority women. *Cultural Diversity and Ethnic Minority Psychology, 21,* 380–90. doi:1099-9809/15/$12.00

Boone, M. R., Cook, S. H., & Wilson, P. A. (2016). Sexual identity and HIV status influence the relationship between internalized stigma and psychological distress in Black gay and bisexual men. *AIDS Care, 28*(6), 764–70. doi:10.1080/09540121.2016.1164801

Bostwick, W. B., Boyd, C. J., Hughes, T. L., West, B. T., & McCabe, S. E. (2014). Discrimination and mental health among lesbian, gay, and bisexual adults in the United States. *American Journal of Orthopsychiatry, 84,* 35–45. doi:10.1037/h0098851

Bostwick, W., Hughes, T., Steffen, A., Veldhuis, C., & Wilsnack, S. (2019). Depression and victimization in a community sample of bisexual and lesbian women: An intersectional approach. *Archives of Sexual Behavior, 48,* 131–41. doi:10.1007/s10508-018-1247-y

Bowleg, L. (2012). The problem with the phrase "women and minorities": Intersectionality—an important theoretical framework for public health. *American Journal of Public Health, 102*(7), 1267–73. doi:10.2105/AJPH.2012.300750

Bowleg, L. (2013). "Once you've blended the cake, you can't take the parts back to the main ingredients": Black gay and bisexual men's descriptions and experiences of intersectionality. *Sex Roles, 68*(11), 754–67. doi:10.1007/s11199-012-0152-4

Bowleg, L., Brooks, K., & Ritz, S. F. (2008). "Bringing home more than a paycheck:" An exploratory analysis of Black lesbians' experiences of stress and coping in the workplace. *Journal of Lesbian Studies, 12,* 69–84. doi:10.1080/10894160802174342

Bowleg, L., Huang, J., Brooks, K., Black, A., & Burkholder, G. (2003). Triple jeopardy and beyond: Multiple minority stress and resilience among Black lesbians. *Journal of Lesbian Studies, 7,* 87–108. doi:10.1300/J155v07n04_06

Calabrese, S. K., Meyer, I. H., Overstreet, N. M., Haile, R., & Hansen, N. B. (2015). Exploring discrimination and mental health disparities faced by Black sexual minority women using a minority stress framework. *Psychology of Women Quarterly, 39,* 287–304. doi:10.1177/0361684314560730

Consolacion, T. B., Russell, S. T., & Sue, S. (2004). Sex, race/ethnicity, and romantic attractions: Multiple minority status adolescents and mental health. *Cultural Diversity & Ethnic Minority Psychology, 10*(3), 200–14. doi:10.1037/1099–9809.10.3.200

Cook, S. H., Valera, P., Calebs, B. J., & Wilson, P. A. (2017). Adult attachment as a moderator of the association between childhood traumatic experiences and depression symptoms among young Black gay and bisexual men. *Cultural Diversity and Ethnic Minority Psychology, 23*(3), 388–97. doi:10.1037/cdp0000119

Cooperman, N. A., Simoni, J. M., & Lockhart, D. W. (2003). Abuse, social support, and depression among HIV-positive heterosexual, bisexual, and lesbian women. *Journal of Lesbian Studies, 7,* 49–66. doi:10.1300/J155v07n04_04

Corliss, H. L., Rosario, M., Birkett, M. A., Newcomb, M. E., Buchting, F. O., & Matthews, A. K. (2014). Sexual orientation disparities in adolescent cigarette smoking: Intersections with race/ethnicity, gender, and age. *American Journal of Public Health, 104,* 1137–47. doi:10.2105/AJPH.2013.301819

Crissman, H. P., Berger, M. B., Graham, L. F., & Dalton, V. K. (2017). Transgender demographics: A household probability sample of US adults, 2014. *American Journal of Public Health, 107,* 213–5. doi:10.2105/AJPH.2016.303571

DeBlaere, C., Brewster, M. E., Bertsch, K. N., DeCarlo, A. L., Kegel, K. A., & Presseau, C. D. (2014). The protective power of collective action for sexual minority women of color: An investigation of multiple discrimination experiences and psychological distress. *Psychology of Women Quarterly, 38*(1), 20–32. doi:10.1177/0361684313493252

Dibble, S. L., Eliason, M. J., & Crawford, B. (2012). Correlates of wellbeing among African American lesbians. *Journal of Homosexuality, 59*, 820–38. doi:10.1080/00918369.2012.694763

Dodge, B., Schnarrs, P., Malebranche, D., Martinez, O., Reece, M., . . . Fortenberry, J. (2012). The significance of privacy and trust in providing health-related services to behaviorally bisexual men in the United States. *AIDS Education and Prevention, 24*(3), 242–56. doi:10.1521/aeap.2012.24.3.242

Drabble, L. A., Veldhuis, C. B., Riley, B. B., Rostosky, S., & Hughes, T. L. (2017). Relationship of religiosity and spirituality to hazardous drinking, drug use, and depression among sexual minority women. *Journal of Homosexuality, 65*, 1734–57. doi:10.1080/00918369.2017.1383116

Duckworth, A., Peterson, C., Matthews, M., & Kelly (2007). Grit: Perseverance and passion for long-term goals. *Journal of Personality and Social Psychology, 92*(6), 1087–101. doi:10.1037/0022–3514.92.6.1087

Earnshaw, V. A., Reed, N. M., Watson, R. J., Maksut, J. L., Allen, A. M., & Eaton, L. A. (2019). Intersectional internalized stigma among Black gay and bisexual men: A longitudinal analysis spanning HIV/sexually transmitted infection diagnosis. *Journal of Health Psychology* [E-pub ahead of print]. doi:10.1177/1359105318820101

Feinstein, B., Turner, B., Beach, L., Korpak, A., & Phillips, G. (2019). Racial/ethnic differences in mental health, substance use, and bullying victimization among self-identified bisexual high school-aged youth. *LGBT Health, 6*(4), 174–83. doi:10.1089/lgbt.2018.0229

Feldman, M. B., & Meyer, I. H. (2007). Eating disorders in diverse lesbian, gay, and bisexual populations. *International Journal of Eating Disorders, 40*, 218–26. doi:10.1002/eat.20360

Follins, L. D. (2017). Preface. In L. D. Follins & J. M. Lassiter (Eds.), *Black LGBT health in the United States: The intersection of race, gender, and sexual orientation* (1st ed., pp. ix—xiii). Lanham, MD: Lexington Books.

Follins, L. D., & Lassiter, J. M. (Eds.). (2017). *Black LGBT health in the United States: The intersection of race, gender, and sexual orientation.* Lanham, MD: Lexington Books.

Follins, L. D., Walker, J., & Lewis, M. K. (2014). Resilience in Black lesbian, gay, bisexual, and transgender individuals: A critical review of the literature. *Journal of Gay & Lesbian Mental Health, 18*, 190–212. doi:10.1080/19359705.2013.828343

Friedman, M., Bukowski, L., Eaton, L., Matthews, D., Dyer, T., Siconolfi, D., & Stall, R. (2019). Psychosocial health disparities among Black bisexual men in the U.S.: Effects of sexuality nondisclosure and gay community support. *Archives of Sexual Behavior, 48*(1), 213–24. doi:10.1007/s10508-018-1162-2

Garret-Walker, J., & Longmire-Avital, B. (2018). Resilience and depression: The roles of racial identity, sexual identity, and social support on well-being for Black LGB emerging adults. *Journal of Black Sexuality and Relationships, 4*(4), 1–15. doi:10.1353/bsr.2018.0008

Ginicola, M. M. (2017). Counseling intersex clients. In M. M. Ginicola, C. Smith, & J. M. Filmore (Eds.), *Affirmative counseling with LGBTQI+ people* (pp. 241–50). Alexandria, VA: American Counseling Association.

Ginther, D., Schaffer, W., Schnell, J., Masimore, B., Liu, F., . . . Kington, R. (2011). Race, ethnicity, and NIH research awards. *Science, 33*, 1015–9. doi:10.1126/science.1196783

Graham, L. F., Braithwaite, K., Spikes, P., Stephens, C. F., & Edu, U. F. (2009). Exploring the mental health of Black men who have sex with men. *Community Mental Health Journal, 45*(4), 272–84. doi:10.1007/s10597-009-9186-7

Grant, J. M., Mottet, L. A., Tanis, J., Harrison, H., Herman, J. L., & Keisling, M. (2011). *Injustice at every turn: A report of the national transgender discrimination survey.* Washington, DC: National Center for Transgender Equality and National Gay and Lesbian Task Force.

Haynes, T., & Dale, S. (2017). Shades of Black: A psychotherapy group for Black men who have sex with men. In L. D. Follins & J. M. Lassiter (Eds.), *Black LGBT health in the United States: The intersection of race, gender, and sexual orientation* (1st ed., pp. 151–68). Lanham, MD: Lexington Books.

Hergenrather, K. C., Geishecker, S., Clark, G., & Rhodes, S. D. (2013). A pilot test of the HOPE intervention to explore employment and mental health among African American gay men living with HIV/AIDS: Results from a CBPR study. *AIDS Education and Prevention, 25*(5), 405–22. doi:10.1521/aeap.2013.25.5.405

Huang, Y.-P., Brewster, M. E., Moradi, B., Goodman, M. B., Wiseman, M. C., & Martin, A. (2010). Content analysis of literature about LGB people of color: 1998–2007. *The Counseling Psychologist, 38*, 363–96. doi:10.1177/0011000009335255

Jones, J. (2003). TRIOS: A psychological theory of the African legacy in American culture. *Journal of Social Issues, 59*(1), 217–42. doi:10.1111/1540–4560.t01-1–00014

Jones, T. (2018). Intersex studies: A systematic review of international health literature. *SAGE Open, 8*(2), 215824401774557. doi:10.1177/2158244017745577

Kertzner, R. M., Meyer, I. H., Frost, D. M., & Stirratt, M. J. (2009). Social and psychological well-being in lesbians, gay men, and bisexuals: The effects of race, gender, age, and sexual identity. *American Journal of Orthopsychiatry, 79*, 500–10. doi:10.1037/a0016848

Lassiter, J. M. (2014). Extracting dirt from water: A strengths-based approach to religion for African American same-gender men. *Journal of Religion and Health, 53*(1), 178–89. doi:10.1007/s10943-012-9668-8

Lassiter, J. M. (2016). Religious participation and identity salience of Black men who have sex with men: Findings from a nationally recruited sample. *Psychology of Sexual Orientation and Gender Diversity, 3*(3), 304–12. doi:10.1037/sgd0000176

Lassiter, J. M. (2017). Introduction: For us, by us: A manifesto of Black SGL and trans health. In L. D. Follins & J. M. Lassiter (Eds.), *Black LGBT health in the United States: The intersection of race, gender, and sexual orientation* (1st ed., pp. 1–9). Lanham, MD: Lexington Books.

Mays, V., Cochran, S., & Roeder, M. (2003). Depressive distress and prevalence of common problems among homosexually active African American women in the United States. *Journal of Psychology & Human Sexuality, 15*(2/3), 27–46. doi:10.1300/J056v15n02_03

McAllister, C. (2014). Toward an African-centered sociological approach to Africana lesbian, gay, bisexual, transgender, queer, and intersexed identities and performances: The Kemetic model of the cosmological interactive self. *Critical Sociology, 40*(2), 239–56. doi:10.1177/0896920512455935

Meyer-Bahlburg, H. F. L., Khuri, J., Reyes-Portillo, J., Ehrhardt, A. A., & New, M. I. (2017). Stigma associated with classical congenital adrenal hyperplasia in women's sexual lives. *Archives of Sexual Behavior, 47*, 943–51. doi:10.10007/s10508-017-1003-8

Meyer, I., Dietrich, J., & Swartz, S. (2008). Lifetime prevalence of mental disorders and suicide attempts in diverse lesbian, gay, and bisexual populations. *American Journal of Public Health, 98*(6), 1004–6. doi:10.2105/AJPH.2006.096826

Morris, J. F., & Balsam, K. F. (2003). Lesbian and bisexual women's experiences of victimization: Mental health, revictimization, and sexual identity development. *Journal of Lesbian Studies, 7*, 67–85. doi:10.1300/J155v07n04_05

Munoz-Laboy, M. (2019). Ethnic and racial specificity, or not, in bisexuality research: A practical commentary. *Archives of Sexual Behavior, 48*, 317–25. doi:10.1007/s10508-018-1318-0

Ports, K., Lee, R., Raiford, J., Spikes, P., Manago, C., & Wheeler, D. (2017). Adverse childhood experiences and health and wellness outcomes among Black men who have sex with men. *Journal of Urban Health, 94*(3), 375–83. doi:10.1007/s11524-017-0146-1

Poteat, T. C., & Follins, L. D. (2017). Narratives of health among Black trans men: An exploratory intersectional analysis. In L. D. Follins & J. M. Lassiter (Eds.), *Black LGBT health in the United States: The intersection of race, gender, and sexual orientation* (pp. 73–86). Lanham, MD: Rowman & Littlefield.

Poteat, T., German, D., & Flynn, C. (2016). The conflation of gender and sex: Gaps and opportunities in HIV data among transgender women and MSM. *Global Public Health, 11*, 835–48. doi:10.1080/17441692.2015.1134615.

Ramsey, F., Hill, M. J., & Kellam, C. (2010). *Black lesbians matter: An examination of the unique experiences, perspectives, and priorities of the Black lesbian community*. Sacramento, CA: Zuna Institute.

Reed, S. J., & Valenti, M. T. (2012). "It ain't all as bad as it may seem": Young Black lesbians' responses to sexual prejudice. *Journal of Homosexuality, 59*, 703–20. doi:10.1080/00918369.2012.673940

Reisner, S., Biello, K. B., White Hughto, J. M., Kuhns, L., Mayer, K. H., Garofalo, R., & Mimiaga, M. J. (2016). Psychiatric diagnoses and comorbidities in a diverse, multicity cohort of young transgender women. *JAMA Pediatrics, 170*, 481–6. doi:10.1001/jamapediatrics.2016.0067

Santos, C. E., & VanDaalen, R. A. (2018). Associations among psychological distress, high-risk activism, and conflict between ethnic-racial and sexual minority identities in lesbian, gay, bisexual racial/ethnic minority adults. *Journal of Counseling Psychology, 65*(2), 194–203. doi:10.1037/cou0000241

Seelman, K. L., Adams, M. A., & Poteat, T. (2016). Interventions for healthy aging among mature Black lesbians: Recommendations gathered through community-based research. *Journal of Women & Aging, 29*, 530–42. doi:10.1080/08952841.2016.1256733

Smallwood, S. W., Spencer, S. M., Ingram, L. A., Thrasher, J. F., & Thompson-Robinson, M. V. (2017a). Different dimensions: Internalized homonegativity among African American men who have sex with men in the Deep South. *Journal of Homosexuality, 64*(1), 45–60. doi:10.1080/00918369.2016.1172869

Smallwood, S. W., Spencer, S. M., Ingram, L. A., Thrasher, J. F., & Thompson-Robinson, M. V. (2017b). Examining the relationships between religiosity, spirituality, internalized homonegativity, and condom use among African American men who have sex with men in the Deep South. *American Journal of Men's Health, 11*(2), 196–207. doi:10.1177/1557988315590835

Teti, M., Martin, A., Ranade, R., Massie, J., Malebranche, D., Tschann, J., & Bowleg, L. (2012). "I'm a keep rising. I'm a keep going forward, regardless": Exploring black men's resilience amid sociostructural challenges and stressors. *Qualitative Health Research, 22*(4), 524–33. doi:10.1177/1049732311422051

Villarosa, L. (2017). America's hidden H.I.V. epidemic. *New York Times*, June 6. https://www.nytimes.com/2017/06/06/magazine/americas-hidden-hiv-epidemic.html

Wade, R., & Harper, G. (2017). Young Black gay/bisexual and other men who have sex with men: A review and content analysis of health-focused research between 1988 and 2013. *American Journal of Men's Health, 11*(5), 1388–405. doi:10.1177/1557988315606962

Walker, J. J., & Longmire-Avital, B. (2013). The impact of religious faith and internalized homonegativity on resiliency for Black lesbian, gay, and bisexual emerging adults. *Developmental Psychology, 49*(9), 1723–31. doi:10.1037/a0031059

Winiker, A. K., Tobin, K. E., Davey-Rothwell, M., & Latkin, C. (2019). An examination of grit in Black men who have sex with men and associations with health and social outcomes. *Journal of Community Psychology, 47*(5), 1095–104. doi:10.1002/jcop.22176

Wilson, B. D. M. (2009a). Widening the dialogue to narrow the gap in health disparities: Approaches to fat Black lesbian and bisexual women's health promotion. In E. Rothblum & S. Solovay (Eds.), *The fat studies reader* (pp. 54–64). New York, NY: New York University.

Wilson, B. D. M. (2009b). Black lesbian gender and sexual culture: Celebration and resistance. *Culture, Health, and Sexuality, 11*, 297–313. doi:10.1080/13691050802676876

Wilson, B., Okwu, C., & Mills, S. (2011). Brief report: The relationship between multiple forms of oppression and subjective health among Black lesbian and bisexual women. *Journal of Lesbian Studies, 15*, 15–24. doi:10.1080/10894160.2010.508393

Wilson, P., Valera, P., Martos, A., Wittlin, N., Munoz-Laboy, & Parker, R. (2016). Contributions of qualitative research in informing HIV/AIDS interventions targeting Black MSM in the United States. *Journal of Sex Research, 53*(6), 642–54. doi:10.1080/00224499.2015.1016139

Wilton, L. (2017). Criminal justice system and transgender people. In K. L. Nadal (Ed.), *The SAGE encyclopedia of psychology and gender* (pp. 388–90). Los Angeles, CA: Sage Publications.

Wilton, L., Chiasson, M., Nandi, V., Lelutiu-Weinberger, C., Frye, V., Hirshfield, S., . . . Koblin, B. (2018). Characteristics and correlates of lifetime suicidal thoughts and attempts among young Black men who have sex with men (MSM) and transgender women. *Journal of Black Psychology, 44*, 273–90. doi:10.1177/0095798418771819

Woody, I. (2015). Lift every voice: Voices of African American lesbian elders. *Journal of Lesbian Studies, 19*, 50–8. doi:10.1080/10894160.2015.972755

Zimmerman, L., Darnell, D. A., Rhew, I. C., Lee, C. M., & Kaysen, D. (2015). Resilience in community: A social ecological development model for young adult sexual minority women. *American Journal of Community Psychology, 55*, 179–90. doi:10.1007/s10464-015-9702-6

CHAPTER

16 Latinx Sexual and Gender Minority Mental Health

Alison Cerezo, Juan Camarena, *and* Amaranta Ramirez

Abstract

Sexual and gender diverse (SGD) Latinxs are a vibrant, heterogenous community that can trace their heritage to various countries in Latin America. This chapter describes how socio-historical trends in the United States and Latin America have shaped the social and health conditions of SGD Latinxs, including the impact of colonialism and recent state-sanctioned discriminatory violence. An intersectionality framework is used in this chapter to consider how race and ethnicity, immigration, language, sexual orientation, and gender identity function interdependently to impact the lives of SGD Latinxs in the United States and around the world. The authors also discuss trends in SGD Latinx research in the United States and Latin America, with a focus on mental health and substance abuse.

Keywords: Latinx, Latina/o, Latinx mental health, intersectionality, religion and spirituality, immigration, acculturation

Latinxs[1] are an immensely rich and diverse community that reside in the United States and around the world. Latinxs make up 18 percent of the total U.S. population and represent individuals of many races, including black/African heritage, indigenous heritage, and white/European heritage (U.S. Census Bureau, 2018). Latinxs' connection to the United States is complex. Many have family lineage that dates to the 1800s when the U.S. was formerly México (California, Nevada, Utah, Arizona, Colorado, New Mexico, and Texas), while others have more recent migration stories. The Latinx community is heterogeneous both within and between nationalities, hailing from various regions of Latin America that include México, Central and South America, and the Caribbean (Casas & Ryan, 2010).

This chapter presents an overview of key cultural issues as they relate to the mental health of sexual and gender diverse (SGD) Latinxs. Given the vast within-group differences among Latinxs in the U.S. and around the world, it is critical that mental health researchers and providers understand and embrace an intersectional framework when working with the Latinx community (see Bowleg, 2008; Cole, 2009; Crenshaw, 1991). Thus, this chapter is based on the premise that the mental health of SGD Latinxs is rooted in their lived experiences related to race, ethnicity, sexual orientation, gender identity, and other cultural dimensions, which place them at increased risk of social and health disparities. This heterogeneity also provides unique opportunities for resilience, connection, and empowerment (Oquendo et al., 2005).

Latinx: The Power of Language and Identity

The term *Latinx* has become more widely used in the recent past, emerging in popular media and the social sciences in 2014 and 2015, as an ethno-racial identifier used to describe individuals of Latin American

[1] Latinx is a non-gendered term used to describe people of Latin American descent.

descent (see Scharrón-del Río & Aja, 2015). As described by Santos (2017),

> Latinx, often pronounced as "La-teen-ex," is a descriptor for individuals in the U.S. who have roots in Latin America which explicitly acknowledges diversity in forms of gender identity and expression via use of "x" in lieu of the gendered articles "a" or "o." Use of Latinx, coupled with an understanding of the reasons for adopting it, may be viewed as a form of solidarity with individuals whose gender identity and expression might differ from binary classifications of men and women and who must navigate spaces of heteronormativity, or social settings that normalize heterosexuality. (p. 12)

The identifier *Latinx* has become more readily embraced in the mental health field, as evidenced by an increased use of the term in journal outlets of the American Psychological Association (APA; Cardemil, Millán, & Aranda, 2019) and the name change of both the National Latinx Psychological Association and the *Journal of Latinx Psychology* (previously Latina/o). Conversations about the use of *Latinx* have also hit major media outlets, thereby centering dialogs about gender identity, and often sexual orientation, front and center in the Latinx community.

Scholars contend that the origins of the term *Latinx* emerged in the early 2000s within queer online communities in Latin America (de Onís, 2017; Santos, 2017). Use of the "x" can be traced to political strategies employed by activists in the black and African American community (e.g., Malcolm X) and Xicana feminist circles (de Onís, 2017). Authors argue that the political use of "x" makes the term Latinx a tribute to people of black and indigenous heritage—two communities that have faced generations of trauma and oppression in Latin America and around the world.

While the term *Latinx* has garnered increased support in the social sciences and popular media, there have also been critiques of the term. Most notably, opponents argue that Latinx is based in the U.S., hard to pronounce, and erases the richness of the Spanish language. Furthermore, critics also call on a long history of attacks on the Spanish language in U.S. culture as well as the term overlooking the importance of some historical scholarship that is intentionally gendered (Lazo, 2018). Proponents of the term *Latinx* have responded to these critiques by noting that the Spanish language itself is tied to the colonization of indigenous and African peoples throughout Latin America, that language is ever-evolving, and that the term emerged from SGD community spaces in Latin America (Cardemil et al., 2019; Santos, 2017; Scharrón-del Río & Aja, 2015). Social change is often coupled with resistance. In this chapter we use the term *Latinx* to embrace an intersectional approach that recognizes how race, ethnicity, sexual orientation and gender identity, and many other cultural dimensions intersect to impact the social and health experiences of SGD Latinxs.

The Complexity of Race and Racial Diversity among Latinxs

The Colonial era of the fifteenth and sixteenth centuries has had a tremendous impact on what is considered in today's world to be Latin America. Although colonialism was carried out by several nations, regions designated as making up Latin America include countries that were under Spanish and Portuguese rule. Thus, the descriptor *Latin America* designates countries where Spanish and Portuguese are formally spoken.

Colonialism in Latin America resulted in the extinction of many Indigenous tribes as well as the importing of African slaves when the exploitation of indigenous people was not possible. As a result, colonial rule resulted in the erasure of many indigenous cultural traditions and languages. Racial shifts also occurred across Latin America with the arrival of Spanish and Portuguese settlers, African slaves, and indigenous communities who were native to the land.

Many Latinxs identify as *mestizo*, a term meant to signify mixed ancestry of Spanish (white/European) and indigenous heritage. While *mestizo* is commonly used in Latin America to describe one's ethno-racial background, the term serves to minimize the presence of Latinxs who have African/black heritage as well those who are indigenous (non-white). The term *Afro-Latinx* describes individuals whose roots trace back to Africa and Latin America (Vargas & Kuhl, 2008) and/or Spanish-speaking individuals of African descent residing in a territory of the United States (Higgins, 2007). Many individuals embrace the identifier *Afro-Latinx* to illuminate the racial heterogeneity of Latin America and to honor the cultural influence of Africa in Latin America (Flores & Roman, 2009; Ramos, Jaccard, & Guilamo-Ramos, 2003; Roman & Flores, 2010).

Afro-Latinx have been largely ignored in health research, practice guidelines, and policy efforts. This invisibility is tied to anti-black sentiment in Latin America and the U.S., which increases negative disparities in social and health domains for this community (Camarena, 2018). Many Afro-Latinx reside in the Dominican Republic, Cuba, and Puerto Rico, regions where the slave trade was more heavily based during the Colonial era. In fact, the first permanent European settlement in the New World was in the Dominican Republic; it served as the first region in the Americas to import slaves from Africa (Gates, 2011).

Afro-Latinx have a rich and diverse experience in the world, tracing their lineage to Africa, Spain, and indigenous roots. That said, many Afro-Latinx also face anti-black racism, often referred to as *colorism*, that leads to barriers in Latin America and on migration to the U.S. (Chavez-Dueñas, Adames, & Organista, 2014; Montalvo, 2009). These challenges expand to the larger SGD community: Afro-Latinx bisexual and gay men report experiencing high rates of objectification within the gay community (Muñoz-Laboy & Severson, 2018). An intersectionality approach is particularly useful when considering the interplay of race and ethnicity among SGD Latinxs. Further research is needed that addresses the diversity of race and ethnicity among SGD Latinxs, particularly how SGD individuals perceive multiple consciousness and identities (Camarena, 2018).

Events and Laws Impacting SGD Latinxs

The various countries that make up Latin America each develop and enforce laws related to sexual orientation and gender identity according to their own sociocultural and historical norms, thus contributing to divergent perceptions of acceptance and safety throughout the region (Russell, Bohan, McCarroll, & Smith, 2011). The past decade has witnessed an improvement in the passage of antidiscrimination laws throughout Latin America related to sexual orientation and gender identity. A major victory for SGD Brazilians occurred in 2019 when the Brazilian Supreme Court—in an opinion strongly criticized by President Jair Bolsonaro—included sexual orientation under workplace protections. In 2010, Argentina became the first country in Latin America to permit same-sex marriage, followed by Colombia, Brazil, Uruguay, Ecuador, and México City and twelve other states across México. Further, Chile passed legislation allowing civil unions that provided legal rights and protections to many same-sex couples.

While progress for SGD communities has improved in the legal realm in the recent past, violent anti-SGD rhetoric in some South American countries continues to be a cause for concern (Inter-American Commission on Human Rights, 2015). In South America, crimes against SGD people are severely underreported due to support of these acts from law enforcement (see Davis et al., 2019). There continues to be active persecution and violence against many SGD Latinxs in Latin America, including disproportionate killings of transgender women. Bolsonaro's presidential campaign was notorious for being anti-gay and anti-women; he famously stated, "I'd rather die than my son be gay." Bolsonaro's anti-SGD sentiments are echoed by many citizens of Brazil, with the country leading the world in rates of violence against sexual minorities. Thus, it is important to understand the conditions faced by the SGD Latinxs from these countries, and why many seek refuge in the U.S.

SGD Latinxs in the U.S. have also faced violence in the past. On the evening of June 12, 2016, a man proclaiming allegiance to the extremist group ISIS opened fire on the patrons inside of Pulse, a gay nightclub in Orlando, Florida, that was hosting a "Latin Pride Night." Fifty-three people were injured and forty-nine were killed; those killed were mostly young Latinx men in their twenties and thirties. Scholars have since criticized the media's role in ignoring the fact that the largest mass murder in U.S. history targeted the SGD Latinx community (see Hancock & Halderman, 2017; Stults, Kuprat, Krause, Kapadia, & Halkitis, 2017). Following the tragedy, Ramirez, Gonzalez, and Galupo (2017) interviewed ninety-four participants, all of whom identified as SGD and persons of color, and identified a series of themes, including the lack of representation of multiple identities in the media coverage following the shooting as well as an acknowledgment that violence toward SGD persons of color is nothing new. As described by Ramirez et al. (2017), the Pulse massacre reminded many SGD Latinxs of the intersectional dangers they regularly face in society at large as both Latinx and SGD.

This incident was not unique, though. A month prior, May 22, 2016, three armed men forced their way inside La Madame, a gay bar in Veracruz, Xalapa, México. They killed seven and injured twelve. However, it wasn't until after the incident in Orlando that the Veracruz shooting reached Western media. The lack of information and awareness comes also from the fear many in the SGD community feel when it comes to reporting incidents of violence in Latin American countries, where there is a culture of minimizing these events

(Davis et al., 2019; Inter-American Commission on Human Rights, 2015).

Immigration

At the time of the writing of this chapter, the U.S. has undergone significant political shifts, resulting in an increase in hate crimes and white terrorism under the administration of Donald Trump. Researchers have found a growing acceptance of bias toward members of certain social groups during the Trump administration (Crandell, Miller, & White, 2018). These incidents of bias carry severe consequences for SGD Latinxs. As of July 2019, two transgender Latinas have died in Immigration and Customs Enforcement (ICE) custody, and in March 2019, a grievance was submitted to ICE officials by several civil and legal rights organizations, including the American Civil Liberties Union, chronicling discriminatory treatment faced by a group of twelve gay men and transgender women in ICE. Included in this grievance was a description of ongoing discriminatory treatment directed toward SGD Latinx detainees, including physical and psychological harms from ICE staff and other detainees in ICE custody (Moore, 2019).

According to a nationwide poll carried out by the Williams Institute, approximately 900,000 Latinx immigrants who reside in the U.S. identify as SGD (Garcia, 2013). Of these individuals, 30 percent are undocumented. Compared to the general immigrant community, SGD Latinxs are more likely to be male and under the age of thirty. Approximately 48,000 SGD Latinx immigrants are in a same-sex relationship where either one or both partners are not U.S. citizens, and many of these couples are raising children. The potential for family separation is a real threat to many SGD Latinx immigrants, especially in light of stricter immigration policies and enforcement. In 2019, birthright citizenship was denied to several children born overseas to same-sex parents; this places many SGD Latinx families at risk of separation. In one case involving two married women, one a U.S. citizen and the other an Italian national, the U.S. State Department denied the child U.S. citizenship because he did not have a biological relation to his U.S. mother (Tillman, 2019).

Many SGD Latinxs experience forced migration in an attempt to flee violence and oppression in their home country—a process known as *sexual migration* (Toro-Alfonso, Ortiz, & Lugo, 2012). Several scholars have determined that SGD Latinxs are migrating to the U.S., regardless of documentation status, for opportunities to work, to increase their quality of life, and to experience freedom to express their sexual orientation and gender identity (American Psychological Association, 2019; Cerezo, Morales, Quintero, & Gebhardt, 2014; Hwang et al., 2019; Toro-Alfonso et al., 2012).

SGD Latinx immigrants regularly face hardship when attempting to attain legal status to reside and/or work in the U.S. The easiest method of entering the U.S. is via temporary visa programs that allow individuals to visit, study, and work. However, when applying for a temporary visa, individuals must provide evidence of their plans to return home once their visa expires (Morales, 2013). This process is particularly challenging for many SGD Latinx immigrants who migrate to the U.S. as a means to escape oppression in their home countries. Family and employer sponsorships, the two most popular routes to gaining U.S. citizenship, require documentation of support from one's immediate family or employer. This process is burdensome to many SGD Latinx immigrants, who are commonly arriving to the United States via sexual migration and therefore do not have these systems of support readily available to them during the application process.

Seeking refugee status in the U.S. via political asylum is a common path to attaining legal residency for many SGD immigrants (American Psychological Association, 2019; Morales, 2013). To be granted political asylum, applicants must prove that returning to their home country would result in persecution, a threat that the government in their home country cannot protect them against. While seeking asylum is a common process of attaining legal residency among many SGD immigrants, the process itself is idiosyncratic; applicants must plead their case to authority figures who determine whether the anti-SGD status described by an applicant is a serious and real threat to their livelihood (Reading & Rubin, 2011). The Trump administration has threatened to terminate asylum to the United States altogether, placing many SGD immigrants' lives at risk (Moore, 2019).

Culture and Identity

Family plays a key role in many SGD Latinxs' identity formation and lived experience. Pastrana (2015) examined factors that contributed to a person's choice to be out as a sexual minority in a nationwide sample of 1,159 SGD Latina/os. The author found that family support, the belief that one's sexual orientation is an important part of one's identity, and having a connection to the SGD community were positive predictors of being out. In fact, family support was the strongest predictor of one's decision to be out. Examining differences by immigration background, Pastrana (2015) found that being born outside of the U.S. (migrating to the U.S.) was a negative predictor of outness.

The role of family in transgender and gender nonconforming (TGMC) Latinxs' lives has also been shown to be an important factor in the developmental process. Cerezo et al. (2014) found that family members provided instrumental supports in the form of financial assistance and emotional encouragement for transgender Latinas migrating to the U.S. Participants noted how the support provided by their families of origin was key to their ability to access medical and social services needed to live as transgender women in the U.S. free from the violence faced in their home countries.

The potential loss of family support upon coming out is particularly stressful for many SGD Latinxs who rely on family relations to access linguistic and cultural traditions that are central to their sense of self. In a twenty-year review of her scholarship on Latina lesbians, Espín (2011) described the unique gendered pressures faced by Latinas at the intersection of ethnicity, sexual orientation, and gender. Specifically, Espín (2011) described how many Latina lesbians stand to lose family and community ties upon coming out, which in turn impacts their ability to contribute to the betterment of their immediate and extended communities.

The role of religion is also vital to consider in SGD Latinxs' identity development and decisions around disclosure. However, while religion is a cultural dimension important to many Latinxs in the U.S., the link between religious background and outness is inconsistent in the research literature (Potoczniak, Crosbie-Burnett, & Salzburg, 2009; Schope, 2002). Across the U.S., there has been a growing trend for Latinxs to indicate *no* traditional religious affiliation (Navarro-Rivera, Kosmin, & Keysar, 2010). The percentage of Latinxs in the U.S. who indicated "no religion" in a nationwide sample grew from 900,000 in 1990 to 4 million in 2008. Thus, the link between religion and outness may continue to diminish for future generations of SGD Latinxs.

Many of the values held by the greater Latinx culture have been substantially influenced by religion. This includes a culture of homophobia driven by Catholicism from the Colonial era that results in the narrowing of gender roles and gender expression (Barbosa, Torres, Silva, & Kahn, 2010). There is also stronger enforcement of what is considered acceptable behavior across genders (Barbosa et al., 2010). For Latinx women, the concept of *marianismo* has been shaped by the religious ideals of the Virgin Mary, where women are socialized to be subservient, self-sacrificing, pure, and nurturing (Barbosa et al., 2010; Miville, Mendez, & Louie, 2017). These traditional female roles are ascribed to women regardless of age, race, and other cultural dimensions and have been associated with depression and eating disorders in young Latinas (Miville et al., 2017) as well as SGD Latinas' sexual orientation disclosure decisions (Espín, 2011). Further, *marianismo* posits that for women, sex should be connected solely to procreation, not pleasure. This makes talking about a same-sex relationship especially difficult for many SGD Latinx women whose sexual orientation is regarded as deviant and unacceptable in the context of *marianismo*, adding to feelings of alienation (Barbosa et al., 2010; Hussain, Leija, Lewis, & Sanchez, 2015).

Understanding the impact of *machismo* on identity development is a crucial aspect of SGD Latinx men's health. In the social science literature, *machismo* is ascribed to Latinx men to explain gender role values and behaviors that include aggressiveness, bravado, being controlling, and so forth (Torres, Solberg, & Carlstrom, 2002). However, many scholars argue that popular narratives of *machismo* have been one-dimensional, stereotypical, and pathological (Falicov, 2010). While roots of the concept are patriarchal, *machismo* also implies positive characteristics such as being hardworking and proud and providing for one's family (Falicov, 1998). Other terms like *contemporary machismo* and *caballerismo* imply valuing positive ethnic affiliation, being emotionally expressive, and navigating masculinity in a nuanced manner (Arciniega, Anderson, Tovar-Blank, & Tracey, 2008; Torres et al., 2002).

Identifying as a gay, bisexual, or queer man does not mean that *machismo* and traditional constructions of gender are abandoned (Estrada, Rigali-Oiler, Arciniega, & Tracey, 2011). Rather, Latinx cultural beliefs shape the sexual decisions of many SGD Latinx men (Muñoz-Laboy, 2004, 2008). This includes fears of being perceived as not "masculine enough" that can drive risk behaviors that include a lack of openness about sexual identity to one's family and community (Diaz, 1998). Further, this lack of openness can contribute to engagement in unsafe sex practices that place Latinx men, and often their long-term partners, at risk for sexually transmitted diseases and other health complications (Hirsch, Higgins, Bentley, & Nathanson, 2002). Latinx men who were less likely to conform to socially acceptable gender norms experience increased levels of mental distress (Sandfort, Melendez, & Diaz, 2007), and those who exhibit increased scores on *machismo* scales also report increased levels of internalized homophobia and engagement in risky sex (Estrada et al., 2011).

The concept of "conflict of allegiance" has been used to describe the perceived incompatibility that many individuals experience when reconciling their sexual orientation and ethno-racial identity as a person of color (Sarno, Mohr, Jackson, & Fassinger, 2015). In fact, this perceived incompatibility exacerbates existing experiences of marginalization and then contributes to psychological distress (Santos & VanDaalen, 2016). In a qualitative study of first- and second-generation SGD Latinxs, participants described facing struggles in balancing connectedness to the SGD community and connectedness to the Latinx community (Gray, Mendelsohn, & Omoto, 2015). As noted by Jamil, Harper, and Fernandez (2009), SGD Latinx immigrant youth face especially hard challenges in their sexual identity development. For example, immigrants often do not have the same access to resources, language, and other forms of social capital that are critical to healthy and positive identity development experiences.

Myriad sociocultural factors shape the lived experiences of SGD Latinxs in the U.S. and around the world. In the next section we will cover trends in health research, with a focus on substance abuse and mental health.

Research Trends in the United States

As noted by the Institute of Medicine (2011), SGD people in the U.S. "have unique health experiences and needs, but as a nation, we do not know exactly what these experiences and needs are" (p. 4). The committee stressed the need for research on racial and ethnic SGD subgroups to better understand health disparities at the intersection of race, sexual orientation, and gender identity.

Despite calls to diversify SGD health research, focus on race and ethnicity has been severely neglected for some time. In 2002, Boehmer conducted a meta-analysis of health research on SGD populations and found that approximately 85 percent of published empirical research omitted demographic questions related to race and ethnicity altogether. Thus, it is unknown whether the majority of the available health data that guide policy and practice for SGD populations are based on representative samples (Alderson, 2003). This is especially troublesome when one considers the significant health disparities in SGD Latinx communities. In fact, across SGD ethno-racial groups, Latinx transgender women and Latinx men who have sex with men (MSM) experience the highest rates of HIV and AIDS in the U.S. (Wohl et al., 2010). Attention on the social and health needs of SGD Latinxs is paramount.

It is well documented that SGD persons of color face marginalization in multiple social domains that is detrimental to their overall health. This includes racism in SGD communities (Giwa & Greensmith, 2012; Loiacano, 1989) and heterosexism and transphobia in Latinx community spaces (Cerezo et al., 2014). The Centers for Disease Control and Prevention (n.d.) defines health disparities as "preventable differences in the burden of disease, injury, violence or opportunities to achieve optimal health that are experienced by socially disadvantaged populations." Health disparities differ across gender. While research on SGD health has focused on HIV among Latinx MSM, research on SGD Latinx women is severely lacking.

A large body of research has established the detrimental impact of minority stress on mental health (Hatzenbuehler, 2009; Meyer, 1995, 2003). Hurd, Varner, Caldwell, and Zimmerman (2014) found that discrimination is associated with increased symptoms of anxiety, and the impact of discrimination is stronger for women than men. Several studies have suggested that SGD Latinx women suffer more psychological distress than SGD white women for reasons that include racism, acculturative stress, and issues with acceptance from family (Diaz, Ayala, Bein, Henne, & Marin, 2001, Rodriguez, Eaton, & Pachankis, 2019). Further, racial discrimination, like sexual orientation discrimination, is also associated with increased rates of substance abuse, contributing to further disparity between SGD Latinx and white women (Swann, Stephens, Newcomb, & Whitton, 2019). In a national sample of Latinx adults, Otiniano Verissimo, Gee, Ford, and Iguchi (2014) found that 30 percent of Latinas reported daily experiences of discrimination regarding race, gender, and socioeconomic status. Thus, SGD Latinx women contend with discrimination and bias outside of sexual orientation and gender identity that also impact their lived experiences and consequent health needs.

Research carried out in the past decade illustrates that SGD women of color face serious health disparities. When within-Latinx group differences were assessed, Rodriguez et al. (2019) found that participants who identified as Hispanic and sexually diverse (lesbian, gay, or bisexual) exhibited worse mental health than those who identified as Hispanic and heterosexual. The authors attributed these differences to the way traditional Latinx values (e.g., *marianismo*) negatively impact SGD Latinx women.

Specific to the area of substance abuse, research has shown a higher prevalence of tobacco and alcohol use in SGD women across ethno-racial backgrounds (Gruskin, Hart, Gordon, & Ackerson, 2001, 2017). There are inconsistent findings on whether SGD Latina women reporter higher rates of drinking than their peers. A recent study by Jeong, Veldhuis, Aranda, and Hughes (2016) found that Latina and African American women reported higher rates of twelve-month alcohol dependence than white women. Jeong et al. (2016) suggested that differences in drinking were due to intersectional factors of bias and discrimination faced by this group related to sexual orientation. Cerezo, Williams, Cummings, Ching, and Holmes (2019) found that drinking behaviors of SGD Latinx and African American women were primarily linked to chronic stress; participants reported having to navigate ongoing stigma and discrimination related to race, ethnicity, and sexual orientation and gender identity. These findings are alarming when one considers the physical, social, and psychological risks SGD women expose themselves to when consuming large amounts of alcohol.

With respect to TGNC individuals, research has begun to determine the higher prevalence of binge drinking in this community compared to the non-TGNC population. The rate of binge drinking among TGNC women greatly outweighs the national average for binge drinking in cisgender women at 51 percent to 8 percent, respectively (James et al., 2016). To our knowledge, no published research has examined the prevalence of alcohol misuse in transgender Latinxs. Another area of recent attention is peer substance abuse norms in SGD communities.

Mental health difficulties (e.g., social alienation, low self-esteem, and psychological distress) experienced by SGD Latinx men have been linked to homophobia, poverty, and racial discrimination (Diaz et al., 2001; Sandfort et al., 2007; Zea, Reisen, & Diaz, 2003). In a study examining factors that impact SGD Latinx mental health, Sandfort et al. (2007) found that substance use, provider bias, and difficulty connecting to the various communities in which SGD Latinxs hold membership were negatively associated with mental health outcomes. When considering the importance of belongingness and health, researchers have found that SGD Latinxs experience racial discrimination from both the larger dominant society and from the white gay community (Guarnero, 2007; Ocampo, 2012). In addition to racism, many SGD Latinxs must also contend with xenophobic bias and discrimination. In a study of SGD Latinx immigrants (specifically gay men, MSM, and transgender individuals) residing in a rural Southern region of the U.S., Rhodes et al. (2013) found that nearly one in three reported perceived day-to-day discrimination, one in four participants reported being treated unfairly, and one in six reported experiencing lifetime victimization upon arriving in the U.S. These findings demonstrate the importance of considering within-group variability for the SGD Latinx community.

In addition to mental health, the relationship between substance use and sexual risk behavior has been an area of concern given the high rates of HIV and AIDS in SGD Latinx men and transgender women (Shoptaw et al., 2009). However, the underlying causes that link substance use and sexual risk behaviors are not clear. Bruce, Ramirez-Valles, and Campbell (2008) found significant associations between racial stigma and the internalization of homosexual stigma, elevated substance use, and unprotected sex. Thus, Bruce et al. (2008) were able to determine that racial stigma played a key role in engaging in risk behaviors. In a subsequent study of behaviorally bisexual Latinx men who recently migrated to the United States, elevated substance use was related to discrimination, lack of access to services, and isolation because of migration, family separation, and lack of social community (Martinez et al., 2011). Participants in the Martinez at al. (2011) study also reported that they abused substances during sexual activity. Similarly, Shoptaw et al. (2009) found that internalized homonegativity was positively associated with substance use and risk behaviors in SGD Latinx men. The prevalence of substance abuse among SGD Latinxs appears to be tied to a reduction of negative emotions, thereby demonstrating a strong link between substance abuse and mental health.

SGD Latinxs are a diverse and rich community. When considering the social and health needs of this community, it is important to consider the intersection of race, ethnicity, sexual orientation, and gender identity. This includes determining shared meanings of behavior and context between practitioners, researchers, and SGD Latinxs themselves. Achieving validity in SGD health research is impossible without consideration of myriad cultural dimensions that impact SGD Latinxs' lives.

Research Trends in Latin America

A review of SGD health research in Latin America over the past few years demonstrates a focus on improving (a) basic human rights and protections and (b) HIV prevention efforts. Notably, the connection between human rights and research is strong in Latin America; data are carefully collected and disseminated to advance ongoing advocacy efforts. This includes research that documents state-sanctioned violence directed toward SGD communities, particularly MSM, in Central America. Davis et al. (2019) carried out twenty in-depth interviews with MSM in El Salvador regarding their perceptions of anti-gay violence from public security forces (e.g., state and federal authorities). Nearly all of the participants reported being targeted by public security forces in relation to their gender expression and/or perceived sexual orientation. Participants reported suffering physical, emotional, sexual, and/or economic violence, with no opportunities to report or seek protection. Further, participants stated that because the violence they endured was perpetrated by public security forces, reporting would result in continued, perhaps escalated, violence. With respect to health outcomes, violence endured was linked to emotional distress, depression, and lasting physical injuries.

Researchers have also made the case for improved access to health prevention programs for transgender women throughout Latin America. Transgender women face the highest incidence of HIV in Latin America, with prevalence estimates ranging from 18 to 38 percent (Silva-Santisteban, Eng, de la Inglesia, Falistocco, & Mazin, 2016). In a large-scale review that included governmental reports from seventeen Latin American countries and interviews with key stakeholders throughout Latin America, Silva-Santisteban et al. (2016) found that transgender women faced limited access to HIV prevention services throughout Latin America. These barriers were related to negative perceptions of transgender women that permeated social, health, and legal sectors.

Wundram Pimentel and Leonardo Segura (2018) traced the complexity of a gender identity law that is being considered by legal authorities in Guatemala. The law would afford Guatemalan citizens the ability to change their sex designation on government documents. The authors note how the law represents both a win for TGNC rights and a source of stress for many TGNC Guatemalans. Choosing to change one's gender documents would result in formal tracking by Guatemalan officials in a social climate that does not support TGNC people. Thus, TGNC Guatemalans face serious challenges to their emotional and physical well-being if and when they choose to change legal documents to match their authentic gender identity.

Future Directions

A review of health research trends for SGD Latinxs in the U.S. and Latin America reveals a wide range of topics and trends. In Latin America, scholarship is often tied to building cases for legal protections for SGD communities related to sexual orientation and gender identity. This includes the opportunity to receive HIV care and to access legal processes for TGNC communities. Similar to trends in U.S.-based SGD research with Latinxs, the great majority of scholarship in Latin America is centered on MSM and individuals who face the highest risk of HIV. As a result, Latinx women, older adults, and other underrepresented communities continue to receive little attention in the SGD Latinx research literature.

There are many opportunities for novel, innovative topics and research approaches in the consideration of SGD Latinx health. This includes identifying social factors that contribute to resilience and positive mental health outcomes in several social spheres such as family, friends, and other community spaces. Furthermore, researchers should explore the protective role of siblings in the coming-out process. Latinx heterosexual siblings may play an especially important role in SGD Latinxs' lives given their ability to buffer negative messages and/or behaviors from parents and other adult family and community members. Empirical research with older Latinx adults is also sorely needed. In 2016, the National Hispanic Council on Aging (NHCOA) carried out a qualitative needs assessment of the socioeconomic and health challenges faced by SGD older Latinxs. The report highlighted a dearth of empirical research on this community that prevents proper understanding and programming. Further, NHCOA reported a severe need for cultural and linguistic services to meet the needs of older SGD Latinxs.

When reviewing the SGD Latinx health research, it is important to note that many studies include measures that were not developed for Latinxs in mind. Thus, many SGD Latinxs, including those who are less acculturated to U.S. customs and values, may interpret psychological and related constructs in manners that are not adequately captured by existing measures (Zea et al., 2003). Researchers should embark on developing measures born from the SGD Latinx experience to assess whether commonly held psychological constructs hold true for this community. This includes perceptions of bias, discrimination, identity formation, coping, resilience, and many other culturally laden constructs. Furthermore, practitioners and researchers should be aware that the common use of convenience sampling poses serious challenges to collecting samples that accurately represent the larger SGD Latinx population. Thus, targeted and/or probability sampling should be used when possible that accounts for racial difference, immigration history, English language acquisition, and acculturation, among other topics.

Conclusion

SGD Latinxs are a rich, vibrant community who reside both in the U.S. and around the world. The Colonial era of the fifteenth and sixteenth centuries resulted in significant shifts across Latin America with respect to race, ethnicity, language, religion, and many other cultural dimensions. The impact of Latin America's Colonial era is still felt today where Latinxs of indigenous and African ancestry remain the most oppressed in the region. Despite the disparities Latinxs experience in social and health realms, there is also immense resilience within the community. Practitioners and researchers should employ intersectional strategies that allow SGD Latinxs to recognize and embrace the strength and well-being that is garnered from all aspects of their social identities. Specific strategies include fostering pride in one's gender identity, sexual orientation, and ethno-racial identity; negotiating the realities of SGD and ethnic and racial oppression; negotiating family relationships; accessing healthcare and financial resources; connecting with SGD social and activist spaces; and cultivating spirituality and/or hope for the future.

References

Alderson, K. (2003). The ecological model of gay male identity. *Canadian Journal of Human Sexuality, 12*, 75–85. https://psycnet.apa.org/record/2004-11679-001

American Psychological Association (2019). LGBTQ asylum seekers: How clinicians can help. https://www.apa.org/pi/lgbt/resources/lgbtq-asylum-seekers.pdf

Arciniega, M. G., Anderson, T. C., Tovar-Blank, Z. G., & Tracey, T. J. G. (2008). Toward a fuller conception of machismo: Development of a traditional machismo and caballerismo scale. *Journal of Counseling Psychology, 55*, 19–33. doi:10.1037/0022–0167.55.1.19

Barbosa, P., Torres, H., Silva, M. A., & Khan, N. (2010). Agapé Christian reconciliation conversations: Exploring the intersections of culture, religiousness, and homosexual identity in Latino and European Americans. *Journal of Homosexuality, 57*, 98–116. doi:10.1080/00918360903445913

Boehmer, U. (2002). Twenty years of public health research: Inclusion of lesbian, gay, bisexual, and transgender populations. *American Journal of Public Health, 92*, 1125–30. doi:10.2105/ajph.92.7.1125

Bowleg, L. (2008). When Black + lesbian + woman ≠ Black lesbian woman: The methodological challenges of qualitative and quantitative intersectionality research. *Sex Roles, 59*, 312–25. doi:10.1007/s11199-008-9400-z

Bruce, D., Ramirez-Valles, J., & Campbell, R. T. (2008). Stigmatization, substance use, and sexual risk behavior among Latino gay and bisexual men and transgender persons. *Journal of Drug Issues, 38*, 235–60. doi:10.1177/002204260803800111

Camarena, J. F. (2018). Afro-Latino same-sex attracted men: Ethnic identity importance, gay community identification, and internalized homonegativity. *Journal of Black Sexuality and Relationships, 5*, 1–22. doi:10.1353/bsr.2018.0018

Cardemil, E. V., Millán, F., & Aranda, E. (2019). A new, more inclusive name: The *Journal of Latinx Psychology*. *Journal of Latinx Psychology, 7*, 1–5. doi:10.1037/lat0000129

Casas, F. J, & Ryan, C. S. (2010). How Latinos are transforming the United States: Research, theory, and policy. *Journal of Social Issues, 66*, 1–10. doi:10.1111/j.1540–4560.2009.01629

Centers for Disease Control and Prevention (n.d.). https://www.cdc.gov/healthyyouth/disparities/index.htm

Cerezo, A., & Morales, A., Quintero, D., & Gebhardt, S. (2014). Trans-migrations: A qualitative exploration of life at the intersection of transgender identity and immigration. *Psychology of Sexual Orientation and Gender Diversity, 1*, 170–80. doi:10.1037/sgd0000031

Cerezo, A., Williams, C., Cummings, M., Ching, D., & Holmes, M. (2019). Minority stress and drinking: Connecting race, gender and sexual orientation. *The Counseling Psychologist* [E-pub before print]. doi: 10.1177/0011000019887493

Chavez-Dueñas, N., Adames, H., & Organista, K. (2014). Skin-color prejudice and within-group racial discrimination: Historical and current impact on Latino/a populations. *Hispanic Journal of Behavioral Sciences, 36*, 3–26. doi:10.1177/0739986313511306

Cole, E. R. (2009). Intersectionality and research in psychology. *American Psychologist, 64*, 170–80. doi:10.1037/a0014564

Crandall, C. S., Miller, J. M., White, M. H. (2018). Changing norms following the 2016 U.S. presidential election: The Trump effect on prejudice. *Social Psychological and Personality Science, 9*, 186–92. doi:10.1177/1948550617750735

Crenshaw, K. (1991). Mapping the margins: Intersectionality, identity politics, and violence against women of color. *Stanford Law Review, 43*, 1241–99. doi:10.2307/1229039

Davis, D. A., Morales, G. J., Ridgeway, K., Mendizabal, M., Lanham, M., Dayton, R...Evens, E. (2019). The health impacts of violence perpetrated by police, military and other public security forces on gay, bisexual and other men who have sex with men in El Salvador. *Culture, Health & Sexuality, 8*, 1–16. doi:10.1080/13691058.2019.1582801 de Onís, M. C. (2017). What's in an "x"?: An exchange about the politics of "Latinx". *Chiricu Journal: Latino/a Literatures, Arts and Cultures*, *1*(2), 78–91. doi:10.2979/chiricu.1.2.07

Diaz, R. (1998). *Latino gay men and HIV: Culture, sexuality, and risk behavior*. Boston, MA: Routledge.

Diaz, R., Ayala, G., Bein, E., Henne, J., & Marin, B. (2001). The impact of homophobia, poverty, and racism on the mental health of gay and bisexual Latino men: Findings from 3 US cities. *American Journal of Public Health*, *91*(6), 927–32. https://www.ncbi.nlm.nih.gov/pmc/articles/PMC1446470/

Espín, O. M. (2011). "An illness we catch from American women"? The multiple identities of Latina lesbians. *Women & Therapy*, *35*, 45–56. doi:10.1080/02703149.2012.634720

Estrada, F., Rigali-Oiler, M., Arciniega, G. M., & Tracey, T. J. G. (2011). Machismo and Mexican American men: An empirical understanding using a gay sample. *Journal of Counseling Psychology*, *58*(3), 358–67. doi:10.1037/a0023122

Falicov, C. J. (1998). *The Guilford family therapy series. Latino families in therapy: A guide to multicultural practice*. New York, NY: Guilford Press.

Falicov, C. J. (2010). Changing constructions of machismo for Latino men in therapy: "The devil never sleeps." *Family Process*, *49*, 309–29. doi:10.1111/j.1545- 5300.2010.01325.x

Flores, J., & Roman, M. (2009). Triple-consciousness? Approaches to Afro-Latino culture in the United States. *Latin American and Caribbean Ethnic Studies*, *4*(3), 319–28. doi:10.1080/17442220903331662

Garcia, A. (2013). The facts on immigration today. http://www.americanprogress.org/issues/immigration/report/2013/04/03/59040/the-factson-immigration-today-3/

Gates, H. L. (2011) Dominicans in denial. https://www.theroot.com/dominicans-in-denial-1790865156

Giwa, S., & Greensmith, C. (2012) Race relations and racism in the LGBTQ community of Toronto: Perceptions of gay and queer social service providers of color, *Journal of Homosexuality*, *59*, 149–85, doi:10.1080/00918369.2012.648877

Gray, N. N., Mendelsohn, D. M., & Omoto, A. M. (2015). Community connectedness, challenges, and resilience among gay Latino immigrants. *American Journal of Community Psychology*, *55*, 202–14. doi:10.1007/s10464-014-9697-4

Gruskin, E. P., Hart, S., Gordon, N., & Ackerson, L. (2001). Patterns of cigarette smoking and alcohol use among lesbians and bisexual women enrolled in a large health maintenance organization. *American Journal of Public Health*, *91*, 976–9. https://www.ncbi.nlm.nih.gov/pmc/articles/PMC1446478/

Guarnero, P. (2007). Family and community influences on the social and sexual lives of Latino gay men. *Journal of Transcultural Nursing*, *18*(1), 12–18. doi:10.1177/1043659606294195

Hancock, A., & Halderman, D. C. (2017). Between the lines: Media coverage of Orlando and beyond. *Psychology of Sexual Orientation and Gender Diversity*, *4*, 152–9. doi:10.1037/sgd0000228

Hatzenbuehler, M. L. (2009). How does sexual minority stigma "get under the skin"? A psychological mediation framework. *Psychological Bulletin*, *135*(5), 707–30. doi:10.1037/a0016441

Higgins, S. (2007). Afro-Latinos: An annotated guide for collection building. *Reference & User Services Quarterly*, *47*(1), 10–15. https://www.jstor.org/stable/20864790?seq=1#page_scan_tab_contents

Hirsch, J. S., Higgins, J., Bentley, M. E., & Nathanson, C. A. (2002). The social constructions of sexuality: Marital infidelity, sexually transmitted disease-HIV risk in a Mexican migrant community. *American Journal of Public Health*, *92*, 1227–37. doi:10.2105/ajph.92.8.1227

Hurd, N. M., Varner, F. A., Caldwell, C. H., & Zimmerman, M. A. (2014). Does perceived racial discrimination predict changes in psychological distress and substance use over time? An examination among Black emerging adults. *Developmental Psychology*, *50*, 1910–18. doi:10.1037/a0036438.

Hussain, K. M. Leija, G. S., Lewis, F., Sanchez, B. (2015). Unveiling sexual identity in the face of Marianismo. *Journal of Feminist Family Therapy*, *27*, 72–92. doi:10.1080/08952833.2015.1030353

Hwang, S. J., Allen, B., Zadoretzky, C., Barber, H., McKnight, C., & Jarlais, D. D. (2019). Alternative kinship structures, resilience and social support among immigrant trans Latinas in the USA. *Culture, Health & Sexuality*, *21*, 1–15, doi:10.1080/13691058.2018.1440323

Institute of Medicine. (2011). *The health of lesbian, gay, bisexual, and transgender people: Building a foundation for better understanding*. http://thefenwayinstitute.org/research/iom-report/

Inter-American Commission on Human Rights. (2015). *Violence against lesbian, gay, bisexual, trans and intersex persons in the Americas*. http://www.oas.org/es/cidh/lgtbi/informes/anuales.asp

James, S. E., Herman, J. L., Rankin, S., Keisling, M., Mottet, L., & Anafi, M. (2016). *The report of the 2015 U.S. transgender survey*. Washington, DC: National Center for Transgender Equality. https://www.transequality.org/sites/default/files/docs/USTS-Full-Report-FINAL.PDF

Jamil, O., Harper, G., & Fernandez, I. (2009). Sexual and ethnic identity development among gay/bisexual/questioning (GBQ) male ethnic minority adolescents. *Cultural Diversity and Ethnic Minority Psychology*, *15*, 203–14. doi:10.1037/a0014795

Jeong, Y. M., Veldhuis, C. B., Aranda, F., & Hughes, T. L. (2016). Racial/ethnic differences in unmet needs for mental health and substance use treatment in a community-based sample of sexual minority women. *Journal of Clinical Nursing*, *25*, 3557–69. doi:10.1111/jocn.13477

Lazo, R. (2018). Before Latinx: X and *cartas de un Americano*. *English Language Notes*, *56*, 48–50. doi:10.1215/00138282-6960724

Loiacano, D. K. (1989). Gay identity issues among Black Americans: Racism, homophobia, and the need for validation. *Journal of Counseling and Development*, *68*, 21–5. doi:10.1002/j.1556–6676.1989.tb02486.x

Martinez, O., Dodge, B., Reece, M., Schnarrs, P., Rhodes, S., Goncalvez, G., . . . Fortenberry, D. (2011). Sexual health and life experiences: Voices from behaviorally bisexual Latino men in the Midwestern USA. *Culture, Health & Sexuality*, *13*, 1073–89. doi:10.1080/13691058.2011.600461

Meyer, I. H. (1995). Minority stress and mental health in gay men. *Journal of Health and Social Behavior*, *36*, 38–56. doi:10.2307/2137286

Meyer, I. H. (2003). Prejudice, social stress, and mental health in lesbian, gay, and bisexual populations: Conceptual issues and research evidence. *Psychological Bulletin*, *129*(5), 674–97. doi:10.1037/0033–2909.129.5.674

Miville, M. L., Mendez, N., & Louie, M. (2017). Latina/o gender roles: A content analysis of empirical research from 1982 to 2013. *Journal of Latina/o Psychology*, *5*(3), 173–94. doi:10.1037/lat0000072

Montalvo, F. (2009). Ethnoracial gap in clinical practice with Latinos. *Clinical Social Work Journal, 37*(4), 277–86. https://link.springer.com/article/10.1007/s10615-009-0241-1

Moore, R. (2019). Gay, transgender detainees allege abuse at ICE facility in New Mexico. *Washington Post,* March 25. https://www.washingtonpost.com/immigration/gay-transgender-detainees-allege-abuse-at-ice-facility-in-new-mexico/2019/03/25/e33ad6b6-4f10-11e9-a3f7-78b7525a8d5f_story.html

Morales, E. (2013). Latino lesbian, gay, bisexual, and transgender immigrants in the United States. *Journal of LGBT Issues in Counseling, 7,* 172–84. doi:10.1080/15538605.2013.785467

Muñoz-Laboy, M. (2004). Beyond "MSM": Sexual desire among bisexually-active Latino men in New York City. *Sexualities, 7,* 55–80. doi:10.1177/1363460704040142

Muñoz-Laboy, M. (2008). Familism and sexual regulation among bisexual Latino men. *Archives of Sexual Behavior, 37*(5), 773–82. doi:10.1007/s10508-008-9360-y

Muñoz-Laboy, M., & Severson, N. (2018). Exploring the roles of race, ethnicity, nationality, and skin color in the sexual partner choices of bisexual Latino men. *Archives of Sexual Behavior, 47,* 1231–9. doi:10.1007/s10508-017-1043-0

Navarro-Rivera, J., Kosmin, B. A., & Keysar, A. (2010). *U.S. Latino religious identification 1990–2008: Growth, diversity & transformation. A report based on the American religious identification survey 2008.* Hartford, CT: Institute for the Study of Secularism in Society & Culture.

Ocampo, A. C. (2012). Making masculinity: Negotiations of gender presentation among Latino gay men. *Latino Studies, 10,* 448–72. doi:10.1057/lst.2012.37

Oquendo, M. A., Dragatsi, D., Harkavy-Friedman, J., Dervic, K., Currier, D., Burke, A. K... Mann, J. J. (2005). Protective factors against suicidal behavior in Latinos. *Journal of Nervous and Mental Disease, 193*(7), 438–43. doi:10.2097/01.nmd.0000168262.06163.31

Otiniano Verissimo, A. D., Gee, C. G., Ford, C. L., & Iguchi, M. Y. (2014). Racial discrimination, gender discrimination, and substance abuse among Latina/os nationwide. *Cultural Diversity and Ethnic Minority Psychology, 20,* 43–51. doi:10.1037/a0034674

Pastrana, A. J. (2015). Being out to others: The relative importance of family support, identity and religion for LGBT Latina/os. *Latino Studies, 13,* 88–112. doi:10.1057/lst.2014.69

Potoczniak, D., Crosbie-Burnett, M., & Saltzburg, N. (2009). Experiences regarding coming out to parents among African American, Hispanic, and White gay, lesbian, bisexual, transgender, and questioning adolescents. *Journal of Gay and Lesbian Social Services, 21,* 189–205. doi:10.1080/10538720902772063

Ramirez, J. L., Gonzalez, K. A., & Galupo, P. (2017). "Invisible during my own crisis": Responses of LGBT people of color to the Orlando shooting. *Journal of Homosexuality, 65,* 579–99. doi:10.1080/00918369.2017.1328217

Ramos, B., Jaccard, J., & Guilamo-Ramos, V. (2003). Dual ethnicity and depressive symptoms: Implications of being Black and Latino in the United States. *Hispanic Journal of Behavioral Sciences, 25,* 147–73. doi:10.1177/0739986303025002002

Reading, R., & Rubin, L. R. (2011). Advocacy and empowerment: Group therapy for LGBT asylum seekers. *Traumatology, 17,* 86–98. doi:10.1177/1534765610395622

Rhodes, S. D., Martinez, O., Song, E-Y., Daniel, J., Alonzo, J., Eng, E., Duck, S... Reboussin, B. (2013). Depressive symptoms among immigrant Latino sexual minorities. *American Journal of Health Behavior, 37,* 404–13. doi:10.5993/AJHB.37.3.13

Rodríguez-Seijas, C., Eaton, N. R., & Pachankis, J. E. (2019). Prevalence of psychiatric disorders at the intersection of race and sexual Orientation. Results from the National Epidemiologic Survey of Alcohol and Related Conditions-III. *Journal of Consulting and Clinical Psychology, 87,* 321–31. doi:10.1037/ccp0000377

Roman, M. J., & Flores, J. (2010). *The Afro-Latino reader: History and culture in the United States.* Durham, NC: Duke University Press.

Russell, G. M., Bohan, J. S., McCarroll, M. C., & Smith, N. G. (2011). Trauma, recovery, and community: Perspectives on the long-term impact of anti-LGBT politics. *Traumatology, 17,* 14–23. doi:10.1177/1534765610362799

Santos, C. E. (2017). The history, struggles, and potential of the term Latinx. *Latinx Psychology Today Bulletin, 4,* 7–14. https://www.nlpa.ws/assets/docs/newsletters/final%20lpt%20volume_4_no_2_2017%20low%20res.pdf

Santos, C. E., & VanDaalen, R. A. (2016). The associations of sexual and ethnic–racial identity commitment, conflicts in allegiances, and mental health among lesbian, gay, and bisexual racial and ethnic minority adults. *Journal of Counseling Psychology, 63,* 668–79. doi:10.1037/cou0000170

Sandfort, T. G. M., Melendez, R. M., & Diaz, R. M. (2007). Gender nonconformity, homophobia, and mental distress in Latino gay and bisexual men. *Journal of Sex Research, 44*(2), 181–9. doi:10.1080/00224490701263819

Sarno, E. L., Mohr, J. J., Jackson, S. D., & Fassinger, R. E. (2015). When identities collide: Conflicts in allegiances among LGB people of color. *Cultural Diversity and Ethnic Minority Psychology, 21,* 550–9. doi:10.1037/cdp0000026

Scharrón-del Río, M. R., & Aja, A. A. (2015). The case FOR "Latinx": Why intersectionality is not a choice. *Latino Rebels.* http://www.latinorebels.com/2015/12/05/the-case-for-latinx-why-intersectionality-is-not-a-choice/#sthash.6e7Pzb7M.dpuf

Schope, R. D. (2002). The decision to tell: Factors influencing the disclosure of sexual orientation by gay men. *Journal of Gay and Lesbian Social Services, 14,* 1–22. doi:10.1300/J041v14n01_01

Shoptaw, S., Weiss, R. E., Munjas, B., Hucks-Ortiz, C., Young, S. D., Larkins, S., ... Gorbach, P. M. (2009). Homonegativity, substance use, sexual risk behaviors, and HIV status in poor and ethnic men who have sex with men in Los Angeles. *Journal of Urban Health: Bulletin of the New York Academy of Medicine, 86,* 577–92. doi:10.1007/s11524-009-9372-5

Silva-Santisteban, A., Eng, S., de la Iglesia, G., Falistocco, C. & Mazin, R. (2016). HIV prevention among transgender women in Latin America: Implementation, gaps and challenges. *Journal of the International AIDS Society, 19,* 1–10. doi:10.7448/IAS.19.3.20799

Stults, C. B., Kupprat, S. A., Krause, K. D., Kapadia, F., & Halkitis, P. N. (2017). Perceptions of safety among LGBTQ people following the 2016 Pulse Nightclub shooting. *Psychology of Sexual Orientation and Gender Diversity, 4,* 251–6. doi:10.1037/sgd0000240

Swann, G., Stephens, J., Newcomb, M. E., & Whitton, S. W. (2019). Effects of sexual/gender minority and race-based enacted stigma on mental health and substance use in female assigned at birth sexual minority youth. *Cultural Diversity and Ethnic Minority Psychology* [E-pub ahead of print]. doi:10.1037/cdp0000292

Tillman, Z. (2019). The State Department is denying citizenship to some kids born to same-sex couples overseas: Judges aren't happy. https://www.buzzfeednews.com/article/zoetillman/state-department-citizenship-children-same-sex-couples

Toro-Alfonso, J., Ortiz, M. L., & Lugo, K. N. (2012). Sexualidades migrantes: La emigración de hombres dominicanos gay (Sexual migrants: Emigration of Dominican gay men). *Caribbean Studies, 40,* 59–80. doi:10.1353/crb.2012.0017

Torres, J. B., Solberg, S. H., & Carlstrom, A. H. (2002). The myth of sameness among Latino men and their machismo. *American Journal of Orthopsychiatry, 72,* 163–81. doi:10.1037//0002–9432.72.2.163

U.S. Census Bureau. (2018). *Population estimates, American Community Survey.* https://www.census.gov/quickfacts/fact/table/US/PST045218

Vargas, M., & Kuhl, P. (2008). Bridging the communication gap between Afro-Latino and African American individuals: An interdisciplinary curriculum initiative. *Journal of Hispanic Higher Education, 7*(4), 336–45. doi:10.1177/1538192708321650

Wohl, A. R., Galvan, F. H., Myers, H. F., Garland, W., George, S., Witt, M., . . . Carpio, F. (2010). Social support, stress and social network characteristics among HIV-positive Latino and African American women and men who have sex with men. *AIDS and Behavior, 14,* 1149–58. doi:10.1007/s10461-010-9666-3

Wundram Pimentel, A., & Leonardo Segura, M. (2018). Paradoxes of visibility: The proposed Guatemalan gender identity law. *Transgender Studies Quarterly, 5,* 83–99. doi:10.1215/23289252-4291538

Zea, M. C., Reisen, C. A., & Diaz, R. M. (2003). Methodological issues in research on sexual behavior with Latino gay and bisexual men. *American Journal of Community Psychology, 31*(3/4), 281–91. doi:10.1023/A:1023962805064

CHAPTER

17 Asian American and Pacific Islander Sexual and Gender Minority Mental Health

Emily Hunt *and* Cindy Y. Huang

Abstract

Psychological research on sexual and gender minority (SGM) people of color has grown in recent years; however, little is still understood about the experiences of Asian American and Pacific Islander SGMs. The purpose of this chapter is to synthesize the current research that examines the intersections of the racial identity of Asian Americans and Pacific Islanders, SGM identity, and the mental health of Asian American and Pacific Islander SGMs. Historical contexts of attitudes toward SGMs in Asian and Pacific Island countries as well as in the United States are provided to contextualize the specific sociocultural issues faced by Asian American and Pacific Islander SGMs in the United States. The authors also discuss the role of specific Asian American and Pacific Islander cultural values such as gender norms, family values, and loss of face in the development and expression of SGM identity. This chapter also examines the unique mental health risks faced by Asian American and Pacific Islander SGMs through the lens of double minority stress. The authors conclude with recommendations for directions of future research.

Keywords: Asian American, Asian Pacific Islander, Asian gender and sexual minority, cultural factors, double minority stress, Asian gender norms

Researchers over the past few decades have acknowledged that sexual and gender minority people of color have distinct experiences compared to sexual minority white individuals (Choi & Israel, 2016). Understanding the intersectionality of sexual and gender identity and racial/ethnic identity is important, as it is a core part of psychological well-being for individuals who hold multiple marginalized identities (Cole, 2009; Moradi & Grzanka, 2017; Velez, Polihoronakis, Watson, & Cox, 2019). However, there is still a dearth of research that addresses mental health issues for Asian American and Asian Pacific Islander sexual and gender minorities.

The term *Asian* or *Asian American* encompasses people from a diverse range of over forty ethnic backgrounds, including East Asian, South Asian, and Southeast Asian Americans (Harley, 2016; Sue & Sue, 2013). According to the U.S. Census Bureau (2012a), the term *Asian Pacific Islander* includes people of Native Hawaiian, Guamanian or Chamorro, Fijian, Tongan, Marshallese, Melanesian, Micronesian, and Polynesian descent. Collectively, Asian Americans and Asian Pacific Islanders (AAPIs) make up 5 percent of the U.S. population (U.S. Census Bureau, 2012b). In the United States, the six largest Asian ethnic groups by population are Chinese, Filipino, Indian, Korean, Vietnamese, and Japanese, in that order (Yamane, 2018). Between 2000 and 2010, the AAPI population was the fastest-growing minority group, and numbers are predicted to rise over the next fifty years (U.S. Census Bureau, 2012b).

AAPIs are racial minority groups that have experienced systemic racism throughout U.S. history; however, due to a common racial narrative of these groups, being viewed as "model minorities" who "have succeeded in society and are otherwise immune to social problems," sometimes there is an assumption, especially by the dominant white society, that AAPIs do not experience negative racial discrimination (Choi, Israel, & Maeda, 2017; Wong & Halgin, 2006). Public opinion polls show that many people in the United States perceive AAPIs with significant anti-Asian sentiments and social distance (Gee, Ro, Shariff-Marco, & Chae, 2009). Additionally, the National Latino and Asian American Study revealed that 62 percent of Asians reported experiences of racial discrimination (Chae et al., 2011).

Despite a growing focus on studying the mental health of AAPIs, research on the mental health of AAPI LGBTQ individuals remains scarce. Scholars have found that the experiences of individuals in the AAPI LGBTQ community are similar to the discrimination and marginalization that AAPI people have faced historically in the U.S. (Dang & Vianney, 2007).

This chapter provides a review of the current literature on the mental health of sexual and gender minority AAPIs in the United States. Given the diversity among both Asian American and Asian Pacific Islander populations and sexual and gender minority (SGM) populations, this chapter paints a broad overview of issues in mental health pertaining to these groups with the intention of contextualizing a framework from which to understand this population. First, this chapter explores both past and present attitudes toward SGM populations in AAPI cultures to gain an understanding of how culturally specific views may affect the mental health of AAPI SGMs. Second, research on mental health in this population is discussed through specific sociocultural factors that affect the intersectional identities of this population, such as minority stress and experiences of discrimination and violence. Then, cultural factors relevant to AAPIs are explored, such as family values and loss of face, as well as how they influence attitudes and behaviors toward their SGM identities. Lastly, directions for future studies are presented.

History of SGM Issues in Asia

Historically, same-sex relations and sexual fluidity were widely accepted in many AAPI cultures (Ching, Lee, Chen, So, & Williams, 2018). In early China, India, and Japan, same-sex sexuality was not condemned as long as "social status" and social class hierarchies were maintained—for example, laws in China during the Qing Dynasty stated that the masculinity of a man was maintained if he had sex with a male of lower status (Loos, 2009). Additionally, in Hawaii, records showed that men who were attracted to men held cultural status and power (Choi & Israel, 2016; Morris, 1990).

In a recent literature review on SGM AAPIs, Choi and Israel (2016) observed that historically, many AAPI cultures found same-sex sexuality less important than the maintenance of a social order. This meant that enactments of same-sex sexuality were tolerated as long as they were not "public" and cultural expectations were maintained through the reinforcement of gender roles and norms, such as heterosexual marriage. These attitudes are still reflected in AAPI communities today—sexuality outside of heterosexual marriage is a highly private topic that is rarely discussed openly (Chng, Wong, Park, Edberg, & Lai, 2003; Choi & Israel, 2016; Kanuha, 2000). Scholarship has found that Western imperialism and colonization greatly influenced a shift in acceptable sexual practices and identities in Asian cultures, from a wider range of acceptable practices to a more delegitimizing, pathologizing view on non-heterosexual orientations (Laurent, 2005; Loos, 2009). Today, quantitative and qualitative studies have found that SGM AAPIs perceive heterosexism and homophobia to be much stronger in Asian American cultures than in mainstream U.S. culture (Kimmel & Yi, 2004; Sung, Szymanski, & Henrichs-Beck, 2015). Malaysia, Singapore, and India still consider homosexual acts to be illegal and punishable offenses (Chung & Singh, 2009). Over the past few decades, some countries have taken strides to be more accepting of homosexuality and bisexuality. For example, in 2001 China removed homosexuality from the list of psychiatric disorders in the Chinese *Diagnostic and Statistical Manual of Mental Disorders* (Chu, 2001; Kwok & Wu, 2015). Additionally, on May 17, 2019, Taiwan became the first country in Asia to legalize same-sex marriage (Ramzy, 2019).

The existence of transgenderism has also been recorded throughout Asian history. Throughout many communities in Southeast Asia, "transgendered ritual specialists," or male-bodied individuals who dressed in female attire, performed prestigious spiritual rituals for royal families because they were believed to possess spiritual powers (Chung & Singh, 2009; Peletz, 2006). In China, the word *bianxing* translates to "one who changes sex," but it does not exclude transgender people who do not seek sex reassignment surgery (Chung & Singh, 2009). In India, those who claim to be neither female or male are known as "hijras," or the "third gender," and they have a history of being both revered and marginalized in their communities (Jain, 2018).

AAPI SGMs in the United States

Few studies have collected socio-demographic data on the LGBTQ population within the AAPI community in the United States. In 2007, the National LBGTQ Task Force conducted a national survey with AAPI LGBTQ individuals in order to address the dearth in collection of quantitative demographic data on this population (Dang & Vianney, 2007). Out of 860 participants, 47 percent identified as gay, 19 percent as lesbian, 9 percent as bisexual, 10 percent as transgender, and 20 percent as queer. They also found that almost all of the participants (98 percent) had experienced at least one form of discrimination or harassment: 85 percent reported that they experienced discrimination or harassment based on their race, and 75 percent reported discrimination or harassment based on their sexual orientation, while 69 percent of the transgender participants reported discrimination or harassment because of their transgender identity (Dang & Vianney, 2007). These findings suggest that experiences of SGM AAPIs are shaped by their status as both racial minorities and gender/sexual minorities, and understanding these experiences requires an intersectional approach (Tan et al., 2016).

Minority Stress

SGM AAPIs are at higher risk for mental health issues when compared to non-SGM AAPIs, non-Asian SGMs, and majority groups. Results from the National Latino and Asian American Survey on psychiatric disorders showed that about 22 percent of Asian and Latinx lesbian/bisexual women met criteria for a recent mental health and/or substance use disorder compared to 15 percent of heterosexual women (Cochran, Mays, Alegria, Ortega & Takeuchi, 2007). Similarly, gay and bisexual men were significantly more likely to report a recent suicide attempt (Cochran et al., 2007). AAPI lesbian and bisexual women had higher levels of trauma (both physical and sexual violence in childhood and adulthood, as well as discrimination-based verbal and physical violence) compared to their white counterparts (Morris & Balsam, 2003).

One possible explanation for the increased mental health risks for AAPI SGMs is minority stress (Meyer, 2003), which postulates that people from oppressed groups experience chronic stress and negative life events due to having a marginalized or nondominant status. Minority stress can then contribute to adverse behavioral and mental health outcomes, including depression, psychological distress, and perceived stress (Balsam, Molina, Beadnell, Simoni, & Walters, 2011; Chen & Tryon, 2012; Choi & Israel, 2016; Szymanski & Gupta, 2009b; Szymanski & Sung, 2010). Minority stress is distinguished as a unique form of distress because it is perpetrated by underlying social and cultural systems and institutions beyond the individual's control (Szymanski & Sung, 2010). Meyer (2003) further theorizes that minority stress comprises both proximal and distal, or external and internalized, stressors. Distal or external stressors consist of experiences of prejudice, discrimination, harassment, and violence as a result of one's minority statuses, while proximal or internal stressors include internalized forms of oppression such as internalized heterosexism or internalized racism, concealment of sexual identity, and perceptions of stigma (Sandil, Robinson, Brewster, Wong & Geiger, 2015; Szymanski & Sung, 2010; Velez et al., 2019). Proximal stressors have been found to be mediators between the relationship of distal stressors and negative mental and behavioral health outcomes (Ching et al., 2018; Pitonak, 2017).

Given the prevalence of discrimination and harassment, and the robust evidence supporting theories of minority stress, it is surprising that only a handful of studies have examined the relationships between multiple minority stress and psychological distress in SGM AAPIs (Diplacidio, 1998; Huang et al., 2010; Landrine, Klonoff, Gibbs, Manning, & Lund, 1995; Sandil et al., 2015; Szymanski & Gupta, 2009a, 2009b). Similar to patterns in research on SGM persons of color in general, a majority of studies on SGM AAPIs focus on HIV/AIDS and other sexual and physical health risks, especially among AAPI gay men (Huang et al., 2010; Dang & Vianney, 2007).

The few studies that have examined experiences of SGM AAPIs have found that, similar to SGM persons of color as a whole, multiple minority stressors were additively related to psychological distress (Szymanski & Meyer, 2008; Szymanski & Sung, 2010; Velez et al., 2019). That is, the AAPI racial/ethnic identity and SGM identity may exist and function independently for AAPI SGMs, which may impact experiences of racism and heterosexism differently. Certain proximal and distal stressors seemed to be better predictors of psychological distress than others. For instance, experiences of racist discrimination and internalized heterosexism were associated with psychological distress; however, heterosexist discrimination and internalized racism were not (Szymanski & Gupta, 2009b; Velez et al., 2019). Heterosexism in communities of color, race-related dating and relationship problems in the LGBTQ community, internalized heterosexism, and outness were the only unique predictors of psychological distress (Szymanski & Sung, 2010). These findings were applicable to South Asian LGBTQs as well, but for South Asians, outness seemed to moderate the relationship between racist events and psychological distress, while this was not the case for AAPI SGMs in general (Sandil et al., 2015). In other words, South Asians who experienced racist events were found to experience higher levels of psychological distress if they had higher levels of outness as LGBTQ as well. Multiple minority stressors also have been found to specifically contribute to both mental and behavioral health. For example, in a study with AAPI gay men, experiences of racism (but not heterosexism) were associated with higher levels of depressive symptoms, and higher levels of discrimination were associated with higher rates of HIV risk behavior (Yoshikawa, Wilson, Chae, & Cheng, 2004). All of these findings suggest that various forms of oppression affect the psychological health of AAPI SGMs in different ways.

Discrimination, Harassment, and Violence

AAPI SGMs face the challenge of managing multiple minority statuses (i.e., racial, sexual, and/or gender minorities) and often face higher levels of discrimination and violence due to their multiple minority statuses. In one study, AAPI SGMs were found to experience more racial/ethnic and sexual microaggressions than African American and Latinx SGMs (Balsam et al., 2011). AAPI SGMs may encounter discrimination toward their sexual or gender minority status within mainstream society, as well as within the closer AAPI community, or they may be discriminated against within the LGBTQ community for their racial or ethnic identity. For example, the National LGBTQ Task Force found that 89 percent of AAPI participants reported that homophobia and/or transphobia were problems in the broader AAPI community, and 75 percent said that they experienced racism within the LGBTQ community (Dang & Vianney, 2007). Additionally, AAPI LGBTQ youth experience more familial physical abuse compared to LGBTQ youth from other ethnic groups, potentially due to their LGBTQ identity (Balsam, Lehavot, Beadnell, & Circo, 2010; Ching et al., 2018).

AAPI SGM men often face discrimination within the LGBTQ community due to their racial or ethnic identities and are often stereotyped as effeminate, submissive, passive, and unmasculine. These stereotypes are similar to how society perceives Asian men in general (Ching et al., 2018; Choi & Israel, 2016; Han, 2008a; 2008b, Phua, 2007). They are frequently eroticized and fetishized in derogatory ways, especially by white men, due to these stereotypes (Choi & Israel, 2016; Han, 2006; Phua, 2007). These stereotypes and forms of discrimination may lead to perceived power differences in intimate relationships that perpetuate intimate partner abuse and violence (Poon, 2000).

Furthermore, in the context of larger U.S. culture, AAPI SGM women often feel their racial and ethnic identities, stereotyped as "exotic," are sexually objectified, which then get conflated with assumptions about lesbian or bisexual behaviors. For example, one participant in a study by Sung et al. (2015) noted that "there are a lot of sexual stereotypes about Asian women which emphasize exotic behaviors, and people associate being a lesbian with those kinds of fantasies—that is, do not take Asian lesbians seriously as people with real lives." Another participant shared that "I experience people fetishizing my race as well as my sexuality. I don't like the idea of 'fulfilling' the freaky Asian woman stereotype that I often see in films, so I am extra wary of choosing partners that won't expect certain things because of my race, gender or sexuality" (Sung et al., 2015, 57–58). The intersecting fetishization of race and sexual identity may put lesbian SGM AAPIs at risk for sexual violence and abuse. In fact, Morris and Balsam (2003) found that almost 40 percent of lesbian and bisexual AAPI women had experienced physical and/or sexual abuse, with 30 percent reporting the abusers as female partners or general acquaintances.

Cultural Factors

Recent literature suggests that cultural norms and stigma play a significant role in the experiences of SM AAPI individuals (Ching et al., 2018; Choi & Israel, 2016). While it is crucial to note that there is substantial heterogeneity within the AAPI population, and scholars highlight the importance of examining specific intersections of SGM AAPIs (Choi & Israel, 2016), there are some similarities across AAPI groups in cultural values such as collectivism, familism, family obligation, and a relational orientation (Yee, DeBaryshe, Yuen, Kim, & McCubbin, 2007). These cultural values are found to be applicable to Chinese, Japanese, Filipino, Southeast Asian, South Asian, Hawaiian, and Samoan cultures (Yee et al., 2007). These values promote family and community interdependence and have been shown to be protective factors against racial and ethnic discrimination (Harley, 2016). For LGBTQ individuals, these norms may also serve as barriers for SM AAPIs as they navigate their sexuality in private and in public (Choi & Israel, 2016; Kimmel & Yi, 2004; Sullivan, 2001).

Gender Norms and Family Values

Cultural gender norms still play a large role in the challenges that SGM AAPI individuals face as they navigate their sexual and gender identities. In many Asian cultures, gender norms tend to be rigid and binary, with men viewed as the dominant figure and women being seen as submissive and in service to men (Liu, 2002; Pyke & Johnson, 2003). These strict binaries leave little room for those who do not fall into traditional gender roles and presentations. In a qualitative study with Chinese Americans, gender was the most salient way in which participants perceived their attitudes toward LGBTQ individuals, and gender nonconformity or nonadherence to traditional gender characteristics was described as the main definition of being LGBTQ (Tseng, 2011).

A primary reason why sexual and gender minority identities are so marginalized in Asian cultures is because of cultural values rooted in the interaction of gender norms with values of collectivism, familism, and family obligation. Filial piety, or loyalty and obedience to one's family, is a particularly salient aspect of Asian culture that highlights adherence to strict gender roles (Bridges, Selvidge, & Matthews, 2003). Identifying as a member of an SGM can be seen as a dishonor to the family because it can interfere with family obligations such as marriage, having children, and maintaining the family reputation (Ching et al., 2018; Choudhury et al., 2009). The act of disclosing one's sexual orientation is seen as a disrespectful and deviant behavior because it is a rejection of one's familial and cultural obligation to continue the family line, which then brings shame and blame to the parents (Szymanski & Sung, 2010). Identifying as transgender can be considered "inappropriate" and "counterproductive" for similar reasons (Chan, 1989; Chung & Katayama, 1998; Chung & Singh, 2009).

For (cisgender) gay men, disclosure of a homosexual identity is seen as a threat to the continuation of the family and is thus seen as a selfish act. In East Asian cultures such as those of China, Japan, and Korea, Confucian tradition prescribes clear gender roles in which men are expected to cultivate domestic virtue before public virtue—they can be seen as strong public leaders only if they have raised a harmonious family (Sohng & Icard, 1996). As noted by one queer male participant (Kumashiro, 1999), coming out as queer is not only rejecting familial obligation, but is also a rejection of Asian culture since it reenacts individualism, which is typically associated with white U.S. society. Because men are often traditionally seen as more dominant in AAPI cultures, attitudes tend to be more negative and critical toward gay or bisexual men than for women (Harley, 2016; Tseng, 2011). This could be because identifying as gay or bisexual as a man is perceived as relinquishing one's dominant status both in the family and in society.

For AAPI lesbian or bisexual women, gender roles that enforce a patriarchal structure further create a culture in which their identities as women and sexual minorities are marginalized and devalued (Chan, 1989; Chung & Szymanski, 2006; Greene, 1994; Kimmel & Yi, 2004; Liu & Chan, 1996; Sung et al., 2015). Therefore, a woman identifying as non-heterosexual is perceived as dismissing these expectations, as well as rejecting continuation of the family line due to beliefs that lesbian women do not want to procreate (Bridges, Selvidge, & Matthews, 2003).

Internalized Oppression

Experiences of racist and heterosexist discrimination from families, AAPI communities, LGBTQ communities, and society at large can contribute to the internalizations of the oppressive messages AAPI SGMs receive from their environment, especially from the dominant majority group. Internalized oppression can have dire consequences for mental health by causing feelings of self-hatred, decreased self-worth, and lower self-esteem. For example, David and Okazaki (2006) found that Filipino Americans who reported high levels of internalized oppression, also referred to as colonial mentality, were more likely to endorse poorer attitudes toward their own and others' Filipino qualities, including feeling shame or resentment about being Filipino. Additionally, higher levels of internalized oppression predicted higher levels of depression and decreased personal and collective self-esteem (David & Okazaki, 2006). Because of the intersection of racial, ethnic, sexual, and gender identities, AAPI SGMs may have higher levels of internalized oppression than other groups. For example, Ratti, Bakeman, and Peterson (2000) found greater levels of internalized heterosexism in AAPI gay men compared to white men.

Interestingly for AAPI SGMs, racist discrimination and internalized heterosexism are positively associated with psychological distress, but not heterosexist discrimination and internalized racism, meaning that for this population, outward experiences of racism may be more psychologically damaging than internalized racial oppression, but internalized experiences of heterosexism caused more distress than experiences of heterosexist discrimination (Szymanski & Gupta, 2009a; Szymanski & Meyer, 2008; Velez et al., 2019). This may be due to the influence of the previously discussed cultural factors unique to the AAPI experience. For example, more adherence to Asian cultural values has been found to be linked with higher levels of internalized heterosexism (Szymanski & Sung, 2010). Additionally, adherence to cultural gender norms and pressure to fulfill familial obligations may increase AAPI SGMs' concealment of their identities, which then could increase internalized heterosexism and transphobia. Because the discrimination that SGM AAPIs face from more intimate support systems (i.e., family) is often related to their sexual or gender identity (as opposed to their racial or ethnic identity), internalization of heterosexist or transphobic messages may be more psychologically damaging than internalized racism.

Some studies have found that internalized racism may impact the mental health of AAPI SGMs as well. For example, Ratti et al. (2000) found that the discrimination and objectification that AAPI gay men experience in dating and intimate relationships due to their race or ethnicity creates internalized racial oppression in which they accept decreased self-worth and distorted self-images, as well as reenact discrimination in terms of considering other AAPI men unattractive and undesirable as partners.

Coming Out and Saving Face

Coming out, or disclosing one's sexual orientation to others, is viewed by AAPI communities as a Western practice. This is evidenced by the fact that there are no words or phrases in any Asian language that describe the coming-out process (Dang & Vianney, 2007). For AAPIs, the concept of coming out is associated with mixed feelings due to the need to juggle conflicting norms between mainstream U.S. and AAPI values, and also struggling to describe this concept in an Asian language.

In many AAPI cultures, outward or public development and self-disclosure of identity (e.g., coming out as SGM, openly sharing one's struggles) is often seen as unnecessary and attention-seeking. Sexual identity in particular is seen as something to be developed privately and internally (Choi & Israel, 2016; Hom, 1994; Li & Orleans, 2001). Interestingly, several Asian cultures tolerate displays of same-sex affection if there is no open disclosure of same-sex identity. Coming out publicly as a sexual or gender minority goes against the AAPI value of "saving face," defined as maintaining dignity or a certain reputation, avoiding humiliation and shame, and preserving a social order within their community (Nadal & Corpus, 2013). Thus, coming out draws the focus to the individual and the individual's needs rather than the needs of one's family/community, and may bring loss of face to the parents, who may feel humiliated by their child's disclosure to the community (Nadal & Corpus, 2013). This directly conflicts with the collectivistic values of Asian cultures; therefore, AAPI SGMs who choose to come out may have higher levels of acculturation than those who do not. In one study by Singh, Chung, and Dean (2006), SGM AAPI women who identified with more Western cultural views or as more bicultural were more likely to publicly disclose their sexual and/or gender identity.

Because of the value of "saving face" and maintaining the social order in AAPI communities, concealing sexual and/or gender orientation is not necessarily distressing for AAPIs. The relationship between internalized heterosexism and psychological distress was not found to be mediated by outness (Szymanski & Sung, 2010). Thus, the decision to not come out may be related to their family's potential loss of face within their community rather than AAPIs having negative feelings about their identities. While not coming out may be less psychological distressing for AAPI SGMs, it may prevent them from seeking medical and psychological help. AAPIs and SGMs (as two distinct groups) have the lowest rates of help-seeking behaviors for mental health services in the United States and are underserved for mental health problems (Matsuoka, Breaux, & Ryujin, 1997; Smalley, Warren, & Barefoot, 2016). Therefore, the intersections of these identities (i.e., AAPI and SGM) may contribute to even more avoidance in seeking treatment. AAPI gay men have much lower rates of seeking HIV treatment and getting tested, with 21 percent of them being undiagnosed as compared to 13 percent in the total U.S. population (Centers for Disease Control and Prevention, 2017).

Alternatively, the cultural value of "saving face" may actually help mitigate the potentially destructive effects of coming out. In other words, collective values (that focus on family loyalty), and the family's desire to "save face" and present as a united family, may serve to encourage AAPI parents to eventually accept their children who come out as SGM (Choi & Israel, 2016).

Directions for Future Research

Research on SGM persons of color is increasing due to a growing recognition of the unique mental health experiences and needs of this community. Despite this growth, AAPIs continue to be underrepresented in this research (Sandil et al., 2015). To better understand the mental health concerns of the AAPI SGM community, future research needs to focus on the cultural factors specifically relevant for AAPIs' mental health. These factors include loss of face (or the inability to "save face"), self-disclosure (i.e., disclosing personal information to strangers), acculturation, and enculturation (i.e., alignment with the values of one's culture of origin) and are related to the underutilization of mental health services in the general AAPI population (Huang & Zane, 2019). These same factors may also act as barriers to mental health for AAPI SGMs. More specifically, little is known about how these cultural factors may influence identity development and mental health outcomes (psychologically and behaviorally) of AAPI SGMs. For example, current literature suggests that AAPI SGMs who are more acculturated to U.S. culture are more likely to come out. However, coming out did not predict more positive psychological outcomes for this population, unlike in other racial groups. Future research needs to examine the dynamics behind this relationship, and how culturally relevant constructs such as acculturation and enculturation may act as protective factors while also serving as psychological barriers. Because many AAPI individuals in the United States often come from immigrant families or first-generation immigrant families, it is crucial to examine immigrant status (e.g., those who are newly or first-generation immigrants vs. those who are second-generation or later immigrants) and family dynamics (e.g., acceptance of SGM youth). Little is also understood about how AAPI SGMs navigate their conflicting identities and cultural values through the use of both helpful and harmful coping strategies. Examples of adaptive coping strategies include engaging with the SGM or AAPI community, using cognitive self-talk, or learning about sexual and gender identities, while examples of harmful coping strategies may include substance use, self-harm, and distancing from one's community. Ultimately, addressing the existing research gaps will promote the development of culturally sensitive, culturally tailored mental health interventions to better help this underserved population.

References

Balsam, K. F., Lehavot, K., Beadnell, B., & Circo, E. (2010). Childhood abuse and mental health indicators among ethnically diverse lesbian, gay, and bisexual adults. *Journal of Consulting and Clinical Psychology, 78*(4), 459–68. doi:10.1037/a0018661

Balsam, K. F., Molina, Y., Beadnell, B., Simoni, J., & Walters, K. (2011). Measuring multiple minority stress: The LGBT People of Color Microaggressions Scale. *Cultural Diversity and Ethnic Minority Psychology, 17*, 163–74. doi:10.1037/a0023244

Bridges, S. K., Selvidge, M. M. D., & Matthews, C. R. (2003). Lesbian women of color: Therapeutic issues and challenges. *Journal of Multicultural Counseling and Development, 31*, 113–30. doi:10.1002/j.2161-1912.2003.tb00537.x

Centers for Disease Control and Prevention. (November, 2017). *HIV Surveillance Report, 2016*. http://www.cdc.gov/hiv/library/reports/hiv-surveillance.html

Chae, D. H., Takeuchi, D. T., Barbeau, E. M., Bennett, G. G., Lindsey, J., & Krieger, N. (2011). Unfair treatment, racial/ethnic discrimination, ethnic identification, and smoking among Asian Americans in the National Latino and Asian American Study. *American Journal of Public Health, 98*(3), 485–92. doi:10.2105/AJPH.2006.102012

Chan, C. (1989). Issues of identity development among Asian American lesbians and gay men. *Journal of Counseling and Development, 68*, 16–20. doi:10.1002/j.15566676.1989.tb02485.x

Chen, Y. C., & Tryon, G. S. (2012). Dual minority stress and Asian American gay men's psychological distress. *Journal of Community Psychology, 40*, 539–54. doi:10.1002/jcop.21481

Ching, T. H. W., Lee, S., Chen, J., So, R., & Williams, M. T. (2018). A model of intersectional stress and trauma in Asian American sexual and gender minorities. *Psychology of Violence, 8*(6), 657–68. doi:10.1037/vio0000204

Chng, C. L., Wong, F. Y., Park, R. J., Edberg, M. C., & Lai, D. S. (2003). A model for understanding sexual health among Asian American/Pacific Islander men who have sex with men (MSM) in the United States. *AIDS Education and Prevention, 15*, 21–38. doi:10.1521/aeap.15.1.5.21.23611

Choi, A. Y., & Israel, T. (2016). Centralizing the psychology of sexual minority Asian and Pacific Islander Americans. *Psychology of Sexual Orientation and Gender Diversity, 3*(3), 345–56. doi:10.1037/sgd0000184

Choi, A. Y., Israel, T., & Maeda, H. (2017). Development and evaluation of the Internalized Racism in Asian Americans Scale (IRAAS). *Journal of Counseling Psychology, 64*(1), 52–64. doi:10.1037/cou0000183

Choudhury, P. P., Badhan, N. S., Chand, J., Chhugani, S., Choksey, R., Hussainy, S., . . . Wat, E. C. (2009). Community alienation and its impact on help-seeking behavior among

LGBTIQ South Asians in Southern California. *Journal of Gay and Lesbian Social Services, 21*, 247–66. doi:10.1080/10538720902772196

Chu, H. (2001, March 6). Chinese psychiatrists decide homosexuality isn't abnormal. *Los Angeles Times*. Retrieved from https://www.latimes.com/archives/la-xpm-2001-mar-06-mn-33985-story.html

Chung, Y. B., & Katayama, M. (1998). Ethnic and sexual identity development of Asian-American lesbian and gay adolescents. *Professional School Counseling, 1*, 21–5.

Chung, Y. B., & Singh, A. A. (2009). Lesbian, gay, bisexual and transgender Asian Americans. In N. Tewari & A. N. Alvarez (Eds.), *Asian American psychology: Current perspectives* (pp. 233–46). New York, NY: Taylor & Francis Group.

Chung, Y. B., & Szymanski, D. M. (2006). Racial and sexual identities of Asian American gay men. *Journal of LGBT Issues in Counseling, 1*(2), 67–93. doi:10.1300/J462v01n02_05

Cochran, S. D., Mays, V. M., Alegria, M., Ortega, A. N., & Takeuchi, D. (2007). Mental health and substance use disorders among Latino and Asian American lesbian, gay, and bisexual adults. *Journal of Counseling and Clinical Psychology, 75*, 785–94. doi:10.1037/0022-006X.75.5.785

Cole, E. R. (2009). Intersectionality and research in psychology. *American Psychologist, 64*, 170–80. doi:10.1037/a0014564

Dang, A., & Vianney, C. (2007). *Living in the margins: A national survey of lesbian, gay, bisexual and transgender Asian and Pacific Islander Americans*. New York, NY: National Gay and Lesbian Task Force Policy Institute.

David, E. J. R., & Okazaki, S. (2006). The Colonial Mentality Scale (CMS) for Filipino Americans: Scale construction and psychological implications. *Journal of Counseling Psychology, 53*(2), 241–52. doi:10.1037/0022–0167.53.2.241

Diplacidio, J. (1998). Minority stress among lesbians, gay men, and bisexuals: A consequence of heterosexism, homophobia, and stigmatization. In G. M. Herek (Ed.), *Stigma and sexual orientation: Understanding prejudice against lesbians, gay men, and bisexuals* (pp. 138–59). Thousand Oaks, CA: Sage. doi:10.4135/9781452243818.n7 .

Gee, G. C., Ro, A., Shariff-Marco, S., & Chae, D. (2009). Racial discrimination and health among Asian Americans: Evidence, assessment, and directions for future research. *Epidemiologic Reviews, 31*, 130–51. doi:10.1093/epirev/mxp009

Greene, B. (1994). Ethnic-minority lesbians and gay men: Mental health and treatment issues. *Journal of Counseling and Clinical Psychology, 62*(2), 243–51. doi:10.1037/0022006X.62.2.243

Han, C. S. (2006). Being an Oriental, I could never be completely a man: Gay Asian men and the intersection of race, gender, sexuality, and class. *Race, Gender & Class, 13*(3), 82–97. https://www.jstor.org/journal/racegenderclass

Han, C. S. (2008a). No fats, femmes, or Asians: The utility of critical race theory in examining the role of gay stock stories in the marginalization of gay Asian men. *Contemporary Justice Review, 11*, 11–22. doi:10.1177/0896920508095101

Han, C. S. (2008b). Sexy like a girl and horny like a boy: Contemporary gay "Western" narratives about gay Asian men. *Critical Sociology, 34*, 829–50. doi:10.1177/0896920508095101

Harley, D. A. (2016). Asian American and Native Pacific Islander LGBT elders. In D. Harley & P. Teaster (Eds.), *Handbook of LGBT elders* (pp. 159–76). Cham, Switzerland: Springer. doi:10.1007/978-3-319-03623-6_8

Hom, A. Y. (1994). Stories from the home front: Perspectives of Asian American parents with lesbian daughters and gay sons. *Amerasia Journal, 20*, 19–32. doi:10.17953/amer.20.1.fw4816q23j815423

Huang, C. Y., & Zane, N. W. (2019). Culture and psychological interventions. In D. Matsumoto & H. C. Hwang (Eds.), *Oxford handbook of culture and psychology* (2nd ed.). New York, NY: Oxford University Press.

Huang, Y. P., Brewster, M., Moradi, B., Goodman, M., Wiseman, M., & Martin, A. (2010). Content analysis of literature about LGB people of color: 1998–2007. *The Counseling Psychologist, 38*, 363–96. doi:10.1177/0011000009335255

Jain, R. (2018). Education for the Hijras: Transgender persons of India. *Knowledge Cultures, 6*(1), 51–61. doi:10.22381/KC6120185

Kanuha, V. K. (2000). The impact of sexuality and race/ethnicity on HIV/AIDS risk among Asian and Pacific Islander lesbian and queer women's relationships. *Violence Against Women, 19*, 1175–96. doi:10.1177/1077801213501897

Kimmel, D. C., & Yi, H. (2004). Characteristics of gay, lesbian, and bisexual Asians, Asian Americans, and immigrants from Asia to the USA. *Journal of Homosexuality, 47*, 143–72. doi:10 0.1300/J082v47n02_09

Kumashiro, K. K. (1999). Supplementing normalcy and otherness: Queer Asian American men reflect on stereotypes, identity, and oppression. *International Journal of Qualitative Studies in Education, 12*, 491–508.

Kwok, D. K., & Wu, J. (2015). Chinese attitudes towards sexual minorities in Hong Kong: Implications for mental health. *International Review of Psychiatry, 27*(5), 444–54. doi:10.3109/09540261.2015.1083950

Landrine, H., Klonoff, E. A., Gibbs, J., Manning, V., & Lund, M. (1995). Physical and psychiatric correlates of gender discrimination. *Psychology of Women Quarterly, 19*, 473–92. doi:10.1111/j.1471–6402.1995 .tb00087.x

Laurent, E. (2005). Sexuality and human rights: An Asian perspective. *Journal of Homosexuality, 48*(3–4), 163–225. doi:10.1300/J082v48n03_09

Li, L., & Orleans, M. (2001). Coming out discourses of Asian American lesbians. *Sexuality & Culture: An Interdisciplinary Quarterly, 5*, 57–78. doi:10.1007/s12119-001-1018-z

Liu, P., & Chan, C. S. (1996). Lesbian, gay, and bisexual Asian Americans and their families. In J. Laird & R. J. Green (Eds.), *Lesbians and gays in couples and families: A handbook for therapists* (pp. 137–52). San Francisco, CA: Jossey-Bass.

Liu, W. M. (2002). Exploring the lives of Asian American men: Racial identity, male role norms, gender role conflict, and prejudicial attitudes. *Psychology of Men & Masculinity, 3*(2), 107–18. doi:10.1037/1524–9220.3.2.107

Loos, T. (2009). Transnational histories of sexualities in Asia. *American Historical Review, 114*, 1309–24. doi:10.1086/ahr.114.5.1309

Matsuoka, J. K., Breaux, C., & Ryujin, D. H. (1997). National utilization of mental health services by Asian Americans/Pacific Islanders. *Journal of Community Psychology, 25*, 141–5. doi:10.1002/(SICI)1520–6629(199703)25:20

Meyer, I. H. (2003). Prejudice, social stress, and mental health in lesbian, gay, and bisexual populations: Conceptual issues and research evidence. *Psychological Bulletin, 129*, 674–97. doi:10.1037/0033–2909.129.5.674

Moradi, B., & Grzanka, P. R. (2017). Using intersectionality responsibly: Toward critical epistemology, structural analysis, and social justice activism. *Journal of Counseling Psychology, 64*, 500–13. doi:10.1037/cou00000203

Morris, J. F., & Balsam, K. F. (2003). Lesbian and bisexual women's experiences of victimization: Mental health,

revictimization, and sexual identity development. *Journal of Lesbian Studies, 7*, 67–85. doi:10.1300/J155v07n04_05
Morris, R. J. (1990). Aikane: Accounts of Hawaiian same-sex relationships in the journals of Captain Cook's third voyage (1776–80). *Journal of Homosexuality, 19*, 21–54. doi:10.1300/J082v19n04_03
Nadal, K. L., & Corpus, M. J. H. (2013). "Tomboys" and "baklas": Experiences of lesbian and gay Filipino Americans. *Asian American Journal of Psychology, 4*(3), 166–75. doi:10.1037/a0030168
Peletz, M. (2006). Transgenderism and gender pluralism in Southeast Asia since early modern times. *Current Anthropology, 47*(2), 309–40. doi:10.1086/498947
Phua, V. C. (2007). Contesting and maintaining hegemonic masculinities: Gay Asian American men in mate selection. *Sex Roles, 57*, 909–18. doi:10.1007/s11199-007-9318-x
Pitonak, M. (2017). Mental health in non-heterosexuals: Minority stress theory and related explanation frameworks review. *Mental Health & Prevention, 5*, 63–73. doi:10.1016/j.mhp.2016.10.002
Poon, M. K. (2000). Inter-racial same-sex abuse. *Journal of Gay & Lesbian Social Services, 11*(4), 39–67. doi:10.1300/J041v11n04_03
Pyke, K. D., & Johnson, D. L. (2003). Asian American women and racialized femininities: "Doing" gender across cultural worlds. *Gender & Society, 17*(1), 33–53. doi:10.1177/0891243202238977
Ramzy, A. (2019). Taiwan legislature approves Asia's first same-sex marriage law. *New York Times*, May 17. https://www.nytimes.com/2019/05/17/world/asia/taiwan-gay-marriage.html
Ratti, R., Bakeman, R., & Peterson, J. L. (2000). Correlates of high-risk sexual behaviour among Canadian men of South Asian and European origin who have sex with men. *AIDS Care, 12*(2), 193–202. doi:10.1080/09540120050001878
Sandil, R., Robinson, M., Brewster, M. E., Wong, S., & Geiger, E. (2015). Negotiating multiple marginalizations: Experiences of South Asian LGBQ individuals. *Cultural Diversity and Ethnic Minority Psychology, 21*(1), 76–88. doi:10.1037/a0037070
Singh, A. A., Chung, Y. B., & Dean, J. K. (2006). Acculturation level and internalized homophobia of Asian American lesbian and bisexual women. *Journal of LGBT Issues in Counseling, 1*(2), 3–19. doi:10.1300/J462v01n02_02
Smalley, K. B., Warren, J. C., & Barefoot, K. N. (2016). Differences in health risk behaviors across understudied LGBT subgroups. *Health Psychology, 35*(2), 103–14. doi:10.1037/hea0000231
Sohng, W. H., & Icard, L. D. (1996). A Korean gay man in the United States: Toward a cultural context for social service practice. *Journal of Gay and Lesbian Social Services, 5*, 115–37.
Sue, D. W., & Sue, D. (2013). *Counseling the culturally diverse: Theory and practice* (6th ed.). Hoboken, NJ: John Wiley & Sons.
Sullivan, G. (2001). Variations on a common theme? Gay and lesbian identity and community in Asia. *Journal of Homosexuality, 40*, 253–69. doi:10.1300/J082v40n03_13
Sung, M. R., Szymanski, D. M., & Henrichs-Beck, C. (2015). Challenges, coping, and benefits of being an Asian-American lesbian or bisexual woman. *Psychology of Sexual Orientation and Gender Diversity, 2*, 52–64. doi:10.1037/sgd0000085
Szymanski, D. M., & Gupta, A. (2009a). Examining the relationship between multiple internalized oppressions and African American lesbian, gay, and bisexual persons' self-esteem and psychological distress. *Journal of Counseling Psychology, 56*, 110–8. doi:10.1037/a0013317
Szymanski, D. M., & Gupta, A. (2009b). Examining the relationship between multiple oppressions and Asian American sexual minority persons' psychological distress. *Journal of Gay and Lesbian Social Services, 21*, 267–81. doi:10.1080/10538720902772212
Szymanski, D. M., & Meyer, D. (2008). Racism and heterosexism as correlates of psychological distress in African American sexual minority women. *Journal of LGBT Issues in Counseling, 2*(2), 94–108, doi:10.1080/15538600802125423
Szymanski, D. M., & Sung, M. R. (2010). Minority stress and psychological distress among Asian American sexual minority persons. *The Counseling Psychologist, 38*, 848–72. doi:10.1177/0011000010366167
Tan, J. Y., Xu, L. J., Lopez, F. Y., Jia, J. L., Pho, M. T., Kim, K. E., & Chin, M. H. (2016). Shared decision making among clinicians and Asian American and Pacific Islander sexual and gender minorities: An intersectional approach to address a critical care gap. *LGBT Health, 3*(5), 327–34. doi:10.1089/lgbt.2015.0143
Tseng, T. (2011). Understanding LGBT bias: An analysis of Chinese-speaking Americans' attitudes toward LGBT people in Southern California. *LGBTQ Policy Journal at the Harvard Kennedy School, 1*, 73–83. http://lgbtq.hkspublications.org/wp-content/uploads/sites/20/2015/10/LGBT_3-14-11_Final.pdf#page=79
U.S. Census Bureau. (2012a, May). The Native Hawaiian and Other Pacific Islander population: 2010. https://www.census.gov/prod/cen2010/briefs/c2010br-11.pdf
U.S. Census Bureau. (2012b, March). The Asian population: 2010. https://www.census.gov/prod/cen2010/briefs/c2010br-11.pdf
Velez, B., Polihoronakis, C. J., Watson, L. B., & Cox, R. (2019). Heterosexism, racism, and the mental health of sexual minority people of color. *The Counseling Psychologist, 47*(1), 129–59. doi:10.1177/0011000019828309
Wong, F., & Halgin, R. (2006). The "model minority": Bane or blessing for Asian Americans? *Journal of Multicultural Counselzing and Development, 34*(1), 38–49. doi:10.1002/j.2161-1912.2006.tb00025.x
Yamane, L. (2018). Biracial Asian and white: Demographic and labor market status. *Theoretical and Applied Economics, 4*(617), 47–62. https://www.researchgate.net/profile/Linus_Yamane/publication/329428665_Biracial_Asian_and_white_Demographic_and_labor_market_status/links/5c084e65a6fdcc494fdca03d/Biracial-Asian-and-white-Demographic-and-labor-market-status.pdf
Yee, B. W. K., DeBaryshe, B. D., Yuen, S., Kim, S. Y., & McCubbin, H. I. (2007). Asian American and Pacific Islander families: Resiliency and life-span socialization in a cultural context. In F. T. L. Leong, A. Ebreo, L. Kinoshita, A. G. Inman, & L. H. Yang (Eds.), *Handbook of Asian American psychology* (2nd ed., pp. 69–86). Thousand Oaks, CA: Sage.
Yoshikawa, H., Wilson, P. A.-D., Chae, D. H., & Cheng, J. F. (2004). Do family and friendship networks protect against the influence of discrimination on mental health and HIV risk among Asian and Pacific Islander gay men? *AIDS Education and Prevention, 16*, 84–100. doi:10.1521/aeap.16.1.84.27719

CHAPTER

18 Indigenous American/Two-Spirit Mental Health

Naomi Bird *and* Margaret Robinson

Abstract

While many Indigenous languages have terms for individuals who combine masculinity with femininity in some way, Indigenous *gender* minority people have increasingly come to self-identify using the pan-Indigenous term "two-spirit." This chapter examines key factors shaping the mental wellness of two-spirit people, such as the negative impact of residential and boarding school incarceration, and highlights available data on anxiety, depression, posttraumatic stress disorder, suicidality, and substance use. Reducing the mental health disparities that two-spirit people face is made more challenging by the lack of culturally informed and supportive health services. The authors describe factors that may buffer the minority stressors that lead to negative mental health outcomes and may increase wellness. The chapter concludes with a discussion of promising directions for future research.

Keywords: two-spirit, Indigenous, Indigenous language, colonialism, intergenerational trauma, mental health, well-being, intersectionality

Prior to European contact, many Indigenous nations on Turtle Island (North America) framed gender in ways that were social, ceremonial, and fluid rather than biological and binary (Fieland, Walters, & Simoni, 2007). Many Indigenous languages had terms for individuals who shifted gender from masculine to feminine or vice versa, or whose gender exceeded a binary framework (e.g., third gender individuals). The A'shwi (Zuni), for example, refer to some individuals who mixed masculine and feminine as *lhamana*, a term that has been translated as "man–woman" (Basaldu, 1999, p. 107; Roscoe, 1988, p. 56). Similarly, the Diné (Navajo) call those who mix masculine and feminine *nadleeh*, meaning "one in a constant state of change" (Thomas, 1997, p. 171). Today Indigenous people who combine masculine and feminine often self-identify using the English term *two-spirit*. While most stories place the origin of the term in 1990, at the Third Annual Inter-Tribal Native American/First Nations Gay and Lesbian American Conference held near Beausejour, Manitoba, Canada, some assert the identity emerged in San Francisco as early as the 1960s (Meyer-Cook & Labelle, 2004).

Nehiyaw (Cree) educator Harlan Pruden argues that in a "traditional setting," the term two-spirit is an *analysis* of gender, not a gender identity or sexual orientation (2019, p. 7). Although Pruden is correct, the influence of settler frameworks that focus heavily on identity has led two-spirit to be taken up as a way to describe sexuality as well, sometimes to the exclusion of gender. The Risk & Resilience study of bisexual mental health, for example, found that 29 percent of participants in the Canadian province of Ontario who self-identified as First Nations, Métis, or Inuit used 'two-spirited' to describe their gender, while 39 percent used the term to describe their sexuality (Robinson, Plante, MacLeod, Cruz, & Bhanji, 2016, p. 2). Regardless of whether it historically applied to gender or sexuality, two-spirit distinguishes itself from identities such as LGBTQ by prioritizing an individual's connection to their Indigenous nation, identity, and culture. Fieland et al. note that the label two-spirit "denotes an individual with specific spiritual, social, and cultural roles" in their Indigenous culture (2007, p. 271). As a pan-Indigenous term, two spirit provides a convenient way to express gender or sexual difference *and* cultural connection, especially since Indigenous language terms, such as *lhamana* or *nadleeh*, may be unfamiliar outside of one's own language group. Indigenous people may also use multiple identity labels. For example, Fieland et al. report that one Navajo activist refers to himself as gay when among LGBTQ settlers, as two-spirit when with Indigenous non-Navajo, and as *nadleeh* among other Navajo (2007, p. 271).

In a study by Ristock, Zoccole, and Passante, one participant described two-spirit identity as "a new word for a very old feeling" (2010, p. 14). Many Indigenous nations historically recognized individuals who exhibited a balance of qualities considered masculine and feminine. Tafoya (1997) estimates that 168 Indigenous languages in the United States have terms for differently gendered people. This cultural recognition also holds true for Indigenous nations north of the colonial border between Canada and the United States. Halverson (2013) reports that the Ojibwe, for example, have a four-gender system consisting of masculine males (*inini*), feminine females (*okwe*), feminine males (*agokwe*), and masculine females (*agowinini*). Accounts of *agokwe* by early colonists reveal settler discomfort with gender shifting and with what they construed as same-sex attraction. One settler describing Ozawwendib, a famous *agokwe*, as "one of those who make themselves women and are called women by the Indians," noting that "this creature" made "disgusting advances" that shamed the settler—to the delight of his Indigenous allies (Tanner, 1830, p. 105).

Indigenous nations often value balance and may have viewed people who combine masculinity and femininity as uniquely positioned to represent and serve their communities. Some two-spirit people functioned as counselors due to their "ability to mediate between and see through the eyes of both sexes" (Meyer-Cook & Labelle, 2004, p. 31). This type of role can be seen in a creation story of the Diné, which features an acrimonious separation between men and women to the detriment of both that is ended by the intervention of a two-spirit person (Roanhorse, 2005). Two-spirit people are also said to have performed tasks that were social (e.g., matchmaking), ceremonial (e.g., naming, coming of age rites), and economic (e.g., mastering both masculine and feminine work) (Newcomb 1964; Pruden, 2019).

While frameworks of gender and sexuality vary across Indigenous nations, they are constantly subjected to what Driskill calls "heteropatriarchal, gender polarised colonial regimes" that position two-spirit people in opposition to colonial powers (2010, p. 69). Argüello and Walters argue that two-spirit self-understanding is a "decolonizing and re-/Indigenizing standpoint" and "an active critique of White supremacy and heteropatriarchal structures from outside and within Native communities" (2018, p. 108). Two spirit identity frames gender and sexuality from an Indigenous perspective, rejecting imposed Eurocentric concepts of binarized sexualities and genders (Argüello & Walters, 2018; Walters, Evans-Campbell, Simoni, Ronquillo, & Bhuyan, 2006). Although a neologism, the term two-spirit points to a historical period of inclusion and respect and serves as a placeholder until Indigenous language terms describing gender and sexuality can be reclaimed, rediscovered, or reimagined.

Two-Spirit Mental Health

An understanding of the mental health of two-spirit people requires an understanding of what constitutes mental well-being. The World Health Organization (WHO) defines mental health holistically as "a state of well-being in which the individual realizes his or her own abilities, can cope with the normal stresses of life, can work productively and fruitfully, and is able to make a contribution to his or her community" (2001, p. 1). Indigenous nations take an even broader view of mental wellness by including elements such as one's connection to spiritual beings, territory, and animal life. As the term itself implies, two-spirit is a spiritual identity, which may entail roles in Indigenous ceremonies or manifest in spiritual gifts. This distinguishes two-spirit from queer settler identities such as gay and lesbian, which define themselves as secular against a historically antagonistic European Christian tradition (Robinson, 2017). Indigenous nations may also take a broader view of gender, expanding beyond "his or her" (WHO, 2001, p. 1) to include an expectation of cultural contributions from third, fourth, or nonbinary community members.

Prior to European contact, two-spirit people lived healthy lives as integral and respected members of their Indigenous nations. Today, however, the mental wellness of two-spirit people is negatively impacted by a number of mutually supporting oppressions. Primary among these is colonialism, "the formal and informal methods (behaviors, ideologies, institutions, policies, and economies) that maintain the subjugation or exploitation of [I]ndigenous Peoples, lands, and resources" (Wilson & Bird, 2005, p. 2). The ongoing trauma that results as colonists displace Indigenous nations from their territory, replace their traditional governments, destroy their economies, criminalize their spiritual practices, and eliminate their languages affects all Indigenous people. Some traumas may impact two-spirit people more heavily due to how the Christian value systems embraced by colonists historically vilified gender and sexual minority people. Losing one's respected role in traditional government, for example, may have negatively impacted the mental wellness of two-spirit people for multiple generations.

The health disparities currently experienced by two-spirit people can be partially explained by Meyer's minority stress theory (2003), which posits that mental health problems among a minority population increase when the stress burden exceeds what can be managed using the available resources and supports. Minority stress has been shown to have negative impacts on sexual minority people across their lifespans (King, 2010; Meyer, 2003; Pascoe & Smart Richman, 2009; Selvidge, Matthews, & Bridges, 2008). As members of Indigenous nations, two-spirit people experience stressors such as political, cultural, or economic oppression, and they also face stressors such as sexism, cissexism, transphobia, homophobia, biphobia, or transphobia as members of a gender or sexual minority. The Honor Project, a study of 447 two-spirit people from seven urban areas in the United States, found that while 53 percent of participants had an educational attainment of secondary school or greater, 59 percent were unemployed and 75 percent were living on a household income below $18,000 per year (Walters, 2010). Similarly, Our Health Counts, the largest study of urban Indigenous people in Canada, found that although 48 percent of two-spirit adults in Toronto had completed secondary school or a postsecondary degree, 83 percent lived below the low income cut-off, 63 percent were unemployed, and 33 percent had experienced homelessness (Seventh Generation Midwives Toronto, 2018).

These socioeconomic disparities are not due to colonialism alone but are the result of a number of oppressions working in tandem. Intersectionality theory argues that "major systems of oppression are interlocking" (Combahee River Collective, 1977), and Davis (1981) and Lorde (1978) have noted how systems of racism, sexism, and homophobia connect to negatively impact the lives of black lesbian women. Crenshaw (1989) coined the term *intersectionality* to describe the phenomena of interlocking oppression, rejecting an approach that views oppression as merely additive. An intersectional approach suggests that the mental health of two-spirit people is stressed by a system of mutually reinforcing homophobic/sexist/colonial racism that can exhaust even the most resilient person.

Indigenous populations on Turtle Island are small relative to the settler population. In Canada, 4.9 percent of the population identifies as First Nations, Inuit, or Métis (Statistics Canada, 2017), and studies in the United States have found that 2 percent of the population identifies as American Indian or Alaskan Native (U.S. Department of Health and Human Services, 2019). There is some evidence that Indigenous people are more likely than their settler peers to identify as a sexual minority person. The First Nations Regional Health Survey, a national study of Indigenous people living on reserves in Canada, found that 3.3 percent of First Nations people aged eighteen or older identified as two-spirit or a related sexual identity (2012), a rate over twice that for the Canadian population as a whole (1.5 percent; Statistics Canada, 2004). Younger people are more likely to self-identify with a sexual or gender minority; 5.2 percent of those aged eighteen to twenty-four identified as two-spirit or a related sexual identity, compared to only 0.9 percent of those aged fifty to fifty-nine (First Nations Information Governance Centre, 2012). The percentage of two-spirit people in urban centers is much higher; the Our Health Counts study found that 23 percent of Indigenous adults in Toronto identified as two-spirit (Seventh Generation Midwives Toronto, 2018).

Because they are a minority within a minority, accurate and respectful information about two-spirit people and their mental health is limited. Most studies fail to recruit sufficient numbers of Indigenous people to enable within-group comparisons or sophisticated data analysis of factors impacting mental health. This chapter examines the best of the available literature to highlight mental health outcomes for two-spirit people in relation to anxiety, depression, posttraumatic stress disorder (PTSD), suicidality, and substance use. Since academic sources and community members often use two-spirit to refer to both diverse gender and sexual identities, that is how we operationalize the term in this chapter.

Negative Impact of Boarding and Residential Schools

The Truth and Reconciliation Commission of Canada (2015) has stressed the urgent need to repair the damage done to Indigenous people and their communities by Indian residential schools. Through forcibly confining Indigenous children to residential schools in Canada (c.1884 to 1996) and boarding schools in the United States (c.1819 to 2007), colonial governments forcibly assimilated generations of Indigenous people into settler religion, language, culture, gender, and sexuality (Ansbergs, 2014). Indian residential schools separated children, some as young as three, from their families in an effort to "kill the Indian in the child" (Royal Commission on Aboriginal Peoples, 1996, p. 3). Residential and boarding schools were rife with physical, emotional, mental, and sexual abuse, and had an alarmingly high death rate due to overcrowding, lack of adequate heating and sanitation, malnutrition, overwork, violence, and infectious disease (Mosby, 2013; Royal Commission, 1996). By 1930, three quarters of First Nations children in Canada had been through the system (Fournier & Crey, 1997), and Barkan (2003) estimates that over 150,000 Indigenous children in Canada were forced to attend.

The schools imposed European understandings of gender directly upon arrival. As a two-spirit participant from a study by Wilson recalls:

> The first thing they did was divide us by boy/girl. Girl go this way, boy go this way. Girl wear pinafores. Boy wear pants. All hair cut... It was like a little factory—one priest shaved my head while the other tore off my clothes. I was so scared. I covered my area. It didn't take long for them to notice.... That was my first beating. (2008, pp. 194–195)

Asserting settler cultural practices as divinely ordained and enforcing them on generations of Indigenous children did much to erase Indigenous gender systems and instill animosity toward two-spirit people (Garrett & Barret, 2003). Forcing students to speak English or French only, for example, erased Indigenous ways of describing gender. Meyer-Cook and Labelle (2004) also note how heterosexuality and gender conformity were connected to economic survival, with children being trained not only to perform European gender roles but to perform them within a capitalist system built on gendered oppression(s). A book detailing the history of St. Michael's Residential Missionary School, operated by the Anglican Church of Canada from 1929 to 1975, explains how gender was enmeshed with compulsory heterosexuality and European capitalism:

> The older boys were expected to build a small house on a piece of land chosen for them by the church before they could get out of school. The girls in the meantime were often placed in non-Native homes to work as servants, "to wait as house maids" for their future husbands. Academic studies had little place within these schools. (Le Chevralier, 1944, p. 29)

Meyer-Cook and Labelle assert that "those with diverse gender/sexual orientation didn't disappear, rather went underground" (2004, p. 35), demonstrating the active and ongoing resistance to colonization by many Indigenous people, which continues in the present day.

Forced assimilation to European Christianity led many Indigenous communities to devalue and even violently reject two-spirit people (Brotman, Ryan, Jalbert, & Rowe, 2002; Fieland et al., 2007). In the Risk & Resilience study in Ontario, 60 percent of bisexual First Nations, Métis, or Inuit participants reported that the faith of their family of origin was unfriendly toward LGBTQ people (Robinson et al., 2016). Oppressions resulting from forced Christianization have been identified as a factor pressuring two-spirit people to leave their Indigenous communities. As one participant in a 2017 study noted, "[A]t one time Two Spirited people, we had a special place in the community, but in modern times, we're looked on as trash even by our people, 'cause of the European mainstream influence" (Ristock, Zoccole, Passante, & Potskin, 2017, p. 13).

The negative impacts of residential and boarding schools are an ongoing concern because so many members of Indigenous communities were incarcerated in a residential or boarding school themselves or were raised by those who were. In a study of two-spirit health by Walters (2010), 18 percent of participants had attended boarding school and 39 percent had a family member who had attended. In the Risk & Resilience study, 24 percent of bisexual First Nations, Métis, and Inuit participants had a parent or caregiver who attended a residential school (Robinson et al., 2016). Wilson (2008) notes that while only two participants in her study of two-spirit identity attended residential schools, all eight participants suffered effects from the residential school experience. Some participants in Wilson's study reported "being sexually, emotionally, and/or culturally abused by family members and others," as well as "their own struggles with depression, anger, and self-destructive behaviours" (2008, p. 195). Wilson's participants connected these problems directly to colonial trauma; as one participant who did not attend a boarding school noted, "All the residential school shit was repeated on [us]!" (Wilson, 2008, p. 195).

The full impact of these colonial school systems is still emerging, with new traumas being revealed as the social stigma against reporting lessens. In the Honor Project, 34 percent of those forced to attend boarding school indicated they had been physically harmed there and 28 percent had been sexually harmed (Walters, 2010). The abuse perpetrated by these carceral systems has damaged generations of Indigenous people, often in ways that are easily and unintentionally passed on to subsequent generations.

Mental Health Disparities of Two-Spirit People

The Our Health Counts study identified several mental health disparities for two-spirit people compared to Indigenous people who did not identify as two-spirit. For example, while 29 percent of two-spirit adults in Toronto rated their mental health as "very good" or "excellent," the rate for those who did not identify as two-spirit was higher, at 32 percent (Seventh Generation Midwives Toronto, 2018). Sixty-two percent of two-spirit people in Toronto had been diagnosed with a mental health problem, and of those, 58 percent noted that "their condition(s) limited the kinds or amounts of activities in which they could engage" (Seventh Generation Midwives Toronto, 2018, p. 2). Since Indigenous people may not always access health services, the actual rate of mental health disparities can be assumed to be higher.

Anxiety is a common mental health problem for two-spirit people, with available statistics elevated far above the norm for both Indigenous and non-Indigenous people. Parker, Duran, and Walters (2017) report that two-spirit people who experienced bias-related victimization such as assault, harassment, or stalking had significantly higher levels of generalized anxiety disorder (42.9 percent) compared to two-spirit individuals who had not experienced such victimization (23.1 percent). By contrast, only 5.7 percent of the adult population of the United States has been found to experience generalized anxiety disorder in their lifetime (Harvard Medical School, 2005). The frequency of anxiety disorders may also be a result of intergenerational trauma. An analysis of data from the Honor Project, examining only those two-spirit participants who attended boarding school or who were raised by someone who attended, revealed that 48.9 percent of those raised by a survivor had a general anxiety disorder, as did 39.0 percent of those who attended themselves (Evans-Campbell, Walters, Pearson, & Campbell, 2012). Gilley (2006) notes that being out to others as two-spirit may prevent individuals from being accepted into Indigenous communities, further separating them from cultural connection and belonging and the mental health supports that accompany such belonging.

Another significant mental health disparity among two-spirit people is depression. The Our Health Counts study found that 23 percent of two-spirit participants had been diagnosed with major depression by a healthcare provider, with 25 percent screening positive for depression on measures within the survey itself (Seventh Generation Midwives Toronto, 2018). By comparison, 18 percent of other Indigenous people in the same survey had a depression diagnosis, and the rate for Ontario adults as a whole has been placed at 11 percent, demonstrating the elevated rates for two-spirit people (Seventh Generation Midwives Toronto, 2018). In some sexual minority populations the elevated risk for depression nearly approaches that of two-spirit people themselves. In the Risk & Resilience study, for example, 39 percent of First Nations, Métis, or Inuit bisexuals had depression scores suggestive of moderate to severe depression, as did 35.4 percent of bisexuals in Ontario as a whole (Robinson et al., 2016; Ross et al., 2014). Walters (2010) found that historical traumas such as the loss of traditional lands and forcible confinement in the residential school system, and related historical trauma responses, are associated with depression among two-spirit people. Ongoing exposure to stress results in elevated rates of cortisol, which may be the causal link between experiences of trauma and outcomes on measures of depression. Minority stress has been found to increase cortisol production, predicting depression scores in young sexual minority adults (Parra, Benibgui, Helm, & Hastings, 2016).

Some mental health issues arise as a result of violent victimization. While Indigenous people as a whole report high rates of colonial trauma and violence (Burnette & Figley, 2016), two-spirit people are at even greater risk. A study by Balsam et al. (2004) found that 40 percent of two-spirit people had experienced sexual abuse in childhood, compared to 25.8 percent of other Indigenous participants

(2004). Given such findings, it is not surprising that several studies of two-spirit mental health have noted elevated rates of PTSD. Walters (2010) found that 7.17 percent of two-spirit people in her study had been diagnosed with PTSD. By contrast, a study of mental health surveys by the World Health Organization found that the global lifetime prevalence of PTSD was 3.9 percent (Koenen et al. 2017).

There are significant discrepancies in diagnosis rates for PTSD. The Our Heath Counts study found that 48 percent of two-spirit Indigenous adults in Toronto scored positive on measures of PTSD, yet only 12 percent had been diagnosed with PTSD by a medical professional. This is slightly higher than the PTSD diagnosis rate for other Indigenous people in the survey (11 percent) and significantly higher than the rate for adults in Ontario as a whole (2 percent) (Seventh Generation Midwives Toronto, 2018). Similarly, the Honor Project found that 86 percent of two-spirit participants exhibited symptoms consistent with PTSD but only 7 percent had received such a diagnosis (Evans-Campbell et al., 2012). Evans et al. (2012) found that PTSD symptoms were more common among two-spirit people who were raised by someone who attended boarding school (90.3 percent) and that the PTSD diagnosis rate in this same group was lower (6.3 percent).

While most mental health conditions impair well-being, suicidality—defined as thoughts about killing oneself, or attempts to do so—poses a threat to two-spirit life itself. Suicidality among two-spirit people must be contextualized within the ongoing Indigenous suicide epidemic. The suicide rate for First Nations communities in Canada, for example, is twice that for the non-Indigenous population, and some First Nations have suicide rates that are 800 times the national average (Chandler & Lalonde, 1998). Researchers have consistently found disproportionately high numbers of suicide attempts among two-spirit people. A study conducted in Minnesota showed that 23.2 percent of American Indian and Alaskan Native adolescent men with exclusive same-sex attractions had attempted suicide, compared with 11.1 percent of their straight peers (Barney, 2003). A national study of trans people in the United States found that 56 percent of American Indian and Alaskan Native participants had attempted suicide, compared with 41 percent of trans participants as a whole (National Gay and Lesbian Task Force and National Center for Transgender Equality, 2012). In the Trans PULSE study, conducted in Ontario, 48 percent of First Nations, Métis, or Inuit participants had attempted suicide (Scheim et al., 2013). In Toronto rates were even higher, with 60 percent of two-spirit people having attempted suicide, compared to 42 percent of Indigenous people who did not identify as two-spirit (Seventh Generation Midwives Toronto, 2018).

Rates for considering suicide (sometimes called suicidal ideation) are also alarmingly elevated for two-spirit people. The Our Health Counts study found that 70 percent of two-spirit adults in Toronto had considered suicide, compared with 50 percent of other Indigenous participants (Seventh Generation Midwives Toronto, 2018). Similarly, 71 percent of the First Nations, Métis, or Inuit participants in the Risk & Resilience study had considered suicide compared to 18.8 percent of bisexuals in Ontario as a whole (Robinson et al., 2016; Ross et al., 2014). Trans PULSE found that 76 percent of two-spirit participants had considered suicide (Scheim et al., 2013). The Honor Project found that the overwhelming majority of two-spirit people who attended boarding school (92.5 percent) or were raised by someone who attended (94.6 percent) had suicidal thoughts in their lifetime, compared to 88.2 percent of those who did not attend boarding school, and 85.4 percent of those whose caretaker did not attend boarding school (Evans-Campbell et al., 2012). In a Minnesota-based study Barney found that 47.3 percent of American Indian and Alaskan Native adolescent men with exclusive same-sex attractions had considered suicide, compared with 23.6 percent of their straight peers (2003). The rates of suicidality above are all based on self-reporting. Reliable statistics on *completed* suicide among gender and sexual minority people are unavailable since such information is often not recorded or not known. As a result, the numbers reported above, while alarmingly high, are also likely under-estimated (Robinson, 2013).

Despite the high rates of mental health problems reported by two-spirit people, access to support services is low. Walters (2010) found that 16.62 percent of two-spirit participants required mental health treatment they did not receive, 65 percent of First Nations, Métis, or Inuit participants in the Risk & Resilience study had an unmet mental health need in the past year, and 16 percent had forcibly received mental health treatment they did not want (Robinson et al., 2016). The Our Health Counts study found that 38 percent of two-spirit participants thought that suicide prevention services were inadequate and 34 percent considered mental health services in general to be inadequate for serving Indigenous people (Seventh Generation Midwives Toronto, 2018). Participants in a study focused on gay, bisexual, and two-spirit men and suicidality described healthcare providers as "throwing pills at situations" instead of providing the referrals to counseling asked for by participants (Ferlatte et al., 2019, p. 1190).

Considering the high rate of mental health issues reported by two-spirit people, taken together with a low rate of access to culturally appropriate and supportive mental health services, it is unsurprising to see people using substances as a coping mechanism. A study of 179 American Indians and Alaska Natives in the New York City area found that 78.3 percent of two-spirit participants had used illicit drugs for nonceremonial purposes, compared with 56 percent of heterosexual participants (Balsam et al., 2004). In Canada, the Risk & Resilience study found that 36 percent of First Nations, Métis, or Inuit participants reported experiences that suggest problem drinking, and 55 percent had used recreational drugs in the past year (Robinson et al., 2016).

Substance use among two-spirit people may be exacerbated by migration to urban centers because settler-dominated LGBTQ communities also have high rates of substance use. In urban queer communities, many of which formed when 'homosexuality' was criminalized, bars have long served as a meeting point (Ristock, Zoccole, & Passante, 2010). As a result, LGBTQ events often involve alcohol and drugs (O'Brien Teengs & Travers, 2006). The combination of frequent substance use and economic and social precarity can put two-spirit youth at risk for a number of negative outcomes, as O'Brien Teengs and Travers note:

> When two- spirit youth are in a situation where survival depends on other people's generosity, or where harmful amounts of alcohol or drugs are used as coping strategies, these youth become vulnerable to HIV. Moreover, when housing, food, money and personal safety are more immediate and urgent concerns, the ability or desire to protect oneself in risk situations lessens. Taken in combination, these factors must be attended to in order to lessen HIV vulnerability among two-spirit youth. (2006, pp. 23–4)

Balsam et al. (2004) note that, on average, two-spirit participants report having their first drink of alcohol at age twelve, while their Indigenous heterosexual peers took their first drink at age fourteen. That study found a statistically significant difference between measures of drinking to improve social skills (3.39 percent of two-spirit people vs. 2.01 percent of heterosexuals) and drinking to manage mood (3.61 percent vs. 1.98 percent) (Balsam et al., 2004).

Several studies have related substance use to experiences of colonial trauma. Evans-Campbell et al. (2012) found that among two-spirit people who had been forced to attend boarding school, 58.5 percent had a diagnosis of alcohol abuse or dependence, compared with 44.6 percent who did not attend. Similar differences in rates of past-year use were found for cocaine (65.4 percent in boarding school attendees vs. 48.4 percent in those who did not attend), narcotics (92.3 percent of boarding school attendees vs. 48.4 percent of non-attendees), and "club drugs" (78.9 percent vs. 38 percent) (Evans-Campbell et al., 2012). Although there were elevated levels of marijuana and methamphetamine use among boarding school survivors, when compared to those who did not attend boarding school the difference was not statistically significant (Evans-Campbell et al., 2012). Similarly, Yuan, Duran, Walters, Pearson, and Evans-Campbell (2014) noted that for two-spirit men, attending an Indian boarding school and being placed in foster care were associated with past-year alcohol dependence (increasing the likelihood of dependence more than threefold), past-year hazardous and harmful alcohol use (a threefold increase), and past-year drinking binges (a sixfold increase). For women, experiences of physical neglect and emotional abuse in childhood were associated with past-year drinking binges (Yuan et al., 2014).

A number of studies have found high rates of smoking among two-spirit people. In the Honor Project, Walters (2010) found that 78 percent of two-spirit men, 88 percent of two-spirit women, and 85 percent of trans-identified participants reported being current smokers. In the Risk & Resilience study, 19 percent of First Nations, Métis, or Inuit participants were daily smokers (Robinson et al., 2016). Walters found a significant association between the historical losses suffered by Indigenous people due to colonial occupation of their territories and smoking rates among two-spirit people, with "each unit increase in historical loss being associated with 3.5 times the odds of current smoking" (2010, p. 33). Johnson-Jennings et al. (2014) found experiences of racial discrimination to be strongly correlated with nonceremonial tobacco use.

While these studies depict elevated rates of substance use, not all two-spirit people use substances. Eleven percent of the First Nations, Métis, or Inuit people in the Risk & Resilience study had consumed no alcohol at all within the past year (Robinson et al., 2016). The Honor Project found that 39.69 percent of two-spirit people had no alcohol dependency at all (Walters, 2010), and Simoni, Walters, Balsam, and Meyers (2006) revealed that, contrary to expectations, no significant differences were found between heterosexual and two-spirit people on measures of substance use in the past year, and high levels of sobriety were noted overall.

Difficulty Accessing Support

Despite elevated rates of substance use, two-spirit people do not report easy access to addiction treatment services. Trans PULSE found that only 29 percent of Indigenous participants who thought they needed addiction treatment were able to access such services (Scheim et al., 2013). Walters (2010) found that 9.72 percent of Honor Project participants reported needing but not receiving treatment for alcohol or drug use. Complicating the issue, Robinson et al. (2016) found that 5 percent of First Nations, Métis, or Inuit participants in the Risk & Resilience study had been forcibly treated in a substance use facility.

Two-spirit experiences of health services are often saturated in discrimination. Indigenous people using non-Indigenous HIV/AIDS services, for example, report experiencing racism, being talked down to, and being mistreated by pharmacists (Ristock et al., 2011). Moreover, due to the long history of justifiable Indigenous mistrust toward healthcare systems and government institutions, some two-spirit people hesitate to seek assistance from health services administered by or connected with colonial governments. In the Our Health Counts study, 70 percent of two-spirit participants reported delaying or avoiding healthcare due to discrimination (Seventh Generation Midwives Toronto, 2018). In the Risk & Resilience study, only 36 percent of First Nations, Métis, or Inuit participants reported using mental health services, and of those who did access treatment, only 67 percent were satisfied with the care they received (Robinson et al., 2016). Twenty-four percent of the participants named mistrust in the medical system as their reason for not seeking the help they needed (Robinson et al., 2016).

Protective Factors

A number of studies have stressed the value of Indigenous culture and tradition in protecting against adverse mental health outcomes. Early studies of Indigenous youth suicide revealed "self-continuity," defined as the ability to see oneself as continuous through time, as a protective factor against suicide (Chandler, Lalonde, Sokol, & Hallett, 2003). Chandler and Lalonde (1998) analyzed suicidality in First Nations communities in British Columbia and found six indicators of "cultural continuity" that act as protective factors against suicide. Similar to self-continuity, cultural continuity refers to the ability to view one's culture as flourishing, with indicators including being self-governed; having made a land claim against the colonial government; having independent control of the community's education, health, police, and fire services; and possessing a cultural facility building in which to host community events (Chandler & Lalonde, 1998). The presence of each individual factor reduced youth suicide rates to varying degrees, and when all six factors were present youth suicide rates dropped to zero (Chandler & Lalonde, 1998). A later study also identified Indigenous language competence as a protective factor; communities with high fluency averaged 13 suicides per 100,000—well below the provincial average for both Indigenous and non-Indigenous youth—whereas communities with lower or no Indigenous language fluency "had 6 times the number of suicides (96.59 per 100,000)" (Hallett, Chandler & Lalonde, 2007, p. 396).

Participation in spiritual, ceremonial, and cultural activities is important to many two-spirit people (Balsam et al., 2004). In a study by Ferlatte et al. (2019), two-spirit men described a return to traditional practices such as smudging as taking away thoughts of suicide. In the Our Health Counts study, 79 percent of two-spirit people reported participating in a traditional Indigenous ceremony, 57 percent used traditional medicines or healing practices, 81 percent felt a strong sense of belonging to an Indigenous community, and 99 percent felt good about their Indigenous heritage (2018). The final statistic is notable because a study from the United States suggests that positive self-identity and group identity might serve as a "psychological buffer against stress associated with racial discrimination" (Chae & Walters, 2009, p. 8144). Fieland et al. suggest that "the very aspects of Native culture targeted by colonial persecution (i.e., identity, spirituality, traditional health practices) may serve as sources of resistance and resilience" (2007, p. 284).

Forced Christianization of Indigenous communities means that cultural and community support may not be available to all two-spirit people. Qualitative research in Saskatchewan and Manitoba, for example, found that two-spirit people who came out risked violence, rejection, and expulsion from their communities of origin (Alaers, 2010). Indigenous cultural inclusion and support facilitate the development and claiming of two-spirit identity, leading to positive self-esteem, self-affirmation, healing, and mental wellness (Brotman, Ryan, Jalbert, & Rowe, 2002). Elders play a crucial role in affirming that two-spirit people always have and still do belong in their Indigenous nations. Due to colonial assimilation practices and processes, however, not all elders are willing or able to support two-spirit people. Alaers reports the frustration felt by one two-spirit person over "seeking two-spirit teachings from Elders who themselves were never taught the teachings" (2010, p. 73). Two-spirit people have stressed the need for visible role models who can educate health professionals and Indigenous communities (Brotman et al., 2002), yet this demands a lot of emotional labor from two-spirit people, most of whom already face multiple stressors.

In a Winnipeg-based study, 33 percent of two-spirit participants reported feeling forced out of their Indigenous community due to their gender or sexual identity (Ristock et al., 2010). In leaving their Indigenous communities, individuals may lose their primary support systems against racism and colonialism (Brotman et al., 2002; Ristock et al., 2010; Walters et al., 2006). In a Vancouver-based study of two-spirit migration, participants reported visiting the West End (a gay neighborhood) but identified the community's racism as a barrier to living there (Ristock et al., 2011). In the Risk & Resilience study, only 54 percent of First Nations, Métis, or Inuit participants reported feeling connected to the LGBTQ community, and of those only 34 percent felt supported there (Robinson et al., 2016).

Markers of LGBTQ community belonging such as specific clothing or hairstyles, may have different, even negative, connotations for two-spirit people. Getting a 'dyke haircut,' for example, may reinscribe trauma from boarding or residential school, where Indigenous children had their hair forcibly cut off. Even for those who did not attend residential or boarding school, the act may not signal liberation from norms of femininity because cutting one's hair signifies mourning in many Indigenous nations. LGBTQ cultural expectations may also conflict with Indigenous cultural practices. Coming out, which is depicted as necessary for queer identity development, may clash with Indigenous philosophies of humility and egalitarianism wherein one refrains from drawing attention to oneself (Walters et al., 2006; Wilson, 1996). As Gilley notes, "If the goal of coming out is to set oneself apart from the mainstream, then this would fail Two-Spirit goals," which are more of a desire to be "incorporated into cultural practices" and to be "brought into the circle," not to be excluded further from it (2006, p. 66).

Wilson terms the process of embracing a two-spirit identity as "coming in," in which all aspects of one's identity (sexuality, gender, community, spirituality, and relationship to land) come together (2008, p. 197). Wilson proposes that two-spirit identity is about "circling back to where we belong, reclaiming, reinventing, and redefining our beginnings, our roots, our communities, our support systems, and our collective and individual selves" (2008, p. 198). For some, two-spirit gatherings are vital for making sense of their identities. As one two-spirit participant reports, two-spirit gatherings are "the only time in the year I get to be my whole self in one place... to me it's healing" (Walters et al., 2006, p. 134).

Multiple scholars have stressed the need for culturally sensitive healthcare services, practitioners, and professionals to consider two-spirit people in their historical, sociopolitical, and cultural contexts (Balsam et al., 2004). Western mental health models, for instance, focus on the individual and their distinct experience(s) of trauma (Balsam et al., 2004), contrasting sharply with Indigenous needs for treatment of intergenerational and historical trauma. Evans-Campbell et al. stress that since Indigenous trauma "occurs to the collective" it is also "potentially healed though the collective" (2012, p. 426).

The changes needed to support two-spirit people within colonial health care systems cannot function in isolation, and work must also address issues stemming from colonialism itself, such as poverty, housing crises, racism, food insecurity, and lack of sovereignty recognition(s), among others (O'Brien Teengs & Travers, 2006). Colonialism is a fundamental determinant of Indigenous health, and eliminating the stressors associated with it include self-determination over unceded, dispossessed, and treaty lands; the full recognition of Indigenous governance structures; and Indigenous control over community institutions, including healthcare systems (Scheim et al., 2013).

References

Alaers, J. (2010). Two-spirited people and social work practice: Exploring the history of Aboriginal gender and sexual diversity. *Critical Social Work, 11*(1), 63–79. http://www1.uwindsor.ca/criticalsocialwork/sites/uwindsor.ca.criticalsocialwork/files/alaerspdf.pdf

Ansbergs, D. (9 December 2014). Overview of Indian residential school system & gender—A visual content analysis. https://www.academia.edu/8872417/Overview_of_Indian_Residential_School_System_and_Gender–A_Visual_Content_Analysis

Argüello, T., & Walters, K. (2018). They tell us "we don't belong in the world and we shouldn't take up a place": HIV discourse within two-spirit communities. *Journal of Ethnic & Cultural Diversity in Social Work, 27*(2), 1–17. doi:10.1080/15313204.2017.1362616

Balsam, K. F., Huang, B., Fieland, K. C., Simoni, J. M., & Walters, K. L. (2004). Culture, trauma, and wellness: A comparison of heterosexual and lesbian, gay, bisexual, and two-spirit Native Americans. *Cultural Diversity and Ethnic Minority Psychology, 10*(3), 287–301. doi:10.1037/1099–9809.10.3.287

Barkan, E. (2003). Genocides of Indigenous peoples: Rhetoric of human rights. In R. Gellately & B. Kiernan (Eds.), *The specter of genocide: Mass murder in historical perspective* (pp. 130–1). New York, NY: Cambridge University Press.

Barney, D. D. (2003). Health risk-factors for gay American Indian and Alaska Native adolescent males. *Journal of Homosexuality, 46*(1), 137–57. doi:10.1300/J082v46n01_04

Basaldu, R. C. (1999). Hopi hova: Anthropological assumptions of gendered otherness in Native American societies. Retrieved from http://arizona.openrepository.com/arizona/bitstream/10150/278711/1/azu_td_1398033_sip1_m.pdf

Brotman, S., Ryan, B., Jalbert, Y., & Rowe, B. (2002). Reclaiming space-regaining health: The health care experiences of two-spirit people in Canada. *Journal of Gay & Lesbian Social Services, 14*(1), 67–87. doi:10.1300/J041v14n01_04

Burnette, C. E., & Figley, C. R. (2016). Historical oppression, resilience, and transcendence: Can a holistic framework help explain violence experienced by indigenous people? *Social Work, 62*(1), 37–44. doi:10.1093/sw/sww065

Chae, D. H., & Walters, K. L. (2009). Racial discrimination and racial identity attitudes in relation to self-rated health and physical pain and impairment among two-spirit American Indians/Alaska Natives. *American Journal of Public Health, 99*(S1), S144–S151. doi:10.2105/AJPH.2007.126003

Chandler, M. J., & Lalonde, C. (1998). Cultural continuity as a hedge against suicide in Canada's First Nations. *Transcultural Psychiatry, 35*, 191–219. doi:10.1177/136346159803500202

Chandler, M. J., Lalonde, C. E., Sokol, B., & Hallett, D. (2003). From self-continuity to cultural continuity: Aboriginal youth suicide. *Monographs of the Society for Research in Child Development, 68*(2), 61–76.

Combahee River Collective (1977). Combahee River Collective statement. In B. Guy-Sheftall (Ed.), *Words of fire: An anthology of African American feminist thought* (pp. 232–40). New York, NY: New Press.

Crenshaw, K. W. (1989). Demarginalizing the intersection of race and sex: A Black feminist critique of antidiscrimination doctrine. *Feminist Theory and Antiracist Politics* (pp. 139–67). Chicago, IL: University of Chicago Legal Forum.

Davis, A. (1981). *Women, race, and class*. New York, NY: Random House.

Driskill, Qwo-Li. (2010). Doubleweaving two-spirit critiques: Building alliances between native and queer studies. *GLQ: A Journal of Lesbian and Gay Studies, 16*(1–2), 69–92. doi:10.1215/10642684-2009-013

Evans-Campbell, T., Walters, K. L., Pearson, C. R., & Campbell, C. D. (2012). Indian boarding school experience, substance use, and mental health among urban two-spirit American Indian/Alaska Natives. *American Journal of Drug and Alcohol Abuse, 38*(5), 421–7. doi:10.3109/00952990.2012.701358

Ferlatte, O., Oliffe, J., Louie, D., Ridge, D., Broom, A., & Salway, T. (2019). Suicide prevention from the perspectives of gay, bisexual, and two-spirit men. *Qualitative Health Research, 29*(8), 1186–98. doi:10.1177/1049732318816082

Fieland, K. C., Walters, K. L., & Simoni, J. M. (2007). Determinants of health among Two-Spirit American Indians and Alaska Natives. In I. H. Meyer & M. E. Northridge (Eds), *The health of sexual minorities: Public health perspectives on lesbian, gay, bisexual and transgender populations* (pp. 268–300). New York, NY: Springer. doi: 10.1007/978-0-387-31,334-4_11

First Nations Information Governance Centre. (June 2012). *First Nations Regional Health Survey (RHS) phase 2 (2008/10): National report on adults, youth and children living in First Nations communities*. Ottawa: First Nations Information Governance Centre.

Fournier, S., & Crey, E. (1997). *Stolen from our embrace: The abduction of First Nations children and the restoration of Aboriginal communities*. Toronto, Canada: Douglas and McIntyre.

Garrett, M. T., & Barret, B. (2003). Two spirit: Counseling Native American gay, lesbian, and bisexual people. *Journal of Multicultural Counseling and Development, 31*(2), 131–42. doi:10.1002/j.2161–1912.2003.tb00538.x

Gilley, B. J. (2006). *Becoming two-spirit: Gay identity and social acceptance in Indian country*. Lincoln, NB: University of Nebraska Press.

Hallett, D., Chandler, M. J., & Lalonde, C. E. (2007). Aboriginal language knowledge and youth suicide. *Cognitive Development, 22*(3), 392–9. doi:10.1016/j.cogdev.2007.02.001

Halverson, E. N. (2013, December 14). *Agokwe. Agokwewin (The way of the continuum woman). The Ojibwewanishinaabe of gender identity*. https://enhalverson.wordpress.com/tag/ojibwe-language/

Harvard Medical School (2005). National Comorbidity Survey (NCS). https://www.hcp.med.harvard.edu/ncs/index.php

Johnson-Jennings, M. D., Belcourt, A., Town, M., Walls, M. L., & Walters, K. L. (2014). Racial discrimination's influence on smoking rates among American Indian Alaska Native two-spirit individuals: Does pain play a role? *Journal of Health Care for the Poor and Underserved, 25*(4), 1667–78. doi: 10.1353/hpu.2014.0193

King, S. D. (2010). *Midlife and older gay men and their use of physical and mental health services: Exploring the effects of health enablers, health need, psychosocial stress and individual health coping*. Ohio State University. http://rave.ohiolink.edu/etdc/view?acc_num=osu1257437705

Koenen, K. C., Ratanatharathorn, A., Ng, L., McLaughlin, K. A., Bromet, E. J., Stein, D. J.,…Atwoli, L. (2017). Posttraumatic stress disorder in the world mental health surveys. *Psychological Medicine, 47*(13), 2260–74. doi:10.1017/S0033291717000708

Le Chevralier, J. (1944). *St. Michael's School: Trials and progress (sic) of an Indian school 1894–1944*. Duck Lake, Canada: Provincial Archivist of the Oblate Fathers of Alberta and Saskatchewan.

Lorde, A. (1978). Uses of the erotic: The erotic as power. In A. Lorde, *Sister outsider: Essays and speeches*. Berkeley, CA: Crossing Press. http://mamagenas.com/wp3/wp-content/uploads/2016/M16/Uses_of_the_Erotic.pdf

Meyer, I. H. (2003). Prejudice, social stress, and mental health in lesbian, gay, and bisexual populations: Conceptual issues and research evidence. *Psychological Bulletin, 129*(5), 674–97. doi:10.1037/0033-2909.129.5.674

Meyer-Cook, F., & Labelle, D. (2004). Namaji: Two-spirit organizing in Montreal, Canada. *Journal of Gay & Lesbian Social Services, 16*(1), 29–51. doi:10.1300/J041v16n01_02

Mosby, I. (2013). Administering colonial science: Nutrition research and human biomedical experimentation in Aboriginal communities and residential schools, 1942–1952. *Histoire sociale/Social history, 46*(1), 145–72. doi:10.1353/his.2013.0015

National Gay and Lesbian Task Force and National Center for Transgender Equality (2012). *Injustice at every turn: A look at American Indian and Alaskan Native respondents in the U.S. National Transgender Discrimination Survey*. Washington, DC: National Gay and Lesbian Task Force. http://www.thetaskforce.org/reports_and_research/ntds_nativeamerican_respondents

Newcomb, F. J. (1964). *Hosteen Klah: Navaho medicine man and sand painter*. Norman, OK: University of Oklahoma Press.

O'Brien Teengs, D., & Travers, R. (2006, summer). "River of life, rapids of change": Understanding HIV vulnerability among two-spirit youth who migrate to Toronto. *Canadian Journal of Aboriginal Community-Based HIV/AIDS Research, 1*, 17–28.

Parker, M., Duran, B., & Walters, K. (2017). The relationship between bias-related victimization and generalized anxiety disorder among American Indian and Alaska Native lesbian, gay, bisexual, transgender, two-spirit community members. *International Journal of Indigenous Health, 12*(2), 64–83. doi:10.18357/ijih122201717785

Parra, L. A., Benibgui, M., Helm, J. L., & Hastings: D. (2016). Minority stress predicts depression in lesbian, gay, and bisexual emerging adults via elevated diurnal cortisol. *Emerging Adulthood, 4*(5), 365–72. doi:10.1177/2167696815626822

Pascoe, E. A., & Smart Richman, L. (2009). Perceived discrimination and health: A meta-analytic review. *Psychological Bulletin, 135*(4), 531–54. doi:10.1037/a0016059

Pruden, H. (29 January 2019). What & who is two-spirit?: A (re) learning and (re)claiming respect and honour. Presentation to the Institute Advisory Board of the CIHR Institute of Indigenous Peoples' Health.

Ristock, J., Zoccole, A. & Passante, L. (2010). Aboriginal Two-Spirit and LGBTQ migration, mobility and health research project, Winnipeg. http://www.2spirits.com/PDFolder/MMHReport.pdf

Ristock, J., Zoccole, A., Passante, L., & Potskin, J. (2017). Impacts of colonization on Indigenous Two-Spirit/LGBTQ Canadians' experiences of migration, mobility and relationship violence. *Sexualities, 22*(5-6), 1–18. doi:10.1177/1363460716681474

Ristock, J., Zoccole, A. & Potskin, J. (2011). Aboriginal Two-Spirit and LGBTQ migration, mobility and health research project, Vancouver. http://www.2spirits.com/PDFolder/2011%20Vancouver%20full%20report%20final.pdf

Roanhorse, S. (27 September 2005). *The Advocate* Report. First Person: Sherrick Roanhorse: A traditional Navajo. *The Advocate*, 26.

Robinson, M. (2013). LGBT youth suicide. Fact sheet. Toronto, ON: Rainbow Health Ontario. http://rainbowhealthontario.ca/wp-content/uploads/woocommerce_uploads/2013/08/RHO_FactSheet_LGBTYOUTHSUICIDE_E.pdf

Robinson, M. (2017). Two-spirit and bisexual people: Different umbrella, same rain. *Journal of Bisexuality, 17*(1), 7–29. doi:10.1080/15299716.2016.1261266

Robinson, M., Plante, I., MacLeod, M., Cruz, L., & Bhanji, N., (2016). On behalf of Re:searching for LGBTQ Health. Experiences of aboriginal people in the Risk & Resilience study [Fact sheet]. Toronto: Centre for Addiction and Mental Health. https://lgbtqhealth.ca/projects/docs/riskresiliencebisexual-factsheet-aboriginal-community.pdf

Roscoe, W. (1988). The Zuni man-woman. *Outlook, 1*(2), 56–67.

Ross, L. E., Bauer, G. R., MacLeod, M. A., Robinson, M., MacKay, J., & Dobinson, C. (2014). Mental health and substance use among bisexual youth and non-youth in Ontario, Canada. *PLoS One, 9*(8), e101604. doi:10.1371/journal.pone.0101604

Royal Commission on Aboriginal Peoples. (1996). *Looking forward, looking back: Report of the Royal Commission on Aboriginal Peoples* (Vol. 1). Ottawa, Canada: Communication Group.

Scheim, A. I., Jackson, R., James, L., Dopler, T. S., Pyne, J., & Bauer, G. R. (2013). Barriers to well-being for Aboriginal gender-diverse people: Results from the Trans PULSE Project in Ontario, Canada. *Ethnicity and Inequalities in Health and Social Care, 6*(4), 108–20. doi:10.1108/EIHSC-08-2013-0010

Selvidge, M. M. D., Matthews, C. R., & Bridges, S. K. (2008). The relationship of minority stress and flexible coping to psychological well-being in lesbian and bisexual women. *Journal of Homosexuality, 55*(3), 450–70. doi:10.1080/00918360802345255

Seventh Generation Midwives Toronto. (2018). Our Health Counts Toronto: Two-Spirit Mental Health [Fact sheet]. http://www.wellllivinghouse.com/wp-content/uploads/2018/02/Two-Spirit-Mental-Health-OHC-Toronto-1.pdf

Simoni, J. M., Walters, K. L., Balsam, K. F., & Meyers, S. B. (2006). Victimization, substance use, and HIV risk behaviors among gay/bisexual/two-spirit and heterosexual American Indian men in New York City. *American Journal of Public Health, 96*(12), 2240–5. doi:10.2105/AJPH.2004.054056

Statistics Canada. (2004). Sexual orientation and victimization. Canadian Centre for Justice Statistics, catalogue no.85F0033M—no. 016. https://www150.statcan.gc.ca/n1/en/pub/85f0033m/85f0033m2008016-eng.pdf?st=f4X7Huky

Statistics Canada. (2017). Aboriginal peoples in Canada: Key results from the 2016 Census [The Daily]. https://www150.statcan.gc.ca/n1/daily-quotidien/171025/dq171025a-eng.htm

Tafoya, T. (1997). Native gay and lesbian issues: The two-spirited. In B. Greene (Ed.), *Ethnic and cultural diversity among lesbians and gay men* (pp. 1–10). Thousand Oaks, CA: Sage Publications.

Tanner, J. (1830). *Narrative of the captivity and adventures of John Tanner*, edited by E. James. New York, NY: Garvil. https://archive.org/details/McGillLibrary-104462-121

Thomas, W. (1997). Navajo cultural constructions of gender and sexuality. In S. E. Jacobs, W. Thomas, & S. Lang (Eds.), *Two-spirit people: Native American gender identity, sexuality, and spirituality* (pp. 156–73). Champaign, IL: University of Illinois Press.

Truth and Reconciliation Commission of Canada. (2015). *Honouring the truth, reconciling for the future: Summary of the final report of the Truth and Reconciliation Commission of Canada*. Winnipeg, MB: Truth and Reconciliation Commission of Canada.

U.S. Department of Health and Human Services. (2019). The Office of Minority Health. Profile: American Indian/Alaska Native. https://minorityhealth.hhs.gov/omh/browse.aspx?lvl=3&lvlid=62

Walters, K. (2010). Critical issues and LGBTQ-two spirit populations: Highlights from the HONOR project study. Presentation to the Institute of Medicine. http://iom.edu/~/media/Files/Activity%20Files/SelectPops/LGBTQHealthIssues/Walters%20presentationl.pdf

Walters, K. L., Evans-Campbell, T., Simoni, J. M., Ronquillo, T., & Bhuyan, R. (2006). My spirit in my heart: Identity experiences and challenges among American Indian two-spirit women. *Journal of Lesbian Studies, 10*(1–2), 125–49. http://www.haworthpress.com/web/JLS. doi:10.1300/J155v10n01_07

Wilson, A. (1996). How we find ourselves: Identity development and Two-Spirit people. *Harvard Educational Review, 66*(2), 303–17. doi:10.17763/haer.66.2.n551658577h927h4

Wilson, A. (2008). N'tacimowin inna nah': Our coming in stories. *Canadian Woman Studies, 26*(3/4), 193–9. https://cws.journals.yorku.ca/index.php/cws/article/viewFile/22131/20785

Wilson, A. C., & Bird, M. Y. (2005). *For indigenous eyes only: A decolonization handbook*. Santa Fe, NM: School of American Research.

World Health Organization. 2001. Strengthening Mental Health Promotion (Factsheet No. 220). Geneva: World Health Organization. https://www.who.int/news-room/fact-sheets/detail/mental-health-strengthening-our-response

Yuan, N., Duran, B., Walters, K., Pearson, C., & Evans-Campbell, T. (2014). Alcohol misuse and associations with childhood maltreatment and out-of-home placement among urban two-spirit American Indian and Alaska Native people. *International Journal of Environmental Research and Public Health, 11*(10), 461–79. doi:10.3390/ijerph111s010461

CHAPTER

19 Biracial and Bi-Ethnic Sexual and Gender Minority Mental Health

Lauren E. Reid *and* Vanessa S. Stay

Abstract

Biracial and bi-ethnic sexual and gender minorities represent a diverse population, and limited research has been conducted on these identities. Since this population does not fit neatly into racial, gender, and sexual orientation categories, it is often excluded from larger studies of health. This chapter examines these identities in context, recognizes sociocultural influences, and couches the research in the current socio-political climate. Because this population is fluid in terms of racial, gender, and sexual identities, this chapter is limited by methodological approaches. The election of Barack Obama as U.S. president in 2009 ignited a boom in biracial/multiracial research in the United States, and today an increasing amount of research is being done that reflects the lived experience of people with multiple identities.

Keywords: biracial, bi-ethnic, multiracial, LGBT+, biracial mental health, biracial identity

This chapter reviews the literature on the mental health of biracial and bi-ethnic sexual and gender minorities (SGMs). It is important to note that language and ways of understanding this population are continually changing.

"Who Are You?" Biracial SGM Terminology

SGMs who identify as biracial may describe their racial identity in a variety of ways. Biracial individuals, people with parentage from two or more races, may express their identity as mixed race, multiracial, or multiple heritage, or by naming their racial ancestry. Oikawa and Yoshida (2007) highlighted the similarities between biracial individuals and bi-ethnic individuals in Japan at a time when the number of international marriages are on the rise. Valles, Bhopal, and Aspinall (2015) noted some of the challenges public health officials have experienced while trying to gather data on mixed-race populations in the United States, the United Kingdom, and New Zealand due to a lack of common terminology. There are significant differences in each country's racial history and racial classification policies. For example, the U.S. Census separates ethnicity and race; thus, an individual of Hispanic origin may be multiethnic and not multiracial (Valles et al., 2015). Clinical research points out the importance of reflecting the expressed identity language of individuals seeking mental health treatment (Edwards & Pedrotti, 2008; Kich, 1996). Therefore, if clients describe themselves as biracial and bisexual, practitioners would use that terminology when referring to the clients' social identities.

Review of the Existing Literature

Sociocultural Influences on Identity

While the recognition of fluidity is increasing, there is still a preference toward classification and categorization in psychological research. The research is limited by the continued application of checkboxes to assess the mental health needs of people with fluid identities. Ecological models of identity development acknowledge the sociocultural and contextual influences on racial, gender, and sexual identity development, yet the extant literature is mostly single-time-point quantitative studies (Shih & Sanchez, 2009). Further, there is limited information to contextualize the data, so research on biracial individuals stays focused on race while mostly neglecting other intersecting identities (Caballero, 2014). The following review of the literature should be couched within sociopolitical histories of these populations: the LGBT+ community's centering of whiteness; the presumption of categorical racial, gender, and sexual identities; and ongoing discrimination and institutional bias.

Biracial and Bisexual

While research on biracial SGMs is limited, the majority of the research has focused on the intersecting identities of biracial and bisexual women. This is due in part to the researchers' conceptualizing the potentially similar experiences of fluidity and in-group/out-group experiences in both identities (Ross et al., 2018). Due to this commonality, Ross et al. (2018) assert that there could be benefit to "shared spaces where these socially marginalized identities can be supported and made more visible, as well as opportunities for learning from other communities' struggles and successes" (p. 451). Similarly, Firestein (2007) noted that:

> Both biracial and bisexual individuals (and particularly women who are both biracial and bisexual) must learn to balance living in multiple, simultaneous cultural contexts. Many bisexual women, for example, must learn to live successfully in both lesbian culture and heterosexual society. Biracial and multiracial women must balance loyalties to multiple heritages, families, and communities. (p. 96)

Further, learning to navigate monoracial and heterosexual culture and having similar in-group/out-group experiences in both racial and sexual identity realms may lead to developing coping skills in the face of discrimination. This link was supported empirically in Friedman et al.'s (2014) validation study of the Bisexualities: Indiana Attitudes Survey (BIAS), which explores the relationship between biphobia and sexual identity in the United States. Freidman et al. (2014) administered the survey online in two forms: BIAS-m (n = 645), surveying attitudes toward bisexual men, and BIAS-f (n = 631), surveying attitudes toward bisexual women. A small portion of each sample identified as biracial/multiracial: 4.8 percent and 3.9 percent respectively. One of the key findings of their study is that identifying as biracial/multiracial was associated with having lower binegativity scores.

Recounting her personal experiences as a "biracial bisexual feminist psychologist," Israel (2004) described her identity development and shared her meaning-making process as a biracial (Chinese/Jewish American) and bisexual woman growing up in a community where her identities were not represented. Grounded in her own experience, Israel made recommendations for the field, encouraging the development of spaces that invite conversations around bi-ness: in clinical work with clients and at professional conferences by including conversations that may dismantle the categories. Israel argued that verbalizing experiences and promoting dialog around how these experiences fit into dynamics of privilege and oppression will inherently start to break down the social structures. For example, therapists should not rely solely on checkbox forms but rather should explore clients' identity narratives around race, ethnicity, and sexuality. Israel called out therapists' tendency to assume clients' identities based on the pronouns used when describing partners rather than ask how the client identifies and whether that has changed over time.

SOCIALIZATION

In a qualitative study with six college-aged, female participants who identified as biracial/multiracial and bisexual/pansexual, King (2013) found three primary agents of socialization as the participants reflected on their experiences in pre-college and college contexts:

1. Family upbringing was impactful in both racial and sexual identity development. In particular, the openness of discussions about race and positive messages about the LBGT+ community influenced how the women saw themselves. Relationships with family members were also integral in the women's identity development, regardless of whether family members were non-heterosexual or instilled a sense of cultural identity.
2. Friends/peers played a significant role in the participants' identity development. Participants described having inclusive or excluding experiences based on their appearance or determined belongingness to a particular racial group. Further, their friendship groups determined whether they felt comfortable exploring their bisexuality or coming out as bisexual. A common theme was being questioned as to whether they were "enough" whether in their racial community or the LGBT+ community.
3. With regard to pre-college contexts, school was a significant influence in participants' racial and sexual identity development. It was notable

that biracial and bisexual people were not included in the curriculum. Also, depending on the school system, participants felt fearful of coming out because some schools were explicit in their homonegative messages.

Overall, King's (2013) study highlighted how participants developed their biracial identity and bisexual identity separately. Yet what was similar about the development of these two identities was that their family/parents may not share their identity and the participants were influenced both by representation and other contextual factors mentioned above. Additionally, King (2013) pointed out the invisibility of multiracial identity and bisexuality: participants voiced feeling "frustrated by not being recognized as multiracial . . . [and] that having their sexual identity ignored added another layer of frustration and anxiety" (p. 320).

POSITIVE EXPERIENCES

A recent study used an online survey to reach a larger sample of people who identified as biracial and bisexual (Galupo, Taylor, & Cole, 2019). With 107 participants ranging in age from eighteen to thirty-six years, the study demonstrated the diversity of this population in terms of self-expression of identity. The authors reported that

> With regard to primary sexual identity, 60 individuals identified as bisexual, 16 pansexual, 22 queer, 4 fluid, and 5 individuals who identified using other terms, including "pansensual/ pandemisexual, omni/panromantic, grey-polyromantic, demi-homoromantic, submissive." With regard to race/ethnicity, all participants identified with two or more identities. Participants indicated partial identification with the following: 14 sAmerican Indian/Alaska Native, 42 Asian/Asian American, 39 Black/African American, 35 Hispanic/ Latinx, 5 Middle Eastern, 7 Native Hawaiian/Pacific Islander participants, 97 White/Euro American, and 7 participants identified other more specific racial identities such as Indian and Indigenous." (p. 155)

While the majority of participants (73.8 percent) identified a positive aspect of dual bi-identity, thirty-eight participants indicated that they could not think of anything positive. Using thematic analysis, Galupo et al. identified the following themes: (1) uniqueness of being, (2) multiplicity of experience, (3) community connections, and (4) strengths and impact. In light of research that indicated the possibility for multiple minority stress (Ferguson, 2016), this study highlighted how people may feel positively about their experience despite multiple oppressions. Therapists are encouraged to consider the potential strengths their biracial bisexual clients may feel they possess.

THERAPY WITH BIRACIAL/BISEXUAL PEOPLE

Research in this area is scant. There is a focus on either biracial identity (Edwards & Pedrotti, 2008) or bisexual people (Firestein, 2007), but not the intersection of these identities. However, Dworkin (2002) identified some implications for therapy based on her qualitative study with bisexual women. She noted that "a few" of the women from her study were of mixed race and focused her article on the voices of these individuals with intersecting identities. She noted that individuals who identify as female, bisexual, and biracial/bicultural may experience sexism, racism, and ethnocentrism, and that therapists should be open to exploring these issues. Dworkin acknowledged how feminist theory may be beneficial in thinking about how political beliefs inform identity expression. Generally, individuals who identify as biracial or bicultural and bisexual felt that their multiple identities helped them with self-acceptance, but they also experienced multiple oppressions.

Lesbian Biracial Women

There are no empirical studies focusing on lesbian biracial women; published literature on this population consists of dissertations, examination of identity development models, and case studies (Collins, 2000; Stanley, 2004, Thompson, 2012). Monoracial identity development models are overgeneralized to include biracial or multiracial individuals; gender identity models are largely normed on white, middle-class, cisgender women; and certain LGBT identity models group all members of the community together, ignoring class, race, or gender differences (Stanley, 2004). The overgeneralization of these single-identity models can contribute to the marginalization of individuals with multiple intersecting identities by reinforcing the idea that their specific experiences are not worth examining or studying.

IDENTITY-BASED VISIBILITY

An individual's self-identity can be very different from how others perceive their identity (Stanley, 2004). When someone does not fit into an existing category, society often chooses one for them, usually based on appearance (Stanley, 2004; Thompson, 2012). Lesbian biracial women frequently find themselves in positions where they have to disclose or hide a part of their identity, depending on the social context, in order to safely and/or successfully navigate a situation (Bing, 2004). Hiding aspects of identity can lead to feelings of invisibility and isolation for lesbian women of color, while also causing them to internalize feelings of shame and deceitfulness for not being "honest" about who they are (Bing, 2004; Thompson, 2012). Many biracial and multiracial lesbian women reported not feeling represented within their chosen communities and felt as though their experiences are either ignored or commodified by the dominant group (Stanley, 2004; Thompson, 2012).

FAMILY

Family is often seen as a source of support and understanding, but that is not always the lived reality of biracial or multiracial lesbian women (Stanley, 2004). Monoracial and heterosexual parents have not had the same experiences as their biracial and lesbian children and cannot always offer relevant resources, support, or advice. For example, a biracial or multiracial woman who had familial support with regard to her racial identity may find herself receiving a negative reaction for coming out as anything other than heterosexual (Collins, 2000; Stanley, 2004).

FRIENDS

Friends are an important part of the identity development of lesbian biracial women and often serve as a buffer from societal devaluation and rejection (Stanley, 2004). These friendships can be sources of support and affirmation and can often contribute to the development of positive self-identity (Stanley, 2004). However, friendships can also be sources of prejudice based on homophobic or racial distrust. A biracial or multiracial lesbian woman might find acceptance within her chosen racial community but may be rejected for being lesbian. Conversely, a non-white lesbian or bisexual woman may be expected to "leave her racial identity at the door" in order to fit into a white LGBT space (Thompson, 2012).

COMMUNITY

Marginalized individuals seek out a community of people with similar experiences and history; however, identity-based communities are usually focused on a singular identity or unifying factor, leaving little room for intersecting or multiple identities (Thompson, 2012). This expectation to unify under a single identity may pressure biracial SGM individuals to choose between an ethnic/racial community that does not accept their sexuality and a (predominantly white) LGBT community (Allman, 1996; Thompson, 2012). Furthermore, there are prejudices within these individual communities (homophobia, racism, sexism, transphobia) that can contribute to the isolation and estrangement of biracial lesbian women (Stanley, 2004).

Black/White Biracial Lesbian Women

Black/white biracial individuals hold a unique place in U.S. society due to a history of slavery, personal and institutionalized racism, and civil unrest between Blacks and whites, all of which continue to occur and affect interactions to this day (Bing, 2004). According to Bing (2004), white individuals in the United States "find people of color easier to accept if their background is not African American" (p. 187), which reinforces a racial hierarchy in which Black individuals are at the bottom. This racialized hierarchy impacts biracial individuals of African origins specifically and can influence how they develop a sense of racial identity and community (Bing, 2004; Thompson, 2012). When the dimensions of sexuality and sexual identity are added, Black/white biracial women must contend with difficult and sometimes conflicting messages about identity and community (Thompson, 2012).

Racial and lesbian identity models contain three similar stages: (1) internalization of the views of the dominant culture; (2) embracing the minority identity and social immersion in the culture; and (3) identity synthesis, which involves accepting and rejecting parts of both cultures to form an identity (Bing, 2004). However, though similar, these models do not occur concurrently or without conflict. For Black/white lesbian women, exploring and accepting their racial identity can impair exploration of their sexual identity. Other lesbian women may find that exploring their sexual identity comes at the detriment of fully accepting their racial identity (Bing, 2004; Comeau, 2012). This process of forming a dual identity can be a resource for some individuals, but the process can often be confusing, conflicting, and emotionally exhausting for those involved.

Black/white biracial lesbian women can often feel a sense of displacement in their communities or lack community. This sense of displacement comes from experiences of both racism in white lesbian spaces and homophobia in African American communities (Bing, 2004; Comeau, 2012). Black/white biracial lesbian women often do not have a specific biracial community to connect with and as a result exist within both African American heterosexual communities and white LGBT spaces (Bing, 2004).

Many lesbian women of African descent report experiencing violence and racism in white lesbian communities and as a result believe that the African American community is the only place where they will feel safe and accepted. However, as we noted earlier, homophobia, sexism, and transphobia in the Black community can make it an unsafe space for anyone who is not heterosexual or cisgender (Bing, 2004; Comeau, 2012). While existing in multiple communities, Black/white lesbian women may face prejudice and must make choices based on their everyday safety.

THERAPEUTIC CONSIDERATIONS FOR BLACK/WHITE BIRACIAL LESBIAN WOMEN

Black/white biracial lesbian women are a population that would benefit from treatment that is "culturally, socially, and politically informed" (Bing, 2004, p. 196). Therapists must be prepared to explore topics like race, gender, and sexuality with the client, while also being mindful of their own internal biases and reactions to these issues. Self-definition is a key component in this process, and therapists should use whatever terms clients use to describe themselves (Kich, 1996). Additionally, it would be beneficial for therapists to be aware of how their own racial identity influences how their clients perceive them. Bing (2004) outlines how the race of the therapist can be a potential therapeutic barrier for black/white biracial lesbian women:

> Similarly, if the therapist is White, what concerns are there for the patient about the therapist's own position of privilege and her ability to understand and empathize with the concerns that the patient brings? For the therapist of color, particularly African American therapists, the Black-White biracial individual may question whether or not it is safe to even bring out the fact that they are part White. What if the therapist has negative feelings toward individuals who are products of interracial unions? What if the therapist feels that the patient is "passing," or somehow negating her own African ancestry? What if the African American therapist is homophobic as is common in a number of African American communities? Is it safer to seek out a therapist from the White community that is believed to be more tolerant of gays and lesbians? (p. 198)

Furthermore, when working with Black/white biracial lesbian women, therapists should be culturally aware of the significance of "race mixing" to both white and Black Americans and ready to explore what "race mixing" means to the client. Finally, being aware of racially charged terms like mulatto and high yellow and understanding how the "one-drop rule" historically and currently disenfranchises Black Americans will be useful for fostering a positive and beneficial relationship with the client.

Biracial Gay Men

Research focusing on biracial gay men is nonexistent. DeMarco, Ostrow, and DiFranceisco (1999) used the term biracial to describe their sample; however, the participants were described as white or African American, not biracial. Their study examined general and AIDS-related stress in "biracial" men; out of the 297 white and African American self-identified gay men, none were specified as biracial. Two hundred fifteen white non-Hispanic men and 82 Black non-Hispanic men participated in a study that examined the psychological and behavioral patterns of men at risk for contracting AIDS. Because biracial gay men were not explicitly mentioned, the results are not necessarily applicable to them. More research is needed for a comprehensive understanding of this population.

Multiracial, Intersex, and Transgender Identity

There has been no research focused on individuals who are both multiracial and transgender or gender nonconforming (Dunham & Olson, 2016). Singh and Chun (2012) outlined the experiences of one biracial transgender man in a case study and noted that the client had similar experiences to cisgender biracial individuals with regard to his racial identity. He presented as a person of color and chose Black/African American when "forced" to provide an identity but preferred checking "other" when given the choice. The client experienced various levels of acceptance from his family and friends with regard to his gender identity but reported feeling lonely as the only transgender man of color in his community. His experiences echo that of other biracial SGMs, but more research on the transgender portion of this population is needed. There has been no research found on individuals who are multiracial and intersex.

Gender Identity and Biracial Children

Most children can identify their race and gender by age five, with the age being slightly younger for children from racial and ethnic minorities (Rogers &

Meltzoff, 2017). In addition, young children demonstrate knowledge of behaviors and characteristics specific to racial and gender groups (Rogers & Meltzoff, 2017). These social identities can have a large impact on children's development and self-esteem, and children with multiple intersecting (or minority) identities can be particularly at risk for internalizing negative messages. Rogers and Meltzoff (2017) studied racial and gender identity in 222 U.S. children aged nine and ten (136 girls, 86 boys). There were 54 Black monoracial children, 83 white children, and 85 mixed-race children. The "mixed-race" sample included 36 Black/white children, 21 Hispanic/white children, 9 Asian/white children, 6 Hispanic/Black children, and 13 multiracial children. Participants were interviewed to collect data and "Me/Not Me" was used to determine children's racial and gender identifications. Analysis of data revealed that all children, regardless of race, rated gender identity as the most important aspect of their identity. Mixed-race children rated "racial identity importance" at similar rates as monoracial Black peers but differed in that they also rated family as very important to their identity. These results suggest that multiracial and monoracial children go through similar stages of gender identity development.

Mind the Gap: Review of Extant Literature

Sexual Orientation

While reviewing existing literature for this chapter, we noticed that the majority of research focused on bisexual or lesbian sexual orientations. A study by King (2013) included pansexuality and DeMarco et al. (1999) included Black/white biracial gay men, but specific research on gay, pansexual, or queer identity among biracial SGMs is nonexistent.

Gender Identity

There is a consistent gender discrepancy in research literature, with cisgender women often being the primary subject area. Research on biracial gay men is scarce, and biracial transgender individuals are missing almost entirely from the literature. Due to the increase of individuals identifying as transgender or gender nonconforming, it is important to have them represented in future scientific research.

Specific Racial and Ethnic Minorities

There is limited research exploring minority/minority biracial sexual and gender minorities. Most of the research focuses on individuals with one white parent. Given the increase in biracial individuals across the world, it is important to explore the diversity of this population (Valles et al., 2015). Biracial SGM individuals who have parents from marginalized communities may have different experiences from individuals who have a white parent.

Populations in the Global South

There was no research found on individuals who are from the Global South. This is another population that needs to be studied as the intersection of race, sexuality, and socioeconomic status may have important differences in experiences and mental health needs from those individuals in existing literature.

Future Directions

This chapter reviewed the literature on biracial and bi-ethnic sexual and gender minorities, which is an understudied population. Alternative methodologies are needed to capture the lived experiences of this population and their mental health needs. Future research could explore the following areas.

Other Gender Identities

There are other prevalent gender identities that have not been studied. As of 2016, 1.4 million adults in the United States identified as transgender (Flores, Herman, Gates, & Brown, 2016). This number is expected to grow as more adolescents and young adults begin to identify as transgender or otherwise gender nonconforming (Flores et al., 2016). Given this population's growth and vulnerability, increasing relevant scientific literature is a necessity.

Since 2013, 164 transgender women have been murdered in the United States, 80 percent of them transgender women of color (Human Rights Campaign, 2019). Given the relatively small population size, this is an exponential rate of violence. There are multiple factors that potentially contribute to this level of violence; according to the Human Rights Campaign (2019), "intersections of racism, sexism, homophobia, biphobia and transphobia conspire to deprive them of employment, housing, healthcare and other necessities, barriers that make them vulnerable." The existing studies seemed to assume that participants were cisgender by using language such as "participants were female," with no other explanation, or did not include transgender women at all. This lack of visibility continues a cissexist narrative that contributes to the marginalization and violence of transgender identities by further "othering" them.

Alternative Methodologies

Most of the existing studies are qualitative. Alternative methodologies could help shed light on the mental health and needs of this population. There is increased recognition of the reality of identity fluidity, yet empirical approaches have not caught up. Further, epidemiological literature on mental health neglects intersectionality. There needs to be a movement toward nonbinary assessments of race, gender, and sexual orientation (Aspinall & Song, 2013). Studies with larger samples often use categorical demographic measures that may not accurately capture how the individuals identify. When participants are faced with a forced choice to describe their identity, it may not reflect the totality of their experience. Additionally, population-specific studies only focus on identity factors and rarely explore mental health. Though identity development will continue to be an integral part of understanding and working with this population, continued lack of guidance regarding mental health will leave biracial SGMs in a position where they are not receiving current and relevant empirically supported treatments.

Additional Concepts

The existing research points to the need to explore concepts that have been explored in monoracial LGBT+ People of Color (Ferguson, 2016) and multiracial heterosexual populations (Shih & Sanchez, 2009). For example, while bicultural self-efficacy and cognitive flexibility were identified as important factors in the mental health of bisexual People of Color, Brewster, DeBlaere, Moradi, and Velez (2013) suggested that future studies could explore the impact of these variables on the mental health of biracial SGMs. This is noteworthy as studies of biracial populations indicate that similar constructs (e.g., malleability) are relevant to biracial mental health (Pauker, Meyers, Sanchez, Gaither, & Young, 2018).

Conclusion

Overall, research on this population is limited. There are some qualitative studies that have begun exploring identity experiences of this population, but there are limited mental health data. Many studies are needed to understand the mental health needs of this growing population, particularly studies of populations outside of the United States and the United Kingdom. Also, it is striking how many dissertations there are on this population in contrast to how few peer-reviewed publications there are, which may point to a need for a special issue looking at fluid, multiple identities. We are in the beginning of a cultural shift toward the affirmation of nonbinary and fluid identity, yet research lags behind in its methodological approaches to capture the complexity, and epidemiological research still focuses on larger populations while grouping nonconforming populations into other.

References

Allman, K. M. (1996). (Un)natural boundaries: Mixed race, gender, and sexuality. In M. P. P. Root (Ed.), The multiracial experience: Racial borders as the new frontier (pp. 263–76). Thousand Oaks, CA: Sage Publications, Inc.

Aspinall, P. J., & Song, M. (2013). Is race a "salient . . ." or "dominant identity" in the early 21st century: The evidence of UK survey data on respondents' sense of who they are. Social Science Research, 42(2), 547–61. doi:10.1016/j.ssresearch.2012.10.007

Bing, V. M. (2004). Out of the closet but still in hiding: Conflicts and identity issues for a Black-White biracial lesbian. Women & Therapy, 27(1–2), 185–201. doi:10.1300/J015v27n01_13

Brewster, M. E., DeBlaere, C., Moradi, B., & Velez, B. L. (2013). Navigating the borderlands: The roles of minority stressors, bicultural self-efficacy, and cognitive flexibility in the mental health of bisexual individuals. Journal of Counseling Psychology, 60(4), 543–56. doi:10.1037/a0033224

Caballero, C. (2014). Mixed emotions: Reflections on researching racial mixing and mixedness. Emotion, Space and Society, 11, 79–88. doi:10.1016/j.emospa.2013.07.002

Collins, J. F. (2000). Biracial-bisexual individuals: Identity coming of age. International Journal of Sexuality & Gender Studies, 5(3), 221–53. doi:10.1023/A:1010137025394

Comeau, D. L. (2012). Label-first sexual identity development: An in-depth case study of women who identify as bisexual before having sex with more than one gender. Journal of Bisexuality, 12(3), 321–46. doi:10.1080/15299716.2012.702611

DeMarco, F. J., Ostrow, D. G., & DiFranceisco, W. (1999). General and AIDS-specific stress, coping, and psychological distress in the biracial coping & change study cohort of gay men. AIDS and Behavior, 3(3), 177–86. doi:10.1023/A:1025496209190

Dunham, Y., & Olson, K. R. (2016). Beyond discrete categories: Studying multiracial, intersex, and transgender children will strengthen basic developmental science. Journal of Cognition and Development, 17(4), 642–65. doi:10.1080/15248372.2016.1195388

Dworkin, S. H. (2002). Biracial, bicultural, bisexual: Bisexuality and multiple identities. Journal of Bisexuality, 2(4), 93–107. doi:10.1300/J159v02n04_06

Edwards, L. M., & Pedrotti, J. T. (2008). A content and methodological review of articles concerning multiracial issues in six major counseling journals. Journal of Counseling Psychology, 55(3), 411–8. doi:10.1037/0022-0167.55.3.411

Ferguson, A. D. (2016). Cultural issues in counseling lesbians, gays, and bisexuals. In I. Marini & M. A. Stebnicki (Eds.), The professional counselor's desk reference (2nd ed., pp. 159–62). New York, NY: Springer Publishing Company.

Firestein, B. A. (2007). Cultural and relational contexts of bisexual women: Implications for therapy. In K. J. Bieschke, R. M. Perez, & K. A. DeBord (Eds.), Handbook of counseling and psychotherapy with lesbian, gay, bisexual, and transgender clients (2nd ed., pp. 91–117). Washington, DC: American Psychological Association.

Flores, A. R., Herman, J. L., Gates, G. J., & Brown, T. N. T. (2016, June). How many adults identify as transgender in the United States. https://williamsinstitute.law.ucla.edu/research/how-many-adults-identify-as-transgender-in-the-united-states/

Friedman, M. R., Dodge, B., Schick, V., Herbenick, D., Hubach, R. D., Bowling, J., . . . Reece, M. (2014). From bias to bisexual health disparities: Attitudes toward bisexual men and women in the United States. LGBT Health, 1(4), 309–18. doi:10.1089/lgbt.2014.0005

Galupo, M. P., Taylor, S. M., & Cole Jr., D. (2019). "I am double the bi": Positive aspects of being both bisexual and biracial. Journal of Bisexuality, 19(2), 152–68. doi:10.1080/15299716.2019.1619066

Human Rights Campaign. (2018). Violence against the transgender community in 2018. https://www.hrc.org/resources/violence-against-the-transgender-community-in-2018

Human Rights Campaign. (2019). Violence against the transgender community in 2019. https://www.hrc.org/resources/violence-against-the-transgender-community-in-2019

Israel, T. (2004). Conversations, not categories: The intersection of biracial and bisexual identities. In A. R. Gillem & C. A. Thompson (Eds.), Biracial women in therapy: Between the rock of gender and the hard place of race (pp. 173–84). New York, NY: Haworth Press.

Kich, G. K. (1996). In the margins of sex and race: Difference, marginality, and flexibility. In M. P. P. Root (Ed.), The multiracial experience: Racial borders as the new frontier (pp. 263–76). Thousand Oaks, CA: Sage Publications, Inc.

King, A. (2013). Mixed messages: How primary agents of socialization influence adolescent females who identify as multiracial–bisexual. Journal of LGBT Youth, 10(4), 308–27. doi:10.1080/19361653.2013.825198

Oikawa, S., & Yoshida T., (2007). An identity based on being different: A focus on biethnic individuals in Japan. International Journal of Intercultural Relations, 31(6), 633–53. doi:10.1016/j.ijintrel.2007.05.001

Pauker, K., Meyers, C., Sanchez, D. T., Gaither, S. E., & Young, D. M. (2018). A review of multiracial malleability: Identity, categorization, and shifting racial attitudes. Social and Personality Psychology Compass, 12(6), e12392. doi:10.1111/spc3.12392

Rogers, L. O., & Meltzoff, A. N. (2017). Is gender more important and meaningful than race? An analysis of racial and gender identity among Black, White, and mixed-race children. Cultural Diversity and Ethnic Minority Psychology, 23(3), 323–34. doi:10.1037/cdp0000125

Ross, L. E., Salway, T., Tarasoff, L. A., MacKay, J. M., Hawkins, B. W., & Fehr, C. P. (2018). Prevalence of depression and anxiety among bisexual people compared to gay, lesbian, and heterosexual individuals: A systematic review and meta-analysis. Journal of Sex Research, 55(4/5), 435–56. doi:10.1080/00224499.2017.1387755

Shih, M., & Sanchez, D. T. (2009). When race becomes even more complex: Toward understanding the landscape of multiracial identity experiences. Journal of Social Issues, 65(1), 1–11. doi:10.1111/j.1540–4560.2008.01584.x

Singh, A. A., & Chun, K. Y. S. (2012). Multiracial/multiethnic queer and transgender clients: Intersections of identity and resilience. In S. H. Dworkin & M. Pope (Ed.), Casebook for counseling lesbian, gay, bisexual, and transgender persons and their families (pp. 197–209). Alexandria, VA: American Counseling Association.

Stanley, J. L. (2004). Biracial lesbian and bisexual women: Understanding the unique aspects and interactional processes of multiple minority identities. In A. R. Gillem & C. A. Thompson (Eds.), Biracial women in therapy: Between the rock of gender and the hard place of race (pp. 159–71). New York, NY: Haworth Press.

Thompson, B. Y. (2012). The price of "community" from bisexual/biracial women's perspectives. Journal of Bisexuality, 12(3), 417–28. doi:10.1080/15299716.2012.702623

Valles, S. A., Bhopal, R. S., & Aspinall, P. J. (2015). Census categories for mixed race and mixed ethnicity: Impacts on data collection and analysis in the US, UK and NZ. Public Health (Elsevier), 129(3), 266–70. doi:10.1016/j.puhe.2014.12.017

CHAPTER

20 Sexual and Gender Minority Mental Health among Children and Youth

Jessica N. Fish, Laura Baams, *and* Jenifer K. McGuire

Abstract

Sexual and gender minority (SGM) young people are coming of age at a time of dynamic social and political changes with regard to LGBTQ rights and visibility around the world. And yet, contemporary cohorts of SGM youth continue to evidence the same degree of compromised mental health demonstrated by SGM youth of past decades. The authors review the current research on SGM youth mental health, with careful attention to the developmental and contextual characteristics that complicate, support, and thwart mental health for SGM young people. Given a large and rapidly growing body of science in this area, the authors strategically review research that reflects the prevalence of these issues in countries around the world but also concentrate on how mental health concerns among SGM children and youth are shaped by experiences with schools, families, and communities. Promising mental health treatment strategies for this population are reviewed. The chapter ends with a focus on understudied areas in the SGM youth mental health literature, which may offer promising solutions to combat SGM population health disparities and promote mental health among SGM young people during adolescence and as they age across the life course.

Keywords: LGBTQ youth, sexual and gender minority youth, sexual orientation, gender identity, mental health

Contemporary Sexual and Gender Minority Youth

Within the span of a single generation, LGBTQ people emerged from veritable invisibility to inequitable but prominent representation in media, politics, culture, and civic life—at least, in many Western countries. Changing social acceptance of LGBTQ people (Kuyper, Iedema, & Keuzenkamp, 2013; Pew Research Center, 2017) and the decline in the age of coming out (Bishop, Mallory, Fish & Russell, 2019; Russell & Fish, 2016) have led to a rapidly growing and dynamic research and practice landscape with regard to sexual and gender minority (SGM) children and youth and their mental health.

The changing cultural milieu around SGM identities has created a historically new possibility for SGM youth to forge and find LGBTQ-related communities and resources that are accepting of and relevant to them. Modern semblances of the "LGBTQ community" have been present for nearly a century, as has our understanding of mental health disparities for LGBTQ individuals. However, these concepts have historically not centered youth. Some of the more prominent evidence of the influence of SGM youth on LGBTQ (and broader) culture is in the use of language. Young people today have expanded up on longstanding identities (e.g., lesbian, gay, bisexual, transgender) to include a wide and varied array of dynamic sexual and gender identities (e.g., pansexual, demisexual, agender, transmasc/transfem, genderqueer, nonbinary) but have also reified and concretized language that captures experiences at the intersection of race, immigrant status, (dis)ability, class, and other (often marginalized) social identities (e.g., quare, transmisogynoir, Latinx; queer crips; Johnson, 2001; Kafer, 2013; Santos, 2017).

SGM young people represent a new wave of LGBTQ activism and liberation in ways that push back on homonormative perspectives of equality and center those who have been at the margins of the modern LGBTQ civil rights narrative—namely queer and trans people of color, SGM immigrants, and LGBTQ people who are economically disadvantaged (Gandy-Guedes & Paceley, 2019), and diverse with respect to gender expression (McGuire, Beek, Catalpa, & Steensma, 2018) and neurological abilities (Strang et al., 2018). In their study of rural young people engaged in queer and trans coalition building, Gandy-Guedes and Paceley (2019) found that issues related to intersectionality—including immigration and criminal justice reform, pay inequality, and trans rights—ranked highest among a long list of concerns.

The proliferation and visibility of LGBTQ youth communities and culture reflect a resilience strategy among contemporary cohorts of SGM young people, who feel empowered to assert who they are in the face of longstanding stigma and oppression and in ways that challenge hetero- and cisnormativity, but also racism, xenophobia, ableism, and other intersecting forms of oppression. Interestingly, despite research supporting the importance of the LGBTQ community for SGM adult mental health (Frost & Meyer, 2012; Meyer, 2015), LGBTQ youth community and empowerment are rarely recognized, integrated, or explicitly interrogated in the broader SGM mental health literature (cf. Frost, Fine, Torre, & Cabana, 2019). Similarly, much of the SGM mental health research has not prioritized understanding how LGBTQ youth experiences intersect with race/ethnicity, immigration and documentation status, and social disadvantage (Santos & Toomey, 2018; Toomey, Huynh, Jones, Lee, & Revels-Macalinao, 2017).

At the same time, there has been a swift propagation of resources for both SGM youth and those who seek to support them (i.e., parents, teachers, therapists, doctors). The increasing visibility of transgender youth, in particular, has brought newfound attention to how families, schools, communities, and providers can affirm gender-diverse young people (Gridley et al., 2016; Kosciw et al., 2018). For example, crowdsourcing efforts have led to community-developed resources for LGBTQ youth and their families to be more informed consumers of mental and medical health care in their communities. Yet, these SGM-affirming services are often geographically restricted and overburdened and may not be affordable. Even youth whose LGBTQ identity is generally affirmed in their day-to-day lives and in prominent contexts (e.g., with family, at school) are likely to encounter discrimination and microaggressions across various other environments (e.g., doctors' offices, restaurants) and structural forms of stigma through broader macrosystemic systems that reinforce hetero- and cisnormativity as well as deny privileges and rights (Hatzenbuehler & Pachankis, 2016).

Theoretical and Developmental Perspectives of SGM Youth Mental Health

As with adults, the prevailing theory to understand the compromised mental health of SGM youth has been the minority stress framework, which describes distal stressors as experiences with oppression and victimization from others, and proximal stressors as the internalization of negative cognitions (i.e., internalized oppression, vigilance, and concealment; Meyer, 2003). These minority stressors have all, separately and in interaction with one another, been associated with mental and physical health outcomes for sexual minority youth (Hatzenbuehler, 2009; Hatzenbuehler & Pachankis, 2016; Russell & Fish, 2016). The minority stress framework has also been expanded to incorporate perspectives more relevant to transgender and gender-diverse people (Hendricks & Testa, 2012; Hughto, Reisner, & Pachankis, 2015) as well as sexual minority youth (Goldbach & Gibbs, 2017; Hatzenbuehler, 2009). In particular, youth applications of minority stress must consolidate normative ontogenetic developmental processes along with SGM-specific experiences to understand how minority stress shapes SGM youth mental health.

Developmental Perspectives of SGM Youth and Their Mental Health and Well-Being

SGM youth development, experiences, and mental health must be considered in the context of normative child and adolescent development in addition to frameworks that help to explain the unique developmental experiences of SGM youth.

Perspectives of Gender (Identity) Development

Some children will display signs of gender diversity in early childhood, although this is not true for all persons who later identify as transgender. Studies of children's development have identified some biological (Berenbaum & Beltz, 2011), cognitive (Olson & Selin, 2018), and social (Steensma, McGuire, Kreukels, Beekman, & Cohen-Kettenis, 2013) indicators that distinguish gender-diverse children from their peers. For example, gender-diverse children approach basic developmental tasks such as the understanding of gender as an individual trait with some essential stability over time in ways that are distinct from peers (Olson & Selin, 2018). In longitudinal studies, children who eventually sought puberty suppression were, at initial childhood assessment, more likely to make statements asserting that they "were" a gender other than their assigned sex rather than they "wished to be" a gender other than their assigned sex (Steensma et al., 2013). There are also some social distinctions between assigned sexes. For children assigned male, beginning social transition behaviors (e.g., clothing, name change) represented a stronger indicator of future treatment requests than corresponding behaviors for assigned females.

Biologically, some early studies have begun to show distinctions in brain structures, otoacoustic emissions, and hormone levels. For example, trans girls (aged five to sixteen) with gender dysphoria who had received no medical intervention were found to have otoacoustic emissions comparable to cisgender girls and lower than cisgender boys, suggesting prenatal hormonal contributions to gender (Burke, Menks, Cohen-Kettenis, Klink, & Bakker, 2014). Further studies found that trans boys who were receiving puberty suppression had frontal cortex activation during mental rotation similar to cisgender boys and different from cisgender girls, suggesting a prenatal contribution to brain function. After ten months of testosterone treatment, trans boys changed in frontal cortex activation similarly to cisgender boys, whereas cisgender girls' patterns did not change over time, suggesting additional pubertal contribution to brain function (Burke, Kreukels, Cohen-Kettenis, Veltman, Klink, & Bakker, 2016). These data and other converging evidence suggest there may be both organizational (i.e., prenatal) and activational (i.e., pubertal) hormonal contributors to gender development that serve to enhance gender diversity among youth at different points in child development and in different ways for different assigned sexes.

Children with gender diversity do not report major mental health concerns at a rate different than the typical population (de Vries et al, 2014; Durwood, McLaughlin, & Olson, 2017; Olson, Durwood, Demeules, & Mclaughlin, 2016) with the possible exception of autism, which has been shown to be disproportionately represented among gender-diverse youth (see Strang et al., 2018, for a summary). Research drawn from clinical referrals at centers for gender-affirmative care shows markedly different mental health indicators than community-based research on youth and young adults who identify as transgender (Collier, Van Beusekom, Bos, & Sandfort, 2013). The distinction between these samples is related to many contributing factors, including the nature of children who have access to clinical care in the United States versus those who do not, and how that capacity to access gender-affirmative care varies across countries.

Perspectives on Sexual (Identity) Development

Sexual interest in peers usually does not start until early adolescence. Pubertal development is often what spurs romantic and sexual interests in others, and this might result in a first crush or the start of sexual behavior (Baams, Dubas, Overbeek, & van Aken 2015). Most of our knowledge about adolescent sexual development comes from research among primarily heterosexual, cisgender samples, or studies in which sexual orientation and gender identity or expression (SOGI/E) are not the main foci. Thus, we have a limited understanding of how SGM youth experience sexual development and first intimate relationships or even how pubertal development impacts their sexual and romantic interests.

Sexual identity development milestones are a useful framework to understand the stages of sexual (identity) development that most sexual minority youth go through (e.g., first awareness of same-sex attraction, first initiation of same-sex romantic/sexual behavior, first labeling as LGBQ, first disclosure of LGBQ identity to family and friends; Bishop et al., 2019). To our knowledge, only one study has explored the connection between pubertal timing and sexual milestones of LGB youth. Among females, younger age at menarche was associated with a younger age at coming out, but not with other sexual milestones. For males, the age of spermarche was associated with having all sexual milestones at younger ages: same-sex attraction, recognition of attraction, self-identification, same-sex sexual fantasies, and coming out (Grossman, Foss, & D'Augelli, 2014).

SGM Development in Context

Changing social attitudes and policies regarding LGBTQ issues and people have created the possibility for SGM people to understand their identities at younger ages and to come out in the contexts of their families, schools, and communities. Indeed, emerging research shows that SGM youth are coming out at younger ages than in previous generations (Bishop et al., 2019; Russell & Fish, 2016). However, the declining age of coming out now coincides with a unique developmental period characterized by heightened self-consciousness, peer conformity, elevated rates of victimization, and social and self-regulation—particularly around the areas of sexuality and gender (Brechwald & Prinstein, 2011; Payne & Smith, 2016). SGM people who come out at younger ages are more likely to be emotionally and financially dependent on their parents, which heightens the impact of family rejection if youth's SOGI/E are not accepted by their families. Notably, adolescence is also a critical period for the onset and progression of mental health and substance use behaviors, the patterns of which set the stage for health and well-being across the life course (Kessler et al., 2012; Kim-Cohen, Caspi, Moffitt, Harrington, Mine, & Poulton, 2003). Emerging trend research over the past five years has demonstrated that even amid improved social attitudes, contemporary sexual minority youth in the United States and Canada continue to experience health disparities equal to, and sometimes greater than, those of sexual minority youth a decade ago (Fish et al., 2017; Fish & Baams, 2018; Peter et al., 2017). Thus, the confluence of normative developmental susceptibilities with unique developmental tasks of contemporary SGM youth (e.g., earlier SOGI/E milestones) creates distinct vulnerabilities for SGM young people today (see Russell & Fish, 2016, 2019).

SGM Youth and Mental Health

SGM youth mental health research originated with documenting the high prevalence rates of suicidal behavior and suicide risk among gay and lesbian youth in the late 1980s (Gibson, 1989; Rotheram-Borus & Fernandez, 1995). Since that time, research has expanded to address the mental health of transgender youth in clinical care (Cohen, De Ruiter, Ringelberg, & Cohen-Kettenis, 1997; Cohen-Kettenis & Van Goozen, 1997; de Vries et al, 2014) and elevated rates of various mental health concerns, including depression (Lucassen, Stasiak, Samra, Frampton, & Merry, 2017), anxiety (Kuyper, de Roos, Iedema, & Stevens, 2016), and suicidality (Salway et al., 2019) for SGM youth. The following synthesis is largely based on studies that capture self-reported mental health symptomatology, relative to diagnostic methods and measures (cf. Mustanski, Garofalo, & Emerson, 2010). Each individual study contains threats to validity, and most are not directly comparable to one another; however, the sheer proliferation of research paints a strikingly clear picture of strained mental health for SGM youth across multiple continents.

Depression

Research on sexual orientation disparities in depression is consistent in its findings: SGM youth report higher levels of depressive symptoms and are more often diagnosed with having a major depressive episode or other mood disorders when compared to heterosexual youth (Plöderl & Tremblay, 2015). A recent meta-analysis of twenty-three population-based studies confirmed these disparities, showing that sexual minority youth had higher rates of depressive symptoms and depressive disorders than heterosexual youth (Lucassen et al., 2017). Furthermore, longitudinal and cross-sectional population-based studies from the United Kingdom (Irish et al., 2019), the Netherlands (La Roi, Kretschmer, Dijkstra, Veenstra, & Oldehinkel, 2016), and the United States (Fish & Russell, 2019) indicate that sexual orientation disparities in depressive symptomatology are present as early as age ten and eleven. Research documenting gender identity–related differences in depression shows similar, albeit more severe, disparities. For example, in a community sample of LGBT youth, 20 percent of transgender youth met the criteria for major depression (Mustanski et al., 2010), and compared to cisgender youth, transgender youth were more likely to experience a major depressive episode (in Canada; Veale et al., 2017) and depressive symptoms (in New Zealand; Clark et al., 2014). However, a small but important set of studies of transgender youth supported in their identities have found similar levels of depression, self-worth, and quality of life to cisgender peers in both the United States and the Netherlands (de Vries et al, 2014; Durwood et al., 2017; Olson et al., 2016).

Anxiety

Although anxiety is often cited as an example of internalizing symptoms that are likely affected by minority stress (Meyer, 2003), evidence of SGM-related disparities in anxiety among youth is mixed and less consistent than studies documenting SGM-related risk for depression. This may be related to several methodological issues. Anxiety as a disorder is difficult to diagnose in childhood and adolescence because anxiety symptoms will often present as (psycho)somatic symptoms. For example, a study among adolescents from the Netherlands showed sexual orientation disparities in psychosomatic complaints generally linked with anxiety, including stomachaches, sleep problems, and headaches (Kuyper et al., 2016). Large school-based data-collection studies rarely include questions about anxious feelings; however, a number of school-based studies have documented SGM students' lack of feelings of safety and missed school due to feeling unsafe (Kosciw et al., 2018; McGuire, Anderson, Toomey, & Russell, 2010). Transgender children who have socially transitioned also report slightly elevated levels of anxiety (Durwood et al., 2017; Olson et al., 2016). Anxiety is a critical area of research because symptoms of anxiety—worry, nervousness, and fear—are shown to be related to minority stress, in particular the expectation of rejection or vigilance (Hendricks & Testa, 2012). Understanding the prevalence and correlates of anxiety among SGM youth is an important future research direction.

Suicidality and Self-Harm

Perhaps the best-known indicator of SGM mental health inequities is suicidality (Haas et al., 2010). A 2011 meta-analysis found that sexual minority youth had almost three times the odds of reporting suicidality (i.e., suicide ideation, plans or intent, and/or attempt) compared to heterosexual youth and that disparities were particularly severe for bisexual youth (Marshal et al., 2011). A more recent meta-analysis of forty-six studies showed that bisexual women and adolescents, relative to lesbian and gay peers, had 1.5 times the odds of suicide ideation or attempt in the prior year (Salway et al., 2019). There have been criticisms of current meta-analytic studies on sexual minority individuals' risk for suicidality—that psychological autopsy studies have found limited support for sexual orientation disparities in fatal suicides, self-reports of past attempts may be biased, and assessments of suicide attempts often lack a clear definition. However, a meta-analytic study by Plöderl et al. (2013) applied different analytical procedures accounting for these potential biases and still found disparities in suicidality for sexual minority individuals relative to heterosexual people.

To our knowledge, there are currently no meta-analytic studies examining differences in suicidality between cisgender and transgender youth; however, several population-based studies show appreciable disparities. A population-based study from California showed that transgender adolescents had almost three times the odds of reporting past-year suicidal ideation compared to adolescents who did not endorse a transgender identity (Perez-Brumer, Day, Russell, & Hatzenbuehler, 2017). Recent studies also demonstrate within-group variability in risk for attempted suicide among transgender youth (Toomey, Syvertsen, & Shramko 2018): female-to-male transgender youth reported the highest rates of suicide attempt (50 percent), followed by youth who did not report either male or female identities (42 percent), male-to-female transgender youth (29.9 percent), questioning youth (27.9 percent), cisgender female youth (17.6 percent), and cisgender male youth (9.8 percent), respectively.

In addition to suicidal ideation and behavior, self-harm or non suicidal self-injury is more common among SGM youth than among heterosexual, cisgender youth. A recent population-based study among U.K. adolescents shows that at ages sixteen and twenty-one, sexual minority youth had 4 to 4.5 times the odds of reporting self-harm behavior in the previous year than heterosexual youth (Irish et al., 2019). In Canada, transgender boys/men and nonbinary youth were also more likely to report self-harm compared to the general population (Veale et al., 2017).

Social Contexts Related to SGM Mental Health

With well-established SGM-related health disparities, researchers have become increasingly interested in understanding the processes implicated in SGM youth mental health. Although not comprehensive, the following sections help to contextualize the vulnerability and resilience of SGM young people across the various contexts that they traverse in their day-to-day lives, including school, family, community, and the broader sociopolitical climate.

School

School climate and interpersonal experiences of support, rejection, discrimination, and victimization within school contexts constitute a large degree of the literature attempting to understand SGM youths' elevated rates of poor mental health. These studies are critically important when we consider that school attendance is mandatory for many young people. The bulk of these studies are U.S.-based, although findings are similar across U.S. (Kosciw et al., 2018), Dutch (Pizmony-Levy, 2018), and Mexican (Baruch-Dominguez, Infante-Xibille, & Saloma-Zuñiga, 2016) contexts. Importantly, a large number of studies across countries show a strong connection between experiences of victimization, bullying, or homophobic/transphobic harassment and mental health symptoms (Collier et al., 2013).

School climate and policy have also received attention (Day, Snapp, & Russell, 2016; Russell, Day, Ioverno, & Toomey, 2016). Studies suggest that school, district, and state policies that enact enumerated antibullying policies, which explicitly mention SOGI/E in a list of protected class statuses, are associated with reduced bullying and victimization (Hatzenbuehler, Schwab-Reese, Ranapurwala, Hertz, & Ramirez, 2015) and suicide attempts for sexual minority youth (Hatzenbuehler & Keyes, 2013). In schools with gender-affirming policies or guidelines, rates of discriminatory practices were almost halved: more students were able to use their chosen name or pronoun and the bathroom or locker room that aligned with their gender identity and to express themselves through clothing (Kosciw et al., 2018).

Factors that influence LGBTQ youths' perceptions of school climate include the presence of LGBT-inclusive curricula (Snapp, McGuire, Sinclair, Gabrion, & Russell, 2015) and LGBT-focused school clubs, such as Gender and Sexuality Alliances (formerly Gay–Straight Alliances [GSAs]). Schools with these features have been shown not only to protect LGBTQ students through decreased victimization and bullying but are also related to better mental health and well-being among LGBTQ students (Poteat, Yoshikawa, Calzo, Russell, & Horn, 2017). In addition, being able to use one's chosen name (Russell, Pollitt, Li, & Grossman, 2018) and having access to gender-appropriate bathrooms on campus and in campus housing (Seelman, 2016) is associated with better mental health for gender minority youth.

Family

Despite the fundamental understanding that families are important to youth mental health, there remains a dearth of research investigating the ways in which the family environment and the processes therein contribute to the well-being of SGM youth. Most research studies on the role of family for SGM youth mental health focus on the independent roles of support and/or rejection (Baiocco et al., 2015; Ryan et al., 2009, 2010; van Beusekom, Bos, Overbeek, & Sandfort, 2015). In two separate studies, Ryan et al. (2009, 2010) found that the degree to which families rejected or accepted SGM youth was related to SGM youth mental health and substance use. Others show that among many forms of support (family, friend, and community), family support appears to be the most strongly associated with positive well-being (Snapp, Watson, Russell, Diaz, & Ryan, 2015). An in-depth analysis of transgender youths' discussion of suicide attempts revealed belongingness and thwarted belongingness as co-occurring themes suggesting complex family relationships (Hunt, Morrow, & McGuire, 2019) that may be better interpreted through a lens focused on the ambiguous nature of family relationships (McGuire, Catalpa, Lacey, & Kuvalanka, 2016).

Preliminary measurement work around family support suggests that parental behaviors that broadly reflect support and rejection are unique constructs that are either weakly correlated or uncorrelated (McGuire & Fish, 2018; Pollitt, Fish, & Watson, 2019). Exploratory work that seeks to document patterns of support and rejection within the family environment show that the majority of transgender, genderqueer, and nonbinary people in their sample report an equal presence of both support and rejection, which likely reflects inconsistent and ambiguous family processes around gender identity. Importantly, gender minority youth who reported the presence of both supportive and rejecting behaviors were those most at risk for compromised mental health, more so than those who reported outright rejection (Allen, Fish, Leslie, & McGuire, 2019). Others who include both acceptance and rejection in models with outcomes of depression also find that rejection emerges as the prominent predictor of (poor) health (McGuire & Fish, 2018).

Continued focus on SGM youths' family context is critical. As youth come out at younger ages, they will be spending longer amounts of time in the context of their immediate family as they navigate their gender and sexual identity developmental processes in childhood and adolescence. However, parental support, alone, has not shown consistent protection for LGB youth: results often reflect that parental support is not enough to buffer the negative influence of peer victimization on poor mental health (Feinstein, Wadsworth, Davila, & Goldfried, 2014; Poteat et al., 2011). Thus, research that provides a more nuanced understanding of the familial context of SGM youth will likely identify other important family processes that undermine and support SGM young people, but also the resources parents and families need to help their SGM children thrive.

Community

The immediate community and region in which SGM youth grow up is a contributing factor to their mental health, in both positive and negative ways. A U.S.-based study by the Williams Institute showed that independent of demographics, LGBTQ youth living in rural areas of California reported a more negative school climate and lower levels of perceived school safety than LGBTQ youth in urban areas of the state (Choi, Baams, & Wilson, 2017). Data from the 2017 National School Climate Survey show that SGM youth in rural/small towns heard more homophobic language, experienced more victimization, had more anti-LGBTQ discriminatory school policies and practices, and reported fewer LGBTQ school resources than SGM youth in urban areas (Kosciw et al., 2018).

In addition to these negative experiences in school, SGM youth in nonmetropolitan areas are less likely to find support outside of their school context (Paceley, Thomas, Toole, & Pavicic, 2018) in, for example, LGBTQ community centers (Rickard & Yancey, 2018). Their lack of access to resources and support may explain the increased mental health problems among SGM youth from nonmetropolitan areas compared to urban areas, including suicidality (Poon & Saewyc, 2009) and substance use (Choi et al., 2017; Poon & Saewyc, 2009). A study among rural and non-rural transgender adults found similar disparities. Transmen living in rural areas reported higher mental health problems, including depression and anxiety, compared to transmen living in non-rural areas; however, there were no statistical differences between transwomen living in rural and non-rural areas (Horvath, Iantaffi, Swinburne-Romine, & Bockting, 2014).

The community resources that SGM youth have access to can also protect them and play a positive role in their lives. SGM community resources are particularly important for accessing supportive peers and adults, creating visibility of SGM identities and SGM peers, providing SGM-specific information and education, and advocating for SGM-inclusive policies, such as antidiscrimination laws (Paceley et al., 2018). In particular, LGBTQ community-based organization have been shown to serve many of the needs of SGM youth in both rural and urban contexts (Allen et al., 2012; CenterLink & Movement Advancement Project, 2018), although there remains a dearth of research on these programs.

SGM Youth and Global Variation

Even in our attempts to bring a global perspective to SGM youth mental health, there is notable overrepresentation of samples from the United States, Australia, the United Kingdom, and several countries in Western Europe (e.g., the Netherlands, Italy, Norway). Largely absent from the literature are perspectives on the mental health of SGM youth in the Global South. The countries in these regions represent a vast array of policies and practices regarding same-sex attraction and behavior that range from growing social acceptance (e.g., Israel, Mexico) to conflicted social and policy environments (e.g., Guatemala, Brazil), imprisonment (e.g., Somalia, Pakistan), and even death (e.g., Iran, Nigeria). It is also important to note that, unlike many countries shaped by Western Christianity and colonization, there are countries and cultural practices that are more accepting of transgender and gender-diverse people relative to sexual minorities (e.g., Iran, India). Initial studies in these diverse contexts have begun to document disparities in the mental health and well-being of SGM youth in these contexts and the mechanisms through which they come to exist (Baruch-Dominguez et al., 2016; Cook, Sandfort, Nel, & Rich, 2013; Manalastas, 2016). It is likely that as countries become more accepting, and with increased access to (unregulated) social media, we will continue to understand geographic and cultural variability in the experiences of SGM young people around the world.

Mental Health Treatment for SGM Youth

SGM populations engage in mental health treatment at higher rates than their heterosexual and cisgender peers (Baams, De Luca, & Brownson, 2018; Lucassen et al., 2011). Fortunately, SGM identities and issues have made their way into the ethical guidelines and standards of care for most major mental health accrediting organizations (e.g., American Psychological Associations, American Association of Marriage and Family Therapy, American Counseling Association, National Association of School Psychologists). However, research in the area of clinical intervention has been largely adult-focused, although more recent studies point to key psychological mechanisms and processes that are relevant to the treatment of SGM young people (Hatzenbuehler & Pachankis, 2016). This work emphasizes the importance of cognitive (e.g., rumination, emotion regulation, appraisals) and interpersonal processes. For example, Hatzenbeuhler (2009) notes that the link between stigma and psychological distress is stronger for those who report greater rumination. In another study, Baams et al. (2015) noted that the association between minority stress and mental health (i.e., depression and suicide ideation) was mediated by perceived burdensomeness—a well-established mechanism from the interpersonal psychological theory of suicide (Joiner et al., 2009). Despite knowledge of underlying factors, adaptations of evidence-based treatments for SGM-specific concerns are lacking.

Burgeoning research shows the promise of affirmative cognitive-behavioral therapy (A-CBT; Austin, Craig, & D'Souza, 2018; Craig, Austin, & Alessi, 2019). At the core, A-CBT methods look to change problematic thoughts and maladaptive behavior while at the same time validating youths' SGM identities and acknowledging the impact of discrimination on mental health. Therapeutic practices often aim to disrupt the meaning that youth ascribe to stressful events and increase their coping and emotional regulation—mechanisms through which minority stress perpetuates poor mental health among SGM youth (Hatzenbuehler, 2009; Hatzenbuehler & Pachankis, 2016). CBT models adapted to fit sexual minority adult men's needs (Effective Skills to Empower Effective Men [ESTEEM]; Pachankis et al., 2015) have also shown efficacy in clinical randomized controlled trials. Specifically, participants in the treatment group reported larger decreases in depressive symptoms and alcohol use but also reduced internalized homophobia, rumination, sensitivity to rejection and increased emotion regulation and perceived social support. Findings suggest CBT models tailored for SGM populations might be particularly adept at addressing some of the underlying cognitive, affective, and behavioral mechanisms through which SGM stressors impact mental health.

The research studies highlighting the role of parental rejection and acceptance in SGM youth mental health (Ryan et al., 2009, 2010) also emphasize the importance of including parents and families in treatment. Attachment-based family therapy (ABFT; Diamond, Russon, & Levy, 2016) and relational-focused therapy (RFT-SGM; Diamond, Boruchovitz-Zamir, Gat, & Nir-Gootlieb, 2019), which were originally designed and applied to address sexual minority youth depression and suicidality, focus on strengthening the relationship between SGM children and their parents. Through attachment-based therapeutic approaches, the treatment is aimed at strengthening "loving, supportive, mutually respectful, meaningful relationships in which the [child] can authentically and openly express all aspects of their identity without fear of rejection or of being negatively judged" (Diamond et al., 2019, p. 432).

For transgender and gender-nonconforming youth, a distinction exists between the need for gender-affirmative medical care and gender-supportive mental health support. Early European studies of successful gender-affirmative medical care existed within the context of substantial gender-supportive mental health care for youth and families (de Vries et al., 2014, Steensma et al., 2013). Countries vary with regard to the age of assent for medical care, and in particular for any kind of gender or sexual care (e.g., contraception, sexually transmitted infection testing, abortion). Likewise, age of assent for gender-affirmative care varies considerably across countries: twelve years is a common age for youth to be considered competent to understand the implications of medical intervention and participate in assent for treatment. Although research into the benefits of puberty suppressants for adolescent mental health is still in its beginning stages, the first cohort of youth to receive puberty suppression is now in adulthood and reporting psychosocial functioning at or above the level of same-age peers in the general population (de Vries et al., 2014).

In the U.S. context, gender-affirmative medical care is more likely to be distinct from mental health support and may or may not occur in coordinated care models (Gridley et al., 2016). The rights of minors to consent to treatment without the approval of parents, or with approval from only one parent, vary across countries, but also across states within the United States. The most restrictive states require written approval of two parents until a youth is age eighteen. Given links between mental health, minority stress, medical treatment, and quality of life, provision of gender-supportive mental health care remains a top priority for the well-being of transgender youth.

Despite the increase in quality and accessibility of mental health care for SGM youth, disparities remain (Baams et al., 2018). A New Zealand–based study showed that same-sex–attracted and both-sex–attracted secondary school students were more likely to have seen mental health professionals, but they also indicated that they had more difficulty "getting help" for emotional worries (Lucassen et al., 2011). For SGM youth, access to mental health care may be problematic if care is not affirming of their SOGI/E. In fact, most licensed care providers do not receive explicit training on culturally competent work with LGBTQ youth. There is also consistent evidence of the harmful effects of sexual orientation and gender identity change efforts for the mental health of SGM youth (Ryan, Toomey, Diaz, &

Russell, 2020), and despite calls to ban these practices in the United States, bans often do not apply to religious providers.

Gaps and Future Directions

Despite enormous progress in the field of SGM youth development and health, there remain critical gaps. This section highlights future directions for researchers and considerations for practitioners and advocates of SGM youth.

SGM Youth and Understudied Systems

FOSTER CARE AND HOMELESSNESS

Most of the research on SGM youth is focused on contextual factors in the school and family environment, meaning that other systems that SGM youth navigate require focused attention. For example, representative studies of California (Baams, Wilson, & Russell, 2019; Wilson & Kastanis, 2015) and the United States (Fish, Baams, Wojciak, & Russell, 2019) indicate that SGM youth are more likely to experience foster care, out-of-home placement, homelessness, and transitional housing. Although we currently know little about the pathways through which SGM youth enter foster care or out-of-home placements, available research shows that SGM youth are more likely to experience abuse and neglect by their parents (Baams, 2018; Friedman et al., 2011) and report being "pushed out" of their home into homelessness (Pearson, Thrane, & Wilkinson, 2017). Among a sample of LGBTQ young adults experiencing homelessness (Shelton et al., 2018), the majority (70.3 percent) reported being kicked out of their family home; this experience was even more likely among transgender youth (75.3 percent). Transgender youth also reported being kicked out of foster homes (26.2 percent) or a relative's home (31.1 percent), and multiply marginalized youth, such as Black and Latinx LGBTQ youth, were more likely to be kicked out of their family and foster homes than white LGBTQ youth (Shelton et al., 2018). Importantly, SGM youth in foster care demonstrate greater odds of depressive symptoms and suicidal thoughts than SGM youth not involved in foster care and heterosexual foster youth (Baams et al., 2019), suggesting that growing up in care does not necessarily provide SGM youth with the protections and resources they need to thrive.

JUVENILE PUNISHMENT

Experience with unsupportive school climates, housing instability, child welfare, and family rejection contribute to SGM youths' elevated risk for involvement with the juvenile punishment system (Irvine & Canfield, 2016; Snapp, Hoenig, Fields, & Russell, 2015). It has become clear that SGM youth are overrepresented in all layers of juvenile punishment, from being stopped by the police to juvenile arrest and conviction (Himmelstein & Brückner, 2011). Research on the school-to-prison pipeline explains the pathway from school to juvenile punishment systems: several studies document that SGM youth are more likely to be suspended or expelled from school as a result of their diverse sexual and gender expression, thus contributing to the increasingly observed school-to-prison pipeline for SGM youth (Snapp et al., 2015). Findings from the National Survey of Youth in Custody, a representative sample of adjudicated youth in juvenile correction facilities, showed that sexual minority youth—especially sexual minority girls of color—were overrepresented in custody, spent more time in custody, and experienced more sexual victimization by other youth in custody compared to heterosexual youth. Furthermore, most facilities often place transgender youth with their assigned-sex peers, putting them at increased risk for sexual victimization (Wilson et al., 2017). Given the overrepresentation of SGM youth in custody and the documented risks to SGM youth in those systems, juvenile justice is likely a loci of exacerbated mental health risk for SGM youth.

SGM Youth and the Internet

An area of increasing interest is how SGM youths' use of new media (e.g., websites, web-based news, social media, social networking) influences their mental health and well-being (Craig & McInroy, 2014). Although the majority of contemporary youth use the internet, research shows that SGM youth are more likely to engage in new media than their heterosexual, cisgender peers (GLSEN, CiPHR, & CCRC, 2013). In studies of Dutch and Canadian SGM youth, findings showed that the internet provided them the opportunity to access resources, explore their identities, find like others, and come out in a digital space, which in some cases facilitated coming out and cultivating social resources offline (Baams, Jonas, Utz, Bos, & van der Vuurst, 2011; Craig & McInroy, 2014). *Children 404* provides another exciting example of online SGM youth social resistance in Russia as a response to government limitations on expression. This cyberspace provided online community, identity validation, foster care placement, and mental health resources, in the face of Russian anti-propaganda laws making it illegal to be gay (GLAAD, 2015).

However, along with studies that document the resilience-cultivating features of new media use by SGM young people (Ceglarek & Ward, 2016; Craig & McInroy, 2014), there are well-established disparities in cyberbullying and its relationship with poor mental health (e.g., depression, psychological distress, suicidal ideation and attempts) among SGM young people (McConnell, Clifford, Korpak, Phillips, & Birkett, 2017; Sinclair, Bauman, Poteat, Koenig, & Russell, 2012). Emerging evidence also suggests that identity management across online and offline contexts may be an added stressor for SGM youth (McConnell et al., 2017; McConnell, Neray, Hogan, Korpak, Clifford, & Birkett, 2018). Considering the amount of time that young people spend engaged with new media, this space reflects an important but largely unstudied context for SGM youth as it relates to their mental health.

Intersecting and Dynamic Identities

Contemporary SGM youth face complex social environments that uniquely challenge the many distinct features of their identities (Santos & Toomey, 2018). For example, rituals that historically marked the coming of age of adolescents (e.g. menarche, driver's license, Bar Mitzvah, first sexual intercourse) are influenced by a host of intersectional factors that will shape the way an SGM young person engages with these milestones (e.g., assigned sex, race, puberty suppression, sex of partner, religious acceptance). In order to care for the mental health of SGM youth, we must first be able to identify, acknowledge, and validate the multifaceted nature of their.

Recently, the National Institute of Health (2019) has called for better measures in SOGI/E research. This will improve understanding of complex identities, the links between sexual orientation and gender identity, and the ability to intervene in support of enhanced mental health treatment. When youth see themselves in these measures, they are validated in their identities. By developing measures that are informed by research, clinical work is informed by a broader and more accurate picture of youth experiences. For decades, care in gender dysphoria has been guided by measures with a binary focus on gender and gender transition. For example, nonbinary measures of gender are becoming more available (McGuire et al., 2018; McGuire et al., in press) and have the power to transform the ways in which gender dysphoric youth and adults are assessed and treated.

Large-Scale Prevention and Intervention

Given the degree to which contemporary cohorts of SGM youth evidence compromised mental health (Plöderl & Tremblay, 2015; Russell & Fish, 2019) there is overwhelming need for large-scale prevention and intervention strategies that curtail the negative effect of anti-LGBT stigma (e.g., policies) but also actively promote health and resilience among SGM young people. Adolescence reflects a critical developmental time for mental health and substance use onset, experiences that set vulnerabilities for mental illness and substance use disorders at later points in the life course (Schulenberg, Sameroff, & Cicchetti, 2004). Thus, large-scale prevention efforts will have downstream effects for current cohorts of SGM youth as they age into adulthood. Unfortunately, there remain few mental health promotion programs specifically for SGM youth.

A recent systematic review of SGM youth interventions—which included behavioral, psychological, educational, pharmacological, medical, and policy—identified only nine interventions for SGM youth mental health, although they predominantly represented individual-level psychological and pharmacological/medical treatment strategies (e.g., ABFT, puberty suppression; Coulter et al., 2019). Increased focus on developing and implementing large-scale prevention and intervention programs like GSAs, which are positively associated with SGM youth mental health (Poteat et al., 2017), should be a priority for researchers, practitioners, and advocates moving forward. For example, many communities have LGBTQ-focused community-based organizations (CenterLink & Movement Advancement Project, 2018) and affirmative 4-H programs, which have been shown (anecdotally) to play a role in promoting health and resilience among SGM young people but have been veritably invisible in the SGM youth mental health literature.

We also lack understanding of resilience among SGM youth (Meyer, 2015). In fact, despite persistent and seemingly intransigent inequities, many SGM young people thrive. Research focused on the factors that cultivate resilience among SGM youth will be particularly helpful in developing and implementing programs to promote the mental health of SGM young people as they age into adulthood. For example, Toomey et al. (2018) found that sexual minority youth who engaged in LGB-specific coping strategies as adolescents (e.g., involvement with LGBT organizations) had better psychosocial adjustment in young adulthood. Continuing to identify these strategies will be critical as the field of SGM youth mental health moves toward translating a large and growing evidence base into applied settings.

Conclusions

Despite coming of age during a time of enormous social awareness of LGBTQ lives and changing social attitudes toward sexual and gender diversity, SGM youth carry the burden of longstanding inequality, bias, and abuse in society. On the one hand, LGBTQ people are more prominent in media and politics and have secured basic protections and more or less equal rights, at least in many Western countries. Yet, contemporary cohorts of SGM youth continue to demonstrate disproportionately compromised mental health, and gender minority youth still face considerable hurdles to affirmative gender-informed care. Prevention and intervention strategies explicitly designed to improve SGM youth mental health are slow to develop but are a necessary accompaniment to policies that protect and affirm LGBTQ people; so are research, programs, and practices that recognize and support the inherent resilience of SGM young people and their growing communities around the world. When the lens of equity for SGM youth is focused on the outcomes of mental health, it is clear that substantial mitigation and intervention is still necessary.

References

Allen, K. D., Hammack, P. L., & Himes, H. L. (2012). Analysis of GLBTQ youth community-based programs in the United States. *Journal of Homosexuality, 59*, 1289–306. doi:10.1080/00918369.2012.720529

Allen, S. H., Fish, J. N., Leslie, L. A., & McGuire, J. K. (May, 2019). *Transgender family environment heterogeneity and associations with health outcomes: A latent profile analysis.* Paper presented at the LGBTQ Research Symposium, Urbana-Champaign, Illinois.

Austin, A., Craig, S. L., & D'Souza, S. A. (2018). An AFFIRMative cognitive behavioral intervention for transgender youth: Preliminary effectiveness. *Professional Psychology: Research and Practice, 49*(1), 1–8. doi:10.1037/pro0000154

Baams, L. (2018). Disparities for LGBTQ and gender nonconforming adolescents. *Pediatrics, 141*, e20173004.

Baams, L., De Luca, S. M., & Brownson, C. (2018). Use of mental health services among college students by sexual orientation. *LGBT Health, 5*, 421–30. doi:10.1089/lgbt.2017.0225

Baams, L., Dubas, J. S., Overbeek, G., & van Aken, M. A. (2015). Transitions in body and behavior: A meta-analytic study on the relationship between pubertal development and adolescent sexual behavior. *Journal of Adolescent Health, 56*, 586–98. doi:10.1016/j.jadohealth.2014.11.019

Baams, L., Jonas, K. J., Utz, S., Bos, H. M. W., & van der Vuurst, L. (2011). Internet use and online social support among same-sex–attracted individuals of different ages. *Computers in Human Behavior, 27*(5), 1820–7. doi:10.1016/j.chb.2011.04.002

Baams, L., Wilson, B. D., & Russell, S. T. (2019). LGBTQ youth in unstable housing and foster care. *Pediatrics, 143*, e20174211.

Baiocco, R., Fontanesi, L., Santamaria, F., Ioverno, S., Marasco, B., Baumgartner, E., . . . Laghi, F. (2015). Negative parental responses to coming out and family functioning in a sample of lesbian and gay young adults. *Journal of Child and Family Studies, 24*(5), 1490–500.

Baruch-Dominguez, R., Infante-Xibille, C., & Saloma-Zuñiga, C. E. (2016). Homophobic bullying in Mexico: Results of a national survey. *Journal of LGBT Youth, 13*, 18–27. doi:10.1080/19361653.2015.1099498

Berenbaum, S. A., & Beltz, A. M. (2011). Sexual differentiation of human behavior: Effects of prenatal and pubertal organizational hormones. *Frontiers in Endocrinology, 32*, 183–200. doi:10.1016/j.yfrne.2011.03.001

Bishop, M. D., Mallory, A. M., Fish, J. N., Russell, S. T. (2019, April). *Generational differences in sexual identity milestones in a nationally representative sample of LGB people.* Poster presented at the Population Association of America Annual Meeting, Austin, Texas.

Brechwald, W. A, & Prinstein, M. J. (2011). Beyond homophily: A decade of advances in understanding peer influence processes. *Journal of Research on Adolescence, 21*(1), 166–79. doi:10.1111/j.1532-7795.2010.00721.x

Burke, S. M., Kreukels, B. P., Cohen-Kettenis, P. T., Veltman, D. J., Klink, D. T., & Bakker, J. (2016). Male-typical visuospatial functioning in gynephilic girls with gender dysphoria: Organizational and activational effects of testosterone. *Journal of Psychiatry & Neuroscience, 41*, 395–404. doi:10.1503/jpn.150147

Burke, S. M., Menks, W. M., Cohen-Kettenis, P. T., Klink, D. T., & Bakker, J. (2014). Click-evoked otoacoustic emissions in children and adolescents with gender identity disorder. *Archives of Sexual Behavior, 43*, 1515–23. doi:10.1007/s10508-014-0278-2

Ceglarek, P. J. D., & Ward, L. M. (2016). A tool for help or harm? How associations between social networking use, social support, and mental health differ for sexual minority and heterosexual youth. *Computers in Human Behavior*, 65, 201–9. doi:10.1016/j.chb.2016.07.051

CenterLink & Movement Advancement Project. (2018). *2018 LGBT community center survey report: Assessing the capacity and programs of lesbian, gay, bisexual, and transgender community centers.* Fort Lauderdale, FL.

Choi, S. K., Baams, L., & Wilson, B. D. M. (2017). *LGBTQ youth in California's public schools: Differences across the state.* Los Angeles, CA: The Williams Institute.

Clark, T. C., Lucassen, M. F., Bullen, P., Denny, S. J., Fleming, T. M., Robinson, E. M., & Rossen, F. V. (2014). The health and well-being of transgender high school students: results from the New Zealand adolescent health survey (Youth '12). *Journal of Adolescent Health, 55*, 93–9. doi:10.1016/j.jadohealth.2013.11.008

Cohen, L., De Ruiter, C., Ringelberg, H., & Cohen-Kettenis, P. T. (1997). Psychological functioning of adolescent transsexuals: Personality and psychopathology. *Journal of Clinical Psychology, 53,* 187–96.

Cohen-Kettenis, P. T., & Van Goozen, S. H. (1997). Sex reassignment of adolescent transsexuals: A follow-up study. Journal of the American Academy of Child & Adolescent Psychiatry, *36,* 263–71. doi:10.1097/00004583-199,702,000-00017

Collier, K. L., Van Beusekom, G., Bos, H. M., & Sandfort, T. G. (2013). Sexual orientation and gender identity/expression related peer victimization in adolescence: A systematic review of associated psychosocial and health outcomes. *Journal of Sex Research, 50,* 299–317.

Cook, S. H., Sandfort, T. G. M., Nel, J. A., & Rich, E. P. (2013). Exploring the relationship between gender nonconformity and mental health among Black South African gay and bisexual men. *Archives of Sexual Behavior, 42*(3), 327–30. doi:10.1007/s10508-013-0087-z

Coulter, R. W. S., Egan, J. E., Kinsky, S., Friedman, M. R., Eckstrand, K. L., Frankeberger, J., Folb, B. L., Mair, C., Markovic, N., Silvestre, A., Stall, R., & Miller, E. (2019). Mental health, drug, and violence interventions for sexual/gender minorities: A systematic review. *Pediatrics, 144*(3), e20183367.

Craig, S. L., Austin, A., & Alessi, E. J. (2019). Cognitive-behavioral therapy for sexual and gender minority youth mental health. In J. E. Pachankis & S. A. Safren (Eds.), *Handbook of evidence-based mental health practice with sexual and gender minorities* (pp. 25–50). New York, NY: Oxford University Press.

Craig, S. L., & McInroy, L. (2014). You can form a part of yourself online: The influence of new media on identity development and coming out for LGBTQ youth. *Journal of Gay & Lesbian Mental Health, 18,* 95–109. doi:10.1080/19359705.2013.777007

Day, J. K., Snapp, S. D., & Russell, S. T. (2016). Supportive, not punitive, practices reduce homophobic bullying and improve school connectedness. *Psychology of Sexual Orientation and Gender Diversity, 3,* 416–25. doi:10.1016/j.jsp.2015.10.005

De Vries, A. L. C., McGuire, J. K., Steensma, T. D., Wagenaar, E., Doreleijers, T., & Cohen-Kettenis, P. T. (2014). Prospective young adult outcomes of puberty suppression in transgender adolescents. *Pediatrics, 134,* 696–704. doi:10.1542/peds.2013–2958

Diamond, G., Boruchovitz-Zamir, R., Gat, I., & Nir-Gottlieb, O. (2019). Relationship-focused therapy for sexual and gender minority individuals and their parents. In J. E. Pachankis & S. A. Safren (Eds.), *Handbook of evidence-based mental health practice with sexual and gender minorities* (pp. 25–50). New York, NY: Oxford University Press.

Diamond, G., Russon, J., & Levy, S. (2016). Attachment-based family therapy: A review of the empirical support. *Family Process, 55*(3), 595–610.

Durwood, L., McLaughlin, K. A., & Olson, K. R. (2017). Mental health and self-worth in socially transitioned transgender youth. *Journal of the American Academy of Child and Adolescent Psychiatry, 56*(2), 116–123.e2. doi:10.1016/j.jaac.2016.10.016

Feinstein, B. A., Wadsworth, L. P., Davila, J., & Goldfried, M. R. (2014). Do parental acceptance and family support moderate associations between dimensions of minority stress and depressive symptoms among lesbians and gay men? *Professional Psychology: Research and Practice, 45*(4), 239–46. doi:10.1037/a0035393

Fish, J. N., & Baams, L. (2018). Trends in alcohol-related disparities between heterosexual and sexual minority youth from 2007 to 2015: Findings from the Youth Risk Behavior Survey. *LGBT Health, 5,* 359–67. doi:10.1089/lgbt.2017.0212

Fish, J. N., Baams, L., Wojciak, A. S., & Russell, S. T. (2019). Are sexual minority youth overrepresented in foster care, child welfare, and out-of-home placement? Findings from nationally representative data. *Child Abuse & Neglect, 89,* 203–11. doi:10.1016/j.chiabu.2019.01.005

Fish, J. N., & Russell, S. T. (2019, March). *Age trends in sexual-orientation-related disparities in homophobic bullying and its association with depressive symptoms.* Paper presented at the Society for Research in Child Development Biennial Meeting in Baltimore, MD.

Fish, J. N., Watson, R. J., Porta, C. M., Russell, S. T., & Saewyc, E. M. (2017). Are alcohol-related disparities between sexual minority and heterosexual youth decreasing? *Addiction, 112,* 1931–41. doi:10.1111/add.13896

Friedman, M. S., Marshal, M. P., Guadamuz, T. E., Wei, C., Wong, C. F., Saewyc, E. M., & Stall, R. (2011). A meta-analysis of disparities in childhood sexual abuse, parental physical abuse, and peer victimization among sexual minority and sexual nonminority individuals. *American Journal of Public Health, 101,* 1481–94. doi:10.2105/AJPH.2009.190009

Frost, D. M., Fine, M., Torre, M. E., & Cabana, A. (2019). Minority stress, activism, and health in the context of economic precarity: Results from a national participatory action survey of lesbian, gay, bisexual, transgender, queer, and gender non-conforming youth. *American Journal of Community Psychology, 63*(3–4), 511–26. doi:10.1002/ajcp.12326

Frost, D. M., & Meyer, I. H. (2012). Measuring community connectedness among diverse sexual minority populations. *Journal of Sex Research, 49*(1), 36–49. doi:10.1080/00224499.2011.565427

Gandy-Guedes, M. E., & Paceley, M. S. (2019). Activism in Southwestern queer and trans young adults after the marriage equality era. *Affilia, 34*(4), 439–60. doi:10.1177/0886109919857699

Gibson, P. (1989). Gay and lesbian youth suicide. In M. R. Feinlieb (Ed.), *Prevention and intervention in youth suicide, report of the Secretary's Task Force on Youth Suicide* (vol. 3). Washington, DC: U.S. Department of Health & Human Services.

GLAAD. (2015). https://www.glaad.org/tags/children–404–0

GLSEN, CiPHR, & CCRC. (2013). *Out online: The experiences of lesbian, gay, bisexual and transgender youth on the internet.* New York, NY: GLSEN.

Goldbach, J. T., & Gibbs, J. J. (2017). A developmentally informed adaptation of minority stress for sexual minority adolescents. *Journal of Adolescence, 55,* 36–50. doi:10.1016/j.adolescence.2016.12.007

Gridley, S. J., Crouch, J. M., Evans, Y., Eng, W., Antoon, E., Lyapustina, M., . . . McCarty, C. (2016). Youth and caregiver perspectives on barriers to gender-affirming health care for transgender youth. *Journal of Adolescent Health, 59,* 254–61. doi:10.1016/j.jadohealth.2016.03.017

Grossman, A. H., Foss, A. H., & D'Augelli, A. R. (2014). Puberty: Maturation, timing and adjustment, and sexual identity developmental milestones among lesbian, gay, and bisexual youth. *Journal of LGBT Youth, 11,* 107–24. doi:10.1080/19361653.2014.846068

Haas, A. P., Eliason, M., Mays, V. M., Mathy, R. M., Cochran, S. D., D'Augelli, A. R., . . . Russell, S. T. (2010). Suicide and suicide risk in lesbian, gay, bisexual, and transgender populations: Review and recommendations. *Journal of Homosexuality, 58,* 10–51. doi:10.1080/00918369.2011.534038

Hatzenbuehler, M. L. (2009). How does sexual minority stigma "get under the skin"? A psychological mediation framework. *Psychological Bulletin, 135,* 707–30. doi:10.1037/a0016441

Hatzenbuehler, M. L., & Keyes, K. M. (2013). Inclusive anti-bullying policies and reduced risk of suicide attempts in lesbian and gay youth. *Journal of Adolescent Health, 53,* S21–S26. doi:10.1016/j.jadohealth.2012.08.010

Hatzenbuehler, M. L., & Pachankis, J. E. (2016). Stigma and minority stress as social determinants of health among lesbian, gay, bisexual, and transgender youth: Research evidence and clinical implications. *Pediatric Clinics, 63,* 985–97. doi:10.1016/j.pcl.2016.07.003

Hatzenbuehler, M. L., Schwab-Reese, L., Ranapurwala, S. I., Hertz, M. F., & Ramirez, M. R. (2015). Associations between antibullying policies and bullying in 25 states. *JAMA Pediatrics, 169*(10), e152411. doi:10.1001/jamapediatrics.2015.2411

Hendricks, M. L., & Testa, R. J. (2012). A conceptual framework for clinical work with transgender and gender nonconforming clients: An adaptation of the minority stress model. *Professional Psychology: Research and Practice, 43,* 460–7. doi:10.1037/a0029597

Himmelstein, K. E., & Brückner, H. (2011). Criminal-justice and school sanctions against nonheterosexual youth: A national longitudinal study. *Pediatrics, 127,* 49–57. doi:10.1542/peds.2009–2306

Horvath, K. J., Iantaffi, A., Swinburne-Romine, R., & Bockting, W. (2014). A comparison of mental health, substance use, and sexual risk behaviors between rural and non-rural transgender persons. *Journal of Homosexuality, 61,* 1117–30. doi:10.1080/00918369.2014.872502

Hughto, J. M., Reisner, S. L., & Pachankis, J. E. (2015). Transgender stigma and health: A critical review of stigma determinants, mechanisms, and interventions. *Social Science & Medicine (1982), 147,* 222–31. doi:10.1016/j.socscimed.2015.11.010

Hunt, Q. A., Morrow, Q. J., & McGuire, J. K., (2019). Experiences of suicide in trans-identified youth: A qualitative community based study. *Archives of Suicide Research* [E-pub ahead of print]. doi:10.1080/13811118.2019.1610677

Irish, M., Solmi, F., Mars, B., King, M., Lewis, G., Pearson, R. M.,... Lewis, G. (2019). Depression and self-harm from adolescence to young adulthood in sexual minorities compared with heterosexuals in the UK: A population-based cohort study. *Lancet Child & Adolescent Health, 3,* 91–8. doi:10.1016/S2352-4642(18)30343–2

Irvine, A., & Canfield, A. (2016). The overrepresentation of lesbian, gay, bisexual, questioning, gender nonconforming and transgender youth within the child welfare to juvenile justice crossover population. *Journal of Gender, Social Policy & the Law, 24,* 243–61.

Johnson, E. P. (2001). "Quare" studies, or (almost) everything I know about queer studies I learned from my grandmother. *Text and Performance Quarterly, 21,* 1–25. https://doi.org/10.1080/10462930128119

Joiner Jr., T. E., Van Orden, K. A., Witte, T. K., Selby, E. A., Ribeiro, J. D., Lewis, R., & Rudd, M. D. (2009). Main predictions of the interpersonal–psychological theory of suicidal behavior: Empirical tests in two samples of young adults. *Journal of Abnormal Psychology, 118,* 634–46. doi:10.1037/a0016500

Kafer, A. (2013). *Feminist, queer, crip.* Bloomington, IN: Indiana University Press.

Kessler, R. C., Avenevoli, S., Costello, E. J., Georgiades, K., Green, J. G., Gruber, M. J.,... Merikangas, K. R. (2012). Prevalence, persistence, and sociodemographic correlates of DSM-IV disorders in the National Comorbidity Survey replication adolescent supplement. *Archives of General Psychiatry, 69*(4), 372–80. doi:10.1001/archgenpsychiatry.2011.160

Kim-Cohen, J., Caspi, A., Moffitt, T. E., Harrington, H., Milne, B. J., & Poulton, R. (2003). Prior juvenile diagnoses in adults with mental disorder: Developmental follow-back of a prospective-longitudinal cohort. *Archives of General Psychiatry, 60,* 709–17. doi:10.1001/archpsyc.60.7.709

Kosciw, J. G., Greytak, E. A., Zongrone, A. D., Clark, C. M., & Truong, N. L. (2018). *The 2017 National School Climate Survey: The experiences of lesbian, gay, bisexual, transgender, and queer youth in our nation's schools.* New York, NY: GLSEN. https://www.glsen.org/sites/default/files/GLSEN-2017-National-School-Climate-Survey-NSCS-Full-Report.pdf

Kuyper, L., de Roos, S., Iedema, J., & Stevens, G. (2016). Growing up with the right to marry: Sexual attraction, substance use, and well-being of Dutch adolescents. *Journal of Adolescent Health, 59,* 276–82. doi:10.1016/j.jadohealth.2016.05.010

Kuyper, L., Iedema, J., & Keuzenkamp, S. (2013). *Towards tolerance: Exploring changes and explaining differences in attitudes towards homosexuality in Europe.* The Hague, The Netherlands: Netherlands Institute for Social Research.

La Roi, C., Kretschmer, T., Dijkstra, J. K., Veenstra, R., & Oldehinkel, A. J. (2016). Disparities in depressive symptoms between heterosexual and lesbian, gay, and bisexual youth in a Dutch cohort: The TRAILS study. *Journal of Youth and Adolescence, 45,* 440–56. doi:10.1007/s10964-015-0403-0

Lucassen, M. F., Merry, S. N., Robinson, E. M., Denny, S., Clark, T., Ameratunga, S.,... Rossen, F. V. (2011). Sexual attraction, depression, self-harm, suicidality and help-seeking behaviour in New Zealand secondary school students. *Australian & New Zealand Journal of Psychiatry, 45,* 376–83. doi:10.3109/00048674.2011.559635

Lucassen, M. F., Stasiak, K., Samra, R., Frampton, C. M., & Merry, S. N. (2017). Sexual minority youth and depressive symptoms or depressive disorder: A systematic review and meta-analysis of population-based studies. *Australian & New Zealand Journal of Psychiatry,* 51, 774–87. doi:10.1177/0004867417713664

Manalastas, E. J. (2016). Suicide ideation and suicide attempt among young lesbian and bisexual Filipina women: Evidence for disparities in the Philippines. *Asian Women, 32,* 101–20.

Marshal, M. P., Dietz, L. J., Friedman, M. S., Stall, R., Smith, H. A., McGinley, J.,... Brent, D. A. (2011). Suicidality and depression disparities between sexual minority and heterosexual youth: A meta-analytic review. *Journal of Adolescent Health, 49,* 115–23. doi:10.1016/j.jadohealth.2011.02.005

McConnell, E., Clifford, A., Korpak, A. K., Phillips, G., & Birkett, M. (2017). Identity, victimization, and support: Facebook experiences and mental health among LGBTQ youth. *Computers in Human Behavior, 76,* 237–44. doi:10.1016/j.chb.2017.07.026

McConnell, E., Néray, B., Hogan, B., Korpak, A., Clifford, A., & Birkett, M. (2018). "Everybody puts their whole life on Facebook": Identity management and the online social networks of LGBTQ youth. *International Journal of Environmental Research and Public Health, 15*, 1078–97. doi:10.3390/ijerph15061078

McGuire, J. K., Anderson, C. R., Toomey, R. B., & Russell, S. T., (2010). School climate for transgender youth: A mixed method investigation of student experiences and school responses. *Journal of Youth and Adolescence, 39*, 1175–88. doi:10.1007/s10964-010-9540-7

McGuire, J. K., Beek, T. F., Catalpa, J. M., & Steensma, T. D. (2018). The Genderqueer Identity (GQI) scale: Measurement and validation of four distinct subscales with trans and LGBQ clinical and community samples in two countries. *International Journal of Transgenderism, 20*(2–3), 289–304. doi:10.1080/15532739.2018.1460735

McGuire, J. K., Catalpa, J. M., Lacey, V., & Kuvalanka, K. (2016). Ambiguous loss as a framework for interpreting gender transitions in families. *Journal of Family Theory and Review, 8*, 372–85. doi:10.1111/jftr.12159

McGuire, J. K., & Fish, J. N., (2018, November). *Family gender environment links to psychological well-being*. Paper presented at the National Council on Family Relations Annual Conference, San Diego, California.

McGuire, J. K., Rider, N. G., Berg, D., Catalpa, J. M., Steensma, T. D., & Cohen-Kettenis, P. T. (in press). Utrecht Gender Dysphoria Scale—Gender Spectrum (UGDS-GS). In T. D. Fisher, C. M. Davis, W. L. Yarber, & S. L. Davis (Eds.), *Handbook of sexuality-related measures*. New York, NY: Routledge.

Meyer, I. H. (2003). Prejudice as stress: conceptual and measurement problems. *American Journal of Public Health, 93*, 262–5. doi:10.2105/AJPH.93.2.262

Meyer, I. H. (2015). Resilience in the study of minority stress and health of sexual and gender minorities. *Psychology of Sexual Orientation and Gender Diversity, 2*, 209–13. doi:10.1037/sgd0000132

Mustanski, B. S., Garofalo, R., & Emerson, E. M. (2010). Mental health disorders, psychological distress, and suicidality in a diverse sample of lesbian, gay, bisexual, and transgender youths. *American Journal of Public Health, 100*, 2426–32.

National Institutes of Health. (2019). *Methods and measurement in sexual & gender minority health research: Developing a research agenda and identifying research opportunities*. Bethesda, MD: National Institutes of Health Sexual & Gender Minority Research Office.

Olson, K. R., Durwood, L., DeMeules, M., & McLaughlin, K. A. (2016). Mental health of transgender children who are supported in their identities. *Pediatrics, 137*, 1–8. doi:10.1542/peds.2015–3223

Olson, K. R., & Selin, G. (2018). Early findings from the TransYouth Project: Gender development in transgender children. *Child Development Perspectives, 12*, 93–7. doi:10.1111/cdep.12268

Paceley, M. S., Thomas, M. M., Toole, J., & Pavicic, E. (2018). "If rainbows were everywhere": Nonmetropolitan SGM youth identify factors that make communities supportive. *Journal of Community Practice, 26*, 429–45. doi:10.1080/10705422.2018.1520773

Pachankis, J. E., Hatzenbuehler, M. L., Rendina, H. J., Safren, S. A., & Parsons, J. T. (2015). LGB-affirmative cognitive-behavioral therapy for young adult gay and bisexual men: A randomized controlled trial of a transdiagnostic minority stress approach. *Journal of Consulting and Clinical Psychology, 83*, 875–89. doi:10.1037/ccp0000037

Payne, E., & Smith, M. J. (2016). *Gender policing*. In N. M. Rodriguez, W. J. Martino, J. C. Ingrey, & E. Brockenbrough (Eds.), *Critical concepts in queer studies and education* (pp. 127–36). New York, NY: Palgrave Macmillan.

Pearson, J., Thrane, L., & Wilkinson, L. (2017). Consequences of runaway and thrownaway experiences for sexual minority health during the transition to adulthood. *Journal of LGBT Youth, 14*, 145–71. doi:10.1080/19361653.2016.1264909

Perez-Brumer, A., Day, J. K., Russell, S. T., & Hatzenbuehler, M. L. (2017). Prevalence and correlates of suicidal ideation among transgender youth in California: Findings from a representative, population-based sample of high school students. *Journal of the American Academy of Child & Adolescent Psychiatry, 56*, 739–46. doi:10.1016/j.jaac.2017.06.010

Peter, T., Edkins, T., Watson, R., Adjei, J., Homma, Y., & Saewyc, E. (2017). Trends in suicidality among sexual minority and heterosexual students in a Canadian population-based cohort study. *Psychology of Sexual Orientation and Gender Diversity, 4*, 115–23. doi:10.1037/sgd0000211

Pew Research Center. (2017). Changing attitudes on gay marriage. Pew Research Center: Religion & Public Life. http://www.pewforum.org/fact-sheet/changing-attitudes-on-gay-marriage/

Pizmony-Levy, O. (2018). *The 2018 Dutch National School Climate Survey Report*. New York, NY: Teachers College, Columbia University.

Plöderl, M., & Tremblay, P. (2015). Mental health of sexual minorities. A systematic review. *International Review of Psychiatry, 27*, 367–85. doi:10.3109/09540261.2015.1083949

Plöderl, M., Wagenmakers, E. J., Tremblay, P., Ramsay, R., Kralovec, K., Fartacek, C., & Fartacek, R. (2013). Suicide risk and sexual orientation: A critical review. *Archives of Sexual Behavior, 42*, 715–27. doi:10.1007/s10508-012-0056-y

Pollitt, A., Fish, J. N., & Watson, R. J. (2019, March). *Being out matters for the measurement equivalence of family acceptance and rejection among LGBTQ+ youth*. Paper presented at the Society for Research in Child Development Biennial Meeting in Baltimore, MD.

Poon, C. S., & Saewyc, E. M. (2009). Out yonder: Sexual-minority adolescents in rural communities in British Columbia. *American Journal of Public Health, 99*, 118–24. doi:10.2105/AJPH.2007.122945

Poteat, V. P., Mereish, E. H., DiGiovanni, C. D., & Koenig, B. W. (2011). The effects of general and homophobic victimization on adolescents' psychosocial and educational concerns: The importance of intersecting identities and parent support. *Journal of Counseling Psychology, 58*, 597–609. https://doi.org/10.1037/a0025095

Poteat, V. P., Yoshikawa, H., Calzo, J. P., Russell, S. T., & Horn, S. (2017). Gay-straight alliances as settings for youth inclusion and development: Future conceptual and methodological directions for research on these and other student groups in schools. *Educational Researcher, 46*, 508–16. doi:10.3102/0013189X17738760

Rickard, A., & Yancey, C. T. (2018). Rural/non-rural differences in psychosocial risk factors among sexual minorities. *Journal of Gay & Lesbian Social Services, 30*, 154–71. doi:10.1080/10538720.2018.1444525

Rotheram-Borus, M. J., & Fernandez, M. I. (1995). Sexual orientation and developmental challenges experienced by gay and lesbian youths. *Suicide and Life-Threatening Behavior, 25*, 26–34. doi:10.1111/j.1943-278X.1995.tb00487.x

Russell, S. T., Day, J. K., Ioverno, S., & Toomey, R. B. (2016). Are school policies focused on sexual orientation and gender identity associated with less bullying? Teachers' perspectives. *Journal of School Psychology, 54*, 29–38. doi:10.1037/sgd0000195

Russell, S. T., & Fish, J. N. (2016). Mental health in lesbian, gay, bisexual, and transgender (LGBT) youth. *Annual Review of Clinical Psychology, 12*, 465–87. doi:10.1146/annurev-clinpsy-021815–093153

Russell, S. T., & Fish, J. N. (2019). Sexual minority youth, social change, and health: A developmental collision. *Research in Human Development, 16*, 5–20. doi:10.1080/15427609.2018.1537772

Russell, S. T., Pollitt, A. M., Li, G., & Grossman, A. H. (2018). Chosen name use is linked to reduced depressive symptoms, suicidal ideation, and suicidal behavior among transgender youth. *Journal of Adolescent Health, 63*, 503–5. doi:10.1016/j.jadohealth.2018.02.003

Ryan, C., Huebner, D., Diaz, R. M., & Sanchez, J. (2009). Family rejection as a predictor of negative health outcomes in white and Latino lesbian, gay, and bisexual young adults. *Pediatrics, 123*, 346–52. doi:10.1542/peds.2007–3524

Ryan, C., Russell, S. T., Huebner, D., Diaz, R., & Sanchez, J. (2010). Family acceptance in adolescence and the health of LGBT young adults. *Journal of Child and Adolescent Psychiatric Nursing, 23*, 205–13. doi:10.1111/j.1744–6171.2010.00246.x

Ryan, C., Toomey, R. B., Diaz, R. M., & Russell, S. T. (2020). Parent-initiated sexual orientation change efforts with LGBT adolescents: Implications for young adult mental health and adjustment. *Journal of Homosexuality, 67*(2), 159–73. doi:10.1080/00918369.2018.1538407

Salway, T., Ross, L. E., Fehr, C. P., Burley, J., Asadi, S., Hawkins, B., & Tarasoff, L. A. (2019). A systematic review and meta-analysis of disparities in the prevalence of suicide ideation and attempt among bisexual populations. *Archives of Sexual Behavior, 48*, 89–111. doi:10.1007/s10508-018-1150-6

Santos, C. E. (2017). The history, struggles, and potential of the term Latinx. *Latina/o Psychology Today, 4*, 7–14.

Santos, C. E., & Toomey, R. B. (2018). Integrating an intersectionality lens in theory and research in developmental science. *New Directions for Child and Adolescent Development, 161*, 7–15. doi:10.1002/cad.20245

Schulenberg, J. E., Sameroff, A. J., & Cicchetti, D. (2004). The transition to adulthood as a critical juncture in the course of psychopathology and mental health. *Development and Psychopathology, 16*, 799–806. doi:10.10170S0954579404040015

Seelman, K. L. (2016). Transgender adults' access to college bathrooms and housing and the relationship to suicidality. *Journal of Homosexuality, 63*, 1378–99. doi:10.1080/00918369.2016.1157998

Shelton, J., DeChants, J., Bender, K., Hsu, H. T., Maria, D. S., Petering, R., . . . Barman-Adhikari, A. (2018). Homelessness and housing experiences among LGBTQ young adults in seven US cities. *Cityscape, 20*, 9–34.

Sinclair, K. O., Bauman, S., Poteat, V. P., Koenig, B., & Russell, S. T. (2012). Cyber and bias-based harassment: Associations with academic, substance use, and mental health problems. *Journal of Adolescent Health, 50*, 521–3. doi:10.1016/j.jadohealth.2011.09.009

Snapp, S. D., Hoenig, J. M., Fields, A., & Russell, S. T. (2015). Messy, butch, and queer: LGBTQ youth and the school-to-prison pipeline. *Journal of Adolescent Research, 30*, 57–82. doi:10.1177/0743558414557625

Snapp, S. D., McGuire, J. K., Sinclair, K. O., Gabrion, K., & Russell, S. T. (2015). LGBTQ-inclusive curricula: Why supportive curricula matter. *Sex Education, 15*, 580–96. doi:10.1080/14681811.2015.1042573

Snapp, S. D., Watson, R. J., Russell, S. T., Diaz, R. M., & Ryan, C. (2015). Social support networks for LGBT young adults: Low-cost strategies for positive adjustment. *Family Relations, 64*, 420–30.

Steensma, T. D., McGuire, J. K., Kreukels, B. P. C., Beekman, A. J., & Cohen-Kettenis, P. T. (2013). Factors associated with desistence and persistence of childhood gender dysphoria: A quantitative follow-up study. *Journal of the American Academy of Child and Adolescent Psychiatry, 52*, 582–90. doi:10.1016/j.jaac.2013.03.016

Strang, J. F., Janssen, A., Tishelman, A., Leibowitz, S. F., Kenworthy, L., McGuire, J. K., . . . Anthony, L. G. (2018). Revisiting the link: Evidence of the rates of autism in studies of gender diverse individuals. *Journal of the American Academy of Child and Adolescent Psychiatry, 57*, 885–7. doi:10.1016/j.jaac.2018.04.023

Toomey, R. B., Huynh, V. W., Jones, S. K., Lee, S., & Revels-Macalinao, M. (2017). Sexual minority youth of color: A content analysis and critical review of the literature. *Journal of Gay & Lesbian Mental Health, 21*(1), 3–31. doi:10.1080/19359705.2016.1217499

Toomey, R. B., Syvertsen, A. K., & Shramko, M. (2018). Transgender adolescent suicide behavior. *Pediatrics, 142*, e20174218.

van Beusekom, G., Bos, H. M. W., Overbeek, G., Sandfort, T. G. M. (2015). Same-sex attraction, gender nonconformity, and mental health: The protective role of parental acceptance. *Psychology of Sexual Orientation and Gender Diversity, 2*, 307–12. doi:10.1037/sgd0000118

Veale, J. F., Watson, R. J., Peter, T., & Saewyc, E. M. (2017). Mental health disparities among Canadian transgender youth. *Journal of Adolescent Health, 60*, 44–9. doi:10.1016/j.jadohealth.2016.09.014

Wilson, B. D., Jordan, S. P., Meyer, I. H., Flores, A. R., Stemple, L., & Herman, J. L. (2017). Disproportionality and disparities among sexual minority youth in custody. *Journal of Youth and Adolescence, 46*, 1547–61. doi:10.1007/s10964-017-0632-5

Wilson, B. D. M., & Kastanis, A. A. (2015). Sexual and gender minority disproportionality and disparities in child welfare: A population-based study. *Children and Youth Services Review, 58*, 11–17. doi:10.1016/j.childyouth.2015.08.016

CHAPTER

21 Sexual and Gender Minority Mental Health among Older Adults

Sandra S. Butler

Abstract

This chapter reviews existing literature on mental health issues among sexual and gender minority older adults. Current LGBTQ older adults lived their formative years prior to the gay liberation movement of the 1970s; a lifetime of discrimination and concealment affects their mental health today. While early studies of sexual and gender minority older adults were largely based on small, relatively restricted samples, two recent national studies out of the University of Washington have improved on sample diversity and generalizability of results. Findings from these larger studies and several others are reviewed, highlighting what is known about positive and negative mental health conditions among LGBTQ older adults and related practice implications. The chapter concludes with a look at ongoing gaps in knowledge about mental health issues confronting sexual and gender minority older adults and best practices for serving them.

Keywords: older adults, LGBTQ older adults, SGM older adults, LGBTQ mental health, LGBT aging, LGBT seniors, well-being among LGBTQ older adults

Introduction

This chapter examines what is known about sexual and gender minority (SGM) mental health issues among older adults in the United States. What constitutes "older" varies in the literature and in public conversation. The age of eligibility for Medicare and, formerly, Social Security—sixty-five—has often been used to designate the start of "old age," but AARP—a large national organization of older adults—begins soliciting membership at age fifty-five and, on the other end of the spectrum, many people remain employed into their seventies and sometimes eighties. This broad range for what can be considered an "older adult" has led to the designations of "young old" for those age sixty-five to eight-five, and the "old old," for those over age eight-five. In the literature on older LGBTQ, samples often include individuals in middle age (forty-five to sixty-four), in addition to those older than sixty-four, because accessing SGM older individuals for study samples has typically been quite challenging. The largest national, longitudinal study to date on the health and well-being of SGM older adults—the Aging with Pride: National Health, Aging and Sexuality/Gender Study (NHAS)—includes study participants who are age fifty and older. Studies reviewed in this chapter will thus reflect this broad definition of older adults, with specific sample age ranges identified.

The Aging with Pride NHAS estimates that 2.4 percent of adults fifty and older in the United States self-identify as LGBTQ—this was about 2.7 million people in 2014. This number is expected to double by 2060 (Fredriksen-Goldsen & Kim, 2017). Yarns, Abrams, Meeks, and Sewell (2016) estimate that there were close to one million LGBTQ adults sixty-five and older in 2015. Due to the ongoing stigma, many older adults who engage in same-sex behavior, are attracted to members of the same sex, and/or experience gender variance do not self-identify as LGBTQ. Including such individuals would quadruple the estimate of SGM adults fifty and older in 2060 to 20 million (Fredriksen-Goldsen & Kim, 2017).

Historical Context

Early baby boomers (those born between 1945 and 1955) and the Greatest Generation that preceded them lived their formative years prior to the gay liberation movement of the 1970s. They grew up in an environment in which homophobia, heterosexism, and transphobia were far more pervasive than they are today and the risks of self-disclosure were extreme. It was illegal to be homosexual in the United States and most other nations at the time, with sodomy laws existing throughout the country. Although some U.S. states began to repeal such laws in the 1960s and 1970s, the Supreme Court upheld Georgia's sodomy law as recently as 1986 in its *Bowers v. Hardwick* decision. It was not until 2003 that this decision was overturned in *Lawrence v. Texas*, thereby striking down the remaining sodomy laws that existed in fourteen states (American Civil Liberties Union, 2003).

Not only were LGBTQ individuals considered criminals during this era, they were also seen as deviant and mentally ill due to their sexual and/or gender nonconformity. In early editions of the *Diagnostic and Statistical Manual of Mental Disorders* (DSM), SGM individuals were classified as child molesters, exhibitionists, voyeurs, and people who committed destructive and antisocial crimes (Hidalgo, Peterson, & Woodman, 1985). Homosexuality was not removed from the list of DSM disorders until 1973. It was not until 2013—forty years later—that the DSM-5 replaced the diagnosis "gender identity disorder" with "gender dysphoria" and the American Psychiatric Association affirmed its support of transgender rights. Unfortunately, "transvestic fetishism" was replaced with "transvestic disorder," a diagnosis that remains stigmatizing for gender minorities, as it classifies gender variance as a psychiatric disease (National LGBTQ Task Force, n.d.).

Early Studies

In the late 1990s, a review of studies reporting empirical findings on older gay, lesbian, and bisexual individuals uncovered only fifty-eight papers (Gabbay, 1997, as cited in D'Augelli, Grossman, Hershberger, & O'Connell, 2001). These studies tended to have small samples made up of white, well-educated, middle-class individuals. Many were focused on debunking myths that portrayed older gay men as sad, isolated, and lonely and older lesbian women as bitter, self-destructive, and lonely (D'Augelli et al., 2001). Very few studies included older bisexual or transgender individuals, a trend that continues today. Mental health issues were rarely examined in the early literature on SGM older adults.

Providing one example of this early literature, Dorfman et al. (1995) conducted a study to examine the commonly held belief that gay men and lesbian women were more depressed and isolated than their heterosexual counterparts. Through a non-probability sample in Southern and Central California, they surveyed fifty-two heterosexual and fifty-six homosexual adults, age sixty and older, on depression and social support. They found no significant differences between the non-gay and gay subsamples in levels of depression. Fifteen percent of the full sample scored in the mild to major depression ranges of the Geriatric Depression Scale, which was consistent with other samples of older adults (Dorfman et al., 1995). Moreover, no significant differences were found between the two subsamples in terms of social support, though the gay and lesbian respondents were more likely to include friends in their networks, while the heterosexual respondents relied more on family. The authors concluded: "Thus older homosexuals and heterosexuals are equally likely to be depressed and to have social supports. This is in contrast to the myth that older gay men and lesbian women are sadder and more isolated that their heterosexual cohorts" (Dorfman et al., 1995, p. 39).

The early literature on older bisexual adults is particularly scarce (Scherrer, 2017), as is the literature on mental health among bisexuals of any age (Dodge & Sandfort, 2007). Only recently has the concept of bisexuality emerged into social and political advocacy efforts; prior to the 1980s, it was a term used rarely outside of academic scholarship. As stated by Scherrer (2017), "the term bisexual has only recently become *culturally available* to adopt as an identity. Because of this history, older adults who grew up before the 1980s are likely to have spent more of their lives being unaware about bisexuality" (p. 47; italics in the original). As a consequence of this relatively recent emergence of the term, older bisexual adults may be reluctant to adopt that identity, leading to increased invisibility and possibly internalized stigma. The early literature rarely distinguished bisexual individuals from their gay and lesbian counterparts, though some authors suggested bisexual individuals experienced more stressors and had greater mental health problems—across the lifespan—than gay and lesbian individuals (Dodge & Sandfort, 2007).

One significant early study on the mental health of sexual minority older adults did include bisexual participants, although only 8 percent of the sample identified as bisexual and bisexual status was not included in reported analyses. In the late 1990s, D'Augelli et al. (2001) surveyed 416 LGB individuals aged sixty to ninety-one through agencies in the United States (n = 18) and Canada (n = 1); this represented the largest study of LGB older adults to that date. Like most early studies, there was little racial diversity, with 95 percent of the participants identifying as white. The large majority (84 percent) reported good or excellent mental health. Those who had partners, had a higher income, or were parents were more likely to report better mental health. Better health and cognitive functioning and more positive views of their sexual orientation were also related to better mental health. Diminished mental health was related to older age, reported worse physical health and cognitive functioning, higher levels of loneliness, and lower self-esteem. One in ten study participants had had suicidal thoughts, and for 29 percent of those individuals, such thoughts were a result of their sexual orientation. Nine percent of the sample had sought counseling to stop feelings of attraction to the same sex. Lower levels of internalized homophobia and greater numbers of people knowing their sexual orientation were related to less lifetime suicidal ideation (D'Augelli et al., 2001; Grossman, 2006).

Although transgender aging has frequently been included in the larger discussions of LGBTQ aging—particularly in the past twenty years—little scholarship has focused on issues facing transgender older adults (Witten, 2014). Much of the early literature on transgender individuals dealt with defining terms and estimating prevalence (Witten, 2003). Early samples of transgender adults revealed that they experienced high levels of abuse, with two out of three reporting abuse in social settings (Witten, 2003). The violence and stigma experienced by transgender adults throughout their lives was considered to negatively impact their aging experience in this early literature. Moreover, data collected in the 1990s indicated that transgender elders had a high likelihood of living alone (nearly 50 percent) and a low likelihood of having children (10 percent; Witten, 2003), leading to compromised social support. Lifetime experiences of violence, stigma, isolation, and inequity of healthcare treatment for transgender older adults began to surface in the early literature on this population, indicating the potential for poor mental health outcomes for later years.

Call for More Research

In 2011, the Institute of Medicine (now called the National Academy of Medicine) published *The Health of Lesbian, Gay, Bisexual and Transgender People: Building a Foundation for Better Understanding*, which included the chapter "Later Adulthood." The report came as a response to a request from the National Institutes of Health (NIH) to assess the current state of knowledge about the health of LGBT individuals, to identify gaps in the research, and to formulate a research agenda that could guide NIH in enhancing and focusing research on the topic (Institute of Medicine, 2011). The chapter on older LGBT in this report noted that research to date had found elevated levels of depression and suicidality among older lesbian women and gay men but that less was known about bisexual and transgender older adults. Research reviewed in the chapter identified risk factors impacting the health of older SGM individuals such as lifetime experiences of discrimination; stigma; and victimization, including violence. The reviewed research also revealed that LGB older adults had higher rates of alcohol and tobacco use than their heterosexual peers, though less was known about transgender older adults. Despite these risk factors, reviewed research indicated LGBTQ elders to be less likely to seek health services than the general population, in part because they did not believe they would receive respectful care (Institute of Medicine, 2011).

The report recommended increased research in general on SGM older adults, with an emphasis on the inclusion of bisexual and transgender older adults. Also suggested was the need to examine experiences of LGBT populations age eighty-five and older, given the lack of research. The report called for both cross-sectional and longitudinal studies to

> explore the demographic realities of LGBT aging in an intersectional and social ecology framework, to allow an understanding of the mechanisms of both risk and resilience in LGBT elders, and to identify appropriate interventions for working effectively with this cohort. (Institute of Medicine, 2011, p. 283)

The report recommendations related to mental health suggested a research focus on depression and suicidality, the effects of discrimination and stigma, and the experiences of and preparation for late life among this population (Institute of Medicine, 2011).

Recent National Studies

CAP Study

Just prior to the publication of the Institute of Medicine's report, a team of researchers from the University of Washington, led by Karen Fredriksen-Goldsen, received NIH funding for a national study on the health of LGBT older adults. The Caring and Aging with Pride (CAP) study was groundbreaking both in its support from NIH on a previously taboo topic and for the reach and size of the study's sample. *The Aging and Health Report: Disparities and Resilience among Lesbian, Gay, Bisexual, and Transgender Older Adults* (Fredriksen-Goldsen et al., 2011) launched an era of considerably more empirical research on the health and well-being of late-middle-age and older SGM adults. This initial cross-sectional CAP study, of 2,560 study participants, preceded the longitudinal Aging with Pride NHAS mentioned earlier in the chapter. Study participants were SGM adults aged fifty and older, recruited through eleven cooperating agencies from across the United States. Each participant completed either a mailed or online survey covering a number of topics related to health, including mental health (Fredriksen-Goldsen et al., 2011).

NHAS Longitudinal Study

In 2014, Fredriksen-Goldsen and her colleagues initiated a longitudinal study of LGBT older adults—the NHAS—and publications beginning in 2017 have drawn on the first wave of cross-sectional data. The sample of 2,450 SGM older adults was recruited from seventeen agencies across the United States. The longitudinal design was designed to allow for an investigation of "changes in health and well-being over time and to assess temporal relationships between psychological, social, behavioral, and biological processes and health and well-being of LGBT older adults" (Fredriksen-Goldsen & Kim, 2017, p. S4).

Findings from these two studies and others published since the 2011 Institute of Medicine report are explored next as they relate to the mental health of SGM older adults.

Mental Health Disparities among SGM Older Adults

There is a growing body of literature indicating that LGBTQ older adults experience higher rates of psychological distress than their non-LGBTQ counterparts (Zelle & Arms, 2015). For example, a statewide survey in California in 2007 found more than one in four LGB (27.9 percent) adults aged fifty to seventy report needing help with emotional and mental health problems as compared to 14 percent of older heterosexual adults (Wallace, Cochran, Durazo, & Ford, 2011). Lifetime exposure to discrimination and societal stigma has been identified as a major contributor to these disparities (Tinney et al., 2015). Meyer (2003) attributed the greater prevalence of mental disorders among LGB individuals, of any age, to a constellation of factors he termed "minority stress." This model suggests that sexual prejudice—and ultimately gender identity prejudice, though not studied by Meyer in 2003—is stressful and may lead to diminished mental health. Recent studies have sought to explore both positive and negative mental health conditions among SGM older adults.

General Mental Health

Using a 100-point scale measuring general mental health (0 = very poor to 100 = excellent), the mean score for all participants in the CAP study was 70.8 (Fredriksen-Goldsen et al., 2011). Score averages varied among groups, with lesbian women and gay men having higher scores (71.8 and 71.7 respectively) and bisexual women (65.6), bisexual men (65.6), and transgender older adults (62.7) reporting lower levels of general mental health. Lower scores for bisexual men and women were explained in part by age, income, and education; this was not true for transgender study participants (Fredriksen-Goldsen et al., 2011).

Using a successful aging framework, Fredriksen-Goldsen, Kim, Shiu, Goldsen, and Emlet (2015) explored differences in perceived quality of life (QOL) among the youngest study participants (aged fifty to sixty-four), the middle-age group (aged sixty-five to seventy-nine), and the oldest study participants (age eighty and older) in the CAP study of SGM older adults; there were 274 individuals in the oldest category. Mental health QOL was measured through items of the SF-8 Health Survey assessing vitality, social functioning and roles, and mental health (Fredriksen-Goldsen et al., 2015). The authors found mental health QOL was highest for the middle-old group. For all age groups, mental health QOL was negatively associated with lifetime victimization and discrimination, identity disclosure, and chronic health conditions. Mental health QOL was positively associated with social network size, social support, physical and leisure activity, positive sense of sexual identity, routine health checkups, substance nonuse, higher income, being employed, being male, and transgender identity (Fredriksen-Goldsen et al., 2015).

Using data from the NHAS, Fredriksen-Goldsen, Kim, Bryan, Shiu, and Emlet (2017) examined pathways by which study participants experienced marginalization, risk, and resilience and their relationship to attaining positive mental health. Identity affirmation and social resources (defined as social support, social participation, community engagement, and relationship status) were associated with positive mental health. Marginalization across the life-course was negatively linked to social resources and mental health. Good mental health was related to good physical health through behaviors that can be targeted in interventions to improve the mental health of this population. For example, increased physical and leisure activities were related to positive mental health, while smoking and insufficient food intake were related to poorer mental health (Fredriksen-Goldsen, Kim, et al., 2017).

Depression and Suicidal Ideation

Nearly a third (31 percent) of the CAP sample reported depressive symptoms at a clinical level as measured by the Center for Epidemiologic Studies Depression Scale (CESD-10). These levels also varied by group with 27 percent of lesbian women, 29 percent of gay men, 35 percent of bisexual women, 36 percent of bisexual men, and 48 percent of transgender older adults indicating high depressive symptoms. Over half the study participants with elevated depression scores on the CESD-10 (53 percent) had been told by a doctor that they had depression. Among the whole sample, nearly one in four (24 percent) had been told by a doctor that they had anxiety; for transgender older adults, nearly two in five (39 percent) had been diagnosed with anxiety (Fredriksen-Goldsen et al., 2011).

The CAP study revealed high levels (39 percent) of suicidal thoughts among LGBTQ older adults, particularly among transgender individuals (71 percent). Among those who had contemplated suicide, a significant minority (39 percent) indicated that their suicidal thoughts were related to sexual orientation or gender identity (Fredriksen-Goldsen et al., 2011). Witten (2014) also reported on this high level of suicidal thoughts among later-life transgender individuals as found in the Trans MetLife Survey on Later-Life Preparedness and Perceptions in Transgender-Identified Individuals (TMLS; n = 1,963). One participant described these thoughts as they accompanied the fear of losing autonomy in old age: "I'd personally rather commit suicide than go into the elderly care 'I can afford' due to exceptionally poor quality of it & the extremely high incidences of sexual/physical/mental abuse that happens there" (as cited in Witten, 2014, p. 26).

Many of the demographic factors related to poor mental health among non-SGM older adults were found to be similarly associated to poor mental health among older SGMs in the CAP study. For example, Latinx and Native American SGM older adults reported lower levels of general mental health, more stress, and higher rates of depression than did white study participants. Native American study participants were also more likely to report being anxious or lonely and to have suicidal thoughts than other ethnic/racial groups. The youngest (aged fifty to sixty-four) and oldest (aged eighty and older) study participants reported lower levels of general mental health and were more likely to experience stress and depression than participants aged sixty-five to seventy-nine. Those aged sixty-five and older were more likely to report anxiety, suicidal ideation, and loneliness than the younger participants. Those with lower incomes and lower education levels were also more likely to report lower levels of general mental health and a higher incidence of depression and loneliness than those with higher incomes and more education (Fredriksen-Goldsen et al., 2011).

In further examining the risk factors for mental health among LGB older adults in the CAP study, Fredriksen-Goldsen et al. (2013) found that financial barriers to healthcare, smoking, lifetime victimization, and internalized stigma increased the odds of depression. Protective factors that decreased the odds of depressive symptomology included physical activities, higher levels of social support, and larger social networks. In focusing on the bisexual older adults in the CAP study (n = 174), Fredriksen-Goldsen, Shiu, Bryan, Goldsen, and Kim (2017) found them to have poorer mental health as compared to the lesbian and gay participants. Higher levels of internalized stigma, lower levels of identity disclosure, lower levels of social support and community involvement, and lower income and educational levels at least partially explained these poorer health outcomes for bisexual older adults.

The researchers (Fredriksen-Goldsen et al., 2014) also examined the risk factors for poor mental health among the 174 transgender older adults in the CAP study. A number of risk factors were associated with higher levels of depression and perceived stress, including concealment of gender identity, internalized stigma, victimization, financial barriers to health services, fear of accessing health services, obesity, and lack of physical activity. Social support and positive feelings of LGBTQ community belonging were associated with lower levels of depressive symptomatology and perceived stress among the transgender participants (Fredriksen-Goldsen et al., 2014).

Hoy-Ellis and Fredriksen-Goldsen (2016) examined the associations among chronic health conditions, minority stress factors, and depression for LGB participants in the NHAS. While the incidence of depression generally decreases in the general population as people age, this is not true for SGM older adults. Consistent with the minority stress model (Meyer, 2003), Hoy-Ellis and Fredriksen-Goldsen (2016) found that concealment of sexual orientation, internalized heterosexism, and chronic health conditions accounted for 76 percent of the variance in depression for older LGB participants in their study.

An interesting analysis of the 183 transgender older adults in the NHAS study found those with military service (n = 43) had lower levels of depression and higher levels of psychological QOL (as measured by the World Health Organization Quality of Life-BREF; Hoy-Ellis et al., 2017). The authors explain this unexpected finding by suggesting that military service may foster resilience through adversity, growth of internal strengths and group cohesion, and/or new life opportunities after military service (Hoy-Ellis et al., 2017).

SGM Older Adults of Color

As stated by Kim, Acey, Guess, Jen, and Fredriksen-Goldsen (2016), "Despite growing racial and ethnic diversity among lesbian, gay, bisexual, transgender, and queer (LGBTQ) older adults in the United States, LGBTQ older adults of color largely are invisible in aging services, research, and public policy" (p. 49). Analysis of racial disparities among study participants in the CAP study revealed that LGBTQ older adults of color experienced higher risk of depression, stress, self-neglect, and suicide ideation. Latinx study participants in the CAP study reported lower levels of both social support and mental health (Kim et al., 2016). Although overall psychological quality of life for African Americans and Latinx individuals was comparable with that of non-Latinx whites in the NHAS study, factors associated with decreased psychological quality of life were higher among participants of color. These included lower income, educational attainment, identity affirmation, and social support (Kim, Jen, & Fredriksen-Goldsen, 2017). On the other hand, Latinx and African American participants indicated higher spirituality, which was associated with increased psychological QOL (Kim et al., 2017).

A recent study based on the Behavior Risk Surveillance System data from 21 U.S. states compared mental health of lesbian and bisexual women over age sixty-five (n = 346) with their heterosexual counterparts (n = 34,361). One particularly interesting finding of this study—and one that the author had not hypothesized—was that sexual minority women of color had 4.17 lower odds of frequent mental health distress than white sexual minority women (Seelman, 2019). In sum, it appears the association between race/ethnicity and mental health for SGM older adults is complex and warrants further study. In the meantime, a few programs exist specifically to address the needs of LGBTQ older adults of color, three of which will be mentioned here.

Increasing opportunities for social engagement can reduce some risk of poorer mental health among older adults in general, and a few such programs have been initiated for SGM older adults of color. Established in 1995, GRIOT Circle in New York City is one of the first organizations in the United States devoted to the well-being of LGBTQ older adults of color. It is a service and advocacy organization "committed to the dignity, well-being, and quality of life of LGBTQ people of color as they age" (Kim et al., 2016, p. 50). Initiatives include the GRIOT Buddy-2-Buddy program, which fosters connections between older SGM individuals of color for mutual support and respect.

Linscott and Krinsky (2016) report on a second example, in Boston, where the LGBT Aging Project of Fenway Health has recently increased its efforts to reach providers of aging services in communities of color. The authors describe the process of meeting community leaders and building relationships over time, ultimately deciding to initially target African Americans, with outreach to Latinx and Asian communities in future years. They held an event called "Flashback Sunday: Honoring the Legacy of LGBT of Color," which drew more than a hundred people. This catalyzed a group to form that has raised funds to expand programming to increase social activities, meal programs, and resource materials for older African American LGBTQ in the city (Linscott & Krinsky, 2016).

A third large U.S. city, Los Angeles, has also deemed outreach to SGM older adults of color a priority. The Los Angeles Gay & Lesbian Center—the largest LGBTQ community center in the world (Gratwick, Jihanian, Holloway, Sanchez, & Sullivan, 2014)—has had aging-specific services since 2008. In the center's attempts to reach the diverse racial, cultural, and linguistic communities of the city, it launched Communidad Latina, a social and cultural group for Latinx LGBTQ adults aged fifty and older. The group hosts monthly social gatherings and workshops on health and legal issues and has stimulated an increase in requests for Spanish-language case management (Gratwick et al., 2014).

These three examples of successful programming for LGBTQ older adults of color illustrate that it is possible—at least in large cities—to reach out to a population that has been largely marginalized in the past.

Practice Implications

Social Resources as a Protective Factor

It is well established that social resources, in the form of social support and social networks, serve as an important protective factor for positive mental health among SGM older adults. Social resources are important to all adults as they age, but the experiences of older LGBT are unique due to the unaccepting context within which the group grew up. Many faced hostility from their families when they disclosed their sexual orientation or gender identity, leading some to become estranged from their families of origin and to create "families of choice" (de Vries, 2014). Such families of choice include partners, ex-partners, friends, neighbors, and/or coworkers (Orel & Coon, 2016).

Numerous studies have found that the presence of social support can ease the stresses of the aging process and is related to better physical, psychological, and emotional health (Masini & Barrett, 2008). Not all LGBTQ older adults have access to social support, thereby compromising their mental and emotional well-being. The CAP study revealed that significant proportions of older SGM individuals lack social support: 33 percent reported that they did not have someone to help with daily chores if they were sick, and 29 percent said they did not have someone to love and make them feel wanted. Nearly three in five of the study participants (59 percent) reported lacking companionship, and over a half said they felt isolated (53 percent) and/or left out (53 percent; Fredriksen-Goldsen et al., 2011).

Social networks, similar to social support, are also related to increased health and well-being (Kim, Fredriksen-Goldsen, Bryan, & Muraco, 2017). Social networks can be seen as social capital in which both size and diversity are important (Erosheva, Kim, Emlet, & Fredriksen-Goldsen, 2015). Among older adults in the general population, determinants of larger social networks include being married, having children, and having access to senior centers and neighbors (Erosheva et al., 2015). The determinants for LGBTQ older adults are likely different and impacted by the issue of identity disclosure. While disclosing one's identity may help older LGBTQ adults build relationships in the LGBTQ community, concealment has served as a protective factor against discrimination and victimization outside that community (Erosheva et al. 2015; Kim et al., 2017).

Kim et al. analyzed data from the first wave (2017) of the longitudinal NHAS study to investigate the diversity of social networks among SGM older adults. They found five social network types with varying degrees of access to social support: diverse, diverse/no children, immediate family-focused, friend-centered/restricted, and fully restricted. Those LGBT older adults in this study with the least diverse and most restricted social networks reported poorer mental health (Kim et al., 2017). Hoy-Ellis, Altor, Kerr, and Milford (2016) point out that the success of the modern LGBTQ rights movement may have contributed to the isolation of some SGM older adults. The authors suggest that as the LGBTQ population becomes more assimilated, former historic gay enclaves, such as the Castro in San Francisco, have become less prominent. They state, "The geographic dispersion that has accompanied LGBTQ assimilation may make it more difficult to sustain social networks, contributing to loneliness and isolation" (Hoy-Ellis et al., 2016, p. 57). Furthermore, they point out that LGBTQ community centers have often been located in these districts and may be difficult to access for older adults who may have been displaced to more affordable outlying neighborhoods with limited transportation options. Older SGM adults may also experience ageism within the LGBTQ communities that originally provided them refuge from a hostile society; such communities tend to be youth-oriented and less than welcoming to older adults (Hoy-Ellis et al., 2016).

Programming to Combat Isolation and Meet Mental Health Needs

GRIOT Circle in New York City, the LGBT Aging Project in Boston, and Communida Latina in Los Angeles, described earlier in the chapter, are examples of programs to reduce isolation among LGBTQ older adults of color and break down barriers to accessing services (Gratwick et al., 2014; Kim et al., 2016; Linscott & Krinsky, 2016). Houston, Texas, offers another example of a program specifically created to address social isolation, depression, and resistance to traditional mental health and other services for SGM older adults (Hoy-Ellis et al., 2016). The local LGBTQ organization, the Montrose Center, partnered with a federally qualified community health center to create the program, Seniors Preparing for Rainbow Years (SPRY):

> From the outset, SPRY was clear that this particular generation of LGBTQ older adults would be distrustful of anything "mental health," and with good reason. Decades of either inadequate or abusive, reparative treatment by mental health professionals; discrimination in general in the elder services industry; fear of being labeled as "crazy"; and continued discrimination even in today's world of marriage equality, is often enough to keep LGBTQ elders from seeking services. (Hoy-Ellis et al., 2016, p. 60)

The program uses trained LGBT peer support workers to engage isolated older adults and then connect them to a welcoming social environment (support groups and social gatherings); mental health therapy and case management are available, but not required. The peer outreach workers provide screening for depression, suicide, and substance use risks. Some SPRY participants have begun to rely less on clinical interventions and more on peer support programs, while for others the social programs have provide a low-barrier entry into needed mental health and case management services (Hoy-Ellis et al., 2016).

Despite such promising programs, many LGBTQ older adults do not live in large cities housing LGBTQ centers, much less programming targeting older adults. Mainstream aging services have traditionally lacked motivation and/or knowledge regarding how best to serve SGM older adults, often claiming to "treat everyone equally" (Butler, 2017; Hoy-Ellis et al., 2016). Progress has been made toward providing resources to such organizations through the establishment in 2010 of the federally funded National Resource Center on LGBT Aging (www.lgbtagingcenter.org/). The center provides technical assistance to health and service providers and community organizations with the goal of improving the quality of service available to SGM older adults (Wallace et al., 2011).

Gaps in Literature and Future Directions

The research reviewed in this chapter took place predominantly in the United States. Research on the experiences of SGM older adults in the United Kingdom (e.g., Guasp, 2011), Australia (e.g., Tinney et al., 2015), and Canada (e.g., Brotman, Ryan, & Cormier, 2003) also exists, with similar findings with regard to the negative consequences of lifelong discrimination and the higher incidence of mental health issues among LGBTQ older adults as compared to their heterosexual counterparts. No research published in English was found pertaining to SGM older adults in the Global South, much less research on the particular mental health issues for this population. Given the limited research infrastructure and social and political contexts that cause SGM individuals to remain hidden in many countries in the Global South, significant barriers will need to be overcome before such studies can take place.

Restricted Samples

Early studies of SGM older adults were based on small studies of urban, white, "young-old" lesbian women and gay men. More recently there has been a greater effort to diversify samples and to include bisexual and transgender individuals. While progress has been made, there is still a long way to go. The CAP study (Fredriksen-Goldsen et al., 2011) was disproportionately non-Hispanic white (87 percent), with other racial and ethnic groups more poorly represented: Hispanics at 4 percent, African Americans at 2 percent, Asian/Pacific Islanders at 2 percent, Native Americans/Alaska Natives at 2 percent, and other races or ethnicities at 2 percent. The more recent longitudinal NHAS study was successful in recruiting a slightly more racially diverse sample: white (82 percent), black (9.3 percent), other (8.8 percent), and Hispanic (6.9 percent; Fredriksen-Goldsen & Kim, 2017). Because these national samples were recruited through existing agencies serving LGBTQ older adults—and such agencies tend to be found in more urban areas—these samples are more likely to be representative of urban populations. More isolated, rural SGM older adults with little access to such specialized organizations are therefore underrepresented in these two samples. Efforts must continue to ensure samples that are as representative as possible of the true diversity of the SGM older population.

It has always been difficult to access the oldest-old for research samples. This is also true for studies of non-SGM older adults. But compounding the barriers of frail health, which may keep older non-SGM adults from participating in research studies, is the history of concealment that today's oldest

LGBTQ have lived with and their understandable resistance to identifying themselves for such studies. The CAP and NHAS studies both made progress in recruiting adults over age sixty-five into their samples, as compared to earlier studies on SGM older adults. While they sampled people as young as age fifty, study participants age sixty-five and older made up more than half the NHAS sample (55 percent; Fredriksen-Goldsen & Kim, 2017). Moreover, as mentioned earlier in the chapter, the CAP study had 274 study participants age eighty and older (Fredriksen-Goldsen et al., 2015). Going forward, as baby boomers—who have lived more of their lives after gay liberation than earlier generations—move into the oldest-old category, it may be easier to recruit members of this age category in future inquiries into the mental health and life experiences of SGM older adults. Every effort should be made to make sure to do so.

Broaden Range of Mental Health Issues Explored

The literature reviewed for this chapter did not include studies on the full range of mental health issues that older adults may confront. General mental health and mental health QOL, suicidal ideations, anxiety, stress, and loneliness were the constructs most typically measured. Little is known about the incidence of more severe mental illness among SGM older adults. The *Journal of Gay & Lesbian Mental Health* has existed since the late 1990s, and in 2011 it featured three articles focused on LGBT older adults based on the 2010 annual symposium of the Association of Gay & Lesbian Psychiatrists (AGLP). After a short introductory article (Kertzner, Barber, & Schwartz, 2011), the other two articles in the issue focused on a single case study of an older gay man who sought therapy (Hicks, 2011; Rubin & Ortmann, 2011), with presenting problems of depression, loneliness, and substance abuse. Rubin and Ortmann (2011) were the treating clinicians of the case—a psychiatrist and clinical social worker—and explored the clinical issues presented by their older gay client. Hicks (2011), a psychiatrist with AGLP, used the same case as the basis for his review of psychiatric, physical, social, spiritual, and emotional aspects of mental health among SGM older adults, concluding that working with this population requires a holistic approach in which all components are considered. Kertzner and coauthors generalize that mental health care for SGM older adults builds on clinical expertise and awareness of the life experiences, vulnerabilities, and available resources of the population. Although this is helpful information, it is quite general. More specific information regarding SGM older adults' experiences with severe mental illness and guidance for best practices in treatment is not currently available and should be one focus of future research.

Substance use disorders occur nearly two times more frequently among LGB individuals than among their heterosexual counterparts (Yarns et al., 2016). Transgender adults also appear to be at elevated risk of substance use disorders. While the incidence of substance use disorders tends to decline with age, they remain a great concern for SGM older adults (Yarns et al., 2016). As stated by Kertzner et al. (2016):

> Several historical age-cohort effects contribute to increased risk of substance misuse in this population, including shame over and concealment of sexual identity, stress linked to sexual orientation discrimination, stigma associated with ageism within society at large as well as within youth-oriented LGBT communities. (p. 337)

They further submit that substance use disorders among LGBTQ older adults represent a "hidden epidemic" as sexual identity may be hidden; rates of substance use disorders in this population are understudied; substance use disorders may go undetected if older LGBTQ individuals avoid medical care for fear of discrimination; or if living alone, as many SGM older adults do, such individuals may have no one who would notice their impairment (Kertzner et al., 2016).

While research exists on this topic, small samples (e.g., Rowan & Butler, 2014) limit the generalizability of many. More recently, the NHAS examined high-risk drinking among its sample of 2,351 LGB older adults, finding that risk and protective factors differed for men and women. While greater day-to-day discrimination was a risk factor for men, it was not for women; unexpectedly, greater social support increased the likelihood of high-risk drinking for women. Older age was a protective factor for women but not men. The longitudinal nature of the NHAS will allow for an examination of LGB older adults' drinking trajectories over time in order to continue to tease out these gender differences (Bryan, Kim, & Fredriksen-Goldsen, 2017). Given the high prevalence of substance use disorders among SGM older adults, this should be a priority focus in future studies of this population.

While not a mental health disorder, dementia in older age is of concern to LGBTQ older adults, as it is in the general population. In 2012, the Alzheimer's Association estimated that there were 350,000 LGBTQ individuals living with dementia and produced its first brochure targeting caregivers of these individuals (Yarns et al., 2016). Limited research exists on the experiences of SGM older adults receiving long-term services and supports, as they and their caregivers cope with dementia. Nonetheless, evidence of "heterosexist norms" leading to increased social isolation, anxiety, confusion, and stress has surfaced (McGovern, 2014). As the population of LGBTQ older adults continues to increase, so will the number of SGM older adults with dementia. Cognitive impairment is being measured in the longitudinal NHAS. One in ten study participants reported severe cognitive impairment in the first wave of the study, 38 percent reported moderate cognitive impairment, and 77 percent reported mild cognitive difficulties (Fredriksen-Goldsen, Jen, Bryan, & Goldsen, 2018). It is imperative to learn more on how to best serve these very vulnerable adults in their final years.

Conclusion

There has been a considerable increase in literature on SGM older adults in the United States over the past decade. This has resulted in an expansion in our understanding of how stigma and discrimination across the life course can impact this population's mental health in their later years. This new knowledge offers mental health practitioners the opportunity to more effectively meet the psychological needs of older LGBTQ adults. Gaps in the research that future inquiries should address include studies in the Global South; samples with greater racial and geographic diversity; a focus on the oldest old; a greater emphasis on the experiences of bisexual and transgender older adults; and increased examination of severe mental illness, substance use disorders, and dementia among SGM older adults.

References

American Civil Liberties Union. (16 June 2003). *History of sodomy laws and the strategy that led to today's decision.* www.aclu.org

Brotman, S., Ryan, B., & Cormier, R. (2003). The health and social service needs of gay and lesbian elders and their families in Canada. *The Gerontologist, 43*, 192–202. doi:10.1093/geront/43.2.192

Bryan, A. E. B., Kim, H-J., Fredriksen-Goldsen, K. I. (2017). Factors associated with high-risk alcohol consumption among LGB older adults: The role of gender, social support, perceived stress, discrimination and stigma. *The Gerontologist, 57*(S1), S95–S104. doi:10.1093/geront/gnw100

Butler, S. S. (2019). Social networks and social isolation among LGBT older adults. In L. W. Kaye & C. M. Singer (Eds.), *Social isolation of older adults: Strategies to bolster health and well-being* (pp. 181–95). New York, NY: Springer.

D'Augelli, A. R., Grossman, A. H., Hersberger, S. L., & O'Connell, T. S. (2001). Aspects of mental health among older lesbian, gay, and bisexual adults. *Aging & Mental Health, 5*(2), 149–58. doi:10.1080/713650002

de Vries, B. (2014). LG(BT) persons in the second half of life: The intersectional influences of stigma and cohort. *LGBT Health, 1*(1), 18–23. doi:10.1089/lgbt.2013.0005

Dodge, B., & Sandfort, T. G. M. (2007). A review of mental health research on bisexual individuals when compared to homosexual and heterosexual individuals. In B. A. Firestein (Ed.), *Becoming visible: Counseling bisexuals across the lifespan* (pp. 28–51). New York, NY: Columbia University Press.

Dorfman, R., Walters, K., Burke, P., Hardin, L., Karanik, T., Raphael, J., & Silverstein, E. (1995). Old, sad and alone: The myth of the aging homosexual. *Journal of Gerontological Social Work, 24*(1/2), 29–44. doi:10.1300/J083V24N01_4

Erosheva, E. A., Kim, H-J., Emlet, C., & Fredriksen-Goldsen, K. I. (2015). Social networks of lesbian, gay, bisexual and transgender older adults. *Research on Aging, 38*(1), 98–123. doi:10.1177/0164027515581859

Fredriksen-Goldsen, K. I., Cook-Daniels, L., Kim, H-J., Erosheva, E. A., Emlet, C. A., Hoy-Ellis, C. P., . . . Muraco, A. (2014). Physical and mental health of transgender older adults: An at-risk and underserved population. *The Gerontologist, 54*(3), 488–500. doi:10.1093/geront/gnt021

Fredriksen-Goldsen, K. I., Emlet, C. A., Kim, H-J., Muraco, A., Erosheva, E. A., Goldsen, J., & Hoy-Ellis, C. P. (2013). The physical and mental health of lesbian, gay and bisexual (LGB) older adults: The role of key health indicators and risk and protective factors. *The Gerontologist, 53*(4), 664–75. doi:10.1093/geront/gns123

Fredriksen-Goldsen, K. I., Jen, S., Bryan, A. E. B., & Goldsen, J. (2018). Cognitive impairment, Alzheimer's disease, and other dementias in the lives of lesbian, gay, bisexual and transgender older adults and their caregivers: Needs and competencies. *Journal of Applied Gerontology, 37*(5), 545–69. doi:10.1177/0733464816672047

Fredriksen-Goldsen, K. I., & Kim, H-J. (2017). The science of conducting research with LGBT older adults: An introduction to Aging with Pride: National Health, Aging, and Sexuality/Gender Study (NHAS). *The Gerontologist, 57*(S1), S1–S14. doi:10.1093/geront/gnw212

Fredriksen-Goldsen, K. I., Kim, H-J., Bryan, A. E. B., Shiu, C., & Emlet, C. A. (2017). The cascading effects of marginalization and pathways of resilience in attaining good health among LGBT older adults. *The Gerontologist, 57*(S1), S72–S83. doi:10.1093/geront/gnw170

Fredriksen-Goldsen, K. I., Kim, H-J., Emlet, C. A., Muraco, A., Erosheva, E. A., Hoy-Ellis, C. P., . . . Petry, H. (2011). *The aging and health report: Disparities and resilience among lesbian, gay, bisexual and transgender older adults.* Seattle, WA: Institute for Multigenerational Health. http://age-pride.org/wordpress/published-articles/

Fredriksen-Goldsen, K. I., Kim, H-J., Shiu, C., Goldsen, J., & Emlet, C. A. (2015). Successful aging among LGBT older adults: Physical and mental health-related quality of life by age group. *The Gerontologist, 55*(1), 154–68. doi:10.1093/geront/gnu081

Fredriksen-Goldsen, K. I., Shiu, C., Bryan, A. E. B., Goldsen, J., & Kim, H-J. (2017). Health equity and aging of bisexual older adults: Pathways of risk and resilience. *Journal of*

Gerontology: Social Sciences, 72(3), 468–78. doi:10.1093/geronb/gbw120

Gratwick, S., Jihanian, L. J., Holloway, T. W., Sanchez, M., & Sullivan, K. (2014). Social work practice with LGBT seniors. *Journal of Gerontological Social Work, 57*(8), 889–907. doi:10.1080/01634372.2014.885475

Grossman, A. H. (2006). Physical and mental health of older lesbian, gay, and bisexual adults. In D. Kimmel, T. Rose, & S. David (Eds.), *Lesbian, gay, bisexual and transgender aging: Research and clinical perspectives* (pp. 53–69). New York, NY: Columbia University Press.

Guasp, A. (2011). *Lesbian, gay and bisexual people in later life.* London: Stonewall. www.stonewall.org.uk

Hicks, D. W. (2011). Case discussion of treatment of an 83-year-old gay white male. *Journal of Gay and Lesbian Mental Health, 15*(4), 392–400. doi:1080/19359705.2011.606069

Hidalgo, H., Peterson, T. L., & Woodman, N. J. (1985). Introduction. In H. Hidalgo, T. L. Peterson & N. J. Woodman (Eds.), *Lesbian and gay issues: A resource manual for social workers* (p. 106). Silver Spring, MD: NASW, Inc.

Hoy-Ellis, C. P., Ator, M., Kerr, C., & Milford, J. (2016). Innovative approaches address aging and mental health needs in LGBTQ communities. *Generations, 40*(2), 56–62.

Hoy-Ellis, C. P., & Fredriksen-Goldsen, K. I. (2016). Lesbian, gay, and bisexual older adults: Linking internal minority stressors, chronic health conditions, and depression. *Aging & Mental Health, 20*(11), 1119–30. doi:10.1080/13607863.2016.1168362

Hoy-Ellis, C. P., Shiu, C., Sullivan, K. M., Kim, H-J., Sturges, A. M., & Fredriksen-Goldsen, K. I. (2017). Prior military service, identity, stigma, and mental health among LGBT older adults. *The Gerontologist, 57*(S1), S63–S71. doi:10.1093/geront/gnw173

Institute of Medicine. (2011). *The health of lesbian, gay, bisexual, and transgender people: Building a foundation for better understanding.* Washington, DC: National Academies Press.

Kertzner, R. M., Barber, M. E., & Schwartz, A. (2011). Mental health issues in LGBT seniors. *Journal of Gay & Lesbian Mental Health, 15*(4), 535–8. doi:10.1080/19359705.2011.606680

Kim, H-J., Acey, K., Guess, A. Jen, S., & Fredriksen-Goldsen, K. I. (2016). A collaboration for health and wellness: GRIOT Circle and Caring and Aging with Pride. *Generations, 40*(2), 49–55.

Kim, H-J., Fredriksen-Goldsen, K. I., Bryan, A. E. B., & Muraco, A. (2017). Social network types and mental health among LGBT older adults. *The Gerontologist, 57*(S1), S84–S94. doi:10.1093/geront/gnw169

Kim, H-J., Jen, S., & Fredriksen-Goldsen, K.I. (2017). Racial/ethnicity and health-related quality of life among LGBT older adults. *The Gerontologist, 57*(S1), S30–S39. doi:10.1093/geront/gnw172

Linscott, B., & Krinsky, L. (2016). Engaging underserved populations: Outreach to LGBT elders of color. *Generations, 40*(2), 34–7.

Masini, B. E., & Barrett, H. A. (2008). Social support as a predictor of psychological and physical well-being and lifestyle in lesbian, gay, and bisexual adults aged 50 and over. *Journal of Gay & Lesbian Social Services, 20*(1–2), 91–110. doi:10.1080/10538720802179013

McGovern, J. (2014). The forgotten: Dementia and the aging LGBT community. *Journal of Gerontological Social Work, 57*(8), 845–57. doi:10.1080/01634372.2014.900161

Meyer, I. H. (2003). Prejudice, social stress, and mental health in lesbian, gay, and bisexual populations: Conceptual issues and research evidence. *Psychological Bulletin, 129*(5), 674–97.

National LGBTQ Task Force. (n.d.). *(In)validating transgender identities: Progress and trouble in the DSM-5.* www.thetaskforce.org/invalidating-transgender-identities-progress-and-trouble-in-the-DSM-5/

Orel, N. A., & Coon, D. W. (2016). The challenges of change: How can we meet the care needs of the ever-evolving LGBT family? *Generations, 40*(2), 41–5.

Rowan, N. L., & Butler, S. S. (2014). Resilience in attaining and sustaining sobriety among older lesbians with alcoholism. *Journal of Gerontological Social Work, 57*(2–4), 176–97. doi:10.1080/01634372.2013.859645

Rubin, H. C., & Ortmann, D. M. (2011). "Today is not a good day": Psychotherapy and psychiatric treatment with an 83-year-old gay man. *Journal of Gay and Lesbian Mental Health, 15*(4), 382–91. doi:1080/19359705.2011.606066

Scherrer, K. S. (2017). Stigma and special issues for bisexual older adults. In K. M. Hash & A. Rogers (Eds.), *Annual review of gerontology and geriatrics: Contemporary issues and future directions in lesbian, gay, bisexual and transgender aging* (vol. 33; pp. 43–57). New York, NY: Springer.

Seelman, K. L. (2019). Differences in mental, cognitive, and functional health by sexual orientation among older women: Analysis of the 2015 Behavior Risk Surveillance System. *The Gerontologist, 59*(4), 749–59. doi:10.1093/geronto/gnx215

Tinney, J., Dow, B., Mande, P., Purchase, R. Whyte, C., & Barrett, C. (2015). Mental health issues and discrimination among older LGBTI people. *International Psychogeriatrics, 27*(9), 1411–6. doi:10.1017/S1041610214002671

Wallace, S. P., Cochran, S. D., Durazo, E. M., & Ford, C. L. (2011). *The health of aging lesbian, gay and bisexual adults in California.* Policy Brief: Center for Health Policy Research. https://www.ncbi.nlm.nih.gov/pmc/articles/PMC3698220/

Witten, T. M. (2003). Transgender aging: An emerging population and an emerging need. *Sexologies, 12*(4), 15–20.

Witten, T. M. (2014). It's not all darkness: Robustness, resilience, and successful transgender aging. *LGBT Health, 1*(1), 24–33. doi:10.1089/lgbt.2013.0017

Yarns, B. C., Abrams, J. M., Meeks, T. W., & Sewell, D. D. (2016). The mental health of older LGBT adults. *Current Psychiatry Report, 18*(6), 60. doi:10.1007/s11920-016-0697-y

Zelle, A., & Arms, T. (2015). Psychosocial effects of health disparities of lesbian, gay, bisexual and transgender older adults. *Journal of Psychosocial Nursing, 53*(7), 25–40. doi:10.3928/02793695-20150623-04

CHAPTER

22 Mental Health of Sexual and Gender Minority Immigrants and Refugees

Edward Ou Jin Lee, Sarilee Kahn, Edward J. Alessi, *and* Abelardo Leon

Abstract

This chapter aims to provide a critical review of the literature that addresses the ways in which sexual and gender minorities (SGMs) with migration experience navigate mental health issues. There has been a recent growth in public interest and scholarship in Canada and the United States about the realities of SGMs with migration experience. However, there are scholarly debates and tensions in relation to how key terms related to sexuality, gender, and migration have been mobilized within this field of knowledge. This chapter thus aims to map out the ways in which knowledge about SGMs with migration experience has been categorized through migrant status, race, and ethnicity. In addition, this chapter provides a synthesis of the latest research findings on the relationship between this population and mental health issues. This chapter also critically reflects on various policy and practice implications of these findings and considers future directions for content, theories, and methodologies of research about this population.

Keywords: migration, sexuality, gender, mental health, refugee, forced migration, newcomer

This current era is marked by a global flux of migrations and, in particular, forced migrations, whereby people are compelled to leave their country of origin due to social, economic, and geopolitical forces of war, dictatorship, persecution, overdevelopment, resource extraction, natural disaster, and human rights violations (Castles, De Haas, & Miller, 2014). Among the increasing number of people who migrate annually are people with diverse and non-normative sexual and gender expressions and identities who encounter varying levels of acceptance, exclusion, and violence both in their country of origin and their host country (Abu-Assab, Nasser-Eddin, & Greatrick, 2017; Carroll & Ramon Mendos, 2017). Throughout the migration process, sexual and gender minorities (SGMs) navigate many challenges on both interpersonal and structural levels, including issues related to mental health.

There has also been a growth in public interest in Canada and the United States about the realities of SGMs with migration experience, coinciding with an increase in knowledge produced about this population. Over the past two decades, there has been an increase in scholarship about SGMs with migration experience, with a particular focus in Canada on refugees and in the United States on binational marriage sponsorship and undocumented people. Although this body of literature has explored the legal, psychosocial, structural, and political dimensions related to the realities of this population, only more recently have studies focused specifically on mental health and SGMs with migration experience.

This chapter will provide a critical review of the empirical literature that addresses the various ways in which SGMs with migration experience navigate mental health issues, as well as proposed clinical frameworks for mental health service delivery for this population. Upon tracing the literature, key gaps in knowledge are identified as well as future clinical, theoretical, and methodological directions for researchers and practitioners interested in advancing knowledge in this area. Before turning to the literature review, we briefly discuss the ways in which knowledge about SGMs with migration experience has been categorized. Indeed, researchers have inconsistently mobilized migrant categories (e.g., economic-class immigrant, refugee, family-class sponsorship). These inconsistencies result in a lack of clarity about how various types of migration categories actually shape SGM experiences.

The Challenge of Categorizing Race, Ethnicity, and Migration

Commonly used SGM population categories that include those with migration experience are often based on race and/or ethnic group such as Black/African American, Latinx, and Asian/Pacific Islander as well as the category of "people of color." While this body of literature most likely includes SGMs with and without migration experience, some studies do not clarify how many participants within their sample have migration experience. Most (but not all) scholarship focused on SGM Latinx and Asian/Pacific Islander populations has included measures to assess the number of participants in their sample who were migrants (e.g., questions related to place of birth, years living in Canada or the United States) (Lee, 2015). In contrast, many (but not all) studies related to SGM Black/African American communities did not include these measures, and yet there has been significant migration to Canada and the United States from African countries (Lee, 2015).

The mobilization of these categories for research with various SGM communities is certainly useful and relevant for SGM people with migration experience. However, some of these studies do not attend to the specific ways in which the migration process shapes every facet of the lives of SGMs, including its impact on mental health. Although anti-Black racism impacts all Black SGMs, the ways in which a Black SGM person who has lived in Canada or the United States for many generations navigates, for example, mental health services in a hospital will differ (due to the historical legacy of slavery) from the experiences of a Black SGM person who migrated to Canada or the United States. Certainly, all chapters overlap with each other to some degree, as SGM people with migration experience include those who are asexual, pansexual, intersex, trans, nonbinary, polyamorous, and so forth. However, we especially encourage readers to engage with this chapter in close conversation with the chapters in this book focused on Black/African-American, Asian/Pacific Islander, and Latinx SGM mental health (Chapters 15, 16, and 17). Our aim is to complement these chapters by focusing on the literature in which all or most of the participant samples are SGM people with migration experience.

Unpacking Migrant Categories and Implications for Research about SGMs

The international migration process entails an individual or group leaving one nation-state and entering another (Castles et al., 2014). According to Castles et al. (2014), "the tendency of migration studies [is] to focus on the consequences of immigration in wealthy, migrant-receiving societies, and to ignore the causes and consequences of migration in origin countries" (p. 26). The migration process of SGMs, especially those from the Global South, to Canada and the United States are thus informed by global historical, economic, and geopolitical forces.

In Canada and the United States, migrant categories such as "immigrant" and "refugee" are often assumed to have always existed, with people divided between those who "choose" versus those who are "forced" to migrate. However, scholars have critiqued the ways in which migrant categories are socially produced, with the Canadian and U.S. governments having historically constructed immigration/colonization laws in racialized, gendered, and sexualized ways in order to justify the surveillance, deportation, and exclusion of certain groups of people (Castles et al., 2014; Lee, 2018; Luibheid, 2008a, 2008b). Migrant categories have shifted and changed over time, resulting in the various inclusion and/or exclusion of certain people, based not only on the circumstances of individual migrants but also on the desires and will of governments to control migration.

It is certainly outside the scope of this chapter to provide a more detailed overview of this historical context and shifts and changes over time within Canadian and U.S. migration law (see Cantu, 2009; Lee, 2018; Luibheid, 2008b; Shah, 2011). Thus, our intent for this chapter is to draw from key migrant categories to organize and assess the literature while also attending to the ways in which SGMs navigate migrant categories that do not neatly fit the circumstances that led them to migrate. For example, thousands of Syrians, including those who are SGMs, have migrated to Canada over the past few years, mostly as refugees. However, some Syrians have also arrived in Canada under temporary status (e.g., visitor, student, temporary worker) and subsequently filed refugee claims or applied to become permanent residents, while others have had the financial and educational means to be classified by the government as an "economic class" immigrant. Syrians thus accessed various migrant categories, based on how these categories were organized, as well as their socioeconomic positions and the particular ways in which the Syrian war shaped each of their lives.

Moreover, the migrant categories produced by the Canadian and U.S. governments have been taken up in various ways by researchers focusing on SGMs with migration experience. Researchers have also mobilized non–state-produced terms that emerged from academic and community milieus. As a result, researchers have mobilized an array of migrant categories, such as newcomer, immigrant, refugee, migrant, forced migrant, migrant with precarious status, undocumented, and so forth. These categories are used by scholars in ways that are often inconsistent with their formulation by the government. In some cases, asylum seekers and undocumented people were included in studies that focused on SGM newcomers and immigrants. Therefore, for this chapter, we have chosen to use the term *migrant* as an umbrella term to include all SGMs with migration experience.

At the same time, this chapter will place an emphasis on SGMs who were compelled or forced to migrate to Canada and/or the United States. This decision is mostly due to there being very few studies that focus solely on SGMs who migrated to Canada or the United States without being compelled to and solely based on accessing an economic-based immigration pathway due to their individually based work, educational, and financial means. Forced migration is defined as the coerced movement of people due to war, political violence, development projects, environmental change (e.g., climate change, natural disasters), human rights violations, and trafficking (Castles, 2003; Crépeau et al., 2006; Nassari, 2009). The term *forced migration* also includes the refugee category, while also recognizing the limitations of its international legal definition that does not fully capture the complex set of factors that compel and/or facilitate coerced movements (Crépeau et al., 2006). Indeed, the economic, political, and social positioning that shapes forced migrations makes it more or less difficult for each particular forced migrant to access the refugee claim process that results in a successful decision (of being named a refugee) (Castles & Van Hear, 2005; Lee, 2015). Moreover, forced migration is influenced by a multitude of factors, some of which do not neatly fit as "forced" or "not voluntary" (Castles & Van Hear, 2005). Forced migrants with financial and educational means can access pathways to permanent residency even when they are compelled to leave their country due to the fear of persecution. This critical literature review is thus informed by the complex ways in which the state, academia, and communities themselves mobilize various migrant categories.

In addition, most studies of SGM migrants include mental health issues as one element, among many, such as access to healthcare and social services, integration within general society and various communities (e.g., immigrant, SGM), and so forth. For this set of literature, our aim is to synthesize the sections of these studies that address the ways in which the migration process shapes mental health outcomes. This chapter will also highlight the key findings from emerging studies in which the mental health issues faced by SGM migrants or clinical frameworks for mental health service delivery for this population were the central objectives of the study. We conclude with presenting key knowledge gaps and exploring future directions for research.

From Psychosocial to Mental Health Research on SGM Migrants

Empirical research on the mental health of SGM migrants has expanded over the past several years. The earliest literature on SGM migrants predominantly focused on the importance of meeting the psychosocial needs of SGM newcomers (Chavez, 2011; Heller, 2009). In terms of psychological symptoms, the majority of research has focused on SGM immigrants from Latin America (e.g., Choi, Paul, Ayala, Boylan, & Gregorich, 2013; Cochran, Mays, Alegria, Ortega, & Takeuchi, 2007; Diaz, Ayala, Bein, Henne, & Marin, 2001; Gilbert, Barrington, Rhodes, & Eng, 2016). For example, one study revealed that experiences of discrimination based on multiply marginalized identities (sexual orientation/gender identity *and* ethnic or racial identity) were linked to depression for Latino and Latina SGM immigrants living in the United States (Sun et al., 2016). Increasingly, however, researchers are turning their attention to the mental health of immigrants from other countries as well. For example, depression has also been shown to associate with substance abuse and posttraumatic stress disorder (PTSD) among African men who recently migrated to the United States and who suffered abuse in their countries of origin as well as in the host country (Ogunbajo, Anyamele Restar, Dolezal, & Sanfort, 2019).

In addition to research on SGM immigrants, a growing body of literature has highlighted the mental health of SGM forced migrants. In one of the first practice-based publications on the topic, Reading and Rubin (2011) described a therapy group for SGM forced migrants, informed by Judith Herman's (1997) trauma and empowerment framework. Indeed Shidlo and Ahola's (2013) work revealed that SGM forced migrants have been subjected to severe and prolonged traumatic events motivated by stigma and discrimination in their countries of origin and that this exposure was related to mental health disorders such as PTSD and complex PTSD. Individuals with complex PTSD frequently manifest all of the symptoms of PTSD but also present with more severe symptoms, including alteration in affect and impulses, severe dissociation, alterations in self-perception and perception of the perpetrator, difficulty relating with others, and somatization (Pelcovitz et al., 1997).

Empirical Research on the Mental Health of SGM Forced Migrants

Since the publication of Shidlo and Ahola's (2013) article, empirical studies on the mental health of SGM forced migrants have emerged. Quantitative studies seek to document the scope of mental health needs for SGM forced migrants. The focus of extant quantitative studies can be divided into four categories: (1) psychological symptoms, (2) traumatic and stressful events and their impacts; (3) promising treatment modalities; and (4) frameworks for clinical practice. In three studies that used an analysis of documents, researchers have found that SGM forced migrants frequently contend with anxiety, depression, substance abuse, PTSD, and suicidal ideation and attempts.

Of these studies, Piwowarczyk, Fernandez, and Sharma (2017) and Gowin, Taylor, Dunnington, Alshuwaiyer, and Cheney (2017) reported a notably high prevalence of mental health disorders for PTSD (70 percent and 100 percent), depression (76 percent and 93 percent), anxiety (28 percent and 60 percent), and substance use (2 percent and 36 percent), respectively. Two studies—Gowin et al. (2017) and Hopkinson et al. (2017)—reported past or present suicidality (56 percent and 72.1 percent), respectively. The sample sizes were relatively small (N = 45 for Gowin et al., 2017; N = 50 for Piwowarczyk et al., 2017; and N = 61 for Hopkinson et al., 2017), and the sample in Hopkinson et al.'s (2017) study was predominately cis men and did not include transgender participants. By way of comparison, in Piwowarczyk et al.'s (2017) study, 56 percent were cis women, and that study also did not include transgender participants. In contrast, participants in the Gowin et al. (2017) study reportedly were all trans women asylum seekers. Despite the limitations of these studies, the rates of psychological symptoms are nonetheless striking in that they are higher than those found in either cis or heterosexual SGM migrant populations (White, Cooper, & Lawrence, 2019).

Qualitative studies highlighting the lived experiences of pre- and post-migration traumatic events for SGM forced migrants can shed light on the reasons for the mental health problems in this population. These studies have shown that by the time SGM individuals arrive in host countries, they have experienced severe and prolonged trauma, precipitated by physical, sexual, and emotional abuse; forced hospitalization; and wrongful imprisonment (Alessi, Kahn, & Chatterji, 2016; Alessi, Kahn, & Van Der Horn, 2017; Alessi, Kahn, Woolner, & Van Der Horn, 2018; Hopkinson et al., 2017; Jordan, 2009; Kahn, Alessi, Kim, Olivieri, & Woolner, 2017). Victimization had begun in childhood and continued into adolescence and adulthood, and the violence had been perpetrated by family, community members, school officials, and state actors (Alessi et al, 2016, 2017; Jordan 2009). Although not focused solely on mental health, there is a growing body of literature that describes how SGM forced migrants respond to interpersonal and state violence both in their countries of origin and their host countries by defending their rights (El-Hage & Lee, 2016; Terriquez, 2015) and mobilizing informal support networks (Lee, 2019; Padilla, Rodriguez-Madera, Varas-Dias, & Ramos-Pibernus, 2016).

As we have discussed, these experiences of victimization may contribute to PTSD and complex PTSD. To make matters worse, when SGM individuals had sought protection from police in their countries of origin, either they were blamed for bringing abuse on themselves because of their sexual orientation or gender identity, or they were further victimized by those presumably charged with protecting citizenry (Alessi et al., 2016, 2017; Jordan, 2009; Kahn et al., 2017). Situations such as these have the potential to exacerbate the trauma SGM forced migrants have experienced by family and community members as well as state actors (Alessi et al., 2016). Taken together, these circumstances have prompted SGM forced migrants to attempt suicide to escape from feelings of utter despair and hopelessness (Alessi et al., 2016; Kahn & Alessi, 2018).

Findings from these qualitative studies are consistent with those employing quantitative measures to identify psychiatric symptoms and suicidality (see Gowin et al., 2017; Hopkinson et al., 2017).

However, a recent scoping review of the SGM migrant literature, as well as scholarship on the realities of SGM people living in the Global South, suggests that the kinds of homophobic and transphobic violence that compel SGM people to flee are intimately tied to national and regional political climate (e.g., civil unrest, generalized violence), a patriarchal social order, and economic inequalities on a global scale (Lee et al., 2017). This report suggests that research on the mental health of SGM migrants should be further contextualized to take into account the broader social and political forces that shape psychiatric symptoms, depression, suicidality, and so forth (Lee et al., 2017). Tourki, Lee, Baril, Hébert, and Pullen Sansfaçon (2018) accomplished this by situating the negative mental health outcomes of trans migrant youth from Syria and Guatemala within a complex historical, geopolitical, and cisnormative context.

Mental Health Consequences in Relation to the Refugee Process

Although the application of international and national refugee law in Canada, the United States, and the European Union (EU) does not fully capture the complex factors that shape forced migration, studies demonstrate that these laws directly shape the ways in which refugee claimants navigate mental health issues (Alessi, Kahn, Greenfield, Woolner, & Manning, 2020; Heller, 2009; Jordan, 2009; Lee & Brotman, 2011). Lee and Brotman (2011) describe how heteronormative and cisnormative processes embedded within the Canadian refugee process result in the retraumatization of SGM people due to being compelled to out themselves to various actors (e.g., doctor, bank employee, social worker), resulting in marked vulnerability to homophobia and transphobia. However, very few empirical studies have traced the mental health consequences for SGM forced migrants seeking asylum.

In one qualitative study focused on the mental health consequences of bureaucratic asylum-seeking processes for SGM claimants (Kahn & Alessi, 2018), findings suggest that premature disclosure of a history of sexual violence, rushed deadlines for filing a refugee claim, and being "forced" to come out could contribute to mental health crises and identity disorientation for SGM claimants, which could possibly persist long after a positive asylum claim decision. Beyond these asylum-seeking processes, researchers underscore that existing psychological symptoms may be exacerbated by multiple stressors associated with all aspects of settlement, acculturation, and/or managing precarious immigration status (Alessi, 2016; Kahn, 2015a). Studies have demonstrated that SGM forced migrants are exposed not only to the stressors experienced by other asylum seekers but also those related to their sexual orientation and gender identity (Alessi, 2016; Kahn, 2015a). In addition to facing discrimination based upon multiply marginalized identities (Fuks, Smith, Pelàez, De Stefano, & Brown, 2018), all SGM migrants must navigate this discrimination while securing safe housing, gainful employment, healthcare, and a social network (Lee & Brotman, 2011).

Research has shown that stressors related to one's sexual orientation or gender identity, known as minority stress (Hendricks & Testa, 2012; Meyer, 2003), accounts for the disparity in the prevalence of mental illness for SGM individuals in general, which may also include SGM migrants. Furthermore, it has been well documented that SGM migrants are often distanced from their families and diaspora communities (Kahn, 2015b; Lee & Brotman, 2011). SGM migrants may find that these losses are even more painful than the homophobic and transphobic abuse they have suffered (Reading & Rubin, 2011). Without a strong social network, SGM migrants in all categories may lack the social support necessary for well-being (Hynie, Crooks, & Barragan, 2011) and social integration (Alessi & Kahn, 2017).

To date, one empirical study (Alessi, 2016) has identified factors that promoted resilience in SGM forced migrants; these included sustaining a positive and hopeful outlook, connecting with one's spirituality or faith, leveraging legal and community-based services, "doing whatever it takes," giving back to one's community, and locating and using social support. Various study findings also showed that resilience could coexist with distress in this population; in other words. SGM refugees and asylum seekers navigated the challenges of asylum seeking and resettlement while they continued to be affected by anxiety, depression, and traumatic stress (Alessi, 2016; Lee & Brotman, 2011, 2013).

Mental Health Consequences for SGM Migrants with Precarious Status

This section includes studies that include SGM migrants with precarious status, meaning that their migrant status is temporary and conditional, resulting in uneven access to services, resources, public goods, and rights (Goldring & Landolt, 2013). Precarious status includes visitor, international student, temporary worker, family or spouse sponsorship, refugee claimant/asylum seeker, protected person, as well as persons detained or undocumented. In particular, this section aims to focus on scholarship that explores the mental health consequences for SGM migrants who are detained and/or undocumented. This section also includes studies that focus on immigrants and/or newcomers but set the parameters of their participant samples to include those with precarious status, such as refugee claimants and undocumented people (Lee et al., 2017; Melendez, Zepeda, Samaniego, Charavarty, & Alaniz, 2013; Morales, 2013; Rhodes et al., 2015). Overall, these studies tend to focus less on particular immigration and/or refugee policies and more on broader issues of housing, employment, education, HIV risk, community belonging, mental health, and so forth.

The studies that include the experiences of SGM migrants who are detained after migration (e.g., after submitting a refugee claim, becoming undocumented) suggest that detention is detrimental to one's mental health (Bachmann, 2016; Cowen, Stella, Magahy, Strauss, & Morton, 2011; Lee & Brotman, 2011). In Lee and Brotman's (2011) study, even after leaving detention, a participant "continued to live with negative psychological and physical health consequences, including those stemming from the frustration with not being provided a clear rationale for decisions being made throughout the process" (p. 257). Studies, mostly from the United States, that include the realities of SGM undocumented migrants also link undocumented status to reduced or denial of access to essential health and social services, resulting in negative mental health consequences (Cisneros, 2015; Cruz, 2008; Jordan, 2009). Cisneros (2015) suggests that SGM undocumented people are living in a "constant state of vulnerability" (p. 150), resulting in social isolation and, for some, suicidality.

Recently, a study examined the realities of trans migrant and racialized youth in Quebec, suggesting a linkage between various structural barriers related to the medical, social, and legal transition process and negative mental health outcomes (Tourki et al., 2018). In their study, one trans migrant youth described the psychological distress experienced due to not being able to afford the costs related to their medical transition (e.g., paying for hormone therapy, gender-confirming surgery) and not being able to access mental health services, because of their precarious status and the lengthy wait period before becoming a permanent resident. Not being able to change one's legal name or gender marker in Quebec until becoming a citizen also resulted in negative mental health consequences.

Specialized Mental Health Service Delivery for SGM Migrants

There remains a lack of studies that provide a more in-depth examination on how the migration process shapes the mental health of SGM migrants with precarious status. Empirical studies of the effectiveness of particular treatments and interventions for SGM migrants are just emerging. In a 2016 qualitative study evaluating the experience of group therapy support for SGM newcomers, Logie et al. (2016) found that participation in a social support group fostered improved mental health and self-acceptance; increased social connection; reduced stigma; and increased networking opportunities in locating housing, employment, secure immigration status, and healthcare.

Other case-based studies discussed group therapy approaches as important modalities to facilitate community, provide psychoeducation, and build resilience for SGM forced migrants (Beaudry, 2018; Nerses, Kleinplatz, & Moser, 2015; Reading & Rubin, 2011). Applying an intersectional and trauma-informed approach, Beaudry (2018) described facilitating a support group with mostly SGM refugees, with group members being able to process difficult mental health–related challenges such as depression, anxiety, and suicide through dialog and mutual support. Through the group process, members strengthened ties to build and foster a "chosen family" (Hicks, 2011) as a way to resist intersectionally informed heteronormative and cisnormative forces while also building collective empowerment (Beaudry, 2018).

To support clinicians serving SGM migrants in their quest to provide culturally competent and affirmative services, researchers have begun to discuss best practices for working with this population. In their guidelines for medical and psychiatric evaluation of SGM forced migrant patients, Hopkinson and Keatley (2017) urged medical providers to allow enough time to build trust in order to conduct a thorough physical and mental health assessment, provide SGM forced migrant patients with strategies for managing the overwhelming feelings that may result during history taking, and attend to the hierarchy of needs for this patient population (e.g., ensuring access to food, shelter, and clothing).

Alessi and Kahn (2017) offered a detailed practice framework specifically for clinicians providing treatment to SGM asylum seekers. Building on the concepts of complex trauma (Courtois, 2004; Herman, 1997), minority stress (Meyer 2003), integration (Ager & Strang, 2008), and resilience (Luthar, Cicchetti, & Becker, 2000), Alessi and Kahn (2017) suggest using a culturally competent, affirmative, trauma-informed framework. Implementation involves building trust, establishing environmental (external) safety and emotional (internal) safety for SGM asylum-seeking clients, promoting practical and emotional skills for managing the asylum claims process, connecting with others, and developing a sense of purpose and meaning.

Best practices, of course, are meaningless if SGM migrants cannot access clinical services. As Chen, Li, Fung, and Wong (2015) suggest, "migrants in search of health care are often deterred by the lack of culturally or linguistically appropriate services, the complexity of Canadian health care system, and a fear that service use would jeopardize the outcome of immigration or refugee claims" (p. 510). Nakamura and Kassan (2013) present a multicultural feminist counseling framework for clinical practice with cis immigrant sexual minority women who migrated to the United States through same-gender couple sponsorship. This framework suggests taking into account a person's multiple and intersecting identities through a cultural identity model that includes individual counseling with advocacy.

Research on access to mental health care for SGM migrants remains scant. In one study of facilitators and barriers to SGM forced migrants' access to mental health care, Kahn, Alessi, Kim, Olivieri, and Woolner (2018) found that it is often difficult to locate competent mental health providers who also understand the psychosocial impacts of intersecting identities for SGM asylum seekers and refugees, and who were both SGM-affirmative and culturally sensitive. Moreover, the study demonstrated that stigmatization of mental health problems, perceptions that mental health practitioners may be untrustworthy (as they were in the country of origin), and structural factors, such as no or limited health insurance coverage, could prevent the population from accessing care. They recommended both culturally sound individual counseling and community-based support. Others have discussed how holding racialized and marginalized sexual orientation and/or gender identities negatively impacts SGM migrants' perceptions of access to healthcare services (Tanner et al., 2014). Although not focused on mental health delivery, Lee and Brotman (2013) suggested that a core feature of engaging in anti-oppressive practice included accompaniment of SGM migrants: "by making visible the hidden structural dimensions that contribution to the oppression, social workers can begin to co-construct narratives of resistance with queer and trans people with refugee experiences" (citing Heller, 2009, p. 174).

Knowledge Gaps and Future Directions for Research

While the research discussed in this chapter has helped to move knowledge on the mental health of SGM forced migrants forward, there remain significant knowledge gaps. For example, the majority of studies to date involved samples composed mostly of cis gay men, with fewer cis lesbian women, cis bisexual men and women, and trans individuals (White et al., 2019). One exception is Gowin et al.'s (2017) study, which focused on trans asylum seekers. Tourki et al.'s (2018) study suggests that an intersectional lens to tracing the ways in which the migration process shapes the social, legal, and medical transitions of trans migrants points to areas for future research on the mental health consequences of migration laws on trans-specific health and social services.

Researchers must make a concerted effort to recruit cis lesbian women, cis bisexual men and women, and trans individuals to ensure that their specific mental health needs are identified and their lived experiences are prioritized when developing practice frameworks and mental health intervention for SGM migrants. As it has been clearly established with non-refugee SGM populations, within-group differences must be accounted for, as lumping all SGM individuals into one group may miss the complexities of their experiences as well as particular nuances that must be considered when developing mental health interventions. For example, lesbian refugees and asylum seekers may be less likely to participate in research because of fear of further abuse or exploitation by authority figures and/or hesitation to disclose their sexual orientation. The violence experienced in their countries of origin may have been perpetrated by families who forced them to enter heterosexual marriages, only complicating their refugee process as they attempt to prove they are "actually lesbian" (Lewis, 2014; Millbank, 2002). Cis queer and lesbian women and trans people may not feel comfortable in group interventions that include predominantly gay cis men due to sexism and transphobia (Lee & Brotman, 2011).

Other knowledge gaps also exist with respect to SGM migrants. There remain very few studies that focus on the mental health of SGM migrants, either how pre- and post-migration processes inform mental health or issues related to access to mental health services, and, in particular, hospital and/or acute care in relation to mental illness. While scholars have begun to identify best practices with this population and research has demonstrated that a combination of individual, group, and community-based support is helpful for dealing with mental health issues, evidence-based treatments do not exist for this population, making it difficult to know what treatments work better than others. Although a number of mental health interventions have been designed to treat traumatic stress among refugees (e.g., narrative exposure therapy), no treatments have been developed for SGM migrants. This is an issue warranting immediate attention because interventions used to treat refugees may not account for issues related to persecution based on sexual orientation or gender identity. At the same time, affirmative psychotherapy interventions for SGM individuals may overlook the complexities surrounding forced migration and integration. It may also be helpful to compare the mental health intervention strategies mobilized specifically for SGM migrants versus SGM ethnic-racial communities and/or Indigenous peoples.

Finally, further studies should be conducted that focus on how SGM migrants both individually and collectively foster, build, and promote their mental health and resilience. For example, there is a need for studies that can pay attention to the ways in which SGM migrants respond to various forms of structural violence (Lee, 2018) in order to further trace how they navigate and manage various mental health–related symptoms. This also points to the ways in which peer-based intervention models may be useful for this population.

Future Directions for Theories and Methodologies

Informed by the critical literature review, we present some key theories and methodologies that should be integrated into future research projects that advance knowledge about SGM migrants. Although intersectionality has been mobilized for research about SGM migrants (Lee & Brotman, 2011), it has not yet surfaced in scholarship that focus on mental health and trauma, with some exceptions (Beaudry, 2018; Kahn et al., 2018). Research on the mental health of SGM migrants using an intersectional lens illuminates how issues related to race/ethnicity, migration status, social class, sexual orientation, and gender identity and expression interact to increase risk and resilience for this population. Intersectionality also requires that researchers further examine the ways in which social structures operate, resulting in differing levels of power and privilege afforded to normative bodies (Collins, 2002; Crenshaw, 1991; Lee & Brotman, 2013).

In addition, mental health–focused studies with SGM migrants can also apply a holistic health model in order to attend to the ways in which physical, mental, behavioral, and sexual health are interconnected and shaped by various interpersonal, environmental, and structural stressors (Gilbert et al., 2016). Gilbert et al. (2016) suggest that research on Latino men who have sex with men (MSM) migrants must expand beyond sexual behaviors and HIV risk and "recognize that sexual health is a key component of MSM health, [but] they urge caution against perpetuating a narrow focus that disregards other health domains" (p. 523).

As described in the previous section, more research should be done that adapts, implements, and evaluates various intervention strategies, such as the treatment of traumatic stress while also being SGM-affirmative. In addition, peer-based intervention models, such as those developed for street-involved youth or people living with mental health challenges, can be adapted, implemented, and evaluated to address the particular needs and challenges faced by SGM migrants. Peer-based practice models further develop the capacity of directly impacted community members, community organizations, and service providers who value and wish to promote the further participation of SGM migrants in the provision of mental health services and/or accompaniment to improve access to these services.

Studies about this topic should also critically reflect on the ways in which directly impacted people can be involved in the research process, not only as research participants. Various community-based and participatory research methodologies can be mobilized in order to ensure that SGM migrants contribute to the research design (i.e., as part of an advisory committee), work as research assistants, and contribute to data collection and synthesis. The involvement of directly impacted people not only enhances how a project is designed but also supports longer-term community capacity building (Lee, 2018; Lee & Miller, 2014; Tourki et al., 2018). Over time, directly impacted people can also be supported to take leadership roles within research projects.

Case Study: ÉTRANGEr: Fostering Collective Empowerment through Community-Based Research among MSM Latino Immigrants

This is a case study of a current research project titled "ÉTRANGEr" that is applying community-based and participatory methodologies to foster the collective empowerment of MSM Latino migrants living in Montreal; mental health is a core part of the project. Dr. Abelardo Leon and Dr. Edward Lee conducted the study with community partner REZO, a Montreal-based organization whose mission favors a holistic approach to health promotion by delivering services and programs for MSM. Funded by the Social Sciences and Humanities Research Council, this project used the Photovoice research methodology and qualitative interviews with MSM Latino migrants living in Montreal with the aim of highlighting community perspectives and improving access to REZO's programs and services. As a participatory methodology, Photovoice brings together six to eight participants. Each takes a series of photos and then shares them with the group in a series of workshops to develop collective themes and identify key policy and practice recommendations (Wang & Burris, 1997).

Some of the topics addressed related to MSM Latino migrant realities (e.g., migration, homophobia, racism) and perspectives (e.g., HIV stigma), and mental health emerged as a central theme. For some participants, the migration process resulted in unexpected social isolation, leading to anxiety and depression. For example, some participants disclosed having to deal with social isolation, anxiety, depression, and panic attacks for the first time in their lives after migrating to Montreal. Other participants had difficulties in accessing mental health services due to a bureaucratic medical system and the lack of culturally and linguistically appropriate services. One participant described how even within the MSM Latino community, he experienced HIV-related discrimination, contributing to isolation:

> I was dating a person... My friends took the opportunity to tell the person that I had AIDS. When I came back into the room, he [the person I dated] had disappeared from the house. I went out to look for this man. I couldn't find him, his car was gone... it hurt a lot, I entered into a deep depression because I felt so bad, since people were leaving me for having HIV.[1]

This quote highlights the ways in which MSM Latino migrants living with HIV must navigate multiple layers of stigma and discrimination. It also points to the relevance of an intersectional analysis in order to produce knowledge about SGM migrants that takes into account multiple sources of marginalization.

Conclusion

This chapter aimed to provide a critical review of the empirical scholarship focusing on the ways in which SGM migrants live with mental health consequences due to interpersonal and/or structural violence related to both pre- and post-migration and/or experience barriers to mental health service delivery. More recently, there are studies emerging that focus on implementing and evaluating specialized mental health services for SGM migrants. However, there continues to be a lack of research that centers the experiences of cis queer and lesbian as well as trans migrants.

Our literature review suggests that additional research should be done that includes mental health as central to the study research question and objectives. We also suggest the adaptation, implementation, and evaluation of intervention-based projects that advance the capacity of community organizations and health and social service providers to provide specialized services for SGM migrants. Studies that mobilize peer-based intervention strategies may also result in the creation of innovative practices that build the capacity of directly impacted people. Finally, we suggest that researchers should also apply community-based and participatory principles into their research design, including data collection, analysis, and knowledge mobilization, in order to foster the direct involvement of directly impacted people throughout the research process.

[1] Original quote: «Yo estaba saliendo con una persona... En ese momento mis amigos aprovecharon la oportunidad de contarle a la persona que yo estaba viendo que yo tenía SIDA. Cuando yo regresé él había desaparecido de la casa. Y yo salí a buscar a este señor, ya no lo encontré, ya no estaba su carro. Y a mí me dolió mucho, me dolió mucho. Y yo tuve una gran depresión porque yo me sentí muy mal, ya que me estaban dejando por tener VIH."

References

Abu-Assab, N., Nasser-Eddin, N., & Greatrick, A. (2017). *Conceptualising sexualities in the MENA region: Undoing* LGBTQI categories: Implications for rights-based advocacy approaches. London: Centre for Transnational Development and Collaboration.

Ager, A., & Strang, A. (2008). Understanding integration: A conceptual framework. *Journal of Refugee Studies, 21*, 166–91. doi:10.1093/jrs/fen016

Alessi, E. J. (2016). Resilience in sexual and gender minority forced migrants: A qualitative analysis. *Traumatology, 22*, 203–13. doi:10.1037/trm0000077

Alessi, E., & Kahn, S. (2017). A framework for clinical practice with sexual and gender minority asylum seekers. *Psychology of Sexual Orientation and Gender Diversity, 4*, 383–91. doi:10.1037/sgd0000244

Alessi, E. J., Kahn, S., & Chatterji, S. (2016). The darkest times of my life: Recollections of child abuse among forced migrants persecuted because of their sexual orientation and gender identity. *Child Abuse & Neglect, 51*, 93–105. doi:10.1016/j.chiabu.2015.10.030

Alessi, E. J., Kahn, S., & Van Der Horn, R. (2017). A qualitative exploration of the premigration adult victimization experiences of sexual and gender minority refugees and asylees in the United States and Canada. *Journal of Sex Research, 54*, 936–48. doi.org/10.1080/00224499.2016.1229738

Alessi, E. J., Kahn, S., Woolner, L., & Van Der Horn, R. (2018). Traumatic stress among sexual and gender minority refugees from the Middle East, North Africa, and Asia who fled to the European Union. *Journal of Traumatic Stress, 31*, 805–15. doi:10.1002/jts. 22346

Alessi, E. J., Kahn, S., Greenfield, B., Woolner, L., & Manning, D. (2020). A qualitative exploration of the integration experiences of LGBTQ refugees who fled from the Middle East, North Africa, and Central and South Asia to Austria and the Netherlands. *Sexuality Research and Social Policy, 17*, 13–26. doi:10.1007/s13178-018-0364-7

Bachmann, C. L. (2016). *No safe refuge: Experiences of LGBT asylum seekers in detention.* UK Lesbian & Gay Immigration Group: Stonewall. http://www.stonewall.org.uk/media-centre/media-release/no-safe-refuge-for-lgbt-asylum-seekers

Beaudry, C. (2018). "Le groupe, c'est ma famille": La famille choisie selon l'intersectionnalité poststructurelle et l'approche informée par le trauma auprès d'un groupe pour minorités sexuelles et de genre migrantes. *Interventions, 148*, 17–27.

Cantu, L. (2009). *The sexuality of migration: Border crossings and Mexican immigrant men.* New York, NY: New York University Press.

Carroll, A., & Ramon Mendos, L. (2017). State-sponsored homophobia: A world survey of sexual orientation laws: criminalization, protection and recognition. International Lesbian, Gay, Bisexual, Trans and Intersex Association (ILGA). https://ilga.org/state-sponsored-homophobia-report-2017-ILGA

Castles, S. (2003). Towards a sociology of forced migration and social transformation. *Sociology, 37*(1), 13–34.

Castles, S., De Haas, H. & Miller, M. J. (2014). *The age of migration: International population movements in the modern world* (5th ed.). New York, NY: Guilford Press.

Castles, S., & Van Hear, N. (2005). *Developing DFID's policy approach to refugees and internally displaced persons.* Report to the Conflict and Humanitarian Affairs Department. Oxford, UK: Refugee Studies Centre.

Chavez, K. (2011). Identifying the needs of LGBTQ immigrants and refugees in southern Arizona. *Journal of Homosexuality, 58*, 189–218. doi:10.1080/00918369.2011.540175

Chen, Y. B., Li, A. T. W., Fung, K. P. L., & Wong, J. P. H. (2015). Improving access to mental health services for racialized immigrants, refugees, and non-status people living with HIV/AIDS. *Journal of Health Care for the Poor and Underserved, 26*(2), 505–18. doi:10.1353/hpu.2015.0049

Choi, K. H., Paul, J., Ayala, G., Boylan, R., & Gregorich, S. E. (2013). Experiences of discrimination and their impact on the mental health among African American, Asian and Pacific Islander, and Latino men who have sex with men. *American Journal of Public Health, 103*(5), 868–74. doi:10.2105/AJPH.2012.301052

Cisneros, J. (2015). *Undocuqueer: Interacting and working within the intersection of LGBTQ and undocumented.* PhD dissertation, Arizona State University. https://repository.asu.edu/items/34804

Cochran, S. D., Mays, V. M., Alegria, M., Ortega, A. N., & Takeuchi, D. (2007). Mental health and substance use disorders among Latino and Asian American lesbian, gay, and bisexual adults. *Journal of Consulting and Clinical Psychology, 75*(5):785–94. doi:10.1037/0022-006x.75.5.785.

Collins, P. H. (2002). *Black feminist thought: Knowledge, consciousness, and the politics of empowerment.* New York, NY: Routledge.

Courtois, C. A. (2004). Complex trauma, complex reactions: Assessment and treatment. *Psychotherapy: Theory, Research, Practice, Training, 41*, 412–25. doi:10.1037/0033–3204.41.4.412

Cowen, T., Stella, F., Magahy, K., Strauss, K. & Morton, J. (2011). *Sanctuary, safety and solidarity: Lesbian, gay, bisexual, transgender asylum seekers and refugees in Scotland.* Scotland: Equality Network BEMIS and GRAMNet. https://www.equality-network.org/wp-content/uploads/2015/04/Sanctuary-Safety-Solidarity-Report-Summary-Version-March-2011.pdf

Crenshaw, K. (1991). Mapping the margins: Intersectionality, identity politics and violence against women of color. *Stanford Law Review, 43*(6), 1241–99.

Crépeau, F., Nakache, D., Collyer, M., Nathaniel, H. G., Hansen, A., Modi, R., . . . Willigen, L. H. M. (2006). *Forced migration and global processes: A view from forced migration studies.* Lanham, MD: Rowman & Littlefield Publishers Inc.

Cruz, C. (2008). Notes of immigration, youth and ethnographic silence. *Theory into Practice, 47*(1), 67–73. doi:10.1080/00405840701764797

Díaz, R. M., Ayala, G., Bein, E., Henne, J., & Marin, B. V. (2001). The impact of homophobia, poverty, and racism on the mental health of gay and bisexual Latino men: Findings from 3 US cities. *American Journal of Public Health, 91*(6), 927–32. doi:10.2105/ajph.91.6.927.

El-Hage, H., & Lee, E. O. (2016). LGBTQ racisés: Frontières identitaires et barrières structurelles. *Alterstice: Revue Internationale de la Recherche Interculturelle, 6*(2), 13–27. doi:10.7202/1040629ar

Fuks, N., Smith, N., Pelàez, S., De Stefano, J., & Brown, T. (2018). Acculturation experiences among lesbian, gay, bisexual, and transgender immigrants in Canada. *The Counseling Psychologist, 46*(3), 296–332. doi:10.1177/0011000018768538

Gilbert, P. A., Barrington, C., Rhodes, S. D., & Eng, E. (2016). *Saliendo adelante*: Stressors and coping strategies among immigrant Latino men who have sex with men in a nontraditional settlement state. *American Journal of Men's Health, 10*(6), 515–25. doi:10.1177/1557988316647704

Goldring, L., & Landolt, P. (2013). The conditionality of legal status and rights: Conceptualizing precarious non-citizenship in Canada. In L. Goldring & P. Landolt (Eds.), *Producing and negotiating non-citizenship: Precarious legal status in Canada* (pp. 3–30). Toronto: University of Toronto Press.

Gowin, M., Taylor, E. L., Dunnington, J., Alshuwaiyer, G., & Cheney, M. K. (2017). Needs of a silent minority: Mexican transgender asylum seekers. *Health Promotion Practice, 18*(3), 332–40. doi:10.1177/1524839917692750

Heller, P. (2009). Challenges facing LGBT asylum-seekers: The role of social work in correcting oppressive immigration processes. *Journal of Gay & Lesbian Social Services, 21,* 294–308. doi:10.1080/10538720902772246

Hendricks, M. L., & Testa, R. J. (2012). A conceptual framework for clinical work with transgender and gender nonconforming clients: An adaptation of the minority stress model. *Professional Psychology: Research and Practice, 43,* 460–7. doi:10.1037/a0029597

Herman, J. (1997). *Trauma and recovery.* New York, NY: Basic Books.

Hicks, S. (2011). *Lesbian, gay and queer parenting: Families, intimacies, genealogies.* New York, NY: Palgrave Macmillan.

Hopkinson R., & Keatley, E. S. (2017). LGBT forced migrants. In K. L. Eckstrand & J. Potter (Eds.), *Trauma, resilience, and health promotion for LGBT patients: What every healthcare provider should know* (pp. 121–32). New York, NY: Springer.

Hopkinson, R. A., Keatley, E., Glaeser, E., Erickson-Schroth, L., Fattal, O., & Nicholson Sullivan, M. (2017). Persecution experiences and mental health of LGBT asylum seekers. *Journal of Homosexuality, 64,* 1650–66. doi:10.1080/00918369.2016.1253392

Hynie, M., Crooks, V. A., & Barragan, J. (2011). Immigrant and refugee social networks: Determinants and consequences of social support among women newcomers to Canada. *Canadian Journal of Nursing Research, 43*(4), 26–46.

Jordan, S. R. (2009). Un/Convention(al) refugees: Contextualizing the accounts of refugees facing homophobic or transphobic persecution. *Refuge, 26*(2), 165–82. https://refuge.journals.yorku.ca/index.php/refuge/article/view/32086

Kahn, S. (2015a). Cast out: "Gender role outlaws" seeking asylum in the West and the quest for social connections. *Journal of Immigrant & Refugee Studies, 13,* 58–79. doi:10.1080/15562948.2014.894169

Kahn, S. (2015b). Experiences of faith for gender role non-conforming Muslims in resettlement: Preliminary considerations for social work practitioners. *British Journal of Social Work, 45,* 2038–55. doi:10.1093/bjsw/bcu060

Kahn, S., & Alessi, E. J. (2018). Coming out under the gun: Exploring the psychological dimensions of seeking refugee status for LGBT claimants in Canada. *Journal of Refugee Studies, 31,* 22–41. doi:10.1093/jrs/fex019

Kahn, S., Alessi, E., Kim, H., Olivieri, C., & Woolner, L. (2017). Promoting the wellbeing of lesbian, gay, bisexual, and transgender forced migrants in Canada: Providers' perspectives. *Culture, Health & Sexuality, 19,* 1165–79. doi:10.1080/13691058

Kahn, S., Alessi, E. J., Kim, H., Olivieri, C., & Woolner, L. (2018). Facilitating mental health support for LGBT forced migrants in Canada: A qualitative inquiry. *Journal of Counseling & Development, 96,* 316–26. doi:10.1002/jcad.12205

Lee, E. O. (2015). The social organization of queer/trans migrations: The everyday experiences of queer and trans migrants with precarious status. PhD Dissertation. Montréal: McGill University.

Lee, E. O. (2018). Tracing the coloniality of queer and trans migrations: Resituating heterocisnormative violence in the Global South and encounters with migrant visa ineligibility to Canada. *Refuge: Canada's Journal on Refugees, 34*(1), 60–74. doi:10.7202/1050855ar

Lee, E. O. (2019). Responses to structural violence: The everyday ways in which queer and trans migrants with precarious status respond to and resist the Canadian immigration regime. *International Journal of Child, Youth & Family Studies, 10*(1), 70–94. doi:10.18357/ijcyfs101201918807

Lee, E., & Brotman, S. (2011). Identity, refugeeness, belonging: Experiences of sexual minority refugees in Canada. *Canadian Review of Sociology/Revue canadienne de sociologie, 48,* 241–74. doi:10.1111/j.1755-618x.2011.01265.x

Lee, E. O., & Brotman, S. (2013). Speak Out! Structural intersectionality and anti-oppressive practice with sexual minority refugees in Canada. *Canadian Social Work Review, 30*(2), 157–83.

Lee, E. O., Hafford-Letchfield, T., Pullen Sansfaçon, A., Kamgain, O., Gleeson, H., & Luu, F. (2017). *The state of knowledge about LGBTQI migrants living in Canada in relation to the global LGBTQI rights agenda.* Montréal: Université de Montréal.

Lee, E. O., & Miller, L. (2014). Collaborative media making with queer and trans refugees: Social locations, competing agendas and thinking structurally. In H. M. Pleasants & D. E. Salter (Eds.), *Community-based multiliteracies and digital media projects: Questioning assumptions and exploring realities.* New York, NY: Peter Lang Publishing.

Lewis, R. A. (2014). Gay? Prove it: The politics of queer anti-deportation activism. *Sexualities, 17*(8), 958–75. doi:10.1177/1363460714552253

Logie, C. H., Lacombe-Duncan, A., Lee-Foon, N., Ryan, S., & Ramsay, H. (2016). "It's for us—newcomers, LGBTQ persons, and HIV-positive persons. You feel free to be": A qualitative study exploring social support group participation among African and Caribbean lesbian, gay, bisexual and transgender newcomers and refugees in Toronto, Canada. *BMC International Health & Human Rights, 16*(1), 18. doi:10.1186/s12914-016-0092-0

Luibheid, E. (2008a). Queer/migration: An unruly body of scholarship. *GLQ: A Journal of Lesbian and Gay Studies, 14*(2–3), 169–90. doi:10.1215/10642684-2007-029

Luibheid, E. (2008b). Sexuality, migration and the shifting line between legal and illegal status. *GLQ: A Journal of Lesbian and Gay Studies, 14*(2–3), 289–315. doi:10.1215/10642684-2007-034.

Luthar, S. S., Cicchetti, D., & Becker, B. (2000). The construct of resilience: A critical evaluation and guidelines for future work. *Child Development, 71,* 543–62. doi:10.1111/1467–8624.00164

Melendez, R. M., Zepeda, J., Samaniego, R., Chakravarty, D., & Alaniz, G. (2013). "La Familia" HIV prevention program: A focus on disclosure and family acceptance for Latino immigrant MSM to the USA. *Salud Publica de Mexico, 55*(Suppl. 4), S491–S497.

Meyer, I. H. (2003). Prejudice, social stress, and mental health in lesbian, gay, and bisexual populations: Conceptual issues and research evidence. *Psychological Bulletin, 129,* 674–97. doi:10.1037/0033–2909.129.5.674

Millbank, J. (2002). Imagining otherness: Refugee claims on the basis of sexuality in Canada and Australia. *Melbourne University Law Review, 26*, 144–77. http://www5.austlii.edu.au/au/journals/MelbULawRw/2002/7.html

Morales, E. (2013). Latino lesbian, gay, bisexual, and transgender immigrants in the United States. *Journal of LGBT Issues in Counseling, 7*(2), 172–84. doi:10.1080/15538605.2013.785467

Nakamura, N., & Kassan, A. (2013). Understanding the experiences of immigrant sexual minority women through a cultural identity model. *Women and Therapy, 36*(3–4), 252–67. doi:10.1080/02703149.2013.797848

Nassari, J. (2009). Refugees and forced migrants at the crossroad: Forced migration in a changing world. *Journal of Refugee Studies, 22*(1), 1–10. doi:10.1093/jrs/fen050

Nerses, M., Kleinplatz, P. J., & Moser, C. (2015). Group therapy with International LGBTQ+ clients at the intersection of multiple minority status. *Psychology of Sexualities Review, 6*(1), 99–109.

Ogunbajo, A., Anyamele, C., Restar, A. J., Dolezal, C., Sandfort, T. G. (2019). Substance use and depression among recently migrated African gay and bisexual men living in the united states. *Journal of Immigrant and Minority Health, 21*(6), 1224–32. doi:10.1007/s10903-018-0849-8

Padilla, M. B., Rodriguez-Madera, S., Varas-Dias, N., & Ramos-Pibernus, A. (2016). Trans-migrations: Border-crossing and the politics of body modification among Puerto Rican transgender women. *International Journal of Sexual Health, 28*, 261–77. doi:10.1080/19317611.2016.1223256

Pelcovitz, D., Van der Kolk, B., Roth, S., Mandel, F., Kaplan, S., & Resick, P. (1997). Development of a criteria set and a Structured Interview for Disorders of Extreme Stress (SIDES). *Journal of Traumatic Stress, 10*, 3–16. doi:10.1002/jts.2490100103

Piwowarczyk, L., Fernandez, P., & Sharma, A. (2017). Seeking asylum: Challenges faced by the LGB community. *Journal of Immigrant and Minority Health, 19*(3), 723–32. doi:10.1007/s10903-016-0363-9

Reading, R., & Rubin, L. R. (2011). Advocacy and empowerment: Group therapy for LGBT asylum seekers. *Traumatology, 17*(2), 86–98. doi:10.1177/1534765610395622

Rhodes, S. D., Alonzo, J., Mann, L., Simàn, F., Garcia, M., Abraham, C., & Sun, C. J. (2015). Using Photovoice, Latina transgender women identify priorities in a new immigrant-destination state. *International Journal of Transgenderism, 16*(2), 80–96. doi:10.1080/15532739.2015.1075928

Shah, N. (2011). *Stranger intimacy: Contesting race, sexuality and the law in the North American west.* Berkeley, CA: University of California Press.

Shidlo, A., & Ahola, J. (2013). Mental health challenges of LGBT forced migrants. *Forced Migration Review, 42*, 9–11. http://www.fmreview.org/sites/fmr/files/FMRdownloads/en/fmr42full.pdf

Sun, C., Ma, A., Tanner, A., Mann, L., Reboussin, B., Garcia, M., Alonzo, J., & Rhodes, S. (2016). Depressive symptoms among Latino sexual minority men and Latina transgender women in a new settlement state: The role of perceived discrimination. *Depression Research and Treatment*, Article 4972854. doi:10.1155/2016/4972854

Tanner, A., Reboussin, B., Mann, L., Ma, A., Song, E., Alonzo, J., & Rhodes, S. (2014). Factors influencing health care access perceptions and care-seeking behaviors of immigrant Latino sexual minority men and transgender individuals: Baseline findings from the HOLA intervention study. *Journal of Health Care for the Poor and Underserved, 25*(4), 1679–97. doi:10.1353/hpu.2014.0156

Terriquez, V. (2015). Intersectional mobilization, social movement spillover, and queer youth leadership in the immigrant rights movement. *Social Problems, 62*(3), 343–62. doi:10.1093/socpro/spv010

Tourki, D., Lee, E. O., Baril, A., Hébert, W., & Pullen Sansfaçon, A. (2018). Au-delà des apparences: Analyse intersectionnelle d'exprériences de jeunes trans migrants et racisés au Québec. *Revue Jeunes et Société, 3*(1), 133–53.

Wang, C. C., & Burris, M. (1997). Photovoice: Concept, methodology, and use for participatory needs assessment. *Health Education and Behaviour, 24*(3), 369–87. doi:10.1177/109019819702400309

White, L. C. J., Cooper, M., & Lawrence, D. (2019). Editorial: Mental illness and resilience among sexual and gender minority refugees and asylum seekers. *British Journal of General Practice, 69*(678), 10–1. doi:10.3399/bjgp19X700349

CHAPTER

23 Bisexual Mental Health

Wendy B. Bostwick *and* Elizabeth A. Harrison

Abstract

Bisexual people, or those who identify as having sexual and romantic attractions to more than one sex or gender, have emerged as a sexual minority group with unique mental health concerns and inequities. This chapter provides an overview of the extant literature related to a host of mental health disorders, highlighting findings among bisexual women and men in comparison to both lesbian/gay and heterosexual counterparts. The authors briefly note potential methodological issues that have not been previously discussed. The chapter then turns to relevant explanatory frameworks, and how these may be used to inform an understanding of mental health inequities among bisexual groups. Finally, suggestions are offered for areas of future research.

Keywords: bisexual, bisexual women, mental health, sexual and gender minorities, LGBT health

Introduction

As has been established throughout this book, the mental health needs, behaviors, and outcomes of lesbian, gay, bisexual, transgender, queer, intersex, and asexual populations—also referred to as sexual and gender minorities (SGMs)—often differ in significant ways from heterosexual and/or cisgender populations. In most areas, though not all, it is SGM groups who fare the worst. Even within SGM groups, however, there are differences of note. This chapter is dedicated specifically to the health of bisexual people, given the increasing body of evidence that points to health inequities among this group, over and above those experienced by lesbian and gay, and heterosexual groups.

Bisexuality is often still defined as attraction to both women and men (*Merriam-Webster*, n.d.). This definition, however, has been critiqued as reinforcing a gender binary and not adequately capturing attraction to those who are gender nonconforming or who otherwise do not identify as men or women (Flanders, 2017). Thus, a more inclusive and acceptable definition of bisexuality or a bisexual person is someone with sexual or romantic attraction to more than one sex or gender (Bisexual Resource Center, n.d.). Attraction, however, is only one dimension of sexual orientation (Laumann, Gagnon, Michael, & Michaels, 1994). Identity (or self-labeling as bisexual) and sexual behavior (or sexual activity with people of more than one sex or gender) are also facets of sexual orientation. In this chapter, "bisexual persons" are those who identify as such.

The Literature to Date on Sexual Orientation and Health

Given that bisexual identity is just as common as a gay or lesbian identity, and in some instances at least twice as common (Gates, 2010), and even more so among younger cohorts of women (Chandra, Copen, & Mosher, 2013), it's curious that bisexual groups have been so frequently overlooked in "LGBT" health research. One reason for this is the historically low base-rate of sexual minority persons in the general population, which in turn has resulted in many population-based studies creating a single "sexual minority" category in order to have sufficient statistical power when comparing to "sexual majority" groups. Another stems from health-related research that was primarily rooted in the context of sexual health, specifically the transmission of HIV, such that behavior-based categories (i.e., men who have sex with men and women who have sex with women) emerged and, in turn, erased sexual identities (Young & Meyer, 2005). In addition, these designations did not account for bisexual sexual behavior but simply lumped together *any* person who had engaged in same-sex sexual behavior, disregarding their sexual behavior with a different sex entirely.

Undergirding both of these circumstances, however, is a larger social and cultural context of epistemic erasure of bisexual persons (Yoshino, 2002), wherein binaristic thinking disallows bisexuality to exist as a stable and knowable concept. Certainly, scientific inquiry is not immune from employing such an epistemological lens, implicitly or explicitly, and such thinking informed research around sexuality, sexual orientation, and the connections between sexual orientation and health for most of the twentieth century (Angelides, 2001; Rust, 2002). Thankfully, as conceptions of sexuality and sexual orientation have continued to evolve and expand, the field of SGM health has grown as well, and the specific health concerns of bisexual-identified persons have received increasing attention. As bisexual groups have finally started to be considered as distinct from lesbian and gay persons in research and study samples, the health disparities specific to them have become visible.

In our overview of the literature, we focus on this century, unless referring to earlier foundational works. We also generally prioritize quantitative studies using probability samples, either at the state or national level, as those data are generalizable. If no probability studies exist, we discuss convenience-based samples. We report findings separately for women and men; however, as most probability surveys do not explicitly capture those who identify as transgender, gender nonconforming, and/or nonbinary, the gender identity of subgroups is not known.

Mood and Anxiety Disorders

One of the most consistent findings to date relates to heightened mood and anxiety disorders among bisexual persons. In particular, when assessing depression, anxiety, or related symptomology, it is most often bisexual women who fare the worst compared to both heterosexual and lesbian women. This finding has been shown across a number of countries, including the United States (Bostwick, Boyd, Hughes, & McCabe, 2010), Australia (Sabia, Wooden & Nguyen, 2018), Canada (Pakula, Shoveller, Ratner, & Carpiano, 2016; Steele, Ross, Dobinson, Veldhuizen, & Tinmouth, 2009), and France (Lhomond, Saurel-Cubizolles, Michaels, & CSF Group, 2014). While bisexual men demonstrate poorer mental health than their heterosexual counterparts (Bostwick et al., 2010; Lhomond et al., 2014; Steele et al., 2009), the pattern of difference is less consistent in comparison to gay men, with a number of studies showing no difference between bisexual and gay men.

The persistent and troubling pattern of mental health inequities among bisexual groups is crystalized in a meta-analysis of previous studies of sexual orientation and mental health (Ross et al., 2018). This analysis pooled studies that assessed both depressive and anxiety disorders and symptoms. In total, the pooled prevalence estimates of current depression and current anxiety among bisexual groups was the highest. Additionally, bisexual groups had significantly higher odds of both current depressive and anxiety symptomology than both heterosexual and gay/lesbian groups (Ross et al., 2018).

Findings also highlight sex/gender differences in the presence and magnitude of disparities (Ross et al., 2018). For example, when analyses were done separately by sex/gender, current depressive symptoms were 75 percent more likely among bisexual women as compared to lesbians, while comparisons of bisexual to gay men were not statistically significant (Ross et al., 2018). However, a comparison of current anxiety found that both bisexual women and men had higher odds of anxiety than lesbian and gay individuals. Sex-stratified analyses for anxiety and depressive symptoms showed significantly higher prevalence among both bisexual women and men compared to heterosexuals.

As least one national study in the United States, using criteria from the fifth edition of the *Diagnostic and Statistical Manual of Mental Disorders* (DSM-5; American Psychiatric Association, 2013), found no differences in the odds of any mood or anxiety disorder among either bisexual men or women in comparison to their gay/lesbian counterparts (Kerridge et al., 2017). Differences between bisexual and heterosexual counterparts, however, were pronounced, findings that are similar to earlier work describing sexual orientation differences in DSM-IV mental health disorders (Bostwick et al., 2010).

Substance Use Disorders

Another heavily researched non–sexual health issue among SGM populations concerns substance use and abuse, and this, too, is an area in which extant literature points to disparities among bisexual groups, with evidence showing bisexual women as being especially at risk (Medley et al., 2016), a pattern of risk that was first explicitly noted over fifteen years ago (McCabe, Hughes, & Boyd, 2004). The literature often considers use (of any kind) of alcohol, tobacco, and/or other drugs and disorders simultaneously. Though substance use, even in the absence of a diagnosed disorder, has clear mental health implications, this section will focus on disorders (conditions assessed by a diagnostic process), as the more expansive literature on substance use is covered in other chapters in this volume.

ALCOHOL USE DISORDERS

Alcohol use disorders (AUDs) are more common among sexual minorities than their heterosexual peers (Kerridge et al., 2017; McCabe, Hughes, Bostwick, West, & Boyd, 2009; Medley et al., 2016), yet the extent to which differences exist within sexual minority groups is not entirely consistent. In some studies reporting on past-year AUDs (Kerridge et al., 2017; McCabe et al., 2009) and lifetime AUDs (Kerridge et al., 2017), bisexual men had a higher prevalence of AUDs than gay and heterosexual men during the past year and during their lifetime, though in another study (Medley et al., 2016), past-year prevalence of AUDs was highest among gay men, though not significantly different than heterosexual men. When adjusting for demographic differences, bisexual and gay men both had significantly higher odds of AUD in one study (McCabe et al., 2009), and only gay men had higher odds as compared to heterosexual men in another (Kerridge et al., 2017). When directly comparing bisexual and gay men (Kerridge et al., 2017) over both lifetime and past year, accounting for sociodemographic characteristics, there were no significant differences in the odds of AUDs between bisexual and gay men.

Bisexual and lesbian women also differ significantly from their heterosexual counterparts in studies of AUDs, with a larger magnitude of difference in prevalence than seen among men, and with both groups of women at significantly higher odds of an AUD than heterosexual women (Kerridge et al., 2017). Bisexual women had higher odds of meeting criteria for AUDs in comparison to heterosexuals for both past-year (Kerridge et al., 2017; McCabe et al., 2009; Medley et al., 2016) and lifetime (Kerridge et al., 2017) timeframes. Direct comparisons of bisexual and lesbian women showed no significant differences in AUDs (Kerridge et al., 2017).

DRUG USE DISORDERS

Illicit drug use disorders are also more prevalent among sexual minority groups than heterosexuals (Medley et al., 2016). "Illicit" drugs typically include marijuana, cocaine, heroin, hallucinogens, inhalants, as well as prescription drugs used nonmedically (e.g., recreational use of prescription opioids) (Lipari & Van Horn, 2017). Because the base rate of single-substance use disorders, other than marijuana disorders, is so low in the general population, such disorders are typically aggregated into a single "illicit drug use disorder" category. One major U.S. study (Medley et al., 2016) found that past-year marijuana use disorders were significantly higher among both gay and bisexual men compared to heterosexual men, with no significant differences in any other category of drug use disorders. Past-year opioid use disorders have been shown to be significantly more likely among both gay and bisexual men as well (Duncan, Zweig, Hambrick, & Palamar, 2019). When reporting drug use disorders in the aggregate (i.e., "any drug use disorder"), bisexual and gay men both differed significantly from heterosexual men in the past year in some studies (McCabe et al., 2009; Medley et al., 2016) but not every study (Kerridge et al., 2017). Direct comparisons of bisexual to gay men yielded no significant differences in drug use disorder over the past year or lifetime (Kerridge et al., 2017).

While patterns of drug use disorders among bisexual men do not unequivocally demonstrate that bisexual men are at highest risk, findings among bisexual women show a more consistent concentration of risk related to drug use disorders. Studies show that bisexual women are most at risk for past-year opioid disorders (Duncan et al., 2019) and have significantly higher odds of past-year and lifetime drug use disorders (Kerridge et al., 2017). Bisexual women have the highest prevalence of lifetime drug use disorders of any group, irrespective of sex/gender—a full 30 percent of adult bisexual women met criteria for a drug use disorder (Kerridge et al., 2017). Across three age cohorts, bisexual women consistently had significantly higher odds of past-year alcohol or drug use disorders (Schuler, Rice, Evans-Polce, & Collins, 2018). In a study that reported on the prevalence of seven separate categories of drug use disorders, bisexual women had the highest prevalence on six of the seven, all of which were significantly higher than heterosexual women—lesbian women only reported significantly higher rates of two disorders (Medley et al., 2016).

NICOTINE USE DISORDERS

In studies that have reported on nicotine use disorders, prevalence was highest among both bisexual men and women, and both bisexual and gay/lesbian groups had significantly higher odds of nicotine use disorders than heterosexual women and men (Kerridge et al., 2017; McCabe et al., 2018). Though there were no significant differences between bisexual and lesbian/gay groups in direct comparisons (Kerridge et al., 2017), when data were stratified by age, bisexual women and men were the most likely of all groups to have a nicotine use disorder as older adults (55 years and older) (McCabe et al., 2018).

Suicide

Suicidality, or thoughts of, attempts at, or actually taking one's own life, is demonstrably higher among sexual minority populations (Haas et al., 2011). Some studies that considered bisexual groups separately (Bolton & Sareen, 2011; Conron, Mimiaga, & Landers, 2010) found lifetime suicide attempts and past-year suicidal ideation were significantly more common among bisexual women compared to heterosexuals, with bisexual women reporting the highest prevalence of suicide attempts of all groups. Reports of past-year suicidal ideation among bisexual women were ten times higher than lesbian or heterosexual women (Conron et al., 2010), and bisexual women had significantly higher odds of suicidal ideation than heterosexuals, while gay and lesbian groups did not differ from heterosexuals (Conron et al., 2010).

Recent meta-analytic work on the topic of suicidality provides much-needed insight into suicidality among bisexual persons specifically, in comparison to both heterosexual and lesbian/gay counterparts (Salway et al., 2019). As noted by the authors, suicidal ideation and attempt rates occurred along a consistent gradient wherein bisexual groups fared the worst, then gay/lesbian groups, then heterosexuals. Across a variety of measures, heightened risk was consistently concentrated among bisexual women. For example, in comparisons of bisexual to gay/lesbian groups, stratified by sex/gender, only bisexual women had significantly higher odds of lifetime and past-year suicidal ideation and attempt—no differences were found among bisexual men (Salway et al., 2019).

Posttraumatic Stress Disorder

Diagnosis of posttraumatic stress disorder (PTSD) requires exposure to a precipitating traumatic event, such as actual or threatened death, serious injury, or sexual violence (American Psychiatric Association, 2013). This disorder is unique in that it is conditionally linked to an event rather than being defined solely by a cluster of symptoms (Pai, Suris, & North, 2017). Because sexual minority persons, especially bisexual women, often report higher levels of physical or sexual assault, both as children and adults (McGeough & Sterzing, 2018; Roberts, Austin, Corliss, Vandermorris, & Koenen, 2010), it is logical to expect higher rates of PTSD among bisexual groups. And, in fact, studies point to notable disparities. Roberts et al. (2010) found that PTSD prevalence was highest among bisexual women, and it was significantly higher than in heterosexual women. Bisexual men did not differ significantly from heterosexuals, whereas gay men did (Roberts et al., 2010). In later work (Kerridge et al., 2017), a familiar pattern emerged wherein bisexual women reported the highest prevalence of PTSD of all groups—though in direct comparisons to heterosexuals, both lesbian/gay and bisexual groups had significantly higher odds of PTSD diagnoses across both the past year and lifetime. When comparing within sexual minority groups, the only significant difference was among bisexual women, who had nearly 2.5 times the odds of past-year PTSD compared to lesbians (Kerridge et al., 2017).

Other Disorders

A national study found that both bisexual women and men had a higher prevalence and odds of any lifetime and past-year personality disorders as compared to both heterosexual and lesbian/gay women and men, (Kerridge et al., 2017). The same study found significantly higher odds of bipolar disorder among bisexual women, but not bisexual men (Kerridge et al., 2017).

One probability study reported on schizophrenia and whether respondents had ever been diagnosed by a healthcare provider with "schizophrenia or psychotic episode or illness" (Bolton & Sareen, 2011, p. 37). Bisexual women were more likely to report this and to have significantly higher odds of such a diagnosis than heterosexual women; bisexual men did not differ from heterosexual men, and gay but not bisexual men had significantly higher odds of receiving such a diagnosis (Bolton & Sareen, 2011).

Literature focusing on eating disorders among sexual minority adults is predominantly from convenience samples and rarely considers bisexual groups as distinct from lesbian or gay groups. Additionally, the focus is less on disorders per se and more frequently on body image, weight, and/or disordered eating behaviors. One racially/ethnically diverse study that assessed full-syndrome and subclinical eating disorder by race, gender, and sexual orientation found that the prevalence of eating disorders was higher among sexual minority men, though bisexual and gay men were combined in a single category (Feldman & Meyer, 2007). Another study that surveyed women across thirty-three healthcare sites found that bisexual women were significantly more likely to report that they had ever had an eating disorder (Koh & Ross, 2006), and they differed significantly from lesbian, though not heterosexual, women.

The Global South

The few English-language studies of mental health among sexual minorities from the Global South (Asia, Africa, Latin America, and the Caribbean) that disaggregated bisexual groups were all convenience samples. A study in southwest China that tested the validity of a measure of internalized "homophobia" (Xu, Zheng, Xu, & Zheng, 2017) did not report differences between gay and bisexual men on psychological distress, but internalized homophobia was higher among bisexual men, and, in turn, psychological distress and internalized homophobia were significantly and positively associated. A large study of health disparities among sexual minorities in South Korea (n = 2,335) reported comparatively higher rates of depressive symptoms among bisexual and lesbian/gay women and men, as compared to heterosexuals, with the highest rates of depressive symptoms among bisexual women (Yi, Lee, Park, Choi, & Kim, 2017). Suicidal ideation and attempts were also higher among all sexual minority groups, compared to general population estimates, and bisexual women most frequently endorsed past-year suicidal ideation (Yi et al., 2017).

A scoping review of studies about sexual minority women in Latin America and the Caribbean (Caceres, Jackman, Ferrer, Cato, & Hughes, 2019) included twenty-two articles and noted that most were focused on sexual health. One study that reported on mental health separately for bisexual women found that they reported higher depression and anxiety than lesbians (Ramírez-Aguilar, Calderón, & Rebollar, 2016). A similar review of women in South Africa (Muller & Hughes, 2016) found even fewer studies (n = 15), and none appeared to report findings separately for bisexual women.

As has been noted throughout this brief discussion, there appears to be a least one consistent finding when reviewing mental health disorders among bisexual populations: *bisexual women fare the worst.* And while any one finding related to pronounced prevalence and odds of a mental health disorder among bisexual groups would be dispiriting, taken in total, with repeated patterns of concentrated risk across multiple disorders, the findings for bisexual women are somewhat harrowing. Before moving to our discussion of explanatory frameworks, it is necessary to highlight some methodological, and perhaps philosophical, issues and concerns vis-à-vis the extant literature and current research.

Methodological Considerations and Concerns

The literature reviewed so far largely, though not exclusively, reports on disorders as defined and assessed by the DSM (American Psychiatric Association, 2013). Leaving aside critiques of the DSM, using a diagnostic threshold, whether through survey assessments or as determined by a clinician, likely underestimates the extent to which people experience mental health problems. Findings are likely the lower-end estimates of the prevalence of mental health concerns and disorders. Additionally, comparisons across different versions of the DSM may be compromised by changes to disorder classifications and criteria that occurred in the DSM-5 especially (e.g., PTSD, Pai et al., 2017).

One concern, particularly in the area of psychotic and personality disorders, is the extent to which stereotypes about bisexual people factor into diagnostic criteria and processes. Individuals who write the DSM are influenced by discourses about ab/normality and set guidelines to define behaviors and characteristics that they believe fall outside of the norm (Crowe, 2000). The inclusion of homosexuality and gender identity disorder in previous versions of the DSM serves as a salient example of such defining of normal versus abnormal ways of being. Judgments about sexual abnormality are woven into diagnostic criteria for mental disorders. For example, "sexual indiscretions" are listed as possible symptoms of mania (associated with bipolar disorder) (Substance Abuse and Mental Health Services Administration, 2016), and impulsive "unsafe sex" is identified as a symptom of borderline personality disorder (National Alliance on Mental Illness, 2017)—both of which disorders are more prevalent among bisexual women (Kerridge et al., 2017). Given societal stereotypes of bisexual people as "sexually irresponsible" (Brewster & Moradi, 2010), it is possible that clinicians could be more likely to judge bisexual sexual behavior as risky or impulsive and, in turn, as symptoms associated with certain disorders. One study of ninety-seven graduate trainees found that their attitudes about bisexuality were significantly related to their clinical assessments of a fictional bisexual patient (Mohr, Israel, & Sedlacek, 2001).

Another issue to be mindful of is pathologizing responses to trauma as mental health disorders, when mental distress is an expected and understandable response to trauma. Feminist Mad Studies scholars have argued that often behaviors or characteristics labeled as "mental illness" stem from the trauma of violence, particularly sexist violence (Briggs & Cameron, 2015; Filson, 2016). Bisexual people experience childhood abuse at high rates (Friedman et al., 2011; Hughes, McCabe, Wilsnack, West, & Boyd, 2010) and as such might reasonably be expected to exhibit signs of disorders that are highly associated with childhood abuse. If this is the case, mental health professionals and researchers should reflect critically on the usefulness of ascribing a diagnosis to a person exhibiting expected responses to trauma. To the extent that such diagnoses assist people in accessing helpful and desired treatment, they may serve a useful purpose. However, this phenomenon also risks individualizing what should be seen as a societal problem.

Conceptual and Explanatory Frameworks

A number of frameworks are useful in describing how social, political, and cultural systems and structures influence the mental health of SGM persons. A report by the Institute of Medicine (2011) laid out four specific models and theories useful to understanding LGBT health issues writ large. We briefly review these here, noting how they are relevant to bisexual persons' mental health specifically. Readers should also consider how such frameworks may assist in better understanding the concentration of poor health outcomes among bisexual women. We also offer thoughts on the utility of additional perspectives that have not traditionally been employed in SGM health research.

Minority Stress Model

The minority stress model posits that minority groups face stressors associated with their minority status(es) that are unique and additive to everyday life stressors. In turn, the associated excess stress results in health disparities, particularly mental health disparities (Meyer, 2003). Minority stressors include enactments of discrimination, prejudice, and stigma. While this model is employed frequently as the primary explanatory framework for sexual minority health inequities (e.g., Institute of Medicine, 2011), the majority of work related to sexual minority stressors and mental health has presumed that experiences of lesbian, gay, and bisexual groups are the same, with inattention to how minority stressors might differ among sexual (and gender) minority groups. A growing body of work has explicitly taken up the issue of bisexual-specific minority stressors, such as anti-bisexual attitudes or prejudice, including microaggressions; rejection or exclusion from both heterosexual *and* lesbian gay communities; internalized biphobia and fear of being "out" as bisexual; and the lack of support from an identifiable bisexual community (Brewster & Moradi, 2010; Dyar & London, 2018; Mereish, Katz-Wise, & Woulfe, 2017; Molina et al., 2015). To date, findings are mixed regarding if or how such stressors influence mental health outcomes for bisexual persons. More research is needed to determine if bisexual-specific minority stressors are in fact the drivers of bisexual health inequities, or if they are but one piece of a more complex puzzle.

Social Ecological Model

The social ecological model highlights the importance of considering the individual as well as the social, cultural, and physical environment in which they are situated, and the interplay among multiple levels of influence (McLeroy, Bibeau, Steckler, & Glanz, 1988). The social ecological model considers five levels of influence: intrapersonal (e.g., beliefs and behaviors), interpersonal (e.g., family and peer relationships), institutional (e.g., policies and norms within schools, religious institutions), community (e.g., geographic neighborhood and networks), and policy (e.g., state and federal laws), which all affect and are affected by one another. There are a handful of studies that have employed a social ecological perspective to help explicate bisexual persons' mental health and related experiences (cf., Flanders, Dobinson, & Logie, 2015; Flanders, Robinson, Legge, & Tarasoff, 2016; Ross, Dobinson, & Eady, 2010; Ross et al., 2016), and they provide instructive examples of how ecological perspectives are useful to understanding mental health inequities among bisexual groups. For example, in framing the social determinants of bisexual mental health, Ross et al. (2010) identified relevant examples at the micro-level, such as individual struggles with identity and self-acceptance; the meso-level, such as un/supportive relationships, including with the "LGBT" community; and the macro-level, such as biphobia and monosexism (the cultural privileging of and assumptions related to single-gender–attracted persons), all of which are interwoven and mutually reinforcing. Using a social ecological framework to contextualize and categorize factors associated with bisexual mental health can also be useful in identifying types of interventions to address or prevent disparities, such as those at an individual level, which might address internalized biphobia, or more macro or structurally oriented interventions, which could seek to dismantle biphobic stereotypes and attitudes (Feinstein, Dyar, & Pachankis, 2019; Ross et al., 2010).

Life Course Perspective

The life course perspective takes a longitudinal look at the causes of health disparities over a person's entire life and posits three central tenets: critical periods, accumulation of risk, and intergenerational effects (Braveman & Barclay, 2009). Evidence suggests that there are critical periods, particularly in childhood, during which negative life events can have lasting effects on health throughout the lifetime, including neurologically (Lipina & Colombo, 2009). A large body of research shows that adverse childhood events impact adult health (Braveman & Barclay, 2009). This is of particular relevance to bisexual groups, as they often experience such events at high rates, or in higher numbers, than both heterosexual and lesbian/gay persons (Andersen & Blosnich, 2013; Austin, Herrick, & Proescholdbell, 2016). The life course perspective also considers the accumulation of risk, whereby trauma, discrimination, poverty, and other risk factors have cumulative effects on mental health over the lifetime (Braveman & Barclay, 2009). Accumulation of risk is relevant for bisexual populations, particularly women, given their high rates of co-occurring trauma, violence, and victimization (Bostwick, Hughes, Steffen, Veldhuis, & Wilsnack, 2019). Poverty is also disproportionately concentrated among bisexuals (Badgett, Durso, & Schneebaum, 2013; Gorman, Denney, Dowdy, & Medeiros, 2015; Ross et al., 2016). The interplay of these risk factors, why they should be so heavily concentrated among bisexual persons (women in particular), and how such risks operate over the life course, is a relatively unexplored area of inquiry. A life course approach requires more longitudinal research among SGM groups and would assist in teasing apart temporal ordering of risk and emergence of health disorders and disparities.

Another useful aspect of the life course perspective is the explicit acknowledgment of cohort effects, wherein shifting cultural and social contexts across generations are considered. As younger generations are reporting more sexual fluidity, and more bisexuality specifically (Ballard, 2018), and as societal attitudes become less negative toward bisexual groups (Dodge et al., 2016), we may start to see concomitant shifts in the health status of bisexual groups.

Finally, the life course perspective draws attention to the importance of studying the health of LGBTQ+ elders, which remains underresearched, especially among bisexual persons.

Intersectionality

Intersectionality posits that systems of power and oppression, such as racism, sexism, and heterosexism, are interlocking, intersecting, and overlapping (Combahee River Collective, 1978; Crenshaw, 1991). Thus, one cannot fully understand the effects of one system (e.g., heterosexism) without considering others (e.g., racism, sexism). When experiencing discrimination, an individual with multiple marginalized identities cannot always tell if the discrimination is based on their sexuality, race, gender, ability status, other factors, or all of the above (Crenshaw, 1991). The larger SGM literature has been largely inattentive to how intersecting minority identities may influence health behaviors and outcomes, either positively or negatively, and this is particularly true for women and bisexual groups. More research is needed, both quantitative and qualitative, to draw out the complexities of intersecting identities among bisexual groups, and how multiple minority statuses are associated with mental health outcomes. Intersectional perspectives may be especially helpful in contextualizing how gender and sexism are at play in producing such heightened mental health inequities among bisexual women.

Additional Frameworks for Consideration

Mad Studies

While dominant cultural discourse considers mental health disorders to be dysfunctions worthy of treatment and cure, this is not the only way to understand mental health conditions. The academic discipline of Mad Studies and the Mad Pride and consumer/survivor/ex-patient (c/s/x) activist movements present alternative views of mental wellness and mental distress (see LeFrançois, Menzies, & Reaume, 2013). Mad Studies and c/s/x movements highlight the impacts of sanism (discrimination and bias against people with mental illness) and discuss psychiatry and psychology as tools of power and social control. The Mad Pride movement uplifts the voices of individuals who are proud of their mental differences and find their disorders neither negative nor dysfunctional. A full discussion of Mad Studies and mad movements is far beyond the scope of this chapter, but we mention it here to suggest that not all people will view mental distress and/or mental disorders in the same way. Researchers and clinicians should take note of mental health disparities, as they are often markers of mental distress that bisexual people experience as a result of minority stress, discrimination, and trauma. However, it is certainly not the case that all mental health disorders are negative or inherently dysfunctional ways of being that should be eliminated. Finally, in discussing mental health disparities, scholars and clinicians must take care to not contribute to sanist discourses about mental illness, and must also carefully consider the social construction of what is considered normal.

Complex Embodiment

Disability embodiment theories offer a possible new avenue for thinking about bisexual mental health. Tobin Siebers's (2008) theory of complex embodiment describes that the social construction of identities happens through and onto bodies. Thus, the social construction of bisexuality can be considered akin to literal construction of a building—whereby cultural meanings ascribed to bisexuality are built onto bodies. Representations of bisexuality become part of the bodies and minds of bisexual people. Similar to the minority stress model, complex embodiment theory offers an explanation for how biphobia and discrimination can impact the bodies of bisexual people. One of several productive differences between the models is that complex embodiment also describes the importance of representation (Siebers, 2008). Thus, images, ideas, and messages about bisexuality in society, media, policies, organizations, and discourses have tangible impacts on the bodies and minds of bisexual people. Negative or nonexistent representations of bisexual people become a bodily matter rather than an abstract political concern. This theory would predict that cultural interventions such as improving bisexual visibility, increasing realistic and positive bisexual representation, and changing biphobic discourses could positively impact bisexual mental health. Given that many posit a lack of visibility of bisexuality as a contributor to mental health issues and disparities, complex embodiment may be an especially generative theory vis-à-vis bisexual mental health.

Future Directions

Protective Factors

Understanding the determinants of poor mental health among bisexual people is vital to designing effective interventions to prevent, reduce, and resolve disparities, yet an exclusive focus on disorders and disparities among marginalized groups runs the risk of reinscribing and reaffirming assumptions of pathology or dysfunction as essential or "natural" among that group (Bostwick & Hequembourg, 2013). To counter this, research should also be directed at determining those factors that promote health and well-being, or that buffer against potentially negative effects of discrimination or victimization. The work to date on protective factors specific to bisexuals has predominantly been among youth, although there is work showing that "positive" events associated with bisexuality, particularly affirmations and acceptance of bisexuality from others, can be protective against depressive or anxiety symptoms (Dyar & London, 2018; Flanders, Tarasoff, Legge, Robinson, & Gos, 2017). There is also evidence to suggest that involvement in LGBTQ (Craney, Watson, Brownfield, & Flores, 2018) or bisexual-specific communities (Lambe, Cerezo, & O'Shaughnessy, 2017) may be protective factors for bisexual women's mental health. Finally, while there is rather robust work demonstrating that supportive and equitable policies at the state level in the United States also serve as protective against mental health problems among SGM populations (Hatzenbuehler, Keyes, & Hasin, 2009), little of this work sorts out if or how such policies influence bisexual groups' mental health specifically.

Qualitative and/or Participatory Research

Qualitative research offers an opportunity for bisexual people to define their needs, strengths, and identities on their own terms and in their words (Callis, 2013; Dodge et al. 2012; Ross et al., 2010). Qualitative research also lends itself to more nuanced answers to questions than fixed quantitative survey options may offer. In the realm of mental health, an emerging body of qualitative research has offered some insights on how bisexual people perceive their own mental health and better illustrated the ways bisexual people perceive biphobia/anti-bisexual discrimination to have a strong impact on their mental health (cf. Flanders et al., 2015; Ross et al., 2010). Qualitative research on community priorities, bi-affirming environments, and bi-positive experiences is useful in considering interventions to improve bisexual mental health. Future qualitative research on bisexual mental health could further elucidate complexities of bisexual health, including the interplay between minority stressors, trauma, physical health, and mental health.

One particularly compelling possibility for future research is the methodology of participatory action research. Such research engages participants as co-researchers and co-creators of knowledge, and also encourages participants to take action together (Baum, MacDougall, & Smith, 2006). Such research could allow bisexual people to define their own issues and take steps toward unique solutions. As researchers grow to recognize the importance of interventions to address bisexual mental health disparities and move to propose possible solutions, it is crucial that these solutions be founded on the knowledge and desires of the community. Participatory action research could represent one method of moving toward community-generated solutions.

Diversification of Study Samples

Bisexual people exist on every continent, are old and young, are found across all racial and ethnic groups and all genders, and have been around for centuries. Yet many have quite legitimately critiqued the body of bisexual health research to date as monolithic, most especially with regard to race/ethnicity (Ghabrial & Ross, 2018), despite evidence that bisexual people are anything but homogenous (Bostwick & Dodge, 2019). Evidence also demonstrates that a large percentage of transgender people identify as bisexual (Meyer, Brown, Herman, Reisner, & Bockting, 2017), yet few studies include transgender people and/or provide adequate information about gender identity. Research on nonbinary and gender-nonconforming bisexual people is also extremely scarce. Future research should intentionally include bisexual transgender and gender-nonconforming people, and bisexual people of color, oversampling when necessary.

Research on bisexual people living outside the Global North is lacking. Although our understanding of this literature may be limited by relying solely on English-language literature, such research is still scarce. Findings on bisexual mental health may not be applicable to cultures and communities outside North America, Europe, and Australia and/or non–English-speaking countries. Studies by researchers from the Global South should be supported and highlighted.

An additional emphasis for future research is exploration of the wide variety of identities included under the non-monosexual umbrella. People take on differing non-monosexual identity labels—such as bisexual, pansexual, fluid, queer—for a variety of reasons (Flanders, 2017), and it is possible that individuals with differing identities have different experiences of mental health. Research that groups all sexual minority people who experience sexual and romantic attractions to people of multiple genders under one label (bisexual) can obscure intra-group differences. Qualitative research may be particularly useful in exploring the differing experiences and identities of those under the non-monosexual label.

Beyond Mental Health

A final area for future exploration is the interplay between physical and mental health among bisexual populations. Some physical health conditions, such as chronic pain, may be particularly intertwined with bisexual mental health concerns. Some preliminary data suggest that biphobic discrimination could be linked to pain, particularly among transgender bisexual people (Katz-Wise, Mereish, & Woulfe, 2017). In non-bisexual-specific populations, intimate partner violence (Breiding, Chen, & Black, 2014) and mood and anxiety disorders (Lerman, Rudich, Brill, Shalev, & Shahar, 2015; McWilliams, Cox, & Enns, 2003) have been shown to be associated with higher rates of chronic pain. Given that bisexual women experience high rates of intimate partner violence (Walters, Chen, & Breiding, 2013) and mood and anxiety disorders (see the section earlier in this chapter), pain may be a particularly relevant issue for bisexual women. Future research should further explore the interplay of chronic pain and other physical conditions with bisexual mental health.

Conclusion

Mental health disorders are highly prevalent among bisexual women and men, with the most pronounced disparities consistently residing within bisexual women, as compared to both lesbian and heterosexual groups. This pattern of disparity repeats itself across a range of disorders, such as mood and anxiety, personality, and substance use. Additionally, evidence suggests that risk factors associated with such disorders, such as victimization in both childhood and adulthood, are also quite high among bisexual women. With the preponderance of risk fairly well established, future work must focus on designing interventions to mitigate, resolve, and, ultimately, prevent such extraordinary inequities from arising in the first place. Additionally, the larger body of work devoted to bisexual mental health would benefit from additional study of both risk and protective factors for bisexual groups specifically, while also working to intentionally expand research to be more inclusive of a diverse array of genders, racial/ethnic identities, ages, geographies, and countries of origin.

References

Andersen, J. P., & Blosnich, J. (2013). Disparities in adverse childhood experiences among sexual minority and heterosexual adults: Results from a multi-state probability-based sample. *PLoS One, 8*(1), e54691. doi:10.1371/journal.pone.0054691

American Psychiatric Association. (2013). *Diagnostic and statistical manual of mental disorders* (5th ed.). Arlington, VA: Author.

Angelides, S. (2001). *A history of bisexuality*. Chicago, IL: University of Chicago Press.

Austin, A., Herrick, H., & Proescholdbell, S. (2016). Adverse childhood experiences related to poor adult health among lesbian, gay, and bisexual individuals. *American Journal of Public Health, 106*(2), 314–20. doi:10.2105/AJPH.2015.302904

Badgett, M. V., Durso, L. E., & Schneebaum, A. (2013). New patterns of poverty in the lesbian, gay, and bisexual community. Los Angeles, CA: Williams Institute, UCLA School of Law. https://escholarship.org/uc/item/8dq9d947.pdf.

Ballard, J. (2018). More young Americans now identify as bisexual. https://today.yougov.com/topics/relationships/articles-reports/2018/06/18/more-young-americans-now-identify-bisexual

Baum, F., MacDougall, C., & Smith, D. (2006). Participatory action research. *Journal of Epidemiology & Community Health, 60*(10), 854–7. doi:10.1136/jech.2004.028662

Bisexual [Def. 2]. (n.d.). *Merriam-Webster Online*. https://www.merriam-webster.com/dictionary/bisexual

Bisexual Resource Center. (n.d.). Labels. https://biresource.org/bisexuality-101/labels/

Bolton, S. L., & Sareen, J. (2011). Sexual orientation and its relation to mental disorders and suicide attempts: Findings from a nationally representative sample. *Canadian Journal of Psychiatry, 56*(1), 35–43. doi:10.1177/070674371105600107

Bostwick, W. B., Boyd, C. J., Hughes, T. L., & McCabe, S. E. (2010). Dimensions of sexual orientation and the prevalence of mood and anxiety disorders in the United States. *American Journal of Public Health, 100*(3), 468–75. doi:10.2105/AJPH.2008.152942

Bostwick, W. B., & Dodge, B. (2019). Introduction to the special section on bisexual health: Can you see us now? *Archives of Sexual Behavior, 48*(1), 79–87. doi:10.1007/s10508-018-1370-9

Bostwick, W., & Hequembourg, A. L. (2013). Minding the noise: Conducting health research among bisexual populations and beyond. *Journal of Homosexuality, 60*(4), 655–61. doi:10.1080/00918369.2013.760370

Bostwick, W. B., Hughes, T. L., Steffen, A., Veldhuis, C. B., & Wilsnack, S. C. (2019). Depression and victimization in a community sample of bisexual and lesbian women: An Intersectional approach. *Archives of Sexual Behavior, 48*(1), 131–41. doi:10.1007/s10508-018-1247-y

Braveman, P., & Barclay, C. (2009). Health disparities beginning in childhood: A life-course perspective. *Pediatrics, 124*(S3), S163–S175. doi:10.1542/peds.2009-1100D

Breiding, M. J., Chen, J., & Black, M. C. (2014). *Intimate partner violence in the United States—2010*. Atlanta, GA: Centers for Disease Control and Prevention.

Brewster, M. E., & Moradi, B. (2010). Perceived experiences of anti-bisexual prejudice: Instrument development and evaluation. *Journal of Counseling Psychology, 57*(4), 451–68. doi:10.1037/a0021116

Briggs, S., & Cameron, F. (2015). Psycho-emotional disablism, complex trauma, and women's mental distress. In H. Spandler, J. Anderson, & B. Sapey (Eds.), *Madness, distress and the politics of disablement* (pp. 99–112). Bristol, UK: Policy Press.

Caceres, B. A., Jackman, K. B., Ferrer, L., Cato, K. D., & Hughes, T. L. (2019). A scoping review of sexual minority women's health in Latin America and the Caribbean. *International Journal of Nursing Studies, 94*, 85–97. doi:10.1016/j.ijnurstu.2019.01.016

Callis, A. S. (2013). The black sheep of the pink flock: Labels, stigma, and bisexual identity. *Journal of Bisexuality, 13*(1), 82–105. doi:10.1080/15299716.2013.755730

Chandra, A., Copen, C. E., & Mosher, W. D. (2013). Sexual behavior, sexual attraction, and sexual identity in the United States: Data from the 2006–2010 National Survey of Family Growth. In A. K. Baumle (Ed.), *International handbook on the demography of sexuality* (pp. 45–66). Dordrecht, NL: Springer. doi:10.1007/978-94-007-5512-3_4

Combahee River Collective. (1978). A black feminist statement. Reprinted in *WSQ: Women's Studies Quarterly, 42*(3–4), 271–80. doi:10.1353/wsq.2014.0052

Conron, K. J., Mimiaga, M. J., & Landers, S. J. (2010). A population-based study of sexual orientation identity and gender differences in adult health. *American Journal of Public Health, 100*(10), 1953–60. doi:10.2105/AJPH.2009.174169

Craney, R. S., Watson, L. B., Brownfield, J., & Flores, M. J. (2018). Bisexual women's discriminatory experiences and psychological distress: Exploring the roles of coping and LGBTQ community connectedness. *Psychology of Sexual Orientation and Gender Diversity, 5*(3), 324–37. doi:10.1037/sgd0000276

Crenshaw, K. (1991). Mapping the margins: Intersectionality, identity politics, and violence against women of color. *Stanford Law Review, 43*(6), 1241–99. doi:10.2307/1229039

Crowe, M. (2000). Constructing normality: A discourse analysis of the DSM-IV. *Journal of Psychiatric and Mental Health Nursing, 7*(1), 69–77. doi:10.1046/j.1365-2850.2000.00261.x

Dodge, B., Herbenick, D., Friedman, M. R., Schick, V., Fu, T.-C. (Jane), Bostwick, W., . . . Sandfort, T. G. M. (2016). Attitudes toward bisexual men and women among a nationally representative probability sample of adults in the United States. *PLoS One, 11*(10), e0164430. doi:10.1371/journal.pone.0164430

Dodge, B., Schnarrs, P. W., Reece, M., Martinez, O., Goncalves, G., Malebranche, D., . . . Fortenberry, J. D. (2012). Individual and social factors related to mental health concerns among bisexual men in the Midwestern United States. *Journal of Bisexuality, 12*(2), 223–45. doi:10.1080/15299716.2012.674862

Duncan, D. T., Zweig, S., Hambrick, H. R., & Palamar, J. J. (2019). Sexual orientation disparities in prescription opioid misuse among U.S. adults. *American Journal of Preventive Medicine, 56*(1), 17–26. doi:10.1016/j.amepre.2018.07.032

Dyar, C., & London, B. (2018). Longitudinal examination of a bisexual-specific minority stress process among bisexual cisgender women. *Psychology of Women Quarterly, 42*(3), 342–60. doi:10.1177/0361684318768233

Feinstein, B. A., Dyar, C., & Pachankis, J. E. (2019). A multilevel approach for reducing mental health and substance use disparities affecting bisexual individuals. *Cognitive and Behavioral Practice, 26*(2), 243–53. doi:10.1016/j.cbpra.2017.10.003

Feldman, M. B., & Meyer, I. H. (2007). Eating disorders in diverse lesbian, gay, and bisexual populations. *International Journal of Eating Disorders, 40*(3), 218–26. doi:10.1002/eat.20360

Filson, B. (2016). The haunting can end: Trauma-informed approaches in healing from abuse and adversity. In J. Russo & A. Sweeney (Eds.), *Searching for a rose garden: Challenging psychiatry, fostering Mad Studies* (pp. 20–4). Monmouth, UK: PCCS Books.

Flanders, C. E. (2017). Under the bisexual umbrella: Diversity of identity and experience. *Journal of Bisexuality, 17*(1), 1–6. doi:10.1080/15299716.2017.1297145

Flanders, C. E., Dobinson, C., & Logie, C. (2015). "I'm never really my full self": Young bisexual women's perceptions of their mental health. *Journal of Bisexuality, 15*(4), 454–80. doi:10.1080/15299716.2015.1079288

Flanders, C. E., Robinson, M., Legge, M. M., & Tarasoff, L. A. (2016). Negative identity experiences of bisexual and other non-monosexual people: A qualitative report. *Journal of Gay & Lesbian Mental Health, 20*(2), 152–72. doi:10.1080/19359705.2015.1108257

Flanders, C. E., Tarasoff, L. A., Legge, M. M., Robinson, M., & Gos, G. (2017). Positive identity experiences of young bisexual and other nonmonosexual people: A qualitative inquiry. *Journal of Homosexuality, 64*(8), 1014–32. doi:10.1080/00918369.2016.1236592

Friedman, M. S., Marshal, M. P., Guadamuz, T. E., Wei, C., Wong, C. F., Saewyc, E. M., & Stall, R. (2011). A meta-analysis of disparities in childhood sexual abuse, parental physical abuse, and peer victimization among sexual minority and sexual nonminority individuals. *American Journal of Public Health, 101*(8), 1481–94. doi:10.2105/AJPH.2009.190009

Gates, G. J. (2010). Sexual minorities in the 2008 General Social Survey: Coming out and demographic characteristics. https://williamsinstitute.law.ucla.edu/wp-content/uploads/Gates-Sexual-Minorities-2008-GSS-Oct-2010.pdf

Ghabrial, M. A., & Ross, L. E. (2018). Representation and erasure of bisexual people of color: A content analysis of quantitative bisexual mental health research. *Psychology of Sexual Orientation and Gender Diversity, 5*(2), 132–42. doi:10.1037/sgd0000286

Gorman, B. K., Denney, J. T., Dowdy, H., & Medeiros, R. A. (2015). A new piece of the puzzle: Sexual orientation, gender, and physical health status. *Demography, 52*(4), 1357–82. doi:10.1007/s13524-015-0406-1

Haas, A. P., Eliason, M., Mays, V. M., Mathy, R. M., Cochran, S. D., D'Augelli, A. R., . . . Clayton, P. J. (2011). Suicide and suicide risk in lesbian, gay, bisexual, and transgender populations: Review and recommendations. *Journal of Homosexuality, 58*(1), 10–51. doi:10.1080/00918369.2011.534038

Hatzenbuehler, M. L., Keyes, K. M., & Hasin, D. S. (2009). State-level policies and psychiatric morbidity in lesbian, gay, and bisexual populations. *American Journal of Public Health, 99*(12), 2275–81. doi:10.2105/ajph.2008.153510

Hughes, T., McCabe, S. E., Wilsnack, S. C., West, B. T., & Boyd, C. J. (2010). Victimization and substance use disorders in a national sample of heterosexual and sexual minority women and men. *Addiction, 105*(12), 2130–40. doi:10.1111/j.1360-0443.2010.03088.x

Institute of Medicine. (2011). *The health of lesbian, gay, bisexual, and transgender people: Building a foundation for better understanding.* Washington, DC: National Academies Press. doi:10.17226/13128

Katz-Wise, S. L., Mereish, E. H., & Woulfe, J. (2017). Associations of bisexual-specific minority stress and health among cisgender and transgender adults with bisexual orientation. *Journal of Sex Research, 54*(7), 899–910. doi:10.1080/00224499.2016.1236181

Kerridge, B. T., Pickering, R. P., Saha, T. D., Ruan, W. J., Chou, S. P., Zhang, H., . . . Hasin, D. S. (2017). Prevalence, sociodemographic correlates and DSM-5 substance use disorders and other psychiatric disorders among sexual minorities in the United States. *Drug and Alcohol Dependence, 170*, 82–92. doi:10.1016/j.drugalcdep.2016.10.038

Koh, A. S., & Ross, L. K. (2006). Mental health issues: A comparison of lesbian, bisexual, and heterosexual women. *Journal of Homosexuality, 51*(1), 33–57. doi:10.1300/J082v51n01_03

Lambe, J., Cerezo, A., & O'Shaughnessy, T. (2017). Minority stress, community involvement, and mental health among bisexual women. *Psychology of Sexual Orientation and Gender Diversity, 4*(2), 218–26. doi:10.1037/sgd0000222

Laumann, E. O., Gagnon, J. H., Michael, R. T., & Michaels, S. (1994). *The social organization of sexuality: Sexual practices in the United States.* Chicago, IL: University of Chicago Press.

LeFrançois, B. A., Menzies, R. J., & Reaume, G. (Eds.). (2013). *Mad matters: A critical reader in Canadian Mad Studies.* Toronto, ON: Canadian Scholars Press Inc.

Lerman, S. F., Rudich, Z., Brill, S., Shalev, H., & Shahar, G. (2015). Longitudinal associations between depression, anxiety, pain, and pain-related disability in chronic pain patients. *Psychosomatic Medicine, 77*(3), 333–41. doi:10.1097/PSY.0000000000000158

Lhomond, B., Saurel-Cubizolles, M.-J., Michaels, S., & CSF Group (2014). A multidimensional measure of sexual orientation, use of psychoactive substances, and depression: Results of national survey on sexual behavior in France. *Archives of Sexual Behavior, 43*(3), 607–19. doi:10.1007/s10508-013-0124-y

Lipari, R. N., & Van Horn, S. L. (2017). Trends in substance use disorders among adults aged 18 or older. In *The CBHSQ report.* Rockville, MD: SAMHSA.

Lipina, S. J., & Colombo, J. A. (2009). *Poverty and brain development during childhood: An approach from cognitive psychology and neuroscience.* Washington, DC: American Psychological Association.

McCabe, S. E., Hughes, T. L., Bostwick, W. B., West, B. T., & Boyd, C. J. (2009). Sexual orientation, substance use behaviors and substance dependence in the United States. *Addiction, 104*(8), 1333–45. doi:10.1111/j.1360-0443.2009.02596.x

McCabe, S. E., Hughes, T. L., & Boyd, C. J. (2004). Substance use and misuse: Are bisexual women at greater risk? *Journal of Psychoactive Drugs, 36*(2), 217–25. doi:10.1080/02791072.2004.10399732

McCabe, S. E., Matthews, A. K., Lee, J. G. L., Veliz, P., Hughes, T. L., & Boyd, C. J. (2018). Tobacco use and sexual orientation in a national cross-sectional study: Age, race/ethnicity, and sexual identity–attraction differences. *American Journal of Preventive Medicine, 54*(6), 736–45. doi:10.1016/j.amepre.2018.03.009

McGeough, B. L., & Sterzing, P. R. (2018). A systematic review of family victimization experiences among sexual minority youth. *Journal of Primary Prevention, 39*(5), 491–528. doi:10.1007/s10935-018-0523-x

McLeroy, K. R., Bibeau, D., Steckler, A., & Glanz, K. (1988). An ecological perspective on health promotion programs. *Health Education Quarterly, 15*(4), 351–377. doi:10.1177/109019818801500401

McWilliams, L. A., Cox, B. J., & Enns, M. W. (2003). Mood and anxiety disorders associated with chronic pain: An examination in a nationally representative sample. *Pain, 106*(1), 127–33. doi:10.1016/S0304-3959(03)00301–4

Medley, G., Lipari, R. N., Bose, J., Cribb, D. S., Kroutil, L. A., & McHenry, G. (2016). *Sexual orientation and estimates of adult substance use and mental health: Results from the 2015 National Survey on Drug Use and Health.* https://www.samhsa.gov/data/sites/default/files/NSDUH-SexualOrientation-2015/NSDUH-SexualOrientation-2015/NSDUH-SexualOrientation-2015.pdf

Mereish, E. H., Katz-Wise, S. L., & Woulfe, J. (2017). Bisexual-specific minority stressors, psychological distress, and suicidality in bisexual individuals: The mediating role of loneliness. *Prevention Science, 18*(6), 716–25. doi:10.1007/s11121-017-0804-2

Meyer, I. H. (2003). Prejudice, social stress, and mental health in lesbian, gay, and bisexual populations: Conceptual issues and research evidence. *Psychological Bulletin, 129*(5), 674. doi:10.1037/0033–2909.129.5.674

Meyer, I. H., Brown, T. N. T., Herman, J. L., Reisner, S. L., & Bockting, W. O. (2017). Demographic characteristics and health status of transgender adults in select US regions: Behavioral Risk Factor Surveillance System, 2014. *American Journal of Public Health, 107*(4), 582–89. doi:10.2105/ajph.2016.303648

Mohr, J. J., Israel, T., & Sedlacek, W. E. (2001). Counselors' attitudes regarding bisexuality as predictors of counselors' clinical responses: An analogue study of a female bisexual client. *Journal of Counseling Psychology, 48*(2), 212–22. doi:10.1037/0022–0167.48.2.212

Molina, Y., Marquez, J. H., Logan, D. E., Leeson, C. J., Balsam, K. F., & Kaysen, D. L. (2015). Current intimate relationship status, depression, and alcohol use among bisexual women: The mediating roles of bisexual-specific minority stressors. *Sex Roles, 73*(1–2), 43–57. doi:10.1007/s11199-015-0483-z

Muller, A., & Hughes, T. L. (2016). Making the invisible visible: A systematic review of sexual minority women's health in Southern Africa. *BMC Public Health, 16*(1), 307. doi:10.1186/s12889-016-2980-6

National Alliance on Mental Illness. (2017). Borderline personality disorder. Retrieved from https://www.nami.org/learn-more/mental-health-conditions/borderline-personality-disorder

Pai, A., Suris, A., & North, C. (2017). Posttraumatic stress disorder in the DSM-5: Controversy, change, and conceptual considerations. *Behavioral Sciences, 7*(1), 7. doi:10.3390/bs7010007

Pakula, B., Shoveller, J., Ratner, P. A., & Carpiano, R. (2016). Prevalence and co-occurrence of heavy drinking and anxiety and mood disorders among gay, lesbian, bisexual, and heterosexual Canadians. *American Journal of Public Health, 106*(6), 1042–48. doi:10.2105/AJPH.2016.303083

Ramírez-Aguilar, M. A., Calderón, G. O., & Rebollar, C. R. (2016). Funciones cognoscitivas en la orientación sexual. *Revista Chilena de Neuropsicología, 11*(1), 30–4. doi:10.5839/rcnp.2016.11.01.06

Roberts, A. L., Austin, S. B., Corliss, H. L., Vandermorris, A. K., & Koenen, K. C. (2010). Pervasive trauma exposure among US sexual orientation minority adults and risk of posttraumatic stress disorder. *American Journal of Public Health, 100*(12), 2433–41. doi:10.2105/AJPH.2009.168971

Ross, L. E., Dobinson, C., & Eady, A. (2010). Perceived determinants of mental health for bisexual people: A qualitative examination. *American Journal of Public Health, 100*(3), 496–502. doi:10.2105/AJPH.2008.156307

Ross, L. E., O'Gorman, L., MacLeod, M. A., Bauer, G. R., MacKay, J., & Robinson, M. (2016). Bisexuality, poverty and mental health: A mixed methods analysis. *Social Science & Medicine, 156*, 64–72. doi:10.1016/j.socscimed.2016.03.009

Ross, L. E., Salway, T., Tarasoff, L. A., MacKay, J. M., Hawkins, B. W., & Fehr, C. P. (2018). Prevalence of depression and anxiety among bisexual people compared to gay, lesbian, and heterosexual individuals: A systematic review and meta-analysis. *Journal of Sex Research, 55*(4–5), 435–56. doi:10.1080/00224499.2017.1387755

Rust, P. C. (2002). Bisexuality: The state of the union. *Annual Review of Sex Research, 13*(1), 180–240.

Sabia, J. J., Wooden, M., & Nguyen, T. T. (2018). Sexual identity, same-same relationships, and health dynamics: New evidence from Australia. *Economics & Human Biology, 30*, 24–36. doi:10.1016/j.ehb.2018.02.005

Salway, T., Ross, L. E., Fehr, C. P., Burley, J., Asadi, S., Hawkins, B., & Tarasoff, L. A. (2019). A systematic review and meta-analysis of disparities in the prevalence of suicide ideation and attempt among bisexual populations. *Archives of Sexual Behavior, 48*(1), 89–111. doi:10.1007/s10508-018-1150-6

Schuler, M. S., Rice, C. E., Evans-Polce, R. J., & Collins, R. L. (2018). Disparities in substance use behaviors and disorders among adult sexual minorities by age, gender, and sexual identity. *Drug and Alcohol Dependence, 189*, 139–46. doi:10.1016/j.drugalcdep.2018.05.008

Siebers, T. (2008). *Disability theory.* Ann Arbor, MI: University of Michigan Press.

Steele, L. S., Ross, L. E., Dobinson, C., Veldhuizen, S., & Tinmouth, J. M. (2009). Women's sexual orientation and health: Results from a Canadian population-based survey. *Women & Health, 49*(5), 353–67. doi:10.1080/03630240903238685

Substance Abuse and Mental Health Services Administration. (2016). Table 11, DSM-IV to DSM-5 manic episode criteria comparison. https://www.ncbi.nlm.nih.gov/books/NBK519712/table/ch3.t7/

Walters, M. L., Chen, J., & Breiding, M. J. (2013). *The national intimate partner and sexual violence survey: 2010 findings on victimization by sexual orientation.* Atlanta, GA: U.S. Centers for Disease Control and Prevention. https://www.cdc.gov/violenceprevention/pdf/nisvs_sofindings.pdf

Xu, W., Zheng, L., Xu, Y., & Zheng, Y. (2017). Internalized homophobia, mental health, sexual behaviors, and outness of gay/bisexual men from Southwest China. *International Journal for Equity in Health, 16*(1), 36. doi:10.1186/s12939-017-0530-1

Yi, H., Lee, H., Park, J., Choi, B., & Kim, S.-S. (2017). Health disparities between lesbian, gay, and bisexual adults and the general population in South Korea: Rainbow Connection Project I. *Epidemiology and Health, 39*, e2017046. doi:10.4178/epih.e2017046

Yoshino, K. (2002). The epistemic contract of bisexual erasure. *Stanford Law Review, 52*, 353–461. doi:10.2307/1229482

Young, R. M., & Meyer, I. H. (2005). The trouble with "MSM" and "WSW": Erasure of the sexual-minority person in public health discourse. *American Journal of Public Health, 95*(7), 1144–9. doi:10.2105/ajph.2004.046714

CHAPTER

24 Transgender Mental Health

Laura E. Kuper, Danna Bismar, *and* Whit Ryan

Abstract

Research on transgender mental health has dramatically increased over the past decade. While initial studies were limited to small clinic-based or geographically limited convenience samples, larger internet and multi-clinic samples as well as increasing inclusion of gender identity questions in regional, national, and probability-based surveys have started to open new avenues for research. Broadly, disparities appear to exist across a broad range of mental health symptoms and diagnoses. However, significant variations exist across studies and intersectional and integrative approaches have started to shed light on some of these variations. This chapter provides an overview of studies examining the prevalence of mental health–related conditions within transgender samples followed by a synthesis of risk and protective factors that appear to underlie mental health disparities. Approaches to conceptualizing and measuring the size of the transgender population, ethical considerations, and implications and future directions are also discussed.

Keywords: transgender, gender diverse, mental health, risk factors, protective factors, health disparities

Over the past several decades, *transgender* has been readily adopted as a term used to refer to the spectrum of individuals who identify as a gender other than, or in addition to, their sex assigned at birth (Valentine, 2007). In contrast, the term *cisgender* is commonly used to refer to individuals whose identity is the gender associated with their sex assigned at birth. The American Psychological Association (APA) Committee on Lesbian, Gay, Bisexual, and Transgender Concerns (2014, p. 1) defines gender identity as "a person's internal sense of being male, female or something else."

More recently, *gender diverse*, *gender expansive*, and *gender nonconforming* have also gained popularity as terms used to refer to individuals whose gender expression diverges from expectations typically associated with one's sex assigned at birth. Gender expression is defined by the APA Committee (2014, p. 1) as "the way a person communicates gender identity to others through behavior, clothing, hairstyles, voice or body characteristics." Some individuals who experience themselves as gender diverse identify with the gender identity associated with their assigned sex. Others identify with terms such as *nonbinary*, *genderqueer*, *agender*, or *gender fluid.* Across time and cultures, a diversity of gender identities and expressions have existed, reflecting an even greater variation in language and conceptualizations of gender (Herdt, 1994). Unfortunately, due to the dominant Eurocentric focus of current research, these experiences are currently not well integrated into transgender health research.

Similar to homosexuality, gender diversity was initially conceptualized by professionals through a lens of pathology; however, it is now viewed as a natural variation in human experience (APA, 2015). For some individuals, the discrepancy between characteristics associated with their sex assigned at birth and their gender identity leads to distress that is relieved by gender-affirming medical care (GAMC, e.g., feminizing or masculinizing hormone therapy and/or surgeries), which is considered medically necessary as reflected in the field's standards of care (Coleman et al., 2012). *Gender dysphoria* is a clinical term used to describe this distress, but it remains controversial due to similar concerns regarding pathologization (Lev, 2013).

These terms and their interrelationships are actively evolving. Due to the personal and contextual nature of gender, it is important to note that while these descriptions refer to general trends articulated within the literature, no universal definitions exist. Further, transgender and gender-diverse individuals appear to commonly identify with more than one identity (e.g., nonbinary trans male), and the strength of these identities also exists on a spectrum (Kuper, Nussbaum, & Mustanski, 2012). With these caveats in mind, the present chapter adopts the term *transgender* to best reflect the current practices within the field. Chapter 25 focuses more specifically on the mental health of *nonbinary* individuals.

Prevalence

Goodman et al. (2019) identified forty-three studies spanning seventeen countries conducted between 1968 and 2018 that have estimated the size of the transgender population. Most studies were from Europe (n = 22) or the United States (n = 12), but Japan, Taiwan, New Zealand, Iran, Australia, and Singapore were also represented. Three subsets of studies examined the amount of people seeking GAMC (n = 9), those who had a gender-related diagnosis such as gender dysphoria (n = 18), and those who applied for legal name or gender marker change (n = 3). Compared to the general population size, these studies produced the smallest estimates of less than 0.01 percent. In population-based studies where respondents self-reported their gender identities or transgender status (n = 9), estimates were higher, ranging from 0.3 to 0.6 percent. In several studies where participants were asked more general questions (e.g., feeling equally as a man and woman, wishing or feeling like someone of a different sex), estimates were even higher, ranging from 1.9 to 7.0 percent. Recent estimates from school-based population studies of adolescents (n = 4) have ranged from 1.3 to 2.7 percent. Using U.S. data, Meerwijk and Sevelius (2017) estimated that there has been a 0.026 percent increase in transgender identification each year between 2007 and 2015. While earlier studies documented ratios favoring transgender females, newer studies have found more even sex ratios, or ratios that favor transgender males.

Ethics

While the past two decades have witnessed a substantial shift away from pathological approaches to transgender research, only recently have researchers begun to articulate ethical considerations relevant to this work. In their guidelines for research, both the APA (2015) and the American Counseling Association (Burnes et al., 2010) highlight the importance of collaborating with transgender community members, being thoughtful and inclusive of the diversity of ways transgender people experience their gender, developing research questions that address the greatest needs within the community (e.g., improvement in care and outcomes), and ensuring research findings are accessible to the community. Vincent (2018) draws on feminist and intersectional perspectives to further articulate these ethical themes. Given the ways that past research has been harmful to transgender communities, Vincent calls for increased transparency in the goals of research, greater consideration of the emotional labor provided by participants and the historical power imbalances present within the field (e.g., research participation requests coming from clinics where transgender people are receiving care), and reflection on how research findings may be misused or misinterpreted by others. While community-based participatory research approaches have been gaining popularity, many of the existing research studies have failed to fully incorporate these ethical themes into their approach and/or have not provided information on how the researchers attempted to do so. It is important to keep this in mind when interpreting existing findings and conceptualizing future directions.

Overview

Research on transgender mental health has dramatically increased over the past decade. While initial studies were limited to small clinic-based or geographically limited convenience samples, the internet has provided a powerful platform for recruiting larger national samples. Increasing inclusion of gender identity questions in large regional, national, and probability-based surveys and synthesis of cross-clinic electronic medical record data have started to open new avenues for research (Reisner, Conron et al., 2016). With larger sample sizes and more diverse sampling strategies, consideration of the influence of intersecting identities and experiences (e.g., age, race/ethnicity, socioeconomic status, geographic location) has become more possible. However, these advancements in understanding remain in their infancy, and the vast majority of existing studies have been based in the United States or Europe. Given variations in population and sampling approaches, assessment methods (e.g., self-report surveys, clinician diagnosis), and conceptualizations of mental health constructs, making comparisons across studies is challenging. Lack of longitudinal research has also prevented identification of causal pathways.

Depression

In comparison to the general population, increased rates of depression have been consistently documented within transgender samples from the United States, Europe, and several additional countries (e.g., India, Iran, Taiwan, Australia, New Zealand) (Reisner, Poteat et al., 2016). A recent review identified fifty U.S. studies that have examined depression symptoms or diagnoses (Valentine & Shipherd, 2018). Clinical elevations on self-report questionnaires of depressive symptoms have ranged between 23 and 69 percent, and lifetime history of clinician diagnoses of major depression has ranged between 2 and 58 percent (Hoshiai et al., 2010; Spack et al., 2012; Veale, Watson, Peter, & Saewyc, 2017). In comparison, within U.S. probability surveys, lifetime prevalence estimates of major depression have ranged from 8 to 16 percent and past-year prevalence estimates have ranged from 6 to 8 percent (Richards, 2011).

While higher rates of depression are typically found among cisgender females in comparison to cisgender males across countries (Seedat et al., 2009), gender differences within the transgender population appear more mixed. Within a large U.S. probability-based sample, rates of a lifetime diagnosis of a depressive disorder were 31 percent for transgender males and 24 percent for transgender females (Downing & Przedworski, 2018). In contrast, within a large U.S. online survey, self-report of clinically significant symptoms of depression was higher for transgender females (49 percent) versus transgender males (37 percent) (Bockting et al., 2013). However, within some studies, no gender differences were found (Reisner, Vetters, et al., 2015; Veale et al., 2017; Witcomb et al., 2018). Population-based estimates suggest the peak age of onset for major depression occurs in adolescence and early adulthood (Richards, 2011). Several studies suggest that there are higher rates of depression among younger transgender individuals (Nuttbrock et al., 2014; Reisner, Biello, et al., 2016), although at least one study found higher rates among older transgender individuals (Witcomb et al., 2018). In one of the only longitudinal studies to date, gender nonconformity in childhood was prospectively linked to depressive symptoms in adolescence (Roberts, Rosario, Slopen, Calzo, & Austin, 2013).

Not enough studies exist to identify variations in depression by other characteristics. In one sample of students presenting to college counseling centers located in the United States, Canada, and England, transgender and gender-nonconforming students of color had the highest initial depression scores and their symptoms of anxiety and depression remitted more slowly (Lefevor, Janis, Franklin, & Stone, 2019). In contrast, within a large study of U.S. veterans as well as a study of young transgender women, African American participants had lower rates of depression than their white peers (Brown & Jones, 2014; Reisner, Biello, et al., 2016). In one U.S. community sample of transgender adults, those with a depression diagnosis or symptoms had less education and lower income on average (Katz-Wise, Reisner, Hughto, & Budge, 2017).

Anxiety

Recent reviews have identified twenty to twenty-five studies that have examined anxiety symptoms or diagnoses within the transgender population. These studies have been conducted primarily in the United States and Europe, although two studies have been conducted in Iran and Japan (Valentine & Shipherd, 2018). Most studies have used self-report of anxiety symptoms, with Millet, Longworth, and Arcelus (2017) estimating that clinical elevations have ranged from 17 to 68 percent. A smaller handful of studies examining rates of anxiety disorder diagnosis among individuals attending clinics providing GAMC found lifetime rates ranging from 27 percent (Reisner, Vetters, et al., 2015) to 36 percent (Mazaheri Meybodi, Hajebi, & Ghanbari Jolfaei, 2014). Within two studies, rates of possible or probable anxiety disorder among individuals who had not yet received GAMC were particularly high (61 and 70 percent) (Millet et al., 2017). In comparison, cross-national prevalence rates for any lifetime anxiety disorder are around 18 percent (Somers, Goldner, Waraich, & Hsu, 2006).

Prevalence rates for other anxiety disorders also appear variable but generally elevated in comparison to the general population. Rates of posttraumatic stress diagnoses have ranged from 2.3 percent within a sample of adolescents presenting for GAMC in the United States (Spack et al., 2012) to 10 percent in a U.S. multi-city sample of young transgender women (Reisner, Biello, et al., 2016) and 24 percent in a large Veterans Affairs sample (Blosnich et al., 2016). Rates of generalized anxiety have ranged from 3 to 49 percent, while rates of social anxiety disorder have ranged from 3 to 31 percent and rates of panic disorder have ranged from 5 to 13 percent (Millet et al., 2017).

Like depression, gender differences in anxiety are more variable within transgender samples (Millet et al., 2017) in contrast to prevalence rates within the general population that are generally higher for cisgender females (Somers et al., 2006). Within several samples of transgender adolescents and adults, no differences by age have been found (Bouman et al., 2017; Budge, Adelson, & Howard, 2013), which may reflect the relatively earlier age of onset for anxiety disorders in general. Variations by other characteristics have been even more limited, although several have also failed to find differences in anxiety by race or ethnicity (Brown & Jones, 2014; Reisner, Biello, et al., 2016).

Substance Abuse

Most studies of substance abuse within the transgender population rely on self-report and the majority have focused on alcohol use. Within a recent review, self-reports of binge drinking ranged between 7 and 61 percent (Gilbert, Pass, Keuroghlian, Greenfield, & Reisner, 2018). Studies from Peru and Brazil have produced estimates on the higher end of this range (Herrera et al., 2016; Kerr-Corrêa et al., 2017). Within the U.S. Transgender Survey (n = 27,715), self-report of past-month binge drinking (27 percent) was only slightly higher than the rate found in a general survey of the U.S. adult population (25 percent) (James et al., 2016). However, within a smaller Canadian sample, monthly heavy episodic drinking (33 percent) was 1.5 times greater than in the Canadian population (Scheim, Bauer, & Shokoohi, 2016). In the only two studies identified that used clinician diagnoses, one study of U.S. veterans found 26 percent had a documented diagnosis of alcohol use disorder (Blosnich et al., 2017), and within one study of young transgender women, 11 percent met criteria for alcohol dependence (Reisner, Biello, et al., 2016).

Disparities in marijuana use were more pronounced in the U.S. Transgender Survey, with 64 percent reporting lifetime marijuana use and 25 percent reporting past-month marijuana use, in comparison to U.S. population estimates of 47 and 8 percent. However, past-month nonmedical use of prescription drugs (7 percent) and illicit drug use (4 percent) were similar to population estimates (James et al., 2016). Within the Canadian sample referenced earlier, rates of nonmedical use of prescription drugs were similar (6 percent), but rates were higher for illicit drug use (12 percent) (Scheim, Bauer, & Shokoohi, 2017). While the U.S. Transgender Survey did not report substance use by gender, within the Canadian sample, transgender males were more likely than transgender females to report heavy episodic drinking (42 vs. 23 percent) and less likely to report use of crack cocaine (1 vs. 5 percent) (Scheim et al., 2016, 2017).

Data from a representative sample of high school students in California as well as from a national U.S. survey of transgender youth found disparities in substance abuse similar to or greater than transgender adults (Day, Fish, Perez-Brumer, Hatzenbuehler, & Russell, 2017; Reisner, Greytak, Parsons, & Ybarra, 2015). Transgender youth were more likely than their cisgender peers to endorse lifetime and recent use of alcohol, cigarettes, and marijuana, and reported initiating use of these substances at younger ages. Rates of recent nonmedical use of prescription drugs, illicit drug use, and polysubstance use were also elevated in comparison to their cisgender peers.

While not enough research is available to identify clear patterns, within the U.S. Transgender Survey, past-month binge drinking was highest among Black, Latino/a, and Middle Eastern participants (30 to 32 percent). Drug use was more prevalent among younger individuals as well as those with a history of job loss, homelessness, or underground economy work (James et al., 2016). In contrast, within the Canadian sample, heavy episodic drinking did not vary by race/ethnicity, employment status, or education, although illicit drug use was more common among White participants and those living in urban settings (Scheim et al., 2016, 2017).

Disordered Eating

Estimates of eating disorder (ED) diagnoses and disordered eating behaviors appear potentially elevated in the transgender population; however, not all studies have found such an effect and rates have varied based on assessment method. Lifetime prevalence estimates for ED diagnoses among the general U.S. population are around 0.6 percent for anorexia nervosa, 1 percent for bulimia nervosa, and 4 percent for binge eating disorder (Hudson, Hiripi, Pope Jr, & Kessler, 2007). Within a U.S. sample of transgender adult patients drawn from a large healthcare system, lifetime prevalence rates of any

ED diagnosis were around 4 percent for both transgender adolescents and adults (Goodman & Nash, 2018). Within two adult studies where transgender participants were asked whether they had been diagnosed with an ED in the past year, rates were 5 to 16 percent (Diemer, Grant, Munn-Chernoff, Patterson, & Duncan, 2015; Diemer et al., 2018); in the former study 7 percent of participants felt that they had an undiagnosed ED.

In an online study that included roughly 450 transgender youth, rates of self-reported lifetime ED diagnoses were particularly high: 40 percent of transgender males and 12 percent of transgender females. However, recruitment may have been skewed given the survey was administered by organizations with a focus on eating disorders and LGBT youth suicide (The Trevor Project, the National Eating Disorders Association, and Reasons Eating Disorder Center, 2018). Nonetheless, this gender difference was consistent with Diemer et al.'s (2018) findings. In contrast, rates of EDs are generally higher in cisgender females versus males (Hudson et al., 2007). Rates of disordered eating among transgender youth also appear high (e.g., losing weight by vomiting [4 to 25 percent]; losing weight by fasting [28 to 53 percent]) (Watson, Veale, & Saewyc, 2017), but these behaviors appear similarly common in samples of cisgender young adults. Despite somewhat mixed findings overall, within qualitative studies, transgender participants frequently describe how their disordered eating behaviors stemmed from a desire to influence their body shape to be more in line with their gender identity (Ålgars, Alanko, Santtila, & Sandnabba, 2012).

Autism Spectrum Disorder

In recent years, increasing attention has been paid to a possible relationship between gender dysphoria and autism spectrum disorder, particularly among transgender children and adolescents presenting for care. In a study of children and adolescents referred to a gender clinic in the Netherlands, 8 percent met criteria for autism spectrum disorder using a semistructured assessment (DISCO-10) (de Vries, Noens, Cohen-Kettenis, van Berckelaer-Onnes, & Doreleijers, 2010) in comparison to European prevalence estimates of 1 to 2 percent (Baxter et al., 2015). However, rates were lower for patients with a gender dysphoria diagnosis (2 to 6 percent) in comparison to patients who only expressed some features of gender dysphoria (13 to 38 percent). In a larger sample from this clinic, children and adolescents had more elevated scores on a parent report of autism spectrum symptoms than a nonclinical sample across all six groups of symptoms (15 vs. 4 percent meeting cutoff) (van der Miesen, de Vries, Steensma, & Hartman, 2018). Within an adult clinic sample, transgender males but not females scored higher on a self-report of autism traits (Jones et al., 2012). As discussed by Turban and van Schalkwyk (2018), these findings should be interpreted with caution as autism spectrum features may, in fact, be manifestations of gender dysphoria in some cases. For example, discomfort with being perceived as one's birth sex may influence the course of social development and ability to think flexibly.

Other Mental Health Conditions

Studies of other mental health conditions remain sparse and have typically been limited to samples of transgender adults from clinics providing GAMC. Several studies have reported prevalence rates of bipolar and psychotic disorders that are generally consistent with population rates (Dhejne, Van Vlerken, Heylens, & Arcelus, 2016; Heylens et al., 2014). In contrast, several studies have found increased rates of dissociative diagnoses and/or symptoms. In one study, elevated rates of dissociative symptoms were driven by high endorsement of items about one's body not belonging to them (Kersting et al., 2003), suggesting dissociative symptoms may stem primarily from experiences of gender dysphoria and/or traumatic stress.

Suicide Ideation, Attempt, and Non Suicidal Self-Injury

Suicide ideation and attempt have become an increasing focus of research. Four recent review articles identified a total of thirty to forty-five studies examining suicide ideation and/or attempt. Most studies have been conducted in the United States, although a handful have been conducted in Canada, the United Kingdom, several European countries, and several additional countries (Australia, Japan, Brazil). Rates have been consistently elevated compared to the general population, with estimates of lifetime suicide ideation ranging from 37 to 95 percent (average around 50 to 60 percent) and estimates of lifetime suicide attempt ranging from 10 to 46 percent (average around 30 percent) (Adams, Hitomi, & Moody, 2017; Marshall, Claes, Bouman, Witcomb, & Arcelus, 2016; McNeil, Ellis, & Eccles, 2017; Wolford-Clevenger, Frantell, Smith, Flores, & Stuart, 2018). In comparison, cross-national studies have produced population-based estimates of suicide ideation ranging from 2 to 18 percent and estimates of suicide attempt ranging from 0.5 to 6 percent (Nock et al., 2008).

While most studies have relied on self-reports from convenience samples, studies relying on chart reviews of individuals presenting for GAMC tended to find lower rates of suicide attempt (10 to 21 percent) (Adams et al., 2017; McNeil et al., 2017). Two studies have attempted to estimate rates of death due to suicide using national registries. Elevated rates were found for both transgender males and females in a Swedish study (2.7 vs. 0.1 percent) (Dhejne et al., 2011) and for transgender females (1.6 percent) in a study from Holland (Van Kesteren, Asscheman, Megens, & Gooren, 1997).

Two large U.S.-based samples of transgender adults found higher rates of suicide attempt among transgender males, American Indian or multiracial, and younger participants. Participants with lower educational attainment, lower income, disabilities, and/or a history of homelessness also reported higher rates (Haas, Rodgers, & Herman, 2014; James et al., 2016). These patterns mirror demographic differences in suicide attempt found within the general population, although findings across other studies of transgender people have been somewhat more mixed (Kuper, Adams, & Mustanski, 2018; McNeil et al., 2017).

Less research exists on non suicidal self-injury (NSI), although studies have documented similarly high rates, with lifetime reports ranging from 21 to 55 percent. One study specifically examined types of NSI and found that while cutting was the most common, other forms of NSI (e.g., hitting, punching self) were also prevalent (dickey, Reisner, & Juntunen, 2015). Several but not all studies found higher rates of NSI in younger and transgender male participants (Marshall et al., 2016). More focus on NSI within the transgender population is particularly important given NSI has been identified as an important predictor of suicide attempt (Wolford-Clevenger et al., 2018).

Risk and Protective Factors

Risk and protective factors for mental health have been identified that span the full range of socio-ecological levels from broad structural factors to individual variations in how people experience the world and navigate stressors. However, not all studies have found significant relationships, particularly when other variables are included that may be overlapping, interacting with, or mediating effects.

Structural Factors

While historical, cultural, and societal contexts have often rendered transgender people invisible and/or marginalized, a number of cultures and societies across time have incorporated gender diversity into the larger social fabric (Herdt, 1994). As facilitated by increased visibility in media, public knowledge and understanding of transgender people has also increased dramatically within the past several decades. Nonetheless, transgender people continue to face structural barriers that influence health.

Although these macro-level factors are often most difficult to study, initial research has demonstrated relationships between mental health and the general social and political climate, legal protections, institutional policies, and access to GAMC. Within a U.S.-based survey of approximately fifty thousand LGBT youth following the 2016 election, 55 percent reported witnessing bullying/harassment associated with gender and approximately half of transgender youth reported often feeling hopeless and/or worthless (Human Rights Campaign, 2017). In another large U.S.-based study of transgender adults, a measure of structural stigma was associated with suicide attempt (Perez-Brumer, Hatzenbuehler, Oldenburg, & Bockting, 2015), and within a large sample of U.S. veterans, living in a state without employment nondiscrimination protections was associated with higher rates of mood disorders and NSI (Blosnich et al., 2016). Lack of access to facilities (e.g., bathrooms) consistent with one's gender identity has been associated with greater incidence of sexual assault of transgender youth (Murchison, Agénor, Reisner, & Watson, 2019) and suicide attempt among transgender adults (Seelman, 2016).

Interpersonal Factors

Discrimination and victimization have become two of the most studied forms of minority stress. The U.S. Transgender Survey documented high rates of lifetime housing discrimination (23 percent), lifetime job loss, (13 percent), and past-year denial of equal treatment (14 percent) based on transgender status. Past-year verbal harassment was reported by 46 percent, and 9 percent reported being physically attacked. Within school-based surveys of transgender youth, rates of bullying and violence are consistently higher than cisgender peers (Clark et al., 2014; Eisenberg et al., 2017). Transgender adults also report greater harassment by the police, mistreatment at work, and negative experiences in public settings (e.g., public transportation, restaurants). Both experiences of discrimination and victimization have been associated with increased risk of depression, anxiety, posttraumatic stress disorder, substance abuse, and suicide (Nuttbrock et al., 2014; Reisner, Greytak, et al., 2015; Roberts et al., 2013; Scandurra, Amodeo, Valerio, Bochicchio, & Frost, 2017; Wolford-Clevenger et al., 2018).

A number of studies have found relationships between both family and friend support or rejection and mental health outcomes such as depression, anxiety, suicide, substance abuse, and self-esteem across both youth (Gower et al., 2018; Kuper et al., 2018) and adult samples (Bockting et al., 2013; James et al., 2016; Scandurra et al., 2017). Greater transgender community belongingness has also been associated with greater well-being (Barr, Budge, & Adelson, 2016), and contact with LGBT peers has been associated with less psychological distress (Bariola et al., 2015). However, greater connection with the transgender community (Bradford, Reisner, Honnold, & Xavier, 2013) and engagement in transgender-related activism (Breslow et al., 2015) have also been associated with more experiences of discrimination.

Ability to express one's gender openly and take steps in social transition has been conceptualized as an important protective factor. Increased congruence between one's gender identity and expression has been linked to reduced rates of major depression and NSI (Chodzen, Hidalgo, Chen, & Garofalo, 2019; Jackman, Dolezal, & Bockting, 2018), and preliminary research with children who have socially transitioned suggests that their mental health is comparable to cisgender peers (Durwood, McLaughlin, & Olson, 2017). Within a sample of transgender youth, being called by one's chosen name in more contexts was associated with lower depression, suicidal ideation, and suicidal behavior (Russell, Pollitt, Li, & Grossman, 2018). In contrast, concealment or nondisclosure of one's gender identity has been linked to poorer mental health (Bockting et al., 2013; Testa, Michaels, et al., 2017).

Unfortunately, experiences with unsupportive or uneducated providers remain commonplace. Within the U.S. Transgender Survey, of those who ever shared their gender with a professional (e.g., counselor), 18 percent reported that the professional "tried to stop them from being transgender." These experiences have been linked to substance abuse, depression, and suicide (Kattari, Walls, Speer, & Kattari, 2016; Romanelli, Lu, & Lindsey, 2018; Seelman, Colón-Diaz, LeCroix, Xavier-Brier, & Kattari, 2017). Within qualitative studies, participants have further described experiences of feeling burdened by the need to educate providers, feeling a need to prove the authenticity of their gender in order to access GAMC, and providers making incorrect assumptions surrounding their experiences of gender (Mizock & Lundquist, 2016).

Intrapersonal Factors

As expected, more positive feelings about one's gender have been associated with lower rates of depression (Bockting et al., 2013). In contrast, internalized transphobia (e.g., negative beliefs about one's gender, transgender people, and/or gender diversity) has been linked to higher rates of depression, anxiety, and suicide ideation (Chodzen et al., 2019; Lehavot, Simpson, & Shipherd, 2016; Scandurra et al., 2017). Higher ratings on general measures of self-esteem and resilience have also been linked to lower rates of depression, anxiety, and suicide ideation (Breslow et al., 2015; Witcomb et al., 2018) while use of avoidant coping styles has been linked to higher rates (Budge et al., 2013). Additional protective intrapersonal themes that have emerged through qualitative research have included increased agency in self-definition, feelings of personal growth, gaining a new perspective, developing hope for the future, and greater connection to one's religion (Riggle, Rostosky, McCants, & Pascale-Hague, 2011; Yarhouse & Carrs, 2012).

Impact of GAMC

A growing number of studies have consistently documented the positive mental health impact of receiving GAMC. A review of studies found that feminizing/masculinizing hormone therapy was consistently linked with fewer symptoms of depression and anxiety and better quality of life (Rowniak, Bolt, & Sharifi, 2019). Studies of participants receiving gender-affirming surgery (e.g., mastectomy, breast enhancement, vaginoplasty, metoidioplasty, phalloplasty, facial feminization) have also documented better mental health functioning, including suicide ideation (Tucker et al., 2018) and ED symptomatology (Testa, Rider, Haug, & Balsam, 2017). Reduced distress with physical features has also been associated with both hormone therapy and surgery (Owen-Smith et al., 2018). More recently, use of puberty suppression for transgender youth starting to experience changes associated with puberty has been incorporated into the field's standards of care following a landmark longitudinal study demonstrating the positive impact of this intervention on psychological functioning (de Vries et al., 2014).

Integrative Models

Tests of mediating and moderating effects provide an avenue to further deepen understanding of the processes influencing mental health. Within several studies, measures of social support have moderated relationships between risk factors (e.g., discrimination, victimization) and mental health (Bockting et al., 2013; Romanelli et al., 2018). Avoidant coping was identified as a partial mediator of the relationship between victimization and depressive symptoms in one study (White Houghto et al., 2017) and of the relationship between social support and depression and anxiety symptoms in a second (Budge, 2013). Within a third study, the serial relationship between gender identity non-affirmation (e.g., not being perceived by others as one's gender identity) and body-related satisfaction mediated the relationship between receipt of GAMC and ED symptoms (Testa, Rider, et al., 2017).

While many studies identify risk and protective factors that provide general support for the minority stress model, few have explicitly tested the specific pathways implicated in this model. In one study, stigma awareness (i.e., perception that others view one's gender negatively) partially mediated the relationship between discrimination and psychological distress. However, internalized transphobia did not mediate this relationship, and resilience did not moderate the relationship between these predictors and distress (Breslow et al., 2015). One study integrated the minority stress model with one of the leading theories of suicide and found that two important risk factors for suicide identified by the interpersonal theory, thwarted belongingness and perceived burdensomeness, mediated the relationships between internalized transphobia and expectations of negative treatment and suicide ideation (Testa, Michaels, et al., 2017).

Implications and Future Directions

Broadly, there exists a need for ethically grounded and translationally oriented research that reflects goals of working collaboratively with transgender populations to improve the quality and accessibility of gender-affirming healthcare. Over the past decade, there has been a proliferation of clinical resources developed to assist clinicians in providing gender-affirming care (Chang, Singh, & dickey, 2018; Keo-Meier & Ehrensaft, 2018). These approaches share a client-centered focus that strives to be sensitive to the diversity of transgender people's experiences and the larger social and structural contexts that shape these experiences with the goal of assisting clients in affirming their experiences of gender and navigating associated minority stressors. Clinicians have also provided guidance on how to adapt cognitive-behavioral (Austin & Craig, 2015), dialectical behavior (Sloan, Berke, & Shipherd, 2017), and interpersonal (Budge, 2013) therapies to meet the needs of transgender clients. However, research has yet to examine the implementation and effectiveness and of these interventions. The Trans Collaborations Clinical Check-In is a promising tool for assisting transgender clients in providing such feedback (Holt et al., 2019). Further, while research has been conducted on methods for incorporating transgender health into medical education and their effectiveness (Dubin et al., 2018), no such efforts were identified in reference to mental health provider training.

Further development of integrative and intersectional frameworks that incorporate a more nuanced understanding of structural, interpersonal, and intrapersonal dynamics and their interactions are likely to improve the provision of care. The Gender Minority Stress and Resilience Scale is a promising measurement tool that reflects nine key constructs consistent with minority stress theory (Testa, Habarth, Peta, Balsam, & Bockting, 2015). More broadly, greater consideration of race and ethnicity, socioeconomic status, and geographic location is needed to inform the tailoring of practices to subsets of the larger transgender population. Continued efforts to include gender identity within large population-based surveys are particularly important in this regard, and guidance exists on how to do so (Reisner, Conron, et al., 2015). Within-person clustering of mental health difficulties has been largely unexamined. While syndemics theory was initially developed to elucidate mechanisms driving disparities in HIV infections, tenets of the theory are likely to prove useful within the field of mental health. In their review of syndemics theory, Tsai, Mendenhall, Trostle, and Kawachi (2017) explored how improved knowledge of the clustering of social and structural factors with health outcomes assists in identifying targets of intervention that are likely to have the greatest impact. Longitudinal studies are also needed to elucidate causal relationships and pathways.

Growing attention is being given to gender affirmation at the structural level. As regions begin to adopt policies such as those addressing discrimination and access to legal gender recognition, continued documentation of the benefits of such policies is likely to assist in further adoption. Within the United

States, the Human Rights Campaign Foundation has developed healthcare (2018) and corporate (2019) LGBTQ equality indexes that provide ratings across a number of identified best practices (e.g., nondiscrimination policies, insurance coverage of GAMC, staff training, community outreach and engagement efforts). Studying the implementation and effectiveness of these efforts is needed to further strengthen their impact. Given ongoing shifts, researchers will need to regularly update their knowledge on the political, legal, and social landscape.

References

Adams, N., Hitomi, M., & Moody, C. (2017). Varied reports of adult transgender suicidality: Synthesizing and describing the peer-reviewed and gray literature. *Transgender Health, 2*(1), 60–75. doi:10.1089/trgh.2016.0036

Ålgars, M., Alanko, K., Santtila, P., & Sandnabba, N. K. (2012). Disordered eating and gender identity disorder: A qualitative study. *Eating Disorders, 20*(4), 300–11. doi:10.1080/10640266.2012.668482

American Psychological Association. (2015). Guidelines for psychological practice with transgender and gender nonconforming people. *American Psychologist, 70*(9), 832–64. doi:10.1037/a0039906

American Psychological Association, Committee on Lesbian, Gay, Bisexual, and Transgender Concerns. (2014). *Answers to your questions about transgender people, gender identity, and gender expression.* Washington, DC: American Psychological Association.

Austin, A., & Craig, S. L. (2015). Transgender affirmative cognitive behavioral therapy: Clinical considerations and applications. *Professional Psychology: Research and Practice, 46*(1), 21. doi:10.1037/a0038642

Bariola, E., Lyons, A., Leonard, W., Pitts, M., Badcock, P., & Couch, M. (2015). Demographic and psychosocial factors associated with psychological distress and resilience among transgender individuals. *American Journal of Public Health, 105*(10), 2108–16. doi:10.2105/AJPH.2015.302763

Barr, S. M., Budge, S. L., & Adelson, J. L. (2016). Transgender community belongingness as a mediator between strength of transgender identity and well-being. *Journal of Counseling Psychology, 63*(1), 87. doi:10.1037/cou0000127

Baxter, A. J., Brugha, T., Erskine, H., Scheurer, R., Vos, T., & Scott, J. (2015). The epidemiology and global burden of autism spectrum disorders. *Psychological Medicine, 45*(3), 601–13. doi:10.1017/S003329171400172X

Blosnich, J. R., Marsiglio, M. C., Dichter, M. E., Gao, S., Gordon, A. J., Shipherd, J. C., . . . Fine, M. J. (2017). Impact of social determinants of health on medical conditions among transgender veterans. *American Journal of Preventive Medicine, 52*(4), 491–98. doi:10.1016/j.amepre.2016.12.019

Blosnich, J. R., Marsiglio, M. C., Gao, S., Gordon, A. J., Shipherd, J. C., Kauth, M., . . . Fine, M. J. (2016). Mental health of transgender veterans in US states with and without discrimination and hate crime legal protection. *American Journal of Public Health, 106*(3), 534–40. doi:10.2105/AJPH.2015.302981

Bockting, W. O., Miner, M. H., Swinburne Romine, R. E., Hamilton, A., & Coleman, E. (2013). Stigma, mental health, and resilience in an online sample of the US transgender population. *American Journal of Public Health, 103*(5), 943–51. doi:10.2105/AJPH.2013.301241

Bouman, W. P., Claes, L., Brewin, N., Crawford, J. R., Millet, N., Fernandez-Aranda, F., & Arcelus, J. (2017). Transgender and anxiety: A comparative study between transgender people and the general population. *International Journal of Transgenderism, 18*(1), 16–26. doi:10.1080/15532739.2016.1258352

Bradford, J., Reisner, S. L., Honnold, J. A., & Xavier, J. (2013). Experiences of transgender-related discrimination and implications for health: Results from the Virginia Transgender Health Initiative Study. *American Journal of Public Health, 103*(10), 1820–9. doi:10.2105/AJPH.2012.300796

Breslow, A. S., Brewster, M. E., Velez, B. L., Wong, S., Geiger, E., & Soderstrom, B. (2015). Resilience and collective action: Exploring buffers against minority stress for transgender individuals. *Psychology of Sexual Orientation and Gender Diversity, 2*(3), 253. doi:10.1037/sgd0000117

Brown, G. R., & Jones, K. T. (2014). Racial health disparities in a cohort of 5,135 transgender veterans. *Journal of Racial and Ethnic Health Disparities, 1*(4), 257–66. doi:10.1007/s40615-014-0032-4

Budge, S. L. (2013). Interpersonal psychotherapy with transgender clients. *Psychotherapy, 50*(3), 356. doi:10.1037/a0032194

Budge, S. L., Adelson, J. L., & Howard, K. A. (2013). Anxiety and depression in transgender individuals: The roles of transition status, loss, social support, and coping. *Journal of Consulting and Clinical Psychology, 81*(3), 545. doi:10.1037/a0031774

Burnes, T. R., Singh, A. A., Harper, A. J., Harper, B., Maxon-Kann, W., Pickering, D. L., & Hosea, J. (2010). American Counseling Association: Competencies for counseling with transgender clients. *Journal of LGBT Issues in Counseling, 4*(3–4), 135–59. doi:10.1080/15538605.2010.524839

Chang, S. C., Singh, A. A., & dickey, l. m. (2018). *A clinician's guide to gender-affirming care.* Oakland, CA: New Harbinger Publications, Inc.

Chodzen, G., Hidalgo, M. A., Chen, D., & Garofalo, R. (2019). Minority stress factors associated with depression and anxiety among transgender and gender-nonconforming youth. *Journal of Adolescent Health, 64*(4), 467–71. doi:10.1016/j.adohealth.2018.07.006

Clark, T. C., Lucassen, M. F., Bullen, P., Denny, S. J., Fleming, T. M., Robinson, E. M., & Rossen, F. V. (2014). The health and well-being of transgender high school students: Results from the New Zealand adolescent health survey (Youth'12). *Journal of Adolescent Health, 55*(1), 93–9. doi:10.1016/j.jadohealth.2013.11.008

Coleman, E., Bockting, W., Botzer, M., Cohen-Kettenis, P., DeCuypere, G., Feldman, J., . . . Meyer, W. J. (2012). Standards of care for the health of transsexual, transgender, and gender-nonconforming people, version 7. *International Journal of Transgenderism, 13*(4), 165–232. doi:10.1080/15532739.2011.700873

Day, J. K., Fish, J. N., Perez-Brumer, A., Hatzenbuehler, M. L., & Russell, S. T. (2017). Transgender youth substance use disparities: Results from a population-based sample. *Journal of Adolescent Health, 61*(6), 729–35. doi:10.1016/j.jadohealth.2017.06.024

de Vries, A. L. C., McGuire, J. K., Steensma, T. D., Wagenaar, E. C., Doreleijers, T. A., & Cohen-Kettenis, P. T. (2014). Young adult psychological outcome after puberty suppression and gender reassignment. *Pediatrics, 134*(4), 696–704. doi:10.1542/peds.2013-2958 de Vries, A. L. C., Noens, I. L., Cohen-Kettenis, P. T., van Berckelaer-Onnes, I. A., & Doreleijers, T. A. (2010). Autism spectrum disorders in gender dysphoric children and adolescents. *Journal of Autism and Developmental Disorders, 40*(8), 930–6. doi:10.1007/s10803-010-0935-9

Dhejne, C., Lichtenstein, P., Boman, M., Johansson, A. L., Långström, N., & Landén, M. (2011). Long-term follow-up of transsexual persons undergoing sex reassignment surgery: Cohort study in Sweden. *PloS One, 6*(2), e16885. doi:10.1371/journal.pone.0016885

Dhejne, C., Van Vlerken, R., Heylens, G., & Arcelus, J. (2016). Mental health and gender dysphoria: A review of the literature. *International Review of Psychiatry, 28*(1), 44–57. doi:10.3109/09540261.2015.1115753

dickey, l. m., Reisner, S. L., & Juntunen, C. L. (2015). Non-suicidal self-injury in a large online sample of transgender adults. *Professional Psychology: Research and Practice, 46*(1), 3. doi:10.1037/a0038803

Diemer, E. W., Grant, J. D., Munn-Chernoff, M. A., Patterson, D. A., & Duncan, A. E. (2015). Gender identity, sexual orientation, and eating-related pathology in a national sample of college students. *Journal of Adolescent Health, 57*(2), 144–9. doi:10.1016/j.jadohealth.2015.03.003

Diemer, E. W., White Hughto, J. M., Gordon, A. R., Guss, C., Austin, S. B., & Reisner, S. L. (2018). Beyond the binary: Differences in eating disorder prevalence by gender identity in a transgender sample. *Transgender Health, 3*(1), 17–23. doi:10.1089/trgh.2017.0043

Downing, J. M., & Przedworski, J. M. (2018). Health of transgender adults in the US, 2014–2016. *American Journal of Preventive Medicine, 55*(3), 336–44. doi:10.1016/j.amepre.2018.04.045

Dubin, S. N., Nolan, I. T., Streed Jr, C. G., Greene, R. E., Radix, A. E., & Morrison, S. D. (2018). Transgender health care: Improving medical students' and residents' training and awareness. *Advances in Medical Education and Practice, 9*, 377. doi:10.2147/AMEP.S147183

Durwood, L., McLaughlin, K. A., & Olson, K. R. (2017). Mental health and self-worth in socially transitioned transgender youth. *Journal of the American Academy of Child and Adolescent Psychiatry, 56*(2), 116–23.e112. doi:10.1016/j.jaac.2016.10.016

Eisenberg, M. E., Gower, A. L., McMorris, B. J., Rider, G. N., Shea, G., & Coleman, E. (2017). Risk and protective factors in the lives of transgender/gender nonconforming adolescents. *Journal of Adolescent Health, 61*(4), 521–6. doi:10.1016/j.jadohealth.2017.04.014

Gilbert, P. A., Pass, L. E., Keuroghlian, A. S., Greenfield, T. K., & Reisner, S. L. (2018). Alcohol research with transgender populations: A systematic review and recommendations to strengthen future studies. *Drug and Alcohol Dependence, 186*, 138–46. doi:10.1016/j.drugalcdep.2018.01.016

Goodman, M., Adams, N., Cornell, T., Kreukels, B., Motmans, J., & Coleman, E. (2019). Size and distribution of transgender and gender nonconforming populations: A narrative review. *Endocrinology and Metabolism Clinics, 48*(2), 303–21. doi:10.1016/j.ecl.2019.01.001

Goodman, M., & Nash, R. (2018). *Examining health outcomes for people who are transgender.* Washington, DC: Patient-Centered Outcomes Research Institute.

Gower, A. L., Rider, G. N., Brown, C., McMorris, B. J., Coleman, E., Taliaferro, L. A., & Eisenberg, M. E. (2018). Supporting transgender and gender diverse youth: Protection against emotional distress and substance use. *American Journal of Preventive Medicine, 55*(6), 787–94. doi:10/1016/j.amepre.2018.06.030

Haas, A. P., Rodgers, P. L., & Herman, J. L. (2014). *Suicide attempts among transgender and gender non-conforming adults.* American Foundation for Suicide Prevention and the Williams Institute.

Herdt, G. (1994). *Third sex, third gender: Beyond sexual dimorphism in culture and history.* New York, NY: Zone Books.

Herrera, M., Konda, K., Leon, S., Deiss, R., Brown, B., Calvo, G., . . . Klausner, J. (2016). Impact of alcohol use on sexual behavior among men who have sex with men and transgender women in Lima, Peru. *Drug and Alcohol Dependence, 161*, 147–54. doi:10.1016/j.drugalcdep.2016.01.030

Heylens, G., Elaut, E., Kreukels, B. P., Paap, M. C., Cerwenka, S., Richter-Appelt, H., . . . De Cuypere, G. (2014). Psychiatric characteristics in transsexual individuals: Multicentre study in four European countries. *British Journal of Psychiatry, 204*(2), 151–6. doi:10.1192/bjp.bp.112.121954

Holt, N. R., Huit, T. Z., Shulman, G. P., Meza, J. L., Smyth, J. D., Woodruff, N., . . . Hope, D. A. (2019). Trans Collaborations Clinical Check-In (TC3): Initial validation of a clinical measure for transgender and gender diverse adults receiving psychological services. *Behavior Therapy, 50*(6), 1136–49.

Hoshiai, M., Matsumoto, Y., Sato, T., Ohnishi, M., Okabe, N., Kishimoto, Y., . . . Kuroda, S. (2010). Psychiatric comorbidity among patients with gender identity disorder. *Psychiatry and Clinical Neurosciences, 64*(5), 514–9. doi:10.1111/j.1440–1819.2010.02118.x

Hudson, J. I., Hiripi, E., Pope Jr, H. G., & Kessler, R. C. (2007). The prevalence and correlates of eating disorders in the National Comorbidity Survey Replication. *Biological Psychiatry, 61*(3), 348–58. doi:10.1016/j.biopsych.2006.03.040

Human Rights Campaign. (2017). *Post-election survey of youth.* https://assets2.hrc.org/files/assets/resources/HRC_PostElectionSurveyofYouth.pdf

Human Rights Campaign Foundation. (2018). *Healthcare Equality Index 2018.* https://www.hrc.org/hei

Human Rights Campaign Foundation. (2019). *Corporate Equality Index 2019.* https://www.hrc.org/campaigns/corporate-equality-index

Jackman, K. B., Dolezal, C., & Bockting, W. O. (2018). Generational differences in internalized transnegativity and psychological distress among feminine spectrum transgender people. *LGBT Health, 5*(1), 54–60. doi:10.1089/lgbt.2017.0034

James, S., Herman, J., Rankin, S., Keisling, M., Mottet, L., & Ana, M. (2016). *The report of the 2015 US Transgender Survey.* Washington, DC: National Center for Transgender Equality.

Jones, R. M., Wheelwright, S., Farrell, K., Martin, E., Green, R., Di Ceglie, D., & Baron-Cohen, S. (2012). Brief report: Female-to-male transsexual people and autistic traits. *Journal of Autism and Developmental Disorders, 42*(2), 301–06. doi:10.1007/s10803-011-1227-8

Kattari, S. K., Walls, N. E., Speer, S. R., & Kattari, L. (2016). Exploring the relationship between transgender-inclusive providers and mental health outcomes among transgender/gender variant people. *Social Work in Health Care, 55*(8), 635–50. doi:10.1080/00981389.2016.1193099

Katz-Wise, S. L., Reisner, S. L., Hughto, J. M. W., & Budge, S. L. (2017). Self-reported changes in attractions and social determinants of mental health in transgender adults. *Archives of Sexual Behavior, 46*(5), 1425–39. doi:10.1007/s10508-016-0812-5

Keo-Meier, C., & Ehrensaft, D. (2018). *The gender affirmative model: An interdisciplinary approach to supporting transgender and gender expansive children.* Washington, DC: American Psychological Association.

Kerr-Corrêa, F., Júnior, P., Leal, F. M., Martins, T. A., Costa, D. L. d. C., Macena, R. H. M.,...Kendall, C. (2017). Hazardous alcohol use among transwomen in a Brazilian city. *Cadernos de Saúde Publica, 33*(3), e00008815.

Kersting, A., Reutemann, M., Gast, U., Ohrmann, P., Suslow, T., Michael, N., & Arolt, V. (2003). Dissociative disorders and traumatic childhood experiences in transsexuals. *Journal of Nervous and Mental Disease, 191*(3), 182–9. doi:10.1097/01.NMD.0000054932.22929.5D

Kuper, L. E., Adams, N., & Mustanski, B. S. (2018). Exploring cross-sectional predictors of suicide ideation, attempt, and risk in a large online sample of transgender and gender nonconforming youth and young adults. *LGBT Health, 5*(7), 391–400. doi:10.1089/lgbt.2017.0259

Kuper, L. E., Nussbaum, R., & Mustanski, B. (2012). Exploring the diversity of gender and sexual orientation identities in an online sample of transgender individuals. *Journal of Sex Research, 49*(2–3), 244–54. doi:10.1080/00224499.2011.596954

Lefevor, G. T., Janis, R. A., Franklin, A., & Stone, W.-M. (2019). Distress and therapeutic outcomes among transgender and gender nonconforming people of color. *The Counseling Psychologist, 47*(1), 34–58. doi:10.1177/0011000019827210

Lehavot, K., Simpson, T. L., & Shipherd, J. C. (2016). Factors associated with suicidality among a national sample of transgender veterans. *Suicide and Life-Threatening Behavior, 46*(5), 507–24. doi:10.1111/sltb.12233

Lev, A. I. (2013). Gender dysphoria: Two steps forward, one step back. *Clinical Social Work Journal, 41*(3), 288–96. doi:10.1007/s10615-013-0447-0

Marshall, E., Claes, L., Bouman, W. P., Witcomb, G. L., & Arcelus, J. (2016). Non-suicidal self-injury and suicidality in trans people: A systematic review of the literature. *International Review of Psychiatry, 28*(1), 58–69. doi:10.3109/09540261.2015.1073143

Mazaheri Meybodi, A., Hajebi, A., & Ghanbari Jolfaei, A. (2014). Psychiatric Axis I comorbidities among patients with gender dysphoria. *Psychiatry Journal, 2014.* doi:10.1155/2014/971814

McNeil, J., Ellis, S. J., & Eccles, F. J. (2017). Suicide in trans populations: A systematic review of prevalence and correlates. *Psychology of Sexual Orientation and Gender Diversity, 4*(3), 341. doi:10.1037/sgd0000235

Meerwijk, E. L., & Sevelius, J. M. (2017). Transgender population size in the United States: A meta-regression of population-based probability samples. *American Journal of Public Health, 107*(2), e1–e8. doi:10.2105/AJPH.2016.303578

Millet, N., Longworth, J., & Arcelus, J. (2017). Prevalence of anxiety symptoms and disorders in the transgender population: A systematic review of the literature. *International Journal of Transgenderism, 18*(1), 27–38. doi:10.1080/15532739.2016.1258353

Mizock, L., & Lundquist, C. (2016). Missteps in psychotherapy with transgender clients: Promoting gender sensitivity in counseling and psychological practice. *Psychology of Sexual Orientation and Gender Diversity, 3*(2), 148. doi:10.1037/sgd0000177

Murchison, G. R., Agénor, M., Reisner, S. L., & Watson, R. J. (2019). School restroom and locker room restrictions and sexual assault risk among transgender youth. *Pediatrics, 143*(6) [E-pub before print]. doi:10.1542/peds/2018-2902

Nock, M. K., Borges, G., Bromet, E. J., Alonso, J., Angermeyer, M., Beautrais, A.,...Gluzman, S. (2008). Cross-national prevalence and risk factors for suicidal ideation, plans and attempts. *British Journal of Psychiatry, 192*(2), 98–105. doi:10.1192/bjp.bp.107.040113

Nuttbrock, L., Bockting, W., Rosenblum, A., Hwahng, S., Mason, M., Macri, M., & Becker, J. (2014). Gender abuse and major depression among transgender women: A prospective study of vulnerability and resilience. *American Journal of Public Health, 104*(11), 2191–8. doi:10.2105/AJPH.2013.301545

Owen-Smith, A. A., Gerth, J., Sineath, R. C., Barzilay, J., Becerra-Culqui, T. A., Getahun, D.,...Millman, A. (2018). Association between gender confirmation treatments and perceived gender congruence, body image satisfaction, and mental health in a cohort of transgender individuals. *Journal of Sexual Medicine, 15*(4), 591–600. doi:10.1016/j.jsxm.2018.01.017

Perez-Brumer, A., Hatzenbuehler, M. L., Oldenburg, C. E., & Bockting, W. (2015). Individual- and structural-level risk factors for suicide attempts among transgender adults. *Behavioral Medicine, 41*(3), 164–71. doi:10.1080/0896489.2015.1028322

Reisner, S. L., Biello, K. B., Hughto, J. M. W., Kuhns, L., Mayer, K. H., Garofalo, R., & Mimiaga, M. J. (2016). Psychiatric diagnoses and comorbidities in a diverse, multicity cohort of young transgender women: Baseline findings from project LifeSkills. *JAMA Pediatrics, 170*(5), 481–6. doi:10.1001/jamapediatrics.2016.0067

Reisner, S. L., Conron, K. J., Baker, K., Herman, J. L., Lombardi, E., Greytak, E. A.,...Matthews, A. K. (2015). "Counting" transgender and gender-nonconforming adults in health research: Recommendations from the Gender Identity in US Surveillance Group. *Transgender Studies Quarterly, 2*(1), 34–57. doi:10.1215/23289252-2848877

Reisner, S. L., Greytak, E. A., Parsons, J. T., & Ybarra, M. L. (2015). Gender minority social stress in adolescence: Disparities in adolescent bullying and substance use by gender identity. *Journal of Sex Research, 52*(3), 243–56. doi:10.1080/00224499.2014.886321

Reisner, S. L., Poteat, T., Keatley, J., Cabral, M., Mothopeng, T., Dunham, E.,...Baral, S. D. (2016). Global health burden and needs of transgender populations: A review. *The Lancet, 388*(10042), 412–36. doi:10.1016/S0140-6736(16)00684-X

Reisner, S. L., Vetters, R., Leclerc, M., Zaslow, S., Wolfrum, S., Shumer, D., & Mimiaga, M. J. (2015). Mental health of transgender youth in care at an adolescent urban community health center: A matched retrospective cohort study. *Journal of Adolescent Health, 56*(3), 274–9.

Richards, D. (2011). Prevalence and clinical course of depression: A review. *Clinical Psychology Review, 31*(7), 1117–25. doi:10.1016/j.cpr.2011.07.004

Riggle, E. D., Rostosky, S. S., McCants, L. E., & Pascale-Hague, D. (2011). The positive aspects of a transgender self-identification. *Psychology & Sexuality, 2*(2), 147–58.

Roberts, A. L., Rosario, M., Slopen, N., Calzo, J. P., & Austin, S. B. (2013). Childhood gender nonconformity, bullying victimization, and depressive symptoms across adolescence and early adulthood: An 11-year longitudinal study. *Journal of the American Academy of Child and Adolescent Psychiatry, 52*(2), 143–52. doi:10.1016/j.jaac.2012.11.006

Romanelli, M., Lu, W., & Lindsey, M. A. (2018). Examining mechanisms and moderators of the relationship between discriminatory health care encounters and attempted suicide among US transgender help-seekers. *Administration and Policy in Mental Health and Mental Health Services Research, 45*(6), 831–49. doi:10.1007/s10488-018-0868-8

Rowniak, S., Bolt, L., & Sharifi, C. (2019). The effect of cross-sex hormones on the quality of life, depression and anxiety of transgender individuals: A quantitative systematic review. *JBI Database of Systematic Reviews and Implementation Reports, 17*(9), 1826–54. doi:10.11124/JBISRIR-2017-003869

Russell, S. T., Pollitt, A. M., Li, G., & Grossman, A. H. (2018). Chosen name use is linked to reduced depressive symptoms, suicidal ideation, and suicidal behavior among transgender youth. *Journal of Adolescent Health, 63*(4), 503–5. doi:10.1016/j.jadohealth.2018.02.003

Scandurra, C., Amodeo, A. L., Valerio, P., Bochicchio, V., & Frost, D. M. (2017). Minority stress, resilience, and mental health: A study of Italian transgender people. *Journal of Social Issues, 73*(3), 563–85. doi:10.1111/josi.12232

Scheim, A. I., Bauer, G. R., & Shokoohi, M. (2016). Heavy episodic drinking among transgender persons: Disparities and predictors. *Drug and Alcohol Dependence, 167*, 156–162. doi:10.1016/j.drugalcdep.2016.08.011

Scheim, A. I., Bauer, G. R., & Shokoohi, M. (2017). Drug use among transgender people in Ontario, Canada: Disparities and associations with social exclusion. *Addictive Behaviors, 72*, 151–8. doi:10.1016/j.addbeh.2017.03.022

Seedat, S., Scott, K. M., Angermeyer, M. C., Berglund, P., Bromet, E. J., Brugha, T. S., . . . Jin, R. (2009). Cross-national associations between gender and mental disorders in the World Health Organization World Mental Health Surveys. *Archives of General Psychiatry, 66*(7), 785–95. doi:10.1001/archgenpsychiatry.2009.36

Seelman, K. L. (2016). Transgender adults' access to college bathrooms and housing and the relationship to suicidality. *Journal of Homosexuality, 63*(10), 1378–99. doi:10.1080/00918369.2016.1157998

Seelman, K. L., Colón-Diaz, M. J., LeCroix, R. H., Xavier-Brier, M., & Kattari, L. (2017). Transgender noninclusive healthcare and delaying care because of fear: Connections to general health and mental health among transgender adults. *Transgender Health, 2*(1), 17–28. doi:10.1089/trgh.2016.0024

Sloan, C. A., Berke, D. S., & Shipherd, J. C. (2017). Utilizing a dialectical framework to inform conceptualization and treatment of clinical distress in transgender individuals. *Professional Psychology: Research and Practice, 48*(5), 301. doi:10.1037/pro0000146

Somers, J. M., Goldner, E. M., Waraich, P., & Hsu, L. (2006). Prevalence and incidence studies of anxiety disorders: a systematic review of the literature. *Canadian Journal of Psychiatry, 51*(2), 100–13. doi:10.1177/070674370605100206

Spack, N. P., Edwards-Leeper, L., Feldman, H. A., Leibowitz, S., Mandel, F., Diamond, D. A., & Vance, S. R. (2012). Children and adolescents with gender identity disorder referred to a pediatric medical center. *Pediatrics, 129*(3), 418–25. doi:10.1542/peds.2011–0907

Testa, R. J., Habarth, J., Peta, J., Balsam, K., & Bockting, W. (2015). Development of the Gender Minority Stress and Resilience Measure. *Psychology of Sexual Orientation and Gender Diversity, 2*(1), 65. doi:10.1037/sgd0000081

Testa, R. J., Michaels, M. S., Bliss, W., Rogers, M. L., Balsam, K. F., & Joiner, T. (2017). Suicidal ideation in transgender people: Gender minority stress and interpersonal theory factors. *Journal of Abnormal Psychology, 126*(1), 125. doi:10.1037/abn0000234

Testa, R. J., Rider, G. N., Haug, N. A., & Balsam, K. F. (2017). Gender confirming medical interventions and eating disorder symptoms among transgender individuals. *Health Psychology, 36*(10), 927. doi:10.1037/hea0000497

The Trevor Project, the National Eating Disorders Association, and Reasons Eating Disorder Center. (2018). *Eating disorders among LGBTQ youth*. Retrieved from: https://www.nationaleatingdisorders.org/

Tsai, A. C., Mendenhall, E., Trostle, J. A., & Kawachi, I. (2017). Co-occurring epidemics, syndemics, and population health. *Lancet, 389*(10072), 978–82. doi:10.1016/S0140-6736(17)30403-8

Tucker, R. P., Testa, R. J., Simpson, T. L., Shipherd, J. C., Blosnich, J. R., & Lehavot, K. (2018). Hormone therapy, gender affirmation surgery, and their association with recent suicidal ideation and depression symptoms in transgender veterans. *Psychological Medicine, 48*(14), 2329–36. doi:10.1017/S0033291717003853

Turban, J. L., & van Schalkwyk, G. I. (2018). "Gender dysphoria" and autism spectrum disorder: Is the link real? *Journal of the American Academy of Child and Adolescent Psychiatry, 57*(1), 8–9.

Valentine, D. (2007). *Imagining transgender: An ethnography of a category*. Durham, NC: Duke University Press.

Valentine, S. E., & Shipherd, J. C. (2018). A systematic review of social stress and mental health among transgender and gender non-conforming people in the United States. *Clinical Psychology Review, 66*, 24–38. doi:10.1016/j.cpr.2018.03.003

van der Miesen, A. I., de Vries, A. L., Steensma, T. D., & Hartman, C. A. (2018). Autistic symptoms in children and adolescents with gender dysphoria. *Journal of Autism and Developmental Disorders, 48*(5), 1537–48. doi:10.1007/s10803-017-3417-5

Van Kesteren, P. J., Asscheman, H., Megens, J. A., & Gooren, L. J. (1997). Mortality and morbidity in transsexual subjects treated with cross-sex hormones. *Clinical Endocrinology, 47*(3), 337–343. doi:10.1046/j.1365-2265.1997.2601068.x

Veale, J. F., Watson, R. J., Peter, T., & Saewyc, E. M. (2017). Mental health disparities among Canadian transgender youth. *Journal of Adolescent Health, 60*(1), 44–9. doi:10.1016/j.jadohealth.2016.09.014

Vincent, B. W. (2018). Studying trans: Recommendations for ethical recruitment and collaboration with transgender participants in academic research. *Psychology & Sexuality, 9*(2), 102–16. doi:10.1080/19419899.2018.1434558

Watson, R. J., Veale, J. F., & Saewyc, E. M. (2017). Disordered eating behaviors among transgender youth: Probability profiles from risk and protective factors. *International Journal of Eating Disorders, 50*(5), 515–22. doi:10.1002/eat.22627

White Hughto, J. M., Pachankis, J. E., Willie, T. C., & Reisner, S. L. (2017). Victimization and depressive symptomology in transgender adults: The mediating role of avoidant coping. *Journal of Counseling Psychology, 64*(1), 41. doi:10.1037/cou0000184

Witcomb, G. L., Bouman, W. P., Claes, L., Brewin, N., Crawford, J. R., & Arcelus, J. (2018). Levels of depression in transgender people and its predictors: Results of a large matched control study with transgender people accessing clinical services. *Journal of Affective Disorders, 235*, 308–15. doi:10.1016/j.jad.2018.02.051

Wolford-Clevenger, C., Frantell, K., Smith, P. N., Flores, L. Y., & Stuart, G. L. (2018). Correlates of suicide ideation and behaviors among transgender people: A systematic review guided by ideation-to-action theory. *Clinical Psychology Review, 63*, 93–105. doi:10.1016/j.cpr.2018.06.009

Yarhouse, M. A., & Carrs, T. L. (2012). MTF transgender Christians' experiences: A qualitative study. *Journal of LGBT Issues in Counseling, 6*(1), 18–33. doi:10.1080/15538605.2012.649405

CHAPTER

25 Gender Nonbinary Mental Health

lore m. dickey

Abstract

In this chapter the author explores the mental health of those with nonbinary gender identities and focuses on the issues they face. The author defines nonbinary identities and discusses how these identities are different than people who have binary identities. There is a summary of the extant psychological literature focusing on people with nonbinary identities. Attention is also brought to how racial and ethnic minority individuals, including Native American people, conceptualize nonbinary identities. The chapter ends with information about the lack of attention to the Global South and the need for additional research and training in the mental health of those with nonbinary identities.

Keywords: nonbinary, gender identity, two-spirit, mental health, health disparities

Gender diversity is not a new concept. The presence of trans people is becoming more frequent in the media, in day-to-day life, and in people's personal lives. Given the prevalence of trans people, it is not uncommon to meet someone who is trans or who knows another person who is trans, but meeting and knowing a person with a nonbinary identity is less common. In this chapter I explore people with nonbinary identities and focus on the issues they face.[1]

Definitions

It is important to begin by defining some terms that will be used in this chapter. *Gender* is a social construct in which roles and rules for behavior are assumed based on the sex one is believed to be. For instance, if a person is perceived as male others may expect them to act aggressively, to be physically stronger than people who are assumed to be female, and to dress in a manner that is associated with being male (e.g., pants, shirt, maybe a necktie). On the other hand, if a person is assumed to be female they are permitted to have emotional interactions, they are more likely to be a social person, and their clothing has a much wider range than that of a man and includes being able to wear dresses without there being negative social implications. A person does not need to be a trans person to be "policed" by others about their attire or behavior. Gender role transgressions are a common source of bullying behavior. For nonbinary people this mistreatment can have lasting traumatic effects.

The *gender binary* is the concept that there are two, and only two, immutable genders (Hyde, Bigler, Joel, Tate, & van Anders, 2018), masculine or feminine, and there is nothing that exists between those poles. In recent years people have talked about gender as being on a spectrum. This means that there are many places between the poles of masculine and feminine. People who identify on the gender binary may or may not recognize and honor the fact that gender is on a spectrum.

Gender nonbinary is a relatively recent term even though people with nonbinary identities have

[1] As the author this chapter, I identify as a trans man. I live and present with a binary identity. I am aware that I have privilege in that identity and it is possible that I have overlooked important elements of the lives of people with nonbinary identities.

existed across history (Chang, Singh, & dickey, 2018). There are other terms that are used to express the gender identity of a person who does not associate themselves with the gender binary. These include gender nonconforming, gender fluid, gender diverse, gender variant, gender atypical, gender creative, genderqueer, neutrois, agender, and more. When working with a person who has a nonbinary identity it is important to use the terminology that fits for that person. Equally important is the need to remember that the labels, or identity markers, a person uses may change over time.

When thinking about people with nonbinary identities, it can be difficult to quantify how many trans people use a nonbinary identity as compared to those who adhere to binary identities. Harrison, Grant, and Herman (2012) explored the results of the National Transgender Discrimination Survey (Grant et al., 2011) and reported the responses to a question in which participants selected the option "a gender not listed here." Thirteen percent of over 6,400 people indicated a gender not listed here. This resulted in 860 written responses that Harrison et al. analyzed. In this sample, people who were assigned female at birth were more likely to endorse a nonbinary identity than were those who were assigned male at birth. Those who identified as nonbinary in the study were more likely to live in the lowest income category (less than $10,000 a year). Similar discrepancies were seen for other social determinants of health across the sample, including the myriad ways people were victimized. Interestingly, Klein and Golub (2016) found that suicide risk and alcohol or drug misuse were more likely in trans people with a binary identity.

Galupo, Pulice-Farrow, and Ramirez (2017) conducted a qualitative study exploring the identity labels that were used by people who chose either gender variant or agender in response to a question asking about their primary gender identity. Participants (n = 161), all with a primary, nonbinary identity, named thirty-two different identities that fell into the categories of binary, nonbinary, fluid, agender, and trans identities. It may seem contradictory for a person with a nonbinary identity to endorse a binary label. However, participants explained this as some days they are male and some days they are female. It was also used as a way to describe what their gender is not. This research study exemplifies the many labels or terms that people with nonbinary identities hold.

Nonbinary People

Nonbinary identities are not a new concept. Nonbinary people have existed throughout history (Chang et al., 2018). In recent times, there has been a resurgence in the numbers of people who identify as nonbinary. Many health and mental health providers, regardless of their own gender identity, are finding themselves in a place where their beliefs about gender are stretched in new ways. In this section I will explore some of the challenges faced by people with nonbinary identities. This process is complicated by the fact that people with nonbinary identities are often "lumped" together with other transgender people, including those who have a binary identity. Where possible, information specific to nonbinary people will be highlighted.

Bockting et al. (2016) conducted a review of the literature to understand the ways that transgender and gender-nonconforming people are adversely impacted as they develop their identity. One of the reasons why Bockting et al. conducted this review was to highlight research that focused on something other than HIV prevalence in the trans community. There were two important findings in the research. First, researchers found that trans and nonbinary people are adversely impacted by discrimination and stigma. This resulted in health disparities, including psychological distress (Bockting, Miner, Swinburne Romine, Hamilton, & Coleman, 2013). When conceptualizing stressors in the framework of the Minority Stress Model (Hendricks & Testa, 2012; Meyer, 1995, 2003) it is clear that trans and nonbinary people experience distal and proximal stressors. Research has shown that this can result in a decrease in the quality of life (Hendricks & Testa, 2012). Second, trans and gender nonbinary people are resilient (Bockting et al., 2016; Singh, Hays, & Watson, 2011). Resilience, the ability to bounce back when faced with adversity (Singh, 2012), is an individual and a community attribute (dickey, 2017; Perrin & Tabaac, 2017; Singh et al., 2011). Individually, people with nonbinary identities are able to marshal their resources to face adversities. On a community level, nonbinary people may participate in support groups or pride events as a means of developing connections with others.

Budge, Rossman, and Howard (2014) explored the ways in which social support moderated coping and psychological distress. Notable about their study is that the participants all identified as genderqueer. Genderqueer was defined as "a label used within the broader transgender community and is defined as a gender identity that is outside the binary construct of male and female" (Budge et al., 2014, p. 95). This study is one of the first, if not the first, to explore the psychological well-being of people with nonbinary identities.

Budge et al. found that the genderqueer people (n = 64) reported high (clinical) levels of depression and anxiety. The results indicated that avoidant coping was associated with higher levels of depression. Facilitative coping was found to be associated with lower levels of anxiety. Finally, the results indicated that having social support led to decreased levels of distress. It seems unusual to need the results of a research study to understand the importance of social support. Yet, when thinking of the many challenges faced by nonbinary people (e.g., violence, discrimination, institutional barriers), it is clear that social support is needed to survive everyday challenges and difficulties.

Scandurra et al. (2019) conducted a systemic review exploring the health of nonbinary and genderqueer people. Health differences were explored in comparison to trans people with binary identities and to cisgender people. Articles reviewed by Scandurra et al. were primarily cross-sectional, used non-probability sampling, and had relatively small sample sizes. Results of the comparisons were mixed: in some cases nonbinary people had worse health outcomes and in other cases they had better health outcomes (Scandurra et al., 2019). This exemplifies the need for additional research with people who have nonbinary identities. Notable in this study, the articles that were reviewed had all been published since 2016. This a new field of inquiry that is in need of attention. Scandurra et al. also reported that people with nonbinary identities received more medical care, were less likely to attempt suicide, and had greater levels of well-being. Although these positive aspects existed, nonbinary people were less likely to have support from family and friends and to have negative health outcomes. This is consistent with the work of dickey, Reisner, and Juntunen (2015), who found that people with nonbinary identities were more likely to engage in nonsuicidal self-injury. Scandurra et al. were also interested in the ways in which medical interventions impacted the lives of people with nonbinary identities. They found a study that reported that nonbinary people who were assigned female at birth reported improved quality of life after having had chest surgery (Esmonde et al., 2018). Some people hold the belief that nonbinary people are not interested in medical interventions. This assumption may not be true for all nonbinary individuals as each person will make the decision about whether they want medical interventions.

Galupo, Pulice-Farrow, Clements, and Morris (2019) conducted a study that explored the ways that microaffirmations in romantic relationships help to provide support to people with nonbinary identities. Four themes were derived from the qualitative study: (a) identity validations (being seen as a nonbinary person), (b) identity endorsements (using affirmative language), (c) active learning (partner engages in their own learning about nonbinary people), and (d) active defense (partner actively defends their partner's identity). Galupo et al. (2019) found that daily microaffirmations from a romantic partner had a positive effect on the nonbinary person. Microaffirmations were especially important for validating nonbinary identities. Given that people often question nonbinary identities (even within the transgender community), this knowledge helps shed light on the importance of verbal demonstrations of support. For example, transgender people who are not supportive may hold the belief that a person with a nonbinary identity is "not transgender enough."

Mental Health of Nonbinary People

There is a small body of research, most of which has come under the direction of Stephanie Budge and her research teams (Budge et al., 2014; Matsuno & Budge, 2017). In a recent review of the literature, Matsuno and Budge (2017) acknowledge the nonbinary identities across cultures. Even with support, nonbinary people are likely to experience more negative mental health outcomes (Matsuno & Budge, 2017). These risks include higher rates of self-injury (dickey et al., 2015), higher rates of suicide attempts (Matsuno & Budge, 2017; Tebbe & Moradi, 2016), and higher rates of depression and anxiety (Budge et al., 2014). These research studies are described in this section.

Budge et al. (2014) conducted a quantitative study of sixty-four genderqueer individuals. Fifty-four (86 percent) of the sample identified as white. The majority of the sample (n = 41, 64 percent) identified their sexual identity as queer. The majority of the sample (n = 40, 63 percent) reported earning less than $30,000 a year. The following scales were used in the study: Multidimensional Scale of Social Support (MSPSS), Center for Epidemiologic Studies Depression Scale (CES-D), Burns Anxiety

Inventory (BAI), and Ways of Coping (revised; WOC-R). Data for this study came from a larger data set that included people with binary identities. The authors of the study hypothesized that genderqueer people would experience higher rates of anxiety and depression than the general population.

The authors tested their hypothesis using two hierarchical multiple regression analyses, first with depression as the dependent variable and second with anxiety as the dependent variable. Results showed that genderqueer people experience higher levels of distress as measured by depression (50 percent of the sample) and anxiety (39 percent). In the general population about 17 percent of people experience depression and about 29 percent experience anxiety (Kessler, Berglund, Demler, Jin, & Walters, 2005). The results also indicated that coping was significant for the sample related to how people addressed depression and anxiety in their life. The results also shed light on the importance of social support: genderqueer people who had higher levels of social support experienced less anxiety and depression.

A study conducted by dickey et al. (2015) found that people with nonbinary identities were more likely to engage in nonsuicidal self-injury (NSI). In this study of 773 self-identified transgender people, 12.9 percent (n = 109) of the sample had a nonbinary identity. Fifty-two of these people reported a history of NSI. A total of 324 people (41.9 percent) from the full sample had a history of NSI. Participants completed the Body Investment Scale, Inventory of Statements about Self-Injury Scale, and the Depression Anxiety Stress Scales (DASS-21). Of the people who identified as genderqueer or other nonbinary identities, 47.7 percent had a history of NSI. When considering the various ways in which a person might engage in NSI, genderqueer and other nonbinary people had some of the highest rates of cutting, banging or hitting self, punching, interfering with wound healing, severe scratching, burning, pulling hair, biting, sticking self with needles, and carving. The rates at which people with nonbinary identities engaged in these behaviors was at least 5 percent higher than the full sample (dickey et al., 2015).

Tebbe and Moradi (2016) applied the Minority Stress Theory in an effort to understand suicide risk in the transgender community. There were 335 transgender people in the sample, 128 of whom had a nonbinary identity. Participants ranged in age from eighteen to sixty-six years, with 78.5 percent of the participants being between the ages of eighteen to twenty-nine. Nearly 82 percent of participants identified as White. The authors used modified versions the subscales of the Daily Heterosexist Experiences Questionnaire (DHEQ); the Internalized Homonegativity subscale of the Lesbian, Gay, and Bisexual Identity Scale; the Gender-Related Fears subscale of the Transgender Adaptation and Integration Measure; the Family, Friend, and Significant Other subscales of the Multidimensional Scale of Perceived Social Support; the Brief Drug Abuse Screening Test; the Alcohol Use Disorders Identification Test; the CES-D; and the Suicidal Behaviors Questionnaire-Revised. Results of the study indicated that experiences of minority stress as mediated by depression were predictive of suicide risk. Tebbe and Moradi conducted an exploratory comparison of the gender groups (binary and nonbinary groups) and found no significant differences in the groups.

Matsuno and Budge (2017) conducted a literature review for the purpose of understanding people with nonbinary or genderqueer identities. They point out the challenges associated with people not having a good understanding of people with nonbinary identities. The lack of knowledge about nonbinary people occurs in spite of the fact that nonbinary people have existed throughout history (Chang et al., 2018; Matsuno & Budge, 2017). Matsuno and Budge comment on the need for the creation of developmental models as existing models tend to be linear and do not acknowledge the ways that some nonbinary people may return to earlier developmental experiences as they come to know their identity. In addition to the challenges associated with developmental models is the concern that mental health providers, even if they have received training in work with transgender people, may have little or no education about nonbinary identities. As a result, nonbinary people who seek care may not get their needs met. Worse yet, they may not seek care at all because they cannot find a provider who understands their concerns. These concerns may arise from the day-to-day stressors associated with living in a society that is structured around binary identities. For example, from restrooms to clothing to demographic forms to the use of pronouns, most structures are defined by the gender binary. A final area of concern addressed by Matsuno and Budge is the fact that nonbinary people may have different conceptions of what it means to transition and whether they will want to engage in medical aspects of transition. They caution providers about the importance of allowing nonbinary people to develop their own identity and to be respectful when those identities are different than a person might typically expect.

Matsuno (2019) conducted a study of nonbinary people as a means of bringing to light the many challenges faced by this subset of the trans community. Their[2] work uses Minority Stress Theory as a means of understanding mental health outcomes. They report that nonbinary people are at heightened risk of experiencing mental health concerns and that they are less likely to have access to mental health services. Matsuno then recommends a number of interventions at the micro-, mezzo-, and macro-levels. At the micro-level, Matsuno discusses the importance of empowering the client (American Psychological Association, 2015). The next intervention discusses the importance of using gender-neutral pronouns. Matsuno acknowledges the challenges that arise when people attempt to use new pronoun terms or existing terms in a new way. However, in order to empower the client, it is critical that providers use language that mirrors the client's lived identity. Using gender-neutral language is the next micro-level recommendation. The use of gender-neutral language should be part of all aspects of the therapy setting. This means that whether a person is answering the phone, greeting a client at the front desk, or escorting a patient to the examination room, gender-neutral language should be used.

Case conceptualization is a critical aspect of the work performed by mental health providers. Matsuno (2019) sees this as a micro-level intervention wherein providers allow themselves to be curious about the ways that gender-related distress is experienced by their clients. Related to this is the need to work with clients to develop the ability to externalize and reject negative messages. If a person is unable to do this, they are likely to experience internalized stigma or prejudice (Perez-Brumer, Hatzenbuehler, Oldenburg, & Bockting, 2015).

Matsuno (2019) explains that mezzo-level interventions are those that attempt to make change within social systems that impact the person's life. There are a number of systems that impact a nonbinary person's life; most salient for this work are those that impact the healthcare setting. Changes to the ways in which a provider gathers demographic data, especially about sex, gender, name, pronouns, or marital status, are relatively simple whether one works from paper intake forms or an electronic health record (Deutsch et al., 2013). Another method that can be very helpful in the healthcare setting is the use of symbols such as a genderqueer flag in waiting room spaces (Webb, Matsuno, Budge, Krishnan, & Balsam, 2017). Finally, an important mezzo-level intervention is the use and establishment of all-gender or gender-inclusive restrooms.

Matsuno (2019) goes on to describe macro-level interventions. These interventions are developed in an effort to change societal, environmental, or institutional systems and practices that serve to promote an anti-trans bias (Trickett et al., 2011). Macro-level interventions suggest that psychologists and other providers engage in research and advocacy as a means of effecting social change. This approach to change has been suggested by others (American Psychological Association, 2015; Chang et al., 2018; dickey, Singh, Chang, & Rehrig, 2017). Matsuno notes that advocacy can happen on local, state, and national levels. For example, a psychologist might advocate for a client by working with their local school district to establish policies about restroom use. At the state level, advocacy might involve contacting a state legislator about proposed legislation that either is supportive or not of the lives of nonbinary people. Similar action can be taken on the federal level. It is important when contacting legislators to be sure to provide information about the reason for making contact and the supporting psychological data.

Matsuno's work extends the American Psychological Association's (2015) *Guidelines for Psychological Practice with Transgender and Gender Nonconforming People.* Most importantly, Matsuno describes the ways to work with people with nonbinary identities. Their work is grounded in their own life experience and in relevant psychological research.

Sexual Orientation and Nonbinary People

People with a nonbinary identity may identify as straight, gay, pansexual, or asexual (to name a few identities). Pansexual is an identity term that is often used by people with nonbinary identities as it indicates that a person is attracted to someone else regardless of their gender identity and is indicative of not adhering to the gender binary. Pansexual is also used by people who have a binary identity yet are attracted to people regardless of their gender identity.

One aspect of sexuality is that it can be fluid for a person, so there may be shifts or other changes in

[2] Matsuno uses the gender-neutral pronouns of they/them/their. For more information about this type of pronoun usage visit *Pronouns Matter* at www.mypronouns.org.

how a person identifies. Regardless of how a person identifies, it is important to be flexible and not make assumptions about who a person should or could be attracted to. This also means that as a client talks about sexuality it is important to dispel preconceived notions about how a person might identify. This can be challenging for people who have a heterosexual identity, who rarely spend time thinking about their own sexual orientation. Some nonbinary people may have heterosexual identities, but it is problematic to begin with that assumption.

Intersecting Identities

Intersectionality is the "the idea that social identities . . . interact to form qualitatively different meanings and experiences" (Warner, 2008, p. 454). Being a gender minority (e.g., a transgender or nonbinary person) and adding other marginalized identities is going to increase the likelihood that a person will experience additional stressors and disparities related to health conditions, housing, employment, food, and ways that a person lives their life (American Psychological Association, 2015).

People with nonbinary identities often experience their lives as being invisible to others (Budge et al., 2014), so that other people are not willing or are unable to see and respect their gender. When adding another marginalized identity (e.g., race, age, disability, immigration status) the experiences of discrimination and other types of mistreatment quickly become overwhelming. Mental health providers need to be aware of the challenges faced by nonbinary clients who have intersecting identities. It is also important for the provider to spend time exploring the ways that their own identities might unwittingly complicate these situations. For example, I am a white trans male. As such, I benefit from male and white privilege. It does not matter that I did nothing to gain this privilege; what matters is that I am willing and able to engage in conversations with my clients with the purpose of understanding how my privilege impacts them.

Race and Ethnicity

A common complaint, anecdotally, is that the labels that are used for lesbian, gay, bisexual, and transgender people were created by and for white people. As a result, trans People of Color often feel out of place in transgender and nonbinary spaces. For example, some nonbinary African American people who were assigned female at birth use the term "stud" as an identity label (Kamau, 2008).

Another challenge faced by nonbinary people of color is when white people choose a name for them. One example is the offensive label *berdache*, a French term for male prostitute (Epple, 1998), which was used to describe some Native American tribes that recognized multiple genders, even as many as five different gender roles (Brayboy, 2017). The term *two-spirit* is most often used across Native American cultures in North America (Jacobs, Thomas, & Lang, 1997). Two-spirit was coined in 1990 at a Native American/First Nations conference in Winnipeg, Manitoba (Jacobs et al., 1997). Although this seems basic, it is critical that mental health providers ask their clients which label (if any) they use to describe their gender. It is important to know that a person who identifies as two-spirit may be transgender, gay or lesbian, or a spiritual leader.

Although not every tribe recognizes two-spirit people, in general when they do these individuals are revered (House, 2016). House describes his/her (the pronouns used by House) life experiences growing up in the Diné (Navajo) culture. House begins by describing those roles that were commonly performed by men, stating that some of those roles were impacted by colonialism, including "assimilation, Christianity, and Indian Relocation Programs" (House, 2016, p. 325). Diné culture has a strong matrilineal emphasis. Women in Diné tribes "had voice over land, wealth, livestock, and family" (p. 325). House describes a childhood that was disrupted through relocation and he/she engaged in activities that were intended for boys. House states that family members were supportive of House being a boy and now a man. This support was strongest through House's maternal family, including his/her grandmother. It has been important for House to keep the name he/she was given at birth as it is a strong tie to his/her family and tribe.

House was trained in medicinal practices and reports having connections to the Holy People in the Diné culture. He/she was a protector of others, beginning at a young age when House would protect other children who were subjected to bullying. House discusses some of the challenges with the term *two-spirit*. He/she states that it can mean both gay and being of more than one gender. Often it is used because it simplifies an understanding of what can be a complex identity. House is most concerned about those people who use *two-spirit* as an identity label and are not of Native American descent: co-opting this terminology is problematic and disrespectful.

Blackwood (1997) argues that labels, especially the many options used by or for Native Americans, are problematic, and some have no real meaning (e.g., not-man/not-woman, man-woman, third gender, fourth gender). Jacobs (1997) discusses the ways that the multiplicity of labels can be confusing, even for those who live in the culture where the labels are used. For example, Cromwell (1997) explains the ways the term *berdache* is centered on masculine experiences, and therefore trans masculine people (assigned female at birth) do not identify with the term.

Populations in the Global South

Little has been written about transgender and gender nonbinary people in the Global South. It is important that nonbinary people be recognized in this part of the world. If one reviews the names and location of trans people who were murdered in the past year (www.tdor.info), people who live in the Global South will be over-represented. This is especially true for those who live in South America. In general, trans people, including those with nonbinary identities, are rarely afforded any protection under the laws of their country. As such, they are often mistreated (at best) and murdered (at worst).

Future Directions

There is scant literature on the lives of people with nonbinary identities. What is troublesome about this is that this makes it easier to erase the existence of nonbinary people. It is not uncommon for a provider who is engaging in clinical work with a nonbinary person to attempt to force them into a binary identity. This happens, in part, because providers receive little to no training in affirmative approaches to working with this client group. For nonbinary people, as for trans people before them, this leads to a feeling that they are alone with their identity. As a result, they may be more likely to experience disparities across social domains (e.g., housing, healthcare, education, employment).

Nonbinary people have existed throughout history and across cultures but still tend to be misunderstood by others to the point where they are effectively erased from reality. By highlighting the lives of people with nonbinary identities, it is hoped that others will begin to grasp and respect people with nonbinary identities. This should help to ensure that nonbinary people are treated with dignity.

References

American Psychological Association. (2015). Guidelines for psychological practice with transgender and gender nonconforming people. *American Psychologist, 70*, 832–64. doi:10.1037/a0039906

Blackwood, E. (1997). Native American gender and sexualities: Beyond anthropological models and misrepresentations. In S. Jacobs, W. Thomas, & S. Lang (Eds.), *Two-spirit people: Native American gender identity, sexuality, and spirituality* (pp. 284–94). Chicago, IL: University of Illinois Press.

Bockting, W., Coleman, E., Deutsch, M. B., Guillamon, A., Meyer, I., Meyer, W, III, . . . Ettner, R. (2016). Adult development and quality of life of transgender and gender nonconforming people. *Current Opinion in Endocrinology, Diabetes and Obesity, 23*, 188–97. doi:10.1097/MED.0000000000000232

Bockting, W., Miner, M. H., Swinburne Romine, R. E., Hamilton, A., & Coleman, E. (2013). Stigma, mental health, and resilience in an online sample of the US transgender population. *American Journal of Public Health, 103*, 943–51. doi:10.2105/AJPH.2013.301241

Brayboy, D. (2017). *Two spirits, one heart, five genders*. https://newsmaven.io/indiancountrytoday/archive/two-spirits-one-heart-five-genders-9UH_xnbfVEWQHWkjNn0rQQ/

Budge, S. L., Rossman, H. K., & Howard, K. A. S. (2014). Coping and psychological distress among genderqueer individuals: The moderating effect of social support. *Journal of LGBT Issues in Counseling, 8*, 95–117. doi:10.1080/15538605.2014.853641

Chang, S. C., Singh, A. A., & dickey, l. m. (2018). *A clinician's guide to gender-affirming care: Working with transgender and gender nonconforming clients*. Oakland, CA: Context Press.

Cromwell, J. (1997). Traditions of gender diversity and sexualities: A female-to-male transgendered perspective. In S. Jacobs, W. Thomas, & S. Lang (Eds.), *Two-spirit people: Native American gender identity, sexuality, and spirituality* (pp. 119–42). Chicago, IL: University of Illinois Press.

Deutsch, M. B., Green, J., Keatley, J., Mayer, G., Hastings, J., & Hall, A. M. (2013). Electronic medical records and the transgender patient: Recommendations from the World Professional Association for Transgender Health EMR working group. *Journal of the American Medical Informatics Association, 20*, 700–3. doi:10.1136/amiajnl-2012-001472

dickey, l. m. (2017). Gender nonconformity and transgender issues: Overview. In K. L. Nadal (Ed.), *The SAGE encyclopedia of psychology and gender* (pp. 692–7). Thousand Oaks, CA: Sage. doi:10.4135/9781483384269.n

dickey, l. m., Reisner, S. L., & Juntunen, C. L. (2015). Nonsuicidal self-injury in a large online sample of transgender adults. *Professional Psychology: Research and Practice, 46*, 3–11. doi:10.1037/a0038803

dickey, l. m., Singh, A. A., Chang, S. C., Rehrig, M. (2017). Advocacy and social justice: The next generation of counseling and psychological practice with transgender and gender nonconforming clients. In A. A. Singh & l. m. dickey (Eds.), *Affirmative counseling and psychological practice with transgender and gender nonconforming clients* (pp. 247–62). Washington, DC: American Psychological Association. doi:10.1037/14957–013

Epple, C. (1998). Coming to terms with Navajo Nádleehí: A critique of berdache, "gay," "alternate gender," and "two-spirit."

American Ethnologist, 25, 267–90. doi:10.1525/ae.1998.25.2.267

Esmonde, N., Heston, A., Ramly, E., Jedrezsewski, B., Annen, A., Guerriero, J., . . . Berli, J. (2018). What is "non-binary" and what do I need to know? A primer for surgeons providing chest surgery for transgender patients. *Aesthetic Plastic Surgery, 39*(5), NP106–NP112. doi:10.1093/asj/sjy166/5051325

Galupo, M. P., Pulice-Farrow, L., Clements, Z. A., & Morris, E. R. (2019). "I love you as both and I love you as neither": Romantic partners' affirmations of nonbinary trans individuals. *International Journal of Transgenderism, 20*(2–3), 315–27. doi:10.1080/15532739.2018.1496867

Galupo, M. P., Pulice-Farrow, L., & Ramirez, J. L. (2017). "Like a constantly flowing river": Gender identity flexibility among nonbinary transgender individuals. In J. D. Sinnott (Ed.), *Identity flexibility in adulthood: Perspectives in adult development* (pp. 163–78). Cham, Switzerland: Springer.

Grant, J. M., Mottet, L. A., Tanis, J., Harrison, J., Herman, J. L., & Keisling, M. (2011). *Injustice at every turn: A report of the National Transgender Discrimination Study.* Washington, DC: National Center for Transgender Equality and National Gay and Lesbian Task Force. https://transequality.org/sites/default/files/docs/resources/NTDS_Report.pdf

Harrison, J., Grant, J., & Herman, J. L. (2012). A gender not listed here: Genderqueers, gender rebels, and otherwise in the National Transgender Discrimination Survey. *LGBTQ Public Policy Journal at the Harvard Kennedy School, 2*(1), 13–24. doi:scholarship.org/uc/item/2zj46213

Hendricks, M. L., & Testa, R. J. (2012). A conceptual framework for clinical work with transgender and gender nonconforming clients: An adaptation of the Minority Stress Model. *Professional Psychology: Research and Practice, 43*, 460–67. doi:10.1037/a0029597

House, C. (2016). Blessed by the Holy People. *Journal of Lesbian Studies, 20*, 324–41. doi:10.1080/10894160.2016.1151242

Hyde, J. S., Bigler, R. S., Joel, D., Tate, C. C., & van Anders, S. M. (2018). The future of sex and gender in psychology: Five challenges to the gender binary. *American Psychologist, 74*, 171–93. doi:10.1037/amp0000307

Jacobs, S. (1997). Is the "North American berdache" merely a phantom in the imagination of Western social scientists? In S. Jacobs, W. Thomas, & S. Lang (Eds.), *Two-spirit people: Native American gender identity, sexuality, and spirituality* (pp. 21–43). Chicago, IL: University of Illinois Press.

Jacobs, S., Thomas, W., & Lang, S. (1997). Introduction. In S. Jacobs, W. Thomas, & S. Lang (Eds.), *Two-spirit people: Native American gender identity, sexuality, and spirituality* (pp. 1–8). Chicago, IL: University of Illinois Press.

Kamau, A. (2008). *Stud: Dispelling the myths.* Sherman Oaks, CA: Glover Lane Publishing.

Kessler, R. C., Berglund, P., Demler, O., Jin, R., & Walters, E. E. (2005). Lifetime prevalence and age of-onset distributions of DSM-IV disorders in the national comorbidity survey replication. *Archives of General Psychiatry, 62*(6), 593–602. doi:10.1001/archpsyc.62.6.593

Klein, A., & Golub, S. A. (2016). Family rejection as a predictor of suicide attempts and substance misuse among transgender and gender nonconforming adults. *LGBT Health, 3*(3), 1–7. doi:10.1089/lgbt.2015.0111

Matsuno, E. (2019). Nonbinary-affirming psychological interventions. *Cognitive and Behavioral Practice* [E-pub before print]. doi:10.1016/j.cbpra.2018.09.003

Matsuno, E., & Budge, S. L. (2017). Non-binary/genderqueer identities: A critical review of the literature. *Current Sexual Health Reports, 9*, 116–20. doi:10.1007/s11930-017-0111-8

Meyer, I. H. (1995). Minority stress and mental health in gay men. *Journal of Health and Social Behavior, 36*, 38–56. doi:10.2307/2137286

Meyer, I. H. (2003). Prejudice, social stress, and mental health in lesbian, gay, and bisexual populations: Conceptual issues and research evidence. *Psychological Bulletin, 129*, 674–97. doi:10.1037/0033–2909.129.5.674

Perez-Brumer, A., Hatzenbuehler, M. L., Oldenburg, C. E., & Bockting, W. (2015). Individual- and structural-level risk factors for suicide attempts among transgender adults. *Behavioral Medicine, 41*, 164–71. doi:10.1080/08964289.2015.1028322

Perrin, P. B., & Tabaac, A. R. (2017). Transgender people and resilience. In K. L. Nadal (Ed.), *The SAGE encyclopedia of psychology and gender* (pp. 1712–4). Thousand Oaks, CA: Sage.

Scandurra, C., Mezza, F., Maldonato, N. M., Bottone, M., Bachicchio, V., Valerio, P., & Vitelli, R. (2019). Health of non-binary and genderqueer people: A systemic review. *Frontiers in Psychology, 10*, article 1453. doi:10.3389/fpsyg.2019.01453

Singh, A. A. (2012). Transgender youth of color and resilience: Negotiating oppression and finding support. *Sex Roles, 68*, 690–702. doi:10.1007/s1119-012-0149-z

Singh, A. A., Hays, D. G., & Watson, L. S. (2011). Strength in the face of adversity: Resilience strategies of transgender individuals. *Journal of Counseling & Development, 89*, 20–7.

Tebbe, E., & Moradi, B. (2016). Suicide risk in the trans population: An application of minority stress theory. *Journal of Counseling Psychology, 63*, 520–33. doi:10.1037/cou0000152

Trickett, E. J., Beehler, S., Deutsch, C., Green, L., Hawe, P., McLeroy, K., . . . Trimble, J. E. (2011). Advancing the science of community-level interventions. *American Journal of Public Health, 101*, 1410–9. doi:10.2105/AJPH.2010.300113

Warner, L. R. (2008). A best practice guide to intersectional approaches in psychological research. *Sex Roles, 59*, 454–63. doi:10.1007/s11199-008-9504-5

Webb, A., Matsuno, E., Budge, S. L., Krishnan, M. C., & Balsam, K. F. (2017). *Nonbinary gender identities.* https://www.apadivisions.org/division-44/resources/advocacy/non-binary-facts.pdf

CHAPTER

26 Intersex Mental Health

Katrina Roen *and* Tove Lundberg

Abstract

This chapter takes a critical psychology approach to reviewing research on psychological distress among people with variations of sex characteristics. The focus is on depathologizing emotional distress and developing affirming and empowering approaches to healthcare. Affirming approaches to psychosocial healthcare can be undertaken by health professionals who have enough knowledge about intersex, diverse sex development, or variations of sex characteristics to be able to support positive adaptation to bodily variation and facilitate non-stigmatizing talk about the experience of living with a diagnosis. There is room for significant development here, particularly research addressing psychosocial well-being in ways that are non-medicalized and culturally relevant in diverse global regions.

Keywords: Variations of sex characteristics, intersex, disorders of sex development, diverse sex development, mental health, psychosocial well-being, critical psychology

The topic of intersex or variations of sex characteristics (VSC) is fraught with contested terminology. The present chapter works across terms that we have chosen to respect the integrity of people living with VSC. The first part of this chapter introduces readers to medical and diagnostic terminology and describes shifts in medical intervention, activism, and human rights claims. We introduce a critical psychology framework that prioritizes a depathologizing approach. The main body of this chapter is a critical review of intersex mental health research with emphasis on affirmative healthcare. We situate intersex psychosocial well-being in the context of GLBTIQ+ mental health and related intersectional questions. This chapter concludes with consideration of research gaps and ways forward.

Intersex or VSC can be understood as an ordinary aspect of human diversity (Roen, 2015). Conversely, disorders of sex development (DSD) (as set out in Hughes, Houk, Ahmed, & Lee, 2006) or diverse sex development (dsd) are usually understood in terms of rare medical phenomena that, collectively, are present in approximately 1.7 percent of live births (Blackless et al., 2000). This framing of bodily variation as ordinary or as pathological underlies questions about the mental health and well-being of people living with VSC.

For the purpose of this chapter, we set out the scope of variations that could be relevant. The point here is to extend the focus beyond narrowly defined diagnoses of sex development. The bodily diversity relevant here includes that relating to chromosomal configurations other than XX or XY, such as Turner and Klinefelter syndrome; hormonal response, such as reduced sensitivity to androgens as in complete or partial androgen insensitivity syndrome (CAIS or PAIS); adrenal function as in congenital adrenal hyperplasia (CAH); gonadal development and location, such as gonads that are neither clearly ovaries nor clearly testes (gonadal dysgenesis), and testes that are not located in the scrotum; the size and appearance of the penis/clitoris (including chordee, micropenis, and clitoromegaly); the location of the urethral opening (hypospadias); the development of the vagina, uterus, and fallopian tubes (including vaginal agenesis and conditions such as Swyer syndrome and Mayer-Rokitansky-Küster-Hauser syndrome [MRKH]); the unexpected presence or absence of menstrual bleeding; the timing of puberty, including puberty that is unusually early or late or does not happen spontaneously at all; and the occurrence of breast development, including that which occurs at any point in the life course of boys/men and that which does not occur as expected in girls/women.

In establishing this wide-ranging description, we are defining VSC in a way that is not limited to specific medical diagnoses, or to genital ambiguity, or to particular medical interventions. Instead, we highlight experiences of—and effects of—living with bodily difference coded as relating to "sex development," where "sex" might be chromosomal, hormonal, or anatomical. Some common threads run through this experience from a psychosocial perspective, relating to the shame, stigma, and secrecy; the difficulty of finding words to talk comfortably about the difference; and the difficulty of finding frameworks of understanding that accommodate the difference. These common threads relate to the need for significant others (including parents and loved ones) and health professionals to have the capacity to be understanding and caring in the face of something that might be outside their usual field of experience. These common threads of experience relate to the psychosocial aspects of living with VSC and therefore have a bearing on emotional well-being and mental health.

Critical Psychology and Psychosocial Well-Being: A Way Forward

We use critical psychology as a conceptual foundation because this offers a way to examine the insights from psychological research on "intersex mental health" while maintaining a careful distance from the pathologizing frameworks of understanding (Roen, 2019). Critical psychology provides a way to work strategically with psychological research, rethinking the subject of psychology (Henriques, Hollway, Urwin, Venn, & Walkerdine, 1984; Marecek et al., 2002) and drawing attention to power relations and social justice issues. Critical work within psychology opens up space for thinking about sex, gender, and sexuality as complex concepts that do not fit into the binary frameworks of male/female and normal/abnormal (Barker & Richards, 2015; Clarke & Peel, 2007).

Psychological research that investigates mental health and well-being among people with diagnoses of sex development typically takes one of three approaches: a psychiatric or psycho-pathologizing approach, an approach that focuses on quality of life and other psychometric measures, or an approach that is explicitly depathologizing or psychosocial. In the current chapter, we work with each of these approaches while privileging a depathologizing interpretation.

Challenges of Producing Evidence-Based Knowledge on Intersex Mental Health

During the 1990s, the medical protocol suggested by Money et al. (Money & Ehrhardt, 1972; Money, Hampson, & Hampson, 1955) was criticized by stakeholders (Davis, 2015; Karkazis, 2008). One main criticism was that the recommended interventions were not evidence-based (Diamond & Sigmundson, 1997) but rested on normative assumptions that equated well-being with having a typically sexed body and having heterosexual penetrative sex (Kessler, 1998). Activists with lived experience of VSC also questioned the efficacy of the protocol. The Intersex Society of North America (ISNA) argued, for example, that interventions caused harm rather than promoting well-being. During the 1990s, it became clear that more research was needed in order to provide an evidence base that could inform more effective guidelines. In 2006, the first medical consensus statement was published, presenting as an international standard a biomedically driven approach to intersex healthcare (Lee, Houk, Ahmed, & Hughes, 2006). This statement influences medical practice and frames psycho-pathologizing approaches to intersex well-being.

Since the 1990s, commentators have continued to critically discuss whether the endeavor of evidence-based medicine will contribute to the well-being of people with VSC. Some suggest that research on psychological endpoints has focused heavily on hormonal effects (Stout, Litvak, Robbins, & Sandberg, 2010) and this has not helped people understand their variation or given them meaningful support in their everyday life (Lundberg, Lindström, Roen, & Hegarty, 2017; Stout et al., 2010). Researchers have also questioned how research recruitment is framed (Ansara, 2016), how aspects such as gender identity (Liao, Audi, Magritte, Meyer-Bahlburg, & Quigley, 2012; Schweizer, Brunner, Handford, & Richter-Appelt, 2014) as well as mental health (D'Alberton et al., 2015) are conceptualized, what statistical methods are used (Stout et al., 2010), and how results should be interpreted (Lee et al., 2016). In a global update on DSD healthcare (Lee et al., 2016), the psychosocial section concluded that

> Any causal link between a diagnosis and a single psychometric measure is flawed, since the effects of a diagnosis on well-being depend on a wide range of intrinsic and extrinsic factors across time... Well-being may be affected in highly specific ways at certain times, such as at the initial diagnosis, during the developmental stage, at symptom control, during fertility treatment or at the beginning and end of an important relationship. (p. 167)

When studies are done from a psychiatric or psychopathologizing perspective, social norms typically go unquestioned (Roen, 2019), including binary understandings of gender, heteronormative assumptions underpinning understandings of well-being, and the assumption that bodily variation might affect mental health negatively (Carpenter, 2016). Such concerns should be considered while reviewing studies on intersex mental health.

Commentators suggest that evidence-based knowledge needs to be complemented with person-centered and value-driven care (Liao & Simmonds, 2014; Lundberg, Roen, Hirschberg, & Frisén, 2016). This means showing patients respect, understanding and validating people's perspectives, and promoting self-determination as a driver of clinical practice. Some argue that qualitative research makes an important contribution here because of the diverse contextually shaped experiences and concerns that people with VSC might have (Guth, Witchel, Witchel, & Lee, 2006; Lundberg et al., 2016; Schönbucher et al., 2010; Stout et al., 2010). The idea of value-driven care (Liao & Simmonds, 2014) also acknowledges the ethical and human rights–related aspects of research and healthcare. Human rights advocates have, during the past two decades, raised important concerns as to what norms and values are driving healthcare, and whether these are ethical and in accordance with human rights principles (European Union Fundamental Rights Agency, 2015; Travis, 2015; United Nations Human Rights Council, 2013). For example, the United Nations (2013) has stated that elective surgery to "normalize" the appearance of genitals can be understood as inhumane treatment that violates physical integrity and bodily autonomy. Ethicolegal commentators have argued that current psychiatric or psycho-pathologizing frameworks might not ensure human rights such as the importance of self-determination, protection from discrimination, and access to justice and reparations (reviewed in, e.g., Carpenter, 2016; Monro, Crocetti, Yeadon-Lee, Garland, & Travis, 2017). Much work remains to ensure that clinical practice and research on intersex mental health are driven by values based on human rights (Carpenter, 2016).

According to some, people with VSC have affinities with LGBTQ+ people in the sense that heteronormative and cisgenderist understandings have led similarly to the pathologization, stigmatization, and minoritization of these experiences in recent decades. However, there is a concern that adding "intersex" to create the acronym LGBTIQ risks focusing on challenges related to gender identity or sexual orientation only, rather than to sex characteristics (Carpenter, 2018; Cools et al., 2016). It is important that the specific challenges of people with VSC are not subsumed and made invisible.

Importance of a Depathologizing Framework

Psychologists who undertake research on the mental health and well-being of LGBTIQ people must negotiate tensions that arise from the historical and ongoing pathologization, stigmatization, and minoritization that is woven through LGBTIQ lives (McDermott & Roen, 2016). There are specific points of negotiation to consider here. First, when a group of people has been explicitly pathologized—rendered diagnosable by medical science—it is no simple matter to assign further pathologizing terms, such as mental illness terms, to those people. It is ethically questionable to undertake research whose purpose is to psychiatrically diagnose LGBTIQ people without critically reflecting on the likelihood that this further stigmatizes an already stigmatized group. Second, when a group of people has been systematically stigmatized and minoritized over generations, it is never a straightforward question to ask about the mental health of that group. Such questions inevitably sit at a point of tension between possible interpretations: a pathologizing interpretation that positions the minority group as (perhaps inherently) mentally ill, and an alternative interpretation that postulates minoritization as a cause of (perhaps unavoidable) psychological distress. Each of these interpretations risks reinscribing minoritizing realities rather than benefiting those concerned. Each risks positioning the people concerned as inevitably mentally ill or perpetually on the edge of psychological distress (McDermott & Roen, 2016).

Some researchers write about psychological distress and well-being with a focus on empowerment-centered and LGBTIQ-friendly service provision (e.g., Harper & Singh, 2014; Roen & Groot, 2019). If we approach the topic of intersex from this perspective, we would not ask how many people with a given diagnosis of sex development might also be psychiatrically diagnosable. Instead, we would ask: Given the ways that living with a VSC can be distressing (including distress that is caused within health services), how might attention best be directed toward promoting psychosocial health and well-being? Such a question would direct attention to a much broader conception of "mental health" than would usually be considered. It would direct attention to concepts such as experience: What kinds of experiences, within healthcare, families, and other relationships, are likely to foster well-being among people with VSC? It would also direct attention to concepts such as emotion: What is the role of emotion and emotional distress in the context of living with a VSC, and managing the healthcare and familial relationships? Such questions about experience and emotion direct attention away from psychopathology, allow for the possibility that emotional distress is sometimes to be expected, and draw respectful attention to the subjective perspectives of the people concerned. Some mental health professionals put concepts of emotion and experience at the center and take this affirming and non-pathologizing approach to the well-being of people with VSC (e.g., Alderson, Madill, & Balen, 2004; Carmichael & Alderson, 2004; Chadwick, Smyth, & Liao, 2014; Gough, Weyman, Alderson, Butler, & Stoner, 2008; Liao, 2007, 2015).

Critical Review of Intersex Mental Health Research

A few researchers have undertaken reviews of intersex/dsd mental health literature (e.g., Bohet et al., 2019; Nordenström, 2015; Schützmann, Brinkmann, Schacht, & Richter-Appelt, 2009). For the purpose of this chapter, we draw principally on studies identified within the two reviews that jointly span 1956 to 2016. The first of these two papers was published in 2009 and reviews the eleven studies available at that time (Schützmann et al., 2009). The second of these papers was published in 2019 and reviews eighteen more recent studies (Bohet et al., 2019). In both reviews, the authors note that there is a very slim evidence base with sparse studies of variable quality.

Schützmann et al.'s literature review focuses on psychological distress across various DSD diagnoses, citing studies published between 1956 and 2005. The best-quality study they could find relating to children included fifty-nine children and reported no psychological problems in 42 percent of the sample and mild psychological problems in 19 percent; a further 39 percent met diagnostic criteria in the fourth edition of the American Psychiatric Association's *Diagnostic and Statistical Manual of Mental Disorders* (Slijper, Drop, Molenaar, & de Muinck Keizer-Schrama, 1998). Another study they consider of high quality focuses on fifty adults and two clinical comparison groups with unrelated diagnoses (Warne et al., 2005). According to this study, there were no differences between groups in mental health, depression, or current anxiety. There were differences, however, in relation to trait anxiety, self-esteem, and interpersonal problems, with the DSD group producing poorer scores than one of the comparison groups.

Schützmann et al. extracted findings from the literature they reviewed specifically in relation to people with CAH (total N = 268), noting consistent findings suggesting that people with CAH tend to be psychologically well adjusted and present psychological distress rates comparable to nonclinical reference groups. They speculate that this might be at least partially attributable to the tendency for researchers to recruit participants from hospitals, therefore excluding from study participants who are sufficiently traumatized to avoid hospitals and clinician-led research.

One paper they review offers a useful point of contrast. This study, by Diamond and Watson (2004), included fifty-seven adults with AIS and reported significant levels of distress, including shame, stigma, and identity problems in addition to suicidal thoughts (61 to 62 percent of the sample), and suicide attempts (17 to 23 percent of the sample). Schützmann et al. explain that these high levels of distress could be attributed to the fact that Diamond and Watson recruited participants from support groups.

The more recent review to examine the relationship between people with DSD and mental disorders does not problematize psycho-pathologization and does explicitly exclude qualitative studies (Bohet et al., 2019). The studies they identified were published between 2006 and 2016. These reviewers suggest that people with DSD face an increased risk of affective disorders, especially anxiety and depressive disorders and interpersonal difficulties. In addition, people with CAH exhibit an increased rate of alcohol consumption. Research with people with complete androgen insensitivity, however, suggested that there was not an increased rate of psychological distress in this group.

Schützmann et al.'s (2009) own empirical study is interesting in that it combines participants from clinical settings and nonclinical settings in an attempt to avoid the sampling issues that may have affected previous findings. They suggest that "psychological distress, especially interpersonal insecurities, suicidal tendencies, and self-harming behaviour, are more frequent in DSD than generally assumed" (p. 32). We suggest there are a few things to be wary of, and these are more or less indicated by Schützmann et al. The first is that not all studies use measures that are sensitive to the particular kinds of distress experienced by people with VSC. Quality-of-life (QOL) studies appear to be particularly poor at discerning the distresses related to VSC and treatment experiences for DSD. Second, as Schützmann et al. point out, clinical studies are unlikely to be able to recruit people who are sufficiently distressed to avoid clinical settings. In combination, these two issues plausibly lead to a significant overestimate of psychological well-being on the part of clinical researchers.

As the topic of intersex has gained wide currency, it has become increasingly possible for community-based and online surveys to be carried out, broadly assessing the well-being of people who identify as intersex or having different sex development. In recent years, this has produced nonacademic literature that can usefully feed into our understanding of intersex mental health. The U.K.-based organization *dsdfamilies* has published online a report based on research with 194 people in the United Kingdom, including children, young people, and families living with different sex development (dsd families, 2019). This report identifies key issues for the well-being of people with different sex development as including psychological and social issues that related to struggling to find people with similar experiences, struggles with self-acceptance, struggles to talk with others about the different sex development, and the desire for access to psychological support with these issues. Also in the United Kingdom, but focusing on a different kind of sample, the Government Equalities Office undertook a national survey of LGBT people that received responses from more than 100,000 people, 2 percent of whom identified as intersex (Government Equalities Office, 2018). Survey respondents were asked about their experiences of mental health services. Compared with other respondents, those who identified as intersex reported more difficulty in accessing mental health services. Thirteen percent of intersex respondents indicated that they had tried to access mental health services within the past twelve months and been unsuccessful. This compares with 8 percent of non-intersex (LGBT) respondents who reported being unsuccessful in accessing mental health services over the same period. When they did manage to access mental health services, 27 percent of intersex respondents reported that the service was "mainly or completely negative." This compares with 21 percent of non-intersex (LGBT) respondents who found the mental health service negative. These very high levels of negative experiences with mental health services deserve attention. It is imperative that mental health service providers develop the skills and knowledge needed to work well with people with VSC.

An Australian online survey posed similar questions about how intersex people experienced mental health services (Jones et al., 2016). Of the 117 participants who responded to a question about how well mental health service providers responded to their variation, 19 percent said "well or very well," 30 percent selected "neutral or mixed," and 23 percent indicated that service providers had responded "badly or very badly." This rate of poor experiences in mental health services is strikingly similar across the U.K. and Australian studies, and the Australian study offers helpful details. Those who wrote comments about the difficulties they experienced with mental health service providers described scenarios where the health professional did not believe that the client had an intersex variation, the health professional lacked knowledge and seemed unwilling to learn about intersex, the health professional mistook intersex as something to do with sexual fetish or sexual disorder, and the health professional did not understand that having an intersex variation could impact psychosocial well-being and therefore was not willing to discuss the issues that were important. Those who wrote comments describing positive experiences with mental health services described professionals who were actively interested and willing to learn about intersex, professionals who saw their role as empowering and enabling clients to seek the healthcare they wanted, and professionals who helped clients come to terms with their own bodies. From this study, it seems clear that promoting intersex mental health means training a wide range of health professionals in ways of working that are sensitive to, and informed about, the realities of living with a VSC.

The Australian study participants (n = 272) were asked about any suicidal thoughts or actions, or self-harming behavior, they had experienced on the basis of issues related to living with a VSC. Twenty-six percent indicated having engaged in self-harm, 60 percent indicated they had thought about suicide, and 19 percent indicated that they had attempted suicide (Jones et al., 2016). This compares with Australian population statistics where fewer than 3 percent of people report having considered or attempted suicide.

Participants in the Australian survey were asked whether health professionals had used counseling, training, or had otherwise pressured participants to act in a more feminine or more masculine way; 44 percent indicated that they had experienced this from health professionals (Jones et al., 2016). The many comments participants offered on this topic detail how being expected and coached to conform to gender-normative and heteronormative ways of being was at best misguided and unprofessional, did not lead to productive healthcare relationships, and did not contribute positively to the client's well-being. It has been clearly established within the trans healthcare literature that it is neither appropriate nor helpful to use methods aimed at gender conformity, yet there is little or no published critique of such practices within intersex healthcare. Promoting intersex mental health requires health professionals to understand that people with VSC are reasonably likely to inhabit or explore nonbinary gender possibilities (Schweizer, Brunner, Handford, & Richter-Appelt, 2014), and there is research evidence showing that pressure to conform to gender norms is not associated with psychological well-being (Egan & Perry, 2001; Langer & Martin, 2004). Being supported in the gender expression one is comfortable with, which may or may not be a binary gender expression, is associated with psychological well-being.

While these community-based surveys present a useful overview of well-being among large samples of people with VSC, much of the small body of research investigating intersex mental health is clinically based and takes a psycho-medical approach. Engberg et al. (2015) undertook a study of psychiatric diagnoses of girls and women with CAH based on Swedish national register data from people born between 1950 and 2010. This is the largest study of psychiatric morbidity of girls and women with CAH. Key findings were that those with CAH (n = 335) were twice as likely as the control sample to have any psychiatric disorder, twice as likely to have stress-related and adjustment disorders, and almost three times more likely to have a record of alcohol misuse.

Engberg et al. seek to understand the levels of anxiety and substance misuse by focusing on genetic and biochemical factors and, in doing so, they do not consider the lifetime experiences that people with CAH go through in relation to the process of diagnosis, treatment, and ongoing management of health issues and stigma. Rather than presuming genetic and biochemical explanations for their data, it would be relevant to consider how the experiences of illness and treatment might lead people to psychological distress that might well take the form of anxiety and might well lead to self-medication that gets classified as alcohol abuse or substance misuse. One risk of relying on a biomedical interpretation of mental health data is that this can lead to a failure to consider how life experiences affect how people feel. This is one example of what happens when a psychiatric and biomedical approach is taken and the researchers lose sight of concepts such as emotional well-being and life experience.

One Dutch study also took a biomedical approach, identifying 130 participants with DSD diagnoses and comparing them with a reference group of 372 people with fibromyalgia (de Neve–Enthoven et al., 2016). It is not clear how this particular comparison might be useful. The researchers used a variety of measures focusing on, for instance, subjective fatigue and self-esteem, QOL, and psychopathology. They concluded that participants "reported good psychosocial wellbeing; they generally reported a good HRQoL [health-related QOL], no serious emotional problems... compared to reference groups" (p. 60). The authors explain that clinical management in the Netherlands has included psychosocial expertise on DSD since the late 1970s. We might read this study to suggest that people with VSC in the Netherlands have enough psychosocial support that they tend not to experience serious emotional problems, or we might consider that the measurement tools and points of comparison do not help us to draw useful conclusions from the data.

One Turkish study focused on a clinical sample of 51 children seen by a Turkish multidisciplinary team (Özbaran et al., 2013). This study provides a striking example of how a psycho-pathologizing approach to research frames people with VSC. The participants in this study were aged between one and eighteen years, with 47 percent of them being in preschool. Despite the very young age of most participants, the researchers report with apparent confidence on their "sense of being male or female," adding that "40 patients (78.4 percent) . . . did not have gender dysphoria; 9 of these patients had a psychiatric disorder" (p. 231). These clinicians focused on matching (binary) gender identity with karyotype, and used a psychiatric framework to evaluate people whose chromosomes and identities did not seem to match during these first years of life. These researchers reported that 54.9 percent "of the patients did not show any psychiatric symptoms," but those who did are described as having depression, anxiety disorder, attention-deficit/hyperactivity disorder, or adjustment disorder. This is an example of a study whose psychiatric framing makes it difficult to avoid pathologizing children with VSC and children who might come to question binary gender.

Krupp et al. (2014) present findings from fifty women with MRKH syndrome and eleven people with complete androgen insensitivity syndrome, focusing on QOL and psychological distress. Just over 54 percent of the sample was found to have a significant level of psychological distress, based on the Global Severity Index of the Brief Symptom Inventory, and the prevalence rates of suicide attempts were found to be significantly higher than national nonclinical population data. The reported rate of attempting suicide was slightly higher than that reported by Schützmann et al. (2009) and fell in the range that has previously been reported for people with mental health disorders such as major depressive episodes and panic disorder. The fact that QOL scores placed participants in an average range for the general population suggests that this is one of a number of studies where QOL scores do not accurately reflect the emotional distress experienced. By contrast, the Brief Symptom Inventory scores gave a more detailed picture of psychological distress. The authors of this article consider the diverse findings, across studies, and question what is happening when psychological distress is not reported. Such a line of questioning provides a platform for querying all clinical studies that treat mental health somewhat superficially, rely on measures that fail to reflect the particular distresses that can be associated with living with a VSC, and do not take into account the distress that is repeatedly reported by those who have undergone clinical interventions relating to DSD. Reviewing this literature through a critical psychology lens means questioning how intersex mental health is conceptualized.

Promoting Health and Well-Being via Lived Experience: Implications for Healthcare

Some researchers argue that the *lived experience* of people with intersex variations needs to be a central focus in order to champion intersex mental health (Liao & Simmonds, 2014; Lundberg, 2017; Preves, 2003; Roen, 2019). These studies explore the everyday challenges people experience and how they navigate those challenges. By drawing on such research, it is possible to develop interventions to improve the living conditions of people with VSC at a structural level, including interventions directed to specific individuals as well as communities (as suggested by, e.g., Meyer, 2015). The remainder of this chapter focuses on interventions that can promote individual mental health from a person-centered and value-based perspective (Liao & Simmonds, 2014), building on human rights values.

Research focusing on lived experience shows that important challenges include making sense of one's body, negotiating questions of identity, coming to understand and learning to talk about these experiences, and connecting with others (Alderson, Madill, & Balen, 2004; Danon, 2015; Davis, 2015; Ernst et al., 2016; Guntram, 2013, 2014; Karkazis, 2008; Lundberg et al., 2016; Preves, 2003; Sanders, Carter, & Lwin, 2015). While some people find strategies to navigate these challenges in everyday life on their own, others find community support and professional psychosocial input useful. Support can be provided by significant others, support or activist groups, or healthcare providers, including psychosocial professionals (Sani et al., 2019). Research exploring the themes taken up in professional psychosocial healthcare points to the importance of making sense of and accepting one's embodiment, talking about medical interventions, connecting with others, and talking about sexual health (Dessens et al., 2017). These psychosocial studies, like the community-based research showing that people have difficulty accessing appropriate professional psychosocial healthcare (dsd families, 2019; Government Equalities Office, 2018), highlight the need to develop affirmative psychosocial healthcare in order to promote psychosocial well-being.

Providing Affirmative Healthcare

For decades, commentators have argued that intersex healthcare protocols build on problematic assumptions about normality and well-being (Kessler, 1990, 1998; Liao, 2015; Lundberg, 2017; Roen, 2008). First, well-being has historically been assumed to be possible only when a person's body, identity, and sexual practices conform to heterosexual and cisgender norms. Erasing and normalizing difference has thus been a priority in healthcare (Kessler, 1990, 1998; Roen, 2008). From an LGBTIQ-historical perspective, these normative assumptions are not new. Similar ideas have underpinned earlier psychopathological thinking on, for example, reparative therapies for people experiencing same-sex attraction (American Psychiatric Association, 2000). In contrast to such pathologization, LGBTQ-affirmative psychosocial practices have grown since the 1980s (Harrison, 2000). Such affirmative approaches highlight the need to counteract any negative effects of sociocultural norms and pressures (Johnson, 2012). Affirmative practice builds on the understanding that the person seeking support must be able to trust the psychosocial professional. Being able to build rapport and a therapeutic alliance involves having professional skills, having enough understanding and knowledge to be able to validate the patient's experiences, and being able to work with the client to affirm and, when appropriate, to celebrate difference (Johnson, 2012; King, Semlyen, Killaspy, Nazareth, & Osborn, 2007).

Psychosocial commentators suggest that health providers should stop regarding normalizing surgical and hormonal interventions that erase difference as standard intersex healthcare (Danon, 2015; Preves, 2003; Roen, 2019). Instead, health professionals should offer psychosocial care that affirms difference. Such healthcare could also be understood as "normalizing" in the sense that it involves normalizing the experience of being different as very common. It is "normal" to be different in one way or another (Guntram, 2013), and coming to understand this is a significant step on the path to addressing stigma and shame. Data from the report of the Government Equalities Office (2018) further support this understanding. Survey respondents reported positive healthcare experiences with mental health professionals who saw their role as empowering and enabling clients, and supporting clients to come to terms with their body. This is very much in line with an affirmative approach.

Many commentators have further critiqued the assumption that bodily differences can be erased through medical intervention, and that this will avert emotional suffering (Liao, 2015; Roen, 2019). We follow Liao's reasoning that medical interventions cannot "bypass emotional suffering" and are not "without emotional cost" (2015, p. 63). Instead of trying to avoid negative feelings, emotions should be addressed and worked with respectfully. LGBTIQ-affirmative psychosocial approaches recognize that affirming difference, instead of trying to erase it, is not necessarily easier and does not simply avert distress. However, the sources of distress and ways of dealing with distress are understood from a different perspective that builds on human rights–based values of self-determination and bodily integrity. Providing affirmative care is not a matter of imposing a certain kind of affirmative agenda on the client (Johnson, 2012). Rather, it is about taking a person-centered approach where the client's specific way of living with a VSC is addressed, and where that person is able to explore what helps them to make sense of themselves and find ways of relating and communicating with others that are useful in their everyday life (Liao, 2012; Lundberg, Hegarty, & Roen, 2018). In order to make sense of and come to terms with one's body, a person might usefully explore different ways of talking about bodily characteristics and experiences. In other words, reaching for self-determination and exploring terminology might go hand in hand.

Self-Determination and Terminology

Taking an affirmative and person-centered approach means de-emphasizing the terminology that reflects professionals' ideas of what is important, and finding out what terminology has day-to-day relevance for people with VSC (Lundberg et al., 2018). Continuing to privilege medical terminology has been described in terms of "hermeneutical injustice" (Carpenter, 2016, p. 79).

While representatives of the medical perspective often use the term *DSD* in research and practice (Pasterski, Prentice, & Hughes, 2010), some argue that "differences" should be used instead of "disorders" (Ahmed et al., 2015) or that the specific diagnostic term might better be used (Cools et al., 2018) when communicating with clients and their families. Studies examining the language preferences of people with VSC suggest that only a minority of participants prefer the term *DSD* (Bennecke & De Vries, 2016; Davis, 2015; Johnson et al., 2017; Jones et al., 2016; Lin-Su, Lekarev, Poppas, & Vogiatzi, 2015; Lundberg et al., 2018; Monro et al., 2017). These studies also show that many prefer to use *intersex* (Jones et al., 2016), while others also think *intersex* is a problematic term (Lundberg et al., 2018). In the study by Johnson et al. (2017), participants preferred *Intersex* or *differences* or *variations* of sex development/characteristics. In one of our studies (Lundberg et al., 2018), participants preferred descriptive language that explained how their body had developed or looked.

Promoting self-determination and providing person-centered and affirmative healthcare could mean supporting the person to explore the diverse ways of understanding VSC and exploring different ways of making sense and talking about these experiences (Lundberg et al., 2018). Having diverse ways of understanding one's body might help a person to know their body as well as talk and connect with others.

Identifying Research Gaps and Looking Forward

In conclusion, we identify areas of research that have not yet been addressed, and we point to conceptual frameworks that might inform researchers wanting to address these gaps. Intersectional thinking has been a key conceptual development within humanities and social sciences in recent decades, stemming from the work of scholars and others concerned with the social injustices that fail to be addressed at the intersections of gender and race inequalities (Crenshaw, 1989). Researchers concerned with LGBTIQ and psychosocial well-being also highlight the importance of considering intersecting identities and social positions (Zeeman et al., 2019) and acknowledging the heterogeneity of people with VSC (Carpenter, 2018). Further work is needed to ensure that intersex research informs understanding about psychosocial well-being across age groups, geographic locations, and sociocultural and economic contexts.

People with VSC are likely to have substantially different experiences according to their age because healthcare protocols for informing people about their variation have changed substantially from not disclosing information (Natarajan, 1996) to giving full age-appropriate information (Lee et al., 2006). Those who were children during the era of secrecy are more likely to have been excluded from conversations about their own healthcare, and to have been unable to ask for support or find similar others.

Culture and geographic location are intersectional considerations that are mostly absent from existing research. Most studies cited in this chapter are done in Europe, the United States, and Australia, and do not offer insights into cultural differences. However, there is a growing body of work in Asian and South American countries, for example (see, e.g., Dessens et al., 2018; Gilban, Junior, & Beserra, 2014; Zainuddin, Grover, Shamsuddin, & Mahdy, 2013), and there appears to be a tendency for these studies to take a psycho-pathologizing approach. One example is a study with Indonesian participants, where Dessens et al. (2018) concluded that adults with VSC experienced more negative emotions compared to controls and that these findings are similar to results found in China and in Western countries. However, they also point out that the Indonesian participants had received minimal medical care and that this had a negative effect on their bodily development as well as their understanding of their body. These researchers conclude that the participants experienced stigma in culturally specific ways. However, they do not elaborate on how these unique lived challenges faced by the participants are understood to have influenced the research results. Further, they also used a generic QoL measure that was not developed in an Indonesian context. Clearly, producing research that informs the psychosocial well-being of people in non-Western countries means developing research tools and approaches appropriate to each cultural context.

In Western countries, there are currently two competing stories, or ways of making sense of VSC: one from a social or human rights–based perspective and one from a biomedical or pathologizing perspective (Monro et al., 2017). It is not clear how or whether (Western) biomedically focused approaches contribute insights on how to promote psychosocial well-being for people with VSC in Indonesia. The authors conclude that what is needed in Indonesia is the same medical model used across various Western countries (Dessens et al., 2018). However, Wieringa (2015), a social science scholar connected to this research project, critically discusses the biomedical agenda it prioritizes. As a supporter of a social understanding of why people with VSC might experience psychosocial distress, Wieringa (2015) proposes that stories designed to reduce stigma could help people make sense of their variation better than biomedical explanations.

A postcolonial critique would suggest that, regardless of attempts to improve research knowledge and healthcare provision, no real change has occurred in how Western researchers engage with the Global South. An exotifying and othering perspective in anthropological intersex case studies has been replaced by a biomedical approach that effectively colonizes by imposing Western understandings on people with VSC (Kraus, 2013). We know from human rights literature that advocating for LGBTQ rights globally is not a project that escapes postcolonial critique (Ali, 2017; Kollman & Waites, 2009). Both perspectives on VSC, the social or human rights–focused and the biomedical psycho-pathological perspective, need to be critically examined and discussed in terms of their colonizing effects (Rubin, 2015).

In conclusion, research could focus on community-based interventions that promote well-being rather than endorsing hospital-based interventions that can add to shame, stigma, and disempowerment. Working with diverse stakeholders, support groups, organizations, and communities is important for building an evidence base that might foster psychosocial well-being and promote human rights for people with VSC.

Finally, commentators suggest that we also need more research on lay people's understandings of VSC (Liao & Simmonds, 2014; Lundberg, Dønåsen, Hegarty, & Roen, 2019). As Liao and Simmonds note, "[i]t is peculiar that academics, journalists and programme makers alike should assume that the only way to understand DSD is via research on affected people. It is as if the non-DSD world had nothing to do with how DSD is experienced" (2014, p. 96). Some research on lay people has been done in this topic area in recent years (Hegarty, Bogan-Carey, & Smith, 2019; Lundberg et al., 2019; Streuli, Vayena, Cavicchia-Balmer, & Huber, 2013). However, we share the view of Liao and Simmonds (2014) that popular understandings circulating in the general public play an important role in framing the lived experience of people with VSC. In order to foster intersex psychosocial well-being, we need to know more about shifting the understanding of the public in general, to encourage supportive rather than stigmatizing responses, and to promote human rights.

References

Ahmed, S. F., Achermann, J. C., Arlt, W., Balen, A. H., Conway, G. S., Edwards, Z., . . . Willis, D. (2015). Society for Endocrinology UK guidance on the initial evaluation of an infant or an adolescent with a suspected disorder of sex development (revised 2015). *Clinical Endocrinology, 84*(5), 771–88. doi:10.1111/cen.12857

Alderson, J., Madill, A., & Balen, A. (2004). Fear of devaluation: Understanding the experience of intersexed women with androgen insensitivity syndrome. *British Journal of Health Psychology, 9*(1), 81–100. doi:10.1348/135910704322778740

Ali, M.-U. A. (2017). Un-mapping gay imperialism: A postcolonial approach to sexual orientation-based development. *Reconsidering Development, 5*(1). https://pubs.lib.umn.edu/index.php/reconsidering/article/view/907

American Psychiatric Association. (2000). Therapies focused on attempts to change sexual orientation (reparative or conversion therapies). http://media.mlive.com/news/detroit_impact/other/APA_position_conversion%20therapy.pdf

Ansara, Y. G. (2016). Psychological effects in surgical decision-making: Evidence, ethics and outcomes. In S. J. White & J. A. Cartmill (Eds.), *Communication in surgical practice* (pp. 68–93). Sheffield, UK: Equinox eBooks Publishing.

Barker, M. J., & Richards, C. (Eds.). (2015). *The Palgrave handbook of the psychology of sexuality and gender.* Basingstoke, UK: Palgrave.

Bennecke, E., & De Vries, A. (2016). *European research project "dsd-LIFE."* Paper presented at the conference "After the recognition of Intersex human rights," University of Surrey, Guildford, UK.

Blackless, M., Charuvastra, A., Derryck, A., Fausto-Sterling, A., Lauzanne, K., & Lee, E. (2000). How sexually dimorphic are we? Review and synthesis. *American Journal of Human Biology, 12*(2), 151–66.

Bohet, M., Besson, R., Jardri, R., Manouvrier, S., Catteau-Jonard, S., Cartigny, M., . . . Medjkane, F. (2019). Mental health status of individuals with sexual development disorders: A review. *Journal of Pediatric Urology, 15*(4), 356–66. doi:10.1016/j.jpurol.2019.04.010

Carmichael, P., & Alderson, J. (2004). Psychological care in disorders of sexual differentiation and determination. In A. H. Balen (Ed.), *Paediatric and adolescent gynaecology* (pp. 158–78). Cambridge, UK: Cambridge University Press.

Carpenter, M. (2016). The human rights of intersex people: Addressing harmful practices and rhetoric of change. *Reproductive Health Matters, 24*(47), 74–84. doi:10.1016/j.rhm.2016.06.003

Carpenter, M. (2018). The "normalization" of intersex bodies and "othering" of intersex identities in Australia. *Journal of Bioethical Inquiry, 15*(4), 487–95. doi:10.1007/s11673-018-9855-8

Chadwick, P. M., Smyth, A., & Liao, L.-M. (2014). Improving self-esteem in women diagnosed with Turner syndrome: Results of a pilot intervention. *Journal of Pediatric and Adolescent Gynecology, 27*(3), 129–32. doi:10.1016/j.jpag.2013.09.004

Clarke, V., & Peel, E. (2007). *Out in psychology: Lesbian, gay, bisexual, trans and queer perspectives.* Chichester, West Sussex, England: John Wiley & Sons.

Cools, M., Nordenström, A., Robeva, R., Hall, J., Westerveld, P., Flück, C., . . . Pasterski, V. (2018). Caring for individuals with a difference of sex development (DSD): A consensus statement. *Nature Reviews Endocrinology, 14*(7), 415–29. doi:10.1038/s41574-018-0010-8

Cools, M., Simmonds, M., Elford, S., Gorter, J., Ahmed, S. F., D'alberton, F., . . . Hiort, O. (2016). Response to the Council of Europe Human Rights Commissioner's Issue Paper on Human Rights and Intersex People. *European Urology, 70*(3), 407–9. doi:10.1016/j.eururo.2016.05.015

Crenshaw, K. W. (1989). Demarginalizing the intersection of race and sex: A black feminist critique of antidiscrimination doctrine, feminist theory and antiracist politics. *University of Chicago Legal Forum, 1989*, 139–67.

D'Alberton, F., Assante, M. T., Foresti, M., Balsamo, A., Bertelloni, S., Dati, E., . . . Mazzanti, L. (2015). Quality of life and psychological adjustment of women living with 46, XY differences of sex development. *Journal of Sexual Medicine, 12*(6), 1440–9. doi:10.1111/jsm.12884

Danon, L. M. (2015). The body/secret dynamic: Life experiences of intersexed people in Israel. *SAGE Open, 5*(2), 2158244015580370.

Davis, G. (2015). *Contesting intersex: The dubious diagnosis.* New York, NY: New York University Press.
de Neve-Enthoven, N. G. M., Callens, N., van Kuyk, M., van Kuppenveld, J. H., Drop, S. L. S., Cohen-Kettenis, P. T., & Dessens, A. B. (2016). Psychosocial well-being in Dutch adults with disorders of sex development. *Journal of Psychosomatic Research, 83,* 57–64. doi:10.1016/j.jpsychores.2016.03.005
Dessens, A., Ediati, A., Verrips, E., Juniarto, A. Z., Faradz, S. M., & Drop, S. (2018). Quality of life in late-treated patients with disorders of sex development: Insights for patient-centered care. *Frontiers in Pediatrics, 6,* 434.
Dessens, A., Guaragna-Filho, G., Kyriakou, A., Bryce, J., Sanders, C., Nordenskjöld, A.,... Faisal Ahmed, S. (2017). Understanding the needs of professionals who provide psychosocial care for children and adults with disorders of sex development. *BMJ Paediatrics Open, 1*(1), e000132–2. doi:10.1136/bmjpo-2017-000132
Diamond, M., & Sigmundson, H. K. (1997). Sex reassignment at birth. *Archives of Pediatrics & Adolescent Medicine, 151*(3), 298. doi:10.1001/archpedi.1997.02170400084015
Diamond, M., & Watson, L. A. (2004). Androgen insensitivity syndrome and Klinefelter's syndrome: Sex and gender considerations. *Child and Adolescent Psychiatric Clinics of North America, 13*(3), 623.
dsd families. (2019). *"Listen to us": Consultations with children, young people and families living with different sex development.* http://www.dsdfamilies.org/application/files/8015/5447/3715/reportdsdf-2019.pdf
Egan, S. K., & Perry, D. G. (2001). Gender identity: A multidimensional analysis with implications for psychosocial adjustment. *Developmental Psychology, 37*(4), 451–63. doi:10.1037/0012-1649.37.4.451
Engberg, H., Butwicka, A., Nordenström, A., Hirschberg, A. L., Falhammar, H., Lichtenstein, P.,... Landén, M. (2015). Congenital adrenal hyperplasia and risk for psychiatric disorders in girls and women born between 1915 and 2010: A total population study. *Psychoneuroendocrinology, 60,* 195–205. doi:10.1016/j.psyneuen.2015.06.017
Ernst, M. E., Sandberg, D. E., Keegan, C., Quint, E. H., Lossie, A. C., & Yashar, B. M. (2016). The lived experience of MRKH: Sharing health information with peers. *Journal of Pediatric and Adolescent Gynecology, 29*(2), 154–8. doi:10.1016/j.jpag.2015.09.009
European Union Fundamental Rights Agency. (2015). The fundamental rights situation of intersex people. http://fra.europa.eu/sites/default/files/fra-2015-focus-04-intersex.pdf
Gilban, D. L. S., Junior, P. A. G. A., & Beserra, I. C. R. (2014). Health-related quality of life of children and adolescents with congenital adrenal hyperplasia in Brazil. *Health and Quality of Life Outcomes, 12*(1), 107.
Gough, B., Weyman, N., Alderson, J., Butler, G., & Stoner, M. (2008). "They did not have a word": The parental quest to locate a "true sex" for their intersex children. *Psychology & Health, 23*(4), 493–507. doi:10.1080/14768320601176170
Government Equalities Office. (2018). *National LGBT survey: Research report.* https://assets.publishing.service.gov.uk/government/uploads/system/uploads/attachment_data/file/721704/LGBT-survey-research-report.pdf
Guntram, L. (2013). "Differently normal" and "normally different": Negotiations of female embodiment in women's accounts of "atypical" sex development. *Social Science and Medicine, 98,* 232–8. doi:10.1016/j.socscimed.2013.09.018
Guntram, L. (2014). *Ambivalent ambiguity? A study of how women with "atypical" sex development make sense of female embodiment.* Linköping Studies in Arts and Science No. 633, Dissertations on Health and Society No. 25. Linköping University, Sweden.
Guth, L. J., Witchel, R. I., Witchel, S. F., & Lee, P. A. (2006). Relationships, sexuality, gender identity, gender roles, and self-concept of individuals who have congenital adrenal hyperplasia: A qualitative investigation. *Journal of Gay & Lesbian Psychotherapy, 10*(2), 57–75. doi:10.1300/J236v10n02_04
Harper, A., & Singh, A. (2014). Supporting ally development with families of trans and gender nonconforming (TGNC) youth. *Journal of LGBT Issues in Counseling, 8*(4), 376–88. do i:10.1080/15538605.2014.960127
Harrison, N. (2000). Gay affirmative therapy: A critical analysis of the literature. *British Journal of Guidance & Counselling, 28*(1), 37–53.
Hegarty, P., Bogan-Carey, T., & Smith, A. (2019). Stigma as framed on YouTube: Effects of personal experiences videos on students' beliefs about medicalizing intersex. *Journal of Applied Social Psychology, 49*(3), 133–44.
Henriques, J., Hollway, W., Urwin, C., Venn, C., & Walkerdine, V. (1984). *Changing the subject: Psychology, social regulation, and subjectivity.* London: Methuen.
Hughes, I. A., Houk, C., Ahmed, S. F., & Lee, P. A. (2006). Consensus statement on management of intersex disorders. *Archives of Disease in Childhood, 91*(7), 554–63.
Johnson, E. K., Rosoklija, I., Finlayson, C., Chen, D., Yerkes, E. B., Madonna, M. B.,... Cheng, E. Y. (2017). Attitudes towards "disorders of sex development" nomenclature among affected individuals. *Journal of Pediatric Urology, 13*(6), 608. doi:10.1016/j.jpurol.2017.03.035
Johnson, S. D. (2012). Gay affirmative psychotherapy with lesbian, gay, and bisexual individuals: Implications for contemporary psychotherapy research. *American Journal of Orthopsychiatry, 82*(4), 516.
Jones, T., Hart, B., Carpenter, M., Ansara, G., Leonard, W., & Lucke, J. (2016). *Intersex: Stories and statistics from Australia.* Cambridge, UK: Open Book Publishers.
Karkazis, K. (2008). *Fixing sex: Intersex, medical authority, and lived experience.* Durham, NC: Duke University Press.
Kessler, S. J. (1990). The medical construction of gender: Case management of intersexed infants. *Signs, 16*(1), 3–26.
Kessler, S. J. (1998). *Lessons from the intersexed.* New Brunswick, NJ: Rutgers University Press.
King, M., Semlyen, J., Killaspy, H., Nazareth, I., & Osborn, D. (2007). A systematic review of research on counselling and psychotherapy for lesbian, gay, bisexual & transgender people. Lutterworth, Leicestershire, UK: British Association for Counselling and Psychotherapy.
Kollman, K., & Waites, M. (2009). The global politics of lesbian, gay, bisexual and transgender human rights: an introduction. *Contemporary Politics, 15*(1), 1–17. doi:10.1080/13569770802674188
Kraus, C. (2013). Hypospadias surgery in a West African context: The surgical (re-) construction of what? *Feminist Theory, 14*(1), 83–103.
Krupp, K., Fliegner, M., Brunner, F., Brucker, S., Rall, K., & Richter-Appelt, H. (2014). Quality of life and psychological distress in women with Mayer-Rokitansky-Küster-Hauser syndrome and individuals with complete androgen insensitivity syndrome. *Open Journal of Medical Psychology, 3*(3), 212–21.

Langer, S. J., & Martin, J. I. (2004). How dresses can make you mentally ill: Examining gender identity disorder in children. *Child & Adolescent Social Work Journal, 23*(5–6), 533–55.

Lee, P. A., Houk, C. P., Ahmed, S. F., & Hughes, I. A. (2006). Consensus statement on management of intersex disorders. *Pediatrics, 118*(2), e488–e500. doi:10.1542/peds.2006-0738

Lee, P. A., Nordenstrom, A., Houk, C. P., Ahmed, S. F., Auchus, R., Baratz, A., . . . The Global DSD Update Consortium. (2016). Global disorders of sex development update since 2006: Perceptions, approach and care. *Hormone Research in Paediatrics, 85*(3), 158–80. doi:10.1159/000442975

Liao, L.-M. (2007). Towards a clinical-psychological approach to address the heterosexual concerns of intersexed women. In V. Clarke & E. Peel (Eds.), *Out in psychology: Lesbian, gay, bisexual, trans and queer perspectives* (pp. 391–408). Chichester, West Sussex, England: John Wiley & Sons.

Liao, L.-M. (2012). Diversity of sex development. In the Professional Practice Board of the British Psychological Society (Ed.), *Guidelines and literature review for psychologists working therapeutically with sexual and gender minority clients.* Leicester, UK: British Psychological Society.

Liao, L.-M. (2015). Stonewalling emotion. *Narrative Inquiry in Bioethics, 5*(2), 143–50. doi:10.1353/nib.2015.0045

Liao, L.-M., Audi, L., Magritte, E., Meyer-Bahlburg, H. F. L., & Quigley, C. A. (2012). Determinant factors of gender identity: A commentary. *Journal of Pediatric Urology, 8*(6), 597–601. doi:10.1016/j.jpurol.2012.09.009

Liao, L.-M., & Simmonds, M. (2014). A values-driven and evidence-based health care psychology for diverse sex development. *Psychology & Sexuality, 5*(1), 83–101. doi:10.1080/19419899.2013.831217

Lin-Su, K., Lekarev, O., Poppas, D., & Vogiatzi, M. (2015). Congenital adrenal hyperplasia patient perception of "disorders of sex development" nomenclature. *International Journal of Pediatric Endocrinology, 2015*(1), 1–7. doi:10.1186/s13633-015-0004-4

Lundberg, T. (2017). *Knowing bodies: Making sense of intersex/DSD a decade post-consensus.* Doctoral dissertation, University of Oslo, Norway. https://www.duo.uio.no/handle/10852/55654

Lundberg, T., Dønåsen, I., Hegarty, P., & Roen, K. (2019). Moving intersex/DSD rights and care forward: Lay understandings of common dilemmas. *Journal of Social and Political Psychology, 7*(1), 354–77.

Lundberg, T., Hegarty, P., & Roen, K. (2018). Making sense of "intersex" and "DSD": How laypeople understand and use terminology. *Psychology & Sexuality, 9*(2), 161–73. doi:10.1080/19419899.2018.1453862

Lundberg, T., Lindström, A., Roen, K., & Hegarty, P. (2017). From knowing nothing to knowing what, how and now: Parents' experiences of caring for their children with congenital adrenal hyperplasia. *Journal of Pediatric Psychology, 42*(5), 520–9. doi:10.1093/jpepsy/jsw001

Lundberg, T., Roen, K., Hirschberg, A. L., & Frisén, L. (2016). "It's part of me, not all of me": Young women's experiences of receiving a diagnosis related to diverse sex development. *Journal of Pediatric and Adolescent Gynecology, 29*(4), 338–43. doi:10.1016/j.jpag.2015.11.009

Marecek, J., Henriques, J., Hollway, W., Urwin, C., Venn, C., Walkerdine, V., . . . Bayer, B. M. (2002). A reappraisal of changing the subject: Psychology, social regulation and subjectivity. *Feminism & Psychology, 12*(4), 423–61.

McDermott, E., & Roen, K. (2016). *Queer youth, suicide and self-harm: Troubled subjects, troubling norms.* Basingstoke, UK: Palgrave Macmillan.

Meyer, I. H. (2015). Resilience in the study of minority stress and health of sexual and gender minorities. *Psychology of Sexual Orientation and Gender Diversity, 2*(3), 209.

Money, J., & Ehrhardt, A. A. (1972). *Man & woman, boy & girl: The differentiation and dimorphism of gender identity from conception to maturity.* Baltimore, MD: Johns Hopkins University Press.

Money, J., Hampson, J. G., & Hampson, J. L. (1955). Hermaphroditism: Recommendations concerning assignment of sex, change of sex and psychologic management. *Bulletin of the Johns Hopkins Hospital, 97*(4), 284–300.

Monro, S., Crocetti, D., Yeadon-Lee, T., Garland, F., & Travis, M. (2017). Intersex, variations of sex characteristics, and DSD: The need for change. http://eprints.hud.ac.uk/id/eprint/33535/

Natarajan, A. (1996). Medical ethics and truth telling in the case of androgen insensitivity syndrome. *Canadian Medical Association Journal, 154*(4), 568–70.

Nordenström, A. (2015). Psychosocial factors in disorders of sex development in a long-term perspective: What clinical opportunities are there to intervene? *Hormone and Metabolic Research, 47*(5), 351–6. doi:10.1055/s-0034-1398562

Özbaran, B., Özen, S., Gökşen, D., Korkmaz, Ö., Onay, H., Özkinay, F., . . . Darcan, Ş. (2013). Psychiatric approaches for disorders of sex development: Experience of a multidisciplinary team. *Journal of Clinical Research in Pediatric Endocrinology, 5*(4), 229–35. doi:10.4274/Jcrpe.1044

Pasterski, V., Prentice, P., & Hughes, I. A. (2010). Consequences of the Chicago consensus on disorders of sex development (DSD): Current practices in Europe. *Archives of Disease in Childhood, 8*(95), 618–23. doi:10.1136/adc.2009.163840

Preves, S. E. (2003). *Intersex and identity: The contested self.* New Brunswick, NJ: Rutgers University Press.

Roen, K. (2008). "But we have to do something": Surgical "correction" of atypical genitalia. *Body & Society, 14*(1), 47–66. doi:10.1177/1357034x07087530

Roen, K. (2015). Intersex/DSD. In M. J. Barker & C. Richards (Eds.), *The Palgrave handbook of the psychology of sexuality and gender* (pp. 183–97). Basingstoke, UK: Palgrave.

Roen, K. (2019). Intersex or diverse sex development: Critical review of psychosocial health care research and indications for practice. *Journal of Sex Research, 56*(4–5), 511–28. doi:10.1080/00224499.2019.1578331

Roen, K., & Groot, S. (2019). Trans* and gender diverse youth: Applied and critical psychology working in the margins. In K. O'Doherty & D. Hodgetts (Eds.), *The SAGE handbook of applied social psychology.* Thousand Oaks, CA: Sage.

Rubin, D. A. (2015). Provincializing intersex: US intersex activism, human rights, and transnational body politics. *Frontiers: A Journal of Women's Studies, 36*(3), 51–83.

Sanders, C., Carter, B., & Lwin, R. (2015). Young women with a disorder of sex development: Learning to share information with health professionals, friends and intimate partners about bodily differences and infertility. *Journal of Advanced Nursing, 71*(8), 1904–13. doi:10.1111/jan.12661

Sani, A. M., Soh, K. L., Ismail, I. A., Arshad, M. M., Mungadi, I. A., Yau, S. L., & Soh, K. G. (2019). Experiences of people living with disorders of sex development and sex reassignment: Meta-ethnography of qualitative studies. *Journal of Advanced Nursing, 75*(2), 277–90.

Schönbucher, V., Schweizer, K., Rustige, L., Schützmann, K., Brunner, F., & Richter-Appelt, H. (2010). Sexual quality of life of individuals with 46, XY disorders of sex development. *Journal of Sexual Medicine, 9*(12), 3154–70. doi:10.1111/j.1743-6109.2009.01639.x

Schützmann, K., Brinkmann, L., Schacht, M., & Richter-Appelt, H. (2009). Psychological distress, self-harming behavior, and suicidal tendencies in adults with disorders of sex development. *Archives of Sexual Behaviour, 38*(1), 16–33.

Schweizer, K., Brunner, F., Handford, C., & Richter-Appelt, H. (2014). Gender experience and satisfaction with gender allocation in adults with diverse intersex conditions (divergences of sex development, DSD). *Psychology & Sexuality, 5*(1), 83–101. doi:10.1080/19419899.2013.831216

Slijper, F., Drop, S., Molenaar, J., & de Muinck Keizer-Schrama, S. (1998). Long-term psychological evaluation of intersex children. *Archives of Sexual Behaviour, 27*(2), 19.

Stout, S. A., Litvak, M., Robbins, N. M., & Sandberg, D. E. (2010). Congenital adrenal hyperplasia: Classification of studies employing psychological endpoints. *International Journal of Pediatric Endocrinology, 2010*, 191520. doi:10.1155/2010/191520

Streuli, J. C., Vayena, E., Cavicchia-Balmer, Y., & Huber, J. (2013). Shaping parents: Impact of contrasting professional counseling on parents' decision making for children with disorders of sex development. *Journal of Sexual Medicine, 10*(8), 1953–60. doi:10.1111/jsm.12214

Travis, M. (2015). Accommodating intersexuality in European union anti-discrimination law. *European Law Journal, 21*(2), 180–99. doi:10.1111/eulj.12111

United Nations Human Rights Council. (2013). Report of the Special Rapporteur on Torture and other cruel, inhuman or degrading treatment or punishment, Juan E. Méndez (A/HRC/22/53). http://www.ohchr.org/Documents/HRBodies/HRCouncil/RegularSession/Session22/A.HRC.22.53_English.pdf

Warne, G., Grover, S., Hutson, J., Sinclair, A., Metcalfe, S., Northam, E., & Freeman, J. (2005). A long-term outcome study of intersex conditions. *Journal of Pediatric Endocrinology and Metabolism, 18*(6), 555–67.

Wieringa, S. (2015). Discursive contestations concerning intersex in Indonesia. In L. R. Bennett & S. G. Davies (Eds.), *Sex and sexualities in contemporary Indonesia: Sexual politics, health, diversity, and representations* (pp. 169–82). London: Routledge.

Zainuddin, A., Grover, S., Shamsuddin, K., & Mahdy, Z. (2013). Research on quality of life in female patients with congenital adrenal hyperplasia and issues in developing nations. *Journal of Pediatric and Adolescent Gynecology, 6*, 296–304.

Zeeman, L., Sherriff, N., Browne, K., McGlynn, N., Mirandola, M., Gios, L., . . . Amaddeo, F. (2019). A review of lesbian, gay, bisexual, trans and intersex (LGBTI) health and healthcare inequalities. *European Journal of Public Health, 29*(5), 974–80. doi:10.1093/eurpub/cky226

CHAPTER

27 Mental Health for Asexual Individuals

Esther D. Rothblum

Abstract

The present chapter focuses on the mental health of individuals who identify as asexual, defined as not having feelings of sexual attraction for other people. It focuses on population-based studies of the prevalence of asexuality and demographic characteristics of asexual respondents in these surveys. The author describes the stigma of asexual identity as perceived by asexual individuals and by society, as well as the advantages that asexual individuals cite. The author also reviews how low sexual desire is described in the current *Diagnostic and Statistical Manual of Mental Disorders*. The chapter reviews the (scant) literature on asexual mental health and ends with some implications for future research.

Keywords: asexual, asexual mental health, asexual identity, research methods for asexual mental health, asexual stigma

When Kathy Brehony and I co-edited a book on lesbian women who were in partnered relationships but not having sex (Rothblum & Brehony, 1993), we reclaimed the term "Boston marriage," which referred to unmarried women who lived together in past centuries (Faderman, 1981). We noted that women in such relationships who were sexual would have kept their sexual relationships hidden. In contrast, we found that contemporary lesbian women who were not having sex often kept their *lack* of sexuality a secret from friends and community. As D'Emilio and Freedman (1997) have written, by the late 1960s, "Aided by the values of a consumer culture and encouraged by the growing visibility of sex in the public realm, many Americans came to accept sexual pleasure as a legitimate, necessary component of their lives, unbound by older ideals of marital infidelity and permanence. Society was indeed becoming sexualized" (p. 327). Within a relatively short time span, Western cultures moved from being "sex negative" to "sex positive," especially regarding attitudes toward women (International Society for Sexual Medicine, 2019).

It is important to remember that radical feminists in the 1960s and anarchist women even earlier, who saw sexual behavior and sexual orientation as a political choice, often questioned whether sexual activity benefited women because men exercised power over women (Fahs, 2010). Przybylo and Cooper (2014, p. 307) too review this history of the women's liberation movement: "Responding to the so-called sexual revolution and permissive sexual turn, political asexuality and political celibacy were articulated as theoretically and politically viable feminist strategies for challenging the institution of heterosexuality, asserting women's independence, and ending women's oppression." Instead, these feminists urged women to focus their energies on nonsexual relationships in their work, political activism, and connections with other women.

In what I have termed the "culture of sex" (Rothblum, 1999, p. 75), Przybylo (2011, p. 444) has termed "sexusociety," and Chasin (2011, p. 723) has termed "sexual normativity," sexual desire, attraction, activity, and relationships are now foregrounded. Sex and romance are the themes of advertisements and commercials, advice columns, television and film, songs, and even products for children (Disney movies, fairy tales). Thus, not only are Western societies "sex positive," but it is difficult to escape the emphasis on sex. In middle school and high school, students talk to each other about who they are attracted to and whether they are in a relationship. Holland and Eisenhart (1990) have written about how women in college are "educated in romance"—how the campus peer culture values their sexual attractiveness more than academics. This focus on sex is also the case in nonacademic settings. In the work setting we often know the relationship status of our coworkers, community organizations may exist for people to find potential romantic partners, and religious institutions focus on what is appropriate sexual behavior (cf. Rothblum, Heimann, & Carpenter, 2019b). Even jokes and humor often have sexual content (Bogaert, 2012b).

The present chapter focuses on the mental health of individuals who identify as asexual, defined as not having feelings of sexual attraction for other people. It will focus on population-based studies of the prevalence of asexuality and demographic characteristics of asexual respondents in these surveys. I will describe the stigma of asexual identity as perceived by asexual individuals and by society, as well as the advantages that asexual individuals cite. I will also review how low sexual desire is described in the current (2013) edition of the American Psychiatric Association's *Diagnostic and Statistical Manual of Mental Disorders* (DSM-5). I will review the (scant) literature on asexual mental health and end with some implications for future research.

Asexual Identity and Terminology

Przybylo (2012) describes how asexuality was "discovered" in the current century, with a focus on legitimizing and depathologizing asexual identity. Beginning with Bogaert's (2004) UK national probability sample as well as the founding of the Asexuality Visibility and Education Network (AVEN, www.asexuality.org) website in 2001 by David Jay, there has been an explosion of studies on asexuality, especially in the past decade. As Przybylo (2012, p. 232) states, "It seemed that, at last, asexuality had come out of the shadows of indifference and entered the limelight of scientific and sexual concern."

The asexual community has created an array of new terms (cf. asexuality.org, wiki.asexuality.org). Asexuals often refer to themselves as *ace*. The opposite of asexual is *allosexual*, referring to people who do experience sexual attraction. *Gray asexuals* are on the continuum from asexual to allosexual, and *demisexual* refers to sexual attraction that can develop over time, or after forming an emotional connection. In a recent survey of members of AVEN with 14,210 respondents, 49.2 percent identified as asexual, 11.1 percent as demisexual, 16.2 percent as gray asexual, and 23.4 percent as other (Ginoza, Miller, & AVEN Survey Team, 2014). Asexuals can be *sex-indifferent* or *sex-averse* (Carrigan, 2011; Carrigan, Gupta, & Morrison, 2013. *Sapiosexual* refers to being attracted to someone's mind rather than their body, and *autocorissexual* refers to having sexual fantasies but not wanting physical sex.

One major dimension is whether asexuals experience romantic attraction or not (*romantic* vs. *aromantic*; cf. Chasin, 2011). They can be heteroromantic, biromantic, homoromantic, or polyromantic (Carrigan et al., 2013). Romantic attraction is also on a continuum, so individuals can be *gray romantic*. *Demiromantic* refers to romantic attraction that can develop over time or after forming an emotional connection. In the survey of AVEN members (Ginoza et al., 2014), 19 percent identified as aromantic, 19.8 percent as panromantic, 22 percent as heteroromantic, 12.4 percent as biromantic, and 5.1 percent as homoromantic, among other identities. As Mitchell and Hunnicutt (2018) have pointed out, these dimensions indicate that love and sex are overlapping but not synonymous dimensions. Finally, asexuality is not synonymous with celibacy, defined as voluntary abstinence from sex. Thus someone could be celibate but not asexual, and also asexual but not celibate.

Is Asexual Identity a Sexual Orientation? Is It Queer?

Canning (2015) has examined whether asexuality can be considered "queer." On the one hand, queer includes any non-normative sexual and gender identities. On the other hand, asexual individuals feel isolated from other sexual identities that focus on sex, and/or may not feel that they are queer. Cerankowski and Milks (2010) also add that some asexuals consider their relationships and desires entirely conventional. Przybylo and Cooper (2014) argue that queer theory has not paid much attention to asexuality. But Gressgård (2013 p. 188) views asexuality as queer "insofar as it serves to destabilize the sexual regime (of truth) that privileges sexual relationships against other affiliations."

The homepage of AVEN states that asexuality is a sexual identity (Pacho, 2013), and in Gupta's (2017) qualitative study of respondents recruited from AVEN and other websites, many respondents described or referred to asexuality as a sexual orientation. In contrast, in a qualitative study by Scott, McDonnell, and Dawson (2016) of fifty asexual interviewees recruited via AVEN, many respondents viewed asexuality as marginal, rather than central, in their lives. Mollet and Lackman (2018) asked college students recruited from the AVEN website whether asexual identity should be included in the LGBTQ community. The majority (87 percent) said yes, but only 62 percent identified with the LGBTQ community themselves. Students mentioned feelings of connection to other marginalized sexual and gender minorities, but also felt erasure and marginalization. In Miller's (2012) analysis of the Asexual Awareness Week Community Census, 41 percent of the 3,436 respondents reported that they considered themselves part of the LGBT community, and a further 38 percent said they were an ally. In AVEN's own survey of its members (Ginoza et al., 2014), 26.6 percent identified as straight, 26.1 percent as bisexual, 16.4 percent as pansexual, 11 percent as queer, 8.4 percent as lesbian, 4.6 percent as gay, and 6.9 percent as other. When asked if they felt welcomed in the LGBTQ+ or queer communities, 52.1 percent said yes, 17.8 percent said "yes, but only as an ally," 15.4 percent said "no, but I wish I could be," 8.9 percent said "no, and I don't wish to be," and 5.8 percent said other (p. 13). Given these disparate results, Bogaert (2006) presents arguments for and against considering asexuality a sexual orientation.

Chasin (2015, p. 171) has also pointed out that asexual individuals are assumed to be non-heterosexual by virtue of the fact that they are not engaging in "hetero*sexual* flirting, dating, and/or sexual behaviours; dressing to be (hetero) 'sexy.'" Similarly, asexual individuals are read as transgender because they do not have a gender-conforming expression.

Research on the Prevalence of Asexuality

It is paradoxical that much information about the prevalence of asexuality has come from surveys of *sexual* behavior. The Kinsey Survey (Kinsey, Pomeroy, & Martin, 1948; Kinsey, Pomeroy, Martin, & Gebhard, 1953) indicated that less than 2 percent of individuals reported no sexual attraction to men or women, but since then most studies of asexuality have been conducted in the twenty-first century. In a probability sample of households in the United Kingdom (Bogaert, 2004), about 1 percent of respondents (57 males and 138 females) reported never feeling sexual attraction toward anyone. Aicken, Mercer, and Cassell (2013) examined the National Surveys of Sexual Attitudes and Lifestyles in the United Kingdom in 1990–1991 and 2000–2001 and found that 0.4 percent and 0.9 percent of participants had never experienced sexual attraction, respectively, with no age or sex differences between people with and without attraction. In the Second Australian Study of Health and Relationships (Richters et al., 2014), 0.3 percent of men and 0.4 percent of women indicated that they were sexually attracted to no one. No comparable population-based study in the United States has asked about lack of sexual attraction, although Poston and Baumle (2010) found that 0.7 percent of males and 0.8 percent of females responded *not sure* about their sexual attraction in the U.S. National Survey of Family Growth. A limitation of these population-based studies is that *asexual* was not included as an identity or sexual orientation, so findings from previous studies have not captured the experiences of asexual-identified individuals specifically.

A major exception is the New Zealand Attitudes and Values Study (Greaves et al., 2017, p. 2419), which included the open-ended item "How would you describe your sexual orientation?" The authors focused on respondents who specifically wrote in "asexual" (0.4 percent of the total sample) as opposed to identities such as "non-existent" or "not applicable" (p. 2419). Of these forty-four asexual respondents, 88 percent were women, 15.9 percent men, and 6.8 percent non-cisgender. More recently, Rothblum, Krueger, Kittle, and Meyer (2019c) surveyed 1,523 LGB respondents recruited via Gallup polling and found that 1.66 percent wrote in "asexual" as a sexual identity.

A number of studies that have focused on sexual behavior and relationships among asexual individuals found, not surprisingly, that asexuals had lower levels of sexual desire and sexual activity than sexuals (Brotto, Knudson, Inskip, Rhodes, & Erskine, 2010; Prause & Graham, 2007; Yule, Brotto, & Gorzalka, 2015) and were less likely to be in a partnered relationship (Greaves et al., 2017).

Research on Demographic Characteristics of Asexual Individuals

Population-based studies consistently show that more women identify as asexual compared to men (Bogaert, 2004; Greaves et al., 2017; Richters et al., 2014; Rothblum et al., 2019). In the survey of AVEN members (Ginoza et al., 2014), 62.1 percent identified as women/female and only 13.3 percent as men/male. Reasons that have been given for this gender difference include the fact that women have more flexible and fluid sexuality than men, that there is less pressure for women to be sexual than for men, and that it may be easier for women to admit that they are asexual than it is for men (cf. Bogaert, 2004; Van Houdenhove, Gijs, T'Sjoen, & Enzlin, 2014, for reviews). To this end Przybylo (2014) interviewed asexual-identified men and found themes of the "sexual imperative" (p. 228)—for men, sex is a main topic of discussion, a means of male bonding and belongingness, and a core part of coming of age.

Asexual identity is also much higher among transgender and genderqueer nonbinary individuals than among cisgender men (e.g. Greaves et al., 2017; Miller, 2012; Parent & Ferriter, 2018; Rothblum et al., 2019). Greaves et al. (2017) found that non-cisgender respondents were 149 times more likely to identify as asexual than were cisgender respondents. In the AVEN member survey (Ginoza et al., 2014), 8.5 percent identified as agender, 7.3 percent as genderqueer, 6 percent as other, 1.6 percent as neutrois, and 1.2 percent as bigender. In MacNeela and Murphy's (2015) qualitative survey of AVEN members, nearly one third of respondents rejected traditional gender identities. As Chasin (2011) has stated, "It is possible that sexual attractiveness standards govern gender presentations and behaviors, and that without the desire to attract a sexual partner, asexual people may have more freedom to explore their own genders." This is supported by quotes such as "Realizing I was asexual made me begin to think about my gender in a way I never had" and "It is also likely that my asexuality has shaped and aided my deconstruction of gender and what it means as I was never invested in the high school ritual of shaping my gender identity in order to meet a social approval to engage in sexual activities" (MacNeela & Murphy, 2015, p. 807). Sumerau, Barbee, Mathers, and Eaton (2018) compared fifty-seven asexual transgender and forty-two heterosexual transgender respondents. Those in both groups avoided biological sex markers when experiencing their own genders or those of others. Chasin (2015, p. 170) has pointed out that "being *read as* lesbian and gay (and bisexual to the extent that this is possible) is primarily about interpreting gender presentation," whereas this is not the case when identifying as asexual.

Asexual identity is also more common among younger respondents (Parent & Ferriter, 2018; Rothblum et al., 2019). The median age in the AVEN survey of its members (Ginoza et al., 2014) was twenty-one. In MacNeela and Murphy's (2015) qualitative survey, older respondents described how they had no language for their asexuality before the onset of the internet and sites such as AVEN. One exception is Bogaert's (2004) U.K. population-based survey (which asked about lack of sexual attraction rather than asexual identity), in which older respondents were more likely to indicate that they had no attraction to either sex. It is possible that online surveys attract younger respondents, and also that older respondents are not familiar with, or less likely to use, asexual as an identity.

Owen (2014) describes how asexuality and hypersexuality have been used historically when describing various racial and ethnic groups. Current studies have generally not found differences in asexual identity by race or ethnicity, but this is confounded by the fact that studies often have few respondents of color. In the survey of AVEN members (Ginoza et al., 2014), 77.3 percent identified as white, non-Hispanic. One exception is the New Zealand population-based survey by Greaves et al. (2017), in which asexual respondents were less likely to be of Pacific descent than were heterosexual, lesbian, or gay respondents. Another is the U.K. population-based study by Aicken et al. (2013), in which lack of sexual attraction was more often reported by respondents of Indian or Pakistani ethnicity, who were also more likely to be Muslim. More recently, Foster, Eklund, Brewster, Walker, and Candon (2018) interviewed eleven asexual women of color; ten of them felt like outsiders in the racial/ethnic and asexual communities due to their intersectional identities.

Studies also find asexual respondents to be nonreligious (Brotto et al., 2010; Rothblum et al., 2019b). In Miller's (2012) analysis of the Asexual Awareness Week Community Census, 64 percent of the 3,436 respondents were atheist, agnostic, or nonreligious. In AVEN's survey of its members (Ginoza et al., 2014, p. 4), 27.2 percent were atheist, 20.9 percent were agnostic, 10.5 percent were "other non-religious," and 11.3 percent were unsure. Again, an exception is Bogaert's U.K. population-based survey, which asked about lack of sexual attraction (rather than asexual identity) and found asexual respondents to be more likely to attend religious services.

Methodological Challenges in Research on Asexual Identity

Studying what Borgogna, McDermott, Aita, and Kridel (2018) have termed an "emerging identity" (p. 54) presents some challenges. Population-based surveys do not include asexual as a sexual identity category, so results are limited to respondents who write in asexual under "other." Respondents who identify as LGBTQ in addition to asexual may select one of the other sexual identity terms when asexual is not listed. Prause and Graham (2007) found that 22 of 1,146 respondents wrote in "asexual" in an open-ended question, but later on in the survey when "asexual" was included in a list of sexual orientation categories, 40 respondents checked that identity, indicating that write-in options are not as useful as more comprehensive lists of identities.

An additional challenge is lack of knowledge of the term or concept of asexuality. Respondents may lack sexual attraction but be unfamiliar with asexuality as an identity. Also, as Hinderliter (2009) has pointed out, individuals who have never felt sexual attraction may not easily be able to understand its lack. Similarly, when researchers ask about sexual behavior and sexual relationships, asexual respondents may have a broader interpretation of "sex." As I have discussed elsewhere (Rothblum, 1999), sex is often defined as heterosexual intercourse, which is problematic when describing sexual activity among sexual minorities. Other forms of sexual activity may not "count" as "real"—and in fact people tend to "count" sexual partners in a way they rarely count other types of relationships, such as friendships. This narrow, genitally focused definition of sex has implications for asexual individuals, who may not consider sex an important part of a partner relationship yet who may feel pressure to have sex in order to be considered in a "real" partnered relationship.

Qualitative researchers have overwhelmingly recruited respondents from the AVEN website, and this has been criticized (Carrigan et al., 2013; Hinderliter, 2009; Wong, 2015). As McDonnell, Scott, and Dawson (2016) have mentioned, online communities tend to have respondents who are female, highly educated, middle class, white, and from the United States.

Wong has written about how the AVEN website has an essentialist understanding of asexuality. Similarly, Przybylo and Cooper (2014, p. 301) state: "AVEN, then, as the public face or voice of asexuality, and as part of the vernacular archive, frequently (though certainly not always if we take its forums into account), rehearses a biologically bound definition of asexuality." Yet, as Scherrer (2008) has pointed out, an essentialist view may help to legitimize asexuality just as essentialist notions helped to legitimize gay and lesbian identities in the recent past by arguing that individuals were "born that way" and thus that their sexual orientation is not a "choice" or a transitory phase.

The Stigma of Asexuality

Asexual individuals face obstacles when asserting their identity, given the focus on sexual attraction and sexual relationships in most aspects of Western societies. When asked about asexuality, a sex therapist on the television program *20/20* stated: "You might as well label yourself not curious, unadventurous, narrow-minded, blind to possibilities. That's what happens when you label yourself as sexually neutered" (Kim, 2011, p. 488). Pinto (2014) described some of the stereotypes about asexuals, including that they have chosen to be asexual, cannot fall in love, are survivors of sexual abuse, just need to "find the right person," are sexually deviant, do not masturbate, are sociopaths, are denying their feelings, or that asexuality is not real (p. 334). Similarly, the AVEN webpage on "FAQ for family & friends" (http://www.asexuality.org/home/?q=family.html) lists many questions familiar to LGBT individuals in past decades, such as "Is this just some rebellious phase?" "Do you think it's caused by sexual abuse?" "Did I do something wrong as a parent to cause this?" and "Does this mean they are incapable of love?" MacNeela and Murphy (2015, p. 800) speculate that the stigma of asexuality may have similarities with the stigma of bisexuality, in that individuals receive "delegitimizing responses that include denial, positioning it as a transitory state, or as concealed homosexuality." Pacho (2013, p. 29) states, "While homosexual people may experience being called shameful, asexuality is seen as a state of being incomplete or underdeveloped."

In our population-based study of sexual minorities, asexual respondents felt more stigma than non-asexual women and men, and asexual respondents reported more everyday discrimination than did non-asexual men (Rothblum et al., 2019c). Gupta (2017) interviewed thirty respondents recruited from AVEN and other websites about stigmatization; over half indicated that they had been stigmatized or marginalized, and everyone mentioned at least one negative incident. Half the respondents had been pathologized, such as getting medical or psychological explanations when they came out to family or friends, being told to seek medical or psychological treatment, or consulting a health professional themselves in order to find an explanation for their asexuality. Two thirds felt alienated from social events, classroom discussions about sex, conversations with friends, or media programs or advertising. One third, all women, had engaged in unwanted sex due to pressure from a partner or social expectations. But respondents also challenged and resisted these norms. They mentioned advantages of asexuality, such as freedom from sexual relationships, greater capacity for friendships, enjoyment of aloneness, and greater acceptance of diversity.

The stigma of asexuality prevents some individuals from coming out to others. Robbins, Low, and Query (2016) interviewed members of AVEN and other online communities about the coming-out experience. Some of the themes included being misunderstood, disbelieved, or pathologized. MacNeela and Murphy (2015) similarly found themes of social invisibility, denial of legitimacy, and limited disclosure to others, although respondents also reported that asexual identity was a good fit and integral to their self-image.

In the only study to compare bias toward asexual individuals compared with other groups, MacInnis and Hodson (2012) asked 148 Canadian heterosexual college students to rate their liking of heterosexuals, homosexuals, bisexuals, and asexuals. Heterosexuals received the most positive evaluations, followed by homosexuals, bisexuals, and last of all asexuals. Asexuals were also rated most negatively when this study was replicated with an online community survey.

Despite the focus on sex, there are two communities that are *desexualized* by society: people with disabilities and the elderly. Kim (2011) states that some of the earliest uses of the term "asexual" appeared in scholarship about people with disabilities, who were viewed and treated as asexual individuals. This has resulted in extensive scholarship affirming the sexuality and rights of people with disabilities (cf. early books such as Browne, Connors, & Stern, 1985; Deegan & Brooks, 1985), to the extent that Kim (2014) points out that asexual individuals now dissociate themselves from disability and disability activists dissociate themselves from asexuality. As one blogger on the autistic spectrum wrote: "saying I am asexual in the disabled community can be interpreted as my affirming and reinforcing those stereotypes, which tends to make people rather angry" (cited in Kim, 2011, p. 482). Similarly, older people are perceived to be asexual by clinicians (Gott & Hinchcliff, 2003) and the popular media (Bogaert, 2012b). Kenny (2013) theorized that the preponderance of young bodies as sexually attractive in the media, the association of aging with physical changes such as menopause and erectile dysfunction, and the fact that older people are more likely to be widowed contribute to these stereotypes.

Sexual Disorders in the DSM

The DSM-5 (American Psychiatric Association, 2013) includes the diagnoses of "female sexual interest/arousal disorder" (p. 433) and "male hypoactive desire disorder" (p. 440). Diagnostic criteria indicate persistent reduced or lack of sexual interest or arousal for at least six months, causing significant distress for the individual. The DSM also states that "If a lifelong lack of sexual desire is better explained by one's self-identification as 'asexual,' then a diagnosis of female sexual interest/arousal disorder would not be made" (p. 434), and it contains a similar statement for male hypoactive sexual desire disorder (p. 443). In that regard, asexual identity is ego-syntonic and not distressing. As Bogaert (2006) has pointed out, asexual identity is often viewed as lifelong, whereas this is rarely the case in hypoactive sexual desire disorder (HSSD).

In the only study comparing asexuality to HSSD (Yule, Brotto, & Gorzalka, 2014), participants were recruited from AVEN, university subject pools, and announcements posted in the offices of sex therapists. Criteria for HSSD were from the revised fourth edition of the DSM (DSM-IV-TR; American Psychiatric Association, 2000). Participants were considered to have HSSD if they met the following criteria: (a) experiencing persistently or recurrently deficient (or absent) sexual fantasies and desire for sexual activity; (b) this deficiency/absence of sexual fantasies and desires causes marked distress or interpersonal difficulty; and (c) this deficiency/absence of sexual fantasies and desire for sexual activity is not better accounted for by a mental health disorder (e.g., depression), a drug (legal or illegal), or some other medical condition. Participants who met criterion (a) but not (b) or (c) were placed into the low sexual desire group. Of the total sample, 534 respondents were considered asexual, 87 as having HSSD, 78 as having low sexual desire, and 187 as the sexual comparison group. Asexual and sexual participants were younger than those with HSSD. Asexual respondents were less likely to indicate that they masturbated at least monthly (56 percent) than respondents with HSSD (65 percent), respondents with low sexual desire (75 percent), and sexual respondents (82 percent). Similarly, asexual respondents were most likely to report that they had never had a sexual fantasy (40 percent) compared with 8 percent of respondents with HSSD, 1 percent of those with low sexual desire, and 2 percent of sexual respondents. The results also indicate that 11 percent of asexual respondents, but very few of respondents in the three other groups, reported that their sexual fantasies did not involve other people, which Yule et al. (2014) speculate might involve masturbation as a form of tension release or physical pleasure alone.

Research on Asexual Mental Health

Given the social stigma of asexuality in a society that focuses on sexual attraction and sexual behavior, it is not surprising that studies of mental health have found higher levels of psychological distress among asexuals. In many ways the studies on mental health of asexuals bear a strong resemblance to studies comparing "homosexuals" to heterosexuals in the middle of the twentieth century. These articles will be reviewed in chronological order by publication date.

In one of the few studies conducted with asexual respondents before the current century, Nurius (1983) compared a convenience sample of 689 heterosexual, homosexual, bisexual, and asexual U.S. college students; 46.1 percent were white and 40.1 percent were Asian American. Asexual respondents (n = 56, with twice as many women as men) were defined as those who scored low on both homosexual and heterosexual items on a scale of sexual activity and preferences. Heterosexual respondents had the lowest scores on depression and highest scores on self-esteem, followed in ranked order by homosexual, bisexual, and asexual respondents. Nevertheless, Nurius mentions that the differences in means between groups were quite small.

Bogaert (2012a) referred to autochorissexualism as sexual fantasies that are removed from one's identity (e.g., fantasizing about fictional characters, or people disconnected from their own identity) and defined this tendency as a paraphilia (an atypical sexual attraction listed in the DSM). He uses quotes about sexual fantasies from the AVEN website as examples of this phenomenon. This corresponds with the research of Yule et al. (2014) described earlier in the chapter that 11 percent of asexual respondents reported that their sexual fantasies did not involve other people, compared with very few sexual respondents.

Yule, Brotto, and Gorzalka (2013) compared asexual respondents mostly recruited from AVEN with heterosexual and non-heterosexual respondents recruited from university students (the authors only analyzed the results for the white respondents because a large percentage of respondents were Asian American and the authors wanted to "avoid differences in ethnic groups," p. 138). The resulting sample of 806 white respondents included 54 asexual individuals. Asexual women and men were more likely to say "yes" to the two items about mood disorders and anxiety disorders than were heterosexual women and men, respectively. On the Brief Symptom Inventory, asexual men had higher scores on depression than heterosexual men, higher scores on somatization than non-heterosexual men, and higher scores on psychoticism than both heterosexual and non-heterosexual men. Asexual women had higher scores on phobic anxiety and psychoticism than heterosexual women and lower scores on hostility than non-heterosexual women. Asexual respondents also scored higher on the two suicidality items than heterosexual respondents.

Carvalho, Lemos, and Nobre (2017) recruited AVEN members who could read English (68 women and 19 men) and compared them with non-asexual respondents recruited from online advertisements matched on age, education, and relationship status. Asexual women reported higher levels of depression, phobic anxiety, and interpersonal sensitivity than non-asexual women, and asexual men reported higher levels of psychoticism than non-asexual men. This study is limited by a small sample size, particularly for male respondents.

The population-based New Zealand Attitudes and Values Study (Greaves et al., 2017) included the Kesler-6, a six-item measure of psychological distress. There were no differences between asexual, lesbian, gay, bisexual, or heterosexual respondents on this measure.

Parent and Ferriter (2018) used the Healthy Minds Study of U.S. college students to examine self-reported posttraumatic stress disorder (PTSD) and a history of sexual trauma in the past year. Asexual was not listed as a sexual identity, so respondents had to write it in under "other." The survey included 228 asexual-identified students (197 female, 31 male). In the general sample 1.9 percent reported PTSD and 2.4 percent reported a history of sexual trauma in the past year; corresponding rates for asexual respondents were 6.6 percent and 3.5 percent. The authors indicate that these rates, while elevated for asexual individuals, are still low.

A study by Borgogna et al. (2018) similarly used data on depression and anxiety from the Healthy Minds Study of U.S. college students to compare heterosexual with sexual minority respondents, including those who identified as "emerging minorities" that included bisexual, questioning, and (via a write-in option) pansexual, asexual, demisexual, and questioning. When compared with heterosexuals, pansexual and demisexual respondents had the highest levels of depression and anxiety, and those who identified as gay or lesbian had the smallest differences from heterosexuals. Respondents who were transgender/gender nonconforming also had higher levels of depression and anxiety compared with cisgender respondents, and those who were both sexual and gender minorities had the highest levels of depression and anxiety. One major limitation of this study is that the article does not list the numbers of respondents in each group, so it is not possible to know the frequency of write-ins for asexual versus demisexual identities. However, the results indicate the importance of assessing separate sexual minority categories, including emerging minorities such as asexual and demisexual.

Lack of Research on the Global South

Most of the research has focused on the United States, Europe, and Australia, so there is a paucity of studies on the Global South (Asia, Africa, Latin America, and the Caribbean). In a recent article in *The Atlantic,* Julian (2018) cited data that adolescents in a number of countries are waiting longer to have sex, adding: "And some people today may feel less pressured into sex they don't *want* to have, thanks to changing gender mores and growing awareness of diverse sexual orientations, including asexuality." Julian goes on to describe the term *sekkusu shinai shokogun* ("celibacy syndrome") in Japan. Similarly, Kobayashi (2017) refers to *soushokukei* ("herbivores"), a term referring to Japanese men who have lost interest in sexual activity. In a survey of residents of Osaka, Japan (Kamano, 2019), 0.8 percent were asexual, defined as "not having sexual/romantic feelings for anyone."

Wong (2015) conducted thirty online interviews and also analyzed 1,000 postings of members of an asexual marriage site (www.w920.net or *wuxing jiu-ai-ni*) in China, which claims to have 200,000 members. The site is for individuals who seek marriage or companionship without sex. In China in the past the focus of a good marriage was happiness, but, as the result of a recent sexual revolution, having sex and satisfying one's partner sexually are now key elements of a good marriage. Wong states (p. 105), "It is ironic that when the sexual revolution reaches China and everyone begins talking about sex, asexual individuals are unable to talk openly about their situation." So asexual individuals search online for a partner who also does not want sex.

Galeano (2017) used convenience sampling to survey sixty-four asexual-identified respondents (68.8 percent women) from Argentina, Chile, Honduras, Mexico, Peru, Spain, and Uruguay. On the International Personality Disorder Examination Test, the respondents scored highest on the trait of social inhibition, hypersensitivity, and feelings of incompetence.

Batričević and Cvetić (2016) conducted interviews about asexuality in Croatia and Serbia and found that the general public was unaware of the term. Furthermore, Muslim leaders were "promoting pro-natalist policies" that put pressure on women to get married and have children (p. 89).

Conclusion: Asexual Activism and Need for Further Research

In sum, the general public, the media, and health professionals hold negative stereotypes about and pathologize asexuality. Though research has not focused on mental health professionals' attitudes about asexuality, there is evidence that asexual individuals often have to educate their therapists about asexual identity and politics (Batričević & Cvetić, 2016). Pinto (2014) has written about how counselors need to be allies to asexual individuals, which includes counselors becoming aware of asexual identity, to forming a positive attitude, knowledge, and respect in order to become better therapists for asexual clients. Foster and Scherrer (2014) applied multicultural competence strategies to provide a safe space for asexual clients in therapy. There is a need for research on how mental health professionals view and respond to asexual clients in affirming ways.

It is also important to conduct research on how members of sexual and gender minority groups respond to asexual members of the queer communities. Many of the rights gained by sexual minorities have come about through more liberal societal attitudes about sex—how does this include asexuals? Given that asexual individuals are far more likely to identity as non-cisgender, how accepted are they by the gender minority communities? As this chapter has indicated, asexual people often have an ambivalent connection with LGBTQ communities.

It is striking that a number of studies have found asexuals to be introverted (Carvalho et al., 2017; Rothblum et al., 2019b), to have small community networks (Rothblum et al., 2019b), and to be higher on interpersonal sensitivity (Carvalho et al., 2017), social withdrawal (Brotto et al., 2010), interpersonal problems (Yule et al., 2013), social inhibition, and hypersensitivity (Galeano, 2017). Is there a connection between disinterest in social relationships and lack of sexual attraction? Or, conversely, do asexuals drift into social isolation because so many social events are thinly masked events for flirtation and ways to find sexual partners? More research is needed in this area.

Given these negative attitudes and experiences, it is not surprising that the limited research on mental health has found that asexual individuals are more likely to have mental health problems. It is also possible that individuals who are willing to be open about such a stigmatized identity may also be more honest about mental health problems, which are, after all, completely based on self-report.

Gupta (2017, p. 995) defines sexuality as "shaped by social, cultural, economic, and political influences." In Gupta's (2017) qualitative study, nearly every respondent described relief upon learning about the asexual community. Similarly, surveys describe the excitement of respondents when they found out that there is a term for their identity (Robbins et al., 2016) as well as a community (Carrigan, 2011). Given their small numbers, the internet and sites such as AVEN are vital for asexuals to feel part of a community.

Even more than group identity, it is important for newer identities such as asexuality to have increased attention from sexual and gender minorities, the media, and the general public. In Gupta's (2017) study, respondents wanted increased visibility for asexual identity. In Otto's (2017) interviews of the AVEN community in Denmark, respondents indicated how young children are taught about LGBT issues in school but not about asexuality. They wanted more reflection of asexuality in the media. Hopefully this marginalized identity will receive increased recognition and acceptance in the near future.

Finally, it is remarkable that the members of this stigmatized and invisible population are finding each other and forming social connections online. As one asexual respondent stated (Rothblum et al., 2019a), "Even in the trans/non-binary communities I've never seen the level of support you get in asexual circles. I also think it's really important for anyone who feels lost regarding their sexuality to look to our community. Because there is a certain diversity under the ace umbrella that you really don't see in the other letters of the LGBTQ+."

References

Aicken, C. R., Mercer, C. H., & Cassell, J. A. (2013). Who reports absence of sexual attraction in Britain? Evidence from national probability surveys. *Psychology & Sexuality, 4*, 121–35. doi:10.1080/19419899.2013.774161

American Psychiatric Association. (2000). *Diagnostic and statistical manual of mental disorders* (4th ed., text revision). Washington, DC: Author.

American Psychiatric Association. (2013). *Diagnostic and statistical manual of mental disorders* (5th ed.). Washington, DC: Author.

Batričević, M., & Cvetić, A. (2016). Uncovering an A: Asexuality and asexual activism in Croatia and Serbia. In B. Bilić & S. Kajinić (Eds.), *Intersectionality and LGBT activist politics* (pp. 77–103). London: Palgrave Macmillan.

Bogaert, A. F. (2004). Asexuality: Prevalence and associated factors in a national probability sample. *Journal of Sex Research, 41*, 279–87. doi:10.1080/00224490409552235

Bogaert, A. F. (2006). Toward a conceptual understanding of asexuality. *Review of General Psychology, 10*, 241–50. doi:10.1037/1089-2680.10.3.241

Bogaert, A. F. (2012a). Asexuality and autochorissexualism (identity-less sexuality). *Archives of Sexual Behavior, 41*, 1513–14. doi:10.1007/s10508-012-9963-1

Bogaert, A. F. (2012b). *Understanding asexuality*. Lanham, MD: Rowman & Littlefield.

Borgogna, N. C., McDermott, R. C., Aita, S. L., & Kridel, M. M. (2018). Anxiety and depression across gender and sexual minorities: Implications for transgender, gender nonconforming, pansexual, demisexual, asexual, queer, and questioning individuals. *Psychology of Sexual Orientation and Gender Diversity, 6*, 54–63. doi:10.1037/sgd0000306

Brotto, L. A., Knudson, G., Inskip, J., Rhodes, K., & Erskine, Y. (2010). Asexuality: A mixed-methods approach. *Archives of Sexual Behavior, 39*, 599–618. doi:10.1007/s10508-008-9434-x

Browne, S. E., Connors, D., & Stern, N. (1985). *With the power of each breath: A disabled women's anthology*. Pittsburgh, PA: Cleis Press.

Canning, D. A. (2015). Queering asexuality: Asexual-inclusion in queer spaces. *McNair Scholars Research Journal, 8*(1), 55–74. http://commons.emich.edu/mcnair/vol8/6

Carrigan, M. (2011). There's more to life than sex? Difference and commonality within the asexual community. *Sexualities, 14*, 462–78. doi:10.1177/1363460711406462

Carrigan, M., Gupta, K., & Morrison, T. G. (2013). Asexuality special theme issue editorial. *Psychology & Sexuality, 4*, 111–20. doi:10.1080/19419899.2013.774160

Carvalho, J., Lemos, D., & Nobre, P. J. (2017). Psychological features and sexual beliefs characterizing self-labeled asexual individuals. *Journal of Sex & Marital Therapy, 43*, 517–28. do i:10.1080/0092623X.2016.1208696

Cerankowski, K. J., & Milks, M. (2010). New orientations: Asexuality and its implications for theory and practice. *Feminist Studies, 36*, 650–64. https://www.jstor.org/stable/pdf/27919126.pdf

Chasin, C. D. (2011). Theoretical issues in the study of asexuality. *Archives of Sexual Behavior, 40*, 713–23. doi:10.1007/s10508-011-9757-x

Chasin, C. D. (2015). Making sense in and of the asexual community: Navigating relationships and identities in a context of resistance. *Journal of Community & Applied Social Psychology, 25*, 167–80. doi:10.1002/casp.2203

Deegan, M. J., & Brooks, N. A. (1985). *Women and disability: The double handicap*. New Brunswick, NJ: Transaction Books.

D'Emilio, J., & Freedman, E. (1997). *Intimate matters: A history of sexuality in America* (2nd ed.). Chicago, IL: University of Chicago Press.

Faderman, L. (1981). *Surpassing the love of men: Romantic friendship and love between women from the Renaissance to the present*. New York, NY: Morrow.

Fahs, B. (2010). Radical refusals: On the anarchist politics of women choosing asexuality. *Sexualities, 13*, 445–61. doi:10.1177/1363460710370650

Foster, A. B., Eklund, A., Brewster, M. E., Walker, A. D., & Candon, E. (2018). Personal agency disavowed: Identity construction in asexual women of color. *Psychology of Sexual Orientation and Gender Diversity, 6*, 127–37. doi:10.1037/sgd0000310

Foster, A. B., & Scherrer, K. S. (2014). Asexual-identified clients in clinical settings: Implications for culturally competent practice. *Psychology of Sexual Orientation and Gender Diversity, 1*, 422–30. doi:10.1037/sgd0000058

Galeano, A. G. (2017). Personality traits in asexual people. *Journal of Sexual Medicine, 14*, e298–e299. doi:10.1016/j.jsxm.2017.04.435

Ginoza, M. K., Miller, T., & AVEN Survey Team (2014). The 2014 AVEN community census: Preliminary findings (pp. 1–19). https://asexualcensus.files.wordpress.com/2014/11/2014censuspreliminaryreport.pdf

Gott, M., & Hinchliff, S. (2003). Barriers to seeking treatment for sexual problems in primary care: A qualitative study with older people. *Family Practice, 20*, 690–5. doi:10.1093/fampra/cmg612

Greaves, L. M., Barlow, F. K., Huang, Y., Stronge, S., Fraser, G., & Sibley, C. G. (2017). Asexual identity in a New Zealand national sample: Demographics, well-being, and health. *Archives of Sexual Behavior, 46*, 2417–27. doi:10.1007/s10508-017-0977-6

Gressgård, R. (2013). Asexuality: From pathology to identity and beyond. *Psychology & Sexuality, 4*, 179–92. doi:10.1080/19419899.2013.774166

Gupta, K. (2017). "And now I'm just different, but there's nothing actually wrong with me": Asexual marginalization and resistance. *Journal of Homosexuality, 64*, 991–1013. doi:10.1080/00918369.2016.1236590

Hinderliter, A. C. (2009). Methodological issues for studying asexuality. *Archives of Sexual Behavior, 38*, 619–21. doi:10.1007/s10508-009-9502-x

Holland, D. C., & Eisenhart, M. A. (1990). *Educated in romance: Women, achievement, and college culture*. Chicago, IL: University of Chicago Press.

International Society for Sexual Medicine (2019). What does "sex positive" mean? https://www.issm.info/sexual-health-qa/what-does-sex-positive-mean/

Julian, K. (December 2018). Why are young people having so little sex? *The Atlantic*, https://www.theatlantic.com/magazine/archive/2018/12/the-sex-recession/573949/

Kamano, S. (2019). Preliminary results from the "Survey on Diversity of Work and Life, and Coexistence among the Residents of Osaka City." http://www.ipss.go.jp/projects/j/SOGI/index.asp

Kenny, R. (2013). A review of the literature on sexual development of older adults in relation to the asexual stereotype of older adults. *Canadian Journal of Family and Youth, 5*, 91–106. doi:10.29173/cjfy18949

Kim, E. (2011). Asexuality in disability narratives. *Sexualities, 14*, 479–93. doi:10.1177/1363460711406463

Kim, E. (2014). Asexuality and disability: Mutual negotiation in *Adams vs. Rice* and new directions for coalition building. In K. J. Cerankowski & M. Milks (Eds.), *Asexualities: Feminist and queer perspectives* (pp. 283–301). New York, NY: Routledge.

Kinsey, A. C., Pomeroy, W. R., & Martin, C. E. (1948). *Sexual behavior in the human male*. Philadelphia, PA: Saunders.

Kinsey, A. C., Pomeroy, W. B., Martin, C. E., & Gebhard, P. H. (1953). *Sexual behavior in the human female*. Philadelphia, PA: Saunders.

Kobayashi, J. (2017). Have Japanese people become asexual? Love in Japan. *International Journal of Japanese Sociology, 26*, 13–22. doi:10.1111/ijjs.12067

MacInnis, C. C., & Hodson, G. (2012). Intergroup bias toward "Group X": Evidence of prejudice, dehumanization, avoidance, and discrimination against asexuals. *Group Processes & Intergroup Relations, 15*, 725–43. doi:10.1177/1368430212442419

MacNeela, P., & Murphy, A. (2015). Freedom, invisibility, and community: A qualitative study of self-identification with asexuality. *Archives of Sexual Behavior, 44*, 799–812. doi:10.1007/s10508-014-0458-0

McDonnell, L., Scott, S., & Dawson, M. (2016). A multidimensional view? Evaluating the different and combined contributions of diaries and interviews in an exploration of asexual identities and intimacies. *Qualitative Research, 17*, 520–36. doi:10.1177/1468794116676516

Miller, T. (2012). Analysis of the 2011 Asexual Awareness Week Community Census. *Age, 13*(15), 5–13.

Mitchell, H., & Hunnicutt, G. (September 2018). Challenging accepted scripts of sexual "normality": Asexual narratives of non-normative identity and experience. *Sexuality & Culture*, 1–18. doi:10.1007/s12119-018-9567-6

Mollet, A. L., & Lackman, B. R. (2018). Asexual borderlands: Asexual collegians' reflections on inclusion under the LGBTQ umbrella. *Journal of College Student Development, 59*, 623–8. doi:10.1353/csd.2018.0058

Nurius, P. S. (1983). Mental health implications of sexual orientation. *Journal of Sex Research, 19*, 119–36. doi:10.1080/00224498309551174

Otto, J. C. (April 2017). The asexual experience and community in Denmark. Proceedings of the National Conference on Undergraduate Research (NCUR), Memphis, TN.

Owen, I. H. (2014). On the racialization of asexuality. In K. J. Cerankowski & M. Milks (Eds.), *Asexualities: Feminist and queer perspectives* (pp. 119–35). New York, NY: Routledge.

Pacho, A. (2013). Establishing asexual identity: The essential, the imaginary, and the collective. *Graduate Journal of Social Science, 10*(1), 13–35.

Parent, M. C., & Ferriter, K. P. (2018). The co-occurrence of asexuality and self-reported post-traumatic stress disorder diagnosis and sexual trauma within the past 12 months among US college students. *Archives of Sexual Behavior, 47*, 1277–82. doi:10.1007/s10508-018-1171-1

Pinto, S. A. (2014). ASEXUally: On being an ally to the asexual community. *Journal of LGBT Issues in Counseling, 8*, 331–43. doi:10.1080/15538605.2014.960130

Poston, D. L., & Baumle, A. K. (2010). Patterns of asexuality in the United States. *Demographic Research, 23*, 509–30. doi:10.4054/DemRes.2010.23.18

Prause, N., & Graham, C. A. (2007). Asexuality: Classification and characterization. *Archives of Sexual Behavior, 36*, 341–56. doi:10.1007/s10508-006-9142-3

Przybylo, E. (2011). Crisis and safety: The asexual in sexusociety. *Sexualities, 14*, 444–61. doi:10.1177/1363460711406461

Przybylo, E. (2012). Producing facts: Empirical asexuality and the scientific study of sex. *Feminism & Psychology, 23*, 224–42. doi:10.1177/0959353512443668

Przybylo, E. (2014). Masculine doubt and sexual wonder: Asexually-identified men talk about their (a)sexualities. In K. J. Cerankowski & M. Milks (Eds.), *Asexualities: Feminist and queer perspectives* (pp. 225–46). New York, NY: Routledge.

Przybylo, E., & Cooper, D. (2014). Asexual resonances: tracing a queerly asexual archive. *GLQ: A Journal of Lesbian and Gay Studies, 20*, 297–318. doi:10.1215/10642684-2422683

Richters, J., Altman, D., Badcock, P. B., Smith, A. M., de Visser, R. O., Grulich, A. E.,... Simpson, J. M. (2014). Sexual identity, sexual attraction and sexual experience: The Second Australian Study of Health and Relationships. *Sexual Health, 11*, 451–60.

Robbins, N. K., Low, K. G., & Query, A. N. (2016). A qualitative exploration of the "coming out" process for asexual individuals. *Archives of Sexual Behavior, 45*, 751–60. doi:10.1007/s10508-015-0561-x

Rothblum, E. D., & Brehony, K. A. (1993). *Boston marriages: Romantic but asexual relationships among contemporary lesbians*. Boston, MA: University of Massachusetts Press.

Rothblum, E. D., Carpenter, K., & Heimann, K. (March 2019a). *Asexual women: Identity, societal roles, and community*. Paper presented at the annual convention of the Association for Women in Psychology, Providence, RI.

Rothblum, E. D., Heimann, K., & Carpenter, K. (2019b). The lives of asexual individuals outside of sexual and romantic relationships: Education, occupation, religion and community. *Psychology & Sexuality, 10*, 83–93. doi:10.1080/19419899.2018.1552186

Rothblum, E. D., Krueger, E. A., Kittle, K. R., & Meyer, I. H. (2019c). Asexual and non-asexual respondents from a U.S. population-based study of sexual minorities. *Archives of Sexual Behavior* [E-pub ahead of print]. doi:10.1007/s10508-019-01485-0

Rothblum, E. D. (1999). Poly-friendships. *Journal of Lesbian Studies, 3*, 68–83. doi:10.1300/J155v03n01_08

Scherrer, K. S. (2008). Coming to an asexual identity: Negotiating identity, negotiating desire. *Sexualities, 11*, 621–41. doi:10.1177/1363460708094269

Scott, S., McDonnell, L., & Dawson, M. (2016). Stories of non-becoming: Non-issues, non-events and non-identities in asexual lives. *Symbolic Interaction, 39*, 268–86. doi:10.1002/symb.215

Sumerau, J., Barbee, H., Mathers, L., & Eaton, V. (2018). Exploring the experiences of heterosexual and asexual transgender people. *Social Sciences, 7*, 162–78. doi:10.3390/socsci7090162

Van Houdenhove, E., Gijs, L., T'Sjoen, G., & Enzlin, P. (2014). Asexuality: Few facts, many questions. *Journal of Sex & Marital Therapy, 40*, 175–92. doi:10.1080/0092623X.2012.751073

Wong, D. (2015). Asexuality in China's sexual revolution: Asexual marriage as coping strategy. *Sexualities, 18*, 100–16. doi:10.1177/1363460714544812

Yule, M. A., Brotto, L. A., & Gorzalka, B. B. (2013). Mental health and interpersonal functioning in self-identified asexual men and women. *Psychology & Sexuality, 4*, 136–51. doi:10.1080/19419899.2013.774162

Yule, M. A., Brotto, L. A., & Gorzalka, B. B. (2014). Sexual fantasy and masturbation among asexual individuals. *Canadian Journal of Human Sexuality, 23*, 89–95. doi:10.3138/cjhs.2409

Yule, M. A., Brotto, L. A., & Gorzalka, B. B. (2015). A validated measure of no sexual attraction: The Asexuality Identification Scale. *Psychological Assessment, 27*, 148–60. doi:10.1037/a0038196

CHAPTER

28 Mental Health for Individuals with Pansexual and Queer Identities

M. Paz Galupo

Abstract

There is a growing need to articulate a framework for exploring mental health disparities among individuals with pansexual and queer identities. This chapter provides an overview of the methodological challenges for researching plurisexuality in general, and pansexual and queer identities in particular. Challenges include the conceptualization of sexuality on a continuum, assumptions of alignment normativity, and the use of multiple labels. The author discusses the strategic use of pansexual and queer identity labels and their relation to current health-related research. The author outlines the scant research on pansexual and queer mental health disparities and offers considerations for moving a larger research agenda forward.

Keywords: bisexual, gender diversity, pansexual, plurisexual, queer, LGBTQ health

Minority stress theory (Meyer, 1995, 2003, 2015) has been the predominant framework from which to understand sexual and gender minority health disparities in the literature. Minority stress is conceptualized as the excess stress experienced based on having a marginalized identity. It has been suggested that sexual (Meyer, 2003) and gender minority (Meyer, Hendricks & Testa, 2015) individuals experience unique distal and proximal stressors. Distal stressors including discrimination and harassment introduce stress based on their *external* impact on the individual (Meyer, 2003). Proximal stressors, in contrast, can be defined as subjective internalizations of negative events and attitudes (Meyer, 2003). These stressors are dependent upon self-identity and take the form of internal processes following perceived stressful events (Meyer, 2003).

Past literature has highlighted the mental health disparities experienced by sexual minority individuals when compared to their heterosexual counterparts (Bostwick, Boyd, Hughes, & McCabe, 2010; Cochran, Sullivan, & Mays, 2003; Hatzenbuehler, Keyes, & Hasin, 2009; Hatzenbuehler & McLaughlin, 2017; Lewis, Derlega, Griffin, & Krowinski, 2003; Meyer, 1995, 2003). Within-group differences across identity are almost exclusively focused on differentiating unique experiences of bisexual-identified individuals using heterosexual and lesbian/gay comparison groups (see Chapter 23 in this volume). Unique stressors for bisexual individuals are understood as resulting from assumptions of monosexuality and anti-bisexual prejudice (Bostwick & Hequembourg, 2014; Feinstein & Dyar, 2017; Flanders, Robinson, Legge, & Tarasoff, 2016) directed toward bisexual individuals from heterosexual individuals as well as lesbians and gay men (Brewster & Moradi, 2010; Wandrey, Mosack, & Moore, 2015). Thus, mental health disparities for bisexual individuals are dually constructed around hetero-cisnormative and mononormative assumptions. Bisexual identities are often characterized by sexual fluidity (Diamond, 2008; Flanders, LeBreton, Robinson, Bian, & Caravaca-Morera, 2017; Mereish, Katz-Wise, & Woulfe, 2017), as complicating binary constructions of gender/sex and sexuality (Callis, 2014; Galupo, Davis, Grynkiewicz, & Mitchell, 2014), and can be best understood as nonbinary sexual identities existing on the sexual borderlands

(Callis, 2014; Ghabrial, 2019; Pallotta-Chiarolli, 2006, 2010, 2011). As a minority within a minority, bisexuality is often defined by what it is not, is poorly defined in the literature (Swan, 2018), and is often conflated with other borderland identities such as pansexual and queer.

As a researcher with a focus on experiences across identity, I have found it increasingly difficult to be both inclusive and specific with the available scientific terminology when addressing nonbinary sexual identities. We introduced *plurisexual* into the academic literature in 2014 (Galupo, Davis, et al., 2014) to refer to identities that are not explicitly based on attraction to one gender/sex (e.g., bisexual, pansexual, queer, fluid) and/or for individuals who leave open the potential for attraction to more than one gender/sex (e.g., bi-curious, heteroflexible, mostly heterosexual, mostly gay/lesbian, nonlabeled). A number of researchers have similarly begun using the term *plurisexual* (Flanders, Anderson, Tarasoff, & Robinson, 2019; Manley, Legge, Flanders, Goldberg, & Ross, 2018; Ross, Goldberg, Tarasoff, & Guo, 2018; Ross, Tarasoff, Goldberg, & Flanders, 2017). Although non-monosexual is used in the literature in a similar way, we intentionally use the term *plurisexual* because it does not linguistically assume monosexual as the ideal conceptualization of sexuality from which to make comparisons (in the same way that we avoid referring to lesbian, gay, bisexual, and queer individuals as simply non-heterosexual). To truly advance an understanding of plurisexual mental health disparities, however, it is necessary to explore within-group differences. Using language that is not referential/deferential to the monosexual norm conceptually shifts the focus on plurisexual experience. Because bisexuality has long been conceptualized as a midpoint between monosexual poles, adding plurisexual into the lexicon strategically centers its purview outside of the continuum extending between same and other-sex desire. No longer tethered to the continuum, plurisexuality as a term allows for other identities such as pansexual and queer to become visible. However, there is a dearth of literature focusing on the mental health outcomes for these other articulations of plurisexual identity beyond bisexual.

Given that identity is central to the theory of minority stress, it is likely that within-group differences may exist among sexual minority individuals across self-identity. Recent literature has documented the way that bisexual individuals conceptualize and negotiate their identity differently from those who identify as pansexual or queer (Galupo, Ramirez, & Pulice-Farrow, 2017). It makes sense, then, that mental health outcomes may also differ across these sexual identity groups. In an effort to articulate a framework for exploring mental health disparities among individuals with pansexual and queer identities, the present chapter (1) considers the methodological challenges for researching plurisexuality in general (and pansexual and queer identities in particular); (2) explores the strategic use of pansexual and queer identity labels; and (3) outlines considerations for incorporating pansexual and queer into the larger research agenda for understanding mental health disparities.

Unique Methodological Considerations for the Study of Plurisexuality

Sexual orientation is understood as an internal mechanism that directs both sexual/erotic and romantic/nurturant interests (Diamond, 2003; Rosario & Schrimshaw, 2014; van Anders, 2015). That sexual orientation is multidimensional, encompassing attraction, behavior, and identity (Laumann, Gagnon, Michael, & Michaels, 1994; Wolff, Wells, Ventura-DiPersia, Renson, & Grov, 2017), poses methodological challenges for researchers. Which dimensions researchers use to recruit participants into studies, to define group membership for analysis, and to measure outcomes has a tremendous impact on the knowledge produced and reported (Sell, 1997). In addition, the diversity of terminology, measurement, and approaches represented in the current literature makes it difficult to interpret findings or make comparisons across studies.

I will discuss three specific methodological challenges presented to sexual health researchers that complicate our understanding of pansexual and queer mental health: (1) the conceptualization of sexuality on a continuum; (2) the reliance upon alignment normativity; and (3) the use of multiple sexual identity labels.

The Sexual Continuum: Implications for Pansexual and Queer Identities

The conceptualization and measurement of sexuality on a continuum has narrowed our definitions of plurisexuality while also implicitly suggesting a hierarchy of experience. This research has been used to establish "degrees" of plurisexuality that implicitly suggest a "pure," "true," or somehow more "substantial" bisexual typology. This same continuum renders pansexual and queer identities invisible and undefined.

Kinsey et al. (Kinsey, Pomeroy, & Martin, 1948; Kinsey, Pomeroy, Martin, & Gebhard, 1953) developed one of the most recognized and used research measures of sexual orientation. Conceptualized on a single continuum, the seven-point scale allows an individual to rate their sexuality numerically between *exclusively heterosexual* (0) and *exclusively homosexual* (6). Kinsey et al. focused on sexual behavior and interests and intentionally disaggregated their measurement from sociocultural identity labels (e.g., gay, lesbian) (Drucker, 2010, 2012). It is ironic, then, that raw scores on the Kinsey Scale are most often used in research to separate individuals into three identity-based categories (i.e., heterosexual, bisexual, lesbian/gay). With this categorization system, the middle five points on the seven-point scale are grouped together under the label of bisexual (Savin-Williams, 2014) and are often treated by researchers as a homogenous group.

Savin-Williams's (2010) Sexual Orientation Label scale (seven-point version) offers an adaptation of the Kinsey Scale where sexual orientation is still conceptualized on a continuum but incorporates more contemporary language and labels. Composed of a single continuum with *exclusively heterosexual* and *exclusively gay/lesbian* at the extreme points, middle points are labeled *mostly heterosexual, bisexual leaning heterosexual, bisexual, bisexual leaning gay/lesbian*, and *mostly gay/lesbian*. Arguing that the three-identity model (heterosexual, bisexual, lesbian and gay) is not adequate for capturing the range of sexuality experienced, Savin-Williams et al. have embarked on a series of studies to consider whether intermediary sexual identity labels such as *mostly heterosexual* (Savin-Williams, Rieger, & Rosenthal, 2013), *mostly gay*, and *bisexual leaning gay* (Savin-Williams, Cash, McCormack, & Rieger, 2017; Vrangalova & Savin-Williams, 2012) represent distinct orientations. This conceptualization has inspired a whole line of research aimed at understanding how experience may differ for *mostly heterosexuals* with regard to a number of mental health outcomes, including substance use and sexual risk (e.g., Corliss, Austin, Roberts, & Molnar, 2010; Hughes, Wilsnack, & Krisjanson, 2015; Kuyper & Bos, 2016), where *mostly heterosexual* is considered an identity distinct from both heterosexual and bisexual experience.

It is noteworthy that the majority of the research inspired by Savin-Williams's theoretical reframe on sexual orientation continuum (2014) has focused on the *mostly heterosexual* group. Enough research has been conducted on this specific group that several review articles (Savin-Williams & Vrangalova, 2013; Vrangalova & Savin-Williams, 2012) and a special issue (McCormack, 2018) have focused on the research on this group. While I do not question whether further focus on individuals who are *mostly heterosexual* is an important undertaking, it is also not surprising that it has garnered the most interest of all the intermediary groupings. A focus on this group reinforces the dominant interest in heteronormative (or in this case *mostly* heteronormative) experiences. It also effectively diverts interest (both conceptually and linguistically) from exploring the range of plurisexual experience.

Although the conceptualization of sexual orientation on a continuum invites a welcome complexity, this shift in language and research approach has evolved in recent years without much comment on the way definitions and demarcations of bisexuality are impacted. By focusing in on *mostly heterosexual* and *mostly lesbian/gay* groupings (previously considered by many as bisexual), bisexuality becomes more narrowly conceptualized. Not only does bisexuality span a shorter range across the continuum within this model, but the definition of bisexuality becomes more rigid. This is made explicit in Savin-Williams's seven-point label scale (2010), where the midpoint is labeled *Bisexual* and is then operationalized as "*more or less equally sexually attracted to females and males.*" This narrowing of bisexuality recalls stereotypes about bisexual individuals as needing to reflect an equal attraction to women and men (Gonzalez et al, 2017) to be truly bisexual. In addition to narrowing the conceptualization of bisexuality, it is important to consider how these groupings may set up a linguistic hierarchy of bisexualities where, for example, individuals scoring as *bisexual* are regarded as "more" bisexual or truly bisexual when compared to *bisexual leaning heterosexual*.

In addition to compacting notions of bisexuality, continuum-based conceptualizations of sexuality do not always resonate with lived experience. Community definitions are more expansive, are much less likely to place bisexuality as a midpoint on a continuum between heterosexual and lesbian/gay experience, and do not mandate equal degrees of attraction to women and men (Gonzalez, Ramirez, & Galupo, 2017). And when sexual minority individuals critique the way traditional scales (i.e., Kinsey; the Klein Sexual Orientation Grid; Klein, Sepekoff, & Wolf, 1985) conceptualize sexuality, they express concerns regarding how well traditional scales capture their experience of sexuality. Sexual minority individuals question whether a single continuum could capture the complexity and fluidity of their sexuality. They also critique the fact that traditional scales are anchored on binary dimensions of gender/sex and object to the way same- and other-sex attraction are measured in opposition to each other (Galupo, Mitchell, Grynkiewicz, & Davis, 2014). This is particularly important for health researchers concerned with understanding within-group differences as plurisexual and transgender individuals are the least likely to feel that sexual orientation scales capture their lived experience of sexuality (Galupo, Mitchell, et al., 2014).

It is important to note that sexual identity labels that conceptually parallel the continuous nature of sexual attraction (e.g., *mostly heterosexual* or *bisexual leaning gay/lesbian*; Savin-Williams, 2010) are distinct from the sexual identity labels that are used in a community/social context that are discrete and nominal in conceptualization (Pega, Gray, Veale, Binson, & Sell, 2013). Community-based labels (e.g., *pansexual, queer, fluid*) are not easily conceptualized on a continuum and are often chosen to specifically challenge continuous and binary notions of sexuality (Callis, 2014; Flanders, 2017; Galupo, 2018; Galupo, Ramirez, & Pulice-Farrow, 2017; Mereish et al., 2017; Rust, 2000). Thus, use of sexual orientation scales to measure sexual or romantic attraction is a common limitation in plurisexual health research that introduces significant bias toward pansexual and queer individuals.

Alignment Normativity: Implications for Pansexual and Queer Individuals

It has been consistently noted that sexual attraction, behavior, and identity are not coincident (Bauer & Brennan, 2013: Bauer & Jairam, 2008; Sell, 1997). For example, two individuals may identify as queer yet report very different patterns of sexual attraction. Similarly, two individuals may report the same behavioral or attraction patterns, yet one may identify as bisexual and another as pansexual or queer (Baldwin et al., 2016; Galupo, Ramirez, & Pulice-Farrow, 2017). In the context of research Pega et al. (2013) note that sexual attraction is often conceptualized as a continuous variable (measured by degree) while sexual behavior and sexual identity are more often conceptualized as categorical (distinguished as discrete experiences). It is likely that the difference in measurement approach contributes to the way sexual attraction, behavior, and identity do not neatly coincide in the research literature (Galupo, 2018). Beyond differences in measurement, the way that branched experiences are viewed among the three should be critically evaluated. The value placed on symmetry (Halperin, 2009) and congruence (Baldwin et al., 2016; Schick, Rosenberger, Herbenick, Calabrese, & Reece, 2012) has also seeped into research approaches. Researchers often use the terms *aligned/misaligned* or *congruent/incongruent* in order to describe the relationship among these three dimensions. However, these terms are not value free. The alternative terms *coincident* and *branched* have been introduced as a way to remove the implicit suggestion that it is more authentic somehow for attraction, behavior, and identity to coincide (van Anders, 2015). van Anders (2015) discusses the way alignment normativity is inherent to our conceptualization of sexuality where alignment among the different dimensions is presumed to be expected and ideal.

It is important to note the unique ways the tripartite model of sexual orientation in conjunction with alignment normativity has been applied to specifically undermine plurisexuality and to reinforce the pervasive negative stereotypes about bisexual individuals specifically. Bisexual individuals are often negatively stereotyped as being untrustworthy, confused, and promiscuous (Kleese, 2011). These negative attitudes are often attributed to shifts in behavior, partner choice, or relationship status (Gonzalez et al., 2017). Plurisexual identities (inclusive of bisexual, pansexual, and queer) have similarly been stereotyped as not valid or stable (Dyar & Feinstein, 2018; Gonzalez et al., 2017).

Despite the distinction between behavior and identity, sexual minority individuals are often held to a behavioral standard for justifying their non-heterosexuality (Boyer & Galupo, 2015; Greenesmith, 2010; Israel & Mohr, 2004; Richter, 2011). For plurisexual people this equates to unrealistic expectations of being simultaneously engaged with multiple individuals of different gender/sexes in order to justify their self-identification. This behavioral standard functions to impose an external measure of authenticity for sexual minority identities through behavioral experience or performance (Boyer & Galupo, 2015). Bauer and Brennan (2013) note that one problem with research using behavioral measures is that at least two sex partners (often one "male" and one "female") are required for a bisexual classification while only one is required within the same time period for a monosexual classification (lesbian/gay or heterosexual). This literal double standard for bisexual individuals is an artifact of the way participant groups are operationalized, conflates sexual identity with number of sexual partners (Bauer

& Brennan, 2013), and simultaneously recalls and contributes to stereotypes of bisexual promiscuity. No research has similarly operationalized pansexual or queer, and it is not clear how a behavioral measure could meaningfully map onto these identities.

Use of Multiple Labels in Different Social Contexts

The earlier sections on the conceptualization of sexual orientation on a continuum and on alignment normativity illustrate biases in the way behavior and attraction have been used in research at the expense of plurisexual identity. However, an overreliance on participant self-identification is not without its own concern. Sexuality researchers commonly use self-identification in order to group participants, but these practices may also disproportionately skew data from those who endorse plurisexual identity labels. When compared to lesbians and gay men, plurisexual individuals are less likely to feel that their sexual identity label fully captures their sexuality (Dyar, Feinstein, & London, 2015), are more likely to provide additional explanation and context around their sexual identity labels (Galupo, Mitchell, & Davis, 2015), and are more likely to endorse multiple labels (Barker, Bowes-Catton, Iantaffi, Cassidy, & Brewer, 2008; Galupo, Mitchell, & Davis, 2015; Rust, 2000). Plurisexual individuals may use multiple labels because they find the existing labels limiting and/or other people's understandings of the labels to be limited (Barker et al., 2008: Galupo et al., 2015, Galupo, Lomash, & Mitchell, 2017; Gonel, 2013; Rust, 2000). Individuals who use multiple labels strategically switch labels across different situational contexts based on acceptance level and safety, parsimony, or out of exhaustion in having to explain them (Belmonte & Holmes, 2016; Flanders, Dobinson, & Logie, 2015; Galupo, 2011; Galupo, Taylor, & Cole, 2019; Ghabrial, 2019; Gonzalez et al., 2017; Kolker, Taylor, & Galupo, 2019).

Understanding Pansexual and Queer Identity Labels

Language is ever-evolving and new labels are often created to counter misconceptualizations and to more accurately define plurisexual attraction and experience (Better, 2014; Galupo, 2018). Just as the scientific literature has placed an emphasis on understanding continuum-based identity labels that mirror sexual orientation measurement scales (such as *mostly heterosexual, mostly lesbian-gay, bi-leaning heterosexual*), qualitative research has described the emergence of identity labels that are more categorical in nature. Only recently has the literature begun to incorporate community-based plurisexual labels such as pansexual and queer (Callis, 2014; Elizabeth, 2013; Galupo, Davis et al., 2014; Morgan, 2013). However, there has not been a singular approach to how these new identities have been studied.

Several studies have allowed a comparison across bisexual, pansexual, and queer participants (Callis, 2014; Galupo, Mitchell, & Davis, 2015; Galupo, Ramirez, & Pulice-Farrow, 2017; Mitchell, Davis, & Galupo, 2015; Morandini, Blaszczynski, & Dar-Nimrod, 2017). Sometimes these comparisons include lesbian and gay individuals (Galupo et al., 2015; Morandini et al., 2017). Other researchers have allowed for a direct comparison between pairs of identity labels such as bisexual-pansexual (Flanders et al., 2017) and bisexual-queer (Barker, Richards, & Bowes-Catton, 2009; Gray & Desmarais, 2014; Mereish et al., 2017). Others still have explored the meaning of these labels singularly (including pansexual: Belous & Bauman, 2017; Gonel, 2013; and queer: Fox & Ralston, 2016; Kolker et al., 2019; Miller, Taylor, & Rupp, 2016). In addition, it is important to note the limitations of labels in general, as some individuals prefer no label at all (Galupo, Ramirez, & Pulice-Farrow, 2017). Although many of these research samples acknowledge gender diversity, several studies have specifically considered bisexual/plurisexual identities among transgender and gender diverse individuals (Galupo, Henise, & Mercer, 2016; Katz-Wise, Reisner, Hughto, & Keo-Meier, 2016). Collectively, this research is instructive when trying to understand how individuals use different identity labels to communicate their experiences and to think through when and how these distinctions may be important questions of minority stress and health research.

Pansexual Identity: Sexuality as Transcending Gender/Sex

Because pansexual is often seen as being a subtype of bisexual (Belous & Bauman, 2017; Flanders, 2017; Galupo, 2018), the research on pansexuality has often included comparisons between the two. Bisexual and pansexual individuals report similar patterns of sexual and romantic attraction, sexual behavior, and partner gender (Morandini et al., 2017). Given these similarities, for some health-related topics the distinction may not be warranted.

Despite similarities, it is important to understand how the label pansexual is understood by those who endorse it. Bisexuality is often stereotyped as reinforcing the gender binary (Serano, 2013; Weiss, 2003) that has served as a source of community tension in the way bisexual and pansexual are often defined and debated (Gonel, 2013). Existing research suggests that although bisexual individuals may use binary terminology to describe their own attractions, they are just as likely to use nonbinary language as their pansexual and queer counterparts (Flanders et al., 2017; Galupo, Ramirez, & Pulice-Farrow, 2017). Therefore binary/nonbinary distinctions of gender/sex are not central to differentiating bisexual and pansexual identities. Instead, the distinction may rest in the way that pansexual identity is more centrally defined as transcending gender/sex altogether (Galupo, Ramirez, & Pulice-Farrow, 2017; Gonel, 2013).

Pansexual identity is conceptualized in a way that explicitly deconstructs not just the binary nature of gender/sex, but the reliance of defining sexual attraction upon gender/sex more generally. As a component of bisexuality (Belous & Bauman, 2017; Flanders, 2017), pansexual identity can be understood to highlight specific articulations of plurisexual desire. Pansexual identity is used to describe a sexuality that transcends gender/sex. For pansexual individuals, then, sexual attraction is primarily based on other (individually determined) factors. When used to mark transcendence of gender/sex, pansexual cannot be conceptualized as an interval or even a specific range on the traditional sexual orientation continuum (Galupo, Mitchell, et al., 2014).

Because sexual identity nomenclature relies on gender identity labels for both self and others to whom one is attracted, and given that pansexuality centers on the transcendence of gender/sex, it makes sense that pansexual identities are more likely to be endorsed by transgender and gender nonconforming individuals (Galupo et al., 2016: Katz-Wise et al., 2016; Morandini et al., 2017). Pansexual as a label, then, may be particularly useful for exploring plurisexual desire in a way that acknowledges transgender and gender nonconforming identities (for both self and others).

Queer Identity: Transcending Monosexual/Plurisexual Dichotomies

Although some researchers have explored queer identity alongside bisexual and pansexual identities or under a bisexual umbrella (e.g., Callis, 2014; Galupo, Mitchell, et al., 2014; Rust, 2000), this grouping has been met with mixed results (Galupo et al., 2015; Kolker et al., 2019; Morandini et al., 2016). When describing their sexuality, individuals who endorse queer identities sometimes conceptually align with bisexual individuals (e.g., in stating preferences in their attractions) and sometimes align with pansexual individuals (e.g., in specifying inclusion criteria for their attraction; Galupo, Ramirez, & Pulice-Farrow, 2017). However, patterns of sexual attraction for queer individuals often map onto those within the lesbian or gay range.

Queer as a label has a unique history within the larger LGBT community and has been used by some individuals as an umbrella label for the entire community (inclusive of monosexual/plurisexual identities) (Barker et al., 2009; Gray & Desmarais, 2014; Kolker et al., 2019; Morandini et al., 2017). This suggests that queer labels may not be easily incorporated into sexual orientation distinctions based on either monosexual or plurisexual conceptualizations (Galupo et al., 2015). *Queer* may specifically be used by individuals to transcend the monosexual/plurisexual dichotomy in a way that neither bisexual or pansexual conveys. *Queer* is also unique in that it is often used as a single label to reference both a queer sexual and gender identity (Kolker et al., 2019).

Pansexual and Queer Identity Labels and Mental Health Research

Although plurisexual labels may be used interchangeably by individuals, research suggests subtle differences in the way each is understood. In comparison to other labels, *bisexual* is more often used by individuals to describe attractions that hold specific preferences or exist to different degrees (Galupo et al., 2017). In contrast, a pansexual label may be used to communicate plurisexual desire as it transcends gender/sex (Galupo et al., 2017; Gonel, 2013) and highlights gender diversity (Galupo et al., 2016: Katz-Wise et al., 2016; Morandini et al., 2017). The label *queer* may better highlight plurisexual desire where distinctions between monosexual/plurisexual are less salient (Galupo et al., 2015) and when individuals identify both their sexual and gender identities as queer (Kolker et al., 2019).

Qualitative research has captured a wide diversity of sexual identity labels and described their multiple meanings. Although this research has been successful in delineating overlap and identifying distinctions across plurisexual identities, this information is not easily applied to health disparity research that relies on simple and discrete methods for grouping. Despite the apparent simplicity of the three-group system (lesbian/gay, bisexual, heterosexual) researchers maintain that these traditional labels remain relevant (Russell, Clarke, & Clary, 2009). Although pansexual and queer individuals are likely to choose a traditional label (heterosexual, bisexual, lesbian/gay) when those are the only options given, it is important to note that they might not resonate with the language used in the same way as someone who identifies closely with those labels. This may impact the way they view the research, determine its relevance, and interpret demographic questions as well as items on standardized questionnaires.

Pansexual and Queer Identities: Considerations for Health Disparity Research

To date, there are only a few research studies that explicitly explore pansexual and queer individuals, their mental health outcomes, and minority stress. Among sexual minorities, pansexual individuals report higher rates of self-harm, and queer individuals report higher rates of alcohol consumption than lesbian, gay, and bisexual individuals (Smalley, Warren, & Barefoot, 2016). Among sexual minority women (including lesbian and bisexual), pansexual and queer women report the highest rates of perceived stress, distress, and depression (McNair & Bush, 2016). In a study of plurisexual individuals, Mitchell et al. (2015) found that pansexual/queer/fluid individuals report less sexual prejudice from lesbian/gay individuals and higher connection to the LGBT community than bisexual individuals. And, in a study of emerging identities, Borgogna, McDermott, Aita, and Kridel (2018) found that pansexual individuals report the highest levels of depression and demisexual individuals report the highest levels of anxiety.

Even though the research on pansexual and queer minority stress and mental health outcomes is in its infancy, these studies collectively provide useful instruction for moving forward. First, these studies have established that there are some unique minority stressors and mental health disparities for both pansexual and queer individuals, suggesting that additional research in this area is warranted. Given the predominance of continuum-based models of sexual orientation (e.g. Savin-Williams, 2014), it makes sense that the most recent trend in sexual minority health disparity research has focused on mostly heterosexual individuals. However, the differences across continuum-based groupings (e.g., heterosexual, mostly heterosexual, heterosexual leaning bisexual) are incremental and based on degree of attraction. Categorical sexual identity groupings (e.g., pansexual, queer), in contrast, have emerged from within the community, are conceptually distinct, and hold particular relevance within a social context. Because identity is central to minority stress theory, it makes sense that models of minority stress should also be developed around pansexual and queer identity groups.

Second, studies exploring pansexual and queer minority stress incorporate gender diversity in their samples and/or intentionally frame the work to understand nonbinary sexual identities alongside transgender/nonbinary gender identities. For example, Borgogna et al. (2018) framed their sample as "emerging identities" inclusive of transgender, gender nonconforming, pansexual, demisexual, asexual, queer, and questioning. Smalley et al. (2016) framed their study as one of understudied LGBT subgroups and specifically found evidence that subgroups that are typically collapsed into one group (e.g., pansexual with bisexual, or genderqueer and nonbinary participants with transgender) exhibit different risk factors when studied independently. McNair and Bush's (2016) sample focused on same-sex–attracted women and trans and gender people. Their findings highlighted the fact that gender diverse, queer, and pansexual individuals were the most likely to experience barriers to help seeking, including discrimination and lack of LGBTI sensitivity. And, in their study of plurisexual identities (i.e., bisexual, pansexual, queer, fluid), roughly one third of Mitchell et al.'s (2015) sample was transgender or gender diverse. This points to an important context for framing a pansexual/queer research agenda moving forward.

The reliance of gender diversity as an important context when studying pansexual and queer experiences makes sense both demographically and conceptually. Research approaches that incorporate pansexual or queer may be particularly relevant to transgender and gender diverse individuals as these labels allow for sexual identities that are less tied to binary gender designations for self or partner (Galupo, Henise, & Mercer, 2016; Galupo et al., 2016; Katz-Wise et al., 2016). It will be important for any research agenda moving forward to make visible the intersection between sexual and gender identity. Finally, because of the way plurisexual identities (as with any sexual identity) are socially negotiated, it will be important for future researchers to consider cultural, situational, or environmental contexts that impact mental health (Cohen, Casazza, & Cottrell, 2018).

References

Baldwin, A., Dodge, B., Schick, V., Hubach, R. D., Bowling, J., Malebranche, D.,... Fortenberry, J. D. (2016). Sexual self-identification among behaviourally bisexual men in the Midwestern United States. *Archives of Sexual Behavior, 44*(7), 2015–26. https://dx.doi.org/10.1007%2Fs10508-014-0376-1

Barker, M., Bowes-Catton, H., Iantaffi, A., Cassidy, A., & Brewer, L. (2008). British bisexuality: A snapshot of bisexual representation and identities in the United Kingdom. *Journal of Bisexuality, 8*(1–2), 141–62. doi:10.1080/15299710802143026

Barker, M., Richards, C., & Bowes-Catton, H. (2009). "All the world is queer save thee and me...": Defining queer and bi at a critical sexology seminar. *Journal of Bisexuality, 9*, 363–79. doi:10.1080=15299710903316638

Bauer, G. R., & Brennan, D. J. (2013). The problem with "behavioral bisexuality": Assessing sexual orientation in survey research. *Journal of Bisexuality, 13*(2), 148–65. doi:10.1080/15299716.2013.782260

Bauer, G. R., & Jairam, J. A. (2008). Are lesbians really women who have sex with women (WSW)? Methodological concerns in measuring sexual orientation in health research. *Women & Health, 48*(4), 383–408. doi:10.1080/03630240802575120

Belmonte, K., & Holmes, T. R. (2016). Outside the LGBTQ "safety zone": Lesbian and bisexual women negotiate sexual identity across multiple ecological contexts. *Journal of Bisexuality, 16*(2), 233–69. doi:10.1080/15299716.2016.1152932

Belous, C. K., & Bauman, M. L. (2017). What's in a name? Exploring pansexuality online. *Journal of Bisexuality, 17*(1), 58–72. doi:10.1080/15299716.2016.1224212

Better, A. (2014). Redefining queer: Women's relationships and identity in an age of sexual fluidity. *Sexuality & Culture, 18*, 16–38. doi:10.1007/s12119-013-9171-8

Borgogna, N. C., McDermott, R.C., Aita, S. L., & Kridel, M. M. (2018). Anxiety and depression across gender and sexual minorities: Implications for transgender, gender nonconforming, pansexual, demisexual, asexual, queer, and questioning individuals. *Psychology of Sexual Orientation and Gender Diversity, 6*(1), 54–63. http://dx.doi.org/10.1037/sgd0000306

Bostwick, W. B., Boyd, C. J., Hughes, T. L., & McCabe, S. E. (2010). Dimensions of sexual orientation and the prevalence of mood and anxiety disorders in the United States. *American Journal of Public Health, 100*(3), 468–75.

Bostwick, W. B., & Hequembourg, A. (2014). "Just a little hint": Bisexual-specific microaggressions and their connection to epistemic injustices. *Culture, Health & Sexuality, 16*(5), 488–503. doi:10.1080/13691058.2014.889754

Boyer, C. R., & Galupo, M. P. (2015). "Prove it!" Same-sex performativity among sexual minority women and men. *Psychology & Sexuality, 6*(4), 357–68. https://doi.org/10.1080/19419899.2015.1021372

Brewster, M. E., & Moradi, B. (2010). Perceived experiences of anti-bisexual prejudice: Instrument development and evaluation. *Journal of Counseling Psychology, 57*, 451–68. doi:10.1037/a0021116

Callis, A. S. (2014). Bisexual, pansexual, queer: Non-binary identities and the sexual borderlands. *Sexualities, 17*, 63–80. doi:10.1177/1363460713511094

Cochran, S. D., Sullivan, J. G., & Mays, V. M. (2003). Prevalence of mental disorders, psychological distress, and mental health services use among lesbian, gay, and bisexual adults in the United States. *Journal of Consulting and Clinical Psychology, 71*(1), 53–61. doi:10.1037/0022-006X.71.1.53

Cohen, T. J., Casazza, S. P., & Cottrell, E. M. (2018). The mental health of gender and sexual minority groups in context. In K. B. Smalley, J. C. Warren, & K. N. Barefoot (Eds.), *LGBT health: Meeting the needs of gender and sexual minorities* (pp. 161–79). New York, NY: Springer Publishing Company.

Corliss, H. L., Austin, S. B., Roberts, A. L., & Molnar, B. E. (2010). Sexual risk in "mostly heterosexual" young women: Influence of social support and caregiver mental health. *Journal of Women's Health, 18*(12), 2005–10. doi:10.1089/jwh.2009.1488

Diamond, L. M. (2003). What does sexual orientation orient? A biobehavioral model distinguishing romantic love and sexual desire. *Psychological Review, 110*(1), 173–92. doi:10.1037/0033-295X.110.1.173

Diamond, L. M. (2008). Female bisexuality from adolescence to adulthood: Results from a 10-year longitudinal study. *Developmental Psychology, 44*(1), 5–14. doi:10.1037/0012-1649.44.1.5

Drucker, D. J. (2010). Male sexuality and Alfred Kinsey's 0–6 scale: "A sound understanding of the realities of sex." *Journal of Homosexuality, 9*, 1105–23. doi:10.1080/00918369.2010.508314

Drucker, D. J. (2012). Marking sexuality from 0–6: The Kinsey scale in online culture. *Sexuality & Culture, 16*(3), 241–62. doi:10.1007/s12119-011-9122-1

Dyar, C., & Feinstein, B. A. (2018). Binegativity: Attitudes toward and stereotypes about bisexual individuals. In D. J. Swan & S. Habibi (Eds.), *Bisexuality: Theories, research, and recommendations for the invisible sexuality.* (pp. 95–112) Cham, Switzerland: Springer.

Dyar, C., Feinstein, B. A., & London, B. (2015). Mediators of differences between lesbians and bisexual women in sexual identity and minority stress. *Psychology of Sexual Orientation and Gender Diversity, 2*(1), 43–51. doi:10.1037/sg0000090

Elizabeth, A. (2013). Challenging the binary: Sexual identity that is not duality. *Journal of Bisexuality, 13*, 329–37. doi:10.1080/15299716.2013.813421

Feinstein, B. A., & Dyar, C. (2017). Bisexuality, minority stress, and health. *Current Sexual Health Report*, 9(1), 42–9.

Flanders, C. E. (2017). Introduction to the special issue: Under the bisexual umbrella of identity and experience. *Journal of Bisexuality, 17*(1), 1–6. https://doi.org/10.1080/15299716.2017.1297145

Flanders, C. E., Anderson, R. E., Tarasoff, L. A., & Robinson, M. (2019). Bisexual stigma, sexual violence, and sexual health among bisexual and other plurisexual women: A cross-sectional survey study. *Journal of Sex Research, 56*(9), 1115–27. https://doi.org/10.1080/00224499.2018.1563042

Flanders, C. E., Dobinson, C., & Logie, C. (2015). "I'm never really my full self": Young bisexual women's perceptions of their mental health. *Journal of Bisexuality, 15*(4), 454–80. doi:10.1080/15299716.2015.1079288

Flanders, C. E., LeBreton, M. E., Robinson, M., Bian, J., & Caravaca-Morera, J. A. (2017). Defining bisexuality: Young bisexual and pansexual people's voices. *Journal of Bisexuality, 17*(1), 39–57. doi:10.1080/15299716.2016.1227016

Flanders, C. E., Robinson, M., Leggee, M. M., & Tarasoff, L. A. (2016). Negative identity experiences of bisexual and other non-monosexual people: A qualitative report. *Journal of Gay*

& Lesbian Mental Health, 20(2), 152–72. doi:10.1080/19359705.2015.1108257
Fox, J., & Ralston, R. (2016). Queer identity online: Informal learning and teaching experiences of LGBTQ individuals on social media. *Computers in Human Behavior, 65*, 635–42. https://doi.org/10.1016/j.chb.2016.06.009
Galupo, M. P. (2011). Bisexuality: Complicating and conceptualizing sexual identity. *Journal of Bisexuality, 11*(4), 545–9. doi:10.1080/15299716.2011.620866
Galupo, M. P. (2018). Plurisexual identity labels and the marking of bisexual desire. In D. J. Swan & S. Habibi (Eds), *Bisexuality: Theories, research, and recommendations for the invisible sexuality* (pp. 61–76). Cham, Switzerland: Springer.
Galupo, M. P., Davis, K. S., Grynkiewicz, A., & Mitchell, R. C. (2014). Conceptualization of sexual orientation identity among sexual minorities: Patterns across sexual and gender identity *Journal of Bisexuality, 14*(3–4), 433–56. doi:10.1080/15299716.2014.933466
Galupo, M. P., Henise, S. B., & Mercer, N. L. (2016). "The labels don't work very well": Transgender individuals' conceptualizations of sexual orientation and sexual identity. *International Journal of Transgenderism, 17*, 1–12. doi:10.1080/15532739.2016.1189373
Galupo, M. P., Lomash, E., & Mitchell, R. C. (2017). "All of my lovers fit into this scale": Sexual minority individuals' responses to two novel measures of sexual orientation. *Journal of Homosexuality, 64*(2), 145–65. doi:10.1080/00918369.2016.1174027
Galupo, M. P., Mitchell, R. C., & Davis, K. S. (2015). Sexual minority self-identification: Multiple identities and complexity. *Psychology of Sexual Orientation and Gender Diversity, 2*, 355–64. doi:10.1037/sgd0000131
Galupo, M. P., Mitchell, R. C., Grynkiewicz, A. L., & Davis, K. S. (2014). Sexual minority reflections on the Kinsey Scale and the Klein Sexual Orientation Grid: Conceptualization and measurement. *Journal of Bisexuality, 14*, 404–32. doi:10.1080./15299716.2014.929553
Galupo, M. P., Ramirez, J. L., & Pulice-Farrow, L. (2017). "Regardless of their gender": Descriptions of sexual identity among bisexual, pansexual, and queer identified individuals. *Journal of Bisexuality, 17*(1), 108–24. doi:10.1080/15299716.2016.1228491
Galupo, M. P., Taylor, S. M., & Cole, D. (2019). "I am double the bi": Positive aspects of being both bisexual and biracial. *Journal of Bisexuality, 19*(2), 152–68. https://doi.org/10.1080/15299716.2019.1619066
Ghabrial, M. A. (2019). "We can shapeshift and build bridges": Bisexual women and gender diverse people of color on invisibility and embracing the borderlands. *Journal of Bisexuality, 19*(2), 169–97.
Gonel, A. H. (2013). Pansexual identification in online communities: Employing a collaborative queer method to study pansexuality. *Graduate Journal of Social Science, 10*(1), 36–59.
Gonzalez, K. A., Ramirez, J. L., & Galupo, M. P. (2017). "I was and still am": Narratives of bisexual marking in the #StillBisexual Campaign. *Sexuality & Culture, 21*(2), 493–515. doi:10.1007/s12119-016-9401-y
Gray, A., & Desmarais, S. (2014). Not all one and the same: Sexual identity, activism, and collective self-esteem. *Canadian Journal of Human Sexuality, 23*(3), 116–22. doi:10.3138/cjhs.2400
Greenesmith, H. (2010). Drawing bisexuality back into the picture: How bisexuality fits into LGBT legal strategy 10 years after bisexual erasure. http://works.bepress.com/heron_greenesmith/3
Halperin, D. M. (2009). Thirteen ways of look at a bisexual. *Journal of Bisexuality, 9*, 451–5. https://doi.org/10.1080/15299710903316679
Hatzenbuehler, M., Keyes, K., & Hasin, D. (2009). State-level policies and psychiatric morbidity in lesbian, gay, and bisexual populations. *American Journal of Public Health, 99*(12), 2275–81 7p. doi:10.2105/AJPH.2008.153510
Hatzenbuehler, M. L., & McLaughlin, K. A. (2017). Sex, sexual orientation, and depression. In R. J. DeRubeis & D. R. Strunk (Eds.), *The Oxford handbook of mood disorders* (pp. 49–59). Oxford, UK: Oxford University Press.
Hendricks, M. L., & Testa, R. J. (2012). A conceptual framework for clinical work with transgender and gender nonconforming clients: An adaptation of the Minority Stress Model. Professional Psychology: Research and Practice, *43*(5), 460–467. http://dx.doi.org/10. 1037/a0029597
Hughes, T. L., Wilsnack, S. C., & Kristjanson, A. F. (2015). Substance use and related problems among U.S. women who identify as mostly heterosexual. *BMC Public Health, 15*, 803. doi:10.1186/s12889-015-2143-1
Israel, T., & Mohr, J. J. (2004). Attitudes toward bisexual women and men: Current research, future directions. *Journal of Bisexuality, 4*(1–2), 117–34. doi:10.1300/J159v04n01_09
Katz-Wise, S., Reisner, S. L., Hughto, J. W., & Keo-Meier, C. L. (2016). Differences in sexual orientation diversity and sexual fluidity in attractions among gender minority adults in Massachusetts. *Journal of Sex Research, 53*(1), 74–84. doi.10.1080/00224499.2014.1003028
Kinsey, A., Pomeroy, W. B., & Martin, C. E. (1948). *Sexual behavior in the human male*. Philadelphia, PA: Saunders.
Kinsey, A. C., Pomeroy, W. B., Martin, C. E., & Gebhard, P. H. (1953). *Sexual behavior in the human female*. Philadelphia, PA: Saunders.
Kleese, C. (2011). Shady characters, untrustworthy partners, and promiscuous sluts: Creating bisexual intimacies in the face of heteronormativity and biphobia. *Journal of Bisexuality, 11*(2–3), 227–44. https://doi.org/10.1080/15299716.2011.571987
Klein, F., Sepekoff, B., & Wolf, T. J. (1985). Sexual orientation: A multi-variable dynamic process. *Journal of Homosexuality, 11*, 35–49. doi:10.1300=J082v11n01_04
Kolker, Z. M., Taylor, P. C., & Galupo, M. P. (2019). "As a sort of blanket term": Qualitative analysis of queer sexual identity marking. *Sexuality & Culture*. https://doi.org/10.1007/s12119-019-09686-4
Kuyper, L., & Bos, H. (2016). Mostly heterosexual and lesbian/gay young adults: Differences in mental health and substance use and the role of minority stress. *Journal of Sex Research, 53*(7), 731–41. doi:10.1080/00224499.2015.1071310
Laumann, E., Gagnon, J. H., Michael, R. T., & Michaels, S. (1994). *The social organization of sexuality: Sexual practices in the United States*. Chicago, IL: University of Chicago Press.
Lewis, R. J., Derlega, V. J., Griffin, J. L., & Krowinski, A. C. (2003). Stressors for gay men and lesbians: Life stress, gay-related stress, stigma consciousness, and depressive symptoms. *Journal of Social & Clinical Psychology, 22*(6), 716–29.

Manley, M. H., Legge, M. M., Flanders, C. E., Goldberg, A. E., & Ross, L. E. (2018). Consensual nonmonogamy in pregnancy and parenthood: Experiences of bisexual and plurisexual women with different-gender partners. *Journal of Sex & Marital Therapy, 44*(8), 721–36. doi:10.1080/0092623X.2018.1462277

McCormack, M. (2018). Mostly straights and the study of sexualities: An introduction to the special issue. *Sexualities, 21*(1–2), 3–15. https://doi.org/10.1177%2F1363460716679378

McNair, R. P., & Bush, R. (2016). Mental health help-seeking patterns and associations among Australian same-sex-attracted women, trans and gender diverse people: A survey-based study. *BMC Psychiatry, 16*, 209. http://dx.doi.org/10.1186/s12888-016-0916-4

Mereish, E. H., Katz-Wise, S. L., & Woulfe, J. (2017). We're here and we're queer: Sexual orientation and sexual fluidity differences between bisexual and queer women. *Journal of Bisexuality, 17*(1), 125–39. doi:10.1080/15299716.2016.1217448

Meyer, I. H. (1995). Minority stress and mental health in gay men. *Journal of Health and Social Behavior, 36*(1), 38–56. doi:10.2307/2137286

Meyer, I. H. (2003). Prejudice, social stress, and mental health in lesbian, gay, and bisexual populations: Conceptual issues and research evidence. *Psychological Bulletin, 129*(5), 674. doi:10.1037/0033-2909.129.5.674

Meyer, I. H. (2015). Resilience in the study of minority stress and health of sexual and gender minorities. *Psychology of Sexual Orientation and Gender Diversity, 2*(3), 209. http://dx.doi.org/10.1037/sgd0000132

Miller, S. D., Taylor, V., & Rupp, L. J. (2016). Social movements and the construction of queer identity. In J. E. Stets & R. T. Serpe (Eds.) *New directions in identity theory and research* (pp. 443–70). New York, NY: Oxford University Press. https://psycnet.apa.org/doi/10.1093/acprof:oso/9780190457532.003.0016

Mitchell, R. C., Davis, K. S., & Galupo, M. P. (2015). Comparing perceived experiences of sexual prejudice among plurisexual individuals. *Psychology & Sexuality, 6*(3) 245–57. doi:10.1080/19419899.2014.940372

Morandini, J. S., Blaszczynski, A., & Dar-Nimrod, I. (2017). Who adopts queer and pansexual sexual identities? *Journal of Sex Research, 54*(7), 911–22.

Morgan, E. M. (2013). Contemporary issues in sexual orientation and identity development in emerging adulthood. *Emerging Adulthood, 1*(1), 52–66. doi:10.1037/a0014572

Pallotta-Chiarolli, M. (2006). On the borders of sexuality research: Young people who have sex with both males and females. *Journal of Gay and Lesbian Issues in Education, 3*(2–3), 79–86.

Pallotta-Chiarolli, M. (2010). *Order sexualities, border families in schools.* New York, NY: Rowman & Littlefield.

Pallotta-Chiarolli, M. (2011). You're too queer for the straights and now too queer for the gays? *Journal of Bisexuality, 11*(4), 566–70. doi:10.1080/15299716.2011.620872

Pega, F., Gray, A., Veale, J. F., Binson, D., & Sell, R. L. (2013). Toward global comparability of sexual orientation data in official statistics: A conceptual framework of sexual orientation for health data collection in New Zealand's official statistics system. *Journal of Environmental and Public Health, 2013*, Article 473451. doi:10.1155/2013/473451

Richter, N. (2011). Ambiguous bisexuality: The case of a shot at love with Tila Tequila. *Journal of Bisexuality, 11*(1), 121–41. doi:10.1080/15299716.2011.545316

Rosario, M., & Schrimshaw, E. W. (2014). Theories and etiologies of sexual orientation. In D. L. Tolman & L. M. Diamond (Eds.), *APA handbook of sexuality and psychology, Vol 1: Person-based approaches* (pp. 555–96). Washington, DC: American Psychological Association. http://dx.doi.org/10/1037/14193-018

Ross, L. E., Goldberg, A. E., Tarasoff, L. A., & Guo, C. (2018). Perceptions of partner support among pregnant plurisexual women: A qualitative study. *Sexual and Relationship Therapy, 33*(1–2), 59–78. https://doi.org/10.1080/14681994.2017.1419562

Ross, L. E., Tarasoff, L A., Goldberg, A. E., & Flanders, C.E. (2017). Pregnant plurisexual women's sexual and relationship histories across the life span: A qualitative study. *Journal of Bisexuality, 17*(3), 257–76. https://doi.org/10.1080/15299716.2017.1344177

Russell, S. T., Clarke, T. J., & Clary, J. (2009). Are teens "post-gay"? Contemporary adolescents' sexual identity labels. *Journal of Youth and Adolescence, 38*(7), 884–90. doi:10.1007/s10964-008-9388-2

Rust, P. C. (2000). Two many and not enough: The meaning of bisexual identities. *Journal of Bisexuality, 1*, 31–68. doi:10.1300/J159v01n01_04

Savin-Williams, R. C. (2010). Sexual orientation label (7-point), http://www.human.cornell.edu/hd/sexgender/research.cfm

Savin-Williams, R. C. (2014). An exploratory study of the categorical versus spectrum nature of sexual orientation. *Journal of Sex Research, 51*(4), 446–53. doi:10.1080/00224499.2013.871691

Savin-Williams, R. C., Cash, B. M., McCormack, M., & Rieger, G. (2017). Gay, mostly gay, or bisexual leaning gay? An exploratory study distinguishing gay sexual orientations among young men. *Archives of Sexual Behavior, 46*(1), 265–72. doi:10.1007/s10508-016-0848-6

Savin-Williams, R. C., Rieger, G., & Rosenthal, A. M. (2013). Physiological evidence of a mostly heterosexual orientation among men. *Archives of Sexual Behavior, 42*(5), 697–9. doi:10.1007/s10508-013-0093-1

Savin-Williams, R. C., & Vrangalova, Z. (2013). Mostly heterosexual as a distinct sexual orientation group: A systematic review of the empirical evidence. *Developmental Review, 33*, 58–88. doi:10.1016/j.dr.2013.01.001

Schick, V., Rosenberger, J. G., Herbenick, D., Calabrese, S. K., & Reece, M. (2012). Bidentity: Sexual behavior/identity congruence and women's sexual, physical and mental well-being. *Journal of Bisexuality, 12*(2), *178–97.* https://doi.org/10.1080/15299716.2012.674855

Sell, R. L. (1997). Defining and measuring sexual orientation: A review. *Archives of Sexual Behavior, 26*(6), 643–58. doi:10.1023/A:1024528427013

Serano, J. (2013). *Excluded: Making feminist and queer movements more inclusive.* Berkeley, CA: Seal Press.

Smalley, K. B., Warren, J. C., & Barefoot, K. N. (2016). Differences in health risk behaviors across understudied LGBT subgroups. *Health Psychology, 35*, 103–14. http://dx.doi.org/10.1037/hea0000231

Swan, D. J. (2018). Defining bisexuality: Challenges and importance of and toward a unifying definition. In D. Joye Swan & S. Habibi (Eds.), *Bisexuality: Theories, research, and recommendations for the invisible sexuality.* Cham, Switzerland: Springer.

van Anders, S. M. (2015). Beyond sexual orientation: Integrating gender/sex and diverse sexualities in sexual configurations theory. *Archives of Sexual Behavior, 44*(5), 1177–213. doi:10.1007/s10508-015-0490-8

Vrangalova, Z., & Savin-Williams, R. C. (2012). Mostly heterosexual and mostly gay/lesbian: Evidence for new sexual orientation identities. *Archives of Sexual Behavior, 41*(1), 85–101. doi:10.1007/s10508-012-9921-y

Wandrey, R. L., Mosack, K. E., & Moore, E. M. (2015) Coming out to family and friends as bisexually identified young adult women: A discussion of homophobia, biphobia, and heteronormativity. *Journal of Bisexuality, 15*(2), 204–29. doi: 10.1080/15299716.2015.1018657

Weiss, J. T. (2003). GL vs. BT: The archaeology of biphobia and transphobia in the U.S. lesbian and gay community. *Journal of Bisexuality, 3,* 25–55. doi:10.1300/J159v03n03_02

Wolff, M., Wells, B., Ventura-DiPersia, C., Renson, A., & Grov, C. (2017). Measuring sexual orientation: A review and critique of U. S. data collection efforts and implications for health policy. *Journal of Sex Research, 54*(4–5), 507–31. doi:10.1080/00224499.2016.1255872

CHAPTER

29 Mental Health for Men Who Have Sex with Men (MSM) and Women Who Have Sex with Women (WSW)

Anna C. Salomaa *and* Jes L. Matsick

Abstract

This chapter reviews mental health research of sexual minorities who are defined by their same-gender sexual behavior. Women who have sex with women (WSW) and men who have sex with men (MSM) encompass not only those who identify as LGBQ+ but also people who identify as heterosexual or are unsure of their sexual orientation. The authors discuss the implications of this broad categorization on the study of mental disorders and psychological distress and present the typical rates of risk for WSW and MSM overall and within subgroups (e.g., heterosexual-identified WSW, Black MSM). This area of research is often hindered by the multiple ways in which MSM and WSW groups can be defined and the vast heterogeneity of people who fall within these categories. Further, because of the origins of WSW/MSM-terminology in HIV/AIDS research, there is a gendered imbalance in allocation of research funding toward MSM over WSW. Future research should address the limitations of this categorization system in understanding mental health by including multiple measures of sexuality to create a fine-grained understanding of which experiences of WSW/MSM transfer risk and by addressing the paucity of research on WSW and their mental health.

Keywords: sexual behavior, identity discordance, sexual identity, mood disorders, sexual minorities, heterosexual

The terms sexual minorities use to identify themselves are abundant, dynamic, and, most importantly, self-determined. In contrast to the challenge of cataloguing the vastness of queer identities, the labels *women who have sex with women* (WSW) and *men who have sex with men* (MSM) can provide researchers relief with their simplicity. Beyond ease of use, these categories capture a broader swathe of people who may not otherwise count themselves or be included in research analyses as sexual minorities. In this chapter, we focus on the current trends and implications of studying the mental health of sexual minorities from the perspective of their same-sex sexual behavior. Given the typically high mental health risks related to belonging to the sexual minority category, it is important that the manner in which this population is defined is inclusive of all of those experiencing detriments to mental health via minority stress. This chapter will (a) evaluate the use of WSW and MSM terminology across research approaches; (b) review mental health issues in the WSW and MSM literature; (c) analyze how WSW and MSM mental health patterns differ across sexual orientation, gender identity, race, ethnicity, and culture; and (d) look forward to future areas of inquiry regarding the mental health of WSW and MSM populations.

Defining Sexual Minorities by Sexual Behavior

Why and when should researchers identify sexual minorities as WSW and MSM rather than by their self-identified sexual orientation? The WSW and MSM terminology is most often used when the focus is on public health and epidemiology—when sexual behavior and its repercussions for health are at the center of the research question. *MSM* was coined by researchers in the 1980s as a way to identify men who have sex with men in the context of HIV/AIDS research (Boellstorff, 2011; Young & Meyer, 2005). Under this lens, how these men identified—whether as heterosexual, gay, or bisexual—did not matter when the focus was tracking disease transmission; only same-gender sexual behavior with other high-risk men was considered of import (Boellstorff, 2011). Further, later efforts to reach these men for intervention that only focused on self-identified gay or bisexual men would exclude those who did not count themselves as part of the gay community, which was overrepresented by White, middle-class men; thus, many at-risk men would be underserved by intervention efforts. Using the term *MSM*, therefore, created a space for a wider variety of men who were overlooked and underserved by researchers. The term *WSW*, too, came from the field of public health; however, it would not emerge until the mid-1990s (Boellstorff, 2011), and the WSW group remains far more understudied than MSM. For example, MSM appears as a keyword approximately four times as often in 2018 scientific literature than WSW (Sullender, 2019).

Sexual health remains a focus of studies that use WSW/MSM identification given the prioritization of sexual behavior in this categorization system; however, the use of these terms has spread to other domains as well, including mental health. One strength of focusing on sexual behavior in the context of mental health is that it leads to broader groupings of people that are inclusive of gay, bisexual, and queer people, as well as people who identify as heterosexual but engage in same-gender sexual behavior. In other words, the categories are not restricted by an individual's social identity labels (e.g., pansexual, lesbian). When sampling from a population by first using WSW/MSM criteria, this inclusive sampling procedure then allows for further post–data collection groupings by identity and attraction to be made if necessary (Salomaa & Matsick, 2019). However, this is not the case when researchers first restrict their population to participants' self-identification with LGBQ+ labels (e.g., sampling participants who only identify as lesbian, gay, or bisexual). Many people with same-gender sexual behavior would be excluded by this approach: for example, researchers would overlook the health risks and outcomes of heterosexual-identified people with same-gender sexual behavior when behavior is not part of the inclusion criteria. Put simply, recruitment efforts that target the behavioral categories of WSW and MSM may yield a more inclusive and wider net of participants for studying sexuality and mental health.

Critiques of WSW/MSM Language

Despite the apparent strength of WSW/MSM terms as more inclusive of non-LGBQ-identified, non-Western, or non-White people's experiences and language, some researchers argue that WSW/MSM terms are reductionistic and particularly problematic in the context of certain cultures, such as South Asia (Khan & Khan, 2006). For example, for some South Asian people, the act of penetration shapes a person's gender identity—the person being penetrated is not seen as male, and therefore the MSM or WSW qualifiers could not adequately describe this population. Further, it creates gray areas for people who have sex with *hijras* (eunuchs and intersex or transgender people), as *hijras* exist outside of a gender binary and are therefore not captured with either MSM or WSW. Thus, there remain cultural considerations researchers must attend to in their choice of language.

Other issues include the lack of shared vocabulary between researcher and participant—rarely does a person self-identify as a "woman who has sex with women," despite their classification in a study as such. Further, as previously described, WSW/MSM also inherently highlights sexual practices over sexual identities; while this may be appropriate for certain kinds of research, WSW/MSM terms are often used as an easy oversimplification for researchers grasping at a shortcut at the expense of a fuller understanding of their participants. Though two people engage in similar same-gender behavior, their identities may contribute to how they construe or reflect on these sexual experiences; for example, same-gender behavior among a lesbian woman may present fewer internal conflicts than does the same-sex behavior of a heterosexual-identified man. These terms also exclude sexual minorities who have not had sex with their same gender, such as individuals who are not sexually active or women who exclusively have sex with men and are attracted to women.

WSW/MSM terminology is overly broad and, without further description of the sample, refers to a wide variety of experiences with important implications (e.g., people who have sex with one vs. more than one gender; all people who have same-sex behavior vs. only those who do not identify as LGBQ+). Without defining specifically who counts as WSW/MSM, it is impossible to compare across studies. This is not a monolithic identifier, and despite its apparent simplicity, it can create greater confusion. Two primary approaches are typically used in studies of WSW/MSM: (1) defining WSW/MSM to include any women or men with same-gender sexual behavior or (2) defining WSW/MSM to include only those who do *not* identify as LGBQ+ (DNI-WSW/MSM) but engage in same-gender sexual behavior. However, it should be noted that these terms are sometimes conflated with identity, such as when participants who identify as LGB are coded as WSW or MSM (e.g., Brown, Masho, Perera, Mezuk, & Cohen, 2015).

Using only WSW/MSM language, therefore, is not a perfect solution for researchers seeking a simple question to add to questionnaires to assess sexual orientation. However, in situations in which the goal is to recruit across the range of sexual minority experiences, it is likely that sampling any people with same-gender sexual experiences is a useful strategy if supplemented with further sampling around self-identification, attraction, and context—allowing researchers to create more nuanced groupings than WSW/MSM.

Who Are WSW/MSM?

Estimates of same-gender sexual behavior are regularly higher than prevalence of LGBQ-identified individuals, with ranges of prevalence of WSW/MSM from 6.9 percent (Australian Longitudinal Study of Health and Relationships, 2005; Gates, 2011) to 8.8 percent (National Survey of Family Growth, 2006–2008; Gates, 2011). In the United States, approximately 5.7 percent of men and 3.9 percent of women report past-year same-gender sexual partners (Fu et al., 2018). Another epidemiologic survey from 2004 had a far lower estimate, reporting that 1.5 percent of U.S. adults had only had sex with the same gender, and 1.9 percent had sex with both men and women (Bostwick, Boyd, Hughes, & McCabe, 2010). A nationally representative sample of the United Kingdom found that 5.9 percent of men and 7 percent of women had had same-gender sexual partners in their lifetime (Hayes et al., 2012). These numbers are contrasted to the estimated 3.5 percent of individuals in the United States who identify as lesbian, gay, or bisexual (Gates, 2011) and suggest that there are as many or more heterosexual-identified people with same-gender sexual behaviors than those who would claim a sexual minority identity. The terms *WSW* and *MSM* encompass most, if not all, of these individuals.

WSW

Of the approximately 7 percent of U.S. women who have had sex with women, half self-identify as heterosexual, 32 percent as bisexual, and 18 percent as gay/lesbian (Xu, Maya, & Markowitz, 2010a). Of U.S. women between the ages of twenty and forty-four, an estimated 7.9 percent both identify as heterosexual and report having had a female sexual partner in their lifetime (Bauer, Jairam, & Baidoobonso, 2010). When defined as those who have had any same-sex behavior but did *not* self-identify as LGBQ+ (DNI-WSW), DNI-WSW were highly likely to report that they were primarily attracted to men, had only had a single female sexual partner in their lifetime, and had a greater number of overall sexual partners compared to other women, when considering a representative sample of U.S. adults (Bauer et al., 2010). In a California sample, WSW were on average of similar age compared to lesbian WSW and heterosexual-identified women who have sex with men (WSM), and older than the average bisexual WSW (Blosnich, Nasuti, Mays, & Cochran, 2016). When comparing DNI-WSW to WSM, these groups had similar rates of marriage, but DNI-WSW fell in between the WSM and LGB-WSW on demographic categories such as racial diversity, education level, and church attendance, as well as rates of discrimination experiences (Gattis, Sacco, & Cunningham-Williams, 2012).

MSM

Slightly fewer men report having a same-gender sexual experience than women in the United States (5 percent); of these MSM, roughly equal numbers identified as either heterosexual (40 percent) or gay (38 percent), whereas only 22 percent identified as bisexual (Xu, Maya, & Markowitz, 2010b). Similarly, Schick et al. (2016) found that 73 percent of all MSM self-identified as heterosexual in their U.S. sample. Heterosexual-identified MSM are typically older than gay- and bisexual-identified MSM, and heterosexual men who have sex with women, perhaps reflecting cultural trends that pressured older generations to maintain a visibly heterosexual lifestyle (Blosnich et al., 2016). This group is about as likely as men who have sex with women (MSW) to be married and attend church, but three times more likely to report past-year experiences of discrimination (Gattis et al., 2012). This suggests that while outwardly there may be few visible signs of difference between these groups, the impact of homophobia or discrimination is still present for heterosexual-identified MSM.

Mental Health among WSW/MSM

The minority stress model guides current understanding of how sexual minority status is linked to increases in psychopathology and poorer well-being (King et al., 2008; Meyer, 2003; Meyer & Frost, 2013). A central tenet of this theory is that the stigma experienced by non-majority members of society increases stress, via experiences of discrimination, aggression, and internalized homophobia. Minority stress has well-documented effects on the health of sexual minorities, including WSW and MSM (e.g., Przedworski, McAlpine, Karaca-Mandic, & VanKim, 2014; Wong, Schrager, Holloway, Meyer, & Kipke, 2014). However, in the case of WSW/MSM, the application of this model becomes complicated by the high proportion of individuals in these groups who do not self-identify as a sexual minority, and therefore may not relate to or experience the common stressors experienced by LGBQ+-identified individuals. Simultaneously, non-LGBQ+ WSW/MSM do not have the same level of access to LGBQ+ communities, which may increase their vulnerability to stressors. Factors such as outness or discordance between identity and behavior play heavily into understanding how a marginalized sexual practice contributes to increased minority-based stress, and given this heterogeneity within WSW/MSM, it is important to consider subgroups when predicting mental health.

General Trends in Mental Health Outcomes

The well-documented pattern of poor mental health in LGBQ+ populations spans from youth (Russell & Fish, 2016) to older adults (Fredriksen-Goldsen et al., 2013) and across mood disorders (Lytle, De Luca, & Blosnich, 2014), trauma (Smith, Cunningham, & Freyd, 2016), and substance use (Lee, Gamaerel, Bryant, Zaller, & Operario, 2016). When taking a broad look at all WSW and MSM, the same general levels of risk emerge. Further, as described later in this section, this pattern extends to and changes for sexual minorities identified as WSW/MSM, with inconsistently both less and more extensive risk experienced by WSW/MSM who do not identify as LGBQ+.

Mood and Anxiety Disorders

Compared to heterosexual WSM and MSW, there is a preponderance of evidence to suggest that WSW and MSM at a broad level are more likely to report symptoms of mood and anxiety disorders (e.g., major depressive disorder, generalized anxiety disorder; Cochran & Mays, 2000a, 2000b; Pyra et al., 2014; Salomon et al., 2009. Further, both WSW and MSM are more likely to report use of mental health services in the past year (Cochran & Mays, 2000a). Similarly, DNI-WSW were more likely to report recent psychological distress and past-year major depression than heterosexual women (Blosnich et al., 2016).

While many studies focused on WSW and MSM compare those who identify as heterosexual to those with an LGBQ+ identification, far fewer examine the relevance of having sex with more than one gender (i.e., WSWM/MSWM, or bisexual behavior). However, concurrent with studies of bisexual identity and mental health risks, individuals who have had sex with both men and women are at higher risk for mood disorders, both across their lifetime and within the past year, when compared to those with only heterosexual behavior (Bostwick et al., 2010; Pyra et al., 2014). Echoing the importance of capturing the "WSWM" group distinctly from WSW-only, the relative risk of WSW, WSWM, and WSM is inconsistent across studies when mood is examined across these three groups (compared to the typical two WSW/WSM groups). Major depression was experienced by 52 percent of WSWM in their lifetime, 27 percent of WSM, and only 15 percent of WSW (Pyra et al., 2014); this suggests that collapsing into a single WSW group obscures a lower-risk group and dampens the ability to identify WSWM as a particularly high-risk group.

Suicidality

Rates of suicide-related experiences in WSW and MSM are closely linked to self-identification of sexual orientation and gender (Blosnich et al., 2016). Heterosexual-identified WSW are found twice as likely as heterosexual WSM to report lifetime suicidal ideation or suicidal attempts, which was on par with lesbian-identified WSW and less than bisexual-identified WSW. Heterosexual-identified MSM were four times more likely than heterosexual MSW to have suicidal ideation and seven times more likely to have made a suicide attempt; unlike WSW, these rates were higher than for gay- and bisexual-identified MSM. Comparatively, gay and bisexual-identified MSM experience similar rates of past-year suicidal ideation as heterosexual MSW, while heterosexual-identified MSM were nearly eight times more likely. A potential cause of this remarkably heightened risk for suicidality in heterosexual MSM could be the lowered access to LGBQ+ communities and outreach, given the lack of identification as a sexual minority.

Consistent with U.S. samples, French WSW reported more physical violence and suicide attempts compared to WSM, although they notably did not report heightened general psychological distress (Lhomond & Saurel-Cubizolles, 2006). Similar patterns of suicidality were found in a Dutch sample, in which sexually active MSM had greater suicide symptoms (death ideation, death wishes, suicidal ideation, suicide attempts) and WSW had greater suicidal ideation compared to non-MSM and non-WSW (de Graaf, Sandfort, & ten Have, 2006). In a sample of Norwegian WSW/MSM youth, only same-gender sexual behavior was found to predict an increase in suicide attempts, but same-gender attraction and self-identification as LGBQ+ did not compared to heterosexual youth (Wichstrøm & Hegna, 2003). Suicidality is also high in Estonian MSM (Rüütel, Valk, & Lõhmus, 2017).

Interactions between Sexual and Mental Health

Sexual and mental health are deeply entwined for both MSM and WSW, given the etiology of these groupings in HIV/AIDS research. However, the focus of sexual and mental health research for MSM is on HIV/AIDS, while research on WSW tends to focus on general sexually risky behaviors and is sparser overall. Given that WSW and MSM experience high rates of mental health disorders, it is important to understand the link between mental health problems and increased risk of sexual health problems, such as HIV risk behaviors and engagement in prevention programs (e.g., Safren, Blashill, & O'Cleirigh, 2011).

Among WSW, increases in minority stress and mental health problems may be linked to avoidance of sexual health information, preventive care, and routine checkups; further, WSW are more likely to be uninsured if they hold a sexual minority identity (Baptiste-Roberts, Oranuba, Werts, & Edwards, 2017; Kerker, Mostashari, & Thorpe, 2006; Knight & Jarrett, 2017; Przedworski et al., 2014; Reisner et al., 2010). Despite this increased need for study and service, research on WSW and sexual health receives far less funding because of the lower HIV transmission rate in women compared to MSM. As a large portion of funding for LGBQ+ research comes from HIV prevention, other health concerns, such as mental health, are often understudied and underserved (Lenke & Piehl, 2009). This has led some to argue that WSW are therefore the most at risk for poor sexual health, given the paucity of research and subsequent intervention development and implementation (Johnson, 2009, as cited in Henderson, Cloete, & van Zyl, 2011). This assertation is supported by research, as the evidence suggests that WSW are more likely to have sexually transmitted infections and engage in sexually risky behaviors compared to WSM (Bauer et al., 2010; Fethers et al., 2000). However, the greatest degree of risk may be for WSW who identify as heterosexual or bisexual (Everett, 2013; Koh, Gomez, Shade, & Rowley, 2005).

While representing only a small portion of the U.S. population, half of those living with HIV/AIDS are MSM (O'Cleirigh et al., 2013). Among MSM, minority stress and mental health problems are linked to HIV risk and vulnerability, as well as the additional burden of HIV-related stigma (Chong, Mak, Tam, Zhu, & Chung, 2017). This link is not necessarily linear, as moderate levels of depression in HIV-infected MSM were found to predict poorer response to treatment of sexual risk-taking behaviors, compared to those with mild or severe depression (O'Cleirigh et al., 2013). This finding parallels studies of general suicide risk, suggesting that while severe depression dampens motivation to engage in any behaviors, including sexual behaviors, moderate levels confer enough energy to act out maladaptive coping behaviors. Beyond the impact of mood disorders, MSM have extremely high rates of childhood sexual abuse and current posttraumatic stress disorder (PTSD), which leads to heightened risk for substance use and sexual risk behaviors (Boroughs et al., 2015). Further, having PTSD symptoms predicted an increased likelihood of having engaged in risky sexual behaviors among MSM (Reisner et al., 2009).

Mental health problems are further entangled with sexual health in MSM. Being HIV-positive doubles the risk of depression for MSM (Ciesla & Roberts, 2001). Younger MSM are particularly at risk, as they are more likely to report depressive symptoms and alcohol/drug use and less likely to use mental health services than older MSM; simultaneously, this group is also more likely to engage in sexually risky behavior (Salomon et al., 2009). Further, MSM who are HIV-positive and experience trauma and depression are more likely to not adhere to antiretroviral treatment medications (Gonzalez, Batchelder, Psaros, & Safren, 2011), perhaps because these symptoms reduce the likelihood of self-care behaviors and perceived self-efficacy (Kavanagh & Bower, 1985; Rabkin, 2008, as cited in White, Gordon, & Miniaga, 2014). This pattern has been replicated in prospective samples, where it was also found that HIV-related stigma perceptions increased transmission risk behaviors (Hatzenbuehler, O'Cleirigh, Mayer, Mimiaga, & Safren, 2011).

Substance Use

The gender of women's sexual partner(s) is a strong predictor of drug use. Women who have sex either only with men or only with women have similar rates of drug use to each other; however, women whose sexual partners include both men and women have comparatively higher rates of substance use and dependence across multiple substances (e.g., Lhomond & Saurel-Cubizolles, 2006; McCabe et al., 2009). This same pattern was found for MSMW, such that partners of multiple genders led to far higher rates of substance use and abuse (Friedman et al., 2019).

A meta-analysis of substance dependence revealed that while MSM and WSW are both at higher risk compared to those with only different-gender sexual partners, WSW have a remarkably higher level of risk than MSM (King et al., 2008). However, these trends also depend on individuals' sexual orientations. For example, heterosexual-identified WSW are four times as likely to use cannabis as WSM (Trocki, Drabble, & Midanik, 2009), and heterosexual-identified MSM are more likely to engage in sexual acts while intoxicated compared to both MSW and LGB-identified MSM (Pathela et al., 2006). Other results paint another picture, where rates of substance use by heterosexual-identified WSW and MSM lie between heterosexual WSM/MSW and LG-identified WSW/MSM (Gattis et al., 2012). Once dependent on substances, heterosexual-identified MSM are also less likely to complete substance use treatment compared to both heterosexual MSW and gay and bisexual men, a difference attributed to negative affectivity surrounding their same-gender activity (Senreich, 2015).

These differences are conceptually concordant with the minority stress model (Meyer, 2003), as it is expected that those with higher rates of environmental stressors and lower access to community supports would be more likely to seek out maladaptive coping strategies, such as alcohol and drug use. Despite their lack of identification as a sexual minority, because heterosexual-identified MSM and WSW are less likely to have access to community support, it follows that they experience stressors that are often coped with through substances. The inconsistencies in where the rates of this substance use lie in comparison with LG-identified individuals is likely explained by the variety of experiences within the heterosexual-identified WSW/MSM groups—such as degree of internalized homophobia, same-gender attraction, or chronicity of behavior (i.e., the timing of being currently or previously sexually active with members of the same gender). Other individual differences such as personality have been explored to predict substance use in MSM; those who are dependent on methamphetamines are higher in neuroticism and lower in openness, agreeableness, and conscientiousness (Solomon, Kiang, Halkitis, Moeller, & Pappas, 2010). All of these components, and other individual difference variables, should be explored in greater depth in future research to more accurately identify risk within the vast categories of WSW and MSM.

Intersecting Identities and Mental Health

Because WSW/MSM groupings are deliberately broad, it is necessary to understand how specific intersections of identity can overlap with behavior to create unique challenges for mental health. Here, the overarching ways that sexual orientation, gender, and race/ethnicity relate to psychopathology and well-being are explored each in separate sections. However, the interactions across each of these domains will also be noted throughout—given that, for example, the typical experiences of a Black lesbian WSW that culminate to impact mental health are likely to be instrumentally different than those of a Latino bisexual MSM.

Sexual Orientation

Being "out" as a sexual minority is to be publicly identified as a lesbian, bisexual, gay, or queer individual. It would be easy to label heterosexual-identified WSW/MSM as LGBQ+ individuals who are simply not out and are concealing their "true" identity; however, this assumes that their heterosexual identity is false. Outcomes for specific identifiers (e.g., lesbian, bisexual) are explored elsewhere in this chapter and in this *Handbook*. However, given the broad umbrella of the terms *WSW* and *MSM*, examining the intersection of self-identification and gender of sexual partners is a fruitful approach to further dividing these groups in meaningful ways. In particular, the idea of sexual identity and behavior discordance and concordance has been demonstrably important to reveal differences in mental health within WSW/MSM (Kerker et al., 2006). Discordance refers to the assumed "mismatch" between self-reports of sexual orientation and sexual behavior (e.g., identifying as heterosexual but reporting same-gender sexual behaviors), whereas concordance refers to the congruity between these components of sexuality (e.g., identifying as lesbian and reporting only female sexual partners; Gattis et al., 2012).

While discordance/concordance language, along with synonyms such as alignment or incongruence, is used extensively in studies of sexual behavior and identity (Brewster & Tillman, 2012; Korchmaros, Powell, & Stevens; 2013), these terms have also been critiqued as having inherent researcher judgment of what are "correct" or "natural" combinations of behavior and identity (van Anders, 2015). While beyond the scope of this chapter, sexual configurations theory (SCT; van Anders, 2015) is a comprehensive model of sexuality and its numerous moving parts that provides a useful alternative to terms such as "discordant." Instead, SCT proposes using "coinciding" and "branching" terminology to describe without value statements the manner in which sexual identity and behavior (as well as attraction, status, partner number, and other components) may combine to form an individual's unique configuration of sexuality.

Across studies, identity–behavior discordance (or branching) uniquely predicts rates of mental health disorders and substance use (Gattis et al., 2012; Horn & Swartz, 2019; Krueger & Upchurch, 2019). The discordant/branching group is typically heterosexual-identified but engages in sex with either the same gender or multiple genders, and is sometimes referred to as "closeted" (e.g., Pachankis, Cochran, & Mays, 2015). Overall, discordant/branching MSM have rates of substance use (e.g., stimulants, cannabis, hallucinogens) and mental health disorders (major depressive disorder, general anxiety disorder, PTSD) that lie above those of coinciding heterosexual men and below coinciding gay men (Gattis et al., 2012). Discordant/branching WSW typically experienced the same pattern of substance use and mental health disorders as concordant/coinciding WSW; however, differences in risk are often found to be greater for WSW than MSM. Application of the minority stress model to these findings would suggest that the discordant/branching MSM/WSW do not experience the full extent of social stressors as LGB-identified MSM/WSW because they do not claim a marginalized identity, but are still harmed by expectations of social rejection or internalized homophobia linked to their discordant/branching experiences. This is supported by findings that heterosexual-identified MSM often experience and express shame regarding sex with men (Reback & Larkins, 2010).

Bisexual identity and behavior are consistent risk factors for substance use and dependence in women. Lesbian-identified WSW and WSW who have only had female sexual partners use substances at lower rates than bisexual- or heterosexual-identified WSW and WSW with both male and female sexual partners (McCabe et al., 2009; Przedworski et al., 2014). Similarly, identifying as heterosexual while having a history of same-gender sexual partners is a profile of branching sexuality in women linked to higher risk in substance use and sexually risky behaviors (Bauer et al., 2010). Given the elevated health risks associated with discordant/branching sexualities, future research should better identify the psychological mechanisms that play a role in the relationship between discordant/branching status and health.

Gender Identity

As detailed earlier in the chapter, there are consistent yet diverging patterns in mental health outcomes between WSW and MSM—demonstrating that gender plays a moderating role in the transmission of risk via the minority stress model. However, a bias in the literature toward focusing on MSM over WSW limits our ability to fully compare these two populations; for example, a review of keywords used in Google Scholar reveals that in 2018, WSW was used approximately 6,000 times, but MSM was used about 23,000 times (Sullender, 2019).

Another central issue with gender is that WSW and MSM categories inherently reinforce a gender binary: while one benefit of the WSW and MSM terminology is that the terms are quite broad, these categories often make invisible people or partners outside of man/woman labels. In doing so, researchers are overlooking subgroups of WSW/MSM that are likely at the greatest levels of mental health risk: transgender or gender nonbinary individuals (Su et al., 2016). There is also a problem with the conflation of gender and sex that is not adequately addressed via these labels, which fails to account for contemporary understanding of gender/sex and theories of sexuality (see SCT; van Anders, 2015). Further, it has been common practice to either overlook transgender participants in studies of WSW/MSM or to group cisgender MSM with transgender women who have sex with men, in studies published as recently as 2015 (Muessig, Baltierra, Pike, LeGrand, & Hightow-Widman, 2014; Peacock, Andrinopoulos, & Hembling, 2015; Zea et al., 2015, as cited in Poteat, German, & Flynn, 2016).

Racial and Ethnic Minorities

Using WSW/MSM sidesteps Global West–centric assumptions that sexuality is defined by fixed identities; therefore, some argue that these flexible terms can better encompass the sexual practices found in other cultures (Blackwood, 2000). WSW and MSM of color in the United States and elsewhere experience high levels of discrimination, which impact mental health; however, the pathways of sexual minority stress differ across different race/ethnicity groups. Overall, homophobia expressed by the surrounding LGBQ+ community and from friends leads to poorer well-being in WSW/MSM of color; interestingly, homophobia from family members was not found to impact the well-being of MSM (Choi et al., 2013).

BLACK WSW/MSM

The consequences of using the term "MSM" are particularly problematic for Black MSM, many of whom use self-identification labels that do not decontextualize or further reinforce the minority status given to this group; some have suggested using "same-gender-loving" or "SGL" in place of MSM (Truong, Perez-Brumer, Burton, Gipson, & Hickson, 2016). Unique identifiers used by men of color who do not identify as gay or bisexual (e.g., "same-gender-loving," "on the down low") may impede efforts to target this population for mental (and sexual) health interventions when not accounted for. While large-scale epidemiological research can help researchers and health providers understand general risks for this group, our understanding would be incomplete without supplementation of qualitative-driven studies that can account for subjective experiences and information outside of researcher-identified questions.

Interviews with Black MSM support other evidence that this group experiences depression and anxiety at high rates, for reasons related to rejection from family and community, cultural messages about expectations of Black men, experiences of violence and discrimination, and high rates of involuntary early sexual experiences (Graham, Braithwaite, Spikes, Stephens, & Edu, 2009). Further, the internalized conflicting expectations of their gender, race, and sexuality often complicated the process of identity formation: it was difficult for some men to integrate hegemonic masculinity with the feminine stereotypes of having sex with men. Notably, participant descriptions of poor mental health were typically characterized by somatic symptoms and irritability, rather than cognitive or emotional experiences. Black MSM also face additional burdens, particularly that of a disproportionally high HIV infection rate (Centers for Disease Control and Prevention, 2013), which in turn increases the burden of mental illness via additional experiences of stigma. The experiences HIV-positive Black men have with stigma predict both depression and PTSD (Galvan, Landrine, Klein, & Sticklor, 2011).

Black MSM in African countries may experience a heightened burden in their mental health. Approximately half of a sample of South African MSM met criteria for depression, suicidality, and alcohol and drug use disorders; they also experienced increased rates of personality and neuropsychiatric disorders (Stoloff et al., 2013). Gender nonconformity in Black South African MSM has an unexpected relationship to anxiety and depression: contrary to findings in Western countries, feminine South African MSM do not experience a higher risk of depression or anxiety despite more experiences with discrimination (Cook, Sandfort, Nel, & Rich, 2013; Sandfort, Bos, Knox, & Reddy, 2016). It was suggested that because gender-nonconforming MSM were less likely to be perceived as having dissonant gender and sexual identities, they experienced less internal distress compared to gender-conforming MSM who may be more likely to try to pass as straight.

LATINX WSW/MSM

Beyond quantitative, epidemiological data on Latina WSW, interviews with Puerto Rican women with severe mental illness illuminate the tangled nature of their difficulties with intimate partner violence, religiosity, and identity (Loue & Mendez, 2006). Common themes emerged from this qualitative study, including historical and current experiences of physical and sexual abuse from men, which motivated some women to seek exclusive or near-exclusive sexual behavior with women. Many of the women were Christian and relied on their religiosity to manage their mental health symptoms. However, having sex with women in conjunction with high religious values was reported to be a source of distress, particularly given the role that Christianity plays in Latina communities. These women reported that they were reluctant to identify as lesbian or bisexual because these identities were not consistent with the expectations of their families.

SOUTH AND EAST ASIAN WSW/MSM

The experiences of South and East Asian WSW/MSM are understudied, particularly those of WSW;

however, there are a few studies that indicate this diverse population is subject to unique stressors that impact mental health (das Nair & Thomas, 2012). For example, same-gender sex is still subject to stigma in China through conflict with traditions around marriage, gender roles, and childbearing (Liu & Choi, 2006), which contributes to an estimated 16 million gay men in marriages with women (Juan, 2012, in Ren, Howe, & Zhang, 2019). In Chinese MSM, minority stress is experienced through the process of anticipated stigma leading to increases in avoidant coping strategies, which in turn predicted greater anxiety and depressive symptoms (Choi, Steward, Miege, Hudes, & Gregorich, 2016). Similarly, Indian MSM also experience greater rates of suicidal ideation and mood disorders (Sivasubramanian et al., 2011). Interestingly, South and East Asian MSM in the United Kingdom were found to report having mostly White sexual partners (57 percent), and 17 percent did not identify as gay or bisexual (das Nair & Thomas, 2012).

Summary and Conclusions

While the very names of these groups provide seemingly comprehensive definitions, WMW and MSM are broad populations containing a vast expanse of experiences, whose only overlapping quality is their history of sexual behaviors with same-gender partners. When attempting to understand the trends in mental health in WSW/MSM, issues with these terms being both too broad and too narrow emerge, as does the problem of heterogeneity of defining further parameters on these categories. Sampling men and women with same-gender sexual behavior may include both LGBQ+ and heterosexual-identified people, but also excludes sexual minorities who have not engaged in same-gender sexual behaviors and people whose gender (or gender of sexual partners) falls outside binary lines. These terms make room for some culturally specific experiences that LGBQ+ language fails to encapsulate while simultaneously excluding other culturally bound practices where defining acts within female/male language limits understanding. These problems culminate in the variety of qualifiers used to define WSW/MSM in research; some studies sample any people who have same-gender experiences, and others limit samples to those who do not identify as LGBQ+. This variation makes comparisons across research difficult, as differing rates of outness and identity likely impact the degree and manner in which minority stress affects mental health.

Despite these difficulties, important trends across studies emerge to outline typical problems WSW and MSM experience with their mental health. While often these trend lines fall in parallel to those of LGBQ+-identified individuals, some important discrepancies emerge when LGBQ+-identified people are contrasted with heterosexual-identified WSW/MSM. For example, heterosexual-identified WSW/MSM are often likely to experience mental health disorders at the same rate as or lower than LGBQ+-identified WSW/MSM, and consistently more often than WSM and MSW. However, having sex with both men and women increases this level of risk beyond that of people who have sex with only one gender regardless of self-identification.

Future Directions

As detailed in this chapter, predicting specific mental health outcomes may depend on the way sexual minorities are defined. Using behavior as a measure of sexual minority status is clearly important for predicting rates of mental disorders; however, it is unlikely to be sufficient as the sole marker of sexuality. More research is needed to know which groupings are most predictive in which areas of mental health (e.g., chronicity of behavior, identity). One trend identified in this literature is that, typically, DNI-WSW/MSM experience risk at rates lower than LGBQ+-identified groups, but higher than WSM and MSW. Whether there is a protective quality to identifying as heterosexual while having a history of same-gender sexual experiences, and whether there are subgroups within DNI-WSW/MSM for whom the risk transferred by minority stress is minimal and who therefore obscure others with much higher levels of risk, are questions that cannot yet be answered. To do so, researchers must consistently take a fine-grained approach to examining mental health and the variety of intersections within sexual identity and experiences.

Not unlike much of health research, there is a historical and contemporary bias toward studying and funding research centered on men over those that focus on women. The distribution of funding around HIV prevention in MSM has increased this bias toward studying men; however, this has resulted in a paucity of research around WSW and their particular experiences surrounding minority stigma and mental health. As such, future research cannot continue to overlook WSW—greater efforts should be made to increase our knowledge of the unique struggles experienced by women with same-gender sexual partners, especially as the intersection of gender and sexuality places this group under the influences of multiple types of stressors. Similarly, WSW and MSM of color and across cultural and racial groups demand more focus in research. The use of WSW/MSM language may be particularly helpful in this area, as defining sexual minorities by sexual behaviors negates the need to rely solely on language that may fail to capture non-Western experiences of sexuality.

References

Baptiste-Roberts, K., Oranuba, E., Werts, N., & Edwards, L. V. (2017). Addressing health care disparities among sexual minorities. *Obstetrics and Gynecology Clinics, 44*(1), 71–80. doi:10.1016/j.ogc.2016.11.003

Bauer, G. R., Jairam, J. A., & Baidoobonso, S. M. (2010). Sexual health, risk behaviors, and substance use in heterosexual-identified women with female sex partners: 2002 US National Survey of Family Growth. *Sexually Transmitted Diseases, 37*(9), 531–7. doi:10.1097/OLQ.0b013e3181d785f4

Blackwood, E. (2000). Culture and women's sexualities. *Journal of Social Issues, 56*(2), 223–38. doi:10.1111/0022-4537.00162

Blosnich, J. R., Nasuti, L. J., Mays, V. M., & Cochran, S. D. (2016). Suicidality and sexual orientation: Characteristics of symptom severity, disclosure, and timing across the life course. *American Journal of Orthopsychiatry, 86*(1), 69–78. doi:10.1037/ort0000112

Boellstorff, T. (2011). But do not identify as gay: A proleptic genealogy of the MSM category. *Cultural Anthropology, 26*(2), 287–312. doi:10.1111/j.1548-1360.2011.01100.x

Boroughs, M. S., Valentine, S. E., Ironson, G. H., Shipherd, J. C., Safren, S. A., Taylor, S. W., . . . O'Cleirigh, C. (2015). Complexity of childhood sexual abuse: Predictors of current post-traumatic stress disorder, mood disorders, substance use, and sexual risk behavior among adult men who have sex with men. *Archives of Sexual Behavior, 44*(7), 1891–902. doi:10.1007/s10508-015-0546-9

Bostwick, W. B., Boyd, C. J., Hughes, T. L., & McCabe, S. E. (2010). Dimensions of sexual orientation and the prevalence of mood and anxiety disorders in the United States. *American Journal of Public Health, 100*(3), 468–75. doi:10.2105/AJPH.2008.152942

Brewster, K. L., & Tillman, K. H. (2012). Sexual orientation and substance use among adolescents and young adults. *American Journal of Public Health, 102*(6), 1168–76. doi:10.2105/AJPH.2011.300261

Brown, M. J., Masho, S. W., Perera, R. A., Mezuk, B., & Cohen, S. A. (2015). Sex and sexual orientation disparities in adverse childhood experiences and early age at sexual debut in the United States: Results from a nationally representative sample. *Child Abuse & Neglect, 46*, 89–102. doi:10.1016/j.chiabu.2015.02.019

Centers for Disease Control and Prevention. (September 2011). HIV and AIDS among gay and bisexual men. CDC Fact Sheet (pp. 1–3). www.cdc.gov/nchhstp/newsroom/docs/fastfacts-msm-final508comp.pdf

Choi, K. H., Paul, J., Ayala, G., Boylan, R., & Gregorich, S. E. (2013). Experiences of discrimination and their impact on the mental health among African American, Asian and Pacific Islander, and Latino men who have sex with men. *American Journal of Public Health, 103*(5), 868–74. doi:10.2105/AJPH.2012.301052

Choi, K. H., Steward, W. T., Miège, P., Hudes, E., & Gregorich, S. E. (2016). Sexual stigma, coping styles, and psychological distress: A longitudinal study of men who have sex with men in Beijing, China. *Archives of Sexual Behavior, 45*(6), 1483–91. doi:10.1007/s10508-015-0640-z

Chong, E. S., Mak, W. W., Tam, T. C., Zhu, C., & Chung, R. W. (2017). Impact of perceived HIV stigma within men who have sex with men community on mental health of seropositive MSM. *AIDS Care, 29*(1), 118–24. doi:10.1080/09540121.2016.1201190

Ciesla, J. A., & Roberts, J. E. (2001). Meta-analysis of the relationship between HIV infection and risk for depressive disorders. *American Journal of Psychiatry, 158*(5), 725–30. doi:10.1176/appi.ajp.158.5.725

Cochran, S. D., & Mays, V. M. (2000a). Relation between psychiatric syndromes and behaviorally defined sexual orientation in a sample of the US population. *American Journal of Epidemiology, 151*(5), 516–23. doi:10.1093/oxfordjournals.aje.a010238

Cochran, S. D., & Mays, V. M. (2000b). Lifetime prevalence of suicide symptoms and affective disorders among men reporting same-sex sexual partners: Results from NHANES III. *American Journal of Public Health, 90*(4), 573–8. doi:10.2105/AJPH.90.4.573

Cook, S. H., Sandfort, T. G., Nel, J. A., & Rich, E. P. (2013). Exploring the relationship between gender nonconformity and mental health among black South African gay and bisexual men. *Archives of Sexual Behavior, 42*(3), 327–30. doi:10.1007/s10508-013-0087-z

das Nair, R., & Thomas, S. A. (2012). Politics of desire: Exploring the ethnicity/sexuality intersectionality in South Asian and East Asian men who have sex with men (MSM). *Psychology of Sexualities Review, 3*(1), 8–21.

De Graaf, R., Sandfort, T. G., & ten Have, M. (2006). Suicidality and sexual orientation: Differences between men and women in a general population-based sample from the Netherlands. *Archives of Sexual Behavior, 35*(3), 253–62. doi:10.1007/s10508-006-9020-z

Everett, B. G. (2013). Sexual orientation disparities in sexually transmitted infections: Examining the intersection between sexual identity and sexual behavior. *Archives of Sexual Behavior, 42*(2), 225–36. doi:10.1007/s10508-012-9902-1

Fethers, K., Marks, C., Mindel, A., & Estcourt, C. S. (2000). Sexually transmitted infections and risk behaviours in women who have sex with women. *Sexually Transmitted Infections, 76*(5), 345–9. doi:10.1136/sti.76.5.345

Fredriksen-Goldsen, K. I., Kim, H. J., Barkan, S. E., Muraco, A., & Hoy-Ellis, C. P. (2013). Health disparities among lesbian, gay, and bisexual older adults: Results from a population-based study. *American Journal of Public Health, 103*(10), 1802–9. doi:10.2105/AJPH.2012.301110

Friedman, M. R., Bukowski, L., Eaton, L. A., Matthews, D. D., Dyer, T. V., Siconolfi, D., & Stall, R. (2019). Psychosocial health disparities among black bisexual men in the US: Effects of sexuality nondisclosure and gay community support. *Archives of Sexual Behavior, 48*(1), 213–24. doi:10.1007/s10508-018-1162-2

Fu, T. C., Herbenick, D., Dodge, B., Owens, C., Sanders, S. A., Reece, M., & Fortenberry, J. D. (2018). Relationships among sexual identity, sexual attraction, and sexual behavior: Results from a nationally representative probability sample of adults in the United States. *Archives of Sexual Behavior*, 1–11. doi:10.1007/s10508-018-1319-z

Gates, G. J. (2011). How many people are lesbian, gay, bisexual and transgender? The Williams Institute. https://williamsinstitute.law.ucla.edu/research/census-lgbt-demographics-studies/how-many-people-are-lesbian-gay-bisexual-and-transgender/

Gattis, M. N., Sacco, P., & Cunningham-Williams, R. M. (2012). Substance use and mental health disorders among heterosexual identified men and women who have same-sex partners or same-sex attraction: Results from the national epidemiological survey on alcohol and related conditions. *Archives of Sexual Behavior*, *41*(5), 1185–97. doi:10.1007/s10508-012-9910-1

Gonzalez, J. S., Batchelder, A. W., Psaros, C., & Safren, S. A. (2011). Depression and HIV/AIDS treatment nonadherence: A review and meta-analysis. *Journal of Acquired Immune Deficiency Syndromes*, *58*(2), 181–7. doi:10.1097/QAI.0B013E31822D490A

Graham, L. F., Braithwaite, K., Spikes, P., Stephens, C. F., & Edu, U. F. (2009). Exploring the mental health of black men who have sex with men. *Community Mental Health Journal*, *45*(4), 272–84. doi:10.1007/s10597-009-9186-7

Hatzenbuehler, M. L., O'Cleirigh, C., Mayer, K. H., Mimiaga, M. J., & Safren, S. A. (2011). Prospective associations between HIV-related stigma, transmission risk behaviors, and adverse mental health outcomes in men who have sex with men. *Annals of Behavioral Medicine*, *42*(2), 227–34. doi:10.1007/s12160-011-9275-z

Hayes, J., Chakraborty, A. T., McManus, S., Bebbington, P., Brugha, T., Nicholson, S., & King, M. (2012). Prevalence of same-sex behavior and orientation in England: Results from a national survey. *Archives of Sexual Behavior*, *41*(3), 631–9. doi:10.1007/s10508-011-9856-8

Henderson, J., Cloete, A., & van Zyl, M. (2011). *"We women are women with a different manner:" Sexual health of WSW in four Western Cape communities.* Capetown, South Africa: Triangle Project and HSRC.

Horn, K., & Swartz, J. A. (2019). A comparative analysis of lifetime medical conditions and infectious diseases by sexual identity, attraction, and concordance among women: Results from a national US survey. *International Journal of Environmental Research and Public Health*, *16*(8), 1399. doi:10.3390/ijerph16081399

Johnson, C. A. (2009). What we know about same-sex practising people and HIV in Africa. In V. Reddy, T. Sandfort, & L. Rispel (Eds.), *From social silence to social science: Same-sex sexuality, HIV & AIDS and gender in South Africa* (pp. 126–36). Capetown, South Africa: HSRC Press.

Juan, S. (2012). Millions of wives wed to gay men: Expert. *China Daily*, 3 February. http://www.chinadaily.com.cn/china/2012-02/03/content_14528838.htm

Kavanagh, D. J., & Bower, G. H. (1985). Mood and self-efficacy: Impact of joy and sadness on perceived capabilities. *Cognitive Therapy and Research*, *9*(5), 507–25. doi:10.1007/BF01173005

Kerker, B. D., Mostashari, F., & Thorpe, L. (2006). Health care access and utilization among women who have sex with women: Sexual behavior and identity. *Journal of Urban Health*, *83*(5), 970–9. doi:10.1007/s11524-006-9096-8

Khan, S., & Khan, O. A. (2006). The trouble with MSM. *American Journal of Public Health*, *96*(5), 765–6. doi:10.2105/AJPH.2005.084665

King, M., Semlyen, J., Tai, S. S., Killaspy, H., Osborn, D., Popelyuk, D., & Nazareth, I. (2008). A systematic review of mental disorder, suicide, and deliberate self-harm in lesbian, gay and bisexual people. *BMC Psychiatry*, *8*(70), 1–17. doi:10.1186/1471-244X-8-70

Knight, D. A., & Jarrett, D. (2017). Preventive health care for women who have sex with women. *American Family Physician*, *95*(5), 314–21.

Koh, A. S., Gómez, C. A., Shade, S., & Rowley, E. (2005). Sexual risk factors among self-identified lesbians, bisexual women, and heterosexual women accessing primary care settings. *Sexually Transmitted Diseases*, *32*(9), 563–9. doi:10.1097/01.olq.0000175417.17078.21

Korchmaros, J. D., Powell, C., & Stevens, S. (2013). Chasing sexual orientation: A comparison of commonly used single-indicator measures of sexual orientation. *Journal of Homosexuality*, *60*(4), 596–614. doi:10.1080/00918369.2013.760324

Krueger, E. A., & Upchurch, D. M. (2019). Are sociodemographic, lifestyle, and psychosocial characteristics associated with sexual orientation group differences in mental health disparities? Results from a national population-based study. *Social Psychiatry and Psychiatric Epidemiology*, *54*(6), 755–70. doi:10.1007/s00127-018-1649-0

Lee, J. H., Gamarel, K. E., Bryant, K. J., Zaller, N. D., & Operario, D. (2016). Discrimination, mental health, and substance use disorders among sexual minority populations. *LGBT Health*, *3*(4), 258–65. doi:10.1089/lgbt.2015.0135

Lenke, K., & Piehl, M. (2009). Women who have sex with women in the global HIV pandemic. *Development*, *52*(1), 91–4. doi:10.1057/dev.2008.77

Lhomond, B., & Saurel-Cubizolles, M. J. (2006). Violence against women and suicide risk: The neglected impact of same-sex sexual behaviour. *Social Science & Medicine*, *62*(8), 2002–13. doi:10.1016/j.socscimed.2005.08.026

Liu, J. X., & Choi, K. (2006). Experiences of social discrimination among men who have sex with men in Shanghai, China. *AIDS and Behavior*, *10*(1), 25–33. doi:10.1007/s10461-006-9123-5

Loue, S., & Méndez, N. (2006). I don't know who I am: Severely mentally ill Latina WSW navigating differentness. *Journal of Lesbian Studies*, *10*(1–2), 249–66. doi:10.1300/J155v10n01_13

Lytle, M. C., De Luca, S. M., & Blosnich, J. R. (2014). The influence of intersecting identities on self-harm, suicidal behaviors, and depression among lesbian, gay, and bisexual individuals. *Suicide and Life-Threatening Behavior*, *44*(4), 384–91. doi:10.1111/sltb.12083

McCabe, S. E., Hughes, T. L., Bostwick, W. B., West, B. T., & Boyd, C. J. (2009). Sexual orientation, substance use behaviors and substance dependence in the United States. *Addiction*, *104*(8), 1333–45. doi:10.1111/j.1360-0443.2009.02596.x

Meyer, I. H. (2003). Prejudice, social stress, and mental health in lesbian, gay, and bisexual populations: Conceptual issues and research evidence. *Psychological Bulletin*, *129*(5), 674–97. doi:10.1037/0033-2909.129.5.674

Meyer, I. H., & Frost, D. M. (2013). Minority stress and the health of sexual minorities. In C. J. Patterson & A. R. D'Augelli (Eds.), *Handbook of psychology and sexual orientation* (pp. 252–66). New York, NY: Oxford University Press. doi:10.1093/acprof:oso/9780199765218.003.0018

Muessig, K. E., Baltierra, N. B., Pike, E. C., LeGrand, S., & Hightow-Weidman, L. B. (2014). Achieving HIV risk reduction through HealthMpowerment.org, a user-driven eHealth intervention for young black men who have sex with men and transgender women who have sex with men. *Digital Culture & Education, 6*(3), 164–82.

O'Cleirigh, C., Newcomb, M. E., Mayer, K. H., Skeer, M., Traeger, L., & Safren, S. A. (2013). Moderate levels of depression predict sexual transmission risk in HIV-infected MSM: A longitudinal analysis of data from six sites involved in a "prevention for positives" study. *AIDS and Behavior, 17*(5), 1764–9. doi:10.1007/s10461-013-0462-8

Pachankis, J. E., Cochran, S. D., & Mays, V. M. (2015). The mental health of sexual minority adults in and out of the closet: A population-based study. *Journal of Consulting and Clinical Psychology, 83*(5), 890–901. doi:10.1037/ccp0000047

Pathela, P., Hajat, A., Schillinger, J., Blank, S., Sell, R., & Mostashari, F. (2006). Discordance between sexual behavior and self-reported sexual identity: A population-based survey of New York City men. *Annals of Internal Medicine, 145*(6), 416–25. doi:10.7326/0003-4819-145-6-200609190-00005

Peacock, E., Andrinopoulos, K., & Hembling, J. (2015). Binge drinking among men who have sex with men and transgender women in San Salvador: Correlates and sexual health implications. *Journal of Urban Health, 92*(4), 701–16. doi:10.1007/s11524-014-9930-3

Poteat, T., German, D., & Flynn, C. (2016). The conflation of gender and sex: Gaps and opportunities in HIV data among transgender women and MSM. *Global Public Health, 11*(7–8), 835–48. doi:10.1080/17441692.2015.1134615

Przedworski, J. M., McAlpine, D. D., Karaca-Mandic, P., & VanKim, N. A. (2014). Health and health risks among sexual minority women: An examination of 3 subgroups. *American Journal of Public Health, 104*(6), 1045–7. doi:10.2105/AJPH.2013.301733

Pyra, M., Weber, K. M., Wilson, T. E., Cohen, J., Murchison, L., Goparaju, L., . . . Cohen, M. H. (2014). Sexual minority women and depressive symptoms throughout adulthood. *American Journal of Public Health, 104*(12), e83–e90. doi:10.2105/AJPH.2014.302259

Rabkin, J. G. (2008). HIV and depression: 2008 review and update. *Current HIV/AIDS Reports, 5*(4), 163–71. doi:10.1007/s11904-008-0025-1

Reback, C. J., & Larkins, S. (2010). Maintaining a heterosexual identity: Sexual meanings among a sample of heterosexually identified men who have sex with men. *Archives of Sexual Behavior, 39*(3), 766–73. doi:10.1007/s10508-008-9437-7

Reisner, S. L., Mimiaga, M., Case, P., Grasso, C., O'Brien, C. T., Harigopal, P., . . . Mayer, K. H. (2010). Sexually transmitted disease (STD) diagnoses and mental health disparities among women who have sex with women screened at an urban community health center, Boston, Massachusetts, 2007. *Sexually Transmitted Diseases, 37*(1), 5–12. doi:10.1097/OLQ.0b013e3181b41314

Reisner, S. L., Mimiaga, M. J., Safren, S. A., & Mayer, K. H. (2009). Stressful or traumatic life events, post-traumatic stress disorder (PTSD) symptoms, and HIV sexual risk taking among men who have sex with men. *AIDS Care, 21*(12), 1481–9. doi:10.1080/09540120902893258

Ren, Z., Howe, C. Q., & Zhang, W. (2019). Maintaining "mianzi" and "lizi": Understanding the reasons for formality marriages between gay men and lesbians in China. *Transcultural Psychiatry, 56*(1), 213–32. doi:10.1177/1363461518799517

Russell, S. T., & Fish, J. N. (2016). Mental health in lesbian, gay, bisexual, and transgender (LGBT) youth. *Annual Review of Clinical Psychology, 12*, 465–87. doi:10.1146/annurev-clinpsy-021815-093153

Rüütel, K., Valk, A., & Lõhmus, L. (2017). Suicidality and associated factors among men who have sex with men in Estonia. *Journal of Homosexuality, 64*(6), 770–85. doi:10.1080/00918369.2016.1236578

Safren, S. A., Blashill, A. J., & O'Cleirigh, C. M. (2011). Promoting the sexual health of MSM in the context of comorbid mental health problems. *AIDS and Behavior, 15*(1), 30–34. doi:10.1007/s10461-011-9898-x

Salomaa, A. C., & Matsick, J. L. (2019). Carving sexuality at its joints: Defining sexual orientation in research and clinical practice. *Psychological Assessment, 31*(2), 167. doi:10.1037/pas0000656

Salomon, E. A., Mimiaga, M. J., Husnik, M. J., Welles, S. L., Manseau, M. W., Montenegro, A. B., Mayer, K. H. (2009). Depressive symptoms, utilization of mental health care, substance use and sexual risk among young men who have sex with men in EXPLORE: Implications for age-specific interventions. *AIDS and Behavior, 13*(4), 811–21. doi:10.1007/s10461-008-9439-4

Sandfort, T., Bos, H., Knox, J., & Reddy, V. (2016). Gender nonconformity, discrimination, and mental health among black South African men who have sex with men: A further exploration of unexpected findings. *Archives of Sexual Behavior, 45*(3), 661–70. doi:10.1007/s10508-015-0565-6

Schick, V. R., Rosenberger, J. G., Herbenick, D., Collazo, E., Sanders, S. A., & Reece, M. (2016). The behavioral definitions of "having sex with a man" and "having sex with a woman" identified by women who have engaged in sexual activity with both men and women. *Journal of Sex Research, 53*(4–5), 578–87. doi:10.1080/00224499.2015.1061632

Senreich, E. (2015). Self-identified heterosexual clients in substance abuse treatment with a history of same-gender sexual contact. *Journal of Homosexuality, 62*(4), 433–62. doi:10.1080/00918369.2014.983375

Sivasubramanian, M., Mimiaga, M. J., Mayer, K. H., Anand, V. R., Johnson, C. V., Prabhugate, P., & Safren, S. A. (2011). Suicidality, clinical depression, and anxiety disorders are highly prevalent in men who have sex with men in Mumbai, India: Findings from a community-recruited sample. *Psychology, Health & Medicine, 16*(4), 450–62. doi:10.1080/13548506.2011.554645

Smith, C. P., Cunningham, S. A., & Freyd, J. J. (2016). Sexual violence, institutional betrayal, and psychological outcomes for LGB college students. *Translational Issues in Psychological Science, 2*(4), 351–60. doi:10.1037/tps0000094

Solomon, T. M., Kiang, M. V., Halkitis, P. N., Moeller, R. W., & Pappas, M. K. (2010). Personality traits and mental health states of methamphetamine-dependent and methamphetamine non-using MSM. *Addictive Behaviors, 35*(2), 161–3. doi:10.1016/j.addbeh.2009.09.002

Stoloff, K., Joska, J. A., Feast, D., De Swardt, G., Hugo, J., Struthers, H., . . . Rebe, K. (2013). A description of common mental disorders in men who have sex with men (MSM) referred for assessment and intervention at an MSM clinic in Cape Town, South Africa. *AIDS and Behavior, 17*(1), 77–81. doi:10.1007/s10461-013-0430-3

Su, D., Irwin, J. A., Fisher, C., Ramos, A., Kelley, M., Mendoza, D. A. R., & Coleman, J. D. (2016). Mental health disparities within the LGBT population: A comparison between transgender and nontransgender individuals. *Transgender Health, 1*(1), 12–20. doi:10.1089/trgh.2015.0001

Sullender, C. (2019). Scholar Plotr. www.csullender.com/scholar/
Trocki, K. F., Drabble, L. A., & Midanik, L. T. (2009). Tobacco, marijuana, and sensation seeking: Comparisons across gay, lesbian, bisexual, and heterosexual groups. *Psychology of Addictive Behaviors, 23*(4), 620–31. doi:10.1037/a0017334
Truong, N., Perez-Brumer, A., Burton, M., Gipson, J., & Hickson, D. (2016). What is in a label? Multiple meanings of "MSM" among same-gender-loving black men in Mississippi. *Global Public Health, 11*(7–8), 937–52. doi:10.1080/17441692.2016.1142593
van Anders, S. M. (2015). Beyond sexual orientation: Integrating gender/sex and diverse sexualities via sexual configurations theory. *Archives of Sexual Behavior, 44*(5), 1177–213. doi:10.1007/s10508-015-0490-8
White, J. M., Gordon, J. R., & Mimiaga, M. J. (2014). The role of substance use and mental health problems in medication adherence among HIV-infected MSM. *LGBT Health, 1*(4), 319–22. doi:10.1089/lgbt.2014.0020
Wichstrøm, L., & Hegna, K. (2003). Sexual orientation and suicide attempt: A longitudinal study of the general Norwegian adolescent population. *Journal of Abnormal Psychology, 112*(1), 144–51. doi:10.1037/0021-843X.112.1.144
Wong, C. F., Schrager, S. M., Holloway, I. W., Meyer, I. H., & Kipke, M. D. (2014). Minority stress experiences and psychological well-being: The impact of support from and connection to social networks within the Los Angeles House and Ball communities. *Prevention Science, 15*(1), 44–55. doi:10.1007/s11121-012-0348-4
Xu, F., Sternberg, M. R., & Markowitz, L. E. (2010a). Women who have sex with women in the United States: Prevalence, sexual behavior and prevalence of herpes simplex virus type 2 infection—Results from National Health and Nutrition Examination Survey 2001–2006. *Sexually Transmitted Diseases, 37*(7), 407–13. doi:10.1097/OLQ.0b013e3181db2e18
Xu, F., Sternberg, M. R., & Markowitz, L. E. (2010b). Men who have sex with men in the United States: Demographic and behavioral characteristics and prevalence of HIV and HSV-2 infection: Results from National Health and Nutrition Examination Survey 2001–2006. *Sexually Transmitted Diseases, 37*(6), 399–405. doi:10.1097/OLQ.0b013e3181ce122b
Young, R. M., & Meyer, I. H. (2005). The trouble with "MSM" and "WSW": Erasure of the sexual-minority person in public health discourse. *American Journal of Public Health, 95*(7), 1144–9. doi:10.2105/AJPH.2004.046714
Zea, M. C., Reisen, C. A., María del Río-González, A., Bianchi, F. T., Ramirez-Valles, J., & Poppen, P. J. (2015). HIV prevalence and awareness of positive serostatus among men who have sex with men and transgender women in Bogotá, Colombia. *American Journal of Public Health, 105*(8), 1588–95. doi:10.2105/AJPH.2014.302307

CHAPTER

30 Mental Health for Sexual and Gender Minority Couples and Families

Samantha L. Tornello

Abstract

The majority of sexual and gender minority (SGM) people want to be in a romantic relationship and desire parenthood in the future. SGM couples and parents often have similar experiences compared to their cisgender heterosexual peers; however, SGM people experience higher rates of mental health challenges. For SGM people, romantic partners buffer the negative impacts of sexual and gender-related stigma, along with providing social support that is lacking from family, friends, and the wider community. According to minority stress theory, sexual and gender-related negative experiences can be detrimental to the well-being of SGM individuals, with particularly distinctive influences on SGM couples and parents. Understanding the couple and co-parenting dynamics and experiences of SGM couples provides great insight into how to improve the mental health outcomes of all SGM people. This chapter will explore the experiences of SGM couples and parents, examine the positive and negative influences on mental health, and discuss ways to improve the experiences of SGM people through the context of romantic and co-parenting relationships.

Keywords: sexual minority, gender minority, mental health, relationship functioning, parenting, co-parenting

The majority of sexual and gender minority (SGM) people report wanting to be in a committed, monogamous relationship (Balzarini et al., 2018; D'Augelli, Rendina, Sinclair, & Grossman, 2007), and many want to have children in the future (e.g., Riskind & Tornello, 2017). There have been some attempts to determine the number of SGM couples and the rates of cohabitation and/or marriage among these couples. Researchers have found that 52.2 percent of same-sex couples in the United States are legally married (Goldberg & Conron, 2018), and approximately 40 percent of self-identified sexual minority adults reported being either married or in a cohabiting romantic relationship (Gates, 2014). In addition, researchers have found that SGM couples, compared to their cisgender heterosexual peers, are more likely to be racially diverse and interracial, to have greater geographic mobility, and to live in an urban area compared to their cisgender heterosexual peers (e.g., Flores, Brown, & Herman, 2016; Rosenfeld & Byoug, 2005). To date, little is known about dissolution rates among SGM couples, although rates seem to be similar to cisgender and heterosexual couples (Gates, Badgett, & Ho, 2008).

The purpose of this chapter is to review the existing literature on mental health and well-being of SGM people in the context of romantic relationships, both with and without children. Researchers have consistently found that SGM people, and in turn couples, have higher rates of mental health problems compared to their cisgender and heterosexual peers (e.g., Downing & Predworski, 2018; Plöderl & Tremblay, 2015). Researchers are beginning to understand the reasons for these mental health disparities and ways to decrease these rates among SGM people (e.g., Meyer, 2003). Understanding the experiences of SGM couples and parents provides great insight into the mental health disparities of SGM people.

Measurement Challenges

Sexual minority couples have typically been counted based on an array of dimensions such as sexual identity, attraction, and/or behavior of one individual or both members of the couple. In addition, sexual minority people are sometimes not identified based on their self-reported sexual identity, attraction, or behavior, but instead by their couple sex/gender design. Couples are identified based on each individual's sex assigned at birth (i.e., physical characteristics, hormones, and/or genetics; noted on an individual's birth certificate) or gender (i.e., how an individual self-identifies their gender, which may or may not align with their sex assigned at birth). Identifying couples by sex/gender design can result in incorrectly assuming a participant's sexual identity (e.g., cisgender woman in a different-sex couple assumed to be heterosexual).

Similar to sexual identity, the measurement of gender identity also lacks standardization. Researchers need to ask participants both their gender identity and sex assigned at birth (Tate, Ledbetter, & Youssef, 2013). In addition, options for these two questions should include multiple sex/gender options (e.g., genderqueer, transgender, intersexed), not just the sex/gender binary of male/man or female/woman. These inconsistencies in categorization—and challenges with data collection—make defining and counting SGM couples and parents difficult.

SGM Romantic Relationships and Mental Health

Commitment

For all couples, a stronger sense of commitment between partners is associated with better individual well-being and couple functioning (e.g., Baams, Bos, & Jonas 2014; Bauermeister et al., 2010; Liu & Wilkinson, 2017; Rodrigues, Huic, & Lopes, 2018). Cohabitation and legal recognition status are two ways in which couples' relationship commitment can be expressed. SGM individuals who are cohabitating with a romantic partner report better mental health outcomes, along with feeling less lonely, compared to their single peers (Grossman, D'Augelli, & Hershberger, 2000). SGM people with poorer mental health are more likely to perceive their romantic relationship as unstable; this is stronger among those with greater commitment to their romantic partner (Otis, Riggle, & Rostosky, 2006; Whitton & Kuryluk, 2014). There are a number of additional couple-level factors that can impact the mental health and well-being of SGM individuals in the context of romantic relationships.

Sexual Satisfaction

For all couples, regardless of sexual or gender identity, sexual satisfaction in romantic relationships is associated with psychological health (e.g., Holmberg, Blair, & Phillips, 2010). In a comparison of cisgender women in same-sex and different-sex relationships, sexual satisfaction was an important factor in individual well-being, although the relationship was stronger for women in different-sex relationships (Holmberg et al., 2010). Sexual satisfaction did not differ among sexual minority individuals based on whether the couple was cohabiting, married, or in a committed relationship (Ritter, Morris, & Knox, 2018). This topic has not been explored among gender minority individuals in great detail. In sum, regardless of an individual's sexual and gender identity, couple-level factors, such as relationship commitment and sexual satisfaction, play an important role in individual mental health and well-being.

Social Support

Another important factor in the psychological functioning of SGM couples is the amount of social support received from family, friends, and the romantic partner. A lack of social support from family and friends among gay, lesbian, and heterosexual couples is linked with diminished well-being (Graham & Barnow, 2013). Less is known about the impact of social support on gender minority couples, but there is evidence that family rejection is associated with negative mental health outcomes (e.g., Grant et al., 2011).

Support from a romantic partner may be particularly crucial for SGM individuals. For example, in a study of Dutch same-sex–attracted youth, those who expressed greater rejection of their sexual identity from their family reported greater mental health difficulties, although this was not the case for those in romantic relationships (Baams et al., 2014). For SGM couples, partners have a buffering effect against the negative impact of external stressors such as sexual identity–related stigma (e.g., Rostosky, Riggle, Gray, & Hatton, 2007). In a qualitative analysis of same-sex women and men couples, Rostosky et al. (2007) found that partners assist in reframing negative experiences and assist in affirming the relationship. When a partner reframes the couple's negative experiences, this could foster a stronger and more positive relationship between the partners and better individual functioning (Frost, 2014). Some couples report that sharing negative experiences results in feeling closer to their partner (Stewart, Frost, & LeBlanc, 2019). In all, SGM couples who receive more support from their partners experience better outcomes (e.g., Baams et al., 2014; Blair & Holmberg, 2008; Graham & Barnow, 2013).

Consensual Non-monogamy

SGM individuals are more likely to be open to discussing and practicing non-monogamy than cisgender heterosexual individuals (e.g., Balzarini et al., 2018; Levine, Herbenick, Martinez, Fu, & Dodge, 2018). To date, there is little information about the functioning and well-being of individuals in non-monogamous relationships, but overall, SGM couples who practice non-monogamy have similar relationship quality compared to monogamous couples (e.g., Rubel & Bogaert, 2015; Séguin et al., 2017). In a study of cisgender Canadian gay men, Séguin et al. (2017) compared couples who were in monogamous, open, and polyamorous relationships and found no differences in relationship quality across the groups. In a literature review, Rubel and Bogaert (2015) found no differences in relationship quality and individual well-being regardless of relationship agreement. In sum, SGM people are more likely than their cisgender heterosexual peers to engage in non-monogamy, but these relationships are similar to monogamous relationships.

Stigma, Discrimination, and Romantic Relationships

Minority stress theory (Meyer, 2003) has been used to understand and explain the mental health disparities among SGM people as compared to their cisgender heterosexual peers. According to this theory, individual experiences of minority stressors, such as stigma or discrimination, can impact both the individual and the couple (Meyer, 2003). Although research exploring the mental health of SGM couples has greatly increased over the past two decades, there are still significant deficits in what is known about different dimensions of these relationships, with even less known about a number of SGM subgroups (e.g., self-identified bisexual, asexual, gender nonbinary).

Among SGM couples, greater internalized stigma is negatively associated with relationship satisfaction (Doyle & Molik, 2015; Feinstein, McConnell, Dyar, Mustanski, & Newcomb, 2018). Minority stressors have been found to be associated with psychological aggression among SGM couples. Individual experiences of minority stressors can distort the individual's cognitive processes and can impact their sense of relationship satisfaction, resulting in greater psychological aggression in the couple (Lewis, Milletich, Derlega, & Padilla, 2014). Sexual minority women with higher internalized homophobia were also more likely to engage in psychological aggression toward their partner (Pepper & Sand, 2015).

As is the case for sexual minority couples, gender minority couples who experience greater stigma or discrimination report poorer relationship quality and individual mental health outcomes (e.g., Gamarel, Reisner, Laurenceau, Nemoto, & Operario, 2014; Iantaffi & Bockting, 2011). In a study of transgender women and cisgender men couples, transgender women reported that both their and their partner's experiences with relationship stigma were linked to decreased relationship quality (Gamarel et al., 2014). However, among cisgender men in this study, only their partner's experiences of relationship stigma predicted poorer relationship quality (Gamarel et al., 2014).

Legal Relationship Recognition

The availability of legal relationship recognition for SGM couples (see Badgett & Herman, 2013, for history of U.S. law; Patterson, Riskind, & Tornello, 2014, for international law) is often dictated by state and local laws. In many countries around the world, there has been a positive shift in the availability of and public opinion on access to legal marriage for same-sex couples. In a recent Pew Research Center report (2019), support for marriage between individuals of the same sex in the United States was at an all-time high, with the majority supporting marriage rights for SGM people (61 percent). However, this is a relatively recent shift. Before 2011, the majority of people in the United States opposed extending legal marriage to same-sex couples (Pew Research Center, 2019). It is important to note that the marriage debate has predominately focused on same-sex couples and has not included all self-identified SGM people in romantic relationships. For gender minority people, legal relationship recognition is a bit more complex. If both members of the couple have gender markers that note the couple as different sex or opposite sex, they can get married legally regardless of whether marriage extends to same-sex couples. Gender minority couples with sex/gender markers that imply the couple is same sex would have similar challenges to their cisgender same-sex coupled peers.

Benefits of Legal Relationship Recognition

For many couples, marriage is seen as an important reflection of relationship commitment and recognition, along with providing access to a number of legal protections. Legal marriage has positive impacts on relationship commitment and stability (Manning, Brown, & Stykes, 2016). After legal marriage was extended to include same-sex couples in Massachusetts, the majority of SGM people (85 percent) cited obtaining legal recognition of their relationship as a major incentive for getting married (Ramos, Goldberg, & Badgett, 2009). SGM individuals in legally recognized relationships report a greater sense of commitment to their partner, more support from family and friends, less stress, and specific financial benefits as a result of the obtaining legal recognition (e.g., Elwood, Irvin, Sun, & Breen, 2017; Liu & Wilkinson, 2017; Manning et al., 2016; Ramos et al., 2009). There is a direct association between legal relationship recognition and availability of health insurance (e.g., Elwood et al., 2017), affecting access to mental health services and thus individual psychological well-being.

Legal relationship recognition has been found to be associated with improvements in individual mental health and well-being (e.g., LeBlanc, Frost, & Bowen, 2018; Wight et al., 2013). Among a representative sample of adults in California, LGB adults in legal marriages reported better mental health compared to their LGB and heterosexual peers who were not legally married (Wight, LeBlanc, & Badgett, 2013). Similarly, when comparing same-sex couples who are legally married to those who are in legal domestic partnership or civil unions, being legally married was associated with better mental health outcomes (LeBlanc et al., 2018). In the largest study to date of gender minority couples, Liu and Wilkinson (2017) compared the experiences of transgender-identified couples who were legally married to couples who were unmarried, cohabiting, or divorced/separated. They found that married transgender individuals reported lower rates of discrimination compared to the nonmarried groups and that this was quite pronounced among married transgender women (Liu & Wilkinson, 2017). While there is limited research on the mental health benefits of legal relationship recognition for gender minority people, the experiences seem to be similar regardless of individual sexual and gender identity.

Negative Impacts of Social and Political Debates

Anti-SGM legislation or discourse, such as bans on legal marriage for same-sex couples, has negative impacts on the functioning of SGM couples and individuals (e.g., Frost & Fingerhut, 2016; Hatzenbuehler, McLaughlin, Keyes, & Hasin, 2010; Manning et al., 2016; Pachankis & Branstrom, 2018). For same-sex couples who reside in areas with constitutional bans prohibiting legal married recognition, relationship stability is lower among these couples (Manning et al., 2016). Sexual minority couples who were exposed to negative campaigns and messages discussing legal marriage bans for same-sex couples reported lower relationship satisfaction, along with negative impacts on individual well-being (Frost & Fingerhut, 2016).

For SGM people living in areas with active marriage debates and bans, rates of mood disorders, anxiety disorders, and alcohol use disorders were dramatically higher (Hatzenbuehler et al., 2010). These trends have also been seen internationally. In a study of sexual minority adults from twenty-eight European countries, unsupportive laws and policies towards sexual minority people were associated with poorer individual psychological outcomes (Pachankis & Branstrom, 2018). For sexual minority adults, living in areas with sexuality-related structural stigma results in greater sexual identity concealment and, in turn, poorer well-being (Pachankis & Branstrom, 2018). In addition to the negative impact of these sociocultural debates, residing in areas with unsupportive laws can have a harmful impact on individual mental health.

Sexual minority couples who reside in U.S. states with no legal relationship recognition reported greater psychological distress (e.g., Ogolsky, Monk, Rice, & Oswald, 2019; Riggle, Wickham, Rostosky, Rothblum, & Balsam, 2017). In one study, same-sex couples reported poorer psychological outcomes, more frequent experiences of stigma, and less family support prior to the legalization of marriage between same-sex couples in the United States (Ogolsky et al., 2019). In addition, sexual minority individuals who live in states with marriage recognition report more positive sexual identity development, less identity concealment, and less concern or isolation due to their sexual identity (Riggle et al., 2017). The destructive impact of negative sociopolitical debates and restrictive marriage laws is clear among sexual minority people, but the impact of these specific experiences on gender minority people is largely unknown.

SGM Couples as Parents and Mental Health

Desires and Intentions for Parenthood

We know that many SGM youth report that future parenthood is likely (D'Augelli et al., 2007), but not all SGM couples want to become parents. Consistently, researchers have found that fewer SGM people desire and intend to become parents compared to their cisgender heterosexual peers. Both in the United States (Riskind & Patterson, 2010; Riskind & Tornello, 2017) and internationally (e.g., Baiocco & Laghi, 2013; Leal, Gato, & Tasker, 2018), gay men and lesbian women are less likely to become parents compared to their heterosexual and bisexual peers. Specifically, cisgender gay men are least likely to become parents (e.g., Riskind & Patterson, 2010; Riskind & Tornello, 2017). Very limited research has explored the parenting intentions and desires of gender minority people and sexual minority individuals who do not self-identify as gay, lesbian, or bisexual (see review by Stotzer, Herman, & Hasenbush, 2014).

Rates of Parenthood

It is unclear exactly how many SGM couples are currently rearing children. Some have estimated that over 6 million people in the United States have been reared by an SGM parent, with between 2 and 3.7 million of these children being under eighteen years of age (Gates, 2014, 2015). Rates of parenthood among different-sex cisgender couples are significantly higher than same-sex couples (Goldberg & Conron, 2018) and gender minority couples (Stotzer et al., 2014). According to the 2014–2016 American Community Surveys, 16.2 percent of same-sex couples are currently raising children, with male same-sex couples (8.1 percent) being less likely compared to female same-sex couples (23.9 percent; Goldberg & Conron, 2018). Researchers have found variations in parenting rates among SGM couples by race/ethnicity; specifically, black female same-sex couples were just as likely as their heterosexual peers to be raising children (Dang & Frazer, 2005). For gender minority people, rates of parenthood vary greatly across studies (25 to 75 percent; Stotzer et al., 2014), with transgender women being more likely to have children compared to their gender minority peers (Stotzer et al., 2014; Tornello, Babic, & Riskind, 2019). In sum, there are many SGM parents, along with many SGM people wanting to become parents in the future (e.g., Gates, 2014; Riskind & Patterson, 2010; Riskind & Tornello, 2017; Stotzer et al., 2014).

Timing of Parenthood

There also has been a generational shift among SGM people regarding the timing of parenthood. This shift reflects a number of younger SGM people becoming parents within the context of an SGM identity, while older SGM people are more likely to have become parents within the context of a former relationship prior to SGM identity discovery and/or disclosure (Gates, 2015; Tornello & Patterson, 2015; Tornello et al., 2019). These generational trends in timing of parenthood among sexual minority people has been seen both in the United States and internationally (Patterson & Tornello, 2011). Similar trends have occurred among gender minority parents. Older gender minority parents were more likely to have had biological children (with a former partner prior to gender transition) and more likely to identify as transgender women (Tornello et al., 2019). In contrast, younger gender minority parents were more likely to have children after gender transition, within the context of their current gender identity, and self-identify as transgender men or nonbinary (Tornello et al., 2019).

Pathways to Parenthood

Along with the generational shifts in the timing of parenthood, there have been major changes in family creation options for SGM couples (Pathways to Parenthood for LGBT People, n.d.). The majority of SGM parents, across all generations, are raising biological children. Among older SGM parents, children were more often conceived in the context of a former cisgender heterosexual romantic relationship through sexual intercourse. Younger generations of SGM people are more likely to become parents within the context of an SGM identity and through the use of assisted reproductive technology and/or adoption (e.g., Goldberg & Conron, 2018; Tornello & Patterson, 2015; Tornello et al., 2019). For example, the majority of same-sex couples (women 68 percent; men 67 percent) are raising biological children, but both are more likely to have a child through adoption (21 percent) than their heterosexual peers (3 percent; Goldberg & Conron, 2018; Tornello & Patterson, 2015). In a study of transgender and nonbinary parents, the majority of parents were biologically related to their children (73 percent), with very few using adoption or foster care to become parents (4.6 percent; Tornello et al., 2019). Decisions regarding how to create a family among SGM couples are often based on reproductive ability and accessibility of options.

For many SGM people, future parenthood includes unique barriers and difficulties. These challenges may help explain the discrepancies in parenting desires and intentions, along with lower rates of parenthood among SGM people. The most important barrier to parenthood is reproductive ability (Tornello & Bos, 2017). For couples who lack the necessary "tools" to produce children, such as functioning eggs, sperm, and/or uterus, parenthood is less likely. The majority of SGM couples desire biological parenthood (e.g., Tornello & Bos, 2017). For many couples, becoming parents through reproductive technologies or adoption is desired but due to cost or accessibility is unattainable.

Using the minority stress framework, sexual and gender-related stigma and discrimination can explain some of the discrepancies in parenting rates across sexual and gender identity. For example, bans on legal marriage for same-sex couples have been associated with less desire to become parents and poorer psychological health (Bauermeister, 2014). Specifically, for young cisgender gay men residing in areas with these bans, the desire to be a father in the future was associated with greater depressive symptoms and lower self-esteem. For cisgender gay men who reside in areas without these bans, parental aspirations are associated with better mental health outcomes (Bauermeister, 2014). Similarly, among Italian cisgender lesbian women and cisgender gay men, future parenthood was seen as more likely if the individual had fewer personal experiences of stigma (Scandurra et al., 2019). For gender minority people, the association between minority stress and parenthood is largely unknown. In sum, SGM people are less likely to become parents, which can be a result of a combination of barriers and unique challenges related to being an SGM individual.

Transition to Parenthood

The transition to parenthood is seen as a stressful and exciting change-filled time for new parents (Cowan & Cowan, 1992), regardless of sexual or gender identity. Transitioning to parenthood can have both positive and negative impacts on the mental health and functioning of SGM people, regardless of how or when they become parents. Many of the changes and challenges occurring over the transition to parenthood are not unique for SGM couples, although there are some differences worth exploring.

Becoming a parent has been associated with greater individual mental health and couple difficulties. Increases in depression before and after the birth of a child are common among heterosexual cisgender couples, especially cisgender women. Ross, Steele, Goldfinger, and Strike (2007) explored the rates of depression among lesbian and bisexual cisgender women as they transition to parenthood. They found that not only were cisgender lesbian and bisexual women more likely to experience depression, but that the rates of depression in this sample were significantly higher than their heterosexual cisgender peers (Ross et al., 2007). Couples who described having romantic relationships with greater difficulties (Goldberg & Garcia, 2015; Goldberg & Smith, 2011) and mental health issues (Goldberg & Smith, 2011) prior to becoming parents also reported greater problems after parenthood. In a study examining experiences of cisgender lesbian couples over the transition to parenthood, researchers found that, on average, feelings of love decreased and conflict increased during the transition to parenthood (Goldberg & Sayer, 2006). Among cisgender gay men, the transition to parenthood was associated with decreased partner attention but increased commitment (Huebner, Mandic, Mackaronis, Beougher, & Hoff, 2012).

Some research has also indicated positive changes over the transition to parenthood. In a study of forty gay cisgender father couples who became parents through surrogacy, becoming a parent resulted in better relationships with their family of origin and greater self-esteem (Bergman, Rubio, Green, & Padron, 2010). These findings have also been replicated outside the United States. In a study conducted in Israel, cisgender gay fathers reported better well-being and functioning than their heterosexual peers (Erez & Shenkman, 2016; Shenkman & Shmotkin, 2013). Some of these positive mental health outcomes among sexual minority parents could be due, in part, to the fact that SGM people may have planned and/or prepared for parenthood for a longer period of time compared to their heterosexual peers.

Limited research exists on the experiences of parents of additional sexual and gender identities, such as bisexual or gender nonbinary parents (e.g., Ross & Dobinson, 2013). Ross et al. (2012) explored the mental health of self-identified lesbian and bisexual mothers and found that bisexual mothers had greater mental health challenges compared to lesbian mothers. In addition, sexual minority women becoming parents with a male partner were less likely to use mental health services. To the best of my knowledge, there are no studies exploring the transition to parenthood among gender minority couples.

Parenting Stress

All couples with children experience parenting stress, which can be described as the strain and anxiety unique to the individual's role as a parent, such as feeling overwhelmed or distressed in the responsibilities of parenthood or by the child's behavior (Abidin, 1992). For SGM parents, parenting stress can be caused by both common and unique factors compared with their heterosexual peers (e.g., Farr, 2017; Farr, Forssell, & Patterson, 2010; Goldberg & Garcia, 2015; Tornello, Farr, & Patterson, 2011). Among adoptive SGM parents, adopting older children (Farr et al., 2010; Goldberg & Garcia, 2015; Tornello et al., 2011) and being less prepared for the adoption process (Goldberg & Garcia, 2015) were associated with negative couple and individual functioning. In addition, having children with greater behavioral problems is associated with negative parental functioning (e.g., Farr, 2017; Farr et al., 2010). These factors are similar across all sexual and gender identities, although there are some experiences unique to SGM parents. Among gay adoptive fathers, a greater stigma sensitivity, or how often the father thought or worried about the negative impacts of being a sexual minority individual, was associated with greater parenting stress (Tornello et al., 2011). In sum, the transition to parenthood is challenging for anyone, but there are unique minority stressors that have been found to negatively impact the functioning of SGM people.

Co-parenting and Division of Labor

Co-parenting, or the coordination between parents in how a couple works together as a team to fulfill the responsibilities of parenthood (McHale & Irace, 2011), can impact the mental health and well-being of SGM individuals. Division of labor, or how a couple designates and performs unpaid household tasks (e.g., washing dishes, doing laundry) and childcare duties (e.g., changing diapers, getting up with the child at night), is an important dimension of the co-parenting relationship (Cowan & Cowan, 1992). In general, SGM couples report being more egalitarian in their division of labor compared to their cisgender heterosexual peers (e.g., Tornello, 2019; Tornello et al., 2015), although this has been found to vary among SGM couples (Carrington, 1999; Moore, 2008). Moore (2008) explored the division of labor of black lesbian couples and found that black stepmothers performed less of the childcare division of labor. This has also been found among cisgender gay men, with stepfathers performing less childcare than their partner (Tornello et al., 2015).

Although the division of unpaid labor may vary across couples, the level of satisfaction with this division, not the actual tasks performed, is associated with individual mental health (Lachance-Grzela & Bouchard, 2010; Tornello, Sonnenberg, & Patterson, 2015). For example, among cisgender gay fathers, greater satisfaction with the division of their unpaid labor was associated with fewer depressive symptoms (Tornello et al., 2015). Although research is limited among gender minority parents, the impact of dissatisfaction on individual well-being appears to be similar (Tornello, 2019). Becoming parents can bring an array of positive and negative changes for any couple, although there are specific aspects of being a SGM person that should be acknowledged.

Stigma, Discrimination, and Parenthood

SGM parents experience sexual and gender-related stressors along with parent-related stressors that negatively impact their well-being (e.g., Goldberg & Smith, 2011). Unsupportive policies or laws may disproportionally impact same-sex racial and ethnic minority couples (Cahill, Battle, & Meyer, 2003. Researchers found that cisgender same-sex adoptive parents with significant internalized homophobia, particularly those who lived in geographic areas with unsupportive policies or laws toward SGM people, reported more frequent symptoms of depression and anxiety (Goldberg & Smith, 2011). There is very little research examining the experiences of gender minority parents, stigma, and mental health outcomes. In one study of seventy-three transgender parents, negative parental experiences within their own families and personal perception of their family roles were associated with poorer individual mental health (Veldorale-Griffin & Darling, 2016). Researchers are beginning to examine the role of SGM-related stressors on mental health functioning of SGM parents, but more research is needed.

Lack of Research on the Global South

Much of the research on SGM couples and parents has focused on the Global North, specifically the United States, Europe, and Australia, with very little attention to SGM couples from the Global South (Asia, Africa, Latin America, and the Caribbean). Cultural views and legal standing of SGM individuals, couples, and parents vary greatly across these countries (see Chiam, Duffy, & Gill, 2017; International Lesbian, Gay, Bisexual, Trans, & Intersex Association, 2019, for summaries of legal protections and criminalization of SGM people). Although many countries in the Global South criminalize and do not extend legal recognition to same-sex couples, some SGM couples find alternative ways of obtaining these rights. For example, Japanese same-sex couples will legally adopt their romantic partner in order to obtain legal protections and inheritances, although this process is complex and contains a number of issues (Maree, 2004).

In the Global South there are very few estimates of SGM people, couples, and parents. In Latin America, prevalence rates of same-sex couples are lower than those in the Global North—Argentina (3.3 percent), Chile (2.7 percent), Uruguay (2.3 percent), and Brazil (1.8 percent) (Goldani, Esteve, & Turu, 2013). There is even less information about the rates of parenthood among SGM couples in the Global South. For example, parenthood among SGM couples in Taiwan may be rare (Pai, 2013). In Brazil and Uruguay, same-sex couples are less likely to be parents; specifically, men in same-sex relationships are the least likely to be parents (5.2 percent and 3.8 percent, respectively) compared to women in same-sex couples (31.3 percent and 21.5 percent). In a study of lesbian women in China, Chinese women reported being less likely to desire future parenthood (50 percent) than their cisgender heterosexual peers (79.1 percent; Lo, Chan, & Chan, 2016).

Laws and policies regarding relationship recognition, availability of reproductive technologies, and accessibility of legal parental rights varies extensively across cultures for SGM couples. In South Africa, SGM couples were given the right to adopt children but are still unable to marry their partner (Butler & Astbury, 2005). Due to the variations in cultural norms and laws regarding SGM couples and parents in the Global South, we know very little about the functioning and well-being of SGM people in these countries.

Future Directions

There are a number of gaps in our knowledge regarding the experiences and mental health of SGM couples and parents. First, there is a dearth of representative samples, along with consistent definitions of SGM couples. Due to a lack of measuring sexual and gender identity in large nationally representative samples, there is little information about the broader SGM population. Being able to identify SGM people in representative samples would provide researchers with a more accurate description and prevalence rates of SGM couples and families. Standardization of measurement would allow for consistency across studies, along with providing an accurate representation of SGM people (e.g., Meyer & Wilson, 2009).

Due to the high prevalence rates of stigma/discrimination, along with a lack of legal protections and social acceptance, SGM couples and parents are a hidden population. In turn, SGM people are typically difficult to recruit, especially those who are most vulnerable, such as members of unrepresentative populations or parents with young children. SGM samples are also quite homogenous in nature, typically white, upper middle class, from the United States, and living in larger, more accepting geographic locations (e.g., Sullivan & Losberg, 2003). Yet researchers estimate that SGM couples are more likely to be interracial and quite diverse (Flores et al., 2016; Rosenfeld & Byoug, 2005). In addition, little research has explored the experiences of SGM people from the Global South. There is a lack of research exploring the experiences of SGM people across racial and ethnic identities, socioeconomic statuses, countries, and cultures, with very limited research examining the role of intersexuality. Future research should ensure participants are recruited from across all underrepresented and hidden groups by employing innovative recruitment techniques and sampling methodologies (Meyer & Wilson, 2009).

Third, the majority of research focuses on sexual identity or couple design, not gender identity. Due to a lack of standardization and inclusion of measurement of gender identity along with sex assigned at birth, there is a basic lack of information about gender minority people. In addition, current research focuses on SGM groups that have more social acceptance (e.g., Roberts, Horne, & Hoyt, 2015) and often are binary in nature (e.g., Matsuno, 2019). For example, nonbinary-identified individuals report experiencing greater frequencies of misgendering and discrimination, which could lead to greater mental health issues compared to their binary peers (Goldberg, Kuvalanka, Budge, Benz, & Smith, 2019; Matsuno, 2019). To gain a more accurate picture of SGM couples and parents it is imperative to examine the experiences of all SGM people.

Although research on SGM individuals, couples, and families has greatly increased, little research has examined couple-level dynamics. The lack of attention paid to *both* members of the couple provides us with only one perspective (for exceptions see Feinstein et al., 2018; Otis et al., 2006), with little research exploring couple-level dynamics and mental health (Umberson, Thomeer, Kroeger, Lodge, & Xu, 2015). Future research should explore the experiences of both members of the couple, as well as the impact of these dynamics on each member of the couple.

Finally, the majority of research on SGM couples is focused on child-free individuals, with a lack of attention on SGM co-parents. Although there is overlap, there are also unique aspects to the couple's relationship when children are present. In all, research on SGM couples and parents has dramatically increased, but much more work needs to be done.

Conclusions and Implications

Increasing knowledge of SGM couples and parents provides great insight into and understanding of the experiences of SGM people. With the large prevalence of mental health issues among SGM people, it is important for practitioners and professionals working with SGM couples and parents to recognize and account for the unique strengths and difficulties of this group (Scott, Whitton, & Buzzella, 2019). For SGM people, support from romantic partner, family of origin, and friends can have positive impacts on mental health, but SGM stressors can have detrimental effects. Healthcare professionals must understand SGM people in the context of their romantic relationships and family systems. In addition, laws and policies that are positive toward SGM couples and parents are vital for improving the mental health and well-being of SGM people. Future research must increase attention to understudied and underrepresented groups within the SGM community, examine both members of the couple, and account for all external and internal factors related to the experiences of SGM people. Further understanding the experiences and mental health of SGM couples and parents will improve the mental health and well-being of all SGM people and their families.

References

Abidin, R. R. (1992). Presidential address: The determinants of parenting behavior. *Journal of Clinical Child Psychology, 21,* 407–12. doi:10.1207/s15374424jccp2104_12

Baams, L., Bos, H. M. W., & Jonas, K. (2014). How a romantic relationship can protect same-sex attracted youth and young adults from the impact of expected rejection. *Journal of Adolescence, 37,* 1293–302. doi:10.1016/j.adolescence.2014.09.006

Badgett, M. V. L., & Herman, J. L. (2013). Patterns of relationship recognition by same-sex couples in the United States. In A. K. Baumle (Eds.), *International handbook on the demography of sexuality* (pp. 331–62). New York, NY: Springer.

Baiocco, R., & Laghi, F. (2013). Sexual orientation and the desires and intentions to become parents. *Journal of Family Studies, 19*(1), 90–8.

Balzarini, R. N., Dharma, C., Kohut, T., Holmes, B. M., Campbell, L., Lehiller, J. J., & Harman, J. J. (2018). Demographic comparison of American individuals in polyamorous and monogamous relationships. *Journal of Sex Research, 56* (6), 681–94. doi:10.1080/00224499.2018.1474333

Bauermeister, J. A. (2014). How statewide LGB polices go from "under our skin" to "into our hearts": Fatherhood aspirations and psychological well-being among emerging adult sexual minority men. *Journal of Youth Adolescence, 43,* 1295–305. doi:10.1007/s10964-013-0059-6

Bauermeister, J. A., Johns, M. M., Sandfort, T. G. M., Eisenberg, A., Grossman, A. H., & D'Augelli, A. R. (2010). Relationship trajectories and psychological well-being among sexual minority youth. *Journal of Youth Adolescence, 39,* 1148–63. doi:10.1007/s10964-010-9557-y

Bergman, K., Rubio, R. J., Green, R.-J., & Padron, E. (2010). Gay men who become fathers via surrogacy: The transition to parenthood. *Journal of GLBT Family Studies, 6,* 111–41. doi:10.1080/15504281003704942

Blair, K. L., & Holmberg, D. (2008). Perceived social network support and well-being in same-sex romantic relationships. *Journal of Social and Personal Relationships, 25*(5), 769–91. doi:0.1177/0265407508096695

Butler, A. H., & Astbury, G. (2005). South African LGBT youth. In James T. Sears (Ed.), *Youth, education, and sexualities: An international encyclopedia* (pp. 814–817). Westport, CT: Greenwood Publishing Group.

Cahill, S., Battle, J., & Meyer, D. (2003). Partnering, parenting, and policy: Family issues affecting Black lesbian, gay, bisexual, and transgender (LGBT) people. *Race & Society, 6,* 85–98.

Carrington, C. (1999). *No place like home: Relationships and family life among lesbians and gay men.* Chicago, IL: The University of Chicago Press.

Chiam, Z., Duffy, S., & Gil, M. G. (2017). Trans legal mapping report. https://ilga.org/downloads/ILGA_Trans_Legal_Mapping_Report_2017_ENG.pdf

Cowan, C. P., & Cowan, P. A. (1992). *When partners become parents: The big life change for couples.* New York, NY: Basic Books.

Dang, A., & Frazer, S. M. (2005). Black same-sex couples household in the 2000 U.S. census: Implications in the debate over same-sex marriage. *Western Journal of Black Studies, 29*(1), 521–30.

D'Augelli, A. R., Rendina, H. J., Sinclair, K. O., & Grossman, A. H. (2007). Lesbian and gay youth's aspirations for marriage and raising children. *Journal of LGBT Issues in Counseling, 1*(4), 77–98. doi:10.1300/J462v01n04_06

Downing, J. M., & Predworski, J. M., (2018). Health of transgender adults in the U.S. 2014–2016. *American Journal of Prevention Medicine*, 55(3), 336–44. doi:10.1016/j.amepre.2018.04.045

Doyle, D. M., & Molik, L. (2015). Social stigma and sexual minorities' romantic relationship functioning: A meta-analytic review. *Personality & Social Psychology Bulletin*, *41*(10), 1361–81. doi:10.1177/0146167215594592

Elwood, W. N., Irvin, V. L., Sun, Q., & Breen, N. (2017). Measuring the influence of legally recognized partnerships on the health and well-being of same-sex couples: Utility of the California Health Interview Survey. *LGBT Health*, *4*(2), 153–60. doi:10.1089/lgbt.2015.0085

Erez, C., & Shenkman, G., (2016). Gay dads are happier: Subjective well-being among gay and heterosexual fathers. *Journal of GLBT Family Studies*, *12*(5), 451–67. doi:10.1080/1550428X.2015.1102668

Farr, R. H. (2017). Does parental sexual orientation matter? A longitudinal follow-up of adoptive families with school-age children. *Developmental Psychology*, *53*(2), 252–64. doi:10.1037/dev0000228

Farr, R. H., Forssell, S. L., & Patterson, C. J. (2010). Gay, lesbian, and heterosexual adoptive parents: Couple and relationship issues. *Journal of GLB Family Studies*, *6*, 199–213. doi:10.1080/15504281003705436

Feinstein, B. A., McConnell, E., Dyar, C., Mustanski, B., & Newcomb, M. E. (2018). Minority stress and relationship functioning among young male same-sex couples: An examination of actor–partner interdependence models. *Journal of Consulting and Clinical Psychology*, *85*(5), 416–26. doi:10.1037/ccp0000296.

Flores, A. R., Brown, T. N, & Herman, J. L. (2016). Race and ethnicity of adults who identify as a transgender in the United States. https://williamsinstitute.law.ucla.edu/wp-content/uploads/Race-and-Ethnicity-of-Transgender-Identified-Adults-in-the-US.pdf

Frost, D. M. (2014). Redemptive framings of minority stress and their associations with closeness in same-sex relationships. *Journal of Couple and Relationship Therapy*, *13*, 219–39. doi:10.1080/15332691.2013.871616

Frost, D. M., & Fingerhut, A. W. (2016). Daily exposure to negative campaign messages decreases same-sex couples' psychological and relational well-being. *Group Processes and Intergroup Relations*, *19*(4), 477–92. doi:10.1177/1368430216642028

Gamarel, K. E., Reisner, S. L., Laurenceau, J.-P., Nemoto, T., & Operario, D. (2014). Gender minority stress, mental health, and relationship quality: A dyadic investigation of transgender women and their cisgender males partners. *Journal of Family Psychology*, *28*(4), 437–47. doi:10.1037/a003717

Gates, G. J. (2014). LGB families and relationships: Analyses of the 2013 national health interview survey. https://williamsinstitute.law.ucla.edu/wp-content/uploads/lgb-families-nhis-sep-2014.pdf

Gates, G. J. (2015). Marriage and family: LGBT individuals and same-sex couples. *Future of Children*, *25*(2), 67–87.

Gates, G. J., Badgett, L. M. V., & Ho, D. (2008). Marriage, registration and dissolution by same-sex couples in the US. https://williamsinstitute.law.ucla.edu/wp-content/uploads/Gates-Badgett-Ho-Couples-Marr-Regis-Dissolution-Jul-2008.pdf

Goldani, A., Esteve, A., & Turu, A. (2013). Coming out in the 2010 census: Same-sex couples in Brazil and Uruguay. Presented at the XXVII IUSSP International Population Conference, Busan, Korea (Vol. 26).

Goldberg, A. E., & Garcia, R. (2015). Predictors of relationship dissolution in lesbian, gay, and heterosexual adoptive parents. *Journal of Family Psychology*, *29*(3), 394–404. doi:10.1037/fam0000095

Goldberg, A. E., Kuvalanka, K. A., Budge, S. L., Benz, M. B., & Smith, J. Z. (2019). Health care experiences of transgender binary and nonbinary university students. *The Counseling Psychologist*, *47*(1), 59–97. doi:10.1177/0011000019827568

Goldberg, A. E., & Sayer, A. (2006). Lesbian couples' relationship quality across the transition to parenthood. *Journal of Marriage & Family*, *68*, 87–100.

Goldberg, A. E., & Smith, J. Z. (2011). Stigma, social context, and mental health: Lesbian and gay couples across the transition to adoptive parenthood. *Journal of Counseling Psychology*, *58*(1) 139–50. doi:10.1037/a0021684

Goldberg, S. K., & Conron, K. J. (2018). How many same-sex couples in the US are raising children? https://williamsinstitute.law.ucla.edu/wp-content/uploads/Parenting-Among-Same-Sex-Couples.pdf

Graham, J. M., & Barnow, Z. B. (2013). Stress and social support in gay, lesbian, and heterosexual couples: Direct effects and buffering models. *Journal of Family Psychology*, *27*(4), 569–78. doi:10.1037/a0033420

Grant, J. M., Mottet, L. A., Tanis, J., Harrison, J., Herman, J. L., & Keisling, M. (2011). *Injustice at every turn: A report of the national transgender discrimination survey*. Washington, DC: National Center for Transgender Equality and the National Gay and Lesbian Task Force.

Grossman, A. H., D'Augelli, A. R., & Hershberger, S. L. (2000). Social support networks of lesbian, gay, and bisexual adults 60 years of age and older. *Journal of Gerontology*, *55*(3), 171–9. doi:10.1093/geronb/55.3.P171

Hatzenbuehler, M. L., McLaughlin, K. A., Keyes, K. M., & Hasin, D. S. (2010). The impacts of institutional discrimination on psychiatric disorders in lesbian, gay, and bisexual populations: A prospective study. *American Journal of Public Health*, *100*(3), 452–9.

Holmberg, D., Blair, K. L., & Phillips, M. (2010). Women's sexual satisfaction as a predictor of well-being in same-sex versus mixed-sex relationships. *Journal of Sex Research*, *47*(1), 1–11. doi:10.1080/00224490902898710

Huebner, D. M., Mandic, C. G., Mackaronis, J. E., Beougher, S. C., & Hoff, C. C. (2012). The impact of parenting on gay male couples' relationships, sexuality, and HIV risk. *Couple Family Psychology*, *1*(2), 106–19. doi:10.1037/a0028687

Iantaffi, A., & Bockting, W. O. (2011). Views from both sides of the bridge? Gender, sexual legitimacy, and transgender people's experiences of relationships. *Culture, Health & Sexuality*, *13*(3), 355–70. doi:10.1080/13691058.2010.537770

International Lesbian, Gay, Bisexual, Trans, & Intersex Association. (2019). Sexual orientation laws in the world. https://ilga.org/downloads/ILGA_Sexual_Orientation_Laws_Map_2019.pdf

Lachance-Grzela, M., & Bouchard, G. (2010). Why do women do the lion's share of housework? A decade of research. *Sex Roles*, *63*, 767–80. doi 10.1007/s11199-010-9797-z

Leal, D., Gato, J., & Tasker, F. (2018). Prospective parenting: Sexual identity and intercultural trajectories. *Culture, Health & Sexuality*, *21*(7), 757–73. doi:10.1080/13691058.2018.1515987

LeBlanc, A. J., Frost, D. M., & Bowen, K. (2018). Legal marriage, unequal recognition, and mental health among same-sex couples. *Journal of Marriage and Family*, *80*, 397–408. doi:10.1111/jomf.12460

Levine, E. C., Herbenick, D., Martinez, O., Fu, T., & Dodge, B. (2018). Open relationships, nonconsensual nonmonogamy, and monogamy among U.S. adults: Findings from the 2012 national survey of sexual health and behavior. *Archives of Sexual Behavior, 47*(5), 1439–50. doi:10.1007/s10508-018-1178-7

Lewis, R. J., Milletich, R. J., Derlega, V. J., & Padilla, M. A. (2014). Sexual minority stressors and psychological aggression in lesbian women's intimate relationships: The mediating roles of rumination and relationship satisfaction. *Psychology of Women Quarterly, 38*(4), 535–50. doi:10.1177/0361684313517866

Liu, H., & Wilkinson, L. (2017). Marital status and perceived discrimination among transgender people. *Journal of Marriage and Family, 79*(5), 1295–313. doi:10.1111/jomf.12424

Lo, I. P. Y., Chan, C. H. Y., & Chan, T. H. Y. (2016). Perceived importance of childbearing and attitudes toward assisted reproductive technology among Chinese lesbians in Hong Kong: implications for psychological well-being. *Mental Health, Sexuality, and Ethics, 106*(5), 1221–9. doi:10.1016/j.fertnstert.2016.06.042

Manning, W. D., Brown, S. L., & Stykes, J. B. (2016). Same-sex and different-sex cohabiting couple relationship stability. *Demography, 53*, 937–53. doi:10.1007/s13524-016-0490

Maree, C. (2004). Same-sex partnerships in Japan: Bypasses and other alternatives. *Women's Studies, 33*(4), 541–9, doi:10.1080/00497870490464396

Matsuno, E. (2019). Nonbinary-affirming psychological interventions. *Cognitive and Behavioral Practice, 26*(4), 617–28. doi:10.1016/j.cbpra.2018.09.003

McHale, J. P., & Irace, K. (2011). Coparenting in diverse family systems. In J. McHale & K. Lindahl (Eds.), *Coparenting: A conceptual and clinical examination of family* systems (pp. 15–37). Washington, DC: American Psychological Association.

Meyer, I. H. (2003). Prejudice, social stress, and mental health in lesbian, gay, and bisexual populations: conceptual issues and research evidence. *Psychological Bulletin, 129*(5), 674–97. doi:10.1037/0033-2909.129.5.674

Meyer, I. H., & Wilson, P. A. (2009). Sampling lesbian, gay, and bisexual populations. *Journal of Counseling Psychology, 56*(1), 23–31. doi:10.1037/a0014587

Moore, M. R. (2008). Gendered power relations among women: A study of household decision making in black lesbian stepfamilies. *American Sociological Review, 73*, 335–56.

Ogolsky, B. G., Monk, J. K., Rice, T. M., & Oswald, R. F. (2019). Personal well-being across the transition to marriage equality: A longitudinal analysis. *Journal of Family Psychology, 33*(4), 422–32. doi:10.1037/fam0000504

Otis, M. D., Riggle, E. D. B., & Rostosky, S. S. (2006). Impact of mental health on perceptions of relationship satisfaction and quality among female same-sex couples. *Journal of Lesbian Studies, 10*(1–2), 267–83. doi:10.1300/J155v10n01_14

Pachankis, J. E., & Branstrom, R. (2018). Hidden from happiness: Structural stigma, sexual orientation concealment, and life satisfaction across 28 countries. *Journal of Consulting and Clinical Psychology, 86*(5), 403–15. doi:10.1037/ccp0000299

Pai, E. (2013). *Making lesbian families in Taiwan*. Unpublished doctoral dissertation, University of York, United Kingdom.

Pathways to Parenthood for LGBT People. (n.d.). https://www.lgbthealtheducation.org/wp-content/uploads/Pathways-to-Parenthood-for-LGBT-People.pdf

Patterson, C. J., Riskind, R. G., & Tornello, S. L. (2014). Sexual orientation, marriage and parenthood: A global perspective. In A. Abela & J. Walker (Eds.), *Contemporary issues in family studies: Global perspectives on partnerships, parenting and support in a changing world* (pp. 189–202). Chichester, UK: Wiley-Blackwell.

Patterson, C. J., & Tornello, S. L. (2011). Gay fathers' pathways to parenthood: International perspectives. *Journal of Family Research, 22*, 103–16. doi:10.2307/j.ctvdf0csb.11

Pepper, B. I., & Sand, S. (2015). Internalized homophobia and intimate partner violence in young adult women's same-sex relationships. *Journal of Aggression, Maltreatment & Trauma, 24*(6), 656–73. doi:10.1080/10926771.2015.1049764

Pew Research Center (2019). Attitudes on same-sex marriage. https://www.pewforum.org/fact-sheet/changing-attitudes-on-gay-marriage/

Plöderl, M., & Tremblay, P. (2015). Mental health of sexual minorities: A systematic review. *International Review of Psychiatry, 27*, 367–85. doi:10.3109/09540261.2015.1083949

Ramos, C., Goldberg, N. G., & Badgett, M. (2009). The effects of marriage equality in Massachusetts: A survey of the experiences and impact of marriage on same-sex couples. https://escholarship.org/uc/item/9dx6v3kj

Riggle, E. D. B., Wickham, R. E., Rostosky, S. S., Rothblum, E. D., & Balsam, K. F. (2017). Impact of civil marriage recognition for long-term same-sex couples. *Sexuality Research & Social Policy 14*, 223–32. doi:10.1007/s13178-016-0243-z

Riskind, R. G., & Patterson, C. J. (2010). Parenting intentions and desires among childless lesbian, gay, and heterosexual individuals. *Journal of Family Psychology, 24*(1), 78–81. doi:10.1037/a0017941

Riskind, R. G., & Tornello, S. L. (2017). Sexual orientation and future parenthood in a 2011–2013 nationally representative United States sample. *Journal of Family Psychology, 31*, 792–8. doi:10.1037/fam0000316

Ritter, L. J., Morris, H. R., & Knox, D. (2018). Who's getting the best sex? A comparison by sexual orientation. *Sexuality and Culture, 22*, 1466–89. doi:10.1007/s12119-018-9538

Roberts, T. S., Horne, S. G., & Hoyt, W. T. (2015). Between gay and a straight place: Bisexual individuals' experiences with monosexism. *Journal of Bisexuality, 15*, 554–69, doi:10.1080/15299716.2015.1111183

Rodrigues, D. L., Huic, A., & Lopes, D. (2018). Relationship commitment of Portuguese lesbian and gay individuals: Examining the role of cohabitation and perceived social support. *Journal of Social and Personal Relationships* [E-pub before print]. doi:10.1177/0265407518798051

Rosenfeld, M. J., & Kim, B. (2005). The independence of young adults and the rise of interracial and same-sex unions. *American Sociological Review*, 70(4), 541–62. www.jstor.org/stable/4145376.

Ross, L. E., & Dobinson, C. (2013). Where is the "B" in LGBT parenting? A call for research on bisexual parenting. In A. E. Goldberg & K. R. Allen (Eds.), *LGBT-parent families: Innovations in research and implications for practice* (pp. 87–103). New York, NY: Springer.

Ross, L. E., Siegal, A., Dobinson, C., Epstein, R., & Steele, L. S. (2012). "I don't want to turn totally invisible": Mental health, stressors, and support among bisexual women during the perinatal period. *Journal of GLBT Family Studies, 8*(2), 137–54. doi:10.1080/1550428X.2012.660791

Ross, L. E., Steele, L., Goldfinger, C., & Strike, C. (2007). Perinatal depressive symptomatology among lesbian and bisexual women. *Archives of Women's Mental Health, 10*, 53–9. doi:10.1007/s00737-007-0168-x

Rostosky, S. S., Riggle, E. D. B., Gray, B. E., & Hatton, R. L. (2007). Minority stress experiences in committed same-sex couple relationships. *Journal of Professional Psychology Research and Practice, 38*(4), 392–400.

Rubel, A. N., & Bogaert, A. F. (2014). Consensual nonmonogamy: Psychological well-being and relationship quality correlates. *Journal of Sex Research, 59*(9), 1–22. doi:10.1080/00224499.2014.942722

Scandurra, C., Bacchini, D., Esposito, C., Bochicchio, V., Valerio, P., & Amodeo, A. L. (2019). The influence of minority stress, gender, and legalization of civil unions on parenting desire and intention in lesbian women and gay men: Implications for social policy and clinical practice. *Journal of GLBT Family Studies, 15*(1), 76–100. doi:10.1080/1550428X.2017.1410460

Scott, S. B., Whitton, S. W., & Buzzella, B. A. (2019). Providing relationship interventions to same-sex couples: Clinical considerations, program adaptations, and continuing education. *Cognitive and Behavioral Practice, 26*, 270–81. doi:10.1016/j.cbpra.2018.03.004

Séguin, L. J., Blais, M., Goyer, M., Adam, B. D., Lavoie, F., Rodrigue, C., & Magontier, C. (2017). Examining relationship quality across three types of relationship agreements. *Sexualities, 20*(1–2), 86–104. doi:10.1177/1363460716649337

Shenkman, G., & Shmotkin, D. (2013). "Kids are joy": Psychological welfare among Israeli gay fathers. *Journal of Family Issues, 35*(14), 1926–39. doi:10.1177/0192513X13489300

Stewart, S. F., Frost, D. M., & LeBlanc, A. J. (2019). Understanding how emerging same-sex couples make meaning of minority stress: A narrative approach. *Journal of Family Psychology, 33*(2), 183–93. doi:10.1037/fam0000495

Stotzer, R. L., Herman, J. L., & Hasenbush, A. (2014). Transgender parenting: A review of existing research. https://williamsinstitute.law.ucla.edu/wp-content/uploads/transgender-parenting-oct-2014.pdf

Sullivan, G., & Losberg, W. (2003). A study of sampling in research in the field of lesbian and gay studies. *Journal of Gay & Lesbian Social Services, 15*, 147–62.

Tate, C. C., Ledbetter, J. N., & Youssef, C. P. (2013). A two-question method for assessing gender categories in the social and medical sciences. *Journal of Sex Research, 50*, 767–76. doi:10.1080/00224499.2012.690110

Tornello, S. L. (2019). *Division of labor among transgender and gender non-binary parents: Association with individual, couple, and child behavioral outcomes.* Manuscript in preparation.

Tornello, S. L., Babic, A., & Riskind, R. G. (2019). Transgender and gender non-binary parents' pathways to parenthood. *Psychology of Sexual Orientation and Gender Diversity, 6*(2), 232–41. doi:10.1037/sgd0000323

Tornello, S. L., & Bos, H. (2017). Parenting intentions among transgender individuals. *LGBT Health, 4*, 115–20. doi:10.1089/lgbt.2016.0153

Tornello, S. L., Farr, R. H., & Patterson, C. J. (2011). Predictors of parenting stress among gay adoptive fathers in the United States. *Journal of Family Psychology, 25*(4), 591–600. doi:10.1037/a0024480

Tornello, S. L., & Patterson, C. J. (2015). Timing of parenthood and experiences of gay fathers: A life course perspective. *Journal of GLBT Family Studies, 11*(1), 35–56. doi:10.1080/1550428X.2013.878681

Tornello, S. L., Sonnenberg, B. N., & Patterson, C. J. (2015). Division of labor among gay fathers: associations with parent, couple, and child adjustment. *Journal of Sexual Orientation and Gender Diversity, 2*(4), 365–75. doi:10.1037/sgd0000109

Umberson, D., Thomeer, M. B., Kroeger, R. A., Lodge, A. C., & Xu, M. (2015). Challenges and opportunities for research on same-sex relationships. *Journal of Marriage & Family, 77*, 96–111. doi:10.1111/jomf.12155

Veldorale-Griffin, A., & Darling, C. A. (2016). Adaptation to parental gender transition: Stress and resilience among transgender parents. *Archives of Sexual Behavior, 45*, 607–17. doi:10.1007/s10508-015-0657-3

Whitton, S. W., & Kuryluk, A. D. (2014). Associations between relationship quality and depressive symptoms in same-sex couples. *Journal of Family Psychology, 28*(4), 571–6. doi:10.1037/fam0000011

Wight, R. G., LeBlanc, A. J., Badgett, L. M. V. (2013). Same-sex legal marriage and psychological well-being: Findings from the California health interview survey. *American Journal of Public Health, 103*(2), 339–45. doi:10.2105/AJPH.2012.301113

CHAPTER

31

Mental Health for Sexual and Gender Minority Polyamorous and Consensually Non-monogamous Individuals

Maria Pallotta-Chiarolli

Abstract

This chapter covers four areas. First, the author introduces, defines, and briefly describes how sexual and gender minority (SGM) polyamorous and consensually non-monogamous (poly/CNM) individuals, families, and communities have been researched in mental health studies. Second, the author reviews the available evidence-based research on poly/CNM SGMs and mental health, and mental health service provision. Third, the author reviews absences and erasures in research pertaining to the mental health of poly/CNM SGMs, particularly in relation to whether an intersectional lens has been applied in service provision such as in relation to age and to racial and ethnic minorities. In the final section, the author identifies and proposes future directions in the content and methodologies of research on poly/CNM SGM mental health, and recommendations for more effective mental health service provision.

Keywords: consensual non-monogamy, custody and child welfare, intersectionality, multiple-minority stress, pathologization, polyaffirmation, polyamory, polyfamilies, polynegativity

Polyamory, a combination of the Greek term for "many" and the Latin term for "love," is defined as the practice of engaging in multiple romantic, intimate, loving relationships simultaneously and is a specific form of consensual non-monogamies (CNMs) (Klesse, 2006). It is defined in research and by poly/CNM people as a relationship orientation (Jordan, 2018), a behavior (Barker & Langdridge, 2010), or a lifestyle and identity (Henrich & Trawinski, 2016). Poly/CNM individuals and families identify with any sexual or gender orientation; are of diverse cultures and social classes; and may or may not cohabitate, share finances, or expect sexual exclusivity among a group larger than two (Pallotta-Chiarolli, 2010a; Pallotta-Chiarolli, Sheff, & Mountford, 2020; Sheff, 2016a). Those who agree to be in sexual relationships only with each other and closed to relationships outside the group are *polyfidelitous*. Many *polycules*—chosen family networks of people associated through poly/CNM SGM relationships (Creation, 2019)—have members that maintain *polyaffective* relationships that are emotionally intimate and nonsexual (Sheff, 2016b). Most polycules include sexual and gender minority (SGM) members, and research has documented an especially strong link between bisexuality and polyamory (Pallotta-Chiarolli, 2010a, 2014, 2016a).

While poly/CNMs are becoming increasingly popular among both SGM and heterosexual populations in the twenty-first century (Moors, 2017), the hidden status of many poly/CNM SGMs makes it difficult to quantify how many experience mental health concerns (Graham, 2014). The increasing populist attention that poly/CNM SGMs has garnered reveals the growing need for mental health awareness, especially when considering the increase in poly/CNM self-help and relational guidebooks and workshops (Ritchie, 2010). Recent studies have highlighted the dearth of research on poly/CNM SGMs in the mental health literature and have called for a recognition of the urgency to better understand the unique mental health stressors, experiences, needs, and resiliency of this population, and ways to respond with more expertly resourced health services (Bairstow, 2017; Kisler & Lock, 2019; Raab, 2018; Torres, 2019; Williams & Prior, 2015).

A brief search of research literature published between 2013 and 2017 revealed no significant increase on the topic of poly/CNM in family therapy (Jordan, Grogan, Muruthi, & Bermúdez, 2017). As Jordan writes, "In a feedback loop, journals are not publishing articles on polyamory; thus, clinicians are not introduced to this relationship system" (2018, p. 4). There is also a lack of valid empirical measures to support treatment, which impairs clinicians' ability to properly assess mental health (Girard & Brownlee, 2015). Many common relationship assessments used in couple and family therapy, such as the Dyadic Adjustment Scale (Spanier, 1976) or the Marital Adjustment Test (Locke & Wallace, 1959), are designed for heterosexual married couples. The review conducted by Rubel and Bogaert (2015) is rare in its focus on psychosocial well-being and relationship quality as correlates and outcomes associated specifically with poly/CNM relationships. Given the limitations in research methods and participant homogeneity in the reviewed literature, they found that CNMs have similar psychological well-being and relationship quality as monogamists.

Throughout this chapter, attention will be paid not only to poly/CNM SGMs as clients seeking mental health service provision but also to how they are affirmed or problematized by mental health service providers. Decades of research have demonstrated the importance of accessibility and affirmation in mental health care to client outcomes (Lambert & Barley, 2001), with strong clinician/client relationships as one of the most salient predictors of positive outcomes in mental health. Thus, the skills, insights, and expectations of mental health service providers need to be evaluated in relation to poly/CNM SGM mental health. Indeed, as this chapter will demonstrate, there is a dearth of data on the mental health issues specifically pertaining to poly/CNM SGMs.

"When Your Relationship Isn't Recognized by Relationship Services": Poly/CNM SGMs in Mental Health Studies

The title of this section comes from a participant in my study of women with bisexual male partners that included poly/CNM relationships (Pallotta-Chiarolli, 2016a, p. 438). There are four larger issues that form the backdrop for mental health scholars and clinical conversations about poly/CNM SGMs. These are very similar and often interwoven with the concerns I summarized in Pallotta-Chiarolli (2016b) in relation to bisexualities in health and education policies and practice: erasure, exclusion by inclusion, absence of intersectionality, and pathologization. Before presenting these four issues, it is important to understand that misattribution and misrecognition often occur when it is assumed that poly/CNM SGM clients experience mental health issues and seek services as a result of being a poly/CNM SGM. In their thematic analysis based on interviews with twenty poly/CNM participants in an online forum in the United States, Kisler and Lock (2019) found two main themes that emerged as predominant and interconnected challenges for both poly/CNM SGMs and their health service providers: dealing with external stigma, navigating the specific internal machinations of polyamory. The majority of poly/CNM SGM clients do seek mental health services for the same reasons as monogamous clients (Girard & Brownlee, 2015). If being in a poly/CNM relationship is identified by the clients as causing mental distress, depression, and suicidality, there are some specific considerations for working with poly/CNM SGM individuals regarding the internal machinations and navigations of their relationships. These may include the negotiation of "new rules, no rules, old rules, and our rules" in relation to fidelity, jealousy, safer sex practices, and parenting, as I found in my research (Pallotta-Chiarolli, 2014), and communication, boundary setting, and maintenance (Zimmerman, 2012). In her work with poly/CNM SGM clients, Weitzman (2006) identified several polyamory-related mental health milestones, including coming out to oneself, coming out to a partner, deciding how out to be, and including additional partners in the primary relationship. At each milestone, mental health service providers could offer support and strategies while remaining nonjudgmental and affirming of clients' relationship choices. Within this framework of polyaffirmation, Weitzman stressed the importance of identifying mental health issues caused distinctly by the mismanagement of poly/CNM relationships in order to support navigation through difficulties and make informed choices, encourage communication, and assist with managing emotions. Thus, what Davidson calls "the shadow side of polyamory" must be attended to (2002, p. 3). This may include coerced consent, manipulation, dishonesty, family violence, or other dysfunctional patterns that are no more representative of healthy polyamory than healthy monogamy.

Erasure

As introduced earlier in the chapter, the following four forms of constructing poly/CNM identities and relationships as the "problem" or the "deficit" in mental health care are particularly concerning. First, the *erasure* of poly/CNM SGMs in mental health discourse continues to reflect and influence the similar erasure and ignorance of poly/CNM SGMs in mental health policies, programs, and practices (Graham, 2014). The challenge is for mental health researchers and service providers to foster awareness of the ongoing erasure and stigmatization of poly/CNM SGMs and advocate for affirmation in mental health policy, programming, and practice (Conley, Moors, Matsick, & Ziegler, 2012).

Exclusion by Inclusion

Some scholars and practitioners adapt to the absence of theory and data about poly/CNM SGMs by using research on monogamous and/or same-sex parent families (Sheff, 2011). This then becomes part of the second issue of *exclusion by inclusion*, which is also problematic because the experiences of poly/CNM SGMs are often distinct and multiple, with even more heightened levels of invisibility and stigmatization compared to monogamous SGMs. This subsuming or incorporation of poly/CNM SGM mental health issues into the overarching SGM framework has become even more apparent as the latter achieve increasing cultural legitimation through legislation and social acceptance of same-sex monogamous couple-marriages, which are often critiqued as assimilating to heteromonogamist norms (Aviram & Leachman, 2015; Marsh, 2011). As Klesse writes, many proponents of same-sex marriage have distanced themselves from polyamory, while poly activists have refrained from demanding polymarriage equality because it is seen as "damaging the realization" of such a drawn-out and widely resisted change for SGMs (2018, p. 12). Thus, all SGMs are presumed to be monogamous, and the examination of the heteropatriarchal structures and systems that promote mononormativity and marginalize and harm alternative relationship formations are excluded from the marriage debates (Zimmerman, 2012). Mental health service providers should examine and challenge the mental health effects of society privileging monogamy, and the construction of new hierarchies between the "good gays" seeking monogamy and marriage and the "bad queers" refuting mono-assimilationism (Eades & Vivienne, 2018).

Exclusion by inclusion is also evident in the lack of studies that distinguish different forms of CNM and different identities within SGMs, which then elicit varying health service judgments (Grunt-Mejer & Campbell, 2015; Weitzman, 2006). For example, bisexual and transgender individuals have increased negative mental health outcomes compared to other sexualities and cisgenders (Bolton & Sareen, 2011; Durso & Meyer, 2013; Eady, Dobinson, & Ross, 2011). There is also some evidence that all SGMs face specific obstacles in navigating the healthcare system and accessing mental health services (Simeonov, Steele, Anderson, & Ross, 2015). This heteronormativity and gender normativity are exacerbated when adding poly/CNM to SGM (Girard & Brownlee, 2015; Jordan, 2018).

Absence of Intersectionality

The third factor is linked to exclusion by inclusion as it leads to research severely limited by its reliance on narrow samples that are white and middle class. In my research (Pallotta-Chiarolli, 2010b), this *absence of intersectionality* is recognized as a major limitation, reflecting the ongoing concern that most research methods fail to access larger representations of people of diverse and intersectional socioeconomic, cultural, and religious locations, as well as transgender, intersex, and gender diverse identities (see also Cardoso, 2019; Haritaworn, Chin-ju, & Klesse, 2006; Noel, 2006; Sheff & Hammers, 2011). To date, the only systematic review and critique of the methodology used in CNM research was conducted by Sizemore and Olmstead, who found there has been "little improvement with regard to addressing methodological limitations" since 1974 (2017, p. 4). Most participants in poly/CNM SGM research continue to be white, middle-class, college-educated individuals who identify as cisgender male or female and LGB. They also have high levels of cyberliteracy that allows them to participate in online social and support groups, and thereby are easier for researchers to locate. While my own research and writings (Pallotta-Chiarolli, 2008, 2010a, 2016a, 2018) provide specific sections and stories on cultural and religious diversity, it is important to acknowledge the impact that a predominantly homogeneous privileged group of people has on research findings and the implications for mental health knowledge and practice. Kisler and Lock (2019) emphasise how the lack of racial and educational diversity in their research participant pool, where eighteen out of twenty participants identified as white or Caucasian, means the results are not generalizable to the larger population of poly/CNM SGM people. If clients are already contending with other marginalizations and manifestations of prejudice, they may have less mental capacity and emotional energy, as well as economic, cultural, and educational capital, to take on the additional hostility of polyphobia being directed toward them.

To date, Balzarini et al. (2018) are the only researchers to undertake a comparative demographic analysis of individuals in poly/CNM (N = 2,428) and monogamous (N = 539) relationships in the United States. They found the former were more likely to have minority sexual identities; less likely to identify as religious; and more likely to be in a civil union, be divorced, earn less income, and be in multiracial relationships. In relation to poly/CNM and nonconsensual non-monogamy (NCNM), data analyzed by Levine, Herbenick, Martinez, Fu, and Dodge (2018) from the 2012 National Survey of Sexual Health and Behavior (*n* = 2,270) found that of the 4 percent who reported CNM, males, gay/lesbian individuals, bisexual individuals, and those who identified as "other, non-Hispanic" were more likely to report CNM. Of the 8 percent who reported NCNM, bisexual individuals and black, non-Hispanic participants were the more numerous. Participants in CNM relationships reported more frequent condom use for anal intercourse and lower relationship satisfaction than monogamous participants, while NCNM participants reported more HIV testing and lower relationship satisfaction.

It has also been argued that CNM looks very different across various life course stages (Conley et al., 2012; Sizemore & Olmsted, 2017); thus, grouping these participants together without adequate consideration for age or other cohort differences presents an important limitation. Some researchers have suggested that different life stages may actually be more conducive to a CNM lifestyle, such as the life course stage of young or emerging adulthood.

Pathologization

The fourth issue is the ongoing *pathologization* of poly/CNM that has not been alleviated by the ongoing de-pathologizing of SGM. Pathologization and problematization of poly/CNM SGM individuals, families, and communities by legal, welfare, and health service providers and government agencies, and the lack of substantial research into what they require from these services and systems, have represented continuing dilemmas (Firestein, 2007; Weitzman, 2006, 2007). Early mental health studies pathologized poly/CNM SGMs as having personality and mental health disorders and commitment-phobia, and advocated that service providers should focus on monogamizing their relationships (Hymer & Rubin, 1982; Knapp, 1975). In more recent studies, mental health practitioners report wariness and unease with the relationship goals of their poly/CNM clients (Finn, Tunariu, & Lee, 2012), often openly expressing their beliefs that poly/CNM is unsustainable and an excuse for infidelity (Sullivan, 2017; Witherspoon, 2015). Drawing from the experiences of their own polyamorous families, Henrich and Trawinski (2016) reported on the pernicious effects of therapeutic bias and sex negativity with poly/CNM clients.

The following is an overview of the very limited data that have been documented in relation to the mental health of poly/CNM individuals, families, and communities. Duplassie and Fairbrother (2018) studied the critical incidents that assist or hinder people from developing healthy and self-affirming poly/CNM identities. Based on their interviews in the United States with fourteen participants (three male and eleven female) with no further specifics provided apart from stating that participants were recruited via word of mouth and two polyamory listservs, the researchers found that communication, community, support, and resources minimized detrimental effects on mental health. The mental health effects of endings and transitions in poly/CNM relationships and polyfamily resilience and protective factors have also been documented in the largest and longest study to date: Sheff's fifteen-year qualitative, ethnographic study on polyamorous families with children living in the United States. From approximately 1996 through 2012, Sheff interviewed 131 children (aged five years and older) and adult members of polyamorous families and conducted serial observations of 500 polyamorous family members of all ages (Sheff, 2014, 2016b).

There has also been some exploration of the strategies required of polyfamilies in the navigation and management of their external worlds, particularly in relation to their children's safety and well-being (Pallotta-Chiarolli, 2010a, 2010b). However, as Bevacqua concludes, there is currently no published research suggesting that "growing up in a poly/CNM family, in and of itself, would be a contributor to or cause for aberrant mental health development or onset of mental health pathology" (2018, p. 492). Based on a case study of a child growing up in a polyfamily, Bevacqua (2018) provided instructions and guidelines to equip nurses who want to provide competent and informed care for children from polyfamilies. A theme that has consistently arisen in research since the 1970s that is linked to mental distress is the question of whether disclosure may risk children being taken away from their families by child protective services (see Anapol, 2010; Watson & Watson, 1982). Child welfare and mental health service providers could benefit from additional education regarding children of SGM polyfamilies as well as the mental health impacts of such hypervigilance and fear (Pallotta-Chiarolli et al., 2020).

Multiple-Minority Stress and Mental Health

The four difficulties outlined in the previous section lead to poly/CNM SGM individuals undertaking stress-inducing and energy-consuming strategies of editing, scripting, and concealing their lives for protection and the ability to live out relationship and family realities with little external surveillance or interference. Strategies of compartmentalization, whereby specific identities are either made publicly visible or given importance, or concealed or undermined depending on the context, necessity, or safety, are also negotiated daily.

The convoluted navigation and negotiation of multiple temporal, spatial, psychological, and social lifeworlds may result in compounded discrimination and isolation, which is then further perpetuated within their healthcare journeys. As Cyrus writes,

> [T]he evidence is now overwhelming that discrimination negatively impacts both the physical and mental health of minority groups. Members of multiple-minority groups... are more likely to be exposed to experiences of stigmatization, discrimination, and fear of rejection. Research to date attempts to address the relationship of stress as a minority and health outcome through examining the role of microaggressions, exploring the concepts of risk and resilience, and most notably the creation of the minority stress model.
> (2017, p. 194)

The minority stress model (Meyer, 2006) is absolutely relevant to poly/CNM SGMs in its analysis of the complex relationship between external (discrimination/prejudice) and internal (self-doubt/guilt/shame) stressors that shape the experiences of multiple-minority groups. This has implications not only for their risk of interconnected physical, mental, and emotional illness but also for their access to healthcare and the quality of care they receive. Health service providers need to consider "the impact of hypervigilance, personal identification with minority status, and negative self-perceptions on their clients in developing policies" (Cyrus, 2017, p. 195). Three main forms of microaggressions described by Sue et al. (2007) are micro-assaults (overt verbal or nonverbal insults and behaviors), micro-insults (stereotypical statements or actions that may slight or demean a person's marginalized identities), and micro-invalidations (moments when perceptions of discrimination are considered unfounded by others and the realities of multiple marginalization and subsequent health concerns are refuted).

The minority stress model also hypothesizes that nondominant groups suffer from health disparities due to the chronic stress of interaction with dominant cultural groups (Meyer, 2006). The intersectionality of two or more identity factors, such as being poly/CNM and SGM, leads to a resulting identity that is often more complex due to the interaction of the individual components, "with risk of competition for saliency, conflict over incongruent values and beliefs, and unique lived experiences that are not fully understood by either [or any] group" (Dominguez, 2017, p. 210). It is also important to understand the relevance of "vicarious trauma," whereby "members of a non-dominant group must witness attacks on other group members" (Dominguez, 2017, p. 212). Shared narratives of psychological and physical harm that peers have experienced, and the further trauma inflicted by inappropriate or blaming/shaming healthcare, means poly/CNM SGM individuals are reminded of the constant threats they face.

Torres (2019) calls for the application of relational cultural theory in mental health care for poly/CNM SGMs that situates psychological distress within the context of disconnections stemming from relational and cultural processes (see also Jordan, 2009). As relationships are central to psychological development, health and well-being, and personal growth, and as individuals desire to connect with others, relational and sociocultural disconnections can have deleterious effects on mental health, especially in social relationships where there is an imbalance of power. This theory is inherently associated with the experiences of poly/CNM SGM individuals who hold less power than heterosexual and monogamous SGM people and experience discrimination across various levels. Disconnection and oppression in personal and social relationships may affect poly/CNM SGM individuals' perception of themselves, engender internalized polyphobia, and result in harmful effects on psychological and physical health.

More attention to the role that shame plays in poly/CNM SGM interpersonal relationships and health outcomes also needs to be undertaken. There is a link between shame and decreased mental and physical health functioning (Kim, Thibodeau, & Jorgensen, 2011). Minority stressors including concealment and internalized polyphobia also have a positive association with shame (Meyer, 2013). People who identify as poly/CNM SGMs may internalize society's harmful views of them, which then may lead to a mentally debilitating sense of shame (Hartling, Rosen, Walker, & Jordan, 2004). For example, when poly/CNM SGM people feel shameful, they may attempt to conceal parts of their identities to prevent being ostracized or rejected. This may elevate feelings of disconnection and lead to isolation and withdrawal from community connections (Hartling et al., 2004). Chronic experiences of relational disconnection and depression may also lead to a decreased quality of intimate relationships and poor health functioning (Jordan, 2009). Some clarity in the mental health literature is needed to elucidate the relational factors that might provide an explanation regarding how multiple-minority stress may influence polyrelationships and feelings of loneliness.

Mental Health Care Access and Utilization

These consistent but extremely scant findings across studies raise a major question that requires further research and awareness of its implications for mental health service providers: To what extent is the low rate of visibility of poly/CNM SGMs in mental health data due to their concealment from outside structures such as health and family services for fear of the ramifications of disclosure? Certainly, family and mental health training and provision have been expanding to include a variety of family forms (Seedall, Holtrop, & Para-Cardona, 2014). Feminist and queer theorists in mental health provision have challenged hegemonic patriarchal and heteronormative frameworks (Jordan et al., 2017). However, compulsory monogamy and coupledom still predominate in mental health research and provision (McDowell, Emerick, & Garcia, 2014). Negative attitudes in mental health service providers toward CNM have been associated with more conservative political views and higher religiosity, requiring awareness of how unconscious biases may impede professionalism (Hutzler, Giuliano, Herzelman, & Johnson, 2016). Clients have also reported "therapeutic voyeurism" and intrusive curiosity (Weitzman, Davidson, & Phillips, 2009).

Future Directions and Recommendations in Poly/CNM SGM Mental Health Studies and Service Provision

Given the issues and concerns that perpetuate mental ill-health in poly/CNM SGMs and prevent effective mental health service provision, the following are recommendations for future development and directions.

Fund and Prioritize Research Projects and Mental Health Promotion Activities

Much more research is required in order to understand causation and experience in mental health stressors for poly/CNM SGMs. This research can then be used to develop health promotion activities on community, societal, and national levels. Related to the need to undertake this work via an intersectional lens is the need to adopt a decolonizing approach in countries in the Global South, which may have had their precolonial diversity of genders, sexualities, and familial relationships erased or stigmatized in historical colonialism and contemporary neocolonialism (Pallotta-Chiarolli, 2020).

Affirm Poly/CNM SGM Resilience and Adopt Strengths-Based Mental Health Care Approaches

Resilience theory is a strengths-based perspective that emphasizes the role of communication, flexibility, and emotional intimacy as key elements that distinguish poly/CNM SGMs who are able to face significant hardship and come through stronger together, from those who experience detachment, distress, depression, and suicidality during or after facing similar heartache (Patterson, 2002). Mainstream and SGM mental health service providers need to consider how a poly/CNM minority identity could "be a source of strength if it is associated with opportunities for support that can offset the impact of stress" and their role in nurturing those strengths and creating supportive opportunities (Cyrus, 2017, pp. 195–6). The resilience hypothesis posits that because of experiences with other marginalizations such as racism and homo/bi/trans phobia, poly/CNM individuals may have "a greater capacity to cope with the minority stress they experience" (Cyrus, 2017, p. 197). Thus, it is important to explore how poly/CNM SGMs address and manage other minority stresses.

However, a focus on poly/CNM SGM individual and community resilience and strategic agency does not excuse or decrease structural and institutional responsibility and culpability. The concept of "situated agency" (Pallotta-Chiarolli & Pease, 2014, p. 35) allows for the scrutiny of interwoven cultural, religious, political, economic, social, and health systems and their constraints within which poly/CNM SGMs are trying to nurture a healthy self.

Diversify Research Methodologies

Accessing the mental health experiences and needs of a larger diversity of poly/CNM SGMs necessitates different recruitment and sampling strategies (Sizemore & Olmstead, 2017). Methodological limitations include the use of convenience samples, with the most frequent form of recruitment being internet based, such as online surveys. These run the risk of repeated participation and multiple submissions from homogenous cohorts, which may be particularly true for online surveys that offer monetary compensation. As Kisler and Lock state, and as I found in my own in-person interview research (Pallotta-Chiarolli, 2010; 2016a), while online data collection can afford participants anonymity when disclosing sensitive information, future research may benefit from in-person interviews to "enrich the process of participants' sharing their stories and enable the researchers to develop a deeper understanding of participants' experiences and insights" (Kisler & Lock, 2019, p. 55).

It is strongly recommended to adopt and create research designs with an intersectional lens that addresses the interweavings of genders, sexualities, ethnicities, indigeneities, socioeconomic status, age, and (dis)abilities, as well as various types of CNM (Sizemore & Olmstead, 2017). Pallotta-Chiarolli et al. (2020) also recommend challenging Anglocentrism in research publications and a stronger engagement with the innovative and groundbreaking research being undertaken beyond the Australian, Canadian, U.K., and U.S. assemblage.

Undertake Self-Reflexivity and Self-Learning

The cornerstone of providing culturally competent mental health care is based on knowledge, awareness, and skills (Ivey, Ivey, & Zalaquett, 2018), with particular attention to cultural sensitivity. Clinicians should seek education by reading research and attending professional development sessions, speaking with poly/CNM SGM people, learning about the benefits of polyamory, and being aware of relevant terminology (Hutzler et al., 2016; Williams & Prior, 2015). Self-reflexive questions such as the Monogamous Privilege Checklist (Davis, 2011) facilitate an exploration of value systems, messages received about what is "natural" in relationships, media representations of monogamy and non-monogamy, and how religious and political institutions have valued and rewarded monogamy (McGeorge & Carlson, 2011).

Provide Poly-Aware and Polyaffirmative Mental Health Services

Some practitioners and academics have used the term *bi-affirmative* or *SGM-affirmative* therapy (Firestein, 2007; see also Pallotta-Chiarolli, 2011), which can be expanded to incorporate poly/CNM. Just as homophobia and biphobia refer to aversions, discrimination, or negative stereotyping, there needs to be language such as polyerasure, polydiscrimination, polyphobia, and polynegativity.

There are four main polyaffirmations to take into consideration when working with poly/CNM SGMs, based on similar tasks recommended by Bradford (2006) in relation to bi-affirmation for bisexual clients. The first is acknowledging that their struggles are located within the social context of oppression. The second is to conduct a thorough assessment at the beginning of mental health care of the many factors that influence mental health and how they may pertain to, or may be exacerbated or avoided by, poly/CNM. The third is creating space for clients to self-ascribe their identity and describe their poly/CNM experiences, which can encompass a wide range of healthy and protective behaviors. The fourth is the facilitation of dialog around issues specific to the mental health needs of clients such as trust, jealousy, polyparenting, legalities, safer sex, and issues that might test the boundaries and expectations of their relationships (Pallotta-Chiarolli, 2014). Feminist theory can be applied in order to assist poly/CNM SGM clients in critiquing how their relationships might be unconsciously mirroring gendered hegemonic power dynamics that benefit men while disadvantaging women (Ziegler, Matsick, Moors, Rubin, & Conley, 2014). Careful attention to the use of language is warranted, such as asking: "How many people are part of your current relationship?" This immediately begins to reduce mental distress as poly/CNM SGMs feel heard, understood, and respected (Sparks, Kisler, Adams, & Blumen, 2011; Torres, 2019).

Improve Schooling and Graduate Training

Graduate programs should better integrate mental health research on poly/CNM and a variety of nontraditional family formations throughout their courses and practicums in an effort to better prepare clinicians to treat a diversity of clients (Graham, 2014;

Schechinger, Sakaluk, & Moors, 2018; Weitzman et al., 2009; Zimmerman, 2012). Due to the limited research and clinical literature available or made accessible to students, graduate faculty training programs are left without the necessary knowledge and skills to adequately prepare and supervise future mental health policymakers and practitioners (Haupert, Gesselman, Moors, Fisher, & Garcia, 2017).

Healthy relationship diversity education should also be incorporated into schools so that young people grow up with polyaffirmative discourses. In my research, many young people who identified as poly/CNM SGM or had grown up in polyfamilies emphatically pointed out how relationship diversity education would have ameliorated some of the debilitating anxiety of feeling like "an X-file":

> Sex education shouldn't be about you can be gay or you can be straight, but it should be about different types of relationships. You can have monogamous relationships, you can have nonmonogamous relationships.
> (*Joanne*, adolescent research participant in Pallotta-Chiarolli, 2010a, p. 466)

This then becomes a form of harm minimization, equipping young people with familiarity and confidence in becoming aware of and undertaking poly/CNM SGM lives, thereby reducing the potential for post-school mentally harmful life circumstances that result in the need for crisis management.

"Okay to Talk about the Unspoken Things": Conclusion

> I think if we had a service where it [being poly/CNM] was okay to talk about the unspoken things . . . the health issues so it's written out there so that people see it.
> (*Hannah*, research participant in Pallotta-Chiarolli, 2016a, p. 465)

Health services as sites of power and gatekeeping must not do what Pitt and Britzman describe as refusing "difficult knowledge" (2003, p. 758). The exploration of the very limited research into the mental health of poly/CNM SGMs and their mental health service providers asks two fundamental questions that require far more extensive and intensive interrogation: (1) What happens when "putting down the two faulty maps—the essentialist script and the monogamy script—that the culture has given them and exploring the territory of their loves and desires on their own"? (Swan & Benack, 2012, p. 65) and (2) What kinds of alternative mentally healthy kinship stories are possible that are not organized by the desire for reproduction, or the desire to be like other families, or by the promise of happiness in "being like" the norm? (Ahmed, 2010, p. 114).

> Our clients are no longer coming to us because they want to be normal, they are coming to us because they want to be whole. . . . Our job is no longer to help those who seek our assistance to achieve the cultural ideal, the mythical norm of well-adjusted middle class heterosexual adulthood.
> (*Firestein*, 2007, preface page)

References

Ahmed, S. (2010). *The promise of happiness*. Durham, NC: Duke University Press.

Anapol, D. (2010). *Polyamory in the 21st century: Love and intimacy with multiple partners*. New York, NY: Rowman and Littlefield.

Aviram, H., & Leachman, G. M. (2015). The future of polyamorous marriage: Lessons from the marriage equality struggle. *Harvard Women's Law Journal, 38*, 269–336.

Bairstow, A. (2017). Couples exploring non-monogamy: Guidelines for therapists. *Journal of Sex & Marital Therapy, 43*(4), 343–53. doi:10.1080/0092623X.2016.1164782.

Balzarini, R. N., Dharma, C., Kohut, T., Holmes, B. M., Campbell, L, Lehmiller, J. J., & Harman, J. J. (2018). Demographic comparison of American individuals in polyamorous and monogamous relationships. *Journal of Sex Research, 56*(6), 681–94. doi:10.1080/00224499.2018.1474333

Barker, M., & Langdridge, D. (2010). *Understanding non-monogamies*. London: Routledge.

Bevacqua, J. (2018). Adding to the rainbow of diversity: Caring for children of polyamorous families. *Journal of Pediatric Health Care, 32*, 490–3. doi:10.1016/j.pedhc.2018.04.015

Bolton, S. L., & Sareen, J. (2011). Sexual orientation and its relation to mental disorders and suicide attempts: Findings from a nationally representative sample. *Canadian Journal of Psychiatry, 56*(1), 35–43. doi:10.1177/070674371105600107

Bradford, M. (2006). Affirmative psychotherapy with bisexual women. *Journal of Bisexuality*, 6(1–2), 13–25. doi:10.1300/J159v06n01_02

Cardoso, D. (2019). The political is personal: The importance of affective narratives in the rise of poly-activism. *Sociological Research Online, 24*, 1–18. doi:10.1177/1360780419835559

Conley, T. D., Moors, A. C., Matsick, J. L., & Ziegler, A. (2012). The fewer the merrier? Assessing stigma surrounding consensually non-monogamous romantic relationships. *Analyses of Social Issues and Public Policy, 13*(1), 1–30. doi:10.1111/j.1530-2415.2012.01286.x

Creation, K. (2019). *This heart holds many: My life as the nonbinary millennial child of a polyamorous family*. Portland, OR: Thorntree Press.

Cyrus, K. (2017). Multiple minorities as multiply marginalized: Applying the minority stress theory to LGBTQ people of color. *Journal of Gay & Lesbian Mental Health, 21(3)*, 194–202. doi:10.1080/19359705.2017.1320739

Davidson, J. (2002). Working with polyamorous clients in the clinical setting. *Electronic Journal of Human Sexuality*, 5, 8. http://www.ejhs.org/volume5/polyoutline.html

Davis, C. (2011). *Monogamous privilege checklist.* www.eastportlandblog.com/2011/04/05/monogamous-privilege-checklist-by-cory-davis/

Dominguez, M. L. (2017). LGBTQIA people of color: Utilizing the cultural psychology model as a guide for the mental health assessment and treatment of patients with diverse identities. *Journal of Gay & Lesbian Mental Health, 21*(3), 203–20. doi:10.1080/19359705.2017.1320755

Duplassie, D., & Fairbrother, N. (2018). Critical incidents that help and hinder the development and maintenance of polyamorous relationships. *Sexual and Relationship Therapy, 33*, 421–39. doi:10.1080/14681994.2016.1213804

Durso, L., & Meyer, I. (2013). Patterns and predictors of disclosure of sexual orientation to healthcare providers among lesbians, gay men, and bisexuals. *Sexuality Research and Social Policy, 10*(1), 35–42. doi:10.1007/s13178-012-0105-2.

Eades, Q., & Vivienne, S. (2018). *Going postal: More than 'Yes' or 'No': One year on: Writings from the marriage equality survey.* Melbourne, Australia: Brow Books.

Eady, A., Dobinson, C., & Ross, L. E. (2011). Bisexual people's experiences with mental health services: A qualitative investigation. *Community Mental Health Journal, 47*(4), 378–89. doi:10.1007/s10597-010-9329-x

Finn, M. D., Tunariu, A. D., & Lee, K. C. (2012). A critical analysis of affirmative therapeutic engagements with consensual non-monogamy. *Sexual and Relationship Therapy, 27*(3), 205–16. doi:10.1080/14681994.2012.702893;

Firestein, B. A. (Ed.). (2007). *Becoming visible: Counseling bisexuals across the lifespan.* New York, NY: Columbia University Press.

Girard, A., & Brownlee, A. (2015). Assessment guidelines and clinical implications for therapists working with couples in sexually open marriages. *Sexual and Relationship Therapy, 30*(4), 462–74. doi:10.1080/14681994.2015.1028352

Graham, N. (2014). Polyamory: A call for increased mental health professional awareness. *Archives of Sexual Behavior, 43*(6), 1031–4. doi:10.1007/s10508-014-0321-3.

Grunt-Mejer, K., & Campbell, C. (2015). Around consensual non-monogamies: Assessing attitudes toward nonexclusive relationships. *Journal of Sex Research, 53*, 1–9. doi:10.1080/00224499.2015.1010193

Haritaworn, J., Chin-ju, L., & Klesse, C. (2006). Poly/logue: A critical introduction to polyamory. *Sexualities, 9*, 515–29. doi:10.1177/1363460706069963

Hartling, L. M., Rosen, W. B., Walker, M., & Jordan, J. V. (2004). Shame and humiliation: From isolation to relational transformation. In J. V. Jordan, M. Walker, & L. M. Hartling (Eds.), *The complexity of connection* (pp. 103–28). New York, NY: Guilford Press.

Haupert, M. L., Gesselman, A. N., Moors, A. C., Fisher, H. E., & Garcia, J. R. (2017). Prevalence of experiences with consensual nonmonogamous relationships: Findings from two national samples of single Americans. *Journal of Sex & Marital Therapy, 43*(5), 424–40. doi:10.1080/0092623X.2016.1178675

Henrich, R., & Trawinski, C. (2016). Social and therapeutic challenges facing polyamorous clients. *Sexual and Relationship Therapy, 31*, 376–90. doi:10.1080/14681994.2016.1174331

Hutzler, K. T., Giuliano, T. A., Herselman, J. R., & Johnson, S. M. (2016). Three's a crowd: Public awareness and (mis) perceptions of polyamory. *Psychology & Sexuality, 7*, 69–87. doi:10.1080/19419899.2015.1004102

Hymer, S. M., & Rubin, A. M. (1982). Alternative lifestyle clients: Therapists' attitudes and clinical experiences. *Small Group Behavior, 13*, 532–41. doi:10.1177/104649648201300408.

Ivey, A. E., Ivey, M. B., & Zalaquett, C. P. (2018). *Intentional interviewing and counseling: Facilitating client development in a multicultural society* (9th ed.). Pacific Grove, CA: Thomson/Brooks/Cole.

Jordan, J. V. (2009). *Relational-cultural therapy.* Washington, DC: American Psychological Association.

Jordan, L. S. (2018). "My mind kept creeping back…this relationship can't last": Developing self-awareness of monogamous bias. *Journal of Feminist Family Therapy, 30*(2), 109–27. doi:10.1080/08952833.2018.1430459.

Jordan, L. S., Grogan, C., Muruthi, B., & Bermúdez, J. M. (2017). Polyamory: Experiences of power from without, from within, and in between. *Journal of Couple & Relationship Therapy, 16*(1), 1–19. doi:10.1080/15332691.2016.1141135.

Kim, S., Thibodeau, R., & Jorgensen, R. (2011). Shame, guilt, and depressive symptoms: A meta-analytic review. *Psychological Bulletin, 137*(1), 68–96. doi:10.1037/a0021466

Kisler, T., & Lock, L. (2019). Honoring the voices of polyamorous clients: Recommendations for couple and family therapists. *Journal of Feminist Family Therapy, 31*(1) 1–19. doi:10.1080/08952833.2018.1561017

Klesse, C. (2006). Polyamory and its "others": Contesting the terms of non-monogamy. *Sexualities, 9*(5), 565–83. doi:10.1177/1363460706069986

Klesse, C. (2018). Bisexuality, slippery slopes, and multipartner marriage. *Journal of Bisexuality, 18*(4), 1–19. doi:10.1080/15299716.2017.1373264

Knapp, J. J. (1975). Some non-monogamous marriage styles and related attitudes and practices of marriage counselors. *Family Coordinator, 24*, 505–14. doi:10.2307/583034.

Lambert, M. J., & Barley, D. E. (2001). Research summary on the therapeutic relationship and psychotherapy outcome. *Psychotherapy: Theory, Research, Practice, Training, 38*(4), 357–61. doi:10.1037/0033-3204.38.4.357.

Levine, E. C., Herbenick, D., Martinez, O., Fu, T. C., & Dodge, B. (2018). Open relationships, nonconsensual nonmonogamy, and monogamy among U.S. adults: Findings from the 2012 National Survey of Sexual Health and Behavior. *Archive of Sexual Behavior, 47*, 1439–50. doi:10.1007/s10508-018-1178-7

Locke, H. J., & Wallace, K. M. (1959). Short marital-adjustment and prediction tests: Their reliability and validity. *Marriage & Family Living, 21*, 251–5. doi:10.2307/348022

Marsh, V. (Ed). (2011). *Speak now: Australian perspectives on same-sex marriage.* Melbourne, Australia: Port Campbell Press.

McDowell, T., Emerick, P., & Garcia, M. (2014). Queering couple and family therapy education. *Journal of Feminist Family Therapy, 26*(2), 99–112. doi:10.1080/08952833.2014.893805.

McGeorge, C. R., & Carlson, T. S. (2011). Deconstructing heterosexism: Becoming an LGB affirmative heterosexual couple and family therapist. *Journal of Marital & Family Therapy, 37*(1), 14–26. doi:10.1111/j.1752-0606.2009.00149.x

Meyer, I. H. (2006). Minority stress and mental health in gay men. *Journal of Health and Social Behavior, 36*(1), 38–56. doi:10.2307/2137286

Meyer, I. H. (2013). Prejudice, social stress, and mental health in lesbian, gay, and bisexual populations: Conceptual issues

and research evidence. *Psychology of Sexual Orientation and Gender Diversity, 1,* 3 26. doi:10.1037/2329-0382.1.S.3
Moors, A. C. (2017). Has the American public's interest in information related to relationships beyond "the couple" increased over time? *Journal of Sex Research, 54,* 677–84. http://dx.doi.org/10.1080/00224499.2016.1178208
Noel, M. J. (2006). Progressive polyamory: Considering issues of diversity. *Sexualities, 9,* 602–20. doi:10.1177/1363460706070003
Pallotta-Chiarolli, M. (2008). *Love you two.* Sydney, Australia: Random House.
Pallotta-Chiarolli, M. (2010a). *Border families, border sexualities in schools.* New York, NY: Rowman & Littlefield.
Pallotta-Chiarolli, M. (2010b). To pass, border or pollute: Polyfamilies go to school. In M. Barker & D. Langdridge (Eds.), *Understanding non-monogamies* (pp. 182–7). London: Routledge.
Pallotta-Chiarolli, M. (2011). "Inclusion with specificity": A review of *Becoming Visible: Counseling Bisexuals across the Lifespan* by Beth Firestein. *Journal of Bisexuality, 11*(1), 141–3. doi:10.1080/15299716.2011.545319
Pallotta-Chiarolli, M. (2014). "New rules, no rules, old rules or our rules": Women designing mixed-orientation marriages with bisexual men. In M. Pallotta-Chiarolli & B. Pease (Eds.), *The politics of recognition and social justice: Transforming subjectivities and new forms of resistance* (pp. 91–108). London: Routledge.
Pallotta-Chiarolli, M. (2016a). *Women in relationship with bisexual men: Bi men by women.* New York, NY: Rowman & Littlefield.
Pallotta-Chiarolli, M. (Ed.). (2016b). *Bisexuality in education: Erasure, exclusion by inclusion, and the absence of intersectionality.* London: Routledge.
Pallotta-Chiarolli, M. (Ed.). (2018). *Living and loving in diversity: An anthology of Australian multicultural queer adventures.* Adelaide, South Australia: Wakefield Press.
Pallotta-Chiarolli, M. (2020). Pre-colonial actualities, post-colonial amnesia and neo-colonial assemblage. In Z. Davy, A. C. Santos, C. Bertone, R. Thoreson, & S. Wieringa (Eds.), *Handbook of global sexualities.* London: Sage.
Pallotta-Chiarolli, M., & Pease, B. (2014). Recognition, resistance and reconstruction: An introduction to subjectivities and social justice. In M. Pallotta-Chiarolli & B. Pease (Eds.), *The politics of recognition and social justice: Transforming subjectivities and new forms of resistance* (pp. 1–24). London: Routledge.
Pallotta-Chiarolli, Sheff, E., & Mountford, R. (2020). Polyamorous parenting in contemporary research: Developments and future directions. In K. Allen & A. Goldberg (Eds.), *LGBT-parents.* London: Sage.
Patterson, J. M. (2002). Understanding family resilience. *Journal of Clinical Psychology, 58,* 233–46. doi:10.1002/jclp.10019
Pitt, A., & Britzman, D. (2003). Speculations on qualities of difficult knowledge in teaching and learning: an experiment in psychoanalytic research. *International Journal of Qualitative Studies in Education, 16*(6), 755–76. doi:10.1080/09518390310001632135
Raab, M. (2018). Care in consensually non-monogamous relationship networks: Aspirations and practices in a contradictory field. *Graduate Journal of Social Science, 14,* 10–27.
Ritchie, A. (2010). Discursive constructions of polyamory in mono-normative media culture. In M. Barker & D. Langdridge (Eds.), *Understanding non-monogamies* (pp. 46–54). New York, NY: Routledge.
Rubel, A. N., & Bogaert, A. F. (2015). Consensual nonmonogamy: Psychological well-being and relationship quality correlates. *Journal of Sex Research, 52,* 961–82. doi:10.1080/00224499.2014.942722
Schechinger, H. A., Sakaluk, J. K., & Moors, A. C. (2018). Harmful and helpful therapy practices with consensually non-monogamous clients: Toward an inclusive framework. *Journal of Consulting and Clinical Psychology, 86*(11), 879–91. doi:10.1037/ccp0000349
Seedall, R. B., Holtrop, K., & Parra-Cardona, J. R. (2014). Diversity, social justice, and intersectionality trends in C/MFT: A content analysis of three family therapy journals, 2004–2011. *Journal of Marital and Family Therapy, 40*(2), 139–51. doi:10.1111/jmft.12015
Sheff, E. (2011). Polyamorous families, same-sex marriage, and the slippery slope. *Journal of Contemporary Ethnography, 40,* 487–520. doi:10.1177/0891241611413578
Sheff, E. (2014). Not necessarily broken: Redefining success when polyamorous relationships end. In T. S. Weinberg & S. Newmahr (Eds.), *Selves, symbols, and sexualities: An interactionist anthology* (pp. 201–14). Thousand Oaks, CA: Sage.
Sheff, E. (2016a). *When someone you love is polyamorous.* Portland, OR: Thorntree Press.
Sheff, E. (2016b). Resilient polyamorous families. In P. Karian (Ed.), *Critical & experiential: Dimensions in gender and sexual diversity* (pp. 257–80). Eastliegh, UK: Resonance Publications.
Sheff, E., & Hammers, C. (2011). The privilege of perversities: Race, class and education among polyamorists and kinksters. *Psychology & Sexuality, 2,* 198–223. doi:10.1080/19419899.2010.537674
Simeonov, D., Steele, L. S., Anderson, S., & Ross, L. E. (2015). Perceived satisfaction with mental health services in the lesbian, gay, bisexual, transgender, and transsexual communities in Ontario, Canada: An Internet-based survey. *Canadian Journal of Community Mental Health, 34*(1), 31–44. doi:10.7870/cjcmh-2014-037
Sizemore, K. M., & Olmstead, S. B. (2017). A systematic review of research on attitudes towards and willingness to engage in consensual non-monogamy among emerging adults: Methodological issues considered. *Psychology & Sexuality, 8*(1–2), 4–23, doi:10.1080/19419899.2017.1319407
Spanier, G. B. (1976). Measuring dyadic adjustment: New scales for assessing the quality of marriage and similar dyads. *Journal of Marriage and the Family, 38*(1), 15–28. doi:10.2307/350547
Sparks, J. A., Kisler, T. S., Adams, J. F., & Blumen, D. G. (2011). Teaching accountability: Using client feedback to train effective therapists. *Journal of Marital and Family Therapy, 37*(4), 452–67. doi:10.1111/j.1752-0606.2011.00224.x
Sue, D. W., Capodilupo, C. M., Torino, G. C., Bucceri, J. M., Holder, A. M. B., Nadal, K. L., & Esquilin, M. (2007). Racial microaggressions in everyday life: Implications for clinical practice. *American Psychologist, 62(4),* 271–86. doi:10.1037/0003-066X.62.4.271
Sullivan, S. M. (2017). *Marriage and family therapists' attitudes and perceptions of polyamorous relationships.* Doctoral dissertation, Purdue University.
Swan, T. B., & Benack, S. (2012). Renegotiating identity in unscripted territory: The predicament of queer men in

heterosexual marriages. *Journal of GLBT Family Studies, 8*(1), 46–66. doi:10.1080/1550428X.2012.641371

Torres, J. G. (2019). A biopsychosocial perspective on bisexuality: A review for marriage and family therapists. *Journal of Bisexuality, 19*(1), 51–66. doi:10.1080/15299716.2019.1596863

Watson, J., & Watson, M. A. (1982). Children of open marriages: Parental disclosure and perspectives. *Alternative Lifestyles, 5*(1), 54–62.

Weitzman, G. D. (2006). Therapy with clients who are bisexual and polyamorous. *Journal of Bisexuality, 6*(1–2), 138–64. doi:10.1300/J159v06n01_08

Weitzman, G. D. (2007). Counseling bisexuals in polyamorous relationships. In B. A. Firestein (Ed.), *Counseling bisexuals across the lifespan* (pp. 312–35). New York, NY: Columbia University Press.

Weitzman, G., Davidson, J., & Phillips, Jr., R. A. (2009). What psychology professionals should know about polyamory. National Coalition on Sexual Freedom, *7*, 1–28. https://secureservercdn.net/198.71.233.68/9xj.1d5.myftpupload.com/wp-content/uploads/2019/12/Poly_Booklet_2014_09_27_2014-10-09.pdf [Retrieved 5th February, 2020]

Williams, D. J., & Prior, E. E. (2015). Contemporary polyamory: A call for awareness and sensitivity in social work. *Social Work, 60*(3), 268–70. doi:10.1093/sw/swv012.

Witherspoon, R. G. (2015). *Stigmatization of polyamory: Perceptions, predictors, and clinical implications.* Symposium presented at the 2015 American Psychological Association Annual Convention, Toronto, Canada. ryanwitherspoon.com/research .

Ziegler, A., Matsick, J. L., Moors, A. C., Rubin, J. D., & Conley, T. D. (2014). Does monogamy harm women? Deconstructing monogamy with a feminist lens. *Journal für Psychologie, 22*(1), 1–18.

Zimmerman, K. J. (2012). Clients in sexually open relationships: Considerations for therapist. *Journal of Feminist Family Therapy, 24*, 272–89. doi:10.1080/08952833.2012.648143.

CHAPTER

32 The Intersections of Physical and Mental Health among Sexual and Gender Minority Populations

Michele J. Eliason

Abstract

There is considerable evidence of health disparities among sexual and gender minority (SGM) populations in the areas of physical health and disability, mental health and suicidality, substance use and abuse, and access to care. However, little research has considered the possibility that disorders might concentrate in subgroups of SGMs with the greatest levels of minority stress over time or those who have experienced the greatest number of adverse childhood events. This chapter examines the scant evidence that physical and mental health disorders coexist in some SGM individuals and offers some critique of the existing research. Future directions for research are proposed.

Keywords: SGM, LGBT, health disparity, comorbidity, co-occurring disorders, minority stress, syndemics

In the past thirty years, a large body of research has revealed both mental and physical health disparities in sexual and gender minority (SGM) populations, and the predominant theory to explain the disparities has been the minority stress model (Institute of Medicine, 2011). Early research focused on "homosexuality" itself as a disease. Even after its removal from the American Psychiatric Association's *Diagnostic and Statistical Manual of Mental Disorders* in 1973, most of the research on SGM health in the 1970s through 1980s focused on rates of sexually transmitted infections, and increased dramatically with the advent of HIV/AIDS (Valdiserri, Holtgrave, Poteat, & Beyrer, 2019). A line of research started to highlight the appalling disparities in depression, anxiety disorders, suicide behaviors, and substance use and abuse (King, et al., 2008), much of it focused on the intersections of substance abuse and HIV/AIDS (Coulter, Kenst, Bowen, & Scout, 2014). The idea of SGM identities as a disease slowly shifted to a perspective of blaming stigma for health disorders (Eliason & Chinn, 2018).

Since the early 2000s, when large-scale health surveillance instruments used by states or federal agencies started adding sexual identity questions (but only rarely gender identity questions), disparities related to physical health disorders other than HIV and other sexually transmitted infections can be more accurately identified. To date, most of this research has been descriptive, citing incidence of diagnosed mental and physical health problems in cross-sectional data sets, but only rarely looking at whether these conditions coexisted in the same individual. In the general population, there is evidence that co-occurring disorders (i.e., some combination of mental and physical health problems) exist in large segments of the population (Druss & Walker, 2011; Walker, McGee, & Druss, 2015). Most of this general population research examines the co-occurrence of substance abuse and mental health disorders (Kushner, 2014) or studies how mental health disorders such as depression increase the risk for chronic physical health disorders (Walker et al., 2015). There are many reasons to hypothesize that mental and physical health disorders might be concentrated in certain individuals. For example, many health disorders share underlying risk factors such as stress, nutritional factors, lack of exercise, smoking, adverse childhood experiences, toxic environmental exposures, and others. In particular, minority stress stemming from stigma associated with SGM identities has been proposed to underlie most disparities in adverse health outcomes (Meyer, 2013; Slater, Godette, Huang, Ruan, & Kerridge, 2017). Second, having one disorder may increase the risk for another—for example, having a nicotine dependence disorder increases the chances of lung disorders and cancer. Third, treatment of some conditions may increase the risk for other problems, such as medication-related kidney or liver disorders or effects of chemotherapy or radiation on mood and anxiety. Finally, normal aging processes and wear and tear on the body increase the chance of several chronic disorders, making age a factor. Stress may accelerate the aging process for some individuals with marginalized identities.

This chapter explores the likelihood that high levels of stress underlie risk for both mental and physical health problems in SGM populations. The chapter will begin with an examination of some of the challenges in answering this question about co-occurring disorders, then briefly review the literature on the most common or striking physical health disparities, and then finally address a few studies that have attempted to document co-occurring disorders in SGM populations. The chapter ends with some recommendations for future research.

Measurement and Research Design Issues

There are many challenges to studying health disparities in general, as well as studying the presence or frequency of co-occurring disorders. We will discuss three main categories of research design challenges: definitions/measurement of terms and concepts related to sex, gender, and sexual orientation; research design issues such as sampling and analysis; and theoretical framework considerations.

Definition of Terms and Measurement Issues

Social constructs like sex, gender, sexual identity and race, are constantly evolving concepts and the labels change over time. There are no direct or biological measures of any of these concepts, leaving researchers to develop self-report items or questions to assess these constructs. As of yet, there are no standardized methods for asking questions about sex, gender, or sexuality; thus, existing survey research has used a wide variety of question formats, and we cannot ascertain whether the findings might be comparable across these different forms of measures (Patterson, Jabson, & Bowen, 2017). Sexual orientation is generally understood to be composed of several factors (Diamond, 2008): attraction patterns (who one fantasizes about), sexual behaviors (actual sex partners and specific behaviors), and sexual identities (how one thinks of one's sexuality, including the terms or labels that individuals use to describe their sexuality). These are not always congruent. People with strong same-sex attractions may never act on them but experience a great deal of stress because of the feelings and may have deeply internalized shame and guilt, even though they have not experienced any external discrimination events. Others engage in same-sex behaviors yet never consider themselves other than heterosexual. Those who use one of the common sexual identity terms like lesbian, gay, or bisexual may be the most likely to have a strong connection to a sexual minority community, which may confer some protection against mental and physical health disorders but which makes them more visible and thus at higher risk for experiencing discrimination.

Most health surveys have used fixed categories to measure only one component of sexual orientation, typically identity, with options of gay, lesbian, bisexual, and heterosexual being the most common. This type of item forces a choice among these categories. For individuals who use terms like *queer*, *nonbinary sexuality*, or *fluid*, or refuse to label their sexuality at all, which label would they choose—or would they not answer the question? In recent years, some studies have added choices such as "mostly heterosexual" or "not entirely heterosexual" to the sexual identity questions (e.g., Drabble, Trocki, Hughes, Korcha, & Lown, 2013; Vrangalova & Savin-Williams, 2012). This raises the methodological challenge of whether to group "mostly heterosexual" individuals with the heterosexual or the LGB group if cell sizes are not large enough for analysis of all sexual identity categories.

Patterson et al. (2017) conducted a systematic review of health surveillance instruments with sexual and/or gender identity items to explore what kind of information has been collected. They found forty-three studies that represented local, state/regional, and national data sets: twenty-one from U.S. national surveys, fifteen from U.S. regional or state surveys, and seven international datasets (United Kingdom, Australia, Canada, New Zealand). Most (77 percent) measured sexual identity and 58 percent included sexual behavior questions. Only 14 percent measured identity, behavior, and attraction; 37 percent measured two of the three (most often identity and behavior). The timeframe of these questions varied, with the most common being past twelve months and lifetime. Thirty-two percent of the studies asked about sex of the partner, and four studies relied only on this measure, thus including only coupled and/or cohabitating LGB individuals.

Sex and gender constructs are equally confusing. In the 1970s, feminist scholars attempted to distinguish sex as the biological factors that define male or female bodies (e.g., hormones, reproductive organs, genitalia) from gender as the social construct that determines how a person assigned male or female should behave, talk, dress, wear their hair, accessorize, and select careers (Jordan-Young, 2010). These scholars in Western countries emphasized that sex, gender, and sexual identity were independent factors. However, even in the early days, information from other cultures indicated that sex/gender and sexuality were interdependent, such as studies about two-spirit identities in Native American communities in the United States and gender variations in other parts of the world (Driskill, 2010; Sheppard & Mayo, 2013).

Gender identity was originally defined as the degree to which a person felt that their sex and gender were aligned, such as identifying as both female and feminine. Over time, gender identity has come to mean a personal identity as male, female, masculine, feminine, transgender, or somewhere outside of or beyond these categories. The terms *cisgender*, defined as consistency between sex assigned at birth and current gender identity, and *transgender*, defined as some level of disconnect between assigned sex and gender identity, have been used in literature about SGM populations but are still not widely used or understood in general health research. A mind-boggling array of terms are found in the literature to refer to gender identity: transsexual, transgender, genderqueer, nonbinary, gender variant, gender nonconforming, gender atypical, male-to-female (MTF), female-to-male (FTM), transmasculine, and many more. When healthcare systems are deeply binary in their understandings of gender, healthcare providers experience consternation when someone with a masculine name and appearance shows up for a Pap test, or a person with no cervix comes to a women's health center.

One notable U.S. national health survey conflates sexual and gender identities, complicating the interpretation of the data. The National Health Interview Survey (NHIS) underwent extensive field testing of a sexual identity question and launched it in 2013 (Dahlhamer, Galinsky, Joestl, & Ward, 2014; Miller & Ryan, 2011). The item had two parts:

Which of the following best represents how you think of yourself?

- Lesbian or gay;
- Straight, that is, not lesbian or gay;
- Bisexual;
- Something else;
- I don't know the answer.

If you answered "something else": What do you mean by something else?

- You are not straight, but identify with another label such as queer, trisexual, omnisexual or pansexual;
- You are transgender, transsexual or gender variant;
- You have not figured out or are in the process of figuring out your sexuality;
- You do not think of yourself as having sexuality;
- You do not use labels to identify yourself;
- You mean something else.

Without separate questions on gender identity, this item lumps SGM individuals together into one group. One cannot merely separate out those who check "transgender, transsexual, or gender variant" to identify gender identity, because some people on the trans spectrum identify simply as men or women and may have checked one of the sexual identity options in the first part of the question. And what do we make of those who respond "something else" to both questions?

Recent studies suggest that sex/gender and sexual identities are not as mutually exclusive as previously thought even in Western samples, and studies that do not measure both sex/gender and sexuality are not able to address SGM health adequately. In two different samples that answered the problematic NHIS question about sexual identity, a significant number of SGM respondents selected "something else," often on both parts of the question: in Eliason, Radix, McElroy, Garbers, and Haynes (2016), 7 percent selected "something else" and in Eliason and Streed (2017), 18 percent selected "something else." Eliason and Streed (2017) found that respondents who identified on the transgender or nonbinary spectrum (using the two-question sex assigned at birth and current gender) were most likely to label their sexual identity as "something else" or "queer" rather than use the terms lesbian, gay, or bisexual. A gender transition often prompts a reconsideration of one's sexual identity (Rowniak & Chesla, 2013), and many trans spectrum individuals may believe that terms based on "same-sex" attractions are inadequate to explain their experience.

In Patterson et al.'s (2017) systematic review of forty-three studies, only 19 percent of the health surveys included gender identity questions and most had only a single item, such as "do you identify as male, female, or transgender?" None of the forty-three studies used the recommended best practice of a two-part gender assessment of sex assigned at birth and current gender identification (GenIUSS Group, 2014).

Another factor, assuming that minority stress and stigma drive health disparities, is to consider how individuals are identified as SGM by others. Presumably, discrimination and harassment by strangers such as healthcare professions occur only if a person is known or perceived to be an SGM. Visible differences are typically based on gender cues—a person who does not appear clearly male or female, or whose appearance, mannerisms, interests, or activities do not conform with societal norms for their sex will encounter more discrimination. This is another way that sex, gender, and sexuality are conflated. A lesbian with a "masculine" appearance or a trans man who needs gynecological care or contraception counseling will often experience discrimination and harassment if they present at OB/GYN or women's clinics (Harb, Pass, DeSoriano, Zwick, & Gilbert, 2019; Wingo, Ingraham, & Roberts, 2018). Most large-scale health studies have not included measures of gender-related physical appearance or "outness." Nor has appearance or outness been considered as a factor in health outcomes in large-scale population-based studies.

Finally, recent attention to intersecting marginalized identities on health and well-being has emphasized the need for a more holistic approach to measurement and analysis (Bowleg, 2012). If samples are divided only on the basis of sexual or gender identity, potential effects of racism, sexism, classism, ableism, xenophobia, ageism, and other forms of stigma that affect health outcomes are obscured. Analytic methods that consider one variable at a time do not allow for this complexity. These identities intersect in many ways: for example, racism, heterosexism, and gender normativity may affect an adolescent's ability to achieve at school and increase dropout rates, substantially decreasing the chance of achieving economic stability in the future and increasing barriers to quality healthcare.

Research Design Issues

Early studies on SGM populations used nonrepresentative, local convenience samples with all the inherent biases in those designs. However, large random-sample population studies have their own limitations. First, when stigma is still very high in society, particularly among more vulnerable populations such as SGM people of color, those with disabilities, and poor populations, supposedly random samples may still be overrepresented by more economically privileged white gay and lesbian individuals. Sampling frames and recruitment methods used in research studies might also contribute to this bias. Many of the studies use random-digit dialing procedures tied to landline phones, leaving out populations with disproportionate numbers of SGM individuals, such as those who are homeless or incarcerated, and whose families are not accepting (e.g., the family member answering the phone may not reveal the presence of an SGM family member). Studies of school populations miss dropouts and absent and truant students who are often SGM students responding to a hostile climate (Thapa, Cohen, Higgins-D'Alessandro, & Guffey, 2012).

Large population studies provide a broad-stroke picture of population health in order to track the development of illness/disease in subgroups; thus, the demographic and social environment questions are kept to a minimum. Often there is only one question about sexuality (most often limited to sexual identity category) and one question about binary sex/gender (male or female). Only rarely is gender identity measured. All questions are by necessity self-report and ask something like "Have you ever been diagnosed by a healthcare professional with XX disorder?" SGM populations are more likely to avoid healthcare settings or not have a medical home and thus may have undiagnosed conditions (Dahlhamer, Galinsky, Joestl, & Ward, 2016; Lewis, Derlega, Clarke, & Kuang, 2006; Lunn et al., 2017; Matthews, Hughes, Osterman, & Kodl, 2005; Ward, Dahlhamer, Galinsky, & Joestl, 2014). There is also a timeframe problem with some questions. If the timeframe is "ever," a person who was diagnosed with a situational depression in their teens and who never experienced depression symptoms again in a lifetime is still coded in the depression category. These large-scale surveys are only good for epidemiological purposes—tracking disease/disorder in populations—but not for exploring theoretical reasons for the concentration of disorders in individuals or subgroups. They provide suggestions about associations of demographic and risk factors with disorder but cannot address causation.

Even in the largest studies, the size of the SGM population is relatively small, making comparisons by sex/gender and sexual identity categories and other important marginalized identities such race/ethnicity and disability status difficult. This results in knowing about health disparities in a very general fashion, such as having data indicating the rate of lifetime or past-year depression or diabetes, but without understanding the subpopulations that are most affected (by age, ethnicity, sexual identity category, gender identity category, religion, disability status, etc.). When the cell sizes are small, researchers tend to lump together disparate groups, such as all LGB or all LGBT participants. Sometimes trans spectrum individuals are grouped with sexual minority groups even if they identify as heterosexual. For some health disparities that cut across all these categories, such as depression or suicide behaviors, this lumping together may be appropriate, but yet it may obscure important subgroup differences. For example, trans people may have health issues related to hormone use or gender-affirming surgeries that cisgender LGBQ people do not experience.

Sample size issues are illustrated in a recent article by Gonzalez and Zinone (2018) that used NHIS data from 2013 to 2016 to study cancer diagnoses by sexual identities. On the surface, this looks like a robust data set with large numbers: over 129,000 heterosexual and 3,400 LGB adults. The sample contained 1,029 lesbians, 1,213 gay men, 780 bisexual women, and 335 bisexual men. Many respondents were omitted from the analyses because they identified their sexuality as "something else" (n = 389) or "don't know" (n = 798) or refused to answer the sexual identity question (n = 808). How many SGM individuals might have been lost to the analysis because they checked one of these boxes? Because age is associated with most cancers, the sample was divided by five age groups, further reducing cell sizes. For example, only forty-three bisexual men were aged sixty-five or older. This study also collapsed all types of cancer together rather than tracking rates of specific types of cancer. Some cancers are related to sex assigned at birth (breast, testicular, prostate), but those nuances are not presented in the data. The study reported that any cancer diagnosis by group was 8 percent in heterosexual men, 8.6 percent in gay men, 5 percent in bisexual men, 9.6 percent in heterosexual women, 8.9 percent in lesbians, and 7.2 percent in bisexual women. So are bisexual people less likely to get cancer? Once data were corrected for age (the bisexual groups were younger), bisexual women in every age group had a greater likelihood of cancer. This highlights the need to adjust data for factors associated with risk for the disorder under study.

Finally, there is a huge gap in knowledge about health disparities in non-Western countries and the Global South, particularly where SGM identities are not just stigmatized but often also criminalized. Stress related to one's SGM status is considerably greater in those countries, and health studies are unlikely to ask questions about sexuality and gender. Even if they did, because of the high risks involved, most respondents would not identify themselves. Thus, the data in the findings section reflect what is known in the United States and a few other Western countries.

Theoretical Framework Issues

One of the problems with the existing research is that the studies are mostly descriptive or present associations rather than providing the kind of data that would allow for testing theories or providing explanation. In SGM health disparity research, the prevailing theoretical framework is the minority stress model (Meyer, 2013). This theory suggests that people with stigmatized identities experience stressors that are above and beyond the everyday forms of stress experienced by the majority of the population. These minority stressors include having actual experiences of or anticipation of discrimination, harassment, invalidation, and/or violence related to the stigmatized identity. For some SGM people, particularly those from conservative religious backgrounds, negative stereotypes may be internalized, resulting in shame, guilt, and fear. Some may feel the need to conceal their SGM identities to feel safe. The distressing emotional states that result from minority stress can underlie mental health problems, suicide behaviors, and substance use, which in turn may contribute to physical health disorders. Several studies have studied how people with emotional distress are likely to "self-medicate" with alcohol, tobacco, drugs, or food (e.g., Johnson, et al., 2013; Mason & Lewis, 2015). Sources of minority stress can be close to the individual, such as parents, family, and peers, or more distal, such as state and national political campaigns and laws. Minority stress can also manifest somewhat differently in couples than in individuals (Frost et al., 2017).

The minority stress model has been a positive contribution to understanding SGM health disparities. However, stress is such a vague, subjective, and complicated construct that measurement of any type of stress becomes challenging. The influence of structural oppression (laws, state policies, overall climate) is often invisible to the individual and hard to measure, so studies tend to focus on the individual-level aspects of stress, such as number of discrimination events or presence of internalized shame and guilt. Questions that attempt to get at experiences of discrimination and harassment are plagued by questions of intersectionality. How does the transmasculine lesbian of color determine whether poor treatment by an employer was due to racism, sexism, heterosexism, gender normativity, or something else? The theory of minority stress seems to imply that there is "normal" stress and then on top of it for some people "minority stress." Yet all the categories of "normal" stress, such as intimate partner relationships, family, work, finances, housing, food security, and others, are also hugely influenced by living with a marginalized sexual or gender identity. The role of religion has been understudied. As the main driver of anti-LGBTQ+ attitudes in the world, religion is often a protective factor against health problems in heterosexual populations (Koenig, McCullough, & Larson, 2001) but a risk factor for SGM individuals (Drabble, Veldhuis, Riley, Rostosky, & Hughes, 2017; Eliason, Burke, van Olphen, & Howell, 2011). How does stress related to one's internalized views of religion and belief in a sin orientation affect the health of SGM populations? Internalized religious condemnation may be a risk factor for health outcomes for some SGM individuals. Finally, another problem is that the theories tend to focus on risk factors and ignore potential protective factors or resiliency as moderators of health.

Minority stress studies often lack a developmental perspective—early childhood experiences have profound effects on adult health, and general stage of development at the time that a person "comes out" as SGM may also affect their long-term health (Friedman, Marshal, Stall, Cheong, & Wright, 2008). Most chronic physical health disorders become more prevalent with age and take years to develop before diagnosable symptoms are present. Before inferring whether minority stress causes disorders, longitudinal studies are needed that account for age of coming out or transition as well as the varieties of stress in different developmental stages. A case in point is the experience of adverse childhood experiences, which are usually defined as physical, sexual, and/or emotional abuse; death or loss of a parent; or having a parent who had a mental health problem or was incarcerated. SGM populations are more likely to report such experiences (Friedman et al., 2011; Schneeberger, Dietal, Muenzenmaier, Huber, & Lange, 2014), but these studies are not methodologically designed to address whether the individual's perceived sexual or gender identity was a source of childhood adversity, thus missing out on a potent form of trauma for many SGM individuals who were aware of their identities early in life. General population studies find that adverse childhood experiences are associated with a wide array of mental and physical health disorders, including depression, anxiety, suicide behaviors, substance use, and elevated weight (Hughes et al., 2017; Kalmakis & Chandler, 2015). It is possible that the greatest health disparities among SGM populations are within those who have experienced adverse childhood experiences related to SGM or in general. For example, Austin, Herrick, and Proescholdbell (2015) found that when health outcomes were adjusted for the presence of adverse childhood experiences in sexual minority adults, the effect of sexual identity was attenuated or even eliminated. Without adjustment, sexual identity was associated with poor physical health, poor mental health, depression, disability, current smoking, asthma, binge drinking, and HIV risk factors, but with adjustment for adverse childhood experiences, there were no sexual identity effects on poor physical health, smoking, or binge drinking, and the other relationships were attenuated.

In public health, several studies have used "biosocial syndemic theory" (Singer & Clair, 2003), which proposes that psychosocial problems often combine and interact over a lifetime to increase the chances of adverse health outcomes. Some of the psychosocial factors include co-occurring disorders that interact with each other to create a greater health burden than any single disorder alone. This theory has been used to understand HIV risk among men who have sex with men (Dyer et al.; 2012; Kurtz, Buttram, Surratt, & Stall, 2012; Mustanski, Garafalo, Herrick, & Donenberg, 2007; Parsons, Grov, & Golub, 2012; Stall et al., 2003) and sexual minority women's health, in particular looking at the role of childhood abuse experiences on later health outcomes (Coulter, Kinsky, Herrick, Stall, & Bauermeister, 2015; Valentine et al., 2015).

Health Disparities and Co-Occurring Disorders in SGM Populations

Common Physical Health Disparities

Other chapters in this book address the wide range and prevalence of mental health and substance use disorders, so this section focuses on chronic physical health disorders in SGM populations. The early research was somewhat misleading because it focused on risk factors for physical health disorders rather than the actual prevalence or incidence of the disorder, leading to some exaggerated claims about health risks (e.g., breast cancer among lesbians).

The most common physical health disparities for which substantial data exists include (1) asthma in sexual minority populations (Blosnich, Lee, Bossarte, & Silenzio, 2013; Fredriksen-Goldsen et al., 2013a; Heck & Jacobsen, 2006); (2) disability in all SGM subgroups (Cochran & Mays, 2007; Fredriksen-Goldsen et al., 2011, 2013b; Gonzales & Henning-Smith, 2015; Siorda, 2015; Streed, McCarthy, & Haas, 2018; Witten, 2014), (3) HIV in men and trans women (Baral et al., 2013; Centers for Disease Control and Prevention, 2013; Herbst et al., 2008; Herman, Wilson, & Becker, 2017), and (4) elevated body weight in sexual minority women and trans people (Eliason et al., 2015; VanKim et al., 2014; Velho, Fieghera, Ziegelmann, & Spritzer, 2017).

There are also several chronic disorders for which data are currently contradictory or partial but may represent SGM health disparities. These include (1) hypertension (Clark et al., 2015; Everett & Mollborn, 2013; Hatzenbuehler, Slopen, & McLaughlin, 2014), (2) cardiovascular disease (Blosnich, Farmer, Lee, Silenzio, & Bowen, 2014; Garland-Forshee, Fiala, Ngo, & Moseley, 2014; Lick, Durso, & Johnson, 2013; Meyer, Brown, Herman, Reisner, & Bockting, 2017; Wierckx et al., 2013), and (3) type 2 diabetes (Beach, Elasy, & Gonzales, 2018; Feldman et al., 2016; Fredriksen-Goldsen et al., 2013b; Liu, Chen, Wilkinson, Pearson, & Zhang, 2019). Cancer studies are more complicated: Blosnich et al. (2014) found higher rates of prostate cancer in sexual minority men, but other studies have not; Boehmer, Miao, & Ozonoff (2011) found higher rates of cancer overall in sexual minority men but not women. Quinn et al. (2015) reviewed several types of cancer and found evidence of increased rates of anal cancer in gay/bisexual men, especially those with HIV, but no strong evidence for any other form of cancer disparity. Simoni, Smith, Oost, Lehavot, and Fredriksen-Goldsen (2017), in a systematic review of sexual minority women's health, found evidence of disparities in asthma, elevated weight, arthritis, and cardiovascular disease, but no differences from heterosexual women for cholesterol, hypertension, cancer, or diabetes.

Co-Occurring Disorders

HIV

A large body of literature has examined how psychosocial factors, mental health, and substance use are associated with HIV risk. In particular, experiences of violence, alcohol and drug use, depression, economic instability, ethnicity, and increased experiences of discrimination are all associated with higher HIV risk in men who have sex with men and transgender women (Brennan et al., 2012; Gilbert et al., 2015; Hart et al., 2017; Wilson et al., 2014). In a study in Jamaica, where discrimination is very high because of the criminalization of same-sex activity, researchers found a very high correspondence between victimization experiences, binge drinking, and depression with number of sexual partners, self-efficacy about condom use, and perceived HIV risk (Logie et al., 2019). HIV is associated with a wide range of other health problems, including cancer (Robbins et al., 2015).

ELEVATED WEIGHT

In recent years, there has been increased attention to the role of heavier weight on health. Although there is still controversy as to whether weight per se causes other health problems, or whether increased weight is a proxy for stress, minority stress (external experiences of discrimination and internalized shame and guilt), nutritional factors, exercise factors, cultural norms, and/or environmental issues (Eliason & Fogel, 2015), many studies have studied weight and body mass index (BMI) in SGM populations. Unlike some health disparities that affect all LGBTQ populations fairly equally, such as depression, posttraumatic stress disorder, and suicide behaviors, weight is distributed differently across SGM subgroups.

Mason and Lewis (2015), in a study of over seven hundred coupled lesbians aged eighteen to thirty-five, found that women who were more "out" and had more depressive symptoms, lower consensus in their relationships, and higher levels of drinking were significantly more likely to be in the "overweight" or "obese" categories. This group also had lower educational levels and lower income, were more likely to have children, and were more likely to live in rural areas—all factors also associated with more health problems.

Data from the California Health Interview Survey (CHIS) were pooled over several years (2003 to 2012) to study how differences in BMI might be associated with chronic physical health disorders. For men (Stupplebeen, Eliason, LeBlanc, & Sanchez-Vasnaugh, 2019), with a sample size over 72,000, in general sexual minority men had lower BMI and more were "normal weight" (48 percent of sexual minority men vs. 33 percent of heterosexual men). However, when men were divided by the classifications often used in medical research—overweight and obese—sexual minority men with higher BMIs had a greater likelihood of reporting heart disease, hypertension, and type 2 diabetes than heterosexual men at the same weight classes. This was despite the fact that the sexual minority group had more white men, higher education levels, and higher income levels, which are generally associated with lower health risks. For example, an "obese" heterosexual man had 6.6 times higher odds of having diabetes than his "normal-weight" counterpart, whereas an "obese" sexual minority man was 13.5 times more likely to report diabetes than a "normal-weight" sexual minority man. This suggests that some subsets of sexual minority men have a greater likelihood of having both elevated weight and chronic health problems. This study was not designed to examine potential intersections of mental health and substance use with these physical health problems and did not collect information on adverse childhood experiences, stress, or experiences of discrimination. Minority stress may be associated with weight gain and accelerated progression of chronic disease for some men.

For women, previous research had consistently demonstrated a pattern of higher BMI in sexual minority women than heterosexual women (Eliason et al., 2015), yet the first studies of chronic physical disorders in the national data sets with sexual identity questions did not show a corresponding increase in heart disease, diabetes, hypertension, or cancer (Eliason, 2014). In the CHIS study (Eliason, Sanchez-Vasnaugh, & Stupplebeen, 2017), almost 98,000 heterosexual women and 2,800 sexual minority women were studied. In the overall sample, sexual minority women had a higher mean BMI (27.1) than heterosexual women (26.3), but sexual minority women were less likely to report diabetes (2.9 percent) than heterosexual women (4.8 percent). The only disorder that was higher in sexual minority women in the unadjusted sample was asthma (22 percent in sexual minority women vs. 14 percent in heterosexual women). However, when the sample was adjusted for age, ethnicity, income, and other factors, heterosexual and sexual minority women showed similar patterns of increased prevalence of diabetes, heart disease, and hypertension as weight increased. These studies cannot tell us whether elevated weight causes chronic health problems like diabetes, only that they are associated with each other in a similar fashion for sexual minority and heterosexual women, unlike the divergent pattern observed for men.

DISABILITY

As noted earlier in the chapter, many studies find higher rates of disability in SGM individuals. In one study of over 370 older sexual minority women, 31 percent had any disability and 25 percent had a physical disability. Women with physical disabilities were more likely to have a BMI of over 35 (64 percent) than nondisabled women (34 percent), and they reported poorer physical quality of life (Eliason, McElroy, Garbers, Radix, & Toms-Barker, 2017). In a subset of this study (Eliason, Martinson, & Carabez, 2015), where more health data were available, women with physical disabilities were more likely to have posttraumatic stress disorder, other anxiety disorders, drug dependence, chronic obstructive pulmonary disease, asthma, arthritis, and diabetes than nondisabled sexual minority women. Disabled sexual minority women had also experienced much more discrimination in their lives. In a cross-sectional study, no causal relationships can be explored, and the timing of adopting a sexual identity and developing a disability could not be examined.

MEDICAL VISITS IN SEXUAL MINORITY WOMEN

Valentine et al. (2015) studied the medical records of 341 sexual minority women who were patients at an urban LGBT community health clinic. They found that four syndemic indicators—childhood sexual abuse, intimate partner violence, substance use, and mental health disorders—were highly interrelated and affected healthcare utilization for both mental and physical health care visits and medical costs over a seven-year period. Of these syndemic indicators, 55 percent of the sample reported none of them, 21 percent had only one, 16 percent had two, and 8 percent had three or four. Although no physical health conditions were reported in this study, visits for medical services over the seven-year study period were as follows: no indicators, 8.8 visits; one indicator, 10.5 visits; two indicators, 15.3 visits;

three or four indicators, 19.8 visits. The study suggests that sexual minority women with mental health problems stemming from trauma were more likely to have physical health problems later.

Future Directions

One descriptive model that is useful in identifying the wide diversity of potential influences on health is the ecosocial model. With the individual nested in the center, circles of influences on the individual from interpersonal relationships, to local communities and institutions, to the broader societal-level policies and procedures can be mapped. SGM health can never be understand at the individual person level alone, and research that takes a broader view and/or puts their study into this context will further the field. Table 32.1 shows some of the influences on health suggested by the literature, and these factors need to be considered when studying whether and how mental and physical health problems overlap in some individuals.

Some particular issues that urgently need further exploration in SGM health disparities research include examining the role of adverse childhood events in the development of mental and physical health disorders. It is quite possible that SGM health disparities are concentrated in subsets of the population that have experienced such events. SGM research would benefit from including measures of adverse childhood events and, for both SGM and general population research on these events, from expanding the categories of childhood adversity to include experiencing stigma related to sexual and gender identities or expressions.

Second, as large-scale population health studies increasingly include items about SGM status, researchers will have access to larger sample sizes and greater statistical power to examine the role of intersectional marginalized identities. This may necessitate different analytic models that do not add one factor at a time but that can shed light on how stigma manifests differently depending on the type and number of marginalized identities. In the meantime, SGM advocacy groups need to continue to press governmental agencies and researchers to include both sexual and gender identity questions, and sexual behavior and gender expression questions when possible, on health surveys and on electronic medical records to maximize the possibility of tracking disorders singly and in combination and study their interactions with other marginalized identity categories.

There is a critical need for longitudinal studies and those that take age into account, since many chronic physical health disorders, such as cancer, heart disease, and type 2 diabetes, are much more age-related than mental health disorders such as depression. Any study of chronic physical conditions needs to be adjusted for age, but other developmental considerations that might affect health outcomes include the age of coming out (the younger the person, the fewer psychological resources they have and the greater the years of experiencing accumulated minority stress).

Table 32.1. Ecosocial Model of Health for SGM Populations

Level	Examples of Influences on Health
Individual (intrapersonal)	Adverse childhood experiences, genetics, intersecting identities, age of coming out or transitioning, developmental stage, psychological resources and coping, resilience, educational level, income level, residence, health insurance coverage, religiosity, risk behaviors (smoking, alcohol/drug use, risky sexual activities, high levels of stress), internalized oppression
Interpersonal	Family support or rejection, peer support, experiences of exclusion, invalidation, rejection, harassment, discrimination, or violence, types and level of social support, significant other support, presence of close social networks
Community	Neighborhood factors such as rates of hate crimes, safety, acceptance of SGM, inclusive churches, levels of racism, heterosexism, gender normativity in local leaders and communities; levels of pollution, crime; geographic location
Institutional	Presence of inclusive and welcoming climate in schools, healthcare institutions, churches, local agencies; healthcare providers' level of knowledge of SGM health; workplace climates and protections; presence of SGM-specific agencies, advocacy groups, social and recreational communities
Societal/Policy	State or federal laws; political campaigns; religious persecution at highest levels of religious organizations (pope, church doctrines); media coverage of SGM people

If minority stress continues to be the predominant theory for explaining health disparities, there needs to be more testing of the theoretical model to explain underlying mechanisms and a commitment to start adding direct measures of stress into health studies rather than using minority sexual, gender, or ethnic identities as the proxies for minority stress. Stress research in general proposes that adverse situations have an impact on both psychological state and physiological processes such as immune system impairments; hence, it makes sense that minority stress could cause both physical and mental health disorders. Studies that examine biological markers of stress reactions would be helpful—thus far, those studies have focused mostly on adolescents and young adults (e.g., Hatzenbuehler & McLaughlin, 2014). Syndemic and ecosocial models are also promising ways to expand the concept of how stress impacts health outcomes.

In conclusion, it is highly likely that mental and physical health disorders develop simultaneously or sequentially in populations that experience high levels of stress stemming from the stigma associated with marginalized identities, and from the accumulated stress of adverse childhood experiences. There is already considerable evidence of co-occurring mental health and substance use disorders in SGM populations, but less research has focused on whether chronic physical health disorders such as cardiovascular disease, cancer, and diabetes are also more common in SGM populations, and whether or how they are linked to minority stress and mental health disorders.

References

Austin, A., Herrick, H., & Proescholdbell, S. (2015). Adverse childhood experience related to poor adult health among lesbian, gay, and bisexual individuals. *American Journal of Public Health, 106*(2), 314–20.

Baral, S. D., Poteat, T., Strömdahl, S., Wirtz, A. L., Guadamuz, T. E., & Beyrer, C. (2013). Worldwide burden of HIV in transgender women: A systematic review and meta-analysis. *Lancet Infectious Diseases, 13*(3), 214–22.

Beach, L. B., Elasy, T. A., & Gonzales, G. (2018). Prevalence of self-reported diabetes by sexual orientation: Results from the 2015 Behavioral Risk Factor Surveillance System. *LGBT Health, 5*(2), 121–30.

Blosnich, J. R., Farmer, G. W., Lee, J. G. L., Silenzio, V. M. B., & Bowen, D. J. (2014). Health inequalities among sexual minority adults: Evidence from ten U.S. States, 2010. *American Journal of Preventive Medicine, 46*(4), 337–49. http://doi.org/10.1016/j.amepre.2013.11.010

Blosnich, J. R., Lee, J. G., Bossarte, R., & Silenzio, V. M. (2013). Asthma disparities and within-group differences in a national, probability sample of same-sex partnered adults. *American Journal of Public Health, 103*(9), e83–e87.

Boehmer, U., Miao, X., & Ozonoff, A. (2011). Cancer survivorship and sexual orientation. *Cancer, 117*(16), 3796–804.

Bowleg, L. (2012). The problem with the phrase women and minorities: intersectionality—an important theoretical framework for public health. *American Journal of Public Health, 102*(7), 1267–73.

Brennan, J., Kuhns, L. M., Johnson, A. K., Belzer, M., Wilson, E. C., & Garofalo, R. (2012). Syndemic theory and HIV-related risk among young transgender women: The role of multiple, co-occurring health problems and social marginalization. *American Journal of Public Health, 102*(9), 1751–7.

Centers for Disease Control and Prevention. (2013). HIV surveillance report: Diagnoses of HIV infection and AIDS in the United States and dependent areas, Vol. 25. http://www.cdc.gov/hiv/pdf/g-l/hiv_surveillance_report_vol_25.pdf

Clark, C. J., Borowsky, I. W., Salisbury, J., Usher, J., Spencer, R. A., Prsedworski, J., . . . Evenson-Rose, S. A. (2015). Disparities in long-term cardiovascular disease risk by sexual identity: The National Longitudinal Study of Adolescent to Adult Health. *Preventive Medicine, 76*, 26–30.

Cochran, S. D., & Mays, V. M. (2007). Physical health complaints among lesbians, gay men, and bisexual and homosexually experienced heterosexual individuals: Results from the California Quality of Life Survey. *American Journal of Public Health, 97*(1), 2048–55.

Coulter, R. W., Kenst, K. S., Bowen, D. J., & Scout. (2014). Research funded by the National Institutes of Health on the health of lesbian, gay, bisexual, and transgender populations. *American Journal of Public Health, 104*(2), e105–e112.

Coulter, R. W., Kinsky, S. M., Herrick, A. L., Stall, R. D., & Bauermeister, J. A. (2015). Evidence of syndemics and sexuality-related discrimination among young sexual-minority women. *LGBT Health, 2*(3), 250–7.

Dahlhamer, J. M., Galinsky, A. M., Joestl, S. S., & Ward, B. W. (2014). Sexual orientation in the 2013 National Health Interview Survey: A quality assessment. *Vital Health Statistics, 2*(169), 1–32.

Dahlhamer, J. M., Galinsky, A. M., Joestl, S. S., & Ward, B. W. (2016). Barriers to health care among adults identifying as sexual minorities: A U.S. national study. *American Journal of Public Health 106*(6), 1116–22.

Diamond, L. M. (2008). *Sexual fluidity.* Cambridge, MA: Harvard University Press.

Drabble, L., Trocki, K., Hughes, T. L., Korcha, R. A., & Lown, A. (2013). Sexual orientation differences in the relationship between victimization and hazardous drinking among women in the National Alcohol Survey. *Psychology of Addictive Behavior, 27*, 639–48.

Drabble, L., Veldhuis, C. B., Riley, B. B., Rostosky, S., & Hughes, T. L. (2017). Relationship of religiosity and spirituality to hazardous drinking, drug use, and depression among sexual minority women. *Journal of Homosexuality, 65*(13), 1734–57.

Driskill, Q. L. (2010). Doubleweaving two-spirit critiques: Building alliances between native and queer studies. *GLQ: A Journal of Lesbian and Gay Studies, 16*(1–2), 69–92.

Druss, B. G., & Walker, E. R., (2011). Mental disorders and medical comorbidity. *The Synthesis Project: Research Synthesis Report, 21*, 1–26.

Dyer, T. P., Shoptaw, S., Guadamuz, T. E., Plankey, M., Kao, U., Ostrow, D., . . . Stall, R. (2012). Application of syndemic theory to black men who have sex with men in the

Multicenter AIDS Cohort Study. *Journal of Urban Health, 89*(4), 697–708.

Eliason, M. J. (2014). Chronic physical health problems in sexual minority women: A review of the literature. *LGBT Health, 1*(3), 259–68.

Eliason, M. J., Burke, A., Van Olphen, J., & Howell, R. (2011). Interactions of sexual identity, sex/gender, and religious/spiritual beliefs on college student substance use. *Sexuality Research & Social Policy, 8*, 117–25.

Eliason, M. J., & Chinn, P. L. (2018). *LGBTQ cultures: What health care professionals need to know about sexual and gender diversity*. Philadelphia, PA: Wolters Kluwer.

Eliason, M. J., & Fogel, S. C. (2015). An ecological framework for sexual minority women's health: Factors associated with greater body mass. *Journal of Homosexuality, 62*(7), 845–82.

Eliason, M. J., Ingraham, N., Fogel, S. C., McElroy, J. A., Lorvick, J., Mauery, D. R., & Haynes, S. (2015). A systematic review of the literature on weight in sexual minority women. *Women's Health Issues, 25*(2), 162–75.

Eliason, M. J., Martinson, M., & Carabez, R. M. (2015). Disability among sexual minority women: Descriptive data from an invisible population. *LGBT Health, 2(*2), 113–20.

Eliason, M. J., McElroy, J. A., Garbers, S., Radix, A., & Toms-Barker, L. (2017). Comparing women with and without disabilities in five-site "Healthy Weight" interventions for lesbian/bisexual women over 40. *Disability and Health Journal, 10*, 271–8.

Eliason, M. J., Radix, A., McElroy, J. M., Garbers, S., & Haynes, S. (2016). The "something else" of sexual orientation: Measuring sexual orientation identities of older lesbian and bisexual women using National Health Interview Survey (NHIS) questions. *Women's Health Issues*, 26(S1), 71–80.

Eliason, M. J., Sanchez-Vasnaugh, E. V., & Stupplebeen, D. (2017). Relationships between weight and health outcomes in women by sexual orientation. *Women's Health Issues, 27(*5), 600–6. doi:10.1016/j.whi2017.04.004

Eliason, M. J., & Streed, C. G., Jr., (2017). Choosing "something else" as a sexual identity: Evaluating response options on the NHIS. *LGBT Health, 4*(5), 376–9. doi: 10.1089/lgbt.2016.0206

Everett, B., & Mollborn, S. (2013). Differences in hypertension by sexual orientation among U.S. young adults. *Journal of Community Health, 38*, 588–96.

Feldman, J., Brown, G. R., Deutsch, M. B., Hembree, W., Meyer, W., Meyer-Bahlburg, H. F., . . . Safer, J. D. (2016). Priorities for transgender medical and health care research. *Current Opinion in Endocrinology, Diabetes, and Obesity, 23*(2), 180–7.

Fredriksen-Goldsen, K. I., Cook-Daniels, L., Kim, H. J., Erosheva, E. A., Emlet, C. A., Hoy-Ellis, C. P., . . . Muraco, A. (2013b). Physical and mental health of transgender older adults: An at-risk and underserved population. *The Gerontologist, 54*(3), 488–500.

Fredriksen-Goldsen, K. I., Kim, H. J., Barkan, S. E., Muraco, A., & Hoy-Ellis, C. P. (2013a). Health disparities among lesbian, gay, and bisexual older adults: Results from a population-based study. *American Journal of Public Health, 103*(10), 1802–9.

Fredriksen-Goldsen, K. I., Kim, H. J., Emlet, C. A., Muraco, A., Erosheva, E. A., Hoy-Ellis, C. P., & Petry, H. (2011). *The aging and health report: Disparities and resilience among LGBT older adults*. Seattle, WA: Institute for Multigenerational Health.

Friedman, M. S., Marshal, M. P., Guadamuz, T. E., Wei, C., Wong, C. F., Saewyc, E. M., & Stall, R. (2011). A meta-analysis of disparities in childhood sexual abuse, parental physical abuse, and peer victimization among sexual minority and sexual nonminority individuals. *American Journal of Public Health, 101*(8), 1481–94. http://doi.org/10.2105/AJPH.2009.190009

Friedman, M. S., Marshal, M. P., Stall, R., Cheong, J., & Wright, E. R. (2008). Gay-related development, early abuse and adult health outcomes among gay men. *AIDS Behavior, 12*(6), 891–902.

Frost, D. M., LeBlanc, A. J., de Vries, B., Alston-Stepnitz, E., Stephenson, R., & Woodyatt, C. (2017). Couple-level minority stress: An examination of same-sex couples' unique experiences. *Journal of Health and Social Behavior, 58*(4), 455–72.

Garland-Forshee, R. Y., Fiala, S. C., Ngo, D. L., & Moseley, K. (2014). Sexual orientation and sex differences in adult chronic conditions, health risk factors, and protective health practices, Oregon, 2005–2008. *Preventing Chronic Disease, 11*, E136.

GenIUSS Group. (2014). Best practices for asking questions to identify transgender and other gender minority respondents on population-based surveys. https://williamsinstitute.law.ucla.edu/research/census-lgbt-demographics-studies/geniuss-report-sept-2014/

Gilbert, L., Raj, A., Hien, D., Stockman, J., Terlikbayeva, A., & Wyatt, G. (2015). Targeting the SAVA (substance abuse, violence, and AIDS) syndemic among women and girls: A global review of epidemiology and integrated interventions. *Journal of AIDS, 69*(2), S118.

Gonzales, G., & Henning-Smith, C. (2015). Disparities in health and disability among older adults in same-sex cohabiting relationships. *Journal of Aging and Health, 27*(3), 432–53.

Gonzales, G., & Zinone, R. (2018). Cancer diagnoses among lesbian, gay, and bisexual adults: Results from the 2013–2016 National Health Interview Survey, *Cancer Causes & Control*, 29(9), 845–54. doi:10.1007/s10552-018-1060-x

Harb, C. Y., Pass, L. E., De Soriano, I. C., Zwick, A., & Gilbert, P. A. (2019). Motivators and barriers to accessing sexual health care services for transgender/genderqueer individuals assigned female sex at birth. *Transgender Health, 4*(1), 58–67.

Hart, T. A., Noor, S. W., Adam, B. D., Vernon, J. R. Brenna, D. J., Gartner, S., . . . Myers, T. (2017). Number of psychosocial strengths predicts reduced HIV sexual risk behaviors above and beyond syndemic problems among gay and bisexual men. *AIDS Behavior, 21*(10), 3035–46.

Hatzenbuehler, M. L., & McLaughlin, K. A. (2014). Structural stigma and hypothalamic-pituitary-adrenal axis reactivity in LGB young adults. *Annals of Behavioral Medicine, 47*(1), 39–47.

Hatzenbuehler, M. L., Slopen, N., & McLaughlin, K. A. (2014). Stressful life events, sexual orientation, and cardiometabolic risk among young adults in the United States. *Health Psychology, 33*, 1185–94.

Heck, J. E., & Jacobson, J. S. (2006). Asthma diagnosis among individuals in same-sex relationships. *Journal of Asthma, 43*(8), 579–84.

Herbst, J. H., Jacobs, E. D., Finlayson, T. J., McKleroy, V. S., Neumann, M. S., Crepaz, N., & HIV/AIDS Prevention Research Synthesis Team. (2008). Estimating HIV prevalence and risk behaviors of transgender persons in the United States: A systematic review. *AIDS and Behavior, 12*(1), 1–17. http://doi.org/10.1007/s10461-007-9299-3

Herman, J. L., Wilson, B. D., & Becker, T. (October 2017). Demographic and health characteristics of transgender adults in California: Findings from the 2015–2016 California Health Interview Survey. *Policy Brief (UCLA Center for Health Policy Research)*, (8), 1–10.

Hughes, K., Bellis, M. A., Hardcastle, K. A., Sethi, D., Butchart, A., Mikton, C., . . . Dunne, M. P. (2017). The effect of multiple adverse childhood experiences on health: A systematic review and meta-analysis. *Lancet Public Health*, *2*(8), e356–e366.

Institute of Medicine. (2011). *The health of lesbian, gay, bisexual, and transgender people: Building a foundation for better understanding*. Washington, DC: National Academies Press. http://www.iom.edu/Reports/2011/The-Health-of-Lesbian-Gay-Bisexual-and-Transgender-People.aspx

Johnson, T. P., Hughes, T. L., Cho, Y. I., Wilsnack, S. C., Aranda, F., & Szalacha, L. A. (2013). Hazardous drinking, depression, and anxiety among sexual-minority women: Self-medication or impaired functioning? *Journal of Studies on Alcohol and Drugs*, *74*(4), 565–75.

Jordan-Young, R. M. (2010). *Brain storm: The flaws in the science of sex differences*. Cambridge, MA: Harvard University Press.

Kalmakis, K. A., & Chandler, G. E. (2015). Health consequences of adverse childhood experiences: A systematic review. *Journal of the American Association of Nurse Practitioners*, *27*(8), 457–65.

King, M., Semlyen, J., Tai, S. S., Killaspy, H., Osborn, D., Popelyuk, D., & Nazareth, I. (2008). A systematic review of mental disorder, suicide, and deliberate self-harm in lesbian, gay and bisexual people. *BMC Psychiatry*, *8*, 70. http://doi.org/10.1186/1471-244X-8-70

Koenig, H. G., McCullough, M., & Larson, D. B. (2001). *Handbook of religion and health: A century of research reviewed*. New York, NY: Oxford University Press.

Kurtz, S. P., Buttram, M. E., Surratt, H. L., & Stall, R. D. (2012). Resilience, syndemic factors, and serosorting behaviors among HIV-positive and HIV-negative substance-using MSM. *AIDS Education and Prevention*, *24*(3), 193–205.

Kushner, M. G. (2014). Seventy-five years of comorbidity research. *Journal of Studies on Alcohol & Drugs, Supplement 17*, 50–8.

Lewis, R. J., Derlega, V. J., Clarke, E. G., & Kuang, J. C. (2006). Stigma consciousness, social constraints, and lesbian well-being. *Journal of Counseling Psychology*, *53*(1), 48.

Lick, D. J., Durso, L. E., & Johnson, K. L. (2013). Minority stress and physical health among sexual minorities. *Perspectives on Psychological Science*, *8*, 521–48.

Liu, H., Chen, I.-C., Wilkinson, L., Pearson, J., & Zhang, Y. (2019). Sexual orientation and diabetes during the transition to adulthood. *LGBT Health*, *6*(5), 227–34. doi.org/10/1089/lgbt2018.0153

Logie, C. H., Want, Y., Marcus, N., Levermore, K., Jones, N., Ellis, T., & Bryan, N. (2019). Syndemic experiences, protective factors, and HIV vulnerabilities among lesbian, gay, bisexual and transgender persons in Jamaica. *AIDS & Behavior*, *23*(6), 1530–40. doi.org/10.1007/s10461-018-2377-x

Lunn, M., Cui, W., Zack, M. M., Thompson, W. W., Blank, M. B., & Yehia, B. R. (2017). Sociodemographic characteristics and health outcomes among lesbian, gay, and bisexual U.S. adults using Healthy People 2020 leading health indicators. *LGBT Health*, *4*(4), 283–94.

Mason, T. B., & Lewis, R. J. (2015). Minority stress, depression, relationship quality, and alcohol use: Associations with overweight and obesity among partnered young adult lesbians. *LGBT Health*, *2*(4), 333–40.

Matthews, A. K., Hughes, T. L., Osterman, G. P., & Kodl, M. M. (2005). Complementary medicine practices in a community-based sample of lesbian and heterosexual women. *Health Care for Women International*, *26*(5), 430–47.

Meyer, I. H. (2013). Prejudice, social stress, and mental health in lesbian, gay, and bisexual populations: Conceptual issues and research evidence. *Psychology of Sexual Orientation and Gender Diversity*, *1-S*, 3–26. http://doi.org/http://dx.doi.org/10.1037/2329-0382.1.S.3

Meyer, I. H., Brown, T. N., Herman, J. L., Reisner, S. L., & Bockting, W. O. (2017). Demographic characteristics and health status of transgender adults in select US regions: Behavioral Risk Factor Surveillance System, 2014. *American Journal of Public Health*, *107*(4), 582–9.

Miller, K., & Ryan, J. M. (2011). *Design, development, and testing of the NHIS sexual identity question*. Washington, DC: National Center for Health Statistics, Office of Research and Methodology, Questionnaire Design Research Laboratory.

Mustanski, B., Garofalo, R., Herrick, A., & Donenberg, G. (2007). Psychosocial health problems increase risk for HIV among urban young men who have sex with men: Preliminary evidence of a syndemic in need of attention. *Annals of Behavioral Medicine*, *34*(1), 37–45.

Parsons, J. T., Grov, C., & Golub, S. A. (2012). Sexual compulsivity, co-occurring psychosocial health problems, and HIV risk among gay and bisexual men: Further evidence of a syndemic. *American Journal of Public Health*, *102*(1), 156–62.

Patterson, J. G., Jabson, J. M., & Bowen, D. J. (2017). Measuring sexual and gender minority populations in health surveillance. *LGBT Health*, *4*(2), 82–105.

Quinn, G. P., Sanchez, J. A., Sutton, S. K., Vadaparampil, S. T., Nguyen, G. T., Green, B. L., . . . Schabath, M. B. (2015). Cancer and lesbian, gay, bisexual, transgender/transsexual, and queer/questioning (LGBTQ) populations. *CA: A Cancer Journal for Clinicians*, *65*(5), 384–400.

Robbins, H. A., Pfeiffer, R. M., Shiels, M. S., Li, J., Hall, H. I., & Engels, E. A. (2015). Excess cancers among HIV-infected people in the United States. *Journal of National Cancer Institute*, *107*(4). doi:10.1093/jnci/dju503

Rowniak, S., & Chesla, C. (2013). Coming out for a third time: Transmen, sexual orientation, and identity. *Archives of Sexual Behavior*, *42*(3), 449–61.

Schneeberger, A. R., Dietal, M. F., Muenzenmaier, K. H., Huber, C. G., & Lange, U. E. (2014). Stressful childhood experiences and health outcomes in sexual minority populations: A systematic review. *Social Psychiatry and Psychiatric Epidemiology*, *49*, 1427–45.

Sheppard, M., & Mayo Jr, J. B. (2013). The social construction of gender and sexuality: Learning from two spirit traditions. *Social Studies*, *104*(6), 259–70.

Simoni, J. M., Smith, L., Oost, K. M., Lehavot, K., & Fredriksen-Goldsen, K. (2017). Disparities in physical health conditions among lesbian and bisexual women: A systematic review of population-based studies. *Journal of Homosexuality*, *64*(1), 32–44.

Singer, M., & Clair, S. (2003). Syndemics and public health: Reconceptualizing disease in bio-social context. *Medical Anthropology Quarterly*, *17*(4), 423–41.

Siorda, C. (2015). Disability estimates between same- and different-sex couples: Microdata from the American

Community Survey (2009–2011). *Sex and Disability, 33*(1), 107–21.

Slater, M. E., Godette, D., Huang, B., Ruan, W. J., & Kerridge, B. T. (2017). Sexual orientation-based discrimination, excessive alcohol use, and substance use disorders among sexual minority adults. *LGBT Health, 4*(5), 337–44.

Stall, R., Mills, T. C., Williamson, J., Hart, T., Greenwood, G., Paul, J., . . . Catania, J. A. (2003). Association of co-occurring psychosocial health problems and increased vulnerability to HIV/AIDS among urban men who have sex with men. *American Journal of Public Health, 93*(6), 939–42.

Streed, C. G., Jr, McCarthy, E. P., & Haas, J. S. (2018). Self-reported physical and mental health of gender nonconforming transgender adults in the United States. *LGBT Health, 5*(7), 443–8.

Stupplebeen, D., Eliason, M. J., LeBlanc, A. J., & Sanchez-Vasnaugh, E. V. (2019). Differential influence of weight status on chronic diseases by reported sexual orientation identity. *LGBT Health, 6*(3), 126–37.

Thapa, A., Cohen, J., Higgins-D'Alessandro, A., & Guffey, S. (August 2012). *School climate research summary, 2012.* New York, NY: National School Climate Center, School Climate Brief No. 3.

Valdiserri, R. O., Holtgrave, D. R., Poteat, T. C., & Beyrer, C. (2019). Unraveling health disparities among sexual and gender minorities: A commentary on the persistent impact of stigma. *Journal of Homosexuality*, 66(5), 571–89, doi:10.1080/00918369.2017.1422944

Valentine, S. E., Elsesser, S., Grasso, C., Safren, S. A., Bradford, J. B., Mereish, E., & O'Cleirigh, C. (2015). The predictive syndemic effect of multiple psychosocial problems on health care costs and utilization among sexual minority women. *Journal of Urban Health, 92*(6), 1092–104.

VanKim, N. A., Erickson, D. J., Eisenberg, M. E., Lust, K., Rosser, B. R., & Laska, M. N. (2014). Weight-related disparities for transgender college students. *Health Behavior and Policy Review, 1*(2), 161–71.

Velho, I., Fighera, T. M., Ziegelmann, P. K., & Spritzer, P. M. (2017). Effects of testosterone therapy on BMI, blood pressure, and laboratory profile of transgender men: A systematic review. *Andrology, 5*(5), 881–8.

Vrangalova, Z., & Savin-Williams, R. C. (2012). Mostly heterosexual and mostly gay/lesbian: Evidence for new sexual orientation identities. *Archives of Sexual Behavior, 41*, 85–101.

Walker, E. R., McGee, R. E., & Druss, B. G. (2015). Mortality in mental disorders and global disease burden implications: a systematic review and meta-analysis. *JAMA Psychiatry, 72*, 334–41.

Ward, B. W., Dahlhamer, J. M., Galinsky, A. M., & Joestl, S. S. (15 July 2014). Sexual orientation and health among U.S. adults: National Health Interview Survey, 2013. *National Health Statistics Report, 77*, 1–10.

Wierckx, K., Elaut, E., Declercq, E., Heylens, G., De Cuypere, G., Taes, Y., . . . T'Sjoen, G. (2013). Prevalence of cardiovascular disease and cancer during cross-sex hormone therapy in a large cohort of trans persons: A case–control study. *European Journal of Endocrinology, 169*, 471–8.

Wilson, P. A., Nanin, J., Amesty, S., Wallace, S., Cherenack, E. M., & Fullilove, R. (2014). Using syndemic theory to understand vulnerability to HIV infection among Black and Latino men in New York City. *Journal of Urban Health, 91*(5), 983–98.

Wingo, E., Ingraham, N., & Roberts, S. C. (2018). Reproductive health care priorities and barriers to effective care for LGBTQ people assigned female at birth: A qualitative study. *Women's Health Issues, 28*(4), 350–7.

Witten, T. M. (2014). End of life, chronic illness, and trans-identities. *Journal of Social Work in End-of-Life & Palliative Care, 10*, 34–58.

CHAPTER

33 HIV/AIDS and Mental Health among Sexual and Gender Minority Populations

Molly Silvestrini, Colleen C. Hoff, Y. Darin Witkovic, *and* Crystal Madriles

Abstract

HIV/AIDS is a disease that significantly affects the health outcomes of sexual and gender minorities (SGMs) and the LGBTQ community globally. HIV is frequently associated with mental health issues among many vulnerable populations, such as depression, anxiety, stigma, substance abuse, and discrimination. In addition, risk factors for HIV acquisition often include mental health problems, lack of social support, and experiences of stigma and discrimination. This chapter focuses on the history of HIV/AIDS, current HIV health disparities in SGM communities in the United States and globally, mental health among HIV-positive vulnerable and understudied populations, and future directions for the improvement of HIV prevention programs and mental health interventions. Understudied populations include women who have sex with women, transgender men, and SGM belonging to racial and ethnic minority groups. This chapter aims to summarize the interaction of HIV/AIDS and mental health over the past two decades in order to demonstrate the importance of this subject in current research.

Keywords: HIV, AIDS, mental health, sexuality, depression, anxiety, MSM, SGM

Introduction and History of HIV/AIDS

Human immunodeficiency virus (HIV) is a virus that invades the CD4 cells, a type of T cell that assists in suppressing infections, diseases, and cancers by interrupting their reproduction process. The most advanced stage of HIV infection is acquired immunodeficiency syndrome (AIDS). An AIDS diagnosis indicates a critically lowered immune system and a CD4 cell count below 200 cells per cubic millimeter (Centers for Disease Control [CDC], 1992). The medical community recognized the cases of AIDS in 1981 with immunosuppression responses in homosexual men in Los Angeles and New York City (CDC, 1981). HIV is transmitted through blood, specifically with sexual contact, by sharing needles to inject drugs, and through an HIV-positive mother to baby during pregnancy, birth, or breastfeeding (CDC, 2018). Although scientists have developed antiretroviral medications to inhibit the virus, mutations often occur that can enable HIV to thrive despite the presence of medication in the body. However, with proper medical care and adherence to antiretroviral medications, HIV can be controlled and the medications can increase life expectancy for an individual living with HIV. Within the United States, AIDS is increasingly viewed as a chronic condition rather than a terminal illness; however, there is no cure for HIV/AIDS, and people still die from complications of AIDS. Challenges to HIV prevention, care, and treatment among low-income communities may include lack of financial resources, lack of education about HIV prevention, and limited access to quality healthcare.

Because the first identified patients were homosexual men during the AIDS epidemic in the early 1980s, a connection to the gay community seemed evident. During this time, HIV/AIDS was known as gay-related immunodeficiency (GRID; Gottlieb, Schroff, Fligiel, Fahey, & Saxon, 1982) and colloquially as "gay cancer" before it was labeled AIDS. (We will use the term *HIV/AIDS* for the duration of this chapter given that one can be infected with

HIV without having an AIDS diagnosis.) The medical community worked tirelessly to investigate what caused HIV/AIDS and how it was transmitted. In the early days of the epidemic, new information and research was languidly developed, making it difficult to know what was safe and what should be done to prevent becoming infected. The discovery of how the virus was transmitted was key to beginning prevention efforts.

Despite the severe health outcomes associated with the development of HIV/AIDS, government support to address HIV/AIDS as a public health crisis was not immediate. Although HIV/AIDS had entered public awareness in the United States by mid-1983, public opinion polls at the time showed relatively little concern that AIDS would reach epidemic proportions (Cook & Colby, 1992). A 1985 poll revealed that 50 percent of people in the United States were in favor of quarantining people with HIV/AIDS, 48 percent supported issuing special identification, and 15 percent wanted infected individuals to be tattooed so they could be identified (Associated Press, 1994). Initially, HIV/AIDS was ignored by the public and government agencies due to the perception that it was a "gay disease" (Padgug & Oppenheimer, 1992). As a result, gay men infected with HIV/AIDS were stigmatized, not given treatments, and faced a very high likelihood of dying. Moreover, gay men who survived the HIV/AIDS epidemic in the United States are uniquely impacted because they are likely to have experienced mass deaths in their social circles (Hammack, Frost, Meyer, & Pletta, 2018). A U.S. study of HIV-positive participants reported an average of 43 friends and significant others who died from AIDS-related complications (Sikkema et al., 2006). Six years after the discovery of AIDS, the pharmaceutical company Burroughs Wellcome gained approval from the U.S. Food and Drug Administration (FDA) to distribute azidothymidine (AZT). It was the first antiretroviral drug to treat HIV/AIDS. AZT gained the fastest approval in FDA history, but it cost $10,000 a year to take, more than any other drug in history at that time.

In 1996, highly active antiretroviral therapy (HAART) became the new standard of HIV/AIDS care. It largely consists of a minimum of two active drugs from two classes to manage HIV and drug resistance. The availability of HAART changed the disease progression so that many were able to live with HIV/AIDS for years rather than die from it within months (Torres & Barr, 1997). Despite this groundbreaking shift in the epidemic, the disease continues to represent a health disparity for gay men, sexual and gender minorities (SGMs), and the LGBTQ community globally (Halkitis, Wolitski, & Millet, 2013).

HIV infection is frequently associated with mental health issues among many vulnerable populations. This chapter summarizes the research that has been conducted on the mental health issues associated with HIV/AIDS since the availability of HAART in 1996. SGM populations continue to be disproportionately affected by the disease worldwide, with high rates of HIV prevalence and risk behaviors. Consequently, it is vital to understand the healthcare needs of this population in order to improve quality of life and limit HIV infection, as well as develop informed HIV prevention and intervention programs.

HIV/AIDS and Men Who Have Sex with Men Outside the United States

Gay, bisexual, and other diversely identified men who have sex with men (MSM) continue to be the most affected by HIV/AIDS consistently across both developed and developing countries (Saavedra, Izazola-Licea, & Beyrer, 2008). HIV and AIDS in China emerged differently than in the United States. The virus likely entered China in 1985 but became apparent during the first outbreak of HIV among injection drug users between the rural borders of China and Myanmar in 1989 (Wu, Rou, & Cui, 2004). Thus, movement occurred from rural to urban areas. From 1985 to 1996, six out of twenty-eight cases of HIV/AIDS confirmed by a major hospital in Beijing occurred in MSM (Zhang, Hu, Li, Shi, & Liu, 2002). Today, Chinese MSM are at higher risk for HIV infection with rates due to risky sexual behaviors (Zhang & Chu, 2005) and represent the second-highest HIV risk group after injection drug users (Zhang et al., 2002). Low- and middle-income countries in Asia (e.g., Thailand), Africa (e.g., Dakar, Senegal), Latin America (e.g., Peru), and the former Soviet Union are experiencing emerging HIV epidemics among MSM exacerbated by homophobia, discrimination, and criminalization of same-sex behavior (Baral, Sifakis, Cleghorn, & Beyrer, 2007; Saavedra et al., 2008).

HIV/AIDS and Mental Health in MSM and Men Who Have Sex with Men and Women

The AIDS epidemic continues to affect the mental health of gay and bisexual men today. Current research suggests that HIV status is associated with severe mental health risks, especially for SGM groups. Interpersonal violence and mental health problems play a significant role in the health of people living with HIV/AIDS (Pantalone, Hessler, & Simoni, 2010). In a study focusing on the mental health concerns of gay and bisexual men, researchers found that the mental health problems of HIV-positive MSM and men who have sex with men and women (MSMW) presenting for treatment are similar to the types of problems reported in general epidemiological studies of psychiatric disorders (Berg, Mimiaga, & Safren, 2004). Examining client-provided information about persisting problems, psychosocial history, and clinician assessments allows researchers to gain insight into the mental health care needs of this population.

Stigma and discrimination are common experiences among people with HIV/AIDS, especially those who are also from an SGM. Internalized homophobia and HIV stigma are significantly related to psychological distress for HIV-positive gay men (Boone, Cook, & Wilson, 2016), and internalized stigma is significantly associated with negative mental health and sexual behavior outcomes (Rendina et al., 2017). Experiences of stigma and discrimination for having HIV/AIDS are a risk factor for elevated mental health concerns and are associated with anxiety, depression, and substance abuse (Heywood & Lyons, 2016). Perceived stress and discrimination among people living with HIV is associated with severe mental health problems and risk behaviors, which highlights the importance of reducing discrimination toward this population (Su et al., 2013). In addition, situational experiences of HIV stigma are associated with increased levels of anger and emotion dysregulation in gay and bisexual men (Rendina, Millar, & Parsons, 2018). Moreover, those experiencing negative mental health symptoms also reported negative physical heath factors such as lower T-cell and CD4 counts (Boone et al., 2016; Heywood & Lyons, 2016). Even among HIV-negative individuals, stigma can play an important role in mental health; associations between HIV status and depression among HIV-negative MSM emphasize the significance of symbolic stigma (Logie, Newman, Chakrapani, & Shunmugam, 2012).

HIV stigma, homophobia, and discrimination may help to explain why MSM and MSMW experience negative mental health outcomes at such high rates. Research suggests that compared to the general population, the prevalence of clinical depression is disproportionately high among gay and bisexual men (King et al., 2008) and two to four times higher in HIV-infected individuals (Ciesla & Roberts, 2001). Depression, the most common neuropsychiatric complication in HIV-infected patients, can significantly limit the quality of life of people living with HIV (Nanni, Caruso, Mitchell, Meggiolaro, & Grassi, 2015). In a study of HIV-positive gay and bisexual men, depression and anxiety were identified as the most prevalent persisting problems in the cohort (Berg et al., 2004). Research suggests that a key protective factor against mental health problems for HIV-positive gay men is access to social support, particularly emotional support (Heywood & Lyons, 2016). Because gay and bisexual men face unique challenges compared to their heterosexual counterparts, additional research and services are needed to address their mental health disparities. Findings suggest that HIV care providers should assess mental health issues for those living with HIV/AIDS in order to make quality care available for this population.

Although gay and bisexual men are often grouped together in studies focusing on HIV, MSMW have health disparities compared to MSM. MSMW exhibit HIV-related health disparities at significantly higher rates than their MSM counterparts (Friedman et al., 2015) and are more likely to be depressed and/or suicidal (Marshal et al., 2011). MSMW who are survivors of childhood sexual abuse and have recent traumatic stress or depression have an even higher risk of HIV transmission (Williams et al., 2013). Further research focusing on the health disparities of MSMW and HIV rates is needed in order to fully examine this population's unique challenges.

HIV in Transgender Women

Transgender women, particularly transgender women of color, are infected with HIV at disproportionate rates compared to the general public and are a highly vulnerable and marginalized population in the United States (Nemoto, Operario, Keatley, Han, & Soma, 2004). The prevalence of HIV among transgender women is anywhere from 11 to 78 percent (Clements-Nolle, Marx, Guzman, & Katz, 2001; Elifson et al., 1993; Gatarri, Spizzichino, Valenzi, Zaccarelli, & Rezza, 1992; Kenagy, 2002; Modan et al., 1992; Simon, Reback, & Bemis, 2000). Despite these alarming HIV rates, there is little research on the risk factors associated with HIV-positive transgender women. A meta-analysis for studies from 1990 to 2003 found that transgender women in the United States had an 11.8 percent prevalence rate for HIV (Herbst et al., 2008). Among transgender women and transgender women sex workers analyzed in twenty-five international studies from 1980 to 2007, the HIV prevalence was approximately 27.3 percent for transgender women sex workers and 14.7 percent for transgender women not identified as sex workers (Operario, Soma, & Underhill, 2008). A systematic review of this topic found that transgender women represent a high-burden population for HIV and need prevention, treatment, and care services (Baral et al., 2013). Despite these outcomes, transgender women have a low perceived risk of HIV acquisition and engage in high-risk activities such as unprotected receptive anal sex, sex under the influence of alcohol and drugs, and sex work (Nemoto, Operario, Keatley, Han, & Soma, 2004; Sausa, Keatley, & Operario, 2007).

Transgender women represent not only one of the highest-risk groups for HIV but also one of the highest at risk for substance abuse and mental health problems, including suicide and suicide ideation (Clements-Nolle et al., 2001; Kellogg, Clements-Nolle, Dilley, Katz, & McFarland, 2001; Nemoto, Operario, Keatley, & Villegas, 2004). Factors associated with the high prevalence for HIV/AIDS among transgender women include engaging in casual sex with more than one partner to assert their gender identity, as well as using substances to cope with stresses associated with sex work and depression (Nemoto, Operario, Keatley, & Villegas, 2004). Transgender women may be more likely to use substances to cope with the stress of sex work and the stigma of being transgender (Nemoto, Operario, Keatley, & Villegas, 2004; Sausa et al., 2007). Mental and social issues such as low self-esteem, intimate partner violence, and victimization, as well as a history of sex work and incarceration, are all associated with a high risk and high prevalence among transgender women. Studies have shown that stigma and discrimination increase transgender women's need for affirmation and validation as women from their sexual partners, which may increase the likelihood of them engaging in risky sexual behavior and reducing condom use (Melendez & Pinto, 2007). A systematic review of HIV-positive transgender women found that this population experiences unique vulnerability to HIV that can be attributed to intersecting factors that influence the HIV treatment and care continuum. The study found that stigma and discrimination, lack of social and legal recognition of their affirmed gender, and exclusion from employment and educational opportunities are factors that increase the risk of HIV in transgender women worldwide (Poteat, Reisner, & Radix, 2014). Finally, gender abuse is a central pillar for HIV exposure, especially for adolescent transgender women, which indicates a need for interventions that focus on psychological impacts and outline ways to reduce and educate society on gender abuse (Nuttbrock et al., 2013).

Research suggests that being younger, using hormones, having some type of gender-confirming procedure, and being Black significantly increase one's likelihood of being engaged in sex work (Sevelius, Reznick, Hart, & Schwarcz, 2009). Transgender women of color particularly are at risk, as they are severely marginalized based on both gender identity and racial identity. Black transgender women experience transphobia and racism at very high rates and may be more vulnerable to employment discrimination and other forms of violence and harassment, contributing to their need to engage in survival sex (Sevelius et al., 2009). This indicates a need for HIV prevention programs and interventions that specifically address issues of race and ethnicity in order to improve outcomes for transgender women of color (Wilson & Miller, 2003).

Because transgender women, particularly transgender women of color, are a high-risk and vulnerable population, there must be special attention paid to their specific issues in treatment interventions. Issues of substance abuse, sex work, gender affirmation, and intersections of transphobia and racism must be addressed in HIV prevention programs for transgender women (Oggins & Eichenbaum, 2002; Sevelius et al., 2009). Fortunately, many HIV prevention agencies that work diligently to serve transgender women do so across race/ethnicities and incorporate intersectional treatment frameworks (Edwards, Fisher, & Reynolds, 2007).

Mental Health Impact of Community-Level Factors Associated with HIV/AIDS

While HIV/AIDS can have detrimental effects on the health and survival of HIV-positive individuals, the disease also has significant implications for HIV-negative people living in communities with high rates of infection. The gay male communities in the United States have experienced the most AIDS-related deaths over the longest period of time; consequently, the burden of grief for these communities is noteworthy and remains largely unaddressed in clinical practice (Mallinson, 1999). Many members of these communities have experienced multiple, repetitive, and sustained losses of persons in their social network to HIV/AIDS (Sikkema, Kochman, DiFranceisco, Kelly, & Hoffmann, 2003). In addition, AIDS is a stigmatized disease that can be associated with homosexuality, sexual promiscuity, and illicit drug use. The effects of AIDS-related loss can result in significant emotional, psychological, physical, and spiritual challenges that must be addressed in the practice, research, and education of HIV/AIDS (Mallinson, 1999). A study examining AIDS-related grief, psychological distress, and coping of individuals affected by HIV found that participants exhibited elevated scores on measures of grief reaction and psychological distress, including depressive symptoms, anxiety, and traumatic stress related to their losses (Sikkema et al., 2003).

The high numbers of AIDS-related deaths in the gay male community may increase rates of survivor guilt, which is a major psychosocial stressor. In research on HIV/AIDS, survivor guilt has been noted among seronegative gay men, children of parents who have died from AIDS, and AIDS caregivers (Brashers et al., 1999). In a study on HIV-positive individuals who may survive due to dramatic treatment developments, participants reported guilt because they have lived longer than friends and loved ones (Brashers et al., 1999). Research indicates that individuals from communities significantly affected by HIV/AIDS may need counseling and services to help them deal with issues such as stigmatizing reactions or rejection from others, survivor guilt, and diminished quality of life (Brashers et al., 1999).

HIV-positive individuals face various forms of community-based discrimination in settings such as healthcare, housing, and employment. During interactions with HIV treatment providers, experiences of discrimination based on race and socioeconomic status are associated with greater levels of depression and posttraumatic stress symptoms, greater severity of AIDS-related symptoms, lower perceived general health, lower adherence to antiretroviral medications, and less healthcare satisfaction (Bird, Bogart, & Delahanty, 2004). Research shows that stigma and discrimination in the healthcare setting contributes to keeping people, including health workers, from accessing HIV prevention, care, and treatment services and adopting key prevention behaviors (Nyblade, Stangl, Weiss, & Ashburn, 2009). HIV discrimination may have adverse mental health sequelae and may prevent people from reducing their risky sexual behaviors (Parker & Aggleton, 2003). This discrimination my affect a person's health as a result of experiencing economic and socially inflicted traumas, such as having to relocate, losing a job, being denied medical care because of HIV status, and being denied housing (Wingood et al., 2008). In addition, HIV discrimination may be underreported because certain populations may internalize the negative views of the dominant culture, with internalized oppression resulting in the belief that the discrimination is deserved (Hooks, 1995). Future research should assess the intensity and frequency of HIV discrimination, examine HIV discrimination among different populations and within different domains, and conduct longitudinal studies on the relationship between HIV discrimination and mental health outcomes (Wingood et al., 2008).

Understudied Issues Associated with HIV/AIDS and SGM Populations

When discussing mental health and HIV/AIDS, it is imperative to examine the challenges that face understudied populations, such as SGM people of color, transgender men, undocumented immigrants, and women who have sex with women (WSW). These populations face unique barriers that contribute to their access to mental health treatment, healthcare services, and HIV prevention; however, there is little research on the challenges facing these understudied communities.

While SGM individuals belonging to racial and ethnic minorities have historically faced marginalization and discrimination in the United States, they now face novel threats to their health and well-being due to attacks on protective health and social legislation under President Donald Trump's administration (Byne, 2017). SGM People of Color face several intersecting forms of inequality: they are societally disadvantaged not only because of their sexual identity but also because of their racial identity. Not all SGM People of Color face the same challenges, and there are diverse experiences tied to different racial and ethnic identities. Black and Latino men are overly represented in the HIV epidemic among MSM (Oster, Johnson, Finlayson, Balaji, & Lansky, 2012). A study examining Black and Latino MSM found that sexual pride exhibited a significant negative effect on instances of condomless anal sex with non-primary partners, while greater sexual pride predicted less sexual risk taking (Corsbie-Massay et al., 2017). Those living in the Black community report particularly high levels of stigma, which is associated with being stereotyped, experiencing separation from others, and feeling a loss of status and support (Galvan, Davis, Banks, & Bing, 2008). HIV-positive black MSM show large disparities in disease outcomes compared to other racial/ethnic and risk groups (Bogart et al., 2017). Asian/Pacific Islander MSM have unique HIV risk factors such as discomfort with sexuality, power dynamics and stereotypes in relationships with white men, and low utilization of health and social services (Nemoto et al., 2003).

Research suggests that SGM People of Color may use coping strategies to combat experiences of homophobia and racism. A study on HIV-positive Black men found that major coping themes included reactive avoidance (using behaviors, cognitions, and emotions to escape from discrimination), a common reaction to racism; proactive avoidance (avoiding situations in which discrimination is anticipated), manifested as selective disclosure of HIV serostatus; external attribution for discrimination (vs. self-blame), used more for sexual orientation and HIV discrimination; and social support seeking, which most often emerged in response to racism (Bogart et al., 2017). Relative to the general population, SGM patients belonging to racial minority groups have worse health outcomes and a higher HIV risk and frequently report negative attitudes among healthcare workers and a lack of skills in SGM health (Wilson & Yoshikawa, 2007). Medical mistrust has been found to be a key mediator in the association between perceived discrimination and adherence to antiretroviral therapy among HIV-positive Latino men, indicating that SGM People of Color may mistrust their healthcare providers (Galvan, Bogart, Klein, Wagner, & Chen, 2017). Further research is needed to examine how to improve healthcare and HIV prevention programs for SGM People of Color in order to address their intersectional needs and challenges.

Accessing quality HIV/AIDS treatment is especially difficult for SGM People of Color who are also undocumented immigrants. HIV-positive Latinos who are undocumented are more likely to enter HIV care with advanced AIDS than Latinos who are documented (Poon, Hartman, Davila, & Giordano, 2010), and foreign-born HIV patients from Latin America are also significantly more likely to receive latent tuberculosis (Dang, Giordano, & Kim, 2012). Those who fear immigration authorities are significantly more likely to delay seeking care despite having symptoms, and undocumented Latino immigrants are less likely to have a usual source of care than their documented counterparts (Berk, Schur, Chavez, & Health, 2000). In addition, Latino immigrants who express a fear of deportation are less likely to seek medical attention and are more likely to experience extrafamilial stress and report worse health status (Berk & Schur, 2001). Studies on this population suggest that barriers to timely HIV care for HIV-positive Latino immigrants include HIV/AIDS stigma, a lack of HIV/AIDS knowledge, language barriers, and confidentiality concerns (Rhodes, Hergenrather, Wilkin, & Alegria-Ortega, 2006). In a qualitative study on the challenges of undocumented immigrants living with HIV, findings suggest that structural barriers to optimal HIV care include dealing with HIV stigma and rejection from family and community, and the experienced and perceived structural barriers in accessing healthcare due to a lack of legal documentation (Dang et al., 2012). This research suggests that undocumented immigrants encounter sociocultural and structural barriers that limit their access to HIV prevention and treatment services, which contributes to fear, stigma, and mental health issues. Future interventions should reflect the reality of undocumented immigrants and address the challenges they face.

Transgender men represent another vulnerable yet understudied population in HIV research. Many transgender men do not have access to healthcare resources and services that address the unique issues they face. HIV research on transgender men is often eclipsed by that on transgender women, because HIV prevalence rates are higher among transgender women (Lemons et al., 2018. A systematic review found that HIV rates and risk behaviors were low among transgender men, with prevalence rates from 0 to 3 percent (Herbst et al., 2008). Another study found that although they may constitute a small proportion of HIV-positive patients, more than one in ten transgender HIV-positive patients were transgender men (Lemons et al., 2018). Some risk factors for transgender men include barriers to sexual negotiation such as unequal power dynamics, low self-esteem, and the need for gender identity affirmation (Sevelius, 2009). Research suggests that transgender men are a vulnerable population lacking evidence-based HIV interventions to address their needs (Lemons et al., 2018).

Although there is little literature focusing on WSW and HIV, studies suggest that this population faces unique health risks. Structural factors have been shown to heighten HIV risk among LBQT women, limit access to HIV prevention, and present barriers to HIV care and support (Logie, Tharo, & Loutfy, 2012). In a cross-sectional study focusing on the prevalence of sexually transmitted diseases and HIV/AIDS in WSW, researchers found that many WSW reported a combination of several potential risk factors for contracting HIV/AIDS and sexually transmitted diseases, which indicates that healthcare professionals need to be educated and sensitive when providing healthcare for WSW (Pinto, Tancredi, Neto, & Buchalla, 2005). Research indicates that interventions that address intersecting forms of marginalization, such as sexual stigma, transphobia, and HIV-related stigma, HIV programming, and HIV research are required to promote health equity among LBQT women (Logie et al., 2012). Further research is needed to fully investigate the health disparities of WSW and HIV risk.

Future Directions and Methodologies

Current research has demonstrated a need for holistic and comprehensive interventions focused on improving the mental health of HIV-positive individuals. Research suggests that cognitive-behavioral interventions are efficient in improving various psychological states of people living with HIV. In a meta-analysis of cognitive-behavioral interventions on the mental health of HIV-positive individuals, HIV-positive people who received training on how to assess and alter irrational thoughts, and gained adaptive coping skills to manage and reduce stress, showed a significant improvement in symptoms of depression, anxiety, anger, and stress compared to those who did not receive the treatment (Crepaz et al., 2008). The HOPE Intervention, which uses social cognitive theory and hope theory to engage with participants, examined factors such as low levels of job-seeking skills, job support, and workplace accommodations; HIV/AIDS stigma; and workplace discrimination among Black men living with HIV/AIDS. The intervention was designed to improve the mental health and employment outcomes in this population. All participants identified improved mental health as a benefit of the intervention, and the study found that increased levels of hope served as a mediator for improved mental health outcomes and employment outcomes for men living with HIV/AIDS (Hergenrather et al., 2013).

Similar to the HOPE Intervention, the LIFT Intervention aimed to examine the traumatic stress of people living with HIV/AIDS who had experienced child abuse. This intervention resulted in the significant reduction of traumatic stress among participants over time (Sikkema et al., 2013). This suggests that a focus on current stressors and improvement of coping skills are important components in addressing traumatic stress for adults living with HIV and childhood sexual abuse. Similarly, a pilot-test intervention that aimed to improve the psychological outcomes of gay and bisexual HIV-positive men resulted in improvements in all psychological outcomes, including sexual compulsivity, depression, and anxiety (Parsons et al., 2017). Decreases in drug use and HIV risk were also observed. The positive outcomes illustrated by these studies indicate that interventions focusing on improving the mental health of people affected by HIV/AIDS can result in significant mental health improvements. Additional interventions are needed to address the mental health burden of HIV-positive individuals, as well as to further examine the effect that mental health interventions can have on this population.

Current research has also identified a need to reduce stigma and discrimination in healthcare settings in order to provide HIV-positive individuals with quality prevention and treatment services, which could in turn lead to better mental health outcomes for vulnerable populations. Studies from different parts of the world reveal that there are three main immediately actionable causes of HIV-related stigma in health facilities: lack of awareness among health workers of what stigma looks like and why it is damaging; fear of casual contact stemming from incomplete knowledge about HIV transmission; and the association of HIV with improper or immoral behavior (Nyblade et al., 2009). Research suggests that the experience or fear of stigma in healthcare settings often results in postponing or rejecting care, seeking care far from home to protect confidentiality, and failing to adhere to the medication regimen. In addition, healthcare providers themselves may not want to access the same testing, care, and treatment they provide to their patients due to a fear of stigma in the workplace and in the community they serve (Gupta & Nyblade, 2007). A review of healthcare models and HIV discrimination indicates that healthcare facilities must focus on the individual, environmental, and policy levels in order to facilitate long-lasting benefits for health workers and HIV-positive patients (Nyblade et al., 2009).

Conclusion

HIV/AIDS is a disease that significantly affects the health outcomes of SGMs and LGBTQ communities globally. Current research suggests that HIV status is associated with serious mental health risks, especially for SGM belonging to racial minority groups. HIV is frequently associated with mental health issues such as depression, anxiety, stigma, substance abuse, and discrimination. Research has demonstrated that internalized homophobia and HIV stigma increase occurrences of psychological distress for HIV-positive gay men, and internalized stigma is significantly associated with negative mental health and sexual behavior outcomes. Experiences of stigma and discrimination for having HIV/AIDS represent a risk factor for elevated mental health concerns and are associated with anxiety, depression, and substance abuse. Current research indicates that the interaction of HIV/AIDS and the mental health of vulnerable populations is a significant problem and must be addressed in healthcare models, community settings, and future research.

Especially vulnerable groups affected by HIV/AIDS and mental health disorders include transgender women, WSW, SGM belonging to racial minority groups, and undocumented immigrants. Transgender women, particularly transgender women of color, are infected with HIV at disproportionate rates compared with the general public and represent a highly vulnerable and marginalized population in the United States. SGM People of Color, particularly Black and Latino men, have worse health outcomes, higher HIV risk, and demonstrate a lack of trust with healthcare workers and primary care providers. Latino immigrants who are undocumented have also been found to have a mistrust of medical providers due to fears of deportation and social stigma. Medical mistrust has been found to be a key mediator in the association between perceived discrimination and adherence to antiretroviral therapy, indicating that SGM People of Color may mistrust their healthcare providers, which can significantly affect their mental and physical health. Further research on understudied populations such as WSW, transgender men, SGM People of Color, and undocumented immigrants is essential in order to fully understand the unique healthcare needs and mental health disparities of these marginalized identities.

Because medical mistrust, stigma, and discrimination in healthcare settings often result in greater levels of depression and posttraumatic stress symptoms, greater severity of AIDS-related symptoms, lower perceived general health, lower adherence to antiretroviral medication regimens, and decreased healthcare satisfaction, it is vital to develop HIV prevention programs and interventions that foster a sense of trust between patient and provider. The reduction of stigma and discrimination in healthcare settings may provide HIV-positive individuals with better-quality prevention and treatment services, and may contribute to improved mental health outcomes for vulnerable communities. In addition, research has demonstrated a need for holistic and comprehensive interventions focused on improving the mental health of HIV-positive individuals, such as cognitive-behavioral interventions like the HOPE Intervention and LIFT Intervention, in order to reduce the severity of mental health problems in communities affected by HIV/AIDS. Finally, special attention must be paid to understudied and marginalized groups affected by HIV/AIDS such as WSW, transgender women, SGM People of Color, and undocumented immigrants in order to improve the treatment and prevention of this disease in especially vulnerable communities.

References

Associated Press. (20 December 1984). Poll indicates majority favor quarantine for AIDS victims. *New York Times*, p. A24.

Baral, S. D., Poteat, T., Stromdahl, S., Wirtz, A. L., Guadamuz, T. E., & Beyrer, C. (2013). Worldwide burden of HIV in transgender women: A systematic review and meta-analysis. *Infectious Diseases*, *13*(3), 214–22. doi:10.1016/S1473-3099(12)70315-8

Baral, S., Sifakis, F., Cleghorn, F., & Beyrer, C. (2007). Elevated risk for HIV infection among men who have sex with men in low-and middle-income countries 2000–2006: A systematic review. *PLoS Medicine*, *4*(12), 1901–11. doi:10.1371/journal.pmed.0040339

Berg, M. B., Mimiaga, M. J., & Safren, S. A. (2004). Mental health concerns of HIV-infected gay and bisexual men seeking mental health services: An observational study. *AIDS Patient Care*, *18*(11), 635–43. doi:10.1089/apc.2004.18.635

Berk, M. L., & Schur, C. L. (2001). The effect of fear on access to care among undocumented Latino immigrants. *Journal of Immigrant Health*, *3*, 151–6. doi:10.1023/A:1011389105821

Berk, M. L., Schur, C. L., Chavez, L. R., & Health, F. M. (2000). Health care use among undocumented Latino immigrants. *Health Affairs*, *19*, 51–64. doi:10.1377/hlthaff.19.4.51

Bird, S. T., Bogart, L. M., & Delahanty, D. L. (2004). Health-related correlates of perceived discrimination in HIV care. *AIDS Patient Care and STDs*, *18*(1), 19–26. doi:10.1089/108729104322740884

Bogart, L. M., Dale, S. K., Christian, J., Patel, K., Daffin, G. K., Mayer, K. H., & Pantalone, D. W. (2017). Coping with discrimination among HIV-positive Black men who have sex with men. *Culture, Health, & Sexuality*, *19*, 723–37. doi:10.1089/108729104322740884

Boone, M. R., Cook, S. H., & Wilson, P. A. (2016). Sexual identity and HIV status influence the relationship between internalized stigma and psychological distress in black gay and bisexual men. *AIDS Care*, *28*(6), 764–70. doi:10.1080/09540121.2016.1164801

Brashers, D. E., Neidig, J. L., Cardillo, L. W., Dobbs, L. K., Russell, J. A., & Haas, S. M. (1999). "In an important way, I did die": Uncertainty and revival in persons living with HIV or AIDS. *AIDS Care*, *11*(2), 201–19. doi:10.1080/09540129948090

Byne, W. (2017). Sustaining progress toward LGBT health equity: A time for vigilance, advocacy, and scientific inquiry. *LGBT Health*, *4*(1), 1–3. doi:10.1089/lgbt.2016.0211

Centers for Disease Control. (1981). Kaposi's sarcoma and pneumocystis pneumonia among homosexual men—New York City and California. *Morbidity and Mortality Weekly Report*, *30*(25), 305–8.

Centers for Disease Control. (1992). 1993 Revised classification system for HIV infection and expanded surveillance case definition for AIDS among adolescents and adults. *Morbidity and Mortality Weekly Report, 41*, 1–19.

Center for Disease Control. (2018). *HIV basics*. https://www.cdc.gov/hiv/basics/whatishiv.html

Ciesla, J. A., & Roberts, J. E. (2001). Meta-analysis of the relationship between HIV infection and risk for depressive disorders. *American Journal of Psychiatry, 158*(5), 725–30. doi:10.1176/appi.ajp.158.5.725

Clements-Nolle, K., Marx, R., Guzman, R., & Katz, M. (2001). HIV prevalence, risk behaviors, health care use, and mental health status of transgender persons: Implications for public health intervention. *American Journal of Public Health, 91*(6), 915–21. doi:10.2105/ajph.91.6.915

Cook, T. E., & Colby, D. C. (1992). The mass-mediated epidemic: The politics of AIDS on the nightly network news. In E. Fee & D. M. Fox (Eds.), *AIDS: The making of a chronic disease* (pp. 84–122). Berkeley, CA: University of California Press.

Corsbie-Massay, C. L., Miller, L. C., Christensen, J. L., Appleby, P. R., Godoy, C, & Read, S. J. (2017). Identity conflict and sexual risk for Black and Latino YMSM. *AIDS and Behavior, 21*(6), 1611–9. doi:10.1007/s10461-016-1522-7

Crepaz, N., Passin, W. F., Herbst, J. H., Rama S. M., Malow, R. M., Purcell, D. W., & Wolitski, R. J. (2008). Meta-analysis of cognitive-behavioral interventions on HIV-positive persons' mental health and immune functioning. *Health Psychology, 27*(1), 4–14. doi:10.1037/0278–6133.27.1.4

Dang, B. N., Giordano, T. P., & Kim, J. H. (2012). Sociocultural and structural barriers to care among undocumented Latino immigrants with HIV infection. *Journal of Immigrant Minority Health, 14*, 124–31. doi:10.1007/s10903-011-9542-x

Edwards, J., Fisher, D., & Reynolds, G. (2007). Male-to-female transgender and transsexual clients of HIV service programs in Los Angeles County, California. *American Journal of Public Health, 97*(6), 1030–3. doi:10.2105/AJPH.2006.097717

Elifson, K. W., Boles, J., Posey, E., Sweat, M., Darrow, W., & Elsea, W. (1993). Male transvestite prostitutes and HIV risk. *American Journal of Public Health, 83*(2), 260–2. doi:10.2105/AJPH.83.2.260

Friedman, M. R., Stall, R., Silvestre, A. J., Mustanski, B., Shoptaw, S., Surkan, P. J., . . . Plankey, M. W. (2015). Stuck in the middle: Longitudinal HIV-related health disparities among men who have sex with men and women. *Journal of Acquired Immune Deficiency Syndrome, 66*(2), 213–20. doi:10.1097/QAI.0000000000000143

Galvan, F. H., Bogart, L. M., Klein, D. J., Wagner, G. J., & Chen, Y. (2017). Medical mistrust as a key mediator in the association between perceived discrimination and adherence to antiretroviral therapy among HIV-positive Latino men. *Journal of Behavioral Medicine, 40*(5), 784–93. doi:10.1007/s10865-017-9843-1

Galvan, F. H., Davis, E. M., Banks, D., & Bing, E. G. (2008). HIV stigma and social support among African Americans. *AIDS Patient Care STDs, 22*(5), 423–36. doi:10.1089/apc.2007.0169

Gattari, P., Spizzichino, L., Valenzi, C., Zaccarelli, M., & Rezza, G. (1992). Behavioural patterns and HIV infection among drug using transvestites practising prostitution in Rome. *AIDS Care, 4*(1), 83–7. doi:10.1080/09540129208251622

Gottlieb, M. S., Schroff, R., Fligiel, S., Fahey, J. L., & Saxon, A. (1982). Gay-related immunodeficiency (GRID) syndrome: Clinical and autopsy observations. *Clinical Research, 30*(2), A349.

Gupta, G., & Nyblade, L. (2007). Turn the tide: Tackling HIV stigma and discrimination. In Commonwealth Secretariat (Ed.), *Commonwealth health ministers book* (pp. 190–3). London: Henley Media Group.

Halkitis, P. N., Wolitski, R. J., & Millett, G. A. (2013). A holistic approach to addressing HIV infection disparities in gay, bisexual, and other men who have sex with men. *American Psychologist, 68*(4), 261–73. doi:10.1037/a0032746

Hammack, P. L., Frost, D. M., Meyer, I. H., & Pletta, D. R. (2018). Gay men's health and identity: Social change and the life course. *Archives of Sexual Behavior, 47*(1), 59–74. doi:10.1007/s10508-017-0990-9

Herbst, J. H., Jacobs, E. D., Finlayson, T. J., McKleroy, V. S., Neumann, M. S., Crepaz, N., & HIV/AIDS Prevention Research Synthesis Team. (2008). Estimating HIV prevalence and risk behaviors of transgender persons in the United States: A systematic review. *AIDS and Behavior, 12*(1), 1–17. doi:10.1007/s10461-007-9299-3

Hergenrather, K., Geishecker, S., Clark, G., & Rhodes, S. D. (2013). A pilot test of the Hope Intervention to explore employment and mental health among African American gay men living with HIV/AIDS: Results from a CBPR study. *AIDS Education and Prevention, 25*(5), 405–22. doi:10.1521/aeap.2013.25.5.405

Heywood, W., & Lyons, A. (2016). HIV and elevated mental health problems: Diagnostic, treatment, and risk patterns for symptoms of depression, anxiety, and stress in a national community-based cohort of gay men living with HIV. *AIDS Behavior, 20*(8), 1632–45. doi:10.1007/s10461-016-1324-y

Hooks, B. (1995). *Killing rage: Ending racism*. New York, NY: Henry Holt and Company.

Kellogg, T. A., Clements-Nolle, K., Dilley, J., Katz, M. H., & McFarland, W. (2001). Incidence of human immunodeficiency virus among male-to-female transgendered persons in San Francisco. *Journal of Acquired Immune Deficiency Syndromes, 28*(4), 380–4. doi:10.1097/00126334-200112010-00012

Kenagy, G. P. (2002). HIV among transgendered people. *AIDS Care, 14*(1), 127–34. doi:10.1080/09540120220098008

King, M., Semlyen, J., Tai, S. S., Killaspy, H., Osborn, D., Popelyuk, D., & Nazareth, I. (2008). A systematic review of mental disorder, suicide, and deliberate self-harm in lesbian, gay and bisexual people. *BMC Psychiatry, 8*(1), 70–86. doi:10.1186/1471-244X-8–70

Lemons, A., Beer, L., Finlayson, T., McCree, D. H., Lentine, D., & Shouse, R. L. (2018). Characteristics of HIV-positive transgender men receiving medical care: United States, 2009–2014. *American Journal of Public Health, 108*(1), 128–30. doi:10.2105/AJPH.2017.304153

Logie, C. H., James, L., Tharao, W., & Loutfy, M. R. (2012). "We don't exist": A qualitative study of marginalization experienced by HIV-positive lesbian, bisexual, queer and transgender women in Toronto, Canada. *Journal of the International AIDS Society, 15*(2), 1–11. doi:10.7448/IAS.15.2.17392

Logie, C. H., Newman, P. A., Chakrapani, V., & Shunmugam, M. (2012). Adapting the minority stress model: Associations between gender non-conformity stigma, HIV-related stigma and depression among men who have sex with men in South India. *Social Science & Medicine, 74*(8), 1261–8. doi: 10.1016/j.socscimed.2012.01.008

Mallinson, K. R. (1999). The lived experience of AIDS-related multiple losses by HIV-negative gay men. *Journal of the Association of Nurses in AIDS Care, 10*(5), 22–31. doi:10.1016/S1055-3290(06)60341–5

Marshal, M. P., Friedman, M. S., Stall, R., Smith, H. A., McGinley, J., Thoma, B. C.,...Brent, D. A. (2011). Suicidality and depression disparities between sexual minority and heterosexual youth: A meta-analytic review. *Journal of Adolescent Health, 49*(2), 115–23. doi:10.1016/j.jadohealth.2011.02.005

Melendez, R., & Pinto, R. (2007). "It's really a hard life": Love, gender and HIV risk among male-to-female transgender persons. *Culture, Health, and Sexuality, 9(3),* 233–45. doi:10.1080/13691050601065909

Modan, B., Goldschmidt, R., Rubinstein, E., Vonsover, A., Zinn, M., Golan, R.,...Gottlieb-Stematzky, T. (1992). Prevalence of HIV antibodies in transsexual and female prostitutes. *American Journal of Public Health, 82*(4), 590–2. doi:10.2105/AJPH.82.4.590

Nanni, N. G., Caruso, R., Mitchell, A. J., Meggiolaro, E., & Grassi. L. (2015). Depression in HIV-infected patients: A review. *Current Psychiatry Reports, 17,* 530. doi:10.1007/s11920-014-0530-4

Nemoto, T., Operario, D., Soma, T., Bao, D., Vajrabukka, A., & Crisostomo, V. (2003). HIV risk and prevention among Asian/Pacific Islander men who have sex with men: Listen to our stories. *AIDS Education and Prevention, 15*(1 Supplement), 7–20. doi:10.1521/aeap.15.1.5.7.23616

Nemoto, T., Operario, D., Keatley, J., & Villegas, D. (2004). Social context of HIV risk behaviours among male-to-female transgenders of colour. *AIDS Care, 16*(6), 724–35. doi:10.1080/09540120413331269567

Nuttbrock, L., Bockting, W., Rosenblum, A., Hwahng, S., Mason, M., Macri, M., & Becker, J. (2013). Gender abuse, depressive symptoms, and HIV and other sexually transmitted infections among male-to-female transgender persons: A three-year prospective study. *American Journal of Public Health, 103*(2), 300–7. doi:10.2105/AJPH.2011.300568

Nyblade, L., Stangl, A., Weiss, E., & Ashburn K. (2009). Combating HIV stigma in health care settings: What works? *Journal of the International AIDS Society, 12*(15), 1–15. doi:10.1186/1758-2652-12-15

Oggins, J., & Eichenbaum, J. (2002). Engaging transgender substance users in substance abuse treatment. *International Journal of Transgenderism, 6*(2), 1–16.

Operario, D., Soma, T., & Underhill, K. (2008). Sex work and HIV status among transgender women: Systematic review and meta-analysis. *Journal of Acquired Immune Deficiency Syndromes, 48*(1), 97–103. doi:10.1097/QAI.0b013e31816e3971

Oster, A., Johnson, C., Le, B., Finlayson, T., Balaji, C., & Lansky, A. (2012). Trends in HIV prevalence and HIV testing among young MSM: Five United States cities, 1994–2008. Presented at International AIDS Conference, Washington, DC.

Padgug, R. A., & Oppenheimer, G. M. (1992). Riding the tiger: AIDS and the gay community. In E. Fee & D. M. Fox (Eds.), *AIDS: The making of a chronic disease* (pp. 245–78). Berkeley, CA: University of California Press.

Pantalone, D. W., Hessler, D. M., & Simoni, J. M. (2010). Mental health pathways from interpersonal violence to health-related outcomes in HIV-positive sexual minority men. *Journal of Consulting and Clinical Psychology, 78*(3), 387–97. doi:10.1037/a0019307

Parker, R., & Aggleton, P. (2003). HIV and AIDS-related stigma and discrimination: A conceptual framework and implications for action. *Social Science Medicine, 57,* 13–24. doi:10.1016/S0277-9536(02)00304–0

Parsons, J. T., Rendina, J. H., Moody, R. L., Gurung, S., Starks, T. J., & Pachankis, J. E. (2017). Feasibility of an emotion regulation intervention to improve mental health and reduce HIV transmission risk behaviors for HIV-positive gay and bisexual men. *AIDS Behavior, 21*(6), 1540–9. doi:10.1007/s10461-016-1533-4

Pinto, V. M., Tancredi, M. V., Neto, A. T., & Buchalla, C. M. (2005). Sexually transmitted disease/HIV risk behaviour among women who have sex with women. *AIDS, 19,* S64–S69. doi:10.1097/01.aids.0000191493.43865.2a

Poon, K. K., Hartman, C., Davila, J. A., & Giordano, T. P. (2010, October). Healthcare disparities: How does race and legal residency affect outcomes in HIV/AIDS? Poster session presented at the 48th Annual Meeting of the Infectious Diseases Society of America.

Poteat, T., Reisner, S. L., & Radix, A. (2014). HIV epidemics among transgender women. *Current Opinion in HIV and AIDS, 9*(2), 168–73. doi:10.1016/S1473-3099(12)70315–8

Rendina, J. H., Gamarel, K. E., Pachankis, J. E., Ventuneac, A., Grov, C., & Parsons, J. T. (2017). Extending the minority stress model to incorporate HIV-positive gay and bisexual men's experiences: A longitudinal examination of mental health and sexual risk behavior. *Annual of Behavioral Medicine, 51*(2), 147–58. doi:10.1007/s12160-016-9822-8

Rendina, J. H., Millar, B. M., & Parsons, J. T. (2018). The critical role of internalized HIV-related stigma in the daily negative affective experiences of HIV-positive gay and bisexual men. *Journal of Affective Disorders, 227,* 289–97. doi:10.1016/j.jad.2017.11.005

Rhodes, S. D., Hergenrather, K. C., Wilkin, A., Alegria-Ortega, J., & Montano, J. (2006). Preventing HIV infection among young immigrant Latino men: Results from focus groups using community-based participatory research. *Journal of the National Medical Association, 98*(4), 564–73.

Saavedra, J., Izazola-Licea, J. A., & Beyrer, C. (2008). Sex between men in the context of HIV: The AIDS 2008 Jonathan Mann Memorial Lecture in health and human rights. *Journal of the International AIDS Society, 11*(1), 1–7. doi:10.1186/1758-2652-11-9

Sausa, L., Keatley, J., & Operario, D. (2007). Perceived risks and benefits of sex work among transgender women of color in San Francisco. *Archives of Sexual Behavior, 36*(6), 768–77. doi:10.1007/s10508-007-9210-3

Sevelius, J. M. (2009). "There's no pamphlet for the kind of sex I have": HIV-related risk factors and protective behaviors among transgender men who have sex with nontransgender men. *Journal of the Association of Nurses in AIDS Care, 20*(5), 398–410. doi: 10.1016/j.jana.2009.06.001

Sevelius, J. M., Reznick, O. G., Hart, S. L., & Schwarcz, S. (2009). Informing interventions: The importance of contextual factors in the prediction of sexual risk behaviors among transgender women. *AIDS Education Prevention, 21*(2), 113–27. doi:10.1521/aeap.2009.21.2.113

Sikkema, K. J., Hansen, N. B., Ghebremichael, M., Kochman, A., Tarakeshwar, N., Meade, C. S., & Zhang, H. (2006). A randomized controlled trial of a coping group intervention for adults with HIV who are AIDS bereaved: Longitudinal effects on grief. *Health Psychology, 25*(5), 563–70. doi:10.1037/0278–6133.25.5.563

Sikkema, K. J., Kochman, A., DiFranceisco, W., Kelly, J. A., & Hoffmann, R. G. (2003). AIDS-related grief and coping with loss among HIV-positive men and women. *Journal of Behavioral Medicine, 26*(2), 165–81. doi:10.1023/A:1023086723137

Sikkema, K. J., Ranby, K. W., Meade, C. S., Hansen, N. B., Wilson, P. A., & Kochman, A. (2013). Reductions in traumatic stress following a coping intervention were mediated by decreases in avoidant coping for people living with HIV/AIDS and childhood sexual abuse. *Journal of Consulting and Clinical Psychology, 81*(2), 274–83. doi:10.1037/a0030144

Simon, P. A., Reback, C. J., & Bemis, C. C. (2000). HIV prevalence and incidence among male-to-female transsexuals receiving HIV prevention services in Los Angeles County. *AIDS, 14*(18), 2953–5. doi:10.1097/00002030-200012220-00024

Su, X., Lau, J., Mak, W., Chen, L., Choi, K. C., Song, J., & Cheng, J. (2013). Perceived discrimination, social support, and perceived stress among people living with HIV/AIDS in China. *AIDS Care, 25*(2), 239–48. doi:10.1080/09540121.2012.701713

Torres, R. A., & Barr, M. (1997). Impact of combination therapy for HIV infection on inpatient census. *New England Journal of Medicine, 336*(21), 1531–3. doi:10.1056/NEJM199705223362118

Williams, J. K., Glover, D. A., Wyatt, G. E., Kisler, K., Liu, H., & Zhang, M. (2013). A sexual risk and stress reduction intervention designed for HIV-positive bisexual African American men with childhood sexual abuse histories. *American Journal of Public Health, 103*(8), 1476–84. doi:10.2105/AJPH.2012.301121

Wilson, B., & Miller, R. (2003). Examining strategies for culturally grounded HIV prevention: A review. *AIDS Education & Prevention, 15*(2), 184–202. doi:10.1521/aeap.15.3.184.23838

Wilson, P. A., & Yoshikawa, H. (2007). Improving access to health care among African-American, Asian and Pacific Islander, and Latino lesbian, gay, and bisexual populations. In I. H. Meyer & M. E. Northridge (Eds.), *The health of sexual minorities* (pp. 607–37). New York, NY: Springer. doi:10. 1007/978-0-387-31334-4_25

Wingood, G. M., DiClemente, R. J., Mikhail, I., Hubbard, D., Davies, S. L., Hardin, J. W., & Saag, M. (2008). HIV discrimination and the health of women living with HIV. *Women & Health, 46*(2–3), 99–112. doi:10.1300/J013v46n02_07

Wu, Z., Rou, K., & Cui, H. (2004). The HIV/AIDS epidemic in China: History, current strategies, and future challenges. *AIDS Education and Prevention, 16*(Supplement A), 7–17. doi:10.1521/aeap.16.3.5.7.35521

Zhang, B. C., & Chu. Q. S. (2005). MSM and HIV/AIDS in China. *Cell Research, 15*(11), 858–64. doi:10.1038/sj.cr.7290359

Zhang, B. C., Hu, T. Z., Li, X. F., Shi, T. X., & Liu, D. C. (2002). The relationship between AIDS high risk behaviors and childhood status, perception of gender orientation and rare experiences/psychology among Chinese gays. *Chinese Journal of Sexually Transmitted Infections, 2*, 1–10.

CHAPTER

34 Mental Health for Sexual and Gender Minority Individuals with Physical or Cognitive Disabilities

Meredith R. Maroney *and* Mallaigh McGinley

Abstract

This chapter explores the mental health experiences and needs of sexual and gender minority individuals with disabilities. The authors review the evidence-based research on mental health, highlighting the role of stigma, discrimination, and barriers to care. Autistic sexual and gender minority individuals are used to illustrate the unique experiences of subgroups. Much of the research on this topic is exploratory or descriptive in nature, focused on the experiences of and prevalence rates of individuals from sexual and gender minorities. The chapter concludes with a discussion of future directions for research, and the importance of centering the voices of sexual and gender minority individuals with disabilities in research and practice whenever possible.

Keywords: disability, physical disability, cognitive disability, mental health, LGBTQ, autistic

There are a number of stereotypes about individuals with disabilities that continue to impact the ways sexual and gender minority (SGM) individuals with disabilities are perceived. Such misconceptions include but are not limited to the following: people with disabilities are not interested in sex, do not experience sexual desire or attraction, may not be capable of identifying their sexual orientation or gender identity, are not in relationships, and are either asexual or hypersexual (see Gougeon, 2010; Noonan & Gomez, 2011). In fact, individuals with disabilities hold a wide range of sexual orientations and gender identities and, relatedly, choose to express their sexuality in a variety of ways (Kattari, 2015).

Prior research has shown that there are higher prevalence rates of disabilities among lesbian, gay, bisexual, and transgender (LGBT) adults as compared to their heterosexual and cisgender counterparts (Fredriksen-Goldsen, Kim, & Barkan, 2012; Fredriksen-Goldsen, Kim, Barkan, Muraco, & Hoy-Ellis, 2013a; Fredriksen-Goldsen et al., 2013b). For instance, one study on LGB adults found that 36 percent of women and 30 percent of men reported having a disability (Fredriksen-Goldsen et al., 2012), while a recent report found that bisexual adults had the highest rates of disability (42 percent of bisexual women and 36 percent of bisexual men) when compared with lesbian, gay, and straight adults (Wolstein, Charles, Babey, & Diamant, 2018). Results from the 2015 U.S. Transgender Survey, which remains the largest study focused solely on transgender or gender diverse (TGD) individuals, showed that approximately 39 percent of respondents endorsed having at least one disability (James, Herman, Rankin, Keisling, Mottet, & Anafi, 2016).

This chapter will discuss the mental health of SGM individuals with physical and cognitive disabilities. The World Health Organization defines disability as:

> An umbrella term, covering impairments, activity limitations, and participation restrictions. An impairment is a problem in body function or structure; an activity limitation is a difficulty encountered by an individual in executing a task or action; while a participation restriction is a problem experienced by an individual in involvement in life situations. (n.d., para. 1)

We begin by reviewing the importance of language and conceptualization of SGM individuals with disabilities. Next, we review the evidence-based research on mental health, particularly highlighting the influence of stigma, discrimination, and barriers to care on the mental health of SGM individuals with disabilities. We use a specific population, autistic SGM individuals, to illustrate the unique experiences of groups within the larger SGM disability community. We conclude by discussing future directions of research content and methodologies and highlighting the importance of asking SGM persons with disabilities about their mental health experiences and needs, as well as involving them in research whenever possible.

Conceptualization of SGM Individuals with Disabilities

Many people have made comparisons between the disability and SGM communities, such as the process of taking back ownership of derogatory terms (e.g., queers and crips), having generally parallel identity processes (Cramer & Gilson, 1999), and experiencing hidden or invisible identities that promote the necessity to continually come out about one's identity (Davidson & Henderson, 2010). As the language used to describe SGM individuals has evolved within the field of psychology (e.g., homosexual, LG, LGB, LGBTI, SOGI; Herek, Kimmel, Amaro & Melton, 1991) with shifts in cultural and the sociopolitical context, we feel it is important to note parallels in language within the disability community, and draw attention to language preferences for those who are living at the intersection of the disability and SGM communities.

Although the American Psychological Association (2010) recommends the use of "person-first" language (e.g., people with disabilities) and some within the disability community prefer the use of this language, it has been suggested that using person-first language in scholarly work may further stigmatize the experience of having a disability (Gernsbacher, 2017). The use of identity-first language (e.g., disabled or disabled person) has emerged as a way to capture the sociopolitical experiences of disability and reduce bias (Dunn & Andrews, 2015) and has been strongly advocated for by disability activists and certain groups within the larger disability community. For instance, in a study on the views of language to describe the autism community in the United Kingdom, results found that the use of "autistic" was preferred by autistic adults, family, and friends, while "person with autism" was more highly endorsed by professionals (Kenny et al., 2016). As such, many choose to integrate person-first and identity-first language in their work, use terms that are preferred by their participants or the population, or explicitly state their decision to use certain language.

The ways in which SGM individuals with disabilities have been defined in the literature has varied. For instance, some have explored this population more generally across categories of disability, sexual orientation, and gender identity, such as LGBT persons living with disabilities (Dispenza, Harper, & Harrigan, 2016), LGBT youth with disabilities (e.g., Duke, 2011; Gutmann Kahn & Lindstrom, 2015), LGBT individuals with intellectual disabilities (e.g., Abbott & Burns, 2007; Wilson et al., 2018), or queer disabled people (Martino, 2017). Others have examined the intersection of more specific SGM identities, including gay and bisexual men with learning disabilities (Thompson, 1994), lesbians with physical disabilities (Hunt, Matthews, Milsom, & Lammel, 2006), or LGB people with intellectual disabilities (Abbott & Burns, 2007; Abbott & Howarth, 2007). Finally, some studies have sought to capture the experience of existing in the world with these identities by defining the interaction as a "minority within a minority" (Bennet & Coyle, 2007, p. 125) or a "double minority," or describing the challenges faced by such individuals (Fraley, Mona, & Theodore, 2007, p. 15). Largely, the experiences of SGM people with disabilities have been missing from literature, as Noonan and Gomez (2011) highlight regarding the experiences of LGBT people with intellectual disabilities.

In this chapter, the language used will vary based on the language used in each study, and to align with the predetermined structure of this book (e.g., SGM individuals with disabilities), when not talking about a specific group within the SGM disability community. But we encourage readers to explore the nuances of each subgroup within the SGM community and to involve individuals whenever possible, which we will discuss in greater detail in the conclusion.

Review of Evidence-Based Research on SGM Persons with Disabilities and Mental Health

LGBT individuals with disabilities have been found to be at increased risk for mental health problems (Leonard, Lyons, & Bariola, 2015). In a national health survey on LGBT Australians (N = 3,853),

LGBT people with disabilities were at an increased (52 percent) risk of developing mental health issues compared to LGBT people without disabilities (37 percent) (Leonard & Mann, 2018). Several U.S. population-based studies have found that older LGB adults are more likely than their heterosexual counterparts to have both a disability and psychological distress (Fredriksen-Goldsen et al., 2013a; Wallace, Cochran, Durazo, & Ford, 2011). It is important to consider differences in gender identities. For instance, older woman in same-sex relationships have been found to have higher rates of poor or fair health, more limitations in functionality, and greater psychological distress than their counterparts in opposite-sex relationships, while older men in same-sex relationships were found to have only higher psychological distress when compared to men in opposite-sex relationships (Gonzales & Henning-Smith, 2015). Finally, older transgender adults have been found to have higher rates of disability, worse physical health, higher rates of depression, and more stress than older cisgender individuals (Fredriksen-Goldsen et al., 2013b).

Stigma and "Double Discrimination"

Many of the studies on SGM individuals with disabilities highlighted the role of stigma and discrimination in the lives of participants. SGM individuals with disabilities often experience "layered stigma" (McCann, Leeb, & Brown, 2016, p. 40), in which they face discrimination for their SGM identity as well as their disability. The impact of stigma on mental health has been well documented for LGBTQ individuals (Hendricks & Testa, 2012; Meyer, 2003) and has been associated with psychological distress among individuals with disabilities (Dagnan & Waring, 2004). Although fewer studies have explored the intersection and how such events differentially impact SGM people with disabilities, LGBT people with disabilities have been found to experience harassment, verbal abuse, physical violence, and sexual assault at higher rates than LGBT people without disabilities (Leonard & Mann, 2018).

A study focused on the experiences of stigma for lesbians with disabilities reported that they had difficulty fitting into both the lesbian community and the disability community, feeling excluded from both (Vaughn, McEntee, Schoen, & McGrady, 2015). Prior research has shown that social support from other sexual minority individuals can be protective and may buffer the impact of stigma for LGB people (Doty, Willoughby, Lindahl, & Malik, 2010). Relatedly, in a study from the Netherlands focused on the lived experiences of gay and individuals with intellectual disabilities, participants reported feelings of loneliness, specifically endorsing difficulty with friendships and generally feeling separate from society (Stoffelen, Kok, Hospers, & Curfs, 2013).

Results from a qualitative study found that LGBT youth with disabilities expressed fears of rejection and experiences of bullying that were amplified by the intersection of their disability and SGM identity (Kahn & Lindstrom, 2015). Likewise, LGBT students with disabilities who reported experiences of victimization had the highest rates of suicidal ideation as compared to their heterosexual peers without a disability (King, Merrin, Espelage, Grant, & Bub, 2018).

A qualitative exploration of subjective health for LGBT people with disabilities found that in addition to the maintenance of physical wellness and ability, emotional vitality (individuals' abilities to manage psychological well-being), and social engagement, including LGBT community involvement, were dimensions of health complicated by the intersection of disability and SGM identity (Dispenza et al., 2016).

Wilson et al. (2018) conducted a narrative analysis of literature on LGBT individuals with intellectual disabilities, finding themes of marginalization and vulnerability, barriers, and attitudes. Their category named marginalization and vulnerability as reflective of the "dual marginalization" experienced by LGBT individuals with intellectual disabilities: "They are initially marginalized by their disability and pushed farther from social 'acceptability' because of their sexual orientation or gender expression" (Wilson et al., 2018, p. 187).

Barriers to Affirmative Care

Given the amount of ongoing stigma experienced by a frequently heterosexist, cissexist, and ableist society, and the role stigma plays in psychological well-being (Hatzenbuehler, 2009), it is no wonder SGM individuals would attempt to seek support from mental health providers. Unfortunately, SGM individuals with disabilities experience a number of barriers to care, and this is a useful topic to explore when considering the impact this has on mental health and overall well-being. Many SGM individuals have reported experiences of bias or negative attitudes from providers, as well as larger systemic issues. Experiences of discrimination were identified as the main reason LGB disabled respondents in one study reported difficulty accessing services, which included themes such as fear of disclosing sexual orientation, perceived assumptions about LGB disabled patients, worry about confidentiality, and blatant homophobia (Brothers, 2003). In a study focused on the counseling experiences of lesbians with physical disabilities (e.g., lupus, ulcerative colitis, arthritis), participants reported that despite finding counselors who were knowledgeable about either their sexual orientation or their disability, it was challenging to find a provider who was competent and aware of the intersection of these two experiences (Hunt et al., 2006). Although participants in this sample (all white lesbians) reported being largely satisfied with their counseling experiences, they noted instances of bias and discrimination from both counselors and office staff (Hunt et al., 2006).

Mann, Horsley, Saunders, Briggs, and Mitchel (2006) explored the experiences of LGB people with intersecting minority identities and found that LGB participants with disabilities endorsed a number of structural barriers accessing both healthcare as well as the LGB community (e.g., walking distance, ramps, literacy skills, transportation, sexual health information). LGBT youth with disabilities under the care of social service providers, special education programs, or supported living facilities have reported feeling compelled to adhere to internal policies that prohibit discussions of SGM identities (Duke, 2011). Finally, providers and staff working with clients with intellectual disabilities were interviewed (N = 71) about their ability to discuss and provide support related to clients' sexuality; the study found that they were particularly lacking confidence and were prejudiced toward LGB clients with intellectual disabilities (Abbott & Howarth, 2007).

Transgender individuals living with a disability face a multitude of barriers to care specific to the intersection of their gender identity and disability status (Ballan, Romanelli, & Harper, 2011). A 2014 literature review examined research on people with a dual diagnosis of a gender identity disorder and autism spectrum disorder and/or learning disability (Wood & Halder, 2014). This review suggests that these individuals may be best supported when caregivers partner with the individuals themselves to collaborate in generating options that enable exploration of gender identity and thus foster increased well-being. Drawing on disability-affirmative (Olkin, 1999, 2016) and transgender-affirmative (Mostade, 2006) therapeutic models, Ballan et al. (2011) propose trans-disability affirmative therapy as an approach that places the intersectionality of a client's experiences as both transgender and disabled at the center of the therapeutic process. Trans-disability affirmative therapists are encouraged to facilitate autonomy and empowerment in their clients by taking their unique histories, contexts, and experiences into consideration and valuing clients as the expert on their own identities, challenges, and experiences.

Autistic SGM Individuals: An Illustration

The experiences of SGM individuals diagnosed with autism spectrum disorder has been an emerging area of research in recent years and provides a helpful illustration of the stigma toward SGM individuals with disabilities. We draw on recent literature to illustrate the unique mental health needs and experiences for individuals who are SGM and autistic, as well as to identify the gaps and biases.

Autism is a heterogeneous spectrum, and the presentation can vary widely across individuals, with core traits related to differences in social communication, social interaction, and restricted or repetitive interests or behaviors (American Psychiatric Association, 2013). Many autistic individuals have co-occurring mental health difficulties including depression, anxiety, attention-deficit/hyperactivity disorder, substance use, trauma, obsessive-compulsive disorder, self-injury, and suicidality (Joshi et al., 2013), which may prompt them to seek treatment. A recent meta-analysis found lifetime prevalence rates of anxiety disorders to be 27 to 42 percent and depressive disorder to be 23 to 37 percent among adults diagnosed with autistic spectrum disorder, although this rate may be inflated due to the high number of samples recruited from clinical settings (Hollocks, Lerh, Magiati, Meiser-Stedman, & Brugha, 2019). In addition, prior to being diagnosed or self-identifying as autistic, many autistic individuals feel overwhelmed, confused, isolated, and misunderstood (Hendrickx, 2015; Zener, 2019). This delayed diagnosis or lack of diagnosis disproportionately impacts women and, we would argue, TGD individuals, who may have adapted to mask or camouflage differences that are more stereotypically thought of as autism (Dean, Harwood, & Kasari, 2017). Autistic individuals may choose therapy to seek answers or a diagnosis or to cope with the stressors of navigating everyday life.

Emerging research has highlighted the diversity of SGM identities among autistic individuals. A growing body of research has focused on the presence of gender dysphoria among autistic individuals, because rates have been found to be significantly higher than those of the general population (George & Stokes, 2018b; Glidden, Bouman, Jones, &

Arcelus, 2016; Van Der Miesen, Hurley, & De Vries, 2016), while others have noted increased likelihood of experiencing gender-nonconforming feelings (Dewinter, De Graaf, & Begeer, 2017). In a study focused on sexual orientation, George and Stokes (2018a) found that approximately 69.7 percent of individuals with autism identified as non-heterosexual, compared with 30 percent of the typically developing participants. Approximately half of the sample in the [Autistic] Women's Sexuality Study identified as transgender or gender diverse (e.g., agender, bigender, nonbinary, gender queer) and 84 percent had a sexual minority orientation (e.g., bisexual, queer, asexual, gay, pansexual; Bush, 2016; Mendes & Bush, 2018). Finally, a population-based study in Sweden found that autistic individuals were more likely to identify as bisexual, as well as more likely to reject identity categories (e.g., heterosexual, homosexual, bisexual) to describe their sexual orientation (Rudolph, Lundin, Ahs, Dalman, & Kosidou, 2018).

Recent research has explored the mental health symptoms of SGM individuals with autism spectrum disorder, finding that individuals with co-occurring autism and traits of gender dysphoria had worse overall mental health, greater stress levels, and lower levels of well-being than individuals with only autism (George & Stokes, 2018c). This is suggestive of the differential impact of multiple minority stress, because individuals with multiple marginalized identities, such as sexual minority and intersecting racial identities, have been found to have worse mental health outcomes (Balsam, Molina, Beadnell, Simoni, & Walters, 2011). SGM individuals with disabilities may be exposed to multiple "-isms" (e.g., heterosexism, cissexism, racism) and more experiences of prejudice due to their minority identities. For instance, autistic SGM individuals may face negative consequences when coming out as both autistic and SGM, such as discrimination in the workplace, unjust labeling, stigma, and stereotypical portrayals of those on the autism spectrum (Davidson & Henderson, 2010), as well as stigma and discrimination related to their SGM identity, which results in detrimental mental health effects (Hendricks & Testa, 2012; Meyer, 2003), particularly for transgender and gender diverse people (Herman, 2013; Kahn, Johnson, Lee, & Miranda, 2018; Kosciw, Greytak, Giga, Villenas, & Danischewski, 2016; Reisner, et al., 2014; Wang, Solomon, Durso, McBride, & Cahill, 2016).

SGM autistic individuals may encounter difficulties finding providers with competence or openness to autism, sexual orientation, and gender diversity. In one study, autistic adults with mental health issues ($N = 200$) reported difficulty accessing appropriate treatment that was tailored to their experiences and needs; providers did not appear to have knowledge on how to best work with autistic clients (Camm-Crosbie, Bradley, Shaw, Baron-Cohen, & Cassidy, 2019). LGBT people with autism spectrum disorder have identified challenges associated with the intersection of their neurodevelopmental disorder and SGM identity, including barriers to appropriate service provision, invalidation of their SGM identity, and alienation from the LGBT community (Hillier et al., 2019). Similarly, LGBTQ autistic individuals reported facing experiences of discrimination and invalidation as a result of their intersecting identities, which was attributed to the many misconceptions about autistic people, despite personally valuing their diverse perspectives (Mendes & Maroney, 2019). Finally, in a qualitative study, TGD autistic individuals endorsed significant difficulty in finding a provider who was knowledgeable about and affirming toward both their autistic and TGD experiences (Maroney & Horne, 2019).

Limitations and Gaps

To our knowledge, there has been limited research on the mental health needs of the following populations: (a) SGM individuals with disabilities who are racial and ethnic minorities, (b) SGM individuals with disabilities from the Global South, (c) TGD individuals with disabilities, (d) bisexual and non-monosexual individuals with disabilities, and (e) asexual individuals with disabilities.

Although a handful of studies from the fields of community and organizational psychology have pointed out the parallels in experiences of racial and ethnic minorities with disabilities and LGBT people with disabilities (Colgan, 2015; McDonald, Keys, & Balcazar, 2007), there continues to be a gap in the literature. A three-year research project exploring same-sex relationships of people with intellectual disabilities (Abbott & Burns, 2007) concluded that further research on the intersectionality of race, SGM identity, and disability status is lacking (Abbott, 2015). Likewise, a recent review highlights the need for future research that examines health disparities for LGBT people with disabilities across racial differences (Leonard & Mann, 2018). Although one study examining the impact of intersecting marginalized identities on peer victimization for high school students with a disability found that both sexual orientation and race/ethnicity contributed to increased rates of peer victimization for students with a disability, this study did not examine the intersection of SGM identity and racial or ethnic minority status for these students (McGee, 2014). Given ongoing calls for the incorporation of intersectionality across race, SGM identity, and ability status in both mental health professional training programs (Smith, Foley, & Chaney, 2008) and international human rights initiatives (D'Elio, 2015), this remains a topic for future research.

The Global South refers broadly to regions of Asia, Africa, Latin America, and Oceania and highlights differences in geopolitical power (Dados & Connell, 2012). While emerging theory from parts of the Global South (e.g., South Africa and Zimbabwe) has begun to explore the intersection of gender, disability, and sexuality more broadly, these preliminary approaches appear to highlight the identities of presumably heterosexual cisgender women (e.g., Majiet 1993; 2013). Although sparse, there have been initial explorations into the experiences of aging LGBT individuals in South Africa (Reygan & Henderson, 2019); however, individuals with disabilities are not specifically highlighted. Although there has been recent interest in exploring experiences of people with a disability from a global perspective (e.g., Shakespeare, 2015), further inquiry into the experiences and unique needs of SGM individuals with disabilities residing in the Global South is called for.

Despite proposed recommendations for treating transgender individuals with disabilities (Ballan et al., 2011; Wood & Halder, 2014), there has been little research on the unique mental health concerns of TGD individuals with a disability. Secondary data analysis of the Trans MetLife Survey (TMLS), a large-scale international survey on end-of-life concerns for transgender adults, found that 27.1 percent of respondents reported having a disability (Witten, 2014). However, as noted by Dispenza et al. (2016), studies examining the intersection of disability status and sexual orientation often failed to differentiate the experiences of transgender individuals from those of cisgender individuals (Conron, Mimiaga, & Landers, 2010; Fredriksen-Goldsen et al., 2013a; Fredriksen-Goldsen, Kim, & Barkan, 2012; Kim & Fredriksen-Goldsen, 2012). Although some authors report focusing solely on sexual orientation in an effort not to compromise the nuanced experiential differences between transgender individuals and cisgender sexual minority individuals (Fraley et al., 2007), there remains a noted gap in the literature around the intersection of transgender identities and disability status (Dispenza et al., 2016). This is particularly important considering evidence that TGD individuals with a disability experience higher rates of discrimination and difficulties in accessing mental health care than those without a disability (Kattari, Walls, & Speer, 2017).

Disability theory highlights the ways in which bisexual/non-monosexual identities and disability status function as a doubly imposed "invisibility" for those at its nexus, becoming subject to both the forces of bisexual erasure and ableist paternalism (Caldwell, 2010). Yet research exploring the experiences of individuals who identify as a sexual minority and have a disability often does not differentiate between the experiences of bisexual individuals and those of gay and lesbian people (e.g., Fraley et al., 2007; Fredriksen-Goldsen et al., 2012). One study that does examine the experiences of bisexual individuals with disabilities focused strictly on the experiences of women and combined the experiences of bisexual and lesbian individuals (Axtell, 1999), reflecting the ways in which bisexuals are overlooked more generally within LGB research (Caldwell, 2010). As bisexual individuals report higher rates of disability than their lesbian and gay peers (Wolstein et al., 2018), more research that explores the unique experiences of bisexual and non-monosexual individuals with disabilities is warranted and should be inclusive of a range of gender identities.

Though the myths about asexuality in and societally ascribed desexualization of the disability community have been identified as damaging to many individuals with a disability (Fraley et al., 2007; Shuttleworth & Mona, 2002), the growing recognition of asexuality as a valid sexual orientation necessitates consideration of individuals with a disability who self-identify as asexual (Lund & Johnson, 2015). Such a recognition, as Lund and Johnson (2015) point out, does not validate generalizations of asexuality within the disability community, though the difficulties of exploring this intersection without contributing to larger narratives of imposed asexuality have been noted (Kim, 2011). This intersection remains underresearched, and further affirming exploration regarding prevalence rates and unique concerns of this population is warranted (Lund & Johnson, 2015), particularly considering evidence that some asexual people with a disability report mental health concerns generated by the tension between these two identities (Cuthbert, 2017).

Future Directions of Research Content and Methodologies

The majority of the studies on SGM individuals with disabilities are exploratory or descriptive in nature (Wilson et al., 2018), noting the prevalence of disability in the SGM community and the diversity of sexual orientation within the disability community. In their review of the literature on LGBT people with disabilities, Leonard and Mann (2018) found a lack of consistency with definitions and terminology used, high rates of violence and abuse, health disparities, and systematic discrimination related to reduced health and overall well-being. At this point, it is clear that SGM individuals with disabilities do exist and do experience disparities in mental health care access and outcomes.

There are a number of case studies and narrative explorations of the experiences of SGM individuals with disabilities (e.g., Thompson, 1994), systematic reviews or meta-analyses (e.g., Duke, 2011; Glidden et al., 2016; Wilson et al., 2018), as well as studies focusing on the perspective of parents or caregivers (e.g., Drummond, 2006). In many of the available studies, the mental health concerns, needs, and treatment experiences emerged in the results but were rarely the focus of the study. The unique experiences and stressors of SGM individuals warrant future study, not just to continue to identify and summarize the co-occurrences or health disparities but to examine how best to support the overall well-being of this multiply marginalized population.

Future research studies should explicitly focus on the mental health concerns of SGM individuals using diverse methodologies, as well as explore ways to buffer the effects of holding these minority identities. There is a need for intervention research to manage the impact of stigma on SGM individuals with disabilities, which has been associated with higher rates of mental health issues. Furthermore, future research should prioritize training and interventions to providers to be more knowledgeable about SGM with disabilities. Providers should be competent in serving SGM individuals with disabilities broadly, as well as SGM individuals with specific disabilities and identities.

It is important to stress the diversity of both the SGM community and the disability community, as experiences will differ by gender, sexual orientation, disability, as well as intersecting identities including race, ethnicity, socioeconomic status, and others. Intersectionality speaks to the need to examine within-group diversity, because the multiple identities are impossible to separate from a person's experience, and the traditional representation of these groups in literature is not representative of the experience of all members (Cole, 2009; Crenshaw, 1990). The treatment experiences and needs of lesbians with physical disabilities may have some overlap with, but will likely vary from, genderqueer autistic individuals, or gay men with learning disabilities. As we have highlighted, there remains a lack of research on bisexual and non-monosexual, transgender, and asexual individuals, which is an important gap for future research. As stated by Shakespeare (1996), "there is a danger of ignoring the fact that disabled people are also men and women, straight and gay, and come from various ethnic groups" (p. 109).

Further research should focus on SGM individuals across the lifespan. In their narrative literature review, Wilson et al. (2018) commented on the "total absence" of research on youth and older adults who are LGBTIQ with intellectual disabilities, which they suggested may be attributed to greater social marginalization (p. 174). Prior research has shown higher rates of psychological distress among SGM individuals with disabilities (Fredriksen-Goldsen et al., 2013a, 2013b), making it important to identify ways to support people as they age.

It is essential that researchers and providers listen to the voices of SGM individuals with disabilities. Researchers should involve SGM individuals with disabilities in research whenever possible. There are books, blogs, and articles that prioritize the experiences of the queer disability population (e.g., Ghauri, 2018; Luckzack, 2015; Mendes & Maroney, 2019), and researchers should make space within the academic literature by explicitly prioritizing the mental health needs and experiences of this population.

Several research collaboratives are partnering with communities, such as the Academic Autism Spectrum Partnership in Research and Education (2019) and the Association of University Centers on Disabilities (2011), and these provide a helpful model for those interested in furthering research in the areas of SGM individuals with disabilities. As first said by James Charlton (2000), and since adopted by many disability organizations, "nothing about us without us."

References

Abbott, D. (2015). Love in a cold climate: Changes in the fortunes of LGBT men and women with learning disabilities? *British Journal of Learning Disabilities*, *43*(2), 100–5. doi:10.1111/bld.12131

Abbott, D., & Burns, J. (2007). What's love got to do with it?: Experiences of lesbian, gay, and bisexual people with intellectual disabilities in the United Kingdom and views of the staff who support them. *Sexuality Research & Social Policy, 4*(1), 27. doi:10.1111/bld.12131

Abbott, D., & Howarth, J. (2007). Still off-limits? Staff views on supporting gay, lesbian and bisexual people with intellectual disabilities to develop sexual and intimate relationships. *Journal of Applied Research in Intellectual Disabilities, 20*(2), 116–26. doi:10.1111/j.1468–3148.2006.00312.x

Academic Autism Spectrum Partnership in Research and Education. (2019). *About.* https://aaspire.org/about/partnership/

American Psychiatric Association. (2013). *Diagnostic and statistical manual of mental disorders* (5th ed.). Washington, DC: Author.

American Psychological Association. (2010). *Publication manual of the American Psychological Association* (6th ed.). Washington, DC: Author.

Association of University Centers on Disabilities. (2011). *Initiatives.* https://www.aucd.org//template/page.cfm?id=426

Axtell, S. (1999). Disability and chronic illness identity: Interviews with lesbians and bisexual women and their partners. *International Journal of Sexuality and Gender Studies, 4*(1), 53–72.

Ballan, M. S., Romanelli, M., & Harper IV, J. N. (2011). The social model: A lens for counseling transgender individuals with disabilities. *Journal of Gay & Lesbian Mental Health, 15*(3), 260–80. doi:10.1080/19359705.2011.582073

Balsam, K. F., Molina, Y., Beadnell, B., Simoni, J., & Walters, K. (2011). Measuring multiple minority stress: The LGBT people of color microaggressions scale. *Cultural Diversity and Ethnic Minority Psychology, 17*(2), 163.

Bennet, C., & Coyle, A. (2007). A minority within a minority: Experiences of gay men with intellectual disabilities. In V. Charles & E. Peel (Eds.), *Out in psychology: Lesbian, gay bisexual, trans and queer perspectives* (pp. 125–53). Chichester, West Sussex, UK: Wiley.

Brothers, M. (2003). It's not just about ramps and Braille: Disability and sexual orientation. In K. Zappone (Ed.), *Re-thinking identity: The challenge of diversity* (pp. 49–67). https://www.ihrec.ie/app/uploads/download/pdf/rethinking_identity_the_challenge_of_diversity.pdf

Bush, H. H. (2016). Dimensions of sexuality among young women, with and without autism, with predominantly sexual minority identities. *Sexuality and Disability, 37*, 275–292. doi:10.1007/s11195-018-9532-1

Caldwell, K. (2010). We exist: Intersectional in/visibility in bisexuality and disability. *Disability Studies Quarterly*, 30(3/4). doi:10.18061/dsq.v30i3/4.1273

Camm-Crosbie, L., Bradley, L., Shaw, R., Baron-Cohen, S., & Cassidy, S. (2019). "People like me don't get support": Autistic adults' experiences of support and treatment for mental health difficulties, self-injury and suicidality. *Autism, 23*(6), 1431–41. doi:1362361318816053.10.1177

Charlton, J. I. (2000). *Nothing about us without us: Disability oppression and empowerment.* Berkeley, CA: University of California Press.

Cole, E. R. (2009). Intersectionality and research in psychology. *American Psychologist, 64*(3), 170–80. doi:10.1037/a0014564

Colgan, F. (2015). Organisational life within a UK "good practice employer": The experiences of black and minority ethnic and disabled LGBT employees. In F. Colgan & N. Rumens (Eds.), *Sexual orientation at work: Contemporary issues and perspectives* (pp. 104–21). New York, NY: Routledge.

Conron, K. J., Mimiaga, M. J., & Landers, S. J. (2010). A population-based study of sexual orientation identity and gender differences in adult health. *American Journal of Public Health, 100*(10), 1953–60. doi:10.2105/AJPH.2009.174169

Cramer, E. P., & Gilson, S. F. (1999). Queers and crips: Parallel identity development processes for persons with nonvisible disabilities and lesbian, gay, and bisexual persons. *International Journal of Sexuality and Gender Studies, 4*(1), 23–37.

Crenshaw, K. (1990). Mapping the margins: Intersectionality, identity politics, and violence against women of color. *Stanford Law Review, 43*, 1241.

Cuthbert, K. (2017). You have to be normal to be abnormal: An empirically grounded exploration of the intersection of asexuality and disability. *Sociology, 51*(2), 241–57. doi:10.1177/0038038515587639

Dados, N., & Connell, R. (2012). The Global South. *Contexts, 11*(1), 12–13. doi:10.1177/1536504212436479

Dagnan, D., & Waring, M. (2004). Linking stigma to psychological distress: Testing a social–cognitive model of the experience of people with intellectual disabilities. *Clinical Psychology & Psychotherapy, 11*(4), 247–54. doi:10.1002/cpp.413

Davidson, J., & Henderson, V. L. (2010). "Coming out" on the spectrum: Autism, identity and disclosure. *Social & Cultural Geography, 11*(2), 155–70.

Dean, M., Harwood, R., & Kasari, C. (2017). The art of camouflage: Gender differences in the social behaviors of girls and boys with autism spectrum disorder. *Autism, 21*(6), 678–89.

D'Elio, F. (2015). Intersectionality in LGBTI advocacy. In A. Carroll & L. P. Itaborahy (Eds.), *State-sponsored homophobia: A world survey of laws, criminalisation, protection and recognition of same-sex love* (pp. 18–22). Geneva, Switzerland: International Lesbian, Gay, Bisexual, Trans and Intersex Association. https://ilga.org/sites/default/files/ILGA_State_Sponsored_Homophobia_2015.pdf

Dewinter, J., De Graaf, H., & Begeer, S. (2017). Sexual orientation, gender identity, and romantic relationships in adolescents and adults with autism spectrum disorder. *Journal of Autism and Developmental Disorders, 47*(9), 2927–34. doi:10.1007/s10803-017-3199-9

Dispenza, F., Harper, L. S., & Harrigan, M. A. (2016). Subjective health among LGBT persons living with disabilities: A qualitative content analysis. *Rehabilitation Psychology, 61*(3), 251. doi:10.1037/rep0000086

Doty, N. D., Willoughby, B. L., Lindahl, K. M., & Malik, N. M. (2010). Sexuality related social support among lesbian, gay, and bisexual youth. *Journal of Youth and Adolescence, 39*(10), 1134–47.

Drummond, E. (2006). Attitudes towards sexuality: A pilot study in Ireland. *Learning Disability Practice, 9*(4), 28–34. doi:10.7748/ldp2006.05.9.4.28.c4283

Duke, T. S. (2011). Lesbian, gay, bisexual, and transgender youth with disabilities: A meta-synthesis. *Journal of LGBT Youth, 8*(1), 1–52. doi:10.1080/19361653.2011.519181

Dunn, D. S., & Andrews, E. E. (2015). Person-first and identity-first language: Developing psychologists' cultural competence using disability language. *American Psychologist, 70*(3), 255–64. doi:10.1037/a0038636

Fraley, S. S., Mona, L. R., & Theodore, P. S. (2007). The sexual lives of lesbian, gay, and bisexual people with disabilities:

Psychological perspectives. *Sexuality Research & Social Policy, 4*(1), 15–26. doi:10.1525/srsp.2007.4.1.15
Fredriksen-Goldsen, K. I., Cook-Daniels, L., Kim, H. J., Erosheva, E. A., Emlet, C. A., Hoy-Ellis, C. P., . . . Muraco, A. (2013b). Physical and mental health of transgender older adults: An at-risk and underserved population. *The Gerontologist, 54*(3), 488–500.
Fredriksen-Goldsen, K. I., Emlet, C. A., Kim, H. J., Muraco, A., Erosheva, E. A., Goldsen, J., & Hoy-Ellis, C. P. (2012). The physical and mental health of lesbian, gay male, and bisexual (LGB) older adults: The role of key health indicators and risk and protective factors. *The Gerontologist, 53*(4), 664–75. doi:10.1093/geront/gns123
Fredriksen-Goldsen, K. I., Kim, H. J., & Barkan, S. E. (2012). Disability among lesbian, gay, and bisexual adults: Disparities in prevalence and risk. *American Journal of Public Health, 102*(1), e16-21. doi:10.2105/ajph.2011.300379
Fredriksen-Goldsen, K. I., Kim, H. J., Barkan, S. E., Muraco, A., & Hoy-Ellis, C. P. (2013a). Health disparities among lesbian, gay, and bisexual older adults: Results from a population-based study. *American Journal of Public Health, 103*(10), 1802–9. doi:10.2105/ajph.2012.301110
George, R., & Stokes, M. A. (2018a). Gender identity and sexual orientation in autism spectrum disorder. *Autism, 22*(8), 970–82. doi:10.1177/1362361317714587
George, R., & Stokes, M. A. (2018b). Sexual orientation in autism spectrum disorder. *Autism Research, 11*(1), 133–41. doi:10.1002/aur.1892
George, R., & Stokes, M. A. (2018c). A quantitative analysis of mental health among sexual and gender minority groups in ASD. *Journal of Autism and Developmental Disorders, 48*(6), 2052–63. doi:10.1007/s10803-018-3469-1
Gernsbacher, M. A. (2017). Editorial perspective: The use of person-first language in scholarly writing may accentuate stigma. *Journal of Child Psychology and Psychiatry, 58*(7), 859–61. doi:10.1111/jcpp.12706
Ghauri, U. (2018). Queer, disabled people like me are excluded from LGBTQ+ spaces—it is dividing our community. *The Independent.* https://www.independent.co.uk/voices/coming-out-lgbt-gay-queer-disabled-disability-twice-sexuality-open-family-friends-a8212431.html
Glidden, D., Bouman, W. P., Jones, B. A., & Arcelus, J. (2016). Gender dysphoria and autism spectrum disorder: A systematic review of the literature. *Sexual Medicine Reviews, 4*(1), 3–14. doi:10.1016/j.sxmr.2015.10.003
Gonzales, G., & Henning-Smith, C. (2015). Disparities in health and disability among older adults in same-sex cohabiting relationships. *Journal of Aging and Health, 27*(3), 432–53. doi:10.1177/0898264314551332
Gougeon, N. A. (2010). Sexuality and autism: A critical review of selected literature using a social-relational model of disability. *American Journal of Sexuality Education, 5*(4), 328–61. doi:10.1080/15546128.2010.527237
Hatzenbuehler, M. L. (2009). How does sexual minority stigma "get under the skin"? A psychological mediation framework. *Psychological Bulletin, 135*(5), 707–30. doi:10.1037/a0016441
Hendricks, M. L., & Testa, R. J. (2012). A conceptual framework for clinical work with transgender and gender nonconforming clients: An adaptation of the minority stress model. *Professional Psychology: Research and Practice, 43*(5), 460–7. doi:10.1037/a0029597
Hendrickx, S. (2015). *Women and girls with autism spectrum disorder.* London: Jessica Kingsley Publishers.
Herek, G. M., Kimmel, D. C., Amaro, H., & Melton, G. B. (1991). Avoiding heterosexist bias in psychological research. *American Psychologist, 46*(9), 957.
Herman, J. L. (2013). Gendered restrooms and minority stress: The public regulation of gender and its impact on transgender people's lives. *Journal of Public Management & Social Policy, 19*(1), 65–80.
Hillier, A., Gallop, N., Mendes, E., Tellez, D., Buckingham, A., Nizami, A., & O'Toole, D. (2019). LGBTQ+ and autism spectrum disorder: Experiences and challenges. *International Journal of Transgenderism* [E-pub before print]. https://doi.org/10.1080/15532739.2019.1594484
Hollocks, M. J., Lerh, J. W., Magiati, I., Meiser-Stedman, R., & Brugha, T. S. (2019). Anxiety and depression in adults with autism spectrum disorder: A systematic review and meta-analysis. *Psychological Medicine, 49*(4), 559–72. doi:10.1017/S0033291718002283
Hunt, B., Matthews, C., Milsom, A., & Lammel, J. A. (2006). Lesbians with physical disabilities: A qualitative study of their experiences with counseling. *Journal of Counseling & Development, 84*(2), 163–73. doi:10.1177/0034355208320933
James, S. E., Herman, J. L., Rankin, S., Keisling, M., Mottet, L., & Anafi, M. (2016). *The Report of the 2015 U.S. Transgender Survey.* Washington, DC: National Center for Transgender Equality. https://www.transequality.org/sites/default/files/docs/USTS-Full-Report-FINAL.PDF
Joshi, G., Wozniak, J., Petty, C., Martelon, M. K., Fried, R., Bolfek, A., . . . Caruso, J. (2013). Psychiatric comorbidity and functioning in a clinically referred population of adults with autism spectrum disorders: A comparative study. *Journal of Autism and Developmental Disorders, 43*(6), 1314–25. doi:10.1007/s10803-012-1679-5
Kahn, E., Johnson, A., Lee, M., & Miranda, L. (2018). *LGBTQ youth report.* Washington, DC: Human Rights Campaign. https://assets2.hrc.org/files/assets/resources/2018-YouthReport-0514-Final.pdf
Kahn, L. G., & Lindstrom, L. (2015). "I just want to be myself": Adolescents with disabilities who identify as a sexual or gender minority. *Educational Forum, 79*(4), 362–76. doi:10.1080/00131725.2015.1068416
Kattari, S. K. (2015). "Getting it": Identity and sexual communication for sexual and gender minorities with physical disabilities. *Sexuality & Culture, 19*(4), 882–99. doi:10.1007/s12119-015-9298-x
Kattari, S. K., Walls, N. E., & Speer, S. R. (2017). Differences in experiences of discrimination in accessing social services among transgender/gender nonconforming individuals by (dis)ability. *Journal of Social Work in Disability & Rehabilitation, 16*(2), 116–40. doi:10.1080/1536710x.2017.1299661
Kenny, L., Hattersley, C., Molins, B., Buckley, C., Povey, C., & Pellicano, E. (2016). Which terms should be used to describe autism? Perspectives from the UK autism community. *Autism, 20*(4), 442–62. doi:10.1177/1362361315588200
Kim, E. (2011). Asexuality in disability narratives. *Sexualities, 14*(4), 479–93. doi:10.1177/1363460711406463
Kim, H. J., & Fredriksen-Goldsen, K. I. (2012). Hispanic lesbians and bisexual women at heightened risk or health disparities. *American Journal of Public Health, 102*(1), e9–e15. doi:10.2105/ajph.2011.300378
King, M. T., Merrin, G. J., Espelage, D. L., Grant, N. J., & Bub, K. L. (2018). Suicidality and intersectionality among students identifying as nonheterosexual and with a disability. *Exceptional Children, 84*(2), 141–58. doi:10.1177/0014402917736261

Kosciw, J. G., Greytak, E. A., Giga, N. M., Villenas, C., & Danischewski, D. J. (2016). *The 2015 national school climate survey: The experiences of lesbian, gay, Bisexual, transgender, and queer youth in our nation's schools.* New York, NY: GLSEN. https://www.glsen.org/sites/default/files/2015%20National%20GLSEN%202015%20National%20School%20Climate%20Survey%20%28NSCS%29%20-%20Full%20Report_0.pdf

Leonard, W., Lyons, A., & Bariola, E. (2015). *A closer look at Private Lives 2: Addressing the mental health and well-being of lesbian, gay, bisexual and transgender (LGBT) Australians* (Report No. 103). Melbourne, Australia: Australian Research Centre in Sex, Health & Society, La Trobe University. https://apo.org.au/node/53996

Leonard, W., & Mann, R. (2018). *The everyday experiences of lesbian, gay, bisexual, transgender and intersex (LGBTI) people living with disability.* Victoria, Australia: La Trobe University. https://www.disabilityrightswa.org/wp-content/uploads/2018/09/GAFLA-Report-Final-Version.pdf

Luczak, R. (Ed.). (2015). *QDA: A queer disability anthology.* Minneapolis, MN: Squares & Rebels.

Lund, E. M., & Johnson, B. A. (2015). Asexuality and disability: Strange but compatible bedfellows. *Sexuality and Disability, 33*(1), 123–32. doi:10.1007/s11195-014-9378-0

Majiet, S. (1993). Disabled women and sexuality. *Agenda: Empowering Women for Gender Equity, 19*, 43–4. doi:10.2307/4065995

Majiet, S. (2013). *"Disabled women must stand up": Exploring the leadership experiences of disabled women in disabled people's organisations in Zimbabwe.* Unpublished doctoral dissertation, University of Cape Town. https://open.uct.ac.za/bitstream/handle/11427/12352/thesis_hsf_2013_majiet_s.pdf?sequence=1&isAllowed=y

Mann, R., Horsley, P., Saunders, M., Briggs, V. & Mitchell, A. (2006). *Swimming upstream: Making places welcoming. A report on the needs of gay, lesbian and bisexual people in "hard to reach" groups.* Gay and Lesbian Health Victoria, La Trobe University, Melbourne. https://www.researchgate.net/publication/242280053_SWIMMING_UPSTREAM_MAKING_PLACES_WELCOMING_A_REPORT_ON_THE_NEEDS_OF_GAY_LESBIAN_AND_BISEXUAL_PEOPLE_IN_'HARD_TO_REACH'_GROUPS

Maroney, M. R., & Horne, S. G. (2019). The experiences and identity development of autistic transgender and gender diverse individuals. Unpublished manuscript.

Martino, A. S. (2017). Cripping sexualities: An analytic review of theoretical and empirical writing on the intersection of disabilities and sexualities. *Sociology Compass, 11*, e12471. doi:10.1111/soc4.12471

McCann, T. E., Leeb, L. & Brown, M. (2016). The experiences and support needs of people with intellectual disabilities who identify as LGBT: A review of the literature. *Research in Developmental Disabilities, 57*, 39–53.

McDonald, K. E., Keys, C. B., & Balcazar, F. E. (2007). Disability, race/ethnicity and gender: Themes of cultural oppression, acts of individual resistance. *American Journal of Community Psychology, 39*(1–2), 145–61. doi:10.1007/s10464-007-9094-3

McGee, M. G. (2014). Lost in the margins? Intersections between disability and other nondominant statuses with regard to peer victimization. *Journal of School Violence, 13*(4), 396–421. doi:10.1080/15388220.2014.894914

Mendes, E., & Bush, H. H. (2018). "Labels do not describe me": Gender identity and sexual orientation among women with Asperger's and autism. http://www.evmendes.com/wp-content/uploads/2015/04/Labels-do-not-final.pdf

Mendes, E. A., & Maroney, M. R. (2019). *Gender identity, sexuality and autism: Voices from across the spectrum.* London: Jessica Kingsley Publishers.

Meyer, I. H. (2003). Prejudice, social stress, and mental health in lesbian, gay, and bisexual populations: Conceptual issues and research evidence. *Psychological Bulletin, 129*(5), 674–97. doi:10.1037/0033–2909.129.5.674

Mostade, J. (2006). Affirmative counseling with transgendered persons. In C.C. Lee (Ed.), *Multicultural issues in counseling: New approaches to diversity* (3rd ed., pp. 303–16). Alexandria, VA: American Counseling Association.

Noonan, A., & Gomez, M. T. (2011). Who's missing? Awareness of lesbian, gay, bisexual and transgender people with intellectual disability. *Sexuality and Disability, 29*(2), 175–80. doi:10.1007/s11195-010-9175-3

Olkin, R. (1999). *What psychotherapists should know about disability.* New York, NY: Guilford Press.

Olkin, R. (2016). Disability-affirmative therapy. In M. A. Stebnicki (Ed.), *The professional counselor's desk reference* (2nd ed., pp. 215–23). New York, NY: Springer Publishing Company.

Reisner, S. L., White, J. M., Dunham, E. E., Heflin, K., Begenyi, J., Cahill, S., & Project VOICE Team. (2014). *Discrimination and health in Massachusetts: A statewide survey of transgender and gender nonconforming adults.* Boston, MA: The Fenway Institute. https://fenwayhealth.org/wp-content/uploads/The-Fenway-Institute-MTPC-Project-VOICE-Report-July-2014.pdf

Reygan, F., & Henderson, N. (2019). All bad? Experiences of aging among LGBT elders in South Africa. *International Journal of Aging and Human Development, 88*(4), 405–21. doi:10.1177/0091415019836929

Rudolph, C. E., Lundin, A., Åhs, J. W., Dalman, C., & Kosidou, K. (2018). Brief report: Sexual orientation in individuals with autistic traits: Population-based study of 47,000 adults in Stockholm County. *Journal of Autism and Developmental Disorders, 48*(2), 619–24. doi:10.1007/s10803-017-3369-9

Shakespeare, T. (1996). Disability, identity and difference. In C. Barnes & G. Mercer (Ed.), *Exploring the divide* (pp. 94–113). Leeds, UK: Disability Press. https://disability-studies.leeds.ac.uk/wp-content/uploads/sites/40/library/Shakespeare-Chap6.pdf

Shakespeare, T. (Ed.). (2015). *Disability research today: International perspectives.* Abingdon, UK: Routledge.

Shuttleworth, R., & Mona, L. R. (2002). Disability and sexuality: Toward a focus on sexual access. *Disability Studies Quarterly, 22*(4), 2–3.

Smith, L., Foley, P. F., & Chaney, M. P. (2008). Addressing classism, ableism, and heterosexism in counselor education. *Journal of Counseling & Development, 86*(3), 303–9. doi:10.1002/j.1556–6678.2008.tb00513.x

Stoffelen, J., Kok, G., Hospers, H., & Curfs, L. M. G. (2013). Homosexuality among people with a mild intellectual disability: An explorative study on the lived experiences of homosexual people in the Netherlands with a mild intellectual disability. *Journal of Intellectual Disability Research, 57*(3), 257–67. doi:10.1111/j.1365–2788.2011.01532.x

Thompson, D. (1994). The sexual experiences of men with learning disabilities having sex with men: Issues for HIV prevention. *Sexuality and Disability, 12*(3), 221–42. doi:10.1007/bf02547909

Van Der Miesen, A. I., Hurley, H., & De Vries, A. L. (2016). Gender dysphoria and autism spectrum disorder: A narrative review. *International Review of Psychiatry, 28*(1), 70–80. doi:10.3109/09540261.2015.1111199

Vaughn, M., McEntee, B., Schoen, B., McGrady, M. (2015). Addressing disability stigma within the lesbian community. *Journal of Rehabilitation, 81* (4), 49–56.

Wallace, S. P., Cochran, S. D., Durazo, E. M., & Ford, C. L. (2011). *The health of aging lesbian, gay and bisexual adults in California* (Policy Brief No. PB2011-2). UCLA Center for Health Policy Research. https://www.ncbi.nlm.nih.gov/pmc/articles/PMC3698220/pdf/nihms472438.pdf

Wang, T., Solomon, D., Durso, L. E., McBride, S., & Cahill, S. (2016). *State anti-transgender bathroom bills threaten transgender people's health and participation in public life.* Boston, MA: Fenway Institute. https://fenwayhealth.org/wp-content/uploads/2015/12/COM-2485-Transgender-Bathroom-Bill-Brief_v8-pages.pdf

Wilson, N. J., Macdonald, J., Hayman, B., Bright, A. M., Frawley, P., & Gallego, G. (2018). A narrative review of the literature about people with intellectual disability who identify as lesbian, gay, bisexual, transgender, intersex or questioning. *Journal of Intellectual Disabilities, 22*(2), 171–96. doi:10.1177/1744629516682681

Witten, T. M. (2014). End of life, chronic illness, and trans-identities. *Journal of Social Work in End-of-Life & Palliative Care, 10*(1), 34–58. doi:10.1080/15524256.2013.877864

Wolstein, J., Charles, S. A., Babey, S. H., & Diamant, A. L. (2018). *Disparities in health care access and health among lesbians, gay men, and bisexuals in California* (Policy Brief No. 9). UCLA Center for Health Policy Research. https://www.ncbi.nlm.nih.gov/pubmed/30358962

Wood, E., & Halder, N. (2014). Gender disorders in learning disability: A systematic review. *Tizard Learning Disability Review, 19*(4), 158–65. doi:10.1108/tldr-01-2013-0004

World Health Organization. (n.d.) *Health topics: Disabilities.* https://www.who.int/topics/disabilities/en/

Zener, D. (2019). Helping autistic women thrive. *Advances in Autism, 5*(3), 143–56. doi:10.1108/aia-10-2018-0042

CHAPTER

35 Stigma and Sexual and Gender Minority Mental Health

Joanne DiPlacido *and* Carolyn R. Fallahi

Abstract

Minority stress and stigma among LGBTQ individuals as a result of oppression from discrimination, heterosexism, and homonegativity has consistently led to poorer mental health outcomes. This chapter outlines the research linking minority stress and stigma to mental health. The authors review Hatzenbuehler's mediational framework to understand the underlying mechanisms to explain why minority stress predicts psychiatric distress. The authors also discuss the role of intersectionality on mental health, recognizing that many LGBTQ individuals deal with multiple oppressions due to not only their sexual orientation or gender identity or expression but also race and ethnicity. This chapter covers minority stress and stigma among more vulnerable populations at higher risk of mental distress, such as transgender, older, and bisexual communities and those living in the Global South. The authors discuss how coping and social support can buffer the negative mental health effects of minority stress and stigma. Methodological issues and future directions are reviewed and suggestions for prevention and treatment interventions are offered.

Keywords: minority stress, stigma, LGBTQ, oppression, mental health, intersectionality, heterosexism, internalized homonegativity, social support

Minority stress in lesbian, gay, bisexual, transgender (LGBT) individuals is posited to result in higher levels of psychiatric disorders, health problems, and maladaptive health behaviors due to the cumulative effects of living in a hostile and discriminatory social environment during their lifetime (Meyer, 2013; Veldhuis, Talley, Hancock, Wilsnack, & Hughes, 2017). As a result of this heterosexism, internalized stigma has been associated with increased disability and mental health symptoms. Importantly, the stress experienced by sexual minorities is not a one-size-fits-all experience, especially when taking into consideration the intersectionality with race, ethnicity, age, and other demographic variables.

Minority Stress/Stigma and Mental Health Research

Much of the research on mental health among LGBTQ populations has relied on Meyer's (2013) minority stress model as a conceptual framework for subsequent research. This model proposes that mental health disparities among sexual minorities can be explained by a lifetime of living in a social environment that is unique, stressful, and hostile, leading to harassment, prejudice, discrimination, and stigma. Further, those stressors are chronic, additive, and socially based, leading to an internalization of negative social attitudes, internalized homonegativity, rejection sensitivity, a failure to disclose sexual orientation and/or gender identity, and the development of different strategies to ameliorate the negative effects of this environment (Dentato, Halkitis, & Orwat, 2013; Meyer, 2013). In an expansion of this model, Herek, Gillis, and Cogan (2015) distinguish between enacted stigma, referring to sexual stigma (overtly expressed), felt stigma (one's awareness of society's homonegative attitudes), internalized stigma (where sexual stigma becomes part of one's identity), and structural sexual stigma (heterosexism). Internalized stigma is associated with lower self-esteem and greater depressive symptoms and state-anxiety (Herek et al., 2015). In support of this model, Lewis, Derlega, Clarke, and Kuang (2006) propose the concept of stigma consciousness, the expectation of prejudice and discrimination as a minority stressor. LGBTQ persons experiencing higher stigma consciousness and alienation from their social network are more likely to experience physical symptoms, intrusive thoughts, and internalized homophobia than those lower in these social constraints.

To understand how minority stress impacts mental health and to better understand prevention and treatment goals, Hatzenbuehler (2009) proposes a mediational model that can help explain the relationship between sexual minority stigma and mental health outcomes. In his psychological mediation framework, distal stigma-related stressors (e.g., objective prejudice, discrimination) may lead to psychological vulnerabilities known to affect mental health. LGBTQ individuals show higher rates of anxiety, depression, suicidality, and other psychiatric disorders. Sexual minority young adults have reported greater symptoms of generalized anxiety disorder, social phobia, panic disorder, post-traumatic stress disorder, and depression compared to their heterosexual peers (Borgogna, McDermott, Aita, & Kridel, 2019). Moreover, concealment of sexual orientation has been found to be related to psychological distress (Cohen, Blasey, Taylor, Weiss, & Newman, 2016; Pachankis, Cochran, & Mays, 2015; Riggle, Rostosky, Black, & Rosenkrantz, 2017).

Griffin et al. (2018) found that exposure to assaults predicted anxiety history, but other forms of discrimination or internalized homophobia did not necessarily predict a history of anxiety, suggesting that there is a difference between discrete external minority stress and internalizations of minority stress and comfort with being out. Greater levels of psychiatric symptoms have been reported by LGBTQ youth who experienced high levels of victimization (Espelage, Merrin, & Hatchel, 2018). Perceptions of school violence, drugs, weapons, and gang activity have been associated with higher levels of suicidality as compared to LGBTQ youth who did not experience those levels of school/neighborhood violence. Nonphysical victimization has been found to also predict depression, stress, and anxiety among LGBTQ youth (Mays & Cochron, 2001). In addition, sexual harassment can be a precursor to depressive symptoms in youth (Hatchel, Espelage, & Huang, 2018). Kelleher (2009) found that heterosexist experiences predicted psychological distress. Sexual minority adolescents have higher-than-average reports of suicidal ideation (Levy, Russon, & Diamond, 2016) related in part to being threatened or harassed at school (Bouris, Everett, Heath, & Elsaesser, 2016) or living in neighborhoods with high levels of hate crimes (Duncan & Hatzenbuehler, 2014), school stigma, early coming-out experiences, and a past history of treatment for anxiety and depression (Rimes et al., 2019).

Several studies report on the high prevalence of parental rejection (Levy et al., 2016) and physical, emotional, and sexual abuse (Balsam, Rothblum, & Beauchaine, 2005; Friedman et al., 2011) and negative mental health outcomes. Friedman et al. (2011) found increased rates of sexual abuse, parental physical abuse, assault at school, and a history of skipping school out of fear for sexual minority children under the age of eighteen. Pachankis, Sullivan, and Moore (2018) found rejection based on sexual minority status to predict both symptoms of depression and social anxiety. Carastathis, Cohen, Kaczmarek, and Chang (2017) conducted a qualitative study on sexual minority individuals who faced rejection from their family because of their sexual orientation. The struggles involved in growing up in a society that was not accepting of sexual minorities led to an early struggle with their identity and ultimately negative feelings about themselves, resulting in significant mental health issues for some. Toro-Alfonso and Rodriguez-Madera (2004) found that younger gay male couples who reported high levels of emotional violence in their relationship reported high levels of violence in their families of origin as well as low conflict resolution skills. Sexual minority youth often relay the belief that they are a burden to their family and friends and in turn experience poorer mental health outcomes (Baams, Dubas, Russell, Buikema, & van Aken, 2018; Baams, Grossman, & Russell, 2015).

Among sexual minority adolescents and adults, shame (Greene, Britton, & Fitts, 2014; Straub, McConnell, & Messman-Moore, 2018), lower self-acceptance among LGBT college students (Woodford, Kulick, Sinco, & Hong, 2014), coping (Kaysen et al., 2014; Salway et al., 2018), and rumination (Szymanski, Dunn, & Ikizler, 2014; Schwartz, Stratton, & Hart, 2016) all have been found to mediate the relationship between minority stress and greater mental distress.

Pachankis, Sullivan, Feinstein, and Newcomb (2018) conducted a longitudinal study using the theory of Herek et al. (2015) to differentiate between external (enacted) and internal (internalized) stigma. They found that enacted stigma was related to greater symptoms of depression and social anxiety, while anticipated and internalized stigma was related to greater social anxiety. Berghe, Dewaele, Cox, and Vincke (2010) found that stigma consciousness (expectation of prejudice and discrimination as a minority stressor), sexual identity distress, and heterosexist experiences all predicted psychological distress among LGB youth in Belgium. Straub et al. (2018) found that among sexual minority women, internalized heterosexism predicted posttraumatic stress disorder symptoms, while Syzmanski et al. (2014) found that multiple forms of discrimination (heterosexist or sexist events) and internalized heterosexism predicted psychological distress. Breslow et al. (2015) found that higher levels of transgender discrimination, internalized transphobia, and stigma awareness (awareness of transgender discrimination) predicted psychological distress. Among transgender persons in Italy, minority stresses (discrimination, shame, and alienation) were related to greater anxiety. Moreover, greater discrimination and shame predicted greater levels of depression and suicidal ideation, whereas pride in their gender identity negatively predicted anxiety.

Hatzenbuehler (2016) suggested that further consideration of the role of structural stigma (societal-level conditions, cultural norms, and institutional policies) is needed when considering the mental health of LGBTQ persons. In a survey across thirty-eight European countries, in more stigmatizing countries, men who have sex with men were less likely to identify as a sexual minority, especially in sparsely populated areas (Pachankis et al., 2017). Pachankis amd Bränström (2018) studied structural stigma across twenty-eight countries and suggested that concealment seems to be a protective factor against discrimination and victimization in high-structural-stigma countries, but was also related to lower life satisfaction.

Hatzenbuehler (2009) asserted the need to examine the mechanisms that link minority stress/stigma and mental health outcomes. Salway et al. (2018) found that among gay and bisexual men, the relationship between anticipated prejudice (rejection sensitivity) and suicide attempts was mediated by depression, the same mechanism found for enacted stigma, but it was smaller in strength. In another study among LGB adults, perceived discrimination was related to depression, anxiety, and stress through greater internalized homophobia (Walch, Ngamake, Bovornusvakool, & Walker, 2016). Similarly, being more closeted was related to greater mental distress through greater internalized homophobia (Baiocco et al., 2014; Hoy-Ellis & Fredriksen-Goldsen, 2017; Schrimshaw, Siegel, Downing, & Parsons, 2013). Moreover, greater structural stigma predicted greater concealment, which in turn predicted lower life satisfaction, among sexual minority adults across twenty-eight European countries (Pachankis & Bränström, 2018).

Intersection of Race, Ethnicity, Sexual Orientation, and Gender Identity/Expression

There is not a lot of research examining the intersection of race and ethnicity with sexual minority status (English, Rendina, & Parsons, 2018). Recognizing that people may experience microaggressions for more than one minority status, Balsam, Molina, Beadnell, Simoni, and Walters (2011) found that these stressors among LGBT people of color predicted greater depression, perceived stress, stigma sensitivity, and internalized homonegativity. Researchers examining multiple types of discrimination (race, ethnicity, gender, sexual orientation) found that people who had experienced sexual orientation discrimination in combination with other types of discrimination had higher odds of a past-year mental health disorder compared to those who experienced only sexual orientation discrimination (Bostwick, Boyd, Hughes, West, & McCabe., 2014).

English et al. (2018) found that in addition to the stigma and discrimination associated with sexual minority status, racial discrimination was associated with emotional regulation difficulties and predicted internalizing psychiatric symptoms and alcohol use in black, Latino, and multiracial sexual minority individuals. Many of these constructs were examined in isolation and therefore do not provide a complete explanation of the problems experienced by sexual minorities. Furthermore, they found that racial discrimination in addition to gay rejection sensitivity impacted individuals more extensively when they occurred together versus separately. Ghabrial and Ross (2018) believe that there are multiple layers of oppression when sexual minorities have multiple identities, such as racism, binegativity, and invisibility. These marginalized identities and experiences of oppression merge and can influence each other. McConnell, Janulis, Phillips, Truong, and Birkett (2018) found that there are differences in the stigma experienced by sexual minority males versus other LGBT individuals. White sexual minority males experienced the lowest levels of racial-ethnic stigma by other LGBT individuals and in their own neighborhoods compared to more racial/ethnic diverse males, with black sexual minority males reporting the highest levels of stigma.

There can also be differences in how individuals from different cultures deal with heterosexism and discrimination. For example, Choi, Han, Paul, and Ayala (2011) conducted focus groups and found that African Americans reported concealment of homosexuality for self-preservation and to protect against ridicule within the larger black community. Latinos concealed their identity because they wanted to be seen as individuals rather than via a sexual label, while Asians were the only group to report actively trying to pass as straight. Ching, Lee, Chen, So, and Williams (2018) proposed an intersectional stress and trauma model among Asian American LGBT persons and found support for this model by discovering that structural/cultural factors were related to mental health outcomes through interpersonal discrimination. In their study interpersonal discrimination also mediated the relationship between structural/cultural factors and internalized oppression and stigma (internalized racism and the model minority stereotype [an assumption that Asians attain greater success than the average population], internalized homophobia and transphobia), which in turn predicted mental health outcomes.

Poorer mental health mediated the relationship between LGBTQ discrimination, but not racial discrimination, and suicidal ideation among LGBTQ people of color, therefore providing an important link to understanding how discrimination is related to suicidal ideation. Both racism and LGBTQ-based discrimination were associated with each other and predicted poorer mental health, suggesting an additive effect of minority stressors (race, sexual orientation, and gender identity) (Sutter & Perrin, 2016). Similarly, Drazdowski et al. (2016) found evidence that LGBTQ discrimination was more damaging on mental health than racism among LGBTQ persons of color. Burks et al. (2018) found that among a largely urban sample of LGB persons of color, lifetime hate crime victimization was related to psychiatric symptoms through internalized sexual minority–specific stress (concerned about how others judge them and internalized homophobia). In contrast, Velez, Watson, Cox, and Flores (2017) found that the relationships between minority stress (rejection sensitivity and disclosure) and poorer mental health outcomes were not different between racial/ethnic sexual minorities and white sexual minorities.

In an exhaustive review of research, Ghabrial and Ross (2018) found bisexual people to be the least studied group among racial/ethnic and SGMs. Researchers are omitting this highly vulnerable population, which experiences biphobia from both heterosexual and lesbian and gay communities and racial/ethnic discrimination, putting them at greater risk of poorer mental health.

Vulnerable Populations

Gender Minorities

Transgender and gender-nonconforming individuals encounter significant stigma and face systematic oppression (Bockting, Miner, Swinburne Romine, Hamilton, & Coleman, 2013; White Hughto, Reisner, & Pachankis, 2015). Gender minorities are more likely to experience an expectation of rejection, self-stigma, and prejudice, leading to psychological distress and rumination (Timmins, Rimes, & Rahman, 2017). They are also more likely to report depression, anxiety, and somatization disorders (Bockting et al., 2013; Yang, Manning, van den Berg, & Operario, 2015). As social stigma increases, so too does psychological distress and bullying victimization (Gower et al., 2018). In a study by Zeluf et al. (2018), transgender people were more at risk for suicidality and attempted suicide. Lehavot and Simoni (2011) found that among sexual minority women, gender expression was related to depression and anxiety through LGB victimization: "A more butch/masculine gender expression was associated with LGB victimization, whereas a more femme/feminine gender expression was associated with greater internalized homophobia and concealment" (p. 167). Borgogna et al. (2019) found that those who identified as gender nonconforming reported the highest levels of anxiety, while those who rated themselves as LGBTQ, pansexual, demisexual, or asexual had higher rates of depression and anxiety compared with heterosexuals, and with gay and lesbian participants. The authors noted that multiple-minority stressors such as both sexual and gender minority combinations have an additive effect.

The greater awareness of LGBTQ issues now than in the past has not always translated to more acceptance of gender diversity in young transgender people. In a study by Jackman, Dolezal, and Bockting (2018), younger trans-feminine individuals reported more psychological distress compared to older trans-feminine individuals. The authors posit that this may be due to internalized transnegativity. Rood et al. (2017) believe this is one of the many underexplored minority stressors for gender minorities, possibly leading to an increase in exposure to negative social messaging and increased internalized stigma. Misgendering (the wrong assumption of someone's gender identity or expression) as a minority stressor for transgender individuals can be stigmatizing (McLemore, 2018).

Hoy-Ellis and Fredriksen-Goldsen (2017) found that perceived general stress had a direct effect on depression, separate from internalized trans-negativity and concealment of gender identity. With the high rates of clinical depressive symptoms in older transgender individuals, the authors concluded that minority stress processes were the etiological explanation. With high rates of discrimination and victimization, especially in employment, this may lead to increased anticipation of further discrimination.

Bisexuals

Research suggests that health disparities are prevalent among bisexual men and women compared to gay men, lesbian women, and heterosexuals (Bostwick et al., 2014; Jorm, Korten, Rodgers, Jacomb, & Christensen, 2002; Ross et al., 2018), and bisexuals are at greater risk of poorer mental health outcomes in large part due to biphobia, whereby bisexual individuals experience discrimination, prejudice, and stigma from both gay/lesbian and heterosexual populations (Brewster & Moradi, 2010; Brewster, Moradi, Deblaere, & Valez, 2013; Dyar & London, 2018; Dyar, Feinstein, & Davila, 2019; Friedman et. al., 2014; Lambe, Cerezo, & O'Shaughnessy, 2017; Salim, Robinson, & Flanders, 2019). Although bisexual individuals are an at-risk group due to minority stress, there is a lack of research on how minority stress/stigma plays a role in mental health outcomes among this population (Lambe et al., 2017).

Older SGM Individuals

Health disparities have also been found to be linked to age in the LGBT population (Butler, 2004). Butler asserts that LGBT individuals who are sixty-five and older endured oppression and discrimination in their younger years, creating secrecy and poor health as they dealt with unwelcoming health and social service systems.

Bradford et al. (2016) conducted a study on older lesbian women and found that they are more likely to experience disability, depression, and other health-related concerns as compared to both heterosexual women and gay men. In part this may be due to financial concerns, because many older lesbian women have experienced lower income across their lifespan and have less financial support from retirement accounts and/or support or benefits from a spouse. They are also less likely to seek healthcare due to concerns about discrimination and cultural competence in their healthcare provider. The women in this study worried about maintaining social support as they grow older and sought to live in communities where they could easily engage with other lesbian women.

In a study on transgender older adults, Fredriksen-Goldsen et al. (2012) found higher rates of lifetime victimization, and internalized stigma predicted poorer physical and mental health. They were more likely to conceal their gender identity and experience lower levels of social support, contributing to high rates of disability, depression, and perceived stress.

Residents of the Global South

There is a dearth of research on LGBTQ minority stress/stigma and mental health in the Global South. Rao and Mason (2018) examined how anti-LGBTQ policies and laws in India impacted sexual minorities. Participants reported increased rates of depressive symptoms through greater concealment stress and less sense of belonging. Participants used negative terms to describe their responses to these laws, like "unsafe, bullied, pathetic and disgusted, suffocated, like a criminal, and like a second-hand citizen" (Rao & Mason, 2018, p. 440). Among transgender women and men who have sex with men in urban areas of India, stigma was related to depression through less resilient coping and social support (Chakrapani et al., 2017).

Nguyen et al. (2016b) studied a sample of young urban-dwelling women on two types of self-stigma (see self as not normal, and self-reproach and wishing away same-sex sexuality) and their own sexual prejudice. While all of these variables correlated with depressive symptoms and lower self-esteem, self-reproach and wishing away same-sex sexuality had the strongest correlations with depressive symptoms and self-esteem. Anticipation of heterosexual marriage was most highly positively related to internalized homophobia (self-stigma). The authors suggest that this type of minority stressor may not be present in countries with more liberal attitudes and laws in support of gay marriage. Nguyen et al. (2016a) found that among sexual minority Vietnamese women, almost 60 percent reported receiving negative treatment from families. In contrast, Shao, Chang, and Chen (2018) did not find minority stress (internalized homophobia, concealment, and rejection sensitivity) to be predictive of psychological maladjustment among self-identified LGB Chinese young adults. They did find that the quality of parent–child relationships may be a more important predictor of well-being of LGB young adults in China than being part of a stigmatized group.

Oginni, Mosaku, Mapayi, Akinsulore, and Afolabi (2018) found that gay male college students in Nigeria had greater depressive symptoms and suicidal ideation and lower resilience compared to heterosexual males. Within the sexual minority male sample, nondisclosure of sexual orientation, perceived stigma, and negative reaction to disclosure of sexual orientation all predicted depression. The authors suggested that disclosure in Nigeria is usually to a small select few; rarely does someone openly take on a sexual minority identity, given the laws and social climate. A qualitative study among men who have sex with men in Cape Town, South Africa, found that those from disadvantaged backgrounds and culturally conservative communities reported more prejudice and psychological distress (McAdams-Mahmoud et al., 2014). Most discussed the prejudice from friends, families, or peers (e.g., experiencing hate speech, violence and expulsions from home and communities), and many talked about living a double life or pretending to be heterosexual in some situations.

To conclude, the study of sexual minorities and psychiatric outcomes continues to be an understudied phenomenon, especially in the Global South. Structural stigma continues to be a significant barrier to the well-being of LGBTQ individuals. Before society can successfully begin to address stigma, oppression, and discrimination and their relationship to adverse mental health outcomes, these discriminatory laws need to change. Laws that increase the level of concealment of one's identity have been associated with poorer mental health outcomes (McAdams-Mahmoud et al., 2014; Nguyen et al., 2016b; Oginni et al., 2018).

Societies across the globe are missing opportunities to educate SGM youth in a number of areas, including health education to prevent sexually transmitted infections (Rose & Friedman, 2017), multiple forms of victimization (Espelage et al., 2018), and programs to promote healthy opportunities for socialization, support, positive role models, and advocacy (Friedman et al., 2011). Finally, the education of professionals in various systems (e.g., educational, health, medical, social service, criminal, child welfare, religious) needs to be improved so that these supportive environments are not associated with SGM abuse.

Methodological Limitations

Most of the studies conducted to identify the mechanisms that link minority stress and stigma have used cross-sectional designs. Tate (2015) argues that to test true mediation, one must determine the timing of the pathways between variables; therefore, longitudinal studies need to be conducted. With cross-sectional designs it is also very difficult to understand the context of how minority stressors are experienced on a daily basis. Daily experience sampling is a method to determine context and temporality. For example, Mohr and Sarno (2016), using daily experience sampling, found that participants who had less internalized stigma and expected rejection experienced more positive affect the next day. Another problem is that most of the studies do not employ probability sampling because of the difficulty finding invisible minorities. In addition, it takes extremely large samples in order to have enough power to determine any significant effects, and nonprobability samples can also bring bias and compromise the internal validity of the research (Fink, 1995). Problems with self-report responses can also introduce bias through social desirability (Zerbe & Paulhus, 1987).

Future Directions

Given the strong relationship between sexual minority stress and negative mental health outcomes, it is important to continue the work of Hatzenbuehler (2009) to understand the mechanisms that explain why minority stress and stigma lead to poorer mental health outcomes. Hatzenbuehler (2016) also advocates for the examination of structural stigma, a broader perspective that includes issues such as laws, social norms, cultural norms, and so forth that provide a culture of oppression for SGMs. But there is a tendency in the literature to examine one type of oppressor in isolation, leaving out the interactions of multiple oppressions (English et al., 2018). There is a need to examine the intersectionality between race and ethnicity with sexual orientation and gender identity and expression. In addition, there is a lack of research on vulnerable populations (e.g., transgender, bisexual, older LGBTQ, and Global South LGBTQ), who are at even higher risk for negative mental health outcomes and oppression.

Better understanding these relationships will result in improved mental health treatment and prevention for SGM. Some innovative recent interventions include expressive writing for gay-related stress (Pachankis & Goldfried, 2010), a mental health prevention model using gay–straight alliances in the schools for LGBTQ youth (Heck, 2015), an LGB-affirmative cognitive-behavioral therapy for young adult men who have sex with men (Pachankis, Hatzenbuehler, Rendina, Safren, & Parsons, 2015), an online intervention to reduce internalized binegativity (Israel et al., 2019), and acculturation strategies among LGB youth (Cox, Vanden Berghe, Dewaele, & Vincke, 2010). These are among the few intervention studies designed to help sexual and gender minorities cope with minority stress and stigma. In addition, intervention and prevention strategies for LGBTQ youth are needed. For example, Heck, Flentjie, and Cochran (2013) found more positive school experiences and mental health outcomes when LGBT youth attended a high school with gay–straight alliances. Rose and Friedman (2017) recognized that schools are missing an opportunity to educate minority youth about their sexual health and increased risk for HIV and other sexually transmitted infections. Espelage et al. (2018) advocate for prevention programs addressing multiple forms of victimization (peer and dating), and Friedman et al. (2011) advocate for an improved multisystemic approach in the treatment of sexual minority youth using various systems (e.g., educational, mental health, medical, social service, criminal, child welfare, religious).

References

Baams, L., Dubas, J. S., Russell, S. T., Buikema, R. L., & van Aken, M. A. G. (2018). Minority stress, perceived burdensomeness, and depressive symptoms among sexual minority youth. *Journal of Adolescence, 66*, 9–18. doi:10.1016/j.adolescence.2018.03.015

Baams, L., Grossman, A. H., & Russell, S. T. (2015). Minority stress and mechanisms of risk for depression and suicidal ideation among lesbian, gay, and bisexual youth. *Developmental Psychology, 51*(5), 688–96. doi:10.1037/a0038994

Baiocco, R., Ioverno, S., Cerutti, R., Santamaria, F., Fontanesi, L., Lingiardi, V., . . . Laghi, F. (2014). Suicidal ideation in Spanish and Italian lesbian and gay young adults: The role of internalized sexual stigma. *Psicothema, 26*(4), 490–6. https://search.ebscohost.com/login.aspx?direct=true&db=psyh&AN=2014-44844-009&site=ehost-live&scope=site

Balsam, K. F., Molina, Y., Beadnell, B., Simoni, J., & Walters, K. (2011). Measuring minority stress: The LGBT people of color microaggressions scale. *Cultural Diversity and Ethnic Minority Psychology, 17*(2), 163–74.

Balsam, K. F., Rothblum, E. D., & Beauchaine, T. P. (2005). Victimization over the life span: A comparison of lesbian, gay, bisexual, and heterosexual siblings. *Journal of Consulting and Clinical Psychology, 73*(3), 477–87, doi:10.1037/0022-006X.73.3.477

Berghe, W. V., Dewaele, A., Cox, N., & Vincke, J. (2010). Minority-specific determinants of mental well-being among lesbian, gay, and bisexual youth. *Journal of Applied Social Psychology, 40*(1), 153–66. doi:10.1111/j.1559–1816.2009.00567.x

Bockting, W. O., Miner, M. H., Swinburne Romine, R. E., Hamilton, A., & Coleman, E. (2013). Stigma, mental health, and resilience in an online sample of the US transgender population. *American Journal of Public Health, 103*, 943–51. doi:10.2105/AJPH.2013.301241

Borgogna, N. C., McDermott, R. C., Aita, S. L., & Kridel, M. M. (2019). Anxiety and depression across gender and sexual minorities: Implications for transgender, gender nonconforming, pansexual, demisexual, asexual, queer, and questioning individuals *Psychology of Sexual Orientation and Gender Diversity, 6*(1), 54–63. doi:10.1037/sgd0000306

Bostwick, W. B., Boyd, C. J., Hughes, T. L., West, B. T., & McCabe, S. E. (2014). Discrimination and mental health among lesbian, gay, and bisexual adults in the United States. *American Journal of Orthopsychiatry, 84*(1), 35–45. doi:10.1037/h0098851

Bouris, A., Everett, B. G., Heath, R. D., & Elsaesser, C. E. (2016). Effects of victimization and violence on suicidal ideation and behaviors among sexual minority and heterosexual adolescents. *LGBT Health, 3*(2), 153–61. doi:10.1089/lgbt.2015.0037

Bradford, J. B., Putney, J. M., Shepard, B. L., Sass, S. E., Rudicel, S., Ladd, H., & Cahill, S. (2016). Health aging in community for older lesbians. *LBGT Health, 3*(2), 109–15. doi:10.1089/lgbt.2015.0019

Breslow, A. S., Brewster, M. E., Velez, B. L., Wong, S., Geiger, E., & Soderstrom, B. (2015). Resilience and collective action: Exploring buffers against minority stress for transgender individuals. *Psychology of Sexual Orientation and Gender Diversity, 2*(3), 253–65. doi:10.1037/sgd0000117

Brewster, M. E., & Moradi, B. (2010). Perceived experiences of anti-bisexual prejudice: Instrument development and evaluation. *Journal of Counseling Psychology, 57*(4), 451–68. https://doi-org.ccsu.idm.oclc.org/10.1037/a0021116

Brewster, M. E., Moradi, B., DeBlaere, C., & Velez, B. L. (2013). Navigating the borderlands: The roles of minority stressors, bicultural self-efficacy, and cognitive flexibility in the mental health of bisexual individuals. *Journal of Counseling Psychology, 60*(4), 543–56. doi:10.1037/a0033224

Burks, A. C., Cramer, R. J., Henderson, C. E., Stroud, C. H., Crosby, J. W., & Graham, J. (2018). Frequency, nature, and correlates of hate crime victimization experiences in an urban sample of lesbian, gay, and bisexual community members. *Journal of Interpersonal Violence, 33*(3), 402–20. doi:10.1177/0886260515605298

Butler, S. S. (2004). Gay, lesbian, bisexual, and transgender (GLBT) elders: The challenges and resilience of this marginalized group. *Journal of Human Behavior in the Social Environment, 9*(4), 25–44. doi:10.1300/J137v09n04_02

Carastathis, G. S., Cohen, L., Kaczmarek, E., & Chang, P. (2017). Rejected by family for being gay or lesbian: Portrayals, perceptions, and resilience. *Journal of Homosexuality, 64*(3), 289–320. doi:10.1080/00918369.2017.1179035

Chakrapani, V., Vijin, P. P., Logie, C. H., Newman, P. A., Shunmugam, M., Sivasubramanian, M., & Samuel, M. (2017). Understanding how sexual and gender minority stigmas influence depression among trans women and men who have sex with men in India. *LGBT Health*, *4*(3), 217–26. doi:10.1089/lgbt.2016.0082

Ching, T. H. W., Lee, S. Y., Chen, J., So, R. P., & Williams, M. T. (2018). A model of intersectional stress and trauma in Asian American sexual and gender minorities. *Psychology of Violence*, *8*(6), 657–68. doi:10.1037/vio0000204

Choi, K.-H., Han, C.-S., Paul, J., & Ayala, G. (2011). Strategies for managing racism and homophobia among U.S. ethnic and racial minority men who have sex with men. *AIDS Education and Prevention*, *23*(2), 145–58. doi:10.1521/aeap.2011.23.2.145

Cohen, J. M., Blasey, C., Taylor, C. B., Weiss, B. J., & Newman, M. G. (2016). Anxiety and related disorders and concealment in sexual minority young adults. *Behavior Therapy*, *47*(1), 91–101. doi:10.1016/j.beth.2015.09.006

Cox, N., Vanden Berghe, W., Dewaele, A., & Vincke, J. (2010). Acculturation strategies and mental health in gay, lesbian, and bisexual youth. *Journal of Youth Adolescence*, *39*, 1199–210. doi:10.1007/s10964-009-9435-7

Dentato, M. P., Halkitis, P. N., & Orwat, J. (2013). Minority stress theory: An examination of factors surrounding sexual risk behavior among gay and bisexual men who use club drugs. *Journal of Gay & Lesbian Social Services*, *25*(4), 509–525. doi:10.1080/10538720.2013.829395

Drazdowski, T. K., Perrin, P. B., Trujillo, M. A., Sutter, M., Benotsch, E. G., & Snipes, D. J. (2016). Structural equation modeling of the effects of racism, heterosexism, and internalized oppression on illicit drug use in LGBTQ people of color. *Drug and Alcohol Dependence*, *159*, 255–62. doi:10.1016/j.drugalcdep.2015.12.029

Duncan, D. T., & Hatzenbuehler, M. L. (2014). Lesbian, gay, bisexual, and transgender hate crimes and suicidality among a population-based sample of sexual-minority adolescents in Boston. *American Journal of Public Health*, *104*(2), 272–8. https://doi-org.ccsu.idm.oclc.org/10.2105/AJPH.2013.301424

Dyar, C., Feinstein, B. A., & Davila, J. (2019). Development and validation of a brief version of the anti-bisexual experiences scale. *Archives of Sexual Behavior*, *48*(1), 175–89. doi:10.1007/s10508-018-1157-z

Dyar, C., & London, B. (2018). Longitudinal examination of a bisexual-specific minority stress process among bisexual cisgender women. *Psychology of Women Quarterly*, *42*(3), 342–60. doi:10.1177/0361684318768233

English, D., Rendina, H. J., & Parsons, J. T. (2018). The effects of intersecting stigma: A longitudinal examination of minority stress, mental health, and substance use among black, Latino, and multiracial gay and bisexual men. *Psychology of Violence*, *8*(6), 669–79. doi:10.1037/vio0000218

Espelage, D. L., Merrin, G. J., & Hatchel, T. (2018). Peer victimization and dating violence among LGBTQ youth: The impact of school violence and crime on mental health outcomes. *Youth Violence and Juvenile Justice*, *16*(2), 156–73. doi:10.1177/1541204016680408

Fink, A. (1995). *How to sample in surveys*. Los Angeles, CA: Sage.

Fredriksen-Goldsen, K. I., Emlet, C. A., Kim, H. J., Muraco, A., Erosheva, E. A., Goldsen, J., & Hoy-Elllis, C. P. (2012). The physical and mental health of lesbian, gay male, and bisexual (LGB) older adults: The role of key health indicators and risk and protective factors. *Gerontologist*, *53*(4), 664–75. doi:10.1093/geront/gns123

Friedman, M. R., Dodge, B., Schick, V., Herbenick, D., Hubach, R. D., Bowling, J., . . . Reece, M. (2014). From bias to bisexual health disparities: Attitudes toward bisexual men and women in the United States. *LGBT Health*, *1*(4), 309–18. doi:10.1089/lgbt.2014.0005

Friedman, M. S., Marshal, M. P., Guadamuz, T. E., Wei, C., Wong, C. F., Saewyc, E. M., & Stall, R. (2011). A meta-analysis of disparities in childhood sexual abuse, parental physical abuse, and peer victimization among sexual minority and sexual nonminority individuals. *American Journal of Public Health*, *101*(8), 1481–94. doi:10.2105/AJPH.2009.190009

Ghabrial, M. A., & Ross, L. E. (2018). Representation and erasure of bisexual people of color: A content analysis of quantitative bisexual mental health research. *Psychology of Sexual Orientation and Gender Diversity*, *5*(2), 132–42. doi:10.1037/sgd0000286

Gower, A. L., Rider, G. N., Coleman, E., Brown, C., McMorris, B. J., & Eisenber, M. E. (2018). Approaches to analysis and associations with bullying victimization and emotional distress. *LGBT Health*, *5*(5), 312–19. doi:10.1089/lgbt.2017.0176

Greene, D. C., Britton, P. J., & Fitts, B. (2014). Long-term outcomes of lesbian, gay, bisexual, and transgender recalled school victimization. *Journal of Counseling & Development*, *92*(4), 406–17. doi:10.1002/j.1556-6676.2014.00167.x

Griffin, J. A., Drescher, C. F., Eldridge, E. D., Rossi, A. L., Loew, M. M., & Stepleman, L. M. (2018). Predictors of anxiety among sexual minority individuals in the Southern US. *American Journal of Orthopsychiatry*, *88*(6), 723–31. doi:10.1037/ort0000363

Hatchel, T., Espelage, D. L., & Huang, Y. (2018). Sexual harassment victimization, school belonging, and depressive symptoms among LGBTQ adolescents: Temporal insights. *American Journal of Orthopsychiatry*, *88*(4), 422–30. doi:10.1037/ort0000279

Hatzenbuehler, M. L. (2009). How does sexual minority stigma "get under the skin"? A psychological mediation framework. *Psychological Bulletin*, *135*(5), 707–30. doi:10.1037/a0016441

Hatzenbuehler, M. L. (2016). Structural stigma: Research evidence and implications for psychological science. *American Psychologist*, *71*(8), 742–51. doi:10.1037/amp0000068

Heck, N. C. (2015). The potential to promote resilience: Piloting a minority stress-informed, GSA-based, mental health promotion program for LGBTQ youth. *Psychology of Sexual Orientation and Gender Diversity*, *2*(3), 225–31. doi:10.1037/sgd0000110

Heck, N. C., Flentje, A., & Cochran, B. N. (2013). Offsetting risks: High school gay-straight alliances and lesbian, gay, bisexual, and transgender (LGBT) youth. *Psychology of Sexual Orientation and Gender Diversity*, *1*(S), 81–90.

Herek, G. M., Gillis, J. R., & Cogan, J. C. (2015). Internalized stigma among sexual minority adults: Insights from a social psychological perspective. *Stigma and Health*, *1*(S), 18–34. doi:10.1037/2376-6972.1.S.18.supp

Hoy-Ellis, C. P., & Fredriksen-Goldsen, K. I. (2017). Depression among transgender older adults: General and minority stress. *American Journal of Community Psychology*, *59*, 295–305. doi:10.1002/ajcp.12138

Israel, T., Choi, A. Y., Goodman, J. A., Matsuno, E., Lin, Y. J., Kary, K. G., & Merrill, C. R. S. (2019). Reducing internalized binegativity: Development and efficacy of an online intervention. *Psychology of Sexual Orientation and Gender Diversity*, *6*(2), 149–59. doi:10.1037/sg0000314

Jackman, K. B., Dolezal, C., & Bockting, W. O. (2018). Generational differences in internalized transnegativity and psychological distress among feminine spectrum transgender people. *LGBT Health*, *5*(1), 54–60. doi:10.1089/lgbt.2017.0034

Jorm, A. F., Korten, A. E., Rodgers, B., Jacomb, P. A., & Christensen, H. (2002). Sexual orientation and mental health: Results from a community survey of young and middle-aged adults. *British Journal of Psychiatry, 180*(5), 423–7. doi:10.1192/bjp.180.5.423

Kaysen, D. L., Kulesza, M., Balsam, K. F., Rhew, I. C., Blayney, J. A., Lehavot, K., & Hughes, T. L. (2014). Coping as a mediator of internalized homophobia and psychological distress among young adult sexual minority women. *Psychology of Sexual Orientation and Gender Diversity, 1*(3), 225–33. doi:10.1037/sgd0000045

Kelleher, C. (2009). Minority stress and health: Implications for lesbian, gay, bisexual, transgender, and questioning (LGBTQ) young people. *Counselling Psychology Quarterly, 22*(4), 373–9. doi:10.1080/09515070903334995

Lambe, J., Cerezo, A., & O'Shaughnessy, T. (2017). Minority stress, community involvement, and mental health among bisexual women. *Psychology of Sexual Orientation and Gender Diversity, 4*(2), 218–26. doi:10.1037/sgd0000222

Lehavot, K., & Simoni, J. M. (2011). The impact of minority stress on mental health and substance use among sexual minority women. *Journal of Consulting and Clinical Psychology, 79*(2), 159–70. doi:10.1037/a0022839

Levy, S. Z., Russon, J., & Diamond, G. M. (2016). Attachment-based family therapy for suicidal lesbian, gay, and bisexual adolescents: A case study. *Australian & New Zealand Journal of Family Therapy, 37*, 190–206. doi:10.1002/anzf.1151

Lewis, R. J., Derlega, V. J., Clarke, E. G., & Kuang, J. C. (2006). Stigma consciousness, social constraints, and lesbian well-being. *Journal of Counseling Psychology, 53*(1), 48–56. doi:10.1037/0022–0167.53.1.48

Mays, V. M., & Cochran, S. D. (2001). Mental health correlates of perceived discrimination among lesbian, gay, and bisexual adults in the United States. *American Journal of Public Health, 91*(11), 1869–76. doi:10.2105/AJPH.91.11.1869

McAdams-Mahmoud, A., Stephenson, R., Rentsch, C., Cooper, H., Arriola, K. J., Jobson, G., & McIntyre, J. (2014). Minority stress in the lives of men who have sex with men in Cape Town, South Africa. *Journal of Homosexuality, 61*(6), 847–67. doi:10.1080/00918369.2014.870454

McConnell, E. A., Janulis, P., Phillips II, G., Truong, R., & Birkett, M. (2018). Multiple minority stress and LGBT community resilience among sexual minority men. *Psychology of Sexual Orientation and Gender Diversity, 5*(1), 1–12, http://dx.doi.org/10.1037sgd0000265

McLemore, K. A. (2018). A minority stress perspective on transgender individuals' experiences with misgendering. *Stigma and Health, 3*(1), 53–64. doi:10.1037/sah0000070

Meyer, I. H. (2013). Prejudice, social stress, and mental health in lesbian, gay, and bisexual populations: Conceptual issues and research evidence. *Psychology of Sexual Orientation and Gender Diversity, 1*(S), 3–26. doi:10.1037/2329–0382.1.S.3

Mohr, J. J., & Sarno, E. L. (2016). The ups and downs of being lesbian, gay, and bisexual: A daily experience perspective on minority stress and support processes. *Journal of Counseling Psychology, 63*(1), 106–18. doi:10.1037/cou0000125

Nguyen, T. Q., Bandeen-Roche, K., German, D., Nguyen, N. T. T., Bass, J. K., & Knowlton, A. R. (2016a). Negative treatment by family as a predictor of depressive symptoms, life satisfaction, suicidality, and tobacco/alcohol use in Vietnamese sexual minority women. *LGBT Health, 3*(5), 357–65. doi:10.1089/lgbt.2015.0017

Nguyen, T. Q., Poteat, T., Bandeen-Roche, K., German, D., Nguyen, Y. H., Vu, L. K.-C., . . . Knowlton, A. R. (2016b). The Internalized Homophobia Scale for Vietnamese sexual minority women: Conceptualization, factor structure, reliability, and associations with hypothesized correlates. *Archives of Sexual Behavior, 45*(6), 1329–46. doi:10.1007/s10508-016-0694-6

Oginni, O. A., Mosaku, K. S., Mapayi, B. M., Akinsulore, A., & Afolabi, T. O. (2018). Depression and associated factors among gay and heterosexual male university students in Nigeria. *Archives of Sexual Behavior, 47*(4), 1119–32. doi:10.1007/s10508-017-0987-4

Pachankis, J. E., & Bränström, R. (2018). Hidden from happiness: Structural stigma, sexual orientation concealment, and life satisfaction across 28 countries. *Journal of Consulting and Clinical Psychology, 86*(5), 403–15. doi:10.1037/ccp0000299

Pachankis, J. E., Cochran, S. D., & Mays, V. M. (2015). The mental health of sexual minority adults in and out of the closet: A population-based study. *Journal of Consulting and Clinical Psychology, 83*(5), 890–901. doi:10.1037/ccp0000047

Pachankis, J. E., & Goldfried, M. R. (2010). Expressive writing for gay-related stress: Psychosocial benefits and mechanisms underlying improvement. *Journal of Consulting and Clinical Psychology, 78*(1), 98–110. doi:10.1037/a0017580

Pachankis, J. E., Hatzenbuehler, M. L., Mirandola, M., Weatherburn, P., Berg, R. C., Marcus, U., & Schmidt, A. J. (2017). The geography of sexual orientation: Structural stigma and sexual attraction, behavior, and identity among men who have sex with men across 38 European countries. *Archives of Sexual Behavior, 46*(5), 1491–502. doi:10.1007/s10508-016-0819-y

Pachankis, J. E., Hatzenbuehler, M. L., Rendina, H. J., Safren, S. A., & Parsons, J. T. (2015). LGB-affirmative cognitive-behavioral therapy for young adult gay and bisexual men: A randomized controlled trial of transdiagnostic minority stress approach. *Journal of Consulting and Clinical Psychology, 83*(5), 875–89. doi:10.1037ccp0000037

Pachankis, J. E., Sullivan, T. J., Feinstein, B. A., & Newcomb, M. E. (2018). Young adult gay and bisexual men's stigma experiences and mental health: An 8-year longitudinal study. *Developmental Psychology, 54*(7), 1381–93. doi:10.1037/dev0000518

Pachankis, J. E., Sullivan, T. J., & Moore, N. F. (2018). A 7-year longitudinal study of sexual minority young men's parental relationships and mental health. *Journal of Family Psychology, 32*(8), 1068–1077. doi:10.1037/fam0000427

Rao, S., & Mason, C. D. (2018). Minority stress and well-being under anti-sodomy legislation in India. *Psychology of Sexual Orientation and Gender Diversity, 5*(4), 432–44. doi:10.1037/sgd0000291

Riggle, E. D. B., Rostosky, S. S., Black, W. W., & Rosenkrantz, D. E. (2017). Outness, concealment, and authenticity: Associations with LGB individuals' psychological distress and well-being. *Psychology of Sexual Orientation and Gender Diversity, 4*(1), 54–62. doi:10.1037/sgd0000202

Rimes, K. A., Shivakumar, S., Ussher, G., Baker, D., Rahman, Q., & West, E. (2019). Psychosocial factors associated with suicide attempts, ideation, and future risk in lesbian, gay, and bisexual youth: The Youth Chances study. *Crisis, 40*(2), 83–92. doi:10.1027/0227–5910/a000527

Rood, B. A., Reisner, S. L., Puckett, J. A., Surace, F. L., Berman, A. K., & Pantalone, D. W. (2017). Internalized transphobia:

Exploring perceptions of social messages in transgender and gender-nonconforming adults. *International Journal of Transgenderism, 18*(4), 411–26. doi:10.1080/15532739.2017.1329048

Rose, I. D., & Friedman, D. B. (2017). Schools: A missed opportunity to inform African American sexual and gender minority youth about sexual health education and services. *Journal of School Nursing, 33*(2), 109–15. doi:10.1177/1059840516678910

Ross, L. E., Salway, T., Tarasoff, L. A., MacKay, J. M., Hawkins, B. W., & Fehr, C. P. (2018). Prevalence of depression and anxiety among bisexual people compared to gay, lesbian, and heterosexual individuals: A systematic review and meta-analysis. *Journal of Sex Research, 55*(4–5), 435–56. doi:10.1080/00224499.2017.1387755

Salim, S., Robinson, M., & Flanders, C. E. (2019). Bisexual women's experiences of microaggressions and microaffirmations and their relation to mental health. *Psychology of Sexual Orientation and Gender Diversity, 6*(3), 336–46. doi:10.1037/sgd0000329

Salway, T., Gesink, D., Ibrahim, S., Ferlatte, O., Rhodes, A. E., Brennan, D. J., . . . Trussler, T. (2018). Evidence of multiple mediating pathways in association between Constructs of stigma and self-reported suicide attempts in a cross-sectional study of gay and bisexual men. *Archives of Sexual Behavior, 47*, 1145–61. doi:10.1007/s10508-017-1019-0

Schrimshaw, E. W., Siegel, K., Downing, M. J., Jr., & Parsons, J. T. (2013). Disclosure and concealment of sexual orientation and the mental health of non-gay-identified, behaviorally bisexual men. *Journal of Consulting and Clinical Psychology, 81*(1), 141–53. doi:10.1037/a0031272

Schwartz, D. R., Stratton, N., & Hart, T. A. (2016). Minority stress and mental and sexual health: Examining the psychological mediation framework among gay and bisexual men. *Psychology of Sexual Orientation and Gender Diversity, 3*(3), 313–24. doi:10.1037/sgd0000180

Shao, J., Chang, E. S., & Chen, C. (2018). The relative importance of parent-child dynamics and minority stress on the psychological adjustment of LGBs in China. *Journal of Counseling Psychology, 65*(5), 598–604. doi:10.1037/cou0000281

Straub, K. T., McConnell, A. A., & Messman-Moore, T. L. (2018). Internalized heterosexism and posttraumatic stress disorder symptoms: The mediating role of shame proneness among trauma-exposed sexual minority women. *Psychology of Sexual Orientation and Gender Diversity, 5*(1), 99–108. doi:10.1037/sgd0000263

Sutter, M., & Perrin, P. B. (2016). Discrimination, mental health, and suicidal ideation among LGBTQ people of color. *Journal of Counseling Psychology, 63*(1), 98–105. doi:10.1037/cou0000126

Szymanski, D. M., Dunn, T. L., & Ikizler, A. S. (2014). Multiple minority stressors and psychological distress among sexual minority women: The roles of rumination and maladaptive coping. *Psychology of Sexual Orientation and Gender Diversity, 1*(4), 412–21. doi:10.1037/sgd0000066

Tate, C. U. (2015). On the overuse and misuse of mediation analysis: It may be a matter of timing. *Basic and Applied Social Psychology, 37*(4), 235–46. doi:10.1080/01973533.2015.1062380

Timmins, L., Rimes, K. A., & Rahman, Q. (2017). Minority stressors and psychological distress in transgender individuals. *Psychology of Sexual Orientation and Gender Diversity, 4*(3), 328–40. doi:10.1037/sgd0000237

Toro-Alfonso, J., & Rodriguez-Madera, S. (2004). Domestic violence in Puerto Rican gay male couples. *Journal of Interpersonal Violence, 19*(6), 639–54. https://doi.org/10.1177/0886260504263873

Veldhuis, C. B., Talley, A., Hancock, D. W., Wilsnack, S. C., & Hughes, T. L. (2017). Alcohol use, age, and self-rated mental and physical health in a community sample of lesbian and bisexual women. *LGBT Health, 4*(6), 419–26. doi:10.1089/lgbt.2017.0056

Velez, B. L., Watson, L. B., Cox, R., & Flores, M. J. (2017). Minority stress and racial or ethnic minority status: A test of the greater risk perspective. *Psychology of Sexual Orientation and Gender Diversity, 4*(3), 257–71. doi:10.1037/sgd0000226

Walch, S. E., Ngamake, S. T., Bovornusvakool, W., & Walker, S. V. (2016). Discrimination, internalized homophobia, and concealment in sexual minority physical and mental health. *Psychology of Sexual Orientation and Gender Diversity, 3*(1), 37–48. doi:10.1037.sgd0000146

White Hughto, J. M., Reisner, S. L., & Pachankis, J. E. (2015). Transgender stigma and health: A critical review of stigma determinants, mechanisms, and interventions. *Social Science & Medicine, 147*, 222–31. doi:10.1016/j.socscimed.2015.11.010

Woodford, M. R., Kulick, A., Sinco, B. R., & Hong, J. S. (2014). Contemporary heterosexism on campus and psychological distress among LGBQ students: The mediating role of self-acceptance. *American Journal of Orthopsychiatry, 84*(5), 519–29. doi:10.1037/ort0000015

Yang, M. F., Manning, D., van den Berg, J. J., & Operario, D. (2015). Stigmatization and mental health in a diverse sample of transgender women. *LGBT Health, 2*(4), 306–12. doi:1089/lgbt.2014.0106

Zeluf, G., Dhejne, C., Orre, C., Mannheimer, L. N., Deogan, C., Hoijer, J., . . . Thorson, A. E. (2018). Targeted victimization and suicidality among trans people: A web-based survey. *LGBT Health, 5*(3), 180–90, doi:10.1089/lgbt.2017.011

Zerbe, W. J., & Paulhus, D. L. (1987). Socially desirable responding in organizational behavior: A reconception. *Academy of Management Review, 12*(2), 250–64. doi:10.2307/258533

CHAPTER

36 The Role of Resilience in Sexual and Gender Minority Mental Health

Dawn M. Szymanski *and* Kirsten A. Gonzalez

Abstract

Many lesbian, gay, bisexual, transgender, and queer (LGBTQ) persons are able to persevere and flourish despite pervasive social stigma and minority stress based on their sexual orientation and gender identity. This chapter reviews the research on LGBTQ resilience that can occur at individual, interpersonal/family, community, and contextual/structural levels. The authors describe qualitative research that has examined pathways to resilience and positive LGBTQ identity. The authors also review quantitative research on LGBTQ resilience via mediator, moderator, and moderated mediation models. Variables are described that have been found to explain or buffer the links between external and internalized minority stressors and mental health outcomes. The authors review the small but growing body of research that has begun to examine the efficacy of therapeutic interventions aimed at promoting LGBTQ resilience. Limitations are discussed and directions for future research are suggested.

Keywords: LGBTQ, heterosexism, cissexism, minority stress, resilience, positive identity

Lesbian, gay, bisexual, transgender, and queer (LGBTQ) resilience refers to the ability to persevere and flourish in the face of harassment, rejection, discrimination, and oppression based on sexual orientation and gender identity that occurs at micro-, meso-, and macro-levels (Meyer, 2015; Riggle, Whitman, Olson, Rostosky, & Strong, 2008). Resilience refers to *successful* adaptation in the face of external (e.g., discrimination, rejection) and internal (e.g., internalized heterosexism/biphobia/transphobia, stigma consciousness) minority stressors (Meyer, 2015). LGBTQ resilience can occur at individual, interpersonal/family, community, and contextual/structural levels. At the individual level, it includes attitudes, characteristics, and/or behaviors that can help a person successfully deal with LGBTQ minority stressors (Meyer, 2015). At the interpersonal/family level, it includes connection to and support from others, as well as the quality of relationships with others (Lira & Morais, 2017). At the community level, it includes community norms and values, access to community and institutional resources and supports, and collective identity and action (Meyer, 2015; Lira & Morais, 2017). Resilience factors at contextual and structural levels include environmental conditions and affirmative LGBTQ practices, policies, and laws (Meyer, 2015).

Historically, LGBTQ resilience research has focused on predicting mental health outcomes, but recent research has begun to examine LGBTQ strengths, positive identity, well-being, and cultural adaptations that emerge within and as a reaction to an oppressive LGBTQ cultural context (e.g., Levitt, 2019; Riggle et al., 2008; Rostosky, Riggle, Pascale-Hague, & McCants, 2010; Szymanski, Mikorski, & Carretta, 2017). Scholars have adopted both qualitative and quantitative methods to study LGBTQ resilience. In terms of qualitative approaches, researchers have identified salient themes and provided rich, contextual understandings of how LGBTQ persons survive and thrive in a sociocultural context of pervasive social stigma toward LGBTQ people. Qualitative and descriptive research has largely focused on pathways to resilience, coping, and/or positive identity development.

In terms of quantitative research, three models of LGBTQ resilience have been put forth: (1) a mediator model, (2) a moderator model, and (3) a moderated mediation model (Hayes, 2013; Meyer, 2015). In a mediation resilience model, a LGBTQ minority stressor triggers the buffer that in turn lessens the effect of the minority stressor on mental health. For example, experiences of LGBTQ discrimination may prompt a gay man to enter counseling, which in turn lessens his depressive symptoms. In a moderator resilience model, an interaction occurs between a minority stressor and resilience variable to alter the impact of a LGBTQ stressor on mental health. For example, self-esteem may buffer the experiences of LGBTQ discrimination on mental health such that the relation between LGBTQ discrimination and depression is weakened or nonsignificant for those with high versus low self-esteem. In a moderated mediation resilience model, a resilience variable alters an indirect effect. For example, the indirect effect of LGBTQ discrimination on depression through internalized heterosexism may be weakened or nonsignificant for those with high versus low sexuality support. A compensatory or direct effects model (any variable, independent of LGBTQ minority stressors, that lessens poor mental health outcomes) is not considered to be a resilience model and is therefore not included in this review (Meyer, 2015; for compensatory models with LGBTQ samples, see Johns, Beltran, Armstrong, Jayne, & Barrios, 2018; Lira & Morais, 2017). Finally, a small but growing body of research has begun to examine the efficacy of therapeutic interventions that aim to promote LGBTQ resilience. In this chapter we review the empirical research in each of these areas and conclude with a discussion of limitations and directions for future research.

Pathways to Resilience and Positive LGBTQ Identity Development

Research on pathways to resilience and positive identity development among LGBTQ persons has largely been qualitative and descriptive. Scholars have asserted that, as a result of dealing with minority stressors based on sexual orientation and gender identity, many LGBTQ people develop coping and resistance skills that transform these negative experiences into attitudes and behaviors that lead to opportunities for personal growth, well-being, and improved functioning (Riggle et al., 2008; Szymanski et al., 2017). Qualitative studies have identified adaptive coping and empowerment strategies that LGBTQ persons use to deal with minority stressors, as well as positive aspects of being LGBTQ. Although there are nuances and complexities, the findings have been fairly consistent across subgroups within the LGBTQ community (e.g., men, women, sexual minority, transgender, racial/ethnic minority LGBTQ people) as well as minority stress experiences at different levels (e.g., interpersonal, familial, political).

Empowerment strategies to cope with pervasive social stigma include confronting internalized heterosexism/transphobia, coming out and unsilencing marginalized identities, using self-care strategies like increasing self-affirmation, expressing feelings of anger and sadness, leaving oppressive environments, creating safe spaces, building social support systems, accessing professional help, externalizing rather than internalizing heterosexism and cissexism, ignoring or dismissing prejudice, confronting perpetrators of oppression, engaging in social activism, and having hope and optimism about the future (Asakura, 2017; Asakura & Craig, 2014; Bowleg, Huang, Brooks, Black, & Burkholder, 2003; Brown & Keller, 2018; Emano, 2007; Erhard & Ben-Ami, 2016; Goldbach & Gibbs, 2015; Kruger, Lubbe-De Beer, & Du Plessis, 2016; Levitt et al., 2016; Moody, Fuks, Peláez, & Smith, 2015; Riggle, Rostosky, Drabble, Veldhuis, & Hughes, 2018; Russell & Richards, 2003; Schmitz & Tyler, 2019; Singh, 2013; Singh, Hays, & Watson, 2011; Singh & McKleroy, 2011; Singh, Meng, & Hansen, 2014; Sung, Szymanski, & Henrichs-Beck, 2015). Quantitative studies have also supported the link between experiences of interpersonal and structural (i.e., anti-LGB marriage amendments) sexual orientation–based discrimination and engagement in LGBTQ activism (Dunn & Szymanski, 2018; Rostosky, Riggle, Horne, & Miller, 2009; Swank & Fahs, 2013).

Maintaining connections to racial/ethnic communities and/or values, connecting to LGBTQ Communities of Color, and engaging in role flexibility were noted as unique sources of strength for dealing with multiple, intersectional identities among LGBTQ People of Color (Bowleg et al., 2003; Gray, Mendelsohn, & Omoto, 2015; Singh, 2013; Singh & McKleroy, 2011; Sung et al., 2015; Wilson & Miller, 2002). Sometimes the main outlet for connecting with LGBTQ Communities of Color and finding LGBTQ People of Color role models were online spaces and social media platforms (Singh, 2013; Sung et al., 2015). Specific to transgender people and transgender People of Color, using self-selected words and definitions to define racial/ethnic and gender identities, accessing reasonably priced transgender-affirming healthcare, and being financially stable help foster resilience in response to discrimination (Singh, 2013; Singh & McKleroy, 2011; Singh et al., 2014, 2011).

Positive aspects of LGBTQ identity often overlapped with coping strategies, and these are not mutually exclusive. They include being genuine and living authentically, having a positive sense of self, having enhanced interpersonal connections, creating loving families of choice, serving as positive role models, having self-awareness, having increased empathy and compassion for others, experiencing freedom from restrictive gender norms and constraints of heterosexuality, creating egalitarian romantic relationships, having increased intimacy in relationships, and having a commitment to social justice (Emano, 2007; Kruger et al., 2016; Moody et al., 2015; Riggle, Rostosky, McCants, & Pascale-Hague, 2011; Riggle et al., 2008; Rostosky et al., 2010; Schmitz & Tyler, 2019; Singh et al., 2011; Sung et al., 2015). Moving beyond binaries, accepting fluidity in terms of both sex and gender, and being congruent in terms of internal gendered feelings and external presentation were also noted as positive aspects of identity among transgender persons (Riggle et al., 2011). In a quantitative study, Rostosky, Cardom, Hammer, and Riggle (2018) found that four aspects of positive LGB identity (authenticity, intimacy, connection to the LGBT community, and commitment to social justice) were associated with one or more dimensions of well-being.

A dearth of empirical research exists on resilience in same-sex parented families. Same-sex parents choosing to have children demonstrate resilience through their choice of children, because having children helps same-sex parents to feel like they fit in socially (Oswald, 2002). Children of same-sex parents report changes in attitudes toward same-sex relationships, openness and acceptance of difference, and exposure to new experiences and knowledge as a result of their nontraditional family (Titlestad & Pooley, 2014). Adult children of same-sex parents are proud of their same-sex family and are equipped to engage in dialogues with others about gay and lesbian families (Oswald, 2002; Tasker & Golombok, 1998; Titlestad & Pooley, 2014). Same-sex families' resilience often manifests as optimism and hope for future societal changes that would reflect a more affirming and welcoming space for all types of families, including same-sex parented families (Kruger et al., 2016).

Mediator Resilience Models

Because qualitative approaches are limited by small sample sizes, generalizability, and an inability to examine associations among variables, researchers have employed quantitative methods to examine LGBTQ resilience. We identified three studies that examined mediator resilience models. Extending qualitative findings on LGB positive identity, Szymanski et al. (2017) found that coping with heterosexist discrimination via education/advocacy (but not via confrontation) mediated the heterosexist discrimination and positive LGB identity links among sexual minority persons. That is, more heterosexist discrimination was linked to more behaviors aimed at raising other people's awareness of discrimination and engaging in social justice efforts to combat heterosexism at micro-, meso-, and macro-levels, which in turn was associated with more self-awareness, genuineness, intimacy in relationships, connection to the LGBTQ community, and commitment to social justice.

Turning to internalized minority stressors, Bruce, Harper, and Bauermeister (2015) found that for gay and bisexual men aged sixteen to twenty-four, sexual orientation concealment during childhood and adolescence was related to more positive sexual minority identity development that resulted from meeting other LGBTQ individuals. Positive identity development was then associated with less internalized heterosexism. Using a longitudinal design, Zimmerman, Darnell, Rhew, Lee, and Kaysen (2015) found that when sexual orientation disclosure to family increased, young adult lesbian and bisexual women in rejecting families showed resilience by increasing LGBTQ community connectedness and collective self-esteem to a greater extent than did lesbian and bisexual women in nonrejecting families twelve months later. That is, they were able to seek out support from their community when it was not available in their families. Future research could examine if these increases in connectedness and self-esteem in turn predict lower levels of psychological distress and greater well-being.

Taken together, these findings suggest that LGBTQ minority stressors may trigger some forms of engagement coping and connection to the larger LGBTQ community that in turn may lessen their negative effects. Research employing mediator resilience models is scant and therefore a fruitful area for future research. A much larger body of research has examined moderator and moderated mediation resilience models, and we review these studies next.

Buffers/Protective Factors in the Face of Minority Stress

Researchers have used moderator and moderated mediation models to examine buffers or protective factors on mental health outcomes when faced with minority stress. We examine the research in this area by first focusing on resilience in the face of external minority stressors and then internalized minority stressors. Within each of these sections, we review LGBTQ resilience moderator variables at individual, interpersonal/family, community, and contextual/structural levels.

External Minority Stressors

INDIVIDUAL FACTORS

Researchers have begun to identify individual characteristics, attitudes, behaviors, and coping responses that might weaken the link between LGBTQ minority stressors and psychological distress. Examining personality via the five-factor model, Livingston et al. (2015) found that LGB adults with adaptive personality styles—consisting of high extraversion, conscientiousness, agreeableness, and openness to experience and lower neuroticism—were less likely to attempt suicide in the face of LGB victimization than those with inverse personality styles. This finding suggests that certain personality trait constellations can confer resilience.

Scholars have theorized that experiences of LGBT external minority stressors may be more easily dismissed by LGBT individuals who hold a stronger sense of their own worth but are more damaging to LGBTQ persons with negative self-evaluations (Szymanski, 2009). Supporting this notion, two studies found that self-esteem buffered the relation between heterosexism and mental health outcomes. Among LGB college students, the relation between heterosexist harassment and risk for alcohol abuse was significant for those with low but not high self-esteem (Woodford, Kulick, & Atteberry, 2015). Similarly, the relation between heterosexist discrimination and psychological distress was significant for gay and bisexual men with low but not high self-esteem (Szymanski, 2009). Contrary to these findings, Hershberger and D'Augelli (1995) found no support for the moderating role of self-acceptance (a composite measure of self-esteem and comfort with one's sexual orientation) in the link between sexual orientation–based victimization and psychological distress and suicidality among LGB youth aged fifteen to twenty-one. This lack of significance might be due to issues related to construct clarity.

Among bisexual adults, Brewster, Moradi, DeBlaere, and Velez (2013) examined cognitive flexibility (i.e., seeing different options in a situation and being able to adapt) and bicultural self-efficacy (i.e., perceived ability to successfully navigate more than one culture) as potential resilience factors in the direct link between anti-bisexual discrimination and both psychological distress and well-being, as well as indirect links through internalized biphobia, stigma consciousness, and outness. They found some support for cognitive flexibility (but not bicultural self-efficacy) as a buffer. Cognitive flexibility moderated both the direct relation between anti-bisexual discrimination and well-being, and the indirect relation between anti-bisexual discrimination and both well-being and psychological distress via stigma consciousness. Bisexual persons with high cognitive flexibility had greater psychological well-being in the face of anti-bisexual discrimination than those with low cognitive flexibility. In addition, bisexual persons with high cognitive flexibility had lower stigma consciousness than those with low cognitive flexibility, but only in the context of low discrimination. This finding suggests that the buffering effect of cognitive flexibility disappears in the context of high discrimination.

For LGB people, having a clear sense of purpose or meaning in one's life buffered the direct effect of heterosexist discrimination and psychological distress link, with the relation being weaker for those with high meaning versus low (Szymanski & Mikorski, 2016). However, the presence of meaning did not moderate the conditional indirect effect of heterosexist discrimination on psychological distress via internalized heterosexism. Using a prospective design, Kwon and Hugelshofer (2010) found that high levels of hope among LGB workers in hostile workplace environments reported higher levels of well-being/life satisfaction than those with low levels of hope.

Research findings provide support for mindfulness (i.e., being attentive to and accepting of one's feelings and experiences) as a resilience factor. Among gay men aged forty and older, higher levels of mindfulness weakened the relation between sexual orientation–based discrimination and psychological distress (Lyons, 2016). Among Latinx LGB high school and college students in the United States, the relationship between sexual orientation–based victimization and depression was significant only for those with low levels of mindfulness (Toomey & Anhalt, 2016).

Resilience, defined as the ability to bounce back after a stressful event, buffered the link between sexist discrimination (but not anti-bisexual discrimination) and psychological distress among bisexual women (Watson, Morgan, & Craney, 2018), with the relation being nonsignificant for those with high versus low levels of resilience. Among a sample of bisexual people, resilience buffered the relationship between sexual minority–based discrimination and suicidal behaviors for those who reported a mental health diagnosis, but not for those without a mental health diagnosis (Miceli, Klibert, & Yancey, 2019). Resilience also buffered the anti-transgender discrimination and depression and suicidality (but not anxiety) links among transgender persons living in Italy, with the associations being significant for those with low (but not high) levels of resilience (Scandurra, Amodeo, Valerio, Bochicchio, & Frost, 2017). In contrast, Breslow et al. (2015) did not find support for the moderating role of resilience in the link between anti-transgender discrimination and psychological distress among transgender people in the United States.

A study examining individual coping styles as resilience factors found mixed support. Ngamake, Walch, and Raveepatarakul (2016) found that LGB adults with lower levels of coping with discrimination via self-blame were less likely to report anxiety and depression when faced with sexual orientation–based discrimination. However other forms of coping with discrimination (e.g., education/advocacy, resistance/confrontation) did not moderate the relation between discrimination and mental health. Turning to religiosity, Szymanski and Carretta (2019) found that having low levels of religiosity buffered the indirect effect of religious-based heterosexist discrimination on both psychological distress and well-being via internalized heterosexism among LGB individuals who were affiliated with a religion. Among LGB college students, exercise buffered heterosexist harassment and risk for anxiety and depression (but not risk for alcohol abuse), with the relation being significant for those with low but not high frequency of exercise (Woodford et al., 2015). Taken together, the research suggests that individual factors play an important role in LGBTQ resilience.

INTERPERSONAL AND FAMILY FACTORS

Numerous studies have documented the direct and beneficial effects of social support on mental health outcomes that are independent of external minority stressors such as LGBTQ discrimination and victimization (e.g., Mustanski, Newcomb, & Garofalo, 2011; Sattler, Wagner, & Christiansen, 2016; Szymanski, 2009). However, research on the protective effects of social support in the link between external minority stressors and poor mental health is less clear.

Among LGB college students, the number of LGB friends buffered the link between heterosexist harassment and alcohol abuse risk, with the relation being significant for those with low but not high numbers of LGB friends (Woodford et al., 2015). Hershberger and D'Augelli (1995) found that family support (a composite variable measured by family acceptance of sexual orientation, family protection from hurt, and level of sexual orientation disclosure and family response) moderated the sexual orientation–based victimization and psychological distress (but not suicidality) link among LGB youth aged fifteen to twenty-one. Family support attenuated the association between victimization and psychological distress, but only when victimization was low. Relatedly, higher levels of sexuality-related support from family and friends (but not general support) buffered the relation between sexuality stress and psychological distress among a small sample ($N = 98$) of LGB young adults aged eighteen to twenty-one (Doty, Willoughby, Lindahl, & Malik, 2010). This relation was significant for those with low sexuality support but not for those with high sexuality support. Among transgender people living in Italy, support from family (but not from friends or significant others) buffered the relation between anti-transgender discrimination and anxiety, with the association being significant for those with low family support but not high family support (Scandurra et al., 2017). However, this moderating effect did not extend to depression or suicidality.

Using a daily diary design, Fingerhut (2018) found that social support from friends (but not family) buffered the link between sexual orientation–based minority stress (a composite of discrimination, internalized heterosexism, and stigma consciousness) and negative affect among adult gay men. Examining legislative processes, Verrelli, White, Harvey, and Pulciani (2019) found that greater social support for same-sex marriage within one's immediate social circle buffered the association between exposure to anti–same-sex marriage media messages and psychological distress among Australian LGB adults, with the relation being weaker for those with high versus low levels of social support.

Social support can also come from romantic relationships. Some research has found support for the protective role of romantic relationships in the link between minority stress and mental health outcomes. Feinstein, Latack, Bhatia, Davila, and Eaton (2016) found that being involved in a romantic relationship (vs. being single) weakened the relation between sexual orientation–based discrimination and both depression and anxiety disorders for bisexual persons but not for lesbian/gay persons. However, they found no support for the moderating role of romantic relationship involvement between LGBTQ victimization and these two mental health disorders. Examining support from spouses, Donnelly, Robinson, and Umberson (2019) found that among married same-sex couples, support from spouses attenuated the relation between discrimination and symptoms of depression.

Other research has not found support for the buffering role of social support in the link between sexual orientation–based discrimination and mental health outcomes. For example, positive peer group relations (Bissonnette & Szymanski, 2019) and number of LGB friends (Woodford et al., 2015) did not moderate the associations between heterosexist discrimination and depression and anxiety among LGB college students. Similarly, general social support did not buffer the link between heterosexist discrimination and poor mental health among LGB individuals with disabilities (Conover & Israel, 2019) and gay and bisexual men living in Germany (Sattler et al., 2016) and the United States (Szymanski, 2009). Examining family supports, Feinstein, Wadsworth, Davila, and Goldried (2014) found that parental acceptance of one's sexual orientation and general family support did not buffer the heterosexist discrimination and depression link among gay men and lesbians. Similarly, Mustanski et al. (2011) found that neither family nor peer support moderated the link between LGB victimization and psychological distress among LGB adolescents and young adults. Kaufman, Baams, and Dubas (2017) found no significant findings for the buffering roles of sexuality-specific acceptance at the time of coming out, nor LGBTQ community connectedness, in the direct link between LGBTQ microaggressions and depressive symptoms. Kaufman et al. (2017) also found an indirect link between microaggressions and depressive symptoms through ruminative thinking among LGB adolescents and young adults.

Scholars have suggested that the mixed findings regarding the moderating role of social supports may be due to a match between the challenges of the stressor and kind of support (Cohen & Wills, 1985; Doty et al., 2010). That is, social support is theorized to be most helpful when the type of support offered is pertinent to the specific type of stress one is encountering. Future research, including meta-analysis, is needed to tease out and understand the conflicting results regarding the moderating role of social support.

COMMUNITY FACTORS

Research on potential buffers at the community level has focused largely on connection to the LGBTQ community and involvement in LGBTQ groups, activities, and activism. The role of connection to the LGBTQ community as a community resilience factor has received mixed support in the link between external minority stressors and mental health, with one study finding a buffering effect and three studies finding no moderating effect. Among bisexual women, LGBTQ community connectedness buffered the direct link between anti-bisexual discrimination and psychological distress (but not the indirect associations via coping), with the relation becoming nonsignificant at higher levels of connection (Craney, Watson, Brownfield, & Flores, 2018). In contrast, connection to the LGBTQ community did not buffer the relation between heterosexist discrimination and psychological distress among sexual minority women (Szymanski & Owens, 2009), sexual orientation–based discrimination and depression among lesbian and gay adults (Fingerhut, Peplau, & Gable, 2010), and sexual orientation–based minority stressors and negative affect link among gay men (Fingerhut, 2018). Contradicting the minority stress buffering hypothesis of community resilience, Swim, Johnston, and Pearson (2009) found opposite effects using a daily diary design. That is, higher levels of LGB identity centrality exacerbated the negative effects of heterosexist discrimination on depression. Differences in measurement and sample characteristics might explain these conflicting findings.

The mere presence of a school gay–straight alliance indirectly attenuated the relation between anti-LGB bullying victimization and suicide attempts among adolescent LGB students through lower levels of hopelessness (Davis, Royne Stafford, & Pullig, 2014). Membership in a high school gay–straight alliance also weakened the relations between LGBQ school victimization and both depression and suicide attempts for those with low levels of victimization, but not high (Toomey, Ryan, Diaz, & Russell, 2011). Participation in college campus leadership buffered the relation between sexual orientation–based microaggressions and depression among White LGBQ (but not racial/ethnic minority) college students, with weaker associations for those who were involved in leadership roles on campus (Kulick, Wernick, Woodford, & Renn, 2017). In contrast, Bissonnette and Szymanski (2019) found that high involvement in LGBTQ campus activities strengthened the link between sexual orientation–based microaggressions and depression.

Turning to involvement in activism, LGBTQ collective action moderated the link between heterosexist discrimination and psychological distress such that there was a positive association between the two variables for racial/ethnic minority lesbians and bisexual women with low levels of LGB collective action but not high (DeBlaere et al., 2014). Relatedly, involvement in feminist collective action buffered against the negative effects of sexist discrimination on psychological distress for sexual minority women, but only when sexist discrimination was low (Szymanski & Owens, 2009). In contrast, Kulick et al. (2017) found that LGBQ collective action strengthened the link between sexual orientation–based victimization and depression among racial/ethnic (but not White) LGBQ college students, with stronger associations for those who were involved in campus LGBQ activism. Finally, four studies found no support for the moderating role of involvement in LGBTQ activism in the direct link between LGBTQ discrimination and psychological distress among transgender people (Breslow et al., 2015), German gay men (Sattler et al., 2016), bisexual women (Watson et al., 2018), and LGB persons (Velez & Moradi, 2016). However, the buffering role of collective action may be more complex. For example, Velez and Moradi (2016) found that involvement in LGBT activism buffered the link between heterosexist discrimination and internalized heterosexism, with the weakest effect at high levels of collective action. Furthermore, they found that LGBT activism buffered the indirect path from heterosexist discrimination to well-being (but not psychological distress) through internalized heterosexism. The buffering effect of LGBT activism was not supported in the direct and indirect relations between heterosexist discrimination and mental health via other internalized minority stressors (i.e., stigma consciousness, outness).

Research has supported internalized minority stressors as mediators in the link between LGBTQ discrimination and poor mental health outcomes (e.g., Brewster et al., 2013; Szymanski & Carretta, 2019; Szymanski & Mikorski, 2016). Furthermore, some researchers have found support for moderating factors in the external and internalized minority stressor links. For example, Mason, Lewis, Winstead, and Derlega (2015) found that greater LGBTQ collective self-esteem and fewer social constraints with LGBTQ friends buffered the negative effects of heterosexist discrimination on internalized heterosexism among lesbian and bisexual women. Future research might extend these findings by examining moderated mediation models to determine if the buffering effects of interpersonal and community resilience factors extend to indirect effects in predicting mental health outcomes. For example, does collective self-esteem buffer the relation between heterosexist discrimination and depression via internalized heterosexism? Future research might also examine different types of activities/involvement LGBTQ people are engaged in (e.g., educative, supportive, entertainment), the contribution of activist burnout, and the effects of the socio-political and cultural climate to see if they shed light on some of the more complex and conflicting findings in this area.

STRUCTURAL/CONTEXTUAL FACTORS

Two studies have examined buffers at contextual and organizational levels. Examining social environments, Tran (2015) found that neighborhood quality buffered the relation between discrimination and psychological distress for LGB (but not heterosexual) adults, with the relations being significant for those with low neighborhood quality and nonsignificant for those with perceived high neighborhood quality. In the school system, Day, Snapp, and Russell (2016) found that supportive (but not punitive) disciplinary strategies attenuated the negative effect of experiencing sexual orientation–based bullying on school connectedness among middle and high school students. Future research might examine whether supportive practices moderate the indirect effect of bullying on mental health outcomes via school connectedness.

Internalized Minority Stressors

INDIVIDUAL FACTORS

Only a handful of studies have examined individual factors that might buffer the link between internalized minority stressors and distress. One study found support for the buffering role of psychological hardiness in the link between stigma consciousness and physical health symptoms but not in the links between stigma consciousness and mental health or subjective physical health among LGB adults (Figueroa & Zoccola, 2015). Another study found that the cognitive strategy of decentering moderated the relation between internalized heterosexism and psychological distress (Puckett, Mereish, Levitt, Horne, & Hayes-Skelton, 2018). That is, the relation was not significant for LGB adults who were high on the ability to see feelings and thoughts as events rather than as facts about the self.

Focusing on United States transgender persons, resilience did not moderate the direct relations between internalized transphobia and stigma consciousness and psychological distress nor the indirect links of anti-transgender discrimination and psychological distress via internalized transphobia and stigma consciousness (Breslow et al., 2015). Scandurra et al. (2018) extended this study by differentiating between two forms of internalized transphobia, alienation and shame, among transgender persons living in Italy. They found that the indirect relation between anti-transgender discrimination and anxiety (but not depression) through trans-alienation was significant only for those with low levels of resilience.

INTERPERSONAL AND FAMILY FACTORS

In contrast to the conflicting evidence concerning the buffering role of social support in the link between external minority stressors and mental health outcomes, research on the role of social support in the link between internalized minority stress and mental health outcomes is more consistent. Examining internalized heterosexism, Mereish and Poteat (2015) found that having a high-quality relationship with a close heterosexual or sexual minority friend was associated with less psychological distress among sexual minority persons with low internalized heterosexism. They also found that having a high-quality relationship with a close sexual minority (but not a heterosexual) friend was associated with less psychological distress among sexual minority people with greater internalized heterosexism. Similarly, Bissonnette and Szymanski (2019) found that positive peer group relations represented a protective factor in the relation between internalized heterosexism and depression among LGBQ college students. That is, internalized heterosexism was linked to depression for students with low levels of positive peer group relations, but not for those with moderate or high levels of positive peer group support. Sattler et al. (2016) found that non-gay social support (but not gay social support) attenuated the relationship between internalized heterosexism and psychological distress among German gay men. In addition, they found that gay social support (but not non-gay social support) was a protective factor in the link between sexual orientation–based rejection sensitivity and psychological distress.

Turning to family support, Feinstein et al. (2014) found that parental acceptance of one's sexual orientation, but not general family support, buffered the relations between both internalized heterosexism and sexual orientation–related rejection sensitivity and depression. That is, relations between internalized minority stressors and depression were significant for gay men and lesbians who experienced less parental acceptance of their sexual orientation but not for those with high parental acceptance. Taken together, these findings largely support the notion of social support as a resilience factor when dealing with internalized minority stressors.

COMMUNITY FACTORS

Among bisexual women, bisexual-specific community involvement buffered the relationship between internalized biphobia and depression (but not self-esteem). That is, the relation between internalization and depression was weaker for those with high versus low community involvement (Lambe, Cerezo, & O'Shaughnessy, 2017). Similarly, Bissonette and Szymanski (2019) found a trend toward the attenuating role of involvement in LGBQ campus activities in the association between internalized heterosexism and depression among LGBQ college students. Among lesbian and gay adults, a sense of belonging to the LGBTQ community buffered the relation between stigma consciousness and depression, with the relation being significant for those with low LGBTQ connection and nonsignificant for those with high LGBTQ connection (Fingerhut et al., 2010).

Breslow et al. (2015) found that involvement in transgender activism exacerbated the link between internalized transphobia and psychological distress. In addition, they found support for moderated mediation where the indirect link between anti-transgender discrimination and psychological distress via internalized transphobia (but not stigma awareness) was significant for those with high collective action but not low. However, Sattler et al. (2016) found no support for the moderating role of involvement in gay rights activism in the link between internalized heterosexism and rejection sensitivity and psychological distress among German gay men. Taken together, the results suggest that connection to and involvement in the LGBTQ community provide sources of resilience, whereas involvement in activism does not.

Treatment Interventions That Foster Resilience

Given the importance of resilience for LGBTQ people, scholars have begun to theorize about possible interventions as well as develop and test the efficacy of interventions designed to intervene with LGBTQ people to reduce minority stress and increase coping, bolster a positive sense of self, and cultivate resilience. Recent scholarship provides important directions for community, group, and individual interventions to bolster resilience for both sexual minority and transgender populations (see Matsuno & Israel, 2018; Zimmerman et al., 2015). A full discussion and analysis of community and group interventions is beyond the scope of this chapter, but we provide a summary of recommendations for community and group interventions before discussing individual-level interventions.

Community-Level Interventions

At the community level, Matsuno and Israel (2018) suggest that psychologists can intervene through providing educational programs, including trainings for healthcare providers to support LGBTQ people. Additionally, psychologists can intervene to create more affirming spaces for transgender people within LGBQ communities (Matsuno & Israel, 2018). These interventions could include consciousness-raising workshops to help LGBQ people better understand transgender feelings of exclusion and isolation when in larger LGBTQ spaces. Finally, psychologists can advocate for laws that provide protections for LGBTQ people as well as advocate for inclusive demographic forms or gender-inclusive restrooms in community centers (Matsuno & Israel, 2018).

Group-Level Interventions

Group interventions to bolster LGBTQ resilience can target social support networks including families, couples, and communities (Matsuno & Israel, 2018; Zimmerman et al., 2015). One way psychologists can intervene at the group level is through developing psychotherapy groups focused on providing support to transgender and sexual minority people (Matsuno & Israel, 2018). Members in these groups could serve as role models for other members in helping to understand how to effectively combat minority stress (Matsuno & Israel, 2018). Finally, psychologists can intervene with family members and couples who, research indicates, can be a huge source of support for LGBTQ people and can foster LGBTQ resilience (Matsuno & Israel, 2018; Zimmerman et al., 2015). Psychologists can work with families and couples to build acceptance of and affirmation for LGBTQ people broadly, and loved ones/family members specifically (Matsuno & Israel, 2018).

Individual-Level Interventions

Scholars have explored effective interventions for reducing sexual minority stress, cultivating positive identity, and enhancing resilience in the face of stress with LGBTQ community members (see Chaudoir, Wang, & Pachankis, 2017, for a recent review of the literature). Many of these interventions use expressive writing exercises (e.g., Pennebaker & Beall, 1986) where LGBTQ people write about their thoughts and emotions in reaction to a stressful event as the mechanism for change. Some interventions using expressive writing exercises are focused specifically on fostering resilience through cultivating positive LGBTQ identities (e.g., Riggle, Gonzalez, Rostosky, & Black, 2014). This scholarship suggests that through writing about a positive aspect of an LGBTQ identity, LGBTQ young adults demonstrate a stronger positive LGBTQ identity as well as improvements in individual and collective self-esteem (Riggle et al., 2014).

Expressive writing interventions are also helpful in bolstering LGBTQ resilience through facilitating more adaptive coping in response to LGBTQ-related stress. In a study on expressive writing with lesbians, Lewis et al. (2005) found that expressive writing interventions are especially effective in helping lesbians with lower levels of outness cope with lesbian-related stress. A study by Pachankis and Goldfried (2010) also found that gay men benefit from expressive writing interventions focused on gay-related stress experiences. Gay men who engaged in expressive writing interventions often experienced more openness about their sexual orientation over time, although this was most pronounced for gay men with lower levels of social support and those whose expressive writing focused on a more distressing topic. These expressive writing interventions can be particularly helpful for gay men with lower levels of social support, as participants in the study with fewer support mechanisms also reported more gay friends three months after the writing intervention (Pachankis & Goldfried, 2010).

Online interventions have also been shown to be effective in reducing minority stress and bolstering resilience for LGBTQ populations who might be a bit harder to reach (Israel et al., 2019; Lin & Israel, 2012). Online interventions that focused on challenging stereotypes, identifying origins of negative messages about sexual minorities, and cultivating positive sexual minority identities effectively reduced internalized heterosexism in a sample of gay and bisexual men (Lin & Israel, 2012). In a follow-up study, Israel et al. (2019) found that an online intervention was also effective in reducing internalized binegativity in a sample of bisexual people. This online intervention expanded on the earlier intervention and included four modules focused on providing information about positive aspects of bisexuality, confronting negative bisexual stereotypes, detecting sources of binegative beliefs, and included an activity where participants wrote a note expressing support to a bisexual person. Online interventions to bolster resilience in response to minority stress seem to be effective for harder-to-reach populations, and the positive effects of these interventions last several months after the intervention takes place. Overall, online interventions might be an effective strategy for targeting LGBTQ communities to enhance a positive sense of self and cultivate resilience.

Research also indicates that interventions building on traditional therapy approaches like cognitive-behavioral therapy and dialectical behavior therapy can be used to effectively increase coping in response to discrimination experiences (see Bogart et al., 2018). One example of interventions using therapy approaches is a pilot intervention for black sexual minority HIV-positive men called *Still Climbin'* (Bogart et al., 2018). This nine-week intervention focused on disseminating information about discrimination, exploring coping strategies in response to discrimination, discussing medical mistrust, brainstorming ways to increase support systems, and addressing systemic discrimination. Results indicated that participants in the *Still Climbin'* intervention experienced improved problem solving and better self-protective coping as a result of participating in the intervention (Bogart et al., 2018).

Finally, interventions in psychotherapy work with LGBTQ clients can combat minority stress while cultivating resilience with LGBTQ people. Budge, Israel, and Merrill (2017) suggest that psychotherapy research with LGBTQ people must include evaluating interventions that will effectively address LGBTQ health disparities. Specifically, they argue for the importance of including measures of resilience, well-being, and pride in psychotherapy outcome research.

Overall, this scholarship suggests that effective strategies exist for combating minority stress while cultivating resilience in LGBTQ people. However, research in this area is in its infancy. Empirically supported interventions to enhance individual, interpersonal, and community/structural variables that have been shown to buffer the links between minority stress and distress are warranted. Future research that uses control groups, follow-up data, and larger sample sizes is needed.

Limitations and Directions for Future Research

Research on LGBTQ resilience has begun to flourish. The studies that have been conducted largely use cross-sectional, correlational designs, and longitudinal studies are needed. Most studies have been based in the United States, and research is needed on LGBTQ samples from other countries, particularly the Global South. Most research has used convenience samples that are predominately White, highly educated, and young. Future research needs to expand resilience research to specific populations such as a community sample of elderly, working-class, and racial/ethnic minority LGBTQ People. Further, more research is needed to understand resilience for transgender, nonbinary, pansexual, asexual, and queer communities, who often face unique forms of discrimination and prejudice. Most of the research to date has focused on discrimination at the individual/interpersonal levels and internalized oppression. Research targeting other minority stressors (e.g., structural stigma, stigma consciousness, sexual orientation and gender identity concealment) is warranted. Future research should also continue to explore support experiences for LGBTQ People of Color and the role of family, romantic, and social support in fostering LGBTQ resilience. Specifically, research must explore how support manifests differently for some members of the LGBTQ community, particularly for bisexual, pansexual, queer, and transgender people, and how resilience is fostered depending on that support. Research has often focused on resilience at the individual and interpersonal levels, and more research is needed at the community and structural/contextual levels. More research is needed to understand how protective and discriminatory state, federal, work-related, and housing policies either hinder or bolster LGBTQ resilience and psychological well-being. Continued research on resilience strategies used by LGBTQ people in oppressive sociopolitical climates and the long-term impact of anti-LGBTQ political climates on LGBTQ psychological well-being is needed. For many LGBTQ people, advocacy and activism often function as a source of resilience. More research is needed to understand the long-term effects of activism and how LGBTQ people can enhance resilience to avoid activist burnout. Additional therapeutic interventions to bolster LGBTQ resilience are needed along with research to examine their efficacy. Interventions at multiple levels of the socioecological system, including the individual, community, and societal levels, should be developed and tested to determine how LGBTQ resilience can be both directly and indirectly cultivated within and outside of LGBTQ communities.

References

Asakura, K. (2017). Paving pathways through the pain: A grounded theory of resilience among lesbian, gay, bisexual, trans, and queer youth. *Journal of Research on Adolescence, 27*, 521–36. doi:10.1111/jora.12291

Asakura, K., & Craig, S. (2014). "It gets better" . . . but how? Exploring resilience development in the accounts of LGBTQ adults. *Journal of Human Behavior in the Social Environment, 24*, 253–66. doi:10.1080/10911359.2013.808971

Bissonette, D., & Szymanski, D. M. (2019). Minority stress and LGBQ college students' depression: Roles of peer group and involvement. *Psychology of Sexual Orientation and Gender Diversity, 6*(3), 308–17. doi:10.1037/sgd0000332

Bogart, L. M., Dale, S. K., Daffin, G. K., Patel, K. N., Klein, D. J., Mayer, K. H., & Pantalone, D. W. (2018). Pilot intervention for discrimination-related coping among HIV-positive Black sexual minority men. *Cultural Diversity and Ethnic Minority Psychology, 24*, 541–51. doi:10.1037/cdp0000205

Bowleg, L., Huang, J., Brooks, K., Black, A., & Burkholder, G. (2003). Triple jeopardy and beyond: Multiple minority stress and resilience among Black lesbians. *Journal of Lesbian Studies, 7*, 87–108. doi:10.1300/J155v07n04_06

Breslow, A. S., Brewster, M. E., Velez, B. L., Wong, S., Geiger, E., & Soderstrom, B. (2015). Resilience and collective action: Exploring buffers against minority stress for transgender individuals. *Psychology of Sexual Orientation and Gender Diversity, 2*, 253–65. doi:10.1037/sgd0000117

Brewster, M. E., Moradi, B., DeBlaere, C., & Velez, B. L. (2013). Navigating the borderlands: The roles of minority stressors, bicultural self-efficacy, and cognitive flexibility in the mental health of bisexual individuals. *Journal of Counseling Psychology, 60*, 543–56. doi:10.1037/a0033224

Brown, C., & Keller, C. J. (2018). The 2016 presidential election outcome: Fears, tension, and resiliency of LGBTQ communities. *Journal of GLBT Family Studies, 1*, 101–29. doi:10.1080/1550428X.2017.1420847

Bruce, D., Harper, G. W., & Bauermeister, J. A. (2015). Minority stress, positive identity development, and depressive symptoms: Implications for resilience among sexual minority male youth. *Psychology of Sexual Orientation and Gender Diversity, 2*, 287–96. doi:10.1037/sgd0000128

Budge, S. L., Israel, T., & Merrill, C. R. S. (2017). Improving the lives of sexual and gender minorities: The promise of psychotherapy research. *Journal of Counseling Psychology, 64*, 376–84. doi:10.1037/cou0000215

Chaudoir, S. R., Wang, K., & Pachankis, J. E. (2017). What reduces sexual minority stress? A review of the intervention "toolkit." Journal of Social Issues, 73, 586–617. doi:10.1111/josi.12233

Cohen, S., & Wills, T. A. (1985). Stress, social support, and the buffering hypothesis. *Psychological Bulletin, 98*, 310–57. doi:10.1037/0033–2909.98.2.310

Conover, K. J., & Israel, T. (2019). Microaggressions and social support among sexual minorities with physical disabilities. *Rehabilitation Psychology, 64*(2), 167–78. doi:10.1037/rep0000250

Craney, R. S., Watson, L. B., Brownfield, J., & Flores, M. J. (2018). Bisexual women's discriminatory experiences and psychological distress: Exploring the roles of coping and LGBTQ community connectedness. *Psychology of Sexual Orientation and Gender Diversity, 5*, 324–37. doi:10.1037/sgd0000276

Davis, B., Royne Stafford, M. B., & Pullig, C. (2014). How gay-straight alliance groups mitigate the relationship between gay-bias victimization and adolescent suicide attempts. *Journal of the American Academy of Child & Adolescent Psychiatry, 53*, 1271–8. doi:10.1016/j.jaac.2014.09.010

Day, J. K., Snapp, S. D., & Russell, S. T. (2016). Supportive, not punitive, practices reduce homophobic bullying and improve school connectedness. *Psychology of Sexual Orientation and Gender Diversity, 3*, 416–25. doi:10.1037/sgd000019

DeBlaere, C., Brewster, M. E., Bertsch, K. N., DeCarlo, A. L., Kegel, K. A., & Presseau, C. (2014). The protective power of collective action for sexual minority women of color: An investigation of multiple discrimination experiences and psychological distress. *Psychology of Women Quarterly, 38*, 20–32. doi:10.1177/0361684313493252

Donnelly, R., Robinson, B. A., & Umberson, D. (2019). Can spouses buffer the impact of discrimination on depressive symptoms? An examination of same-sex and different-sex marriages. *Society and Mental Health, 9*(2), 192–210. doi:10.1177/2156869318800157

Doty, N., Willoughby, B., Lindahl, K., & Malik, N. (2010). Sexuality related social support among lesbian, gay, and bisexual youth. *Journal of Youth and Adolescence, 39*, 1134–47. doi:10.1007/s10964-010-9566-x

Dunn, T. L., & Szymanski, D. M. (2018). Heterosexist discrimination and LGBQ activism: Examining a moderated mediation model. *Psychology of Sexual Orientation and Gender Diversity, 5*, 13–24. doi:10.1037/sgd0000250

Emano, D. M. (2007). Coping with multiple oppressions: Exploring resilience in African American, Latino, and Asian American gay men. *Dissertation Abstracts International: Section B: The Sciences and Engineering*, 4758.

Erhard, R. L., & Ben-Ami, E. (2016). The schooling experience of lesbian, gay, and bisexual youth in Israel: Falling below and rising above as a matter of social ecology. *Journal of Homosexuality, 63*, 193–227. doi:10.1080/00918369.2015.1083778

Feinstein, B., Latack, J., Bhatia, V., Davila, J., & Eaton, N. (2016). Romantic relationship involvement as a minority stress buffer in gay/lesbian versus bisexual individuals. *Journal of Gay and Lesbian Mental Health, 20*, 237–57. doi:10.1080/19359705.2016.1147401

Feinstein, B., Wadsworth, L., Davila, J., & Goldfried, M. (2014). Do parental acceptance and family support moderate associations between dimensions of minority stress and depressive symptoms among lesbians and gay men? *Professional Psychology Research and Practice, 45*, 239–46. doi:10.1037/a0035393

Figueroa, W. S., & Zoccola, P. M. (2015). Individual differences of risk and resiliency in sexual minority health: The roles of stigma consciousness and psychological hardiness. *Psychology of Sexual Orientation and Gender Diversity, 2*, 329–38. doi:10.1037/sgd0000114

Fingerhut, A. W. (2018). The role of social support and gay identity in the stress processes of a sample of Caucasian gay men. *Psychology of Sexual Orientation and Gender Diversity, 5*, 294–302. doi:10.1037/sgd0000271

Fingerhut, A. W., Peplau, L. A., & Gable, S. L. (2010). Identity, minority stress and psychological well-being among gay men and lesbians. *Psychology & Sexuality, 1*, 101–14. doi:10.1080/19419899.2010.484592

Goldbach, J. T., & Gibbs, J. (2015). Strategies employed by sexual minority adolescents to cope with minority stress. *Psychology of Sexual Orientation and Gender Diversity, 2*, 297–306. doi:10.1037/sgd0000124

Gray, N. N., Mendelsohn, D. M., & Omoto, A. M. (2015). Community connectedness, challenges, and resilience among gay Latino immigrants. *American Journal of Community Psychology, 55*, 202–14. doi:10.1007/s10464-014-9697-4

Hayes, A. F. (2013). *Introduction to mediation, moderation and conditional process analysis: A regression based approach*. New York, NY: Guilford Press.

Hershberger, S., & D'Augelli, A. (1995). The impact of victimization on the mental health and suicidality of lesbian, gay, and bisexual youths. *Developmental Psychology, 31*, 65–74. doi:10.1037/0012-1649.31.1.65

Israel, T., Choi, A. Y., Goodman, J. A., Matsuno, E., Lin, Y.-J., Kary, K. G., & Merrill, C. R. S. (2019). Reducing internalized binegativity: Development and efficacy of an online intervention. *Psychology of Sexual Orientation and Gender Diversity, 6*(2), 149–59. doi:10.1037/sgd0000314

Johns, M. M., Beltran, O., Armstrong, H. L., Jayne, P. E., & Barrios, L. C. (2018). Protective factors among transgender and gender variant youth: A systematic review by socioecological level. *Journal of Primary Prevention, 39*, 263–301. doi:10.1007/s10935-018-0508-9

Kaufman, T. M., Baams, L., & Dubas, J. S. (2017). Microaggressions and depressive symptoms in sexual minority youth: The roles of rumination and social support. *Psychology of Sexual Orientation and Gender Diversity, 4*, 184–92. doi:10.1037/sgd0000219

Kruger, L., Lubbe-De Beer, C., & Du Plessis, A. (2016). Resilience in gay and lesbian parent families: Perspectives from the chrono-system. *Journal of Comparative Family Studies, 47*, 343–56. http://www.jstor.org/stable/44109630

Kulick, A., Wernick, L. J., Woodford, M. R., & Renn, K. (2017). Heterosexism, depression, and campus engagement among LGBTQ college students: Intersectional differences and opportunities for healing. *Journal of Homosexuality, 64*, 1125–41. doi:10.1080/00918369.2016.1242333

Kwon, P., & Hugelshofer, D. (2010). The protective role of hope for lesbian, gay, and bisexual individuals facing a hostile workplace climate. *Journal of Gay & Lesbian Mental Health, 14*, 3–18. doi:10.1080/19359700903408914

Lambe, J., Cerezo, A., & O'Shaughnessy, T. (2017). Minority stress, community involvement, and mental health among bisexual women. *Psychology of Sexual Orientation and Gender Diversity, 4*, 218–26. doi:10.1037/sgd0000222

Levitt, H. M. (2019). A psychosocial genealogy of LGBTQ+ gender: An empirically based theory of gender and gender identity cultures. *Psychology of Women Quarterly, 43*(3), 275–97. doi:10.1177/0361684319834641

Levitt, H. M., Horne, S. G., Herbitter, C., Ippolito, M., Reeves, T., Baggett, L. R., . . . Geiss, M. (2016). Resilience in the face of sexual minority stress: "Choices" between authenticity and self-determination. *Journal of Gay & Lesbian Social Services, 28*, 67–91. doi:10.1080/10538720.2016.1126212

Lewis, R. J., Derlega, V. J., Clarke, E. G., Kuang, J. C., Jacobs, A. M., & McElligott, M. D. (2005). An expressive writing intervention to cope with lesbian-related stress: The moderating effects of openness about sexual orientation. *Psychology of Women Quarterly, 29*, 149–57. doi:10.1111/j.1471-6402.2005.00177.x

Lin, Y. J., & Israel, T. (2012). A computer-based intervention to reduce internalized heterosexism in men. *Journal of Counseling Psychology, 59*, 458–64. doi:10.1037/a0028282

Lira, A. N. de, & Morais, N. A. de (2017). Resilience in lesbian, gay, and bisexual (LGB) populations: An integrative literature review. *Sexuality Research & Social Policy, 15*, 272–82. doi:10.1007/s13178-017-0285-x

Livingston, N. A., Heck, N. C., Flentje, A., Gleason, H., Oost, K. M., & Cochran, B. N. (2015). Sexual minority stress and suicide risk: Identifying resilience through personality profile analysis. *Psychology of Sexual Orientation and Gender Diversity, 2*, 321–9. doi:10.1037/sgd0000116

Lyons, A. (2016). Mindfulness attenuates the impact of discrimination on the mental health of middle-aged and older gay men. *Psychology of Sexual Orientation and Gender Diversity, 3*, 227–35. doi:10.1037/sgd0000164

Mason, T. B., Lewis, R. J., Winstead, B. A., & Derlega, V. J. (2015). External and internalized heterosexism among sexual minority women: The moderating roles of social constraints and collective self-esteem. *Psychology of Sexual Orientation and Gender Diversity, 2*, 313–20. doi:10.1037/sgd0000115

Matsuno, E., & Israel, T. (2018). Psychological interventions promoting resilience among transgender individuals: Transgender Resilience Intervention Model (TRIM). *The Counseling Psychologist*, 46, 632–55. doi:10.1177/0011000018787261

Mereish, E. H., & Poteat, V. P. (2015). The conditions under which growth-fostering relationships promote resilience and alleviate psychological distress among sexual minorities: Applications of relational cultural theory. *Psychology of Sexual Orientation and Gender Diversity, 2*, 339–4. doi:10.1037/sgd0000121

Meyer, I. H. (2015). Resilience in the study of minority stress and health of sexual and gender minorities. *Psychology of Sexual Orientation and Gender Diversity, 2*, 209–13. doi:10.1037/sgd0000132

Miceli, M., Klibert, J., & Yancey, C. T. (2019). Minority stress and suicidal behavior: Investigating a protective model through resilience in a bisexual sample. *Journal of Bisexuality, 19*(1), 83–102. doi:10.1080/15299716.2019.1567433

Moody, C., Fuks, N., Peláez, S., & Smith, N. G. (2015). "Without this, I would for sure already be dead": A qualitative inquiry regarding suicide protective factors among trans adults.

Psychology of Sexual Orientation and Gender Diversity, 2, 266–80. doi:10.1037/sgd0000130

Mustanski, B., Newcomb, M. E., & Garofalo, R. (2011). Mental health of lesbian, gay, and bisexual youths: A developmental resiliency perspective. *Journal of Gay & Lesbian Social Services, 23,* 204–25. doi:10.1080/10538720.2011.561474

Ngamake, S. T., Walch, S. E., & Raveepatarakul, J. (2016). Discrimination and sexual minority mental health: Mediation and moderation effects of coping. *Psychology of Sexual Orientation and Gender Diversity, 3,* 213–26. doi:10.1037/sgd0000163

Oswald, R. F. (2002). Resilience within the family networks of lesbians and gay men: Intentionality and redefinition. *Journal of Marriage and Family, 64,* 374–83. http://www.jstor.org/stable/3600111

Pachankis, J. E., & Goldfried, M. R. (2010). Expressive writing for gay-related stress: Psychosocial benefits and mechanisms underlying improvement. *Journal of Consulting and Clinical Psychology, 78,* 98–110. doi:10.1037/a0017580

Pennebaker, J. W., & Beall, S. K. (1986). Confronting a traumatic event: Toward an understanding of inhibition and disease. *Journal of Abnormal Psychology, 95,* 274–81. doi:10.1037//0021-843X.95.3.274

Puckett, J. A., Mereish, E. H., Levitt, H. M., Horne, S. G., & Hayes-Skelton, S. A. (2018). Internalized heterosexism and psychological distress: The moderating effects of decentering. *Stigma and Health, 3,* 9–15. doi:10.1037/sah0000065

Riggle, E. D. B., Gonzalez, K. A., Rostosky, S. S., & Black, W. W. (2014). Cultivating positive LGBTQA identities: An intervention study with college students. *Journal of LGBT Issues in Counseling, 8,* 264–81. doi:10.1080/15538605.2014.933468

Riggle, E. D. B., Rostosky, S. S., Drabble, L., Veldhuis, C. B., & Hughes, T. L. (2018). Sexual minority women's and gender-diverse individuals' hope and empowerment responses to the 2016 presidential election. *Journal of GLBT Family Studies, 1,* 152–73, doi:10.1080/1550428X.2017.1420853

Riggle, E. D. B., Rostosky, S. S., McCants, L. W. E., & Pascale-Hague, D. (2011). The positive aspects of a transgender self-identification. *Psychology & Sexuality, 2,* 147–58. doi:10.1080/19419899.2010.534490

Riggle, E. D. B., Whitman, J. S., Olson, A., Rostosky, S. S., & Strong, S. (2008). The positive aspects of being a lesbian or gay man. *Professional Psychology: Research and Practice, 39,* 210–7. doi:10.1037/0735-7028.39.2.210

Rostosky, S. S., Cardom, R. D., Hammer, J. H., & Riggle, E. D. (2018). LGB positive identity and psychological well-being. *Psychology of Sexual Orientation and Gender Diversity, 5,* 482–9. doi:10.1037/sgd0000298

Rostosky, S. S., Riggle, E. D., Horne, S. G., & Miller, A. D. (2009). Marriage amendments and psychological distress in lesbian, gay, and bisexual (LGB) adults. *Journal of Counseling Psychology, 56,* 56–66. doi:10.1037/a0013609

Rostosky, S. S., Riggle, E. D. B., Pascale-Hague, D., & McCants, L. E. (2010). The positive aspects of a bisexual self-identification. *Psychology & Sexuality, 1,* 131–44. doi:10.1080/19419899.2010.484595

Russell, G. M., & Richards, J. A. (2003). Stressor and resilience factors for lesbians, gay men, and bisexuals confronting antigay politics. *American Journal of Community Psychology, 31,* 313–28. doi:10.1023/A:1023919022811

Sattler, F., Wagner, U., & Christiansen, H. (2016). Effects of minority stress, group-level coping, and social support on mental health of German gay men. *PLoS One, 11,* 1–15. doi:10.1371/journal.pone.0150562

Scandurra, C., Amodeo, A. L., Valerio, P., Bochicchio, V., & Frost, D. M. (2017). Minority stress, resilience, and mental health: A study of Italian transgender people. *Journal of Social Issues, 73,* 563–85. doi:10.1111/josi.12232

Scandurra, C., Bochicchio, V., Amodeo, A. L., Esposito, C., Valerio, P., Maldonato, N. M., . . . Vitelli, R. (2018). Internalized transphobia, resilience, and mental health: Applying the psychological mediation framework to Italian transgender individuals. *International Journal of Environmental Research and Public Health, 15,* 508–25. doi:10.3390/ijerph15030508

Schmitz, R. M., & Tyler, K. A. (2019). "Life has actually become more clear": An examination of resilience among LGBTQ young adults. *Sexualities, 22*(4), 710–33. doi:10.1177/1363460718770451

Singh, A. A. (2013). Transgender youth of color and resilience: Negotiating oppression and finding support. *Sex Roles, 68,* 690–702. doi:10.1007/s11199-012-0149-z

Singh, A. A., Hays, D. G., & Watson, L. B. (2011). Strength in the face of adversity: Resilience strategies of transgender individuals. *Journal of Counseling & Development, 89,* 20–7. doi:10.1002/j.1556–6678.2011.tb00057.x

Singh, A. A., & McKleroy, V. S. (2011). "Just getting out of bed is a revolutionary act": The resilience of transgender people of color who have survived traumatic life events. *Traumatology, 17,* 34–44. doi:10.1177/1534765610369261

Singh, A. A., Meng, S. E., & Hansen, A. W. (2014). "I am my own gender": Resilience strategies of trans youth. *Journal of Counseling & Development, 92,* 208–18. doi:10.1002/j.1556–6676.2014.00150.x

Sung, M. R., Szymanski, D. M., & Henrichs-Beck, C. L. (2015). Challenges, coping, and benefits of being an Asian American lesbian or bisexual woman. *Psychology of Sexual Orientation and Gender Diversity, 2,* 52–64. doi:10.1037/sgd0000085

Swank, E., & Fahs, B. (2013). Predicting electoral activism among gays and lesbians in the United States. *Journal of Applied Social Psychology, 43,* 1382–93. doi:10.1111/jasp.12095

Swim, J. K., Johnston, K., & Pearson, N. B. (2009). Daily experiences with heterosexism: Relations between heterosexist hassles and psychological well-being. *Journal of Social and Clinical Psychology, 28,* 597–629. doi:10.1521/jscp.2009.28.5.597

Szymanski, D. M. (2009). Examining potential moderators of the link between heterosexist events and gay and bisexual men's psychological distress. *Journal of Counseling Psychology, 56,* 142–51. doi:10.1037/0022–0167.56.1.142

Szymanski, D. M., & Carretta, R. F. (2019). Religious-based sexual stigma and psychological health: Roles of internalization, religious struggle, and religiosity. *Journal of Homosexuality* [E-pub before print]. doi:10.1080/00918369.2019.1601439

Szymanski, D. M., & Mikorski, R. (2016). External and internalized heterosexism, meaning in life, and psychological distress. *Psychology of Sexual Orientation and Gender Diversity, 3,* 265–74. doi:10.1037/sgd0000182

Szymanski, D. M., Mikorski, R., & Carretta, R. F. (2017). Heterosexism and LGB positive identity: Roles of coping and personal growth initiative. *The Counseling Psychologist, 45,* 294–319. doi:10.1177/0011000017697195

Szymanski, D. M., & Owens, G. P. (2009). Group-level coping as a moderator between heterosexism and sexism and psychological distress in sexual minority women. *Psychology of Women Quarterly, 33*, 197–205. doi:10.1111/j.1471–6402.2009.01489.x

Tasker, F., & Golombok, S. (1998). Young people's attitudes toward living in a lesbian family. *Journal of Divorce & Remarriage, 28*, 183–202. doi:10.1300/J087v28n01_13

Titlestad, A., & Pooley, J. A. (2014). Resilience in same-sex-parented families: The lived experience of adults with gay, lesbian, or bisexual parents. *Journal of GLBT Family Studies, 10*, 329–53. doi:10.1080/1550428X.2013.833065

Toomey, R. B., & Anhalt, K. (2016). Mindfulness as a coping strategy for bias-based school victimization among Latina/o sexual minority youth. *Psychology of Sexual Orientation and Gender Diversity, 3*, 432–41. doi:10.1037/sgd0000192

Toomey, R. B., Ryan, C., Diaz, R. M., & Russell, S. T. (2011). High school gay-straight alliances (GSAs) and young adult well-being: An examination of GSA presence, participation, and perceived effectiveness. *Applied Developmental Science, 15*, 175–85. doi:10.1080/10888691.2011.607378

Tran, A. G. (2015). In these spaces: Perceived neighborhood quality as a protective factor against discrimination for lesbian, gay, and bisexual (LGB) adults. *Psychology of Sexual Orientation and Gender Diversity, 2*, 345–52. doi:10.1037/sgd0000113

Velez, B. L., & Moradi, B. (2016). A moderated mediation test of minority stress: The role of collective action. *The Counseling Psychologist, 44*, 1132–57. doi:10.1177/0011000016665467

Verrelli, S., White, F. A., Harvey, L. J., & Pulciani, M. R. (2019). Minority stress, social support, and the mental health of lesbian, gay, and bisexual Australians during the Australian Marriage Law Postal Survey. *Australian Psychologist, 54*(4), 336–46. doi:10.1111/ap.12380

Watson, L. B., Morgan, S. K., & Craney, R. (2018). Bisexual women's discrimination and mental health outcomes: The roles of resilience and collective action. *Psychology of Sexual Orientation and Gender Diversity, 5*, 182–93. doi:10.1037/sgd0000272

Wilson, B. D. M., & Miller, R. L. (2002). Strategies for managing heterosexism used among African American gay and bisexual men. *Journal of Black Psychology, 28*, 371–91. doi:10.1177/009579802237543

Woodford, M. R., Kulick, A., & Atteberry, B. (2015). Protective factors, campus climate, and health outcomes among sexual minority college students. *Journal of Diversity in Higher Education, 8*, 73–87. doi:10.1037/a0038552

Zimmerman, L., Darnell, D. A., Rhew, I. C., Lee, C. M., & Kaysen, D. (2015). Resilience in community: A social ecological development model for young adult sexual minority women. *American Journal of Community Psychology, 55*, 179–90. doi:10.1007/s10464-015-9702-6

CHAPTER

37 Epilogue: Challenges in Research Methods and Future Directions on Sexual and Gender Minority Mental Health Research

David M. Frost

Abstract

This chapter is focused on the challenges that face researchers who are investigating the mental health of sexual and gender minority (SGM) individuals. The chapter provides an overview of predominant frameworks and theories guiding research on the mental health of SGM individuals in order to highlight the methodological challenges that stem from these guiding frameworks and theories. Although there are challenges specific to certain subgroups within the broader SGM population, this chapter focuses on common challenges that are widely applicable within the field. The author concludes with suggestions for future research that aims to improve the field's ability to understand and address mental health disparities continuing to face diverse SGM populations.

Keywords: minority stress, social stress, resilience, psychological well-being, social well-being, LGBT, nonbinary, intersectionality

The past several decades have witnessed a proliferation and diversification of theories of and research on sexual and gender minority (SGM) mental health. This chapter highlights some pressing challenges that face researchers working on SGM mental health along with suggestions for future directions that may serve to overcome such challenges. The chapter will begin with a brief overview of predominant frameworks and theories guiding SGM mental health research in order to highlight the methodological challenges that stem from guiding frameworks and theories. Although there are challenges that may be specific to research on subgroups within the broader SGM population, this chapter will focus on common challenges that are widely applicable within the field.

Theories and Frameworks for the Study of SGM Mental Health

Social Stress Theories

The majority of theoretical perspectives applied to the study of SGM mental health can be categorized as social stress theories (Aneshensel, Rutter, & Lachenbruch, 1991), with the most predominant example being minority stress theory (DiPlacido, 1998; Hendricks & Testa, 2012; Meyer, 1995, 2003). As reviewed by DiPlacido and Fallahi in Chapter 35 of this *Handbook*, the central premise of minority stress theory is that the higher prevalence of mental health disorders (i.e., mental health disparities) frequently observed in SGM populations is attributable to the higher levels of social stress that they experience relative to their heterosexual and cisgender peers. The reason for this excess exposure to social stress stems from the socially disadvantaged and stigmatized minority status that societies continue to afford to SGM individuals across the globe. Early models (DiPlacido, 1998; Meyer, 1995) focused on the social psychological manifestations of minority stressors in the form of acute stressful life events related to prejudice (e.g., being fired or kicked out of one's home due to being a SGM person); everyday discrimination and microaggressions (e.g., being treated with less courtesy; being avoided or feared); expectations of rejection; the need to conceal and manage the visibility of one's SGM identity; and the internalization of stigma surrounding being a SGM person (Meyer, 2003). Although the minority stress model (Meyer, 2003) has yet to be tested in its fully articulated form, research has provided evidence for its central premise. For example, Mays and Cochran (2001) found that the differences between sexual minority and heterosexual individuals in mental health observed in population-level data were statistically attenuated when differential exposure to discrimination was accounted for.

Lick, Durso, and Johnson (2013) have identified additional physiological pathways that may explain the connection between exposure to minority stress and negative health outcomes. These pathways include the general physiological pathways linking stress to health in both mental and physical health domains. They contend that minority stress can produce poor health outcomes by disrupting hormone regulation via dysregulation of the hypothalamic–pituitary–adrenal (HPA) axis, thereby suppressing the effectiveness of the autonomic nervous system and diminishing immune function (see Lick et al., 2013, for a review).

Moving from psychological to sociological levels of explanation, theories of structural stigma (e.g., Hatzenbuehler, 2014) contend that discriminatory social structures represent sources of stress at the macrosocial level that put SGM individuals at risk for poorer mental health. Specifically, structural stigma refers to "societal-level conditions, cultural norms, and institutional practices that constrain the opportunities, resources, and wellbeing for stigmatized populations" (Hatzenbuehler & Link, 2014, p. 2). For example, laws and policies that discriminate against SGM individuals (e.g., prohibitions on same-sex marriage, restrictions on changes to official documents allowing for expression of gender identities other than one's sex assigned at birth) represent forms of structural stigma. Research has shown that living in countries, states, and regions that are high in structural stigma can be detrimental to the mental health of SGM individuals in ways that are unique and not detrimental to heterosexual and cisgender individuals (see Hatzenbuehler, 2014, for a review).

Theories of Resilience

Although social stress models arguably represent the most prevalent type of theoretical perspective in research on SGM mental health, a focus on resilience—as positive adaptation to adversity—has emerged over the past decade as outlined by Szymanski and Gonzalez in Chapter 36 in this *Handbook*. Individuals' abilities to be resilient depend on access to a variety of individual and social resilience resources such as mastery, agency, social support, and connection to an affirming community (e.g., Singh, Hays, & Watson, 2011). Resilience frameworks are often used in research on SGM mental health as critical of predominant social stress perspectives (e.g., Meyer, 2015) in order to highlight the many ways in which SGM individuals exercise personal strengths and agency and take advantage of social resources, allowing them to live healthy lives and thrive despite prevailing stigmatizing climates. However, social stress and resilience perspectives need not be positioned in opposition to each other and can more productively be seen as complementary given that resilience in its classic psychological conceptualization is considered a response to stress and trauma (Bonanno, 2012). Thus, emphasizing the complementarity of social stress and resilience approaches stands to benefit research on SGM mental health.

Some recent attempts have been made to explicitly integrate social stress and resilience perspectives (e.g., Frost, 2011a; Meyer, 2015; Fredriksen-Goldsen et al., 2014). For example, the health equity promotion model (Fredriksen-Goldsen et al., 2014) makes an explicit attempt to highlight both adverse and health-promoting pathways linking social context to mental health. As part of the health-promoting pathways, resilience resources are included to account for the ways in which resilience resources can "delink the relationship between stressors in early life and consequential health deterioration in later life" (Fredriksen-Goldsen et al., 2014, p. 5). By accounting for risk as well as resilience, such combined perspectives have utility beyond suggestions for prevention of negative mental health outcomes by targeting the promotion of positive mental health and flourishing among SGM populations (Fredriksen-Goldsen et al., 2014).

Life Course Framework

A focus on social and temporal context via the life course framework has also emerged as useful in the study of SGM mental health (e.g., Fredriksen-Goldsen et al., 2014; Hammack, Frost, Meyer, & Pletta, 2018; Institute of Medicine, 2011). This has been highlighted by what Russell and Fish (2016) have termed a "developmental collision." Specifically, although SGM health disparities persist, there is clear evidence that the social climate for SGM individuals in Western contexts has drastically improved over the past decade. The effects of these social changes on health must be accounted for in disparities research given that their impact on health may not be universally positive. First it remains to be seen whether these changes in public opinion translate to the level of diminished social stress at the interpersonal level for SGM individuals. Just as racism has changed over time from overt to implicit forms, stigma and prejudice against SGM individuals may be changing form as well, and thus new measures may be needed to assess such experiences (Hatzenbuehler, Dovidio, Nolen-Hoeksema, & Phills, 2009; Krieger et al., 2010). Take also, for example, findings that young SGM individuals are coming of age at a time when sexual orientation and sexual minority statuses are potentially not as defining of differentness in lived experience in the ways they have been for previous generations (e.g., Cohler & Hammack, 2007; Ghaziani, 2011; Savin-Williams, 2005). Additionally, SGM seniors are more "out" about their sexual orientation and gender identities within the healthcare system and assisted living contexts, while previous generations have not been as visible (e.g., Hillman & Hinrichsen, 2014). These two examples, drawing on the unique experiences of different age cohorts, highlight the potential importance of using a life course developmental framework in studying SGM health (Fredriksen-Goldsen et al., 2014; Hammack, Frost, Meyer, & Pletta, 2018; Institute of Medicine, 2011).

Intersectionality

Alongside generational differences in how SGM individuals experience social stress, researchers have increasingly called for attention to the ways in which minority stress and resilience are experienced uniquely at the intersection of multiple social identities. As several chapters in this *Handbook* have highlighted, there is a tremendous amount of diversity within the population of SGM individuals with regard to race, ethnicity, geographic region of residence, socioeconomic status, and immigration status, which shape their lived experiences of the risk and resilience factors that influence their mental health. Intersectionality scholars from the fields of critical race theory, feminism, psychology, and public health (Cole, 2009; Crenshaw, 1991; McCall, 2005; Rosenthal, 2016) have called for researchers to interrogate, rather than gloss over, the unique intersectional circumstances that may give rise to important variability in the experience of minority stress and resilience, and the resulting implications for mental health. Take, for example, the experiences of black lesbian women, whose experiences of stress, resilience, and mental health are likely shaped by intersecting forms of oppression that they uniquely experience at the intersection of being (simultaneously) Black, female, and sexual minorities (Bowleg, 2008). Their experiences at the intersection of these social identities cannot be reflected by additive stress or "triple jeopardy" models of mental health risk that consider race, gender, and sexual orientation separately in isolation (Bowleg, 2008). In order to account for these important intersectional experiences of stress and resilience, the study of SGM mental health has increasingly incorporated intersectionality frameworks to varying degrees of success.

Challenges in Linking Frameworks, Theories, and Methods

Between-Group Versus Within-Group Designs

One persistent challenge to attempts to understand and address persistently observed mental health inequalities affecting SGM populations pertains to differences in what it is possible to achieve within research designs focusing on explaining variability in mental health within the SGM population (i.e., within-group studies) or research designs focusing on explaining differences in mental health between SGM individuals and their heterosexual and cisgender peers (i.e., between-group designs). Although often manifested in challenges regarding measurement, conceptual issues arise in attempts to account for factors theorized to explain health disparities. For example, the minority stress model (Meyer, 2003) suggests that health disparities exist between SGM and heterosexual and cisgender populations largely because of the unique stressors that SGM individuals experience, as previously outlined. However, heterosexual and cisgender individuals do not experience or are not exposed to many of these minority stressors, making it difficult to examine whether the lack of those stressors explains their better outcomes. Thus, methodological challenges arise in research involving between-group designs that examine factors unique to one group's experience in explaining a difference in outcomes between the groups (for detailed exploration of this challenge, see Schwartz & Meyer, 2010).

Take, for example, the minority stressor of internalized stigma. Several studies have examined the impact that internalized stigma can have on the health of sexual minority individuals in within-group studies (e.g., Herrick et al., 2013). Internalized stigma is therefore likely a key part of the additional stress burden that sexual minorities are exposed to relative to heterosexuals. However, in a between-group design necessary to directly investigate whether minority stress explains health disparities based on sexual orientation, it is not possible to include internalized stigma in explanatory models given that it cannot be measured among heterosexuals beyond the mere absence of it. Similar problems would arise with regard to constructs like "passing" in investigations of the role of minority stress in health disparities based on gender identity, because cisgender individuals do not experience stress related to passing as cisgender. As a result, the majority of research on minority stress and its impact on SGM mental health has used within-group designs. This approach is useful in understanding the association between minority stress and mental health but cannot examine the extent to which stigma explains a given disparity in mental health (Schwartz & Meyer, 2010).

There are some forms of minority stress that can theoretically be experienced by SGM individuals as well as heterosexuals and cisgender individuals; for example, a cisgender man could theoretically expect to be rejected as a result of his gender depending on the context. Thus, researchers using a disparities frame can adapt measures of minority stress constructs—like expectations of rejection—so that they can account for stress exposure in the form of some minority stressors across heterosexual and cisgender and SGM populations. To illustrate, the everyday discrimination measure by Williams, Yu, Jackson, and Anderson (1997) takes a two-step approach to first assessing how often (i.e., frequency) an individual has experienced various forms of differential treatment (e.g., poor service in stores, being treated in a disrespectful manner), followed by the individual's attribution for that treatment in a second step (e.g., did it happen because of race, gender, sexual orientation). In employing this measure of discrimination, total scores can be computed based solely on responses to the frequency items, regardless of attribution. This would allow for the creation of a total everyday discrimination score that is comparable across all groups in a comparative design (e.g., heterosexual vs. sexual minority individuals, cisgender vs. gender minority individuals). As a result, everyday discrimination can be examined as an explanation for differences in a given mental health outcome or domain between the groups.

Need for Longitudinal Designs in the Study of Resilience

As mentioned previously, resilience has increasingly become the focus of research on SGM mental health (see Chapter 36 in this *Handbook*). However, just as is the case in the broader literature on resilience (Fletcher & Sarkar, 2013), there are a variety of inconsistencies in the ways that researchers investigating resilience in the lives of SGM individuals have defined and operationalized the construct. Methods for studying resilience have relied primarily on qualitative data and/or cross-sectional survey designs, and have often conceptualized resilience as a trait or resource that an individual possesses, such as agency or access to social support. These studies provide evidence of resilience in various forms, such as narrative accounts of the factors that facilitate positive responses to risk factors for mental health (e.g., minority stressors), interaction terms suggesting that resilience resources moderate the association between risk factors and mental health outcomes, and direct associations between measures of resilience resources and mental health outcomes.

Although these studies offer useful suggestive evidence for the role of resilience in determining SGM mental health, they do not provide direct and sufficient evidence for resilience due to retrospective bias and the inability to study adaptation to adversity over time. As Bonanno (2012) argues, resilience is an outcome, not a quality of individuals, that can only be fully understood by examining how individuals react to adversity over time. He has usefully offered the concept of resilience as a trajectory, which can be operationalized in the form of a "relatively stable trajectory of healthy functioning and positive adaption" (Bonanno, 2012, p. 755) over time after a person has experienced adversity (e.g., been exposed to minority stress). This understanding of resilience as a trajectory can only be achieved in longitudinal designs that repeatedly measure mental health outcomes, resilience resources, and risk factors. Thus, there is a need to study resilience as a trajectory in order to accurately understand the psychological and social resources that have been theorized (e.g., Fredriksen-Goldsen et al., 2014; Meyer, 2015) to promote resilience in the context of SGM mental health.

Social Change and the Shifting Definition of SGM Populations

In some parts of the world, policy changes (e.g., equal marriage, recognition of nonbinary gender identities on official documents) and improvements in the social climate (e.g., attitudes toward SGM individuals) have paved the way for new generations of SGM individuals to experience, achieve, and express diverse forms of SGM identities. For example, the emergence of queer, pansexual, asexual, and nonbinary identities challenges and moves beyond the LGBT identities that characterized the majority of individuals in previous SGM generations. Recent polling suggests that adolescents and emerging adults may be more likely to adopt minority sexual and gender identities than previous cohorts (e.g., in the United Kingdom, one out of every two eighteen- to twenty-four-year-olds identifies as other than exclusively heterosexual; Dahlgreen & Shakespeare, 2015). As social and policy climates are shifting to become increasingly more positive for younger generations of SGM individuals, who are adopting increasingly diverse identities, researchers focused on the mental health and well-being of SGM youth need to examine the degree to which predominant theories of stress and resilience apply to such emerging experiences (Svensson & Frost, forthcoming).

For example, a few recent studies have been conducted that have examined the degree to which aspects of the minority stress model explain the lived experiences of "nontraditional" SGM individuals, such as queer, pansexual, and sexually fluid individuals (Goldbach & Gibbs, 2017; Mitchel, Davis, & Galupo, 2015: Shilo, Antebi, & Mor, 2015). These studies support the continued utility of aspects of the minority stress model but also suggest the need to further develop aspects of the model, in order to improve its ability to understand and explain the ways in which stress and resilience processes impact mental health within increasingly diverse communities of SGM individuals. For example, queer and pansexual people experience minority stress stemming from within the broader sexual and gender community (Goldbach & Gibbs, 2017), yet bisexual individuals experience less connection to SGM communities than other "plurisexual" individuals (e.g., pansexual, queer, and sexually fluid individuals; Mitchel et al., 2015).

Despite these important intragroup differences in the experience of minority stress and community, it is clear that emerging generations of SGM individuals continue to experience social stress stemming from prevailing societal stigma, which may continue to explain the persistence of mental health disparities in younger generations of SGM individuals (Russell & Fish, 2016). However, as new forms of identities emerge and proliferate within the broader population of SGM individuals, researchers need to expand definitions of who "counts" as a member of the SGM population in order to monitor if and how the changing social climate impacts their mental health.

Methodological Challenges in Studying Intersectionality and Mental Health

It is widely agreed that researchers need to explore how the intersection of multiple social statuses shapes the experiences of risk and resilience that are theorized to effect the mental health of SGM individuals (Institute of Medicine, 2011). However, public health researchers have long pointed out problems with the predominant quantitative methods used in mental health research for studying intersectionality (e.g., Bowleg, 2008). For example, quantitative analysis models that examine whether individuals with multiply stigmatized minority identities experience incremental risk for negative mental health outcomes are often positioned as investigating intersectionality but are instead looking at additive models such as additive burden or "double jeopardy" hypotheses that do not allow for an understanding of potentially unique experiences at the intersection of given individual and social identities (Bowleg & Bauer, 2016).

Some researchers have proposed novel mixed methods and quantitative methods to bridge these concerns. For example, Stirratt, Meyer, Oullette, and Gara (2008) used hierarchical classes analysis (HICLAS) to understand how aspects of sexual, gender, and racial identity intersectionality among sexual minority individuals relate to mental health. They used a prompt allowing individuals to qualitatively describe their sexual, gender, and racial identities followed by a quantitative rating system involving a series of traits and qualities that described each identity. These identity-specific ratings were then analyzed using the HICLAS procedures to determine the degree to which various identities were connected with one another. For example, a given identity (e.g., sexual identity) could be superordinate, subordinate, overlapping, or disconnected from another given identity (e.g., racial identity). This approach has the potential to overcome the previously described shortcomings of quantitative analyses relying on additive models by investigating the degree to which individual differences in the experienced connection (or lack of connection) between social identities may be related to mental health among diverse groups of SGM individuals. As noted by Bowleg and Bauer (2016), more attention to developing new methods and relying on quantitative, qualitative, and mixed-methods designs are needed to bring the field's methods in line with its interests in investigating the role of intersectionality in SGM mental health.

Future Directions

Identifying New and Unique Forms of Minority Stress and Resilience

As the use of social stress and resilience frameworks proliferates in research on SGM mental health, future research is needed to understand the full "universe" of potential forms of social stress and resilience resources uniquely relevant to SGM individuals affecting the population's risk for mental health problems. This is especially true for gender minority individuals, for whom the minority stress model has only been recently theoretically extended (Bockting, Miner, Swinburne Romine, Hamilton, & Coleman, 2013; Hendricks & Testa, 2012). For example, Johnson, LeBlanc, Deardorff, and Bockting (2019) conducted qualitative research providing insight into the ways in which individuals with nonbinary gender identities (e.g., gender fluid, gender queer) experience gender invalidation. They note how stress emanates from experiences of gender invalidation when others refuse to accept nonbinary gender identities as real or true, thereby imposing a binary definition on individuals who identify outside of the male–female gender binary.

In addition to stressors that result from events or interactions, non-events—anticipated events or experiences that do not come to pass (Gersten, Langner, Eisenberg, & Orzeck, 1974; Neugarten, Moore, & Lowe, 1965)—are also associated with negative mental health and well-being outcomes among SGM individuals (Frost & LeBlanc, 2014). Examples of non-event stressors include hoped-for achievements in life that are delayed or do not happen at all, like not being promoted at work when expected (Neugarten et al., 1965). Non-event stress is experienced across a number of life domains that involve not achieving, or experiencing delays in achieving, widely recognized expectations for the timing of certain milestones like marriage and parenthood. Social stress researchers have widely theorized the importance of non-event stress as a predictor of negative mental health outcomes; however, empirical research on this type of stressor has been plagued by the inability to measure the experience of stress related to an event that does not come to pass. One attempt to measure the impact of non-event stress on SGM mental health and well-being has conceptualized and operationalized non-event stress in the form of frustrated goal pursuits (Frost & LeBlanc, 2014). This work has indicated that non-event stress in the form of frustrated pursuit of goals for relationships (e.g., not being able to marry a partner, having been denied housing when seeking to jointly rent an apartment) may be the result of structural stigma (e.g., Hatzenbuehler, 2014; e.g., exclusion of same-sex couples from legal marriage, discriminatory housing practices), which is associated with negative mental health and well-being outcomes for SGM individuals. Indeed, the frustration of SGM individuals' pursuit of goals as a result of legal barriers can manifest in stress related to the non-achievement of such goals. Thus, non-event stress is likely to contribute to the already exacerbated amount of stress that SGM people experience relative to their heterosexual and cisgender peers in most parts of the world.

In addition to identifying new forms of stress, researchers must also focus on identifying and measuring previously unaccounted for resilience resources. Operating from a stress-coping framework, minority stress research has thus far mainly examined the ways in which individuals use personal and group-level coping strategies, as well as social support. Some emerging research has pointed to the potential role of engagement in activism as a community-level response to experiences of minority stress (e.g., Frost, Fine, Torre, & Cabana, 2019). General research on activism and collective action has indicated that it may indeed be a potent response to oppression (e.g., Campbell & Deacon, 2006; Swank & Fahs, 2006). The activist commitments of SGM individuals have been theorized to arise from "radical marginality" (Hall & Fine, 2005); however, the extent to which involvement in activism represents "positive marginality" (Unger, 2000) in response to minority stress has yet to be explicitly examined. Findings from previous research in the general population have shown relationships between experiences of discrimination and engagement in activism for ethnic minority individuals (Cronin, Levin, Branscombe, van Laar, & Tropp, 2012) and SGM individuals (Swank & Fahs, 2006); however, these studies did not investigate the implications of these associations on mental health. There have been a few studies that examined links between activism and well-being among SGM individuals, but the findings have been mixed (cf. Earnshaw, Rosenthal, & Lang, 2016; Frost et al., 2019). More work is arguably needed on the association between activism involvements and mental health given that research in the broader population indicates a consistent link between engagement in activism (using several indicators, such as behavioral acts, volunteerism) and positive outcomes across several domains of mental health (e.g., Klar & Kasser, 2009; Thoits & Hewitt, 2001).

Incorporating Social Stress and Resilience Frameworks in Integrative Designs

Minority stress and health equity promotion models both offer explanations for why SGM populations experience inequalities in mental health. Accounting for the negative effect of social disadvantage and stigma on health, as well as when individuals are able to thrive despite the negative social climate, is of vital importance to bring research more in line with the holistic reality of SGM individuals' lived experiences (Fine, 2005; Fine & Cross, 2016; Frost, 2011).

Thus, one approach to address this limitation is to consider disparities within a larger model of factors that result in the negative effects of social stress and factors that contribute to stress resistance and resilience (Fredricksen-Goldson et al., 2014; Frost, 2017; Herrick et al., 2013; Meyer, 2015; Singh et al., 2011). This approach would increase the potential of combined frameworks to explain the multitude of factors and mechanisms contributing to mental health inequalities faced by SGMs that may not be explained by excess stress exposure alone (e.g., Frisell, Lichtenstein, Rahman, & Långström, 2010). This approach to SGM mental health research may also help to avoid "blaming the victim" (i.e., faulting those who are not resilient in the face of social disadvantage) by accounting for how disadvantage can affect increased stress exposure as well as diminished access to resilience resources (e.g., Meyer, Schwartz, & Frost, 2008).

Broadening Mental Health Outcomes

Following general models of social stress and health (e.g., Aneshensel et al., 1991), the effects of social stress and resilience on mental health are theorized *not* to be specific to any given disorder or condition and are intended to be extended to mental health as a collective domain of health more generally. For example, the minority stress framework was designed to explain mental health disparities between sexual minorities and heterosexuals as a general domain of health, rather than disparities in specific mental health disorders, such as major depressive disorder or generalized anxiety (Meyer, 2003). This is because the model's hypothesized explanation for health disparities is social stigma, which should (in theory) impact a given domain of health (e.g., mental health) containing multiple indicators in aggregate, as opposed to impacting one indicator (e.g., major depressive disorder) but not another (generalized anxiety disorder). In practice, a disparity in a specific mental health disorder may not be explained by stigma and social disadvantage. However, when such null findings do occur, they cannot be taken to indicate that stigma and social disadvantage can be ruled out as a potential "cause" of observed disparities. A focus on disparities in domains of health rather than specific disorders in isolation would protect against such "false null" findings and the implied conclusion that stigma and social disadvantage do not matter for the health of SGM individuals. Efforts to build transdiagnostic outcomes (e.g., Caspi et al., 2014) may also be of use in efforts to be more inclusive in focusing disparities research on domains of mental health rather than specific disorders (e.g., Eaton, 2014).

When conceptualizing domains of mental health, researchers (e.g., Fredriksen-Goldsen et al., 2014; Kertzner, Meyer, Frost, & Stirratt, 2009) have called for a shift away from focusing exclusively on mental health as either the presence or absence of pathology in the form of disorder or symptoms of disorder, and instead broadening the focus to include positive indicators of mental health in the form of well-being. Conceptualizing and operationalizing mental health in the form of well-being should include forms of psychological and social well-being that emphasize "eudaimonic" dimensions, such as the achievement of autonomy, purpose, and meaning in life, alongside "hedonic" dimensions, such as positive affect, life satisfaction, and happiness (Keyes, 1998; Keyes, Shmotkin, & Ryff, 2002; Ryan & Deci, 2001; Ryff, 1989). By conceptualizing and operationalizing mental health with a focus on both pathology/disorder and well-being, researchers can take advantage of a "two-continua model" of negative *and* positive mental health, which scholars of the social determinants of mental health contend allows for a more holistic understanding of mental health (Kertzner et al., 2009; Keyes, 2002, 2005). This two-continua model for conceptualizing and operationalizing mental health has enormous potential for advancing research and interventions focused on mental health outcomes among SGM populations. As previously stated, research has established that SGM populations evidence higher rates of mental health disorders and symptoms of disorder (e.g., subthreshold depressive symptoms) than their heterosexual and cisgender peers; however, this extensive body of research has yet to account for potential inequalities in the achievement of positive mental health (e.g., thriving) in the form of psychological and social well-being. Just as is the case in the general population, the majority of SGM individuals do not have a mental health disorder (or exhibit high levels of disorder symptoms). However, they may experience low levels of life satisfaction, less meaning in life, and diminished social well-being as a result of social stress stemming from their stigmatized status as SGM individuals (Fredriksen-Goldsen et al., 2014; Kertzner et al., 2009). Thus, research on SGM mental health stands to benefit from expanding its definitions of mental health to include outcomes of psychological and social well-being in addition to outcomes related to mental health problems and disorders.

Understanding Interrelationships Between Structural, Interpersonal, and Intrapersonal Factors

Increasingly, scholars have recognized that the factors influencing SGM mental health are located across individual, social, and structural levels (e.g., Bowleg & Bauer, 2016; Fredriksen-Goldsen et al., 2014; Hatzenbuehler, 2014). Further, calls for interventions to reduce risk, promote resilience, and thereby reduce or eliminate health inequalities faced by SGM persons have also highlighted the need to target change efforts at multiple levels (e.g., Cook, Purdie-Vaughns, Meyer, & Busch, 2014; Hughto, Reisner, & Pachankis, 2015). Despite the increased attention to the relevance of the multi-level pathways linking risk and resilience to SGM mental health, very few empirical investigations have been conducted to demonstrate the existence of such layered pathways. This is likely because of the daunting methodological requirements for studies of multi-level influence. For example, in order to test the theory that discriminatory laws and policies produce increases in interpersonal forms of discrimination, which in turn affect mental health, researchers need to obtain and combine geographically specific data on laws and policies with individually reported experiences of discrimination along with validated measures of mental health outcomes. This would ideally require access to large geographically diverse, representative, and longitudinal data sets. Although many countries have nationally representative population health data that include validated measures of mental health, many lack questions about sexual orientation and gender identity. Those that include such questions often have very small numbers of SGM individuals due to the representative nature of their sampling strategies (Rothblum, Balsam, & Mickey, 2004) and are unlikely to include questions about SGM-specific risk and resilience (e.g., minority stress, community connection). Thus, researchers need to be creative in combining multiple data sources that can, when joined, allow for the testing of the theorized multi-level pathways that influence SGM mental health.

A notable example of such a design can be found in the work of Pachankis and Bränström (2018), who investigated the degree to which structural stigma was associated with higher levels of stigma concealment and the resulting implications for mental health in the form of life satisfaction. Focusing on SGM individuals living across countries in the European Union, they created an index of structural stigma by obtaining information on the laws and policies surrounding SGM rights in each country and combining this information with country-level attitudes toward SGM individuals as measured in the European Social Survey. They next combined these data with data on concealment and life satisfaction from a sample of SGM persons living in each country of the European Union collected in the European Union Lesbian, Gay, Bisexual, and Transgender Survey. Once combined, their analyses of these data provided evidence that individuals living in countries categorized as high in structural stigma were more likely to conceal their sexual identities, which in turn put them at greater risk for diminished life satisfaction. Studies like this, which incorporate cross-national cultural and policy differences in analyses of SGM mental health, are increasingly important, given the lack of research in countries that have the most discriminatory social policies and cultural norms, such as countries in the Middle East, North Africa, and the Global South.

In order to recognize the potential of the theoretical advancements in attempts to explain the multi-level risk and resilience pathways shaping SGM mental health, researchers need to build off examples like these and continue to explore novel integration across multiple forms and levels of data. This will require a continued push for the inclusion of questions to identify SGM individuals in population-level data (e.g., census, public health surveillance systems, electronic medical records) along with sufficient oversample and focus on risk and resilience mechanisms relevant to SGM mental health.

Summary and Conclusion

Over the past several decades, research on SGM mental health has proliferated and diversified in important ways. These include increasingly nuanced frameworks and theories designed to explain persistent mental health inequalities and target interventions, as well as heightened attention to diversity within SGM populations and the mental health concerns they face. The contributions in this *Handbook* collectively attest to the value of these important achievements. However, as this field moves forward, there are important tensions that have arisen when putting new theories and frameworks into practice. This chapter has highlighted several important challenges that those aiming to understand and address the factors shaping SGM mental health continue to contend with. However, within these challenges lie important and exciting new directions for research that, if successful, stand to produce scholarship and interventions with the potential to improve the mental health of SGM individuals.

References

Aneshensel, C. S., Rutter, C. M., & Lachenbruch, P. A. (1991). Social structure, stress, and mental health: Competing conceptual and analytic models. *American Sociological Review, 56*(2), 166–78. doi:10.2307/2095777

Bockting, W. O., Miner, M. H., Swinburne Romine, R. E., Hamilton, A., & Coleman, E. (2013). Stigma, mental health, and resilience in an online sample of the US transgender population. *American Journal of Public Health, 103*, 943–51. doi:10.2105/AJPH.2013.301241

Bonanno, G. A. (2012). Uses and abuses of the resilience construct: Loss, trauma, and health-related adversities. *Social Science and Medicine, 74*(5), 753. doi:10.1016/j.socscimed.2011.11.022

Bowleg, L. (2008). When Black+ lesbian+ woman≠ Black lesbian woman: The methodological challenges of qualitative and quantitative intersectionality research. *Sex Roles, 59*(5–6), 312–25. doi:10.1007/s11199-008-9400-z

Bowleg, L., & Bauer, G. (2016). Invited reflection: Quantifying intersectionality. *Psychology of Women Quarterly, 40*(3), 337–41. doi:10.1177/0361684316654282

Campbell, C., & Deacon, H. (2006). Unraveling the contexts of stigma: From internalisation to resistance to change. *Journal of Community and Applied Social Psychology, 16*(6), 411–7. doi:10.1002/casp.901

Caspi, A., Houts, R. M., Belsky, D. W., Goldman-Mellor, S. J., Harrington, H., Israel, S., . . . Moffitt, T. E. (2014). The p factor: One general psychopathology factor in the structure of psychiatric disorders. *Clinical Psychological Science, 2*(2), 119–37. doi:10.1177/2167702613497473

Cohler, B. J., & Hammack, P. L. (2007). The psychological world of the gay teenager: Social change, narrative, and "normality." *Journal of Youth and Adolescence, 36*(1), 47–59. doi:10.1007/s10964-006-9110-1

Cole, E. R. (2009). Intersectionality and research in psychology. *American Psychologist, 64*(3), 170–80. doi:10.1037/a0014564

Cook, J. E., Purdie-Vaughns, V., Meyer, I. H., & Busch, J. T. (2014). Intervening within and across levels: A multilevel approach to stigma and public health. *Social Science & Medicine, 103*, 101–9. doi:10.1016/j.socscimed.2013.09.023

Crenshaw, K. (1991). Mapping the margins: Intersectionality, identity politics, and violence against women of color. *Stanford Law Review, 43*(6), 1241–99. doi:10.2307/1229039

Cronin, T. J., Levin, A., Branscombe, N. R., van Laar, C., & Tropp, L. R. (2012). Ethnic identification in response to perceived discrimination protects well-being and promotes activism: A longitudinal study of Latino college students. *Group Processes and Intergroup Relations, 15*(3), 393–407. doi:10.1177/1368430211427171

Dahlgreen, W., & Shakespeare, A. E. (2015). 1 in 2 young people say they are not 100% heterosexual. YouGov. https://yougov.co.uk/topics/lifestyle/articles-reports/2015/08/16/half-young-not-heterosexual

DiPlacido, J. (1998). Minority stress among lesbians, gay men, and bisexuals: A consequence of heterosexism, homophobia, and stigmatization. In G. M. Herek (Ed.), *Stigma and sexual orientation: Understanding prejudice against lesbians, gay men, and bisexuals* (pp. 138–59). Thousand Oaks, CA: Sage Publications, Inc. doi:10.4135/9781452243818.n7

Earnshaw, V. A., Rosenthal, L., & Lang, S. M. (2016). Stigma, activism, and well-being among people living with HIV. *AIDS Care, 28*(6), 717–21. doi:10.1080/09540121.2015.1124978

Eaton, N. R. (2014). Trans-diagnostic psychopathology factors and sexual minority mental health: Evidence of disparities and associations with minority stressors. *Psychology of Sexual Orientation and Gender Diversity, 1*(3), 244–54. doi:10.1037/sgd0000048

Fine, M. (2005). Bearing witness: Methods for researching oppression and resistance—A textbook for critical research. *Social Justice Research, 19*(1), 83–108. doi:10.1007/s11211-006-0001-0

Fine, M., & Cross, W. E. Jr. (2016). Critical race, psychology, and social policy: Refusing damage, cataloging oppression, and documenting desire. In A. Alvarez, C. T. H. Liang, & H. A. Neville (Eds.), *The cost of racism for people of color: Contextualizing experiences of discrimination* (pp. 273–94). Washington, DC: American Psychological Association.

Fletcher, D., & Sarkar, M. (2013). Psychological resilience: A review and critique of definitions, concepts, and theory. *European Psychologist, 18*(1), 12. doi:10.1027/1016–9040/a000124

Fredriksen-Goldsen, K. I., Simoni, J. M., Kim, H. J., Lehavot, K., Walters, K. L., Yang, J., . . . Muraco, A. (2014). The health equity promotion model: Reconceptualization of lesbian, gay, bisexual, and transgender (LGBT) health disparities. *American Journal of Orthopsychiatry, 84*(6), 653–63. doi:10.1037/ort0000030

Frisell, T., Lichtenstein, P., Rahman, Q., & Långström, N. (2010). Psychiatric morbidity associated with same-sex sexual behaviour: Influence of minority stress and familial factors. *Psychological Medicine, 40*(2), 315–24. doi:10.1017/S0033291709005996

Frost, D. M. (2011). Social stigma and its consequences for the socially stigmatized. *Social and Personality Psychology Compass, 5*(11), 824–39. doi:10.1111/j.1751–9004.2011.00394.x

Frost, D. M. (2017). The benefits and challenges of health disparities and social stress frameworks for research on sexual and gender minority health. *Journal of Social Issues, 73*(3), 462–76. doi:10.1111/josi.12226

Frost, D. M., Fine, M., Torre, M. E., & Cabana, A. (2019). Minority stress, activism, and health in the context of economic precarity: Results from a national participatory action survey of lesbian, gay, bisexual, transgender, queer, and gender non-conforming youth. *American Journal of Community Psychology, 63*, 511–26. doi:10.1002/ajcp.12326

Frost, D. M., & LeBlanc, A. J. (2014). Nonevent stress contributes to mental health disparities based on sexual orientation: Evidence from a personal projects analysis. *American Journal of Orthopsychiatry, 84*(5), 557. doi:10.1037/ort0000024

Gersten, J. C., Langer, T. S., Eisenberg, J. G., & Orzeck, L. (1974). Child behavior and life events: Undesirable change or change per se? In B. S. Dohrenwend & B. P. Dohrenwend (Eds.), *Stressful life events: Their nature and effects* (pp. 159–70). New York, NY: Wiley.

Ghaziani, A. (2011). Post-gay collective identity construction. *Social Problems, 58*(1), 99–125. doi:10.1525/sp.2011.58.1.99

Goldbach, J. T., & Gibbs, J. J. (2017). A developmentally informed adaptation of minority stress for sexual minority adolescence. *Journal of Adolescence, 55*, 36–50. doi:10.1016/j.adolescence.2016.12.007

Hammack, P. L., Frost, D. M., Meyer, I. H., & Pletta, D. R. (2018). Gay men's health and identity: Social change and the life course. *Archives of Sexual Behavior, 47*(1), 59–74. doi:10.1007/s10508-017-0990-9

Hatzenbuehler, M. L. (2014). Structural stigma and the health of lesbian, gay, and bisexual populations. *Current Directions in Psychological Science, 23*(2), 127–32. doi:10.1177/0963721414523775

Hatzenbuehler, M. L., Dovidio, J. F., Nolen-Hoeksema, S., & Phills, C. E. (2009). An implicit measure of anti-gay attitudes: Prospective associations with emotion regulation strategies and psychological distress. *Journal of Experimental Social Psychology, 45*(6), 1316–20. doi:10.1016/j.jesp.2009.08.005

Hatzenbuehler, M. L., & Link, B. G. (2014). Introduction to the special issue on structural stigma and health. *Social Science & Medicine, 103*, 1–6. doi:10.1016/j.socscimed.2013.12.017

Hendricks, M. L., & Testa, R. J. (2012). A conceptual framework for clinical work with transgender and gender nonconforming clients: An adaptation of the minority stress model. *Professional Psychology: Research and Practice, 43*(5), 460. doi:10.1037/a0029597

Herrick, A. L., Stall, R., Chmiel, J. S., Guadamuz, T. E., Penniman, T., Shoptaw, S., . . . Plankey, M. W. (2013). It gets better: resolution of internalized homophobia over time and associations with positive health outcomes among MSM. *AIDS and Behavior, 17*(4), 1423–30. doi:10.1007/s10461-012-0392-x

Hillman, J., & Hinrichsen, G. A. (2014). Promoting an affirming, competent practice with older lesbian and gay adults. *Professional Psychology: Research and Practice, 45*(4), 269. doi:10.1037/a0037172

Hughto, J. M. W., Reisner, S. L., & Pachankis, J. E. (2015). Transgender stigma and health: A critical review of stigma determinants, mechanisms, and interventions. *Social Science & Medicine, 147*, 222–31. doi:10.1016/j.socscimed.2015.11.010

Institute of Medicine. (2011). *The health of lesbian, gay, bisexual, and transgender people: Building a foundation for better understanding*. Washington, DC: Author.

Johnson, K. C., LeBlanc, A. J., Deardorff, J., & Bockting, W. O. (2019). Invalidation experiences among non-binary adolescents. *Journal of Sex Research* [E-pub ahead of print]. doi:10.1080/00224499.2019.1608422

Kertzner, R. M., Meyer, I. H., Frost, D. M., & Stirratt, M. J. (2009). Social and psychological well-being in lesbians, gay men, and bisexuals: The effects of race, gender, age, and sexual identity. *American Journal of Orthopsychiatry, 79*(4), 500–10. doi:10.1037/a0016848

Keyes, C. L. M. (1998). Social well-being. *Social Psychology Quarterly, 61*, 121–40. doi:10.2307/2787065

Keyes, C. L. M. (2002). The mental health continuum: From languishing to flourishing in life. *Journal of Health and Social Behavior, 43*, 207–22. doi:10.2307/3090197

Keyes, C. L. (2005). Mental illness and/or mental health? Investigating axioms of the complete state model of health. *Journal of Consulting and Clinical Psychology, 73*(3), 539–48. doi:10.1037/0022-006X.73.3.539

Keyes, C. L. M., Shmotkin, D., & Ryff, C. D. (2002). Optimizing wellbeing: The empirical encounter of two traditions. *Journal of Personality and Social Psychology, 82*, 1007–22. doi:10.1037/0022–3514.82.6.1007

Klar, M., & Kasser, T. (2009). Some benefits of being an activist: measuring activism and its role in psychological well-being. *Political Psychology, 30*(5), 755–77. doi:10.1111/j.1467–9221.2009.00724.x

Krieger, N., Carney, D., Lancaster, K., Waterman, P. D., Kosheleva, A., & Banaji, M. (2010). Combining explicit and implicit measures of racial discrimination in health research. *American Journal of Public Health, 100*(8), 1485–92. doi:10.2105/AJPH.2009.159517

Lick, D. J., Durso, L. E., & Johnson, K. L. (2013). Minority stress and physical health among sexual minorities. *Perspectives on Psychological Science, 8*(5), 521–48. doi:10.1177/1745691613497965

Mays, V. M., & Cochran, S. D. (2001). Mental health correlates of perceived discrimination among lesbian, gay, and bisexual adults in the United States. *American Journal of Public Health, 91*(11), 1869–76. doi:10.2105/AJPH.91.11.1869

McCall, L. (2005). The complexity of intersectionality. *Signs, 30*(3), 1771–800. doi:10.1086/426800

Meyer, I. H. (1995). Minority stress and mental health in gay men. *Journal of Health and Social Behavior, 36*(1), 38–56. doi:10.2307/2137286

Meyer, I. H. (2003). Prejudice, social stress, and mental health in lesbian, gay, and bisexual populations: Conceptual issues and research evidence. *Psychological Bulletin, 129*(5), 674. doi:10.1037/0033–2909.129.5.674

Meyer, I. H. (2015). Resilience in the study of minority stress and health of sexual and gender minorities. *Psychology of Sexual Orientation and Gender Diversity, 2*(3), 209. doi:10.1037/sgd0000132

Meyer, I. H., Schwartz, S., & Frost, D. M. (2008). Social patterning of stress and coping: Does disadvantaged social statuses confer more stress and fewer coping resources? *Social Science & Medicine, 67*(3), 368–79. doi:10.1016/j.socscimed.2008.03.012

Mitchell, R. C., Davis, K. S., & Galupo, M. P. (2015). Comparing perceived experiences of prejudice among self-identified plurisexual individuals. *Psychology & Sexuality, 6*(3), 245–57. doi:10.1080/19419899.2014.940372

Neugarten, B. L., Moore, J. W., & Lowe, J. C. (1965). Age norms, age constraints, and adult socialization. *American Journal of Sociology, 70*, 710–17. doi:10.1086/223965

Pachankis, J. E., & Bränström, R. (2018). Hidden from happiness: Structural stigma, sexual orientation concealment, and life satisfaction across 28 countries. *Journal of Consulting and Clinical Psychology, 86*(5), 403. doi:10.1037/ccp0000299

Rosenthal, L. (2016). Incorporating intersectionality into psychology: An opportunity to promote social justice and equity. *The American Psychologist, 71*(6), 474–85. doi:10.1037/a0040323

Rothblum, E. D., Balsam, K. F., & Mickey, R. M. (2004). Brothers and sisters of lesbians, gay men, and bisexuals as a demographic comparison group: An innovative research methodology to examine social change. *Journal of Applied Behavioral Science, 40*(3), 283–301. doi:10.1177/0021886304266877

Russell, S. T., & Fish, J. N. (2016). Mental health in lesbian, gay, bisexual, and transgender (LGBT) youth. *Annual Review of Clinical Psychology, 12*, 465–87. doi:10.1146/annurev-clinpsy-021815–093153

Ryan, R. M., & Deci, E. L. (2001). On happiness and human potentials: A review of research on hedonic and eudaimonic well-being. *Annual Review of Psychology, 52*(1), 141–66. doi:10.1146/annurev.psych.52.1.141

Ryff, C. D. (1989). Happiness is everything, or is it? Explorations on the meaning of psychological well-being. *Journal of Personality and Social Psychology, 57*, 1069–81. doi:10.1037/0022–3514.57.6.1069

Savin-Williams, R. C. (2005). *The new gay teenager* (Vol. 3). Cambridge, MA: Harvard University Press.

Schwartz, S., & Meyer, I. H. (2010). Mental health disparities research: The impact of within and between group analyses on tests of social stress hypotheses. *Social Science & Medicine, 70*(8), 1111–8. doi:10.1016/j.socscimed.2009.11.032

Shilo, G., Antebi, N., & Mor, Z. (2015). Individual and community resilience factors among lesbian, gay, bisexual, queer and questioning youth and adults in Israel. *American Journal of Community Psychology, 55*, 215–27. doi:10.1007/s10464-014-9693-8

Singh, A. A., Hays, D. G., & Watson, L. S. (2011). Strength in the face of adversity: Resilience strategies of transgender individuals. *Journal of Counseling & Development, 89*(1), 20–7. doi:10.1002/j.1556–6678.2011.tb00057.x

Stirratt, M. J., Meyer, I. H., Ouellette, S. C., & Gara, M. A. (2008). Measuring identity multiplicity and intersectionality: Hierarchical classes analysis (HICLAS) of sexual, racial, and gender identities. *Self and Identity, 7*(1), 89–111. doi:10.1080/15298860701252203

Svensson, M. E. D., & Frost, D. M. (forthcoming). Sexual orientations and identities among sexual minority emerging adults. In E. Morgan & M. van Dulmen (Eds.), *Sexuality in emerging adulthood.* New York, NY: Oxford University Press.

Swank, E., & Fahs, B. (2006). An intersectional analysis of gender and race for sexual minorities who engage in gay and lesbian rights activism. *Sex Roles, 68*, 660–74. doi:10.1007/s11199-012-0168-9

Thoits, P. A., & Hewitt, L. N. (2001). Volunteer work and well-being. *Journal of Health and Social Behavior, 42*(2), 115–31. doi:10.2307/3090173

Unger, R. K. (2000). The 1999 SPSSI Presidential Address: Outsiders inside: Positive marginality and social change. *Journal of Social Issues, 56*, 163–79. doi:10.1111/0022–4537.00158

Williams, D. R., Yu, Y., Jackson, J. S., & Anderson, N. B. (1997). Racial differences in physical and mental health socio-economic status, stress and discrimination. *Journal of Health Psychology, 2*(3), 335–51. doi:10.1177/135910539700200305

INDEX

A

C

D

Q

R

S

T

U

V

W

X

Y